Alec Douglas-Home

By the same author

THE UNCROWNED PRIME MINISTERS
A Study of Sir Austen Chamberlain,
Lord Curzon and Lord Butler

SELWYN LLOYD

D. R. THORPE

ALEC DOUGLAS-HOME

POLITICO'S

First published 1996 by Sinclair-Stevenson, an imprint of
Reed International Books Ltd

This edition published 2007 by
Politico's Publishing, an imprint of
Methuen Publishing Limited
11–12 Buckingham Gate
London SW1E 6LB

Methuen Publishing Limited Reg. No. 3543167

A CIP catalogue record for this book is available from the British Library.

1

ISBN-10: 1-84275-191-3
ISBN-13: 978-1-84275-191-6

Set in Ehrhardt
Printed and bound in Great Britain by
The Cromwell Press, Trowbridge, Wiltshire

For Eric and Poppy Anderson

It hath been taught us from the primal state
That he which is was wished until he were;
And the ebbed man, ne'er loved till ne'er worth love,
Comes deared by being lacked.

Antony and Cleopatra (I. iv. 41–4)

Contents

List of Illustrations
Preface xv
Acknowledgments xxv
List of Abbreviations xxvii

1 An Unexpected Prime Minister 1
2 Border Ancestry and English Education 9
3 First Steps in Parliament 34
4 The Chamberlain Years 63
5 Acquiring Identity 108
6 Scotland's Minister 134
7 Binding the Commonwealth Ties 154
8 Working with Macmillan 188
9 Caligula's Horse? 205
10 The Cuban Missile Crisis 231
11 That Was The Year That Was 253
12 Customary Processes 270
13 Top of the Greasy Pole 316
14 The 1964 General Election 362
15 'The Right Moment to Change' 378
16 Return to the Foreign Office 404
17 Last Things 439

Appendices
I The Douglas-Home Procedure for the Selection of the Leader of the Conservative and Unionist Party 465

II Lord Home's address at the Memorial Service for Harold Macmillan 467

Bibliography 470
Notes 489
Index 547

List of Illustrations

First plate section

1 Alec Douglas-Home with his mother, 1903
2 Alec Douglas-Home with his grandfather, 1907
3 Alec Douglas-Home before going away to Ludgrove
4 Alec, Bridget, Henry and Rachel at Springhill
5 At Ludgrove, 1913
6 Lord Dunglass at Eton
7 Alec Dunglass with fellow members of Pop, 1920
8 Top scorer in the Eton-Harrow match, 1922
9 On the MCC tour to Argentina, 1926 *(Marylebone Cricket Club)*
10 Douglas Castle in the 1920s
11 Coming of age, July 1924
12 The family in 1924
13 Inspecting the Boys' Brigade, 1931
14 A speech in Lanark, 1931
15 With the Lanarkshire Yeomanry, 1939
16 Marriage in Durham Cathedral, 3 October 1936

Second plate section

17 On constituency business in Lanark
18 Fund raising with Mrs Neville Chamberlain, 1938
19 Neville Chamberlain on his return from Munich *(Hulton Deutsch)*
20 The Chamberlains at the Hirsel, October 1938
21 With Chamberlain and Halifax in Rome, 1939
22 With Archie Sinclair, May 1940 *(Hulton Deutsch)*
23 Sir John Simon at the Treasury, September 1939 *(Hulton Deutsch)*
24 Eden, Churchill, Attlee and Morrison, 15 August 1945 *(Hulton Deutsch)*

25 With the Queen and Churchill at the christening of Jock and Margaret Colville's daughter, 1953
26 The theft of the Stone of Scone, 1950 *(Hulton Deutsch)*
27 The Coronation Chair after the return of the stone, 1951 *(Hulton Deutsch)*
28 Scottish Nationalism in 1953 *(Hulton Deutsch)*
29 'The Affair of the Handbag', 24 June 1953 *(Hulton Deutsch)*
30 The Alingtons on their Golden Wedding Day
31 In Ceylon, 1955
32 Demonstrations over Suez, 1956 *(Hulton Deutsch)*
33 A delegation at Douglas, 1957

Third plate section

34 With Macmillan and Adenauer, 1960
35 At the United Nations, 1960
36 Protest over Cuba, 1962 *(Hulton Deutsch)*
37 With President Kennedy, 1963
38 With Ambassador Bruce, 1964
39 The Test Ban Treaty, Moscow, August 1963
40 'Goodness, Prime Minister!', Cummings cartoon, January 1961
41 Macmillan in his Bromley constituency, 1963 *(Hulton Deutsch)*
42 'Mind you, Littlehampton!', Osbert Lancaster cartoon, December 1962
43 Tony Benn renounces his peerage, 31 July 1963 *(Popperfoto)*
44 John Boyd-Carpenter and Alec Home at the Blackpool Conference, October 1963 *(Hulton Deutsch)*
45 The Queen at the King Edward VII Hospital, 18 October 1963 *(Hulton Deutsch)*
46 With Elizabeth and David in Downing Street, October 1963
47 'What fight over the leadership?', Cummings cartoon, October 1963
48 Outside Downing Street, November 1963 *(Hulton Deutsch)*
49 At President Kennedy's funeral, November 1963 *(Hulton Deutsch)*
50 With Robert Kennedy, January 1964

Fourth plate section

51 With Rab Butler and Ludwig Erhard, January 1964
52 At the White House, February 1964
53 In Lagos, March 1964
54 In the Kinross constituency, August 1964
55 Canvassing in 1964
56 In Bedford during the 1964 general election *(Hulton Deutsch)*

57 The State Opening of Parliament, November 1964
58 Edward Heath as Conservative leader, 1965 *(Hulton Deutsch)*
59 With King Olav, 1965
60 With Richard Nixon, 1969
61 Alec of Arabia, 1971
62 With Ian Smith in Rhodesia, 1971
63 The ink-throwing episode at the Egmont Palace, January 1972 *(Hulton Deutsch)*
64 In Madrid with Prince Juan Carlos and Antony Acland
65 'Alec where art thou?', Osbert Lancaster cartoon, February 1974
66 Elder statesman in the Lords, 1985 *(Hulton Deutsch)*
67 The opening of the Hirsel golf course, 1980
68 The Hirsel in the summer of 1995
69 Alec and Elizabeth Home, September 1990
70 Alec on his 90th birthday
71 Alec Home in benign old age *(Kate Darby)*

Preface

Alec Home invited me to write his biography on 19 June 1990. Our lunch at the House of Lords had originally been fixed for 21 June, but as the date approached he asked, with characteristic honesty, if it would be all right to bring our meeting forward by two days because the twenty-first was Gold Cup Day at Ascot. It was also the week of the christening of his first great-grandchild and of a dinner, hosted by the Speaker of the House of Commons, for those MPs elected before the Second World War, a dwindling band by 1990. As we talked that summer afternoon, it was clear that Alec Home felt the time had come for the record to be set down of a parliamentary career which had stretched over six decades and had unexpectedly included the premiership.

Not that his involvement in public life was yet over. There was the Gulf War at the end of the year, over which he was consulted, and on 22 November, the day of Elizabeth Home's memorial service at Westminster Abbey, the resignation of Mrs Thatcher as Prime Minister. The ensuing contest for the Conservative Party leadership, conducted under electoral rules established by Alec Home a quarter of a century earlier, before his departure from Downing Street, saw him declaring publicly for Douglas Hurd, one of his successors as Foreign Secretary, whose early career had overlapped with Alec Home's at the Foreign Office in 1960. 1990 was also the fiftieth anniversary of the fall of Neville Chamberlain as Prime Minister and, as Chamberlain's former Parliamentary Private Secretary, Alec Home was much in demand for television retrospectives. There were also dinners and celebrations to mark Churchill's advent to power. At 10 Downing Street Alec Home was at the top table, and at the Other Club, the political dining club founded by Churchill and F.E. Smith in 1911, despite the fact that he had not been a member of the Great Coalition, he gave the speech about the Prime Minister who had given him his first ministerial post (as Under-Secretary at the Foreign Office) in the caretaker government of May to July 1945.

This burst of late activity is hardly surprising. Not only was Alec Home in his late eighties still a man of great energy who followed political developments avidly but, following the death of Harold Macmillan in December 1986, he became the senior member of the exclusive club of former prime ministers. The Treasury benches in the House of Commons may be littered with the bones of future prime ministers ('Whom the gods wish to destroy,' wrote Alec's Eton contemporary Cyril Connolly, 'they first call promising'*) but from the time that Alec Home re-entered the House of Lords in 1974 as a life peer until his death in October 1995 the benches of the Upper House supported five ex-premiers. The 1980s saw the appearance of many biographies of these figures and their contemporaries and rivals. Alistair Horne (Harold Macmillan), Robert Rhodes James (Anthony Eden) and Anthony Howard (Rab Butler) were dubbed by Roy Jenkins the three musketeers of modern Conservative biography. And as a second wave of biographers began to sharpen their pens – John Campbell (Edward Heath and Margaret Thatcher), Austen Morgan, Ben Pimlott and Philip Ziegler (Harold Wilson), and Geoffrey Lewis (Quintin Hailsham) – Alec Home's premiership was the gap in modern political research. There had been two previous books on his career (in addition to his own autobiography), *The Uncommon Commoner* by John Dickie, published shortly after his arrival in Downing Street, followed in 1970 by Kenneth Young's *Sir Alec Douglas-Home*, just after its subject had embarked on his second stint as Foreign Secretary. Public records were not available for the substantive part of his career, though both books were written with his help and co-operation. Nevertheless it was not incorrect for Anthony Seldon to observe:

> Home's is the least-written-about career of any twentieth-century Prime Minister. His premiership has attracted no scholarly study, and his political career before 1963 has failed to excite much interest or comment from historians and biographers. It might be easy, therefore, to dismiss him as a lightweight, but such a conclusion is seriously misleading.†

I had got to know Alec Home slightly in the late 1980s while writing the official life of Selwyn Lloyd. He had been extremely helpful to me (as he was to many historians at that time) and his shrewd observations on the post-war political scene had illuminated many issues. Their careers had overlapped, especially between 1960 and 1962 when they had been Foreign Secretary (Alec Home succeeding Selwyn Lloyd in the post) and Chancellor of the Exchequer in Harold Macmillan's government. In 1963

* Cyril Connolly, *Enemies of Promise*, Penguin Books, Harmondsworth, 1961, p. 121.

† *The Blackwell Biographical Dictionary of British Political Life in the Twentieth Century*, Blackwell, Oxford, 1990, p. 209.

Alec brought Selwyn Lloyd back into the Cabinet as Lord Privy Seal. They served together in government for twelve years and were colleagues in Parliament for twenty-eight years. Home had given the address at Selwyn Lloyd's funeral and, at the request of the family, had read one of the lessons at the Westminster Abbey memorial service. He reviewed my book for the *Scotsman* and was one of the guests at the Garrick Club dinner to mark its publication. There was a certain natural symmetry for me to write his life, a view fortunately shared by Alec Home himself.

Over the next few years I got to know him and his family as friends, staying at the Hirsel to work through the virgin archive of his voluminous papers and to talk over the key moments of his career. The last time I saw him was eight weeks before his death when I was gathering photographs for this book, then nearing completion. The kindness and hospitality afforded me ensured that one of Dr Samuel Johnson's requirements of the biographer was fulfilled: that 'Nobody can write the life of a man, but those who have ate and drunk and lived in social intercourse with him.'* On the first of these occasions in August 1990 I talked for many hours with Elizabeth Home; we chatted between typing sessions in 'Siberia', the unheated wing of the Hirsel, where the Home papers were then housed. Three weeks later, on 3 September, the anniversary of the declaration of war, she died in hospital at Carluke after being taken ill at the family home in Lanarkshire.

Elizabeth Home's influence on this biography is twofold. Not only did I have the benefit of hearing at first hand many episodes from a different perspective, but through her legacy of the 108 family volumes (scrapbooks is an inadequate description of this unique historical archive) and other diaries and journals she kept of their joint lives, she ensured a permanent record of the public and private sides of their partnership.

When Nigel Nicolson wrote his life of Earl Alexander of Tunis he titled it *Alex*, and one of the first decisions in writing the life of Lord Home was whether the biography should simply be called *Alec*, the one common factor in his many changes of names over nine decades. Indeed Elizabeth Home delighted in the fact that she had appeared at one stage in *The Guinness Book of Records* as the woman who had changed her name most often during a single marriage. 'Considering the number of different names I have had in my life,' she said, 'it is surprising how infrequently I've been married!'† The person Elizabeth Home displaced in the records

* Letter to Sir Joshua Reynolds, 31 March 1772

† Cited by Lord Charteris of Amisfield in his address at the Memorial Service for Lady Home, Westminster Abbey, 22 November 1990

was no less than Queen Mary, who, on being told that a much-married woman had changed her name seven times and therefore had a better claim to the record, replied, 'Ah, but whereas mine have been by accident, hers have been by enterprise.'

Elizabeth Home's changes of name from the original Miss Elizabeth Alington were to Lady Dunglass (1936–51), the Countess of Home (1951–63), Lady Douglas-Home (1963–74), and finally Lady Home of the Hirsel (1974–90). Thus mirrored, her husband's career went through many phases, of title as well as political status. For the pre-war generation (even now in talking to survivors of that time) he was Dunglass, the young PPS to Neville Chamberlain. For those who became politically conscious in the 1960s he was Alec Douglas-Home and his administration the Douglas-Home one. But that is over thirty years ago; to present-day commentators he is Lord Home. In all the circumstances it seemed most appropriate to refer mainly to my subject as Alec Home, the name by which he was affectionately known to his friends and colleagues, but to shorten this when suitable to Alec, while making it clear whether the career was in the Dunglass, Home or Douglas-Home phases. As with Winston, Austen, Neville, and Selwyn, the name Alec has a clear political resonance in the history of the last sixty years.

My principal debt to Alec Home is for inviting me to undertake this task in the first place, for affording me unrestricted access to his papers and for his hospitality and friendship over several years. To have had the papers and principal records of one's biographical subject at one end of the house and the subject at the other, ready to go over the details of the day's researches, was of inestimable value in unravelling long-distant events. The Hirsel too was redolent of history and for the biographer the *genius loci* is of more than atmospheric importance. To talk with Neville Chamberlain's Parliamentary Private Secretary about the post-Munich days in the very rooms where Chamberlain had visited Alec Home's father and family in October 1938 provided a special frisson. Similar emotions could be experienced in talking with Enoch Powell about the famous midnight meeting in October 1963 at his house in Eaton Place, while sitting in the chair Iain Macleod had occupied during that meeting, and in discussing in Rab Butler's former London home in Smith Square the events that followed the resignations of Anthony Eden and Harold Macmillan.

Professor Ben Pimlott has rightly commented that lives of public figures used to be 'part of a process of canonisation'. There were many conventions: 'a customary part of the ritual was for the author to declare at the beginning of the book that the co-operation of the family had been provided unconditionally, and that no pressure had been exerted whatsoever.* That this is a biographical commonplace makes it no less true in the present case; Alec Home and his family have been of the utmost help to me, without at any time wishing to influence my interpretation of the material available in public and private archives. I would particularly like to acknowledge the many kindnesses of the present Earl of Home in facilitating access to his father's associates and their records and the Countess of Home in talking to me about her father-in-law. Lady Caroline Douglas-Home has helped me in my many visits to the Hirsel, during which address books have been scoured for useful names, records photocopied and insights given into the family and its life in invaluable and generous measure. I have also benefited from talks with Mr Adrian and Lady Meriel Darby, and Lady Diana Wolfe Murray, at the Hirsel and in London. The Hon Edward Douglas-Home welcomed me to his home in Northumberland and gave me glimpses of family life from pre-war days. In Hampshire I talked with the late Hon William Douglas-Home and corresponded further over family details in his final book, *Old Men Remember*. At the Hirsel the late Lady William Scott spoke to me about her brother as well as giving me illuminating details about their parents, the 13th Earl and Countess of Home. Other members of the family who have talked to me are Miss Kate Darby, Mr Peregrine Douglas-Home, Lady Ian Fraser and Mr Walter Scott. I am grateful to them all.

At the outset of the project I received invaluable help and advice from Lord Charteris of Amisfield, the late Lord Fraser of Kilmorack, Mr Graham C. Greene, Mr Kenneth Rose and Lord Wakeham, and to them I would extend my special gratitude. I am particularly indebted to Lord Home's earlier biographer, John Dickie, for his generous help over so many aspects of my research, not only in scouring his records for otherwise unobtainable material but for his wise counsel in many fruitful talks.

Her Majesty Queen Elizabeth the Queen Mother granted me a private audience at Clarence House. I am conscious of the privilege of such an audience and of hearing about Lord Home's life from Her Majesty and of his association firstly with the Bowes-Lyon family before 1923 and later with the royal family, including his time as Parliamentary Private Secretary to Neville Chamberlain, to the time of his premiership and

* Ben Pimlott, *Harold Wilson*, HarperCollins, 1992, p. xiii

beyond. In this connection I would also like to acknowledge the help of the late Sir Martin Gilliat and Captain Sir Alastair Aird.

The bulk of the book is based upon the papers of the Douglas-Home family and estates, divided between the Hirsel, Coldstream, and HM General Register House, Edinburgh (The National Register of Archives, Scotland). Government records up to the end of the Douglas-Home administration in October 1964 are at the Public Record Office, Kew. Details of these papers and of the many private archives consulted can be found in the bibliography.

Oral evidence has been generously given by a wide cross-section of Lord Home's friends and associates. The flavour of events and the atmosphere of times many decades previous cannot be recaptured by documents alone and such interviews have been central to the research, not least in the way that a chain of evidence is built up by an interviewee suggesting further avenues, as in the memorably laconic suggestion, 'You ought to speak to David Bowes-Lyon's sister.' I am immensely grateful to all those who have spoken to me about Lord and Lady Home and been so generous with their time and hospitality. As many of the interviews were on a non-attributable basis, the reader will find few direct references in the notes but no fact has been included from these sources unless independently corroborated or vouched for unimpeachably. Those who have spoken to me about Lord Home's life and times include:

Sir Antony Acland, Mr Jonathan Aitken, Sir Michael Alexander, the late Lord Amery of Lustleigh, Dr Eric and Mrs Anderson, the Countess of Avon, Mrs Ian Ball, Dr Correlli Barnett, Sir Nicholas Barrington, Sir William and Lady Becher, Dr B.S. Benedikz, Mrs Edna Berresford, the late Mr Humphry Berkeley, Lord Blake, Professor Vernon Bogdanor, Lord Boyd-Carpenter, Lord Briggs, the late Lord Brimelow, Lady Butler of Saffron Walden, Dr David Butler, Lord Callaghan of Cardiff, Dr John Campbell, Sir Matthew Campbell, Lord Carr of Hadley, Lord Carrington, Sir Roger Cary Bt., Lord Charteris of Amisfield, Dr Christopher Coker, Sir David and Lady Cole, the late Lord Colyton, Lady Colyton, Lord and Lady Crathorne, Mr Patrick Croker, Sir Charles Cunningham, Mr and Mrs John Curtis, Sir Robin Day, Lord Deedes, Mr and Mrs John Dickie, Professor David Dilks, Mr Hubert Doggart, Professor James Douglas, Dr David Dutton, Mr Peter Earle, the late Baroness Elliott of Harwood, Dame Eleanor Emery, Lord Fanshawe, Mr Martin Fearn, the Rev. Jonathan Fletcher, Sir Edward Ford, Sir Marcus Fox, the late Lord Fraser of Kilmorack, Lady Fraser of Kilmorack, Mr J.S. Gibson, Lord Glenamara, Miss Sylvia Goodfellow, Sir Philip Goodhart, the late Lord

Goodman, Sir John Graham, Mr Graham C. Greene, Lord Greenhill of Harrow, Sir Eldon Griffiths, Lord Hailsham of St Marylebone, the late Mr R.M. Hamilton, Sir Edward Heath, Sir Nicholas Henderson, Sir James Hennessy, Professor Peter Hennessy, Professor Christopher Hill, Mr Alistair Horne, Mr Anthony Howard, Mr and Mrs Miles Hudson, Sir Alan Hume, Sir David and Lady Hunt, Mr Douglas Hurd, Mr Henry James, Mrs Sylvia James, Miss Sheila Jeffreys, Lord Jenkins of Hillhead, Sir John Johnson, Sir Ronald Johnson, the late Mr Brian Johnston, Sir John and the late Lady Killick, Professor Anthony King, Mr Keith Kyle, Mr Richard Lamb, Lord Lawson of Blaby, Sir John Leahy, Sir Martin Le Quesne, Mr Magnus Linklater, the late Sir Henry Lintott, Lady Lintott, the late Mrs Sheila Lochhead, Dr Christopher Lord, Sir Philip and Lady Mansfield, the late Lord Margadale of Islay, Mr and Mrs John McDonnell, Mr John MacGregor, Miss Peggy Metcalfe, Mr Angus Mitchell, Sir Derek Mitchell, Miss Anthea Montgomery, Mr Andrew Morrison, the late Sir William Murrie, Sir Patrick Nairne, Mr Nigel Nicolson, Professor Philip Norton, Air Vice Marshal Derek O'Hara, Dr Susan Onslow, the late Sir Anthony Parsons, Lady Parsons, Miss Jane Parsons, Mr Edward Pearce, the late Sir Francis Pearson, Sir Michael Palliser, the Earl and Countess of Perth, Sir David Pitblado, Mr George Pottinger, Mr Enoch Powell, Lord Prior, Lord Rawlinson of Ewell, Lord Rees-Mogg, Mr and Mrs Malcolm Reid, Sir Patrick Reilly, Sir Robert and Lady Rhodes James, Mr Peter Riddell, Lord Rippon of Hexham, Sir Frank Roberts, the late Mr Ian Robertson, Mr John Robertson, the late Mrs John Robertson, Mr Kenneth Rose, Mr Ian Samuel, Sir David and Lady Scott, the late Very Rev. Dr Ronald Selby Wright, Dr Anthony Seldon, Mr Donald Shell, Lord Sherfield, Mr Anthony Shone, Mr Christopher Sinclair-Stevenson, Mr Richard Slater, Sir Harold Smedley, the late Sir Arthur Snelling, Lady Soames, Mrs Eila Straker-Smith, Baroness Thatcher of Kesteven, Mr David Twiston Davies, Mr Jeremy Varcoe, Mr George Walden, Sir Michael Walker, Professor Nigel Walker, Sir Denis Walters, Mr Alan Watkins, Lord Weatherill, Lord Whitelaw, Mr and Mrs Compton Whitworth, Maj-General Reginald Whitworth, Sir Michael Wilford, Sir David Innes Williams, the late Sir Edgar Williams, Sir Philip Woodfield and Lord Younger of Prestwick.

The following people corresponded with me about Lord Home: the late Brigadier Peter Acland, Mr David Badenoch, Dr Stuart Ball, Mr Gerald Barber, Mr Glanvill Benn, President George Bush, Mr Sandy Colville, Lord Crathorne, Mr Donald Crichton-Miller, Mrs Ann Dunn (secretary to Mr Dean Rusk), Mr Oliver Everett, Mrs Elizabeth Hill, Professor Alan

James, Mrs Jacquetta James, Dr Henry Kissinger, the Marquess of Lothian, Lady Mitchison, Lady Francis Pearson, Mr R.J. Priestley, Mr Peter Robinson, Sheryl B. Vogt, Mrs John Woodrow and Professor John Young.

I owe a debt of gratitude to the librarians and archivists of many institutions, and would like to acknowledge the help given by the staffs of the Public Record Office, Kew; the John Fitzgerald Kennedy Presidential Library in Boston, Massachusetts, particularly Maura Porter, Reference Archivist; Dr B.S. Benedikz, former Keeper of the Special Collections, and Miss Christine Penney, University Archivist, and the staff of the University Library, Birmingham, for the Chamberlain and Avon papers; Mr Alistair Cooke of the Conservative Research Department; Dr Sarah Street, former Keeper of the Conservative Party Archives; Helen Longley of the Department of Modern Political Papers and the staff of the Bodleian Library, Oxford, for help over the Conservative Party Archives; Jacqueline Kavanagh, Written Archivist, Gwyniver Jones, Deputy Written Archivist, and the staff of the BBC Written Archives Centre at Caversham; Dr Correlli Barnett, former Keeper of the Churchill Collections; Kathryn Beckett, Sophie Cant, Josephine Sykes, Alan Kucia, Archivist, and the staff of the Churchill Archives Centre, Churchill College, Cambridge; Lord Brabourne and the Mountbatten Trustees, Dr Christopher Woolgar, Chief Archivist, Mrs K. Robson, Deputy Archivist, Dr Martin Alexander of the Department of History, and the Staff of the University Library, Southampton, for help over the Mountbatten Papers; Mr Bruno Longmore, Modern Records Branch, and the staff of the Scottish Records Office, Edinburgh; Dr David McKitterick, Librarian of Trinity College, Cambridge, Jonathan Smith and the staff at Trinity College Library; Colonel John Stephenson, former Secretary of the MCC, for access to the archives of the Marylebone Cricket Club, and to Mr Roger Knight, Secretary of MCC, Glenys Williams and the staff in the Library at Lord's Ground; Mr Gerald Barber for access to material at Ludgrove School, Wokingham; Mrs Penny Hatfield, College Archivist in College Library at Eton College, for help over material relating to Lord Home's schooldays and Lady Home's time as a Fellow of Eton; and Mr Michael Ashmore, Chairman, and Mrs Rita Fanshawe, Secretary, for access to material in the archives of the Clydesdale Conservative Association, Lanark. The staff at the Library of the United Oxford and Cambridge University Club, and at Godalming Library have been unfailingly helpful in unearthing out-of-print books and other material. I am also grateful to the Macmillan trustees for access to the voluminous archive of the late Harold Macmillan, 1st Earl of Stockton, while still at the Birch Grove Estate. In connection with this, I would like to thank Mrs Philippa Blake-Roberts of Taylor Joynson Garrett, Mrs Sylvia James, Archivist at Birch Grove, and Air Vice Marshal Derek O'Hara for their help before the papers were transferred to the Bodleian Library.

Others who have helped in various ways and to whom I would like to express my gratitude include Mr Peter Attenborough, Mr James Bayliss, Mr and Mrs Ron Bell, Dr Anthony Bennett, Dr Ian Blake, the late Major Michael Chignell, Mr Richard Crawford, Mr Jim Davies of the Photographic Department of Birmingham University Library for copying material in the Neville Chamberlain Papers, Mr Anthony Day, Mr H.W. Foot (former private secretary to Dr Hastings Banda), Mrs Perina Fordham, Mr Cary Gilbart-Smith, Mr Richard Gilliat, Mr Jonathan Goodwin, Mr Leonard Halcrow, Dr David Holloway, Mr Hector Innes ABIPP (for help in copying photographs in the Home papers), Mr Henry de L'Isle, Mr and Mrs Robert Ingram, Mr John Knight, Mr Tim Law, Miss Zubeen Mehta, Mrs F.M. Myles, Dr Jeff Opland, Mr John Peters, Mrs Sally Russell, Mr S.J. Shuttleworth, Mr Brian Souter, Mrs Carole Tranmer, Mr David Twiston Davies and Dr Ernst Zillekens.

Lord Home's tenure of the Foreign Office and the events of October 1963 are two of the central strands of his life. Over the last twenty years I have spoken with many from the Foreign Service as well as the main participants in the leadership struggle at Blackpool, while researching my earlier books, *The Uncrowned Prime Ministers* and *Selwyn Lloyd*, and their help has been invaluable in unravelling still controversial events. Sadly, many of these figures are no longer alive. Among those who spoke to me earlier I would mention with gratitude: the late Lord Boothby, the late Lord Butler of Saffron Walden, the late Lord Caccia, the late Sir John Colville, the late Sir Knox Cunningham, the late Sir Patrick Dean, the late Lord Devlin, the late Mr Peter Goldman, the late Sir William Gorell Barnes, the late Lord Inchyra, the late Mr Reginald Maudling, the late Colonel Terence Maxwell, the late Sir Evelyn Shuckburgh, the late Lord Soames, the late Earl of Stockton, the late Sir Austin Strutt, the late Lord Thorneycroft, the late Lord Wilson of Rievaulx and the late Sir Philip de Zulueta.

I am grateful to all those who read the book at manuscript stage, particularly the Earl of Home, Lady Caroline Douglas-Home and Mr Graham C. Greene. I would also like to thank Dr Eric Anderson for his comments, especially on passages dealing with Eton College; Sir Frank Roberts for reading the chapter on the Cuban Missile Crisis; Mr Oliver

Everett for checking the chapter on the leadership contest of 1963 and other sections dealing with the royal family; and Sir Robin Butler for reading the chapters containing material within the Thirty Year Rule, particularly that on Sir Alec Douglas-Home's second spell at the Foreign Office from 1970–74.

For their help over the technicalities of computing, I am much indebted to Locland Computers, a Scottish firm which by happy chance is based in East Kilbride, part of Lord Home's former constituency of Lanark.

Finally, I would like to thank Christopher Sinclair-Stevenson, friend, mentor, editor and publisher, who over the last six years has been an unfailing support and without whom this project would not have come to fruition.

While acknowledging with gratitude all the help I have been given, I would add that the views expressed in this book do not, of course, represent the views of those mentioned.

D. R. Thorpe
Godalming, 1996

Acknowledgments

The author and publishers are grateful to the following for permission to quote from copyright material:

Extracts from the Royal Archives and private letters from Her Majesty The Queen to Harold Macmillan and Sir Alec Douglas-Home are published by the gracious permission of Her Majesty The Queen.

Crown copyright material in the Public Record Office is reproduced by permission of the Controller of Her Majesty's Stationery Office.

The late Lord Amery of Lustleigh for extracts from the diaries and writings of the late Leo Amery; the Countess of Avon for extracts from the Avon Papers and for private correspondence of the 1st Earl of Avon; Mr David Badenoch for a letter to *The Times*; the BBC Written Archives Centre for extracts from the BBC Archives, Caversham Park; the Rt Hon. Tony Benn for extracts from his diaries, published by Century Hutchinson Ltd; the late Mr Humphry Berkeley for letters written to Sir Alec Douglas-Home; Mrs Edna Berresford for extracts from letters; The University of Birmingham for extracts from the Neville Chamberlain Papers; the Bodleian Library, Oxford, for extracts from the Papers of Viscount Boyd of Merton, Viscount Crookshank and Lady Emmet; David J. Brown, Inspecting Officer, Goverment Records Office, for extracts from the Scottish Record Office; Lady Butler of Saffron Walden for letters by the late Lord Butler of Saffron Walden; Mr T.S.B. Card for extracts from *Eton Renewed*, published by John Murray; Viscount Chandos for extracts from the papers of the 1st Viscount Chandos; the Master and Fellows of Churchill College, Cambridge, for extracts from collections in the ownership of the Churchill Archive Centre; Lady Margaret Colville for letters by the late Sir John Colville, extracts from published writings and photographic material; the Chairman of the Conservative Party and Mr Alistair Cooke for material in the Conservative Party Archives; Lord Crathorne for letters in the Crathorne papers; Miss Sylvia Goodfellow for correspondence; Mr Robin Gordon-Walker for extracts from the Gordon-Walker papers; Mrs Elizabeth Hill for material by the late Mr B.J.W. Hill; Mr Anthony Howard for extracts from published works; Mr Miles Hudson for extracts from his papers and for a letter to *The Times*; Mr Douglas Hurd for extracts from his diary; Mr Roger Knight, Secretary of the MCC, and the MCC Committee for permission to quote from MCC Minutes; the Trustees of the Selwyn Lloyd estate for extracts from the Selwyn Lloyd papers; the Trustees of the Harold Macmillan Book Trust for extracts from the papers of the 1st Earl of Stockton; Lord Owen for an extract from a letter to Lord Home; Mr Edward Pearce and Mrs Ian Ball for extracts from the papers of the late Lord Pearce; Sir Patrick Reilly for an extract from his papers; Mr Peter Robinson for an extract from a letter to the *Daily Telegraph*; the Richard B. Russell Library for Political Research and Studies at the University of Georgia for a letter from the late Dean Rusk; the Marquess of Salisbury for extracts from letters by the 5th Marquess of Salisbury; Lord Sherfield for extracts from his diary and papers; Christie, Viscountess Simon, for extracts from the Simon Papers; Sir Harold Smedley for extracts from his diary; Baroness Thatcher for letters to Lord Home; extracts from *The Times* obituaries of Dr Cyril Alington, Sir Nicholas Fairbairn, Lord and Lady Home of the Hirsel, and Iain Macleod are published by kind permission of *The Times*; the Master and Fellows of Trinity College, Cambridge, for extracts from Lord Butler of Saffron Walden's Papers; and Dr C.M. Woolgar, Archivist and Head of Special Collections, Hartley Library, University of Southampton, on behalf of the Mountbatten Trustees, for extracts from the papers of Earl Mountbatten of Burma.

Every effort has been made to contact copyright holders. In some cases this has not proved possible. Where any inadvertent infringement of copyright has been made, the publishers and author would crave indulgence and will make the necessary acknowledgements in later editions.

List of Abbreviations

AE	Anthony Eden
ANC	African National Congress
BEF	British Expeditionary Force
BOAC	British Overseas Airways Corporation
CB	Companion, Order of the Bath
CE	Common Entrance
CENTO	Central Treaty Organisation
CIA	Central Intelligence Agency
CND	Campaign for Nuclear Disarmament
CO	Colonial Office
CRD	Conservative Research Department
CRO	Commonwealth Relations Office
CROWS	Commonwealth Relations Office Wives' Society
DBE	Dame Commander of the Order of the British Empire
DCL	Doctor of Civil Law
DDR	Deutsche Demokratische Republik
EEC	European Economic Community
EFTA	European Free Trade Association
FO	Foreign Office
FS	Foreign Secretary
GLC	Greater London Council
HA	Hirsel Archive
HM	Her Majesty
HMG	Her Majesty's Government
H of C	House of Commons
KC	King's Counsel
KGB	Komitet Gosudarstvennoi Bezopasnosti
KT	Knight of the Thistle
LVO	Lieutenant, Royal Victorian Order
MCC	Marylebone Cricket Club

MP	Member of Parliament
NATO	North Atlantic Treaty Organisation
NB	North Britain
NIBMAR	No Independence Before Majority Rule
NOP	National Opinion Poll
OEEC	Organisation for European Economic Co-operation
ONUC	United Nations Force in the Congo
PM	Prime Minister
PPS	Parliamentary Private Secretary
PRO	Public Record Office
RA	Royal Archives
RAB	R. A. Butler
RMS	Royal Mail Steamer
RPM	Resale Price Maintenance
SB	Stanley Baldwin
SCUA	Suez Canal Users' Association
SEATO	South-East Asia Treaty Organisation
SIS	Secret Intelligence Service
SNP	Scottish National Party
TW3	*That Was The Week That Was*
UDI	Unilateral Declaration of Independence
UNFICYP	United Nations Force in Cyprus
UNO	United Nations Organisation
YMCA	Young Men's Christian Association*
ZANU	Zimbabwe African National Union
ZAPU	Zimbabwe African People's Union

* Also used as the nickname for a group of young progressive Conservative backbenchers of the 1920s and 1930s who followed the ideas of Noel Skelton on 'the property-owning democracy'.

I

An Unexpected Prime Minister

Alexander Frederick Douglas-Home was born on 2 July 1903 at 28 South Street, London. A child of the Edwardian age with its illusory certainties, his life spanned the twentieth century from the end of the Boer War to the end of the Cold War. His father was Charles Cospatrick Archibald Douglas-Home, Lord Dunglass, and heir to the Earldom of Home and the Barony of Douglas, whose motto after the linking of the Douglas and Home families in 1875 was 'True to the end'.

Inappropriately nicknamed the unlucky earl when he became the thirteenth of his line in April 1918, 'Charlie' Home was known as a saintly man, who saw sermons in stones and good in everything, even remarking of Adolf Hitler, 'Poor fellow, surrounded by all those generals, and not one of them able to tell him he's got his Sam Browne on the wrong way round.' His wife was the former Lady Lilian Lambton, second daughter of the 4th Earl of Durham, and a great-granddaughter of 'Radical Jack', the 1st Earl of Durham, a driving force behind the Great Reform Bill, and author in 1840 of the famous Durham Report on Dominion Status for Canada. Lady Lilian's unorthodox radicalism never left her and by her sons she was dubbed, only half-jestingly, 'the well-known socialist'.[1] Their marriage on 14 July 1902 had coincided with the retirement as Prime Minister of Lord Salisbury, at the turn of the century a seemingly permanent fixture at the head of the Conservative Party, a scion of the Upper House which in the previous century had produced eleven of Britain's nineteen prime ministers. The twentieth century would produce only one from the House of Lords: Alexander Frederick Douglas-Home.

When Alec (from early childhood he was known by this diminutive) was nine years old the great constitutional battle between the House of

Lords and House of Commons which followed David Lloyd George's People's Budget of 1909 was resolved by passage of the Parliament Act, which severely limited the powers of the Upper House. This had profound implications for politically ambitious peers, for when Lord Curzon was passed over for the premiership in May 1923 in favour of Stanley Baldwin – on the ostensible grounds that a peer would be unacceptable to the Labour opposition in the Commons – the convention that members of the House of Lords could not be prime ministers became the new political reality. Even in the exceptional wartime circumstances of May 1940, on the fall of Chamberlain, Lord Halifax's self-denying ruling that a peer could not be prime minister in a 'People's War' confirmed this constitutional convention. Yet only a few months earlier a curious prophecy had been made in the private office in 10 Downing Street, where one of the secretaries was Miss Edith Watson, a legendary figure, who had served in No. 10 since the days of Lloyd George. Her job in the outer office, which she shared with John Colville and Alec Douglas-Home (then Lord Dunglass), Chamberlain's Parliamentary Private Secretary, was to draft replies to parliamentary questions. One day when Chamberlain was at the House of Commons for Prime Minister's Questions with Lord Dunglass, Miss Watson turned to John Colville. 'You know, Mr Colville,' she said, 'there is hardly anybody here nowadays who understands the House of Commons. The PM doesn't and Sir Horace certainly doesn't. I sometimes think Captain Margesson and Captain Dugdale don't either. The only one who does is Lord Dunglass. He will be Prime Minister one day.' John Colville was surprised by this confident assertion and said, 'Of course you have much more experience of these things than I have, Miss Watson, but long before the time comes that Lord Dunglass could be Prime Minister, he will be Lord Home; and I cannot believe that a peer could ever again be Prime Minister.' Miss Watson was not deflected. 'Well, say what you will, I shall be dead before it happens, but on the day Lord Dunglass becomes Prime Minister I hope you will remember what Miss Watson said.' On 18 October 1963 Colville remembered and penned the letter Miss Watson had predicted he would write.[2]

Edith Watson was not the only person to see such qualities in Lord Dunglass. In *Enemies of Promise* Cyril Connolly has a celebrated description of Alec Dunglass as a fellow member of Pop, the self-electing Eton society of senior boys:

> The other important Pop was Alec Dunglass, who was President and also Keeper of the Field and Captain of the Eleven. He was a votary of the esoteric Eton religion, the kind of graceful, tolerant sleepy boy who is showered with favours and crowned with all the laurels, who is liked by the masters and admired by the boys without any apparent exertion on his part, without experiencing the ill-effects of success himself or arousing the pangs of envy in others. In the eighteenth century he would have become Prime Minister before he was thirty; as it was he appeared honourably ineligible for the struggle of life.[3]

The story of how this unassuming hereditary peer became Prime Minister of Great Britain in the second half of the twentieth century is equivalent to the time when Lord Randolph Churchill famously 'forgot Goschen', who took his place as Chancellor of the Exchequer in December 1886 in Lord Salisbury's government. Alec Home was the Goschen of this century, honourably ineligible in some eyes, but the unfancied tortoise who pipped many political hares to the Prime Minister's office.[4] The generally accepted version of how this happened is that Harold Macmillan personally recommended Alec Home to the Queen to deny Rab Butler the premiership.[5] Home's path to 10 Downing Street was a combination of unique circumstances over the previous three years, involving figures as diverse as Derick Heathcoat Amory from his own party and the second Viscount Stansgate (Tony Benn) from the opposition.

On 18 October 1963 it was announced from Buckingham Palace, 'The Queen has received the Earl of Home in audience and invited him to form an administration.' Lord Home was the first peer to be offered the office of Prime Minister and First Lord of the Treasury since the retirement of Lord Salisbury on 11 July 1902. Though he had not then disclaimed his title, he now took the necessary steps under the new Peerage Act so as to be eligible for election to the House of Commons. For some fifteen days from 23 October until 7 November 1963, when the result of the Kinross and West Perthshire by-election was announced, he was the only Prime Minister of modern times to have no seat in either House of Parliament.

Alec Home was the eighteenth Etonian to become Prime Minister and the third in succession after Anthony Eden and Harold Macmillan. Like Gladstone, Salisbury and Eden, who first gave him Cabinet office in 1955, he was also a product of Christ Church. Also like Eden, he took the direct route from the Foreign Office to No. 10. But when the

Conservatives elected their new leader in November 1990 it was an absolute *disadvantage* to have been educated at Eton. As Douglas Hurd wrote to Alec Home, after coming third in the ballot behind John Major and Michael Heseltine, 'It was particularly good of you to back me up in this very peculiar contest, and *I am most grateful.* I remember that you let me use your name twenty years ago when I was looking for a seat. The handicap of being an Old Etonian seems to have increased since your time!'[6]

John Major was in many respects an unexpected Conservative leader, yet the Party has often turned to a dark horse candidate. Benjamin Disraeli, Edward Heath, Margaret Thatcher and John Major may seem to be the obvious examples of outsiders succeeding to the leadership, yet Bonar Law, Stanley Baldwin, Winston Churchill, Harold Macmillan and Alec Home were by no means expected victors of their respective contests. Of Bonar Law's elevation in November 1911, Lloyd George wryly commented, 'The fools have stumbled on the right man by accident.'[7] (Apart from being the two shortest-serving premiers of the century, Bonar Law and Alec Home had in common a liking for simple and homely fare and a complete unpretentiousness in their life styles.[8]) In May 1923 some, Curzon included, thought that Baldwin was too junior to be the new Prime Minister, and in May 1940 many felt Lord Halifax would receive the summons. In January 1957, most expected Rab Butler to be chosen to succeed Eden. Alec Home has a clear place in this line of initially unforeseen leaders.

Conservative leaders are chosen to win elections and despite all the retrospective affection bestowed on Alec Home, history records that he was one of four this century who never led the Party to victory at the polls, the others being Arthur Balfour, Austen Chamberlain and Neville Chamberlain. He was also one of four twentieth-century prime ministers who succeeded to the premiership during a Parliament and was not subsequently confirmed in office by popular ballot, the others being Balfour (who lost elections in 1906 and in January and December 1910), Neville Chamberlain (who never faced the electorate) and James Callaghan (defeated in May 1979). Not entirely accurate parallels have been drawn between Arthur Balfour, Alec Home and James Callaghan, in that all three became Prime Minister at the end of a long period of domination by their party, only to experience the adverse swing of the political pendulum. Callaghan identified such a process as inevitable. 'You know there are times, perhaps once every thirty years, when there is a sea-change in politics. It then does not matter what you say or what you do,' he said in April 1979, of deceptively encouraging opinion polls. 'There is a shift in what the public wants and what it approves of. I suspect there is now such a sea-change – and it is for Mrs Thatcher.'[9] At such a time the *momentum* is more important than the *mathematics*. Alec Home became leader in 1963 as public opinion was turning against the Conservatives, yet, unlike Balfour or Callaghan, he almost reversed the trend, bringing them to the brink of victory. His achievement in reducing the 11 per cent Labour lead shown by the polls to less than 1 per cent has been obscured by ultimate defeat. One of the few to acknowledge this was Jo Grimond, leader of the Liberal Party at the 1964 election, who wrote, 'In spite of the scoffing of some of the publicists, Sir Alec Douglas-Home impressed many floating voters. He was a thoroughly professional politician for he had been at it all his life ...'[10] Arguably, his best was yet to be. His authority as a former Prime Minister added inestimably to his effectiveness as Foreign Secretary in the 1970s; in all, his career exceeded six decades. From the time as a schoolboy that he heard General Haig talking to his father about the Great War, to his letters as an elder statesman to Margaret Thatcher on foreign affairs, politics was the substance of his professional life. He once partnered Balfour at golf at North Berwick, only to see the former Prime Minister charge the decisive putt on the last green beyond the hole. 'Fancy letting a man who putts like that, run a country like this,' observed his caddy.[11] Though he would claim no expertise as a golfer himself, unlike cricket where he is the only Prime Minister to have played the first-class game, in political terms, Alec Home knew which way the putts broke.

'All political lives unless they are cut off in midstream at a happy juncture, end in failure,' wrote Enoch Powell, 'because that is the nature of politics and human affairs.'[12] Although the February 1974 general election brought Home's second stint as Foreign Secretary to a premature conclusion, he is an exception to Powell's rule. Few twentieth-century leaders have managed their retirements from office smoothly. Herbert Asquith, Lloyd George, Neville Chamberlain and Margaret Thatcher were removed after party strife and controversy. Others, notably Churchill, have lingered too long as the political footman held the coat. Only Harold Wilson and Alec Home, the great rivals of October 1964, departed from the leadership of their parties at an unexpectedly early time of their own choosing.

It could be argued that in the summer of 1965 Alec Home was in a similar position to Eden (in 1957) or Macmillan (in 1963) in that his leadership was the subject of intense scrutiny, especially after the publication of William Rees-Mogg's article 'The Right Moment to Change'.[13] But some felt that his last service to the party should have been to take the obloquy of a second defeat (in the election of March 1966), so that his successor could be launched into the battles of 1970–1 with an unblemished record. So his departure on 22 July 1965 came as a great shock to many by its suddenness (particularly to Elizabeth Home, who felt that her husband should have continued), including those who had urged his departure.

All political leaders are subject to critical comment, even (at times especially) from their own side. Arthur Balfour commented wryly that 'it is not a principle of the Conservative Party to stab its leaders in the back, but I must confess that it often appears to be a practice'.[14] Alec Home was no exception to this harsh truth, but his unique contribution was the formal system of electing the leader. He had emerged by 'the customary process of consultation'; the new rules ensured that the result reflected broadly what the parliamentary party wanted, according to an agreed format. Justice would be done, and would be *seen* to be done. Alec Home and Lord Blakenham, then Party Chairman, took careful advice from Dr David Butler of Nuffield College in December 1964 in establishing these rules, paying particular attention to Butler's point that 'where there is disagreement, there is the double problem, first of making the right choice and then of being seen to make the right choice'.[15] The leadership rules were Home's most important legacy to the Conservative Party and their influence is felt to the present day. In 1974, at the request of Edward Heath, he revised the original rules and the requirement that a candidate should receive '15 per cent more of the votes cast than any other candidate' to win on the first ballot became 15 per cent more of the *eligible* votes, a much stiffer hurdle which brought abstentions into the reckoning, a change immediately and unfairly dubbed by the political wags as 'Alec's revenge'. The new requirement weakened the position of a leader whose support was in decline, by making a second ballot more likely. Home intended the multiple ballots to serve different purposes. The first ascertained whether the Party wanted a change of leader. In 1989 when Sir Anthony Meyer challenged Mrs Thatcher, the answer was negative, though the result (sixty MPs failed to support her) came with the tacit rider that things might not be the same in a year's time. In November 1990, Michael Heseltine secured 152 votes against Mrs Thatcher's 204. With 16 abstentions Mrs Thatcher failed by 4 votes to satisfy the requirement of the revised 15 per cent hurdle. The second ballot then began the process of identifying the new leader. It did not follow that the MP who destabilised the incumbent would prevail. The fall of Mrs Thatcher took place under a general ruling Alec Home had drawn up a quarter of a century before.

Many threads came together in his twenty-one-month leadership of the Conservative Party. Despite his Etonian background he was the unexpected leader, the Bonar Law to Hailsham's Walter Long and Butler's Austen Chamberlain.[16] Like Balfour in 1902 and Callaghan in 1976, he had the misfortune to enter Downing Street as the sea-change in political attitudes was occurring after a long period of one-party domination. He appeared to be a continuation of Macmillan by other means, whereas when John Major became Conservative leader, it was as though there had been a change of government without an election. Such perceptions did not favour Alec Home, and his leasehold on the leadership began to run out. But he kept 'himself proof against calumny'[17] and Harold Macmillan felt that 'even the most bitter opponents or the most critical debaters found beneath an apparently meek demeanour something very firm and tough. He is well able to give a very good account of himself'.[18] It was a judgment which could stand as the embodiment of his career.

However many parallels may be drawn between that career and those of other Conservative leaders, in one thing Alec Home is unique and likely to remain so. There is no precedent for a prime minister disclaiming his peerage to enter the House of Commons, and it is now virtually impossible to envisage circumstances in which a hereditary peer (by the terms of the 1963 Peerage Act life peers may not disclaim titles voluntarily assumed) might give up his – or her – title to enter a formally structured ballot without a seat in the Commons. In the days before a formal party ballot was established, Lord Hailsham announced his intention to disclaim his peerage (a course he honourably followed, even after the premiership had eluded him), to become a candidate for the Conservative leadership. Alec Home gave notice of his intention to disclaim only after he had accepted the Queen's invitation to form an administration. 'He has got the loaves and fishes,' commented Lord Beaverbrook, wily mentor of Bonar Law and king-maker of Conservative leadership contests in 1911 and 1922. 'There is no stopping him now.'[19] And so it proved.

The appointment of the Earl of Home or – as the instrument of disclaimer described him – the Right Honourable Sir Alexander Frederick Douglas-Home, Knight of the Most Ancient and Most Noble

Order of the Thistle, to the position of Prime Minister and First Lord of the Treasury on 19 October 1963 ended an unprecedented eleven days in the history of the Conservative Party. The charges of class preference did not worry him as he took up the post; he felt it more damaging that the Conservative Party had no member of the Commons considered fit to succeed Macmillan. Indeed, after the appearance of Iain Macleod's *Spectator* review of Randolph Churchill's *The Fight for the Tory Leadership*, Home confided his doubts to Harold Macmillan. 'Alec (PM) rang up this morning & asked for advice as to how he should treat it,' wrote Macmillan in his diary on 18 January 1964. 'I thought he w[oul]d be wise to ignore the whole thing. Controversies of this kind (not principles but gossip & personalities) are like fires. They must be fanned if they are to harm.'[20]

Alec Home was born to great riches and an assured position in society. Yet in many ways he was an unconventional representative of the political landowning tradition. There are not many foreign secretaries who would have taken a Soviet counterpart, Andrei Gromyko, to dine at the Carlton Club or been greeted by the strains of the 'Eton Boating Song' in the Great Hall of the People's Republic of China. Nor was his early determination to enter public life the *noblesse oblige* of his class. He was genuinely ambitious in his own right, as he believed that there was a pragmatic purpose to politics, that individual people could make a difference and that the country could be improved by judicious actions. He also knew that politicians could not make that difference unless they controlled the levers of power. Macmillan described him as an 'urbane but resolute character – iron painted to look like wood'.[21] This modesty belied his determination.

In retirement, an elderly lady engaged him in conversation on the Berwick train, and said, 'My husband and I think it was a great tragedy that you were never Prime Minister.' 'As a matter of fact I was,' replied Home, before adding, 'but only for a very short time.'[22] In this, as in other things, he remained true to the end.

2

Border Ancestry and English Education

Journeying north past the site of the battle of Flodden at Branxton Hill and through the Northumberland village of Cornhill the traveller comes to an old toll bridge over the River Tweed which marks the border between England and Scotland. For ninety years after it was opened in 1766 marriages were celebrated at its northern gate; peaceful events in an area known for its centuries of strife. Sir Walter Scott chronicled its warlike character:

> Come from the hills where the hirsels are grazing,
> Come from the glen of the buck and the roe;
> Come to the crag where the beacon is blazing,
> Come with the buckler, the lance and the bow.
> Trumpets are sounding,
> War steeds are bounding,
> Stand to your arms then, and march in good order,
> England shall many a day
> Tell of the bloody fray,
> When the Blue Bonnets came over the Border![1]

Nor was the traffic all southwards. On many occasions the marauding armies of England crossed the ford, following in the footsteps of Edward I in 1296. Today the bridge, over which Robert Burns entered England in 1787, is one of the gentler crossing-points into Scotland. The pilfering borderers are long gone, and spoils are no longer for the picking, but military traditions live on in the town where General Monk raised the Coldstream Guards in 1659. At the eastern approaches of Coldstream a tall column stands as a monument to the political dynasty of Charles Marjoribanks, MP for neighbouring Berwick. Coldstream today is a quiet market town, content as a staging post on the journey north, where the lorries rumble through on their way to Edinburgh. To the north-west, the traveller passes the entrance to the Hirsel estate, associated with another and more famous political name than Marjoribanks, and it is to the Hirsel that local horsemen ride, following the Coldstreamer, young and old alike, to drink the stirrup cup during Civic Week in August, one of the annual rituals and traditions of the Border town. On another day there is a ride-out for a service of remembrance on the site of the Battle of Flodden.

The name hirsel (as used by Scott) derives from an agricultural term denoting particular areas where sheep are grazed. An estate has been on this land from the distant time when Hirsel Law, the hill north-west of Hirsel House, was first occupied, a prehistoric ring enclosure on its summit. In the twelfth century the estate was owned by the Dunbar family, when the rents of the 'Herishille', including one carucate of land (approaching a hundred acres), were given as part of a foundation grant to the Cistercian Priory of Coldstream in 1166. In 1611 the Home family first came into ownership of the estate when it was sold by Sir John Kerr to Alexander, 6th Lord Home. Before that they had lived at Hume Castle, some eight miles from the Hirsel, now a picturesque ruin on the tourist trail. In 1621 the Barony of Hirsel was granted to James, 2nd Earl of Home, and in 1640 his son James, the 3rd Earl, brought his new bride, Lady Jean Douglas, to live at Hirsel House, where the Homes have lived ever since. On 7 November 1974, Alec Douglas-Home incorporated the name into his life peerage, when he became Baron Home of the Hirsel of Coldstream.

Hirsel House, on rising ground beyond Hirsel Lake, is a long, exposed building that has undergone many changes. The original house was extended in the eighteenth century and Regency builders later added a third storey. Lutyens was asked to redesign it in 1893 and a model still exists of his grandiose scheme, which he later said was the most interesting architectural problem he had ever faced.[2] Nothing came of these plans, but other architects added a Victorian wing. At the same time Alec Douglas-Home's grandmother arranged for the building of a private chapel, which was still in use in 1951 at the time of his father's funeral. In the 1950s these Victorian accretions were smoothed away and the private chapel demolished. Not all these changes were easily accomplished; Home admitted after some unsatisfactory building work, 'I should never have trusted that architect, his eyebrows weren't symmetrical' – one of the few occasions when his native shrewdness betrayed him. When Neville Chamberlain came to the Hirsel in October 1938 to rest after the Munich agreement, the sight of grazing sheep met his eyes each morning from the large drawing-room window. 'It is very pleasant', he wrote to his sister Ida, 'in the delightful sitting room allotted to me, with its wide window looking down over green lawns and fields dotted with the big Cheviot sheep and then up again to the corner of a lake backed by high dark woods. There is a strong wind blowing but there are gleams of sun and there is a cheerful air about the place.'[3] The bracing climate was part of the childhood memory of a generation of Homes.

The family name derives from Home in Berwickshire. Although a charter of 1138 records the Home name from Cospatrick and Dunbar stock, and various ancestors were described as being 'of Home', the exact pedigree begins with Sir John Home, father of Sir Thomas Home of that ilk, acquiring the Barony of Dunglass in East Lothian in February 1385 through his marriage with Nichola, heiress of the Pepdie family. From all accounts the family fitted well into the company of marauding brigands and chieftains in a bloody era of Scotland's stormy history. 'Bred to war' was Scott's description of the Borderer: 'He knew the battle's din afar, And joyed to hear it swell.'[4]

One battle fought afar was Verneuil in France in 1424 during the Hundred Years War, in which Sir Alexander Home (the great-grandson of Sir John) was killed fighting in alliance with the French against the English. His son, also Sir Alexander, was ambassador to England in 1459 and was created a Lord of Parliament as the 1st Lord Home in the peerage of Scotland on 2 August 1473. He founded the Collegiate Church of Dunglas in 1450, was twice married and was succeeded by his grandson, Alexander, the 2nd Lord Home, who was also twice married. His first marriage to Isabel Douglas was annulled on grounds of consanguinity; by his second wife, Nichola Ker of Samuelton, he had seven children, two of whom, Alexander (the 3rd Lord) and William, were executed in October 1516 in the confused political situation after Flodden. Though of no lasting strategic importance, Flodden confirmed the English in European eyes as a front-rank power. During the 1950s, when Alec Home was Minister of State at the Scottish Office and the question of Scottish Home Rule was high on the political agenda, Flodden was a past the Scots wished to expunge, but in the highly charged atmosphere of the England versus Scotland football internationals, the banners unfurled on the terraces with the mournful and admonitory slogan 'Remember Flodden' had an honoured place.

Alexander, the 3rd Lord, was joint leader of the van at Flodden with the Earl of Huntly ('many a rugged Border clan, With Huntly, and with

Home' in Scott's words). His marauding raids into Northumberland from Hume Castle led to Henry VIII's sending a retaliatory force northwards in September 1513. The Scottish vanguard took the full weight of the English onslaught by the Earl of Surrey's flank, Lord Home destroying his English opponents. It was the second phase of the battle that led to controversies. In the mists of that September day on the slopes of Branxton Hill, the Earl of Huntly sent for Home's forces to counter the second English attack. But Lord Home had taken his men back to secure the crossing at the Tweed for the Scottish army, and his forces thus survived the slaughter which cost James III of Scotland his life: 'Where's now their victor vanward wing, Where Huntly, and where Home?' In Flodden mythology, Home was written down as a deserter and the lament for the flowers of the field who fell that day resonated down the years.[5]

After Flodden the 3rd Lord Home, as one of the surviving commanders, embraced the English interest against the Regent, Albany. Three years later, visiting the court in 1516, retribution followed. Alexander was arrested with his brother William and arraigned at a hastily arranged trial; his castles and territories had already been seized by Albany. On 8 October the two brothers were executed in Edinburgh and their heads put on public display at the Tollbooth. Their titles and estates were forfeited, although these were restored six years later to George, the 4th Lord, who also died violently, just before the battle of Pinkie in 1547. Alexander, the 5th Lord, was a supporter of Mary, Queen of Scots. For this he too was convicted of treason and in 1573 the lands and titles were forfeited once more.

The 6th Lord, another Alexander, was of special significance. When James VI of Scotland became James I of England in 1603, Alexander travelled south with him, became a privy councillor and trusted adviser and married into the English aristocracy by taking as his second bride Mary Sutton, eldest of the daughters of the 9th Lord Dudley. The union of England and Scotland was established and the turbulent era of Border reivers came to an end. 'The moss-trooper's occupation was gone', wrote G.M. Trevelyan, 'he yielded place, on the moors that had known him, to the shepherd, who could now drive the flocks in security to the very ridge of the Cheviots.'[6] It was the era of Shakespeare's great tragedies in the London playhouses, and of particular relevance to the new political age was *Macbeth*, a play which reflected the Scottish ancestry and political concerns of the new monarch. Like Shakespeare's King Duncan, King James was benevolently generous to his loyal supporters: 'Signs of nobleness, like stars, shall shine/On all deservers.'[7] Prominent among the new creations, on 4 March 1605 (though some records give the year as 1604), was the 5th Lord's son, Alexander, now 1st Earl of Home, Lord Dunglass and Baron of Jedburgh, in the peerage of Scotland, 'with remainder to his heirs male whatsoever'. The Border warriors had become part of the new nobility and political ruling establishment.

Not for nothing had the Border ballads rung with titles such as 'The Lament of the Border Widow' and 'Northumberland Betrayed by Douglas'; the ballads reflected the harsh internecine quarrels and perpetual feuding of the reivers and looters with England over the 'debatable lands'.[8] In these conflicts the ancient family of the Douglases, with whom the Homes were to be linked by marriage in 1832, played a prominent role. The estates of the Douglas and Home families lay in both the west and east of lowland Scotland. Although in Alec Home's time (and that of his grandfather and father) the principal seat was listed in *Debrett's Peerage* as the Hirsel, earlier generations saw Douglas, with ten times the acreage of the Hirsel, as the centre of the family's activities. Indeed it was Douglas which provided Alec Dunglass with the geographical springboard for his entry into politics. The medieval village of Douglas, about thirty miles south of Glasgow, took its name from its most famous family. The name Douglas derives from the Gaelic *dubhghlais*, meaning 'black water', an apt description of Douglas Water which borders the western side of the village.

Black is also the epithet associated with the most famous of the early Douglases, Sir James the Good, who slaughtered a congregation of English in twelfth-century St Bride's Church on Palm Sunday in 1307. The family, like the church, dated from the twelfth century, but Black Douglas was the first to rise to national prominence. Douglas Castle (now a ruin)[9] was the family seat and it was to rid the castle of the occupying English that Black Douglas attacked them while they worshipped. History records that his forces then devoured the meal prepared for the English at the castle. Scott, a sure guide to this stormy period, based his portrait of Castle Dangerous on this Lanarkshire citadel and his poem *Marmion* inspired the name Douglas in Sir Arthur Conan Doyle's *The Valley of Fear*. Black Douglas was a doughty fighter in the armies of Robert the Bruce; he met his death at the hands of the Moors in Spain in 1330, while taking the heart of Robert the Bruce to the Holy Land. His body was brought back to Douglas, where his own heart now lies in a heart-shaped casket in the chancel of Old St Bride's with the remains of other kinsmen.

His death marked the beginning of a period when the Douglases, their line reinforced by well-chosen marriages, became one of the most influential families in Scotland. A fourteenth-century saying was that 'nae man was safe in the country unless he was a Douglas or a Douglas's man.' Another Douglas of that era invited his neighbours to dine and then negotiated for the transfer of their properties to his name. Those who refused were hanged from a tree by the castle windows. As a boy, Alec Home dined off a sideboard made from 'Hangman's Tree'.[10] As Foreign Secretary, Home once said that international diplomacy could not be run on the principle of people seizing what belonged to them in the thirteenth century, adding that if that were the case it would suit himself admirably – a recognition that at times more can be gained by levity than solemnity.[11]

In this Border world the Homes and Douglases played different roles, although both were more concerned with the broader national scene than local family feuding. The Homes were the agents of order, as Wardens of the Eastern marches, pouring what oil they could on troubled waters, often in league with their English counterparts. The Douglases were the scourge of the English. When Alec Home took the Gromykos to Robert Bolt's play, *Vivat Vivat Regina*, the story of Mary Queen of Scots and Rizzio, Gromyko asked in the interval if he were not now in very dangerous company. 'Did I not hear Mary Stuart say, as the dagger went into Rizzio, "And you, Douglas, too?"'[12] For Gromyko, Home was always an uneasy combination of the 'Black' and 'the Good'. 'After talking to him for a while, one realised that something did not quite match his moderate manner,' he recalled. 'Resting now on one leg, now on the other, he would insist – quietly, of course – on expounding his ideas, without stopping, through to the bitter end. If he was obliged to give his partner in conversation a break, he would just be waiting for his side of the tournament to begin again.'[13] He was not alone in finding that there was a Douglas and a Home side to the Border Scot. Alec Home succinctly summed up the differences when he wrote, 'The Douglases had a habit of taking what they wanted, the Homes of conserving what they had got.'[14]

Only in 1832, the year of the Great Reform Bill, in which another of Alec Home's ancestors, Lord Durham, was a prime mover, did the Douglas and the Home families unite by marriage. The intervening years for both families had seen their dramas, none more so than the eighteenth-century dispute over the Douglas succession, beside whose complexities the War of the Spanish succession paled into insignificance. The case hinged on whether the Lady Jane Douglas of the day produced legitimate male twins in Paris at the age of fifty-three, a case that went through the Scottish courts, eventually being decided on appeal in the House of Lords against the Duke of Hamilton, who would otherwise have inherited the Douglas lands and possessions. The feud between the Hamiltons and the Douglases ended only when Alec Home's father, who had succeeded to the Earldom on 30 April 1918, invited the then Duke of Hamilton to Douglas Castle after the Great War.

The line of the Earldom of Home dated from the reign of James I. James, the 2nd Earl, who succeeded his father in 1619, died without issue in 1633. There was much dispute as to the succession and James, the 3rd Earl, received full recognition of his title only in 1636, with new letters patent, with remainder to heirs male granted. The 3rd Earl fought on the Royalist side in the Civil War, with the result that his estates were seized by the Cromwellians; they were restored in 1660. The 3rd Earl occupies a unique place in that his three sons, Alexander, James and Charles, became successively 4th, 5th and 6th Earls. Alexander was a member of Charles II's Privy Council. He died childless as did his younger brother, James. Political considerations came to the fore again with Charles, the 6th Earl, who opposed the Act of Union and was imprisoned in Edinburgh Castle in 1678, as was his son Alexander, the 7th Earl, a representative peer for Scotland, at the outbreak of the rebellion in 1715, until released by the revival of Habeas Corpus the following year.

The 8th Earl, also Alexander and a representative peer for Scotland, was a Hanoverian and fought for the King against Bonnie Prince Charlie in the 1745 war. Alexander, the 9th Earl, was an Anglican clergyman, the only Home to take holy orders. The 10th, yet another Alexander, was the eldest son of his third wife. With his marriage in 1798 to Elizabeth, second daughter of the Duke of Buccleuch and Queensberry, and an inheritance from his mother, the fortunes of the Home family improved materially. To succeed to this inheritance the 10th Earl changed his surname by royal licence to Ramey-Home, and it was with the birth of his son, Cospatrick Alexander, in October 1799, that the modern threads of the Home lineage are discernible. Cospatrick Alexander, the 11th Earl, married Lucy Elizabeth, granddaughter and heiress of Lord Douglas, in 1832. This has been called 'the most significant event in Home history'.[15]

The importance of the 11th Earl's life and career lay in public service. Alec Home's great-grandfather's career resembled his own, in that Cospatrick went south for education at Christ Church before serving in the Foreign Office. The 11th Earl moved from being an attaché in St Petersburg to an under-secretaryship in London in 1828, the first Home to hold government office. To English and political connections was added by marriage a vital third component; in 1859 Lady Home's mother died and the great wealth of the Douglas family devolved upon the Homes. This entailed properties (Douglas Castle being the foremost), with accompanying grouse moors, numerous farms and estates, in addition to the wealth of one of the richest families in eighteenth-century Scotland. On 11 June 1875 the 11th Earl was also created Baron Douglas of Douglas in the County of Lanark. In political terms wealth means independence, and three generations later this independence gave Alec Dunglass a detachment and objectivity which were the source of great political stability.

Alec Home's grandfather, Charles Alexander, succeeded to the title in 1881. Lord Lieutenant of Lanarkshire and Berwickshire, he continued the tradition of public service, though this did not embrace politics. For ten years (from the Golden to the Diamond Jubilees) he was an aide-de-camp to Queen Victoria. These were the years when the Hirsel 'ran on wheels greased with gold'.[16] A private chapel was built on the north side of the house, and red stone stables, crowned with a clock-tower, were built just north of Hirsel Lake for the Earl's thirty-two horses. Almost as many gardeners were employed for the estate's 3000 acres. Including Douglas in Lanarkshire, the 12th Earl owned over 100,000 acres and was the twenty-fifth largest landowner in the country: land income alone brought in £56,000 a year. Each August a private railway train took the entire household to Douglas for the grouse shooting, an annual ritual with carefully guarded traditions and an atmosphere of complex formality, family prayers and footmen. This Edwardian atmosphere has largely vanished, though it was recreated in L.P. Hartley's *The Go-Between* and Isabel Colegate's *The Shooting Party*. Alec Home spent his childhood in this world, not only at Springhill and the Hirsel but with other families in Scotland and farther afield. He met many famous figures at the Hirsel; Douglas Haig from nearby Bemersyde and Lord Robert Cecil, with their talk of the First World War and the League of Nations. The Homes were welcome guests at St Paul's, Walden Bury, where David Bowes-Lyon and his sister Elizabeth were their friends from early childhood.

Grandfather Alexander was the first Douglas-Home, adding the name Douglas to the family surname to honour the 1875 Barony of Douglas. This hyphen was accompanied by a new family motto. The motto of the Homes had been 'A Home, a Home, a Home'; that of the Douglases 'Jamais arrière'. Now came 'True to the end', which was carved in stone over the gateway to the new stables. The 12th Earl had four children, a son (Alec Home's father) and three daughters, by his wife Maria (May), only daughter of a naval officer, Captain Charles Conrad Grey.

Those who knew Alec's father, Charles, the 13th Earl, remembered him for his virtuous qualities. He was, according to Jock Colville, 'as near to being a saint as any uncanonised human being'.[17] The impression was not one of meek naivety but of inner shrewdness and kindliness. 'The only thing I regret is that not enough has been made of your father, who bears quite a heavy responsibility for all this,' wrote Lord Boothby to Alec Home when he was appointed Prime Minister. 'My own father, a good judge, always said he was the nicest man he had ever known.'[18] One neighbour met him carrying a great bundle of sticks and firewood, while the poor woman he had relieved of the burden was taken home in the Earl's chauffeur-driven car.

Charlie, as he was known to the family, was a small, wiry figure, whose size was the only diminutive thing about him. Red-haired and loud of voice, he had the authority that came from force of personality. As was now becoming the family custom he was educated at Eton and later Christ Church, Oxford, taking up a groom and six hunters and spending his time on the hunting field in the season. A countryman at heart, he was never at ease in the bowler hat he wore on visits to Edinburgh or to London. He was of the generation that was permanently marked by the Great War, in his case in the Gallipoli campaign in which he served as a lieutenant-colonel in the Lanarkshire Yeomanry and was mentioned in despatches. It was in the last months of that traumatic conflict that he had succeeded to the Earldom. Other titles and honours followed in a fulfilled and generous life, but he was never a political figure. The political interest in the family lay with his wife, Lady Lilian, whose radicalism extended to the ballot box; it was not only in 1945 that she voted Labour.

The 13th Earl and Countess of Home had seven children: five sons (the brothers who 'knew which way the wind blew') and two daughters.

Alec, the future 14th Earl, was born in 1903. Bridget followed in 1905 and Henry Montagu, who found fame as the 'Bird Man' of BBC radio, was born in 1907. A second daughter Rachel, who married William Montagu Douglas Scott, son of the 7th Duke of Buccleuch, was born in 1910, and the pre-war family was completed by the arrival of William, the future playwright, in 1912. Two younger brothers arrived after the war: Edward Charles, wounded and taken prisoner by the Japanese in the Second World War, was born in 1920, and George Cospatrick in 1922. George was killed on active service with the RAF in Canada in June 1943, a few weeks short of his twenty-first birthday.

The Edwardian age into which Alec Douglas-Home was born was bounded by the death of Queen Victoria and the outbreak of the Great War. The highpoint of Empire – the Diamond Jubilee in 1897 – had passed and the Boer War was over. 'But in the years after the Boer War,' as James Morris has written, 'the ants began to stir.'[19] In the nine decades of Alec Home's life there were three profound changes in the economic and political pattern of Britain, with which his own life was closely bound. When he was born the House of Lords still provided half the Cabinet, and in the years before the Parliament Bill of 1911 Balfour could still boast that whoever was in office the Conservatives were in power. By the 1990s the convention was two peers in Cabinet: the Lord Chancellor and the Leader of the House of Lords. The Parliament Bills of 1911 and 1949 confirmed the House of Commons as the dominating chamber of Parliament.

The second great change was the transition from Empire to Commonwealth. When he was born Britain ruled over the greatest Empire the world had known; the process of decolonisation, with which he was intimately involved, was the accepted and necessary pattern. 'All my policy and all my acts tend to rivet the British rule more firmly on to India and to postpone the longed-for day of emancipation,' wrote the Viceroy of India, Lord Curzon, in the very week of Alec Douglas-Home's birth. 'I am an Imperialist, and Imperialism is fatal to all their hopes.'[20] The political realities had changed by the time Alec Home was Foreign Secretary, and so had the challenges, as he acknowledged when he wrote, 'Anyone can give a country independence without worrying about the result but if the aim is to launch a nation in which there will be law and order and tolerance and justice, a nation which is capable of surviving economically and will conduct its foreign relations according to the code of the good neighbour it all becomes much more complicated. I confess I am not satisfied with the answer that freedom is everything and the rest nothing.'[21]

The third great change, and this in the first twenty years of his life, was the dislodgment of the Liberals as the main party of opposition by the Labour Party. The first general election of Douglas-Home's life, the famous Liberal landslide of January 1906, seemed to presage an era of almost permanent Liberal government. But wiser and shrewder judges saw the real implications of the rise in Labour representation, from two seats in the Khaki election of 1900 to the combined fifty-three seats of the Labour Representation Committee and the trade-union-sponsored MPs, as a truer pointer to the future. 'I am profoundly interested in this new development,' wrote Arthur Balfour, 'which will end, I think, in the break-up of the Liberal Party, and, perhaps, in other things even more important.'[22]

The genesis of these three changes can be traced to the Edwardian age. 'Yes! the Age was passing!' observed John Galsworthy. 'What with this Trade Unionism and Labour fellows in the House of Commons, with continental fiction, and something in the general feel of everything, not to be expressed in words, things were very different.'[23] At the turn of the century, for instance, a London birth certificate was considered a desirable, if not essential, accompaniment to young landed heirs as they embarked on life's journey. So, rather in the manner that those who hoped their sons might play cricket for Yorkshire made sure that their wives gave birth in one of the three Ridings, Charlie Dunglass took the lease of a tall, imposing house, number 28 South Street, for his wife's first confinement, and it was here that Alec Douglas-Home was born. This Mayfair house, just off Park Lane, subsequently went through many different ownerships; it was a source of pleasure to its most famous inhabitant that in the 1960s it became the headquarters of the English Schools Cricket Association, one of whose meetings he attended on his sixty-third birthday, just before becoming President of the MCC. Such ironies and anniversaries amused Alec Douglas-Home, not least that 2 July 1903 also saw the birth at Appleton House, on the Sandringham estate, of Prince Alexander Edward Christian Frederick, the future King Olav V of Norway, whom he always referred to as his twin, to the delight of both men.

In the summer of 1903 the infant Alec was taken back to Springhill, where he spent the first fifteen years of his life, and where he lived after his marriage in 1936. The house, on rising ground above the River Tweed, had the happiest childhood memories for him, and indeed for his children, all of whom were born there. It was an idyllic place for young children; the river wound its way by the foot of the grounds, though its perilous currents and disguised dangers needed reassessing after each winter's travail. Respect for nature brought an awareness of its dangers: ten soldiers were once drowned attempting the shortest crossing during manoeuvres, just downstream from Springhill. The 'Big House', with Grandpapa Alexander, was just a short drive away, though access was more formal than in later generations. One of the earliest photographs of Alec is at the age of four, holding the hand of his grandfather, who seems stern and unbending in his Lord Lieutenant's uniform.

Life was ordered but it was not stern. Alec suffered none of the deprivations of a Churchill, brought up by Nanny Everest and a variety of schoolmasters, or a Curzon, with a governess such as Nurse Paraman. His father took him riding and encouraged him in country pursuits, for which he needed little prompting, either by his parents or by Miss Triplow, his governess from the age of five. He loved playing cricket on the Springhill lawns and had a voracious appetite for books of all kinds. Like many children of the Edwardian age he delved into the volumes of G.A. Henty, with their ochre-coloured covers. Kipling was a favourite, and he was an early devotee of detective stories. Sunday evenings were the time for religious instruction from his mother, and weekday mornings saw a sound grounding in Latin and Greek grammar from Miss Triplow as Ludgrove School loomed. What was instilled into him by his father was the doctrine that privilege brought responsibilities and that service to others was its own reward. Church was an important and central part of the week and each Sunday the family went to St Mary and All Souls, the Scottish Episcopal church on the Lennel Road east of Coldstream; the landmarks of family life were celebrated and commemorated there. The family was divided into pre-war and post-war offspring, so Alec had two spells of being the 'older' brother, first to Bridget, Henry, Rachel and William; later to Edward and George, born in 1922 when Alec (Lord Dunglass by then) was about to go up to Christ Church in his father's footsteps.

In many respects the Douglas-Home children had an isolated upbringing, living cocooned in their world, not lonely but self-contained. Alec spent many hours in boyhood learning the craft of the fisherman, and his first cast into the River Tweed caught an eight-pound salmon, the first of countless from this river over nine decades. He learned, in a Wordsworthian sense, 'to look on Nature' and his countryman's eye never left him. Still at the Hirsel are some of his nature and game books and early drawings of the birds that came in to nest at Hirsel Lake, as well as the faded crushings of butterflies and plants, named and noted in spidery hand. When Roy Plomley invited him on to *Desert Island Discs*, his chosen book was Bannerman's *History of British Birds* in twelve volumes. This love of the countryside was one of his major points of contact with Neville Chamberlain; the two relished spotting scaup ducks on the lake in St James's Park or green woodpeckers in the nesting box at Chequers.

In September 1913, a few weeks after his tenth birthday, his father took him south for his first term at Ludgrove School, then at New Barnet in Hertfordshire.[24] The last summer before going away to school had been spent at Douglas Castle in Lanarkshire, always a fixed point for the grouse shooting, though the uncertain political situation in 1913 led to a truncated season and a break in the normal rhythm.[25] This did not diminish the benign and unworried cheerfulness of his father, who was a great singer of hymns; his guests would hear the refrain break off ('Bright is the morning ... cock to the right') as the sport quickened. Thanks to Miss Triplow, Alec (and later his brother Henry) entered high into Ludgrove and Eton. Education at Springhill had been long mornings of grind, punctuated by intervals for rat-catching when Miss Triplow accompanied the boys into the fields with their Border terrier. Sport of a different kind was the great memory of Ludgrove days. The founding headmaster was Arthur Dunn, a famous amateur international footballer, and when Alec arrived the headmaster was the no less illustrious Corinthian sportsman G.O. Smith, who had played centre-forward for England and had scored a century for Oxford in the University match in 1896.

'Shall I tell him to mind his work, and say he's sent to school to make himself a good scholar?' pondered Squire Brown as Tom Brown set off for Rugby School. 'If only he'll turn out a brave, helpful, truth-telling Englishman, and a gentleman, and a Christian, that's all I want.'[26] Such values were certainly the fabric of Alec's childhood, and were reinforced by the experience of Ludgrove. Work and games had their place. Greek was in the hands of 'Bunco' Brown, who had written the school song:

> But we'll ever be true
> To the flag – white and blue.
> And the fair fame of Ludgrove we'll treasure,
> Play up for Ludgrove.

Alec played up for Ludgrove in football, and, more surprisingly for one brought up in Scotland's climate, as a cricketer. A former Kent cricketer, W.S. Bird, saw in Alec a bowler of talent and encouraged him to develop into an all-rounder. Mr Bird was killed in the war, the shadow of which lay heavily over Alec's time at Ludgrove. Not only was his father away at Gallipoli but the danger of war (as well as its excitement) was brought home vividly to the Ludgrove boys in 1916 when a Zeppelin appeared in the night sky over the school, only to crash in flames near Potters Bar.

Alec spent four fulfilled and happy years at Ludgrove and always retained an affection for the school. Few things gave him greater pleasure in the years of Cabinet office than going down to 'Wokingham' Ludgrove to play in the Fathers' Eleven against the boys, which he was still doing in his fifties. His schooldays confirmed his love of competitive games, particularly football and cricket. They also gave him a solid grounding in classics and literature, and an appetite for books of all kinds. Above all, the private school tradition of Edwardian England dealt in moral absolutes and Lord Dunglass was pleased to have the values of family life reinforced by the school. In 1917 Alec passed his Common Entrance into the Remove at Eton. 'This showed him to be academically bright without being a scholar,' wrote a later Ludgrove headmaster.[27] G.O. Smith wrote to Lady Dunglass, 'I am delighted about Alec and he deserves great credit for having worked with such keenness and perseverance. I shall miss him very much, but I hope he will be very happy and get on well at Eton in every way, which I am sure he will. Alec has won the racquet cup and fives cup, so is ending his career here in a blaze of glory.'[28]

In one respect Ludgrove could have delayed his progress, for by virtue of his age he should have gone to Eton in 1916.[29] Because of his skill at games, he was too valuable in Smith's eyes to be lost to Eton prematurely. Rather in the manner of the celebrated advertisement in the *Church Times* for a Somerset living ('Slow left arm bowler preferred') Ludgrove was unabashed in its motives. But in a hierarchical society such as Eton, he was at a disadvantage compared with many of his contemporaries, who had a head start in seniority. When he left Eton (on 1 August 1922) he was still only halfway up the list of the First Hundred, even though he was by then nineteen.[30] Sir Roger Cary takes up the story. 'What happened to Alec was this. With almost criminal selfishness G.O. Smith kept Alec on at Ludgrove until he was fourteen, simply to help Ludgrove at cricket. It was amazing ... that he ...

recovered from this handicap ... to become Captain of his House and get as high up in school order as the First Hundred. No sludge in brain power and adaptability here. Hardly surprising that he again should have broken through later to become Prime Minister. The two feats have much in common.'[31]

The young Alec had been destined for Eton from the start. There was no question, as with his contemporaries Cyril Connolly and Eric Blair (George Orwell), of attempting a scholarship examination at Wellington first.[32] It was the natural progression. Eton is one of the major strands in Alec Douglas-Home's life. His father was educated there, as were his brothers, his own son and grandsons.

The Hon. Alexander Frederick Douglas-Home (as he appeared on house lists) was taken to Eton by one of his younger aunts (his father was at the war and his mother in Scotland) on 3 May 1917. His address was registered as Lord Dunglass, Springhill, Coldstream, N.B.

In his first summer half, his housemaster was P.V. Broke, a King's Scholar at Eton in the 1870s, and now on the verge of retirement. Alec Douglas-Home's first months were thus something of a false start, so important is the presence and personality of the housemaster in the Eton system, which allowed baronial autonomy to the rulers of each little kingdom. The only advantage of arriving late was avoiding six months of mundane fagging. Edward Lyttelton, headmaster since 1905, had retired in 1916 and been succeeded by Dr Cyril Alington, headmaster of Shrewsbury School for the previous eight years. The new provost was M.R. James, an Eton luminary of the post-war period. In terms of personalities, 1917 was a good time to be entering the college.

'At Eton, the very stones cry out names,' wrote Grizel Hartley.[33] The stones which Alec Douglas-Home first encountered were those of Corner House, overlooking the rat-infested graveyard of the Chapel. The name they evoked was that of his housemaster, A.W. Whitworth, one of the great mentors of his life, and a friend for five decades. (One of the first letters he received on moving into Downing Street in October 1963 was from A.W.W. 'You started it all!' wrote the new Prime Minister in reply, still addressing Aymer Whitworth as 'My dear Tutor', 'Please be one of our first visitors in Downing Street.'[34]) Corner House had been in use as a boys' boarding house since 1596. It was not a welcoming environment, as one later housemaster recalled in 1952:

> The boys' side consisted mostly of Victorian additions built on by various occupants ... A narrow staircase with uneven wooden treads

> worn shiny, smooth and razor-edged by generations of boys led up to three boys' passages. There was little uniformity about either the passages or the boys' rooms. In parts the passages were broad; in other places they were so narrow that two people could pass only by turning sideways ... the appearance of the boys' side was mournful to a degree; in fact taken as a whole it looked like a slum tenement, with two dingy bathrooms with concrete floors at the end of the bottom and middle passages for the use of forty-one boys.[35]

Alec Douglas-Home lived there for four of his five Eton years. Despite the surroundings and the wartime conditions, he had happy memories of Corner House. 'I think one learned to see through shams', wrote Alec Home of his time there. 'It truly was a Pierian spring, at which one refreshed one's values, intellectual, aesthetic and moral.' Unlike many Eton houses, run by bachelor housemasters, Corner House was a family home, with Aymer Whitworth's two young sons very much part of the daily life. Whitworth had a great understanding of human nature, and especially of the young male going through 'the dark tunnel of adolescence', though this caused Alec Douglas-Home few traumas. The impression he made on his contemporaries was of unperturbed equanimity.

The summer of 1917 was a paradoxical interlude in Alec's life. His Eton career, particularly as a sportsman, had hardly begun and the initial loneliness had to be overcome by the resilience and adaptability of a lowland Scot in a strange and bewildering environment. 'I think one did feel, even as a lowland Scot, a sense of England. One felt a part of England. Eton has a southern English atmosphere about it.'[36] There was the contrast, too, between the experience of the evocative, historic surroundings – the grace of Lupton's Tower in School Yard, the ever-present silhouette of Windsor Castle, the arcane and esoteric games played on fields such as Agar's Plough, Mesopotamia, Sixpenny and Strawberry – and the daily reports of the slaughter at the Ypres Salient and Messine Ridge. As his first half came to an end, the news of Passchendaele was like gathering thunder in the benign summertime days of what Cyril Connolly called a Georgian Boyhood.

'Yet another Summer Half is before us and still the world is at war', ran an editorial, 'The Present School Time', in the *Eton College Chronicle*, regretting the fact that there would be 'no procession of boats' and 'no Eton & Harrow at Lords'.[37] It is all too easy to think of Eton, as George Orwell put it, as 'an atmosphere, as it were, of eating everlasting strawberry ices on green lawns to the tune of the Eton

Boating Song'.[38] The reality was more sombre. Younger masters had not yet come back from the war and some of the older generation were about to go into retirement. 'The years 1917 and 1918 were to prove dreary indeed,' Eton's most recent historian has written, 'and the boys often felt cold and hungry.'[39] Alec Douglas-Home's own memories of the food were far from happy: '... It was a fairly austere life, with rationing and all that sort of thing ... the food was disgusting. There was something called Miss Marten's pudding which I remember to this day. It consisted of cold suet and bacon fat. Can you imagine anything worse? You couldn't get it down at all, it was awful.' Despite such discomfort, he did not censure. 'But that wasn't the school's fault; it was just the situation that had to be coped with.'[40]

But there were more important things than food. Friendships were forged for a lifetime, not least with Aymer Whitworth. For many boys this tie with a master would have meant social ruin but, as Cyril Connolly famously pointed out, Alec Dunglass aroused no envy among his schoolfellows. The varied adult company at Springhill made Dunglass responsive and open in company, particularly with those who were open with him. One of his great characteristics was, after his father's manner, to look for good in everyone and to treat each person with unaffected courtesy. He found much goodness in Whitworth, whose talent for getting people to work together was one of his strongest traits.

Aymer Whitworth had implicit trust in Alec Dunglass's integrity and leadership potential. When a notorious bully, who was also the school boxing champion, proved an intractable and awkward member of the house, he turned to Alec to resolve the situation, for he knew that the boy in question would respond to Dunglass's moral pressure. 'He meant more than we can ever tell to me and countless others who were his pupils at Eton, and all our memories of him are happy,' wrote Lord Home when Whitworth died in June 1976. 'He really had a splendid life and faced old age as few are able to do. I think that schoolmastering in those days must have been fun and certainly he and his generation were a vintage lot. He always seemed to extract the maximum enjoyment from every situation in life.'[41]

Prominent among the 'vintage lot' of schoolmasters that Alec Home recalled fifty years on was his future father-in-law, Dr Cyril Alington, headmaster of Eton. Some boys saw Alington as cold and aloof, but conventions and expectations were different then and there is no doubting the impact he made, both on his colleagues and on the boys.

In the opening chapter of *Antic Hay* Aldous Huxley gives a memorable portrait of Alington preaching in Chapel. His evening sermons (like Dr Arnold, he was most imposing in the light of many candles) were particularly memorable, especially his well-timed extinguishing of the candles during the final sentence, as in '... And his name ... was Pontius Pilate'. On one occasion the Conduct of Eton (a priest who read the services in Chapel, now the senior chaplain) was asked to preach at Sandringham and in great concern consulted Alington on what level he should 'pitch' his sermon. 'Quite simple,' came the advice, 'treat it as though one was preaching to the junior boys in Lower Chapel, but with all the difficult bits left out.'

To many boys his fame resided in the fact that he still joined in games of rackets, cricket and fives. His great academic strength, though there were those who never saw him as a true scholar, was as a teacher of Latin prose. He was also very open-minded and liked the kind of philosophical arguments about Christianity that he had with A.J. Ayer. One small boy asked him once if there was a difference between God and the headmaster. 'Yes,' he replied, 'but it is not a difference that will concern you for the next five years.' Alington was also punctilious and in the then Eton manner called his pupils 'Mr'. After a birching, he once said, 'There are two types of argument in this world; one is *a priori* and the other is the one you've just had.' Above all, the Alingtons brought a family atmosphere to Eton; the boys were always welcome in the headmaster's house in the Cloisters, and it was here that Dunglass first met his future wife, whom he visited from Christ Church on festive days such as the Fourth of June. Sunday breakfasts were a special occasion, when Alington made seemingly arbitrary and inconsequential remarks. 'What do you think the prospects are for Nottingham Forest?' he would ask a classical scholar. On one occasion he was dining with Lionel Ford, his opposite number at Harrow, when Ford claimed that if the Duke of Wellington's elder brother had done better at Harrow the great Duke would have followed him there; in which case the Battle of Waterloo would have been won on the playing fields of Harrow. 'Lost, Lionel, lost', Alington replied.

His wife, Hester, was an integral part of the Eton scene in the early 1920s, both maternal and formidable. A daughter of the fourth Lord Lyttelton, she was the youngest of fifteen children. 'She was as good a human being as one could hope to meet,' wrote her half-nephew George Lyttelton. When he once said to her that he found it hard to see why people should believe in God, she replied, 'He certainly did make it very difficult, and at such moments one *mustn't worry* but go desperately on.'[42] She married Cyril Alington in 1904 and was the supporter and stay of his life and career, an example of the wife her daughter Elizabeth was to be for Alec Dunglass. The stories of her time at Eton are legion. When Gandhi came to talk to the Eton Political Society he brought with him his inseparable companion Miss Slade, who was discovered, ayah-like, sleeping across the threshold of the Mahatma's bedroom. Hester Alington surveyed the scene and Miss Slade was despatched to more decorous and comfortable sleeping arrangements with the insistent, 'No, my dear, not while I am a member of the Mothers' Union.'[43]

Many of the characteristics of his future in-laws rubbed off on Alec Dunglass in these formative years. The sense of integrity inherited from his father was reinforced, but also encouraged was an impish sense of humour and the knowledge that there were times for dignity, the importance of the sense of loyalty to family, church and institutions, and the excitements that come from myriad interests, whether the love of crosswords (where Alington solved *Times* crosswords, Alec Dunglass was later to set them), or the delights of travel. In their company, as well as that of Aymer and Alice Whitworth, Alec Dunglass experienced vicarious excellence.

He met excellence in others too. George Orwell's contemporaneous memory of the college had been of its snobbery and money-consciousness;[44] that such things did not occur to Dunglass did not mean they were non-existent, rather that his perspectives were different. Of all the post-war prime ministers, Home was the least pompous, the least self-important, the least prone to pronouncements on patrician values, and the most self-effacing. In a neutral way he was unselfconscious where matters of class were involved. He did not regard Eton with a critical eye; he was too concerned with its opportunities, and, unlike Orwell, he was not politically precocious. Interest in politics came later. In this he was more typical of the public schoolboy of his era, going out into the world with what E.M. Forster called the well-developed body, the fairly developed mind and the undeveloped, though not cold, heart. 'Some of them remain Old Boys and nothing else for the rest of their lives,' but this was never a Dunglass characteristic, golden though his schooldays were.[45]

The fairly developed mind was owing to a variety of complex and interesting personalities whom Alec Dunglass experienced in his five years at Eton, many of whom such as 'Tuppy' Headlam were guests at

Douglas. Headlam tutored Alec in the complexities of Dicey and the Constitution. Of uncertain temper, and at times pessimistic, he was a stimulating and witty figure who once began an early-morning tutorial with the declaration, 'I am told on good authority that there will shortly be an internecine struggle between the white races, the black races and the yellow races. My prayer is that we shall draw a bye in the first round.'[46] A.J. Gow, his Greek Tutor, was another Douglas guest, a man of great historic sense, who brought dead languages alive. Yet neither at Eton, nor later at 'The House' (Christ Church), could academic studies be seen as Alec Dunglass's priority, a characteristic common to many who were comfortably off in those days. His leisure was never a roaring twenties, Brideshead-type of abandonment (at Eton, for instance, he was Secretary of the Musical Society) but he certainly played hard. Cricket was one of his great loves. In a letter many years later to Sir William Becher, one of the stalwarts of the I Zingari cricket club, Alec Home refers to 'Scotland and cricket, the two loves of my life'.[47] Scotland had never been a noted cradle of cricketers (Douglas Jardine apart, and he was born in India), owing to the uncertain weather. Nevertheless, in the Borders a tradition of 'village' cricket was an important thread in Alec's early cricketing experience. There had been good coaches at Ludgrove, notably G.O. Smith, but Eton brought in some of the famous cricketers of the day as coaches, and there were matchless pitches to play on. Real canniness was instilled by the professionals, such as Yorkshireman Matt Wright, who considered it the greatest solecism for a batsman not to reach double figures after a quarter-hour at the crease. Once when Alec Dunglass (in his own words) had been 'scratching about' Wright reprimanded him, 'For God's sake, sir, if you must miss, do it in style.'[48] But the most influential of his coaches was another great Yorkshireman, George Hirst: 'Hirst was so determined that his pupils should succeed that he unconsciously breathed something of his own rare spirit into them and, time and time again, made them play better than they knew.'[49]

Throughout his life Dunglass set great store by the professionals in their field, and George Hirst was one of his first experiences of someone who was supreme in his field and could communicate his expertise without fuss. Alec was always a solid batsman, but Hirst brought on his bowling so that he became the invaluable all-rounder of the Eton eleven in the early twenties. He became a regular member of the team in 1921, playing in the seven-wicket victory match against Harrow on 8 and 9 July and scoring thirty in the first innings. The following year in a rain-affected draw he was top scorer and took four wickets for thirty-seven runs.

Dunglass had a good eye for all ball games and the game of Eton Fives became another of his enthusiasms. As with his cricket he rose to the top, representing the College in the undefeated First Pair for two years with Nico Llewelyn Davies. Contemporary reports are a microcosm of Alec's later career. 'Dunglass was full of promise' recorded the *Eton College Chronicle* in May 1921. 'He did the lion's share and never lost heart. More experience will teach him strategy.'

The pinnacle of an Etonian's career was membership of the Eton Society. Originally a debating society when it was founded in 1811, it took its name 'Pop' from the Latin *popina*, a pastry cook's shop, as the members first met in Mrs Hatton's cake shop in Eton High Street. A self-electing oligarchy with social privileges and disciplinary responsibilities (to be 'pop-tanned' was an awesome experience), they wore garish and multicoloured waistcoats which ensured they were instantly recognisable; a junior boy could be beaten for not knowing their names. 'At that time Pop were the rulers of Eton, fawned on by masters and the helpless sixth form', wrote Cyril Connolly.[50] Alec Dunglass moved smoothly to membership in July 1920, although elections normally went on for hours through successive ballots as the gathering of adolescent cardinals made or blighted the careers of their contemporaries. It was his first taste of *realpolitik*. A year later (the high point of his Eton career) Alec Dunglass was elected President of Pop, the equivalent of reaching the top of Disraeli's 'greasy pole'.

This could be a heady cocktail for the impressionable adolescent, but Alec was not that kind of person, though the position gave him immense power and prestige. Because so much of the school's life was run by the boys, with only an occasional touch on the tiller from Dr Alington and the housemasters, Alec Dunglass and his contemporaries in Pop had an immense training in taking decisions, leadership, guidance, and the need for justice. Power concentrated so firmly in youthful hands can lead to abuses of privilege and ritualised cruelty, or perhaps priggishness. Alec Dunglass, as Connolly and others have testified, avoided the Scylla and the Charybdis. When he reflected later on what Eton had given him, he listed independence, tolerance, self-discipline, responsibility, reticence and a sense of the fun of living; but above all 'a recognition that power and authority must be exercised with restraint'.[51]

The glittering prizes won by Alec Dunglass also came with a levelheadedness that made the summer of 1922 a truly golden time. In July Aymer Whitworth sent his last report on Alec in the customary Eton form of a private letter. 'I have never heard him grumble or criticise harshly anybody or anything since he came here and so he has been head of what I think has all the year been a very happy family.' He reported that his Captain of the House had 'sound ability quite enough to enable him with his other gifts to attain real success and power even in public life. But he is not at present ambitious and not inclined to go out and face storms from which he can stand aside.'[52]

After the customary summer shooting at Douglas, Alec Dunglass went up to Christ Church in October 1922. His arrival at Oxford coincided with the fall from power of Lloyd George, an event which barely impinged on Alec, though he welcomed Baldwin as a calming influence after the frenetic atmosphere of Lloyd George's last years. Strangely, Christ Church was never 'held against him' in later egalitarian times in the way Eton was, yet its traditions were as venerable, its wealth as secure and its exclusivity undoubted. The largest and one of the richest of the Oxford Colleges with a cathedral in its grounds, The House, as it is known, has always had a particular place in the Oxford collegiate system – something of the air of Eton-by-the-Cherwell, though this was by no means the whole picture. Its size meant that it had many different facets, though essentially there were two broad divisions: the impecunious undergraduates, frugal scholars (including those on closed scholarships from Westminster), and a larger category of well-off students, many of them scions of great aristocratic houses, who hunted and joined the Bullingdon.

But underneath the insouciant Brideshead atmosphere, Christ Church was a college where serious work was done and its proportion of Firsts was high. As with Eton, its main characteristic was its freedom. Roger Makins, one of Alec's Wykehamist friends, cannot remember his attending any lectures at all, but tutorials with Keith Feiling, biographer of Neville Chamberlain, and J.C. Masterman were experiences Alec Dunglass long remembered. Both men became his lifelong friends. Masterman guided Alec Dunglass in his course of seventeenth- and eighteenth-century European history and his special period of the reign of William and Mary. Before final schools in the summer of 1925 Masterman took A.L. Rowse and Makins on a vacation reading course. Alec Dunglass was not invited. Masterman knew that Dunglass would not be a candidate for high academic honours and in addition he was suffering from a debilitating and mysterious illness he could not shake off, which coincided with final schools and accounted, according to Masterman, for Alec Dunglass's poor degree. 'The third class he took in his final year is an entirely false rating. He was ill for half his time at Christ Church, and what he did produce never fell short of a second,' Masterman recalled in 1973. 'He would not in my opinion have got a first. He had too many interests. Nor did it really matter to him what sort of academic label he would bear on leaving Oxford.'[53] One of Alec Dunglass's regrets was that he did not work harder at Oxford; the truth is that there were just too many other things to occupy his time.

Even for an Etonian, Christ Church was an emancipation and a reshuffling of the pack of friendship. The Etonian circle had new figures such as Peter Acland, who recalled their friendship over seventy years. 'We were at Eton at the same time but I did not get to know him well there except to a minor extent on the cricket field. He came up to Christ Church in 1922 – one year later than myself and it was there that cricket brought us together ... The main things about Alec then as now were his absolute trustworthiness, his complete lack of side and pomposity, his charming manners and his sense of humour, his kindness and consideration for others.'[54]

To his Etonian circle of friends he added an important Wykehamist strain, which included Roger Makins and Evelyn Baring. He lived in Peck Quad, a member of the 'Peck Gang' with Makins and Alan Lennox-Boyd, a future Cabinet colleague, and Dick Heathcoat-Amory. Over seventy years later Roger Makins said, 'We really did know how to enjoy ourselves.'[55] One of the distinctive characteristics of the Peck Gang was a love of practical jokes, and a result was the Coconut Cricket Club, the principal rule being that a coconut should be bowled as the first ball of every innings. With Heathcoat-Amory, Baring and Makins as fellow founders, Dunglass was also a member of the Aspidistra Society, which required members to destroy immediately any aspidistra encountered, and post the evidence to all other members. 'I and many of my friends seem in retrospect rather immature compared with modern youth,' wrote Roger Makins in an introduction to his diary. An entry for 19 September 1925, describing a birthday party at Micklem Hall, belies his intellectual achievements. Suffering from 'flu, he wrote, 'I felt much worse, but was determined to stay for the birthday party in Micklem. Went and sat between Alec Dunglass and Dick Amory. Alec also had the 'flu. It was a pouring wet night and the champagne was so nasty that it was almost undrinkable. We sat for hours at table and nobody got drunk so the conversation never became general ... then

Dick and I and members of the Society for the destruction of Aspidistras destroyed some with such effect that we covered another room with several inches of mud.'[56] It was a carefree world of hunting, cricket, bridge and champagne, though racing was becoming one of Dunglass's interests at this time. Having heard the scriptural phrase 'and they sent him bread from Heaven' at a service in Christ Church Cathedral, Dunglass and Makins took this as an indication that Manna would win the Derby in 1925, which it promptly did. It was not, however, a world in which women played any part. Like many public schoolboys of his (and later) generations, Alec Dunglass compartmentalised his friendships. Shooting parties at Douglas or house parties at neighbouring grand houses were where the sexes mingled, not at Somerville or Lady Margaret Hall.

With Roger Makins he attended meetings of the Raleigh Club and was a member of the Canning and Carlton, and the Chatham Club at Magdalen, all of which gave him the opportunity to hear important political figures; his political interest was beginning to stir. After he had gone down at the end of the Trinity term 1925, he returned to Christ Church that autumn and revisited the political clubs. In some ways the six months after he had formally gone down were among the most valuable of his time at Oxford. He had met Lord Robert Cecil at the Hirsel and was particularly drawn to the question of the League of Nations, which was Leo Amery's subject at one meeting of the Raleigh Club, as Roger Makins recalled. 'Went to hear Amery ... He pointed out how apt the League of Nations was to take the line of least political resistance irrespective of the pure justice of the case.'[57] He met all manner of political figures during those months, including Philip Kerr, John Buchan and Sir John Simon.

Surprisingly for one who was beginning to take an interest in political developments, the Union Society was not a priority. For many aspiring politicians the Union was the cradle of their hopes and the focus of their activities. Alec Dunglass's indifference to it was shared by Lord Rosebery, Anthony Eden, Clement Attlee and Harold Wilson.

Alec Dunglass's Bachelor of Arts was not his final degree from Oxford. On 22 June 1960, just before taking over as Foreign Secretary, he received an Honorary DCL in Harold Macmillan's first Encaenia as Chancellor of the University. It was the culmination of his association with Oxford, an institution for which he always retained a deep affection. Looking back on his days at The House, he felt he had been introduced to civilised values and that, living and working in the college, he had assimilated something of the traditions of history and the great men of the past. The festal light in Christ Church Hall burnished the portraits of the House's long line of Prime Ministers. When Dunglass left Oxford, the next Christ Church Prime Minister, Anthony Eden, was about to set his foot on the parliamentary ladder as PPS to the Foreign Secretary, Sir Austen Chamberlain. Ten years later Eden would be Foreign Secretary and Alec Dunglass PPS to Austen Chamberlain's younger half-brother, Neville. As Alec Dunglass went out into the world at the end of his formal education, none of his contemporaries would have guessed that the diffident Scottish borderer would become the thirteenth Prime Minister from Christ Church.

3

First Steps in Parliament

When Alec Dunglass left Oxford, one career option was immediately available. His father, who was fifty-two in 1925, would have been happy for him to take over the management of the Hirsel and Douglas estates. The 12th Earl's death in 1918, eight years after Lloyd George's People's Budget had been implemented, entailed heavy death duties, which meant artefacts had to be sold and outlying estates dispersed. Indeed, Douglas Castle was rented out for shooting for three years after the end of the Great War and the growing family holidayed at a house they took in Dunbar. Arthur Balfour lived at neighbouring Whittingehame and Alec Dunglass played golf with him occasionally at North Berwick. There were also tennis parties with Balfour and the Dugdales, his nieces. Kay Tennant, daughter of Sir Charles Tennant and half sister of Margot Asquith, was in this circle too. Later as the wife of Sir Walter Elliot and eventually as Baroness Elliot of Harwood, the first lady peeress in 1958, 'K' Elliot was to be an important strand in Scottish Unionist politics and in Alec Douglas-Home's life.[1]

It was clear that the demands of estate management were going to be very different in the post-war world and, as both Douglas and the Hirsel had professional agents, Alec Dunglass was determined to experience the wider world first. He did not intend to bury himself in estate work at the age of twenty-three; such responsibilities would be shouldered in due course. Nevertheless, in the first two years after Oxford, he familiarised himself with the particular problems and possibilities of agricultural development, especially in the realms of hill farming and forestry. This was characteristic of his initial approach to many later political jobs, particularly his work at the Scottish Office and the Commonwealth Relations Office. He believed in listening to the experts in their field – he was a good listener – and liked learning from those 'on the ground', whether Galloway sheep farmers, his father's ghillie, civil servants in St Andrew's House or district commissioners in the Central African Federation.

There were no pressures, financial or otherwise, to take up an immediate career. After Oxford he took two years off and these were the years when he first travelled abroad. His first major journey abroad was in a cricketing context, when he was invited by Pelham ('Plum') Warner to join an MCC side on a three-month tour of Argentina, Chile, Peru and Uruguay. At this time Dunglass was seen as one of the 'coming men' of the amateur game, then a far more prominent part of the cricketing scene. His photograph began to appear in publications such as *The Cricketer*; he became a member of the MCC in 1926 and was a natural choice for a touring party which included England players such as G.O. ('Gubby') Allen and J.C. White, as well as county and army players. At this time he was an active playing member of many clubs, from the local Coldstream side to the Eton Ramblers, the Free Foresters and I Zingari. All were institutions to which he devoted many active years. He served for eleven years from 1976 to 1987 as governor of I Zingari and was a contributor to its published history.[2] In all these roles he revelled in the opportunities such services gave for encouraging the next generation of cricketers with all their innocent gaucheries.[3]

The visit to South America was an unmissable opportunity for a twenty-three-year-old, known as a useful bowler and stylish stroke player, to see parts of the world known only to intrepid travellers. He travelled to Argentina in December 1926, a seventeen-day voyage of nearly 7000 miles, and arrived in Montevideo just before Christmas. The first match of the tour took place on Christmas Day and Dunglass contributed to the MCC victory by taking four wickets for twenty-six runs. Illness, a recurrent worry of his life – in this case a grumbling appendix – prevented him from playing the middle games, but he finished the tour successfully and by March 1927 was back at Coldstream. Though he developed a taste for travel that was never to leave him, he did not forget that his family life would always be based in the Borders. Edinburgh, where his father was chairman of the British Linen Bank, was another focus, only an hour or so from the Hirsel, and at this time he became a member of the New Club, where his portrait now hangs. The capital city of his native land was connected in so many ways with his ancestry: Moray House in the Canongate, near his beloved Canongate Kirk, was built by the Dowager Countess of Home in 1628.[4]

He and his brother Henry walked many miles over the Douglas

estate, and the game books record the routines of the August days and the labours of Telfer, the head gamekeeper, with his lieutenants, Carr and Bell. A 1926 game book contains the precise paintings with which Alec Dunglass decorated the lists of grouse, snipe, partridge, woodcock and mallard.[5] David Bowes-Lyon, who had been one of his close Eton friends, came from Glamis, and others whom he had met in a cricketing context, such as Cosmo Crawley, became regular house party guests. Henry tended to bring in friends from the point-to-point world and in due course his younger brothers brought schoolfriends from Ludgrove and Eton. The Whitworths continued to be guests with Aymer Whitworth's talents for getting people to work together extending to organising the stragglers on the moors, and members of Dr Alington's family visited too. Elizabeth Alington was a friend of Alec's sister, Rachel, who invited her to both the Hirsel and Douglas. Nearby Lanark races became a focal point and one of the first photographs of Alec Dunglass and Elizabeth Alington is at the racecourse. Where Alec painted the wild life with sensitivity, his youngest brother George was a talented photographer and much of the pre-war world of Douglas and the Hirsel, particularly the topography and the wildlife, is recorded in albums.[6] With his sisters' friends and suitors among the varying population of house guests, there was a cosmopolitan and youthful flavour to the long Douglas summers, which the former factor recalled as 'a haven of peace and contentment'.[7]

If Douglas was the place for shooting, the Hirsel (with the Tweed at hand) was where Alec Dunglass honed his skills at fishing. As a child he had fished for perch in the lakes at Hirsel and Douglas, but the Tweed formed for four miles the southern boundary of the estate at Hirsel, which offered endless possibilities for salmon fishing in the spring and autumn. Even in February and November rich pickings were possible: on 13 November 1926, before the river rose to flood, Alec landed nine 20lb salmon in a morning. 'My most exciting day', he claimed.[8]

The Hirsel was the scene of many memorable days, such as the belated celebrations of his twenty-first birthday before the start of his final year at Oxford. The actual birthday on 2 July had seen family celebrations in London; the September festivities at the Hirsel were a gathering for the tenant communities from the various Home estates. Lunch was served in marquees (Alec Dunglass consumed two of his favourite Scottish delicacies that day, salmon and whisky) and various addresses and presentations followed, including a pair of fine guns from the tenants. A tree was planted to the north of the house.

Local roots had always been important to his father and the pattern was repeated with his son. It was a natural consequence of the position the family occupied in two distinct counties and communities. In 1927 Alec Dunglass began to take up activities in both Lanarkshire and Berwickshire. The links were threefold: literary, religious and military, in addition to his increasing political commitments at local Party functions. No self-respecting Scot living near Alloway could neglect the presence of Robert Burns. Patronage of village Burns' clubs satisfied the innate Scottish sense of celebration, ritual and national identity. The anniversary of Robert Burns's birth on 25 January 1759 was always an important day in Dunglass's calendar. As Foreign Secretary, his knowledge of Burns, 'the Heaven-taught ploughman', impressed Gromyko and Russian delegations at the United Nations. The author of the brotherly sentiments of the ballad 'For A' That and A' That' had cult status in the Soviet Union and the Foreign Secretary could match quotations by many of the Russians.

Church obligations were also important. The Boys' Brigade occupied much of his time, especially in Lanarkshire, where he became president of the West of Scotland district in the 1930s when his father was beginning his term as national president. The Brigade occasionally held parades at the Hirsel and the Boys' Club of the Canongate Kirk in Edinburgh came for summer camps, one of the last things which Alec's father presided over before his death in July 1951. Their next visit was to sing the 23rd Psalm at his funeral. Alec Dunglass continued links with the Canongate Kirk over many years and 'his interest in the Boys Club in Canongate did not diminish when he became Prime Minister'.[9]

His father also encouraged him to join the Lanarkshire Yeomanry; he became a lieutenant in 1924 and was promoted captain in 1928. The most dramatic event in his time as a Territorial officer was in 1926 when the regiment was called out during the General Strike, a formative political experience for many of the post-war generation, and one which focused Dunglass's mind on the problems of the west of Scotland at a time of industrial decline and unrest. Lanarkshire was an area of acute unemployment, particularly in steel and coal, and many of the thousands of unemployed had not worked for ten years. The human misery this represented made a profound impression upon him. In a speech in the House of Commons on 22 July 1936 Aneurin Bevan berated Dunglass, by then MP for Lanark, for speaking of the 'family instinct and pride of the working people of this country', as though he was disqualified by his social position from knowledge of or comment on what Disraeli had called 'the Two Nations'.[10] The truth is more complex.

Alec Dunglass's upbringing was privileged even by the standards of the upper classes of the time, but that did not mean he was ignorant of or insensible to the conditions of life. Douglas was literally founded on coal, and the landscape was studded with the detritus of open-cast mining. The neighbouring villages, with their associative names of Bankend, Coalburn and Stockbriggs, faced a bleak economic future as farm prices fell and employment in the mines contracted. Such was the pattern throughout Scotland, with the centres of heavy industry, such as shipbuilding on the Clyde, badly hit in the great slump of 1929. Coal output had fallen by a third, and in the ten years up to 1931 eighty out of every thousand people emigrated from Scotland. Lanarkshire was worse hit than most areas. Once the mainstay of Scotland's coal production, by 1937 its output was almost halved.[11] 'For anyone with eyes to see,' the Scottish historian Andrew Marr wrote of these grim times, 'the condition of the poor was the most glaring problem facing the country.'[12]

Such conditions placed a heavy responsibility on those in a position to enter political life, whether on a local or national level, and determined Alec Dunglass's choice of direction. Although his father was lukewarm about his son's intention to seek a political career, his mother saw the Lambton blood coming to the fore. Her son's choice of party was, however, a disappointment. At Christ Church, he had been influenced by an undergraduate two years his senior, Ralph Assheton. The Toryism he represented, inspired as it was with a devout Anglicanism, was attractive, and conditioned Dunglass's thinking on the domestic issues of the time. Another Christ Church figure, with more robust views on a wide range of social issues, was 'the Prof', F.A. Lindemann, later Viscount Cherwell, from 1922 a Fellow of the college.

The Tory Party was a natural, if not whole-hearted, choice for Alec Dunglass to make. The problems lay with the alternatives. By the time of the 1929 general election, the climacteric was at hand for the old Liberal Party as British politics realigned. The Lloyd George–Asquith split of 1916 had left a weakened party – more a rump when deprived of Conservative support after 1922 – whose bruised fortunes the pact of 1923 was too late to repair. After Asquith's retirement in 1926, Lloyd George faced financial and organisational difficulties as Labour consolidated its position as the main party of opposition to the Conservatives. Herbert Samuel had been appointed head of the Liberal

Party organisation in February 1927, his main priority being to renew the enervated constituency associations. He had some, but not universal, successes: the glaring exception was in Scotland. By the end of 1928 only thirty-two candidates were in place for the seventy-one constituencies and Scotland, not at that time inimical to Conservatism, seemed to have no place for Liberalism. A wave of nationalism had led to the founding of the National Party of Scotland in February 1928 and the growth of the Labour Party was to marginalise further the Liberal cause north of the border. By the time of the 1924 general election, they were in sharp decline in Scotland, with only eight seats. Their Party – quite apart from the divergence on economic matters such as Protection – was not where the ambitious Alec Dunglass was going to stake his political future.

Surprising though it may seem, he did not immediately rule out standing as a Labour candidate. Oswald Mosley had joined the Independent Labour Party, an affiliate organisation of the Labour Party, in April 1924. This was seen as a great *coup* by Labour leaders, an extension to the predominant class base of the enfranchised and unionised industrial workers. 'MacDonald, the party leader, attached great importance to the adherence of aristocrats,' Mosley's biographer has written. 'They made Labour respectable.'[13] But the Labour Party was never a realistic option for Dunglass. 'He could never have been a Socialist, not because he did not feel for the underprivileged but because it would never have occurred to him to believe in Socialism,' wrote one of his later political advisers. 'He started from an essentially emotional position and then rationalised his beliefs later. But he had an instinctive understanding of people which often eluded those who approached politics in a more intellectual way.'[14]

West of Scotland Labour politics was dominated by the 'Clydesiders' – James Maxton, George Buchanan, James McGovern and David Kirkwood – left-wing firebrands and not natural bedfellows of a future earl. But this was not his main consideration; he had a poor view of the Labour Party's first government in 1924 and felt that the Conservative political programme, vaguely defined and defensive though it may have been under Baldwin in his 'Safety First' guise, gave a better prospect for economic regeneration. One of the later myths that came into being about Alec Douglas-Home was that his experience was limited to the foreign field, an impression given credence by his ill-advised remark to an *Observer* journalist in September 1962: 'When I have to read economic documents I have to have a box of matches and start moving them into position to simplify and illustrate the points to myself.'[15] In fact, it was not until he became Secretary of State for Commonwealth Relations in April 1955 that he made a major contribution to a non-domestic portfolio. His experience in politics from 1928 until 1955, with the exception of nine weeks as Under-Secretary at the Foreign Office during the caretaker government in the summer of 1945, was almost entirely on the domestic front.

In 1928 he let it be known to Sir John Gilmour, MP for Pollok and Secretary of State for Scotland in the second Baldwin administration, and to Noel Skelton, MP for Perth, that he would like to be considered for any vacancy at the forthcoming general election, so as to get his foot on the first rung of political experience. This was before the more formal system of Conservative Central Office lists of approved candidates, the Vice-Chairman of the Party and the Chief Whip then being the conduits to acceptance. Gilmour was a friend of his father's and had often stayed at Douglas, and Dunglass had read Skelton's *Constructive Conservatism* at Oxford. To later generations this may seem a casual and undemocratic way of finding candidates, but word-of-mouth recruitment was the accepted pattern in a wide cross-section of constituencies before the reforms of the Maxwell Fyfe Report of 1948.

Unionist MPs in Scotland had tended to be worthy loyalists who followed the Party line from Westminster, but with the growing sense of national consciousness north of the border many of the younger, progressive element felt a need for a new identity and sense of social purpose. If the Unionist party was to counter the appeal of the National Party of Scotland, and the Labour Party, response to the particular needs of Scotland was required. Within the next three years that process, largely completed by the 1931 general election, had seen the re-establishment of a new two-party system, with the Liberals the losers. That the Unionist Party survived in Scotland as a major force in those days can be attributed to the important contribution made by independent-minded Scottish MPs such as Walter Elliot and Robert Boothby.

In each political generation there is a need for renewal: this was particularly important in Unionist politics in the 1920s. Often its focus is a far-sighted younger figure, and Noel Skelton was Alec Dunglass's inspiration as he embarked on his political career.[16] A strong Unionist, who always described himself as such rather than Conservative, Skelton was a bachelor advocate who lived with his sister in Edinburgh New Town. Although Edinburgh was the focus of his professional life,

Skelton regarded Perthshire as his spiritual home. He attended Trinity College, Glenalmond before going on to Christ Church, and won Perth from the Liberals in 1922 with a majority of six thousand. The following year Anthony Eden won Warwick and Leamington, and the two became close friends and political allies, the focus for progressive, forward-looking Conservatism.

Skelton's reputation had been established by a series of articles in *The Spectator* in 1923, in which he addressed the central question of what the Conservative Party should stand for in the post-war age, and these political essays were published as *Constructive Conservatism.*[17] After the fall of Lloyd George and with the rise of Labour, the Conservative Party under Baldwin had increasingly adopted the stance of representing the status quo, defending the social fabric against whatever assaults the new political left might attempt.[18] For Noel Skelton this was not enough; he believed that where there is no vision the people perish, and he sought to give focus to that vision. The famous phrase about 'the property-owning democracy' is often attributed to Anthony Eden, but it was Skelton who coined the phrase in one of the *Spectator* articles. He developed the theme further in the book: 'Until our educated and politically minded democracy has become a property-owning democracy, neither the national equilibrium nor the balance of the life of the individual will be restored,' he wrote. 'To restore that balance is the master-problem of the era.'[19] To this concept he added the then revolutionary idea of co-partnership between employers and workforce, share options and a greater industrial democracy. 'In urban industrial life the road lies through profit sharing and co-partnership,' he urged. 'The basic institution is, today, democracy. It can be stabilised and maintained by being founded on property owning ... there is, in truth, no other way ... To develop in Britain a property-owning democracy – that, it is submitted, is at once the fundamental task of Conservatism and an objective for the nation consonant with its character and with the natural evolution of its life. That is Conservatism's true answer to Socialism.'[20]

Skelton also advocated an extensive house-building programme. He considered John Wheatley's Housing Act of 1924 a bold and necessary achievement by the first minority Labour government and commended the achievements of Neville Chamberlain as Minister of Health and Housing to the electors of Perth at the 1929 election. 'The building of some 930,000 houses in the last four and a half years is a world record and has greatly relieved the Housing shortage in our cities.' For the election campaign the Perthshire Unionists produced a Skelton acrostic:

> Skelton is the workers' friend;
> Keeps his promise to the end;
> Ever faithful, ever sure,
> Longs to make our joys secure,
> Tries to bring to all content,
> Our 'Ideal' for Parliament,
> None so fit to represent.[21]

After Skelton's death, Eden became the standard-bearer for this philosophy, and before the 1964 election sent Sir Alec a letter reminding him that 'a property-owning democracy is the aim'.[22]

In the close-knit world of Scottish politics Skelton was a centripetal force. As Alec Dunglass moved into his 'public' life, he found himself drawn by Skelton's magnetism – not so much his personality, attractive though that was, but by his vision of how the community could be improved and the fabric of society bound by the wider ownership of property. Although a candidacy was not immediately forthcoming, Dunglass was now firmly 'on the list' and began to participate in the round of speechmaking and political activity in the west of Scotland. He spoke for the 'Junior Imps' (the Junior Imperial League), the Primrose League and for the local Unionist Party in places such as Blackwood, Carluke and Newbiggin, and he did not have an easy ride. Shy and self-effacing, his diffidence did not equip him to deal with the robust heckling, an accepted part of political initiation on which more naturally gifted orators thrived.

Many strands came together in Alec Dunglass's determination to seek a political career. At the height of the controversy over his appointment as Foreign Secretary one of his private secretaries was staying at the Hirsel and asked why he bore all these whips and scorns when there was such a world elsewhere. Rewarding though this life was, he replied, it was not enough, and as the political world was not one he needed to enter, the inevitable criticisms were of no consequence.[23] He had no wish to follow his father into the world of banking, but nor did he wish to abdicate the responsibilities of his position, which afforded a great opportunity for entering public life. No less than King Edward VIII a decade later he believed of Lanarkshire particularly that 'Something ought to be done to find these people employment'.[24] Some of the remedies he advocated, such as the importance of labour mobility, were not popular in small, parochial communities, but his political thinking was developing eclectically. Speeches at the Primrose League reflected his awareness of the rifts in society and the need for the Tory Party to be national. He never believed that economic salvation for Scotland could be achieved by independence from the Westminster Parliament and was wary of those who played the nationalist card. There was a Samuel Smiles element of 'self help' in his approach, and Skelton's property-owning democracy was in the same tradition.

One other influence was important. Although Lloyd George had fallen from office in 1922, he remained a potent force in British politics.[25] Dunglass believed that Lloyd George's Safeguarding of Industry Act (1921) could lead to economic regeneration. 'Safeguarding' may have been 'protection' by another name, with its attendant political difficulties, but as wartime restrictions on imports had lapsed, manufacturing and other bodies had argued that the slump and unemployment could be alleviated by preventing foreign manufacturers 'dumping' their goods in a depressed British market. Dunglass felt that if 'safeguarding' led to domestic recovery, it would be justified, and for the Lanark coalfields it would be one way forward. At the time of the Safeguarding of Industry Act Lloyd George had said that it was up to the new generation to look at things through new eyes. Two months after becoming Prime Minister in 1963, Alec Douglas-Home unveiled the statue of Lloyd George in the lobby of the House of Commons, and recalled how he would probably not have entered politics had it not been for that remark of Lloyd George.[26]

His first attempt to enter the House of Commons at the 1929 election was unsuccessful. In 1928, owing to the patronage of Skelton and the support of Sir John Gilmour, Dunglass was nominated for the candidacy at the Coatbridge and Airdrie Division of Lanark. He had no expectation of victory, but Coatbridge was a challenge that he welcomed. Ten miles east of Glasgow, it was stunted by recession. Although the Labour majority in 1924 had been one of only fifty-seven votes, Labour's position in Scotland had improved considerably since; three successful by-elections had eroded the overall Unionist majority and Labour were now the biggest parliamentary Party north of the border. The constituency, which once produced thirty per cent of Britain's pig-iron, had found the return to peacetime trading difficult and had suffered from over-dependency on a single heavy industry.

Coatbridge was only twenty miles from Douglas and Dunglass began to speak at meetings after adoption, while finding out what he could about the needs of the area apart from employment. His principal opponent was the sitting Labour MP, James C. Walsh, an official of the Lanarkshire Miners' Federation, who had been elected in 1922. He was a doughty champion of the cause of colliery workers and had published several books and poems on life in the coalfield. Known as 'the miners' poet', he was widely respected, not least by Alec Dunglass's father. The Liberal candidate was also a respected local man, very dismissive of Dunglass, so it was going to be uphill all the way.

Nationally, the issue of unemployment dominated the election. Lloyd George had promised that unemployment would be reduced to 'normal' levels within the year by an incoming Liberal administration. *We Can Conquer Unemployment*, born of the famous Keynesian 'Yellow Books', was the central Liberal plank. In the debate between economic orthodoxy and unorthodoxy which lay at the heart of the election – not, as often supposed, the debate between the forces of capital and those of labour – *We Can Conquer Unemployment* was a bold initiative. Labour's main election pamphlet (G.D.H. Cole's *How to Conquer Unemployment: Labour's Reply to Lloyd George*) was defensive rather than original; as Lloyd George observed, 'The Labour Party could not make up its mind whether to treat the Liberal plan as a freak or to claim its paternity.'[27] The Conservative Party was increasingly sidelined: Baldwin's slogan of 'Safety First' was not calculated to set the pulses racing among an electorate which included many newly enfranchised women voters, now touching thirty million nationally.

Parliament was dissolved on 10 May and polling set for 30 May. Dunglass concentrated on a whistle-stop tour of the villages before nomination day. He spoke in the local primary schools and at the YMCA hall in Coatbridge. Heckling was intense, especially when he talked of the need to find work elsewhere if none was forthcoming in Coatbridge. He always believed that this was one way of correcting the imbalance, which was such a marked characteristic of the inter-war period, between chronic unemployment in the areas of the old, heavy industries of the North and the relative prosperity of southern areas with expanding service and light industries.

Many miners had no time at all for Dunglass and his support for industrial transference, and found his speeches unconvincing. 'Probably the rawest and most immature candidate I have ever seen at any time' was one recollection. Another miner remembered him as being 'pathetic on the platform, absolutely pathetic'.[28] In the class politics of the time he was a representative of capital, not labour; in the nationalist context, he was 'English'. These may have been prejudices, but they were deeply rooted in many parts of his constituency. His final meeting, when he tried to talk about derating, was at Coatbridge Town Hall. On the platform with him were his sisters Bridget and Rachel and (an indication of his standing in Unionist circles) the Secretary of State for Scotland, Sir John Gilmour. It was a fiery baptism. Heckling grew so intense that the police sent reinforcements to restore order. Although he did not have to be smuggled from the hall on this occasion, he was left in no doubt that politics could be a rough trade and an uneasy calling. He returned chastened to Douglas to await the outcome, which was J.C. Welsh (Labour) 16,879; Lord Dunglass (Unionist) 9,210; Robert Irvine (Liberal) 4,610 – a Labour majority of 7,669.

In Scotland the Conservative Party lost sixteen seats, including eleven county seats in Lanark and Berwickshire. Labour's representation rose to thirty-seven seats, but nationally the picture was not so clear-cut. Ramsay MacDonald's Labour Party were for the first time the largest party with 288 seats; Baldwin's Conservatives won 260 seats, and the Liberals managed only 59.

In the next forty-five years Alec Dunglass was to fight nine more campaigns. Coatbridge was one of his only two defeats (the other was at Lanark in 1945), but it was a valuable experience fighting a seat in Labour territory. He was only twenty-five and time was on his side. The minority Labour government of 1924 had lasted a mere nine months and although the expectations were that this one would last longer, most political commentators forecast (correctly) that the next general election would be well before 1934, though they did not foresee the circumstances of the financial crisis which caused the government's demise.

The Conservative post-mortems into the defeat were particularly bitter, Baldwin coming under attack for his cautious campaign from the very people who had welcomed it as a tactic. Dunglass took part in the obsequies north of the border and attended the Scottish Unionist Conference in Edinburgh, speaking in the economic debate, where he urged consumers to 'spend imperially'. The most interesting event at the conference, one very much influenced by Noel Skelton, was the motion (for which Dunglass voted) calling upon the party to abandon its Conservative name. The motion which was passed with only three dissentients, read:

> That this Conference of Scottish Unionists is of the opinion that the use of the word 'Conservative' to describe the Unionist Party and Policy is injurious to the interests of the Party, and, agreeing with Lord Balfour that the word 'Unionist' expresses better the things in which 'we most passionately believe', urges that the use of the term 'Conservative', whether in speeches or writings, be discontinued, and the term 'Unionist', which is the correct and official designation in Scotland, be always used.[29]

For his part, Alec Dunglass always thought of himself as a Unionist.

After the false start at Coatbridge, he kept a weather eye open for a new opportunity. The element of luck should never be underestimated in political careers and although his name and position would probably have brought some Scottish candidacy before the next election, fortune favoured him with unexpected suddenness. The intervening constituency between Douglas and Coatbridge was Lanark, county town of the area and one which housed many Home tenants, and in 1930 Stephen Mitchell, the former Unionist MP, who had lost the seat at the 1929 election, resigned to pursue a career in the tobacco industry. As he was only forty-six at the time, this suggested a degree of pessimism about future Unionist prospects, which Alec Dunglass was to confound. Stephen Mitchell thus paved the way for Alec Dunglass's Westminster career.

Alec Dunglass was a suitable replacement on several counts: he was a local man at the outset of his political career, who was becoming increasingly well known in Unionist circles; his speech on Empire Trade at the conference the previous December had been well received, and many Douglas tenants, as well as others who drew their livelihood from agricultural and mining interests associated with the estate, lived in the constituency. In an age more given to deference, his social position was an advantage, and he had financial independence, which was a distinct advantage in winning a nomination. Dunglass was thus adopted and by November 1930 was firmly on the political circuit as prospective candidate for the Lanark division. His contributions to constituency funds were unobtrusive, not least when he waived expenses that would normally have been paid as a matter of course. During the period out of the House of Commons after his 1945 defeat, the Lanark Unionist Association minutes record a generous example over the agent's salary. 'Should there be any doubt in regard to the necessary finance to meet the salary of £500 per annum, Lord Dunglass was prepared to forgo such portion as is necessary of the election expenses which the association is kind enough to raise.'[30]

Although Lanark was classified as a marginal seat, Walter Elliot had held it for the Unionists during the early 1920s and it had been lost in 1929 by only a small margin. In normal circumstances it would be a reasonable prospect, but the circumstances of 1930 were far from normal. Apart from the uncertain economic situation which was threatening to overwhelm the minority Labour government, the Labour Party in Lanark was in difficulties. The Unionists were thus in a fortunate position.

The next election was not long delayed. Against a background of rising unemployment and unremitting financial crisis MacDonald formed a National government on 24 August 1931. It was 'national' in name only, consisting overwhelmingly of Conservatives, Samuelite Liberals (the Lloyd George Liberals, a diminishing band, had broken with Herbert Samuel) and only four National Labour MPs. As with Peel (in 1846) and Gladstone (in 1886), MacDonald split his party for a generation but in the longer term the real losers of the 1931 election were the fragmented sections of the Liberal Party. If the 1929 election had been a battle between financial orthodoxy and unorthodoxy, the 1931 campaign was seen in terms of a 'patriotic' (i.e., the National candidates) and 'unpatriotic' divide. The National government won 554 seats with fourteen and a half million votes. The Labour Party, briefly under the leadership of Arthur Henderson after the expulsion of Ramsay MacDonald, were reduced to 52 seats, their position of a quarter of a century earlier. 'The importance of the election was that it gave the Conservatives, under false colours, an overwhelming strength in Parliament which they could have hardly won unaided.'[31]

Dunglass stood as a National Unionist. His Labour opponent had worked for the Scottish Labour Party since his undergraduate days, and the Liberals did not put up a candidate as they supported the 'National' banner. Demographically, Lanark was a diverse constituency with agricultural, mining and middle-class professional elements. This latter group was lost by Labour when they brought in the principal Clydesider MPs from Glasgow, who inveighed against MacDonald and all his works. Not that Dunglass had an easy ride from the Clydesiders or the mining element. As in 1929, he spoke at village halls and local schools, where the bulk of the electorate was unemployed. Although in some villages he was heard with only average heckling, at Stonehouse, a solid mining community, came the most violent opposition he had yet experienced. With the threat of physical violence, the chairman was forced to abandon the meeting and whisk the candidate to safety via a window. However, the National ticket took Dunglass and countless other first-timers to Westminster when the results were declared:

Lord Dunglass (National Unionist)	20,675
J. Gibson (Labour)	11,815
Majority	8860

This meant there had been a swing of over 10,000 votes from the Labour Party since 1929.[32]

Fifty-seven Conservatives were returned for Scottish seats, a figure not accomplished before or since in this century. Labour and the Liberals won only seven seats apiece. There were several Labour reverses in the Clyde valley, which in later years became synonymous with the Labour Party. The special conditions of the National government blurred these underlying tendencies.

News of Alec's victory at Lanark was telephoned to Douglas, where Collingwood, the butler, was taking down details of the countless messages of congratulation; he eventually ran out of paper and resorted to scratching on a slate in the general excitement.[33] Celebrations began in Lanark, where, befitting a town which turned out annually for the Perambulation of the Marches in Lanimer week ('Lanimer' being derived from the Land Marches, the stones marking the medieval burgh boundaries), the centrepiece was a procession with bands and torchlights. Dunglass was borne in triumph past the statue of Lanark's most famous son, William Wallace; at the age of twenty-eight he was a National Unionist MP with every prospect of holding the 'patriotic' vote for many years.

Lanark had an assured place in Scottish history, its Royal Charter dating from 1140. William Wallace's claim to fame was his attack on Lanark Castle in 1297, then occupied by the English garrison, and the slaying of the governor, Haselrig. With the subsequent establishment of a Scottish Parliament in Lanark, the town has claim to being part of the birth of the nationalist movement north of the border. The town's location, on a prominent plateau in rich farming country and on the main route to England, ensured its continuing importance and growth. In the seventeenth century it had been the focus of the Covenanting Movement and in January 1682 the Test Oath, which required swearing allegiance to the King in civil and church matters, was burnt at the Market Cross. In the late eighteenth century the neighbouring Falls of Clyde were discovered by artists and writers, such as J.M.W. Turner and Sir Walter Scott, and William Wordsworth and Samuel Taylor Coleridge visited at the time of the writing of the Lyrical Ballads.

In the nineteenth century the area was in the vanguard of industrial development. The Glasgow industrialist David Dale had built cotton mills by the Falls of Clyde and when Dale's son-in-law, Robert Owen, took over their management a progressive experiment in creating a model environment for the workforce became one of the outstanding examples of Victorian philanthropy. 'New Lanark' had an Institute for the Formation of Character, a co-operative shop (forty years before the co-operative movement began in Rochdale), nurseries, schools and accommodation for the workers' families. Owen's influence on safety standards in subsequent nineteenth-century Factory Acts was of seminal importance. By the twentieth century Lanark was an important market town, far removed from the bland suburbia of many Conservative MPs' constituency experience, with a colourful past but a none too certain economic future. There was a diversity of rural and industrial activity, but fitful and unequal rewards for the working population. In his time as Lanark MP, Walter Elliot had built up the local livestock market to one of the largest in Scotland, and the surrounding sheltered area is renowned for its soft fruit and tomatoes.

However, the continued recession in the coalfields meant that relative prosperity and great poverty co-existed in the same street. The constituency was dotted with mining villages with their rows of bleak terraced cottages, the backdrop to street gatherings of the long-term unemployed. The documentaries of the Scottish film-maker John Grierson, especially *Industrial Britain* in 1933 and *Coal Face* in 1935, focus on the conditions such ordinary families faced at that time, conditions which were all too common in the mining areas of the constituency. Dunglass did a great deal of parliamentary work on safety in the coal industry, yet it was among this mining community that his greatest political challenge would come, especially when Labour's split over the 1931 economic crisis was resolved.

The new Parliament met on 3 November. Of the 518 candidates who had stood as Conservatives, only 48 failed to be elected.[34] Such domination by one party, reinforced by the National government coalition of which the Conservatives were the overwhelming faction, meant that competition for political preferment in the next decade would be intense. Although the 'career' backbencher, happy to serve the interests of his constituents and to support the government line, was still a feature of the pre-war Parliament, for the ambitious newcomer of 1931 the subsequent years were ones of frustration.[35] Many accepted the political stagnation as an inevitable corollary of all three parties featuring in the National government. 'The average person who went into the House as a young man', Alan Lennox-Boyd said of that period, 'wasn't in the least impatient or annoyed if he was passed over.'[36] The fact that Dunglass did not languish unnoticed on the backbenches is an indication of how well known he had become in Unionist circles, with powerful and influential allies. Not only was he seen as a model of reliability and loyalty, but among the countless 'amateur' newcomers referred to by Harold Macmillan as 'temporary gentlemen', those with an intention of staying the course were in a different category. In the reconstruction of the government after the 1931 election, Noel Skelton invited Alec Dunglass to be his Parliamentary Secretary. His career of public service had begun, as 'a countryman and in exile in London for forty years'.[37]

When the results of the election were known, MacDonald had written to all members asking them to place their Offices at his disposal. Noel Skelton, who had been appointed shortly before the election as Under-Secretary at the Scottish Office, sent an immediate reply acquiescing, and similar letters and telegrams from constituencies in all parts of the country reached MacDonald, who faced a difficult balancing act in forming an administration. Many were retained in their previous posts: Baldwin was Lord President of the Council; as the leader of 470 MPs he was also the real power broker in the coalition. Sir Herbert Samuel, leader of the mainstream Liberals, remained at the Home Office, where he earned the undying enmity of Lloyd George.[38] But there were significant promotions.

Neville Chamberlain moved from the Ministry of Health to the Chancellorship of the Exchequer, a post he had first held in August 1923 ('What a day! two salmon this morning, and the offer of the Exchequer this afternoon.').[39] Sir John Simon replaced Lord Reading at the Foreign Office and Sir Archibald Sinclair retained his post at the Scottish Office, now in the Cabinet, with Noel Skelton once more his Under-Secretary. Sir John Gilmour, who had been so helpful to Alec Dunglass over his candidacies, also entered the Cabinet in his retained post as President of the Ministry of Agriculture and Fisheries. Walter Elliot was to succeed Gilmour in September, but was one of the younger Tories now promoted on Baldwin's recommendation, together with Anthony Eden, Oliver Stanley and Duff Cooper. No room was found for Churchill, partly because of his opposition to Conservative views on the future of India, or Lloyd George. Secondary, safe figures were assuming starring roles; respectability was to the fore.

Dunglass was firmly in the respectable camp, though some of his comments in that Parliament, however, were robustly unorthodox and direct. He had the best of both worlds: trusted, but not entirely predictable, and this commended him to figures both inside and outside government circles. He never trimmed to accommodate current orthodoxies, nor was he easily won. The India Bill and its controversies brought Dunglass into contact with Winston Churchill, who approached the vast mass of newcomers into the 1931 Parliament to get them to join him in opposing the India Bill. What has been described as 'the utter unscrupulousness of Churchill's attack on the government's policy and Hoare as its chief protagonist'[40] did not sway Dunglass: 'He tried to enlist some of us who were young Conservatives to his cause. I could not join him, first because it seemed to me that from the moment when we had set foot in our overseas territories, we had begun to train the native inhabitants in the techniques and arts of government; and secondly, because in India, unlike in Africa, there had been a village democracy for a thousand years, on which a comparatively stable nation could be built.'[41]

Future economic policy was the subject of his maiden speech on 15 February 1932 – on the second reading of the Import Duties Bill – and was a clear indication of these characteristics. He had already begun the habit of lightening the tone of serious speeches, believing that more could be taught by laughter than solemnity, and he now spoke of the dangers of promising instant solutions, like the politician 'who got up and said that all that was wrong with South Africa was that they wanted a better class of settler and a better water supply; and a voice from the back of the hall called out, "Yes, and that is all that is wrong with Hell."'[42] In the atmosphere of 1932 there were not many light touches in the pages of *Hansard*, yet the underlying tone of the speech was assertive and serious. Dunglass said that the Clydesiders – and he paid sincere tribute to Maxton, Buchanan and McGovern and 'the feeling and eloquence which they always put into their appeals' – had no monopoly of concern for the unemployed in the Clyde valley. 'I think sometimes that they give too little credit to honourable members in other parts of the House for ideals that are no less sincerely held than their own, or for being no less backward in their intentions to do what they can to root out the poverty and distress that are in the country.'

Ever since the Safeguarding of Industry Act in 1921, Dunglass had been convinced that a home-based market was a prerequisite of industrial recovery. One of the first acts of the National Government after its overwhelming endorsement was the introduction (in November 1931) of an Abnormal Importations Bill, which gave the Board of Trade the power for six months to impose tariffs *ad valorem* on manufactured goods entering the country in 'excessive' quantities. The short-termism of the November bill had to be addressed before six months had elapsed, and on 4 February 1932 Chamberlain introduced the Import Duties Bill (a further safeguarding of industry measure), which divided the Protectionists and Free Traders within the government. Dunglass's maiden speech capitalised on this element, catching the attention of the Chancellor.

The main thrust of his speech was set against the background of the particular problems of Lanark, where, he reminded his audience, unemployment was running at 32 per cent.

> To honourable Members opposite, it seems that the imposition of a tariff must raise the cost of living; to us equally it seems that in so far as it stimulates employment and gives work, it will increase the purchasing power of the people by substituting wages for unemployment benefit and various reliefs of that kind. It seems to honourable Members opposite that the putting on of a tariff in order to get revenue from it and apply it to the reduction of Income Tax, is to relieve the rich at the expense of the poor; to us, equally truly, it seems that it is absolutely necessary in order to reduce the heavy burden of taxation which is crippling industry, and we can honestly believe that until we can do something to remove that burden, we cannot make any great inroad into the numbers of the unemployed.

In his twenty-minute speech he developed many salient points. The old battles between protection and free trade were subsumed in economic realities. Trade unionists had their responsibilities: 'I suggest that the time has come when we need peaceful pickets, not only at the factory door but at the ports of entry to this country. Nobody can deny that goods made by cheap labour in other countries and brought into this country are just as much a danger to the standard of life of the working people ... as the blackleg who stands outside the door of the factory in this country.' The effect of the speech on Neville Chamberlain had important consequences on Dunglass's career.

Skelton had admired his talents and this speech (Dunglass was not disqualified as an unpaid Parliamentary Secretary from speaking in the Chamber) confirmed him in the wisdom of his choice. Although the post Skelton had offered was the bottom step of the political ladder, it offered the newcomer an insight into the practicalities of a big spending department. The work of the Scottish Office was of absorbing and wide-ranging interest, a fiefdom of its own, with considerable plenipotentiary powers. Since his arrival at Dover House, the headquarters of the Scottish Office in Whitehall, Sir Archibald Sinclair had taken stock with Skelton of the pressing problems of housing, education administration (state education north of the border was the responsibility of his department), Scottish funding and the problems anticipated owing to the upsurge in Scottish nationalism since 1928.[43] Dunglass became part of the team that worked on these and associated problems endemic to Scotland. In the four years that he was with Skelton he learned a great deal about the practicalities of political administration and parliamentary life. Topics in which he became involved included a Medical Service Scheme for the Highlands and Islands, land settlements in Caithness, a Scottish fishery board and legal matters in the City of Inverness.[44]

There was an inevitable air of retrenchment in the Scotland office in the depressed circumstances of 1931. Housing subsidies were cut back and the promised raising of the school-leaving age was postponed.[45] Nevertheless there was a greater consciousness among the government whips that time had to be found for Scottish business at Westminster, especially after Sinclair's resignation owing to the government's protectionist policy. Sir Godfrey Collins – a National Liberal and non-partisan in the Free Trade and Protection argument – became the new Secretary of State in September 1932. Collins appealed to Dunglass, who felt a sense of purpose in working for such a practical figure. There was a continuity in his approach: housing and education were still seen as vital areas of concern which could not be allowed to slip from the political agenda. He capitalised on the mood of goodwill from the Westminster government machine in raising the profile of Scottish affairs and on 24 November 1932 a day was allocated in the debate on the Address which opened the new session of Parliament, an unprecedented move. Dunglass spoke in this debate of the need for government 'to use its international bargaining powers in defence of industry', by which he meant the heavy industries traditionally associated with Clydeside.[46] It was a curious speech for a PPS to make, not that of a government spokesman so much as a campaigning backbencher.

Dunglass's work with Sinclair, and particularly Collins, gave a bi-partisan atmosphere to his first parliamentary years, when there were more cross-party friendships than in later eras, though this did not prevent the Clydesiders from venting their wrath on him when he spoke against Scottish self-government or the importance of the mobility of labour, with families moving to new areas, but he had an unlikely friendship with Jimmy Maxton, fostered by a mutual love of cricket and concern for Clydeside. Dunglass also appreciated the quality of the civil servants, with their traditional virtues of continuity, impartiality and anonymity. He particularly admired Sir David Milne, later Permanent Secretary and author of the pioneering history of the Scottish Office.[47] From 1931 to 1933 Dunglass worked with William Murrie, and from 1933 to 1935 with Charles Cunningham, successive private secretaries to Noel Skelton. Skelton believed in the practice, more common in the 1930s, of the political master and the civil servant meeting informally to seek acceptable solutions to difficult problems. Dunglass's presence added to the feeling of purposeful, friendly co-operation and Murrie remembered him as 'charming and courteous'.[48] When Skelton was absent with illness, Dunglass worked directly to Sir Godfrey Collins, when he was not on constituency business in Lanark.

His conscientious approach to local interests in Lanark puzzled Collins, who gave him the surprising advice that he was spending too much of his time on his constituents. Dunglass asked how often Collins visited his constituency in Greenock. 'Five times in thirty years' was the answer. It was not advice Dunglass took. Walter Elliot had lost the Lanark seat in 1923 by a mere 230 votes and Dunglass was taking nothing for granted. There were many August forays from Douglas to his constituency, not always for political reasons. He invited national figures such as Sir Kingsley Wood, Postmaster-General, and Oliver Stanley, Minister of Transport, to speak, combining this in August 1933 with a garden party and a cricket match between Lord Dunglass's XI and the Lanark team. In February 1934 he brought Noel Skelton to speak. Dunglass also welcomed constituents to London, with generous hospitality and his time. In April 1934 he took a party of constituents around the House of Commons, before travelling with them to Wembley to see the England–Scotland football international. Watching sport at the highest level was a lifetime fascination for Dunglass. In 1930 he had seen Bradman's great test innings of 334 at Leeds, then a world record. Aware of the technicalities involved, he regarded that innings as the consummate example of a skilled batsman who never seemed to lift the ball more than an inch off the ground in accumulating his runs, though its almost total lack of 'big' hitting made it appear as caviare to the general.

A politician's first spell at Westminster is inevitably a learning process, and his bed-rock of pragmatic political understanding stemmed from this period of apprenticeship. With Sinclair, Collins and Skelton, Dunglass found himself a close witness to the executive machinery of government, as well as the distinctive personalities who made that machinery work. Much of the work was dull and repetitive – preparation of answers to parliamentary questions, scrutiny of Scottish bills and long hours in the chamber – but it was vital if, as he hoped, he would one day be a minister in his own right. As in his cricketing days, he began to be talked of as a 'coming man'. 'Lord Dunglass hides a decisive character under the unassuming manner proper to a young man' ran one cutting on 'Parliamentary Personalities'. 'But his steady gaze and the firm line of his mouth tell of unswerving purpose which should take him a long way. When to this is added a manner of singular ease and charm there seems good reason for the prophecy that he is unlikely to remain the modest backbencher who arrived at Westminster in 1931.' The Parliamentary sketchwriter saw one eventual cloud on the horizon. 'Nevertheless, the British constitution being what it is, it may be that, when he succeeds to the ancient Earldom to which he is heir, his gifts may be diverted to the administration of his estates in Scotland, and the local affairs of Lanarkshire which will gain what Britain as a whole will have lost.'[49]

His circle of associates widened. One important friendship was with James Stuart, third son of the Earl of Moray, and MP for Moray and Nairn. His forthright opinions made him a controversial figure and Dunglass later wrote that 'his political enemies could never get the measure of him'.[50]

If Collins had startled Dunglass by his advice on the scarcity value of constituency visits, Stuart's advice to Dunglass as he embarked on his Westminster career was one that Dunglass often recalled, particularly during the 'Poll Tax' rows during the Thatcher premiership. 'Whatever you do,' he told the young MP, 'never, never touch the rating system.'[51] Stuart influenced a whole generation of aspiring Unionist MPs. In February 1950 he was giving advice to the Scottish candidates prior to the general election. 'Do you talk politics to your constituents?' he was asked. 'Certainly not,' he replied, 'they might discover they were Liberals.'[52]

The Scottish flavour was important in Dunglass's inclusion in the political salon which Kay Tennant established in her house in Lord North Street. Many cross-party friendships were cultivated there; it was a group which has been described as 'the stimulating fringes of all parties',[53] and it was here that he met the leftish, unorthodox Tory MP for Stockton-on-Tees, Harold Macmillan, beginning an association of importance in post-war political history. A whole network of influential political friendships was formed at this time, and in 1934 many circles were squared when Kay Tennant married Walter Elliot, whose first wife had been killed in a mountaineering accident. Like Elliot, Dunglass was direct and open in his dealings and cultivated a wide circle of friends, political and otherwise, unlike the prevailing 'Scottish lairdism' of the conventional upper-class Unionist politician. 'The thing about Walter and Alec', Kay Elliot recalled, 'was that they were the same with everyone, whether the man in the street or the Duke of Buccleuch. Both were MPs in their time for Lanark and "Lairdism" would never have been tolerated there.'[54] When Baroness Elliot gave her maiden speech in the House of Lords, it fell to Lord Home, then leader of the Lords, to speak next. He remembered the friendship of many decades, speaking of her 'courage tempered by an acute mind and practical common-sense which she renews every day as she goes about her affairs in contact with people from all walks of life'.[55]

Local constituency activities centred on such things as cricket and racing, as well as the more conventional village-hall meeting. Apart from garden parties at Castlebank, most political activity in Lanark emanated from the (now defunct) Bonnington Hotel, where the local Unionist Association held their Annual General Meetings and conducted constituency business. Unionist Association meetings were held in Reid's tea rooms in Glasgow. Despite its rural appearance and recreational facilities such as the race-course and a classic golf course laid out by Old Tom Morris in 1897 and extended by James Braid in 1926, Lanark was still an area of acute industrial contraction and most of Dunglass's constituency work and correspondence concerned the 'intractable' question of unemployment. The Constituency Association were not slow to let him know what they felt about the response of the National Government. On 1 December 1933 they sent him a letter, setting out their strong views on government responsibilities. 'The question of the Government's attitude towards the grant to be given to Local Authorities in respect of the maintenance of the able-bodied unemployed was discussed ... the Government should bear the full cost of the maintenance of able-bodied unemployed and [we] shall be pleased to learn that the recommendation has your support.'[56] Although Dunglass sympathised, he knew that the palliatives they suggested were but a skin on the ulcerous place and that the problems of the early 1930s would not yield to short-term solutions.

Noel Skelton died of cancer on 22 November 1935. He inspired a whole political generation and among his most fervent admirers was Alec Dunglass. But Dunglass was not with Skelton at the end. Baldwin's accession to the premiership in June 1935 had led to a partial reconstruction of the government, and Colonel Anthony Muirhead, who had been appointed Parliamentary Secretary at the Ministry of Labour, asked Sir John Gilmour and Walter Elliot if they knew of any 'coming man', who might serve as his PPS in his new responsibilities. They both suggested that Dunglass would fit the bill and he was invited to join Muirhead at the Ministry of Labour. A single man and landowner, Muirhead had been at Eton and Magdalen, Oxford, and he listed cricket as his main recreation in *Who's Who*. Dunglass would have had to look hard for a more congenial political master.

The Ministry of Labour represented an important sideways move for him. He had worked for Skelton at the Scottish Office for four years – what he called 'a good innings' – and had been MP for Lanark for the same length of time. There was little doubt that he would be returned at the 1935 election, and he was unanimously adopted as National Unionist candidate. The election was called for 14 November 1935, the only November contest this century, apart from that of 1922, which was also a Conservative landslide. Gibson was again his Labour opponent, though a third candidate emerged in the shape of William Carlin, a former miner, who stood for the Independent Labour Party. There was little doubt about the outcome of the election and the national campaign was muted. The main interest was in the number of seats the Labour Party would recapture after its low-point of 1931. The Lanark campaign was uncharacteristically vigorous and passions ran high. Polling day was wet and turnout was down some 5 per cent from 1931. The result in Lanark was Lord Dunglass (National Unionist) 17,759; J. Gibson (Labour) 10,950; William Carlin (ILP) 2583 – a majority of 6809 votes.

On a 53.7 per cent share of the overall vote, the Conservatives won

432 seats. Labour won 154 seats (37.9 per cent), higher than the 37.1 per cent when they had won power in 1929. Baldwin 'thwarted the opposition', in the vivid phrase of historian Tom Stannage, and the Conservatives seemed set for an extended period as governing party. 'Perhaps most importantly the result of the 1935 general election disguised the growth of class politics', Stannage wrote. 'The 1929 general election had shown the unacceptability of the Conservative Party in areas where working-class Toryism had long been a fact of political life. The elections of 1931 and 1935 cut through this development by making it possible for electors to vote for a National Government rather than a Conservative one. In 1945 consciences could not be appeased in this way, and faced with a clear choice between the Conservatives and Labour, the people affected voted Labour, and in such numbers that the backlog in the development of class politics in the 1930s was fully taken up.'[57] Alec Dunglass's electoral experience, from defeat in Coatbridge in 1929, through victories in Lanark in 1931 and 1935, before going down in the Labour landslide in 1945 is a microcosm of this pattern.

For Dunglass parliamentary responsibilities were now in a new context under Muirhead, but the methods and aims were broadly similar. He had had experience of issues where trade and unemployment had been of major concern, but where the overall Scottish context had always to be considered. Now his work would be on a more specific level. The Ministry of Labour had been created in 1916 as a wartime measure, but it survived and was expanded in the Second World War as the Ministry of Labour and National Service. Dunglass gained knowledge of legislation on trade union matters and conciliation of labour disputes, and worked on the purchase of land in Lanarkshire for the development of industrial estates, a pragmatic continuation of the domestic character of this phase of his career. But involvement in wider issues was not long delayed. David Margesson, the Chief Whip, was looking for one of the younger MPs to take on the job of Chamberlain's PPS at the Treasury, as a preliminary to accompanying the Chancellor to 10 Downing Street as and when Chamberlain succeeded Baldwin as Prime Minister. Soundings revealed that Dunglass would be a popular choice, and Chamberlain was delighted at the prospect of taking on the speaker he had heard in the debate on the Import Duties Bill in 1932. It was a wholly unexpected development for Dunglass, but he relished the prospect of working with the heir apparent; it would be his first, vicarious taste of power. Despite his outward insouciance he never lost his sense of fascination for being at the centre of things. So in February 1936 he moved to the Treasury: the right-hand man to the right-hand man of Baldwin's government. The signs were propitious, but the political symbiosis which was to tie Dunglass so closely to Chamberlain eventually became a millstone for the younger man.

As the eyes and ears of Neville Chamberlain, Dunglass was much in demand by the Party managers as they sought out grass-roots feelings on a variety of issues. His new responsibilities led to his first foray into the field of foreign affairs on 12 March 1936 in the wake of Germany's occupation of the Rhineland, when Baldwin required an account of the meeting of the Foreign Affairs Committee. Dunglass was asked by Thomas Dugdale, Baldwin's PPS, to prepare a report for the Downing Street Secretariat on the feelings of the Party at that meeting. He gave a detailed account to one of Baldwin's secretaries, who prepared a digest of it.

> It was a small meeting, only about 50 members present.
>
> Lord Winterton was the first notable speaker, and said if we condone Germany's action France and the smaller nations will execrate our name – we must therefore make a violent protest and work towards securing a symbolic withdrawal from the Rhineland.
>
> Mr Boothby said he had had a telephone message from Berlin which stated that there were great internal dissensions in Germany and a real rupture between the Civil Government and the General Staff. He concluded that we must accelerate our rearmament programme.
>
> Sir Austen (Chamberlain) asked what would be the next move by Germany if she was allowed to get away with what she had just done. He suggested the following action: submission to the Hague Court of the Franco-Soviet Pact; Germany to be told she had to withdraw troops etc. from the Rhineland; symbolic withdrawal only perhaps, pending the Hague Court's decision.
>
> Sir E. Grigg – 100 per cent for war.
>
> Mr. Churchill. We must fulfil our obligations under the Covenant and follow the procedure it enjoins. It is unthinkable that we should repudiate our signature of Locarno. He drew a dramatic picture of all the countries of Europe hurrying to assist France and ourselves against Germany but said nothing about their military preparedness.
>
> Sir S. Hoare said there exists a strong pro-German feeling in this country – he had been surprised how strong the anti-war feeling had been in France when he was there in the autumn of 1935 but he was convinced it was even stronger in this country. If divisions of

> opinion existed in Germany at present, a dictator could soon put that right if he had to. As regards Winston's reference to all the nations of Europe coming to our aid, he could only say that in his (Sir S.H.'s) estimate these nations were *totally unprepared* from a military point of view ... He added that he did not mean thereby that he was in favour of repudiating our obligations – no reservation whatever should be made in our condemnation of Germany's action but it could be fatal to prejudge or to lay down exact conditions for Germany's withdrawal before the League council had met; therefore at all costs we must keep to the machinery provided in the Covenant of the League. It was all very well to talk of pushing the Germans out of the Rhineland but he had the gravest doubts whether this country could lend effective aid in such an undertaking ...
>
> Sir S. Hoare had the support of almost the whole meeting. At the beginning a substantial proportion of the Committee seemed inclined not to stop short of being prepared to see this country go to war but Sir S. Hoare's speech definitely sobered them down.[58]

This memorandum is of interest for several reasons. Not only does it show the growing (and belated) awareness of a resurgent Germany transgressing the bounds of the Paris Peace Treaty of June 1919 but it reveals the division and tensions within the Conservative Party on such issues as rearmament and Churchill's grasp of reality. Churchill may have been full of fine words, but Dunglass wondered if they added up to much in practical terms. He was to be firmly in the wrong camp for the great shake-up of 1940.

Alec Dunglass was thirty-two when he went to work for Chamberlain. His position in the party as a safe pair of political hands had been consolidated, and he was seen as a serious practitioner for the long haul. At the same time that his political fortunes were being subtly altered, there was an important transformation in his personal life. In the summer of 1936 he became engaged to Elizabeth Alington, the daughter of his headmaster at Eton. Dunglass's contact with the Alington family had been more with the father; the Alington sons and daughters initially made their friendships with Alec's younger brothers and sisters, especially William and Rachel. Elizabeth's close friend in the Home family at that time was Rachel, whom she began to visit at Douglas and the Hirsel in the early 1930s.

Alec saw Elizabeth Alington on many occasions during the late 1920s and early 1930s. The Whitworths' visitors' book has numerous entries recording the visits of Alec and his brothers, Henry and William, usually in connection with some sporting weekend – Fourth of June celebrations, the Caird Fives Cup, matches for the Eton Ramblers.[59] Alice Whitworth, who was perceptive in affairs of the heart, knew that many Eton hostesses gave dinner parties when Alec Dunglass visited, invariably placing him next to Elizabeth Alington, and the general perception was that he would marry her. But the well-intentioned efforts of many to hasten the engagement seemed to hang fire. Alice Whitworth let it be known that it would be better if Elizabeth were not always placed next to Alec Dunglass; indeed it would be better if she were not invited to the formal dinner parties then customary, because this would put the onus on Alec to take the initiative.[60] In 1932 his name featured in the Whitworths' visitors' book – thirteen times in the first few months – and that autumn Elizabeth Alington stayed at Douglas as Rachel's guest. Aymer Whitworth retired in December 1932 and the next year the Alingtons moved to Durham, when Alington became dean of the Cathedral. Durham's proximity to the Hirsel meant that Alec Dunglass and Elizabeth Alington saw each other even more during the parliamentary recess. One of their first joint ventures was the composition of a crossword for *The Times*, which appeared in October 1933. Alec Dunglass became a frequent contributor of crosswords to *The Times* and on one occasion an unknowing travelling companion asked for his help over some clues. With an air of plausible anonymity and appropriate furrowing of the brow, Dunglass completed the crossword for the admiring stranger.

Their engagement was announced in June 1936. They had been to the Oaks at Epsom, where they jointly backed the winner, and on to the gardens of Dropmore House in Buckinghamshire, where Alec Dunglass proposed and was accepted. The news was greeted with great joy by their families and at New College, Oxford, William Douglas-Home told Brian Johnston of the event and later recalled Johnston's response.

'Well, bless my soul,' he said, 'I was engaged to her myself last year at school.'

'Well, why didn't you marry her?' I asked.

'Because', he replied, 'we were in the rhododendrons together one Sunday morning and Dr Alington walked by in his surplice on his way to Chapel and said, "Come out of there, Elizabeth, you can do better than that."'[61]

The Lanark constituency of the Unionist Association sent a formal message of congratulation and their wedding present, subscribed to by the local villages and town branches, was munificent: a silver tea and coffee service, a dinner service and a painting.[62] The wedding was at Durham Cathedral on 3 October 1936. Dr Alington performed the service; the address was given by William Temple, Archbishop of York, and the blessing was pronounced by the Bishop of Durham. At Douglas a fifty-foot bonfire was lit by William Murray, the oldest employee on the estate, and Alec Dunglass said it was 'the happiest event of my life'.[63] His gift to his wife was a garnet necklace and ear-rings; Elizabeth gave her husband field-glasses, and the Earl of Home gave the newly married couple Springhill, Dunglass's boyhood home on the banks of the Tweed.

Their honeymoon took them across Europe, to Cologne, Baden-Baden, Freiburg, Montreux and Locarno. They became aware, especially in Cologne, of the fetid political atmosphere and, through the continental newspapers, of Edward VIII's growing involvement with Mrs Simpson. They returned in time for the new parliamentary session, setting up their first London home at 57 Chester Square.

Alec Dunglass now had the support of an intelligent and far-sighted wife, who was to sustain him in the triumphs and turbulence that lay ahead. This was widely recognised, as were her Christian values. Alec's Christianity was of the heart, not of the pew, a matter of private witness and personal conduct. This was the pragmatic Christianity in which Alec and Elizabeth Dunglass were as one. 'Elizabeth Home faced all eventualities with the same humility,' *The Times* said after her death. 'Its source was the spiritual strength she found in true Christianity … the achievements of Elizabeth Home identify an outstanding example of how a wife can share her husband's statesmanship.'[64] Her political prescience and forceful determination added an element of resolve to her husband, Harold Macmillan once remarking, 'Elizabeth I would have made PM, if I could!'[65] When the Alingtons left Eton for Durham in the summer of 1933 a tree was planted in the headmaster's garden to mark his tenure. On the day of Elizabeth Home's death in September 1990 a storm blew through the garden she had known in her early life and, as the winds abated, a great branch fell from her father's tree.[66]

4

The Chamberlain Years

Even before he became Prime Minister on 28 May 1937, Neville Chamberlain was the dominant figure in the National government. He entered the House of Commons late, being forty-nine before he became MP for the Ladywood Division of Birmingham in the general election of December 1918. In the 1920s he was Postmaster-General, twice Minister of Health (the spell from 1924 to 1929 he thought the most productive of his career and was the one he enjoyed most) and, briefly, Chancellor of Exchequer at the end of 1923.

It was with the formation of the National government in 1931, when he again became Chancellor of the Exchequer, that he was increasingly seen as Baldwin's natural successor to lead the Conservative Party. His influence as director of the Conservative Research Department and his role as Chairman of the Party had given him a firm grasp of both policy and presentation, and Baldwin assumed that the two eventual contenders for the succession would be Douglas Hogg, then Attorney-General, and Neville Chamberlain. Hogg's elevation to the Woolsack in March 1928 removed one contender and with Churchill's decline from political favour after 1931 there was no longer any serious doubt that Chamberlain was the heir apparent.[1]

Chamberlain was under no illusions about the pivotal role he occupied, first under MacDonald and later under Baldwin. His success with the Import Duties Bill in 1932 and his forceful shepherding of Baldwin at the Ottawa Conference later that summer, together with his astute use of the newsreels as a medium for explaining his fiscal measures in successive budgets, gave him a high profile in Westminster and with the public. He was seen as a shrewd and pragmatic political operator, who was now taking the lead on economic matters. With A.J. Balfour in 1902 and Anthony Eden in 1955, Chamberlain is a rarity – a twentieth-century Conservative heir apparent who actually took possession of 10 Downing Street. He also shares with Eden a less happy place in history, clouded by the general censure of one final act, to the detriment and over-shadowing of earlier accomplishment.

But the political skies were clear in February 1936 when Alec Dunglass became his Parliamentary Private Secretary – no longer was he the coming man; he had arrived. Dunglass owed his elevation to David Margesson, described as having 'a commanding influence on political appointments'.[2] As Chamberlain respected the judgment of Margesson, this was to the benefit of Dunglass, and his standing with the Whips Office and Margesson was of importance at this stage of his career. Margesson, the Chief Whip, had taken soundings among a circle of influential Conservative MPs, including James Stuart. As the then Scottish Whip Stuart knew the golden opinions Dunglass was winning among a significant group of thoughtful younger MPs and as Chamberlain's need was for such a young figure who could be his eyes and ears in the Commons Dunglass was a natural and popular choice. For his part, Dunglass admired Chamberlain's record, though he was unaware of some of his traits of personality: aloofness, attention to detail – which some found pernickety – and his public reserve. Other considerations, such as the limiting effect on his freedom of action, did not enter into the equation. Dunglass did not calculate from his own perspective, but from what he could do to serve the Party and justify the trust placed in him.

Chamberlain and Dunglass had many things in common, not least a deep love and knowledge of the countryside. Underneath the forbidding exterior – the Churchill group referred to Chamberlain as 'The Coroner' – Chamberlain was a sensitive and sophisticated aesthete, far more rounded and complex than the historical caricature allows. Not gregarious, he eschewed the London scene whenever he could, preferring to indulge his love of fishing on the River Test with trusted friends. He was an expert in the world of flowers and gardens, and set up bird tables in the gardens of Downing Street and Chequers, wrote articles for *The Countryman* and was a good shot. He much preferred the country peace of Chequers, where he embarked on a programme of planting trees and shrubs, an activity also indulged by Alec Dunglass over the years at Springhill and the Hirsel. The bed-rock of Chamberlain's life was his family, deep religious belief and love of his country. After his death, his widow wrote to Baldwin, 'I always connect a certain part of the garden at Downing Street near the Ilex Tree with a few minutes' walk we had up and down after breakfast the morning before he went to Munich. As we were passing the tree he said, "I would gladly stand up against that wall and be shot if only I could prevent war."'[3] Such was the man to whom Dunglass's immediate political fortunes were bound. In many respects, he could have been an uncle or older brother; their symbiotic relationship was deep. 'In the afternoon I had several long conferences with Alec Dunglass who is a miracle of tact, humour and sound sense', wrote 'Chips' Channon in his diary on 26 April 1936. 'He admires Neville so much he has even come to look like him.'[4]

The role of a Parliamentary Private Secretary may be relatively humble, but it offers great opportunity to experience what Jock Colville later dubbed 'the fringes of power'; 'burgeoning bag-carriers' was one recent pejorative phrase. Whether a PPS was ever more than a mere 'bag-carrier' was considered by Tam Dalyell, who served Richard Crossman in this capacity in the 1960s. In his experience, he wrote to *The Times*, 'Parliamentary Private Secretaries were both valuable to their ministers and gained a great deal of knowledge about administration and the Civil Service that they would not have otherwise gleaned.' No minister could digest four red boxes a night and 'even Crossman in his heyday would hand me official documents for an "independent synopsis"'.[5] For his part, Chamberlain appreciated Dunglass's judgment and the fact that he was succinct; he also came to appreciate that the loyalty shown was of a special kind. When Dunglass was offered the post of Under-Secretary in the Scottish Office in September 1939, he declined so that he could see things through to the end with Chamberlain, conscious of how the Prime Minister's personal and political loneliness would intensify in his remaining months in government.

The main preoccupation when Dunglass arrived was the build-up to the April budget, which gave him an early insight into the pressures of fiscal and monetary policy. The hours were long, especially as Chamberlain was also involved in the preparation of the Defence White Paper for that year. The Chancellor was not in the best of moods, rather grumpy with an attack of gout, and Dunglass ensured that his presence was mollifying. Their first 'public' appearance together was for the 1936 budget, and for the next four years newsreel films of Chamberlain emerging from Downing Street invariably showed Dunglass in the background.

Chamberlain was also concerned about the new King Edward VIII: 'I do hope he "pulls up his socks" and behaves himself now he has such heavy responsibilities for unless he does he will soon pull down the throne,' he had written in January.[6] 'Neither he nor Dunglass was confident of the outcome. Baldwin came to the abdication crisis rested after a quiet autumn, during which Chamberlain had increasingly been in the political limelight. This was more by accident than design, as Baldwin had not been well, but the abdication and its aftermath (notably the Coronation of the new King on 12 May 1937, an event which saw Dunglass and his wife at the Abbey) made the suitable moment to hand over the reins. Chamberlain had been seen as Prime Minister-in-waiting for some time, but at the Conservative Conference of 1936 he was greeted as the next leader when he (instead of Baldwin) addressed the mass rally, which ended the two-day conference.

Chamberlain had returned to the Treasury after his Scottish holiday at Blair Atholl. Although the date of his appointment was now loosely fixed for some time after the coronation, many important economic matters demanded his attention in his final months at the Treasury. Foremost was the Tripartite Agreement between the British, French and United States finance ministers to promote stability in exchange rates by inter-governmental co-operation. Though Dunglass was of necessity concentrating on his day-to-day administrative work, the seeds were being sown of many later difficulties for his political master. Civil war was raging in Spain; Mussolini's son-in-law, Ciano, was at Berchtesgaden for talks with Hitler, and Germany signed an anti-Comintern pact with Japan. But by the beginning of December, even such weighty matters gave way to the abdication crisis.

Through his friendship with Thomas Dugdale, Baldwin's PPS, whom he saw on a daily basis, Dunglass learned a great deal of the way Baldwin threaded a path through the myriad difficulties. What impressed him most about Baldwin's handling of the crisis was the importance the Prime Minister attached to allowing a 'fall-back' position – the morganatic proposal ('Does that mean he marries Mrs Simpson and then does nothing with her?' asked one schoolchild) was both a lifeline and a resolution. The King's hopes of marrying Mrs Simpson and retaining the throne faded when Baldwin received reactions from the Dominions on the issue. The crisis would have ended even sooner had it not been for a delay in receiving New Zealand's reply: 'They could not find out who Mrs Simpson was,' Baldwin recalled in 1947. 'Then the Prime Minister of New Zealand wanted to know what Mrs Simpson would be called if not HRH. When he was told, "Her Grace the Duchess of Windsor", he answered, "and quite enough too!" '[7] Privately, Chamberlain was critical of some aspects of Baldwin's handling of the crisis, wrongly so in Dunglass's recollection of Baldwin's sure touch. He knew from his friendship with the Queen with what distaste her Majesty recollected the events of 1936;[8] Dunglass was clear about his own feelings, even if it meant disagreement with his political master.

After Chamberlain's success at the Conservative conference, Dunglass attempted (not altogether successfully) to bring him into the Smoking Room of the House of Commons to meet the younger members, particularly those elected for the first time in 1935, but it proved difficult to get Chamberlain to relax. This was where James Stuart, the Deputy Chief Whip, was important. He brought a whiff of the atmosphere of White's; as a lover of gossip, a Scottish grandee and a friend of Alec Dunglass, he was an ideal catalyst for these rather embarrassing gatherings at Westminster which took place in the full public gaze of opposition backbenchers. Stuart recalled them ruefully:

> Chamberlain did not follow Baldwin's practice of frequenting the Smoking Room and making contact with back-benchers. One evening Alec Douglas-Home (then Lord Dunglass) asked some of us to look into the Smoking Room before dinner because he was bringing the PM in and wanted a few friendly souls to rally round …
>
> About eight or ten of us gathered together and conversations admittedly dragged a bit, though we managed to get going to some extent on fly-fishing, which was Neville's great love. In spite of our efforts, however, it was not a great success and, as I was leaving the room, my Socialist friend, James Maxton, came up to me and said, 'Ach, Jimmy, ye'll have to do better than that. Anybody could see how unhappy ye all were.'[9]

Knowledge of Chamberlain's social awkwardness was not confined to MPs. 'They had managed to get him to go into the smoking room of the House of Commons a few times,' John Reith wrote, 'but he had just given that up.'[10] Alec Dunglass did not forget that the essential error of these uneasy visits to the Smoking Room was that they were relentlessly regular: backbenchers could set their watches by Chamberlain's appearances. As Prime Minister, and particularly as Leader of the Opposition from October 1964 to July 1965, Alec Douglas-Home was conscious of how he needed to keep in touch with grass-roots opinion (one of the reasons he did not overstay his time), yet aware of the dangers of coming down with clouds descending. In the aftermath of the 1964 election defeat he wrote to the new Conservative Chief Whip, William Whitelaw, to consider his programme. "'How much Smoking Room? lunch? dining room? tea-room? lower bar?!' he wondered. Whitelaw advised, 'The thing to remember is that an *irregular* routine by you creates more contacts with the *regular* habits of Members.'[11] This was not something Chamberlain ever achieved.

Dunglass's personal contacts with his leader were hardly more fruitful. He would put his head round the door of Chamberlain's room in the House, only for the PM to look up and enquire forbiddingly, 'What do you want?' His real understanding of Chamberlain's personality was in a private context, latterly at the Hirsel when the Chamberlains were guests of the family. After Dunglass was appointed chairman of the Junior Imperial League in 1937, he persuaded the Chamberlains to attend some of the functions; photographs show the Dunglasses at the tombola stall with Anne Chamberlain in Park Lane. But the real rapport between the Prime Minister and Dunglass was in their joint love of country things. At the height of the Munich crisis Dunglass received a message to see Chamberlain by one of the bridges in St James's Park. Was it a specially sensitive message from one of the dictators? When Dunglass arrived it was to find that Chamberlain had discovered a rare scaup duck nesting by the bank. Their love of Scotland was also a great bond. Blair Atholl, Dalchosnie and Edzell – these were the places Chamberlain loved; for Dunglass, they were all ones he knew in his native land.

Just before Chamberlain succeeeded Baldwin, he suffered a deep personal blow; on 16 March 1937 his brother Austen died of a heart attack. The emotions he experienced were complex – family sadness inevitably, and perhaps a tinge of guilt that the political cards had fallen for him, not Austen, and that his brother had not lived to see a Chamberlain as Prime Minister. Dunglass saw the episode as intensifying Neville Chamberlain's sense of isolation and deep loneliness.

Quite apart from the dangers brewing in Europe, it was an emotionally vulnerable time for Chamberlain, which contrasted with Dunglass's own personal family happiness. On 27 April his sister Rachel married Lord William Scott, MP for Roxburgh and Selkirk, and Elizabeth was expecting their first child in October. For Chamberlain, on the other hand, matters were not helped by Baldwin's reluctance to name a date for the hand-over. Dunglass experienced vicariously the frustrations of those early months of 1937, but Chamberlain's anxieties proved unfounded. An announcement was made late in February that Baldwin would go after the Coronation. The Coronation on 12 May 1937, which the Dunglasses attended, was one of the last peacetime celebrations on the grand scale, celebrations in which they took a full part, both on the personal and the public levels. On 28 May Neville Chamberlain became Prime Minister and Alec Dunglass went to work full-time at 10 Downing Street.

There were some consequential changes in the new administration, but few material promotions. Sir John Simon became Chancellor of the Exchequer.[12] Eden continued at the Foreign Office, and to Churchill's great delight, Duff Cooper became First Lord of the Admiralty. In retrospect the most debilitating change was the appointment of Leslie Hore-Belisha to the War Office in place of Duff Cooper. Dunglass considered this Chamberlain's worst appointment and many difficulties were to stem from it. However, the team that Chamberlain assembled around him at Downing Street (the first of those that later became known as 'Kitchen Cabinets') was of more importance for Dunglass's immediate future. The political commentators began looking for future stars and Alec was not overlooked in this process, being singled out as one 'who gives the impression of being rather retiring, but who can hold an audience as well as the next'.[13]

At the pinnacle of the team was Sir Horace Wilson, Permanent Secretary at the Ministry of Labour before the age of forty, when Baldwin invited him to join him at Downing Street as a special adviser. Chamberlain came to admire Wilson greatly and asked him to 'stay around for a bit' in the Private Office at 10 Downing Street. He accompanied Chamberlain on his three visits to Germany to see Hitler in September 1938, and this association with 'Munich' blighted unfairly his reputation as one of the outstanding civil servants of his generation. ('Sir Horace' became a soubriquet for an unelected civil servant who presumed to ideas above his station; it influenced the choice of the name 'Sir Humphrey' in *Yes Minister* in the 1980s.) Dunglass never joined in the denigration of Sir Horace – part of the *Guilty Men* school of historical interpretation. When Wilson died in 1978, Home was asked to write his notice for *The Dictionary of National Biography*. This he declined to do, not because he was reluctant to rake over the controversies of the past (for he would have defended Wilson robustly), but because his personal knowledge was limited to the years 1937 to 1940 and thus atypical of his overall career. 'I am afraid I cannot do Horace Wilson as I did not know him at all before he came to Neville,' he wrote in November 1980, 'and the years at the Ministry of Labour were the most important of his life.'[14]

In the Private Office Dunglass did not work directly to Wilson, nor did he come into the orbit of such luminaries as the Cabinet Secretary Sir Maurice Hankey or his successor, Sir Edward Bridges. His main associates in the Private Office were Arthur Rucker and Cecil Syers, who were the two senior Private Secretaries, and the legendary Miss Watson – Chamberlain loyalists all. The Downing Street team was completed, on 10 October 1939, by Jock Colville, who gave a memorable portrait of the times in his diary, *The Fringes of Power*.[15]

Drudgery was an inevitable part of life at Downing Street, as Miss Watson, 'a kind, efficient, unassuming and rather wizened old thing', warned Colville on his arrival. She was soon organising him in the ways of the office. 'Miss Watson came to sit in the same room as me, and the peace of the last ten days vanished,' he wrote in January 1940. The antidote to this was the cheerfulness inspired by Dunglass, 'invariably delightful', and with Rucker and Syers 'the sound of laughter seldom failed to resound in the Private Secretaries' rooms and did much to relieve the gloom of those grey winter days'.[16] And there *was* gloom, not only in the winter days. Chamberlain's relations with his Foreign Secretary, Anthony Eden, were complex and Eden was slow to grasp how the balance was shifting in the conduct of foreign policy. Outwardly things continued on a basis of understanding and even friendship; Eden came to believe that his position with the Prime Minister was one of special intimacy, 'one of the worst mistakes of his life'.[17] Chamberlain was determined to replace Sir Robert Vansittart, Permanent Under-Secretary at the Foreign Office, whom he regarded as defeatist, and did so in 1938 when Sir Alexander Cadogan was appointed. The seeds of conflict between Chamberlain and his Foreign Secretary had been sown; their final break would be dramatic. There was also the problem of the unofficial diplomacy undertaken by the Prime Minister's sister-in-law, Ivy Chamberlain, Sir Austen's widow, who was a great admirer of Mussolini. She communicated private messages on Downing Street writing paper from her brother-in-law to Count Ciano (son-in-law of the Duce), which were a great embarrassment to Chamberlain.

It was over worries such as these that Dunglass was such a reassuring presence. Unlike his later Prime Minister, Harold Macmillan, who was mistakenly renowned for 'unflappability', Dunglass had the inner security and serene calm that came from an assured social position and a rocklike marriage. Chamberlain did not discuss political decision-making with his young PPS – that was never Dunglass's function – but he did confide his worries and anxieties. Shortly after he became Prime Minister, Alec went down to Chequers for an extended weekend visit. In the midst of the Buckinghamshire countryside, they went for walks, observing the wild life with expert eyes while Chamberlain used Dunglass as a sounding board, testing the effectiveness of his ideas and listening keenly to the observations Dunglass made about the younger personalities in the Party. The weekend cemented the bond between the two men and, as Annie Chamberlain and Elizabeth Dunglass got on well together, the two families became close at this time.

Dunglass's influence on Chamberlain's anxious personality was benign. The conventional view of Chamberlain is of public abrasiveness and a stubborn sense of the rightness of his actions, masking a sensitive and kindly person. In neither respect is it an accurate portrait; on cinema newsreels, a medium he used skilfully, he talked sensitively about how opportunities should be opened up for people to develop taste in aesthetic matters ('the wisdom to be found in books'). In its essentials his view was D.H. Lawrence's, 'the human soul needs actual beauty even more than bread'. In private he could be demanding, impatient and the hardest of taskmasters to his staff. It was a real baptism for Dunglass to see the workings of government from the centre and to experience, albeit vicariously, the pressures and strains which the Prime Minister experienced in his efforts at 'shuttle diplomacy', for which Dunglass developed a profound mistrust. Their private friendship drew forth the more sensitive and attractive side latent in Chamberlain's character: his capacity for hospitality, conversation and the delights of the natural world. The Chamberlains were meticulous in their orderliness and Alec's insouciance, not least in the manner of dress, was a mollifying contrast to the stiff exterior of Birmingham nonconformism. On the public level, Dunglass was expert at shielding Chamberlain tactfully from the unwanted pressures of the daily grind. His efficiency was a force for calm and lowering of the temperature.

On 11 October 1937 Elizabeth gave birth to their first child, who was christened Lavinia Caroline in the chapel of the Hirsel, and Aymer Whitworth was among the godparents. One of the first telegrams was from Chamberlain: WARMEST CONGRATULATIONS TRUST ALL GOES WELL. Brother William telegraphed characteristically: HEARTIEST CONGRATULATIONS ON A VERY SUCCESSFUL MORNING'S STORK FLIGHTING.[18] When their second daughter, Meriel, was born in 1939, Annie Chamberlain was among the first with congratulations and, in the last sad months of his life, Neville Chamberlain was a godfather. Alec and Elizabeth Dunglass spent Christmas 1937 at Springhill. With their two-month-old daughter, and the traditional family celebrations at the Hirsel, it was a happy season, the last Christmas for eight years unclouded by public uncertainties or private worries.

The first sign that all was not well when Parliament reassembled was the depressed condition of the Foreign Secretary, who proposed taking a break from his duties on account of ill health. 'AE is hoping to take six weeks' holiday and get to West Indies just after Christmas', wrote his Private Secretary, Oliver Harvey. 'PM to take on FO in his absence. This is rather alarming in view of intrigues, but as PM is now in agreement with AE, perhaps all will be well.'[19] This brief entry contains the genesis of many of the political troubles and misunderstandings Dunglass witnessed in the next few months. Not only were Chamberlain and Eden poles apart temperamentally, but political differences over the conduct of foreign policy were coming to the surface. A meeting at Downing Street on 16 November 1937 (for part of which Dunglass was present) had been particularly strained, with Eden finding Chamberlain obdurate and unhelpful. The disagreement was on Lord Halifax's proposed visit to Hitler, which the press was billing as of special importance. As the newly appointed Lord President of the Council, Halifax was clearly not undertaking a diplomatic initiative when he visited Hitler, but he was a representative of the British government (as well as the Foreign Affairs spokesman in the Lords) and Eden was understandably concerned about the misunderstandings that might follow. 'Before too long', one of his biographers has written, 'Halifax became the involuntary catalyst for the eventual break-up between Prime Minister and Foreign Secretary.'[20]

There had been a series of disagreements that autumn, often on trivial matters, which masked the deeper cause of division, namely, the direction of foreign policy, particularly the negotiations with Mussolini, but this was only the most visible fissure in the deepening rift. Eden's resignation on 20 February was a defining moment in Chamberlain's premiership, and it had a lesson for Alec Dunglass. He saw the dangers that could arise when a strong-willed Prime Minister no longer confided in his Foreign Secretary and it was a lesson he never forgot, especially in the sometimes delicate situation when R.A. Butler was Foreign Secretary from 1963 to 1964. The public damage caused by Eden's resignation was arguably less significant than that caused privately in the Conservative Party as the former Foreign Secretary became the reluctant focus for the disaffected in their ranks, one hundred of whom backed Churchill in his support of Eden at a Foreign Affairs Committee. The subsequent communiqué to Chamberlain calling for a more positive attitude caused David Margesson anguished hand-wringing and a clash with Churchill. The battle lines between the Munichois and their opponents were already being traced on the political map.

There were many groupings within the Party in the inter-war period. Those supporters of Eden, many elected with him in the early 1920s, were known as the YMCA or, less flatteringly, 'The Glamour Boys'. There was also 'The Boys' Brigade', a rival group of younger MPs, including Butler, among others. Chamberlain loyalists were known disparagingly as 'The Old Gang'. One of the things Eden admired about Dunglass was that when it later became fashionable to clamber aboard the anti-Chamberlain bandwagon, Dunglass made no attempt to do so.[21]

The events surrounding Eden's resignation were to be important for Dunglass's later career in two further respects. A new Foreign Office team was now appointed in the persons of Halifax as Foreign Secretary and Butler as Under-Secretary. Dunglass saw some of the difficulties which may arise when someone who is not of the highest rank in Cabinet standing and, in addition, is a member of the House of Lords, is promoted to the post of Foreign Secretary. This next occurred in July 1960 when he became the first Foreign Secretary in the Upper House since Halifax's day. On that occasion, however, Lord Home had the services of a Cabinet Minister in the House of Commons, Edward Heath, as Lord Privy Seal, with particular responsibilities for European matters. No such formal arrangement was made in 1938 and Butler thus had the worst of both worlds, as well as having moved from The Boys' Brigade to The Old Gang. Denied executive authority, he nevertheless received his share of the abundant obloquy discharged after Munich, which was not directed against Dunglass to the same extent.[22] Indeed Chamberlain made it clear after Halifax's appointment that he now intended to answer in the Commons for the Foreign Office. 'As the new Foreign Secretary will be a member of the House of Lords, the Prime Minister proposes himself to deal with all important aspects of Foreign Affairs which are the subject of debate or question in the House of Commons.'[23]

All of this brought extra burdens for Dunglass, but it also gave him new opportunities in a part of the political world that had been largely a closed book. For the remainder of his time with Chamberlain, foreign affairs were the dominant issue. Dunglass never forgot one sentence in Eden's resignation letter: 'It cannot be in the country's interest that those who are called upon to direct its affairs should work in an uneasy partnership, fully conscious of differences in outlook yet hoping that they will not recur.'[24] Chamberlain was saddened by the way the break was now interpreted as a personal rift between himself and Eden, whose integrity he admired. When Iain Macleod published his biography of Chamberlain in 1961, he wrote to Eden, 'You will be particularly interested to see what I have written from Neville Chamberlain's papers about his relationship with you and your resignation. There is not in fact a single line or a word in any of his voluminous diaries, letters and papers, all of which I have had, which has anything but admiration for you, and I hope you will think that ... the account is a fair one.'[25]

Within weeks of Eden's resignation, Hitler's troops had occupied Austria. With the fall of Austria on 12 March, Czechoslovakia was now surrounded on three sides, and the 'Czech question' dominated the next six months. Dunglass worked long hours at Downing Street, as papers and advice poured in to the Prime Minister from all quarters. Three Foreign Office papers were considered on 16 March, all differing on the next course of action but acknowledging that Czechoslovakia was likely to be Hitler's next target. Two days later Chamberlain celebrated his sixty-ninth birthday, an occasion, as Dunglass noted, of much time-consuming ceremonial and celebration with a round robin of congratulation signed by 150 Members, including Churchill, assuring him of their confidence.

Over the summer Dunglass witnessed at first hand the anxieties of Chamberlain. There were twenty-four debates on foreign policy (many on the Spanish civil war). Amid the welter of parliamentary questions (nearly fifteen hundred crossed Miss Watson's desk in the Private Office), Chamberlain pushed ahead with his desire to reach some understanding with Mussolini, with rearmament, and with initiatives such as the Runciman mission to Prague, where the former Liberal Minister would be an 'independent negotiator' between the Czechoslovakian government and the Sudeten Germans. Dunglass concluded that this mission was misbegotten and doomed, in that the French were the allies of Czechoslovakia, not the British. By the time Runciman returned from Prague, Chamberlain had already made his first visit to Hitler.

It was at this juncture that Dunglass found his Lanark constituency at the centre of political attention. Chamberlain's preliminary August foray to Scotland for the fishing had not been a success, owing to severe sinus trouble, which obliged him to return to London for treatment. The traditional visit to the King and Queen at Balmoral, in the aftermath of the successful royal state visit to France in July, was a happier interlude, but Chamberlain was still not in the best of health. The King, in the best traditions of Walter Bagehot, 'encouraged' and cheered his Prime Minister, who was in low spirits, and tried to persuade Chamberlain to stay on for a further day, offering him the use of an aircraft of the royal flight for his return to London. Chamberlain declined, on the grounds that he had not been in a plane before and did not intend to break the habit of a lifetime at this stage.[26] Within a fortnight he embarked on the first of three of the most famous flights in history.

Also in Scotland, for a golfing holiday, was Sir John Simon, the Chancellor of the Exchequer. Dunglass had always been keen to offer his constituency as a platform for national figures, and he was now in a position to do so. He had already invited Simon to attend the Lanark Unionist Association's summer garden fête. Events conspired to make the visit one of the most significant Dunglass arranged for the voters of Lanark. Chamberlain realised that it could be turned into a statement of the government's stance on the current crisis, and agreed with Halifax that Simon should make a statement aimed at the wider international audience. As a former Foreign Secretary, Simon was ideally placed to speak for the government, having considerable influence with Chamberlain and access as Chancellor of the Exchequer, to the inner councils. What he said would be interpreted as the 'official' line and his speech was framed for that purpose.

History has not been kind to Simon, his reputation being that of a cold, calculating lawyer ('There'll be no moaning at the Bar, when he puts out to sea'), but Dunglass judged as he found, not as conventional wisdom declared.[27] He admired Simon's intellect and incisiveness and felt that he was in the presence of a political heavyweight. Dunglass knew of Simon's struggles to establish himself at the Bar, and the sadness of his first wife's premature death when he was unable to afford the medical treatment for her condition. His later wealth and manner were for many distancing factors, when it was said that his smile shone, but like the brass plate on a coffin. As a key figure in 'The Old Gang' he was politically unpopular with those who agreed with Lloyd George that 'Sir John Simon has sat so long on the fence that the iron has entered his soul'. With his innate shrewdness, Dunglass knew that Simon's failing was not one of arrogance but of insecurity and the desire to be loved.

When Dunglass told his Constituency Association that Simon would be speaking on the Czechoslovakian crisis, it was clear that there would be a vastly increased attendance, including the national press. Lanark racecourse was booked, and a vast crowd assembled to meet Sir John and Lady Simon. Simon wrote of the event:

> Aug. 31 North Berwick. I had a long-standing engagement … in Lanark on August 27 and I took the opportunity to deal with the burning topic. Every sentence about Czechoslovakia was, of course, agreed with Halifax, and the 'Lanark speech' has been treated all over the world as an authorised declaration of British policy, and has been given a warm reception everywhere, at home and abroad, except in Germany where it is treated as encouraging the Czechs. The real effect is to warn Hitler that if he uses force it may be impossible to localise the war: and this has had a steadying effect.[28]

After referring to the uncertain state of Neville Chamberlain's health, he declared that the government's intention was 'a positive policy of peace'. His remarks were greeted with great enthusiasm, none more so than when he declared: 'The beginning of a conflict is like the beginning of a fire in a high wind. It may be limited at the start, but who can say how far it would spread, or how much destruction it would do, or how many may be called upon to beat it out.'[29] His speech was a combination of reassurance and firmness. Sir Horace Wilson wrote that the Chancellor's speech at Lanark 'reaffirmed the Prime Minister's statement of the 24th March'.[30]

While the national press concentrated on Simon's speech, the Scottish papers gave a good deal of attention to the local MP, who was seen as the mastermind behind the enterprise: 'Lord Dunglass … spoke briskly. Some people have a warm tip for this young man. Speaking to me of him some weeks ago, P.J. Dollan said "He has brains, that man." That from the Socialist leader about an opponent is equivalent to saying he has the ability to be Premier in good time. To my mind he lacks the showmanship necessary for big-time politicians. Time will talk.'[31] The event typified Dunglass's work nationally and locally in the latter part of the 1930s. Chamberlain had gone to Scotland for a Highlands holiday which was cut short by illness; for the better part of a fortnight, he was laid low in Downing Street. His PPS remained on standby and was the conduit through which government policy was introduced to a wider audience. By virtue of his position at Chamberlain's right hand, Alec Dunglass was now to witness events he would never forget. Munich was the first formative turning-point of his public life.[32]

At this stage Chamberlain conceived his plan to visit Hitler in person. He was aware of the risks that this entailed. 'I fully realise', he wrote to Ida, 'that if eventually things go wrong and the aggression takes place there will be many, including Winston, who will say that the British Government must bear the responsibility and that if only they had had the courage to tell Hitler now that if he used force we should at once declare war that would have stopped him'.[33] He outlined his intentions to the King two days later. 'I have been considering the possibility of a sudden and dramatic step which might change the whole situation. The plan is that I should inform Herr Hitler that I propose at once to go over to Germany to see him. If he assents, and it would be difficult for him to refuse, I should hope to persuade him that he had an unequalled opportunity of raising his own prestige and fulfilling what he has so often declared to be his aim, namely the establishment of an Anglo-German understanding, preceded by a settlement of the Czechoslovakian question.'[34] This initiative, revealed to the Cabinet on 14 September, though discussed in advance with Halifax, was the prelude to his visit to Berchtesgaden on 16 September, the first of Chamberlain's flights to Germany over the next fortnight. Dunglass did not accompany Chamberlain on this visit, or on the second flight to Godesberg on 22 September, but he saw Sir Horace Wilson's copious notes. Constituency matters impinged in the weeks leading up to Munich; on 21 September Dunglass was asked to arrange a diamond jubilee telegram from the King to a Carluke constituent, which he did. On 22 September, the day Chamberlain was at Godesberg, the Lanark Unionist Association wrote to thank Dunglass, adding, 'I do not think it would do any harm if you looked into the executive meeting on the 28th inst.' But other duties were to call that day, one of the most dramatic in Dunglass's life.

Chamberlain's meetings with Hitler at Godesberg had concluded at 1.45 a.m. on Saturday 24 September. The Cabinet met for two hours at 5.30 p.m. that same day and the next morning when Edouard Daladier, French Prime Minister, and Georges Bonnet, Foreign Minister, were invited to London on Sunday 25 September. On 26 September, even after receiving Wilson's gloomy account of an acrimonious meeting with Hitler in Berlin that afternoon, Chamberlain said he was willing to visit Germany again, if it would help to secure peace. At 10.30 p.m. on 27 September, Dunglass was present in Downing Street when another message came from Hitler signifying that he was prepared to look again at his demand that Czechoslovakia should accept the terms of the Godesberg memorandum by 2 p.m. on 28 September. Duff Cooper, First Lord of the Admiralty, had released news of the mobilisation of the fleet. Chamberlain replied that he was sure the essentials could be met without war, before instructing Lord Perth, the British ambassador in Rome, to follow through his earlier suggestion that the Italian Foreign Minister, Count Ciano, might prevail upon Mussolini to temper Hitler's belligerence. David Margesson had already issued his instructions for the next day: '28 September 1938. 2.45. 3 line whip. The Prime Minister will make a statement on the international situation and your attendance by 3 p.m. is most particularly requested.'[35] By 11.30 that morning, the Foreign Office had despatched messages to Hitler, expressing Chamberlain's willingness to attend a four-power conference in Germany, and to Mussolini, urging him to persuade Hitler to agree.

The House of Commons met in an atmosphere of unparalleled apprehension and misgiving. As MPs gathered for the statement, those walking down Whitehall noticed quiet crowds placing flowers at the foot of the Cenotaph. Members of the Royal Family, including Queen Mary and the Duke of Kent, were in the gallery to hear Chamberlain's statement. Shortly after 2.45 p.m. Dunglass took his seat directly behind Chamberlain's place at the Dispatch Box. His instructions from Chamberlain were to keep an eye out for any message. When Chamberlain entered, he was greeted with enthusiasm order papers were waved and applause rang out, but the mood changed to one of solemnity as Chamberlain began his statement, a chronological résumé of the events of August and September. Shortly after 3.30 p.m. Sir Alexander Cadogan, Permanent Under-Secretary at the Foreign Office, appeared in the Peers' Gallery with a message for Halifax, who handed it to Sir Horace Wilson. Dunglass saw that Wilson was signalling to him. The House was so packed that it was difficult for the sheet of paper to be passed but Dunglass leant along the bench and the message was handed to him. He beckoned to Sir John Simon, who quickly read it. As Chamberlain was still in full flow and largely oblivious of the drama going on, the problem was how and when to interrupt the Prime Minister's speech. It is perhaps best to recount events in the words of Sir John Simon, the final link in the transmission of the historic message:

> Halfway through the PM's speech Frank Roberts brought Halifax, who was listening in the Peers' Gallery above the clock, a telegram from Hitler, inviting Chamberlain to fly to Munich the next morning, when Mussolini would be there. Daladier had also been invited. Halifax sent the news down to me, as I was sitting nearest to the PM on the Treasury bench. The problem was how and when to let the speaker know this encouraging and indeed vital fact without disturbing the flow of his discourse. I waited for some time with the necessary sentences on a piece of paper in my hand, for I did not want to interrupt the current of his argument or throw him off his balance by suddenly interjecting this joyful piece of news. At last, during a burst of cheering, I managed to whisper to him that Hitler's answer had come and give him the passage to be inserted later on. This was to give him time to prepare for the announcement, which might make the difference between peace and war, before the actual moment came to make it. The prompting worked without a hitch, and I am told that listeners in the Lords library (a microphone had been placed on the Treasury box for the first time in the history of Parliament) actually heard a few moments later the whispered conversation:
>
> PM to Simon: Is this the place to bring it in?
>
> Simon to PM: Yes.
>
> Then came the passage which suddenly turned gathering gloom into new hope, and indeed may alter the course of the history of the world.
>
> It was incomparably the greatest piece of real drama that the House of Commons has ever witnessed.[36]

Chamberlain announced the news of Hitler's invitation to an exultant House of Commons. 'I need not say what my answer will be,' he declared. 'God has sent him a peroration and it is in time,' remarked Ernest Brown, Minister of Labour.[37] Congratulations poured in from all sides, though much was later made of the fact that Leo Amery, Winston Churchill, Anthony Eden and Harold Nicolson had remained seated. Attlee, the Labour leader, spoke in the warmest terms and, as Chamberlain left the Chamber, Churchill went over to shake the Prime Minister by the hand and wish him 'God speed' on his mission.[38]

The House rose at 4.30 amid scenes of enthusiasm. The departing Royals were cheered as they left Speaker's Court. 'Then I saw Chamberlain's car draw up, and Bill Astor and I rushed up the private staircase he always uses, and met him advancing with Mrs Chamberlain and the faithful Dunglass,' wrote Chips Channon. 'He had walked out of the noisy frantic Chamber alone, and a gulf of his own making seemed to open between him and mankind.'[39] Chamberlain returned to Downing Street through cheering crowds and began to make arrangements for his third flight to Germany. He invited Dunglass to accompany him for the final act of the drama. 'I went with him more as an aide-de-camp than anything else, and because I'd never met Hitler and I very much wanted to see him and get some idea myself as to what he was like and the general feeling.'[40]

The team included the omnipresent Wilson, William Strang of the Foreign Office and Cecil Syers of the Private Office, Frank Ashton-Gwatkin, who had been on the Runciman mission to Prague, and Sir William Malkin, Legal Adviser to the Foreign Office. As Chamberlain busied himself with briefings for his departure the next morning, Dunglass was concerned with more mundane matters. Not noted for his sartorial elegance, he found himself without an appropriate shirt for his journey, so went to the flat which his brother William was sharing with Brian Johnston and borrowed a silk shirt.[41]

The main party assembled at Downing Street before travelling to the airport. Sir John Simon had suggested that the Cabinet should be at Heston to see the Prime Minister off at 8.30. Accordingly an intrepid and unbreakfasted group of ministers, including all shades of opinion from Halifax to Duff Cooper, assembled on the tarmac, to wish Chamberlain well on his mission. Dunglass's air ticket was marked 'Special flight', and Commander Robins, the pilot, kept a photographic record, together with flight plans, which he later gave to Chamberlain. Due attention was paid to the needs of the inner man; luncheon hampers had been provided by the Savoy Hotel, containing grouse sandwiches, plus ample supplies of caviare, pâté and smoked salmon, together with claret, beer and cider.[42] For the return flight, the hampers were restocked by a Munich hotel. When Chamberlain inquired where the food had come from, and was told that it had been provided by the Germans, he said it would give him great satisfaction if the food remained untouched. Those who were hungry on the return flight made do with digestive biscuits.[43]

The noisy Lockheed 14 took off shortly after 8.30 for the bumpy three-hour flight to Munich, lumbering slowly over the London suburbs, watched by a vast crowd, not only at the airport but from the gardens of houses along the arterial roads. On the way out the party spent the time discussing the form the conference would take; despite the joyous send-off at the airport, Dunglass remembers the atmosphere as anxious. Nobody was fooled into thinking that peace was guaranteed; the general impression was that Hitler was too unreliable for any such guarantee. Chamberlain told Dunglass privately that this was his last throw, but that he could not see how it would pay Hitler to push things to the point of war. The plane touched down at Munich airport shortly after 11.30.[44] Joachim von Ribbentrop, German ambassador in London, greeted Chamberlain and his party on behalf of Hitler, who was meeting Mussolini at Kufstein, just over the Austro–German border, 'to give him an overview of the whole problem so that they are on the same side in the talks', as Joseph Goebbels recorded laconically.[45]

In the time before Hitler's return, the British party was installed in the Regina Palace Hotel in Munich and Sir Nevile Henderson, ambassador in Berlin, who had been the main go-between, briefed Chamberlain on the developments of the last forty-eight hours. Dunglass thought Chamberlain looked as though he were dressed for a funeral. The entourage was driven through the streets of Munich to Hitler's house, the Fuehrerhaus in the Königsplatz, an imposing stone building where Hitler stayed when he returned to the heartland of his political power. The British party was ushered into a conference room.

'There behind a dark table was this little, very grey, dull and dour man,' Dunglass recalled. 'He was dressed in ordinary clothes sitting behind this table in a very, very dour mood.'[46] Dunglass noticed at once how the Germans treated the Italian delegation with contempt, and he registered that the British did not treat Daladier's party much better. Though he did not know it at the time, Hitler had nothing but scorn for both Chamberlain and Daladier. 'It is terrible', said Hitler to Ribbentrop as the British and French delegations departed. 'I always have to deal with nonentities.' Eleven months later, when drawing up the plans for the invasion of Poland, he said, 'I have seen these miserable men at Munich.'[47] Goering changed his uniform a number of times to impress everyone, but Chamberlain did not even notice his gaudy strutting. 'He would have impressed Chamberlain far more if he had talked to him about scaup ducks', was Dunglass's recollection.[48] He found Hitler unimpressive physically, his presence defined only by his position. As he walked, his arms moved in tandem, like a primate pacing his cage. 'He was a small man; he strutted along, and obviously had a great idea of his own presence and power over people.'[49]

The substantive part of the conference, which Dunglass did not attend, though he witnessed the signing of the Munich Agreement and of the 'piece of paper', went on for the best part of the next fourteen hours. They were long and unrewarding hours for those on the fringes of the various delegations, left in the corridors of the Fuehrerhaus or sitting in overheated rooms, eating unwanted meals. As the division of the spoils continued – a process to which the Czechs had not been invited – the delays seemed interminable. 'The length of the proceedings was largely due to the inefficiency of the arrangements for the conference made by the Germans,' Chamberlain said in his dictated record at Downing Street the next evening. The final detail was aptly symbolic: 'When the time had come to sign the final Agreements, it had been found that the inkpot into which Herr Hitler dipped his pen was empty.'[50] The Czechs were given until 10 October to vacate the Sudetenland, and claims on Czechoslovakia were to be settled by an international commission. The remaining portions of the country, once new frontiers had been established, would be guaranteed against further aggression by the Four Powers. Mussolini's compromise between the terms of the Godesberg Memorandum and the Anglo–French proposals carried the day.

News filtered through to the BBC in London in a series of tape messages through British United Press, starting at 8.33 p.m. and ending at 1.57 a.m. on Friday 30 September. The final message stated baldly, 'The communiqué specifies that the agreement is between Germany, the United Kingdom, France and Italy, and does not specify Czechoslovakia's agreement.'[51]

At 1 a.m. Chamberlain had asked Hitler if they might have a private conversation. He wanted a separate statement of the peaceful aims of the British and German nations. Hitler agreed and at 2.30 a.m. Dunglass was among those summoned for the signing of the Munich Agreement between the Four Powers, watching from the doorway. The Agreement was dated 29 September, though it was signed in the early hours of the next day. Before he retired to bed, 'pleasantly tired', Chamberlain saw the two Czech representatives, Dr Voytech Mastny and Dr Hubert Masarik, who had been permitted to come to Munich as observers. Frank Ashton-Gwatkin had kept them in touch with developments during an embarrassed evening and was to accompany them back to Prague later that day. In the small hours Chamberlain handed them the text of the Agreement as a *fait accompli*. They had already been told by Ashton-Gwatkin that they would stand alone if they did not accept the terms, and on this note the British delegation returned to their hotel. As Alec Dunglass settled to fitful sleep in Room 316, it was twenty hours since he had left Chester Square.

Later that morning he breakfasted with Chamberlain. The Prime Minister had with him the piece of paper on which he had drafted the famous words:

> We regard the agreement signed last night and the Anglo–German Naval Agreement as symbolic of the desire of our two peoples never to go to war again. We are resolved that the method of consultation shall be the method adopted to deal with any other questions that may concern our two countries, and we are determined to continue our efforts to remove possible sources of difference and thus to contribute to assure the peace of Europe.[52]

Chamberlain's motives in preparing this document, as he assured Dunglass over breakfast, were not to guarantee peace (that was impossible with a man of Hitler's volatility) but to ensure that if war did break out the international community would know on which nation the responsibility would fall. 'If he signs it and sticks to it that will be fine, but if he breaks it that will convince the Americans of the kind of man he is,' he told Dunglass. 'I will give the maximum publicity to it when I return to London.'[53] After breakfast, exhausted from the travelling and the long hours of the previous day and night, Dunglass accompanied Chamberlain once more to the Fuehrerhaus, a last call before travelling to the airport. They were received in Hitler's private flat. Chamberlain recapitulated the main drift of his conversation: 'He would not keep Herr Hitler any longer, but he wished to say that he thought it would be a pity if this meeting passed off with nothing more than the settlement of the Czech question, which had been agreed upon yesterday. What he had in mind was to suggest to Herr Hitler that it would be helpful to both countries and to the world in general if they could issue some statement ... on the desirability of better Anglo–German relations, leading to greater European stability. Accordingly he had ventured to draft a short statement which he would now ask Herr Hitler to read and to consider whether he would be disposed to issue such a statement to the public over the signatures of himself and the Prime Minister. As these observations were translated to Herr Hitler he ejaculated at intervals "Ja! Ja!" and when it was finished he said he would certainly agree to sign this document. When did he wish to do so? The Prime Minister: Immediately. Herr Hitler: Then let us sign. At this point, they both rose, went to a writing table and, without any further words, appended their signatures to the document.'[54]

To Dunglass's consternation, Hitler signed the paper 'with suspicious alacrity', without even a cursory glance at its contents.[55] He and Chamberlain returned to the hotel in contrasting moods. 'I've got it,' Chamberlain exulted to the remainder of the British party, minus Ashton-Gwatkin, who had now departed for Prague, where President Beneš was forced into accepting the terms by noon.[56] Dunglass was not alone in his reservations. The professional diplomats looked askance at the implications of this personal diplomacy.

A crowd outside the hotel called for Chamberlain and did not disperse until he had appeared on the balcony.[57] Flowers from many parts of Germany were stacked high in Chamberlain's hotel suite. Daladier and Chamberlain were taken on a sightseeing tour of Munich where they were cheered by the crowds. After lunch, Chamberlain's party set off for the airport, and the anxious atmosphere returned as the plane took off. Some slept as best they could, but soon the outlines of the coast near Southend could be seen. As Chamberlain looked down on the rows of defenceless terrace houses around the docks, he was aware of the vulnerability of British cities to air attack. In the early evening the plane was seen circling the skies above Heston. It touched down at 5.38 p.m., the restocked hampers untouched. The BBC 'broadcast, televised and recorded' the next ten minutes, breaking into normal programmes.[58] The newsreel cameras recorded Chamberlain's appearance on the tarmac once more, Dunglass appearing just behind him before melting anonymously into the background.[59] The Great West Road outside the airport was jammed with parked cars for a mile in both directions. Police prevented all those without official passes from entering the airport. The only vehicle allowed on the tarmac was the royal car, bringing the Lord Chamberlain, the Earl of Clarendon. After shaking Chamberlain by the hand and offering his congratulations, Clarendon handed over a message from the King. 'My dear Prime Minister,' it read, 'I am sending this letter by my Lord Chamberlain to ask you if you will come straight to Buckingham Palace so that I can express to you personally my most heartfelt congratulations on the success of your visit to Munich. In the meantime this letter brings the warmest of welcomes to one who by his patience and determination has ensured the lasting gratitude of his fellow countrymen throughout the Empire. Yours sincerely and gratefully, George RI.'[60]

Before departing for Buckingham Palace, Chamberlain spoke to the crowd, one of the defining moments of the late 1930s. 'I want to thank the British people for what they have done, and next I want to say that the settlement of the Czechoslovakian problem, which has now been achieved, is in my view only a prelude to a larger settlement in which all Europe may find peace.' He drew from his pocket the piece of paper. 'This morning I had another talk with the German Chancellor, Herr Hitler, and here is a paper which bears his name upon it as well as mine. I would just like to read it to you.' When he reached the phrase 'Never to go to war again' his words were lost in cheers.

Dunglass followed Chamberlain to Buckingham Palace. The crowds pressing forward along the Great West Road to greet the cavalcade and the throngs as the convoy neared central London were an ineffaceable memory. He accompanied the Chamberlains into the palace where the Prime Minister and his wife were received in private audience by the King and Queen. Queen Elizabeth was struck not by the sense of elation that Chamberlain might understandably have exuded but by the awareness of utter exhaustion. Shortly after seven o'clock, the King and Queen appeared on the floodlit balcony with the Prime Minister and Mrs Chamberlain. Dunglass could hear the surge of cheering and singing; it was the first time a commoner had been honoured in this way and was later to be a source of controversy. The most trenchant criticism came in a letter from Taplow in Buckinghamshire: 'To His Majesty the King, I always understood that, in form and theory at any rate, the Crown was non-Party. Why, then, does it depart from its traditional status and lavish praise on a Tory Premier who, far from making permanent peace, has just sown the seeds of prolonged and deadly strife?'[61]

Chamberlain and his party returned to Downing Street, where the BBC had begun a live sound and (for the London area) television outside broadcast.[62] Crowds had broken through the police cordon and Cabinet Ministers and the public clamoured for a sight of the Prime Minister. Dunglass found himself propelled into the lobby of Downing Street and heard someone say to Chamberlain, 'Neville, go up to the window and repeat the historic statement "Peace with Honour".' Even in the bustle of the moment he saw Chamberlain turning upon the man; 'I don't do that kind of thing,' he said, with a flash of anger. Dunglass felt this was the real Chamberlain, not flamboyant or self-seeking. But somewhere on the stairs, where people were packed like sardines, he was persuaded to change his mind. A few moments later Chamberlain appeared at the first-floor window over Downing Street, and spoke to the crowds. Dunglass concluded that it must have been Anne Chamberlain, for from the moment that she was reunited with her husband at Heston, she never left his side during the return to Downing Street. When it was clear that Chamberlain was going to speak, there was a lull. 'The scenes culminated in Downing Street when I spoke to the multitudes below from the same window I believe as that from which Dizzy announced peace with honour 60 years ago,' he wrote.[63] On 14 July 1878, after successfully concluding the Peace of Berlin, Disraeli had announced to the crowds gathered in Downing Street that he had brought back 'Peace with Honour'. This was indeed so, but Disraeli was more cautious in private, writing to his Secretary of State for India that the Government would continue to be popular with the country as long as they believed that it was indeed 'Peace with Honour … but if they find there is no peace they will be apt to conclude there is also no honour'.[64] This became a close parallel in the year ahead, which could not be seen as Chamberlain spoke his fateful lines: 'My good friends. This is the second time in our history that a British statesman has come back from Germany with "Peace with Honour". I believe it is peace for our time. We thank you from the bottom of our hearts. Now I recommend you to go home, and sleep quietly in your beds.'[65]

Dunglass saw Chamberlain as he stepped back into the room. His eyes were full and Dunglass knew that Chamberlain, in his heart, sensed he had made a fatal mistake. Dunglass never forgot the conflicting emotions of these thirty-six hours. He stayed at Downing Street until Chamberlain had finished reporting to a hastily convened Cabinet, a meeting at which Duff Cooper voiced his doubts, and offered his resignation.[66] As he walked with difficulty through the crowds to Chester Square, his feelings were of apprehension that the peace might not hold. Chamberlain had told him that Hitler was the 'nastiest piece of work he had ever had to deal with', and they had both been struck by Hitler's foul mood, particularly towards Mussolini. Dunglass thought Hitler felt upstaged, in that the Italian leader was the only main negotiator who understood all three languages employed – English, French and Italian.[67] As Dunglass turned into Whitehall, unrecognised in the throng, though his photograph now appeared frequently in the press, a souvenir seller approached him with mementoes. Elizabeth Dunglass was building up a set of volumes of their life together and he bought a silk scarf, embroidered with the words 'Souvenir in Commemoration of the Great Peace without Bloodshed'. It was never worn, but placed in the scrapbook for 1938, 'bought in Whitehall, Friday eve 30 September 1938'.[68]

'I must make an effort to get away,' Chamberlain wrote to his sister the next day, 'if only for a week.'[69] Dunglass suggested to the Chamberlains that they should come to the Hirsel once the debate on the Munich Agreement was over. There they could all find some respite.

The first trickle of dissent, which over the years became a torrent, came with the resignation of Duff Cooper. Among the many letters Cooper received over the next few days, commending him for his integrity and courage, was one from Bridget McEwen, wife of John McEwen, MP for Berwickshire.

> Dear Duff,
>
> I am so sorry you have felt you must throw up the Admiralty because I know you liked it and I have always depended upon you to put some ginger into the Navy, but everyone must respect your motives and regret your decision – If you are right you will have all the fun of saying 'I told you so' and if you are wrong you will be the last to mind.[70]

When the House divided on 6 October, thirty Conservatives abstained, thirteen of them remaining in their seats as the voting proceeded. The motion was 'That this House approves the policy of His Majesty's Government by which war was averted in the recent crisis and supports their efforts to secure a lasting peace.' It was carried by 366 to 144 votes. After the debate Chamberlain returned to Downing Street to change for his overnight train journey to Scotland with his wife and Alec Dunglass. They were driven to King's Cross early, so that Chamberlain could retire. The exhaustion that had been apparent to the Queen at Buckingham Palace had now overtaken Chamberlain completely and was widely understood. What Dunglass knew, however, was shared only by an intimate few, and was the reason he had suggested complete seclusion in the Borders. On 2 October Chamberlain had been walking in the woods at Chequers and had suddenly felt that he was experiencing a breakdown. The moment passed but he was deeply worried by the medical implications, as he confided to his sister Ida that day. 'I came nearer there to a nervous breakdown than I have ever been in my life.'[71] Prompted by this news from his son, the Earl of Home at once offered the Hirsel as a refuge for the Chamberlains. Dunglass realised the Prime Minister was completely played out and fielded all press questions the following morning at Berwick-upon-Tweed station. He told a representative of the *Scottish Daily Express* that Chamberlain was in Scotland for a complete rest, adding, 'He intends to fish but that depends greatly on whether the rain may cause the river to flood.' News of the Prime Minister's visit to Coldstream had spread and, despite the early hour, people were standing by the roadside. Alec Dunglass issued an appeal to the press to leave Chamberlain in peace and, apart from a few photographs taken when the two were fishing on the Tweed and clambering on the walls of the ruined Norman keep at Norham, this wish was respected.

The Prime Minister's visit to the Hirsel was a great occasion in the history of the estate, despite its essentially private and recuperative nature.[72] Alec and Elizabeth Dunglass acted as the effective hosts, motoring over from nearby Springhill to co-ordinate the programme. To begin with Chamberlain stayed indoors, but later in the week he went fishing on Birgham Water with Alec and did some desultory shooting with his hosts. By 9 October Chamberlain felt able to say to his sister, 'I have had no return of that brief mental disturbance at Chequers and though I am physically tired I get a bit better each day. I expect to be still here next week.'[73] In the event, he stayed ten days at the Hirsel – the last prolonged social relaxation he and Dunglass had together. These days were the culmination of their relationship and the beginning of its end.

Gradually official boxes began to arrive from London and after a week Chamberlain found the morning and evening occupied by official work; the long Hirsel drawing room became a temporary private office. 'In two days I must go back to work at the numerous problems which lie before me,' Chamberlain wrote to his sister Hilda. 'I have had a very pleasant quiet time here. Salmon have been down or I haven't succeeded in hooking one though I got a nice sea trout yesterday of about $3\frac{1}{2}$ lbs. There is a tearing wind *every* day and heavy showers *most* days. Pouches, telephones and letters keep me fairly busy morning and evening.'[74] The Earl of Home enjoyed Chamberlain's visit, but the open-endedness in the arrangements caused him to exclaim to his son one morning, 'I like this fellow Chamberlain, but when's he going?' The arrangement was that Chamberlain would travel back to London via his sisters' home in Birmingham, when they were ready for him. The letter never seemed to arrive, until one morning Alec Dunglass found a letter some days old that he had bundled into his jacket and forgotten. It was from Ida Chamberlain telling her brother to arrive whenever he wanted. On the last morning photographs were taken of the family and the Chamberlains outside the Hirsel, several showing a smiling Chamberlain with the kilted figure of Alec Dunglass's nephew, Robin Douglas-Home, then seven years old.[75] So ended ten memorable days for all the Homes. 'Your family treated me as one of yourselves and that was just how I felt and still feel about you,' Chamberlain wrote to Lady Home. 'I can't remember the time when I have stayed so long under someone else's roof, but your welcome was so genuine that I feel no remorse at having inflicted myself upon you all these days.'[76]

For Alec Dunglass the contrast between Chamberlain at Munich and when he left the Hirsel could not have been greater. He believed that Chamberlain was now on the path of recuperation, his personal health rebuilt to match the high political esteem he enjoyed. How quickly both expectations were disappointed. Within a few months Czechoslovakia was engulfed by the Nazis and Chamberlain's hopes for peace were dashed; shortly afterwards his health was broken and he was out of office. By the time he lay dying two years later, Dunglass was crippled with a life-threatening illness. As Chamberlain departed from the Hirsel on 19 October, in good spirits and with an overwhelming gratitude to his PPS, he looked forward to the new parliamentary session with optimism. In its place came disappointment and obloquy.

Dunglass had been with Chamberlain for two years and eight months. His spell as Parliamentary Private Secretary had less than two years to run, though he was offered an Under-Secretaryship on the outbreak of war in September 1939, which he declined because he wanted to remain with Chamberlain to the end. His most important role in the immediate post-Munich period – and one of some controversy – was in the notorious Kinross and West Perthshire by-election of December 1938. By one of the repetitive ironies of history, the constituency was the one he fought as Prime Minister, in a by-election twenty-five years later.

By-elections can serve many functions, apart from their necessity to fill a vacancy in Parliament: their psychological impact can often be more important than their statistical one. After Munich there were an unusually large number of by-elections pending, and eight were held between 27 October and 21 December. Three of these – Oxford, Bridgwater and Kinross and West Perthshire – were fought, unusually, on foreign policy and were interpreted as giving the voters an opportunity to express their views on Chamberlain's appeasement policy. Oxford and Bridgwater were *sui generis*, in that the opposition parties withdrew to unite behind independent anti-Munich candidates, A.D. Lindsay (Master of Balliol College) and Vernon Bartlett (broadcaster and former foreign correspondent of *The Times*). Dunglass took no part in either campaign. Quintin Hogg retained Oxford for the Conservatives in a celebrated contest, where in addition to Duff Cooper, four future Conservative premiers – Churchill, Eden, Macmillan and Heath – supported Lindsay. Feelings ran high, one of the anti-Munich slogans being 'A vote for Hogg is a vote for Hitler'. At Bridgwater, Bartlett, standing as an Independent Progressive, overturned a Conservative majority of 10,569 to win by 2332 votes. It is against this background that the Kinross and West Perthshire by-election should be seen.

Kinross and West Perthshire differed from Oxford and Bridgwater in that the anti-Munich candidate was the former Conservative member, the Duchess of Atholl, who had applied for the Chiltern Hundreds in the wake of her de-selection (notwithstanding the presence of the Duke of Atholl in the chair) by 273 votes to 167 by the local constituency association, who wanted a candidate 'who will support the Prime Minister's policy of peaceful understanding in Europe'. The duchess opposed the full weight of the official Tory Party organisation by standing as an independent. She had long been seen as the loose cannon of Scottish Unionist politics.[77] Her first difference with the local Party had come over the India Bill in 1935 (where her stance was right-wing imperialist), but her support for the Republican side in the Spanish Civil War (she feared a Franco victory would have strategic security implications for Britain) gave rise to further tensions and won her the enduring nickname of 'The Red Duchess'. In April 1938 she gave up the government whip for the second time, over Chamberlain's appeasement policies. Her de-selection was the catalyst for the by-election, which was now seen as a further referendum on Chamberlain.

The duchess had been encouraged by Bartlett's success at Bridgwater, but had not reckoned on the powerful campaign now waged against her by the official Party machine, both nationally and locally. The results at Oxford and Bridgwater had indicated that to some extent the jury of public opinion was still out over the Munich policy and it was vital that further anti-Munich expressions should be checked. James Stuart, the Scottish Whip, and his political secretary, Patrick

Blair, co-ordinated a campaign in Kinross and West Perthsire to ensure victory for the official candidate, W. McNair Snadden, a prize-winning breeder of shorthorn cattle and a leading agriculturalist and employer – a fervent supporter of Chamberlain. In short, he would prove a doughty opponent.

'Conservatives have always held that MPs are not the mandated delegates of their associations and have the right to exercise their judgment and follow their conscience,' Stuart Ball has written, 'but in reality this latitude operates within pragmatic limits.'[78] The Duchess of Atholl was now to discover what those limits were in 'one of the dirtiest by-election campaigns of modern times, from which only the duchess emerged with any distinction, and which faithfully reflected one of the most disgraceful periods in the history of the Conservative Party, and Chamberlain's personal vindictiveness against anyone who stood against him'.[79] On the other hand, Kinross has been seen as the most important of the three 'Munich' by-elections, as 'it was the only one to have come about not by the accident of death or promotion, but as a direct result of the controversies over European affairs and as a deliberately staged test of public attitudes on foreign policy'.[80]

Churchill had sent the duchess a letter of support, which infuriated the Party managers, and when Boothby, Unionist MP for East Aberdeenshire, proposed to speak on her behalf, Stuart told him he would lose the whip if he did – a threat also made to Churchill if he dared to participate in the campaign, which at one stage seemed likely. Stuart and Blair now flooded the constituency with big-name campaigners to ensure no repeat of the Bridgwater defeat. The timetable of events, with Christmas approaching, was very tight. The duchess applied for the Chiltern Hundreds on 24 November and the writ for the by-election was moved on 1 December. Nomination day was 12 December and polling day Wednesday 21 December. The crucial weekend was, therefore, the one before polling. On 17 December a group of government MPs was brought in to blitz the constituency, including Sir John Colville, Secretary of State for Scotland, Florence Horsburgh, a leading Scottish Conservative MP, and Ernest Brown, Minister of Labour. Dunglass completed the quartet of 'big names' drafted in and was a pivotal figure in the campaign, largely because he had witnessed the events at Munich. He could give a first hand account of what had happened and put over the official line. Posters appeared around the constituency: COME AND HEAR THE TRUTH

ABOUT MUNICH FROM THE MAN WHO WAS THERE WITH THE PRIME MINISTER.

In atrocious blizzard conditions, Dunglass travelled to Auchterarder where he was billed to speak. 'I was close to the Prime Minister during a part of those critical days,' he told a packed audience. 'I suppose that a full estimate of his achievement will have to be told by history; but during that time he drew his strength and endurance from the knowledge that if he failed, your homes, your future, your happiness, and that of your children would be gone for ever, and that they would perish in a war the causes of which could easily be settled by reasoning and discussion.' He ended by telling how the hotel in Munich had been besieged by Germans as they left for the airport. 'I believe there were none who had not tears of gratitude in their eyes.'[81] The electors should use their votes as a message of encouragement and hope to the Prime Minister in preserving the peace of the world.[82] He then battled through the snow to speak at a hall a few miles from Auchterarder.

Mass Observation, which had been set up in 1937, recorded that 65 per cent of voters in the constituency thought home affairs the most important issue of the day, as opposed to 15 per cent who opted for foreign policy and 20 per cent undecided. This did not reflect indifference to 'Munich', but 'the feeling that the duchess had lost all sense of proportion, had placed too much emphasis on foreign affairs, and had neglected local concerns'.[83] The campaign was one of the first where Mass Observation recorded public attitudes, which reflected the minutiae of the campaign, as in this exchange in Crieff between two women in their fifties:

> 'Oh, the duchess is a fine woman – she is an' all. Ye know she will get in easily. I dinna know much about politics but I do know that if the duchess says Mr Chamberlain is wrong he canna be right.'
>
> 'I am voting for Mr Chamberlain, he saved war. You know, I've always voted for the duchess, but you can't do better than what Mr Chamberlain did, an old man – he went to Germany – why they might have killed him.'[84]

W. McNair Snadden received 11,808 votes and the Duchess of Atholl 10,495, a majority of 1313. The Duke of Atholl went over to Snadden after the results had been declared and said, 'Well, I suppose you are pleased with your majority over my wife.' 'Not quite, your Grace,' Snadden replied. 'I would have liked one more vote, then it would indeed have been Bannockburn.'[85] The collective results of these three by-elections 'demonstrated that the post-Munich situation was still on balance to the government's advantage. The real turning-point did not come until the occupation of the rest of Czechoslovakia in March 1939.'[86]

Dunglass's involvement in the Kinross and West Perthshire by-election, which he does not mention in his memoirs, is an example of an essentially uncontroversial man becoming involved in controversial political events. Unlike many of those who participated, notably Patrick Blair, he emerges with no retrospective obloquy. His was a supportive, loyalist Chamberlain stance, totally in character and conducted with integrity. He believed in the rightness of Chamberlain's position, though he was not without regrets, as he had known the duchess and her husband for many years. His speech at Auchterarder showed passion and emotion, but his role was low-key. He did not play any part behind the scenes before the by-election and during the campaign 'he said nothing exceptional, and indeed was notably mild and circumspect in his involvement in the election'. Nor did the duchess hold it against him: 'I am sure that Dunglass's role ... did not attract any attention or hostility on the part of the Conservative "anti-appeasers".'[87] The by-election could have been a damaging episode for Dunglass and his prospects in the years of the Churchill hegemony. Although Stuart and Churchill made up their quarrel, it was never entirely forgotten or forgiven, but by the time of the Conservative victory in the 1951 general election, Stuart was again one of the kingmakers and Dunglass, by then Earl of Home, one of his protégés. Both Home and McNair Snadden joined Stuart's ministerial team when he became Secretary of State for Scotland, as Minister of State and Under-Secretary respectively.

Kinross showed the ruthless side of the Prime Minister and the Party managers and the premium placed upon Party unity. The by-election had been close run and had made national headlines, and was an indication of the unease surfacing in Conservative ranks. There was a feeling, particularly among those Members who looked to Churchill and Eden for leadership, that relief at the signing of the Munich Agreement was ignoble, in that the relief was for Britain, not for the Czechs.

A less publicised visit than Munich, but one by which Chamberlain set great store, came in January with the journey to Rome for talks with Mussolini. Chamberlain's aim was to drive a wedge between Hitler and Mussolini and, if possible, to draw Mussolini away from any formal alliance with the Fuehrer. In 1935 Ramsay MacDonald and Sir John

Simon had made a similar visit, which had raised real (though equally illusory) hopes that some agreement was possible with the Italian dictator. The visit in January 1939 was even more disappointing, though Chamberlain took excessive comfort from the reactions of the Italian people to his public appearances. Dunglass accompanied Chamberlain and Halifax to Rome, where they stayed for three days, but the substantive talks with Mussolini lasted less than three hours. Much of the time was taken up with purely social and ceremonial detail, and Dunglass was in attendance at all the main events, including factory tours, the laying of wreaths, a visit to the Opera House and banquets at the Palazzo Venezia and at the British embassy. Mussolini made every effort to display his armed forces and the ranks of Blackshirts, with drawn daggers, through which the British delegation had to pass. Dunglass was struck by Mussolini's appalling table manners and his habit of holding his head at an imperious angle to disguise the wart on top of a bald patch. His jutting profile was because of his unwillingness that the blemish be recorded on camera.

Ciano later told Ribbentrop that the political conversations had been 'an innocuous farce'; Chamberlain received no assurances regarding German military activities in the east, which appeared to threaten the Ukraine and Poland.[88] Chamberlain did not achieve his ostensible purpose (in May Hitler and Mussolini signed their 'Pact of Steel'), and Dunglass was relieved when they departed.

What impressed both Chamberlain and Dunglass was the enthusiasm of the ordinary people towards the British delegation, 'The demonstrations in the street went far beyond my wildest anticipations,' Chamberlain wrote. 'My car was always escorted by six special police on motor cycles and the noise of their machines was the only notice people had of my approach ... But wherever I went passers-by stopped and saluted, customers rushed out of the shops, workmen stopped their work to clap and shout "Viva Chamberlain".'[89]

Shortly after the return from Rome, the Dunglasses moved from 57 to 32 Chester Square. It was a happy time: Elizabeth was expecting their second child and Dunglass was in demand on the political scene. In March he made his first radio broadcast, speaking in the slot after the main evening news bulletin on 'Scotland in Parliament'. Later that month he became Vice-Chairman of the Conservative Party's Central Council. With his work for the Junior Imperial League, his daily meetings with Chamberlain and constituency work it was a busy and fulfilled time. But on 15 March feelings of complacency were dispelled by the news that Hitler had entered Prague. This marked the beginning of the end for Chamberlain, although, when he attended the banquet given for him by the 1922 Committee of backbenchers, he was given a 'riotous reception and was cheered and cheered so much so that he was much moved and made no attempt to conceal his emotion'. 'Chips' Channon, his neighbour at table, was pleased to hear that Chamberlain had decided against conscription and Dunglass agreed that it would take 'another dictator's coup to bring that in here'.[90] Not that Dunglass remained uncritical of Chamberlain, who three days later made his statement in the Commons giving unconditional guarantees to Poland. In Dunglass's view this was a hasty pledge and a complete reversal of foreign policy since 1919, which could close off later options. The 'pledge' on conscription made at the banquet went by the board on 26 April to the fury of Attlee and the Labour Party when Chamberlain announced it to the House. Dunglass felt that an election could follow if Labour overplayed their opposition on this issue. He was developing political sensitivity in other areas, noticing how Halifax and Chamberlain were no longer seeing eye-to-eye on all issues; Rab Butler, Under-Secretary at the Foreign Office, was more in tune with Chamberlain on foreign affairs. Since Channon was Butler's PPS, Dunglass was thrown into his company a great deal, which explains his appearing in many entries in Channon's diaries. 'More and more we are being ruled by a small group of thirty or forty people, including myself,' wrote Channon on 11 May, 'for Alec Dunglass and I have woven a net around the PM whom we love and admire and want to protect from interfering, unimportant noodles.'[91]

Mussolini invaded Albania in April and the pact with Hitler followed in May. Chamberlain turned his thoughts to a Grand Alliance between Britain, France and the Soviet Union, plans for which were dragged out and finally dashed dramatically when Germany and the Soviet Union signed a non-aggression pact on 23 August. Parliament had risen on 4 August and Chamberlain had travelled to Scotland for some fishing with the Duke of Sutherland. The Dunglasses spent the first part of the holiday at Springhill, before going to Douglas, but on 21 August Dunglass returned to London to be with Chamberlain. Parliament was recalled on 24 August. The countdown to war had begun. Chamberlain upgraded his pledge to Poland to the status of a treaty, and Hitler delayed his invasion until 1 September. 'Poor Neville!' wrote Bobbety Cranborne on 30 August, 'he has indeed reaped the whirlwind.'[92] Dunglass was at Chamberlain's side continually in these last desperate hours of peace. As at Munich, he was close to all developments, including a message from MI6 that Goering wished to fly to London to see Chamberlain secretly. A security blanket was arranged for Chequers, but no visit ensued.[93] On 31 August Ciano telephoned Halifax proposing a further 'Munich' conference on 5 September. At dawn the next day Hitler invaded Poland.

At 6.30 p.m. on 1 September Dunglass was with Chamberlain when he made his statement to the House: 'It now only remains for us to set our teeth and enter upon this struggle.' But twenty-four hours later it seemed that Chamberlain, clutching at the straw of another conference, was about to reverse his determined stance, which had earned the confidence of Parliament. At 7.42 p.m. Chamberlain entered the Chamber. Thirty-four hours had elapsed since Hitler's invasion of Poland and the pledge had been for immediate guarantees. 'It was evident when he sat down', wrote Harold Nicolson, 'that no decision had been arrived at.'[94] When Arthur Greenwood, acting Labour leader, stood up, there was a unique demonstration from some sections of the Tory benches. 'Speak for England, Arthur,' was the cry attributed to Leo Amery and Robert Boothby.[95] It took the hostility in the Commons, and a Cabinet meeting that night, after a stormy meeting with a delegation of ministers led by Simon, to convince Chamberlain that an ultimatum had to be sent through Nevile Henderson. It would expire at 11 a.m. on Sunday, 3 September.

Chamberlain broadcast to the nation at 11.15 a.m. Dunglass was in the next room at Downing Street, and could hear the message twice, once dully through the door and then on the wireless in the Private Secretaries' room. He believed that his beleaguered master spoke with dignity and that his speech matched the gravity of the hour. Unlike some, he did not think the personal note Chamberlain introduced towards the end jarred: 'It is evil things that we shall be fighting against; brute force, bad faith, injustice, oppression and persecution and against them I am certain that right will prevail.'[96] After the broadcast, Dunglass accompanied Chamberlain to the House of Commons (the first time it had sat on a Sunday), where the Prime Minister made a short statement. The distant sound of air-raid sirens was heard in the Chamber – the all-clear after an earlier false alarm.

Dunglass felt he had to get out of London. He rang his brother Henry and suggested they drive to the South Downs to look for Chalk Blue butterflies. The first hours of war were spent in the countryside they both loved, its tranquillity especially appreciated in this lull. Yet even this was not an oasis of peace. Wandering off into some woods, the brothers were apprehended by a special constable, and it took some time to persuade him that they were not fifth columnists. Alec Dunglass's truthful description of his job as the Prime Minister's Private Secretary ('Yes, and I'm the Queen of Sheba' was the constable's reply) added to the suspicious nature of the two unknown bird-watchers. Only by giving the secret No. 10 telephone number was their story verified. As they journeyed back to London, black-out curtains were going up in windows. Dunglass returned to Downing Street, and when he stood on the steps with Chips Channon, waiting for a thunderstorm to pass, 'I remember that almost simultaneously the words came to us that this was the gods weeping for the folly of man.'[97]

In the aftermath of the declaration of war, Dunglass knew that Chamberlain's days were numbered. 'He will soon go,' wrote Patrick Gordon Walker, future Labour MP and Foreign Secretary, acknowledging that 'many people to hide their cowardice from themselves will vent their shame on Chamberlain'.[98] Dunglass turned his attention to private matters, taking his family back to the Borders where the semi-basement at Springhill was to be given over to evacuees. Their second daughter, Meriel, was born on 27 November, and the first telegram of congratulation was from Anne Chamberlain. Elizabeth and her daughters remained in Scotland during the war; in London, Dunglass shared the house in Chester Square with Evelyn Baring, who had joined the Egyptian Department of the Foreign Office in November. His loneliness in a blacked-out London was alleviated by Baring's presence.

Work for Chamberlain was enlivened by the arrival in the Private Office of Jock Colville, who shared a room with Dunglass and Edith Watson. Each day brought different issues to the fore, in addition to Dunglass's usual work of preparing speeches for the Prime Minister on his frequent appearances before the 1922 Committee. On 7 November Attlee came to Downing Street to discuss rationing; the Labour leader had received an increasing number of letters advocating its introduction. The pressures began to affect Dunglass, an uncharacteristic petulance exacerbated by his general feeling of being run down and tired, an indication of worse problems to come in the new year. After Attlee's visit he remarked to Colville how astonishing it was that people grumbled while one was doing one's best to maintain normal conditions. He felt that a defeatist spirit was growing in the country and was worried lest it spread to the House of Commons. He had no doubt that Hitler was preparing for the long haul, and history taught him that it was a Liverpool not a Pitt, a Lloyd George not an Asquith, who brought the nation out of a lengthy war. Chamberlain was ill at ease as a war leader and Dunglass's last months with him were his unhappiest.

On 15 December, a bitterly cold day just after Parliament had risen for the Christmas recess, he made his last journey overseas with the Prime Minister on the visit to the British Expeditionary Force in France. Dunglass wore his uniform of a major in the Lanarkshire Yeomanry, complete with spurs, 'looking very unmilitary' recorded Colville as the party departed from Downing Street.[99] The instructions issued to the party in utmost secrecy seem in retrospect less than ideal: 'It has been suggested that for the visit to the B.E.F., the most suitable clothing will be shooting kit and, for evening wear, Dinner Jacket.' Travellers were advised to bring a 'British warm' overcoat.[100] Chamberlain was nervous about the whole flight and had a presentiment that the aeroplane was going to crash, though he recorded, 'We flew without incident in rather foggy weather via Shoreham.'[101]

As a fifteen-year-old schoolboy, Alec Dunglass had heard Field Marshal Haig, with his grandfather at the Hirsel, saying that the British must never rely on the French again in a war, as they had been bled white in the one just completed. He told Chamberlain of this as they visited the British troops and then the Maginot Line. Chamberlain needed no persuading; he was profoundly dismayed by what he found. The morale of the British troops was not high, but in the French army morale was at rock bottom. The soldiers were dirty, scruffily equipped and badly led. If France fell Chamberlain believed Italy would join the war for whatever spoils they could get.

Cold and discomfort were Dunglass's main memories of the visit. Chamberlain inspected guards of honour and troops at each stop. 'Lord Dunglass wore a major's uniform, a crown on each shoulder of his British warm, and probably the only pair of spurs in the B.E.F.' ran one press report. Although Chamberlain professed ignorance of the military details, he had an acute awareness of human feeling and felt that the French armed forces were somewhere between preparation and defeat. After lunching in Gamelin's train (hors d'oeuvre, sole, tournedos Rossini, fromages, soufflé au Grand Marnier, fruits) the British party journeyed to Paris, where they were met by Daladier, Halifax and the British ambassador. A dinner for fifty-one guests was held at the War Ministry that evening (consommé, langouste, roulade, fromages, profiteroles, fruits) for which the dinner jackets were necessary. On 18 December a Council was held from nine until one o'clock. After lunch, the party was driven to Le Bourget airport, and Chamberlain's presentiment about safety returned as the flight was all in cloud 'and the last part very low over the houses'.[102] Newsreel film of the visit, highlighting the icy airport parade, was widely shown in British cinemas; it did nothing to reassure the public of Chamberlain's suitability as war leader.

On his return, Chamberlain reported to the Cabinet and told Dunglass that in the New Year his principal theme would be that Britain was approaching a grimmer phase of the war and should prepare accordingly.[103] Dunglass kept Chamberlain in touch with restive feelings in the Commons, and, occasionally, with more encouraging developments. Chamberlain wrote in his diary:

> The H of C which had for a long time been sitting three days a week rose on the 14th for a month. It is an immense relief to me for though I seem always able to carry this House with me it is a great extra strain to be always thinking about it & preparing answers to questions, making statements or debating speeches. The last week provided an example of all these, the statement being made on Thursday, the day we rose, questions every day and the debating speech in the secret session on Wednesday. David Margesson & Alec Dunglass both reported that the speech had pulled the party together after a ragged debate, but of course I had to give the whole afternoon & evening to it.[104]

For Chamberlain the new year was to bring defeat and death. The months of the 'phoney war' were dismal, Chamberlain's melancholy affecting all who served with him. Alec Dunglass was also to experience reversal and a glimpse of death in 1940 – the nadir of his personal and political fortunes. The last echo of the peacetime years was the Easter weekend at Springhill. Alec and Elizabeth entertained a house party, including Roger Makins and Evelyn Baring. It was a happy time, all the more poignant for the knowledge that the crisis for their generation was at hand. In April, Dunglass spent six quiet days fishing in Birgham Upper Water, and recorded Elizabeth's success in landing a salmon.[105]

He returned to the feverish atmosphere of Westminster after the Easter recess, a time described by Baring as 'universal gloom'.[106] News of the Norwegian naval reverses culminated in the fall of Trondheim on 16 April, and an extraordinary episode involving Alec Dunglass. Admiral of the Fleet Sir Roger Keyes, famed for his part in the Zeebrugge raid in 1918, sought command (in his sixty-eighth year) of a special task force to recapture Trondheim.[107] He tried to persuade Churchill, as First Lord, of his claim, suggesting that Chamberlain had not discouraged him. It transpired that Keyes had indeed gone to 10 Downing Street to see the Prime Minister, but Rucker and Dunglass had waylaid him. Dunglass wrote, 'I pointed out that Churchill was, after all, not merely First Lord but Chairman of the Military Co-ordination Committee, and that if he were to bring forward a scheme backed by his full authority, then obviously there would be a very good chance that his word would go with the War Cabinet.' This tactful stalling had been misinterpreted by Keyes as a guarantee from Chamberlain. Dunglass noted that Keyes was 'so excited as to be almost incoherent, and apparently heading for a brainstorm, so he may generally have misunderstood'.[108] Chamberlain was contemplating a change at the Admiralty at this time and used Dunglass as his eyes and ears to tap feelings in the Party, as Channon recorded:

> Dunglass pumped me: did I think that Winston should be deflated? … Ought he to leave the Admiralty? Evidently these thoughts are in Neville's head. Of course he ought to go, but who could we replace him with? Today I heard that chagrined by his failure at the Admiralty, he has now thrown off his mask, and is plotting against Neville, whom up to now he has served loyally; he wants to run the show himself: all this was inevitable, and I am only surprised it did not come before.[109]

At the beginning of May, Makins and Baring told Dunglass that Chamberlain was far too complacent, but Dunglass felt that Chamberlain was the only person who could contain the war situation. He told Baring that the service chiefs 'predicted chaos in the inner circle without Neville'.[110]

Dunglass accompanied Chamberlain to both days of the Norwegian Debate. He was one of the team of whips and private secretaries 'tremendously busy trying to persuade the revolting Unionists to vote for the Government "just once more", promising them that Neville would see them next day and tell them about his plans for reconstruction, even hinting that he might sacrifice Sam Hoare and John Simon to assuage them'.[111] One of the figures, whom Dunglass approached (unsuccessfully) was Paul Emrys-Evans, Conservative member for South Derbyshire, who made it clear that matters had deteriorated too far; Horace Wilson was greatly resented by many backbenchers, as were the strong-arm tactics of the whips under

Alexander Frederick Douglas-Home
in his mother's arms, 1903

'Life was ordered but not stern':
the young Alec with his grandfather in 1907

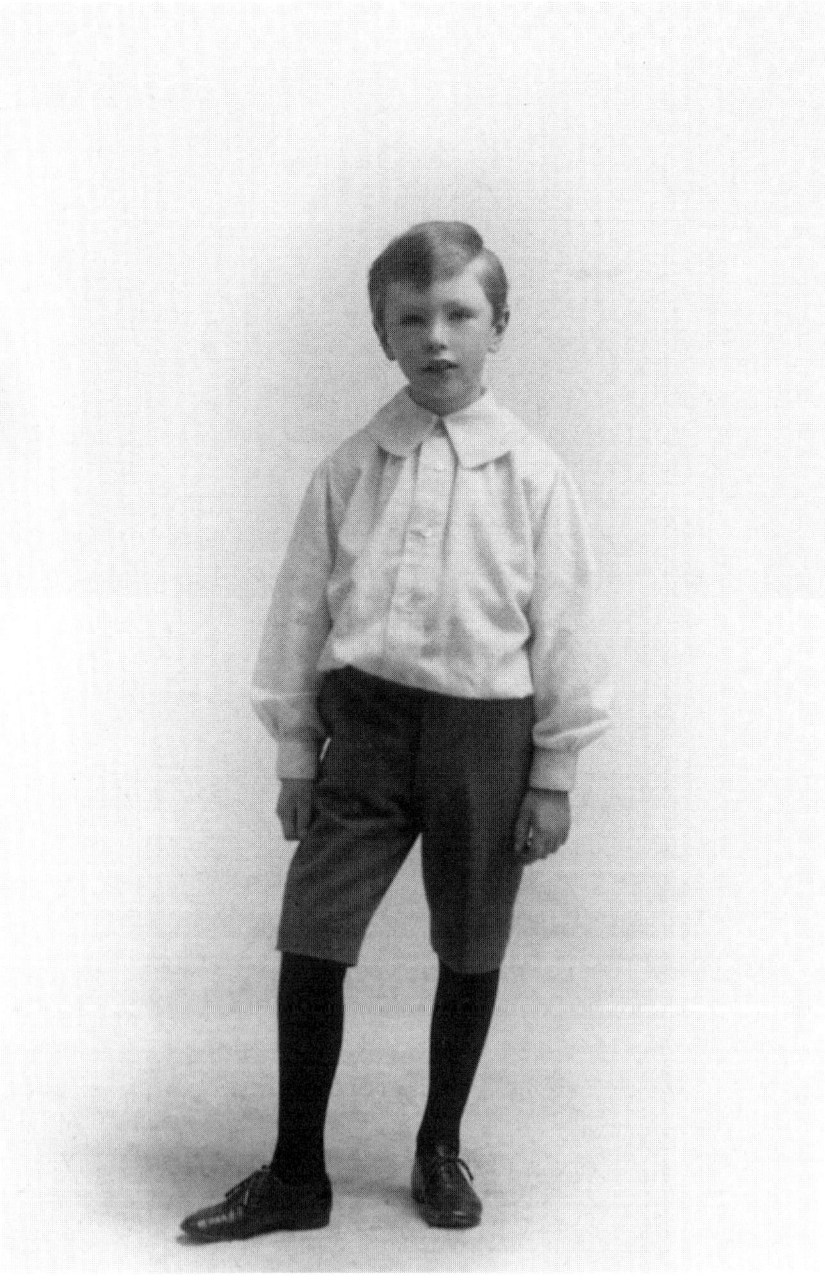

'Shall I tell him to mind his work,
and say he's sent to school to make himself a good scholar?'
Alec Douglas-Home before going away to Ludgrove

Alec, Bridget, Henry and Rachel in the grounds of Springhill:
'It was an idyllic place in which to bring up young children'

'But we'll ever be true/ To the flag – white and blue':
A. F. Douglas-Home (back row, second from right) at Ludgrove School
in the autumn of 1913

Douglas Castle in the 1920s

Alec Dunglass receiving a presentation at his coming-of-age, 1924

The 13th Earl and Countess of Home with their seven children, the Hirsel, 1924

LANARK IN THE 1930s

Inspecting the Boys' Brigade, Motherwell, May 1931

Alec Dunglass addressing a meeting in Lanark, 23 August 1931, the day before the formation of the National Government. His sister Bridget is seated at the table

Captain Lord Dunglass (seated second from right) with the Lanarkshire Yeomanry in the summer of 1939

'The happiest day of my life':
Alec Dunglass leaving Durham Cathedral on 3 October 1936
after his marriage to Elizabeth Alington

Margesson.[112] After this rebuff Dunglass considered Chamberlain's position parlous, and over the next two days he watched despairingly the interventions of Leo Amery (who quoted Cromwell's words to the Long Parliament, 'In the name of God, go'); the antics of Sir Roger Keyes, with a dramatic exposé of the weaknesses of the naval operation; and David Lloyd George, who asked for the Prime Minister's resignation 'because there is nothing that can contribute more to victory in this war than that he should sacrifice the seals of office'.

When it became clear that Labour would divide the House, Alec Dunglass was among those drafted in to put pressure on wavering backbenchers. A three-line whip was of no avail and when it became clear that Chamberlain would not be able to stay in power without a fundamental reorganisation of the government, Dunglass despatched Channon to ascertain the attitude of the Labour Party to joining a national coalition. Attlee and Greenwood soon called at Downing Street to disabuse Chamberlain of any hope he might have entertained of heading a new Coalition Government.

In circumstances of some relevance to the way Dunglass was to become Prime Minister in October 1963, a successor to Chamberlain was sought. There were two possibilities: Lord Halifax and Winston Churchill. The King favoured Halifax and felt that 'his peerage could be put in abeyance for the time being', enabling him to speak in the Commons without disclaiming his title.[113] But the decision for Churchill became inevitable when Halifax declined to be considered on the grounds that 'it would create a quite impossible position' and that he would 'speedily become a more or less honorary Prime Minister, living in a kind of twilight just outside the things that really mattered'.[114]

The next evening, Chamberlain, accompanied by Dunglass, drove to Buckingham Palace to tender his resignation as Prime Minister. They returned to Downing Street at 6.25 p.m., by which time Churchill had already been sworn in as Prime Minister. At 7.15 p.m., Alec Dunglass and Jock Colville 'went over to the FO to explain the position to Rab, and there, with Chips, we drank in champagne the health of "the King over the Water" (not King Leopold, but Mr Chamberlain). Rab said ... that the good clean tradition of British politics – of Pitt as opposed to Fox – had been sold to the greatest adventurer of modern political history'.[115]

Chamberlain's team was swiftly marginalised. 'Horace [Wilson] has been told bluntly that his services at No. 10 are no longer required, and Miss Watson is to be relegated to a back room to deal with "the post".'[116] Dunglass's reaction was bitter. When he found that Wilson's papers and possessions had been unceremoniously dumped outside his office during the lunch hour, he remarked, 'The advance troops are on the sofa.'[117] A few weeks later he was even more forthright, as Nancy Dugdale reported to her husband, 'Alec said in the last fortnight, and indeed since W[inston] came in, the H of C had stunk in the nostrils of decent people. The kind of people surrounding Winston are the scum and the peak came when Brendan [Bracken] was made a P[rivy] C[ouncillor]! For what services rendered heaven knows.' (The first thing Dunglass did on hearing that Bracken was to be 'the new man at Number 10' was to burn all his confidential papers, lest they fell into the wrong hands.) Already the signs of Dunglass's illness, contributing to his uncharacteristic language, were apparent to his friends, as Nancy Dugdale reported in the same letter. 'Alec was not looking at all well, *so* thin and a stye in his eye. I told you he is joining the Home Defence. He told me the Flanders campaign had been such a gigantic muddle that it beggared description.' His anger at Chamberlain's treatment made a deep impression on her.[118]

'He is rather gloomy about Winston as Premier and I have my doubts too,' Baring wrote to his wife. 'Alec says that in the middle of the debate [in the Commons, after which many Conservatives abstained to show their lack of support for Neville Chamberlain] there was a noise like an air raid siren which was Quintin Hogg who leapt to his feet and screamed five times 1000 to one against Neville.' On Whitsunday Baring 'took picnic lunch with Alec beyond Croydon. Three holly blues after a terrific chase to the noise of endless fighters from a neighbouring aerodrome. Alec says he can stand anything provided that Bob Boothby and Harold Macmillan are not put in the Government. [Boothby became PS to Lord Woolton at the Ministry of Food and Harold Macmillan PS to Herbert Morrison at the Ministry of Supply.] He is not very pleased at Anthony Eden's appointment [Secretary of State for War].' Two days later, Baring wrote, 'Alec tried hard not to be catty about the new govt, but could not refrain from saying that Winston had had a very cool and Neville a rapturous reception in the House.' By 23 May Dunglass had said to Baring that 'Neville was in despair yesterday and thought it was because he was not used to war'. Hitler's onslaught, according to intelligence reports, was planned for 6 June. Dunglass got out of London whenever he could. On one occasion he was arrested by the Oxfordshire police, while searching for butterflies in a wood, after a woman had reported his suspicious behaviour (a repeat of his brush with the law on 3 September 1939).[119]

On leaving Downing Street, Chamberlain retained the leadership of the Conservative Party (Churchill became leader only on 9 October 1940, on the resignation of Chamberlain) and was appointed to the War Cabinet as Lord President of the Council. Dunglass moved with him to the Privy Council Office in Whitehall, but it was a melancholy time. Nancy Dugdale kept her husband in touch: 'Alec told me that WC consults NC about NOTHING, neither the small nor the large things and he tells him nothing. Poor N. No wonder he is so low.'[120] Chamberlain, although he did not know it, was mortally ill with cancer, and Alec Dunglass was on the verge of the most serious illness of his life. It was a time for retrenchment. 32 Chester Square was requisitioned for billeting; a newspaper headline proclaimed 'Bombed East-Enders to Stay in Exclusive Belgravia'.[121] As Parliament departed for the summer recess, Dunglass wrote what was to be his last letter to Chamberlain. 'There are many of us who date our hope of victory from the day when you exploded the myth of collective security with the speech on "midsummer madness", and many more who saw in the faces of those people who greeted you in Munich and London a deep longing for peace, the strength of which could not be long denied.' He assured Chamberlain that the younger generation 'would always be grateful to you and will turn to you again for help and guidance in building a better and happier world'.[122] Chamberlain replied, 'I could not see the end of our particular association come without a feeling that something good had gone out of my life which could not be replaced. You have given me all that a PPS should, and I have felt confident, as long as you were there, that I was not missing the main currents of opinion in the House.'[123]

Speculation about Dunglass's future now began to appear in the political columns.

> Lord Dunglass, who was PPS. to Mr Chamberlain when he was Prime Minister, is still in the same service. His technique is not so breezy as Mr Bracken's. Lord Dunglass is a slim, fair-haired young man with a mild manner and an appearance of shyness. These characteristics were at times encouragement to bluffers. They soon discovered how deceptive appearances could be. The shyness disappeared and in firm and polite tones callers were told just what Lord Dunglass wanted them to know.

Chamberlain resigned his post as Lord President on 3 October and went to spend his last weeks at Highfield Park, Heckfield. He was visited by the King and Queen, and Cabinet colleagues such as Halifax. By that stage Dunglass was too ill to visit his former employer as press comment had hinted in speculating whether he would continue as PPS to the new Lord President. 'There is some doubt, however, whether he is medically fit. His indifferent health has been keeping him away lately from the House of Commons … He is ill at the moment, but will doubtless wish to have some field for his activities shortly.' For a short time he was attached to Sir Edmund Ironside's staff and joined the Home Guard, but by the end of September his name began to appear in the 'Invalids' column of *The Times*: 'Lord Dunglass, MP, has just undergone in Scotland a rather serious operation for spinal trouble. Though he is making good progress towards recovery, his convalescence is likely to be protracted.' The *Daily Telegraph* reported that it was not now going to be possible for him to join the Guards: 'He intended to do that immediately Mr Chamberlain resigned his post as Lord President of the Council. Now like Mr Chamberlain himself he is attacked by serious illness.'[124] When Chamberlain heard of Dunglass's illness, though only a few days away from death, he wrote a last letter. 'I trust that you are getting better, but I am afraid your recovery will also be a long business and I hope you won't attempt to take up active work until you are really passed fit to do so.'[125]

Chamberlain died on 9 November. 'He was happy in his soul that last week and was ready to go – and not afraid to die,' wrote his widow. 'No one should fear death less than he.'[126] His death drew one of Churchill's most eloquent tributes to an 'English worthy', though, as he admitted to his secretary, Kathleen Hill, after he had dictated the speech, 'Of course, I could have done it the other way round.'[127] Alec Dunglass, who was devastated by the news, wrote to Anne Chamberlain from Springhill:

> I know you will forgive this very short letter which brings with it my fullest sympathy in your overwhelming sorrow.
>
> Words seem pitifully inadequate to express the sense of loss so real and so lasting which Neville's death has brought and yet it seems almost ungrateful to speak of loss for none could know him without the gain of a fuller and richer life himself.
>
> I shall always remember the generosity with which he gave of his friendship and wisdom to a much younger man.
>
> I shall always remember too the courage and tenacity and faith

> with which he fought for peace for us all and I shall always count it my good fortune that I was with him then and was given a privilege so precious – so rare.[128]

Alec Dunglass's father had written to Mrs Chamberlain, 'We shall always remember his wonderful help and goodness to Alec.'[129]

Dunglass's four and a half years with Chamberlain were to prove the most politically formative time of his life. They gave him insight into the world of foreign affairs, until that time a closed book; more importantly, they gave him understanding of the core operation of the government machine, the diverse pressures on the executive, and the impossibility of accommodating will to circumstance. First at the Treasury and then in Downing Street, he saw the loneliness of the highest offices and the fickleness of public approbation. Looking back on the tragic events of the late 1930s he felt that 'people generally had been lulled into a feeling of security and those years in the 20s must certainly carry a part of the blame. And I should be surprised if those who analyse the events of those years in the future, do not find that it was in the 20s that the seeds of pacifism and complacency were very largely sown.'[130] In his retirement, many historians approached him for recollections of that period; an endearing aspect was the care with which he replied to the young, who were studying Munich at school. One such letter (ironically written on 30 September 1985) is an example of his reflections:

> No one could have been surprised by the outbreak of war, as Mr Chamberlain had taken the possibilities of conciliation and compromise to the limit.
>
> Munich was criticised heavily, but Britain gained a year, and the Hurricanes and Spitfires which saved us arrived on the airfields literally just in time for the Battle of Britain.
>
> I was not surprised at Russia's attitude. They were playing for time. Their alliance with Hitler was totally cynical, but that is the Communist way.
>
> Churchill set great hopes on the French army, but their morale proved to be rotten against the German armour.
>
> The moral for us and our allies is never again to be so weak that an aggressor is tempted to attack.[131]

Dunglass learned many other lessons in his time with Chamberlain, not least the dangers of what later became known as 'shuttle-diplomacy'.

From Munich stemmed his distrust of 'summitry' as a means of diplomatic initiative, with the dangers of public humiliation and failure. Fact-finding missions were less inflexible, and a 'fall-back' position was vital; the dangers of the diplomatic cul-de-sac, coupled with high public expectation, were profound.

The uneasy relationship between Chamberlain and Eden taught him the over-riding importance of trust between the Prime Minister and Foreign Secretary of the day, a characteristic of his two spells at the Foreign Office under very different prime ministers. The Norwegian Debate made him realise that a leader must never underestimate the corrosion of widespread dissent among backbenchers – and even the damage wrought by studied abstention. On reflection he felt that Chamberlain had been guilty of 'playing to the crowd'. He always maintained that the 'appearance on the balcony was completely out of character' and that he was too preoccupied with media exposure.[132] He had understood that one of Simon's fatal flaws was to try to make himself loved, a trap into which Chamberlain latterly fell, as the manifest approval and relief of the public disguised the dangers after Munich. 'He thought there was just a chance that the agreement would hold,' Dunglass said.

Like Thomas Stockmann in Ibsen's *An Enemy of the People*, Dunglass knew that the strongest man is the one who stands alone. This led him, unwisely, to underestimate the importance of the media, which had vastly increased its influence by the time he became Prime Minister. His work with Margesson taught him the importance of the Whips Office; later he never underestimated the roles of Martin Redmayne and Willie Whitelaw. The Kinross and West Perthshire by-election taught him to nurture his constituency, the local agent and his staff. Party Conferences were never Dunglass's favourite time in the political calendar, but he never forgot the solidifying effect Chamberlain's speech had at the 1936 Conference at Margate.

How far did the Chamberlain years hinder Dunglass's career? These years were never forgotten, either by friends or opponents. Hostile commentators (and cartoonists) delighted in evoking the 'spirit of Munich'. When he advised Scots in 1979 to vote against devolution, there were those who said he had begun his career by betraying a small country and ended it by betraying another. 'The accusation was wounding,' wrote Alan Massie, 'but he kept his silence.'[133] In private, Alec Home was always at pains to 'explain' his position over Munich, and was remembered and admired for his loyalty to Chamberlain, not his commitment to a policy. He never wavered from his view that Chamberlain had been right to attempt what he did. In the words of John Maynard Keynes:

> It is our duty to prolong peace, hour by hour, day by day, for as long as we can. We do not know what the future will bring, except that it will be quite different from anything we predict. I have said in another context that it is a disadvantage of 'the long run' that in the long run we are all dead. But I could have said equally well that it is a great advantage of 'the short run' that in the short run we are still alive. Life and history are made up of short runs. If we are at peace in the short run, that is something. The best we can do is to put off disaster, if only in the hope, which is not necessarily a remote one, that something will turn up.[134]

Neville Chamberlain's ashes were buried in Westminster Abbey on 14 November. Alec Dunglass was at Springhill, encased in plaster after his operation for spinal tuberculosis. Owing to the danger of an air raid, the details of the funeral were kept secret; nevertheless the public seats were filled. Churchill led the nation's tribute, and sat just in front of the Chamberlain family with tears streaming down his cheeks throughout the service.[135] Shortly afterwards, a plaque was erected in Chamberlain's memory at Heckfield village church. The epitaph reads:

Write me as one that loves his fellow men.

5

Acquiring Identity

November 1940 was the low point of Alec Dunglass's life. Encased in plaster and isolated from events in London, his career in public affairs seemed to be over. 'Alec does not make very good progress,' reported Horace Wilson to Thomas Dugdale. 'He expects to come to London soon for further examination by the medicos. He wrote cheerfully of the local spirit – as does everybody else, despite loss of home, friends etc.'[1] Nevertheless, he remained Unionist MP for Lanark and his Westminster friends kept in touch, notably Rab Butler, who began a chatty and lively correspondence, informing him of the latest London political gossip.

In retrospect, Dunglass regretted that he had stayed on with Chamberlain, but not because it cost him office as Under-Secretary of State for Scotland or because his wagon had been hitched to a falling star. His regret was that by not rejoining the Lanarkshire Yeomanry in September 1939, he had missed (as events turned out, permanently) the opportunity of active service. Sadder developments lay in store. Towards the end of May 1940 he had taken the first step in what he believed would be a formality prior to donning uniform: a routine examination at the Army Medical Board in Edinburgh. To Dunglass's surprise and annoyance, he was not given immediate clearance. Sir Crisp English, in charge of the board, told him he was completely run down and needed three months of rest and recuperation before a further examination. For many months he had been feeling 'under the weather', and an uncharacteristic tetchiness had been evident as in his comments to Nancy Dugdale about Churchill and his followers.

At the second examination in September there was no improvement in his general condition, and the medical board now advised him to see his own doctor. It was thought that he had a kidney problem and he was examined in Edinburgh by David Band, a leading kidney specialist, but this was not the problem. Dunglass told Band in the course of this consultation that two years earlier he had taken a knock in the lower part of his spine while felling a tree at Springhill. X-rays revealed the severity of his condition: there was a hole in his spine, surrounded by tuberculosis. In the early 1940s advances were being made in the treatment of tuberculosis, once a virtual death sentence. Now there was a glimmer of hope, advanced though his condition was, because the foremost surgeon in this field, Sir John Fraser, was in Scotland and available for consultation. The case was one of the worst Sir John had seen and there was a danger that within six months Dunglass would not be able to walk. He could have a course of injections, which might hold back the disease and allow him some degree of mobility, or he could undergo a risky operation, the only option with a possibility of full recovery.

Dunglass opted there and then for the operation, and Elizabeth, expecting their third child, agreed. His sister, Bridget, was also a source of comfort at this time. Within two days, he was in the Randolph Nursing Home in Edinburgh, and the operation took place on 23 September. It lasted six hours and by the medical standards of the time was one of great complexity. The surgeon had to scrape out the diseased hole and take healthy fragments of bone from the patient's shin to plug the gap in the spine. Characteristically, Dunglass would later joke that he was the only politician to have backbone put into him. Once the operation was completed, he was encased in plaster which was to remain in place for almost two years.

He returned to Springhill by ambulance in the second week of October, and a ramp was constructed at the house to enable him to be wheeled into the garden. Until the plaster was removed, it would be impossible to tell whether the gamble had paid off. 'I had a very down letter from Elizabeth,' wrote Nancy Dugdale to her husband, 'to say that Alec has had a terrible operation to his spine and has to be flat on his back for a year in plaster of Paris, encased in it – he has suffered terribly. Poor Alec.'[2] The only bright spot in an apprehensive and troubled Christmas season was the birth of the Dunglasses' third daughter, Diana, though when the doctor came from the delivery his thumbs were down: the family had wanted an heir.[3] Alec Dunglass's extended recuperation, with the seemingly endless time in plaster ('Isn't it itchy?' he said to a fellow sufferer), was a daunting experience: the pain changed his perception of life and the world about him. Until his tuberculosis, he had felt that he was physically weak, and to a certain extent, despite all his advantages of birth and position, without direction. His illness changed that. He realised that it was an obsessive not a casual disease, and survival depended on patience and resolution, as well as the best medical attention. His illness reinforced his inner strength and gave him a deeper understanding of the kind of person he was. His spiritual side had always been strong, though he never paraded his religious nature. In the years of convalescence, surrounded by a loving and caring family, as well as less flexible nurses, he drew on these springs, which gave him the will to be what he was, through greater self-knowledge. Thereafter he had a fellow-feeling for those who experienced tuberculosis, particularly for Jonathan Aitken, the young son of Sir William Aitken, the MP for Bury St Edmunds, who had fought with tenacity to pull through, with extended treatment and long convalescence in Ireland. When Jonathan Aitken entered the political world he and Lord Home remained close.[4] They were survivors with special strength.

Another who needed comfort and sustenance was Walter Elliot, his old friend and mentor, who suffered a horrific accident at Hawick station in January 1943. Elliot had many virtues, but punctuality was not one of them; he would never leave his estate at Harwood to catch a train earlier than he had to, and used to joke that the train should be given a chance. That morning was bleak and icy and the train was five minutes ahead of its timetabled schedule. Rushing in his hobnail boots on the slippery platform, he slipped into the gap between the platform and the swinging carriage door; his right pelvis was wrenched from its socket and he was grievously injured.[5]

Messages came to Elliot from all over the world, but the most helpful and practical encouragement came from Alec Dunglass, recently released from his plaster casing. He wrote a series of letters to Kay Elliot, with advice on how Walter might minimise his discomfort. One letter, complete with miniature drawings, advised

> (1) There is nothing to compare with the arms if you can get them properly supported. I was on a hard bed and could support them with *hard* pillows ... You want them of several sizes and *hard*, otherwise they become hot and uncomfortable. It may be that Walter has no hard bed surface under him – if not, then one has to try the mechanical devices.
> (2) Devices in general are infuriating to the temper and all the reading desks I had on legs were horrible. They were all very cumbersome and would not negotiate my middle which was slightly

> raised and the book was never at the right angle for reading flat. It would never tip forward without the book falling off and hitting one in the face. If I had not perfected the arm system, I was going to explore the second-hand orchestra music stands and see if I could get one adapted. Of course it would have to be strong. Only a lot of very tiresome experiences can get it right. With the book tipped forward to the necessary angle for comfort, it falls out unless the holding clips are substantial.
>
> There are spectacles which enable you to read with the book lying on the chest. I found them horrible and a great strain on the eyes, but I know others who have used them and found them good.

He concluded, 'Give Walter my love and tell him there are compensations about bed which he will discover, especially the feeling of power when one's wife has to do up one's shoes.'[6]

While he had been incapacitated, Dunglass greatly appreciated how friends kept him in touch with Westminster news. He never lost his fascination with the political scene, even when physically at his most debilitated, and he kept up a busy correspondence with many of his colleagues and he received letters from the local Party organisation. However, his most important correspondence was with Butler. Both had tried in vain to persuade Halifax to take on the premiership, and when Halifax became ambassador in Washington in January 1941 – 'this high and perilous charge', as Churchill had described it – Butler had a brief, and not entirely happy spell at the Foreign Office under Halifax's successor, Anthony Eden, before moving to be President of the Board of Education.[7] Dunglass had written to Butler wishing him well and asking about the Westminster scene. This occasioned one of their longest exchanges, as Butler had recently seen Keith Feiling, one of Alec Dunglass's old tutors from Christ Church.

'You will know that he has been commissioned to write the life of Chamberlain,' Butler wrote. 'He has already seen Halifax and Horace Wilson, and spent a little time with me yesterday. He hopes to go north to see you and I think it important that he should spend a little time with you.' Dunglass was interested to hear Butler's assessment of how history might see Neville Chamberlain; he was also delighted to be kept in touch with Feiling and to be of use. Butler continued, 'Keith Feiling's present view is that Neville's early life on the Sissil [sic] Plantation while his brothers went up to London, made him a lonely figure. He came into power late, fully prepared in reading and preparation, but perhaps not psychologically prepared.' This phrase about being 'fully prepared in reading' struck a chord with Dunglass, who was embarking on such a course himself, to fill the long and vacant hours. Butler was perceptive: 'I told Feiling how I thought Neville was like Saul in one respect and the younger Pitt in another. He was like Saul because he towered head and shoulders above all other members of the Cabinet, and like the younger Pitt because he was definitely a man of peace and the husbander of the nation's resources. I drew Feiling's attention to the speech he made in Birmingham on the Friday after the occupation of Prague. I said that in this Chamberlain had compared himself to the younger Pitt and they both died before they saw the end of their work. They both faced the enemy with resolution, both were reserved in manner. I also told Feiling of the many memories I had of Neville when I saw him off his guard; how he was often doing his best to act a part in history, such as when he harked back to the Berlin Conference and used Disraeli's words when he got back from Munich. You will be able to tell Feiling much more to do justice to a great theme.'

Butler ended, as did many of Dunglass's correspondents, with thoughts on the current Westminster scene: 'You asked me my view on politics. I think that centrifugal tendencies are increasing. I notice a good deal of suspicion of the Party Committee which has been set up. I am doing this Committee [The Post-War Problems Central Committee] and having a job to fit it in with all that there is to be done at the Board of Education. It has shown me how dangerous will be the return to Party politics and yet how likely this may be in the future with the need for having a policy with more principle behind it instead of a hotch potch. It is remarkable, for example, how many Labour Ministers there are on the Home Front and how far we are behind as a Party in preparation for the evolution of the future. I find in Education that much of the drive towards a vaguely progressive future comes from Labour. On the other hand, much of the sense comes from our side. I know I shall enjoy the work there and only hope I have long enough to do some good.'[8]

Dunglass was deeply interested in Butler's analysis of the post-war settlement. His experience was primarily in domestic affairs and he understood the basic concerns of his constituents with the 'New Jerusalem' of the Beveridge Report on Social Insurance and Allied Services. Indeed he always considered, and not just with hindsight, that one of Churchill's gravest tactical errors was in not embracing 'Beveridge' more wholeheartedly, from a point of view of both equity and expedience. Dunglass saw Feiling a few weeks later and they talked in the summer house at Springhill, not only of Chamberlain but of Christ Church, and many memories were evoked. There are many discreet insights in Feiling's biography that Dunglass was uniquely able to provide.

Life at Springhill, after the operation, settled into a regular pattern, comfortable rather than luxurious. Things were arranged pragmatically by Elizabeth. An ingenious ramp was constructed for Alec Dunglass's bed so that he could be out of doors as much as possible. He joined in a correspondence in 1941 in the *Scotsman* about rare butterflies: 'I was on the look-out for a hatch of butterflies up here, as in late June I saw a fine specimen of a female *croceus* travelling in search of a suitable place to lay her eggs. So far, apart from the *hyale* recorded from Gullane, a *croceus* has been seen on the Northumberland coast, and no doubt, if people were on the look-out, many more would be found.'[9] He gained comfort from the natural life around him in the Border country, as the animals came to investigate this strange mute figure. The Cheviot hills were a backdrop to the natural panorama before the invalid, their hues and perspectives reflecting the changing seasons. The Tweed flowed past the bottom of the garden and in 1944 Caroline began to learn the intricacies of salmon fishing. At night the sounds of the natural world were punctuated by the drone of German bombers making their way to the Glasgow shipyards.

For wartime the household lived well, largely on the principle of self-help, as with many country dwellers. There was plenty of salmon and game in season, and an abundance of fresh vegetables. Gradually Dunglass gained weight and one of the major worries, before the plaster cast was removed, was whether his legs would sustain the increased weight of his frame. The house was well staffed also, though the men were elderly. Phyllis Coulson, the family nanny, was a crucial figure who kept Springhill and later the Hirsel running for many years. Mr Hay, the handyman and boilerman, came in early each morning to stoke up the boiler, as hot water was a constant need for Dunglass's team of nurses, led by Sister Wilson. (Patterns of nursing were different in wartime conditions from those that obtained later. After Lord Home's stroke in November 1990, his fear was a return to the inflexible disciplines of the 1940s but half a century later the succession of young nurses, mainly from Australia and New Zealand, became informal extensions of the family at the Hirsel.) Mr Feeney, the gardener, came in each day. In the last year of the war there was a nursery maid, Ellen

Philpott, who died from injuries when she was hit by a car, after collecting milk from the bus on the Kelso road.

The maid was Edna Robson (Mrs Edna Berresford), who came from the Newcastle-on-Tyne area. When Elizabeth Dunglass collected Miss Robson from the Newcastle coach, the fourteen-year-old girl (two pounds a month, all found) was very apprehensive. Elizabeth put her mind to rest on one score: if any china was broken, she should say so at once and not try to conceal or repair it. 'I was always treated with kindness. I usually served coffee to his Lordship in the garden summer house as he was still recovering from an illness, and can well remember the occasion I dropped her Ladyship's dinner tray, complete with dinner, when she had retired early, being pregnant at the time. Not a cross word was said to me.' The Dunglasses were considerate employers in other ways. Dinner was punctually at eight and the family never sat late at table, even when there was company. Edna Robson began work at 6 a.m., pulling open the heavy dining-room curtains to see rabbits scuttling away into the undergrowth at the movement from the house across the dew. 'It wasn't all work, however, and I was soon introduced to the joy of Scottish dancing, being slung about by the local youths in the Eightsome Reel or the Call of the Pipes. Sometimes we would cycle miles to some village, returning home with the moon shining on the River Tweed making it glow like a silver ribbon. Mrs Donaldson, the housekeeper and cook, soon took me, a motherless child, under her wing and gave me my first Bible after packing me off to "Kirk" on a Sunday morning. I also read my first papers of Hansard, which Lord Home left lying around, and would listen intently whenever he played the piano, particularly liking a piece called "Jesu, Joy of Man's Desiring".'[10]

Music was not Alec Dunglass's only consolation at this time. He set about embroidering the dining-room chairs in petit point, but his main activity was reading, now more purposefully. As in prep school days there were three books 'on the go' at any one time: a serious political biography or history, a work of fiction, and perhaps one of his father-in-law's detective stories, though as a devotee of the detective story he did not allow family loyalty to persuade him that Alington was in the top flight. In the early 1940s, his predominant reading was in the first of these categories. John Stuart Mill wrote that the enforced pattern of reading insisted upon in his childhood by his father bestowed on him 'an advantage of a quarter of a century over my contemporaries'.[11]

Dunglass's sustained and serious attempt at self-improvement had a similar effect.

The majority of his generation did not have a 'sabbatical' from war or politics, and Dunglass turned adversity into opportunity: he now read the books which helped to shape and confirm his political thinking, notably his anti-communist beliefs, which remained consistent throughout the Cold War period. He read *Das Kapital* from cover to cover – the only British Prime Minister known to have done so.[12] What disturbed him most about Marx was the negation of family, which Dunglass regarded as the key unit in society; this was one of the reasons he was fervently anti-communist. A book which made a great impression was Dostoevsky's *The Devils*, which warned of the nihilism of Russian society and the importance of seeking spiritual salvation as a corollary to the negative aspects of contemporary life. Arthur Koestler's *Darkness at Noon*, which had been published in 1940, also helped his understanding of the consequences of the Russian revolution. Individual liberty and the repression of the human spirit were issues which he considered deeply at this time; two epigrams which made a particular impact were:

> 'Nobody can rule guiltlessly.'
>
> Saint-Just
>
> 'Show us not the aim without the way.
> For ends and means on earth are so entangled
> That changing one, you change the other too:
> Each different path brings other ends in view.'
>
> Ferdinand Lasselle

He also read works by Engels (*Private Property and the State*) and Lenin. He knew the *Communist Manifesto* almost by heart, useful when he was dealing later with Khrushchev and Gromyko. In 1982 he wrote to his grandson Matthew Darby, then at Eton, 'If you have the patience, I will bombard you with a further series of letters on the development of Communist Russia's international relations following her revolution.' These letters were published in book form and were motivated by Home's wish to hand on his experience to the younger generation. It remains the most successful of his three published works.[13] Dunglass also immersed himself in the 'tombstone' lives of the nineteenth-century grandees in their several volumes: Monypenny and Buckle on Disraeli, Morley's *Gladstone*, Winston Churchill's filial tribute to Lord Randolph (the final paragraph of which one later Prime Minister considered a suitable starting-point for an assessment of Lord Home himself),[14] and works on Melbourne, Peel and Rosebery, as well as the three volumes quarried by J.L. Garvin on Joseph Chamberlain (his ministerial colleague, Julian Amery, later completed it in three more volumes). Anything by or on the Chamberlains fascinated him: Austen Chamberlain's *Down the Years* (1935) and *Politics from Inside* (1936), as well as the two-volume life by Sir Charles Petrie, *The Life and Letters of the Rt. Hon. Sir J. Austen Chamberlain*. He eagerly awaited Feiling's biography. Philip Guedalla on Palmerston, Blanche Dugdale's two volumes on Balfour, Lloyd George's various outpourings, Churchill's *The World Crisis*, Temperley's *History of the Paris Peace Conference* – all found their way on to the ever increasing piles. Of the politicians who came to prominence after the Second World War, only Harold Macmillan and Roy Jenkins had his knowledge of political biography.[15]

His earlier taste in fiction had been for the great storytellers, especially Walter Scott and John Buchan, together with 'middlebrow' authors such as Charles Morgan, Hugh Walpole and Somerset Maugham. Now, with time on his hands, his taste deepened, though it did not encompass 'modernist' authors such as James Joyce or Virginia Woolf: he covered many of the mainstream figures of the nineteenth-century novel – Dickens, George Eliot and the Brontës. Evelyn Waugh, C.P. Snow and his Eton contemporary, Anthony Powell, were writers he admired. Waugh's Paul Pennyfeather (in *Decline and Fall*, which recalled aspects of Christ Church) and Powell's Kenneth Widmerpool (in *A Dance to the Music of Time*) were favourite characters.

Alec was the only one of the brothers to remain at Coldstream during the war. Henry served in Scottish Command; William was a captain in the Royal Armoured Corps. Edward, who was at Balliol, enlisted in the Lanarkshire Yeomanry, and George joined the Royal Air Force on leaving Eton. The sufferings borne by so many in those grim years did not spare the Homes. Edward served in India and Malaya; gravely wounded, he fell into the hands of the Japanese and worked on the Burma Railway for three years. William's name is associated with Le Havre. In August 1944, as an Allied assault was about to be launched on the port, the German commander asked leave to evacuate the civilian population. When this was refused, Captain William Douglas-Home, liaison officer between the tanks and the infantry, also refused to take part in an assault in which upwards of 12,000 civilians were killed. William was court-martialled, cashiered, sentenced to a year's hard labour and imprisoned in Wormwood Scrubs before being transferred to Wakefield Gaol. His prison experiences led him to write what Alec considered his finest play, *Now Barabbas*. For the Earl of Home the conflict of emotions as he visited his son at Wakefield, having travelled by train from Berwick to York, were painful in the extreme. 'What it cost him to call on a disgraced son in prison must have been immeasurable,' wrote William, 'yet in spite of this he came to Wakefield Gaol, a little Lord Lieutenant in a bowler hat, because the love he felt towards his children came before all else.' At the end of the visit, the 13th Earl called on the governor, to 'thank the dear little Governor for having William here'.[16] To the end of his life, William maintained that he could have acted in no other way. Though he fought to clear his name and be granted a pardon, this was never forthcoming from the Army board. Some had harsher fates. John Amery, son of Leo Amery, Secretary of State for India in the wartime coalition, was 'one of the casualties of a world revolution in which the accident of his environment, and his own sincere convictions, found him, at the finish, on the wrong side of the barricades'. He was convicted of treason and hanged in Wandsworth Prison in December 1945.[17]

The greatest sadness for the family was George's death in 1943, killed on active service with the RAF in British Columbia. 'Missing, presumed killed' was the official intimation when his twin-engined bomber failed to return to its base. A year elapsed before the news was confirmed; four weeks later Elizabeth Dunglass's younger brother, Patrick, died of wounds in Italy.

The war affected the Hirsel in other ways. Parts of the building were converted for use as a hospital for crippled children, and Alec's sister, Bridget, worked there as a nurse. An episode which had a profound effect upon Dunglass in this transitional stage was one of the darkest of secrets: as he lay in his plaster cast, he received a white feather. From the start, it was suspected that this was from somebody known to the Dunglasses, and it eventually transpired that it had been sent by a close relation. Although Alec brushed it aside, Elizabeth's wrath was formidable. Deeply wounding though the episode was, and one which hurt Dunglass more than he revealed at the time, it had its positive effect. He became even more determined to do something of value in any bonus years granted to him. For the sake of those who did not survive, he now had obligations he was even more determined to fulfil.[18]

News of the seriousness of Dunglass's illness gradually seeped into the local and national press, to be met with widespread regret. In the Scottish press there were retrospectives, almost political obituaries.

Many considered his career had passed its peak. Generally, it was felt that he had not been up to the rough and tumble of contemporary politics, one paper recalling that in Coatbridge he had been 'handled unmercifully by the tough hecklers of that constituency'.[19] But he was not to be written off so easily. The great day came when the plaster was removed. When the outer casing had been cut away, he was not allowed to move until a new plaster jacket had been fitted; only then did he take his first tentative steps. When his father rang that night from the Hirsel to see how things were, Dunglass was able to give the news himself. Gradually he learned to walk again, but it was a long, slow process. He was able to go to North Berwick for a family holiday that autumn and even took Caroline swimming, a sign of great determination, as he had never passed his swimming test at Eton and water sports were his least favourite.

The press reported the improvement, and that he was keeping in touch with government departments in all matters affecting his constituency. There was a convention during the war that if an MP was killed, his successor would have an unopposed candidacy in the subsequent by-election. Similarly, if an MP were prevented through illness or injury from attending his constituency on a regular basis, there was no pressure to apply for the Chiltern Hundreds. In common with many Conservative associations, constituency activities largely ceased in wartime conditions. Nevertheless, Dunglass wrote to a local Party official, who informed his Constituency Association 'that his doctor will allow him to visit the Constituency in a month's time or so'. This tentative beginning was to see how things went medically. 'Lord Dunglass does not desire the visit to be a political visit but he feels it his duty to meet again some of the workers in the various wartime services and also to deal with any questions which might affect any of his Constituents. The visit will be most informal and I shall be obliged if you, in conjunction with other friends in Douglas, could arrange for such a meeting and let me know what would be the most convenient time.'[20] In December he met members of the Women's Land Army at the Bonnington Hotel in Lanark and presented good service badges. Later he met the provost, magistrates and members of the town council, and attended a meeting of the Fruit Growers' Association in Lanark. In the New Year he attended a parade at Douglas to acclaim the feats of the RAF. In his speech Dunglass stressed that the side which had domination in the air would win the battle.

Gradually political meetings picked up again, as he found he was able to take on more commitments. Financially, the Lanark Association was in poor shape, no subscriptions having been collected since May 1940 when 'the activities of the Association more or less ceased'.[21] With the removal of the cast, Dunglass was able to resume normal life in other ways also. Polish troops were billeted at Douglas Castle and among their number was Count Starzenski, who had been private secretary to Poland's Foreign Minister, Colonel Beck. When Germany and then Russia had invaded Poland, Starzenski and his wife left separately and, when they arrived in Britain, Starzenski enlisted under General Anders. Dunglass soon struck up a friendship with the Starzenskis. Even when Dunglass was still immobile, Starzenski had come over to both Douglas and Springhill (where his uniform made a great impression on the children) and spoken at first hand of the horrors and indignities of the Russian occupation of Poland. Dunglass's feelings about the Yalta summit, concerning which he made a courageous speech on returning to the Commons, grew out of these many evening talks at Springhill. His daughter Caroline remembers the Starzenskis half a century later. 'Count Starzenski came to visit us, and to shoot, quite a lot and so did his wife and they both maintained correspondence with my parents until their deaths … They were charming. She was *very* shy.'[22] Although Dunglass did not feel well enough to venture a journey to London, he increased his appearances in both Lanark and Kelso, and in February 1943 he met Chamberlain's widow, who wrote to Lady Home:

> I just must tell you and Lord Home how wonderful it was to see Alec looking so well the other day – better I think than I have ever seen him. It was a miracle of courage and patience on his part – and on all of yours too … seeing him again with all his *fun* and quickness of mind brought back to me with a vivid rush of thought so many things and what it meant to Neville to have him with him … during those years, in good times and in bad times.[23]

He took to bicycling over to the Hirsel to see his parents, which had the double advantage of building up his stamina and conserving petrol. From Douglas he made forays to his Lanark constituency; his agent wrote to all ward branches: 'Lord Dunglass intends to visit the various parts of his Constituency next week and he has suggested that he would like to visit East Kilbride … owing to his own indisposition … and to the present national emergency matters may not be in such good shape as one would like and I hope you will place your local knowledge at his

Lordship's disposal.' In a general circular, the agent minuted: 'Lord Dunglass, who is now able to attend to matters personally, has been worried about the reorganisation of Unionist Associations after the War and he asked me to write to you and ascertain if you could recommend a suitable person to act as Secretary of such an Association in [Forth].' He had assimilated the concerns of Rab Butler and others about post-war political prospects for the Conservative Party, particularly regarding the local organisations, which were understandably moribund.

On 2 July 1943, Dunglass celebrated his fortieth birthday. For the first time in almost three years, it now seemed that he would be able to resume his political career and he made his first visit to the House of Commons since his operation. But most of his political activity was concentrated north of the border. The autumn had been sad, with the deaths of George and Patrick Alington, but the happiest moment of the wartime years at Springhill followed: the birth, on 20 November 1943, of a son and heir. Mrs Donaldson was beside herself with excitement and when Edna Robson asked her about the infant's name, Mrs Donaldson reeled off the full list – David Alexander Cospatrick – without a pause for breath. When the time came for a christening cake, Mrs Donaldson put a dash of ink into the wartime icing to make it light blue for a boy.[24] The future 15th Earl had been welcomed into the world.

Dunglass returned to London to take his place in Parliament once more – a changed man in the eyes of his colleagues. Gone was the shyness and self-effacing aspect of Neville Chamberlain's PPS; he was a parliamentarian in his own right now, a different kind of Westminster foot-soldier – assiduous, forthright, wide-ranging in his interests. He showed much greater interest in foreign matters, particularly those regarding the Soviet Union, and he began to attend various Party committees, notably the Conservative Private Members' (or 1922) Committee. This was to evolve into a backbench body of considerable king-making (and king-destroying) power, but was not founded – as popular myth has it – by the Conservative backbenchers who had brought down the Lloyd George coalition in October 1922. It was the product of the 'Class of 1922', those MPs who had entered the Commons at the subsequent general election on 15 November. Despite its title, the Committee was in fact founded in 1923.[25] By 1944 it had many functions, not least of which was the scrutiny of government policy through a variety of sub-committees; it also voiced backbenchers' concerns.

In the remaining fourteen months, before he joined the caretaker government on 26 May 1945, as Under-Secretary at the Foreign Office, Dunglass took an active part in 1922 Committee meetings. In November the Committee criticised the role of the Board of Trade and its President, the Labour MP, Hugh Dalton, particularly over price controls. 'Dunglass suggested that an amendment never got rid of a minister,' the minutes read. 'A deputation to the Prime Minister would be better.'[26] A new asperity can be detected in his role in this ginger group, but the political reality was that Churchill would have found it difficult to remove a stalwart of the Labour Party at such a juncture.

Dunglass made what was, in effect, his second maiden speech in the House of Commons on 24 May 1944. The new, almost scholarly, authority was apparent; the speech was that of a man who knew what he was talking about and who weighed his words carefully. As he still found it difficult to stand for a long time, its brevity added to the effect of the speech. He told the House that he had recently had to learn to walk again. 'The time is coming, we hope soon, when foreign policy will have to stand on its own legs, and if those legs are to be sound, then a great deal will depend upon a proper reading of history and upon a comparative and approximately accurate assessment of political tendencies, particularly on the Continent of Europe. For the last four years I have had very little to do but study these problems, and I cannot say that the lessons of history are particularly encouraging.' Eighteen years before Dean Acheson declared that 'Great Britain has lost an empire and has not yet found a role',[27] Dunglass warned that Britain would not be able to depend on the empire as in the past and that its defensive needs would increasingly depend on regional security alliances 'cemented by specific military treaty'. The countries he had in mind were Belgium, Denmark, France, Holland and Norway. This did not mean that we should neglect the United States; he affirmed that 'an almost ideal solution would be if the Americans agreed to integrate their defence policy absolutely with our own'.[28] Even at this early stage in his public pronouncements on international affairs, he thought that the European and the American ties, on which Britain would increasingly depend in the post-war world, should be seen as complementary. On foreign policy, Dunglass was 'that great and true amphibium', living 'in divided and distinguished worlds'.[29]

His speech ended with a clear statement of his view on the Soviet Union: 'Two things are necessary in our dealings with Russia. The one is absolute clear speaking upon moral issues when they arise and when we differ, and the other is to make absolutely clear to Russia, beyond doubt, where our vital interests lie in Europe. If they know where our vital interests lie, then the Russians are realists enough not to run up against them, but if they do not know, there might be a danger of a clash'.[30] Dunglass returned to this Russian theme in a speech on 29 September. The previous day, Churchill, in reviewing Polish-Soviet relations and his forthcoming visit to Stalin in Moscow, had said, 'We recognize our special responsibilities towards Poland and I am confident that I can trust the House not to engage in language which would make our task harder.' To Dunglass, with Count Starzenski's conversations still fresh in his mind, this sounded suspiciously like capitulation before the might of Stalin. He was also conscious that Neville Chamberlain had been the guarantor of Polish independence. Accordingly he declared uncompromisingly, 'If after the defeat of Germany this unhappy people are left in bondage and if this country has failed to do anything that we ought to have done, then our national conscience will be uneasy for generations.'[31]

1944 was a year of transition: the question was no longer whether the war would end in Allied victory, but how long it would take to liberate so many oppressed peoples. General Alexander, one of Dunglass's close friends of the post-war era, entered Rome on 4 June, and in the east, the Russians pushed on towards Warsaw and Belgrade. By comparison, Dunglass's activities at the time were very mundane. Political activity at the constituency level continued to be hampered by petrol rationing and by the general shortage of paper. When Dunglass planned a meeting in February 1944, his agent reported that 'it was illegal to have more than ten bills printed for each meeting owing to paper shortage and a space of 100 yards must be allowed between each Poster when displayed'. But there were hints of a return to peacetime conditions. Alec and Elizabeth managed a visit to the Royal Scottish Academy Exhibition in Edinburgh and in August Dunglass made a speech at a garden fête, where Harry Lauder entertained the guests. In September he was appointed Deputy Lieutenant for Berwickshire. Thoughts of the forthcoming election were never far from his mind. The Unionists would not be able to shelter behind a 'National' label when normal political life resumed and, unlike many in his party, Dunglass was aware of the difficulties that lay ahead. He spoke to his local officials about the unpreparedness of the constituency, becoming more pressing as the war neared its end and a general election loomed.

The subject of Poland had been high on the agenda at Churchill's meetings with Stalin in Moscow in October 1944. By the time of the Yalta Conference of 4–11 February 1945 the Russian army was already in possession of most of eastern Europe, including Poland, the base for the final Soviet invasion of Germany.[32] The Russian occupation of Poland meant that Churchill was in a weak bargaining position. For Roosevelt, free elections in Poland had to be 'Above suspicion, like Caesar's wife'; for Stalin, they meant a government unfriendly to the Soviet Union. The dilemma was not satisfactorily resolved by Stalin's 'assurances'. 'Looking back on Yalta', one of the British delegation has written, 'the only alternative course open to Churchill and Roosevelt would have been to refuse to sign any agreement on Poland and Eastern Europe, on the assumption that Stalin was going to carry out policies there regardless of Western interests or those of the local inhabitants. I cannot see that this would have done much good.'[33] Pragmatism was the order of the day. With the controversies that also surrounded the repatriation agreement on Russian prisoners, Yalta's legacy was a bitter one. Yet initial reaction was favourable, especially in America where Roosevelt ensured that his version of events prevailed. Churchill returned to London to adulation and enthusiasm, but in the meantime James Stuart telegraphed Eden from London, 'for your guidance must warn you of Conservative anxiety over Poland increased by active lobbying by Poles now in progress here'.[34]

Stuart had been told by the 1922 Committee of Conservative concerns about Yalta. At a meeting on 14 February, feelings had run very high. Victor Raikes said that 'Poland had been utterly sold out'. At the same meeting, Dunglass said the agreement was a breach of the Atlantic Charter. 'A substantial proportion of London government should have been included. There must be international supervision of the election in Poland.'[35] At the next meeting of the 1922 Committee, backbenchers discussed tactics for the Yalta Debate. When Churchill addressed the House of Commons on the Yalta Agreement, he was thus aware that there were dissenting voices, and he attempted reassurance. 'The impression I brought back from the Crimea, and from all my other contacts is that Marshal Stalin and the Soviet leaders wish to live in honourable friendship and equality with the Western democracies. I feel also that their word is their bond.'[36] Dunglass interrupted on a point of order to ask whether there was going to be international supervision of the elections. Later in the debate he spoke of Poland's precarious position:

> In 1939, when the people of this country had to make a choice between peace and war they chose war because they were convinced to the point of certainty that so long as appeals to force were the rule in international affairs, there could be no peace, nor progress. Since then, whenever we have had time to lift our eyes for a moment from our self-preservation, we have reaffirmed our intention to rebuild and to restore at least the elementary standards in international behaviour.
>
> ... One reason why there is world concern over the differences between Russia and Poland is because it is the first case – a test case – in the relationship between a Great Power wielding great military might and her smaller, weaker neighbour.[37]

Guy Eden, secretary of the parliamentary lobby journalists, wrote to Home that evening, 'I cannot possibly let your terrific effort pass without saying what a fine speech it was. I have heard a few speeches in my time, as you can imagine, but never a more eloquent or obviously sincere one.'[38] The next day, twenty-one Conservatives (including Dunglass) put down an amendment, which regretted that 'the territory of an Ally' should be transferred 'to another Power'. Although this amendment was lost by 396 votes to 25, the government did not escape unscathed. The Duff Cooper of Yalta was Henry Strauss, Parliamentary Secretary at the Ministry of Town and Country Planning, who resigned in protest at the treatment of the Poles. 'The PM is trying to persuade himself that all is well,' wrote Jock Colville, 'but in his heart I think he is worried about Poland and not convinced of the strength of our moral position.'[39] Nor had the irony of the situation escaped Churchill, as Harold Nicolson noted: 'Winston is as amused as I am that the warmongers of the Munich period have now become the appeasers, while the appeasers have become the warmongers.'[40] A.J.P. Taylor stressed the point five years later. 'The greater the readiness to conciliate Hitler ten years ago, the more determined the resolve to resist the Russians now.'[41]

Dunglass's intervention in the Yalta Debate was an act of great political courage, some would say foolhardiness. Churchill was not notably conciliatory towards those who crossed him, and it could not be predicted which way he would jump over Dunglass's intervention. A caretaker government of Conservative tinge would certainly guide the country in the interim between victory and an election and the spoils would be distributed as Labour left the national coalition. The general expectation was that Churchill would win the subsequent election, and the caretaker government would define the ministerial intake for a generation.

Churchill's Foreign Secretary also had to reply to specific questions from Dunglass in the Yalta Debate, some of the points he made winning grudging acceptance. Yet, within three months of the Yalta debate, Churchill and Eden gave Dunglass his first ministerial post, as Under-Secretary at the Foreign Office in the caretaker government. Plain speaking had not harmed his prospects, possibly because he had the ability to put unpalatable truths in a palatable way. At the time of Churchill's centenary on 30 November 1974, when Lord Home paid tribute to Churchill's memory, he did not skirt the question of Yalta:

> At the time it seemed to me that they [Churchill and Roosevelt] had yielded too easily to what could only be labelled Stalin's blackmail. The Yalta Agreement confirmed me in my belief. In a tense debate on it I criticised our government's capitulation. In it Churchill had used a phrase which I could not let go by. He had seemed to accept a Russian occupation following victory as 'an act of justice' – to use his words. I could recognise it as a fact of power but repudiated any suggestion of an act of justice. I have no doubt, perhaps with the benefit of afterthought, that to ask Churchill to stand up to Stalin virtually alone was to require him to be almost superhuman. And I've no doubt he put up a big resistance. At Yalta Roosevelt was mortally ill and could give no help at all; Churchill had won the war against Germany which was his first duty to the British people, and to ask him to open a quarrel with Communist Russia at that point was to ask too much.[42]

Foreign policy was now emerging as Dunglass's main area of interest and involvement. On 7 February 1945 he had visited Eton to give a talk to the Political Society on 'British foreign policy'. At the 1922 Committee he was one of those whose views were now sought on these matters, a clear change of emphasis from the domestic agenda of his days with Skelton and Muirhead. The end of the war was not long delayed. On 8 May Dunglass was among those Members of Parliament who crossed Old Palace Yard to attend a service of thanksgiving at St Margaret's, Westminster, when the Speaker of the House of Commons read out the names of Members killed on active service. On 23 May, after he had been sworn in as Prime Minister of a caretaker government, Churchill hosted a dinner at 10 Downing Street for those who had served in the grand coalition, to which Anne Chamberlain was thoughtfully invited. A general election was fixed for 5 July.

One bright piece of news shortly after VE-Day was from Rangoon: Edward was among those former Japanese prisoners of war now safe in British hands, and the upbeat of renewal was confirmed with news that Elizabeth's sister, Lavinia Alington, was engaged to be married to Roger Mynors. The legacy of suffering, divorce, accident and sudden death had been a common experience. Dunglass noticed the change that the war had wrought in his parents. There were shocks that his father, in particular, never got over: his eldest son's brush with death; the breakdown of Henry's marriage; Edward's years as a Japanese prisoner; William's incarceration in Wakefield Gaol, but above all the loss of the Benjamin of the family, George. What was unusual with Dunglass was that he had experienced so much suffering away from the shared bond of fighting men. Yet he emerged from his illness stronger and sure of the kind of person he was, with more of what Samuel Johnson called 'bottom', that indefinable gravitas so important in politics. If the world is the vale of soul-making, this was the time when Dunglass came spiritually of age. 'I say Soul Making,' wrote Keats, 'but they are not Souls till they acquire identities, till each one is personally itself.'[43] In the 1940s Dunglass acquired that identity.

On 26 May 1945 he entered the Foreign Office, the department with which he was most associated for the next thirty years, in a ministerial capacity, as Under-Secretary of State. Dunglass owed his preferment primarily to James Stuart. Churchill had written to Stuart, a letter charging Stuart with the task of making a first draft of possible ministers. 'The following is in strict confidence,' Churchill wrote 'and you should not consult anyone about it.'

> If charged to do so by the King, I propose to form the most impressive Government I can before the Election. There will have to be an understanding that this Government is liable to very considerable changes and remodelling after the poll, even though we may have a majority. It seems to me that it would be better now that domestic questions will be so prominent, to form a full Cabinet of 18–20 members.

The letter ended with the clear command, 'I invite you to draw me up, as soon as possible, a list of the new Government, upon which I can work.'[44] Apart from a cautious and hitherto unregarded concern that domestic issues would have to be addressed if the Conservatives were to retain an overall majority, this letter shows Churchill's faith in Stuart's advice, particularly for the intake of talent at the second echelon of power.

Stuart went to work with a will. He replied to Churchill on the following day, 23 May, 'I have included the Minister of Health and Works in view of the importance of their work in the domestic field.' In a further comment, which was to be of significance for Dunglass in October 1951, Stuart added, 'The same argument applies to Scotland, with the addition that to omit the S[ecretary] of S[tate] would encourage Scottish Nationalist feeling.' The Foreign Office was high on Stuart's list of priorities. Eden was obviously going to continue as Secretary of State and wanted the election as soon as possible, for stability in the conduct of foreign affairs. The names initially submitted for Eden's team bear many deletions and arrows in Churchill's distinctive red ink. Eventually, in consultation with Eden, Churchill settled on the National Liberal MP for Huddersfield, Sir William Mabane, as Minister of State (one of many attempts in 1945 and 1951 to cement a Conservative–Liberal understanding), and chose Lord Dunglass and Lord Lovat as the Joint Parliamentary Under-Secretaries; their names were at the head of the list of junior offices submitted to the King on 26 May. (Churchill tended to call people by the name by which he had first known them; even after he had succeeded to his father's earldom, Alec was always known as Dunglass.)

'In 1945 he sent me as Under-Secretary to the Foreign Office,' Lord Home said later. 'In a few months of caretaking that had to be done, during which there was almost nothing which we could achieve, I saw Eden at work on matters of which he was a master and I've always been grateful for that experience.'[45] Dunglass now took over what had once been Rab Butler's job. Lovat had no desire to stay in more than a temporary capacity, as he intended to develop his business interests in Argentina. He formally resigned on 6 July, the day after the election, and on 7 July Colville wrote to Churchill, '... there seems no doubt that Lord Lovat's work in the Foreign Office could well be undertaken by Lord Dunglass'[46] – a tacit acceptance that Dunglass would be the senior Under-Secretary if the Conservatives were confirmed in office. The man who had taken Rab Butler's job was being groomed for high things. There was every reason to expect a five-year spell in office, but the result of the election put such expectations on hold for six years.

In his role in the caretaker government, Dunglass set out on the round of parliamentary, Party and Foreign Office activities with vigour and enthusiasm. The caretaker government did more than caretaking; the war against Japan had still to be won, which meant considerable anxiety for Churchill and Eden, who was so preoccupied that both Dunglass and Lovat were hardly consulted at all. (Dunglass was critical of this lack of communication and decided that, if he returned to the Foreign Office, he would remedy this defect, as he did after July 1960.) The build-up to the Potsdam Conference was Eden's main preoccupation, though electioneering also took up his time. Dunglass was employed on representational work, such as the reception he hosted for delegates of the International Red Cross. On 27 June came news that reopened recent wounds for him. Eden's eldest son, as George Douglas-Home had been, was a pilot in the RAF, and was reported missing in Burma. The same anxious interval ensued, until the wreckage of Simon Eden's plane was found in the Burmese jungle. Dunglass sympathised profoundly with Eden in his grief.

He was too shrewd to take his re-election in Lanark for granted; he knew he could expect a tough fight in his constituency. At a meeting at the Bonnington Hotel, Lanark, on 16 June a resolution was passed: 'That the executive Committee recommend the Lanark Division Unionist Association to adopt Lord Dunglass as Unionist Candidate for the Lanark Division at the ensuing General Election'.[47] The local association saw in their sitting MP a man firmly on the ladder of promotion, a future potential Secretary of State. The battle in Lanark was a straight fight between Dunglass and a new Labour candidate, Tom Steele, a former stationmaster, and was the most bitter he ever fought. A whispering campaign hinted that during his 'illness', he had been away on a secret spying mission. He was accused of being a Nazi sympathiser and threats of physical violence were made against him; telephone calls warned him off visiting nominated wards. Undaunted, Dunglass held meetings the length and breadth of his constituency. Outside one village hall an elderly man asked another why he was not going to Dunglass's meeting; the reply was 'I have voted Conservative all my life and I am no gonna be put off by yon long-haired Lord!'[48] His posters seemed to belong to a gentler age, and the acrostic still remained in fashion as it had been in Noel Skelton's time:

*D*ecide against *U*ncertainty. *N*ation needs *G*ood *L*eadership *A*nd *S*ound *S*tatesmanship.[49]

The Unionist Association was not in fighting trim and much of the voluntary help had evaporated in the difficult social conditions of the return to peace. Petrol shortages were more disadvantageous for the Conservatives, with their traditional reliance on private transport, particularly in rural areas. Nevertheless, Dunglass managed to attend forty-five meetings; his personal expenses, notified as required by electoral law, amounted to £13.[50] Polling was on 5 July, but to allow time for servicemen's postal votes, counting was delayed until 26 July. Churchill's standing in 1945 was a complex matter. Anti-Churchill graffiti appeared in working-class areas, his car was scratched in the East End of London and he was sometimes booed on cinema newsreels. His notorious broadcast of 4 June when he claimed that the Labour Party 'would have to fall back on some form of Gestapo, no doubt very humanely directed in the first instance' was a major miscalculation. Nevertheless, it was the legacy of the past that the electorate turned against – the locust years of unemployment and appeasement rather than Churchill himself. The Conservatives were no match for Labour, who were committed to the post-war goal of full employment and social justice. Aneurin Bevan, the Duke of Devonshire, Emanuel Shinwell and Lord Templewood (the former Sir Samuel Hoare) had actually ventured over the parapet to say as much in advance, 'a splendidly comprehensive democratic quartet' as Anthony Howard has described them, though R.A. Butler had made many private warnings, notably at a Cabinet meeting as early as 1941, when he had been told by Lord Beaverbrook that if he spoke like that he would not be in the next Conservative government. The results, as King George VI noted in his diary, were 'a great surprise to one and all'.[51]

The Labour Party won a landslide victory and twenty-nine ministerial heads rolled as the results became known. Dunglass was not exempt; the figures were Tom Steele (Labour) 17,784; Lord Dunglass (Unionist) 15,900; his opponent had a majority of 1884 votes. In the flush of victory, Steele wrote to the *Daily Worker*, thanking the Communist Party 'for the magnificent part they played in the campaign'.[52] Nothing could have been calculated to infuriate Dunglass more; he quietly filed the cutting away for future use. When the Earl of Home was told that his son had lost, 'Lost what?' was his response. There were no great family post-mortems; life would go on.

On a national level repercussions for the Conservative Party proved shattering. Eden summed up the feelings of many when he wrote to Alec Cadogan, Permanent Under-Secretary at the Foreign Office, 'This whole business has given a great shock to many, but it is Winston for whom I am really sorry. I think that I can understand the varied motives that led the country to vote as it did, but that does not diminish the blow for him, nor the sense of having been scurvily treated which he inevitably feels.'[53]

As in the wake of the great Tory defeats in 1832 and 1906, the Conservatives now submitted to a process of reappraisal in three crucial areas: finance, philosophy and organisation. Absent from the House during these five years of opposition, Dunglass was not involved in the rethinking of party policy under Rab Butler.[54] The centre of gravity of his life shifted to his growing family and his Scottish roots; the year ended with the marriage of Lavinia Alington to Roger Mynors in December. His father was now in his seventy-second year and there was the tacit assumption in some quarters that Dunglass's political career – an interesting interlude – was over and that he would turn his attentions to the legacy and responsibilities that would come his way. But he had no intention of giving up his political activities; his freedom from parliamentary responsibilities meant he could devote more time to Lanark, which he nursed assiduously for the next five years.

The Lanark Unionist Association agreed unanimously to send 'an invitation to Lord Dunglass to stand again as Candidate for the Lanark Division at the next General Election, and to express … the Committee's appreciation of his work at the last election'.[55] The Unionist Party in Scotland was a dispirited band after July 1945. Although they still had a plurality of seats north of the border (29 to Labour's 27), those who survived were now in opposition. The generally accepted leader of the Scottish Conservatives, Walter Elliot, had also lost at Kelvingrove, and the leadership now devolved upon James Reid, MP for Hillhead, an advocate in a party dominated by landowners and lawyers. Dunglass's name was mentioned in some circles for the candidacy at the Hillhead by-election, but Thomas Galbraith was selected. (On Galbraith's death in 1982, the seat was won by Roy Jenkins of the Social Democratic Party.) Dunglass's loyalty to Lanark gave no guarantee of an early return to the Commons; Steele was a powerful figure, with local roots. Later the constituency became a Labour stronghold, with Judith Hart its most famous representative. Even in the late 1940s, the prospect was not promising for the Unionists. Dunglass worked hard behind the scenes and annual general meetings were fixed points in his calendar. Executive meetings took place in Glasgow, and Dunglass took the initiative in setting up a sub-committee to meet on a monthly basis 'to deal with urgent matters', particularly finance and agents' remuneration.[56]

The change of emphasis in Dunglass's priorities became apparent when he was appointed a director of the Bank of Scotland in February 1946. His term with the bank lasted until his return to ministerial office in October 1951; it was never an alternative career, but an opportunity to gain first-hand knowledge of commercial practices. Life branched out in many new directions. He began to contribute regularly to the *New English Review* on political and literary matters. In 1947 he became president of the Scottish Unionist Association. Estate matters demanded his attention and there were many meetings over the partial demolition of the stables at Douglas Castle and the effects of the nationalisation of the coal industry, which ended the coal royalties. But political considerations were never far from his mind. On 5 March 1946 Winston Churchill made his speech on the Iron Curtain; a week later, Dunglass wrote to *The Times*, analysing Russian foreign policy, at a time when the Soviets were unilaterally retaining troops in Persia:

> Recent manifestations of Russian foreign policy prompt me to recall the summer of 1939 and the failure of Mr Chamberlain's government to secure an Anglo-Soviet alliance. Towards the end of protracted talks the price of co-operation was raised until it stood at a demand that Britain should assent to the forcible absorption of the three independent States of Latvia, Lithuania, and Estonia into the Soviet Union. Mr Chamberlain, although he realized to the full the strategic value of such a deal, felt bound to refuse it on those terms.
>
> Apart from the price, another aspect of the negotiations caused much concern. Whenever agreement seemed to be in sight the Soviet delegates found some excuse for delay or introduced some irrelevancy with an irritant value, and they carried this technique so far as to throw serious doubts on their sincerity of purpose. In the event, the Russian–German alliance and the smooth occupation of Poland by the Soviet armies proved that these moves must have been prepared while Anglo–Russian talks were proceeding.
>
> During the war Mr Churchill and Mr Eden made many sacrifices in order to secure Russian co-operation, but no sooner had the common enemy been defeated than the treaties and agreements which they signed were broken in rapid succession. With the peace, Mr Bevin and his party came into office with the declared determination to work with Russia. They have found that the price of co-operation is still on the 1939 level – namely the sacrifice of the sovereignty and political freedom of independent countries. The tactics, too, are unchanged.
>
> Many people in Great Britain censured Mr Chamberlain and the

> Conservative Party, but it is to be hoped that they now have more understanding and will realize that co-operation and friendship with Russia do not depend upon the personality of the British Prime Minister or Foreign Secretary, or the nature of the party in office. Friendship can only grow from action based upon common moral and ethical principles, and so long as Communists direct Soviet foreign policy these are not there.[57]

Such uncompromising directness was not the fashion in the immediate post-war years. But it was an indication of the way Dunglass's views had developed over Soviet policy and methods and it was a repeated theme for the remainder of his public life.

Local party workers appreciate visits from their national leaders, as Dunglass realised when he had invited Sir John Simon to speak at Lanark in 1938, and he took an early opportunity to invite Eden to be the principal speaker at a vast rally at East Kilbride in June 1947. Such meetings were the bedrock of political activity before the days of television and followed a familiar pattern. Not only a fund-raising rally, the gathering combined sporting activities and family entertainments ('Strathaven Junior Unionists Ankle Judging Competition') in a garden party atmosphere with a speech by the guest of honour, on this occasion the glamorous figure of Anthony Eden. Dunglass was an accomplished major-domo for these local events, and so comprehensive were his activities, it passed unnoticed that he was not the MP for Lanark at this time. On occasions when national figures were unavailable, he spoke himself, particularly in the small villages. One of the characteristics of his career was the way he made statements on international events to parochial gatherings, as in July 1948 when a major issue of the time was the Berlin Crisis:

> Dealing with the situation in Berlin, Lord Dunglass stated that it was one phase of a co-ordinated drive to end British influence in Europe and the Mediterranean. Russia might want war now. It was quite likely that Communists in this country had reported to the Russian Government that the British people would not support their leaders if Russia was to fight. 'Such information would be as false as that which Ribbentrop gave to Hitler'.[58]

Dunglass's activities, with Elizabeth's support, meant non-stop travelling and constant meals (at which he formulated his golden rule of hospitality, one glass of water for every glass of wine). In October 1949, one of the Junior Unionist Assocations 'had a short debate on Scottish nationalism, which proved that a few of our members were quite strong supporters of "The Covenant"'. This may not have been what the senior members wanted to hear, but was one of the first indications of simmering nationalistic feelings which erupted in the 1950s.

Dunglass was determined to have the local Party organisation in trim for the next election, and he played his part in the appointment of a new agent, J.C. Teesdale, waiving his expenses so that the money could go towards the salary of a professional agent, which he thought essential.[59] One duty he did not enjoy were Saturday morning meetings (later known as 'surgeries'), even when he was not the MP. He felt he was not cut out to be a glorified social worker; it was not that he did not give pragmatic help, but he was uneasy in the one-to-one interviews, often painful and distressing, and felt that the time available added little to what could be explained and initiated in writing to Teesdale. His preferred method was for the agent to identify constituents' areas of concern and then for him to approach the requisite national or local authority.

On 7 December 1949, reviewing the activities of the last full year before an inevitable general election (Tom Steele had been re-adopted as Labour candidate) Dunglass made a speech to the Executive Committee in Glasgow, in which he said that 'he had held numerous meetings at the small places, so that he could, from now on to the election, concentrate on the larger areas. He advocated hecklers at opposition meetings and gave many hints for his own supporters to practise.'[60]

Though he was no longer an MP he was potentially in a strong position, because he was equipped to take any opportunity presented to him. He had learned a great deal about the ground-work of domestic policy-making and the grass-roots organisation of the local Party machine. Asquith once said that the measure of a man's career was how he developed and flourished during his forties. Alec Dunglass was now in his forty-seventh year, and the years in opposition had been positive and productive.

On 10 January Attlee announced that a general election would be held on 23 February. On the outcome of that contest, Alec Dunglass's future direction depended.

6

Scotland's Minister

The general election of February 1950 was the first winter contest since 1910. By later standards it was also an unusually long campaign, running from 10 January until 23 February. Dunglass was formally adopted as the Unionist candidate for Lanark on Monday 30 January; as in 1945, he faced a straight fight with Tom Steele. Opinions differed as to the national outcome, one of the most perceptive forecasts coming from Hugh Gaitskell, Labour's Minister of Economic Affairs. 'Most of my colleagues seem to be very confident, and expect us to have a majority of 70 to 100,' he wrote in his diary; 'I am not so sanguine. I fear that the Tories will get a lot of Liberal votes and that this, together with redistribution, and some inevitable swing-over will make the contest very even.'[1] So it proved, in Lanark, as well as nationally. The major piece of unfinished business for Attlee's administration was steel nationalisation and this issue was a focus of attention in Lanark.

After his adoption on 30 January, Alec Dunglass (The Lord Dunglass, DL, JP on his leaflets) took to the hustings. In 1945 he had been unprepared for the personal nature of the campaign against him; now he was forearmed. There were not many people with whom Dunglass did not strike up some personal rapport, but Tom Steele was one of the exceptions. Dunglass had neither forgotten nor forgiven the slights of 1945. Three days into campaigning Dunglass's agent issued a leaflet which reprinted Steele's letter of 1945 to the *Daily Worker*, thanking the communists for their invaluable help – and attitudes towards communism were very different in 1950. Steele's reaction betrayed his concern. Legal action was threatened, but Dunglass stood firm. Teesdale was instructed to continue the attack, and the episode was crucial in swaying floating voters from Labour, erosion which Steele's majority was not sufficient to withstand. 'The General Election of 1950 in Lanark seems very far away,' Teesdale wrote to the new

Prime Minister in October 1963, 'but I remember it as one of the most satisfying episodes in which I have ever taken part.'[2]

Dunglass did not confine his attacks to Steele's previous tactics. He stressed how increasing state control – the feeling that 'the gentleman in Whitehall really does know better'[3] – led to less competition and rising prices. He struck a responsive chord in the constituency with his warnings. The Unionist Association was also in better trim, thanks to his work during the last five years, and the professional canvassing, with efficient harnessing of the postal vote, showed understanding of the psephological niceties. The 1950 election was one of the last old-style campaigns, when the three party leaders rejected the BBC's suggestion of televised election broadcasts.[4]

Despite the harsh February weather in many parts of the country (there was drizzle in Lanark, and downpour by evening), the national turn-out was 84 per cent and some constituencies ran out of ballot papers.[5] The reputation of opinion polls, still in their relative infancy, was clouded by memories of the 1948 débâcle in the United States, when Governor Dewey had failed to defeat Truman.[6] Nevertheless, for the 1950 election, the British Institute of Public Opinion (later Gallup) put Labour on 41 per cent and the Conservatives on 40 per cent. In such a close election, postal voting – traditionally felt to favour the Conservatives – was of particular significance. The Representation of the People Act of July 1948 brought significant changes in the provisions for postal voting. This was to make the difference between success and failure for Dunglass.

The postal vote in 1950 undoubtedly benefited the Conservatives, and eighteen Conservative seats may well have been won because of their greater efficiency in using the new postal vote rules. Lanark was the 12th most marginal constituency with a Conservative majority of only 685 votes and a postal vote of 1563, or 4 per cent of the total vote. The majority was thus 43.8 per cent of the total postal vote.[7] The figures were Lord Dunglass (Unionist) 19,890; Tom Steele (Labour) 19,205.

The Parliament to which Alec Dunglass returned was very different from that at the end of the caretaker government. The massive Labour landslide of July 1945 was reduced to single figures: 315 seats to the Conservatives 298; the Liberals took only 9 seats. But it was in the composition of the Conservative Party that the greatest change was apparent. Following the Maxwell Fyfe Reforms of 1948, which limited the amount of money MPs (£50) and candidates (£25) could contribute to their constituencies, there was a meritocratic air about many of the new intake of ninety-three Members. 'The Class of 1950' was famously described by Aneurin Bevan as 'the finest Tory vintage in history'.[8] Although Dunglass was one of 79 Etonians returned (and 29 Christ Church men), the social composition of the parliamentary Party had subtly altered. February 1950 was when Butler's backroom boys came to public notice. Many of them had worked at the Conservative Research Department with David Clarke and Michael Fraser, and over the next fifteen years their influence rendered the old-style, pre-war Tories anachronistic and isolated, a process which was not to leave Dunglass unscathed either.

The Unionist Association in Lanark were well pleased with their work. Victories in marginal seats do not happen by accident and they acknowledged Dunglass's part in this cultivation of the grass roots over the years, often in unfavourable circumstances. Dunglass thanked them all and 'indicated that for the next few months he would not hold political meetings, but would endeavour to attend non-political functions where invited'.[9] With the narrow majority, his time was now increasingly taken up with late-night sittings and divisions; the atmosphere was more partisan and fractious than before. He observed the Labour frontbench in action for the first time (Attlee's rise to ministerial prominence had coincided with Dunglass's illness in 1940) and, as always, judged as he found. His main impression of Attlee was of his waspishness, even of fiery temper when crossed, which he attributed to the grievous disappointment of the 1950 result and having to come to terms with the changed realities of power after the erosion of his landslide majority. There were also the first flickerings of the internal warfare that was to bedevil the Labour Party for many years. Later Dunglass respected Attlee's patriotism and goodness of character, but his first impressions of the beleaguered Prime Minister were not entirely favourable.[10]

He considered Herbert Morrison, Lord President of the Council and supremo on Home Affairs, 'very clever' and was saddened by the way his career was hoist by the Foreign Office petard after March 1951 – the outstanding example, in his recollection, of the square peg in the round hole. He had a lot of time for Arthur Greenwood, and although the former deputy leader was now in decline Dunglass admired his unstinting work for the Labour Party. A.V. Alexander, later Earl Alexander of Hillsborough, was another figure whom Dunglass knew in the 1930s, and of whom he saw a great deal more in the Lords in 1951.

Dunglass thought he was in the very best tradition of public service. Another figure whose quiet dignity he admired was Patrick Gordon Walker, who became Secretary of State for Commonwealth Relations in February 1950. Although he had no personal contact with the colossus of the Attlee government, Dunglass regarded Ernest Bevin as among the front rank of foreign secretaries. He knew how pleased Eden had been in July 1945 ('I am very glad that Bevin is my successor,' Eden had written to Cadogan. 'He is the best man they have.'[11]) and ultimately regarded Sir Edward Grey, Bevin and Eden as the pantheon of the Foreign Office.

The Labour administration had a careworn look about it after the years of austerity and it was in this atmosphere that Churchill decreed 'One More Heave' would oust Labour from office. During the summer recess, many of the new intake had prepared an influential and important Conservative Political Centre booklet, *One Nation*, which echoed Disraeli's famous analysis of the state of England and which became not just a manifesto, but the name of a whole political group.[12] To many of the older Conservatives, such philosophical approaches were profoundly puzzling; these were the privileged figures from a charmed circle, those who thought nothing of steering £10,000 towards the constituency coffers, right-wing figures whose politics were unoriginal and uninspiring. Dunglass was mistakenly perceived by some Labour MPs as being of that camp, a throwback to the 1930s, a man who might, with luck, become Minister of State at the Scottish Office, but who would never be a central player. This view of Dunglass was fundamentally flawed. After his years with Neville Chamberlain, Dunglass never lost his taste for being at the centre and the 1950 General Election was a necessary step in that process of rehabilitation. By background and upbringing, he seemed to belong to the pre-war group, but instinct and an awareness of changing circumstances allied him more closely to the progressive elements than has been realised. According to the recollections of one member of the 'One Nation' group only two MPs went out of their way to welcome the new intake: Alec Dunglass and Selwyn Lloyd.[13]

Selwyn Lloyd, who had been elected as Member for the Wirral in July 1945, was an unexpected friendship for Dunglass: the middle-class lawyer from Liverpool and the aristocrat from the Scottish Borders. Yet Dunglass admired Lloyd's staying power and determination over such things as the establishment of commercial television and the campaign to abolish capital punishment, whereas Lloyd always envied the insouciant calm under pressure that eight hundred years of history gave a fourteenth earl. Their careers were to overlap in the next twenty-five years, not least when Home succeeded Lloyd as Foreign Secretary in July 1960. In a party where the centre of gravity moved increasingly to the Home Counties, Home and Lloyd were important representatives of other areas. 'The trouble with our party is that leaders are S.E. based,' wrote Lloyd in 1968. 'The only real provincials are Alec Douglas-Home and myself.'[14] Anthony Eden, James Stuart, Thomas Dugdale and Oliver Stanley were friends from the pre-war generation, whereas Churchill, whom Dunglass did not see at first-hand in the days of his plenitude and glory, was a figure he treated with caution. He admired Eden, whom he saw as a figure of real stature, a lodestone in a changing and uncertain world, though he was by no means blind, having served at the Foreign Office, to the temperamental failings Eden occasionally exhibited in personal relations.

A particular death in 1950 was to have its effect on Dunglass's career. Viscount Hailsham, the former Lord Chancellor, died after a long illness. His heir was Quintin Hogg, MP for Oxford City since 1938, who regarded his translation to the Upper House with melancholy dismay. Now that the moment had arrived, he wrote to the Prime Minister, asking for a review of the law on hereditary peerages. Hogg was not hopeful of immediate satisfaction over the matter, but was unprepared for the mean-spirited and disingenuous way Attlee treated his approach, as though it were entirely for personal advantage and not as a general reform of peerage law.[15]

Attlee's second administration from February 1950 to October 1951 was bedevilled by internal strife, public resentment at continued austerity and central bureaucratic controls, as well as the worsening international situation after the outbreak of the Korean War. Such a fractious atmosphere was a great opportunity for the Conservative opposition, and Dunglass duly harried the government in the debates, as well as being one of the foot-soldiers of the guerrilla tactics of late-night voting. Two issues caught his attention particularly, the growth of state control and the situation in Korea. In what was to prove his last spell in the House of Commons for thirteen years, he concentrated on the communist threat and the danger of underestimating aggression in 'far away countries'. 'It seems to me', he said in a debate on 29 November 1950, 'that there are three objectives which the Russians have before them. The first is to prevent the western powers from getting the benefit of minerals and other raw materials from south-east

Asia. The second is the possession of Persian oil, the end of Turkish independence and a footing in, and control of, the Eastern Mediterranean. The third, above all, is the possession of Germany.' Of Britain's responsibilities, in alliance with the United States, he had no doubts. 'It is true to say at this moment the United States and Great Britain are standing between civilisation and barbarism, and that should there be any political split in this alliance between America and Britain, the savages will walk in.'[16] Such unvarnished language was typical of his trenchant approach. There was no compromise on what he saw as moral absolutes.

On 11 July 1951 Alec Dunglass inherited the Earldom of Home. His father, who had not been well for some time, had died suddenly at the Hirsel. Alec and Elizabeth Dunglass, now the new Earl and Countess, prepared to leave at once for Berwick by the night train. Before collecting his possessions together for the journey north, Lord House remembered that he had left his spectacles in the House of Commons and went to retrieve them. News of his elevation, however, had spread and he was barred from entry by the door-keepers; he was after all, a member of 'another place'.

There was a genuine sadness in the Border country and far beyond at the passing of a much loved man, who did good by stealth. Tributes poured in from many diverse worlds to Alec Home and his family. Although the elevation of their MP meant a by-election in the constituency (this was subsumed in the general election of 1951), the Lanark Unionist Association '... resolved to ask the Earl of Home to continue his Hon. Presidency of the Association ...' He was to hold the post until his ninetieth year.[17] The Lanark constituency occupies a very special place in the story of Alec Home's life. Although there was an element of lairdism in his relationship with it (as the heir to 30,000 Douglas acres he attracted the deferential vote, so marked in many Conservative constituencies before the war, and which the post-war social revolution of 1945 diminished but did not entirely remove), he had a genuine concern for the mining, agricultural and light industrial base of the area. He understood the nature of rural poverty, with the variations of seasonal income, and knew the anxieties of harvest time, often outside the control of fruitgrowers and farmers, on which so much depended financially.

Although Home was not directly involved in the choice of his successor (Patrick Maitland, Master of Lauderdale), he kept in close contact with the constituency and campaigned in the 1951 election, the timing of which was curious. Attlee did have a majority and could have soldiered on, but the catalyst was the King, who was due to embark early in 1952 on a six-month tour of the Commonwealth (but by which time he had died). On 1 September he had written to Attlee warning that it would be difficult for him to be absent from the country for so long if there were continued political uncertainty. Attlee accordingly asked for a dissolution and announced it on 19 September.[18] With Churchill heading a revitalised Conservative Party, the manifesto commitment to 'Set the People Free' found a responsive chord among those disturbed by the centralist trends of the government and the Conservatives secured an overall majority of 17, winning 321 seats to Labour's 295 and 6 to the Liberals.[19]

Initially Alec Home reconciled himself to an end to his political career. Estate matters were the immediate priority. Probate was granted at nearby Duns, with the estate valued at £267,758, subject to death duties at the rate of 60 per cent. Over the next few years 12,000 acres of land were sold. Although the 13th Earl had set up a family trust in 1946 against the ravages of death duties, his death was a few weeks short of the five-year exemption rule to benefit his heirs. Through primogeniture, Alec Home, in the words of his brother William, 'scooped the pool' and was not always aware of how this left the other brothers. Although Douglas and the Hirsel were of great value, the estates had not been managed very professionally. Home now set about rectifying this when belated rationalisation and a more professional approach were adopted. One of the few nettles not immediately grasped was when the swop would take place from Springhill to the Hirsel. The Hirsel was far too big for the Dowager Countess, and Springhill was becoming too constricted for the new Earl and Countess with their four growing children. It was not until the summer of 1959 that the move took place.[20]

The government Churchill formed in October 1951, as he was about to begin his seventy-eighth year, bore his stamp to a much greater degree than had the caretaker government. But he had little to do with Home's appointment as Minister of State at the Scottish Office. James Stuart had been summoned to Chartwell by Churchill, who promptly appointed him Secretary of State for Scotland. After lunch Stuart was given the names of possible candidates for the new post of Minister of State, which the Conservatives had promised in their 1950 manifesto, incorporating a paper, *Scottish Control of Scottish Affairs*, written by Stuart and Dunglass in 1949. The names did not appeal. 'All right, you get hold of one of my young ladies,' said Churchill 'and get her to write down what you want.'[21] This began Alec Home's effective post-war political career.

'Home, sweet Home', as Churchill referred to the new Minister of State, was sworn a member of the Privy Council, a point Stuart specifically made to the House of Commons as he set out the responsibilities of his new team. The choice had been between Alec Home and Geordie Selkirk (who became a Lord-in-Waiting to the King, and Paymaster-General in 1953), though Lord Clydesmuir's name had also been canvassed in Scottish circles.[22] Alec Home owed a great debt to Stuart, with whom Churchill had resumed a serene relationship after earlier difficulties. If the name Dunglass meant anything to Churchill, it would have been through his association with Chamberlain and his intervention in the Yalta Debate. Home's name would not in all likelihood have suggested itself. Ministers of State were the products of their immediate departmental masters, such as Stuart, and when Home's name came up, either at Chartwell or in Whitehall, reaction invariably centred on his *reliability*. Stuart was generally considered to have chosen wisely.[23]

The new Secretary of State for Scotland was undoubtedly a political heavyweight in the Conservative hierarchy; he was a trusted confidant of the Prime Minister. 'Few ministers reached office if Stuart did not approve,' his private secretary has written.[24] Indeed, in some respects James Stuart had inherited the mantle of Oliver Stanley, as 'he was probably number three in the batting order after Churchill and Eden, a ranking not reached by any Scottish Minister before or since'.[25] He was certainly able to manipulate the levers of political power and little went on that he did not know – one of the reasons he was so effective as Chief Whip.

That James Stuart was Home's first real political patron and that the two of them worked in such close harness in a largely autonomous department, enhanced the Minister of State's position immensely. Stuart's main political ambition had been fulfilled as Chief Whip, so the two had no need to play to either the Westminster or the Calton Hill gallery. They had an intuitive understanding of each other's needs and styles. Stuart disliked being disturbed: on a train journey a member of the public passed a comment on the weather to Stuart and Home. 'Talkative fellow, that,' said Stuart to his Minister of State.[26] Alec Home was perceived by many as a man who had 'been through it' with his illness, was now tougher for the experience, and respected for it. His civil servants found him courteous and fair, but steely on what they called 'pressure issues', the prospective Forth Road Bridge being one of the longest-running. On the Wild Deer Protection Bill, also a perennial issue of the early 1950s, he was extremely tough on commercial poaching, pressing for forfeiture of cars and weapons, something unheard of in Scottish Office memories. The civil servants found him considerate; with his peers he could be very sharp. His membership of the Lords also meant that he was not diverted by constituency problems and was 'able to attend to Scottish business here without the Conservative Whip becoming anxious about the government majority'.[27] Stuart found this invaluable when he was in London for weeks at a time: his Minister of State kept him in touch with St Andrew's House developments, whilst Stuart was the link with the Churchill circle.

The appointment of such an intimate of the Prime Minister (and a descendant from King James V of Scotland) as Secretary of State was a clear sign that Scottish affairs mattered. Indeed the rising tide of Scottish nationalism, which took many forms after the war, exercised both main political parties, though for different reasons. For Labour politicians such as William Ross, a future Secretary of State in the Wilson administrations, the nationalist movement was a threat to Labour's electoral support; to the Conservatives it was a threat to the stability of the United Kingdom and called into question the future of the Act of Union of 1707. Scottish nationalism had become increasingly prominent in the last years of the Attlee government, the movement exhibiting, as so often, a cyclical rhythm, conditioned by economic and political factors beyond Scotland's borders. The Scottish National Party had been born in April 1928, and in April 1949 a covenant was drafted, 'whereby we pledge ourselves, in all loyalty to the Crown and within the framework of the United Kingdom, to do everything in our power to secure for Scotland a Parliament with adequate legislative authority in Scottish affairs'. Eventually two million signatures were collected.[28] But the most dramatic example of nationalist feeling was the removal of the Stone of Scone, the symbol of English authority over Scotland, from beneath the Coronation Chair in Westminster Abbey on Christmas Eve 1950. When the Stone was recovered from Arbroath Abbey in April 1951, it was returned to Westminster Abbey despite Scottish protests. The issue rumbled on into the next reign and the next government. Alec Home, as Minister of State, defended the government's position, in a lightly ironic speech that skilfully defused controversy. 'I must say that if we should be able to snatch and grab back everything that belonged to us in the thirteenth century, it would suit me very well,' he said. He recalled the Act of Union. 'It was agreed that the Crown, the Sceptre and the Sword should be the symbolic articles which might be permitted to remain in Scotland. They were named as the Honours chosen by Scotland to remain in Scotland, and the Stone was not mentioned at all at that time.'[29]

Unionist reaction to this turmoil was far from complacent. At the annual conference in Glasgow in 1949, one of the recommendations was that a Minister of State should be appointed to act as deputy to the Secretary of State, one who would normally work in Scotland. Some six hundred Scottish Unionists emphatically rejected the Scottish Covenant.[30] The main product of a special meeting in November was the policy document, *Scottish Control of Scottish Affairs*, three features of which were incorporated into the 1950 election manifesto: the establishment of a deputy to the Secretary of State with the title and position of Minister for Scotland; the appointment of an extra Parliamentary Under-Secretary of State; and the appointment of a Royal Commission to review the situation between Scotland and England.

Ian Robertson,[31] who became Home's Private Secretary, first met his new boss prior to travelling north on the overnight train. 'I have a happy recollection of going to join the Homes at a hotel in Kensington somewhere … and finding him in his overcoat in the hall of the hotel, waltzing round happily by himself singing the theme song from the film *La Ronde*.'[32] Robertson introduced Home to many of the key figures at St Andrew's House on Calton Hill, and his charm and natural gaiety of spirit made an immediate impression on all who worked with him. Home was now a pivotal figure in the Scottish Office team, overseeing the three Under-Secretaries, though on a loose rein, and communicating their concerns to the Secretary of State. His routine was swiftly established. 'In the mere ten days since he took over his task in St Andrew's House,' ran one contemporary account, 'Lord Home has already established a reputation as the busiest Minister St Andrew's House has known for many years.'[33] He was soon drawn into Edinburgh's social, educational and legal life; indeed, the New Club, where his portrait hangs in the main clubroom overlooking Princes Street, was almost an extension of the Scottish Office, and a great centre of Edinburgh wheeler-dealing.[34]

For those who worked at the Scottish Office, the early 1950s were something of a golden age, if only because of the special relationship between Stuart and Churchill, in the sense that the Office could have written its own ticket as regards expansion. This spirit of optimism did not last. The Balfour Commission on Scottish Affairs in 1954, knowing what was to happen in Scottish industry, marked the end of many hopes; industrialists, trade unions, government ministers and civil servants, failed to foresee the imminent collapse of shipbuilding on the Clyde, on which so much else depended. Home joined the Scottish Office when its shares were riding high; when he left for the Commonwealth Office on Churchill's retirement, the special links with Whitehall did not survive, and Stuart's successor, John Maclay (Viscount Muirshiel) did not carry the same weight with Macmillan. But in 1951 the Scottish Office was 'on the move', an attractive place for ministers and civil servants to work. Although it did not have control of defence, foreign or exchequer affairs, it was in other respects a microcosm of Whitehall. The Scottish Office job was to see the miniature as a whole. Home found that Kirkcaldy often came up on the agenda as a further microcosm: to see things from a Kirkcaldy perspective was to start from the beginning. As Minister of State, he was initially seen as being in an ambiguous position. Was he there to show the flag when Stuart was in London or was he there to take independent decisions? As the Scottish Office was then a federal structure, with Agriculture, Education, Health and the Home Department separate entities, Home's role needed defining and initially he trod warily. 'The Scottish Office', it has been written, 'embracing as it does so many different portfolios, offers ample opportunity for error, upon which the sensitive national conscience is ever willing to swoop.'[35]

Home was not the Secretary of State on a lower level (as Heath in 1960 and Rippon in 1970 were under Alec Home at the Foreign Office), he was the helper of the Secretary of State, the one who gave Stuart a breather. As Minister of State, Alec Home was well served by Ian Robertson, who would often bring Scottish Office business down to Springhill. In 1952 Nigel Walker took over the post, when Robertson became James Stuart's principal secretary, and was with Alec Home for three years. The Permanent Under-Secretary was Sir David Milne, a figure of legendary reputation in Dover House (the Whitehall headquarters of the Scottish Office) and on Calton Hill. Milne was a shrewd defender of Scottish Office interests, never exposing his flank, and made a formidable alliance with James Stuart. Home was the conduit between the junior ministerial team and the Secretary of State, and he was a member of the Highlands and Islands Panel, which brought him into contact with the legal officers of the department. As befitted an autonomous fiefdom serving a significant and over-represented electorate (in 1951 Scotland had 71 MPs for an electorate of 3.4 million; Wales had 36 MPs for 1.8 million voters, and Northern Ireland 12 MPs for 0.8 million),[36] the law officers were important and independent figures in the persons of the Lord Advocate and the Solicitor-General for Scotland. 'Where did Lord Home fit into all this?' pondered a member of the team many years later. 'The irreverent view from the Private Office was that the new Minister was guided initially on to consideration of perennial Highland problems so that he would not stand in the Secretary of State's light!'[37]

At the time of the Unionist decision to create the position of Minister of State for Scotland, a Labour peer had said, 'I understand that we shall not have the privilege of looking on his countenance in this House too often. He will be in St Andrew's House, where he will let not only the civil servants but the people of Scotland feel that there is somebody with a grip upon Scottish affairs.'[38] This welcome in the House of Lords was symptomatic of the feeling of many Conservative peers that the Upper Chamber might be called upon to play a more active role in many different areas of government. James Stuart made a statement on 21 November 1951 about the new arrangements: 'A matter in which I think this arrangement will be of considerable help is in having more or less resident in Scotland a Minister of high rank, what, in my day, when I was Chief Whip, was known as a Minister above the line. It would be a great help in expediting the conduct of Scottish business because the Minister of State would be resident in Scotland and be able to meet … representatives of industry, local authorities and other bodies, such as, for example, the Highland Panel, with very little delay, and be able to hear their views.' He paid a warm tribute to Home. 'I am only too happy to say that I feel myself extremely fortunate in having my noble friend to undertake this important work. We have worked together in the past and I am quite satisfied we can work amicably together in the future.'[39]

The reference to the Highland Panel was indeed an indication of Lord Home's principal activity beyond the confines of St Andrew's House. Stuart had said that he was 'now being asked specially to handle education and the Highlands and Islands' problem',[40] but the disadvantage for Home (residence in Scotland and travel in the Highland region) was that it kept him away from London and the House of Lords, with the result that when he became Secretary of State for Commonwealth

Relations, and a member of the Cabinet in April 1955, many commentators referred to him as an unknown figure, which meant 'unknown to metropolitan commentators'.

Home's maiden speech in the House of Lords as Minister of State for Scotland was made on 20 November 1951, in circumstances charged with emotion as several peers took the opportunity of paying tribute to the memory of his father. Alec Home therefore began his speech at 4.55 p.m. by saying 'I am fully aware that he will be a very difficult man to follow in public life'. His appointment as Minister of State meant that he 'must surely embody one of the quickest fulfilments of an Election pledge in British political history'. His responsibilities, he explained, before resuming his seat at 5.15 p.m., were threefold. 'My office has been charged by the Secretary of State with certain particular responsibilities for the welfare of the Highlands and Islands, and for the orderly development of Scottish industry and for close relations with the local authorities.'[41]

The most important of these responsibilities initially was the Advisory Panel on the Highlands and Islands, a body set up by the Labour government in 1947. Its function was 'to keep under review, and advise the Secretary of State on the carrying out of the approved Programme of Highland Development; and to arrange, in consultation with the Secretary of State, for the investigation of further means of promoting the economic use of capacity and reserves in the Highlands and Islands and the social welfare of the highland people.'[42] The panel was a sounding board, a gadfly and a safety valve, and its members enjoyed considerable autonomy. When Alec Home served, the meetings were held every three months: his first meeting was on 7 December 1951, six weeks after taking office. The panel was bi-partisan in its approach; paying particular attention to the Highlands, it also tried to remember the problems of Scotland as a whole, a parallel with the Minister of State's function, which was to take the broad overview while seeking individual solutions. Home said that he regarded the panel as specialists in Highlands problems and approved its non-party views.

The first practical issue that arose at this meeting – giving some indication of the domestic detail which preoccupied Home for the next three and a half years – was on the withdrawal of steamer services in the Highland region. The Minister of State explained that he had already seen the Minister of Transport on this matter, and described plans to bridge North Ford and establish small industrial units to help stem the depopulation of the Highlands. With the road-building programme in the Highlands and the initial plans for a Forth Road Bridge in the early 1950s, the Ministry of Transport was the Whitehall department with which Home had most of his dealings. From May 1952, the Minister of Transport was Alan Lennox-Boyd, a friend from Christ Church days, with whom Alec Home established a useful working partnership.

The panel contained many figures regarded as leaders in their communities. One of the most colourful (and voluble) of these was the writer Naomi Mitchison, and few meetings went by without a paper from her on some matter of importance. She recalled, 'I think we felt all the time that, although some of the Scottish Office top people were sympathetic and even helped us, they would never back the really big ideas, many of which would have meant taking over land from large (often absent) land owners ... we managed to do a few things, but ... in spite of Edinburgh rather than with its help ... Lord Home was more sympathetic than some of the others.'[43] This first meeting was typical of many in the years ahead. In January 1952 all Highland MPs were invited to serve. In the minutes, 'it was agreed that the Minister of State should preside at meetings of the officials concerned with Highland matters and that the meetings should take place every three months.' Alec Home did not think it appropriate that he should take over the actual chairmanship of the Highland panel. 'His preference was that the Chair should be taken by some strong representative from the Highland local authorities.'[44] There was a feeling of goodwill and the hope that, with the panel as a pressure group, the centralised control from Edinburgh could be broken down. Home said that to encourage tourism he was seeing the chairman of the Hydro-Electric Board about reducing the costs of electric power for industry in the Highlands. In June 1953, he provided details of assistance for recent storm damage, and in May 1954 reported how he and the Secretary of State had travelled 'many hundreds of miles and talked to all and sundry in the crofting counties. Everywhere the theme has been development and the difference which I saw in outlook is that the people are not sitting back and waiting for someone else to do the work of reconstruction, but themselves are willing to take the initiative.'[45]

His travels took him the length and breadth of the country. He went to the Island of Mull, where local government was being reorganised; to the Turnberry Hotel for dinners of the Scottish Farmers' Union; to Edinburgh for meetings of the Educational Institute of Scotland and to Bettyhill on the northernmost coast of the United Kingdom, where in the summer months he could walk at midnight along the silver beaches by the light of the Aurora Borealis. With other members of the Panel, he was instrumental in setting up a Crofting Commission, which helped to reorganise, develop and regulate crofting, perhaps the most tangible achievement of his years at St Andrew's House, a valedictory example of his progressive paternalism.

The prospective Forth Road Bridge (opened by the Queen on 4 September 1964, in the last few weeks of Home's premiership) became an important issue, though in the early 1950s its economic importance and the way it would improve communications were underestimated. Alec Home was not convinced until one foggy day when the South Queensferry ferry was not sailing and he had an urgent meeting in Fife. Next day his secretary apologised for not arranging the longer circuitous road route, but the episode clarified the position. From that time he was a Forth Bridge convert, though he had constant battles with the Treasury over it.[46] In his travels, hotels were a rarity, as he knew so many people around the country that he was usually offered hospitality by local grandees, such as Dame Flora Macleod at Dunvegan Castle, where Alec and Elizabeth Home were always welcomed with open arms and greeted like family relatives. (In many places they were.) 'And who exactly are you?' asked Dame Flora Macleod of Nigel Walker on one such visit to the island of Skye, as though he were some distant great nephew, to whom she had not yet been introduced. But not all his work was 'in the field'. There were regular meetings, particularly with local authorities and representatives of industry at St Andrew's House, where he dealt with working parties on sea transport, road transport, fisheries and textiles, as well as liaising with the four departments at the Scottish Office. After the Balfour Commission of 1954, local electricity boards were set up, responsible for generating and supplying electricity outside the area of the Scotland Hydro-Electric Board, a semi de-nationalisation.

Calton Hill days had their regular pattern. Home arrived from Springhill or the New Club, by which time the duty secretary had sorted the mail into personal and public files. One of the first things the Minister of State did was to check the day's racing news (the Scottish Office was by far the best of his various departments for placing bets). He was especially good at forecasting the five classic races, for they were 'honest' races, which owners, trainers and jockeys wanted to win for reasons of prestige, so it came down to pedigree and breeding, and Home knew about bloodstock lines.[47] After dealing with the mail, he received the day's submissions from the Agriculture, Education, Health and Home Affairs departments. He could be very sharp on legal niceties: once the Agricultural Department submitted a draft proposal for changing arrangements for tied cottages 'by regulation'. The experienced parliamentarian soon had that changed to 'by legislation'.[48] He had an alert eye for potential difficulties and he kept the proprieties with his civil servants. On one occasion, a secretary offered a conversational gambit about problems Herbert Morrison was having as Labour's deputy leader. He was met with a stony stare. The civil servants respected Home's courtesy, though they sometimes preferred to have their submissions dealt with by James Stuart, feeling uneasy about sending the Minister of State (in Aneurin Bevan's colourful phrase) 'naked into the Conference Chamber'.[49] Because they felt he could be talked out of a cast-iron case. To many civil servants he was a strange contradiction. Outwardly, he was the establishment figure nonpareil, yet underneath there was an unorthodox, even rakish, element at odds with this image. But he knew which battles to fight; claims had been prepared for the Chancellor of the Exchequer for additional roads and piers in the Highland region. Stuart submitted the claim: 'We feel it to be very important that this question should be viewed, not merely on traffic grounds, but in the light of the development of this area in the national interest.' He explained that he and Home wanted a Special Highland Programme of £750,000 ('announced by our predecessors in 1950') to be implemented; only £300,000 had been forthcoming from Treasury funds. Eventually, the Scottish Office view prevailed. Many minutes submitted have Home's spidery handwritten additions. The conferences of the Scottish Council of Social Service in Skye seemed worth encouraging. 'How?' he added. On the relationship between Highland agricultural colleges and local authorities, he wrote, 'How can we promote this?' On the Scottish Agricultural Organisation Society providing advisory services for crofters, he asked, 'Ought they to continue? Who pays?' All three issues were resolved at a subsequent meeting.[50]

The London base of the Scottish Office was at Dover House in Whitehall and it was here that Alec Home and his family spent the evening before the coronation. There was not much sleep that night; the crowds already gathering for the festivities. The Homes awakened to the news that a British expedition had achieved the first ascent of the world's highest mountain: THE CROWNING GLORY: EVEREST IS CLIMBED.[51] It was a memorable day on a personal level too, as Lord Dunglass was allowed to act as his father's page. Normally the minimum age was twelve, but the Duke of Norfolk, the Earl Marshal, gave special dispensation.[52] The rehearsals were not without incident. Alec Home had been apprehensive about the Duke of Norfolk, who had four daughters but no sons, allowing a group of young pages to sit unsupervised during the lengthy ceremonial. The unscrewable bobbles on the coronets soon found service in impromptu marble games on the stone steps of the Abbey, much to the horror of the Queen Mother's Treasurer, Sir Arthur Penn.[53]

A week of celebrations followed, with much official entertaining of visiting royals and Commonwealth prime ministers. In Scotland, Alec Home hosted the visit of Queen Salote of Tonga, who, by braving the June rain in an open carriage, had endeared herself to the crowds. On 8 June the Homes attended the premiere of Benjamin Britten's specially commissioned opera *Gloriana*, when a largely non-musical audience received the work with bemused indifference.

The coolness of the reception accorded Britten's coronation opera, though, was as nothing compared with the storm which was to break over 'The Affair of the Handbag', when the Honours of Scotland – Crown, Sceptre and Sword – were presented to the new queen at St Giles's Cathedral, Edinburgh, on 24 June 1953. The Scottish Office had been considering since February 1952 the form of the ceremonial to mark her visit to her Scottish capital in the wake of the coronation. As the Scots, alone among the countries of the United Kingdom, would present their national regalia, James Stuart and Alec Home recommended that it be paraded before Her Majesty in St Giles's Cathedral. What should have been a joyous celebration, a service of national thanksgiving, turned into acrimonious controversy. The Scottish Office assumed that as the Scottish peerage would be there in full court dress so would the royal party. The ministers did not reckon on the advice that the Queen would receive from her English courtiers. In November 1952 it was announced that the ceremony in St Giles's Cathedral would be a 'National Service', and the Queen wore day clothes and carried a handbag. The Queen's Private Secretary, Sir Alan Lascelles, and a Home Office civil servant, Sir Austin Strutt, had so advised. 'His instinct for once played him false', Kenneth Rose has written of Lascelles' advice. 'The congregation, robed and jewelled in their finery, saw it as a Sassenach snub.'[54] The government and the Scottish Office were heavily criticised over the incident, which was said to have exacerbated tensions between the Westminster Parliament and the Scottish people. It was symptomatic of the difficulties St Andrew's

House faced in those days, with a sensitive Scottish population that soon spotted being patronised or treated as less important than England. Home was conscious of the varying strands of nationalist feeling, particularly at the annual rugby or football contests against the 'auld enemy'. At Murrayfield, the more decorous Edinburgh bourgeoisie might limit themselves to good-natured banter against the English, but the sight of the 'Tartan armies' at Hampden Park with their banners, set against a sea of thousands of St Andrew's flags, was an unforgettable demonstration of native pride. For Alec Home, the political demonstration of these feelings, particularly in their educated, middle-class form, was like a Scottish version of Fabianism. These were the so-called Crofters of Drummond Square, often romantic grandees, who had a 'Whisky-Galore' Scottish nationalism, rooted in historic grievances and wreathed in Highland Mist. 'The Affair of the Handbag' brought together both strands, the Hampden hordes and the Drummond Square Crofters, a potent mix of resentment and national pride.

A curious footnote to the episode is the story of the official painting of the scene in St Giles's. Consideration was given to whether the artist should paint the Queen as though she had appeared in Coronation robes. But this might fuel further controversy. Stanley Cursiter, the painter, saved the day. 'Before the completed picture was hung at Holyrood, ... the artist made one small concession to Scottish sentiment. He erased the Queen's handbag.'[55]

'The Affair of the Handbag' showed that Scottish nationalist sentiment was very much alive. James Stuart and Alec Home were diligent about other matters that gave rise to ill-feeling and even acts of vandalism at this time. A potential row blew up over the insignia EIIR on new pillar boxes; for Scots the correct historical numbering was 'EIR' and many decorations, even the icing on cakes in bakers' shops, had been altered during the coronation summer. Stuart and Home arranged that the pillar boxes should have crowns only; these 1953 pillar boxes can still be seen in Scottish cities.[56]

1954 saw no lessening of the pace of Scottish Office work. In February, the Minister of State was involved in plans for the provision of Civil Aviation at both Renfrew and Prestwick, and, with Lord Bilsland, he argued successfully with Alan Lennox-Boyd, the Minister of Transport, against contraction of the two principal west coast airports.[57] In May, at a meeting at the Inverness Town House, he laid the foundation for the provision of remote schools in connection with the new teachers' salary scales, and spoke of the problems of ageing and dwindling populations, a process accelerated by the reluctance of the young to stay and cultivate the soil. For one whose instincts were for the rural rather than the metropolitan, this was a cause of sadness, though he understood the lure of the city and the economic pressures which led to this seemingly irreversible shift in the demographic base.

Whenever Home could see ways of regenerating areas of Scotland he welcomed them, as in the decision to place the Atomic Breeder Reactor Station at Dounreay. 'This project of great, but at present unknown potential, is a major economic gain to Caithness,' he reported to the Highlands and Islands Panel. 'But it is more than that; there is now housed in the Highlands a growing point in industrial research.' Discussions on the Forth Road Bridge occupied much of his time, a three-way battle between the Scottish Office, the Treasury and the Ministry of Transport. The principal event of 1954 was on 16 July when the Royal Commission on Scottish Affairs finally reported.[58] The report was a disappointment to the Scottish Office. The level on which it operated was the control of roads and animal disease, such as the dreaded under-shot jaw in cows, when it should have concerned itself with laying the foundations for the Scottish Office to have control of regional development.

At the end of November 1954 the Homes took part in the celebrations of Churchill's eightieth birthday. It was felt, mistakenly, that his resignation could now not be long delayed but, to Eden's barely disguised chagrin, Churchill stayed until April 1955, with profound consequences on the future course of British political history. 'Anthony Eden was trained to win the Derby in 1938,' Harold Macmillan once noted characteristically, 'but he wasn't let out of the starting stalls until 1955.'[59] On 4 April 1955, the Homes were among those present at the historic dinner, attended by the Queen and the Duke of Edinburgh, to mark Churchill's retirement. After his guests had departed, Churchill was in sombre mood. Jock Colville found him sitting in a darkened upstairs room. He turned to Colville and said, 'I don't believe Anthony can do it.'[60]

After waiting so long for his inheritance, Eden might have been excused for enjoying the moment, but, with unacknowledged political bravery, he prepared at once for a general election and announced several Cabinet changes. One of these was the appointment of Alec Home as Secretary of State for Commonwealth Relations. The appointment had its element of farce. After the Downing Street dinner, Home had returned to Scotland and was on his way to Helensburgh with Nigel Walker when he became conscious of a police car, blue lights flashing, trying to attract their attention. They pulled in at the side of a narrow road and were told that the Minister of State had to get in touch with 10 Downing Street as soon as possible. They were miles from anywhere and so they drove up the coastline, looking for a house. The first sign of an inhabited dwelling was a small roadside inn, so Walker went inside to seek a telephone. He was told that there was a public one, but as that was in the hearing of the interested customers of the inn, Walker explained the situation and asked if there was another. Alec Home was allowed to use a phone in a bedroom upstairs, where a small child was asleep in a cot. He asked Walker to stay, lest the child awoke, while he rang 'Anthony', who invited him to become Commonwealth Secretary.[61] On 12 April he travelled to Windsor to receive his Seals of Office.

7

Binding the Commonwealth Ties

When Alec Home entered the Cabinet in April 1955 he was three months short of his fifty-second birthday. It had been a steady rather than spectacular rise and his reaction to his promotion was characteristically muted. On 7 April he wrote to the new Prime Minister:

> My dear Anthony,
>
> When I talked to you on the telephone last night (from a hotel manager's bedroom in Helensburgh!) my wits were so woolly that I never said how delighted I was to see you as Prime Minister.
>
> Everyone will rejoice to see your devotion to the country's service so richly and rightly rewarded. Well done.
>
> I am grateful indeed for the opportunity you have given me to take on the Commonwealth Office. I will try to help you there to the best of my powers. Anyway you can always give me the sack!
>
> Thank you. I will see you next week.
>
> Yours ever, Alec[1]

Rarely can a new Cabinet Minister have accepted office in more self-effacing terms. His light-hearted reference to his possible sacking must be unique; such correspondence is usually conducted with uneasy formality. In the previous four years, Home had got to know Eden better through their mutual friendship with James Stuart; he had grown to admire his diplomacy, which he regarded as responsible for the ceasefire in Indo-China in 1954, the *annus mirabilis* of Eden's career. The spring of 1955 was an optimistic time and Eden took office with a unanimity of goodwill, Attlee's tribute in the House of Commons being warm and generous. In retrospect, Home considered that the major miscalculation of the period was in not attending the Messina Conference, which left Britain outside the 'Messina Six', largely because the Commonwealth commitment was considered more important than the embryonic Common Market. 'The British public was still too near to the glory of Empire,' Lord Home wrote later, 'to accept the role for Britain of just another country in Europe.'[2]

In April 1955 Gallup Poll showed the Conservatives on 41 per cent, a mere point ahead of Labour, with an eventual prediction of a Conservative lead of 1.7 per cent. With Eden, the Conservatives had relative youth and glamour on their side, though the campaign was one of the dullest of the century. Home was confident of victory. In 1951 the Labour Party had campaigned predominantly on three issues: unemployment would return to pre-war levels under the Tories, the welfare state would be dismantled and (with Churchill's 'finger on the trigger') warmongering would prevail. Four years later, unemployment was down, social services had not been dismantled and there had been no war. The 1955 general election is a classic example of the outcome being influenced not by current canvassing but by the memory of the previous campaign.[3] Expectations of an early election had been fuelled by a very limited government reshuffle, only Swinton (Commonwealth Secretary) and de la Warr (Postmaster-General) not surviving from the Churchill administration.

Some years later Eden wrote down his reasons for the promotion of Selwyn Lloyd and Alec Home:

> When I came to form a government early in 1955, I wanted to select one or two men to bring into the Cabinet who had, as I thought, proved themselves in subordinate offices and might be looked upon to play leading parts in government and party in the future. The two I selected were Mr Selwyn Lloyd in the House of Commons, and Lord Home in the House of Lords. Mr Lloyd had had experience of defence problems as Minister of Supply, a difficult post which he had filled most ably, therefore I decided to appoint him Minister of Defence.
>
> Lord Home had had all round experience at the Scottish Office. It was evident that he could one day become an effective and respected Secretary of State for Scotland. On the other hand, I suspected that he had significant diplomatic gifts and that there was much to be said for giving him a chance now to display them. Moreover, I thought the time had come for a younger man at Commonwealth Relations.
>
> I knew most of the Dominions at first hand myself and I thought that their Governments would welcome a man like Lord Home as Secretary of State and that he would grow to fill the office with

> distinction. This, I felt, could lead to a future career for him in a wider sphere than administration, and so it proved.[4]

Eden's first thought had been to give the post of Foreign Secretary to Lord Salisbury, but the House of Lords obstacle was considered too great, not a consideration that inhibited Macmillan five years later, when Home succeeded Lloyd. In any event, Salisbury saw his main role as Leader in the Lords and his brief spell at the Commonwealth Office in 1952 had not been successful, because of his commitments in the Upper House and at Hatfield. So Macmillan was appointed. The choice of Macmillan, a strong-willed personality of great ambition, proved unhappy but with hindsight it is easy to see how Eden miscalculated the Cabinet appointments in April 1955, as well as later reshuffles. At the heart of the miscalculation was his concern for his Chancellor of the Exchequer, whose wife had died after a long battle with cancer in December 1954. A pre-election budget was due on 19 April, which precluded Butler's immediate move to a different post, after nearly four years at the Treasury, but Eden's sympathy made him flinch from a major reshuffle in the wake of the election victory at the end of May.[5] As a result, Butler continued at the Treasury until December 1955, and the October 'pots and pans' budget (purchase tax was imposed on household utensils) re-introduced much of the pre-election tax burden. His distinguished tenure of the Treasury ended under a cloud, just as larger political questions on the future of the Conservative leadership were over the horizon.

Home's appointment to the Commonwealth Relations Office came as a surprise to him. He felt he might have been appointed Secretary of State for Scotland if James Stuart had gained promotion. But Stuart stayed in Dover House (the peak of his career had passed, though he still remained a figure of influence) and Home's appointment marked him out as a possible successor to the Marquess of Salisbury as Leader of the Lords and was one of the most significant moves of his career. In the Commons he inherited Douglas Dodds-Parker as Parliamentary Under-Secretary, but the dominating personality was Sir Gilbert Laithwaite, the Permanent Under-Secretary, who 'kept the Commons Minister well below the salt, by restricting the information passed to him and usually only calling him in when some item threatened to backfire into the Commons'.[6] This method of working gave Home considerable autonomy and provided another great opportunity. Although regretting Swinton's departure (at seventy-one he was twenty years older than his successor), Macmillan welcomed the infusion of younger blood, noting, 'Lord Home becomes Commonwealth Secretary in place of Lord Swinton, who is now pretty old, though still very clever ... But it is absolutely necessary to promote some younger peers. Someone will eventually be needed to lead the House of Lords.'[7] As deputy leader in the Lords in addition to his Commonwealth responsibilities, Home was well placed for its leadership, which was to come his way sooner than anyone might have expected. Among the younger generation of Conservative peers, he was now outstripping the Earl of Perth (not yet in the government) and Lord Selkirk (Paymaster-General since November 1953) and within two years he was appointed Leader of the Lords by Macmillan.

In any successful political career, a defining moment is the crucial move from a subordinate position to an altogether higher level. Home's promotion to the Commonwealth Office in April 1955 proved the step which made all others possible. The department, which depended so much on personal contacts, fitted him like a glove and was far more broadening than a move to Housing and Health; it paved the way for his move to the Foreign Office five years later. Relationships between the Foreign Office and Commonwealth Relations were subject to intense internal rivalries. Over the next five years Home avoided the manifold pitfalls and established good working relationships with both Harold Macmillan and Selwyn Lloyd and their secretariats. His office was among the grandest in Whitehall, and replicated the architectural grandeur of that occupied by the Foreign Office, his powerful political neighbour. In the fractious circumstances of the time, a connecting door known as 'the hole in the wall' was a 38th Parallel of diplomatic niceties; relations between the Foreign Secretary and the Commonwealth Secretary were gauged by whether it was a frontier or a conduit. When Home became Foreign Secretary in July 1960, old Foreign Office hands meant it as a warm compliment when they said that he had come 'through the hole in the wall'.[8]

The Commonwealth Office had been formed in 1947 by the merger of the India Office and the Dominions Office. Attlee's keen interest in Indian affairs and his concern for the burdens that Bevin, not in the best of health, bore as Foreign Secretary led him to create the new department.[9] Whereas the India Office had dealt with India and Pakistan (members of the Commonwealth since 1947), the Dominions Office maintained contact with the 'old' Commonwealth – Canada, Australia, New Zealand and the Union of South Africa. As new countries joined, their responsibilities were taken over from the Colonial Office by the Commonwealth Office, amid mutual suspicion, which Alan Lennox-Boyd (Colonial Secretary from July 1954) and Alec Home did much to alleviate. A Colonial Affairs Committee was set up to erase or reduce tension between the two offices, and the problem was contained during Eden's premiership and subsequently. 'Alec Home and I were the two ministers during virtually the whole of my period at the CO,' wrote Lennox-Boyd, '… there was considerable jealousy in the two staffs, and indeed the CRO was known in the CO as "the three letter department", which indeed it was; I had to spend a good deal of time trying to build bridges between them. We used to have things out, the Commonwealth Secretary and the Colonial Secretary, at the Colonial Policy committee under the chairmanship of either Kilmuir as Lord Chancellor, or Rab Butler, and Winston would certainly – if the Colonial Secretary & the Commonwealth Secretary had a disagreement which hadn't gone first to the Committee – be very annoyed indeed at what he would call a waste of time.'[10]

By the time Home took office, nine prime ministers attended Commonwealth conferences. (Ceylon had joined in 1948, and the Rhodesian Federation had been affiliated since November 1953.) These meetings were held in the Cabinet Room at Downing Street, already showing signs of its inadequacy as a venue. Alec Home was one of those who negotiated to acquire Marlborough House, formerly the home of Queen Mary, who had died in March 1953, as headquarters for the Commonwealth Secretariat.[11] At his final Cabinet in April 1955, Churchill had expressed the hope that ministers would weave 'still more closely the threads which bound together the countries of the Commonwealth or, as he still preferred to call it, the Empire'.[12]

As with his period at the Scottish Office, Alec Home was fortunate in the possibilities presented by his new department. He became Secretary of State at a time when the move towards de-colonisation, as presaged at the San Francisco Conference of 1945, was gathering pace and he was thus at the epicentre of an important historical development. The central period of the process was the late 1950s and early 1960s, when there was a broad consensus over the value of the Commonwealth ideal. India remained within the Commonwealth after it became a republic in 1950 and the Commonwealth Office was seen as 'the Foreign Office with a family feeling'.[13] Ghana and Malaya became independent in 1957, and by 1970 eighteen other countries in Africa, the Mediterranean and the Caribbean had gained self-rule but were happy to remain within the Commonwealth, which disguised the political reality of the dismantling of Empire.[14]

Although in public esteem the CRO was a 'lesser' Cabinet post, Eden regarded it as an important and prestigious responsibility. By 1955, the concept of 'The Big Three', if it existed, did not include Britain at the highest level, though this reality (in the year before Suez) was still masked. It was the 'Big Thirteen or Fourteen' below the superpower level, where, in Eden's view, the CRO had an important part to play. Britain's role was difficult to formulate; some felt that the future lay with the American relationship; for others, the European ideal fathered by Jean Monnet was the way ahead. Eden never showed much enthusiasm for the European alternative: 'I have constituents in Leamington who have relations in the Commonwealth, but they don't have relations in Europe,' he said.[15] The Commonwealth was for Eden a source of strength within the wider framework, quite apart from its historic associations. 'Everywhere through our Commonwealth and Empire nations are growing up. This places a heavy responsibility on the parent.'[16] That responsibility was now Alec Home's.

The Commonwealth Office was concerned not with administration, but with the conduct of relations with other governments.[17] Its work was diplomatic in character, concerned with consultation, negotiation and representation, and depended heavily on the quality of its personnel. It was a time of consolidation, with the main priority being the build-up of a sense of co-operation between the various governments. Home was conscious that Swinton, with his antipathy to Nehru, had never really seen the Commonwealth as a whole and that his essential task was to encourage trust among the members. Its advisory functions extended to briefing ministers on matters which impinged on their departments, particularly in trade matters, and its supervisory functions included co-ordination of Cabinet decisions over a broad field. It was responsible for Indian Service pensions, as well as the provision of staff for United Kingdom representation throughout the High Commission territories.

Criticism of this function came from Lord Chandos (the former Colonial Secretary, Oliver Lyttelton) who had family ties with New Zealand; 'One aspect worries me a bit, and I don't quite know how to deal with it, and that is the incomparably higher social quality of the people sent here by the USA vis-à-vis their English counterparts. Apart from the High Commissioner himself, who is extremely able and whom I like sincerely, the rest of the High Commissioner's Office consists of pasty-faced intellectuals with little suburban snob wives who make little effort to *like* New Zealand or New Zealanders, and who have none of the easy and affable grace of the Yanks. God knows, the job needs no Talleyrand – only a moderately intelligent ex-public-school boy, who fishes and plays golf and *takes trouble* with the natives.'[18] This letter highlights one of the dilemmas of Home's tenure of the Commonwealth Office, how or whether the expectations of an earlier age could be accommodated to contemporary realities. Later generations would have to worry about jobs for the golf-playing public schoolboys who took trouble with the natives.

Alec Home met his new private secretary, Harold Smedley, at the Travellers' Club, and Smedley introduced him to the staff at the Commonwealth Relations Office.[19] They were among the few who had to adjust to a new minister. The announcement that Home was to be the new Secretary of State came as a bolt from the blue; there were hurried consultations of *Who's Who* and soundings on the grapevine. One of the first people he met, in a dark and gloomy corridor, was Gilbert Laithwaite, whom he initially found a formidable and forbidding bachelor, a martinet whose ideas had been formulated by his Indian service, with its incidental snobberies. He was a mandarin who insisted on the highest standards, and Home was taken aback when Laithwaite turned on a young man in the corridor. 'Do you want to make your way in this office?' he asked the hapless junior, 'then have your hair cut by lunchtime and get a bowler hat'.[20] However, he came to appreciate Laithwaite's insistence that things be done properly; a more emollient person would not have dovetailed so well with Home's very different personality.

Alec Home's relationship with his staff, as counterpoint to Laithwaite, was informal, but assured and no less productive. His greatest skill was perceived as his ability to draft documents: a letter to Sir Roy Welensky was worked on by a high-powered team of advisers, but came back from the Secretary of State with its essence distilled in sharp and skilful revisions, an ability which was much admired in the Office.[21] He read and digested papers quickly, spotting the salient points, and he expressed himself clearly and concisely. He did not dally over decisions when officials presented him with the facts, reversing Swinton's policy on Indian textile imports on his first working day. Nobody claimed that Alec Home was the greatest intellect or the most powerful personality who headed the Commonwealth Office in the post-war period, but his understanding of human nature and ability to get on with people and produce results made him 'the best of the lot'.[22]

He never had to drive people, because they wanted to work for him, and he never kept the long hours which so infuriate and tire staff. He had an intuitive sense of what feelings were on the day-to-day issues, as well as what would be politically feasible. He dealt with memoranda quickly, was prompt with his red boxes, and was known as a civil servant's Secretary of State. He had the ability to work on speeches in unpromising places, often while in transit, in the back of the official car or whilst waiting in draughty railway stations.

For one whose eyes often tired, his appetite for the printed word was extraordinary. His office kept him supplied with reading matter for the long flights to all parts of the globe: heavy philosophical works, which he studied, and paperback detective stories, which he devoured at a ferocious rate. One work of political theory was left behind in Honolulu, but the airport authorities rescued it and sent it on, judging that it must have belonged to Lord Home. 'The outstanding qualities he displayed at the CRO were integrity and fairmindedness. He was totally without meanness in his thoughts or actions; he was concerned solely to be of service without any ulterior motive or thought of personal reward … If he did not probe every problem in great depth … he always understood it in the round …'[23] This could serve as a description of his methods and style throughout his ministerial career.

An air of unreality pervaded Home's first weeks at the Commonwealth Relations Office. He spoke in his first Cabinet on the multilateral guarantee of the security of Formosa, which was under discussion with Foster Dulles in America and Menzies in Australia. The Cabinet authorised Macmillan and Home to co-ordinate further approaches to the governments of Canada and New Zealand.[24] It was a baptism in political agenda far removed from Scottish issues, such as under-shot jaw and the Forth Road Bridge. Until the electorate made their verdict known, there was a provisional air about many of the ministerial meetings, but Eden began sending out his first memoranda to the Cabinet. Home received a missive on the problems of the country which eventually became Malaysia. 'We must consider urgently the problem of [Malcolm] MacDonald's successor as Commissioner-General, South-East Asia, and the future functions and staff of this office,' wrote Eden. 'I think that MacDonald should come home as soon as convenient, both to prepare for his post in India and for consultation about the future of the set-up in Singapore.'[25] This was typical of the businesslike notes Home received over the next eighteen months, which he dealt with in an equally pragmatic manner.

Election day saw Alec and Elizabeth Home in Lanark to support Patrick Maitland. During the campaign Elizabeth's father, Cyril Alington, died; the family gathered for the funeral at Durham, where Alington had been Dean for eighteen years and where in 1936 he had officiated at the marriage of Alec and Elizabeth Dunglass. Alec Home, Roger Mynors and John Wilkes were the three sons-in-law brought together in Durham that early summer, when the ashes were buried in the north transept. 'It is probable that he will be most generally remembered as the Headmaster of Eton,' wrote *The Times* obituarist, adding, 'He was the kindest and most charitably minded of men.'[26] Within a year, there was a further blow with the death at the age of only forty-one of Elizabeth's last brother, Giles Alington, a much respected don at University College, Oxford.

The results of the 1955 election were a vindication of Eden's decision to seek an early mandate. The Conservatives won 344 seats, an increase of 23, and Labour fell back to 277. The two major parties won over 96 per cent of the popular vote. Before the year was out Hugh Gaitskell had replaced the ageing Attlee as Labour leader and in 1956, Jo Grimond took over as Liberal leader from Clement Davies. Politics seemed to some to be entering a new era, but this was a false impression. Not only was the old two-party system more firmly entrenched than ever, but the background of prominent figures was predominantly that of the older public schools and Oxbridge colleges. In 1956, two Etonians and a Wykehamist, from Christ Church, Balliol and New College respectively, led the three main parties and the Marquess of Salisbury still presided in the Upper House. The real sea-change came only eight years later when Harold Wilson succeeded Alec Douglas-Home as Prime Minister.

Eden retained his Cabinet *en bloc*. The newspaper strike had ended, but potentially damaging disputes erupted in industrial action in the docks and on the railways. These difficulties were not Home's concern, though he shared in the Cabinet decisions. His priority was to visit as many Commonwealth countries as possible, and the summer of 1955 was spent preparing for his first major tour. He also prepared a nineteen-page document with Lennox-Boyd on Colonial Immigration, summarising the restrictions on the entry of British subjects into Commonwealth countries and the Irish Republic, and a memorandum on defence co-operation with South Africa with Selwyn Lloyd and J.P.L. Thomas, First Lord of the Admiralty, arguing for retention of the Simonstown naval base.[27] Eden granted him the tenure of

Dorneywood, at Burnham Beeches, given to the nation by Lord Courtauld-Thomson in 1943, where he lived and entertained during the parliamentary sessions. His visitors from the Commonwealth included the Australian cricket team in 1956, when an impromptu match was played on the lawns, with the Commonwealth Secretary in the host side. Of all his official houses during his career it was the one for which he felt the greatest affection. From it he set forth to Heathrow airport on government business or to Ludgrove School for family outings, where he was a regular participant in fathers' cricket matches, and later Eton, where his son David followed him in 1957. Over the next five years, he hosted many important conferences and meetings there, most particularly in May 1960 when the question of South Africa's continued membership of the Commonwealth was discussed ahead of the Commonwealth Prime Ministers' meeting.

In the summer of 1950, one of Alec Home's predecessors at the Commonwealth Relations Office, Patrick Gordon Walker, had undertaken a 41,000-mile tour of the Commonwealth and on his return had reported to Attlee on the desirability of making such journeys a regular feature of the Commonwealth Secretary's remit. 'It will make a lot of difference if visits by various Ministers, especially to Australia and New Zealand, can become a more normal thing,' he wrote. 'I found that there is still great ignorance in Australia and New Zealand about the nature and problems of the new Commonwealth.'[28] Gordon Walker's suggestion had been taken up by Swinton in 1953, when he embarked on a ten-week tour of Australia and New Zealand with visits to India, Pakistan and Ceylon on his return journey, a pattern followed by Alec Home, who was keen to learn the ropes at the earliest opportunity.[29] Arrangements were put in hand within days of his appointment. He wrote to Eden, 'There has been criticism in the Australian Press of my appointment on the grounds of lack of experience of Commonwealth affairs, and an early announcement of my intention to go and see them would help to allay their doubts.' By the time he sought formal approval from Sir Michael Adeane, he was thinking of visiting 'as many as possible of the countries for whose relations I am responsible'.[30]

Home had a detailed briefing from Laithwaite: the subjects suitable for public speeches and those 'not intended for public use but for talk across the table' were discussed. The former included the Commonwealth today, the CRO and its functions, the development of new Commonwealth countries. The colonial responsibilities of the United Kingdom, including assistance in development and progress towards self-government, and information about trouble spots were in the more sensitive category. After Parliament had risen he went to Springhill to work on his speeches, from drafts provided by Laithwaite. Welcoming letters followed him to Scotland when his tour was announced, and requests for guidance on his preferences for off-duty entertainments. Harold Smedley let it be known that 'the Secretary of State is very keen on horse racing and ... would be very glad to have an opportunity of seeing how things are conducted in Australia'. One of his secretaries minuted, 'He would welcome some fishing rather than shooting if the season is right,' which prompted the New Zealand High Commissioner to write, 'Perhaps I could be told the size of the Secretary of State's shoe for the purpose of the provision of waders if necessary.'[31] Eden arranged that Elizabeth Home should join her husband for the return leg, a gesture which was much appreciated.

Home left London on 30 August with Harold Smedley. He carried binoculars, his little joke book, detective stories and a wedge-shaped cushion to support his back. They were to be away until 4 November, an unimaginable absence now, but one that enabled Home to get the feel of the countries. The priorities can be inferred; he was to spend seventeen days in New Zealand, four weeks in Australia, a week in Ceylon, eight days in India, and a week in Pakistan. Their flight took them via New York and San Francisco to Honolulu, and on 4 September they landed at Vita Leva, the largest island of the Fiji group. ('During the night we crossed the Equator and also the International Date Line. So Saturday never existed for us.')[32] In Auckland that night, the Secretary of State gave his first press conference to a group of deferential reporters.

The tour began in earnest the next morning; after lunch at the Auckland Rotary Club 'the Secretary of State spoke on the theme of British recovery from the economic stresses engendered by war and how we were equipped and willing to meet the demands of the twentieth century'. The optimistic tone was well received. There were talks with the head of ICI before an evening reception. The day was typical of the programme over the next few weeks. Sight-seeing, always an opportunity for informal conversations, had given way to the fulsome loyalty of the Empire societies, and the formal civic reception. This contrast between the public ceremonials and the uninhibited openness of the people was one of Home's main impressions of New Zealand. Political talks were businesslike, usually on trade matters, but Home soon realised that his hosts had a great capacity for unstuffy relaxation. At

Government House Sid Holland and the Governor-General, Lord Norrie, embarked on a vigorous game of indoor cricket, with the Secretary of State and other guests. During the next few days, he attended meetings of the Cabinet, broadcast live on New Zealand radio, and visited farms. He went trout fishing in the Tongariro river, toured hydro-electric stations, tried 'radium' baths before breakfast and watched Maori dancing in Whakarewarewa. One meeting which gave him particular pleasure was with Sir Edmund Hillary, conqueror of Everest.

New Zealand reminded Home, geographically and socially, of Scotland, and the visits to sheep farms and other rural outposts were reminiscent of his responsibilities at the Scottish Office. Strategically, 1955 was a good time for a Commonwealth Secretary to visit South-East Asia. The Collective Defence Treaty, binding Australia, New Zealand, Pakistan, the Philippines, Thailand, together with the United Kingdom, the United States and France, had been enacted on 8 September 1954, and Home's travels enabled him to assess the implications of this co-ordinated development.

He flew to Sydney to begin the more substantive second stage of his tour, including talks with Robert Menzies, who became one of his most trusted political friends. Australia entailed dealings in each state with leading figures in political, religious and social life, and, with its cricketing associations, became one of his favourite countries. One of his first meetings was with an old cricketing friend, Jack Fingleton, now making a career as a sporting commentator. New acquaintances included the opposition leader, Dr H.V. Devatt, who showed a Wisden-like recall of cricketing statistics, not that this impressed Robert Menzies, whose disdain for political opponents, even in 'off-duty' matters, was uncompromising. Alec Home was left in no doubt that Robert Menzies was the 'big' man of Australian politics.

As in New Zealand, the tour was a mixture of the formal and the informal. Small talk with local dignitaries who clamoured to be near the Secretary of State at the top tables required special skills. The wife of one university chancellor introduced herself with the words, 'You know I have had a stroke', a conversational gambit not easy to follow. Trade questions were a major preoccupation and great interest was shown by the press in British agricultural policy. He had discussions on the Assisted Passages Scheme, whereby British emigrants could travel to Australia for a minimal fare. He spoke on the work and aims of the Commonwealth Relations Office to members of both Houses of

Parliament at a lunch in Victoria, toured factories and met executives. At the end of September Home managed a four-day visit to Tasmania; on his return to Adelaide he spoke on the peaceful uses of atomic energy and went down a uranium mine. From Perth, he flew to Indonesia en route to Singapore.

The tour was considered a success by the Australian press. When he had arrived, he was an unknown figure on the international scene. He became a minor celebrity and paved the way for Harold Macmillan's visit three years later.

After Singapore, Home and Smedley flew to Colombo, where Elizabeth Home had arrived some hours earlier. The official welcoming party was headed by Sir Cecil Syers, High Commissioner in Ceylon from 1951 to 1957, an old friend from the days of Neville Chamberlain's secretariat, who had travelled on the plane to Munich in September 1938. On the first evening there was an official dinner with the Prime Minister, Sir John Kotelawala, at which Home also met Lester Pearson, whom he was to meet more formally on his Canadian tour in 1956. The next night the Homes were able to relax in the company of old friends; the dinner that Sir Cecil and Lady Syers gave for them proved 'a genial evening', when Syers and Home recalled the far-off Munich days and the Heston flight.

One of the distinguishing features of Alec Home's tenure of the CRO was that 'he set great store by the High Commissioners receiving an account from "the horse's mouth"'.[33] This was not just a question of seeing the High Commissioners on his various tours, as in this case with Syers, but of persuading the relevant ministers (Macmillan, for example, on his return from the Geneva Conference) 'to speak to the Commonwealth High Commissioners and give them a first-hand account of this conference'.[34] The first two days in Ceylon were part of this pattern, but it was a two-way process because Home was able to meet the Commonwealth prime ministers. The overlapping of past networks gave him trusted associates in a myriad of places. Home may not have been well known to the public at this stage, but in the diplomatic and Westminster worlds there were few areas his life had not touched.

There were signs in Ceylon that the questioning of the Secretary of State was to be sharper than in New Zealand and Australia. The *Daily Telegraph* had reported him as saying that the Commonwealth Relations Office would sponsor a Commonwealth immigration plan, whereas Home had said that no such proposal had been put forward, but if it were, it would be considered – a topic which might have proved controversial in Australia if he had confirmed it. The visit to Ceylon provided an introduction to the sterner tests awaiting him when he flew to Bombay, where he was met by Malcolm MacDonald, High Commissioner in India. At Delhi, the following day, 'the Secretary of State stepped from the aircraft straight into batteries of floodlights and photographers'. He also received a battery of contradictory advice from the Prime Minister, Pandit Nehru, on the virtues of Indian 'non-alignment', the value of their entente with China and the necessity for British withdrawal from its last colonial outposts in Africa, while avoiding mention of India's worsening relations with Pakistan over Kashmir. On 22 October, Home addressed the Indian Council of World Affairs, 'a body somewhat equivalent to Chatham House'. He outlined his feelings on the communist threat in South-East Asia and the motivations underpinning the North Atlantic Treaty Organisation and guiding British foreign policy aims. 'The lessons we and our friends in Europe have learned in a bitter school is that weakness invites aggression and that neutrality has no meaning in the context of totalitarian ambition. To match strength with strength has been the policy of risk which to you in Asia might seem unnecessary and dangerous, but the North Atlantic Treaty corresponded to the instinctive and genuine need for self-preservation which was felt in Western Europe.'[35] The response from Nehru was distinctly cool; Home thought him duplicitous on some matters.

Memories of the Raj were evoked by the various Willingdon Clubs in which they were hospitably entertained, but the old imperial ties, nostalgic for the British 'staying on', meant little to the Indian national consciousness, with the result that there was an underlying tension to Anglo–Indian relationships, not helped by the anti-colonial fervour (and ambivalent attitude towards the communist *bloc*) of some Indian politicians, such as Krishna Menon, who proved a persistent thorn in the flesh.[36] The final phase of the tour to Pakistan was quiet, though he still travelled 3000 miles during his short visit. He laid a wreath at the tomb of Jinnah, creator and first Governor-General of Pakistan, journeyed up the Khyber Pass and called in on the test match between Pakistan and New Zealand. On 3 November, the party began the long flight to England. 'We had covered 35,000 miles by air and 3000 miles by road in nearly 2½ months. We felt we had earned a rest, but the Secretary of State at least was not to get it.'[37]

Although Home was to be involved in many further diplomatic

missions over the next twenty years, that Commonwealth tour was of special importance, marking his emergence on to a wider political stage with politicians of global status, such as Robert Menzies and Pandit Nehru. His discussions with Menzies had been of fundamental importance; the Australians felt that the old Commonwealth unities were being eroded. He warned of the opportunities that enlarged Commonwealth Prime Ministers' conferences might give for the ventilation of differences and the advertisement of conflicts.[38] Home now began to understand the coded language of old Commonwealth hands; he had heard people talking of the 'responsible' countries, such as Australia, and of those, such as Canada, which were liable to take an intransigent and independent line. A word much employed was 'robust', the degree of robustness being how far a Commonwealth country could be relied upon to follow the British line. The high priest of 'robustness' was Menzies, which is why he was so popular in Whitehall. The question which was at that time unanswered (though the Suez Crisis offered some resolutions) was whether the more recent Commonwealth countries – such as India and Pakistan, and later the African states – would be 'responsibly robust' or 'intransigently independent' in the face of crisis.

The New Zealand press was 'disarmed by the speed with which he set out to gain a first-hand impression of New Zealand and by the arduous programme which he agreed to carry out'. In Australia, there was approval of 'his clear determination to learn as much as possible about Australia and its problems whatever the personal effort involved'.[39] His understanding of strategy was deepened by his awareness of the *realpolitik* of South-East Asia.

His return to the Lords for the new session of Parliament in November saw his position enhanced among his Cabinet colleagues. The successful induction period in his new job and the publicity for his 'world' tour meant that his opinions were now sought on wider matters, such as the Simonstown naval base, the continuing difficulties in Aden and constitutional advance in Cyprus, particularly by Harold Macmillan as Foreign Secretary and Selwyn Lloyd as Defence Secretary. An example of this arose over the increasingly contentious issue of Commonwealth immigration, which had been discussed in desultory fashion during the last weeks of Churchill's administration and then put aside until the election had been safely negotiated. The Cabinet discussed the question on 30 August, the day Home left on his Commonwealth tour. They had before them a memorandum Home had prepared, warning of repercussions if Britain attempted to legislate on racial grounds. There was danger of retaliatory discrimination against British business interests from India, Pakistan and Ceylon and he felt the governments of India and Pakistan would exercise restraint without legislation (though the numbers of immigrant Indians had increased during the previous year and 'unless checked this could become a menace'[40]). He was prepared to see curbs on West Indian immigration. Though he differentiated between West Indians and other nationalities, Home was regarded as one of the liberal members of the Cabinet on this issue ('emotionally white, but politically neutral'[41]) together with Lennox-Boyd and Macleod. When the issue was discussed in Cabinet in July 1956, Home said he had 'no doubt that any legislation we might enact must apply in form to the Commonwealth as a whole'. He did not believe that this 'would give any rise to any serious consequences in our relations with Commonwealth countries, many of whom under their own laws practised discrimination against immigrants from other parts of the Commonwealth.'[42]

Eden had high regard for Home and saw great promise in him. He took a notably solicitous line towards Home, whose health had not been of the best. 'Don't wear yourself out,' he had warned at the end of 1955, when outline plans for a tour of Canada were known.[43] Macmillan, a shrewd judge of political character, was also impressed by this new arrival. Macmillan shot at Douglas, which became a haven for him beyond the reaches of the press. Another friendship was with Selwyn Lloyd, a lonely figure after the breakdown of his marriage, who joined family suppers at the Homes' London flat. His closest friend in Cabinet remained James Stuart, and other old friends were increasingly found in influential places. Roger Makins was ambassador in Washington, and proposed a stop-over for Home on his way to Canada. 'It would be good for some of the administration leaders and, for that matter, my Commonwealth colleagues, to make your acquaintance.'[44]

Notwithstanding their pre-war friendship, Butler and Home were never quite comrades-in-arms. In his years as a widower (he remarried in October 1959) Butler retreated within himself and the two had drifted apart. Despite being a keen shot, Butler was never invited to Douglas and the Homes were not habitués of Butler's house, Spencers, near Great Yeldham or Stanstead Hall, even though Elizabeth Home and Butler's second wife were old friends. One member of the Cabinet Home could never fathom was Macleod. While Macleod was at the Ministry of Health and Home was at Commonwealth Relations this was not of major importance, but the situation altered when Eden announced a further reorganisation of his Cabinet on 20 December 1995. Although Home continued at the CRO – *The Times* noting 'It would obviously not have been sense to move Lord Home so soon after his Commonwealth tour' – he was not unaffected by the subtle changes in hierarchy and ranking that accompanied Eden's changes. Macleod moved to the Ministry of Labour, a staging post to the Colonial Secretaryship in Macmillan's government in October 1959, and when he and Home overlapped at the Colonial and Commonwealth Offices, the seeds of mutual mistrust were sown. Macleod had little time for Home, who for his part found it difficult to establish a fruitful relationship – a failure on both sides which had important consequences both for the Conservative Party and for British politics.

Foremost among Eden's considerations in his second Cabinet reshuffle was the problem of Harold Macmillan and Rab Butler. In an ironic repetition of the difficulties Eden had experienced at the Foreign Office from May 1937 to February 1938 during Chamberlain's premiership, the relationship between Macmillan and his Prime Minister was far from satisfactory. Their policy differences were manageable – Macmillan felt that Eden had 'missed the European boat' by his coolness towards Messina and there were problems of emphasis over the long-running Arab–Israeli disputes. What was not easy to reconcile was the clash of temperament; Eden was notorious for his inability to delegate and Macmillan's style was one of expansive autonomy. In short, Macmillan wanted to be the boss in foreign affairs and resented interference, even from an expert such as Eden. Many felt that Eden's promotion of the relatively junior Selwyn Lloyd to Foreign Secretary was a clear indication that he wished to wrest back control of foreign policy, an impression not dispelled by the Suez crisis.

Eden had first mooted the Treasury for Macmillan before Butler's 'pots and pans' budget, telling him that if he did move his successor would be Selwyn Lloyd. Macmillan was uneasy on several counts, not least because the Foreign Office was a post he had long wanted and one that was of special challenge and opportunity. In a long letter to Eden he insisted on 'a position in the Government not inferior to that held by the present Chancellor'. The position of Rab Butler in the hierarchy was crucial to Macmillan's hopes of succeeding Eden. 'As Foreign Secretary, I am the head of the Foreign Front, under you as Prime Minister. As Chancellor, I must be undisputed head of the Home Front under you. If Rab becomes Leader of the House and Lord Privy Seal that will be fine. But I could not agree that he should become Deputy Prime Minister ... the presence of a much respected ex-Chancellor with all that this implies in the Cabinet and in Whitehall must somewhat add to my difficulties, however loyal he will try to be. If he were also Deputy Prime Minister, my task would be impossible.'[45] Eden accepted these conditions, and it is now easy to see that the loser in the reshuffle of December 1955 was Rab Butler. Deprived of a power base as Lord Privy Seal and without departmental responsibilities as Leader of the House of Commons, he occupied a nebulous hinterland between seniority and influence. Even before the controversies of the Suez operation, Macmillan had taken a firm step on the road to 10 Downing Street.

There were other winners and losers. Walter Monckton took over at Defence when Lloyd moved to the Foreign Office and Edward Heath became Chief Whip. Eden had been considering the reshuffle for months, but the general reaction was that he had been panicked into making changes because of the election of a new leader of the Labour Party, Hugh Gaitskell, nine years younger than the Prime Minister. As one of the Ministers who remained in his current department, Home consolidated his position and planned his tour of Canada in May and of the African states, including South Africa, in the autumn of 1956, a tour postponed owing to the Suez crisis. Under the outward veneer of insouciant calm, many tensions were contained in the newly reshuffled Cabinet.

Alec and Elizabeth Home were not part of this febrile atmosphere. Lady Home played a full part in the social side of the Commonwealth Relations Office and in the welfare of those whose work meant a greater disruption of family life than was evident in domestic departments. Present generations see such involvement as a Lady Bountiful approach, but nothing was further from the truth in her case. In 1954, the Commonwealth Relations Office Wives' Society (always known as the CROWS) had been established, and, in the years that the Homes were involved, it worked well. It was not just a question of social occasions, but practical help in getting children on their holidays to places where their parents were serving, along with the whole gamut of 'injections, travel and visas' – and emergencies, such as a quick return to Britain when there was family illness or bereavement.

There was no indication as Cabinet business got underway in January that 1956 would blight, make and alter so many careers. At the end of January, Home reported that 'negotiations had been proceeding for some time for the sale of a substantial number of British aircraft to India', and 'it was specially important that this contract should be concluded, as ... the Indians were toying with the alternative of buying bomber aircraft from the Russians ...' Home arranged an acceptable deal and moved on to constitutional talks with an all-party delegation from Singapore.[46]

He left on his second major tour on 9 May, calling at Newfoundland on the way. Elizabeth Home travelled with him from the start, and Smedley was again in attendance. Alec Home found that questions at press conferences were much sharper. The visit of the Russian leaders, Bulganin and Khrushchev, to Britain in April had coincided with the incident of the disappearance of the frogman, Commander Crabb, in Portsmouth Harbour, where Russian warships were moored; together with the earlier defection of Burgess and Maclean in 1951, public interest in the half-world of espionage was at its Cold War height, in Canada as elsewhere. This led to stone-walling, at which point 'Cyprus was also raised by a questioner who clearly had little sympathy with British policy there', as Smedley recorded. The Secretary of State was also questioned about United States investment in Canada. His remarks, 'garbled by the evening paper', led to the headline, UK MINISTER SAYS US CAPITAL NO DANGER TO CANADA.[47] The High Commissioner's Office rang Smedley 'to say that Lord Beaverbrook had launched a bitter attack in the *Sunday Express* on the Secretary of State's remarks on American capital'. The virulence of the attack took Home completely by surprise, but was a sharp reminder of how an unguarded remark could be blown up out of all proportion. The episode had long-term implications: Beaverbrook did not forget and the attitude of his newspapers to Home, as his career developed, was unsympathetic. There was a mischievous streak in Beaverbrook that thrived on the world of telegrams and anger. He liked 'dra-ma', as he pronounced it, and Home would prove good copy over the years.

Alec Home wrote to Selwyn Lloyd on 1 June about the controversy, stressing the importance of maintaining Middle Eastern oil supplies, although his main concern was lest his speech and Beaverbrook's intervention had caused the Foreign Secretary any difficulty:

> Beaverbrook seems to have got his knife into me, which is all right by me but I do hope that nothing he quotes me as saying is inconvenient for you. All the interest here is on our policy in Cyprus and Middle East and the general attitude is one of doubt

> tending to criticism. It has been necessary to try and convince Canadians that our policy in Cyprus and Middle East is not designed to protect our narrow British interests but to safeguard the interests of the free world. I have therefore made points that the oil supplies of Middle East must be protected for the sake of all; that United Kingdom must accept responsibility for Government and constitutional changes in Cyprus; that we were willing to go a very long way towards self-government, but must retain control of internal security and external defence.
>
> I would normally not open my mouth as you know on things outside my own field of operation but press and radio are concentrating all the attention they can spare from the pipe-line on this question. There has been no criticism in Canadian Press of anything I have said. It will be a great help if our information people here can be given any speeches to be made by yourself or Prime Minister on this which emphasise that our policy is inspired by a desire to do our duty by the free world.[48]

Other parts of the tour were less fraught, although the itinerary had a higher political content than his previous tour. Before leaving for Washington, Home had a final meeting with the Prime Minister, Lester Pearson, one of the creators of NATO and then at the height of his influence as leader of one of the 'middle powers' in world affairs. Later in the year when the Suez Crisis broke, Home's main responsibility was maintaining Commonwealth unity; one of the most significant contributions was made by Lester Pearson, which alleviated Home's disappointment at 'the ambivalent attitude' of the Canadians. On this tour he was struck by their defensive independence and breezy lack of deference, certainly not dependably 'robust', and the dourness of many of his fellow countrymen, who had settled around Toronto and Ottawa. Before leaving Heathrow, he had asked his staff for five amusing Canadian stories to include in his little black joke-book. He was solemnly told that five such stories did not exist.[49]

No such dourness was evident in his welcome by Sir Roger Makins at the Washington embassy; it was a meeting of old friends from Aspidistra Club days and the laughter rang loudly and long in the Lutyens corridors that weekend.[50] Its main purpose was for Home to meet some of the decision-makers on Capitol Hill. Foremost among these, of course, was Dwight Eisenhower, shortly seeking a second term, whom Home saw in the White House and came to respect, though there were moments of exasperation. In the absence of John

Foster Dulles, he met Herbert Hoover Jr at the State Department, to be brought up to date with foreign issues. This was Home's first introduction to the world of Washington politics, and his admiration for America and commitment to the 'special relationship' was a consistent theme from those meetings in the summer of 1956. When asked some years later by an American historian if he could define the special relationship, he answered, 'I suppose it is very hard to define and maybe that is one of the things that helps it. It is certainly founded on a common language. And there is also the fact that we have a great respect for your achievements. The United States is an outstanding example of the operation of a free society. We have all that in common. And we fought together in two wars and have developed the habit of working together.' Smiling, he added, 'I suppose we have an affection for you as a former colony. It is a rather intangible thing.'[51]

When he returned to London, one of his shrewdest appointments, on the eve of Suez, was Henry Lintott.[52] Africa was now the major missing link in his Commonwealth travels. Home knew that independence in the African territories was going to be a major concern for his political generation and that the response to this growth of national consciousness would transcend the trading concerns of countries such as New Zealand and Canada. One of the first submissions Home and Lennox-Boyd made to Cabinet in June 1956 was over self-government for the Central African Federation set up in 1953, which they both accepted 'should advance without delay'.[53] Home had therefore been considering a scheme which 'would safeguard the position of the Africans in the Federation territories and maintain the pledges given in Parliament in 1953 that no advance towards full membership of the Commonwealth would be made without the agreement of the inhabitants of the Federation'. The Cabinet agreed that 'it would be both illogical and dangerous to attempt to confer Commonwealth membership on the Federation before it reached the stage of full internal self-government'.[54]

On 26 July 1956, Alec Home was a guest at the state banquet for King Feisal of Iraq, when Eden was given the news that Nasser had nationalised the Suez Canal. Elizabeth Home received a telephone call from her husband telling her that he would be delayed; it was clear that this was a major crisis. Lady Home therefore decided that, although she did not normally keep more than an engagement diary, she ought to keep a record of events as they unfolded. 'It is perhaps worthwhile writing down the extraordinary occurrences in Alec's life ever since on July 26 he went to dine with the PM to meet King Feisal' runs the first (retrospective) heading. The entry reads, 'He telephoned back about 11 p.m. to say he had gone to a meeting & hoped he would not be very long. At 1 he hadn't returned nor at 2 and I was beginning to agitate & at 2.30 he came in flinging off his very incongruous looking white tie and tails & said, "That idiot Nasser has seized the Canal." And that was the end of all peace – world peace or domestic peace.'[55]

Suez was an issue, even before Nasser's nationalisation of the Canal, that had sparked off deep divisions within the Conservative Party. The Defence Secretary, Earl Alexander, and the Secretary of State for War, Antony Head, believed that the nuclear age had made the Suez base redundant, but the 'Suez Group' of dissident backbenchers saw the 1954 evacuation from the base as a dangerous sell-out. When the party establishment asked Churchill for moral support at a 1922 Committee meeting, he quipped, 'I'm not sure I'm on our side.'[56] Such manoeuvrings had bypassed Home, who was involved in Scottish Office matters at the time, but as Commonwealth Secretary he was now involved in the unfolding crisis, the first occasion on which he was embroiled at the highest executive level in an affair of international importance.

His role has been underestimated for two basic reasons. Public attention was focused on Eden in Britain and Nasser in Egypt, the major players. Other figures appeared as the drama unfolded – the trio of Foreign Ministers from Britain, France and Egypt: Selwyn Lloyd, Christian Pineau and Dr Fawzi. To this trio was soon added the US Secretary of State, Foster Dulles, and President Eisenhower, the decisive figure in the Anglo–French withdrawal. Many circles of influence came together in those summer months: the United Nations and its Secretary-General, Dag Hammarskjöld, and Sir Robert Menzies and his Commonwealth 'Mission' to Nasser. Among Eden's inner circle of Cabinet colleagues, Macmillan influenced the decision to withdraw, after pressure from the US Treasury Secretary, and Butler was propelled into being acting head of the government when Eden retired to Jamaica because of ill-health at the end of November. Little attention was paid, either at the time or later, to other Cabinet ministers. Home does not even rate a mention in the index to Anthony Nutting's *No End of a Lesson*, which was seen in 1967 as the fullest (and most controversial) version then available from the British side. He met the same fate in Keith Kyle's *magnum opus* on Suez.[57]

The second reason that little attention was paid to his role is the unrevealing account of Suez in his memoirs. *The Way the Wind Blows* is, however, not a comprehensive account of Home's political career. When first-hand accounts of Suez began to appear, it was to those of Nutting, Lloyd and Macmillan that historians turned; Home was not 'good copy'. However, from the time that the news reached Downing Street during the dinner for King Feisal to the farewells as the Edens set sail for New Zealand on 18 January 1957, Home was at the inner councils.

Within minutes of hearing the news of Nasser's action, Eden summoned Jean Chauvel, the French ambassador, Andrew Foster, the American chargé d'affaires, and the Chiefs of Staff to Downing Street. He told Gaitskell what had happened, and just before midnight, the first of many meetings began in the Cabinet Room. The five Cabinet ministers who had been at the dinner – Eden, Salisbury, Kilmuir, Lloyd and Home – gathered with the two foreign diplomats and the Chiefs of Staff – Lord Mountbatten (Acting Chairman), Sir Gerald Templer (Chief of the Imperial General Staff) and Sir Dermot Boyle (Chief of the Air Staff). The meeting broke up just after 2 a.m. with the Chiefs of Staff instructed to begin preparations for a possible invasion of Egypt, though the diplomatic initiative – a concerted action by the British, French and American governments – was the first priority.

Later that morning, as Harold Macmillan recorded in his diary, Eden 'appointed a "Suez" Committee of the Cabinet – himself, Salisbury, Home and myself'.[58] This so-called 'Suez Committee' became the formally constituted Egypt Committee, with an enlarged membership. Eden now took central charge of the executive machine. Home's attendance at the meeting which authorised contingency plans for invasion may have been fortuitous, in that he was already at Downing Street when the crisis broke, but there was nothing fortuitous about his inclusion in the hastily convened committee. The Commonwealth was going to be a vital backdrop to British actions; nobody could foresee how the different governments would react and it would require special skills to hold the Commonwealth together.

In the Suez Crisis Alec Home played a significant and, owing to his own reticence, largely unrecorded role. He was a pivotal figure in four areas: with Eden; with other members of the Cabinet; with the rank-and-file of the party; and with the Commonwealth. Eden's wish to carry his Cabinet colleagues with him during the crisis led him to value Home, whose 'firmness and discretion' gave reassurance, especially as support became more equivocal.[59] If he was aboard, some sections of the party felt, the operation could not be wholly discreditable.[60] His influence with Mrs Pandit, the Indian High Commissioner, contributed to keeping India within the Commonwealth, despite the malevolent influence of Krishna Menon, who was fervently opposed to the British viewpoint and one of the main agents in the collapse of the Menzies Mission to Nasser.[61] Mrs Pandit, whom Alec kept as fully informed as he was able, was the proper conduit to the Indian government, and they struck up a wry understanding during the crisis. On one occasion, Mrs Pandit assured Alec Home in advance that if she kissed Krishna Menon on his arrival at London Airport it should not be interpreted as a gesture of political solidarity. Home believed there was a tendency at times of crisis for the Commonwealth to divide on colour lines, something he was determined should not happen over Suez.

Although he had not returned home until the early hours of 27 July, Home was at the CRO early that morning to see the High Commissioners of Australia, Canada, Ceylon, India and New Zealand, and, in South Africa's case, the Acting High Commissioner, to inform them of the impending crisis. He wished the governments of the Commonwealth countries to understand how serious a view was taken in London of this issue. 'Our fundamental position was that we could not allow control of the Canal to be in the hands of one irresponsible individual when the economies and prosperity of so many countries were dependent on unrestricted freedom to use it.' In discussion with most high commissioners, he agreed that there were objections to almost any course that might be taken. 'It was hoped to be able to take some form of action in co-operation with the United States and France; and this action might take the form of the use of force.' He warned that this possibility should not be communicated for the time being, as the discussions with the Americans had not yet taken place.[62] It was, however, a clear indication of the way the wind was blowing.

Eden was at this stage encouraged by Gaitskell's description of Nasser's action as 'a totally unjustified step'.[63] Home was much preoccupied with the meetings of the Egypt Committee; he became their eyes and ears in the House of Lords, communicating feelings from the Upper House, particularly from non-Conservative peers, who spoke freely of their concern. Lord Samuel, a Liberal peer, thought Egypt should be brought before the United Nations General Assembly as an aggressor, and that the United Nations could properly be asked to send an international force to take over the Canal.

Events moved swiftly towards the First Suez Conference, chaired by Selwyn Lloyd in London from 16 to 23 August. Home was not a central player in the decision to send the Menzies Mission to Cairo (crippled by Eisenhower's unconditional rejection of the use of force), nor in Dulles's proposal the same day to establish the Suez Canal Users' Association (SCUA), an idea that was almost still-born over the attempt to find a suitable acronym, as most of the suggestions had indelicate associations in some language, usually Portuguese. He was privy to the decision to call up reservists on 2 August, but the debates over the various military options were not his concern. His main perception was the attitudes of Commonwealth members, which crystallised rapidly: 'I have seen the High Commissioners for all the Commonwealth countries; the three Asians in one group and our "old Dominions" in another.' Canada, Australia, New Zealand, South Africa and Ceylon 'would favour the calling of a conference of users'. But all five were 'in doubt as to the methods which could be adopted to induce Nasser to agree'. It was clear 'that all Commonwealth countries would welcome the chance of attending a conference'.[64]

The two constant figures in the months ahead were Menzies, who in Home's opinion acted 'in a masterly manner',[65] and Holland of New Zealand, who declared that 'New Zealand goes and stands where the Mother country goes and stands'.[66] Both the Australian and New Zealand Governments believed that national survival depended on securing the Canal, but by 21 September (the day the second London Conference ended) it was clear that only Australia and New Zealand were full square behind the British position. The Canadian response was one of the most disappointing; Home realised that they were uninterested in the Middle East and not stirred by Nasser's actions. Norman Robertson, the Canadian High Commissioner, expressed his government's grave concern about the possible use of force to compel Nasser to accept international authority for the Canal. Unless Nasser committed some new aggressive act, Robertson's view was that the United Kingdom would be brought before the United Nations as an aggressor and he doubted whether the Commonwealth or the United Nations could survive that. Home sent a note to Eden and a memorandum which included two sentences revealing Canada's ambivalent attitude. 'I then asked him whether if force could not be avoided we could expect support from Canada. For your strictly personal information … he felt the answer would be "No".' Eden sent a bleak response: 'I think that this should be taken up with the Canadian Government – by our High Commissioner with Mr Pearson. It is far worse than anything the United States Government has ever said. AE. August 16.'[67]

Home saw the danger of such an approach which he felt could be too 'committing' for the Canadians at this stage. '... I confess that I feel some doubt as to whether it is wise to try to get a precise definition of their attitude from the Canadian government at this stage. May there not be some danger of their giving us an answer which they might be sorry for later if and when some new aggression by Nasser or his complete failure to respond make the use of force the definite and immediate issue? ...' Eden replied, 'Very well, we will not follow up. But I see no advantage in asking Mr Robertson his opinion any more. AE.'[68] Home continued to see Robertson, and kept the Canadians in the picture.

The South African response was opposition to United Nations intervention in any country's domestic jurisdiction. More worrying was the opposition orchestrated by Menon, and the possibility of India, Pakistan and Ceylon leaving the Commonwealth. Pakistan, whose instincts were with the Muslim side, was a constant worry. The British government warned that 'Pakistan herself would be the principal loser if she left the Commonwealth', while Alec Home was informed that if the United Kingdom did not accept the verdict of the United Nations 'it might well shatter the very concept on which the United Nations was built.'[69] Of the possible defections from the Commonwealth, Alec Home was most relieved that the break with Pakistan was avoided.

From the first Cabinet meeting on the morning of 27 July, it was clear that Eden was willing to employ a military option, which caused Walter Monckton, the Defence Secretary, and Lord Mountbatten much heart-searching. Neither was convinced by Eden's unfolding policy. 'I think it is well known that I personally was opposed to Suez,' Mountbatten wrote in 1965. After Alec Home's meeting on 31 July with the various high commissioners, he told Mountbatten of the Canadian view that the Commonwealth could break up if force were used. Mountbatten subsequently 'made it quite clear that I was convinced India would certainly leave the Commonwealth if we started a war and I thought Ceylon and Pakistan would follow suit'.

He was particularly concerned about Alec Home's news of the Canadian attitude, with which he sympathised. 'I told the First Lord [at that time Viscount Cilcennin] that the Secretary of State for Commonwealth Relations (Lord Home) had, at the Prime Minister's request, informed the Egypt Committee of the Cabinet which the Chiefs of Staff had attended that the High Commissioner for Canada had informed him that in the Canadian view armed intervention by us would cause the break-up of the Commonwealth and the disintegration of the United Nations Organisations.'[70] Monckton was increasingly unhappy as military options solidified. On 22 August, the day before the end of the First London Conference, Duncan Sandys, the Minister for Housing and Local Government, who personally favoured action if necessary, asked Eden for a guarantee that the Cabinet would be consulted before any final decision was taken. Eden wrote to explain that although the nature of the crisis meant that many of the decisions had to be taken by a 'small number of my most senior Cabinet colleagues', the 'final decision' would be submitted to a full meeting of the Cabinet. 'It would not, however, be possible for the Cabinet as a whole to discuss the plans for any military operations that might have to be undertaken. Knowledge of these details must, for obvious reasons of security, be confined within the narrowest possible circle.'[71] Home, Sandys and Butler, another Cabinet Minister who shared many of Monckton's misgivings, discussed privately the implications of this reply. Cilcennin and Mountbatten were at the time concerned with the strategic and political implications of 'Musketeer', which was postponed that day. Home felt that Eden should know of Butler's deep anxieties. He wrote to the Prime Minister on 22 August from the Commonwealth Relations Office:

> I sense that Rab is very unhappy. I know your time is full but if you could see him alone it would be well worthwhile.
>
> He is not against the use of force, but he fears that we have got ourselves into a position where we shall press the button before we have a moral basis for action which will carry conviction in this country, the free world and the Conservative Party. He feels that there should be more flexibility so as to allow time for the fullest diplomatic action the extent of which cannot be foreseen.
>
> I have told him that the pressing of the button is entirely within our control and that an intensive study is being made of the 'casus belli' and justification for armed intervention.
>
> I think his anxiety derives very largely from the fact that he was away for a fortnight and feels that possibly irrevocable decisions have been taken before the full implications of the use of force have been weighed.
>
> I may be wrong about this diagnosis but I am certainly right about his state of mind and I think if you can see him you can put

everything into perspective and he will feel he has had a chance to tell you what he feels.

I am sorry to add this to your preoccupation but I thought you should know ...

Rab, of course, does not know I am telling you of this.[72]

As with his letter accepting Cabinet Office in April 1955, this approach shows a remarkable openness towards his Prime Minister by the Commonwealth Secretary, writing as he does about the preoccupations of one of Eden's most senior colleagues and, at that time, the likeliest heir apparent. Although there is no written record of any meeting between Eden and Butler, Home's letter left the Prime Minister in no doubt about the feelings among some of his Cabinet colleagues. It was against this background that Monckton's patience finally snapped.

During a discussion of the timetable for a further Security Council debate, Macmillan said in a matter-of-fact way that the military option was now a foregone conclusion. Monckton then caused what Salisbury described as a 'painful and rather disturbing' scene. Home was horrified; he was quite clear that such intemperance was not the way to proceed. He was one of several ministers who wrote to Eden.

My dear Anthony,

Even before Walter's outburst at our Committee this morning I had thought that I had better warn you that I see a definite wavering in the attitude of some of our colleagues towards the use of force.

They vary in the intensity of their feeling but the important thing is that they should get these feelings off their chests so that you should know where you are.

Derry Amory, for instance, who is one of the most stable of our colleagues, feels the deepest anxieties, but I think would be ready to face up to it if all the procedures of UNO had been exhausted.

Others, I think, feel that it would divide country, party and Commonwealth so deeply that we should never recover. I had expected a cleavage of opinion in H of C and possibly a few of our supporters dissenting, but this I think represents something more serious.

The anxieties of some, Rab for instance, might be removed if we didn't have to go on thinking in terms of button pushing & dates & had plenty of time for diplomatic manoeuvre.

All this is disturbing. For myself I have no doubts that if we

> cannot make anything of the Security Council, and that largely depends on Dulles, we have no option but to go through with it. I need not say more but I am convinced that we are finished if the Middle East goes & Russia & India & China rule from Africa to the Pacific.
>
> You will know how to handle all this but I am sure you should encourage those who have not been on the Egypt Committee to be frank and outspoken.[73]

This letter – a combination of tact, warning and reassurance – showed that Home could write to Eden on terms of equality, without being concerned whether he might be dismissed. His worry for the Commonwealth and for the unity of the Cabinet in a perilous venture comes over unequivocally. But at the very time that Selwyn Lloyd travelled to France to negotiate the Protocol of Sèvres, Alec Home was out of action with gall bladder trouble.[74] 'On October 23rd and 24th Alec had extensive X-ray examinations & Barium meals,' Elizabeth Home wrote in her diary. 'Everything found to be extremely fine except a gall bladder condition – this necessitates a lot of pills & a diet which excludes all eggs (yolk of) – cream or fatty foods. As he has lived on butter & cream ever since his back trouble this will make for great changes in his life & what *do* we do without eggs.'

On 30 October, after much vacillation, Home's tour to Africa was called off. 'Alec telephoned about mid-day to say that our trip was off on account of Suez troubles', wrote Elizabeth Home. Next day the air raids on Egypt began. 'Wednesday Oct 31. The wireless gave news of the Anglo–French offensive by bomber aircraft against military targets in Egypt.' Now that the button had finally been pushed, a strange calm seemed to settle on Eden, whose fractious nervousness had been obvious in the previous months. The next day Home was due to speak in a Lords debate. Elizabeth listened from the gallery. 'Listened to Lord Henderson opening & to Alec & to Lord Silkin. A. extremely good. Anne Chamberlain was there & I talked to her while we were waiting. A. referred to the Munich time which moved her deeply. A. back with me for supper in the flat.' Afterwards Anne Chamberlain wrote to Elizabeth Home. 'How delighted I was to hear him speak on a big occasion – the first time I have done so – I thought his speech first rate in every way.'[75] At the United Nations on 1 November, Dulles tabled ('with a heavy heart') a resolution urging a ceasefire. His demand for a withdrawal of the invading forces led to a British veto in the Security Council. On 2 November, Alec Home attended two Cabinet meetings.

The first at 4.30 (for which the official records are not available until 2007) heard Lloyd say that 'we could not hope to avoid serious difficulties with the Arab states for more than a very short time longer, certainly not for as long as it would take us to complete an opposed occupation of Egypt'.[76] At a late meeting ministers considered whether referring the matter to the United Nations while continuing the military operation was a feasible or honourable course of action. Alec and Elizabeth Home watched Eden's ministerial broadcast on television. 'Alec and I thought him extremely good. He looked and sounded surprisingly well & robust. A back to meetings at 10.30 & returned ultimately about 1 a.m. Anthony Nutting resigned as Minister of State for Foreign Affairs on disagreement over Government's Suez policy.'

Sunday 4 November was, in Elizabeth Home's words, 'peaceful until 11.30 when Alec was telephoned for a Cabinet'. The rest of the day was one of the most tense of the entire crisis. A succession of telephone calls gave some hint of the slow progress. To the background noise of a Labour Party rally in Trafalgar Square, the Cabinet heard of the possibility of oil sanctions. The stark decision was whether to proceed with the invasion. Eden invited each of his colleagues (eighteen of whom were present at 6.30 p.m.) to give his view on three possible courses: the initial phase of the Anglo–French action to continue, the parachute landings to be postponed for twenty-four hours, or the military action to be postponed indefinitely. The Cabinet minutes record that 'the preponderant opinion in the Cabinet was in favour of the first course'. Salisbury and Buchan-Hepburn 'were inclined to favour the third course, but they made it clear that if a majority of the Cabinet favoured a different course, they would support it'. Monckton 'said that he remained in favour of suspending further military action indefinitely and that if this course did not commend itself to his colleagues he must reserve his position'. Twelve members, including Home, favoured the first course. The collective will of the Cabinet was clear.[77]

On 5 November, as news of the Russian invasion of Hungary spread, the British paratroop drop began at dawn at Port Said. 'I lunched with Alec in the House of Lords & David Kilmuir joined us. He was interesting about the international law aspect of all this. Our paratroopers have landed at Port Said with complete success but there's been a little fighting since … Alec telephoned jubilantly at 6 to say that Port Said had fallen which is terrific.' News of Nutting's resignation was followed by that of Edward Boyle, Economic Secretary to the Treasury, and at this juncture, Home wrote to bolster Eden's confidence. 'The stakes you were playing for yesterday were the highest – to lose all or to win all. We are not yet out of the wood, but we have won a decisive round. If our country rediscovers its soul and inspiration your calm courage will have achieved this miracle.'[78]

The next day brought the news of Eisenhower's re-election and the decision for a ceasefire at 5 p.m.[79] With the ceasefire and the news on 20 November that Eden was 'ill and having to take 3 weeks off', Home also succumbed to the unrelenting schedule. Elizabeth Home's diary is full of references to his low humour: 'Nov 10 We kept him in bed all morning & though he telephoned non stop it was technically a rest. I've never seen him look tireder than when he got up ... Monday 19 A came in with "the miseries". He was feeling very tired indeed & low about the whole situation.'

In Eden's absence the government had a beleaguered air, complicated by the first manoeuvrings for the succession between Macmillan and Butler. There was an atmosphere of suspicion and mistrust when presents began to arrive for government ministers at their various offices. The intelligence advice was to discard edible gifts. On Saturday 24 November Harold Smedley 'put a little note for me in the box to say that a box of broken biscuits had arrived at the office with a sender whose name seemed unknown to us all,' wrote Elizabeth Home. 'This petty poisoner will get us yet.'[80] The last chapter of Suez began with Eden's return from Jamaica on 14 December. Two days earlier Home, as deputy leader in the Lords, had made a speech in defence of government policy. The actions initiated by Eden had four aims: to secure the Suez Canal; to ensure continuity of oil supplies; to topple Nasser; and to keep the Russians out of the Middle East. The results were diametrically opposed to these aims. The Canal was blocked; oil supplies were interrupted; Nasser became the acknowledged leader of Arab nationalism, and the way was left open for Russian intrusion into the Middle East. Home, of course, regarded the fourth of these as the most significant in the long-term perspective, and concentrated his speech on the Soviet threat:

> Since 1945 Russia has adopted the conception of permanent hostility to the West, and her foreign policy has openly been advertised as a policy of world revolution. Your Lordships are familiar with the instruments of that policy; subversion within and military pressure without. I need not remind all those in this House this evening of

> the ruthless and unrelenting probing that there has been against what they conceive to be the weak spots in the structure of the Western world: Iran, Greece, Turkey, Berlin, Malaya – and I could continue the catalogue. The purpose has always been to extend Russian dominion, which is greater today than it was in 1939.[81]

The second aspect that worried Home was the deleterious effect on Commonwealth unity. He had done everything possible to avoid open splits and the crisis ended without defections but the divisions and resentments festered and Home was aware of the retrospective strains that Suez would put on the Commonwealth.

The day after his speech in the Lords, Alec Home wrote a long account of Suez to Lord Lothian, who had kept him in touch with the attitudes of Commonwealth countries at the UN:

> We are obviously round the worst of the strains, relations with the United States have picked up again, the Canadians have been extremely helpful and ... even Krishna, who has been so intolerable at earlier stages, seems to have come out as unexpectedly as usual in the completely new light of a defender of the Commonwealth connection! ... The Pakistanis have been most helpful and good all through this though naturally they have to bear in mind the old consideration of Muslim solidarity and that has inevitably made them a great deal less forthcoming in public than they have been in private ... We have also, as you will have seen, got a kind word for the Commonwealth from Nehru in the last couple of days, though his attitude over Hungary has been deplorable and seems to have done him quite a lot of harm in India. We had two or three busy days of discussions with Bandaranaike on his way through to Ceylon. His real anxiety was to be able to announce as soon as possible that we were giving up our bases there, but for obvious reasons the present would have been a very inappropriate moment to make any announcement of that type.
>
> I very much hope that things will be easier for you now that evacuations have begun and the temperature has dropped ...[82]

Thus Home continued to bind the Commonwealth ties. Although historians do not regard him as a source for Suez information, his colleagues knew otherwise and in the last year of his life Selwyn Lloyd began a long correspondence as he undertook his own account of Suez, published posthumously as *Suez 1956: A Personal Account*. The question of 'collusion' with the Israelis loomed large in this correspondence. 'I suppose at some time I must say something about collusion,' Lloyd admitted on 6 December 1977, 'collusion implies something dishonourable and we were all honourable men!'[83] Home advised frankness, but he had been consulted over a longer span. In July 1965, three days after his retirement from the Conservative leadership, Alec and Elizabeth Home visited Selwyn Lloyd for tea and dinner at his Oxfordshire home. The Edens had been there in the morning and for lunch. As in 1957, the Tories were in the midst of a leadership struggle, but though the talk turned to whether Maudling or Heath would succeed Home, the shadow of Suez weighed over the three-way reunion. Whenever Suez became headline news, a correspondence resumed between old colleagues, as when Nutting's book was published in 1967. 'I would not if I were you comment on Nutting at all,' wrote Alec Home to Eden in June 1967. 'Isn't it better to let him be dealt with by events?'[84]

All entries to office in Downing Street are happy in a largely similar way, but all departures are unhappy in their own individual way. Eden's exit was much more painful than Home's. A defeat at a general election is a clean break, but to be driven from office by ill health and adverse political conditions is particularly hard. Not only was the medical advice firmly against Eden's continuing in office, but his reception at a 1922 Committee meeting on his return from Jamaica had revealed the depths of the political opposition to his doing so. On 8 January Eden informed the Queen of his intention to resign as Prime Minister, and the following day he told the Cabinet.

For Alec Home, Eden's resignation was one of the tragedies of post-war British political life. His whole life had been bound up with foreign affairs; to be brought down on a foreign affairs issue was a poignant irony. Home wrote to his departed leader:

> These are cruel days for you but as your supreme courage has triumphed before so it will over this calamity. There will come to your aid too the knowledge that you have been true to your principles and your convictions.
>
> I am sure that will be so, for now that this has happened the one wish of your friends is that you should find good health and peace of mind and happiness.
>
> I don't believe, given the military limitation in the early days, that there was a perfect way of dealing with the Suez situation, but those of us who have been so intimately associated with you in the

> conduct of policy have been amazed at the tenacity with which you stuck to the main goal – which I personally believe history will say was won. May I send you in all humility my unstinted admiration and my gratitude that you brought me into your government and allowed me to share in its work.
>
> I hope you will not decide quickly about your seat in the House of Commons. I feel sure that with complete rest and freedom from the conduct of public business your health will recover completely and you must not deprive yourself of the most effective platform from which you can give the nation the benefit of your wisdom and experience.
>
> So – for the present – it is goodbye with all my affection to you and to Clarissa. Politics is in some ways a nasty profession but when one is allowed the privilege of witnessing absolute integrity then there is great reward – and it is that that you have brought to all of us. Thank you and God bless you.[85]

Eden was moved by the letter from a man whom he had backed for those very qualities of integrity and principle which Home acknowledged in this letter. Two days before sailing for New Zealand, he replied,

> I cannot thank you enough for all your kindness and help to me. I hope that you have enjoyed the CRO. You have certainly done its work brilliantly. I am so glad you are going on with it.
>
> I am glad that you feel as you do about Suez. I am sure that your analysis is correct, although it continues to be provoking to be told by Dulles that the Americans can't be associated with us in the area. However, they will learn better in time. That is one of their great qualities. I hope you will never again have as difficult months as Suez brought to us. I know, however, that I could not have worked through them without your help. For this and much else besides I shall be everlastingly grateful.[86]

By January 1957 there were no doubts that Home had seized the opportunities Commonwealth Affairs had given to him with enthusiasm, discretion, tact and success. In the short period of Eden's premiership, he had moved to the edge of the front rank in the Conservative hierarchy. Eden's departure did not halt that process. Since April 1955, Home had been able to display his diplomatic gifts in a wider sphere; with Eden's departure, he became one of the Conservative Party's main players.

8

Working with Macmillan

Eden's departure in January 1957 posed a constitutional problem for Buckingham Palace. It was the first peace-time occasion since the resignation of Bonar Law in May 1923 that the governing party had a vacancy in its leadership without an agreed heir apparent. Chamberlain had long been seen as Baldwin's natural successor in May 1937, as Eden had Churchill's in April 1955. The question in both instances was not so much who would succeed, as when the incumbent would step down. Eden's resignation was unexpected and there was neither an agreed procedure for choosing a successor nor agreement about the likely outcome. There were two possible candidates: Harold Macmillan, Chancellor of the Exchequer, and Rab Butler, Lord Privy Seal. By comparison with the events of October 1963, the choice of Macmillan as Prime Minister was relatively uncomplicated. Advice was sought, directly and indirectly, from four separate quarters. The outgoing Prime Minister gave the Queen his views, the Cabinet were then formally consulted; backbenchers were systematically canvassed and the party grandees, headed by Winston Churchill, communicated the results of these consultations to the Queen's Secretary.

The precise nature of Eden's advice to the Queen has been treated with reticence,[1] but the evidence is clear: Eden did not recommend Macmillan. 'Her Majesty spoke of the future and of the difficult choice that lay before her,' wrote Eden. 'I agreed that it was certainly difficult. The Queen made no formal request for my advice but enabled me to signify that my own debt to Mr Butler while I have been Prime Minister was very real and that I thought he had discharged his difficult task during the three weeks while I was away in Jamaica very well.'[2] Eden further suggested that soundings should be taken by a disinterested senior figure, such as Lord Salisbury. After the Cabinet meeting on 9 January, Lord Kilmuir, the Lord Chancellor, and Salisbury, the

Lord President, saw each member of the Cabinet, apart from Butler and Macmillan, in the Privy Council Office.

'Well, which is it?' was Salisbury's famous question. 'Wab or Hawold?' Only Buchan-Hepburn declared in favour of Butler, and that afternoon visited him to commiserate: 'Went to see R.A.B. 10 Jan p.m. 1957. Harold McM [sic] had been to see HM & accepted PM that a.m. R.A.B. very calm and sensible ... He said he would carry on, and make a success of the "middle thing".'[3]

Home had no doubts that Macmillan was the man to lead the Conservative Party and the country in the wake of Suez. Edward Heath, the Chief Whip, and John Morrison, Chairman of the 1922 Committee, took soundings among the rank and file, as did Oliver Poole, the Party Chairman. Many Conservatives, including Robert Boothby, MP for East Aberdeenshire, were away at the Council of Europe meeting at Strasbourg. 'The party was consulted extensively and at every stage,' Boothby recalled, '... they even took the trouble to ring me up to find out who I wanted. There was no doubt the overwhelming majority of the party preferred Macmillan to Butler. If there'd been a vote it would have been exactly the same.'[4] The party managers identified this ground swell of opinion among the backbenchers for Macmillan, as well as a small minority who were implacably opposed to Butler at any price, and Salisbury was so informed before he went to the Palace. On 10 January Churchill, Salisbury, Lord Waverley and Lord Chandos saw Sir Michael Adeane.[5] All four recommended that the Queen should send for Macmillan. Churchill later gave age as an excuse to Butler when he told him, 'Look old cock, we went for the older man.'[6]

Harold Macmillan told the Queen that he did not think his government could last six weeks,[7] but Home was convinced that Macmillan could ride out the storm. From the start he became one of Macmillan's confidants, encouraging him and serving as a sounding board for ideas, particularly on foreign and colonial policy. 'I feel, exactly as you do, that if we can get through the next six weeks we can settle down to work for which the country will bless us in the years ahead. That being so we must stick together in Cabinet and demand and obtain the loyalty of the Party in Parliament – I have a hunch we will bring it off – if not we shall have done our best.'[8] At the end of the year Macmillan wrote, 'I am so grateful to you for all the help you have given me during this year. It has not been easy, but ... I do not think we have made a bad job of it.'[9] A more difficult letter for Home was to Rab Butler:

My dear Rab,

You have been in an intolerably exposed position during the last week and this is just to tell you that all I have seen are unstinted in their admiration of the way you have met it.

May I add my own sincere tribute and my conviction that time will bring the just reward for so much integrity and unselfishness.[10]

Home was soon back to the grindstone of Commonwealth Affairs. The Cabinet reshuffle passed him by. There was no question of promotion; he was getting acquainted with the portfolio and it would have been unproductive to move him. He considered the later trend to short tenures of Office detrimental to good government. Of all his posts, Commonwealth Secretary was where he had the longest continuous spell, and he was grateful.[11] The pace of Commonwealth affairs had not slackened during 1956. Preparations were in hand for his delayed visit to Africa, and at home he instituted a series of Commonwealth Trust education meetings at Rhodes House, Oxford. In addition, he had reported to the Cabinet on subjects as varied as the exiled Seretse Khama; terrorism in Northern Ireland; migration policy on assisted passages to Australia, where Home wanted to extend the Empire Settlement Act of 1952 by continuing to make funds available; the Kashmir dispute between India and Pakistan; and Commonwealth consultation over the development of nuclear power – as comprehensive a *pot-pourri* of responsibilities as faced any Cabinet minister.

Potentially one of the most intractable of these problems was the Bechuanaland Protectorate and the position of Seretse Khama, heir to the chieftainship of the Bamangwato tribe. In 1948, Khama had married an English wife, Ruth Williams, which called into question whether he would be permitted to take up the chieftainship from his uncle, Tshekedi Khama, the acting regent. The Labour Commonwealth Secretary, Patrick Gordon Walker, had sought to resolve the situation, involving future relations between Bechuanaland and South Africa, by exiling Khama and his wife in 1950 (they took up residence in Brighton) 'with a suitable allowance', despite the Bamangwato tribe's having overwhelmingly declared for Seretse rather than his uncle. In 1951 the new Conservative Commonwealth Secretary, Lord Salisbury, had confirmed this non-recognition, and there the matter rested. On 23 October 1956, Home announced in the House of Lords that Seretse Khama had renounced his claim to the chieftainship and was being allowed to return to Bechuanaland as a private citizen to play his part in the affairs of the tribe, the beginning of a rehabilitation which saw Seretse Khama contest the first elections as founder of the Democratic Party, subsequently becoming Prime Minister and finally first President of independent Botswana.[12]

Home's position in the upper ranks of the Cabinet was consolidated both by his response to the Khama question and by his handling of the long-running Cyprus situation, including whether an independent Cyprus would remain within the Commonwealth. In February 1959 Home wrote to Macmillan about its future status:

> The question of Commonwealth Membership for Cyprus was left rather in the air as a result of our Cabinet discussions last week. I am certain that we must not in the present round of negotiations use any language which would suggest that we could agree to full Commonwealth membership … there are powerful reasons both relating to the status of Cyprus herself and to the precedent that would be set for a host of other smaller Colonies why this would be extremely dangerous.
>
> I do not, however, rule out some kind of association, which could comprise some, but not all, of the advantages and responsibilities of membership. Thus Imperial Preference, Sterling Area membership, rights of entry or of citizenship in the UK, attendance at certain non-political Commonwealth Conferences, could be elements in such a status.
>
> This will need very careful examination here because it is quite a new idea and will certainly set a new pattern. But I am particularly concerned that we should not make any step which could possibly appear to prejudice the view of other Commonwealth Governments, who must be fully associated with us in any decision of this kind.[13]

The issue was thrown into sharper focus by the government's decision to release Archbishop Makarios from exile. As terrorism had escalated on the island through the anti-British guerrilla movement EOKA, Macmillan decided that tensions might be eased if Makarios, spiritual leader of the Greek community and political advocate of Enosis (union of Cyprus with Greece), were released from his year-long detention in the Seychelles. This proved too much for Lord Salisbury, who promptly resigned, convinced that a Conservative government could not survive without a Cecil in its ranks. This was a miscalculation. Macmillan accepted the resignation and not a dog barked. The Prime Minister's reputation for 'unflappability' was established, at least in the public eye, by this break with the past. It was as though Macmillan felt he could not be in charge of the Tory Party until he had got rid of a Cecil.

Salisbury's resignation was not the last time Macmillan treated a potential check to his authority as a 'little local difficulty', the phrase he employed when the entire Treasury team of Thorneycroft, Enoch Powell and Nigel Birch resigned the following year. Trouble with Salisbury had been brewing for long enough. He had written to Macmillan about the need for greater representation in the government of the younger generation of peers. 'There are at present twenty-seven senior posts held in the House of Commons, as compared with eight in the House of Lords ... Even given the vastly greater importance of the House of Commons – which I do not dispute – the balance has in my view, swung too far over on the side of the Commons. A young Peer today, if he gives up his time to politics, can have no hope or expectation of a career there; and more and more are finding this out.'[14] Among those he recommended for cultivation was Alec Home. Macmillan promptly promoted his Commonwealth Secretary to the posts of Lord President of the Council and Leader of the House of Lords, the posts Salisbury had vacated. In the correspondence that ensued, the former Lord President was addressed as 'My dear Salisbury', but the Commonwealth Secretary was 'Dear Alec'. Bobbety had burned his boats that day.

'Few men in Cabinet will now wield more power,' ran a newspaper report, 'than this diffident, quiet-voiced Scot.'[15] It was a notable responsibility for one who had entered the Cabinet less than two years earlier, and Macmillan was conscious that it might be too great a burden for his Commonwealth Secretary. He was relieved when the tasks were accepted, writing supportively to Home. Home replied.

> I am glad to do anything I can to help you and will do my best to keep the House of Lords in sympathy with the government's policy. It won't be too easy as Bobbety's authority was unrivalled and we have many fences to take before the summer ends. The knowledge that I can always come to you when trouble looms is a great comfort ...
>
> I have some doubts whether I can double up the jobs of the Commonwealth Secretary and leader of the House of Lords, but we will see how things go and as you know any or all of the jobs I have at present are at your disposal for reshuffle whenever you like.[16]

As Commonwealth Secretary, Home met the new Governor-General of Cyprus, Sir Hugh Foot, and Archbishop Makarios, before the end of the year. 'My concern is not to encourage Makarios to join the Commonwealth but to make sure that if he opts for association that he does so on the basis of a specific plan and that no misunderstandings are possible.'[17] At the Cyprus Conference on 15 January 1960, he assured Makarios that Cyprus would not be put 'in a secondary position in relation to the other Commonwealth countries' if they became an independent republic within the Commonwealth, a status achieved on 16 August 1960.

Apart from his now obligatory daily attendance in the Lords, as Lord President, his responsibilities included the Department of Scientific and Industrial Research, the Medical Research Council, the Agricultural Research Council, and Civil Research. He visited Ghana from 14 to 21 May and the Commonwealth Prime Ministers' Conference was scheduled in London for June and July.

There were also changes in his Private Office. Harold Smedley moved on to the British High Commission in Calcutta; his replacement was David Cole, an old Dominions Office man, who was of some importance in Home's career at this point. Cole's arrival coincided with Home's visit to Australia and New Zealand in March for the SEATO Conference, a trip which became a mini-world tour. Home reassured Richard Casey, Australian Foreign Minister, that the Suez fences were being mended, and at a meeting with Menzies, he 'suggested that Australia, New Zealand, Pakistan, Thailand and the Philippines might help to persuade Malaya to join SEATO, and they might even tackle Malaya on this subject, but it would have to be tactfully done'. His grasp of the subject impressed Menzies who reported to Peter Carrington, the High Commissioner, that the meeting had been 'extremely interesting and valuable, one of the most useful he had ever had with a United Kingdom Minister on this subject'.[18]

The Commonwealth Prime Ministers' Conference began on 26 June. Defence matters again predominated as far as Home's contributions were concerned. At a meeting on 1 July, Welensky (much discomfited that his status as Prime Minister of the Central African Federation placed him in an inferior position to Dr Nkrumah of the newly independent Ghana) had indicated that the government of the Central African Federation wished to make a contribution to Commonwealth defence, which Home accepted as 'most welcome to the United Kingdom Government'.[19] The long delayed visit to Central Africa followed hard upon this, beginning with a private stay with the Barings in Kenya, before the official tour of the Federation. 'I should like, if I may, to take Elizabeth with me. My previous experience has taught me how invaluable it is for the Commonwealth Secretary to have his wife with him on trips like this when social activities play such a large part in the programme.'[20] Macmillan, like Eden, readily concurred, and David Cole was also of the party.

Although there was a limit to what Home was prepared to do in the way of museums and art galleries ('He's had Buddhas' said Elizabeth Home after one visit to an Indian temple), when political considerations or representational duties were foremost such personal feelings were set aside. However, one disconcerting habit indicated his self-effacing nature. Even though the party could claim diplomatic priority, Cole had great difficulty dissuading the Secretary of State from joining the ends of queues for passports and inoculations. Many in the Commonwealth Relations Office could not recall when there was less emphasis on rank. On one occasion a cheering crowd swarmed on to the tarmac at Athens airport to greet a Greek pop star on the same flight, so Alec Home insisted the singer disembark first to receive his plaudits.[21]

His time at the Commonwealth Relations Office brought Alec Home into renewed contact with the royal family – on the political as well as the social level. The Commonwealth was seen in royal circles as a painless way of dismembering the empire, a feeling not entirely shared by the professional diplomats. Some felt that an aligned group of disparate nations owing allegiance to the mother country, in whatever nebulous or 'dignified' a manner, was not a good idea, however comforting the optimistic newsreel coverage of royal visits suggested; it seemed a possible source of difficulty and friction as the emerging nations came to political maturity and independence. Overseas tours with the royal family did not occupy as much time as later, when he was Foreign Secretary, but no week went by during the political year in the late 1950s without at least one private audience.

Relationships with the Foreign Office through 'the hole in the wall' also had to be carefully nurtured; not that there was any difficulty with Selwyn Lloyd and his team, but because of the insecurities Commonwealth Office staff felt at the first stirrings of the idea of 'amalgamation'. Gilbert Laithwaite worked tirelessly to ensure that when the inevitable happened 'his' men would not be at a disadvantage. The succession to the Foreign Office was also a subject for speculation. Macmillan saw, from an early stage, that Home was a potential Foreign Secretary.[22] In some respects it would have made a cleaner break with the past to have amalgamated the two departments in July 1960, for it was inevitable that the Foreign and Commonwealth Offices would merge, just as the three Service Ministries would one day be amalgamated into a unified Ministry of Defence.

Alec Home now pressed ahead with his plans to visit Central and Southern Africa, a vast area of volatile political standing in a stage of crucial transition, that impinged on the British domestic scene to an extent hard to recapture by later generations. British responsibilities extended from Kenya and Uganda in the north to Bechuanaland (Botswana) in the south. Sudan had received its independence in 1956 and Nkrumah's Ghana in 1957, and the strength of African nationalism was an established political fact. Jomo Kenyatta in Kenya, Dr Hastings Banda in Nyasaland, Kenneth Kaunda in Northern Rhodesia and Archbishop Makarios in Cyprus – all were familiar to British newspaper readers. The orderly devolution of responsibilities in Central and Southern Africa tested British diplomatic skills for over forty years. Home was involved longer than any other comparable British figure and at increasingly important levels, culminating in his 1971 attempt at negotiations with Ian Smith over the future of Southern Rhodesia.

One of the most important of these areas in October 1957 was the Central African Federation which had been created on 1 August 1953. By the time Home visited the Federation, Roy Welensky had been Prime Minister for a year. Welensky was a substantial figure in every sense. A former railwayman and heavyweight boxing champion, he had moved from Northern Rhodesia to become Prime Minister of the Federal government based in Salisbury, and was a formidable political operator and shrewd judge of character. On the death in 1957 of the Governor-General, Home was keen that Lord Dalhousie should be appointed as his successor, but he wanted Welensky to stay with the Dalhousies in Scotland first, so that they could get to know each other. This worked triumphantly. Dalhousie's nine-year-old son wanted to know whether it was true that Welensky had been an engine-driver. Welensky confirmed that he had. 'And you gave all that up to be a politician!' said the son. Welensky agreed that Dalhousie was exactly the person to have as Governor-General. On such incidents are personal relationships forged.[23] Alec Home, though very different from Welensky – not least in physical appearance and mode of speech – found in Welensky an honest spirit whom he much respected, not least for the expressed frankness of his views. There was no equivocation, and Home, who disliked weasel words and double standards, knew it.

Responsibility for the Federation was divided between the Colonial Office and the Commonwealth Relations Office. Southern Rhodesia, where Garfield Todd had succeeded Huggins as Prime Minister, was a self-governing colony and thus the responsibility of the Commonwealth Office, whereas Northern Rhodesia (Zambia) and Nyasaland (Malawi) were the responsibility of the Colonial Office. In Ghana, which Home had visited the previous May and which moved to independence with relative ease, a white minority did not hold political power, as they did in the Federation, which the black African states saw as an obstacle to nationalist advance. Home was now well versed in assessing the political climate and was a good listener. He took careful soundings from representatives of the (white) Dominion Party and the Southern Rhodesian Cabinet. But his most substantive meetings were with Welensky. Home's main concern was with the franchise, which he wished to see liberalised by easing the literacy and income qualification to increase the number of black voters, but at their first meeting Welensky was in no mood to compromise on these issues. Towards the end of the tour, Home spoke of the necessity of presenting the House of Commons with evidence of greater African participation. Welensky again argued over the small print and Home finally undertook to emphasise the moderate features in the Federal government's proposals.

On his return to the UK, Home warned his colleagues that Welensky might go to the polls 'on a less liberal franchise, on Dominion Status in 1960 and on general opposition to British interference in Federation affairs'. Lennox-Boyd agreed that this would have but one outcome. 'He would be returned by a huge majority and the European attitude towards the African would have been hardened disastrously. Racial trouble would then be certain. It may be argued that Sir Roy Welensky has missed a chance to … [attract] the support of moderate Africans. But … they insisted that they could not carry their supporters if they suggested such a step.'[24] Home also spelt out the difficulties that lay in the future. 'Politically there is heavier weather ahead. The Africans in the three territories combined outnumber the Europeans by 30 to 1, while the Europeans hold all the wealth and political power. In the future development of the country each is indispensable to the other but each is afraid of the "partnership" which is declared to be the social and political goal of Federation. The African fears that the European will use his experience, wealth and privilege to maintain power for ever and

Elizabeth and Alec Dunglass
in Lanark on constituency business

Alec Dunglass (left) and Elizabeth Dunglass (right) with Mrs Neville Chamberlain at a fund-raising evening of the Junior Imperial League in 1938

'We regard the agreement signed last night and the Anglo–German Naval Agreement as symbolic of the desire of our two peoples never to go to war again': Neville Chamberlain at Heston Airport on his return from Munich, 30 September 1938

'Your family treated me as one of yourselves. Your welcome was so genuine': Neville and Anne Chamberlain at the Hirsel in the week after the Munich Debate, October 1938

'For three days the visitors were fêted at Rome':
Chamberlain, Halifax and Dunglass in Italy to meet Mussolini, January 1939

Alec Dunglass, gas-mask in hand, arriving at 10 Downing Street, with the Liberal leader, Archibald Sinclair, on 10 May 1940, the day of Chamberlain's resignation as Prime Minister

Sir John Simon leaving the sandbagged Treasury to deliver his War Budget, 27 September 1939

Anthony Eden, Winston Churchill, Clement Attlee and Herbert Morrison
on their way to the Thanksgiving Service at St Margaret's, Westminster,
on VJ Day, 15 August 1945

The Queen, Lord Home (second from right) and Winston Churchill
as godparents at the christening of Jock and Margaret Colville's daughter
in February 1953

The Coronation Chair in Westminster Abbey after the theft of the Stone of Scone by Scottish Nationalists on Christmas Eve, 1950; and (below) after the stone had been returned on 13 April 1951. The episode contributed to Churchill's decision to create the new post of Minister of State for Scotland. On 3 July 1996, the Prime Minister, John Major, announced that the Stone of Scone would be returned to Scotland

Members of the Covenant Association before the 'Scottish Coronation'. The controversy over the Queen's title led to Lord Home agreeing a change to the design of Scottish postboxes

'The Affair of the Handbag': the Queen and the Duke of Edinburgh in procession in Princes Street, Edinburgh, on the way to St Giles Cathedral for the Presentation of the Honours of Scotland, 24 June 1953

THE
MID-1950s

Cyril and Hester Alington on their Golden Wedding day in 1954

Alec Home in Ceylon during his Commonwealth Tour, October 1955

Demonstration in Trafalgar Square during the Suez Crisis, 4 November 1956

A delegation from Basutoland at Douglas, August 1957

to exclude him from political responsibility. The European fears that, if the African is admitted to political influence, he will use his weight of numbers to oust the Europeans from the country for which he has done everything and where he considers he lives as of right.' Home also commented that there was 'a tension between the races which is not yet serious but is noticeable and cannot be ignored'.[25]

In Northern Rhodesia, Kenneth Kaunda formed the Zambian African National Congress in 1958, with a manifesto based on that of President Nkrumah, who had led Ghana to independence. In Nyasaland, a black nationalist organisation, the Malawi National Congress was led by Dr Hastings Banda, and these groupings expressed the fears of the African population that they would come under the control of the southern whites. Federation, established by the Europeans, was in the end dismantled by the very ministers Welensky had come to trust.

The 'question of Africa' exercised Macmillan and his government consistently in the late 1950s. The tide of African nationalism that Macmillan was to identify in his 'Winds of Change' speech gave rise to many questions on the long-term future of the British colonies as well as shorter-term strategic decisions as to the pace of decolonisation, issues which concerned Lennox-Boyd and Home and on which they established partnership and tacit understanding. This was particularly valuable when Lennox-Boyd came under criticism over the White Paper on the Hola Camp massacre in Kenya, where eleven Mau-Mau detainees were killed, followed in July 1959 by the Devlin Report on the riots in Nyasaland which had led to the arrest of Hastings Banda. The report concluded that 'Nyasaland is – no doubt temporarily – a police state', which infuriated Macmillan, who felt 'it may well blow this government out of office'.[26] As Lennox-Boyd was on the verge of resignation, though countering the personal attacks mounted in the Commons, Alec Home chose a characteristic way to encourage his colleague. He wrote, 'You were at the top of your form and that reaches the heights! Well done and thank you for your championship of the Federation – I am so glad it went well. Keep it up over Devlin because you have a splendid case and all behind to back you.'[27]

These debates left their scars, however, and contributed to Macmillan's decision to reconsider the balance sheet of Britain's African commitments. The result was the Monckton Commission, which gave legitimacy to Macmillan's dismantling of the Federation and made an unhappy end to Alec Home's five years at the Commonwealth Relations Office.

Iain Macleod, as the new Colonial Secretary after the October 1959 general election, was to see the African problem in a very different light; his brief from Macmillan was to 'get a move on Africa'.[28] Home's main difficulties in the year ahead were to be with Iain Macleod. The fruitful days of understanding with Alan Lennox-Boyd were over. Theirs had been a remarkable partnership over four years; they had similar aims and mutual understanding of problems. Both favoured the idea of federation; both had a belief in the concept of trusteeship, whereby Britain should lead former colonies to independence and help them to take their places in the international community. For Home this was the essence of decolonisation. Their very differences of personality contributed to the success of their partnership. Physically, Lennox-Boyd was a domineering, at times aggressive figure, who figuratively was not averse to knocking heads together. Home complemented this with his ability to get on with all and sundry, and to be reassuring. When Lennox-Boyd left the Colonial Office, Alec Home sent him a letter that went far beyond the conventional valedictory despatch between two colleagues:

> I must tell you what an undiluted joy it has been to me to work with you during these last few years and to benefit as I hope I have done by your wisdom and courage and foresight.
>
> If I can carry on for a bit longer at the CRO I shall feel fortified by the recollection of the many times we have found difficult problems and somehow got by them to live and fight another day. I doubt if any Minister ever had such a series of insoluble problems with which to grapple and your grasp of them and resolution in handling them filled us all with constant admiration and confidence ... Thank you many times – more than I can express for your friendship. Bless you.[29]

Things were very different in the seven months alongside Iain Macleod In addition to their joint membership of the Cabinet from December 1955, when Macleod had become Minister of Labour, they were both on the Conservative Party's Steering Committee which produced the manifesto for the 1959 election. Macleod, as a representative of the younger, progressive Tory generation, was an influential figure in this world of policy-making, chairing the Policy Studies Group. He had clear views on the direction the Party should take on a wide variety of issues and expressed them forcefully. Macmillan had intended the membership of the Steering Committee, 'an exceptionally gifted team of politicians by any standard', to be fairly compact, but during 1958 added further members, including Home for his advice on three areas – the Lords, Scottish affairs and Commonwealth matters.[30] Home attended his first meeting in the wake of the Rochdale by-election defeat for the government in the spring of 1958, and the atmosphere was of fraught concern and pragmatic determination to reverse the tide before the wider political battle was joined. The prospect of a Liberal breakthrough caused Macmillan considerable unease. 'The only thing I fear is over-confidence which might lead to people voting Liberal, thinking they could do so with impunity,' he wrote to Home. 'This must somehow be stopped at an early stage.'[31]

From the start Alec Home's relationship with Macleod was hardly tranquil. Macleod was one of the first beneficiaries of the 1948 Maxwell Fyfe reforms which had paved the way for Conservative candidates to be selected on merit. Underneath his outward confidence, built on undoubted expertise and knowledge of his brief, there was in Macleod an alienation from the Tory generations which had never had to concern themselves with the world of mortgages and babysitters. The contrast between Macleod, who had to cash in a £1500 life insurance policy to help with his expenses as Colonial Secretary, and his two predecessors – Oliver Lyttelton and Alan Lennox-Boyd, both men of financial independence – was marked as it was, of course, with Alec Home.[32] At the Steering Committee, Home advocated a deal with the Liberals. The Lib-Lab Pact in 1906 had contributed to the Conservatives' landslide defeat and the mathematics of alliance were attractive. 'The floating voters are getting fed up with rigid Party attitudes,' he said in discussion. 'If they could see two anti-Socialist Parties trying to get together it would create [a] very good impression.' This was anathema to Macleod. The job of the Conservatives was 'to beat the Liberal Party out of politics in this country'; when Home suggested twelve seats as a preliminary offer, Macleod and Hailsham roundly condemned the idea. Macleod's view prevailed and did nothing to help his confidence in Home: 'Macleod never respected Home's political judgment.'[33]

All in all, the Steering Committee met on seventeen occasions, Home confining his contributions to the three areas where he had direct knowledge, and when the manifesto ('The Next Five Years') was being drafted he was a source of information on Scottish affairs.[34] He was behind the commitment 'to complete the Forth Road Bridge, the two Clyde tunnels and the reconstruction of the Carlisle–Glasgow–Stirling trunk road, and to speed up the programme of Highland road development.'[35] On 7 September, Home wrote to Macmillan from the

Commonwealth Relations Office. 'You have done all that could be done & more to bring us to the starting gate fit to win & it now remains for the people to show they have a sense of true values.' The next day, Macmillan announced the dissolution of Parliament and a general election on 8 October.

As a peer, Home did not have to concern himself with re-election and might have been expected to take a prominent role in the campaign. But the party managers did not consider him 'televisual'. The campaign was to be fought centrally, with television and press and poster advertising playing the major role. The old-style hustings of the small village halls were now a sideshow. Home lacked experience of television campaigning but was billed to appear in a telecast on the subject of 'Britain Overseas'. Edward Heath, the Chief Whip, saw an early version: 'It began with a shot of Lord Home, the Commonwealth Secretary, and Alan Lennox-Boyd, the Colonial Secretary, walking out of Downing Street together. One of them said, "Perhaps we had better talk about these foreign people and the colonies. Where shall we go?" And the other said, "I think we'll go to the Club, old boy, don't you?" And in the next picture they were seated deep in leather chairs with their drinks ... I said, "Look, this can't go on."'[36] The programme was abandoned.

The Conservatives increased their overall majority to a hundred seats; their percentage vote of 49.6 has never subsequently been bettered. In the wake of victory, Macmillan declared that the class war was now dead. 'The great thing', he wrote in his diary, 'is to keep the Tory party on *modern* and *progressive* lines.'[37] The victory gave Macmillan particular pleasure, especially as Gaitskell's speech at Newcastle on 28 September, in which he had promised not to increase the burden of income tax in peace-time conditions, was generally regarded as having been the fatal blunder of the campaign. Alec Home, also, never forgot the special glow of October 1959.[38] Macmillan's main concern was the replacement for Lennox-Boyd, and his choice of Macleod was carefully weighed. Macleod was anxious for a move from the Ministry of Labour, to broaden his overall political experience; he began a correspondence with Macmillan on future African policy and took to appearing on the front bench when Colonial and Commonwealth matters were being debated after Whitsun.

Africa had been relegated to the background by the election campaign, but Macmillan faced a difficult balancing act between the claims of the African leaders, who wanted early independence, and those of the white settlers (not to mention the Tory right), who saw a threat to their political control. Macleod saw things differently from the former Boyd/Home team and, in promoting him, Macmillan gave a message of hope for African self-government in the foreseeable future. In retaining Home at the Commonwealth Office, he gave reassurance to the backbench element who feared a headlong rush to catastrophe.

Other Cabinet changes were minor by comparison: Heath became Minister of Labour; Maudling became President of the Board of Trade, and Sandys took over the Ministry of Supply to form a new Ministry of Aviation. Rab Butler became Party Chairman, not the most crucial post in the wake of an election, but time-consuming in what he called his 'Pooh-Bah' years. Once again, Home was not moved (Macmillan was keeping him for greater things when Amory retired from the Treasury).

Macmillan's determination to make progress on Africa was symbolised by his dramatic four-week visit to Ghana, Nigeria, Nyasaland, Northern and Southern Rhodesia and South Africa in the New Year. In the course of this comprehensive visit he made his famous 'Winds of Change' speech in Cape Town. The strength of African national consciousness was what impressed Macmillan on his tour. 'The wind of change is blowing through this continent, and, whether we like it or not, this growth of national consciousness is a political fact.' The speech had immediate impact, 'Winds of Change' going into the political lexicons as well as providing the title for the first volume of Macmillan's memoirs. Only retrospectively did the phrase appear to Home as melodramatic, one he rather wished had not been used.[39] More important than the semantics of style was the political message, which accorded with Macleod's views on the pace of change and was a veiled warning to Dr Verwoerd, Prime Minister of South Africa; and to Welensky and the white settlers in the Federation that the old certainties were no more.

While Macmillan was in South Africa the conference on the constitutional future of Kenya began in London under Macleod's chairmanship, but the question of Banda's release most exercised the Cabinet. Macmillan telegraphed to Home: 'If we get the release of Banda plus constitutional talks and the beginning of political advance in Nyasaland, this Commission for Southern Rhodesia could be worthwhile.'[40] But it was clear that Welensky wanted the Monckton Commission postponed, and from his point of view with good reason.

Home made every effort over the following months to achieve a compromise between the Federation Cabinet and the British government, but the decision was taken (under a thinly veiled recognition threat from Macleod) to release Banda in April 1960. When the Monckton Commission reported in October, as Welensky feared, it contained the majority conclusion 'that Her Majesty's Government should make a declaration of intention to consider a request from the Government of Nyasaland to secede from the Federation'.[41] By that time it was Home's successor, Duncan Sandys, who was sent out to Salisbury to mollify Welensky. Had Home not been moved to the Foreign Office before the publication of the report, his position would have been very difficult, though, unlike Macleod, he did not trail his possible resignation as a bargaining counter. In one sense, the Monckton Commission was a defeat for him, in another it showed his ability to recognise when history had moved on. 'The Commonwealth is not a centre of power', he said. 'If, as is certain, power is to lie in Europe, then I think it is there that Britain ought to be.'[42]

His greatest achievement at the Commonwealth Office was his ability to hold together the disparate elements of a multifarious family, with its differences, feuds and rivalries. The spotlight in April moved south; South Africa was the focus of world attention after the massacre at Sharpeville township, in which sixty-seven Africans were killed by the police. This was followed by the first attempt on Verwoerd's life. In the last weeks of Home's tenure of the Commonwealth Office, the question of whether South Africa would leave the Commonwealth assumed a new importance in British Cabinet discussions, and was one of the major considerations of his first year at the Foreign Office.

Europe, a divisive issue in the Conservative Party over the next three decades, was the subject of his last major contribution in his old portfolio, when he considered the balance between our European links and our older Commonwealth ones. He said that from the point of view of our future political influence there were strong arguments for joining the EEC. 'We might hope eventually to achieve leadership of it and we could use our influence in it to keep Western Germany independent of the Soviet bloc. On the other hand, our wider interests and influence throughout the world depended … on our links with the Commonwealth; and if, by joining the EEC, we did fatal damage to those we should lose our power to exert our influence on a world scale. We should therefore consider full membership, but seek special terms to meet our fundamental interests and those of the Commonwealth.'[43]

With Heathcoat Amory's departure in the summer of 1960, Macmillan's planned Cabinet changes became reality. On 19 June, when Alec Home had formally agreed to move to the Foreign Office – a decision to be kept secret for over a month – Macmillan wrote to thank him for taking on a perilous charge:

> I cannot tell you how much pleasure your decision has given me. I know you will make a great success of it. The only thing that worries me is that you must on no account injure your health, but I believe that the work can be so arranged as not to be the intolerable burden that it has been recently to Foreign Secretaries.[44]

On 24 July, the Homes gave a farewell dinner party at Dorneywood for the Commonwealth Office. It was mooted, at short notice, as being for David Cole and his wife. Only when the guests arrived did they hear that Lord Home was transferring to the Foreign Office.

His five years at the Commonwealth Relations Office had been the most important of his career to date. He had entered the Cabinet in April 1955, very much a junior partner in a team that included such luminaries as Eden, Salisbury, Crookshank, Woolton, Stuart and Monckton. With Eden's retirement in January 1957, Home's career moved into a new phase. A younger generation now moved into the positions of power or consolidated their growing influence – Sandys, Hailsham, Thorneycroft, Lloyd, Heath and Macleod. Alec Home was not only of this group, but as the one first elected to the House of Commons in 1931 (Sandys had entered the House in 1935 and Hailsham and Thorneycroft in 1938), he was the senior figure by length of service and leadership of the House of Lords. In addition, he was a colleague and a friend with whom Macmillan felt comfortable and at ease. They spoke the same language, they shared the same interests and inhabited the same world. At Douglas Macmillan found 'an atmosphere which is (in these days) truly refreshing and stimulating … a haven from the storm'.[45] Home was, as Macmillan told the Queen in October 1963, 'a right-down regular peer', unlike Lord Hailsham, who, despite his hereditary viscountcy, was seen by Macmillan as a temporary peer, rather in the manner of officers in the First World War, who were 'temporary gentlemen'.[46] Alec Home with eight hundred years of history behind him, was the real thing.

Home's work in Commonwealth Affairs had introduced him to the wider global scene and made him a political equal of figures as diverse as Menzies, Nehru, Pearson, Bandaranaike, Welensky and Nash. In the summer of 1960 there was no figure in the Conservative Cabinet who had the necessary seniority and knowledge of the wider context of foreign affairs to deny Home the succession to the Foreign Office. Butler had the first, but not the second, though as a former Under-Secretary at the Foreign Office he undoubtedly had a claim and would have welcomed the opportunity.[47] Others, such as David Ormsby-Gore and John Profumo, as Under-Secretaries, were in tune with contemporary developments but did not have the seniority. After his meeting with the new President of the United States, John F. Kennedy, in March 1961, Macmillan decided on the appointment of Ormsby-Gore as British ambassador in Washington, an excellent choice which gave Ormsby-Gore special and privileged entrée to the White House, because of the understanding already in place between Alec Home and his former Under-Secretary.

Home's ability to establish productive political relationships was a major factor in Macmillan's decision to appoint him to the Foreign Office. Both Macmillan and Home knew how important it was that there should be unforced rapport between Downing Street and the Foreign Office, so on 27 July 1960, amid criticism from the *Daily Mirror* that it was 'the most reckless political appointment since the Roman Emperor Caligula made his favourite horse a consul',[48] Harold Macmillan made Alec Home Secretary of State for Foreign Affairs. Half-forgotten names (Curzon, Reading and Halifax) were brought forth as comparisons and constitutional issues were considered in the popular newsprints. Even rumours of the appointment had engendered rows. It was 'the biggest Tory backbench revolt he has ever faced as Prime Minister'.[49] With this promotion, Home entered the innermost circle of Macmillan's Cabinet.

9

Caligula's Horse?

After the triumph of the 1959 election, Macmillan could reasonably have expected a tranquil period of consolidation. That this was not the case can be attributed to two contrasting and unlikely figures, Derick Heathcoat Amory and Nikita Khrushchev, Prime Minister of the USSR. Amory's expected resignation as Chancellor of the Exchequer and Khrushchev's precipitate departure from the Paris summit meeting in May 1960, after the shooting down of the American U-2 spy plane over Russia, had important effects upon the course of British politics in the 1960s. Macmillan's subsequent reshuffle of his Cabinet may not have been as dramatic as the Night of the Long Knives two years later when he dismissed seven of his ministers, but the limited reshuffle of July 1960 may have had more significant consequences. It was also the crucial turning point in Home's career.

To trace the origins of this upheaval, it is necessary to go back to the events of 4 November 1959, when Amory had one of his regular meetings with Selwyn Lloyd, the Foreign Secretary, who recorded: 'After my official talk with Derry Amory, he said he wanted to have a serious personal talk with me. He was going to resign within a couple of "months" – he felt that I ought to succeed him – he wanted to talk seriously about this.'[1]

Although neither Amory nor Lloyd mentioned this, within a few weeks the lobby correspondents were speculating on Amory's future. On 22 November, Crossbencher in the *Sunday Express* 'forecast Derry Amory's retirement – and the "durable" Mr Lloyd as his successor, because by then Harold M. will be diverting his attention to home politics again and will want someone to fetch and carry!'[2] After his return from South Africa, Macmillan addressed the question of the reshuffle that would now be necessary. The basic pattern was already taking shape in his mind: if he could persuade Lloyd to go to the

Treasury, then, health permitting, he would ask Home to go to the Foreign Office, a natural escalation of the Commonwealth Secretary's responsibilities.

On 22 May, the papers were full of speculation about Cabinet changes, focusing on whether Lloyd would go to the Treasury. The next day Amory again reiterated that he wished Lloyd to succeed him, though he doubted, in the wake of the unsuccessful Paris summit, whether Macmillan could spare him from the Foreign Office. The failure of the Paris summit the previous week, though it was an unlucky end to Lloyd's years in King Charles Street, was for Macmillan the ideal opportunity to make a fresh start on the foreign front, especially when questions of Britain's application to join the EEC were considered. Macmillan had a long, ruminative talk with Lloyd on 24 May about the future shape of the administration. 'If I go to the Exchequer,' Lloyd wrote, 'did I think Alec could do F.S.? I said that for purely physical reasons I did not think so, and the burden on Harold himself would be too great.'[3] As far as the press was concerned, Home was pencilled in to take over the Scottish Office from John Maclay,[4] but Macmillan was determined to have him at the Foreign Office. So determined was he that he consulted the Permanent Under-Secretary, Sir Frederick Hoyer Millar, among other senior figures, about the physical demands of the job, asking what the Foreign Office could do to lighten the load so that somebody who was not in the best of health could cope with the physical burdens. Macmillan wanted that resolved before the issue was publicised.

The advice he got was that any Foreign Secretary in the Lords, not just Home, already had the built-in advantage of being free from constituency responsibilities, a point Lloyd, with his large constituency in the Wirral, had stressed and an advantage which Macmillan later told the 1922 Committee would allow for travel and the broader view.[5] On Monday 30 May, Macmillan offered Lloyd the Chancellorship. Most of their subsequent talk centred on arrangements for the Foreign Office, as Lloyd recorded. 'I said that could only work if there was another FO minister in the Cabinet – I think there is a lot to be said for Foreign S. in the Lords, but he must have a senior Minister as No. 2 – to take weight off PM and also to help with foreign representatives. We agreed to think it all over after Whit.'[6] On 11 June Macmillan and Lloyd discussed the putative changes again. 'Long talks about other jobs', Lloyd wrote. 'Would Erroll [Minister of State at the Department of Trade] do for the 2nd FO Minister?'[7]

Macmillan eventually decided to ask Edward Heath to take on the role, feeling that a minister already in the Cabinet was essential if the Number 2 post was to be taken seriously. Heath had the foresight to realise the possibilities of such a post, which could lead on to the Foreign Office itself – quite apart from the autonomy he would be granted over his brief on the EEC. He wisely insisted on a real executive role, not just that of a Commons spokesman, and was given the title of Lord Privy Seal, 'specially concerned with European affairs in all their aspects'. As his biographer has written, 'with this appointment Heath found his life's cause'.[8] Although the changes would not be announced until 27 July, the final dispositions were made the following week.

Alec Home considered the implications at some length, talking to Elizabeth about the changes it would mean in their lives. As with the offer of Cabinet rank from Eden, he did not rush into acceptance. Nevertheless, by 22 June all was signed and sealed. It was the day of Macmillan's first encaenia as the new Chancellor of Oxford University. Lloyd and Home, as yet unrevealed as the new Chancellor of the Exchequer and Foreign Secretary, walked in procession as honorary graduands on a golden summer's day. A lunch was held at All Souls and in the evening there was a gaudy at Christ Church; it was one of the happiest days of his public career. Macmillan's introduction of Home, who was to speak before Dr Michael Ramsey, Archbishop of York, was a reference to the portrait of Cardinal Wolsey which hung above the guests. 'Perhaps it is as well in this Hall that we should be reminded of the precedence that the State has over prelates.'[9] The enthusiasm with which Home was greeted was in sharp contrast with the events of 27 July. When the announcement of his appointment was made, there was a predictable outcry. 'There is a furious controversy going on,' Lloyd recorded. 'Comment on my own translation was rather lost in the row about Home.'[10]

Salisbury's request for the Upper House to be given more governmental responsibility had been accomplished in the most unlikely manner; the Lords were pleased that one of theirs was in an important government position. Alec Home was well suited to the serious, considered debates in the Lords – far more disciplined and courteous than those in the Commons; the sheer brutality of the Commons in its uglier moods was absent. When discussions took place in the Lords on complex post-Suez questions such as Egyptian assets, party issues were subsumed in careful analysis of the legal niceties of confiscation and sequestration. Debates on the European issues at this time also had their more dispassionate side in the Upper House. The two main emotions in the Commons at his promotion were amazement on the Conservative benches and anger on those of Labour. The shock for many Conservatives lay in the departure from current practice. When Lord Carrington became Foreign Secretary in 1979 there was no equivalent row – Home's tenure of the post had paved the way. 'As I expected, a great row developed about a Peer going to Foreign Office,' Macmillan wrote. 'There was a premature leak (which on the whole helped the Party, first to get excited and then to calm down). The Opposition had a debate – and Gaitskell made the cleverest and most effective speech I have heard him make. My reply was not too good, but the Party rallied round and we won by a majority of 110 (our paper majority being 94). ... This was a great act of loyalty to me, and several of our chaps came from sick beds and even hospitals to vote.'[11]

Gaitskell realised the potential for the opposition, grateful for any stick to beat the government; Home felt that this was a legitimate tactic by the Labour Party and bore no animus towards Gaitskell. Although the Labour leader thought Home 'generally reactionary and obsessive about communism' (he had told Gaitskell that the UN representative in Elizabethville was 'an American communist'), Gaitskell stressed that the appointment was 'constitutionally objectionable and not good for the conduct of our affairs in the world'.[12] A belief in the centrality of the Commons was also a contributing factor to the row, rather than the qualifications of Alec Home.

The Beaverbrook press predictably led the media onslaught. NEW CABINET: BIG ROW ran the headline in the *Sunday Express*, while its edition north of the border went for the local impact of ROW OVER SCOTS EARL.[13] There was puzzlement in some quarters as to who Home actually was and one paper referred to him as the Earl of Rome. The conventional wisdom was that Macmillan, who had a penchant for aristocrats in his government (other earls included Dundee, Perth and Waldegrave) had now overstepped the constitutional limits. It was one thing having the Marquess of Lansdowne as an Under-Secretary at the Foreign Office, but the Secretaryship of State? For many on both sides of the Commons, Home was an earl too far.

Macmillan had foreseen the objections, but underestimated the virulence of some of the comments, especially from his own side. He wrote apologetically to Home as the row simmered on, 'I am so sorry that the events of the last week have led to some newspapers – and some people who ought to know better – saying a lot of silly things about you.

I know that you have turned these lightly aside but they must have been a worry.'

His new Foreign Secretary, who had considered carefully the pros and cons of accepting the post, replied:

> Thank you so much for your note. I was afraid as you know that I should cause you a lot of trouble but the critics had the field to themselves a bit longer than I thought and while our lips were still sealed. I hope that the haymaking hasn't done too much damage & that Ted & I can confound the pessimists by showing that your idea works very well.
>
> Needless to say I will do all I can to demonstrate that your confidence in me is justified. I am deeply grateful to you for all you have said & done for me.[14]

The partnership of Macmillan and Home was not going to depend for its effectiveness on joint membership of the House of Commons. More significant was whether the diarchy of Home and Heath would cause difficulties in the conduct of foreign business, or whether it would be a profitable and creative partnership. That no problem occurred from 1960 to 1963 was a major factor in defining Home's Foreign Office career, freeing him from an area of policy-making which was not his main interest, though he was well aware of its importance, particularly in the new economic relationship with the Commonwealth, the European Free Trade Association (EFTA) and the European Economic Community (EEC).

The relationship between Edward Heath and Alec Home was of considerable significance to both men: 'Ted made Alec PM and Alec made Ted PM' is the verdict of many of the events of 1963 and 1965. One of the reasons for the efficiency in despatch of business was that there was no sense of demarcation. Edward Heath's work was not exclusively 'European', and there was no sense of Home impinging on the Lord Privy Seal's domain when he discussed the future of the EEC. Briskness was the order of the day. The Egyptian compensation issue, which had bedevilled Selwyn Lloyd's last months in office, was taken to the top of the agenda and the Claims Department of the Foreign Office was working at full stretch. European Free Trade Area negotiations were also an important early issue. Home let Heath have his head, proving himself a Foreign Secretary who trusted his team implicitly, and advice from this team was of the highest calibre.

Many continued to resent Home's unexpected appointment, but

when the dust had settled and unbiased observers realised that Alec Home was not an ineffectual aristocrat but a politician of wide practical experience, far more balanced temperamentally than his Prime Minister, the tune began to change.[15] 'How *wrong* we were about Home', admitted the *Daily Mail*, a reaction many more shared in the coming years, when differences with the opposition were on policy, not deficiencies of personality.[16] Dean Rusk, American Secretary of State after November 1960, considered Home 'one of the ablest foreign ministers he dealt with'.[17] Home admired Rusk immensely, and did not approve of Macmillan's private references to him as 'the biscuit man'. His relationship with Rusk flourished not just because of mutual understanding but because of Home's awareness that Rusk was a kind of permanent under-secretary within the American presidential system. This became clear during the Cuban missile crisis and the important role played by the National Security advisers under Rusk. It was of inestimable benefit to Anglo–American relationships that these two found themselves on the same wavelength. Among the 'new frontier' men of the Kennedy administration, Rusk was in many ways an outsider, but his solidity and dependability were a stabilising influence. Home always regarded Rusk as 'one of us', since he had been a Rhodes scholar at Oxford. When Alec Home's seventieth birthday was celebrated with a dinner at 10 Downing Street, Rusk was unable to attend but sent the Prime Minister, Edward Heath, a message to be read out:

> Alec has long since taken his place among the greatest of British Foreign Secretaries. In the annals of diplomacy there are few who have earned such respect and admiration in the trade union of foreign ministers from all parts of the world. His personal integrity, his intellectual honesty, his eloquent and forceful advocacy of the attitudes of Her Majesty's Government, his simplicity and modesty of manner with high and low, his urbanity in crisis and good humour in disagreement are only a few of the qualities which make him a towering figure of our times. One gets to know a man rather well when one occupies the same foxhole with him. I have had this experience with Alec a number of times, and it is good to have him at your side at moments of danger and difficulty.[18]

The failure of the Paris summit in May 1960 was a grievous blow to Macmillan and the catalyst for the Cabinet reshuffle. The domino effect of a change at the top can be considerable and so it was with Amory's departure. After Lloyd and Home had been placed on their new squares on the board, Macmillan considered the replacement at the Commonwealth Office, with the Monckton Commission due to report later in the year. However, in offering the post to Rab Butler, Macmillan displayed great insensitivity. In the words of Butler's biographer, 'It is hard to think of a more hurtful insult to a man who had, after all, been Chancellor of the Exchequer, when Home was a mere Minister of State at the Scottish Office, than to invite him to step into the shoes of a former junior colleague now about to be elevated (as a peer) to the Foreign Office.'[19] Many, including Butler himself, thought that he had a claim on the Foreign Office, so the offer added insult to injury.[20]

So Duncan Sandys succeeded Home at the CRO, Hailsham became Lord President of the Council and Leader of the Lords, but not before Macmillan had considered a junior figure and had wondered 'whether Lord Hailsham could lead the House of Lords without disaster', hardly a ringing endorsement and ironic in the light of Macmillan's initial preference for Hailsham as his successor in October 1963.[21] The key to Eden's unsatisfactory reshuffle in December 1955 had been Rab Butler, who had been moved to indeterminate and non-departmental responsibilities from the Treasury; the key to Macmillan's reshuffle in July 1960 had also been the Chancellor of the Exchequer, and the outcome was again unsatisfactory for Butler, who, to perceptive observers, had passed the cusp of his career. As early as February 1958, Wedgwood Benn, Labour MP for Bristol South-East, had written, 'Mr Butler is a spent political force who has not one chance in a hundred of succeeding to the premiership.'[22] After Kennedy's election as President in November 1960, the Department of State asked for regular analyses of Macmillan's position. These discounted Butler as a successor. 'Butler has slumped badly in recent weeks,' ran one telegram from Grosvenor Square, 'he is technically Macmillan's deputy in the House, although few Conservatives … consider his chances of succession to be bright.'[23]

The clear winner in the reshuffle was Home, and to a lesser extent Lloyd, though his inheritance was to prove a poisoned chalice. Heath also, although this was not widely seen at the time, had taken the crucial step of his career. Among the many letters of congratulation Home received, one contained a verse from Jock Colville:

Let Khruschev tremble, Gaitskell wail,
  Let Common Marketeers grow pale,
And Nasser shiver in his den,

But one improvement we desire
(Should Harold M at last retire)
To see you back at Number 10.[24]

On his appointment, Home joined the company of those who have served in one of 'the great offices of state'. Two of his predecessors at the Foreign Office – Bevin and Eden – are ranked among the most important foreign secretaries of the century. Although it is difficult to imagine two figures outwardly more dissimilar than Ernest Bevin and Alec Home, there are certain similarities. Both were unconventional in dress, unorthodox in many ways, impatient of restraints and willing to say unpopular things. Heath could depend on Home in the 1970s, just as Bevin had a special position in relation to Attlee. Neither was a *professional* diplomat. This is not to imply that they were amateurish; rather that their contribution was instinctive, with an intuitive feel for what was politically viable, and could be understood by the initiate and the unsophisticated alike. Both were representative of a distinct class, but transcended the narrow base of their classes: both were admired by their Foreign Office staffs. Bevin's seventieth birthday party, when every employee gave sixpence towards the cost – an echo of the famous docker's tanner – is well chronicled.[25] Home also celebrated his seventieth birthday at the Foreign Office.

'There is no more onerous job in the world than that of the British Foreign Secretary', wrote Sir Ivone Kirkpatrick the year before Home's appointment. 'Every Foreign Secretary I have known has been surprised and appalled to discover ... how much he was expected to do.'[26] But Home was under no illusions about the burden he would bear; paradoxically, his membership of the House of Lords was one of his great long-term advantages, and his staff at once noticed the difference from Selwyn Lloyd's routine. No longer were there weekend dashes to the Wirral constituency, with a duty secretary in attendance; mid-week attendance at Commons question time was a thing of the past; there were no late night sittings. Home avoided social commitments for Friday evenings: 'If the Secretary of State is free, he will be in the country' was a blanket response to invitations. Although the political aspects were no less frenetic, with continuing crises on Berlin, the Congo and Laos, as well as East–West relations after the failure of the Paris summit, Alec Home's presence at the Foreign Office brought a centre of calm to the eye of the storm.[27]

Alec Home was at the apex of a pyramid of politically loyal colleagues and a Rolls-Royce generation of diplomats and civil servants. In addition to Edward Heath as Lord Privy Seal, his Minister of State was David Ormsby-Gore; his PPS was Ian Samuel, assisted by Oliver Wright, Antony Acland and Michael Wilmshurst. The number two secretary, Michael Wilford, who moved over to head Heath's office, was the link between the Foreign Office and the Lord Privy Seal's department. In the office of the Permanent Under-Secretary (Sir Frederick Hoyer Millar), was Douglas Hurd and the Deputy Under-Secretaries included Sir Patrick Reilly and Sir Evelyn Shuckburgh. Home clearly had confidence in his ability to do the job, and the role of Elizabeth Home was also important, though largely unseen. He had always depended on his wife to organise day-to-day matters, and she proved invaluable with a new batch of officials who were unaware of the idiosyncrasies of their new Secretary of State. 'I enclose spare spectacles of my husband's,' she wrote to Wilmshurst from Dorneywood. 'He usually loses *about* one pair a fortnight!' She wrote to Antony Acland after a particularly fraught August at Douglas, asking for a further scrambler telephone. 'There's apt to be so much business on the line & *either* President Kennedy can't get on because Meriel is talking to her chums *or* the cook can't order the joint because some of you are fixing the world.'[28] As a result, Home took the world of telegrams and anger philosophically. Elizabeth was there to smooth over the difficulties, as she had done for the CROWS in the 1950s.

Two thousand telegrams a day came into the Foreign Office, of which he would personally deal with upwards of fifty. There were over a hundred foreign and Commonwealth missions. He believed in keeping up as much personal contact as possible with the ambassadors; at least one major meeting a day was customary with his staff and several each week with ministerial colleagues. He saw Macmillan each day. Macmillan recalled this practice in his last letter to Home shortly before he died:

> I often think of the old days when you used to walk over and we settled in a quarter of an hour before lunch matters which might have taken days of correspondence. This is the proper relationship between a Foreign Secretary and a Prime Minister. You were really perfect. I remember the mild row in the H of C when you were appointed but it did not last for you overcame everybody by your skill and charm.[29]

In the midst of serious international diplomacy, Home wanted people to have fun, the word that most often came to mind among those who worked for him at the time. Secretaries were welcomed at Douglas and the Hirsel as friends, and only secondly as operators of scrambler telephones and dispatchers of telegrams. He was particularly good with the children of his secretarial team, who revered him, and had perhaps an exaggerated view of how the Private Office worked. 'Who's going to run Daddy's office now?' asked one, when Home became Prime Minister.[30] He was at ease with the work in a way that was not true of his time at Number 10, and when he returned to the Foreign Office in the summer of 1970, he felt that he was returning home. His Foreign Office years, like Eden's, were his happiest.[31] Underneath his insouciant air of calm, Home possessed an intuitive feel for what was important and what was secondary. Underlying this was his remarkable political skill in knowing what would wash with the Party and what would be acceptable to Parliament. This did not mean that he trimmed for popularity – when it came to push and shove, he could not be pushed in a direction he did not wish to go; he knew when absolutes had to yield to expediency and when, whatever the political dangers, the expeditious would not be considered. Unlike Rab Butler, he did not think that politics was the art of the possible; he regarded it as a choice between the unpalatable and the disastrous. It was instructive to see how foreign ministers from other countries responded to him. The world of professional diplomacy was formal and reserved: 'The Honourable Foreign Minister of such and such' was the customary way of naming a counterpart at the United Nations, but when the British Foreign Secretary, leaning back with his headphones, raised his pencil, the preliminary would be 'Yes, Sir Alec'. The formal rejoinder was somehow redundant.[32]

Alec Home went to the Foreign Office with no preconceptions about the direction of foreign policy. He was not a paid-up member of the European tendency in the Conservative Party; he saw the advantages of closer European union, but not why it had to be *either* Europe *or* the United States. He did not see why it should not be a mixture of both. He was tolerant without being feeble, and had firm ideas on how business should be conducted. He was profoundly suspicious of summits as facilitating diplomatic negotiation, distrusting the expectations aroused and the razzmatazz of media circuses.

He believed his job was to manage foreign affairs from the Foreign Office. Time spent out of London was not usually productive, he felt, outside the regular fixtures, such as the October visits to the United Nations. He believed in conventional diplomacy, not the airport interview. (Memories of Chamberlain died hard.) Nor did he want his energies dissipated by journeys to far-flung embassies. One of his earliest commitments was to visit Portugal, and he was advised that Spain should be included in the itinerary. 'I get more and more concerned at the amount of time a Foreign Secretary has to spend out of London', he minuted. 'I am quite certain this is wrong especially in the present state of the world. I will do this one but I am going on strike soon.'[33]

Many problems awaited the attention of the new Foreign Secretary in the summer of 1960, foremost among them being the former Belgian Congo, Laos and Berlin. British troops were deployed in Aden, Cyprus, Kuwait and Malaya. Home was convinced that the key to the containment of many of these problems lay in better East–West relationships, hence the importance he attached to his relationships with Dean Rusk and with Andrei Gromyko, who formed with him the troika of senior foreign ministers in the early 1960s.

By January 1961 the Kennedy administration was in office, and there was greater continuity in US foreign policy than expected. Kennedy, no less than Dulles, believed in the 'Domino Theory'. This matched with Home's implicit belief that vigilance was the key factor in dealing with the Soviet Union: '... one of the most disconcerting features of communism has been this: that it also lays down the doctrine that conciliation may be used as a tactical weapon; and one of the terrible difficulties of doing business with the Russians has been ... knowing whether their moves towards peace are true, or whether they are manoeuvres in a cold and relentless campaign of aggrandisement.'[34] He returned to this theme on his first visit to America in September, when he spoke to the National Press Club in Washington:

> The first profound conviction which I hold, on taking up my new office, is that if Britain is to fulfil her role as leader of the Commonwealth, as a reliable ally and as a buttress to the free world, that Britain must be strong; economically strong, because solvency is the essential basis of all national enterprise and of all international influence; physically strong because our island holds a strategic position on the continent of Europe and in the Atlantic ... and morally strong because let us have no doubt that in the last analysis communism is going to be beaten by a creed and by principles of

> living which are demonstrated to be more virile and to be more compelling than their own creed.

Such sentiments found ready ears in the Washington of 1960, but more prescient were his remarks about the EEC. 'We welcome the European Economic Community and for two reasons: first because it will bring strength and cohesion economically to Europe; but, secondly, because it will cement the relations between France and Germany. Never let us forget that twice, when France and Germany have fallen apart, Britain has suffered disaster, and in the wake of Britain the United States has been brought into war, and so has the whole Commonwealth of Nations.'[35]

Home was in New York that autumn for the Fifteenth Session of the General Assembly of the United Nations, the largest gathering in its history. Two major issues – disarmament and the Congo – were at the top of the agenda. Khrushchev had attacked the United Nations Secretary-General, Dag Hammarskjöld, over the United Nations Force (ONUC) in the Congo, which had celebrated its independence on 30 June but subsequently descended into anarchy. In July, the Prime Minister, Patrice Lumumba, and the President, Kasavubu, had asked the United Nations for urgent military assistance, but the force of 3000 men was a peace-keeping body not intended to be drawn into the struggle against the secessionist province of Katanga, led by Moise Tshombe. Lumumba thus sought Soviet assistance in his struggle for a united Congo, but the anti-Communist Kasavabu then dismissed Lumumba. Power was seized temporarily by Joseph Mobutu. The West feared Soviet penetration in Africa. A predictable Russian veto in the Security Council led to the issue being debated in the General Assembly, which Home addressed: 'First, my delegation wish to demonstrate beyond any possibility of doubt the strong support of the United Kingdom for the pacific role which the United Nations is seeking to play in the Congo. Secondly, my purpose in speaking is to ask from the Assembly a decisive vote. We ask that the Assembly should declare that they will not tolerate outside intervention designed to subvert the independence of the Congo or indeed of any other state in Africa.'[36] The decisive vote – seventy in favour, none against – was, as Anthony Parsons has written, 'a clear signal to Moscow that, whatever suspicions there might be and however bitter loyalties might be strained, the Africans and Asians were still determined to back the UN operation and not allow Cold War rivalries to open up irreparable splits.'[37]

Vigilance had brought initial results, but the respite was temporary as the Congolese problem – in which Home was to take 'an extremely close interest, closer than Foreign Secretaries are generally able to take in issues which do not directly involve their states'[38] – was to erupt again with even more tragic consequences the following year. When Lumumba was mysteriously murdered in January 1961, the Americans backed a moderate, Cyrille Adoula, as Prime Minister of the central government in Leopoldville. On a mission to Tshombe, to negotiate an understanding between him and Adoula, Dag Hammarskjöld lost his life in an air crash in September. Twice Home tried to bring Tshombe to agreement with the central government, never wavering from his view that 'the United Nations was on a misguided course in being willing to contemplate force to end Katangan secession'.[39] But he was also realistic enough to know that Tshombe's was a volatile political personality, at bottom unreliable, and that the strength of the American hand, when in September 1961 they backed the UN intervention, would be more telling than British wishes. In December 1961 Home wrote to Eden:

> Let me say at once how entirely I agree that to attempt to bring Katanga to heel by force is not statesmanship … We thought that far too little attention was paid in the resolution to conciliation and negotiation and far too much to solution of the problem by force … To give them their due, I do not think that the Americans want to see a solution by force either. But of course they know little about Africans and know little of the patience which is needed when dealing with them. They have on the whole co-operated closely with us and with Roy Welensky in our effort to bring Adoula and Tshombe together …
>
> I have thought a good deal about the possibility of stopping contributing funds to the Congo operation … I said on November 29 … [that if] the United Nations were taking action which was not contributing to the cause of peace, I should feel bound to advise that we should review our present practices. But … so long as there was a chance that the peace-keeping machinery of the UN could in fact help to keep the peace, so long should the United Kingdom support it. I don't want to get right out if we can avoid it because the Americans will go on financing it or if they didn't the Russians would and would begin to call the tune.[40]

Eventually and reluctantly, Britain backed United Nations action in the

Congo. The whole imbroglio made Home increasingly disillusioned with the United Nations; he was also at odds with the Commonwealth countries who provided over half the UN force and resented implicit criticism of their role.

Home remained 'extremely anxious about the extent of the UN operation' in Katanga.[41] He submitted a memorandum to Cabinet on 'United Nations Debates and Resolutions': 'One after another resolutions are put forward containing propositions and clauses which seem to run counter to our policy. The technique is something like this. First, a draft resolution is floated by the Russians or one of the near-communist Afro–Asians. This is then recognised by the moderate Afro–Asians to be totally unacceptable to the West, so they set about trying to amend it behind the scenes to see if they can induce the sponsors to modify the original. They often succeed up to the point where they (the moderates) believe we ought to vote for the modified text but where we are still far from satisfied.'[42] He felt that the United Nations was rapidly becoming a 'place where no-one's votes (except the Communists) mean what they say'.[43]

The most public manifestation of Home's sense of frustration was his 'double standards' speech on 28 December 1961 to a small gathering of the Berwick-upon-Tweed United Nations Association, not a body regularly in the headlines. The speech was precisely calculated and he knew the furore that it would cause. The United Nations had been set up as a peace-keeping force, yet was a pro-active body with an agenda for setting free the peoples of the Congo. What angered him was that nearly ninety nations had not paid their dues to the United Nations, yet this did not stop them exercising their right to vote. A solitary journalist, among a small and frozen group of members of the UNA, became the conduit for the Foreign Secretary's strictures. 'At last my friends, I am come amongst you,' said Gladstone to his supporters at Manchester in 1865, 'and I am come unmuzzled.' Home spoke in a similarly uninhibited way in Berwick on 'the adoption of a double standard of behaviour by many of the newly elected countries'. He asked whether there was 'one rule for the communist countries and another for the democracies?' and 'whether the United Nations of the authors of the Charter had had its day?'[44] Not for the first time in his career, he articulated what many thought.

Macmillan had delayed a decision on whether his presence at the UN Fifteenth Session would be beneficial, or potentially embarrassing, in view of the uncertainties regarding Khrushchev's behaviour after the stormy break-up of the Paris summit in the summer. He asked Home to test the water. Home advised, 'There will be no awkwardness about a meeting between you and Mr. Khrushchev.'[45] His recommendation was that Macmillan should attend: there would be opportunities for informal meetings, and the British presence would be strengthened. 'I think it would be extremely good for Tito and Nasser and others to see you in action,' Home wrote. 'At the moment the limelight is on the eye-catching capers of Castro & Khrushchev, but ... the large majority of the Assembly, including particularly the new members, will soon tire of this and will want to get down to serious business.' Macmillan decided to go, and the visit became the occasion for one of his most celebrated displays of unflappability. When Khrushchev had met Home at a reception, the Russian leader asked what kind of speech Macmillan would give. 'That depends on your speech,' replied the Foreign Secretary. 'You English people are very shrewd and clever,' replied Khruschev, warning Home to fill his pockets with food as his speech was going to be a very long one.[46] It was not only long but immoderate, inflaming Cold War tensions, with attacks, among other things, on Hammarskjöld, Eisenhower, western colonialism and the United Nations. The diatribe lasted for two hours nineteen minutes; by contrast Macmillan displayed studied moderation in his defence of Britain's record over decolonisation (with Nigeria the latest colony on the verge of independence[47]) and his impartial plea for internationally agreed nuclear inspections. The latter proved too much for Khrushchev; when Macmillan reached the point about the presence (and inconvenience) of 'a large number of officials' for such inspections the Russian leader banged his shoe on the table, a noise magnified by the microphones. Macmillan said mildly, 'Well, I'd like it translated if you would, certainly.'[48]

New York's diplomatic community took to this new double act. Home had calculated wisely in urging Macmillan's appearance as a counter to the antics of some delegates. Their meetings with foreign leaders were serious and responsible, as with President Tito of Yugoslavia on 27 September. Home admired Tito's refusal to follow the Moscow line and the way he used his unofficial position as the leading non-aligned ruler. The next day they met Nasser, a situation of some delicacy which Home treated as an opportunity for frankness, not diffidence or disingenuous apology. Macmillan and Nasser agreed that Home and his Egyptian opposite number, Dr Fawzi, 'should carry on their discussion so that a start could be made in improving relations between the two countries'. Other substantive talks were held with the Norwegian Foreign Minister (on the fishing dispute with Iceland), Dr Kwame Nkrumah and King Hussein of Jordan, and Home went out of his way to meet the Polish Foreign Minister. A relaxed dinner was given by Menzies at the Australian embassy, when they discussed 'Ike and Mr K', the Congo and whether the UN Secretary-General should have three deputies.[49]

The visit was regarded as a great success, a fire in Macmillan's car in the Lincoln tunnel notwithstanding. Eisenhower had welcomed Macmillan as an old war-time colleague, and Alec and Elizabeth Home dodged their security guards and walked with Macmillan in New York's Central Park, a counter to the long hours in the United Nations. The American press reacted favourably to the visit. 'This tall, lanky Scottish peer – whom few had known before his appearance here this week – suddenly became an international personality,' said one journal.[50] Home had far-ranging talks with Christian Herter, the US Secretary of State, who wanted to hear of Home's Commonwealth experience in the light of developments in the Congo. For one whose reputation was of rabid anti-communism, Home made an unexpected reply. He told the Secretary of State that for the new African countries being seen to be left-wing was a matter of pride; they equated it with social progress and the West should not necessarily regard it as a sign of communist sympathies. British press coverage was also favourable. 'Lord Home is winning golden, nay platinum, opinions among the Western world and is holding the fort to great advantage,' ran one report. 'So far everything has gone pretty well for our side and we are doing a good deal better than we did in the Olympic Games.'[51]

The most important result of the United Nations conference was the sustained opportunity it gave to meet the Russian leadership. Home had no illusions about Khrushchev and never approached him with unrealistic expectations. Yet he liked him and felt that he was approachable, even amusing at times (though coarse), and that he had an inherent toughness that made his actions understandable, if not predictable. These insights were to be of value during the Cuban missile crisis in October 1962. Home saw Khrushchev as a gambler, pushing to see what he could get away with; but he, too, understood the psychology of gambling, and knew the disarming influence courtesy could have on Khrushchev.

Home's relationship with Andrei Gromyko, the Russian Foreign Minister, was more complex – hardly surprising given Gromyko's personality. There were two sides to him: the official and the personal, and as long as one was aware which *persona* Gromyko was adopting, progress was possible. He could be formidably obstinate; the shutters came down and there was nothing but reiteration of the Kremlin line. Home knew that 'Old Grom' (as he privately referred to him) could be human and amusing on the private level. The relationship over the years between the two was fascinating to the informed observer, especially as some knew that Mrs Gromyko had taken a shine to the man she described as 'The English Lord', which Gromyko joked about with Alec Home in his more informal moments. There were many points of contact between the two men. The first time they met was when Elizabeth Home was present. She had just bought a clockwork bear for a grandchild. Gromyko entered, black-suited (Alec Home never ceased to be amazed at the sight of Gromyko's long-johns tucked into his stockings, even at the height of an English summer), and paused to admire the bear, and even to wind the key.[52] The situation was defused and though both said straightforwardly what they believed, they developed considerable respect and liking for each other. Both were professionally detached. For Gromyko politics was like a game, which he played hard but he could stand above the battle while arguing over detail. In private he spoke English, but when on business confined himself to Russian. Though knowing perfectly well what Home was saying, he waited for the interpreter while he thought out his response, like an icon on a computer screen indicating that calculations are unfolding. He was tough and experienced, but found Home an elusive opponent. No other Russian Foreign Minister has been taken to dine at the Carlton Club, few British foreign secretaries would have chosen to host a meal there. But Home knew that Gromyko was fascinated by tradition. Shooting was one of his main pastimes and he always sought Home's advice on his Purdey guns when he came to London, insisting that his son get the best that the London gunsmiths had to offer, as 'He, silly boy, waits for ducks to fly off lake before shooting them!' Home invited him to stay at Douglas for the shooting, but Gromyko inquired whether Douglas was private land and baulked at acceptance (even though Home, tongue-in-cheek, suggested they could lease the land to Lanark County Council for the day). When Home expelled 105 Russian spies in 1971, Gromyko found it very difficult, despite his apoplectic reaction, to make any headway with his protest. Each knew the other too well and Alec Home had only to say that he thought Gromyko would be grateful, because otherwise people back home in Russia might believe that he was not controlling the KGB. Gromyko gave his verdict on Home in his memoirs. 'I have very lively memories of Douglas-Home,' he wrote. 'He was a mild-mannered man: it was not in his nature to speak harshly, especially to a foreigner ... but he would insist on expounding his ideas ... If he was obliged to give his partner in conversation a break, he would just be waiting for his side of the tournament to begin again. There were no sudden, still less brilliant, breakthroughs in my meetings with Douglas-Home, but at least each one left a civilised impression that made the next meeting easier.'[53]

On 8 October 1960, Home sat next to Khrushchev at a dinner in New York, his last engagement on the American visit. Their talk was a fascinating exchange of communist and western philosophies. 'What is the most important problem standing between us which we ought to resolve?' Home asked. 'Undoubtedly disarmament,' replied Khrushchev. Home's note continues:

H: Our talks then will have been useful but I wish you could help me by identifying the difference between us on inspection. I cannot understand it and wonder if it exists.

K: Oh, that is simple – you want control and will not have any disarmament. Mr Macmillan's speech confirmed me in that view. Arms must be destroyed and on a large scale or how can it be called disarmament?

H: There is clearly confusion. I will put it this way and see if you can agree with me. We feel that actual disarmament and the necessary inspection should run concurrently, hand in hand. Would you agree with that?

K: Yes, but I would put it this way. We should complete the matter in three stages. First, we would make the agreement to disarm. The agreement would cover all weapons but we would *do nothing about it at that stage*. Second, we would work out the agreement on control. I would accept any control you would like to suggest. Third, we would apply the controls we had agreed to the disarmament plan which had been settled in Phase 1.

H: I am grateful for this clarification and I would like to make absolutely sure I have understood it, so I will take the opportunity of talking to Mr Gromyko or your ambassador in London.

K: I shall be very glad. The Americans don't want disarmament. I hope you in Britain do. But disarmament must mean destruction of weapons and there is no certainty of that in your plan, where the control comes first. But we will see.

This extended and informal talk, as far as informality was possible with interpreters, gave some insight into Khrushchev's often enigmatic way of thinking and how his arguments sometimes went off at a tangent. Home summed up the meeting for Macmillan. 'We had a good deal of talk on other subjects, and he said that we must expect complete opposition from Russia on our Colonial Policy "until every Colony was free". He thought our attitude on the Congo completely wrong ... he did not mention Berlin and I left it alone. He was relaxed and full of back chat.'[54]

Home returned for the Conservative Party conference at Scarborough in October, his reputation enhanced by press reports of his days in Washington and New York, and his speech on foreign policy underpinned that reputation. It was uncompromising in its warnings of Soviet intentions. 'No communist propaganda, no threats, no blandishments, will ever shake my belief that fundamentally on the Anglo–United States alliance depends the freedom of mankind.' There was also a lightness of touch in his asides. When one Young Conservative said that criticising a government statement was like grappling with a blancmange, he replied that he had a lifelong aversion to blancmange. If delegates wished to express disapproval, he said, 'the procedure is to bang on the desk'.[55] On 2 November he made a major speech in the House of Lords, concentrating on events at the United Nations and especially the behaviour of the Russian delegation. 'The technique used was a mixture of crude power and blandishment. This particular manoeuvre cannot be said to have succeeded. It was my strong impression that those countries at the United Nations for the first time were alarmed by the bullying nature of the approach.' Summing up, Lord Hailsham said, 'Not since Sir Winston Churchill ceased speaking on great matters of international import have the British public heard more plain speaking than came from Lord Home this afternoon.[56]

On 8 November, news came of Kennedy's election by the narrowest of margins to the American Presidency, a result that meant Macmillan and Home would in future be dealing not with Nixon and Christian Herter but with Kennedy and Dean Rusk. It was a contest that was to cast a long shadow over the 1964 British General Election. Two months would elapse before Kennedy's inauguration, when the major crisis for the new administration was Laos, which the United States chose to regard as the Asian line of defence against the advance of communism, bordering as it did four non-communist states: Burma, Cambodia, South Vietnam and Thailand. The Geneva Conference of 1954 had recognised the right to independence of Cambodia, Laos and Vietnam. By 1960 this neutrality was threatened in Laos by the Pathet Lao communists, who were in conflict with the weak neutralist government of Prince Souvenne Phouma. Kennedy regarded Laos as 'the worst mess the Eisenhower administration left me'.[57] Home would inevitably be involved in Indo-China as Eden had been co-chairman with the Russians of the 1954 Geneva Peace agreement. In parallel with the volatility of the Congolese situation, a localised civil war in South-east Asia could be the spark for a major international conflict if the Americans sent military assistance to Prince Phouma while China, and later Russia, backed the Pathet Lao. At the reconvened Geneva Conference, a cease-fire between the Laos government and the Pathet Lao was arranged, preliminary to the brittle settlement of 23 July 1962, which the Americans were optimistic would hold.

On 16 November 1960, an event occurred which was to have a considerable effect on Alec Home's life. The Labour peer, Viscount Stansgate, died. 'At the moment of his death, in constitutional law and practice,' wrote his eldest surviving son Anthony Wedgwood Benn, 'I succeeded to the peerage and was automatically disqualified.'[58] So began the constitutional struggle, conducted with great persistence and courage by Tony Benn, to enable a hereditary peer to renounce his title. The measure, under the terms of the Peerage Act on 31 July 1963, was the means by which the Earl of Home was able to assume the Premiership. Although Hailsham and Home had accepted the inevitability of their inheritance there was no such acquiescence from Benn.

On the Monday after his father's death, he had a meeting with Butler, the Home Secretary:

> Butler was very cordial, and I was misled by this. He said, 'very interesting case' … I got the idea that he was vaguely on my side, which was clearly quite wrong. He went on: 'By the way, one thing: would your scheme permit Quintin to come back?' So I said, 'Well, no, it wouldn't really.' So he said, 'Ah, well that's all right.' … Possibly if Quintin came back he might represent a threat to Butler's leadership.[59]

Benn's analysis of Butler's motives in expressing reservations was prescient, though neither man could know that the real threat would come not from Quintin Hailsham but from Alec Home.

*

In October 1961 Butler was succeeded as Leader of the House of Commons by Iain Macleod, whose responsibility the peerage question became. Matters were not to be resolved for another twenty-one months. This meant that, apart from the weekly Cabinet meetings, Home's path now rarely crossed that of Macleod. There was little overlap – and potential for differences – on policy, or on party matters, for Macleod was primarily occupied with Commons business, which did not impinge on the Foreign Secretary's domain.

Two events in 1961, however, served further to distance Home and Macleod. On 7 March 1961, the day after Home had returned from a tour of Nepal and Iran,[60] he was present in the House of Lords to hear a debate on Central Africa. Their Lordships were astonished to hear a personal attack by Lord Salisbury on Macleod, then Colonial Secretary, whom he denounced as being 'too clever by half'. It was one of those moments, familiar enough in the House of Commons, but virtually unprecedented in the Lords, when simmering personal antagonisms spill over. The episode did great personal damage to Macleod, who never shed the 'too clever by half' label. But the attack did not enhance Salisbury's standing. Home was embarrassed by the incident and stayed aloof from the subsequent controversies. Home's successor as Leader of the Lords, Viscount Hailsham, wound up the debate by taking the fight to Salisbury, whose insults he described as 'utterly unworthy'. The Earl of Perth, Macleod's Minister of State, made a personal statement the next morning pledging his loyalty to his Secretary of State. What had begun as an attack on Macleod, ended as a battle between the generations. 'It wasn't really about Africa', recalled one peer, 'it was pure class warfare – the upper-class peers against the middle-class peers.'[61] Home's silence may have been interpreted by Macleod as acquiescence in Salisbury's views.[62] If so, he was mistaken. The Foreign Secretary disapproved of Salisbury's attack, which was not the way he felt things should be conducted, but the episode did nothing to bring Home and Macleod closer together.

Nor did a second development, in November 1961, four weeks after Macleod became Leader of the House of Commons. For some time, Macleod had been working in a desultory fashion on a biography of Neville Chamberlain, the first such study since Feiling's pioneering book of 1946. It was a curious book, written largely to help with the expenses of his daughter's coming out, much of it ghosted by Peter Goldman, a former colleague from Conservative Research Department days.[63] What attracted him to the subject was Chamberlain's work at the

Ministry of Health and in the realms of Conservative policy-making, two strands of his own career. But the contentious part of the book was the section written by Goldman, which took a revisionist attitude towards Munich and appeasement. Macleod must have been aware of the hidden agenda in putting his name to such an interpretation, and for a variety of reasons the book duly ruffled many feathers. As the senior surviving figure of Chamberlain's circle, Home was disappointed with the portrait that emerged. Feiling had deliberately withheld some of Chamberlain's more acid criticisms of Stanley Baldwin, and in the immediate aftermath of Chamberlain's death, had generally used the primary material with discretion. The *raison d'être* for a new life should have been the opportunity for fuller revelations from Chamberlain's letters and diaries, seen in the context of a wider historical perspective. This Macleod failed to deliver. Macleod's project, which could have been a bridge between Home and himself, not least because of the basic admiration Macleod had for Chamberlain, was a lost opportunity. Following Salisbury's outburst, it seemed that Macleod had a trait for alienating himself from certain Conservatives of an older generation, though his stoutest champion remained Macmillan.

The Berlin crisis was a major concern for Home in his first spell in King Charles Street. In January 1961 Khrushchev had issued a six-month ultimatum for an end to Allied 'occupation' and for 'free city' status for Berlin. Otherwise, he would sign a separate bilateral treaty with Ulbricht's East German state and the West would have to negotiate with the East Germans for access to Berlin. Kennedy's failure to forge an agreement with Khruschev in Vienna in June 1961 was the prelude to the building of the Berlin Wall in August; of all the crises the West faced in the early 1960s, this was potentially the most serious.

On Home's first day in the Foreign Office, Berlin was on the agenda. 'It's all about zones, isn't it?' he said, an opening remark which caused a few raised eyebrows, but he understood the strategic issues well. The Berlin Wall was duly put in place by the East Germans in August, closing off the 'escape' route to the West and catching the holidaying British establishment off guard. The press finally caught up with Macmillan on the eighteenth fairway at Gleneagles, where his impatience with their questions led to some injudicious remarks. Home, at Douglas for the shooting, advised the Prime Minister to call a proper press conference and Home and his team prepared a statement which

Macmillan delivered at the Gleneagles Hotel. Its main aim was to lower the temperature.

Macmillan confided to a friend that all his colleagues were getting excited 'except my admirable colleague, the Foreign Secretary'.[64] But privately Macmillan was deeply anxious about the developments in Berlin and there was much telephoning of the White House. David Ormsby-Gore had taken up his appointment as British ambassador in Washington in June 1961, and had an excellent relationship with Kennedy. 'It was as if they had powers of telepathic communication.'[65] Ormsby-Gore's despatches to Home over the next two and a half years, on every conceivable topic from Khrushchev's intentions over Cuba to the White House's view on a Hailsham premiership, make fascinating reading with their incisive summaries of complex issues and trenchant views, often amusingly expressed. On Berlin, his summary was to the point: 'He [Kennedy] said that he would be most interested in any suggestions we might have for trying to bring home to Khrushchev the tremendous risks he would be running if he took unilateral action which threatened the security of West Berlin.'[66] Home monitored the Berlin situation and called for reports from those able to give first-hand accounts. The psychological aspects of the Berlin Wall were the ones on which the British Embassy in Bonn concentrated: 'Berlin has lost its function as the meeting place of Germans from all parts of the divided country, and the hope that this special function might ease the way to reunification has been dashed' ran one early despatch. 'Although it is recognised that the Russians have always had the power to seal off the Soviet sector … the fact that they have now plunged after hesitating so long has suggested to many West Berliners that the Russians now feel stronger than the West and are beginning to treat their obligations to the West with corresponding contempt.'[67]

On 19 August 1961, Home wrote to Rusk about developments in Berlin – notably the building of the Wall – since their meeting in Paris:

> I was sure that you were right in insisting in Paris that we must be getting on with positive moves towards negotiation. It does not seem to me that what has happened in Berlin since we met has in any way invalidated this. The prevention of East Berliners getting into West Berlin has never been a *casus belli* for us. We are concerned with Western access to Berlin and it is that we must maintain. Of course, we must do what is necessary to keep up West Berlin morale, but the main objective must be to … [persuade] the Soviets to join tacitly or implicitly in some system which will in fact

> ensure uninterrupted access to Berlin for the Allies and for necessary civilian traffic ... I do not think it impossible that the Russians might be ready to agree to something like the *status quo* in Berlin through channels of negotiation less spectacular than a meeting of Foreign Ministers. This may be a case of the lower the level of contact the greater likelihood there is of concessions and agreement. When you have time send me your views which I value very much.[68]

The fullest exchange of these views was to come at the Bermuda Conference in December, arranged to enable Kennedy and Macmillan to compare notes on their respective meetings with Adenauer and de Gaulle. The meeting with de Gaulle, at which both Berlin and the Common Market were on the agenda, had taken place at Birch Grove at the end of November. 'We must try to convince him that the Berlin situation cannot be allowed to drift or deteriorate,' Home wrote in a memorandum for Cabinet. 'Since 13 August it has changed radically for the worse. West Berlin has now become a liability to the West and it is positively necessary to try to improve it. If nothing is done there is a grave danger that the life of the city will wither away under our eyes. To some extent this is happening already, but the trend will be aggravated if the Western powers remain inactive ... Mr Khrushchev cannot be expected to come forward with proposals as General de Gaulle apparently thinks he should. It would enable us, incidentally, to put forward our own ideas ... for Berlin as an independent German city protected by allied forces, enjoying free communication with the outside world and living a life of its own. If General de Gaulle or Dr Adenauer agree to negotiations, our aim must be to finalise the Western negotiating position without delay. If not, a Western Four-Power meeting will have to be held to resolve our differences.'[69]

De Gaulle's visit to Birch Grove was notable for its security aspects, with much argument over where de Gaulle's supply of blood should be stored (Mrs Bell, the Macmillans' cook, objected to its being kept in the fridge beside the haddock), and for his formidable intransigence over the Common Market. Of this visit Macmillan remarked that the French leader showed 'all the rigidity of a poker without its occasional warmth'.[70] With the Cabinet, Macmillan adopted a more confident air. 'It would be premature to despair since President de Gaulle, like other great men, never yields to argument but occasionally to facts. An argument which appears to be repelled at the moment might sink in later.'[71]

The Bermuda Conference, from 20 to 23 December, was devoted to

Berlin, the Congo and Laos, together with discussions on nuclear tests, the Common Market and the growing mood of anti-colonialism in the United Nations. The pattern was for Kennedy and Macmillan to meet separately, while Rusk and Home discussed the day's agenda, pooling their conclusions in the late afternoon. Home discussed with Rusk the failure of the Security Council to condemn Indian action against Goa and pointed out that 'a large number of member states now disregarded the original objectives of the United Nations and were concerned only to use the Charter against the colonial powers'. At the follow-up meeting that day Kennedy asked Home about access to Berlin. Home said there were four main points on which the West might have to make concessions to get a settlement: first, some *de facto* recognition of the DDR [Deutsche Demokratische Republik]; second, recognition of the Oder-Neisse line; third, the West's occupation rights; and fourth, the links between West Berlin and the Federal Republic. So far as occupation rights were concerned, the West obviously could not give them up but might have to find a way to present the position in West Berlin as that of trustees for the people of the city. 'We might also strengthen our position by proving (by plebiscite or other means) that we were in West Berlin by consent of its people.'[72] On nuclear tests, the divisions were clear. The British were against further atmospheric tests, but wanted underground testing in the Nevada desert of the warhead of the long-range Skybolt missile system (part of the deal Eisenhower had negotiated with Macmillan in return for Polaris bases in Scotland). The Americans wanted access to Christmas Island, a British possession in the Pacific, to which Macmillan reluctantly agreed.

Kennedy's methods of working greatly impressed Home. He believed that Kennedy had made a mistake by meeting Khrushchev so soon in Vienna. 'Khrushchev, being a very shrewd man, probably summed the situation up fairly well, but his advisers almost certainly concluded that here was a young man around whom Khrushchev could make rings. They found out that they were wrong but only after the most anxious months of trial and error and brinkmanship.' But in Bermuda, Home appreciated Kennedy's qualities of stillness. 'He would say little, getting everyone else to talk, then ask a very few pointed, and sometimes awkward questions, never sparing his own advisers, and finally say, "Well, why cannot we do this or that? It seems the commonsense way." And it usually was ... he would not automatically accept a brief, and he always kept in reserve the right to vary or reject its conclusions. But, once the decision was taken, that was that, and there were no second thoughts or regrets.'[73] After Bermuda, Home knew that Kennedy was amenable to reason and essentially open-minded. Home's involvement in the Cuban missile crisis was conditioned by that knowledge.

Macmillan recognised the way Home juggled the various balls of the international situation and depended on him increasingly for advice and reassurance, from dealings with de Gaulle to the reshuffling of his government. On one occasion when Home was not a central confidant – the Night of the Long Knives in July 1962 – the ultimate loser was held to be Macmillan, whose reputation for 'unflappability' was dented. 'Fortunately, I was not too near the arras on that occasion,' Home said.[74]

The Foreign Office felt it was beneficial that the Secretary of State did not have to deal with what one ambassador called 'the tribunes of the people'. Another advantage of Home's appointment was that he knew all the troublemakers from his CRO days and was not browbeaten by them. Berlin, Congo and Laos were enough to try Job, but they were only the most regular of the day-to-day problems. South Africa had left the Commonwealth in May 1961, and become a Foreign Office responsibility. The West Indian Federation had been dissolved and decolonisation continued with the independence of Jamaica in August 1962; difficulties were simmering in British Guiana. Only his absence from the Commons masked his increasing importance in Macmillan's strategy. The Prime Minister acknowledged this gratefully. 'I do not think any Foreign Secretary has had a more difficult task than you,' Macmillan wrote in a 'Top Secret and Personal' letter in April 1962. 'There are so many things going on at the same time and all of them complicated. The world also is full of perfectionists and, I am afraid, of rather slick operators. There is no such thing today as confidence which is respected even between countries nominally allies. The nearest thing to real partnership in this respect is the relationship that you have built up with Rusk and that I seem to have with the President.'[75] That relationship was now to be severely tested: in October 1962 Russian nuclear missiles were detected in Cuba by American reconnaissance aircraft. What Macmillan called 'the world crisis' was at hand.[76]

10

The Cuban Missile Crisis

'If way to the Better there be,' wrote Thomas Hardy, 'it exacts a full look at the Worst.'[1] In October 1962 such a full look was the experience of millions over thirteen days. Although the Cuban missile crisis broke upon an unsuspecting world on 22 October 1962, with President Kennedy's broadcast to the American people that 'within the past week, unmistakable evidence has established the fact that a series of offensive missile sites is now in preparation on that imprisoned island',[2] the situation had been closely monitored by both the American and British governments for some time. Colonel Oleg Penkovsky, the most important Moscow contact of the CIA and MI6, had been supplying intelligence details for the West since April 1961.

The origins of the crisis lay in the overthrow in 1959 of the corrupt US-backed government of Fulgercio Batistá by Fidel Castro. Economic sanctions, backed by western governments and the International Monetary Fund, drove Castro to seek Soviet aid. When Kennedy took office he continued with Eisenhower's plan to allow Cuban supporters of Batistá to prepare an invasion of the island. In the meantime Cuba had sought export markets for its sugar crop, which America now refused to buy, in the Soviet Union. In April 1961 the disastrous Bay of Pigs invasion took place on the southern coast of Cuba. The invasion, which was a grievous blow to the new President's standing, drove Castro into an even more clearly defined anti-American stance. The Cuban leader sought military aid from Russia, which came in the form of intermediate ballistic missiles. A total of twenty-four Soviet SA-2 surface-to-air missiles (SAMs), then the most advanced weapons system, were initially installed in Cuba and as early as February 1962 Warsaw Pact countries were told that the missiles would be used to launch an attack on America if nuclear war broke out.[3] The threat to America's security could not have come in clearer form. Surveillance revealed to Kennedy the extent of the build-up of Russian bases in Cuba. In September 1962 the CIA had received reports from Cuban refugees of the situation on the island. On 16 October an American U2 plane took high altitude photographs of what the CIA positively identified as Russian-built nuclear missile sites in the course of construction, photographs with which Adlai Stevenson was later to confront Ambassador Zorin, at that time President of the Security Council with dramatic effect at the United Nations, a tactic urged upon Kennedy by the British Government. Intelligence reports calculated that the missiles on Cuba had a range of 2000 miles with a potential for killing 80 million Americans. In time, if the build-up was not checked, the range of the missiles would not be to Salt Lake City, but to the furthest reaches of California and even Alaska.

Alec Home was involved in the British response from the start. In 1961, when the overthrow of Castro was being planned, David Bruce, the American ambassador, approached the British government with a request that an airfield 'be available for use, if necessary, in mounting combat operations with tactical aircraft'. It was agreed that the Americans should have access to the island of Mayaguana in the Bahamas, though the condition was that 'nothing is to be put in writing'.[4] In the summer of 1962 Alec Home was consulted over American economic sanctions. On 26 June 1962 the President of the Board of Trade, Frederick Erroll, told the Cabinet that the United States Government was seeking restrictions on trade with Cuba. The Foreign Secretary then reported that he had already told Dean Rusk 'that the United Kingdom Government were doubtful about the efficacy of a general policy of applying economic sanctions to Communist countries; but he would prefer to pursue that argument as a general problem of policy than to adopt a position on Cuba which would not have the support of the other members of the Alliance'.[5] Even before Kennedy had informed Macmillan of the presence of Soviet missile sites, Cuba had been a dominating issue at the October Cabinets in Admiralty House, where Macmillan had moved whilst Downing Street was undergoing renovation. On 9 October, in a survey of the international situation, the Foreign Secretary had reported that current Russian activities in Cuba were causing intense feeling in the United States, where some saw them as a goad to provoke a second Bay of Pigs. President Kennedy 'seemed inclined to believe that the Soviet Government were deliberately increasing the scale of Russian activity in Cuba in order to provoke ... intervention, which they would then use as a pretext for the forcible occupation of West Berlin'. Home thought such a development unlikely: 'It was more likely that they [the Russians] would continue to use the Cuban situation to exacerbate President Kennedy's difficulties and then offer a reduction of tension over Cuba in return for concessions over Berlin.'[6]

The Foreign Secretary was kept abreast of the developing situation through extensive briefings from David Ormsby-Gore in Washington; Sir Frank Roberts, Ambassador in Moscow; and 'our man in Havana', Herbert Marchant.[7] Ormsby-Gore had already given Alec Home an insight into Kennedy's preferred methods of working in a series of letters in November 1961, which were to be of inestimable value in predicting how the President might act under pressure. Of one meeting he attended in the Oval Office, Ormsby-Gore wrote to the Foreign Secretary:

> The Presidential advisers expressed their views in strong terms and it was fascinating to have a ringside view of the President's technique. Although he constantly intervened in the debate with many pointed questions, he never gave anything like a complete summary of his views on any of the points under discussion and no matter how hard he was pressed the decision he was finally likely to take remained wrapped in mystery. This was, as I understand it, very much the same technique as was used by Roosevelt and, of course, there are many respects in which the President tries to model himself on his distinguished predecessor.[8]

Of a private talk with Kennedy on the possibility of nuclear conflict with the Russians, Ormsby-Gore had reported in 1961:

> When I said to him that I thought it was inconceivable that a democratic nation would be prepared to go to the brink of nuclear war without there having been an attempt to talk the matter over with the Russians, he said that he was not sure that this was true of the United States. He personally felt that they ought to think in this way, but the attitude of complete and total distrust of the Russians had been so effectively created by the press and radio that if he cared to tell the people that it was useless to negotiate they would probably agree with him. He did not mean to suggest that he thought that this was in any way a wise thing to do, but he thought it did indicate an important difference in the political climate in our two countries.

Alec Home showed this letter to Macmillan, who minuted: 'This is a very important letter. It is *not* very encouraging.' The seriousness with which Kennedy regarded the Cuban situation was unequivocally spelt out in a further letter to Home eleven days later. Ormsby-Gore wrote: 'On Cuba, he said ... that somehow Castro would have to be brought down ... the present situation was intolerable and they would not cease from exploring every possible means of laying Castro low.' How this was to be achieved was not clear. 'In view of his experience in April [the Bay of Pigs invasion], I do not think we need fear any ill-considered adventure going off at half-cock.'[9]

These communications remained very much in Home's mind when a few months later the Cuban Crisis reached boiling point. He believed that Kennedy was essentially open-minded and was amenable to well-argued, non-partisan argument. But also he was aware that in the end Kennedy might be prepared to launch a nuclear attack. The importance of working on the first characteristic, to avoid the second course of action, was paramount in his discussions with Macmillan on the best course to adopt during the period of the telephone conversations with the White House in October 1962.

Sir Frank Roberts advised on developments in Russia, especially the uncertain state of Khrushchev's health in 1962. 'Khrushchev was clearly ill at New Year's Eve reception', he reported in his first despatch of the year. Though Khrushchev was in better form by March – 'cracking jokes for the best part of a talk lasting nearly two hours' – Roberts felt there were question marks over his long-term position.[10] Some 'big gesture' might yet be attempted. The interpreter Ted Orchard prepared a paper on Khrushchev for Home, which the Foreign Secretary sent on to the Prime Minister.[11] The feeling in the Foreign Office was that Khrushchev's position was by no means secure and that his braggadocio, as at the United Nations, was as much for home consumption as to browbeat other nations. Roberts's insights convinced Home that when the ultimate was reached in the stakes of nuclear confrontation, Khrushchev would back down. Home had the utmost respect for Frank Roberts with his experience of Munich, Yalta, the Berlin air-lift and, as the United Kingdom's Permanent Representative on the North Atlantic Council in 1958, the second Berlin crisis. Roberts reported that Cuba was not the same crisis in Moscow that it was in the West, people were not waking up wondering if the world might end that day. This analysis was confirmed by the Northern Department of the Foreign Office and a senior figure from the Hungarian Embassy at a private lunch with a

British diplomat. 'I don't know what you are worrying about,' the Hungarian said, 'we have lived in Russia's shadow for years in Eastern Europe. Khrushchev will back off.'[12] Alec Home's basic premise was that the situation would lead to nuclear conflict only if the Americans lost their nerve. Those in authority in Moscow knew that Khrushchev would stand back from the Rubicon of all-out nuclear war. Khrushchev's miscalculation was in underestimating the escalation of the stakes and Kennedy's resolve: the man he was now dealing with was not the novice of Vienna. After the announcement of the American naval blockade, the onus was on Khrushchev. From the moment that the first Russian boats were stopped on 24 October, Kennedy had in effect prevailed, however anxious the postlude might prove. When Kennedy's ultimatum was made public Frank Roberts told Alec Home that there was no sign of panic buying in Moscow and that people were going about their business in an orderly manner. The atmosphere both men remembered in London before Munich was notably absent. Censorship of news in Moscow was not a factor. People were aware of what was going on, but there was never the sense of impending armageddon that many experienced in the West.[13] Khruschev had never wanted a war and had to get out of the crisis into which he had plunged the Soviet Union, without disaster. In fact he did better than that in the end by getting a commitment from Kennedy not to attack Castro. The British contribution could best be made by tendering advice that encouraged Kennedy to avoid situations which led to an unacceptable loss of face by Khrushchev. If the Russian leader could, in however small a form, be given some kind of 'bail-out' clause, then the unthinkable could still be avoided. Dean Rusk already felt the same, believing that in negotiation one should always put oneself in the place of one's opponent. How would he feel? What would make him act in the way one might want? George Ball, the American Under-Secretary of State, urged a blockade of Cuba, rather than an invasion. On 24 October Kennedy asked Macmillan, with Home in the room as he was throughout the hot-line telephone conversations, the $64,000 dollar question – 'Should he take out Cuba?' Macmillan said that he would 'like to think about this and send an answer', admitting 'it's just like a revue called "Beyond the Fringe" which takes off the leading politicians'.[14] Fortunately George Ball's blockade option coincided with the advice the President was getting from Robert Kennedy, the Attorney-General, who also had a pivotal, defusing role in his private meetings with Soviet Ambassador Anatoly Dobrynin to end the crisis. Macmillan's telegram on 25

October confirmed American strategic thinking. There would be no nuclear strike.

One who did not receive his due over Cuba was Marchant. Thanks to his perceptive despatches, the crisis was not as unexpected in Britain as Washington thought. What made Marchant's analysis so valuable and even-handed was that he was not anti-Castro, he felt that the western view of Castro as a communist bogeyman was simplistic and flawed. In fact Castro impressed many western diplomats with his social concern for his people and with the immense progress made in Cuba after the 1959 revolution, particularly in the advances towards universal schooling and the provision of a free medical service. Before that the rich had been immensely rich and by western standards the poor had lived in conditions of unimaginable hardship. Castro was also politically astute in that he always watched his flank. He had a sense of pride in what he had achieved, but knew that the 'worms' as he called them, the die-hards who favoured the old regime, were disenchanted with his brave new world. Castro was fiercely proud and independent as a personality, despite the economic conditions which led him to seek shelter under the Soviet umbrella. He did not begin as a Marxist and many of the top Russians were anything but convinced of his 'true faith', seeing him as something of a potential Tito, but one whose proximity to the United States kept him under a modicum of Soviet control. Yet Marchant's admiration was never rose-tinted. His diplomatic experience left him in no doubt that the missile crisis was potentially the most dangerous facing the superpowers since the Berlin air lift of 1948. Marchant wrote to Home during those thirteen days not only about the larger issues, but of ordinary civilian life in Havana. 'Castro issued an order of "war alarm" at 5.40 p.m. yesterday and according to the press, Cuban forces have already been placed on war footing. There is so far very little evidence of this in Havana all is actually calm ... with no sign of enthusiasm or alarm.' The juxtaposition of Marchant's evidence alongside that coming from Moscow gave Alec Home an up-to-date overview of what was happening in the two capitals. For instance, the same day Frank Roberts reported from Moscow: 'It may be worth reporting that the Cuban ambassador, whose call I happened to be returning yesterday, was surprisingly calm over rumours already coming out of Washington. He was very understanding about the problems of an American election and about President Kennedy's present attitude to Cuba.' The next day (24 October) Roberts reported to Home that Khruschev had been seen at the Bolshoi 'applauding an

American singer'.[15] Marchant telegrammed also on that day. 'There is an unnatural calm here as in the edge of a cyclone. This is partly the result of the government's policy to keep the temperature down and morale up by continuing as far as possible business as usual. But it also stems from a mood of dazed anxiety and we have nothing to suggest that the average man and woman – very many of them now in military uniform – has a burning desire to die for the cause.'[16] Home could thus piece together the jigsaw and the 'mood of dazed anxiety' that Marchant so graphically described. For his part, Home remained calm (unlike some of his colleagues), though he was exhausted by the crisis, and the succession of sleepless nights. He used the occasion of a speech to the International Chamber of Commerce in London to outline in fiercely anti-communist terms the British government's response to the crisis:

> The first essential is to recognise that international communism as practised by Russia today is both opportunist and two-faced. We have lately had examples of these two techniques. In the Congo the Russians sought to establish control of that African country, in which few Russians had previously set foot, within a few days of the breakdown of local government. In Cuba they stepped in last year to take advantage of a situation which was already explosive. In Berlin they created a crisis where, but for their action, there was no need for any crisis at all. The purpose of all these adventures is undoubtedly one thing – that is to increase the area of communist domination ... the evidence is overwhelming that that is the communist objective and unless we understand the broad strategy of communism we will come to the wrong decisions when confronted by individual situations.

After this uncompromising opening, the Foreign Secretary turned to the immediate situation in Cuba:

> By putting medium-range and intermediate-range ballistic missiles into Cuba Russia is deliberately placing her own power in a position to do three things – to threaten the United States, to threaten the Caribbean, and beyond those two, to threaten South America. We must recognise that this is plainly an act of power.
>
> At a time when the non-dissemination of nuclear weapons to non-nuclear countries is on the agenda at Geneva, Russia introduces these weapons into new places. At a time when the United Nations, actually this week, is beginning to debate this question and trying to carry on discussions, that is the time when the Russians do what

> they have not (repeat not) done in Eastern Europe – that is, put their offensive weapons on the soil of a Satellite.

Home emphasised the dishonesty of Khrushchev's position:

> Only last week, Mr Khruschev instructed Mr Gromyko to assure President Kennedy that there were no offensive weapons in Cuba and Russia had no intention of putting them there. Within a week, that statement by the architect of Soviet policy proved that those words were only said to deceive …
>
> Meanwhile I can only say to our own countrymen that the Prime Minister and myself, upon whom the main burden of decision must fall, will, once we have checked the present fever, play our full part in an attempt to end the cold war and do everything we possibly can to co-operate with all countries, and the Russians if they will come in, in the creative tasks of peace.
>
> One other alternative is there for us. As I ventured to say to the United Nations only a few weeks ago: 'Man is now at the point of choice and the choice is this: whether we blow ourselves to bits or whether we sit down round the table and negotiate and negotiate again, however long that process lasts.'
>
> That is the choice we have before us today.[17]

In this process, there was no shortage of unsolicited advice from many quarters. Alec Home filtered out what Rudyard Kipling would have called 'the Comforters'. When the crisis broke, one of the figures who rang up offering to help was the osteopath Dr Stephen Ward, who told Home's officials that if they wished he could see the Soviet Naval Attaché, Captain Yevgeny Ivanov, for off-the-record soundings.[18] This was not an offer of which Alec Home availed himself. The Foreign Office knew of Ivanov's intelligence activities, and as early as August 1961 the Cabinet had discussed Ward's position as an intermediary with the Russians.[19] Harold Caccia telegrammed to Frank Roberts in Moscow, letting him know that Captain Yevgeny Ivanov, Assistant Naval Attaché had had meetings with 'a private individual', adding that 'we have always been told the results of these contacts'.[20] Ward and Ivanov were background figures at the time, though before the year was out, their names were to be widely known for other reasons.

For the Foreign Office the abiding memory of the crisis was that it unfolded in two phases. Initially, there was disbelief: the gung-ho

Americans were being American, waiting to replicate the Bay of Pigs. Then the President broadcast details of the photographic evidence and informed opinion changed. Recollection is vivid three decades later for those involved in those anxious times – the quick steps of diplomats crunching along the path from Horseguards Parade; the hidden messages in the tone of Kennedy's speeches and knowing how serious things were from what was not said; the chaos of the new hotline between Number 10 and the White House, the buttons of which neither head of government understood; and the everpresent Alec Home, his suit more dishevelled as the hours ticked by; the lights going on in Whitehall in the October dusk.

The flavour of Alec Home's life during this intense period is best indicated in Harold Macmillan's diary. That Macmillan found the energy to note down, day by day, the unfolding of events shows remarkable stamina. On the day the crisis broke, he had 'a hurried lunch with Alec Home'. By then they knew that the President would be making his speech. David Bruce, the United States ambassador, and Chester Cooper, a CIA veteran, who was later to become Averell Harriman's deputy as America's ambassador-at-large, had promised Macmillan that they would get a copy of the President's speech to him in advance of the broadcast. This was finally telephoned through to Downing Street at 5 p.m. London time.[21] 'Alec Home came over and together we worked out a reply to the President' recorded Macmillan. The Suez analogy weighed heavy on their minds. For Alec Home the parallels of 1940 were also very close. On 4 April 1940 Chamberlain had spoken of Hitler missing the bus. Both felt on reflection that if Kennedy 'missed the bus' then, in Macmillan's words, 'he may never get rid of Cuban rockets except by trading them for Turkish, Italian or other bases'.[22] The worst scenario would be a trading off of Berlin for Cuba. The first telephone contact with Kennedy was at 1.30 a.m. (GMT). Recordings exist of all these conversations, and at times the tone is surprisingly low-key, as though words could not match the gravity of the situation; at others the tense staccato of the dialogue marks the drama and determination. Occasionally, Macmillan breaks off his conversation with the President to ask Home for his views, while Kennedy continues to pour out words.

Did these calls have an impact on the decision-making process? McGeorge Bundy, assistant to the President for National Security Affairs, said the 'Cuba Phone Calls' were 'more to touch a base than because of a sense that he really wanted to know what Macmillan thought about a thing'.[23] The transcripts show that what Kennedy required was 'an assurance that a tough line of interception would … be supported by the British Government'.[24] Peter Thorneycroft, the Defence Secretary, recalls that Alec Home looked 'at how a very difficult hand ought to be played even if he wasn't playing it himself' and then it 'was for President Kennedy to ask any advice that he might want from Macmillan or Home'.[25] Even if Kennedy did not ask for specific policy options (apart from the $64,000 question), Home knew that Kennedy was a good listener and operated eclectically, so the conversations were the chance the British had to lower the temperature and give reassurance. Whatever Macmillan felt inwardly (and at times his diary reflects despair), he spoke with great composure, communicating calm, one of the most important contributions during the crisis Home thought.[26] A problem on the British side was that Kennedy's calls ignored London time. 'We were consulted throughout the whole of the crisis before the final decisions were taken. Indeed, we were so closely consulted that, as the President seemed to forget that midnight – which was the time of his last telephone conversation with me – was 5 a.m. our time, neither Sir Alec Home nor I slept at all during the whole seven days.'[27]

In Cabinet at 10.30 on 23 October, Macmillan brought his colleagues up to date on the position since he had first been warned by Bruce two days earlier that the President had a personal message, 'the first intimation to him of the chain of events which had led to the imposition of the United States blockade of Cuba'. During the first telephone conversation the previous evening President Kennedy 'had reiterated his view that firmness offered the best chance of avoiding the outbreak of a third world war and had recalled the lesson of Hitler'. Alec Home, who was now put in charge of draft changes to the forthcoming Queen's Speech for the State Opening of Parliament on 30 October, told the Cabinet that he 'thought it unlikely that Mr Khrushchev wanted to start a war. It was more probable that he was seeking to improve his bargaining position, particularly in relation to Berlin, and that he wanted the US Government to appreciate from their own experience the Soviet reaction to the presence of US missile bases in Europe close to Russia and their determination to secure their removal'.[28] Macmillan and Home had worked late the previous night on draft messages to Commonwealth prime ministers, and Home now finalised these telegrams. The central point he emphasised was that no connection should be deduced between the Cuban situation and Berlin. 'Where necessary you should say *on-the-record* that Berlin has nothing to do with Cuba. Berlin and Cuba are entirely different subjects. West Berlin threatens nobody and there is no military base in West Berlin.'[29] Later that day, Home gave his speech to the National Committee of the International Chamber of Commerce, a speech from which Sir Patrick Dean was to quote at the United Nations.

An unexpected difficulty now arose in the form of a confidential Memorandum from Lord Dilhorne, the Lord Chancellor, on the legality or otherwise of the American action. 'The imposition of the "quarantine" cannot be justified as "pacific" blockade under international law' wrote Dilhorne. 'In fact, the United States' conduct is not in conformity with international law.'[30] The Lord Chancellor was backed by the Attorney-General, the Solicitor-General and the Chief Legal Adviser to the Foreign Office, and this opinion, if widely disseminated, could have had grave political implications. Sir Frank Soskice, the distinguished lawyer and member of the Shadow Cabinet, was to dissent from this view, as Dilhorne reported to the Prime Minister in a supplementary letter on 25 October.[31] Although Home authorised a Foreign Office Draft on Legality that read 'H.M.G. regret that after careful consideration they are not satisfied as to the legality of the blockade measures to be taken by the United States against Cuba',[32] he was anxious to avoid any public statement. After the State Opening of Parliament, however, questions might well be asked of the Lord Chancellor in the Upper House. Accordingly Home wrote a Memorandum for Macmillan:

Cuba – Legality of the United States Blockade

> Some time before Parliament meets I would like a word about this. I don't much like serving written notice on the United States now but what I am concerned about is what is said in the House of Lords. I should have thought it would be impossible for the Lord Chancellor to refuse to give an opinion if he is directly challenged to do so. But if he has to give an opinion it may be difficult for him to fudge it. And yet I am very anxious that we should not publicly take sides against the United States by saying that Her Majesty's Government doubt whether the blockade is legally justified.[33]

Although he did not copy this Memorandum to anyone other than the Prime Minister, Home told Sir George Coldstream, the Clerk of the Crown and the Lord Chancellor's Private Secretary, of his views.

Dilhorne was thus forewarned of difficulties that might arise after 30 October. By then the moment had passed, but Home was responsive to possible complications. He also kept Buckingham Palace informed of Foreign Office developments through Sir Michael Adeane, the Queen's Private Secretary.

On 24 October, Macmillan wrote, 'A confusing morning, with Lord Home, Harold Caccia and much sending and receiving of telegrams. An anxious day, too. For the first clash will soon begin, if the Russian ships sail on.'[34] One of the telegrams on which Home worked that morning was for the United Kingdom Mission at the United Nations in New York:

> If I am right in assuming that the President's mind is moving in the direction of negotiations before the crisis worsens, I think that the most fruitful course for you to pursue at present might be to try to elicit from him on what lines he may be contemplating a conference, what its scope and purpose might be and whether he has any ideas of how and at what moment to launch a proposal for discussions.
>
> ... One idea that occurs to me is that the President might wish to reconsider his present contention that the crisis arises from a conflict between the Soviet Union and the United States. If he could say that American concern was primarily directed against the situation in Cuba for which he holds Cuba responsible and need not necessarily involve the vital interests of the two major forces, this might well take the heat out of the situation and prepare the way for a conference.
>
> ... A straight bargain about bases has obvious disadvantages. It might strike the neutrals as cynical and involve us in serious difficulties with some N.A.T.O. countries, quite apart from Berlin. It strikes me that a more favourable field from the Western point of view would be that of disarmament and the permanent need for reducing the dangers of nuclear confrontation. What we might work for would be a summons to Heads of Government by the President and Khrushchev to an immediate meeting with the object of deciding that Stage 1 of disarmament as contemplated in the German negotiations should be carried out within a specified time limit. I realise of course that formidable difficulties would arise in the negotiations themselves, where we should be faced immediately with the inspection issue and other basic differences between the Western and the Soviet proposals. The proposal might also break down because the Russians refused to dismantle their weapons in Cuba as a preliminary. But I think it is worth exploring and if you

see no objection I should be grateful if you could sound the President on these lines.[35]

Late that evening, Kennedy asked Macmillan directly on the transatlantic telephone link whether 'he should take out Cuba'. 'A talk with President at 11 p.m., Home and Caccia present', Macmillan recorded laconically of this extraordinary conversation. His considered response was sent in a telegram the next day: 'I have been thinking over the 64,000 dollar question which you posed on the telephone. After much reflection, I think that events have gone too far. While circumstances may arise in which such action would be right and necessary, I think that we are now all in a phase where you must try to obtain your objectives by other means.' Macmillan gave a further reason in his diary for the advice: 'The "guilty" ships seem to be turning away. At least 3 or 4 have done so. We also know (from British intelligence) that a number of Russian ships not so far on in the queue are returning via Baltic to Polish or Russian ports.'[36]

Despite the late call and the discussions following it, Macmillan and Home met at 9.30 on 25 October, St Crispin's Day as Home recalled, to finalise the statement that was to be made in Parliament. 'I told the Cabinet about Cuba,' recorded Macmillan 'which they seem quite happy to leave to me and Alec Home.'[37] In his report to the Cabinet at 2.45 p.m., the Foreign Secretary felt that there were three pre-requisites for a settlement of the dispute: the dismantling of the missile sites in Cuba, the stationing of UN observers in Cuba to witness this dismantling and also in Havana to scrutinise incoming cargoes. 'It did not seem that there was any action that the Prime Minister could usefully take at the present juncture,' Home said. 'An early visit to Washington, for example, could easily be misinterpreted as a mission of appeasement.'[38] Yet Mr Loginov, the Soviet Chargé d'Affaires in London, had suggested to Home that the UK government should intervene in some manner. He could not have bargained for the reception he got. Just before Loginov's arrival at the Ambassador's Entrance of the Foreign Office, Home had received Marchant's latest telegram from Havana. 'The people at large still show neither enthusiasm nor panic, but there is rather more underlying tension.'[39] Home was in no mood to be told what the UK Government should or should not be doing by Loginov, who opened the meeting by telling the Foreign Secretary that the Soviet government 'considered that an extremely dangerous situation had been created by the United States in establishing a blockade off Cuba'. Nothing could have been more calculated to infuriate Alec Home. He asked Loginov why the Russians had put their missiles into Cuba. Loginov replied that he did not know what missiles were there 'but in any case the American government had put missiles in Turkey which were directed against his country'. Privately, Home regarded this as a hopeful sign that Khrushchev was interested in bargaining, not war. But to Loginov he concentrated on the disingenuousness of the Russian approach. 'The Soviet practice of duplicity made immense difficulties for us', he continued. 'Mr Gromyko had been sent by his government on the 18th of October specifically to tell President Kennedy that they did not wish to install these offensive guided weapons in Cuba. Yet within a few days the Americans had discovered that the Russians had already made considerable progress in installing just these weapons. This was what I meant by deception.' Home said that the first step now should be to get United Nations observers into Cuba and then 'to make real progress in a disarmament conference for a general reduction of weapons. Since Mr Khrushchev had sent Mr Gromyko to tell President Kennedy that they did not want these weapons in Cuba, then surely they would have no objection to observers going in to inspect.' He told Loginov that it was up to the Russians to remove the offensive weapons as soon as possible. 'They would be threatening the Canadians next.' He emphasised that there could be no progress until such weapons were reduced. Summing up, the Foreign Secretary said that 'what the Russians had done in Cuba was an act of power which had gone wrong and had done the Russians great damage. We were thinking hard about what we could do to help in this dangerous situation but the Russians must remove these weapons from Cuba before anything could be done.'[40]

October 26 was a day of waiting. 'No early news from America', Macmillan wrote.[41] Home continued to receive up-to-date accounts from Roberts in Moscow and Marchant in Havana. 'There is no longer any real attempt to conceal the American charge of the introduction of missiles into Cuba', telegrammed Roberts on 26 October. From Havana Marchant reported that 'At 0025 hours, October 26, members of my staff saw convoy of about thirty vehicles moving towards city. It was significant that this movement was taking place at night, whereas the convoy described in my telegram No. 463 took place during the day'.[42]

Meanwhile, news of Home's meeting with Loginov had been sent to Washington. David Ormsby-Gore gave Home the American response:

> Mr Rusk telephoned me last night to ask whether I could tell him anything about your conversation with the Soviet Chargé d'Affaires in London yesterday. As you can imagine the Americans are anxious to have every shred of evidence which can help them in assessing Soviet thinking at present.[43]

By Saturday 27 October the crisis had reached a new peak. The American pilot who had provided photographic evidence of the build-up of Soviet missiles was shot down and killed. This led to wild rejoicing in Cuba. The same day Kennedy received two contradictory letters from Khrushchev. The first was, in essence, a capitulation in return for a guarantee that there would no invasion of Cuba; the second, much tougher, demanded negotiations about the American missiles in Turkey. Kennedy's master-stroke was to ignore the second letter and reply to the first.

On the morning of 28 October, Macmillan called a meeting of ministers, including Alec Home, Rab Butler, Peter Thorneycroft and Edward Heath, at Admiralty House to discuss the letter the British government would send to Khrushchev in support of the American demand for the removal of the missiles. The message that was sent at noon urged Khrushchev to turn to disarmament questions. Thorneycroft was later asked if he thought that nuclear war would break out. 'The thought crossed my mind that it might', he said. 'I particularly remember that Sunday morning; Whitehall deserted, it was very quiet, rather a lovely morning, and just walking in there to the Ministry of Defence and thinking "My God, I wonder whether this really is it".'[44] News of Khrushchev's acceptance of Kennedy's terms came while the ministers were having lunch. The Russian leader promised 'to dismantle the weapons' and 'to crate and return them to the Soviet Union'.[45] It was a total *volte-face*. As Macmillan wrote in his diary: 'a complete climb-down (*if* they keep their word)'.[46]

Although there was a sense of euphoria, Home's reaction was one of caution. The Northern Department of the Foreign Office was asked to produce a paper on the origins of the crisis, and he appointed Sir Evelyn Shuckburgh to head an *ad hoc* committee on the aftermath of Cuba. For Shuckburgh one of the central unanswered questions was how far Gromyko had deliberately lied to Kennedy, an issue 'important to our future relations with him'. In a letter to Ormsby-Gore on 29 October, Home warned of the possible ramifications for Berlin:

> The Cuban lesson cannot have increased anybody's confidence in Soviet undertakings. Whatever assurances might be received from Khrushchev at this time, the geographical exposure of West Berlin would remain a fact and we should not be able to feel that the problem was disposed of because of a Soviet promise not to intervene. They possess too many different means of making things difficult for Berlin.[47]

In a further letter of 31 October, Home requested that the question of Gromyko's foreknowledge and untruthfulness about the missiles should be investigated. Meanwhile, the American Department of the Foreign Office provided an initial report on likely developments. 'There is no doubt that the Americans will wish to retain the maximum room for manoeuvre against Castro' ran one section. Another acknowledged that trade questions would be a thorny problem in the months ahead. 'Continuance of a tough American policy towards Cuba will raise problems for H.M.G.'[48] In this lay the genesis of the Leyland Bus controversy of February 1964.

In Moscow, Frank Roberts was coming to the end of his mission as ambassador. In a series of valedictory telegrams, he reflected on the lessons of the missile crisis, certain that Home had played a significant role in the Soviet withdrawal, and on its lessons for Berlin:

> It is clear that Khrushchev feared early US action against Cuba and, in this direct confrontation between the two world powers and two men Khrushchev and Kennedy, your own strong warnings to the Soviet Chargé d'Affaires in London no doubt played a part in bringing Khrushchev to call a halt to his Cuba blackmail, even sooner than I had dared to hope.
>
> So far as Berlin is concerned the significant factor of the Cuba affair is that Khrushchev unquestionably backed off when the chips were seen to be down. We know this; Khrushchev knows it; and a large part of effective world opinion, in neutral and bloc areas as well as in the West, also noted it.[49]

Mending of fences was now the order of the day. Vasily Kuznetsov, First Deputy Minister of Foreign Affairs, was sent as Russian emissary to the United Nations, his brief being to negotiate the final stages of the crisis. Kuznetsov's frankness (he admitted that the Soviets had placed forty-two missiles in Cuba) was an eye-opener for Adlai Stevenson, who said that he 'had been staggered at the size and "enormity" of the Soviet adventure in Cuba'. Its failure would cost the Soviets dear. 'The exposure of Soviet perfidy ... had lost them much of the goodwill which they had painfully built up with the uncommitted nations.'[50] Rusk also told Ormsby-Gore that he would always treasure Alec Home's personal message of congratulation. Without British support from the start there would have been no successful outcome. 'Both sides had been looking into the mouth of the cannon and the Soviets had blinked first.'[51] The considered Foreign Office view was that Cuba had been deleterious to Khruschev. '[It] may well weaken his authority within the Communist bloc and may also weaken to some extent his personal position at home. It will give substance to the Chinese claims that he is ineffective as the leader of world Communism against imperialism.'[52] This view was to prove the correct prognosis. In the Cuban crisis lay the seeds of Khrushchev's downfall, which happened during the 1964 general election in Britain. Ironically, Alec Douglas-Home and Nikita Khrushchev were to surrender power within hours of each other.

On 31 October, the Queen's Private Secretary wrote to the Prime Minister to thank him and the Foreign Secretary for all they had done to keep the Palace informed:

> As I mentioned to you last night, I made a rough note of the various contacts which took place during the last weekend between the Queen on the one hand, and yourself and the Foreign Secretary on the other. These were numerous and as a result Her Majesty was fully and continuously informed of what was going on in the relations between this country, the United States and the U.S.S.R.
>
> The Queen knows very well what a heavy strain both you and Lord Home and your staffs were working under during these days and she wishes you to know how much she appreciates the trouble which was taken in your own office and in the Foreign Office to see that she was kept up-to-date with the rapidly changing news.[53]

The same day Home spoke to the Conference of the Institute of Directors. He could not let the moment pass without alluding to the lessons of the Cuban Crisis. The action that he felt most disquieting was the blatant deception of the Russian Government. 'If, before this incident, verification of Russia's word was necessary, it is now much more necessary.' That is why he felt that the threat would never truly be over until the Russians had kept their word and removed their missiles from Cuba. 'There has been a good deal of speculation about Russia's motives. To me they are quite clear. Their motive was to test the will of the United States and to see how the President of the United States, in particular, would react against a threat of force. If the President had faltered for one moment in a matter which affected the security of the United States, no ally of America would have had confidence in United States protection ever again.'[54]

In a two-day debate in the House of Lords at the beginning of November, Home said that verification was vital in any disarmament agreement with the Soviets, as Cuba had proved that their word was not to be trusted. 'There is one thing that I should like to make plain to the Russians today', he said. 'If in this field of disarmament, as in so many others, they are playing for a win, then they will not get it.'[55] In the winding down period after Cuba, Kennedy continued to ring Macmillan over a range of difficulties, though gradually the continuing problem of Laos took precedence over Cuba. At 10.55 p.m. on 15 November, Kennedy made a long call on both issues. 'I will talk to Alec Home who is here', said Macmillan.[56] Two days later Kennedy wrote suggesting a meeting with Macmillan on 18 and 19 December. Macmillan wished to see de Gaulle over the British application to join the EEC, so it was arranged that Macmillan and Home would meet de Gaulle at Rambouillet on 15 December and travel to Nassau three days later. Both summits were to prove among the most difficult diplomatic occasions that either figure had experienced. Before they went to France, Alec Home invited Macmillan and his wife to Douglas for a rest.

'Dorothy and I came up on on Thursday night [22 November] to Douglas. We have had two very good days shooting, including two little grouse drives yesterday afternoon', Macmillan wrote on 25 November. 'Alec and Elizabeth Home are charming hosts and we had a very agreeable party ... We went this afternoon to the little church in Douglas. The castle is now completely destroyed and the park is rather a sad sight – but it's vy attractive country.'[57] Although Macmillan was exhausted in the aftermath of the Cuban crisis, the house party atmosphere encouraged him to take stock of his strategy for the forthcoming summits and to ruminate with his Foreign Secretary on the way ahead. The Douglas visit confirmed his view that informality should be the keynote of the American meeting, and he wrote to Ormsby-Gore along these lines: 'If we do have a meeting I am anxious that it should be on the Bermuda model, a sort of house party, rather than a formal meeting with a great many people present'.[58]

Macmillan and Home also had time to reflect on the past month.

Both agreed that by any standards the Cuban crisis had been a climacteric in the Cold War. There was quiet satisfaction that the British had been able to play some positive role, however small in the overall perspective, though it was not until the publication of Macmillan's final volume of memoirs in 1973 that the extent of this involvement was first publicly appreciated. From being berated as a neglected ally, whose influence was non-existent (very much the Opposition stance in 1962), Harold Macmillan has emerged as a calming influence on the Kennedy administration. It is important not to exaggerate British influence during the Cuban crisis. Macmillan was not a major player in the decision-making process, but he was a man with whom Kennedy could share his loneliness.[59] Alec Home felt that the British Prime Minister was not somebody to whom the young President turned for advice, but that he served as a sounding board for Kennedy's ideas. Alec Home recalled later that Kennedy 'told me several times how much he valued being able to talk with Mr Macmillan and with the British because he could do so without reserve – something he could not do with any other people'.[60]

If the Prime Minister's role during the Cuban crisis should not be discounted, nor should Alec Home's steadying influence on Macmillan. The Prime Minister, whose personality sometimes led him to betray to his inner circle of confidants a nervous vulnerability that was masked from the public gaze, often sought reassurance. The loyal Sancho Panza to his mercurial Don Quixote varied over the years. During the Moscow visit of February 1959 when Khrushchev was at his most intransigent, this steadying role was provided by his then Foreign Secretary, Selwyn Lloyd, 'always sensible, calm and a steadying influence during the bad times of the visit', as the British ambassador in Moscow at the time, Sir Patrick Reilly, privately recorded.[61] During the long, sleepless hours of October 1962, Alec Home fulfilled a similar role. The Foreign Secretary's role as a go-between was not so much between the British government and the President, as between Macmillan and Dean Rusk, the American Secretary of State. He also played a significant part in influencing the Russian Diplomatic Corps in London. David Bruce attributed the successful outcome to the team work of all involved and 'the confidence reposed by the Prime Minister in his Secretary of State for Foreign Affairs, Lord Home, and by President Kennedy in his Secretary of State Dean Rusk'.[62] They proved a formidable quartet. And Alec Home was by no means the least formidable. For the Foreign Secretary, there were no 'ifs and buts', as he pointed out unhesitatingly to Mr Loginov on 25 October. The missiles had disturbed the balance. They were a new factor. Therefore they would have to go. The missiles in Turkey did not come into it. They already existed and were part of the *status quo*.

In their Douglas talks Macmillan and Home also discussed the responsibilities the superpowers had towards the rest of the world. Brinkmanship was too dangerous and unacceptable as a diplomatic strategy; steps had to be taken urgently to avoid conflict between America and Russia. A hotline with teleprinter facilities was set up between Moscow and Washington, and there was general acceptance that nuclear arms control talks should be held, which achieved some success the following year with the signing of the Nuclear Test Ban Treaty, when the three Foreign Secretaries of the Cuban Crisis – Gromyko, Rusk and Home – met in happier circumstances. Out of the worst, a better had come. The Cuban confrontation was of particular significance in Home's first spell at the Foreign Office. It was the third world crisis of which he had intimate experience, but Cuba was on a different plane. First the consequences of miscalculation were unprecedented for the future of humanity. Secondly, it was a period when Alec Home was at the very heart of the executive machinery of government. For all his involvement in the earlier crises, even Suez, his position then was nevertheless a secondary one. Within the context of the British response – whether in intelligence matters, decoding Penkovsky intercepts, with defence chiefs or the network of ambassadors – the Foreign Secretary was a central player. Such experience should not be discarded lightly. Home's close involvement at Macmillan's side during these fraught days was the best possible preparation for the responsibilities of Prime Ministerial power in the age of Cold War tactics extending the range of his experience of the major world players. Nothing in his year in Downing Street was to match the perils of the Cuban situation.

After the serenity of Douglas, the pace did not relent at Rambouillet and Nassau in December and both summits threatened to blow the Macmillan administration off course. Rambouillet, despite the outward courtesies, was a frustrating experience. De Gaulle would not admit Britain to the EEC. Only on the impending nuclear difficulties with the Americans who wanted to cancel Skybolt, was Macmillan able to satisfy de Gaulle. The denial of entry to the EEC and of Skybolt, which Eisenhower had agreed to sell to the British in 1960, but which the American Defense Secretary now wished to cancel because of its technical deficiencies and costs, was a double disaster which could be seen as marking the beginning of the end for the government.

On 17 December Macmillan, Home and Peter Thorneycroft set out for Nassau. Macmillan, who had advance warning of the Skybolt cancellation, was prepared to argue for Polaris. Without one or other missiles Britain would be forced out of 'the nuclear club'. The arguments were long and bitter and only at the last moment did Kennedy relent. 'I have no doubt that all his advisers were dead against Britain getting the weapon, and they told him so', said Home subsequently. 'I was fairly sure that he would decide in Britain's favour from my knowledge of the man. First, he knew that a country with a record such as we had, could not ... hand over our defence to another power, however friendly. It was something we could not give, and therefore he could not ask it of us. Secondly, he had talked to me earlier about the hideous responsibility which he alone carried for the safety of the free world in that he, as President, carried the sole decision to declare nuclear war if the British Prime Minister was not with him to help and to assist. I believe that he felt relief that there were people in the world in whom he could place absolute trust, who would not let him down, but would do all in their power to help him and his country to share these terrible cares.'[63]

Home proved the conciliatory figure when Kennedy revealed himself hesitant on the question of supplying Polaris. Home said that he did not share the President's anxieties. 'To give Polaris to Britain would have absolutely no effect on the French who would go ahead anyhow with their own plans.' In his view 'the only sensible European arrangement to be envisaged in the immediate future was for the United States, the United Kingdom and France to put some of their nuclear capacity into some NATO framework and to develop the work of the NATO nuclear committee so that the smaller countries felt they had some participation'.[64] In further talks on 21 December (Macmillan had by this time reported to Butler in London that 'things are not at present going very well'), Home was a prominent advocate of inspection, nuclear testing and non-dissemination.[65] He felt that Britain should be realistic and 'was strongly in favour of accepting Kennedy's terms'. He was later to write modestly: 'Macmillan and I certainly influenced him on that'.[66] The resulting agreement was beneficial in the short term, but in the longer term the financial considerations were debilitating. Although France was offered Polaris, de Gaulle turned it down. Nassau convinced him of the need for France to take an independent course, in the light of what he saw as US favouritism towards Britain. Within a few weeks he delivered his resounding '*Non*' to the British application to join the EEC and signed a Franco-German agreement with Adenauer. Polaris was a pyrrhic victory.

Alec Home returned to Scotland from the Bahamas to the worst winter in Britain since the *Annus Horribilis* of 1947. The lake at the Hirsel was frozen over and the Cheviots covered in snow. It was a time for taking stock after an unprecedented period of pressure and anxiety. That Christmas was a bleak time in many ways. Hugh Gaitskell had entered hospital with a mystery virus and was dead within weeks. Of his possible successor, Harold Wilson, Macmillan wrote that he was 'able but dangerous'.[67] An aftermath of the Vassall Affair, when an Admiralty official had been sentenced on espionage charges, had resulted in the imprisonment of two journalists for refusing to name their sources, which soured the government's relationship with the press at the worst possible moment. There were also fences to be mended with the French. On 28 December, Alec Home wrote to Sir Pierson Dixon, the British ambassador in Paris, on the meeting in the Bahamas. 'The agreement would be infinitely better if the French were a party to it and that is what we should very much like to see.'[68] On New Year's Day 1963, Macmillan wrote: 'Can we recover in 1963 and 1964? I don't know. But I mean to have a good try.'[69] At the Hirsel, Alec Home wrote to President Kennedy after a momentous period in Anglo-American relations. 'I wish we were still in the Bahamas,' he concluded, 'as we are snowed in.'[70] It was an apt metaphor for the year that lay ahead.

11

That Was The Year That Was

'All periods of history are periods of transition,' Robert Blake has written, 'but some are more transitional than others.'[1] This truth was never more evident than in the early 1960s. The kind of society that had reacted with optimism to the spirit of the Festival of Britain ten years earlier or stood bare-headed as the train bearing George VI's coffin had passed through the Norfolk countryside on its way to London, was very different from that which bought 60,000 copies of Michael Shanks's *The Stagnant Society* (the most influential of the 'What's wrong with Britain?' books that appeared in 1961) or laughed with Dudley Moore in his sketch from *Beyond the Fringe* when he said there was 'No Royal Personage actually gracing the Royal Box … unless of course they're crouching.'[2] The deferential society had given way to the questioning society. For most people this was long overdue: the 'old' Britain had been class-ridden, economically inefficient and sliding down most significant economic league tables. The reversal of that decline had been Selwyn Lloyd's first preoccupation on moving to the Treasury, a period Samuel Brittan has identified as 'The Great Reappraisal'.[3] 'The absence of equal opportunity and social mobility,' wrote Anthony Crosland, 'is both a denial of democratic rights, and a positive cause of discontent.'[4] A logical panacea was a new meritocracy, the rise of which had already been the subject of a sardonic satire by Michael Young.[5] Even language adapted to reflect this new agenda. Terms such as 'meritocrat' and 'establishment' took on subtler layers of meaning, and fresh coinages, such as 'neophiliac', appeared.[6] What place was there for Eton and its products in this Brave New World? The changing attitudes to the prospect of Eton, even from within, can be seen in two novels, separated by forty years. In 1922 (the year that Alec Dunglass left Eton), Sir

Shane Leslie had published *The Oppidan*, a nostalgic and affectionate novel of his schooldays; in 1962 (the year that his son, David Dunglass, left Eton), David Benedictus published *The Fourth of June*, in part a study of class antagonism towards a scholarship 'guinea pig', and described on its dust-jacket as 'mercilessly irreverent'.[7] Part of the ethos of the times was the pursuit of materialism which Macmillan himself had identified when he said 'Most of our people have never had it so good … What is beginning to worry some of us is, it too good to be true? – or perhaps I should say, is it too good to last?'[8]

Any process of change threatens the established order, of which Macmillan's government was the most obvious representative. It seemed increasingly irrelevant. Even Macmillan's jokes spoke of bygone times: 'Mr Attlee had three Old Etonians in his Cabinet, I have six. Things are twice as good under the Conservatives.'[9] As with so much of Macmillan's *persona*, this was a pose. He was acutely aware of the need for 'The Modernisation of Britain', the subject of countless memoranda to his ministers. With Alec Home he discussed the rationalisation of the Cabinet Committee system, one of the first overhauls of the machinery of government Home instigated when he took over at Number 10. At Christmas 1962 Macmillan confessed to his secretarial team that his administration was at a crossroads and that new ideas were vital. 'I do not know when any government has been so beset by problems at such a stage in its life.'[10]

The problems were, however, long-standing. Evidence of public dissatisfaction with the Conservatives was clear from the dismal run of by-election performances: Orpington on 14 March 1962, followed by Middlesborough West in June. The threat of losing Leicester North-east precipitated the Night of the Long Knives, and Glasgow Woodside and South Dorset fell on 22 November. The last year of his premiership – from the Cuban crisis to his illness in October 1963 – was one of unprecedented upheaval, catastrophe and crisis, internationally as well as in Britain.

Assassination, sudden death, sickness and retirement cut a swathe through the leadership of the world in 1962–3. At the time of the Cuban crisis, Kennedy was President of the United States, Macmillan was Prime Minister of Great Britain and Hugh Gaitksell was Leader of the Opposition. Adenauer was Chancellor of West Germany and Pope John XXIII presided in the Vatican. Just over a year later, the picture was very different. Hugh Gaitskell died on 18 January; in Rome, Pope John XXIII died in June, much mourned. Adenauer retired in October 1963 as Chancellor of West Germany, and on 22 November, President Kennedy was assassinated in Texas. Three other heads of state also met violent deaths during 1963. It was a Shakespearean year in its catalogue of catastrophes and political upheaval.

Politically Britain was in a state of almost permanent turmoil. The long succession of by-election reverses produced the brutal reconstruction of the government in July – a miscalculation by Macmillan of which Selwyn Lloyd wrote with generosity, 'I was sad for him as well as for myself, because I thought he was damaging his own position, perhaps beyond repair.'[11] For Alec Home, it was business as usual during these alarums; he was deeply embroiled in the continuing crisis of Laos, and continuing the disarmament talks in Geneva. Macmillan's diaries for 1962 are full of references to Home. 'I was rung up early by the Foreign Secretary, who told me that Khrushchev had now agreed to the procedure which we and the Americans had proposed for the Geneva Conference, including the prior meeting of the three Foreign Ministers to discuss in particular the nuclear test problem' runs one entry. Alec Home was in a small group who discussed the British application to join the EEC and how best to argue the case with de Gaulle. Three days later, he talked of the Commonwealth, South-east Asia and the Common Market at a supper for Sir Robert Menzies. 'Foreign Secretary and Chief Whip to luncheon,' Macmillan recorded on 22 June after a long Cabinet. 'We discussed the situation in the Party and agreed on its gravity.' After the first session of the new Cabinet on 17 July Macmillan wrote: 'It is very sad not to see dear David Kilmuir sitting opposite me, as for so long. Lord Home (Foreign Secretary) has taken his place.' Early in August the pair had a long private talk about the nuclear test ban and American proposals for Geneva. In the depths of the recess, Macmillan still 'dined with Alec' (22 August). On 10 September, he recorded 'Nehru and Lord Home to luncheon'.[12] A week later they met to consider de Gaulle and the bomb, Soviet maritime activities, and Nasser and the Yemen, as well as reviewing overall strategy.[13] In a Cabinet now weighted towards a younger generation, Macmillan turned increasingly to Home for disinterested advice. The move to Admiralty House had made it less easy for Alec Home to call informally on the Prime Minister and it was at this time that Macmillan vetoed the idea of moving the Foreign Office to a new location, perhaps in the Mall. A car journey from a more distant location was not conducive in Macmillan's view to the kind of relationship he felt should exist between a Prime Minister and a Foreign Secretary.[14]

Despite a spell of poor health, this was a time of great personal happiness for Alec Home. The move to the Hirsel had been accomplished, with much building work and renovation. His son David had left Eton and had moved on to Christ Church, together with Douglas Hogg, son of Lord Hailsham and Jonathan Aitken, son of Sir William Aitken, MP for Bury St Edmunds. (The contest for the Conservative leadership was therefore followed with more than vicarious interest in the college a year later.) Eton had been a particularly happy time for David and thus for Alec and Elizabeth Home also. The Homes' third daughter, Diana, married James Wolfe Murray at Coldstream on 8 June. The Profumo resignation, which had taken place four days earlier, seemed worlds away to the guests who gathered at Hirsel for the festivities.

On 15 October 1962, at the outset of the state visit to Britain of King Olav V of Norway, Alec Home had been installed as a Knight of the Most Noble Order of the Thistle, as had King Olav. Home liked to recall that not only were he and King Olav born on the same day but now they had been 'thistled' together. His banner was placed in the stall in the Chapel in St Giles' Cathedral next to King Olav's.[15] The Thistle service was a fixed point in Alec Home's calendar from then on. If any one moment could be pinpointed as the end of his participation in public life, it was when he was unable to attend Lord Whitelaw's installation into the Order of the Thistle in July 1991 after an 'extension' to his original stroke seven months before.[16] The idea of using the historic backdrop of Edinburgh for this state visit had been Home's. The landing of the royal party from Norway at Leith, the procession through the streets of Edinburgh, the state banquet at Holyrood, the gala performance of a play based on Scott's *Rob Roy* – all combined to make the event memorable. It was the first state visit by a foreign sovereign to Edinburgh since the accession of James VI to the throne of England in 1603. 'London has no street to compare with Princes Street, caparisoned with great flags, shorn of traffic and banked with people,' Home recorded. 'By all accounts King Olav thoroughly enjoyed himself. Certainly his handsome bearing and unassuming friendliness came across well in Scotland and on television throughout the country.' Macmillan travelled to Scotland also and was in notably fine fettle. He lunched with Alec Home on 16 October, before inspecting the site of the Forth Road Bridge, an echo of Home's Scottish Office past, and a project now well on the way to fruition.[17] The Norwegian party much appreciated the backdrop of Scotland's capital and the programme that had been arranged for them. The relaxed atmosphere was felt by the British also, as Home noted. 'At the final banquet on board King Olav's yacht The Queen remarked that she … had enjoyed this state visit more than any other in which she had taken part.'[18]

Yet the very grandeur of such occasions was symptomatic to many people of the way that Britain was living in the past. *Rob Roy* may have been a suitable presentation for a state visit, but it was not the fare of ordinary playgoers, flocking that year to see plays such as Wesker's *Chips with Everything*. On 5 December the former American Secretary of State Dean Acheson spoke about Britain's dilemma at West Point Academy:

> Great Britain has lost an empire and has not yet found a role. The attempt to play a separate power-role – that is, a role apart from Europe, a role based on a 'special relationship' with the United States, a role based on being the head of a 'Commonwealth' which has no political structure, unity, or strength and enjoys a fragile and precarious economic relationship by means of the sterling area and preferences in the British market – this role is about played out.

The speech caused a furore, not least because it touched a raw nerve. Many felt the truth of what he said, but the Institute of Directors described the speech as 'a calculated insult to the British nation'.[19] For Home the speech came in the wake of a major personal miscalculation. Kenneth Harris, the journalist, was conducting an informal interview with Alec Home in September 1962 for a series of major profiles for the *Observer*. In the published article, Alec Home was reported as saying that he doubted he would ever become Prime Minister because 'When I have to read economic documents I have to have a box of matches and start moving them into position to simplify and illustrate the points to myself.'[20] Although the prospect of Home's becoming Prime Minister did not then seem remotely possible, this remark was to be pure gold for his opponents, and the cartoonist Vicky had his defining image for Alec Home. Many phrases go down into political legend. Dean Acheson's remarks about Britain certainly did. Alec Home's 'matchsticks' remark was coupled with similar hostages to fortune by his successors as Prime Minister – Harold Wilson and 'the pound in your pocket', Edward Heath promising to 'cut prices at a stroke', and James Callaghan's 'Crisis, what crisis?'[21] In Home's case, the damage was retrospective, but the remark certainly influenced Harold Wilson's speech at Scarborough in October 1963 when he set out the agenda for the Labour Party's programme:

> For the commanding heights of British industry to be controlled today by men whose only claim is their aristocratic connection or the power of inherited wealth or speculative finance is as irrelevant to the twentieth century as would be the continued purchase of commissions in the armed forces by lordly amateurs. At the very time that even the MCC has abolished the distinction between amateurs and professionals, in science and industry we are content to remain a nation of Gentlemen in a world of Players.[22]

Eighteen days later Home was to be Prime Minister. From that moment the 'matchsticks' comment was a ticking bomb. When it went off, the damage was widespread. The interview affords a prime example of how a remark made in jest is repented at leisure. The Conservatives and Alec Home were to pay a heavy price for it.

More immediate damage was done to the government by a series of reversals in the latter part of 1962 and the early months of 1963. These were bounded by the Vassall and Profumo affairs, though neither was as damaging in the long term as de Gaulle's rejection in January 1963 of the British application to join the EEC: 'Though not unexpected, it fell like a blow upon a bruise.'[23] The Prime Minister's search for a European role was now dashed and the government seemed directionless as the election approached. Although the EEC negotiations were Heath's responsibility, they came within the orbit of the Foreign Office's responsibilities and Home, a late convert to the European ideal, was deeply disappointed, not least for his loyal deputy.

It seemed now that all pigeons were coming home to roost. Macmillan had known of the suspicions regarding Kim Philby after the defection of Burgess and Maclean to Moscow. Early in 1961, the unmasking of the 'Portland Spy Ring' led to the imprisonment of George Blake. The subsequent inquiry was critical of the positive vetting system, and put renewed pressure upon Macmillan to get his security house in order. The arrest of John Vassall in September 1962, and his sentence to eighteen years' imprisonment, was particularly damaging, its main political effect being to turn the press against Macmillan in the spring of 1963, when the government needed any media support it could muster, after jailing two journalists for protecting their sources.

In the midst of this came confirmation that Kim Philby was the 'Third Man', and no sooner had the dust settled after the inquiry into the Vassall case than the Profumo Affair reared its head. The atmosphere of sleaze, incompetence and sheer bad luck was not easy to counter. Even the Great Train Robbery, which followed the suicide of Dr Stephen Ward, an osteopath concerned in the Profumo affair, was seen as a reflection on the competence of the Macmillan government. If in doubt, the press blamed Supermac. But the Profumo affair made it difficult for the Prime Minister to throw in the sponge in its immediate aftermath. It also effectively ruled out a general election in the autumn of 1963, till then a considered option.

In the summer of 1963, however, Macmillan's thoughts turned seriously to the prospect of retirement. A general election was due by the autumn of 1964 and if he were to step down before it he should allow his successor to establish himself. If Macmillan had fallen after the Profumo Affair then the likeliest successor at the time was Reginald Maudling, the Chancellor of the Exchequer. Harry Boyne, the political correspondent of the *Daily Telegraph*, conducted various private polls. The first of these, on 20 June 1963, based on 50 interviews, claimed that if the sample was representative then first choice preferences overall would be 147 for Maudling, 56 for Hailsham, 42 for Heath, 28 for Butler, 21 for Powell, with Macleod and Home level on 7 each; 35 were recorded as being undecided. After Macmillan had spoken to the 1922 Committee on 25 July at the end of session (and as the Test Ban Treaty talks were coming to their successful conclusion in Moscow), Boyne polled 100 Conservative MPs. Of declared preferences, the result was conclusive, 71 supporting Maudling, with 9 for Butler, 5 for Hailsham and 1 for Heath and Powell.[24] The long-term significance of these polls – for Maudling's support melted away like the morning dew – was that two members of the Upper House (even before the passage of the Peerage Bill on 31 July) were 'in the frame'.

The summer of 1963 also saw the culmination of Tony Benn's three-year campaign for the right to disclaim his peerage, which had occupied the government intermittently for two years. On 22 April 1961 Macmillan had written to the Lord Chancellor on the issue of Parliament and Lords Reform:

> I am rather distressed to hear that the proposal is to limit the subject for enquiry for the Joint Select Committee to the question of peers and peeresses becoming eligible for election to the House of

> Commons. This is the Benn point 'pure and simple'. Would it not be better tactics to widen the terms of reference? ... to take the opportunity which is offered to us, not merely to deal with the immediate problem but by widening the scope of the enquiry do something to settle the composition of the House of Lords and perhaps establish it for many years to come?
>
> If we get an enquiry of this kind we shall first of all confuse the Benn issue, which would be a good thing, and secondly lead to a result ... from which we, as a government, can ultimately choose what suits us. We can then claim to be the true reformers of the House of Lords composition, first by the Life Peerages Act, and secondly by any act which might follow from the enquiry.[25]

Not only was it an important issue for Benn; it was becoming increasingly relevant for Alec Home and Quintin Hailsham. Ever since Anthony Howard had published an article entitled 'Mr Home and Mr Hogg?' in the *New Statesman* on 14 December 1962, forecasting with remarkable accuracy how events might unfold if Macmillan resigned before the next general election, the possibility of a Home or Hailsham candidacy had been public gossip in the bars of Westminster.[26] Home suggested a meeting with Hailsham in May 1963 where they discussed what their joint stance should be if they were enabled to renounce by a new Peerage Act. The Upper House was disposed towards granting peers the right to disclaim from the moment the Peerage Bill received the royal assent and not, as the legislation proposed, *after* the next election. If that happened, Home and Hailsham agreed they could not both disclaim, which amounted to a tacit acceptance that one of them might, and agreed that neither would act without consulting or informing the other.[27] In the first months of 1963, events moved quickly and unexpectedly towards their conclusion.

A Cabinet memorandum on 18 January considered the timescale for existing peers and new hereditary peers to decide whether they wished to disclaim their titles, a period fixed at six and twelve months respectively. But the substantive point that legislation should only take effect at the next general election was rejected by the House of Lords. As Leader of the House of Lords, Hailsham was a key figure in a process that would change the course of political history. On 8 May it was decided that 'Surrender should not extinguish the Peerage itself'. If it had, then Alec Home would have refused to allow his name to go forward for the leadership.[28] The Cabinet 'invited the Lord Chancellor to give authority for a Bill to be drafted, with a view to its introduction as soon as possible'.[29] It was this development that sparked off the Home–Hailsham meeting. On 15 May a statement was made in both Houses of Parliament that the measure would be operative after the next election, but a Labour frontbencher in the Commons said the Opposition wanted the measure to be effective there and then.[30] Shortly afterwards Hailsham was confirmed (11 June) as the British representative at the Nuclear Test Ban talks in Moscow.[31] Before he left, Lord Poole, Joint Chairman of the Conservative Party, visited him and told him to prepare himself for the leadership of the Party.[32] In the race of the peers, Hailsham was the early pace-setter. The fact that he was now seriously being considered as a candidate for the leadership (whenever a vacancy might occur) can be seen in a letter from Tim Bligh to Harold Macmillan on 4 July. 'As at present drafted,' Bligh wrote, 'Quintin has to wait until Parliament has dissolved before he can exercise a disclaimer.'[33]

On 27 June the Cabinet resumed discussion about an amendment to the Peerage Bill designed to ensure that the Bill would take effect on receiving the Royal Assent rather than on the dissolution of Parliament. Although the weight of opinion appeared to favour rejection of the amendment it was agreed after a five-minute deliberation, that if an amendment was carried it should be accepted. The Cabinet then moved on to the issue of the Yemen, on which Alec Home addressed them.[34] In retrospect the preceding five minutes were among the most significant of his life. Ironically, Butler was one of those who paved the way for the Reform.[35]

In due course the Lord Chancellor recorded that the opposition in the House of Lords had tabled an amendment designed to bring the bill into operation when it received the royal assent rather than on the dissolution of Parliament. With memories of the conflicts of the past and a desire to see the issue settled, the Cabinet accepted the Lords amendment,[36] and the Bill became law on 31 July. The way was now open for 'Mr Home' and 'Mr Hogg' to offer themselves as candidates for the leadership of the Conservative Party.

Two weeks after the Peerage Bill had entered the statute book, events made a Home premiership possible. Gilmour Leburn, MP for Kinross and West Perthshire had been walking on the moors when he collapsed and died. Although the local constituency association had adopted George Younger as its candidate, the writ for the by-election would not be moved in the recess. Not only was the machinery in place for Home to leave the House of Lords but there was a vacant constituency, one which could hardly have been better had it been handpicked. Though not overly safe in the iconoclastic political climate of the time (there was a distinct concern that a strong Liberal showing could win the seat from the Conservatives), in every other respect it was tailor-made for Scotland's Foreign Secretary.

The most tangible evidence of the ending of the age of deference was the appearance on BBC television of a late night satirical programme, *That Was The Week That Was*, known as *TW3*, and first broadcast on 24 November 1962. Its keynote was one of irreverent and investigative scepticism. Together with *Beyond the Fringe*, still playing to packed houses at the Fortune Theatre, and the satirical magazine *Private Eye*, which first appeared in 1962, *TW3* embodied the abandonment of the old cap-doffing to 'the Establishment'. Few public figures escaped *Private Eye*'s barbs over the next three decades. Alec Home was nicknamed Baillie Vass after a misplaced caption underneath a photograph of the Foreign Secretary.

One of the myths of the satire boom of the 1960s was that the Establishment metaphorically quaked in their beds at night. They did nothing of the kind. *Private Eye*, which Selwyn Lloyd described as the working man's Erskine May, became essential reading, its investigations surreptiously enjoyed, even by some of its intended victims. Saturday night invitations went unaccepted; *TW3* had priority. Reginald Maudling, Chancellor of the Exchequer, was in the studio audience one Saturday for a live broadcast, a risky venture considering the unpredictability of some of the items. Tickets for *Beyond the Fringe* were difficult to come by, but on the Dickens principle that 'it is a hopeless endeavour to attract people to a theatre unless they can be first brought to believe that they will never get into it'[37] this served to encourage even the victims to clamour for admission. Some quick thinking was required when it became known in Whitehall circles that the Queen wished to see the revue, for Her Majesty could hardly go in an 'official' capacity. Her Majesty's Foreign Secretary came to the rescue, and a scheme was devised whereby Her Majesty visited the Fortune Theatre privately in a party hosted by Lord Scarborough.[38] The fact that the Head of State attended at the gathering of the Young Turks hardly heralded the arrival of the tumbrils.

Alec Home was now involved in the dissolution of the Central African Federation and the build-up to the test ban talks, scheduled for Moscow. The Victoria Falls Conference concluded on 4 July 1963, bringing to an end a chapter of colonial history with which he had been involved for eight years. In the long term this conference and the treaty he signed in Moscow in August were among the most important initiatives of the twilight of Macmillan's leadership. The European negotiations having collapsed in January, the pressure for success in the test ban talks was very strong in Macmillan's mind, quite apart from its intrinsic importance in the aftermath of the missile crisis. In April 1963 Alec Home had met with Dean Rusk in Paris for preliminary discussions, especially over the uncertain position of Khrushchev; rumours were circulating that he was about to resign the Russian leadership. Further talks with Rusk followed in Ottawa in May, where Home indicated the views of the British government on nuclear testing. If a comprehensive ban proved politically impossible, he told Rusk, 'an atmosphere ban only, leaving the underground on one side, might be the best agreement with the Russians we could get: it would relieve the world of fall-out and the Russians could represent it as a great victory for humanity'. Rusk indicated that the Americans were thinking on similar lines.[39] On 8 June it was announced that Khrushchev had agreed to talks.

Although Hailsham was to be the British representative for these talks, the Americans made it very clear that he would play a subordinate role to Averell Harriman, the main western negotiator, in Moscow in July. Herein lay some of the later difficulties on the Allied side. But it was not in Hailsham's nature to play a subordinate role and, with hindsight, it might have speeded the process of negotiation if Alec Home (whom Macmillan felt he could not spare) had accompanied Harriman. Much of the preliminary work was done by Home and Rusk, though Julian Amery, the Aviation Minister (and Macmillan's son-in-law), visited Khrushchev on 12 June for talks which were cut short when Amery spoke of the need for full inspection.

Before the plenary sessions in Moscow, Kennedy accepted an invitation to stay with Macmillan at Birch Grove. 'I envy him so much seeing you both again,' Jacqueline Kennedy wrote to Macmillan. 'He is truly looking forward to it and it will be lovely for him to be with friends.'[40] The visit was planned to last three days, but this was reduced after Kennedy decided to visit Ireland to see the haunts of his ancestors and Chatsworth to see the grave of his sister, Lady Hartington. Home and Rusk had talks on 27–28 June at 1 Carlton Gardens, setting out the objectives for the Moscow talks. They agreed that the first objective would be a comprehensive ban on nuclear testing. 'If the Russians refuse to budge on a comprehensive treaty,' they wrote in a joint communiqué, 'our next object should be a *partial treaty* covering tests in all environments except underground with no restrictions on underground tests. This might be offered as something separate, or as the first stage of a further continuous negotiation for a comprehensive treaty.'[41]

Macmillan paints a golden picture of the weekend at Birch Grove in his memoirs, an interpretation later questioned.[42] The truth lies somewhere between. There were difficulties over the agenda and Kennedy found the Prime Minister tired and dispirited in the continuing Profumo crisis, but the warmth of the private letters afterwards testifies to the impact the weekend had on all those who were present. Home was the only other British figure to stay overnight at Birch Grove, which 'spoke volumes' about their relationship, according to Macmillan's biographer.[43] The Prime Minister had set great store by the meeting and was anxious for the talks to go well as a preliminary to Moscow, and to reinforce his image as a world statesman. Certainly he was disappointed that Kennedy was with him for just 24 hours, but much of the preliminary work, which endured, had already been conducted by Home and Rusk in London. In any case, Kennedy crammed a great deal into those 24 hours, even quizzing Philip de Zulueta about the Profumo scandal whilst in the car on the way to early morning Mass at Forest Row, before leaving by helicopter from the grounds of Birch Grove in the late afternoon.[44] In private conversation before the full talks at noon on the Sunday, Kennedy told Macmillan that he would be prepared to go to Moscow to sign any agreement. The directives for Harriman and Hailsham had been established, and Kennedy stressed that the psychological position was very important. 'It was not only the true balance of power that mattered but also the appearance', he said. 'At the time of the Cuban crisis the suggestion that missiles should be placed in Cuba was important not because it really changed the balance of power but because it appeared to do so. That was why if it was impossible to prove that the Russians could not carry out any small clandestine tests it was very important to determine as closely as possible how much they would gain by such cheating.' Kennedy also raised the question of the number of on-site inspections, and Home said he and Rusk had agreed to explain to the Russians the western estimate of the need for on-site inspections before broaching the question of numbers.[45] Kennedy's helicopter then set off down the valley. 'We have been in part equal to the Churchill–Roosevelt relationship at the most critical moment of history,' Macmillan wrote to the President after the visit.[46] He was never to see Kennedy again.

In the days that remained before Harriman came to London to accompany Hailsham to Moscow, Home produced a draft treaty covering tests in the three environments (the atmosphere, in outer space and under water), and at Kennedy's suggestion it was agreed that Rusk and Home would go to Moscow for the signing. The terms of the Test Ban Treaty were eventually agreed on 25 July. After the terms of the Treaty had been agreed, Macmillan began to have second thoughts about retiring, as Ormsby-Gore explained in a letter to the President, three days before the actual signing:

> The Prime Minister is in such a state of euphoria after the Test Ban agreement that Alec doubts whether he now has any intention of resigning. This may lead to trouble as an overwhelming majority of the Conservatives in Parliament are convinced he should make way for a younger man in the shape of Reggie Maudling this autumn. By the way Reggie will be coming to Washington a few days before the Bank and Fund meeting in September and would very much like to see you sometime on Friday the 27th September if you could manage it.[47]

It is indicative of how matters were conducted in palmier times that five days were allotted to the ceremonial signing. Khrushchev sent Macmillan copious quantities of caviare, crabmeat and wine. Alec Home took out in return a modern English cornucopia vase for Khrushchev, together with a large Stilton cheese. The vase bore the motto 'Peace and Prosperity' and was engraved 'To commemorate an agreement – HM to NK July 25 1963'.[48] Relaxation and sightseeing were the order of the day. Dean Rusk and Khrushchev were photographed playing badminton (without a net) at the Soviet leader's villa on the Black Sea. Sir Humphrey Trevelyan, the new British ambassador, pulled off something of a coup by having a church service in the Embassy on Sunday 4 August. As Alec Home read one of the lessons and Ted Heath played the organ, this was considered *très snob* and impressed the Russians inordinately. Alec Home chose a lesson from St Mark's Gospel that ended 'have peace one with another', which was considered a coded message to the listening Muscovites.[49] Douglas Hurd, who had accompanied Home and Caccia, recorded: 'Service in the ambassador's study looking out over the sunny garden and hose playing. The Privy [i.e. Ted Heath] plays the harmonium, the Secretary of State reads the lesson: a full and hearty congregation.' On the Sunday evening there was a big Anglo–American banquet at the American embassy, and the next morning when Home and Heath set out for their various missions, the juniors were left 'hanging about while the great shunted to and fro', the day 'punctuated by bouts of vast eating'. Home met Gromyko to discuss trade prospects and at noon he met Khrushchev, telling him that when Germany was reunified it would not be by war.

The culmination of the day was the Kremlin reception for the signing. In his speech Alec Home spoke of the future health of unborn children, of how the Treaty was a brake on the arms race, and 'a conscious start in demolishing the world of suspicion'. He later went on Soviet television, where he quoted from Burns, always a shrewd move in Moscow.[50] Hurd recorded: 'This is a magnificent white [hall] with gold chandeliers and the uncouth crowd of guzzling Soviets underneath. Immediately after the Test Treaty is signed Khrushchev speaks, small and pink, with China in the back of his mind and Rusk and Home like tutelary angels behind him.' After the grandeur of the ceremony, the next morning was a leisurely affair and Douglas Hurd called on the Secretary of State 'naked to waist, unconcerned in blue pyjamas with his back to the sun'. The contrast with the usual world of Whitehall proprieties was somewhat disconcerting for a young secretary.[51] Alec Home sent a final despatch to Macmillan, giving his impressions of the visit:

> Everything has so far gone off very well. The treaty has been safely signed with much toasting and feasting. Khruschev has been jovial though tired and even Gromyko has tried to look cheerful. Rusk and I have had two good sessions with Gromyko together and each one of us with G. and K. on our own. The atmosphere is remarkably relaxed.

On Berlin, Home reported, 'Whereas Gromyko played the old gramophone records, he had put in a new needle and the effect was comparatively agreeable. We said things about free elections in the Soviet Union etc, and got away with them; last year he would have gone up in smoke.' Khrushchev was 'delighted with your Stilton'.

The meetings had been such a successful new departure that a year later, as Prime Minister, Alec Home wrote to Khrushchev on 5 August. 'Today is the first anniversary of the signature in Moscow of the Nuclear Test Ban Treaty and I recall with pleasure that it was my privilege, as Foreign Secretary, to be in Moscow on that occasion.' The letter was sent on 4 August so that the Russians did not 'beat us to the draw'.[52]

The television satirists talked of the week that was; 1962 3 was the year that was. In the midst of a troubled political time, the Test Ban Treaty was balm indeed for Macmillan's beleaguered administration and a high point of his premiership. It paved the way for important later developments, such as the Non-proliferation Treaty of 1968, and the Strategic Arms Limitation Treaties of the 1980s. In the short term, it had two consequences for British politics. Cheered by the success of the talks, Macmillan began to reconsider his earlier belief that the time had come to retire. The President, warned by Ormsby-Gore, had gained the impression at Birch Grove that Macmillan was in the last phase of his premiership. But the Test Ban success dispelled the Profumo gloom. On 16 June, twelve days after Profumo's resignation, Home had written to Macmillan to warn him of the scheming in the party against his leadership, of which Macmillan was in the event well aware, but the combination of the Treaty in August and the lack of an agreed successor seemed to indicate that he could carry on.

The second factor to emerge from the Moscow meeting was the low opinion the Americans, especially Averell Harriman, had of Hailsham, whom they thought a difficult partner, unwilling to accept his secondary role, and with his lawyer's instinct for the detail of the small print, dragging out negotiation on minor points and almost losing the backing on major points, as though he were trying to persuade three appeal judges to reverse an earlier opinion. The official records of the talks indicate Hailsham's concentration on the semantics. Of a crucial meeting on 24 July, the communiqué reads: 'He [Hailsham] had a suggestion to make, which was to remove all the words in the last sentence after the word "question" and then add: "in the hope that agreement satisfactory to all may be achieved"'. Even the official documentation cannot disguise the true feelings of the Russian delegation. 'Mr Gromyko again proposed reverting to the previous day's text.' So it went on, Gromyko stating at one point 'The suggestion made by Lord Hailsham about using the word "hope" did not help.' Hailsham countered by saying 'that this state of affairs reminded him of the early councils of the Church', not a parallel that would find a ready echo in Moscow. He then explained the importance of 'the indefinite article in English'.[53] When Alec Home heard of this through Ormsby-Gore he felt it was all part of the Hailsham *persona*, understandable to those who had known him for years, but infuriating for those of newer acquaintance. Nevertheless, the episode made a deep impression on Home, who felt that such a temperament was not fitted for the role of Prime Minister, and that if a candidate from the Lords was to enter the fray, it had better be Home himself.[54] The Birch Grove meeting in June had established that Hailsham was to play a secondary role to Harriman when the Moscow talks got underway, but David Ormsby-Gore left the Prime Minister and Alec Home in no doubt about American feelings on Hailsham. This was a grievous disappointment to Macmillan, who had deliberately put Hailsham in the limelight, by nominating him to head the British delegation to Moscow.

That autumn, as the test ban faded from the front pages, Macmillan seemed once more to lose the glint of battle. In a long talk with Alec Home on 18 September, he discussed the succession. Home did not favour a change in the leadership because of the disunity and turmoil a contest would bring, but he assumed a Hailsham candidacy, though Maudling was still the front runner. Home warned that he did not see calmer waters ahead as a result of change. Nevertheless, Macmillan wrote to the Queen two days later to tell her that he would not hold an election in 1963 and that he would not lead the Party into the election in 1964. There the matter might have rested, but vacillation and second thoughts were in the air in a strangely indecisive period. On 3 October Alec Home dined with Macmillan to report on his annual visit to New York and Washington. 'Although there is a certain lull,' Macmillan recorded, 'we are in a great tangle in every part of the world.' Was this the time to step down? On 6 October Macmillan held what was in effect a family conference with his son Maurice and son-in-law Julian Amery. His mind was 'beginning to move [at the last minute] to staying on'.[55] That evening Macmillan dined alone with Alec Home. A speech, one way or another, would be needed by the following Saturday at the closing rally of the Conservative Party Conference. On the Monday, Macmillan returned to Downing Street to discuss the issue further before a final decision. He met senior colleagues, and by the evening had decided to stay; he would announce this at a Cabinet meeting on the Tuesday.

During the night Macmillan was struck down by prostate trouble. His doctor, Sir John Richardson, was on holiday in the Lake District. Dorothy Macmillan summoned Dr Lionel King-Lewis, who was well known in Westminster circles, and doctor to many MPs, including Selwyn Lloyd. Dr King-Lewis arrived at Downing Street at 4 a.m. on Wednesday 8 October. It was the beginning of ten dramatic days in

British political history. Within hours of the news of Macmillan's illness the battle for the Conservative leadership was underway.

12

Customary Processes

'I nearly rang you up about six times during the turmoil, but thought it was not fair to worry you with my concerns. I think it has all come out pretty well, but would love sometime to tell you the whole story – a very strange one – and what is behind Macleod and Powell at this moment, I wonder.'

Selwyn Lloyd to Anthony Eden, 28 October 1963[1]

'The tenor of Macleod's article curiously suggests that he assumed that the *first* choices of the Cabinet Ministers would (and should) be of decisive importance … After more than a decade in the Cabinet, Macleod appears to have forgotten that on the occasion of the choice of a new Leader it is the machinery of *party* and not of *government* which takes precedence.'

Robert McKenzie[2]

'Why, damn it,' said Thomas Young, Lord Melbourne's secretary, 'such a position never was occupied by any Greek or Roman, and, if it only lasts two months, it is well worth while to have been Prime Minister of England.' 'By God that's true', said Melbourne. 'I'll go.'[3]

On 25 October 1961, Alec Home, as Foreign Secretary, gave a speech to the Eton Society at their 150th anniversary dinner. In the course of an anecdotal address, he told the story of how a Field Day umpire discovered a cadet officer in the Eton Corps sleeping peacefully in the Aldershot heather, in a smoke-screen raised by the cigarettes of his company. When the umpire angrily demanded to know what were the agreed tactics most likely to deceive the enemy, the cadet replied, 'Opportunism based on inertia'.[4] By such methods, some might think, did Alec Home become Prime Minister in October 1963. They would be mistaken. Inertia is hardly the favoured way for politicians to enter

10 Downing Street, and opportunism (as Hailsham found) can prove counter-productive.

Alec Home had been in politics for very many years when his opportunity to become Prime Minister presented itself. He knew how the Conservative Party reacted in a crisis, and how its leadership battles were resolved. In the phrase which he used for his memoirs, he knew which way the wind was blowing. He understood that if he were to be a candidate for the premiership under the consultative process then employed, precipitate action would be fatal. He became Prime Minister by keeping his options open and by not wanting the prize too much. But as the example of Melbourne shows, there are few who turn down the opportunity if it comes their way; if chance would have him king, chance could crown him, but there was always a world elsewhere.

There had been three contested battles for the Conservative leadership in Alec Home's lifetime, those of 1911, 1923 and 1957. In each instance the favoured candidates fell at the final hurdle. The same was to apply in 1963, as well as in 1965, 1975 and 1990. The closest parallel to the contest of October 1963 was that of November 1911. Balfour's leadership, albeit of the opposition, was under considerable pressure after the election defeats of January 1906, January 1910 and December 1910. During 1911, dissenting Unionists wore BMG (Balfour Must Go) badges; Balfour succumbed to the pressure and stepped down in November 1911. As in 1963, there was no agreed successor. The two wings of the party were represented by Walter Long and Austen Chamberlain. When it became clear that neither could give the party the unity it needed, Chamberlain suggested that they both step down in favour of Andrew Bonar Law. It is easy, but mistaken, to see this as the triumph of the darkhorse compromise candidate, but Law and Home were perceived as being the best chance of uniting a bitterly divided party. When Bonar Law was acclaimed Conservative leader, Austen Chamberlain called for unity. Rab Butler seconded the election of Alec Douglas-Home as leader after the Kinross and West Perthshire by-election. The message was clear on both occasions: past differences would be buried in the cause of outward unity.

Home's ultimate shortcoming as Conservative leader was not failure to deliver victory in the general election of October 1964, but his inability in the face of significant Party opposition to be the focus for that unity. His tenure of the leadership was one of the shortest of the century[5] but all subsequent leaders were chosen by the system he put in place.[6]

On the evening of Sunday 6 October, Alec Home dined alone with Harold Macmillan at Birch Grove. The Foreign Secretary had just returned from talks with Dean Rusk and Gromyko in New York, where he had what was to prove his last meeting with President Kennedy on 4 October. Macmillan had sent a message to Alec Home in New York inviting him to hear of developments over *detente* and future East-West relationships.[7] After reviewing the Foreign situation in the light of the Test Ban Treaty, Macmillan and Home turned to the central preoccupation of the leadership. The previous day Macmillan had received a letter from James Stuart reassuring him that there was no credible alternative for the leadership. Although he had his supporters there were others who felt he should step down and clearly the moment of decision was now at hand. At the closing rally of the Conservative Party Conference it was tacitly accepted on all sides that the Prime Minister would have to give some indication of his intentions. Macmillan was undecided. The summer of 1963 had been a low time and he genuinely did not know what was for the best. The aftermath of the Profumo Affair had left him debilitated and depressed, but the success of the Test Ban Treaty had temporarily lifted his spirits. Nevertheless, whenever he dined with trusted friends the conversation came back to the same topic. Should he stay or go? On 18 September he had written in his diary, 'When Lord Home was here on Tuesday night [17 September], I talked to him about my own position and about a possible successor. He was very distressed to think that I had any idea of retiring, but could well understand my reasons and thought them sound. As for a successor, he favours Hailsham, but fears that there will be complete disunity in the Party and that great troubles will follow. I may be forced to stay.'[8] This was not the clarion call of a man who was looking forward to leading the party into battle once more. Nor was it even a true reflection of Home's views by that stage and could be an indication of how Macmillan was trying to rationalise what was already forming in his own mind. Home consistently advocated that Macmillan should step down at a moment of his own choosing, but that he should certainly not contest the next election. He had told Macmillan this clearly at his Chequers meeting in September and he now reiterated the message at Birch Grove. That afternoon, during talks with his son Maurice and son-in-law Julian Amery, Macmillan had moved towards a decision to stay. The message he was now receiving was a confusing and disturbing one, as Macmillan respected Alec Home's judgment. Even with an agreed successor, such as Anthony Eden, Churchill had lingered indecisively in office. Now there was no agreed successor and this compounded Macmillan's reluctance to quit the stage irrevocably. Macmillan believed that Butler was fearful of the outcome of the battle for the succession and would be happy for him to stay. The likeliest candidate in the summer had appeared to be Reginald Maudling, but his support was not as well founded as the *Daily Telegraph* polls had suggested. Maudling supporters had fed the paper percentage figures that exaggerated the Chancellor's support because they were projections based on a very low initial base, conducted selectively among sympathetic younger MPs.[9] Many in the Labour Party felt that Maudling could prove to be their most formidable opponent, especially if he showed that he had the pulse of the nation over economic concerns. The decision was not going to be taken by the Labour Party or by a small junior caucus of Tory MPs, but some senior figures on the Conservative side, influenced by the polls and private conversations with Labour MPs, assumed that Maudling would at least be a formidable runner for the succession, or, failing him for any reason, Rab Butler. As Secretary of the 1922 Committee, Philip Goodhart was asked by John Morrison to sound out the younger elements in the party. A more comprehensive survey showed that they were in fact divided between Maudling and Butler.[10] Morrison, however, had already told Butler that 'the chaps won't have you', a judgment that the 1922 Executive confirmed privately.[11] As a result, Butler was under no illusions about his slim chances of success. Indeed when Butler had met Maudling by chance in a London street after his return from the Victoria Falls Conference he said, almost in passing, 'Of course, I'd be very glad to serve under you, Reggie.'[12] But by the time of the Party Conference, Maudling's lack of staying power was all too clear. The strange chemistry of political reputation can dip as inexplicably as shares in the stock market and so it proved for Maudling. He seemed too 'quiet' a figure and some felt him to be indolent, though their numbers did not include those at the Treasury, who knew that Maudling's incisive intellect enabled him to deal with the agenda in half the time it took most people. But as a public figure Maudling did not seem like a prime minister-in-waiting. Macmillan harboured doubts about the succession and found it disconcerting to hear Alec Home's views in the autumn of 1963, particularly after the reassurance he had received from Julian Amery, who had been his eyes and ears during the 1957 leadership contest. Macmillan was confident that his son-in-law could still keep him in touch with grassroots opinion. Home's frank analysis of the disadvantages later that evening – far more cogently and powerfully expressed than Macmillan acknowledged in his diary – now muddied the waters. On two occasions Home had told Macmillan openly that he ought to stand down, if not immediately, then certainly before the Election, for he believed that the Party's chances of victory would best be served under a new leader. This uncompromising message was typical of Home's approach: the unpalatable reality was always preferable to the evasive half-truth. The problem was one of timing, for if Macmillan announced that he would not fight another election campaign, the question of the successor would become the central preoccupation of the party. Judging by precedent, the intervening period was hardly likely to be tranquil. The Party would thus get the worst of both worlds.

Macmillan came back to Downing Street on the morning of Monday 7 October to take further soundings. Despite Home's twice expressed reservations, on the morning of Tuesday 8 October (the fourth anniversary of his election victory of 1959) he telephoned the Queen's assistant private secretary, Sir Edward Ford, with the news that he had decided to stay on.[13] Speculation about Macmillan's long-term future had been a preoccupation of the political commentators since July 1962. The events of the summer of 1963 had intensified this process and the palace had been on a state of 'red alert', lest there was a sudden resignation by the Prime Minister. After Macmillan's telephone call, the state of alert was subconsciously downgraded, ironically just at the moment the crisis was about to erupt. When it became clear that Macmillan was to retire the Queen came down from Balmoral and the instructions from the palace were quite clear. Advice was going to be needed, but this was to be on the basis of YOU CHOOSE, WE SEND FOR; the royal role was to be confirmatory, based on clear notification from Downing Street. By such means the palace would not be embroiled in Party controversy. Indeed Macmillan wrote to the Queen with a résumé of events on 15 October on this very subject: 'I am anxious that everything done so far should be amply recorded in writing and not give rise to the kind of confusion by which previous crises have afterwards been poisoned with very ill effects to all concerned. I believe that all this can be documented from beginning to end.'[14] The system Macmillan proposed to Cabinet (and which was accepted at its meeting on Tuesday 15 October) was based on the precedent of 1957, but allowed for wider and more formal consultation of all levels of the party. Macmillan wrote to Butler, outlining the suggested procedure:

> I think I should record my view that it is right that soundings should be undertaken as follows: the Lord Chancellor will see members of the Cabinet; the Chief Whip will see all other Ministers and Members of the House of Commons; Lord St Aldwyn will see Members of the House of Lords who are regular supporters of the Party and Lord Poole will talk to Lord Chelmer and Mrs Shepherd representing the National Union (and this should include the candidates).
>
> These consultations may take a day or two. I would like to be informed when they have been completed and I will at that time decide according to the state of my health what steps should then be taken.[15]

This minute showed how the procedures of 1963 built on those of 1957, where the secondary level of consultation had been less formal. But now it was not a straight choice between 'Wab or Hawold?', but a more complex consultation, a prelude to the majority alternative vote system from 1965 onwards. What was unique about 1963, apart from the fact that the contest began in the glare of the Party conference, was that a form of 'black-balling' was built into the process of consultation, the kind of input accomplished later only by tactical abstentions or change of allegiance between ballots. All levels of the Party from Cabinet to candidates were asked who was their first choice, who was their second choice, and (tellingly) the names of anyone they would oppose.[16] What the system delegated to Macmillan was the right to interpret this data and to act as sole conduit of the information to the palace, and it is on his role as interpreter and transmitter that controversy has centred.

Macmillan's papers reveal that he felt this controversy intensely. 'I am sorry that the procedure by which I gave advice to the Queen has been so much misrepresented in the press,' he wrote to Lord St Aldwyn on the day Alec Home became Prime Minister, 'but I am sure you can do something to put it right, for you know the immense trouble I took to get information and pass it on.' On the same day he wrote to John Morrison, Chairman of the 1922 Committee, 'The press has tried to represent that Alec Home was my personal choice. You know well the immense trouble I took to get the views of the Cabinet, the House of Commons, the House of Lords and the Conservative Party generally. I think if you can help to get this about among Members it will do a lot of good. I was not really anything more than a convenient recipient of this information, and the means by which this advice could be given to the Queen.' Years later Macmillan was still adding notes to his records of the events of October 1963 when the old controversies flared up. 'I made no attempt to influence the choice of my successor', he wrote after one letter to *The Times* by Humphry Berkeley. 'My sole object was to inform the Queen of the results of the investigations which I had made in the Cabinet, among MPs, among Conservative Peers and within the Party organisation. This result showed an overwhelming support for Sir Alec Douglas-Home. Although Mr Berkeley is of no importance I thought it as well to file this cutting in the appropriate chapter, together with this comment.' Knox Cunningham confirmed the accuracy of this interpretation of events. 'You are well aware,' he wrote to the author in 1975, 'that it is thought that Harold Macmillan made a personal recommendation of his successor in 1963 with a view to preventing Rab from becoming Prime Minister. This is not true. Recently a reference to this occurred in the Press (one can never kill a story such as this) and Harold Macmillan asked me to give him a note of events. This I did and the enclosed memo. refers to two passages in his sixth volume *At the End of the Day* and my unpublished book *One Man Dog*. I told him about your book [*The Uncrowned Prime Ministers*] and he suggested that I should send you the enclosed document for information.'[17] Knox Cunningham's prediction was to prove correct. To use a phrase that Humphry Berkeley employed as the title of a book about the 1931 financial crisis, Macmillan's 'manipulation' of the evidence submitted to him in October 1963 is 'the myth that will not die'. The cause of this is not hard to establish, for as Francis Bacon observed, 'It is hard in all causes when voices shall be numbered but not weighed.'[18]

What Macmillan did not tell Sir Edward Ford when he rang the Palace on the morning of Tuesday 8 October was that during the night he had awakened with severe pains and had been unable to pass water. Macmillan was treated at 4 a.m. by Dr King-Lewis, but it was clear that specialist assistance would be needed. Despite the pain he was experiencing, Macmillan went ahead with his plans to preside at Cabinet the following morning. His colleagues were shocked by his appearance and obvious discomfort. Macmillan said that he planned to stay on to fight the general election but then withdrew to allow the Cabinet to discuss this decision – a curious constitutional development. Enoch Powell was firmly of the opinion that Macmillan should stand aside. The disadvantages of the status quo were rehearsed once again, as Home explained in a note to Macmillan, outlining the discussion in his absence: 'I told the Cabinet that those of us who had been called in by you had felt bound to emphasise the difficulties you would face. I asked anyone who felt this might have been overdone to tell you so firmly as only a few had so far been consulted & all members of the Cabinet who had served with you had just as much right to tell you their view as everyone else. Other views were expressed which I should like to tell you about. What is absolutely sure is that whatever you say will command the maximum effort of us all. I hate all this & know what you must be feeling.'[19]

Dilhorne, the Lord Chancellor, had also sent Macmillan a note, outlining the difficulties if he decided to stay on and pressing for Hailsham as his successor. Neither Home nor Dilhorne told Macmillan that both had offered themselves as sounders of Cabinet opinion in the event of Macmillan's resignation. Dilhorne had said that as he was not a candidate he would be prepared to help in the consultations over a successor. Alec Home had followed suit, disclaiming interest in the succession and offering his services. In retrospect this was a crucial tactical error that was to have serious repercussions for his leadership and the result of the 1964 general election, as both Iain Macleod and Enoch Powell believed he had made a binding commitment that he was in no circumstances a candidate for the premiership. Both refused to serve in his administration, Powell because of this undertaking, Macleod because the 'revoked pledge' was one among other factors. Never is a rash word to use in politics, and less than twenty-four hours later Macmillan was urging Home to be a candidate, something Home had been considering on and off for nearly ten months. The statement that he was not a candidate tacitly paved the way for Hailsham's declaration. Why did Home give this hostage to fortune?

While he declined an interest on Tuesday 8 October, Home felt that his chances of the succession were remote, but it was a mistake to rule himself out in this way; one that his opponents would come back to time and time again. Dilhorne's offer to sound Cabinet opinion had required no seconder; by offering help, Home boxed himself in. When he later reconsidered his options, it was at the cost of unity in the Cabinet and a smooth transition to office. After Dilhorne's statement, several ministers left Cabinet promptly to catch the 1.35 p.m. train for Blackpool. Significantly, one of the Cabinet ministers who was absent from London as the situation now unfolded was Iain Macleod, Leader of the House of Commons and joint Chairman of the Party, who later complained that he had not 'any inkling' of many of the key developments.[20]

Alec Badenoch, a leading neurological surgeon, arrived soon after the Cabinet meeting. After a careful examination, he said that Macmillan was suffering from an inflammation of the prostate gland and that surgery would be required. This was a more serious development than the initial diagnosis had suggested, but Badenoch had no doubt that the prostate was benign. The absence of Sir John Richardson, Macmillan's regular doctor, at this crucial juncture has been the subject of much speculation, for by the time he did arrive, Macmillan had already decided to resign. It is one of the fascinating 'What ifs?' of recent political history. Macmillan's official biographer, Alistair Horne, records that the Prime Minister 'was predisposed to fear the worst' and that if Richardson had been present from the start, Macmillan would not have rushed into a decision he later regretted.[21] A contrary view has been expressed by David Badenoch, Alec Badenoch's son, himself a consultant urological surgeon:

> Alistair Horne disseminates an inaccurate view of events surrounding Harold Macmillan's resignation. In October 1963, Macmillan suffered acute retention of urine. He was attended by my father Alec Badenoch, a leading urological surgeon, and was immediately catheterised at 10 Downing Street prior to admission to King Edward VII's Hospital for Officers, where he underwent urgent surgery by way of retropubic prostatectomy to relieve the obstructing prostate. His recovery was uncomplicated and he led a fruitful life for the following twenty-three years.
>
> Horne suggests that there was a possible cancer of the prostate. This was not the case. The histology of the prostate showed benign hyperplasia and Macmillan was aware of this fact.
>
> At no time was he encouraged to resign by his medical attendants and indeed when he did resign he expressed great relief that he had reason to leave the political crises which he had faced. He termed this 'an act of God'.[22]

The key fact in this letter is that Macmillan was aware that his condition was benign, but the pain he was experiencing, backed by Home's account of the feelings in Cabinet, was the final straw. After so much uncertainty, his decision to resign was a relief, largely because it seemed to have been the 'stroke of fate'. To those who attended him in the aftermath of his operation, Macmillan seemed at ease in his mind, he said that he had been looking for a way out. 'This really might have been providential', he commented.[23]

Home left the Cabinet meeting without being aware of the medical situation and attributed the Prime Minister's state to worries about the leadership; the Foreign Secretary regarded himself as in some way to blame because of his unequivocal recent advice that Macmillan should step down. On his return to the Foreign Office, he wrote to Lady Dorothy Macmillan:

> My dear Dorothy,
> I feel horribly miserable and a very low sort of worm. I could not help but tell Harold truthfully that I felt he should not expose himself to another election campaign. I do not think I would have been repaying his unfailing trust & friendship if I had refrained from doing so. But I fear that anxiety may have made me clumsy & to appear inconsiderate & that I may have caused him extra worry, pain & strain. If I have done so, I do want you at least to know that I would rather be out of everything than be guilty of that. As to the choice before Harold I have made the best judgment I can but there are many who have come to a different conclusion & he must give their views full weight. I know you will make sure that he does so. On no account are you to answer this letter. I see Harold tomorrow & if you are about I will look in on you. But I felt so stricken when I saw him in Cabinet & knew & felt all that he was going through that I had to send you a line.[24]

Macmillan was very reluctant to enter hospital, but his doctors insisted that there was no alternative to an immediate operation. At a party to celebrate the reopening of 10 Downing Street after renovation, Macmillan moved between the guests, his Downing Street secretariat, and his medical advisers. He told Alec Home of his decision, and Home arranged to see him in hospital the next morning. Before the evening was out, Macmillan also told Butler that he would not be able to fight the next election. At this stage they were the only Cabinet members to know of Macmillan's intentions. According to Harold Evans, Macmillan's Press Secretary, Butler 'seemed rather surprised and said that surely this was going rather far, but shrugged his shoulders'.[25] The succession battle which he had so much feared was now at hand. Although Butler would occupy the Prime Minister's suite at the Imperial Hotel in Blackpool, this was no guarantee of a future tenure of 10 Downing Street. Arrangements were put in hand for a news release, the BBC announcing at 9.41 p.m. that Macmillan had entered hospital for an operation for prostatic obstruction. 'It is expected that this will involve his absence from official duties for some weeks and he has asked the First Secretary, Mr R.A. Butler, to take charge of the government while he is away.' The Cabinet Secretary Burke Trend gave instructions that all Prime Ministerial communications should be sent to Butler.[26] The next day's headlines told it all. MAC IN HOSPITAL ran the early editions of the *Daily Mail*. By early afternoon, the *Evening Standard* was proclaiming TORIES ON THE BOIL: CRISIS OVER THE LEADERSHIP HEADS FOR SHOWDOWN.[27]

When the news broke that Macmillan was in hospital, many Conservatives began ringing the palace, as the numbers of Sir Michael Adeane, the Queen's Private Secretary, and the two assistant secretaries, Sir Martin Charteris and Sir Edward Ford were not ex-directory. Although the Prime Minister had not yet announced that he was to stand down, the tacit assumption was that such a course would prove inevitable. Sir Charles Mott-Radclyffe, MP for Windsor and Vice-Chairman of the 1922 Committee, rang from his home in Norfolk to say that Rab Butler could not conceivably be chosen. Other MPs rang with equally strong views which they wished to communicate, setting out why Hailsham, Maudling and – as early as 9 October – Home should not be chosen.[28]

Butler travelled to Blackpool on Wednesday 9 October, and moved into the Prime Minister's Suite (Room 127) at the Imperial Hotel, where he went into immediate consultation with Iain Macleod and Lord Poole, to bring them up to date with developments in London. Macleod was under the mistaken impression that Philip Woodfield's call from Downing Street the previous evening had been a sign that he was in the special confidence of the Prime Minister, whereas he had in fact been told in his capacity as Joint Party Chairman. When further 'special' messages failed to arrive this added to Macleod's sense of discontent, although it was not the method of selecting a successor he objected to, but the result.[29] A poignant photograph appeared in the papers of Mollie Butler sitting in the corridor outside the Prime Minister's Suite whilst consultations took place within. Reports were already circulating that Hailsham might be on the verge of relinquishing his peerage.[30]

Home was meanwhile visiting Macmillan at the King Edward VII Hospital. This meeting on the morning of 9 October was crucial in the leadership crisis. Macmillan was not going to fight the election, but the timing of the announcement would influence the succession. If his resignation was announced during the conference it would favour candidates such as Hailsham, a darling of the constituency associations since his high-profile Chairmanship of the Party in the late 1950s, and, indeed Home himself, who was in the eyes of many activists a latter-day Plantagenet Palliser, 'such a one as justifies to the nation the seeming anomaly of a hereditary peerage and of primogeniture'.[31] If the announcement was delayed until Parliament reassembled, it would favour Butler and Maudling, the leading candidates in the Commons.[32] Overnight Macmillan had prepared a letter in his own hand, which he now showed to Alec Home:

> SECRET AND PERSONAL
> DRAFT LETTER TO MR BUTLER
>
> As you know I am going into Hospital for some weeks to have an operation for prostate trouble. This blow to my health has made me decide that I should, when I am well enough to see The Queen, resign my position as Prime Minister and Leader of the Party. I do not propose to announce this decision at this stage. But I should be grateful if you and any Ministers whom you care to consult would decide how best to apply this decision to resolving the problems which we have discussed, both in relation to the Party Conference at Blackpool and the succession.[33]

The question Macmillan and Butler had briefly considered the previous evening at Downing Street concerned the closing speech at the conference – whether it should be cancelled or whether Butler should speak in his place. It was obviously in Butler's interests to be seen as the leader-in-waiting, a position psychologically strengthened by his occupation of the Prime Minister's suite at the Imperial Hotel. The eventual decision that he should give the final rallying speech, was, however, to rebound on him.

Home now urged Macmillan to put an end to speculation, which was already feverish. The Party would expect some amplifying announcement to the desultory news release on the BBC. As that year's President of the National Union of Conservative Associations (another coincidence which contributed to the eventual outcome), Home was ideally placed to be the bearer of a message from the Prime Minister to the delegates (though supporters of Butler later believed that this placed Home in the conference limelight and that the announcement should have been delivered by the Deputy Prime Minister). The first casualty of the Macmillan/Home meeting was the draft letter to Butler. Had the letter been sent, much of the initiative would have passed to Butler, who had rung Tim Bligh to tell him that it was important for the Prime Minister to remember that the proceedings at Blackpool were more of a rally and that one did not take a serious decision at a rally. He therefore hoped that there would be no reference to the future leadership, a shrewd assessment of the dangers to his position if the conference became the equivalent of an American nominating convention. As it was, Home's presence in London during the first 48 hours of the Conference and his knowledge of Macmillan's intentions placed him at the hub of events. Tim Bligh and Knox Cunningham began work on a new letter, for Home to read out at Blackpool.

While this was being prepared, Macmillan turned to Home's own position. Why should he not make himself available? He was a senior and respected figure, the focus of no animosity and the Peerage Act, combined with the impending by-election at Kinross and West Perthshire, fortuitously afforded him the means to return to the Commons. Such a suggestion was not new; what was interesting was its timing, *preceding* Hailsham's announcement of his intention to disclaim, the action generally accepted as ending his candidature at the very moment of its announcement.

Macmillan's uncertainty about his resignation was coupled with a genuine indecision about the man he would most like to succeed him. He had always considered that successful political partnerships were based on a pairing of complementary opposites. As a result his instinctive preference had been for Hailsham or Macleod, 'the men of real genius in the Party who were the true inheritors of the Disraeli tradition of Tory Radicalism'.[34] Now Macmillan was not so sure. The reports from the Americans of Hailsham's conduct at the test ban negotiations had cooled his enthusiasm, and Macleod was no longer riding high in the Prime Minister's estimation; indeed the disillusion may have come as early as 1961, according to Reginald Bennett, Macleod's PPS: 'As Macleod entered the lobby with Bennett, Macmillan was sitting on the bench opposite. He caught Iain's gaze and his eyes flickered away. At that moment it was clear to Bennett that Macleod no longer had the Prime Minister's full confidence and that he considered his Secretary of State expendable.'[35] Although this cooling was the result of disagreements over the release of Dr Hastings Banda and some rapprochement had been achieved by 1963, doubts still lingered in Macmillan's mind as to Macleod's capacity for unifying the Party.

On the morning of 9 October Home was himself undecided about his candidacy. Hailsham was bound to receive strong initial backing at Blackpool and a crowded field could hardly sustain two peers. He told Macmillan that he would prefer to see how events unfolded, but he rehearsed with him some of his leadership thoughts. The previous week, Home had been at the United Nations General Assembly with Peter Thomas, his Minister of State at the Foreign Office. Although there was no disloyalty, there was a tacit assumption in his conversations with Thomas that the days of the Macmillan government were dwindling. Home felt that Butler would never win the confidence of the Party, and he also thought the disadvantages of Hailsham were manifest. Despite his great political virtues Home felt that Hailsham wore his heart too much on his sleeve, an impression confirmed by subsequent events. (In 1990 he was to find the harrowing personal details recounted in Hailsham's second book of memoirs *A Sparrow's Flight* inappropriate for outsiders to share.) He was in no doubt that Hailsham had the intellectual capacity for the job, but not the right temperament. In his mind, Home discounted both as likely successors to Macmillan, despite the support from different sections of the Party. Macleod he did not even consider. The choice, he told Thomas, would be between Maudling and Heath. He felt that Maudling had the better chance, because Ted Heath's single-mindedness and lack of personal rapport with some backbenchers would disqualify him in many people's eyes (a prophetic foretaste of how Heath's leadership eventually foundered). Never once did he hint to his Foreign Office junior that he might be a candidate himself.

These random thoughts did not strike a chord with Macmillan; the change was too soon for the younger generation; Heath, Maudling and Macleod had all been given their chance in the reshuffle of July 1962, and none had yet established prominence. Macmillan made it clear that a leader in his sixties would be much more likely to command widespread support than a younger man. Indeed Macmillan hinted that the Lord Chancellor, Reggie Dilhorne (born in August 1905), might be preferable to Hailsham. For a time Dilhorne, whose role was to be as a sounder of opinions, a task he fulfilled in Butler's words, 'like a large Clumber spaniel sniffing the bottoms of the hedgerows', was discussed by the two men, though this only served to stengthen Home's position in Macmillan's view.[36] Later John Morrison told Dilhorne not to discount his own candidature as a second dark horse, if Alec Home fell as the first.[37]

Knox Cunningham then brought in the first draft of the letter Alec

Home was to read out to the conference. The initial plan was that this should take place on the Friday afternoon, possibly as a conclusion to the formal business, with the Saturday rally cancelled. When the news came through later that day that the executive of the National Union had agreed to Rab Butler giving the leader's speech, it was decided that Home should make the announcement on arrival in Blackpool on the Thursday (10 October). As to his own position, Home said he would consider the options and let Macmillan know before travelling north.

The next morning, Home's resolve had stiffened significantly. He and Macmillan agreed that there was no bandwagon movement behind an unstoppable candidate. Indeed there could not be, because officially there was no vacancy. Hailsham had made a speech on the Wednesday evening at Blackpool, in which he had said, 'In the Cabinet we are a loyal band of friends and feelings of personal loyalty are really of the stuff of which public life is and ought to be made.'[38] The days ahead were to test that loyalty to the utmost. Home agreed that he would allow his name to be drafted if there were sufficient support for his candidacy, then flew to Blackpool and prepared to address the conference about Macmillan's intentions.

Alec Home had never been a great attender of Party conferences. As a peer he had no constituency responsibilities and during his Lanark days the annual gathering had not been the media circus it later became. Home arrived to find the atmosphere feverish with speculation. From the start of the week, when a young holidaymaker was drowned in the sea opposite the Imperial Hotel, the whole affair had seemed jinxed. Home's appearance in Blackpool on the Thursday afternoon, his name mooted in *The Times* that morning as a possible fourth candidate, was to transform everything from the moment he appeared on the platform in the Winter Gardens, where John Boyd-Carpenter was about to reply to a debate on Local Government Finance. Delegates noticed how the main platform was filling up with party grandees, and rumour spread that an announcement was imminent about Macmillan's future. 'The Debate then reached the point when I was due to reply', Boyd-Carpenter later recalled. 'The disappointment when, as directed by the Chairman, I, rather than Alec, went to the microphone was painfully if politely evident.' Whispered messages from the platform suggested that the Chief Secretary should shorten his speech.[39] After thirty difficult minutes, Boyd-Carpenter sat down and Alec Home, wearing his half-moon spectacles, came to the microphone. The audience were hushed, for instinctively people felt they were about to witness an important moment in British political history. Home duly began to read out the letter, which for many in the Cabinet was their first intimation that Macmillan was retiring. He explained first how he had seen the Prime Minister in hospital and had been asked to read out the letter 'as soon as I could after arriving at Blackpool'.[40] He continued slowly:

> I should be very grateful if you would tell the conference assembled at Blackpool, of which you are President, how sorry I am not to be with them this week. I was especially looking forward to the mass meeting on Saturday, which is a great annual event and on this occasion likely to have special significance.
>
> It is now clear that, whatever might have been my previous feelings, it will not be possible for me to carry the physical burden of leading the Party at the next general election. If the operation which I am to undergo tomorrow proves successful it is clear that I will need a considerable period of convalescence. I would not be able to face all that is involved in a prolonged electoral campaign. Nor could I hope to fulfil the tasks of Prime Minister for any extended period, and I have so informed the Queen.
>
> In these circumstances I hope that it will soon be possible for the customary processes of consultation to be carried on within the party about its future leadership.
>
> I am writing to you as President of the Conference to ask you to announce this at the earliest opportunity.[41]

Turning to Mrs Shepherd, who was presiding, Home said that it was 'a moment of sadness and deep emotion for all Conservatives'.[42]

The letter was a catalyst in the struggle which now ensued. Delegates wanted to start on the process of identifying a new leader; indeed the phrase about 'the customary processes' invited nomination and canvassing, but it simply disguised the fact that there were no customary processes. In the words of Vernon Bogdanor, who has described what now ensued as 'guided democracy', the phrase 'implied precedents where none existed'.[43] Each Conservative leadership struggle had been settled in its own individual way. But Macmillan was establishing guidelines for consultation, which were to be widespread. A further effect of the letter was to draw attention to the fact that Home was President of the National Union: he was now one of the movers and shakers.

On the way back to the Hotel, Hailsham reminded Home of their earlier agreement that the field would support only one peer, indicating some apprehension over Home's favourable reception by the delegates. He was also aware that the *Daily Telegraph* had reported that morning, 'A comparatively new name is beginning to be "talked up" in the conference and hotel lobbies: the Earl of Home, Foreign Secretary. There is clearly a strong move to turn the party's opinion in favour of Lord Home as offering "the highest common factor" of leadership qualities.'[44] Hailsham said he did not think it a good idea for Home to stand, as he had no experience of domestic affairs. Home pointed out his four years' experience at the Scottish Office, apart from his work at the Ministry of Labour. Hailsham said this was not at a senior enough level, his protests indicating his concern that Home might stand, despite his statement at Cabinet two days earlier. Home made no such pledge on this occasion.[45]

The first move came from Hailsham that evening, possibly encouraged by Macmillan's much earlier hints of support and those of Julian Amery and Maurice Macmillan, and by the feeling that he needed to be in the field before Home. At the end of his prepared speech at a fringe meeting Hailsham said he had one other thing to say to his audience. 'I wish to say tonight that it is my intention after deep thought to disclaim my peerage.' The rest of his words were lost in the general enthusiasm that now gripped the body of the hall but was not apparent among the platform party, as one of Hailsham's main aides, Dennis Walters, recorded in his diary: 'Geoffrey Lloyd appeared livid; Keith Joseph embarrassed; Toby Aldington, William Rees-Mogg and Peter Goldman all embarrassed; Peter Thorneycroft supportive; Martin Redmayne, Chief Whip, stony and prefectorial, clearly not best pleased; Michael Fraser rather embarrassed.'[46]

It was a formidable alliance of grandees to have antagonised. He was not helped by Randolph Churchill's distribution of American-style 'Q' buttons, some of which he even offered to Rab Butler, nor by his appearance in the lobby of the Imperial Hotel with his infant daughter Kate and her bottle. 'Never discount the baby food,' said an influential figure to the author, 'as a factor in disqualifying Hailsham.'[47]

Alec Home shrewdly weighed his options as the field of front runners came back towards him. Although his rival from the Lords had a higher public profile, Home was well placed to see off more strongly fancied rivals from the Commons because of the timing of the contest. For Butler 1963 was a contest too far; although he was only seven months older than Home, he was not a 'fresh' face. For the younger generation in their forties, such as Maudling, Heath and Macleod, it was a contest too soon. As Anthony Howard had predicted, the Conservative leadership battle was to be galvanised by the entry of Mr Home and Mr Hogg. They plugged a gap between the Macmillan generation, approaching their seventies, and the 1950 intake, who might block the leadership for too lengthy a period by succeeding to the office of Prime Minister too young.[48] Hailsham and Home were ideally placed to be stop-gap candidates till electoral matters had clarified. For one thing, neither would linger in the post after a general election defeat. There was another advantage that both men had over Butler, as Anthony Howard pointed out in his article:

> The great point of peril in any political career comes at the moment that a powerful figure begins to be thought of as a prospective prime minister. Almost invariably from that moment on things begin to go wrong: unsuspected faults and weaknesses are looked for and discovered, the slightest tactical mistake leads straight to the conclusion that the highest prize must really remain beyond reach and on every side heads are much more ready to shake in dismissal than they are to nod in approval. Mr R.A. Butler knows all about this process – and so, for that matter, does Mr Iain Macleod: they have both had to learn the hard way that the position of 'front-runner' is as unenviable in British politics as it is normally at American conventions. But up to now every British potential prime minister has had to endure this phase – which may possibly explain why there have been so many casualties amongst them. The real advantage that both Lord Home and Lord Hailsham may have available to them over all their rivals is that they may now be, if they want to, the first politicians in British history to make a bid for party leadership without having to survive the customary years of ordeal. Their very membership of the House of Lords (Lord Hailsham's since 1950 and Lord Home's since 1951) may in the end turn out to be the best thing that ever happened to them: it has, as it were, sheltered them throughout the crucial years and then put them down safe and sound within a few yards of the winning post.[49]

In fact, Hailsham, by virtue of his high-profile position as a bell-ringing, dawn-bathing Party Chairman, who was the scourge of TV interviewers such as Robert McKenzie over the Profumo Affair, was not as 'sheltered' as his membership of the Lords might suggest. Temperamentally, Hailsham was no shrinking violet. Home on the other hand had escaped scrutiny, not merely because of his self-effacing character, but because for nine years he had held posts at the Scottish

Office and the Commonwealth Office that had not naturally brought him before the public gaze. Even as Foreign Secretary – the Cuban missile crisis is a key example – he had done good by stealth. The United Nations was his province, not the Lime Grove studios of the BBC. The key phrase in Howard's article was '*if they want to*'. Of Hailsham's 'passionate desire to win, to be the first' (Curzon's self-description[50]) there can be little doubt. Benn's campaign had given him a belated lifeline. There was no such agonising when Alec Dunglass assumed the Earldom of Home in July 1951. Life – and the career – carried on. But the provisions of the Peerage Act of 31 July 1963 applied no less to Alec Home than to Quintin Hailsham. The clause insisted upon by Lord Salisbury in the amendment of 16 July, allowing current peers the opportunity of disclaiming within a period of twelve months, made both Home and Hailsham possible candidates in a leadership contest that took place before 31 July 1964. This left a very narrow window in the timetable if either was to become Prime Minister. If Macmillan decided to lead the Party into the next election, and if he decided to allow the Parliament elected in October 1959 to run its full course, then the cut-off date of 31 July 1964 would have passed for both Home and Hailsham. If he fought (and lost) in the autumn of 1963 or the spring of 1964, the leadership would be handed on to the younger generation in opposition. Home's only chance – and the same applied to Hailsham – would be if Macmillan, for whatever reason, stepped down in the autumn of 1963 when the vacancy would be for both leadership of the party *and* Prime Minister. Rather in the manner of second ballot candidates under the codified system (William Whitelaw in 1975, John Major and Douglas Hurd in 1990), Home and Hailsham would hardly wish to disclaim until there was a vacancy. One of the ironies of the 1963 leadership contest was that Butler was a principal participant in the legislative process that was ultimately to deny him the crown.[51]

When did Alec Home first consider the prospect of the premiership? It was not a consideration that came upon him suddenly. The first recorded instance in his papers of the question being mentioned, albeit light-heartedly, was in the six-line poem Jock Colville sent him in July 1960. Yet Jock Colville has also gone on record as citing Edith Watson's view (as early as 1939) that 'Lord Dunglass' would one day be Prime Minister. The issue did not greatly concern Alec Home, though Kenneth Harris raised the prospect in his interview for the *Observer* profile in September 1962. From the moment Tony Benn began his campaign in earnest to renounce his title after the death of his father, there was the constitutional possibility that Home could eventually be Prime Minister. But if any moment can be identified as the beginning of his journey, it was 14 December 1962. Elizabeth Home had kept scrapbooks of their lives together for nearly thirty years and was compiling Volume 26. She scoured the newsprints for any mention of Alec Home and juxtaposed the subsequent cuttings with family memorabilia; Anthony Howard's article speculating on a Home or Hogg premiership was placed in the appropriate volume. It was percipient and well argued, and made a deep impression on Alec Home.[52] If one is given cogent reasons why one might be Prime Minister before the year is out, it tends to concentrate the mind.

The question, as so often in Conservative leadership struggles, was not how many people were for you, but how many were against you. Dissatisfaction with the available candidates in the Commons made Home's position much stronger. The principle of negative choice would apply in the Upper House also and Hailsham had aroused many antagonisms, which Home had not. If Home had fewer immitigable opponents than other candidates and could be persuaded to run, he could be, according to some early calculations, the inevitable and natural choice. 'I'm an Alec Home man,' Nigel Birch pronounced to all and sundry in Blackpool on Friday 11 October. 'There aren't any other possibilities. He's *going* to get it.'[53] Home's main hurdle was not to disqualify himself from the race (which is why the assurance to Cabinet on 8 October was a mistake), or to arouse widespread antagonisms when he came under scrutiny as a candidate. He had many powerful allies. Martin Redmayne, the Chief Whip, had written to him during the summer, long before Macmillan's resignation, urging him to be a candidate in due course.[51]

Several strands came together in the summer and autumn of 1963 to make such a candidature possible. The government was deeply unpopular in the opinion polls. Privately, the Prime Minister vacillated between retiring and staying. A major constitutional reform of peerage law came into effect. Above all there was a mood of restlessness and anxiety in the parliamentary party as the ever-approaching general election concentrated minds. The prospect of a lost seat is the most powerful inducement to a Conservative backbencher to consider a change in the leadership.

This mood was best identified by David Bruce, the American ambassador in London, when he wrote to Dean Rusk about the British political scene, two days after the Profumo debate in the House of

Commons. In a telegram marked PRIORITY, which coloured Kennedy's view of Macmillan as a tired leader when they met at Birch Grove a fortnight later, Bruce made the following points:

> 1. On past record Conservative Party capable of moving with brutal speed when fountainhead of Leader's authority dries up. Conservatives now beginning actively consider when and by whom Macmillan should be replaced.
> 2. Several factors must be weighed in reaching decision:
> A. Timing. Some believe Macmillan unfairly if inevitably victimized and are willing to give him opportunity to make dignified exit in succeeding months. Others wish to begin reversing disastrous public opinion rating Party as soon as possible by cutting losses through swift change in leadership.
> B. Electoral chances. If judgment reached that Tories have no rpt no chance at all of winning next Election Tories might decide to choose Butler or Hailsham as stop-gap leader to take Party through election and then step aside. Some might think Butler would probably accept the stop-gap role more gracefully than Hailsham. Hailsham cannot enter House of Commons before passage House of Lords Reform Bill.
> C. Need for reassurance. In view of shock and depression Profumo scandal caused among Party faithful, particularly women, many feel need for strong fighting personality. This consideration will strengthen position Hailsham over Butler because former is renowned for his exhortational qualities.
> D. Respectability. Party also feels need for morally impeccable leadership. Both Hailsham and Butler would meet this requirement but Butler's long experience in Cabinet and his political savoir faire may win him some support as 'tried and true'. Strong admirers Heath believe in present atmosphere unmarried man would be at great disadvantage. Seems likely Heath supporters might give their support to Hailsham or Butler rather than Maudling. If Maudling should become Party Leader now it would be difficult to replace him even after defeat in general election unless he grossly mismanaged affairs.
> E. Party image. Some advocate swift creation new image for Party with aim of reducing Labor [sic] gains at general election as far as possible. Even if Labor wins, the strength of its grip on power will clearly depend on size of majority. This emphasises importance of Tories attracting as much of floating vote as possible. It strengthens argument for much younger leadership. On this score Maudling likely to attract support.

3. Macleod does not seem to be in running for leadership – at least for time being.
4. Conservative Party does not select its leaders by ballot but by sounding out opinion influential groups in Party, especially Conservative backbenchers. Consensus must be arrived at by soundings in Lords, Commons, Clubs and Party organisations. At this moment normal focus of Party opinion, the Whips, temporarily discredited owing to Redmayne's role in Profumo affair. This will increase difficulties of reaching consensus. Views of such leading personalities as John Morrison, Chairman 1922 Committee, Party Manager Lord Poole, Members of 'One Nation Group' and other supporters of Tory Modernism, leading Party contributors, top figures in Party Organization like Selwyn Lloyd and Lord Aldington and last but not least Salisbury (once thought to be a king-maker but whose influence is now difficult to calculate) must all be taken into account.
5. No single obvious alternative to Macmillan exists. In past this situation made it easy for Macmillan to quash attempts to replace him. Now that it is accepted that he must go the same factors that worked to Macmillan's advantage will complicate task of party leaders in consolidating support around a single candidate.
6. Picture inevitability Macmillan's replacement strengthened by publication Gallup poll figures (based on sample of 1250) in Daily Telegraph June 19 showing only 23 per cent interviewed thought Macmillan should carry on as PM. Thirty per cent favored [sic] immediate general election, 41 per cent wanted Macmillan to retire.[55]

One of the most interesting points of this perceptive document, concerns the need for 'morally impeccable leadership', a factor not to be discounted in understanding the final outcome. Also noteworthy is the emphasis on the importance of the backbenchers and on the influence of 'top figures in party organization like Selwyn Lloyd'. All three of these factors were to be crucial in the ensuing struggle.[56]

Many preparations were in hand when this moment arrived. As has been noted, the palace were in a state of readiness for any handover of power. Alec Home had been party to some of these talks, as he explained to Macmillan in a letter on 16 June, just before the Profumo Debate in the House of Commons:

My dear Harold,

This is just to wish you every possible good fortune in the debate tomorrow. I am sure that in the country the corner has already been turned and that you will win the day decisively.

I have asked Martin Redmayne to tell you of two private conversations which I have had with Oliver Poole and one with Michael Adeane. I would like to tell you about them myself but I will not bother you until after tomorrow.

From what Oliver told me I am satisfied there is no scheming going on but there is a lot of anxiety about what may happen at the next stage and too many people with bright and rather wild ideas.

I told Oliver two things. First that you must have time to assess the implication of the debate and that you must take charge of the situation and decide what you want to do. No one else can or should try to decide for you although naturally your friends and colleagues would give every help they could if you asked for it.

Secondly there must be enough time so that you and indeed everyone else who is consulted can arrive at the right answer. No one should contemplate hasty decisions.

The rumours from the H of C were so bad on Thursday as to the possible result of a division that I thought that someone ought to be aware of the technicalities should everything go completely wrong. Otherwise there would be total confusion.

Happily people seem to have taken a grip of themselves so I trust my talk with Michael is now happily academic. He would, I know, want to talk to you sometime when you are ready.

I am really no good at situations of this sort but people come along and say I am the only one they can talk to! I hope tomorrow will clear the air a lot but I would like a chance to see you and you know that if it is within my power to help at all you have only to ask.[57]

This letter reveals the real possibility that Macmillan could have been driven from office by an adverse vote in the Profumo Debate. The majority sank to 57; had it been much lower (40 was considered the crucial hurdle), Macmillan might have resigned. Alec Home was consulted, as a figure then aloof from the battle, by Sir Michael Adeane, the Queen's Private Secretary, for his advice as to the constitutional procedures to be adopted if the Prime Minister resigned suddenly. His advice was that the Palace would inevitably become involved in the process, which would not be a matter of political controversy if the Monarch took the advice of the outgoing Prime Minister – the origins of the 'YOU CHOOSE, WE SEND FOR' approach the Palace adopted. By 9 October, Home had again been involved with the Palace when Macmillan sent a formal confirmation of his intention to step down.

'The PM has been discussing with Lord Home this morning the situation caused by his illness', Tim Bligh reported to Sir Edward Ford. 'The PM therefore proposes to make it quite clear that he has no intention of continuing as PM at the next election, even if his recovery is complete.' Macmillan sent a copy of his proposed statement to be read out to the conference at Blackpool and formally sought the Queen's permission for this to be done. In the original draft of the letter, the phrase 'customary processes of consultation to be carried on within the Party' is added in Home's own hand.[58]

In fact, the customary processes had been going on at John Morrison's retreat on the windswept island of Islay, off the West Coast of Scotland. In July, Edward Heath went to stay with the Morrisons, by no means his normal pattern of summer relaxation, as he was more often to be found at cultural events such as the Salzburg Festival or Glyndebourne. But there was a political aspect to the visit. As a former chief whip, Heath discussed with the Chairman of the 1922 Committee possible autumn developments. Morrison told him that he had come to the conclusion with Charles Mott-Radclyffe, Vice-Chairman of the 1922 Committee, and another senior backbencher, Sir Harry Legge-Bourke, that Alec Home should run for the leadership. Morrison was deputed to see Home, who subsequently told him on 31 July, the day the Peerage Act was entered on to the Statute Book, that he would see his doctor, John Henderson. During the Islay holiday, Heath agreed, and from that moment put all his support behind the Foreign Secretary's candidacy.[59]

Home's statement to Hailsham on the afternoon of 10 October, that he was to see his doctor, confirmed what Hailsham had suspected for some time, namely that Home's decision had been made much earlier at the behest of Morrison, backed by Heath.[60]

A stream of visitors now began to call on Alec Home in his hotel room in Blackpool ahead of the Foreign Affairs Debate scheduled for the next morning. Elizabeth Home was travelling up to Blackpool by train that day, having been consulted by her husband at all stages about his possible candidacy. They were in full agreement about the course to be taken if Macmillan retired before 31 July 1964, the 'cut-off date' for disclaiming. On her return to London, Lady Home was consulted by Sir Michael Adeane on 14 October, without her husband's knowledge, about the situation. Adeane wanted to know in confidence if Alec Home would accept the premiership if it were offered. Elizabeth Home knew of the pressures that were mounting, but said that if the situation demanded it, then he would serve.[61]

One of the first visitors to Home's room was Lord Dilhorne, whose enthusiasm for Hailsham had now cooled. He urged Home to be a candidate; ministers such as Duncan Sandys and John Hare added their voices. Backbench MPs such as Sir William Anstruther-Gray, Sir Charles Mott-Radclyffe and Colonel C.G. Lancaster the MP for Fylde, pressed him to stand. Nigel Birch, Treasury Minister until the 'little local difficulties' of 1958, also told Home that he provided the best chance of uniting the Party but doubted that Home would serve. 'He has eaten the King's salt' he kept saying, a phrase taken up by Robin Day to the puzzlement of his broadcasting colleagues.[62]

The pivotal figure in Home's campaign, however, was Selwyn Lloyd, former Foreign Secretary and Chancellor of the Exchequer. He was one of the most senior figures in the Party to urge Home to stand and Home respected his judgment. Following his dismissal as Chancellor of the Exchequer in July 1962, Lloyd had skilfully rehabilitated himself by travelling the country in the worst winter since 1947 to produce a report on party organisation. As a result, many of the rank and file were prepared to listen to what he had to say about the leadership. Lloyd also had influence with Martin Redmayne, the Chief Whip. These three factors were a powerful combination. On three separate occasions Lloyd told Alec Home that the premiership was his for the asking and, in a manner quite dissimilar to Randolph Churchill's advocacy of Hailsham, quietly spread the claims of the Foreign Secretary. By 11 October, the Lord Chancellor, the Chief Whip and the party's senior backbencher all in Home's camp. The three went for a walk along the seafront at Blackpool to discuss the options. Here they were met by a Labour-voting old age pensioner who told them that his Socialist household recognised in Home the qualities to lead the nation. Selwyn Lloyd later recalled that this pensioner represented 'the gnarled voice of truth'.[63]

Alec Home played the part of reluctant candidate to perfection, a fact that key figures in other camps were beginning to recognise and fear. The *New York Times* correspondent, Tony Lewis, told Dennis Walters of the Hailsham camp, that Home's conduct was exactly how compromise candidates behaved at American conventions.[64] He began his speech in the Foreign Affairs Debate on the morning of 11 October with the remark, 'I am offering a prize to any newspaperman this morning who can find a clue in my speech that this is Lord Home's bid to take over the leadership of the Conservative Party.' (At this moment one of the platform party whispered to his neighbour, 'Alec, you're lying!')[65] After surveying his feelings about communism ('deadly poison'), he ended: 'One of our distinguished generals once said when asked for a definition of leadership, "Be yourself plus". My whole plea to the people of our country today is that Britain should be herself plus. If that is the mood of the nation then we will be able to deliver to our people that most elusive of prizes, which is peace, and bring that priceless prize at last within the grasp of men.'[66]

Home sat down to a rapturous reception. On the BBC's *Gallery* programme, Ian Trethowan summed up the mood by saying, 'That was Lord Home – getting the biggest ovation yet from the Conservative conference. In another hectic day of lobbying here at Blackpool he's now emerged as the man who may be drafted into the premiership to break the deadlock between Mr Butler and Lord Hailsham.'[67] The newspapers next day endorsed this view. 'The chandeliers rocked with the applause for the Earl of Home, in crisp fighting form' ran the report in the *Daily Mail*.[68] Maudling's speech in the Economic Debate on that day was received with little enthusiasm and Butler's closing speech failed conspicuously to rouse the Tories. 'In contrast Lord Home's contribution in the debate on foreign affairs was regarded as a considerable success.'[69] The speech had given the Party faithful something to cheer and had pleased the political pundits with its survey of the foreign scene in the aftermath of the Test Ban Treaty, the outstanding achievement of Macmillan's last year in office.

For those who were close observers of the way things were developing, however, it was yet another example of the reluctant candidate keeping his options open. The previous evening Home had been interviewed by Robin Day in the curious, airless underground BBC studio in the Imperial Hotel where waiting politicians took their turn on an upturned orange box. Robin Day attempted to whittle out of Home a confession that he was a runner. He asked him if he was aware that he was widely regarded as an increasingly strong contender, whether he was discouraging people from advocating his candidacy and whether he was going to renounce his title. 'It will be settled by the normal customary processes,' the Foreign Secretary replied. As Home left, Maudling turned to Robin Day, 'Well, Alec is obviously going to run,' he said.[70]

Following the decision of the Executive of the National Union, Rab Butler was due to give the closing speech – a decision made when it had been assumed that Butler would be standing in for a temporarily indisposed leader. What Rab Butler knew was that 'by the time he came to make the speech, he would inevitably be regarded as a declared candidate for the succession'.[71] As President of the National Union, Alec Home was to take the chair. Before the rally, the Homes lunched with the Butlers at the Imperial Hotel, and Home casually introduced what was a bombshell for Butler, who had stayed aloof from all the intrigue of the week and was thus substantially out of touch with the way things were moving. When Home told him that he was seeing his doctor in London the next week, Butler did not grasp the significance of the remark and asked him why. 'Because I have been approached about the possibility of my becoming the Leader of the Conservative Party', replied Home.[72] It is difficult to imagine a more unsettling piece of news for Butler to receive at what was already an anxious and nervous time for him. The fact that the information was imparted in front of Lady Home and Mollie Butler precluded further discussion between the two men. The lunch continued, but Butler's equanimity had been deeply bruised. When they proceeded to the Winter Gardens, Home was again received with enthusiastic applause as he introduced the platform party. His remarks about Butler were generous:

> The Prime Minister being absent the choice to make the speech which winds up our debates falls naturally and properly on Mr Butler. There is no need for me to assure him that he will get the warmest of receptions, for everyone here and in the country knows that there is no one who has given more loyal and unselfish service to the country and there is no one who has done more to design Conservative policy for the modern Britain of which I invite him to talk to you now.[73]

Butler rose to speak at 2.15 p.m. So dramatic was the situation that the BBC kept breaking into its Saturday afternoon *Grandstand* programme for frequent updates. This led to some ironic juxtapositions over the closing stages of the conference, as, in addition to *Grandstand*, scheduled programmes included 'One Enchanted Weekend' and 'The Uneasy Crown'. Sports coverage had begun at 1.15, with boxing's 'Fight of the Week'. At 1.30 there was a two-minute update from Robin Day. 'Here in Blackpool nobody had any idea that another fight of the week had been going on,' he began. 'In half an hour's time we will reach the climax of one of the most fantastic weeks in the history of British politics.' During racing from Kempton Park (Wily Trout and Secret

Step among the favoured runners), short extracts of Butler's speech were transmitted live. Before the rugby league got underway, the BBC returned again to Robin Day and Ian Trethowan for a recording of the end of Butler's speech and a summing up. There was no disguising Butler's failure to stir his audience, noted in the Sunday newspapers.[74] That evening's edition of *That Was The Week That Was* concluded with Willie Rushton (shortly to be one of Home's opponents at the Kinross and West Perthshire by-election), impersonating Macmillan as a faded music-hall star singing 'The party's over'.

Alec Home said later of Butler's speech, 'It was rather a pity really that he just had this one sort of failure, which anyone can have.'[75] How far can Home be blamed for that failure? The news that he was a candidate for the leadership, a fact carefully concealed from the rank and file at Blackpool, despite all the talking-up of his chances, was a grievous blow to Butler, whose chances must have seemed rosier after Hailsham's declaration.

The Conservatives left Blackpool in a state of turmoil. Although the opinion polls were predicting a Butler or Hailsham premiership (they were co-favourites with the bookmakers at 5–4, with Home shortening to 4–1), things were not so simple. Both Butler and Hailsham evoked strong opposition. In the minds of many, the real choice would be between Home and Maudling, not for ideological reasons but on grounds of age. Was the Party prepared to switch over to the next generation, or would it go for the man whom Maudling supporters dubbed 'The Manchurian Candidate'?[76]

Ministers began to assemble in London on the Monday (14 October), knowing that the coming week would resolve the situation. The Queen arrived overnight from Balmoral, and the lobbying that had taken place in Blackpool was replaced by hurried telephone calls, as MPs kept abreast of developments. One minister who travelled to Italy on government business for a couple of days at the beginning of the week, noted how Home was a possibility when he left the country, but that on his return on Wednesday 16 October was seen as a certainty. On Monday Home worked at the Foreign Office in the morning, and lunched privately. Macmillan, who had read the Sunday newspapers, prepared a memorandum for Butler to read out at Cabinet on Tuesday 15 October, outlining the proposed method of consultation of all sections of the Party. Macleod was still considered a possible candidate, and, as Robert McKenzie has commented, 'did not realise the extent to which all possible contenders for the succession are, as it were, kept in a state of semi-purdah while the soundings are conducted'.[77] Butler arrived in London at noon and went to 10 Downing Street, where he saw Dilhorne and Home during the evening to discuss Macmillan's memorandum, before retiring to the St Ermin's Hotel. Apart from this meeting, Home spent most of the day at 1 Carlton Gardens. There were few sightings of Maudling or Hailsham.

The second phase of the Conservative leadership struggle began on Tuesday 15 October.[78] The Cabinet meeting that morning agreed the procedures outlined by Macmillan. This process ensured that the views of the party as a whole would be considered, and despite Macleod's criticisms in his *Spectator* article of the 'magic circle', he said publicly a few days later that a system of consultation was preferable to a formal vote.[79] Robert McKenzie's comments are worth quoting in full, as they explain the process fully:

> The tenor of Macleod's article curiously suggests that he assumed that the *first* choices of the Cabinet Ministers would (and should) be of decisive importance. Martin Redmayne emphasised, however, that those conducting the operation were seeking what might be called 'the highest common factor' of agreement. On this basis, even if Home did not have the largest number of first choices among ministers, he might, if he had overwhelming 'second-choice' strength (and faced little outright hostility), be considered to have the 'strongest' Cabinet backing. Macleod also seems to have been greatly surprised and exasperated that during the decisive period of the enquiries the Cabinet did not meet (presumably to arrive at a collective judgment as to who should succeed to the leadership). With no less than six of its members possible contenders for the succession – including its presiding officer, R.A. Butler – this would have been not only an unprecedented, but very probably an unworkable, procedure. After more than a decade in the Cabinet Macleod appears to have forgotten that on the occasion of the choice of a new leader it is the machinery of *party* and not of *government* which takes precedence.[80]

Home went to see Macmillan in the hospital at 3.30 p.m., staying for an hour. Tim Bligh wrote a 'Top Secret Note for the Record' of this meeting.[81] The Prime Minister was keen to hear at first hand all the happenings at Blackpool and whether Home had decided to be a candidate; he was relieved to hear that Home was seeing his doctor that evening. Three main points were then made: 'David Ormsby Gore had rung up in a great state to say that if Lord Hailsham was made Prime Minister this would be a tremendous blow to Anglo-American relations and would in fact end the special relationship. It was believed that the ambassador had been talking to the President. It was agreed that the Ambassador should be asked to come to London right away. The manifest reason would be something else.'

Macmillan then moved on to the question of Hailsham's reception at Blackpool, of which he had heard conflicting reports. Home said that the incidents at Blackpool had 'alarmed him'. His account of the Q buttons, the meeting at which Hailsham had announced his intention to disclaim, and the baby food in the hotel lobby confirmed Macmillan's suspicions: Hailsham did not have the temperament for the job, which he had already noted in a draft memorandum on the succession. Home told Macmillan that 'he would be prepared to undertake the task if he was asked by the Prime Minister to do so in order to prevent the Party collapsing'. He had been much heartened that morning by a letter from Lord Woolton, the former Party Chairman, delivered by hand to 1 Carlton Gardens. It read:

> My dear Alec,
>
> I trust you will not regard this letter as an impertinence. I am deeply concerned for the country if we have anyone who is not the best available person as Prime Minister.
>
> I have taken no part in the many conversations that have been taking place, but I hear this morning that you are both reluctant to have your name put forward and are hesitant in the matter ... I understand your attitude on both accounts but let me urge you to dispel any views about your suitability for the post: I do not think the view that you have not taken any ministerial part in home affairs should count for a moment. The Prime Minister should not be an expert: he should be a man of detached judgment, who can balance competing views and claims. So far from being a weakness I think this is a strong point: you have the tremendous strength of the complete trust of anyone who has ever worked with you and that will ensure the strength of the country under your guidance. I do beg you to consider it. I think I understand your hesitation: the honour, great as it is, means little to you: it is a task that absorbs a man's whole time and is physically exhausting and a great strain.
>
> For you to take it will mean an enormous sacrifice and I would not lightly write this letter, but I believe you will give the country the strength it needs at this juncture. The very success of your

previous service inevitably makes one pray that you will accept this heavy burden – and so I venture to write to you.

Ever yours,
Fred.

Six days later Alec Home was to write to Woolton from the Cabinet Room in Downing Street:

My dear Fred,
Very many thanks for your letter. Your good opinion is a real encouragement to me and I am most grateful for your offer of advice. Your letter to me influenced me a lot and it was kindness itself to take so much trouble. Come and see me soon as your wisdom and counsel will be invaluable.

Yours ever,
Alec.[82]

Woolton was pushing at an open door as far as Home's candidacy was involved, as Macmillan had gathered from Martin Redmayne. Indeed Home had already told Selwyn Lloyd (the nearest equivalent he had to 'a campaign manager') of his determination to stand:

Tues 15 Oct. Saw Lord Home. He said that he had come to the conclusion that he will accept if the Queen sends for him after all the consultations and it being apparent that most people want him. He said that the opposition to Quintin in the Cabinet was: Heath, Powell, Boyle, Joseph. Sandys was strongly pressing Home to accept, and he thought that Soames, who was his next visitor, also wanted him to do so. Lord Home advised me to get in touch with Lord Chelmer, because Alec understood that the constituency associations, possibly the area chairmen, were nothing like as unanimously for Hailsham as had been represented. It would be a problem if both he, Alec, and Quintin left the House of Lords together, but he thought that by getting Alan Lennox-Boyd that might be solved. He had spoken to Lord Salisbury who thought that the House of Lords aspect could be managed.[83]

Home was the first of the senior ministers that Macmillan saw in a two-day procession to his hospital room. Their talk confirmed that Home would stand, if asked, information that the Palace, through Adeane's private talk with Elizabeth Home, already knew. But the decisive piece of information Home gave the Prime Minister that afternoon, which blackballed Hailsham's candidature in Macmillan's eyes, was the message he had received from David Ormsby-Gore in Washington about the American unease at the prospect of Hailsham as British Prime Minister, the legacy of the Test Ban Treaty.

After Home's visit at 3.30 p.m., the Prime Minister received calls from Maudling, Macleod, Heath and Hailsham, at half hourly intervals, the discussions being minuted by Knox Cunningham. Heath was shrewd enough to see that his chance of the leadership lay in the future, and now told Macmillan that the choice of Home would be the only way of avoiding party disunity. Macmillan decided to begin the second draft of his memorandum to the Queen.

The 'Tuesday memorandum' (or first draft) differs from the final version in its ruminative style and the uninhibited way Macmillan sets down his thoughts about the personalities involved. When the full text of this Memorandum was released at the Public Record Office in January 1995, Professor Peter Hennessy noted, 'It is one of those richly revealing, thinking aloud, deeply personal historical fragments which will be referred to any time a scholar wishes to visit the demise of the Macmillan premiership.'[84] As it was an early draft, a copy was never sent to the Palace. The copy in the Royal Archives is of the final 'Thursday memorandum', with an addendum dated Friday, 18 October 1963, covering the 'midnight meeting' at Enoch Powell's flat, as disaffected Cabinet ministers sought to block the recommendation of Home, which Macmillan handed personally to the Queen on the Friday morning. This memorandum was the third draft and shows Macmillan toning down earlier criticisms of Hailsham, particularly his being 'impulsive, even arrogant'. Its final version is notably even-handed, putting the pros and cons of all candidates.

In the 'Tuesday memorandum', Macmillan summarised his thoughts on Alec Home:

> Lord Home is clearly a man who represents the old, governing class at its best and those who take a reasonably impartial view of English history know how good that can be. He is not ambitious in the sense of wanting to scheme for power, although not foolish enough to resist honour when it comes to him.
>
> Had he been of another generation, he would have been of the Grenadiers and the 1914 heroes. He gives that impression by a curious mixture of great courtesy, and even of yielding to pressure, with underlying rigidity on matters of principle. It is interesting that he has proved himself so much liked by men like President Kennedy and Mr Rusk and Mr Gromyko. This is exactly the quality that the

> class to which he belongs have at their best because they think about the question under discussion and not about themselves.
>
> It is thinking about themselves that is really the curse of the younger generation – they appear to have no other subject which interests them at all and all their books, poems, dramas and all the rest of it are almost entirely confined to this curious introspective attitude towards life, the result no doubt of two wars and a dying faith. Lord Home is free, therefore, from many of the difficulties that beset modern people today. But the very fact that he is free from them makes him in my mind at a disadvantage as well as at an advantage because this strange people, tortured by material success and affluence, are seeking release by some teacher who is himself subject to all these pressures and is not ashamed to break the ordinary rules and conventions suitable to more settled intellectual periods. However, the important fact is that Lord Home's candidature has not been set forward on his own merits but has been thought of as a last minute method of keeping out Mr Butler now that Lord Hailsham has (according to the pundits) put himself out of court by his stupid behaviour in the foyer of the Imperial Hotel at Blackpool.

In the current situation, Home would be an 'effective chief' in Macmillan's opinion, 'the choice of the board if the business is to run quietly, but particularly of a board that did not have to make any difficult appeal to the shareholders and held all the premiums in their pocket'.[85]

On the Tuesday evening, Alec Home underwent a thorough medical examination; it took over an hour, and for a sixty-one-year-old with his record, the results were good, 'disconcertingly so', as Home later put it. However, there was still one aspect that bothered him greatly. His burden as Foreign Secretary entailed a seemingly endless daily round of telegrams and he feared that, as Prime Minister, this would increase. He felt that he could not in all honesty be a runner if his eyes could not withstand the strain. He mentioned this to John Henderson and an appointment was arranged with the distinguished consulting ophthalmic surgeon, Sir Benjamin Rycroft, who pronounced him equal to the task. If the Party wanted him, he would stand.

On the Wednesday morning, Redmayne called on Macmillan with the results of his soundings among the members of the House of Commons and the junior ministers.

> With the help of the Whips I have now canvassed the views of 300 members of the Commons. Opinions have been freely given. Candidates have been assumed to be Heath, Macleod, Maudling, Hailsham, Butler. There has been some doubt whether Home is in the field ... Hailsham, while running third in first preference, has by far the largest number of declared opponents. I have therefore transferred his support elsewhere. Both before and after this transaction the three leaders are Home, Butler and Maudling. The first is always in the lead, though by varying margins; the other two tend to share second and third place, though with some advantage for Butler. In respect of Home's lead account must be taken of the uncertainty about his intentions.

Redmayne reported that the opposition to Hailsham and Butler tended to be outspoken, but with Home it turned solely on the disadvantages arising from his position. There was little personal objection to Maudling, but he failed to get sufficient positive support.

> I have carefully studied the quality of support given to these candidates. Maudling's is almost exclusively from the younger and more junior element. That given to Home and Butler is more mature but Home's covers a far wider cross-section of the Party. I would describe the quality of Hailsham's backing as comparatively unimpressive.
>
> Apart from Home's actual lead, I am impressed by the general good will shown towards him, even by those who give reasons in favour of other candidates, and I cannot fail to come to the opinion that he would be best able to secure united support.
>
> In the meantime there is a considerable amount of positive lobbying, which is having a disruptive effect without achieving much positive result.
>
> In view of this, and of growing criticism from outside, you will agree, I think, that it will be desirable to move towards an early conclusion of this difficult period.'[86]

The first of the second batch of senior ministers to visit Macmillan was Peter Thorneycroft, who told Macmillan he was strongly in favour of either Hogg or Butler, seeing no point in a third choice unless that was the only way to save Party unity, in which case it would be Home, but he did not believe this situation to be the case. He had heard that the Queen might consult senior figures, such as Lord Avon, as in 1957 when the retiring Prime Minister's predecessor had been invited by the palace to give advice. He felt this was hardly necessary but tolerable. (Lord Avon was, of course, canvassed by Lord St Aldwyn in the process approved by Cabinet. His preferences, in order, were Hailsham, Home, Maudling.[87])

Edward Boyle then arrived; he felt that either Butler or Home would attract more liberal, moderate and wavering votes than Hailsham. After the meeting, it occurred to Boyle that he had been too enthusiastic in putting the claims of Home and had a word with Tim Bligh, pointing out that he did not think Home would go very well in Finchley, Orpington and subtopia generally, a point Bligh noted and handed to Macmillan in a written memorandum.

At noon Christopher Soames called. He believed that the imperative was for an early conclusion. Hailsham, perhaps unfairly, would be thought of as a right-winger and might repel the moderates. Then, in a phrase which emerged in Macmillan's memorandum to the Queen, he said that Hailsham was not thought of as a peer in the same way as Lord Home. It would be a mistake to pick a Prime Minister on the uncertain basis that he would win the next election; the main priority was someone who would pull the party together and stop the rows.

When Selwyn Lloyd appeared at 12.30, although he was not in the Cabinet, Macmillan told him that he had 'an important role to play in these discussions'. He said that in the event of a continuing deadlock, he had it in mind to suggest to the Queen that she should see Lloyd. 'He could not think of any other Member of the House of Commons who had my position,' Lloyd recorded. 'He thought it was all very bad luck on Rab, because had he [Macmillan] been run over by a car he assumed that the Queen would automatically have sent for Rab.' As for Hailsham, Macmillan felt he had done a good job as Leader of the Lords and 'had been a very good First Lord of the Admiralty during Suez'. But there was much to be said for Alec Home also. 'The British liked a real aristocrat who could talk to ordinary people – people like the Duke of Devonshire, his [Macmillan's] father-in-law. We talked of the abuse that was thrown at Alec when he was made Foreign Secretary.' Lloyd made it clear that his firm preference was for Home. In the corridor outside Lloyd was less ruminative with Tim Bligh, telling him frankly that from his experience over the previous year going around the constituencies for his party report there was a strong opposition to Mr Butler among many party workers and, for some reason, particularly among the women. He did not know to what cause this should be attributed, but he ensured that Bligh heard his impressions, which were duly reported to Macmillan. He thought Butler would not make a dramatic leader and if there was any question of a deep rift within the party between the Hoggites and the Butlerites the unity of the party was more important, in which case there was a lot to be said for Lord Home. Lloyd concluded by telling Bligh that he also thought that the Opposition in the House of Commons would find Lord Home far more formidable when he got there than they now expected.[88]

John Hare, the Minister of Labour, recognised that there was a growing bitterness towards Hailsham inside Cabinet and elsewhere. He regretted but accepted this and would therefore be happy if Lord Home was chosen. He said that party organisations were very much against Butler, for reasons which he did not understand. Hare was followed at 3.30 by the Home Secretary, Henry Brooke, who nominated Butler as his first choice, but 'next to Rab he would like Alec'. At 4 p.m. Sir Keith Joseph, Minister for Housing and Local Government, arrived. He told Macmillan that he was torn between safety and growth. Butler would be safe in running the government effectively and nothing would go dramatically wrong, especially as Alec Home as Foreign Secretary would be able to exploit advantages from the improved international situation. If for any reason Butler was not acceptable, he favoured a move to the next generation; Hailsham lacked stability.

After a break for tea, Macmillan received Duncan Sandys. He was firmly in favour of Home, not as a compromise between two deadlocked figures, but on his own merits.

At 5.30 p.m. Macleod called with his account of what had transpired at Blackpool. In the light of later developments, it is worth noting that Macleod (in the words of Bligh's minute) 'expressed himself perfectly happy about the arrangement made in my minute (to the First Secretary of State) which he thought was wise, and understood that I had selected Poole because I did not wish to rule him (Mr Macleod) out of a possible candidature.' Macleod was followed by Hailsham, who, among other things, said that there had been a lot of trouble at Blackpool with the press and television, and that his baby had been a diversion rather than a political gimmick. Macmillan had the impression that Hailsham was not conscious of how he had lost ground by this behaviour. Macmillan's final visitor was Edward Heath, who told Macmillan frankly that Poole had made a serious mistake in backing Hailsham and forfeiting his impartial position as Chairman of the Party. The Party had won in 1955 and 1959 with the moderate vote and Hailsham would not increase this but alienate the waverers. Rab Butler had earned the succession and ought by now to have justified it. But the fact was that he had not and would not be an inspiring leader. The only way to prevent a split was by drafting Alec Home. Heath said that he had seen him speak in various places like the United Nations, which were not easy to handle and he would be surprisingly good in the House of Commons. The country regarded him as moderate, an internationalist and a peacemaker, and although some people would think it undemocratic, it would not amount to very much after the first excitements had died down. Macmillan was also in receipt of various letters from the public, putting their views, including one anonymous letter from a serving ambassador (the handwriting was recognised) pleading for Home to be left at the Foreign Office where he was doing such a successful and important job.

On Thursday, 17 October the decision was finally taken for Home. Knox Cunningham arrived at the King Edward VII Hospital shortly after 9 a.m. with Tim Bligh, who had a letter for Macmillan with advice on how the news should be broken to Hailsham. This was to avoid the embarrassments that had occurred when Curzon learned he had been passed over in favour of Baldwin in May 1923, and was a tacit assumption that whatever the decision, it was not going to be for Hailsham. Bligh felt that it was most important for Hailsham to be kept in the boat. He had discussed the problem with Lord Poole, who was willing to help. The suggestion was that Poole should have advance information as to whom the Queen would send for, in order that he could be with Lord Hailsham before there was any chance that he might learn of the decision by other means. Bligh returned to Downing Street and Knox Cunningham became the duty secretary in the hospital room.

> I was alone with the Prime Minister during all the interviews. They came at intervals during the morning – Rab; Lord Poole; Lord Chelmer and Mrs Shepherd came together; the Lord Chancellor; the Chief Whip; Lord St Aldwyn; James Stuart. My job was to take a careful note of all that was said and this I did. In the afternoon he insisted on going downstairs to a larger room where he met a group comprised of the Lord Chancellor, the Chief Whip, Lord Poole and Lord St Aldwyn and heard their views as representatives given in each other's presence. I was there to record what took place.[89]

Knox Cunningham's notes consist of seventeen sheets of Basildon Bond writing paper. The morning meetings were confined to the mathematics of the consultation, an exercise that was later the subject of much controversy. Lord Dilhorne reported that 10 members of the Cabinet were for Home, 4 for Maudling, 3 for Butler and 2 for Hailsham. The exact figures for Maudling were changed by Dilhorne, initially from 3 to 5, and then (in Philip de Zulueta's handwriting) from 5 to 4. Home was not counted as voting for himself. If he were included, his total was 11. Those choosing Home as their first alternative preference included, according to Dilhorne, Iain Macleod. (The other nine, in a count that has been the subject of much controversy, were Boyle, Deedes, Dilhorne, Hare, Heath, Marples, Noble, Sandys and Soames.) When Alistair Horne first revealed Macleod's inclusion, there was considerable puzzlement in the light of his later opposition to Home.[90] Boyle also later made it clear that his preference was for Butler. It is inconceivable that Macleod would have voted for Home, for whom he had little regard; Macleod was one of the few political figures with whom Home had no rapport.

The figures from the Lords prepared by St Aldwyn showed, not surprisingly, a big preponderance for Home. Of those who had expressed a preference, 28 peers had Home as their first choice, and 12 as their second. The figures respectively for Butler were 14 and 13, for Hailsham 10 and 12, and for Maudling 2 and 8. Lord Chelmer and Mrs Shepherd reported that the constituencies were 60–40 in favour of Hailsham (against Butler), but that both evoked strong antagonisms. Significantly, the last person Macmillan saw before the decisive afternoon meeting was James Stuart, whose connections with Alec Home went back to the 1920s, and whose first political mentor he had been. He was strongly in favour of Home assuming the highest office.

The afternoon meeting was the resolution of the leadership question. Macmillan opened the discussion by saying that he thought the Party at large were a little confused. 'They were not on all the horses that were running,' Knox Cunningham noted. Lord Poole explained that at that stage people were not fully informed, to which Macmillan added that a straight Hailsham–Butler contest would probably break 60–40 in Hailsham's favour. Lord Poole felt that if people had thought it a three horse race between Hailsham, Butler *and* Home then Home would have displaced Butler in second place. Poole also added that the more one got away from the centre of Westminster, the more people were in favour of Hailsham. The Young Conservatives, for instance, were 80 or 90 per cent for Hailsham, though he emphasised that this was specifically not the case with the Executive. Hailsham had more support in suburban than in rural areas.

Macmillan asked if people were seeing the contest as exclusively

Butler versus Hailsham. The Lord Chancellor said that if they were the only two runners, the Cabinet would break 12–7 in favour of Butler. If Maudling was a runner, then it would be Butler 8, Maudling 7, Hailsham 5. If Hailsham was not a runner and Home was, then the figures were Home 11 (the original note reads 10, but 11 is added in brackets), Maudling 5, Butler 3. At this point the Chief Whip in the Lords, St Aldwyn, reported that the peers were 2 to 1 in favour of Alec Home, with Rab Butler second and Hailsham a close third. Macmillan then asked the Chief Whip in the Commons for his figures. Redmayne explained that the Whips had been instructed to ask three questions. Who was the first choice, who was the second choice and was there anyone to whom the respondent had 'aversion'. When these questions were put, the first preferences were 'narrow' with Home and Butler the front runners, Maudling third and Hailsham a 'bad fourth'. 'When one came on to the second choices', reported Redmayne, 'Home had much the best of it.' Redmayne concluded by saying that it was perfectly clear in his mind that Home would be the candidate most likely to secure the united support of the Party. Macmillan asked if Butler would be the next most likely, to which Redmayne replied that he would be initially opposed by many more members.

Lord Poole, as Joint Party Chairman, was then asked for his views. He reported that the Party in the country would be in favour of Hailsham. It was difficult to say what ten million voters would make of Maudling or Home, because they were not so widely known. He did think there was a difference between the people in the country and the House of Commons. As Party Chairman he felt that Hailsham would go down well in the country, however the corollary would be a disunited Cabinet, which could be disastrous. He felt it would be equally disastrous to go for Home: he was not widely known and would lead a disunited Cabinet. It seemed that an impasse had been reached.

Macmillan now broke the silence by saying that it was difficult advice he was going to have to give the Queen. He stressed that he saw his role as a collector of views, adding that a good argument for a man was not just that he had no enemies; it might also mean he had no character. Lord Poole, who still pressed for Hailsham, repeated that Home was surprisingly little known. In reply to this, Macmillan moved on to the question of Home's Earldom. Was it a disadvantage? Poole immediately said that it was not an *advantage*, adding that Hailsham was not regarded as a Lord in that he was so much in the hurly-burly (a point which survived into the final Memorandum). In other words, Macmillan said, historical parallels in his mind, he was like Churchill in 1910.

Poole, who dominated the discussion at this stage, moved on to the question of what he called 'a solid block': the only person who suffered from this, apart from Hailsham, was Butler. Macmillan agreed that people in the party machine were not inspired by him. Dilhorne added that he was surprised by what Macmillan had said about the party machine, as he felt that the opposition was more among what he termed 'the middle ground'. Poole agreed, and felt there would be considerable opposition to Butler in the City and in rural areas. 'Should have thought in the UN too', added Macmillan, before the discussion moved on to the views of what Macmillan termed 'the Orpingtonians'. Were these people attracted by Maudling? Lord Poole felt that after six months in the post Maudling would represent 'that class of person' better than Home. Redmayne felt that Maudling's support was almost exclusively among the younger members of the party, adding 'younger in experience and age'.

The discussion had now reached a critical stage. There was a limit to the time five people could go round the possibilities. Macmillan now drew the conversation back to Hailsham – how did he stand in the north-east? In a curiously lateral response, Redmayne said that Home had more widespread support in the country than might be thought. Poole agreed at once that no one who thought of it did not think well of Home, perhaps the tilting moment from Hailsham's most fervent supporter. Macmillan remained cautious. It would all be a tremendous gamble, he suggested. The next six to eight months were crucial. The election would be in June or October. The key thing was for the new Prime Minister to dominate the House of Commons. This was an essential priority. If the new Prime Minister could get the better of Wilson, really defeat him, then that would spread out through television. It was coming down to Home or Hailsham. The advantage of a 14th Earl, said Macmillan, was that he could spread out and become a Palmerstonian figure. The advantage of Hailsham was that he was a Parliamentary performer, though his manner was a little arrogant.

Lord Poole felt that the opinion of people after six months was what would count in the long term. Macmillan restated his basic premise that whoever was chosen must dominate the House of Commons and get a united Cabinet behind him. There must be no bickering and attacking the leadership. Dilhorne said that Home would have that Cabinet backing; it was doubtful if the same could be said of Hailsham.

Macmillan replied that Wilson was six months ahead at the present moment, and Poole agreed that after the choice, the spotlight would be firmly on the Conservatives. Dilhorne added that he doubted whether Hailsham would dominate the Commons, whereas, in his opinion, Home had established a remarkable reputation as Foreign Secretary and was regarded as the bigger man. Macmillan agreed that Home dominated the Party committees more than anyone he had known, yet still flinched from the choice. It was a great gamble, he repeated, saying that he was thinking not only of the Party but of the Queen. Adeane had told him there was no wish for long consultations. The Palace wanted a clear recommendation and an end to the matter.

Macmillan then said that he wished to make two things clear. He proposed to write a final memorandum, relating what he had been told, but that he would destroy all the names. He wanted to protect the Queen from controversy. He would relate what had been said and give his own views if asked. He faced the four men in his room and asked them if that was the right way to proceed. They agreed that it was. Poole asked if the Blackpool conference had made any difference. Macmillan said that it had, as it had produced the idea of Alec Home. He then drew the meeting to its close. He told the others that he would prepare to send his resignation to the Queen that evening. As he was unable to go to the Palace, the Queen would probably come to the hospital the next morning. He would have a memorandum ready to be sent to the Palace for 10.30 a.m. on Friday. He could then see the Queen later in the morning.

The Prime Minister then asked that the news be discreetly disseminated, with the rider that it was for the good of the Party. 'It will be terrible for Rab,' he said. Poole said that Rab considered he had no chance, but the actual moment would still be painful. Macmillan asked to be put through to Home on the telephone. The three vital matters were to settle Hailsham, the Chancellorship and the Foreign Secretaryship, an implicit assumption that Hailsham would not be offered either of the two posts. Macmillan said that he was not keen for Rab to be given the Foreign Secretaryship as there were so many initiatives. It would please Rab, but nothing would happen. He felt the obvious man for Foreign Secretary was Ted Heath. Dilhorne said that difficulties might be avoided if Hailsham could be persuaded, despite his declared intention to disclaim, to stay in the Lords. Home then came on the telephone and Macmillan told him that he would formally be recommending his name to the Queen. The meeting had lasted fifty-six minutes.

The news that the decision was likely to be for Alec Home had already been circulating in Whitehall, after Philip de Zulueta had remarked *sotto voce* at the Cabinet and Defence Staff Mess at lunch that the odds were heavily on the fourteenth Earl. This news was rushed to the Mirabelle restaurant, where Macleod was lunching with Maudling and his wife, and given to them as they emerged into the street half an hour before the meeting began at the King Edward VII Hospital. Macleod received the news with derision. It was not possible. So tightly observed were the main participants that the evening papers were soon ringing up the Treasury and Central Office to ask for information from Maudling and Macleod. Ninety minutes later Dilhorne informed Maudling's office that a document was being prepared for the Queen. Although this telephone call did not specify the nature of the advice to be tendered, Maudling left the Treasury for talks with Macleod and Enoch Powell.

Meanwhile, Macmillan prepared the memorandum for the Queen – a document that he always regretted not printing in full as an appendix to his final volume of memoirs, *At the End of the Day*, in 1973.[91] His main concern was to shield the Queen from political controversy; although he recorded the need to preserve the prerogative,[92] he knew that the Palace was operating on the YOU CHOOSE, WE SEND FOR principle so there could be no ambiguity in his recommendation. Faced with the evidence from all wings of the Party, the only possible recommendation was Lord Home. As Vernon Bogdanor recently commented, 'The outcome, the selection of Lord Home, cannot be said seriously to have misrepresented Conservative opinion at the time.'[93]

The 'Thursday memorandum' begins with a factual outline of the procedures adopted since 14 October for canvassing opinion throughout the Party. It then outlines all the information Macmillan had received, and sets out unequivocally the advocacy of Lord Home, concluding that if the Queen made this choice, she would incur no blame and would be held to have chosen a man generally supported by all the various sections to whom a Minister must look for the support of his administration. He was bound to say that if Lord Home could not be persuaded to undertake this task, as he felt Her Majesty would be able to do, he could think of nobody to whom he would more willingly commit the further stages of the policies which he had tried to pursue during his tenure of office, particularly in the realm of foreign affairs.

It should, of course, be a prerequisite of Home's acceptance of the Queen's nomination that he should seek immediate election to the House of Commons. In Lord Home's case, since the Queen had conferred on him the honour of Knight of the Thistle he was, even when he gave up his peerage, a Knight. He would in future be known as Sir Alec Home, Alec being a well-known diminutive of Alexander in Scotland. Although the pedants of heraldry may make some objection, he felt that 'Sir Alec' would be acceptable.

After receiving Macmillan's telephone call, giving him advance notice that his name would be recommended to the Queen, Alec Home stayed at 1 Carlton Gardens, where he was joined by Selwyn Lloyd and Martin Redmayne, and it was at Carlton Gardens that he first heard of the backlash by supporters of Rab Butler. The first telephone call was from Hailsham, who said (in Selwyn Lloyd's record) that 'it would be a disaster if Alec took the job and he would have to denounce him publicly'. Home received this message with calm politeness. Lloyd spoke to Hailsham from another telephone in Carlton Gardens and said that if Hailsham did speak out it would look like sour grapes. Iain Macleod and Enoch Powell also telephoned with their objections and Elizabeth Home said to her husband, 'It looks rather smelly now, doesn't it?' To Dilhorne, who had now arrived, Home said, 'Well, I was quite prepared to come forward as the candidate to unify the party, accepted by everyone; but if it is said that my coming forward would split the Party, that is a different proposition.' Dilhorne told him that he 'must pay no attention'.[94]

Selwyn Lloyd then drove Redmayne to Enoch Powell's house in South Eaton Place, where the famous 'midnight meeting', attended by Powell, Macleod, Maudling, Erroll and Aldington, was already underway, the culmination of activity in the anti-Home camp since Macleod had heard the rumour that Home was to be summoned. Hailsham had been kept in touch with developments and Butler had been assured of the support of this significant group of Cabinet ministers. Redmayne had been summoned to hear of the support, and he undertook to tell Macmillan the following morning. Powell's main objection was still that Home had agreed to help Dilhorne with canvassing as he was not a candidate. Macleod's objections went deeper, not least the slur the choice of a peer cast on the competence of over 300 Conservatives in the House of Commons. Surrounded by the balloons and streamers of his daughter's birthday party that afternoon in the upstairs drawing room at South Eaton Place, Powell presided over a group whose fervent hope was that Rab would hold out and deny the premiership to Home. 'For becoming a Prime Minister a man must be ready to shoot it out', Powell later remarked.[95] Powell and his colleagues presented Butler with the loaded revolver, but Butler would not fire.

The next morning Martin Redmayne apprised Macmillan of the meeting at South Eaton Place, but 'The Prime Minister was firm and Tim set out for the palace carrying the letter of resignation'.[96] Macmillan and Knox Cunningham prepared an addendum for the Queen to the 'Thursday memorandum' covering the overnight happenings, so that she would be up to date with the current situation. With memories of the political situation from the days of Lord Aberdeen, who had been offered the premiership by Queen Victoria at Osborne on 18 December 1852, but had only kissed hands the following day on securing the agreement of Lord John Russell, whom he regarded as an essential buttress to his administration, to serve as Foreign Secretary, so Macmillan advised that Lord Home should sound out the possibilities of forming a government. If Home failed, then the Queen could entrust the commission to other hands, and there would be no obloquy attached to the Palace.[97]

The Queen, accompanied by Sir Michael Adeane, arrived at the hospital at 11 a.m. Macmillan had put on a silk shirt and saw the Queen in the downstairs room. One of his main concerns was that he should not receive the Queen whilst attached to various tubes and paraphernalia. An elaborate system of signals was worked out for the prompt opening and closing of doors for this private audience. The Queen stayed for forty minutes while Macmillan read the memorandum aloud. The Queen agreed that Lord Home was the candidate most likely to command general support, but asked about the implications of the midnight meeting. Macmillan recommended that Lord Home be summoned to the palace immediately. As the Queen left the hospital, the memorandum was placed in a huge white envelope and given to Michael Adeane, a scene which reminded Knox Cunningham of Tenniel's drawing of the Frog Footman in *Alice in Wonderland*.[98]

Alec Home arrived at the Palace at 12.30 p.m., and the press office put out a statement: 'The Queen has received the Earl of Home in audience and invited him to form an administration.' Alec Home did not kiss hands; he would first see if he could form an administration. But the baton was in his hands and he was in possession of 10 Downing Street, which had been the temporary fiefdom of Rab Butler. 'He has got the loaves and fishes,' said Lord Beaverbrook, old combatant in many a Conservative leadership battle, 'there is no stopping him now.'[99]

Although Home would not be entirely secure until Rab Butler had agreed to serve, the momentum was his. At 2.45 p.m. he saw Butler, who initially reserved his position on the grounds of whether it was right to have a hereditary peer and whether Home could in fact bring unity to the Party. But the very fact that he had accepted Home's invitation to attend at 10 Downing Street was a tacit admission that he no longer held the initiative. If Butler had intended to fire the loaded revolver, then this was the moment. But it was not in his nature. 'I don't know what's happening,' Butler had said to one of the No. 10 Secretariat two days earlier, when he had sat alone at the Cabinet table, adding 'but I do really.' When the secretary asked him what he would do, Butler replied, 'I shall behave with dignity.'[100] A crucial meeting followed at 3.15 when Home saw Reginald Maudling, who also was non-committal. Home said that if he was holding out in the hope that Rab Butler would become Prime Minister, he was mistaken. If Home failed to form an administration, the task would devolve upon the Chancellor of the Exchequer.[101] (Home later came to believe that he could have formed an administration without Butler, but not without Maudling.) Surprisingly, Hailsham was one of the first to crumble as Home continued seeing his colleagues until the late hours, the last being Edward Boyle at 10.30 p.m. The comings and goings by late evening were so complex that 10 Downing Street lost track of the timetable, one of the few certainties being that Maudling had cancelled a private outing with his wife to see the new James Bond film *From Russia with Love*. By the end of the evening, there had been a quadrilateral meeting of Home, Hailsham, Butler and Maudling, at which it became clear that Hailsham would serve. Geoffrey Lloyd tried vainly in the small hours to persuade Butler to hold out. The next morning Maudling said he would continue as Chancellor, and Butler agreed to become Foreign Secretary.[102] Only Macleod and Powell refused to continue.

Lord Home returned to the Palace with the news that he had been able to form an administration. His car drove past the band of the Grenadier Guards, who were playing 'The Longest Day'. On his way to lunch at the Turf Club, Selwyn Lloyd saw the crowds of photographers outside the palace as Home arrived. 'I had thought he was going in the afternoon' he noted, Butler not having been expected to accept office on the Saturday morning.[103] Twenty minutes later came the announcement, 'The Queen this morning received in audience the Earl of Home who kissed hands upon his appointment as Prime Minister and First Lord of the Treasury.' The prophecy of Miss Edith Watson, made in the dark days of 1939, had been fulfilled.

13

Top of the Greasy Pole

'Turning Aside from Progress' was the reaction to Home's appointment in an article by William Rees-Mogg.[1] 'It is incredible that such a thing should have happened,' wrote Tony Benn. 'From the Labour Party's point of view he is much less dangerous than Maudling but I am disturbed that my battle should have paved the way for a Conservative peer to come back as PM.'[2] Harold Wilson was ecstatic at the prospect of facing a 14th Earl who had been out of the Commons for twelve years.[3] The Dowager Countess of Home was telephoned at Springhill for her opinion: 'I am frankly very surprised, I thought it would be Mr Butler – he seemed to deserve it.'[4] His brother Henry thought Alec would not be too pleased because he might miss the partridge shooting. In private, the Dowager Countess was deeply moved by her son's translation to the highest office. 'My many congratulations that you have been chosen', she wrote. 'I only wish Daddy could be here. He would be so proud and happy.'[5] His sister Bridget also wrote from Springhill. 'The reporters and photographers have left us in peace the last two days! They were a nightmare!'[6] The Hirsel was besieged and Caroline Douglas Home gave an interview on the understanding that the reporters would then leave – the undertaking was not respected. The *Daily Herald* used selective quotations from this interview to portray Alec Home as someone out of touch, who did not understand the concerns of ordinary people.[7]

But not everyone had reservations. 'He has graduated gently upwards doing each job that fell to him a good deal better than had been expected,' said a leader in *The Times*. 'He has been an outstandingly successful Foreign Secretary, and his services as Commonwealth Secretary appear in retrospect greater than was appreciated at the time.'[8] David Ormsby-Gore wrote from Washington:

> My dear Alec,
>
> As I told you on the telephone we were overjoyed to hear the news of your appointment as Prime Minister. The criticism it has touched off in England was of course predictable and I judge it to be less than at the time of your appointment as Foreign Secretary. The critics were confounded utterly on that occasion and I have not the slightest doubt that they will [be] again on this. Nevertheless it must be very unpleasant for you both and I expect your blood is frequently on the boil – mine is. Over here the news was received with rapture throughout the Administration. One of your admirers remarked that 'there were not too many "Q" buttons around the White House.'
>
> Yours ever, David.[9]

In a separate telegram, Ormsby-Gore offered to set up an early meeting with the President, but within a month Kennedy was dead and Home's first contact with the American Administration was to be with Lyndon Johnson.

Letters poured in to Downing Street from all corners of the world and from each compartment of Alec Home's earlier life congratulating him on his appointment. The deputy Labour leader, George Brown, who was in New York at the time, said he was not sure that Lord Home would be the easiest candidate to defeat at the general election, adding 'he has great popular appeal and presents a good image to the public'.[10] A personal message from Harold Caccia, the Permanent Under-Secretary at the Foreign Office, was a fitting valediction to Home's three and a half years in King Charles Street. 'You must let me tell you of the inspiration which you have been to the whole Foreign Service over which you presided. Believe me this isn't just diplomatic wordage. The pros know when England has got a real skipper to captain our side. They also know when their Secretary of State really cares for the Service and the conditions in which its members have to work. No wonder that you have won and will always retain the respect and affection of us all.'[11] Richard Crossman wrote, 'Directly I heard Home had been appointed, though I found it hard to believe, I characteristically began to see the advantages to the Tories ... Macmillan's falling off the back of the Tory Party was an enormous relief, that anybody was better than he was, that Home would have a good television personality and that probably he would be good on the hustings too.'[12]

The unexpectedness of the choice made the Conservatives front page news. It was, as Macmillan had acknowledged, an enormous gamble.

The House of Commons was a very different body from that in 1951, when Home had last sat there, but, faced with a resurgent Labour party, many Conservatives were prepared to rally around the new leader. Butler, as he had promised, behaved with great dignity, though his repeated failure to become Prime Minister haunted him for the rest of his life. 'I did do the right thing, didn't I?' he asked old and trusted friends in late night conversations. It was a subject to which he returned with melancholy frequency. 'If I had been less of a gentleman I could have been Prime Minister,' he said to Sir Nicholas Henderson after a dinner in New York on 20 November 1979, before adding, 'or if Alec had been less of a gentleman.'[13] Butler's unwillingness to challenge the concurrence of second preferences was the key to Alec Home's entry into Downing Street. In the end, Rab Butler made Alec Home Prime Minister, not Harold Macmillan. Butler could live with a Home premiership; the two of them had been friends in Parliament for thirty-two years and the friendship between Mollie Butler and Elizabeth Home was even more long-standing. He could take comfort in what remained. 'After all', he said, 'it's not every man who *nearly* becomes Prime Minister of England.'[14] Rab Butler had three opportunities to succeed to the highest post, whereas Alec Home had only one. In other respects, there were many similarities. When Walter Bagehot wrote an introduction to the second edition of his famous book *The English Constitution* in 1872 he considered what requirements best suited the needs of executive government. 'Sensible men of substantial means', he concluded 'are what we wish to be governed by.'[15] Nobody could deny that Alec Home fulfilled these two criteria. Ironically, it was also true of Rab Butler.

Why did Rab Butler fail to become Prime Minister and what does this failure tell us of Alec Home's position in the Conservative Party in 1963? It is simplistic to say that Home appealed to the right wing, whereas Butler aroused their suspicions. The matter was more complex than that. In fact, there were two right wings in the Conservative Party in those days – the old landed gentry, with a paternalistic attitude to society, whose service was in the tradition of public duty; and the younger Monday Club element, who were unwilling to accept the pace of decolonisation. Alec Home appealed to both of these groups, in a way that Rab Butler never did. Butler's supporters in the progressive 'One Nation' group (with the exception of Iain Macleod), never felt the antagonism towards Home that the right-wing groups felt towards Butler. They admired the firmness with which Home had dealt with

Empire loyalist hecklers at the recent conference. Among the constituency workers in the important rural constituencies, he was their idea of heaven, a better shot than any of them, and the kindest and nicest gentleman who ever walked the earth. The 'Orpingtonians' were prepared to give him their support, even though many would have preferred Maudling. As Kilmuir had said, loyalty was the Tories' secret weapon. The Queen wrote to Macmillan on 21 October:

> I have the greatest confidence in Alec Home and this is reinforced by his distinguished record at the Foreign Office and as Leader of the House of Lords; he will be greatly missed in both places as well as by the Foreign Statesmen who have come to trust in his character and skill and I have not the least doubt that as the fourth Prime Minister of my reign he will lead my Government and our country with an equally firm and sure hand.[16]

The question of whether Rab Butler would have won the 1964 election is one of the great conundrums of post-war political history. Harold Wilson believed that he would have done so.[17] Rab Butler's great advantage as Prime Minister in 1963 would have been the lack of the controversies that dogged Alec Home, who later believed that, as the public had seen Rab Butler as the heir apparent, it might have been better in the end for him to have had the job. Anyone else was seen in some sense as an 'unnatural' successor. If Rab Butler was not acceptable then the best thing (as Butler himself conceded in his memoirs) would have been to skip a generation, something that happened within twenty months in any case.[18] In a close election, one that Alec Home nearly won, who is to say that Butler would not have prevailed? However, this did not mean he was better suited to the post of Prime Minister than Alec Home. He knew how Whitehall worked, loved tinkering with the machinery of government and fine-tuning the engine, but this was not the same as taking the wheel of the car in a Grand Prix. The relationship between Home and Butler during the following year, though conducted with perfect courtesy, was not always easy. The Foreign Office, the job Butler had wanted in January 1957, was a consolation, but nobody, least of all Butler, mistook it for the real thing; nor was it Home's long-term intention to keep his great rival in King Charles Street. Before the year was out, Christopher Soames had been promised the reversion privately if the Conservatives were returned at the general election. Rather in the manner of Baldwin, who was obliged to retain Curzon as Foreign Secretary in May 1923 on becoming Prime Minister, but who swiftly demoted him on returning to power after the election victory of October 1924, Home only needed Butler to bolster his immediate position. Butler never deluded himself into thinking himself indispensable, and connoisseurs of his ambiguous conversational style were treated to some vintage Rabbisms over the coming year. In his great room on the first floor of the Foreign Office, he would often comment, by way of a footnote to the issue under discussion, 'Mind you, Alec's a good man really'.[19] Privately he did not think Home had the intellectual calibre to be Prime Minister. Time and again in Cabinet, when a meeting wound down and ministers were mentally preparing to leave their places, Butler would say, 'There is one more thing, Prime Minister', and with an inward sigh, people settled back for twenty minutes' circumlocution. Alec Home showed the patience of Job, for he was by instinct very expeditious in despatching government business, as Burke Trend at once appreciated.[20] Their joint visit to Washington in February 1964 was not considered a great success by those who travelled with them. Some remember Home as having 'a figure of eight mind', with the top circle his personal view and the problem to be solved as the lower one. He knew exactly how much of the sand should trickle through to the bottom half. Yet, for all his decency and integrity, there remained many who felt that Home had interrupted the flow of Conservatism. Eden, with his call for a property-owning democracy, a theme dear to Macmillan's heart, had represented the whole of Conservatism. Alec Home and his two immediate successors, for all their great and varied qualities, only represented a part of Conservatism.

As Prime Minister Home did the things that were expected of him conscientiously and accurately, though without a feel for the wider imaginative role. He was clear-sighted in Cabinet, but without the philosophical flair that so characterised the Macmillan era; he never bestrode the political arena. 'The great man of the age is the one who can put into words the will of his age, tell his age what its will is, and accomplish it', wrote Hegel. 'What he does is the heart and essence of his age; he actualises his age.'[21] That role, fulfilled in the 1960s by Harold Wilson and by Margaret Thatcher in the 1980s, was never Alec Home's. His words to the nation on television on the night he assumed office were patently those of a sincere man. 'I would like to say to you at once that my task is to serve the nation. The second thing I would like to say to you is that you need expect no stunts from me, just plain straight talking.'[22] The speech did not, in later parlance, break the mould of politics.

The formation of his Cabinet, after Butler's acceptance of the Foreign Office and Maudling's agreement to continue at the Treasury, occupied Home's first weekend in Downing Street, though it did not prevent his attendance at Sunday morning service at St James's, Piccadilly. Later he was to say that assembling a Cabinet was worse than trying to raise a side for the Eton Ramblers.[23] As with all incoming Prime Ministers, one of the first priorities was to receive his security briefing, including details of the United Kingdom's nuclear strike force and how to activate it. While the Cabinet was still being formed, he received news of the suicide of Diana Churchill, and in one of his first acts as Prime Minister, sent a message of sympathy to his distinguished predecessor, a letter which crossed with Churchill's own message of congratulation. 'I remember with gratitude that it was you and James Stuart who launched me some years ago', he replied.[24] On 22 October, he met Harold Wilson to discuss the date of the State Opening of Parliament. Wilson told him that the Opposition took the view that the work of the House of Commons 'should not be held up by accident of circumstance, birth or anything else'. It was possible that the Prime Minister might not win the by-election, 'and then what would happen?' Home said that this was a situation that would have to be faced if it arose.[25] The meeting left no doubt that Wilson would be a tactically astute opponent. Wilson later described as an 'impertinence' Home's request (one about which the Prime Minister was much embarrassed) that the date should be put back from 29 October, until he had secured a seat in the House of Commons. So that the Palace should be kept informed, Tim Bligh sent the Queen a memorandum of how events were unfolding:

> In the course of the Saturday afternoon the PM proceeded to form his Cabinet. There were a number of complicating factors. First, the position of Lord Hailsham was uncertain since it was not then known whether he wished to stay in the House of Lords or make himself eligible for election to the House of Commons. Indeed this uncertainty persisted until the middle of Sunday afternoon and the press announcements of the new Cabinet had to be held up until the consequentials of Lord Hailsham's final decision were worked out, including the leadership of the House of Lords. In parenthesis, I should perhaps say that the PM was most anxious in the public interest to announce his Cabinet on the Sunday evening since it

> seemed important to him to demonstrate the basic unity of the Conservative Party and any undue delay in setting up the Cabinet would, in the particular circumstances, have been the cause of much speculation. Secondly, the PM was anxious to improve the machinery of government for dealing with the positive side of the Government's plans for directing industry to the right places, that is, away from the suburban sprawl and into the areas that need development. These problems were also confused by the uncertainty of Mr Macleod's position which, of course, carried with it uncertainty about the leadership of the House of Commons and the chairmanship of the Party.[26]

Alec Home was unable to persuade Enoch Powell and Iain Macleod to serve, but he respected the reasons for Powell's refusal. 'I don't expect, Alec, you expect me to give you a different answer on Saturday from the one I gave you on Friday', said Powell at their second meeting. 'I'd have to go home and turn all the mirrors round.'[27] As Baldwin had brought Austen Chamberlain back into the ministerial fold after the election victory of October 1924, so forty years later Home planned to reinstate Powell in government if the Tories won in 1964, and indeed asked him to help on the manifesto and 'to attend meetings of the Steering Committee as an observer', as early as 4 December 1963.[28] But for Iain Macleod he planned no such early olive branch, though after the election defeat of October 1964 he did invite Macleod to join the Shadow Cabinet as the Conservative spokesman on Labour's plans for steel nationalisation, a shrewd conciliatory move (on both sides) as it gave Macleod a portfolio he particularly wanted, one ideally suited to his adversarial Commons style.

Home's most important decision was to abolish the post of 1st Secretary of State.[29] The functions were subsumed into the enlarged Ministry of Industry, Trade and Regional Development headed by Edward Heath, who was nevertheless disappointed not to have been made Foreign Secretary. Of the importance of regional development, already mentioned in Tim Bligh's memorandum to the Palace, there was no doubt. Alec Home's old tutor from Christ Church, Sir John Masterman, who had moved into the field of industrial training and development after his retirement from the Provostship of Worcester College, Oxford, in 1961, wrote to say that such a department was 'exactly right at this juncture'.[30] Alec Home consulted Masterman a great deal at this time, not only on security matters, but also on industrial relations. As Hailsham felt it incumbent upon himself to disclaim (described by one colleague as paying a bet after the horse had scratched) Home appointed Peter Carrington as Minister without Portfolio, second-in-command to Rab Butler at the Foreign Office and Leader of the House of Lords, a promotion which paved the way for Carrington's later tenure of the Foreign Office. Lord Jellicoe took over at the Admiralty; Quintin Hogg (as he shortly became) continued as Lord President and Minister for Science, and Anthony Barber replaced Enoch Powell as Minister of Health. As Chairman of the Party, Home chose John Hare, ennobled as Viscount Blakenham, with a seat in the Cabinet as Chancellor of the Duchy of Lancaster – a shrewd move, as Blakenham had previously served as Vice-Chairman under Lord Woolton.

Joseph Godber took over as Minister of Labour, but the real winner of the reshuffle was Selwyn Lloyd, without whom Home would probably not have become Prime Minister. Lloyd took over the Leadership of the House of Commons and re-entered the Cabinet as Lord Privy Seal. On the day that Home became Prime Minister Harold Wilson said in a speech, 'After half a century of democratic advance, the whole process has ground to a halt with a 14th Earl.' It was Selwyn Lloyd who suggested the perfect riposte for Alec Home when he was interviewed two days later by Kenneth Harris. 'As far as the 14th Earl is concerned,' said Lord Home, 'I suppose Mr Wilson when you come to think of it, is the 14th Mr Wilson.' He was not to be the 14th Earl for much longer; under the terms of the Peerage Act he disclaimed his various titles on 23 October.[31] His name was Number 3 in the Register of Renunciation, where he was to be followed by Quintin Hailsham. On disclaiming, the Prime Minister of Great Britain was a member of neither House of Parliament, a positively Pirandellian situation, but not a unique one. When Colonel John Seely resigned as Secretary of State for War on 30 March 1914, his place was temporarily taken by the Prime Minister H. H. Asquith. Until 1918 any member of the Commons accepting a Cabinet Office had to seek re-election to Parliament, as Asquith did at East Fife.[32] The timetable of renunciations eventually led to some spirited responses at Christ Church, where events had been keenly followed by David Dunglass and the Hon. Douglas Hogg, undergraduate heirs to the respective titles. When the instruments of renunciation had taken effect, the porters of Christ Church punctiliously set forth to the various staircases, painting out the words 'Lord Dunglass' and substituting 'The Hon. David Douglas-Home', a correct adjustment. However, they rather zealously painted out 'The Hon.' in front of Douglas Hogg's name. Although Douglas Hogg is not a man to stand on ceremony or titles, he did object on the grounds that the dropping of the courtesy title was wrong in his respect, and it was duly reinstated.[33] The story, however, did not end there, and there was much to-ing and fro-ing with official and unofficial paintbrushes until, in the manner of newspaper editors, the authorities declared that this correspondence must now cease.

First impressions count for much, particularly in politics. Alec Home's premiership got off to a particularly unfortunate start, quite apart from the legacy of the Blackpool controversies and their aftermath, of which the *Observer* noted that 'Home was almost certainly chosen as the man who would not rub anyone up the wrong way, whereas in fact he created the most frantic shindig the party has known for decades'.[34] A perfectly routine political commentary on a BBC television news bulletin on 18 October by Robert McKenzie, a person of some authority, served as a biographical introduction of Alec Home to the wider public. In the course of his thumbnail sketch, McKenzie observed that, whatever his great gifts in Foreign Affairs, he knew nothing of the domestic agenda, on which, it was suggested, Harold Wilson was a master. Thus from day one, Alec Home was thought of as 'the man who knew nothing about domestic matters'. Those who had worked with him in the early 1950s knew how untrue this was, and how Eden had moved him to Commonwealth Affairs in April 1955 to *broaden* his knowledge in the field of foreign affairs, but after McKenzie's broadcast the damage was done, as many in the BBC spotted at the time.[35] Perceptions and reality rarely coincided, largely because Alec Home was oblivious to image. He did not 'market' himself in the way that became obsessional with later political generations. One evening, the television was broadcasting a speech by Harold Wilson, asking rhetorically what Home knew about ordinary life and the concerns of families and their children. The duty secretary went to the upstairs flat with some government business and found Home putting his first grandchild to bed in the spare room, as the Wilson speech continued in the same vein on a flickering set.[36] The press continually portrayed him as an antediluvian, inexperienced and anachronistic figure.

The domestic agenda dominated Home's first Cabinet on Tuesday 22 October, and Burke Trend, the Cabinet Secretary, was not the only one to notice a new briskness in the despatch of government business. The agenda was crisply dealt with and rambling monologues were cut short.

Home was determined that the government should not just 'bat out time' (he liked cricketing metaphors), but should have a real agenda to put before the electorate in 1964. The question of the election date occupied a considerable amount of time also, and Home engaged in a long correspondence with Macmillan on the advantages and disadvantages of the only two viable options, the spring of 1964 (the time Eden had won) or the autumn (the time Macmillan had won). He also consulted Lord Avon, who came to visit him from time to time in Downing Street, though on one occasion the former Prime Minister was late, and found that Alec Home was not prepared to reorganise his timetable to accommodate him. Home was totally unfussed; Eden had missed his 'slot' and the Prime Minister had other engagements. But it was a matter of some delicacy for the secretariat, who found an alternative date. 'Once again many apologies for my stupidity in confusing the hour of our meeting', Lord Avon apologised. 'I enjoyed our talk very much.'[37]

Home left no doubt he was the captain of the side and that in the short time remaining only a united effort should win the Party an unprecedented fourth term; he asked for 'the prompt and effective despatch of public business'. All ministers were required ('in the next few days') to submit an outline of plans for their departments, together with an indication of any major problems.

Despite Wilson's objections, the Cabinet agreed that the Opening of Parliament should be postponed until Home was able to take a seat in the Commons.[38] The Prime Minister also presented a memorandum setting out a blueprint for forthcoming strategy. 'Our plans for reform and modernisation must be matched by financial and fiscal responsibility,' he wrote. 'If we cannot manifestly ensure this, we have no effective answer to our opponents' attempts to outbid us. I shall rely on all ministers to continue to keep their departmental programmes under close review in order to maintain the momentum of a positive and forward-looking policy.' He was well aware of the pitch Wilson was making for the progressive vote in the forthcoming contest. Although it is generally thought that Alec Home was the first Tory leader since Bonar Law to lead the party from the right of centre, this was largely owing to his uncompromising anti-communist stance. On the domestic agenda the lessons of Noel Skelton from the 1920s had not been forgotten, as he emphasised to all ministers:

> It is equally important, however, that, provided that we remain

> within the limits prescribed by a sense of economic responsibility, our policies should be, and should be seen to be, positive and constructive. This requires us to identify the points where decisions need to be taken; to take the necessary decisions; to present them as attractively and imaginatively as we can; and to stick to them. I have tried to take the first step in this direction by sending minutes to individual ministers on the topics which seem to me to need special attention or added effort; and I hope that during the next few weeks these questions will be brought forward, through the normal committee machines, and will be dealt with as promptly as possible.[39]

Not only did policy come under sharp scrutiny but the machinery of government itself. The Cabinet Secretary is the crucial lynchpin of the Downing Street machine; Home was fortunate that his term of office coincided with the tenure of Sir Burke Trend, who was preparing a review of the Cabinet Committee system, not publicly acknowledged in the early 1960s.[40] He found a ready supporter in Alec Home when it came to pruning and rationalisation. Trend much admired Home's methods of working, finding him decisive, clear-minded and a good controller of the Cabinet agenda; he thought Home the best Chairman of Cabinet.[41] As Prime Minister Home also had the power to set up both *ad hoc* and standing committees, nominate the members and decide on the Chairman, if he himself was not to head the Committee.

The Macmillan years had seen a steady increase of committees on all subjects, from one on University Population in 1959, a prelude to the Robbins Report on Higher Education in September 1963, through to a committee considering the aftermath of the Profumo Crisis. Many of these had now run their natural course. In February 1936, Thomas Jones, Deputy Cabinet Secretary, had noted in his diary that one minister felt that the Cabinet office was over-machined, breeding committees like rabbits.[42] Although he might not have expressed it in identical terms, Home would very much have agreed with these sentiments. On 1 November Burke Trend wrote to the Prime Minister with proposals for dissolving certain committees. One of the first to be wound up in Home's review was the Post-Brussels Committee, set up to consider the implications of de Gaulle's veto on Britain's application to join the Common Market. Bodies such as the Distribution of Industry Committee, and the Civil Scientific Research and Development Committee, found their functions concentrated into the new Ministry of Industry, Trade and Regional Development. Where Home felt that a committee's usefulness remained, as with the Reorganisation of

Railways Committee, following the Beeching Report of 1962, he retained it. Unlike some of his successors, he was a great traveller by rail, and there were few weeks when he did not pass through Berwick-upon-Tweed station. But there were no sacred cows. The Northern Ireland Committee was subsumed into the Regional Development Committee, already one of the policy priorities of his first days in office. The Farm Price Review Committee (all those endless debates in Scottish Office days on hill cow subsidy) he kept, as well as the Overseas Information Services Committee and Educational Co-operation Overseas Committee. He also agreed with Burke that a Transport Policy Committee should be established. There was talk of ending the Committee on the Press, but Burke Trend advised retention, believing that in the hands of William Deedes, Minister without Portfolio in charge of government information, this still had a useful function in the post-Vassall era.[43] In its quiet way, this reorganisation was symptomatic of the steadying efficiency Home brought to his task.

Home inherited most of his Downing Street team from Macmillan, but two figures on whom he came to depend in the area of public relations were John Groves and Henry James. Knox Cunningham retired with Macmillan and Home was faced with choosing a new Parliamentary Private Secretary. 'I am rather inclined towards Frank Pearson', wrote Redmayne on 12 November, after he and Sir John George, Chairman of the Scottish Unionist Party, had introduced Alec Home into the Commons. 'Admittedly an oldish man but one who is very well respected throughout the Party.'[44] After considering the advantages of a young figure, as he had been for Neville Chamberlain, Home settled on Frank Pearson MP, for Clitheroe, a loyal and experienced backbencher with a reputation for 'no fuss and good manners'. Pearson also represented the electorally important north-west, the area that was the key to victory for Heath in June 1970. Why should he have one of the Young Turks? Pearson was a totally natural choice, just the kind of man the Prime Minister wanted. Although the relationship did not bring all the political dividends Home had hoped, the friendship and trust between the two was of the highest order, and in the resignation honours list Home recommended Pearson for an hereditary baronetcy. Pearson's career went back to his time as ADC to the Viceroy of India in the 1930s, but he saw his time with Alec Home as a greater honour. 'He knew the art of heading a team and getting the best from those who served with him,' Pearson wrote. 'For him leadership was not thumping the table or shouting his beliefs as the only right solution. He had great humility and while appearing detached, missed nothing.[45] It was the kind of assessment Dunglass could have written of Chamberlain. 'He idolised Lord Home', Pearson's widow wrote, 'and the years working as his PPS were really the apex of his life'.[46]

Others also departed from the Downing Street team, notably John Wyndham, who was *sui generis* as far as Macmillan was concerned. His replacement was Malcolm Reid, who came from a Board of Trade background, and was to serve at No. 10 until 1966, before going on to even higher things in the enlarged Department of Trade and Industry. Home struck up a warm friendship with Reid and found much in common, especially with their joint interest in National Hunt racing. When the classic races were run, the lobby always wanted to know which horses the Prime Minister was backing, as his knowledge of bloodstock lines was legendary. The team was to be augmented by the arrival of Oliver Wright, Home's former Counsellor and Private Secretary at the Foreign Office, and Derek Mitchell, from the Treasury, as the Principal Private Secretaries. Both were to serve Harold Wilson, though Mitchell's days under the new regime were blighted by internal wrangles, totally absent from No. 10 under Home.[47] With Philip Woodfield continuing in office, it was a harmonious team that continued the family atmosphere that had been such a part of the Macmillan years. The Garden Room Girls, who were to arouse great suspicion among the incoming Labour entourage in October, who wrongly suspected them all of being 'Tory debs', were led by Jane Parsons, who had first worked at No. 10 with the Attlees. The Macmillan years had been very special for the Garden Room Girls and Alec Home's brief tenure was the end of a particular way of working. Family informality combined with professional efficiency and a sense of happy teamwork, with Alec and Elizabeth Home always remembering birthdays and anniversaries. Elizabeth was very much part of the team, making sure that things worked and thinking nothing of driving up to the Hirsel and back over a weekend with Angela Bowlby, Alec Home's personal secretary, to bring back things that were needed. In Harold Macmillan's time, grandchildren were always part of the scene. With the arrival of Fiona Wolfe Murray, there was a continuation of this same atmosphere, and photos appeared in the papers of Meriel and her friends, often with guitars and in modish dress. This struck an ironic modernity when contrasted with the rather home-spun, almost 1930s domestic hobbies of the Wilson family in Hampstead, with bicycles and stick insects. Meriel's engagement to Adrian Darby, an economics don, later Bursar, at Keble College, Oxford together with the arrival of Diana's daughter, ensured that the year in Downing Street, for all its political vicissitudes, was a time of great personal happiness for Alec and Elizabeth Home. The growing family circle gave more scope for the cartoonists, especially the possibility of Adrian Darby helping the Prime Minister with his 'matchsticks'. Adrian and Meriel's marriage was to take place in Coldstream on 30 March 1964, all hopes for a quiet wedding lost in the scrum of press photographers outside the church. Contrary to the accepted image of stuffiness, No. 10 Downing Street under the Homes was a house that was always open to a variety of young people. On one occasion a group of sea scouts came to the door (this was before the era of security gates), wanting the Prime Minister's autograph as part of an initiative test. Alec Home invited them all in, gave them a tour of the Cabinet room and a buffet lunch. However busy the agenda, he always seemed to have time to spare, doing much of the paper work in the very early morning. He gave regular interviews to figures such as John Dickie, Diplomatic Correspondent of the *Daily Mail*, who was then writing Alec Home's first biography, and to David Butler of Nuffield College, already preparing his book on the forthcoming general election. When Professor Anthony King of Essex University came on academic political business, he was astonished to find that Alec Home found time also to give him a guided tour of the Downing Street complex.[48]

Two figures Home inherited from the Macmillan team were Nigel Lawson and John MacGregor. 'I have been conscious for some time that we could do with more help on the party speeches', Macmillan had written to Rab Butler in May 1963. 'I would like to ask Iain Macleod and Oliver Poole to try and find two good speech writers who would be borne for pay and rations by the Conservative Research Department but who would be available directly to me when I wanted them.'[49] The upshot was the appointment of Lawson and MacGregor, who now became vital figures in the by-election campaign to return Home to the House of Commons. Michael Fraser had recruited John MacGregor, who had been in voluntary political work and on the editorial staff of the archetypal sixties magazine, *New Society*, while Oliver Poole had brought Nigel Lawson from the *Sunday Telegraph*, where he had been the founding city editor. Together with Eldon Griffiths and George Christ (pronounced 'crist') of Central Office, the team was a precursor of the political advisers that became *de rigueur* for serious politicians a decade later. When Alec Home became Foreign Secretary for the second time in 1970, he appointed Miles Hudson specifically to this post, just as his successor, James Callaghan, brought in Tom McNally to complement the work of the Private Office. Before October 1963 Alec Home would never have thought of having a speechwriter, but media attention meant that no speech could be repeated. Though the venues in Perthshire in October 1963 were by and large still village halls, Alec Home had to be primed with different speeches for each location. Lawson and MacGregor, backed up by Central Office, therefore co-ordinated a continuous supply of material, finding that Home was always very punctilious about distinguishing between Party work and government business. It was said that Peter Goldman produced the economics, Eldon Griffiths the Foreign Affairs and George Christ the jokes. When Michael Fraser telephoned to find out how things were going, George Christ replied, 'They say it's a Scotch mist up here, but I think it's raining.' Nigel Lawson pepped up many of the blander statements, adding the famous phrase about Wilson being 'the slick salesman of synthetic science', not entirely the best idea in practice as Alec Home was never good with sibilants, though the phrase stuck. Daphne Shrimpton from the Garden Room Girls became the secretary in attendance in Perthshire as the team began work.

The Kinross and West Perthshire by-election was an anxious time for Home's supporters; despite Gilmour Leburn's majority of 12,248 at the general election in 1959, the Scottish Unionist Party took nothing for granted. Now there was a resurgent Liberal Party, represented by Duncan Millar, a local landowner for whom the future Liberal leader, David Steel, was working. Millar was a strong local candidate who capitalised on the recent controversy over government farming subsidies. A variety of fringe characters completed the list of candidates. The most colourful, in the days before the appearance of Screaming Lord Sutch, was William Rushton, one of the television performers from *That Was The Week That Was*. Hanging over the whole contest for the Unionists was the unmentionable spectre of a shock defeat. So seriously was the possibility considered, that constitutional experts were consulted as to the implications. But there was no alternative seat readily available and if Alec Home could not win a constituency in rural Perthshire, then his premiership was hardly viable. It was the first of the many gambles that Macmillan had envisaged.

Much of the initial grumbling came from the local Constituency Party Association, who had taken immense trouble in selecting George

Younger as their candidate after the sudden death of Gilmour Leburn in August. Such an attractive seat had drawn a wide field of candidates, eventually whittled down to four, including Lord Mansfield, a future government minister. On 10 October, the day Home read out Macmillan's letter at Blackpool, George Younger was chosen by a selection committee representative of every corner of the large constituency, who did not now take kindly to their hard work counting for nothing, even if the replacement candidate imposed upon them was the Prime Minister. The situation was complicated by the fact that nominations closed at noon on Monday 21 October (the by-election had been fixed in *The London Gazette* for 7 November) and John Robertson's wife, Una, rushed the Home papers to Perth after the weekend with only minutes to spare. Younger was the grandson of Viscount Younger of Leckie, with whom Alec Dunglass had worked in Lanark days, heir to both a title and a famous political name. He showed more understanding of the realities than many of his local executive, who were reluctant to release him. In the end the key figures were David Maitland-Gardiner, the local Chairman, who lived at Culdees Castle, Sir John George, Chairman of the Scottish Unionist Party, and his deputy, Sir John Gibson. The first sign that something was in the wind came on Wednesday 16 October (the day before Macmillan began drafting his final memorandum for the Queen) when George Younger was canvassing in the constituency with John Robertson.[50] Telephone calls started coming through from the London press, asking Younger if the rumour was true that he was about to give up his seat for Lord Home. (It was another twenty-four hours before Iain Macleod had any inkling of this development.) This was the first that Younger had heard of the matter and, as he had found some difficulty in winning an adoption, the matter had disturbing implications. It would obviously be very difficult, if not impossible, for him to hold out in the circumstances, though he was assured that his reward would be the next available safe constituency in Scotland. In practice, Younger had little choice, but there were longer-term political advantages (he was then thirty-two) of being cast in the role of sacrificial lamb, though this was emphatically not part of Younger's calculation. The campaign began in earnest on Friday 18 October, with three big meetings the following day. In the early hours of Sunday morning, John Robertson was asked by David Maitland-Gardiner to be at the Conservative Club in Glasgow later that day. When Robertson arrived that morning (20 October), he was ushered in with other delegates through the kitchens lest the press had got wind of the meeting. Sir John George put the stark situation to the local party executive and his erstwhile candidate. 'George, you'll do your duty for your country and your party,' he said. After some talk about what it would mean for the constituents, who appeared very low in the list of priorities, Younger agreed to stand down, but only after releasing Robertson to serve as Home's agent.[51] After that, Alec Home could never do enough for George Younger, and, as Prime Minister, went out of his way to speak personally for Younger in his Ayr constituency at the 1964 General Election, an intervention that crucially tipped the balance towards Younger in a close-fought campaign, according to the local Liberals.

Within forty-eight hours of renouncing his titles, Alec Home left for Berwick on the overnight train. After visiting his mother at Springhill, the first time she had seen him as Prime Minister, Elizabeth drove him to Comrie, where he set up his base at Easter Ross, the house of Major Andrew Drummond-Moray ('Andy's place', the party workers called it). For the next two weeks Easter Ross became both home and a substitute Downing Street, with scrambler telephones for government business. Although the by-election was being used to get Sir Alec (as he was now known) back to the House of Commons, local issues, redolent of his Scottish Office days, were a central preoccupation of the electorate.

Alec Home's first speech of the campaign was at the Auction Mart in Perth on 26 October. He had asked George Younger if he would continue canvassing for him, an exciting political apprenticeship for a future Secretary of State for Scotland, as the small towns and villages of Perthshire became a focus for the world's press, with a significant contingent from the United States. Many of those involved in Home's campaign can remember the incomprehensible transatlantic pronunciations of the names of Scottish villages. 'Say where's this CRY EFF?' became the catchphrase of the campaign. The attention of the TV cameras proved too much for some party workers and in Auchterarder the local lady President ended one packed meeting by excitedly telling the loyal Unionist constituents to go out and vote as they had never voted before. George Younger selflessly acted as warm-up man for the Prime Minister in the village halls. In the course of his campaign, Home made seventy-two different speeches, some to packed halls, others in bustling market squares, one at Glen Lyon to a mere handful. He signed autographs for local children and, with Elizabeth at his side, met as many local people as possible. It was one of the last occasions on which a British Prime Minister was in such concentrated, close contact with ordinary people, talking face to face about local problems. At the Maclaren Hall in Killin on the evening of 1 November, Alec Home was in full flow when a photographer suddenly came down the central aisle. Slowly he unpacked his case and set up a tripod, the attention of the local audience diverted increasingly to these technicalities. He tested the focus and the zoom lens, before training the camera on the platform. A whirring as he took his single photograph was a prelude to the whole elaborate process in reverse, before he disappeared into the night. Heads turned, but Home paid not the slightest attention, never drawing breath as he continued his prepared speech.

Flights back to London were arranged for Cabinet and other meetings, among them a talk with a 'Mr I.D. Smith, the Southern Rhodesian Finance Minister'. His old Commonwealth Relations Office sent a tactful but uncompromising briefing for this meeting, which began, 'The PM will no doubt wish to lead Mr Smith gently to a realisation of the plain facts of the situation today.'[52] Together with the Duke of Devonshire, Minister of State at the Commonwealth Office, Alec Home heard Ian Smith's views on independence for Southern Rhodesia. Pressures were building after the winding-up of the Central African Federation and it would be intolerable in Smith's opinion if Nyasaland got independence first. Home warned that a minimum degree of international support would be indispensable for an independent Southern Rhodesia. Nevertheless Smith said, accurately as events proved, that the Southern Rhodesian government was moving towards a head-on collision with Britain, with the Prime Minister replying that Smith should think seriously about the dangers of isolation and of rejection by the Commonwealth. It had been an uneasy hour, though Ian Smith wrote to the Prime Minister thanking him for seeing him during his election campaign, something he regarded as a great courtesy.[53] At Prime Minister's question time on 28 November, Home reiterated that the principle of majority rule for the Rhodesian franchise was not in dispute. The issue was one of pace. It was seventeen years before 'the issue' was resolved.[54]

Many prominent Scottish supporters came to speak on the Prime Minister's behalf in Kinross. Lady Tweedsmuir, formerly John Robertson's employer, canvassed, as did John Maclay, the former Secretary of State. Sir Fitzroy Maclean attended a meeting at Port of Menteith. Lady McNair Snadden, glad to be back in the political swing, attended many meetings and gave generous hospitality. William

Whitelaw went up to the meeting at Kinross on 31 October, which led to the cancellation of Cabinet, as it was the only day the hall at Kinross was available. The final meeting of the campaign was at the Victoria Hall in Dunblane. The Prime Minister's theme, obviously aimed at the wider national audience, was that socialism and austerity are boon companions. 'Does any wage earner really pine for the days when he was earning less, as he was under the Socialists?' he asked his audience. 'If his average wage increases, as it has under the Conservatives, does he feel thereby debased and debauched?'[55]

Polling Day on Thursday 7 November was a tense affair. There was no telling how disaffected Tories might vote after the events of Blackpool and the strong Liberal showing was a constant worry. The Luton by-election, on the same day resulted in the Tories' loss of the seat. At 9.30 a.m. Alec Home left Easter Ross to tour twenty of the scattered polling stations. He did not sit down for a meal until 9 p.m., after which the company at the Drummond-Morays adjourned to watch the result of the Luton by-election on television. (The count in Perthshire was not due to begin until the Friday morning.) When the result was known, George Christ and Nigel Lawson saw the Prime Minister before he gave a brief statement.

At 9 a.m. on Friday 8 November, Alec and Elizabeth Home left Easter Ross for the count at the Sheriff Court House in Perth. They arrived at 9.45 to find a very formal and disciplined operation under the control of Sheriff Principal George Emslie. The respective piles of votes were soon an indication that Alec Home would be returned. At 11.45 a.m., Sheriff Emslie announced the figures live on national television from the steps of the City Hall:

Sir Alec Douglas-Home (Conservative)	14,147
Alastair Duncan Millar (Liberal)	4,819
Andrew Forrester (Labour)	3,752
Arthur Donaldson (Scottish Nationalist)	1,801
Ian Smith (Independent)	78
William Rushton (Independent)	45
Richard Wort (Independent)	23
Conservative Majority	9,328

The first feeling was one of relief, not least among members of the Cabinet who were watching in different parts of the country. Home gave a short speech to the crowds outside the City Hall and held a press conference at 12.20 p.m. Although he could have flown back to London there and then, he toured the constituency in the afternoon, thanking his supporters and the party workers. Messages of congratulations poured in, one of the most felicitous and generous telegrams being from Rab Butler: MY HEARTIEST CONGRATULATIONS. IT IS A FAMOUS VICTORY FOR YOU AND THE BEST ENCOURAGEMENT IN THE WORLD FOR THE PARTY. THAT CERTAINLY WAS THE WEEK THAT WAS. RAB.[56] On his return to Dorneywood that evening, Alec Home began work on his speeches for the Debate on the Address and for the Lord Mayor's Banquet on 11 November. In the formal surroundings of Guildhall, he struck a new relaxed note, incorporating Butler's gibe at the satirists. 'My Lords, with some nostalgia ...', he began, 'you have proposed the government's health – rather for us an unusual experience – but I should like to say at once that we are very well. We had you see a holiday by the sea at Blackpool, then I took another week in Scotland. That was a week that was.'[57]

His return to the House of Commons proved quite a week also, including as it did the Festival of Remembrance at the Albert Hall, and (on 10 November) his only appearance as Prime Minister at the Cenotaph. His formal election as Conservative leader was at Church House, Westminster, where his name was proposed by Carrington and seconded by Butler, the third time Butler had fulfilled this role. Among the ornate lettering on the ceiling of Church House some noted the words 'They inherit a home of unfading splendour wherein they rejoice with gladness evermore.'[58]

On 12 November the Prime Minister was introduced into the House of Commons, and in his first speech there for over thirteen years, he gave priority to the government's domestic policy, speaking of plans for education, housing, transport and development of depressed areas. On foreign affairs he emphasised the importance of the independent nuclear deterrent, asking Harold Wilson whether he would abandon Polaris. The speech reads well, but its delivery was punctuated by Labour heckling and boos. Prime Minister's speeches were no longer listened to in silence; deference, even politeness, was at a premium. The American ambassador, David Bruce, sent his customary update on the British political scene to the State Department in Washington:

> Prime Minister's first day in Parliament rough going. Subjected to loud and long heckling by Labor backbenchers. He had difficulty in

> developing continuous and coherent presentation. He seemed strained, repetitive and was occasionally at a loss for a word, giving impression of not being thoroughly at home in economic and domestic sections of speech with which he began, his economic presentation seemed oversimplified. He compared poorly with Wilson's thorough command of subject, polish and fluency. When PM came to foreign policy section of speech where he was on more familiar ground he gained greatly in assurance ... At end of day impression of Conservative backbench mood was one of relief, not jubilation ... In Labor oriented *Daily Herald* impression given was that Douglas-Home, while scoring no personal triumph, had demonstrated ability to survive rough and tumble of Commons.[59]

That evening, Home had an audience with the Queen to bring Her Majesty up to date with events since he had kissed hands on 18 October, before returning to the House where he listened to further speeches on the address.

Home's first full week back in London was typical of his programme for the next eleven months. Most days saw tactical meetings with the Chief Whip and the Lord Privy Seal, often on the date of the election, a constant preoccupation. There were functions such as the Chief Whip's Lobby Party and a cricket lunch hosted by the England player Ted Dexter, who was to stand against James Callaghan in the 1964 election. He chaired the Overseas Policy Committee and had meetings on the Robbins Report on Higher Education, as well as addressing all junior ministers in the large Committee Room at the House. He received foreign visitors such as the President of Iceland, and was interviewed at the Lime Grove studios of the BBC.

There was no indication that Friday, 22 November was to be anything out of the ordinary. The day began with a visit to the Campaign for Education Exhibition at the TUC's Congress House. After this he fitted in one of his 'biographical' meetings with John Dickie at No. 10, before seeing Captain Terence O'Neill, Prime Minister of Northern Ireland, for his first talks on the Province. Sir Laurence Helsby, head of the Home Civil Service called on him at 2.35 p.m., followed by a session of official photographs. He set off at 5.15 p.m. with Elizabeth for a weekend with the Duke of Norfolk at Arundel. It was to prove the beginning of one of the most traumatic episodes in his entire premiership. Arriving at Arundel shortly after seven o'clock, he was met by a breathless Duke on the steps of the castle. The Duke told him that President Kennedy had been shot in

Dallas, and at 7.30 it was confirmed that the President was dead. Home's first thought was that he would have to return to London and speak for the nation; the BBC had already made preliminary contact with Arundel Castle. Home took a hurried supper and returned by car to London. Paul Fox, the head of current affairs, was attempting to contact all three party leaders. Harold Wilson was in north Wales and would broadcast from the BBC in Manchester; Jo Grimond, the Liberal leader, was at the Oxford Union. The situation was complicated by the BAFTA Awards Night at the Dorchester, and a hasty rearranging of BBC schedules ensued. Richard Dimbleby, the voice of the BBC on such momentous occasions, was unwell, therefore the tributes were to be co-ordinated by Ian Trethowan who was in charge in Studio H, Lime Grove, with Alun Gwynne Jones.[60] Home was driven directly to the Lime Grove studios to make a live television broadcast, but the lift taking him to the studio jammed and an engineer worked desperately to free the Prime Minister in time for the broadcast. He made it with thirty seconds in hand.

His tribute to the assassinated President was one of his finest and most spontaneous addresses. 'There are times in life when mind and heart stand still and one such is now,' he said. 'And all of you will have felt, as I did, that everything in one cried in protest at the news that President Kennedy was dead at the hand of an assassin.'[61] Memories of the Nassau and Bermuda conferences and the recent visit by the President to Birch Grove were still vivid. Over thirty years later, in a newspaper correspondence on the television performances of Alec Home and Harold Wilson, Mr Peter Robinson wrote: 'Sir Alec certainly outclassed all other politicians who gave televised condolences on the occasion of the Kennedy assassination. In a procession of tributes ranging from the embarrassing to the maudlin, Sir Alec's short appearance on TV shines in my memory as sincere, dignified, very moving and perfectly adapted to the traumatic atmosphere prevailing at that time.'[62] Wilson had made an appropriately dignified broadcast from the BBC's Manchester studios, but the effectiveness of both tributes was overshadowed in the public consciousness by the interview the Deputy Labour Leader, George Brown, gave to Kenneth Harris. Brown was already the worse for wear after the beginnings of a convivial evening at Shoreditch Labour Party, and was now offered further hospitality before the broadcast. His performance, in which he nearly came to blows with another guest, and claimed great personal friendship with the assassinated President, was a severe embarrassment to the Labour Party and claimed all the later headlines.[63]

Through David Ormsby-Gore, Alec and Elizabeth Home sent a personal message to the President's widow. WE ARE HORRIFIED BY THE TERRIBLE NEWS AND SEND YOU OUR DEEPEST SYMPATHY IN YOUR GRIEF. ELIZABETH AND ALEC DOUGLAS-HOME.[64] Home's immediate concern was that the British response to the tragedy should be above all dignified and appropriate. On the morning of 23 November he wrote to Rab Butler, 'I think that a Memorial Service for President Kennedy should be arranged at a very early date. On the precedent of the Service for President Roosevelt it ought to take place within a week of his death if possible. On that occasion the Service was held at St Paul's Cathedral and I think this would again be appropriate.'[65]

The main official British mourners at the Washington funeral were the Prime Minister and the Duke of Edinburgh. So hasty were the arrangements from the American end that the Duke of Edinburgh had not been allocated a ticket for the funeral service in St Matthew's Cathedral, and attended on Lady Home's ticket. The Kennedy rites were a mixture of dignity and spontaneous grief. Tim Bligh, Harold Evans, Philip de Zulueta, and Daphne Shrimpton completed the Downing Street delegation. Home offered seats on the flight to Harold Wilson and Jo Grimond; the Duke and Duchess of Devonshire, related by marriage to the Kennedys, flew on the same plane. The Douglas-Homes were very relaxed during the flight, but formalities were retained at the front end of the plane with the Prime Minister warning Daphne Shrimpton not to turn her back on the Duke of Edinburgh when she came up for dictation. Only the Prime Minister's delegation could be accommodated by the Ormsby-Gores at the British Embassy (Harold Wilson was put up by John Killick, then Head of Chancery in Washington), where they were driven after being met by Dean Rusk at Dulles Airport.

Home knew that he would only have the briefest of meetings with Lyndon Johnson, the new President, but the Foreign Office had sent an advance despatch requesting an appointment, as 'it might look odd if he came to Washington and did not have any time with the President at all'.[66] At 10.30 a.m. on 25 November, the Duke of Edinburgh and the Prime Minister left the British Embassy for the White House, where they joined President Johnson. Home's main memory was of the secret service agents who accompanied the dignitaries. Their eyes were not fixed on the mute crowds lining the streets, but on the roofs of buildings as though they were expecting another high-angle shooting. The visual images stood out: John Kennedy Junior saluting the cortège, de Gaulle's head above the other world leaders, the riderless horse with reversed stirrups. A pontifical Low Mass was held at noon, after which the Duke of Edinburgh and the Prime Minister were driven to Arlington National Cemetery where President Kennedy was buried. At the White House, both had separate meetings with Mrs Kennedy. President Johnson gave a reception at the State Department, at which the two new leaders met for the first time. 'Your presence was a great comfort during these tragic hours', wrote Johnson on a copy of the official photograph of the two leaders.[67] The Duke of Edinburgh flew back to London, while Alec Home returned to the British Embassy for a working dinner with Lester Pearson and other Canadian leaders.

The next morning Home went with Ormsby-Gore to the White House, where he had a half hour meeting with Johnson, the two agreeing to a longer series of talks in February. As so often, a state funeral proved to be a working opportunity. Home gave a lunch for Chancellor Erhard of West Germany and met Anastas Mikoyan, First Deputy Chairman of the Soviet Council of Ministers, after which he gave the Russians a tour of the British Embassy, introducing them to the Devonshires, Elizabeth Home and the ambassador's wife. Many of the Russians he had met in Moscow in August at the signing of the Test Ban Treaty. That evening, the Homes dined at the Residence with Theodore Sorenson, one of the closest of the Kennedy circle, and Joe Alsop of the *Washington Post*. A tragic occasion had in the end done much to establish Home in American eyes as the new British Prime Minister.

On 27 November, the Homes prepared to return to Britain with the Devonshires and Jo Grimond, but as the plane crossed the Atlantic, news was received of thick fog at London Airport. The party was diverted to Manchester's Ringway Airport, where they landed at 9 p.m. GMT. After Home had given a press conference at the airport, it was discovered that the London midnight sleeper was fully booked and a return to the capital was impossible that night. Jo Grimond's impatience at the inconvenience to his plans was clear, leading Elizabeth Home to put things in perspective, by asking, 'Honestly, Jo, if you can't run your personal life, how do you run the Liberal Party?'[68] Humour prevailed in the end. The Devonshires suggested that the entire party stay overnight at Chatsworth, which was already prepared for a visit by Princess Margaret that weekend. 'If I lie very still and don't turn over', said Alec

Home, 'you won't have to change the sheets.'[69] When they arrived at Chatsworth, the Homes were allocated the centre bedroom, the bed of which was so enormous that Tim Bligh suggested it could accommodate the entire Parliamentary Liberal Party. There were times when laughter was the best tonic, and for Alec Home, the dreadful week of Kennedy's assassination was such a time.

The death of Kennedy brought to an end an important era in Anglo–American relationships. The golden days of Mac and Jack were over and a more uncertain period began. Lyndon Baines Johnson, the political bruiser from Texas, and Alec Douglas-Home, the border aristocrat, were temperamentally poles apart. Although there had been courteous sympathy between them in the aftermath of Kennedy's assassination, there was little fellow political feeling. In the last months of his life Kennedy had already had his reservations about the British leadership, but his respect for Macmillan had temporarily sidelined deeper American doubts. Kennedy had inscribed a photograph for Alec Home 'with appreciation for his most useful efforts to bridge the Atlantic',[70] but it is doubtful if Kennedy and Home would have replicated the happy relationship of the Macmillan era. Alec Home, who considered that Robert Kennedy had the greater potential, knew of Kennedy's sharp and critical assessment of Britain's prospects and his wariness about the Test Ban Treaty. Johnson regarded Macmillan's successor as a stop-gap, and was looking to a new relationship with Harold Wilson before the year was out. At the first Cabinet meeting after Kennedy's death, Rab Butler said, 'Our forward plans must inevitably be based on the assumption that United States leadership would now be less positive than hitherto.'[71] Home wrote to Ormsby-Gore, thanking him for the arrangements the embassy had made 'for our very hurried visit', but tacitly accepting that things would now be different. 'You know what a great help your close friendship with the late President has been. I know that in consequence his death has been a very heavy personal blow to you. I am so very sorry and we are all truly grateful for all you are doing and not least for the fortitude with which you have faced all this. I am also grateful for your assurances about the future. No doubt you will be able to talk things over if you can arrange to come here in December.'[72]

Three days after Home's letter to Ormsby-Gore, the by-election at the St Marylebone constituency returned Quintin Hogg to the House of Commons, though with a majority down from 14,771 at the general election to 5,276. The result revived all the controversies of Blackpool;

FIRST DAYS AT THE FOREIGN OFFICE

Alec Home, Harold Macmillan and Konrad Adenauer, Bonn, 10 August 1960

'This tall, lanky Scottish peer suddenly became an international personality': David Ormsby-Gore (studying what the Foreign Secretary thought might have been the *Times* crossword) and Alec Home at the opening of the 15th session of the General Assembly of the United Nations, September 1960

'A mood of dazed anxiety': CND supporters protesting during the Missile Crisis over American policy towards Cuba, 28 October 1962

David Ormsby-Gore and Alec Home with President Kennedy at the White House, 4 October 1963. A fortnight later Alec Home was Prime Minister

Alec Home with David Bruce, the American Ambassador to Britain, February 1964. Bruce's despatches to the State Department in Washington give a vivid picture of British political life in the early 1960s

'Immediately after the Test Treaty is signed, Khruschev speaks, small and pink, with China in the back of his mind, and Rusk and Home like tutelary angels behind him': the signing of the Test Ban Treaty in Moscow, 5 August 1963

Cummings cartoon:
'Goodness, Prime Minister!
Now it's the *English*
demanding independence
and the right to run
their own affairs . . .'

Harold Macmillan in his Bromley constituency
at the time of the Profumo Affair, 22 June 1963

Osbert Lancaster cartoon:
'Mind you, Littlehampton,
I still say that lettin' all those
Scots peers in completely
unvetted is a damn stiff
price to pay for gettin' rid of
Stansgate and Hailsham'

The reluctant peer: Tony and Caroline Benn outside the House of Commons with the Instrument of Disclaimer, 31 July 1963. Benn's campaign to renounce his Peerage paved the way for Alec Douglas-Home to become Prime Minister

'The disappointment when I, rather than Alec, went to the microphone was painfully, if politely, evident': John Boyd-Carpenter addresses the delegates on Local Government Finance at the Conservative Conference, 11 October 1963, whilst Alec Douglas-Home waits to read out Macmillan's letter of resignation

The scene outside the King Edward VII Hospital, 18 October 1963:
'As The Queen left the hospital, the memorandum was placed in a huge white envelope and given to Michael Adeane'

Elizabeth, David and Alec Douglas-Home in 10 Downing Street, October 1963

Cummings cartoon:
'Fight over
the leadership!
What fight over the
leadership?'

Alec Douglas-Home leaving 10 Downing Street, 12 November 1963, to take his seat in the House of Commons after the Kinross and West Perthshire by-election

Alec and Elizabeth Douglas-Home with the Duke of Edinburgh at President Kennedy's funeral, Washington, 25 November 1963

Alec Douglas-Home with Robert Kennedy, Downing Street, 27 January 1964: 'The acute depression into which he was plunged after his brother's assassination has increased his air of dogged determination in his work'

matters were not helped when Hogg began his maiden speech in the Commons, 'My Lords'.[73] Randolph Churchill was known to be nearing completion of his blow-by-blow account of the struggle for the Tory leadership, so a certain apprehension marked the coming of the Christmas season for some Tory MPs.

Another delicate matter, which threatened to revive old controversies, was the forthcoming publication of Lord Kilmuir's memoirs. The former Lord Chancellor had submitted his proposed text to the Cabinet Secretary, Burke Trend, who had given Alec Home advance warning of possible difficulties. 'There are three sections of the book which, for different reasons, give me some concern', Trend had written.[74] These concerned Suez, Eden's resignation and the events leading up to the reconstruction of the Macmillan Government in July 1962, which held such bitter memories for Kilmuir.[75] Kennedy's funeral meant that it was some time before the controversial passages could be fully considered. The book was provisionally entitled *Laborious Days*, though it was to be published as *Political Adventure*, which led one former colleague to decline to review it on the grounds that even the title was inaccurate as the final letter 'r' had been omitted from the end of the second word.[76] When the book was eventually serialised in the *Sunday Times*, Eden sought counsel's opinion and Robert Rhodes James, who had helped Kilmuir in the preparation of his autobiography and was later to be Eden's biographer, had to act as intermediary between the two men.[77] But it was criticisms of serving Cabinet colleagues that most concerned Home. Ever since Kilmuir had been one of the principal victims of Macmillan's Cabinet reconstruction, a sense of festering resentment had fuelled his determination to set down his version. With an impending election Home knew how politically damaging this could prove. The first drafts contained scathing denunciations of Kilmuir's former colleagues, two of whom, R.A. Butler and Selwyn Lloyd, now held senior posts in the Home administration. Trend was also concerned about the constitutional impropriety of disclosing details of Cabinet committees, such as the Egypt Committee during the Suez crisis, and the advice Churchill and Eden gave in January 1957 when Harold Macmillan became Prime Minister. Home read the proofs carefully, but Cabinet office clearance was only sought at a very late stage and serialisation was imminent. It was agreed at a meeting between Trend and the Prime Minister that Home should show Kilmuir marked passages in the drafts which were embarrassing and should be omitted. Home did not take such exception to the Suez chapter, writing to

Kilmuir, 'I have read it once and would not have thought there was more in it than all of us said in Parliament at the time.' What he did take exception to, as did Burke, was a derogatory remark about Butler in 1956/1957 which accounted for his failure, in Kilmuir's opinion, to be chosen as Prime Minister to succeed Eden. In the light of the events of a few weeks earlier this was a sensitive area for Alec Home. The phrase was one about Butler having no one to blame but himself for the sharp decline in his political fortune owing to 'his habit of publicly hedging his political bets'. As a result Alec Home saw Kilmuir, by now Chairman of Plessey, at No. 10 on 5 December. Home stressed the unsuitability of the reference to the Cabinet committee system, especially the Egypt Committee during the Suez crisis. In the published version such references were modified to vaguer phrases about 'a meeting of the inner group of ministers specially concerned with Suez'.[78] On some of the other points the Prime Minister's appeals were not so successful. The record of their meeting continued: 'It would be noticed that he was writing about people who were not only members of the government but were also for a long time his ministerial colleagues. Some of the remarks he made were extremely derogatory including some about ministers now in senior positions, that is to say the Foreign Secretary and the Leader of the House of Commons.' Alec Home emphasised that the remarks would have repercussions both at home, where a general election was imminent, and abroad. Home ended by saying that 'he did not wish to suggest any new form of wording for these passages but just thought it right that Lord Kilmuir should bear in mind the high reputation he at present enjoyed for being a fair-minded man, and that he should look at these chapters again with particular keenness to ensure that he was not open to the criticism of being petty'.[79] On 18 December Kilmuir wrote to Trend saying that 'on the matter of general tone, I hope it may be possible to go some way to meeting the Prime Minister's wishes'.[80] In retrospect this may seem a relatively insignificant episode but in the very different conventions then operating and while a fifty-year rule was still in operation regarding government papers, Alec Home was much concerned about the political fall-out, possessing sharper strategical antennae than he has been credited with. Despite the personal appeal from the Prime Minister, Kilmuir retained the phrase about Butler in the published version.[81] The main damage was to Kilmuir's own reputation and, precisely as Alec Home had warned, he laid himself open to the charge of being petty-minded. But the saga of the Kilmuir memoirs rumbled on and in

August 1992, Robert Rhodes James recalled these events in a correspondence with Lord Hartwell, who had been responsible for the original serialisation, in the *Spectator*. In his recollection of events at the time, including a meeting with Kilmuir shortly after he had left Downing Street on 5 December, Rhodes James was in no doubt that Home had acted both firmly and correctly. 'As a party leader facing a very difficult election, Sir Alec was absolutely justified in his actions to attempt to limit the political impact of Kilmuir's book.'[82] Only under subsequent questioning in the House about whether the government had exerted pressure on Kilmuir was Alec Home (in a later famous phrase) 'economical with the truth'.

For many members of the Cabinet the most important consideration was the date of the election, and two camps were already forming among Alec Home's advisers. Some, such as John Blakenham, the Joint Party Chairman, were in favour of an early contest (this led to him being dubbed in some circles as 'the March Hare'), but Home's instincts told him that the Party's best chance was to allow the full course of the Parliament – 'running up to the buffers' (a phrase current at the time) meant more time for people to tire of Wilson's novelty value. And there was always the possibility of some memorable intervention by George Brown. Lord Avon was also consulted about possible dates, but Alec Home was confirmed in his instinct for an October election (later he regretted not opting for November) by a long correspondence he had with Macmillan on the question and by the row over Randolph Churchill's book, *The Fight for the Tory Leadership*, published in January 1964.

Indications that a major row was about to erupt came with a letter Martin Redmayne received on 6 January from Iain Macleod, now editor of the *Spectator*.

> Dear Martin,
>
> I expect you have read Randolph Churchill's book. It's a dull book and a bad book but what horrifies me is the material he has been given by Harold Macmillan and others. Frankly I regard this as most improper. As you know, both Enoch Powell and myself have been at great pains (and I may add at great cost to ourselves in our constituencies) to say nothing and to refuse interviews to the press and television. Obviously this now becomes an impossible position to maintain. I intend to review Churchill's book at great length in the *Spectator* and to give my account of what happened. Oddly enough, I think both you and Harold Macmillan come a good deal better out

of my account than you do out of Churchill's, but you may not agree. Anyway, you can be quite sure that I will write it as moderately as I can. It will appear in next week's issue.

Yours ever,
Iain.[83]

On 17 January, Macleod's review appeared in the *Spectator* under the title, 'The Tory Leadership'. It is one of the famous polemics of post-war British history. Macleod described Churchill's book as 'Mr Macmillan's trailer for the screenplay of his memoirs' and asserted that 'from the first day of his premiership to the last, Macmillan was determined that Butler, although incomparably the best qualified of the contenders, should not succeed him'. But the phrase that went down into the political lexicon was that about 'the magic circle', the Etonians who conspired to make one of their own the Conservative leader, despite Cabinet backing for other candidates, notably Butler. 'Macleod had realised there would be a row,' wrote Nigel Fisher, his friend and biographer, 'he had not foreseen its scale and duration.'[84]

Alec Home was deeply saddened, not for his own reputation or feelings but by what he considered irreparable damage to the Conservatives' success in the election. He did not consider the phrase about 'the magic circle' the most damaging, but a less regarded point towards the end of the article: 'we have confessed that the Tory Party could not find a Prime Minister in the House of Commons at all.'[85] Despite the evidence, Alec Home regarded the Macleod article as a crucial contribution to the Tory defeat at the election, and on the day he resigned as Prime Minister he was to be seen pacing the drawing-room floor of Selwyn Lloyd's flat at Buckingham Gate, blaming the defeat on Macleod in language those who were present had not heard him use before.[86]

Discussion of the Macleod article took precedence over other political stories, even the Cyprus situation and Home's forthcoming visit to Washington for talks with President Johnson. 'This, of course just suits the press today, most of which loves to attack Eton and the aristocracy', wrote Macmillan. 'It's all great nonsense, but it touches off the "inverted snobbery" emotion wh. is very strong today.' Macmillan felt there would be inevitable, though imprecise, long-term damage. 'What harm this will do is hard to say. Our electoral prospects are *not* good – for natural & normal reasons, 13 years of power. But I'm afraid

Macleod's article will do *some* damage. His statements are, in many respects, just *not* true. But who cares? or how can it be shewn?'[87]

Much of the damage done was to Macleod himself. 'What is boring and irrelevant', wrote Peregrine Worsthorne in the *Sunday Telegraph*, 'is the suggestion of an upper class conspiracy, particularly coming from a man who has sedulously and successfully modelled himself on that class, and whose complaints against the magic circle only began when he failed to square it in his own interests.'[88] The most considered response to Macleod came from the political commentator Robert McKenzie, in an article in the *Observer* on 19 January. Describing Macleod's piece as an 'inflammatory retaliation', McKenzie considered that it 'makes sense at this juncture only if it is seen as the first move in the contest to determine who will lead the party in Opposition'. Macleod's mistaken assumption, according to McKenzie, was in believing that first-choice preferences should be decisive, and that particular weight should be attached to *Cabinet* first-choice preferences. The *Spectator* article made it impossible for Home to establish the prequisite unity for eventual electoral success. It was a turning point also in Macleod's career: 'He was not forgiven', *The Times* wrote on his premature death in 1970, 'for his act of rebellion against the leader thrown up by the customary processes of his party. It was a political failing on his part that he took so long to appreciate that he had disqualified himself for the highest office.'[89]

By chance, a Cabinet meeting was scheduled for the morning of 17 January, when Macleod's article appeared. Butler began the proceedings by making a short statement. The Cabinet minutes state:

> The Foreign Secretary said that he had seen the article but had refused to make any comment upon it. He hoped that all members of the Cabinet would adopt the same attitude. He did not propose to offer any observations to the Cabinet on the substance of the article; and he felt that the Cabinet's right course was to reaffirm their support for the Prime Minister in his efforts to lead the government forward to the general election. The Prime Minister thanked the Foreign Secretary for these remarks. There was no further discussion.[90]

Though the laconic Cabinet minutes do not entirely disguise the ambiguous tone of some of Butler's observations, who privately agreed with many of the points Macleod had made, his timely intervention was much appreciated by Home, who had already begun a correspondence with Macmillan on the possible ramifications.

The Macleod controversy came at a particularly unfortunate time. The debate on the Denning Report on Profumo had taken place in December, a special Cabinet meeting had been held on Christmas Day on the worsening Cyprus crisis, and there was backbench dissent over Resale Price Maintenance. 'You seem to have started something!' Home wrote to Randolph Churchill, thanking him for a copy of the book.[91] But Churchill had not finished, and on 20 January, he wrote to *The Times*, 'My information for the most part came from the winning side who had no need to whine. Mr Macleod's comes from those who, after tardy, miscalculated and unseemly machinations, are now trying to excuse the acts of their own political folly.'[92] It was with some relief that Home visited South Wales on one of his pre-election tours. He toured several factories, and ended the day with a speech in Swansea. 'When we came into office less than one family in three owned their own house,' he said. Now it was nearly half. 'A property-owning democracy is becoming a reality.' Buying a copy of the *South Wales Evening Post* for the return journey, he was surprised to read the prominent headline: SIR ALEC EXQUISITE AS DYLAN THOMAS[93] – a reference to Sir Alec Guinness's one-man performance in *Dylan* in New York. After the week the other Sir Alec had experienced, this was one confusion he could bear.

The Prime Minister returned to London to prepare for a visit by Robert Kennedy, an important preliminary to Home's Washington trip in February, which he acknowledged by clearing a full weekend for the American Attorney-General. 'The most important thing is to ensure that President Johnson is in a receptive frame of mind when you see him in February', wrote Oliver Wright. 'We must send Mr Kennedy home to Washington gratified with his reception in London.'[94] A weekend gathering at Chequers was arranged for Kennedy and his wife Ethel, who arrived at the end of a tour of European capitals, accompanied by David Bruce, the American ambassador. The British delegation for the afternoon talks included Rab Butler, Duncan Sandys, Peter Thorneycroft and Lord Carrington. After lunch there was a comprehensive and constructive survey of foreign affairs, though Home made some sharp points about American policy in Indonesia. The talks continued the next morning at No. 10, and afterwards Home took Robert Kennedy on a personal tour of the house. David Ormsby-Gore reported to Rab Butler later in the week how much Robert Kennedy had appreciated his purposeful and friendly reception in London. 'The acute depression into which he was plunged after his brother's assassination has increased his air of dogged determination in his work.'[95]

Although the atmosphere was congenial, Alec Home knew of the difficulties he would face in Washington over the sale of British Leyland buses to Cuba. The valuable contract predated the missile crisis, and had not been seen as contentious by the Eisenhower administration. This was no longer the case, as Burke Trend had warned Harold Macmillan. 'This is a clash between economic policy on the one hand and a particularly sensitive area of foreign policy on the other hand', he wrote. 'A refusal on our part to supply the buses will not prevent Cuba from obtaining them elsewhere. And buses are hardly strategic weapons ... On the other hand, there is no issue more likely to inflame anti-British sentiment in the United States than official British encouragement to trade with Cuba, especially since it was we who ousted the United States from their monopoly in this Cuban market.'[96]

On 7 January a further five-year contract was announced (on favourable credit terms for the Cubans); Leyland would supply $10m worth of buses, together with $1m worth of spare parts and an option for a further 1000 buses. President Johnson was outraged. He wanted Cuba marginalised and rang Home to express his anger. Johnson found that the Prime Minister was not to be dissuaded from the course decided by the British Cabinet and an agreement freely signed between trading partners. He told Johnson that buses were hardly a nuclear threat to the United States and that trade between Britain and Cuba in 1963 had been a mere £1.9m, as compared with £15m in 1959. Johnson was also incensed when Home said in a BBC interview, 'Nobody of the nature of Castro is brought down by economic sanctions and boycotts.'[97]

The disagreement cast a shadow over the visit to Washington, on which Alec Home and Rab Butler embarked on 9 February, flying first to Canada. Elizabeth Home and Mollie Butler accompanied their husbands on this first extended visit since the events of October 1963, and there were too many unspoken memories for the atmosphere to be entirely easy, though, as always, there was perfect courtesy on both sides. In the words of one of those in the party that week, 'Alec was such a terrific gent'. The Prime Minister and Foreign Secretary were welcomed in Ottawa by Home's old partner from Commonwealth Relations days, Sir Henry Lintott, now British High Commissioner in Canada. As with the 1955 reunion with Sir Cecil Syers in Ceylon, old strands came together as the career moved onwards and upwards. Two days of talks were held on Anglo-Canadian trade and the forthcoming meeting of Commonwealth Prime Ministers, scheduled for July in London. Lester Pearson felt that there were now some members of the Commonwealth who were not particularly desirable colleagues: 'How would one feel if one sat round the table next to Field Marshal Othello?'[98] Pearson also warned Home of Johnson's concern over the Leyland buses, a point taken up by Oliver Wright. 'Everyone seems to agree that you will be in for a rough time at Washington over Cuba', he wrote. 'This is a "no win" situation for us in the States.'[99] The visit ended with a speech by the Prime Minister to the Empire Club of Canada, in which he referred to 'the virtual end of the process of decolonisation', a movement of emancipation that had begun in Canada more than one hundred years ago with the Durham Report.[100] Harry Lintott wrote to the Permanent Secretary at the Commonwealth Relations Office with his impressions:

> Altogether, in his dealings with the Government and the Press and in his speech in Toronto, the Prime Minister completely wiped out any impression of an effete and ineffective aristocrat. As Pearson put it in a speech he made at a House dinner of the Rider Club just after the visit, Sir Alec matched up to all that Canadians expect a British Prime Minister to be, and this feeling was certainly very widely shared.[101]

The reception in America was less comfortable when Home arrived on 12 February. (Butler had gone ahead for talks with U Thant, Secretary-General of the UN, in New York, where pickets were outside the British Consulate.) The extensive agenda included East–West relations, NATO, the world economy, bilateral defence, South-east Asia, Cyprus and the United Nations. Everyone knew that Cuba would be the sticking point; the Texas style, as Oliver Wright had warned, was very different from the Boston style.

Home had a private meeting with Johnson at the White House at 11 a.m. and Johnson brought up at once the difficulties over Cuba. Alec Home 'hoped that the United Kingdom would not be asked by the United States Administration to curtail trade with Cuba'. He told the President that 'to go to the House of Commons and say that the government was taking steps to restrict trade would bring about a strong anti-American feeling, and that would be a very bad thing'. Johnson moved on to other foreign matters – Indonesia, South Vietnam and Kashmir – and nuclear questions were scheduled for the afternoon meeting, when Dean Rusk and Rab Butler joined the discussions. Johnson reaffirmed the agreement Macmillan and Kennedy had framed about 'prior consultation on the use of nuclear weapons'. The following day's private talks centred on contingencies in case of nuclear accident at the Holy Loch base in Scotland, and finally a bland communiqué stated that the two leaders had decided 'to maintain close and continuous personal contact'.[102]

In a telegram to Johnson on his return, Home hoped that 'from now on our agreements will be underpinned by mutual trust and our disagreements softened by friendship and mutual understanding'.[103] After Home's response on the Cuban buses there was no question of a 'special' relationship, which Macmillan had anticipated: 'I expect you have had a gruelling time in Canada and United States & I'm afraid that without Jack (who was such a critical man) there will have been something of a relapse into the old American doubts and misunderstanding of what you are trying to do in the world. I cannot judge of the intense political situation, but I am sure that your calmness and courage are being understood and admired.'[104]

Home received a large correspondence on the Cuban trade question, largely from people protesting at the American attitude. The Prime Minister hoped his reply would draw the line under an episode in which he had showed resolve in doing what was best for Britain:

> There is no question of dictation by the United States Government to this country over commercial relations with Cuba. This is a subject which is decided solely by the British government. The government's policy has been clearly explained to the country, namely that we will continue to trade with Cuba in non-strategic items if we see commercial advantage in doing so. It is, of course, true that trade with Cuba arouses strong feelings in the United States; the Prime Minister is aware of this feeling, and has taken it into account in formulating the policy.[105]

Johnson continued to show his irritation; when Butler visited Washington again in 29 April 1964, the President sarcastically produced a bundle of dollar notes, saying that if Britain was so hard up that she needed to trade with Cuba, he could pay for the cancelled order himself. 'My talk with the President this morning consisted largely of a monologue from him on the deplorable effect upon Anglo-American relations of our attitudes towards trading with Cuba,' Butler noted to the Prime Minister. '... you should be under no illusion as to his preoccupation with this subject.'[106]

The main foreign problem facing the Prime Minister was the long-running situation in Cyprus. As Foreign Secretary, Home had been closely involved with Cyprus since 1960, when an earlier settlement had seemed to offer a pause in the internecine warfare. Now he found himself increasingly in charge of day-to-day decision-making, because of Butler's withdrawal from the political struggle. He was content to let Home act as Foreign Secretary as well as Prime Minister.[107] It was a time when Butler seemed 'to be providing the Tory Party with little sense of direction in any context' and there were backbench murmurings about his lethargy.[108] The continuing emergency in Cyprus caused Butler to interrupt his holiday in Mull briefly in August, but the Foreign Office increasingly turned to No. 10 for resolution of outstanding issues.

In a memorandum to Cabinet in January 1964, after the outbreak of civil war between the Greek majority and the Turkish minority in Cyprus, Home had emphasised that 'we have no intention of allowing ourselves to be manoeuvred into supporting one side or the other'.[109] Indeed one of the positive outcomes of the Washington visit had been Britain's involvement in the United Nations Peace Keeping Force (UNFICYP) that had been sent to Cyprus in March 1964. Under the 1960 Treaty of Guarantee, Britain, together with Greece and Turkey, had undertaken to ensure the independence of Cyprus. The changes unilaterally imposed by Archbishop Makarios in December 1963 outraged Ankara and British troops in the two sovereign bases on the island were drawn into a difficult peacekeeping role, prior to the arrival of UNFICYP. Home had considered in December whether Britain should continue to be involved in Cyprus, and questioned the strategic importance of the sovereign bases, which he assumed would be of use only for Canberra bombers 'to cover Iran in the event of a nuclear attack by Russia or as possibly a staging post in the Near and Middle East'.[110] He therefore found it particularly galling to receive a belligerent letter from Khrushchev on 7 February 1964 accusing Britain of infringing sovereign independence. He wrote to Moscow in blunt terms:

> I will not conceal from you that I have been surprised and disappointed to receive the message which you sent me on 7 February about the situation in Cyprus. I am surprised that the Soviet government should have formed a view of this question which

> is so completely divorced from reality and I am disappointed that, on the basis of that view, you have seen fit to make charges which are as offensive as they are unfounded ... There is no question, as you claim, of infringing the sovereignty, independence and freedom of a small state.[111]

Turkish troops had seized northern Cyprus, expelling all Greek Cypriots. On 4 March the Security Council called on Greece and Turkey to stop the violence and sent the peacekeeping force which was to be on the island for the next thirty years, but Home had no hopes that it was a permanent solution; he was also realistic enough to know that American influence had stayed the Turks.

In January Winston Field, Prime Minister of Southern Rhodesia, had come to London for talks. His Dominion Party had won a majority in the 1963 elections, and he wished to negotiate independence for Southern Rhodesia. Alec Home established that there would be four conditions: progress towards majority African rule (which led to the acronym NIBMAR, No Independence Before Majority Rule); a guarantee against non-progressive amendments to the Constitution of 1961–2; improvement in African rights; and the agreement to independence by the African majority. In April, Field had been ousted from the premiership by Ian Smith, a sign that white attitudes to African nationalism were hardening. Home felt there was a very real danger that Smith might declare independence unilaterally, and on 8 June wrote a 'Secret and Personal' letter to Sir Humphrey Gibbs, Governor General in Salisbury:

> I consider that you, as Governor, would be justified in taking any measures which are open to you to secure respect for the Constitution, of which you are the ultimate guardian. If, in that eventuality [a unilateral declaration of independence], you decided to dismiss your Ministers or dissolve the Legislature, on the grounds that they were infringing the Constitution, you could count on the full public backing of the British Government. In the exceptional situation which you envisage, we would regard ourselves as free to take whatever legislative or executive steps might be necessary to validate your action ... We here have complete confidence in you and we feel that, at this critical moment, it is most important that you should continue to occupy this key position. I hope, therefore, that you will put out of your mind any thought of resigning and that, as you say, you will 'see this thing through'. I am giving

careful consideration to your suggestion that the British government should issue a public statement expressing its opposition to a unilateral declaration of independence. But, before deciding to do so, I want to be sure that this would not provoke the very thing which it is designed to prevent ... If you think there is a serious likelihood of your being placed under arrest, you will ... inform us instantly ... [and] of any decision by you to dismiss your Ministers or dissolve the Legislature.[112]

Four days earlier, Home had written to Ian Smith, who wished to attend the Commonwealth Prime Ministers' Conference as a full delegate, telling him that the meetings were 'confined to representatives of fully independent states'.[113] Nevertheless, he invited Smith to attend for general talks. Although Smith was not to come to London until early September, Rhodesia was never far from the thoughts of the delegates to the Conference, which began on 8 July. Home kept Gibbs informed of developments:

We have been very conscious that Smith might use some action on our part as a pretext to justify a declaration. I have this very much in mind and you may be sure that we shall be very careful not to give any valid pretext for unconstitutional action ... it looks from Smith's latest utterances as if he is ready to play for time. In any case, he has now accepted an invitation to come here for talks on September 4, and I hope that there will be no difficulty in keeping the ball in play until then. I am trying to get through the Commonwealth PMs' meeting without too much of a row. Please send me your private thoughts as to the handling of affairs any time you feel like it. They help a lot.[114]

Home had been preparing for the thirteenth Commonwealth Prime Ministers' Conference since early April. A briefing memorandum of 12 June had spelt out the background on South Africa. 'The hard fact is that since South Africa left the Commonwealth the white population is united as never before, the economy is booming, and Dr. Verwoerd's Government is applying the policy of "separate development", with all the cruelty and discrimination it involves, with ever greater severity.'[115] The Prime Minister also received briefs on Malawi, the world political situation, and the future of the Commonwealth, including the progress towards future independence for Commonwealth countries (Malawi received its independence on 6 July, two days before the Conference opened). His recent visit to Lagos for trade talks with the Nigerian Prime Minister, Alhali Sir Abubaker Tafawa Balewa, had given him firsthand knowledge of development in a recently independent Commonwealth country, as well as an insight into colourful ceremonial not experienced since the days of his visit to Queen Salote's Tonga as Commonwealth Secretary.

He was skilful in bringing together the views represented by seventeen prime ministers and presidents during the five days of talks. Two decisions were the appointment of a Commonwealth Secretary-General (Arnold Smith held the post for ten years from 1965), and the acceptance of the offer of Marlborough House as the headquarters of the Commonwealth Secretariat. In both instances, Home played a prominent part, liaising with Buckingham Palace over the transfer of Marlborough House for its new Commonwealth function. The controversies over Southern Rhodesia were kept in perspective, and the meeting renewed, rather than undermined, the idea of the Commonwealth. Much credit was due to the host Prime Minister.

In the midst of these concerns – other issues of the period included the collapse of contracts to supply the Spanish navy with frigates, a working visit to Delhi for Nehru's funeral in May, and the Plowden Report on Representational Services Overseas – Home retained a sense of perspective and displayed a new confidence in the Commons. He took great pains to improve his performance at the Despatch Box, as well as on television (taking many hints from Robin Day), and displayed a more assured technique. 'Rarely has he been in such command of the House', wrote *The Times* of his performance on 18 February. 'Never has he shown such cheerful confidence and unforced humour.'[116] Macmillan had been famous for unflappability, but the truly unflappable Tory Prime Minister of the post-war era was Home. To his opponents he was a rolling drop of mercury, impossible to pin down, and Harold Wilson did not underestimate the challenge of the general election to come.

Home took wide-ranging advice on the date of the ever-approaching election. For a final decision between a spring or an autumn poll, Home rang Macmillan on 22 March and a meeting was held four days later to discuss the issue. Home told Macmillan how there were those in the Cabinet such as Christopher Soames and Reginald Maudling who wanted a contest in June but that his instincts told him it would be better to wait until October. Macmillan agreed. Macmillan summed up the arguments in a Memorandum:

> 1. I have thought further about the questions which we discussed on March 26th.
> 2. The Budget is an instrument of policy. It should be the servant, and not the master.
> 3. If there is to be an election in *June*, there should be a standstill Budget (except for minor adjustments) – and that is no *increase* and no revision of taxation.
> 4. If the election is to be in *October*, increases in tobacco and spirits are tolerable. Beer is doubtful. No betting tax.
> 5. *Date of Election.* I am coming more and more a partisan for October and for the following reasons:
>
> a) The Party in Parliament has been thoroughly upset by R.P.M. This reacts on the constituencies.
>
> b) Since the Bill cannot be carried till the middle of May, this confusion will injuriously affect a June election.
>
> c) It is always an advantage to an *Opposition* to have Parliament in session. It is therefore an advantage to the Government to have an interval between the end of Parliament and the Election. This was proved in 1959.
>
> d) The decision will ultimately be on almost Presidential lines. Therefore, the longer Wilson has to become i) a bore ii) mistrusted as a crook, the better.
>
> e) *After* a summer holiday, the mood of the people is better. It was in 1959.
>
> 6. *Against* this is the argument 'You are hanging on to the bitter end etc.' But I think you could meet this (at least to some extent) by a clear and simple statement of intentions in April.[117]

Macmillan recommended an announcement before 9 April, the date of the Greater London Council elections, correctly expected to be bad for the government. 'You will lose nothing by this and avoid great difficulty if London goes badly, as it probably will.'[118] Home spoke with Butler after receiving Macmillan's letter and continued to hold ministerial meetings on the election date. The seventh of April was the day of decision: eight separate meetings with all sections of the Party. Late that evening, Home decided firmly on October and the next day informed the Queen that he would not be asking for a dissolution until after the summer recess. He made the announcement before the polls closed on 9 April, which also marked the christening of his first grandchild, Fiona Wolfe Murray, in the Crypt of the House of Commons. The Press statement from Downing Street read, 'In order to remove the present uncertainty about the date of the general election the Prime Minister thinks it right to inform the country of his decision not to ask the Queen to dissolve Parliament before the autumn.'[119] Speculation then shifted to the precise day in the autumn. 5 November was the last possible date legally, but few expected Home to choose such a confining option. (He later regretted that he had not opted for this date, but this was with the hindsight of unforeseeable events in Russia and China.)[120] On 13 April, Tony Benn asked the Prime Minister to confirm that the election would take place after 2 October, because 330,000 first-time 'Y' voters would only be eligible to vote after that date. The Prime Minister observed that not much had been heard about these poor young voters when the opposition were pressing for a June election.[121] Selwyn Lloyd had no doubt of the date, pencilling into his desk diary 'October 15 Election Day (according to newspapers).'[122] So it was to prove.

Five days after the announcement, Maudling presented the budget, which had been prepared in expectation of a June poll. Maudling promised 'expansion without inflation', raising taxes on tobacco and spirits by the then modest amount of £100m. However, the so-called 'dash for growth', which had begun in the 1963 budget, created a serious balance of payments deficit (£800m by the autumn, compared with £35m the year before), out of which the incoming Prime Minister, Harold Wilson, made considerable political capital.

The dominating economic controversy of the early part of the year, however, was not expansion or retrenchment but Edward Heath's bill to abolish resale price maintenance, which was at the heart of the old tensions between free traders and protectionists in the Conservative Party. Modernisers saw a system that legitimised an anti-competitive pricing structure, at levels fixed by the manufacturers of branded goods, as incompatible with the radical business restructuring necessary for Britain's trading survival. Caution was urged by those who had the interests of the traditionally Tory small shopkeepers in mind. Sir Stafford Cripps, President of the Board of Trade, had set up a committee in August 1947 which took two years to report. Outright abolition had been considered in 1959, but there had been powerful opposition within the ranks of Cabinet, and reform had foundered on the reluctance of Harold Macmillan to press the question.

Three factors forced Home's hand which by a strange quirk all occurred on 11 December 1963. A Private Member's Bill was introduced to abolish RPM followed by another to regulate the increasing proliferation of trading stamps such as those offered by Green Shield, seen as a back-door evasion. Faced with imminent debate on the two Private Member's Bills, Heath, president of the enlarged Industry, Trade and Regional Development Ministry, took action. 'Once persuaded, he quickly and characteristically made the issue his own,' his biographer has written. 'He was determined to put his name to some major piece of legislation before the election. If it had to be the abolition of RPM, so be it.'[123] For Home it was a question of backing Heath or moving him to another department. The second option was not politically viable and in any case, encouraged by John Masterman, Home had staked too much on the question of industrial modernisation and development to back off now. He gave Heath every encouragement, though the issue divided Cabinet.[124]

Heath sent his first minute on RPM to the Prime Minister on 17 December 1963 and recommended its abolition. 'This is very difficult', replied Home heeding the views of the Chancellor and Chief Whip, who both emphasised the political difficulties. 'My own view about RPM,' wrote Redmayne, 'is that it is probably on the way out, but that we should not unnecessarily hurry it. Politically, it is the short-term result which must most concern us, and here without question it would seem that a great number of small traders who are mostly our supporters would be hit.' Maudling also emphasised the difficulties of the shopkeepers. 'Of course the political objections are very strong. Many of our supporters feel strongly about it, and for a number of small traders, particularly pharmacists, it arouses the wildest passions.'[125] Despite this unencouraging response, Heath pressed ahead with his campaign. At Cabinet on 14 January 1964 he urged a declaration of policy before the debate on 17 January on Stonehouse's Private Member's Bill. 'The government had committed themselves to a policy of modernising Britain and promoting a more efficient use of resources. This policy would fail to carry conviction if they were to tolerate the continuance of a practice so manifestly at variance with it.' Alec Home promised such a statement the following day. 'RPM represented an uneconomic use of resources and was contrary to the national interest', he told the Cabinet, adding that 'in order to avoid injustice, individuals who believed that in their particular circumstances it could be defended would have an opportunity to argue their case. It would be essential, however, to make it clear that, on the main issue of proscribing RPM, the government intended to act with speed and decision.'[126] One of the crucial decisions of his premiership was thus made.

Cabinet dissidents continued to express their reservations, even before the full-blown revolt of backbenchers in the House of Commons.

One of Home's most sceptical colleagues on the issue was Selwyn Lloyd, whose Wirral constituency contained a high proportion of the small traders who would be adversely affected. 'I am afraid that I must add to your troubles by giving you my impressions of the feelings in the House about the Bill', he wrote on 14 February. 'I have been in the House even more than usual this week and it would be quite wrong for anyone to suggest that the feeling against the Bill has subsided. Indeed the note of bitterness has increased.'[127] Francis Pearson, his Parliamentary Private Secretary, also reported the feelings of misgivings among backbenchers. 'Interest in Committee and in the Smoking Room is concentrated on RPM and the bill is awaited with apprehension.'[128] Home was now in the middle of a growing controversy. The Bill was published on 16 February 1964. When some sort of compromise was suggested by way of partial exemptions, Heath was soon writing to the Prime Minister to disagree. 'I am convinced that we must stand firm against special treatment for any class of goods, such as has been suggested for books and tobacco.'[129] Backbench passions ran high and on 11 March 1964, the Conservative government faced the biggest revolt since the fall of Chamberlain in May 1940, when 22 Conservatives voted against the Second Reading and some 25 abstained. The next day, John Morrison, Chairman of the 1922 Committee, pleaded for some middle way. 'I am very sorry to write this and I like Ted Heath – but somehow he must be made to realise that there must be a little flexibility and compromise.'[130] Redmayne's position as a conciliator was compromised by the knowledge that he was one of the opponents of abolition in Cabinet and further difficulties followed, including a 'victory' by only one vote on the amendment for the exemption of medicines. 'Having given Heath the "brief" of modernisation, it was not in the Prime Minister's nature to desert him when trouble came. Without the Prime Minister's support, it is certain that Heath would never have been able to steamroller the Bill through the Cabinet.'[131] The Bill finally passed its third reading on 13 May, but the whole episode was a bruising experience for its main participants.

Opinion is divided as to the electoral effect of the abolition of resale price maintenance. It is often held up as one of the *cumulative* issues that cost the Conservatives victory in October. John Boyd-Carpenter, Paymaster General at the time, has written that 'a Bill to outlaw RPM in the last months of a dying Parliament seemed to me to have every disadvantage'.[132] John Campbell, however, believes that 'a measure that had the effect of lowering prices was thoroughly popular with everyone except shopkeepers' and that 'RPM cannot really be made the scapegoat for the Tories' defeat'.[133] David Butler and Anthony King have written that 'resale price maintenance figured hardly at all at the election'.[134] The main impact of the abolition of RPM was positive. It showed that the government had not run out of new ideas and was not prepared to have economic policy dictated by vested interest groups, even if these were traditional Conservative supporters, and as such it was the harbinger of even more decisive changes in the future. Another example of this was Home's tough stance on trade unions, giving no legislative help over the Rookes v Barnard case in January 1964, when the House of Lords upheld the right of a BOAC employee at Heathrow Airport to damages for unfair dismissal because of a closed shop policy by the Association of Engineering and Shipbuilding Draughtsmen. He held two weekend policy-making seminars on the trade unions at Chequers, though he knew that the parliamentary position was not strong enough to embark on a programme of major reform. Nevertheless, he made regulation 6 of the 1920 Emergency Powers Act a permanent legislative tool, ironically a great help to Harold Wilson during the 1966 seamen's strike.[135]

For Home and Heath, the abolition of RPM was an indication that they took modernisation seriously, and it remains the most important legislative measure of the Douglas-Home administration. For both men, the issue was one of economic liberation. Heath, in particular, was unrepentantly in favour of reform, though the determined methods he had employed to ensure abolition reaped a bitter harvest in the difficult period from 1973–4. Politically, RPM made Heath many enemies among backbenchers, but he remained grateful to Alec Home for his support. On 25 February 1994 two Heath anniversaries were commemorated. One was a gathering at the Institute of Economic Affairs for the thirtieth anniversary of the bill to abolish RPM, the other a conference at Nuffield College, Oxford, reappraising the Heath government twenty years on. Heath was invited to both gatherings, but the one he chose was the IEA meeting in London, commenting ironically that the abolition of RPM was the only thing he did that the Institute of Economic Affairs had ever approved of.[136]

The summer months were busy in many ways, quite apart from the major Conference of Commonwealth Prime Ministers, in which Home had played such a prominent role. He attended the opening of Churchill College, Cambridge, with the Duke of Edinburgh, Chancellor of Cambridge University, on 5 June. A fortnight later he embarked on a major pre-election tour of Yorkshire, starting in Leeds, but taking in the major towns in the West Riding such as Huddersfield (Harold Wilson's birthplace) and Halifax. In his first six months in office, he had given sixty-four 'full dress' speeches and 150 whistle-stop homilies. Over the next few months the pace quickened even more. Lord Crathorne was his host for the Yorkshire tour (fitting in a visit to the Yorkshire county cricket match against Glamorgan at Headingley) and on 28 June Home wrote with his impressions and thanks, 'I feel I must drop you a line to say how grateful I was to you for having done so much to make my Yorkshire visit so very pleasant and, I hope, so successful. I really felt that the Leeds meeting went extremely well and I came away much encouraged. I found the whistle-stop tour very interesting: Maurice Macmillan tells me that at his meeting at Halifax there were a number of non-Party members among the crowd and that their reaction was very favourable.'[137]

As the opinion polls were now edging the way of the Conservatives, Home continued to believe that victory was possible and that his decision to delay until the autumn would be vindicated. The Devizes by-election had been a welcome fillip with an adverse swing of only 2.8 per cent, the lowest for two years. Home had staked a great deal on the Devizes result, seeing it as an archetypal marginal seat that would be a great pointer to the overall result. He had asked Peter Walker to mastermind the campaign, an example of how he brought on the brightest of the younger generation to infuse new blood and fresh ideas. Peter Walker saw at once that the support of the Beaverbrook press was vital and spoke personally to Beaverbrook about Charles Morrison's candidature and attitude towards the Common Market.[138] The subsequent support of the *Daily Express* was crucial in Morrison's victory by 1,670 votes. It was one of Beaverbrook's last political interventions for he died on 9 June. Home's tribute was a generous and kindly one considering all the invective he had undergone at the hands of the Beaverbrook press, paying particular attention to the Beaver's restless energy which had 'helped us to win the Battle of Britain'.[139]

After Parliament had risen on 31 July (Home was never to address the House of Commons again as Prime Minister), he wrote to Cabinet ministers warning against complacency over the summer period. The legislative programme for 1964–5 needed finalising. 'It is the more important to ensure, therefore, that there is no loss of impetus during the next two months.'[140] Home believed it vital that business should be conducted on the expectation of victory, one of the reasons he did not look for a flat in London, where he had no roof of his own at the time, for if the news of such a purchase leaked, it would appear unduly pessimistic.

One particular ceremony that gave him great pleasure was the opening of the Forth Road Bridge by the Queen on 4 September. Though some of his opponents suggested the timing was a cynical political exercise to drum up electoral support north of the Border, those who had worked with him in the Scottish Office knew he had been concerned with it for many years. The Queen was about to embark on an important tour of Canada, and Home made sure that all the arrangements for the election were meticulously in hand before the Queen left the country. As an example of the attention to detail, when the Queen flew to London from Balmoral on 2 September to be fitted for clothes for the Canadian trip, Sir Michael Adeane made this clear to the press 'in case it should be thought that the return implied an early Dissolution'.[141] The trip to French Canada was a politically sensitive one, against the background of assassination threats, and Home was greatly concerned that the visit should be safe and successful.

Home had his first meetings with Ian Smith on the deepening Rhodesian crisis on Monday 7 September. The threat of UDI was real and Home's main aim was to prevent such precipitate action. Smith had asked 'for a clear and definite statement that, if the government of Southern Rhodesia could satisfy the United Kingdom government that they had the support of a great majority of the population of the Territory, the United Kingdom government would then grant independence without more ado'. Home replied 'that a referendum or some equivalent procedure would be necessary', at which Smith withdrew the threat of UDI. A communiqué was issued on 11 September, saying that the British government looked forward to Southern Rhodesia's eventual independence but had to 'be satisfied that any basis on which it was proposed that independence should be granted was acceptable to the people of the country as a whole'.[142] Within five weeks, Smith had to deal with a new Prime Minister and the march to UDI was underway.

The summer recess was the end of an era in several ways. Many papers pointed out that the Conservatives had been in office for the longest unbroken spell for 134 years – not a point Home wanted stressed in view of the 'time for a change' feeling. It also marked Sir Winston Churchill's retirement from the House of Commons, and one of Alec Home's duties was to attend at Churchill's home to express the gratitude of the Lower Chamber. On 29 July together with Harold

Wilson, Leader of the Opposition, and Jo Grimond, Leader of the Liberal Party, and other dignitaries, he presented a Resolution from the House of Commons to Churchill, who had little idea what was going on. His daughter described it as a 'rather sad, muted occasion'.[143] Lady Soames also outlined the inadequacies of the original Resolution, which appalled Alec Home when he saw the Civil Service jargonese.[144] With Churchill's retirement arrangements were put in hand for Operation 'Hope Not', the procedures to be followed in the event of his death. Home discussed with Redmayne what should happen if Churchill died before the election, or during the campaign, and he was duly issued with draft television speeches and a list of arrangements for the state funeral and its aftermath.[145]

Alec Home's first letter as Prime Minister had been to Churchill on the death of his daughter Diana. The last he wrote before the election on 15 October was to the Queen welcoming her back from her Canadian tour. The election was only twenty-four hours away. Although the expectation was that Wilson would prevail, the outcome was too close to call with any confidence. 'I only hope the visit may have done more good than harm,' wrote the Queen in reply to Home's letter, 'but for the result, one will have to wait and see. Just like tomorrow!!'[146] The next day was to bring to an end thirteen years of Conservative government.

14

The 1964 General Election

'In the life of any government, however safe its majority,' wrote Christopher Booker, 'there comes a moment when the social movements of which it had once been the expression turn inexorably against it.'[1] Such was the difficulty facing Alec Home in the 1964 general election. The Conservatives had been in office for thirteen years and the twin cries of 'Thirteen wasted years' and 'Time for a change' were psychologically difficult to counter, especially when they were advanced with the consummate political skill and wit Harold Wilson showed in his twenty months as Leader of the Opposition.

Another difficulty faced Home as he prepared for the electoral fray. His experience of fighting elections was from a different age and the 1964 election was not going to be won in the streets of Ayr, Bedford or Lancaster where he appeared in support of friends such as George Younger, Christopher Soames and Anthony Nutting, whose seats were less safe than his own. This election was to be dominated by television, at which he had worked hard to accustom himself, but which remained a weakness in his armoury acknowledged by Conservative Central Office.[2] While Reginald Maudling and Edward Heath were the main Party protagonists at the daily press conferences, Alec Home travelled the length and breadth of the country.

The last campaign in which Home had experienced such sustained grass-roots electioneering was in 1950, when, after Parliament had been dissolved on 3 February, the usual moratorium on election coverage under the Fourteen Day Rule was imposed by the radio networks, and the three party leaders declined to use television for their election broadcasts. 'The BBC kept as aloof from the election as if it had been occurring on another planet' wrote H.G. Nicholas. 'Every programme was scrutinised in search of any item, jocular or serious, which might give aid or comfort to any of the contestants, and after February 3rd virtually all mention of election politics disappeared from the British air.' The contemporary view was that this was the right and proper manner in which to conduct such important matters. 'Undoubtedly in view of the enormous power wielded by such a monopolistic instrument the decision to carry neutrality to the lengths of castration was the only right one.'[3]

The world was very different in 1964. The BBC no longer had a monopoly and television was the dominant medium. This campaign was the first to be ruled (and some would say decided) by the extensive television coverage. These were not conditions which worked to Alec Home's advantage. On his return from visiting President Johnson in February, for instance, he had been interviewed on the BBC's *Panorama*, a challenge more daunting as it took place on the 'neutral' ground of Lime Grove studios. He was coached intensively for this appearance by Christopher Chataway, the Conservative MP for Lewisham North, who had considerable television experience, and also by his speechwriter, Nigel Lawson. The interview with Robin Day was recorded on 17 February and Conservative Central Office were relieved by his largely favourable reception.[4] Three days later he did a further recording for independent television's current affairs programme, *This Week*. It was one thing to record an interview prior to transmission; an entirely different matter, however, to appear live in the cut and thrust of a general election, when an unguarded comment could have serious repercussions. Harold Wilson was in his element in the television studio, and 'would have made an admirable participant in a television panel game, for he had a remarkable memory for figures and was quick on the verbal draw'.[5] But both Home and Wilson had intensive programmes of regional tours throughout the spring and early summer, preliminary sparring for the championship contest in October.

The question of the precise date for the election resurfaced during the summer recess and the Prime Minister received a great deal of (largely hostile) correspondence. He wrote to John Blakenham, the Party Chairman, from the Hirsel: 'Are we getting unpopular about not allowing the date of the General Election to be known? … Would it be a good thing for you to write a letter to a newspaper saying why we don't do it, or are not the reasons entirely respectable?'[6] Respectable or not, no announcement was to be made for a further three weeks. Alec Home made many constituency visits during the politically quiet days of August, but behind the scenes he continued to discuss dates with his advisers. The rest of the month he spent at Douglas, and his last engagement in Scotland was the opening of the Forth Road Bridge by the Queen. He returned to London the next day in buoyant mood, addressing a dinner for Conservative candidates that evening, telling the guests not to be diverted by stunts or scares. In a pre-echo of what was to become one of the main motifs of his campaign, the Prime Minister warned that Britain should not disarm unilaterally. If she did so 'she would forfeit her own safety and cease to exercise any influence in matters of peace and war'.[7]

The final decision on the election date was taken at Chequers on Sunday 6 September. The afternoon had been spent mainly on the forthcoming Rhodesian summit, and in the evening Martin Redmayne and John Blakenham arrived to consider the options. There were various complicating factors such as the impending industrial trouble at Her Majesty's Stationery Office, which necessitated the pre-release of election material to Returning Officers. Under current practice the British Olympic team in Tokyo were disenfranchised because of their absence, and Home considered whether postal voting for those 'on holiday' should be allowed, but it proved too late to alter electoral law.[8] The longest discussion was on the constitutional implications of dissolving Parliament without prorogation, which had last happened in 1922. 'In ordinary circumstances I would have advised that both Houses should meet for prorogation and have been prepared to meet an inevitable opposition request for a day or two of debate. I would still regard this as the proper course if the course of talks with Mr Smith was to take a serious turn', the Prime Minister wrote to the Queen. 'But short of this kind of situation developing I would much prefer to dispense with the recall of Parliament and proceed directly to Dissolution by proclamation. My reason is that all other issues will be raised and debated on the hustings within a few days and over three weeks and I believe that this is the proper course and will be recognised to be so.'[9] In 1959 (when the election also followed the long summer recess) Parliament had met to shake hands with Mr Speaker, a move that caused considerable inconvenience and the recall of over a thousand attendants at the Palace of Westminster. Although the Prime Minister's suggestion was a break with tradition, the Palace accepted that in the circumstances it was the practical way to proceed, so long as it was not seen as a precedent. All that remained now was to finalise the actual date. 1 October was never really viable, owing to the disqualification of the Y voters, the Queen's absence in Canada later in the week disqualified 8 October, and the uncertainties of the weather as

November neared, meant that 15 October, as predicted, emerged as the preferred date, five years and one week since the victory of Harold Macmillan in 1959. The Parliament would thus be the longest since the interval between elections had been reduced to five years in 1911.

The Cabinet was informed of the decision at its meeting on 10 September, by which time the Labour and Liberal parties had already published their manifestos. Christopher Soames, the Agriculture Minister, was in the Middlesex Hospital at the time and Alec Home wrote with the news. 'I do hope that you are mending fast. It must be very disappointing to be out of the fray! I will try and call in and am glad to have good news of you.'[10] Not only did the Prime Minister call in to see Soames twice in hospital during the campaign, but he also arranged to speak in Soames's Bedford constituency. Home was particularly anxious for Soames to be returned safely, for during a half-hour visit to the Middlesex on 20 September he promised Soames the reversion to the Foreign Office if the Conservatives were successful on 15 October.[11]

Alec Home flew to Balmoral on 14 September, and had an audience of the Queen the following morning when he asked for a dissolution of Parliament on 25 September. The announcement of the date for the election was made on 18 September, one calendar month before polling. The Conservative manifesto, *Prosperity with Purpose*, was also launched on 18 September, but its impact was dissipated by Wilson's challenge to Sir Alec to debate the issues on television.

The Prime Minister was opposed in Kinross and West Perthshire by his Labour and Scottish Nationalist opponents from the previous November's election, and a new candidate, C.M. Grieve (the poet Hugh MacDiarmid), who stood as a communist, and was subsequently to bring an election petition, challenging the legality of the level of Sir Alec Douglas-Home's expenses during the campaign. Grieve used his candidacy to try for more broadcasting time for the Communist Party: 'We have firmly inserted the thin end of the Marxist wedge into this feudal 8,000 square miles constituency,' Grieve wrote on the eve of polling, 'and must, after Friday, do all we can to hammer it home.'[12] He polled 127 votes. Kinross and West Perthshire was no longer considered marginal; many Liberal votes were confidently expected to be transferred to the Unionist cause. As Prime Minister, Alec Home would only be able to spend a limited amount of time in the constituency, and John Robertson anticipated this in his preliminary election literature to party workers: 'It will be readily understood that Sir Alec's national commitments as Prime Minister and leader of the party necessitate his speaking throughout the length and breadth of the country during the election campaign. His time, therefore, within Kinross & West Perthshire will be limited, but it is hoped that arrangements will be made so that Sir Alec will speak at evening meetings once in each of the four districts of the constituency, highland, central, western and Kinross-shire.'[13] A full programme was nevertheless arranged, starting with Alec Home's adoption meeting at the cinema in Crieff on 25 September, and the Prime Minister devoted the first full campaigning weekend to touring the widespread constituency.

The campaign had not got off to the best of starts for the Conservatives after Home's appearance on the BBC's *Election Forum*, in which Party leaders had answered a variety of questions submitted by viewers in interviews conducted by Robin Day, Kenneth Harris and Ian Trethowan. Harris had been the interviewer when Home had made his remark about the matchsticks in September 1962; now another slip of the tongue had even more damaging consequences. In reply to a question about the level of pensions, the Prime Minister said, 'I think we must always judge in the circumstances of the day the sum of money that we can afford for the basic pension. Now we've made proposals in our manifesto, of course, but over and above the basic pension, in future years, we will give a donation to the pensioners who are over a certain age because they are in the greatest need.'[14] He realised at once his gaffe in referring to pensions as a 'donation', which had all the paternalistic associations of Victorian charity. A Vicky cartoon appeared in the *Evening Standard* of two elderly men reading about the pension scheme. 'Sir Alec says he'll give us a donation when we're a bit older ...' was the caption. It was probably the worst mistake of his entire premiership and 'presented Labour spokesmen with a phrase which they exploited throughout the campaign to illustrate the Conservatives' patronising attitude'.[15]

The pattern of the next three weeks was soon established. Heath and Maudling, who were at the time considered more skilful television performers, took responsibility for the morning press conferences at Central Office, while the Prime Minister took the electoral message to the country. Wednesday, 30 September was described as 'the most exciting day in the whole campaign'.[16] It began with a *Daily Mail* poll that gave the Conservatives a lead of 2.9 per cent and ended with an uncharacteristic mistake by Wilson over the strike at Hardy Spicer, an important supplier of parts to the Midlands car industry. At his morning press conference, Wilson said there was now reason to examine whether such strikes were fomented deliberately at election times to help the Conservative cause, a suggestion not taken seriously, even by Labour voters. Herbert Hill, chairman of Hardy Spicers, issued a writ for libel, which meant that the matter was then *sub judice* and could not be exploited by the government. Anyway, the story soon proved embarrassing to the Conservatives, as Hill described the workers in his factory as 'poor dears', who did not understand such questions. Home had further cause to bury the story. Hill had briefly overlapped with Selwyn Lloyd at Fettes, before going on to Worcester College, Oxford, whose former Provost, Sir John Masterman, in his new role in the field of industrial relations, was now a colleague of Hill in engineering concerns. Lloyd and Masterman were key figures in the Prime Minister's circle, and as, for a few brief hours, Hill symbolised all that was wrong with the attitudes of the managerial class, 'the outdated methods' Wilson claimed he was going to sweep away, Home wanted no guilt by association.

The third big story of 30 September was the balance of payments figures for the second quarter of 1964, showing a deficit of £73m. Wilson naturally devoted the main part of his speech that evening to the economic situation. The contrast between the two leaders' Norwich visits was typical of their different approach. Home's speech had been at an informal meeting in the car park of the church of St Peter Mancroft, close by the statue of Sir Thomas Browne, open to the elements and the hecklers, whereas Wilson's was an orchestrated all-ticket, indoor affair before an audience of vetted supporters, carefully aimed at the television coverage.[17]

The 1964 general election campaign was marked by considerable bitterness and occasional violence. 'Sir Alec mauled by whistle-stop crowd' and 'Lady Home is saved from the crowd' are two of the milder cuttings Elizabeth Home put in her scrapbooks.[18] Alec Home had experienced the rough-and-tumble of election meetings in the thirties, but heckling was now abusive, rather than witty (though, in answer to his rhetorical question 'Why do I emphasise the importance of the Royal Navy?', Wilson provoked the retort, 'Because you're in Chatham'.). The Prime Minister was shouted down in north London and Yorkshire, and fights broke out at a meeting in Stockport. It seemed somehow appropriate that Alec Home should address one meeting from the boxing ring in Watford Town Hall on 8 October. But the uproar at the Birmingham Bull Ring the same evening marked the full flow of this tide. Geoffrey Lloyd, the MP for Sutton Coldfield, had invited the Prime Minister to speak, but had not made the meeting all-ticket. The Prime Minister was systematically shouted down, and his address was inaudible. He pressed on gamely, but the overall impression on television was that the campaign was slipping away from the Conservatives. Macmillan had silenced Khrushchev's interventions at the United Nations with a witty riposte; nobody could legitimately be expected to deal with the sustained chants of 'Tories out' and 'We want Wilson'. Alec Home faced the throng for an hour and afterwards insisted on walking through the jostling, slogan-shouting crowd to the main entrance, though the police had wanted to spirit him out through a back door.[19] 'We go along as well as I could have hoped at this stage', Alec Home had written cheerfully to John Masterman three days earlier. 'Nearly all the opposition at meetings comes from a few teenagers. Very difficult to tell their sex!'[20] The Bull Ring debacle proved an entirely different experience, and led to accusations that Labour were hiring hecklers to disrupt the Prime Minister's meetings, accusations that Lord Blakenham refused to withdraw.

Another damaging episode had Rab Butler at his most indiscreet. The *Daily Express* allocated George Gale, the paper's special and foreign correspondent, to cover Butler's campaigning. The Foreign Office suggested that Gale might like to accompany him on a visit to Tees-side, and on the train journey to Darlington they discussed how things were progressing. The combination of Rab Butler's indiscretions (he was popular among journalists, as his renowned Rabbisms were always considered 'good copy') and Gale's willingness to print what Butler thought were off-the-record remarks proved a potent cocktail. Gale was an old-style foot-in-the-door reporter with an eye for the outright scoop. As Gale was covering a political event, Butler made the mistake of assuming he was a member of the parliamentary Lobby, who would know when things were off-the-record and when they could be quoted directly. But Gale did not feel bound by the conventions of the Lobby. In any case he was given more than enough material to make a very dramatic story, duly published on 9 October as a front-page splash. 'We're running neck and neck', Butler was reported as saying, a true enough statement of the position a week before polling. 'I'll be very surprised if there's much in it – say 20 seats either way. But things might start slipping in the last few days.' Though this was hardly the most optimistic rallying cry, it was the final remark that proved the damaging one: 'They won't slip towards us', a phrase at once enshrined in the mythology of the 1964 campaign, with 'donations' and the 'poor dears'.[21] Privately, Home was furious about this blow to the party's morale. Many detected a sense of *schadenfreude*, as though a subconscious part of Rab Butler found it not entirely displeasing for Alec Home to lose.[22] Whether George Gale was a member of the Lobby or not, such remarks were bound to leak out, as David Ormsby-Gore recognised when he wrote to commiserate with Alec Home after the Conservatives' narrow defeat:

> How tantalising a result. So near and yet so far. Almost anything could have tipped the balance, Khrushchev's removal twelve hours earlier, China's nuclear explosion thirty-six hours earlier or just Rab keeping his mouth shut for once. It is cruel luck after all your superhuman efforts, but nothing can detract from the fact that you took over a dispirited and divided party less than one year ago and only failed by a bee's knee to win a fourth consecutive victory for the Conservatives. You deserve our deepest thanks, although there are sure to be some miserable carpers around. There always are.[23]

The most controversial episode in the election was the defeat of Patrick Gordon Walker, the shadow Foreign Secretary, in his Birmingham constituency of Smethwick. As the campaign was widely believed to have been fought on racial grounds – 'Labour win will mean race riots' was the headline in the *Birmingham Post* on 24 September – Harold Wilson referred to Peter Griffiths, the victorious Conservative MP, in uncompromising terms in the House of Commons on 4 November: 'Smethwick Conservatives can have the satisfaction of having topped the poll, of having sent a member, who until another election returns him to oblivion, will serve his time here as a Parliamentary leper.'[24] The episode was one with implications for Alec Home. On 24 September he deplored the reported remarks in the Birmingham press. 'We should not indulge in statements of this kind,' he said and ordered that no official Conservative candidate should attempt to employ the race card. On 25 September, Patrick Gordon Walker wrote to the Prime Minister, asking him to dissociate the Conservative Party from Alderman Griffiths' alleged comments. Considerable care was taken over the reply on the importance of all British citizens being treated equally, but which concluded, 'I do not, however, feel that a problem of this sort is best dealt with by public correspondence during a general election campaign.'[25] Despite Gordon Walker's defeat, Wilson appointed him Foreign Secretary. The Conservatives did not make an issue of the

Foreign Secretary's non-membership of the House of Commons (a year earlier their leader had been in a similar position) and Gordon Walker's family were grateful for the understanding Home showed to him in this difficult period.[26]

Another spectacular reversal in October 1964 came at Brighton Kemptown. Against all expectations, the Labour candidate, Dennis Hobden, won the seat from David James, the sitting Conservative, by seven votes after seven recounts, marking him the first Labour MP to be elected for a Sussex seat. The final figures were 22,308 to 22,301 with 60 spoilt ballot papers.[27] Many special factors contributed to this defeat, of which Alec Home later said that the name of Kemptown would be to him as that of Calais was to Mary Queen of Scots.[28] A study of the campaign shows by what narrow margins the overall result was determined in the 1964 general election, in which it has been calculated that some 400 votes judiciously redistributed in the Conservatives' favour in the most marginal constituencies would have kept them in office. Four of those votes in Kemptown would have halved Wilson's eventual majority and Hobden made much of his contribution to victory, once beginning a speech to the Parliamentary Labour Party, 'If I was not here there would not be a Labour government, so you had better listen carefully to what I say.'[29] David James has been blamed for losing the seat by his dilatory campaigning and eccentric priorities. It has even been claimed that he spent most of the campaign looking for the Loch Ness Monster.[30] Although it was true that he had gone diving in Loch Ness, he missed canvassing on only one morning of the three-week campaign, after losing his voice.[31] The final straw was the fact that many members of the local Women's Branch of the Conservative Association had, many weeks earlier, arranged an all-day cross-Channel shopping trip to Calais, and were therefore absent during polling hours, which in 1964 ended at 9 p.m. If this trip had not taken place and fourteen voters in Ealing North (where there were fifty-six spoilt ballot papers) had voted Conservative rather than Labour, Wilson would not have had an overall majority.

Wilson knew how important the scheduling of the television programmes in the evening of the election might be to the turn-out of Labour voters. The popular BBC comedy *Steptoe and Son* was scheduled for 8 p.m; Wilson was so concerned that he went to the Director-General, Sir Hugh Greene, to have the programming changed. When Greene asked him what he would like to see transmitted in place of *Steptoe and Son*, Wilson replied, 'I suggest you put on

Oedipus Rex, Greek tragedy.'[32] After some difficulty in agreeing a solution, the programme was moved to 9 p.m. 'Thank you very much, Hugh,' said Wilson, 'that will be worth a dozen or more seats to me.'[33]

Alec Home believed that the Bull Ring episode was the turning point of the campaign. But things remained nail-bitingly close towards the end, so much so that a 'Deadlock File' was kept, in case the palace should have to deal with a hung Parliament for the first time since 1929. In this, three alternative courses of action were outlined. The resignation of a Prime Minister if he was in a minority meant that the Queen could press him to stay on until defeated in the House of Commons; alternatively the Queen could press him to stay on in the hope that he might form a coalition, or (most debatably) 'send for someone who is not the Leader of either major party in the hope that some sort of compromise government could be carried on until it were feasible to have another General Election'.[34] Home took a clearer view of these constitutional niceties: if he failed to win an overall majority, his duty was to resign forthwith. Tucked away in the 'Deadlock File' were preliminary arrangements for Chequers to be made available to him in the event of his resignation.

As the last week of the campaign began, the Prime Minister knew that much would depend on his final television broadcast. Norman Collins, one of the most experienced broadcasting figures, devoted most of Sunday 11 October to coaching Home for his final party political. His main aim was to relax the Prime Minister, and he secretly recorded the rehearsals in the (vain) hope of getting acceptable material to broadcast. It was not to be and a further exhausting series of 'takes' followed at Elstree on 13 October. At Norwich on 30 September, Home had said to his audience, 'I am not a bit like you see me on television, am I?'[35] Although this was true, the toll of the campaign had been a heavy one, and Home was patently exhausted by all the travelling. Wilson, nearly thirteen years his junior, had conserved his energies by avoiding extensive travels to smallish meetings, concentrating his efforts on the well-orchestrated set-piece meetings for evening news bulletins. Furthermore, as Wilson constantly spelled out Labour policies, people referred to 'the Sheffield speech' or 'the Norwich speech' as shorthand guides to the programme.[36]

General elections are fought on several levels but broadly speaking, there are two basic constants – the idealistic level and the materialistic. In 1964, in a way never replicated in subsequent elections, both Party leaders made a pitch for the idealistic vote. With Wilson, this was through an appeal to the twin themes of social justice and modernisation. Against all advice, Home concentrated on the theme that Labour were not fit to govern because their abandonment of the independent nuclear deterrent would leave the country defenceless under the prevailing global conditions. General elections are rarely decided on questions of foreign or international policy; next Friday's grocery bill is a far more potent factor for millions of voters. Less than two years after the Cuban missile crisis, however, and despite the Test Ban Treaty of August 1963, Home believed the survival of the independent nuclear deterrent to be one of the most important questions facing Britain. In short, he ran a Foreign Secretary's campaign, rather than a Prime Ministerial one.

As the campaign drew to an end, Home returned to Scotland to fulfil his longstanding promise to speak for George Younger at Ayr. Without Younger's self-sacrifice a year earlier, he would not have become Prime Minister and he never forgot that fact. In the evening he returned to his constituency, staying at Culdees Castle on the eve of polling. From the start of his premiership Alec Home had refused to act in the belief that his time in Downing Street would be brief. Yet as the last hours of his premiership approached, there was an intuitive feeling that the campaign had slipped away. On the day of the election Elizabeth Home was cheerful, but realistic. 'It isn't the end of the world if we lose,' she said, though a few hours later she was more disappointed than her husband at the cruel suddenness with which the British system despatches its defeated leaders into a political limbo.

On 15 October, Alec Home had seventeen engagements in his constituency, before flying to London from Scone Airport at 6.15 p.m.[37] Unlike the by-election of November 1963, there was at least no anxiety about his personal result and the following day, the Prime Minister had increased his majority to 11,972.

Alec Home followed the election results at Downing Street with his family and staff. The tables groaned with food, for people to help themselves as the night went on, but few had any appetite. Hopes rose and fell with each batch of results, but unlike those who could not bear to leave the television, the Prime Minister retired to bed at 1.30 a.m. News of Khrushchev's fall began to percolate by 6 p.m. on polling day, but was not a headline in the news until after the polls closed. More significant at the time seemed to be the heaviest rainfall for weeks, which was expected to reduce the Labour turn-out, Steptoe or no Steptoe. The first result was declared at Cheltenham, shortly after 10 p.m. The archetypal seat of Billericay, declared shortly afterwards, was held by the Conservatives, and for a time it seemed that they might once more prevail. Marcus Worsley, MP for Keighley, was the first member of the administration to lose his seat, shortly followed by Maurice Macmillan, Economic Secretary to the Treasury. But there were considerable regional variations in the swing. The outcome of one election was in doubt until the afternoon of 16 October, by which time news was being received of the Chinese government's successful testing of an atomic bomb and Harold Wilson secured a majority with the victory at Brecon and Radnor. A late swing to the Liberals in three Highland seats was particularly disappointing. Home's first thought was for the Conservative candidates who had lost and he wrote to all those who were known personally to him. He was particularly saddened by the defeat of his Health Secretary, Anthony Barber in Doncaster, one of two Cabinet Ministers ousted, the other being Geoffrey Rippon. 'I was so sorry that Doncaster went wrong', he wrote 'but I think the odds all over were just stacked too heavily against us.'[38] At 3.20 p.m., Alec Home set out for the Palace and was received by the Queen in the Audience Room. The Palace Press Secretary issued the following statement, 'The Right Honourable Sir Alec Douglas-Home had an audience of The Queen this afternoon and tendered his resignation as Prime Minister and First Lord of the Treasury which Her Majesty was graciously pleased to accept.' He had been Prime Minister for 362 days. A few hours later he left Downing Street, with Elizabeth Home and Francis Pearson, by the garden gate from which Churchill had departed in July 1945. A photograph of their departure, with a typical caption, made the cover of the following week's edition of *Private Eye*. But there was great courtesy from the victor: Wilson at once offered the Homes the hospitality of Chequers. Alec Home accepted the offer with gentility: 'It was good of you to suggest that we might use Chequers until we can make other arrangements. I would like to take advantage of your offer and we propose to go down to Chequers for the weekend. We would like to return briefly to No. 10 early next week, to clear up on Monday but only in the top flat.'[39]

Until the Homes moved into a flat in Whitehall Court (and on 6 May 1965 more permanently to Roebuck House in Palace Street), the Conservative Party arranged accommodation in a penthouse suite in Claridges. Both Wilson, who experienced the bitterness of defeat in June 1970, and Home felt that there should be an official residence for the leader of the opposition to minimise the indignities of sudden eviction from Downing Street. It has yet to materialise.

Despite the expectations earlier in the year, Harold Wilson did not win a substantial majority which, from the Conservative point of view, was a vindication of Home's decision to hold the election in October. Labour's percentage share of the total vote (44.1%) was only 0.3% higher than in October 1959 when they had lost by 100 seats. Wilson always felt that the episode of the Spanish frigates had damaged Labour. In June 1964 Wilson had criticised the Conservatives for making a deal with Franco's Spain, a deal then cancelled by the Spanish government. Wilson's attack pleased the Labour Left, but was roundly condemned by the Prime Minister: 'When everyone else is striving to increase exports he is striving to discourage them.'[40] Subsequent opinion polls showed a movement to the Conservatives, but it was not to prove sufficient. The Liberal leader Jo Grimond wrote, 'During the last Monday and Tuesday I was touring in Aberdeenshire. I heard that the Tories had chosen to finish by putting on some of their more cantankerous spokesmen at the final press conferences. When I heard that one of them had said that anyone who voted Labour must be bonkers, I guessed they would lose.'[41] The rise in the Liberal vote (up from 5.9% in 1959 to 11.2% in 1964) was the really damaging effect, especially in Scotland, where the Conservative vote was well down. But defeat, in the end, is defeat, and the longest continuous spell of one party domination of the century (up to that date), was at an end.

The difference between a landslide victory and a hung Parliament is small in percentage terms: it takes only two to three people in every hundred to change their voting intentions. The final result gave Labour 317 seats (out of a total of 630), the Conservatives 304 and the Liberals, 9. As Elizabeth Home recognised, this was the worst possible result for the Conservatives.[42] A decisive, clear majority for Wilson, leading to a full term, would have given the Party time to reflect on the lessons of defeat, and an opportunity to change their leader in orderly fashion and fight another election four years later with a coherent and well-directed campaign. The initiative was now with Labour; it was only a matter of time before Wilson sought a fresh and fuller mandate, and won an outright majority of 97 seats in 1966. In 1964 Wilson won an arithmetical victory; his triumph in 1966 was one of momentum.

The result naturally reopened the question of the Conservative leadership, quite apart from arguments about the methods of choice. In the short term, Home would have to stay in case there was a snap election. But few expected him to stay for more than a few months. It was widely appreciated that he had fought a dignified campaign. One factor, often discounted in assessing the outcome, was his appeal to a generation that had folk memories of the pre-1914 world. This numerically significant constituency, long since departed, was part of the age in which he had grown up, people for whom decency, patriotism, integrity and restraint were accepted and expected standards of behaviour, for whom Armistice Day was an important anniversary. Even those who opposed his politics recognised his attractive personal characteristics. 'Home had a certain quality about him – it was easy for Wilson to make fun of him, but he had a certain straightness about him – "good old Alec Home",' recalled Tony Benn, who had done more than anyone to make his premiership possible. 'That's why the Tories picked him, they wanted a straight man after a fixer. And he campaigned very powerfully. I think he's a much underestimated figure. He was very competent and hard-working.'[43] Others also felt this undervalue, as Lord Reith wrote in his diary: 'Two bits of news this evening – one that Khrushchev had suddenly disappeared down the oubliette; the other that Harold Wilson is in by a small majority. Of course I have been asked innumerable times what I thought would happen, and I have answered innumerable times that I thought Labour would get in with a majority between 10 and 20. I have always spoken well of Alec Douglas-Home; and I have said that the Labour majority would be more but for him.'[44] In the aftermath of defeat, Alec Home received letters from all over the world. Nearly all commented on his achievement in bringing the party so close to victory and on his personal bearing in adversity. In the midst of all the political comment, there was one letter from Michael Ramsey, Archbishop of Canterbury, that meant a great deal to him. 'I am so grateful for all the care and trouble which you gave to the church matters which came to you, and I have a feeling that you enjoyed that part of your task! You certainly could not have helped me more.'[45]

Downing Street was in many ways an uneasy interlude for Home, whose reputation was made in his other offices. Yet his premiership, despite its brevity, was not insignificant. He brought reforming zeal to the institutions of Whitehall and the system of Cabinet committees, work that would have been continued had he won in October 1964. Enoch Powell would have been appointed to take charge of Civil Service reorganisation, with the aim of cutting back on the Cabinet's workload.[46] Home also had plans for restructuring the Party Organisation, with an enhanced role for Michael Fraser, and when he heard that senior Labour figures were having informal, private talks with Civil Service mandarins during his premiership, he felt this was an eminently sensible move, which should be formalised into 'official' unofficial talks.[47] The 'Douglas-Home rules' governing the meetings of shadow ministers and permanent secretaries meant that future incoming administrations could 'hit the ground running', and were accepted on both sides of the House as promoting better government.

After defeat, Alec Home turned to the question of the Dissolution Honours, but his most generous offer was not accepted. He wrote to Rab Butler, offering to recommend him for an hereditary earldom, the rarest of political honours for a politician who had never been Prime Minister. Although he appreciated the spirit of the offer, Butler was not yet ready to say goodbye to the Commons. Yet within three months, Butler accepted the Mastership of Trinity and with it a life barony. As always, he was more interested in the substance than the style.

The Prime Minister, it has been said, is the loneliest man in England.[48] To a great extent, Alec Home was a lonely political figure in Downing Street. There was no inner circle, such as Macmillan enjoyed in the company of John Wyndham; no 'Kitchen Cabinet', in the manner of the incoming Prime Minister, Harold Wilson. At weekends, the Homes would go when possible to trusted friends outside the political arena; they would entertain at Douglas or the Hirsel. Politics was never the be-all and end-all. As such, Home brought a sense of perspective to his approach, inspiring trust on both sides of the political spectrum. No one questioned his integrity, and though his policies could inspire heated discussion, and his background give rise to inverted snobbery, he never trimmed for easy popularity. Alec Home was not in politics for what he could get out of it personally. His administration was the last example of a certain style of government. It is easy to categorise this as amateurism, to see Home as the most hands-off Prime Minister since Baldwin. In fact few Prime Ministers have suffered more from public misconception about the reality of their role, not only among opponents, but also among erstwhile supporters.

The carping at Home's leadership of the Party in opposition was soon to begin. Jock Colville, doyen of prime ministers' secretaries, had expressed the hope in July 1960 that Alec Home would live in 10 Downing Street, and in October 1964 he had told the new Prime Minister about Edith Watson's prediction in 1939. When Home stepped down from the Conservative leadership in July 1965, Colville wrote an appropriate epitaph to his twenty-one months as Prime Minister and Leader of the Opposition:

> This is a severely professional age. There will probably never again be men who are prepared to subject themselves to all the indignities, disappointments and ingratitudes of public life merely because they want to serve their country. If, as I suspect, you are the last of that breed, this week is a sad one in our history.[49]

15

'The Right Moment to Change'

Alec Home returned to London on 19 October after his weekend at Chequers to a dispirited and demoralised Party. The Conservatives faced an uncertain future and the possibility of a long spell in opposition. Harold Wilson had proved himself an astute tactician in holding together the forces under his control – the Labour Party, as he had observed, was a broad church. His job was to convert Labour into 'the natural governing party of the country', and for this two, or even three, election victories would be needed.

Home's fate could not be separated from that of his Party. The question of the leadership was almost immediately accepted as ripe for consideration. Alec Home had no wish to stay on, but he intended to leave at a moment of his own choosing and only when a new system for choosing his successor was in place. He also wanted to begin the healing process, important as a foundation for electoral success. Home moved swiftly to rehabilitate Enoch Powell and Iain Macleod, both of whom accepted his invitation to join the Consultative Committee. William Deedes had advised that it would not be appropriate to appoint a shadow cabinet to cover Wilson's sprawling administration;[1] as a result, specific portfolios were not to be allocated until the new year, when Powell took on Transport, and Macleod shadowed Labour on steel nationalisation, a task well suited to his combative oratory. Maudling became Shadow Foreign Secretary, and Heath the Shadow Chancellor, a job that enabled him to lead the attack on the new Labour government over its Finance Bill, and lay the ground for his later success over Maudling in the Conservative Party's first formal leadership contest in July 1965.

The question of whether a more formal system of selecting the Conservative leader was desirable had been raised even before the events at Blackpool by Humphry Berkeley, MP for Lancaster, who had advocated such a system the previous March, reinforced by public statements and a letter to *The Times*.[2] On 1 January 1964 Berkeley began a long correspondence with Alec Home on the issue. 'The events of the Blackpool conference and after have, in my view, emphasised this need and would have done so, whoever had emerged as Leader of the Party,' he wrote. 'No doubt there are different views as to what formalised system should be adopted. Some would advocate a secret ballot of MPs voting for openly competing candidates. Others might extend the electoral college by including representatives of the candidates, the National Union and peers in receipt of the Party whip. All these possibilities might be explored. Would you consider, as Leader of the Party, setting up a small committee to consider this matter, hear opinions and make recommendations?'[3]

Some Prime Ministers would have regarded such an overture from one of their junior MPs as bordering on impudence. Not so Alec Home, for the tenor of the letter reflected his own thinking. He wrote back, 'I am not averse to the idea of a private study of the methods which might be used on some future occasion, but I do not think that it would be wise to initiate this before the Election. It would inevitably become known, and would then be taken as evidence of dissatisfaction with the present leadership – although I appreciate your assurance that it does not.'[4] There the matter rested until after the election defeat in October. On 5 November Home addressed a meeting of the Conservative Party's 1922 Committee, saying that he proposed to hold a review of the way in which the leader of the Party was chosen. The next day Berkeley wrote to him again, expressing the hope 'that the younger members of the Party will be adequately represented, since this would be in keeping with your own view of our need to look to the future and not to the past'. Alec Home had already discussed with the Consultative Committee how best that review might begin: 'I am having some talks with Blakenham and others on the machinery for choosing a leader,' he wrote back, 'and will get in touch when our ideas are a little further forward.'[5] On 20 November, a committee, which included Blakenham and Fraser, considered a 'Secret Draft on Possible Methods for Selecting a Leader of the Party', and agreed on various objectives whatever system was adopted. These included:

The predominant voice in the selection must be that of the House of Commons since the Leader's position ultimately depends more on his ability to command the support of the Party in the Commons than on any other single factor.

While in many ways the present procedure is admirably suited to the characteristics of the Conservative Party, a more open and obvious procedure would be more readily intelligible to the Party and the public.

There seems to be no reason why the procedure in office and in opposition should be entirely identical.

The proposal would have to be seconded by, say, seven other Members to avoid the putting forward of entirely frivolous candidates.

The candidate should be nominated by the Commons on the basis of something more than a plurality of votes.[6]

Home indicated that he wished the issue to be settled by mid-February. Opinion was sought, and offered, from several quarters. James Douglas, who worked at Central Office, advocated what he termed the 'Outside Inwards' method; allowing the Party outside the Commons a proper say in the choice, while ensuring that the final choice had the support of the Party inside the Commons. He envisaged MPs consulting their constituents before the poll, rather than after the die was cast. Introduction of the new Party leader at Church House, Westminster, should be a unanimous show of support, acclamation rather than grudging confirmation.[7] On 9 December Home called a meeting 'to continue the discussion on methods of selecting a Party leader', when it was agreed that 'some form of ballot is necessary'. The ballot was in many respects more important than the way it was conducted. 'While no new procedure will retain all the advantages of the old system, some more readily understandable procedure that looks more open is now, in practice, imperative.'[8]

The same day, Home received a letter from David Butler of Nuffield College, whose pioneering studies of general elections had made him the acknowledged expert in psephology. Earlier in the year he had interviewed Home in Downing Street for his book on the 1964 campaign. That he had no personal axe to grind and could give impartial, expert advice made his unsolicited letter welcome, particularly since Butler's basic premiss was what the Consultative Committee were considering in their Secret Draft. 'When there is disagreement,' Butler wrote, 'there is the double problem, first of making the right choice and then of being seen to make the right choice.' Assuming that in future contests more than two candidates would stand, 'The alternative vote is the simplest, quickest and fairest method of ensuring that, when one man has to be chosen out of three or four, the most acceptable leader emerges."[9] The final version of the rules reflected this advice.

As a member of the Shadow Cabinet, Macleod contributed to the issue; indeed his January article in the *Spectator* was the most public opening shot in the movement for change. He outlined his thoughts in a letter to Home for wider consideration: 'The correct procedure is a vote of the Party in the House of Commons, using the transferable vote system. It might be desirable to add the peers who are members of the Cabinet or Shadow Cabinet and perhaps the area Chairmen but I would not myself consider it right to go beyond this.' Under such a system, Butler would almost certainly have prevailed in October 1963. It would not have produced Hailsham, Macmillan's candidate, whose support was in the constituencies rather than at Westminster. Home would not have been the likely victor if such rules had been in place, for his candidacy would have had to be unequivocal from the start, and this would have given time for his opponents to marshal more effective opposition. Macleod also felt that an election might not always be necessary: 'There is one more point. The ideal answer is always that there shouldn't be a contest at all, as for example when Eden followed Churchill, or Chamberlain followed Baldwin. There should then be some provision to take account of this circumstance. Clearly we shouldn't launch into a complicated election unless one is inevitable.'[10]

At a further meeting on the morning of 22 December, at which Macleod was present, Lord Carrington felt that the role of the House of Lords was reduced too much in the new procedures. Fraser suggested that, after a ballot in the House of Commons, the result could be 'put to the Party meeting as at present constituted, giving it the right of veto', but James Douglas had already covered that possibility in the 'Outside Inwards' method. In summing up, Alec Home said that 'it must be seen that the Commons choice was the first process of electing a Leader, and not an independent operation'. All agreed that multiple ballots without elimination, which could otherwise go on indefinitely, should be avoided.[11]

Letters from Humphry Berkeley had now resumed. He declared that 'time is passing by' and let it be known that he wished to submit a memorandum, 'Choosing a Leader', which he was invited to discuss at a meeting on 14 December. 'I am delighted that you accept the three basic principles of procedure outlined in my memorandum – namely that Members of Parliament alone should vote, that they should do so by secret ballot, and that the result should be published,' Berkeley wrote. He was jumping the gun on the first point, for the exact composition of the electoral college had not yet been settled, as Alec Home pointed out: 'It may well be that the final result of our thought on this will be that members of the House of Commons alone shall vote, but at this stage I would not like you to go away with the impression that this is my absolutely firm and final view, or that any other possible variation is entirely ruled out.'[12]

Home showed great patience with Berkeley, but felt now that he should be left to formulate the new rules with his advisers; in later years, he was wary of any new correspondence with Berkeley, which always came back to the same topic. For his part, Humphry Berkeley felt that no backbencher could have been treated more sympathetically.[13] Although he had been opposed to Alec Home's becoming Prime Minister in the autumn of 1963, 'this was not because I thought that he was unfitted to be Prime Minister ... In fact, he turned out to be an excellent Prime Minister because of his shining honesty.'[14]

Discussions continued until the publication in February of the 'Procedure for the Selection of the Leader of the Conservative and Unionist Party'.[15] This document marked an irrevocable change in the way the Conservative Party perceived itself and the way in which power was distributed. In November 1974 at the request of the leader, Edward Heath, Home chaired a committee to bring the rules up to date, though the document of February 1965 remained the template.

There were thirteen provisions in the original document, covering all aspects of the electoral college, the possible three ballots and the final meeting at which the elected leader would be presented to the Party for acclamation. Many similarities with a papal conclave come to mind. Firstly, after consideration of all the possible alternatives, the procedure limited the electoral college to 'the Party in the House of Commons'. The Chairman of the 1922 Committee was given full responsibility for the conduct of the ballot and 'all matters in relation thereto'. Experience showed that this gave him powers to abbreviate a lengthy process, calling a halt to later ballots if the will of the Party had been made clear at an earlier stage. By the strict letter of the rules, neither Edward Heath (in July 1965) nor John Major (in November 1990) was elected according to the constitution, final ballots being abandoned and front runners declared the winner.

Initially, two (anonymous) nominations sufficed for a valid candidature. Victory on the first ballot required an 'overall majority' and '15 per cent more of the votes cast than any other candidate'. If these conditions were not met, a second ballot would be arranged. Previous nominations became invalid and new nominations could be submitted, the so-called 'coward's charter' allowing senior figures to stand without inflicting the initial wound. An overall majority would be sufficient for victory in this ballot. If *those* conditions were not met, the three candidates receiving the highest number of votes at the second ballot would be listed on a ballot paper for a third and final vote. The voter had to specify his first and second preference (the advice of David Butler). 'The scrutineers will proceed to add the number of first preference votes received by each candidate, eliminate the candidate with the lowest number of first preference votes and redistribute the votes of those giving him as their first preference amongst the two remaining candidates in accordance with their second preference. The result of this final count will be an overall majority for one candidate, and he will be elected.'[16] Ironically, this final provision was a close approximation to what had happened in the wake of Macmillan's resignation, in that Home was the concurrence of second preferences. Unlike the later revisions of 1975, this procedure was triggered only on the death or resignation of the incumbent leader, whether Prime Minister or Leader of the Opposition. It did not permit a challenge to a leader whose position was under threat.

The revisions of 1975 weakened the position of an incumbent leader whose popularity was in decline, by making provision for an annual election within twenty-eight days of the opening of a new Parliament (which is why November became the cruellest month) and by requiring the victor to achieve an overall majority plus 15 per cent more of the *available* votes (not 15 per cent of the votes actually cast), a much stiffer hurdle which made abstentions a vital part of the equation. The combined effect of these two amendments ended the ten-year leadership of Edward Heath in February 1975, as the first ballot showed that he had lost the confidence of the Party, though his principal challenger, Margaret Thatcher, did not secure the 15 per cent margin at the first time of asking.[17] The 1975 amendments did not, however, preclude a challenge to an incumbent Prime Minister, which Mrs Thatcher experienced in both November 1989 and November 1990.

Despite the 'openness' of the new system, Home always regretted that the change was necessary – not because he had been the beneficiary of the 'customary processes', but because the flexibility of the previous arrangements suited the different situations between 1911 and 1963. What the system of February 1965 did was to formalise the main characteristics of the two contests of 1911 and 1963 into an agreed procedure, thus precluding the criticism Macleod had made in his *Spectator* article. If everyone knew what the agreed rules were at the outset, however bitter the battle might be, nobody could criticise the result in terms of the method. Macleod had criticised the *method*, though his real quarrel was with the *result*. Home also regretted the weakening of the input from wider sections of the Party, believing that Douglas's 'Outside Inwards' clause did not permit the wider national Party to make a significant contribution. Cabinet Ministers in the Lords, in particular, were marginalised by the new system. However, he acknowledged that a formal system meant that any future Conservative leader would enter into his or her position without the incubus that had bedevilled his tenure. And so it proved. He bequeathed harmony of method, if not always of outcome.

Alec Home's nine months as Leader of the Opposition were a twilight period, but they were not without incident. The Labour government had the briefest of honeymoons, ending with Gordon Walker's failure to hold Leyton in January 1965. The local MP, Reginald Sorenson, had reluctantly accepted ennoblement as Lord Sorenson, the reverse route to that taken by Home in 1963 when George Younger's sacrifice had enabled him to return to the Commons. Gordon Walker was not so fortunate, losing the seat by 205 votes. Alec Home wrote privately to Gordon Walker to commiserate. Ironically, his defeat weakened Home's position, as Martin Redmayne recognised:

> I do not believe that Leyton necessarily helps you personally – or at least only if the dangers of it are seen and met. Some ambitions will become sharper and more urgent as the chance of winning an election seems more real. There are two separate prizes, one the eventual leadership, the other, if at any time it seems practicable, leadership coupled with a successful election (and therefore seized before that election). The devious mind may think that the larger prize is now nearer, and for that reason attacks on the present leadership may increase. The antidote lies not only in an increase of activity in the Shadow Cabinet, but in making sure that that activity is observed in the Party and outside.[18]

In the opinion of many close to Alec Home, the damage to his position was done not by Leyton but by a contest close to his political heartland: Roxburgh, Selkirk and Peebles. On 24 March 1965, David Steel, the future Leader of the Liberal Party, won this formerly safe seat from the

Conservatives. The Unionists had lost their overall majority in Scotland in the 1959 general election, and a further eight seats in 1964. Now the young Edinburgh bourgeoisie epitomised by Steel were turning to Liberalism, and the rural lairds who still chose anglicised upper-class Scots as their Unionist candidates 'saddled the party with a feudal look that was almost a caricature of its English sister'.[19] The resultant feeling was that if the Conservatives could not hold a seat next to Coldstream, what could they hold under Alec Home's leadership? Home realised this too and decided that the new electoral rules he had so carefully formulated should be given their first trial in the near future.

Before Christmas 1964, Harold Wilson had enquired of Rab Butler whether he would be interested in becoming Master of Trinity College, Cambridge, a crown appointment. An imaginative and generous offer, it was recognised as the perfect summation to Butler's career. The appointment came with a life barony (he took the title of Baron Butler of Saffron Walden, after the constituency he had represented for thirty-six years) and was announced on 31 January 1965. Two days earlier, Butler had written to Home, 'These sort of offers come only once and they time themselves.' He added, 'I shall not be far away and shall be frequently down the corridor in another place.'[20] For both men, this ended an uneasy period.

The announcement had been delayed owing to the stroke and subsequent death of Sir Winston Churchill. As Leader of the Opposition, Home was inevitably drawn into the event, but with great reluctance. Harold Wilson made a much publicised visit to 28 Hyde Park Gate on 20 January, when he was received by Churchill's daughter, Mary Soames, Lady Churchill being too exhausted and strained to receive visitors.[21] The feeling in the Conservative Party was that Alec Home should not be left out in this procession and he was duly despatched to 28 Hyde Park Gate. Received also by Mary Soames, he was acutely embarrassed during his short visit. Circumstances had placed him in a position which he instinctively knew was not appropriate and he regretted that the Churchill family had to receive any guests at all, however well intentioned.[22] Churchill died on Sunday 24 January 1965, and the state funeral took place the following Saturday. When the death was announced, Home made a short and appropriate tribute, 'We stand in homage with the nation,' he told the House of Commons.[23]

Few stood in homage to Alec Home at this time. David Steel's entry into the House of Commons became the focus of muttering about the

Conservative leadership. On 26 March, Home was called a 'cretin' on the television programme *Not So Much a Programme, More a Way of Life* by Bernard Levin, an episode that was highly embarrassing to the BBC. Many figures would have sought legal redress. Sir Hugh Greene, Director General of the BBC, was inundated by letters of complaint. He sent Home a transcript of the broadcast and a letter of profuse apology. It had already been announced that the run of the programme was to end on 11 April, but the 'cretin' episode meant that few regretted its demise. The episode evoked a great deal of sympathy for the Conservative leader, but it was a sign that the parameters of possible, if not acceptable, public comment had moved into new, uncharted areas.[24]

'There is quite a lot of snarling about Alec', Selwyn Lloyd wrote to Lord Avon on 14 April, in a review of the political situation, 'but I don't think that the potential successors are particularly distinguishing themselves. I doubt myself whether the mood will change much for another twelve months. Therefore I hope that we do not have an early election.'[25] Such a prospect declined when the Conservatives made 562 gains in the local elections and on 26 June Home was prevailed upon to say that he would continue as leader. Harold Wilson (his majority down to two seats after the Leyton reversal) then announced that there would be no general election in 1965, which put Home's leadership into question once again. A snap general election would have left the Conservatives in an exposed position if they were in the throes of a contest for the leadership, but Wilson's announcement removed this spectre.

The serious contenders for the leadership were Reginald Maudling, shadow Foreign Secretary, and Edward Heath, shadow Chancellor, but, as in the previous leadership battle, Maudling's position had slipped drastically in the preceding few months. Heath's leading the attack on the government's Finance Bill, coupled with an efficient, though discreet, campaign for the leadership, contrasted sharply with Maudling's failure to prepare the ground. On 5 July, a motion signed by twenty-five backbenchers (largely, though not exclusively, Heath supporters) was put to the 1922 Committee, requesting a 'debate' on the leadership. Sir William Anstruther-Gray, who had succeeeded John Morrison as Chairman, agreed to communicate these feelings to the leader, the only way in which a vote could be avoided. Although Home made the ritual noises about staying on, he now knew the new leader would have the chance to play himself in before the next election, so he decided the appropriate time had come.

He was confirmed in his decision by an article by William Rees-Mogg entitled 'The Right Moment to Change', which brought a sense of relief that he was doing the right thing at the right time. Rees-Mogg's article was an analysis of the Conservative Party's dilemma at that time and contained a memorable cricketing analogy of the kind Alec Home appreciated:

> He has in fact played the sort of captain's innings one used to see in county cricket before the war. There were then in most counties good club players, often fresh from the university, who were appointed captain because they were amateurs. They lacked the professional skills and they never had very high averages. But occasionally, when the wicket was taking spin at Canterbury or Weston-super-Mare, they would come in when their side had scored thirty-seven for six and by dint of concentration and a well-coached forward prod survive to make twenty runs or so and see their side past the follow-on.[26]

The detail about Weston-super-Mare (Lord's or Headingley would not have had the same resonance) was so apt that an underlying truth could not be denied. A clinching detail was a National Opinion Poll which narrowly claimed Wilson to be the more sincere of the two main Party Leaders: 'This mass failure to appreciate what his intimates would claim to be his greatest quality was deeply wounding.'[27] There was, however, compensation in the NOP: 'The best joke in it was that I was within a point of H.W. in "intelligence". He won't be pleased!' Home wrote to Peter Thorneycroft.[28] On 20 July he told Elizabeth of his decision only when it was irrevocable, and Selwyn Lloyd, who would have pressed him to stay, was also not told until the die was cast. He asked Lloyd to see him at the House of Commons on Thursday 22 July, the day he was due to speak to the 1922 Committee at their end of session meeting.

Selwyn Lloyd noted, 'When I got to his room in the House of Commons he said "I am going to let you down. I have decided to chuck my hand in and give up the leadership."' He told Lloyd that the 1922 Committee meeting was the last easy chance for him to go. 'At six o'clock the same day he came to the 1922 Committee, looking terribly drawn and ill and made a moving little speech which was received with obvious sadness and sympathy. I then went into the Smoking Room, where several people said how unnecessary they thought it was.'[29] After speaking of the need to strengthen the Party organisation and to rethink policies, and warning that the perennial curse of the Tory Party had been disunity born of rivalry, Alec Home said that he had asked the Chairman of the 1922 Committee to put the new procedures into effect. 'I myself set up the machinery for this change and I myself have chosen the time to use it. It is up to you to see that it is completed swiftly and efficiently, and with dignity and calm. I do not intend to stand for election.'[30] Only Greville Howard, MP for the St Ives Division of Cornwall, stood up and said that this was a sad day for the Party and should not be happening. Most felt that he was bowing to the inevitable. Those who had campaigned behind the scenes for his removal were now the ones who came up to him to say how sorry they were he was going.[31] So ended Alec Home's twenty-one-month leadership of the Conservative Party.

It seemed a disappointingly tame conclusion to his career. Newspaper comment was of a valedictory nature, with speculation rife as to whether he would be made governor-general of Australia.[32] The letters that poured in spoke almost invariably of his service to his country, as though it was a thing of the past and the prelude to a well-deserved retirement. Lord Avon wrote:

> I am very, very sorry at the news. As you know, I think you have done a wonderful job in rescuing the party from the effects of Harold's last phase and Profumo. I could not have expected that you could have run Labour so close last autumn. It was mainly your personal leadership which did it; since then you have not had the true loyalty from the party you deserve. Nobody can reproach you, but some Tories should reproach themselves. You could not have set a higher standard of integrity and fair dealing. Personally I believe that the contrast with Wilson would have been remarkable and effective at the next General Election. Anyway, this is just to say a heartfelt thank you from one of your admirers and well wishers.[33]

Rab Butler wrote generously from Trinity:

> I feel that the Party, having encouraged you to come forward, and having appreciated your own special qualities, should stand by you and see you through. There must now of necessity be considerable lack of confidence as to whether 'the Party', whoever that may mean, will be consecutive and thorough in their loyalty in the future.
>
> You have done a great deal for the organisation and for policy making. You have given a first class example of integrity and this has been enhanced by the manner in which you have taken this

latest decision. I hope you will continue to serve the new leadership in a senior capacity thus ensuring some continuity. If there is a chance at any time of a talk my friendship for you, my regard and my experience will be at your service. Mollie and I are thinking very much of you both and send you both our love.[34]

Home had telephoned Macmillan with advance notice of his decision to go. 'It was a very sad moment when I heard your voice on the telephone ...' Macmillan wrote:

To me, I can assure you, your decision is a great shock and a great grief. It is just two years since it was my duty to advise the Queen about my successor and there was no doubt at all in anybody's mind, whether the Cabinet, the House of Commons, the House of Lords or the Party in the country that you were the right choice. You made a wonderful recovery for the Party and only by a bit of bad luck in the way the cards fell were prevented from getting a majority. Had this happened, there would have been no questioning of your leadership, for you had already shown high qualities as a Prime Minister, and I am sure could have steered us through these difficult years.

Of course, I know that the qualities required for leading an opposition are different. None of the Prime Ministers whom I remember with admiration were good at it; Balfour not at all, nor Baldwin; Churchill was frankly bored by it; I am bound to say I should have found it very distasteful. For, of necessity, the work is destructive and not constructive. Nevertheless, I feel sure that you had the confidence of the Party throughout the country. This is a trouble you had in the House of Commons and due largely to the inexperience of the younger members and their lack of responsibility.

However, I know that you made your choice deliberately and with the certainty that it was right for the country and for yourself. I respect it all the more because I know that nothing weighed with you except to do what was best.

I am afraid this is a very halting letter and does not adequately represent my sorrow and my sympathy. I hope that we may remain in touch. It will give me great pleasure if you would allow our friendship to be continued and even strengthened. My love to Elizabeth.[35]

Alec Home wrote back at once:

I am so grateful for your understanding. It was a decision which I

> could not shift onto anyone else. The feeling had become stronger and stronger that the many younger ones in our party were determined to have one of a new generation and a new type to lead. It is a fashion which will pass, but it is very strong now. Backed by the press they would not settle down and I thought that the only thing was shock treatment to stop the intrigue which was beginning all over again. I don't like the 'professional' because office means too much and that is not good for public life. I pray that I was right and anyhow I have been deeply indebted to you for such success as has come my way in public life and I will continue to lean on you for wisdom. Thank you.[36]

On 25 July, the Sunday before the voting for the new leader, Alec and Elizabeth Home dined with Selwyn Lloyd at his country home. The man who more than any other had persuaded him to stand again let his disappointment be known. 'Elizabeth was very angry that he had done it. She didn't think it at all necessary. I agreed with her. Alec was quite unmoved. We talked about the succession. He made it pretty clear that he himself was going to vote for Heath.'[37] Anthony and Clarissa Avon had lunched with the Lloyds earlier and 'had no particular comment on the crisis,' recorded Lloyd, 'except that Anthony thought that Alec could have continued. He was non-committal as between Heath and Maudling.' Under the old system, Avon could have been one of the main power-brokers and would almost certainly have been asked by the Palace for his views. Now he was sidelined, as was Macmillan, who had left the House of Commons at the 1964 dissolution. Nominations closed on 26 July. To the surprise of many, there was a third candidate: Enoch Powell. Both main camps were apprehensive as to how this might affect a closely fought contest. The possibility of more than two candidates had been considered and there was a great deal of speculation as to who might be the 'Bonar Law'. Selwyn Lloyd, Christopher Soames and Peter Thorneycroft were all mentioned after news had leaked of their tri-partite meeting on 23 July.[38] The big question was whether Macleod would try to put a marker down for the future by standing as a third candidate. Such an intervention could have made a profound difference to the outcome. The vote was held on 27 July. Home took no open part in the contest, though he voted for Heath, whose campaign under Peter Walker proved far too professional for Maudling and his supporters. Heath even had time to attend the opera at Glyndebourne on the evening of Home's announcement. From the start Maudling had a clear lead in the opinion polls (by 44 per cent to 28 per cent at one stage), but the public were not the electorate that mattered. Heath had received 150 votes in the first ballot, Maudling 133 and Powell 15. Heath had thus failed to achieve the 15 per cent margin necessary for outright victory, but the feeling of the Party was clear and Maudling withdrew. The first reaction among many in the Party was relief that the new system had 'worked', and they had been spared the traumas of October 1963. Heath was presented as the new leader at Church House on 2 August. In his farewell speech, Home paid tribute to all the help that Elizabeth had given him over the years. 'The trust and confidence which you have shown in me as your leader, and in my wife who has been my constant ally (I'm not sure she shouldn't have been leader of the Party) has been a sufficient and rich reward for any work which I may have been able to do.'[39]

The 'modern' technocrat had been chosen to defeat Wilson and much was made of the fact that Heath had been educated at Chatham House, a grammar school, whereas his three predecessors had been Etonians. It is easy to exaggerate the difference between Alec Home and his successor. Despite appearances Home was a professional politician to his finger tips and well aware of the importance of organisational and policy reforms. Heath had moved a long way from his lower-middle-class origins (his father had been a carpenter, and his mother in domestic service) and was now a grandee in the Tory Party in his own right – a former Chief Whip, with rooms in Albany and tastes to match. The change to Ted Heath was not so much a change from Eton to Chatham House but from Christ Church (the college of Eden and Home) to Balliol (that of Macmillan and Heath). The public perceptions were of real change however, one of the reasons Heath was chosen. But in July 1965, Home's appointment as shadow Foreign Secretary and the confirmation in office of his appointee as the new Party Chairman, Edward du Cann, gave a sense of continuity to the opposition team, on which Heath shrewdly built.

Nevertheless, there was for Alec Home a sense of *fin de saison* about his retreat to Douglas that August. He cleared out the baggage of many years, winnowing files and papers. He consigned his joke book to the fire, a sign that he really did think the great game was over. His priorities changed. He accepted the Chancellorship of Heriot-Watt University and appeared to be slipping graciously into the role of the elder statesman, with plans for lecture tours in America. At his installation as Chancellor he spoke of his great pleasure that he had been the head of the government 'which accepted the recommendations of the Robbins Committee to create a number of new universities in Great Britain and, in particular, that the Colleges of Advanced Technology in England and the Heriot-Watt College in Scotland should become universities of Technology'.[40] He was awarded an honorary DSc from Heriot-Watt, one of seven degrees he received in the 1960s.[41] As the various parts of Macmillan's memoirs appeared, he read and commented on sections where he had special knowledge, and took advice from Macmillan on publishing memoirs, against the moment when, as he described it, he 'fell'.

But when the new political year began with the Conservative Party conference at Brighton in October, it was clear that he was not going to be allowed to go gently into the political night. He was the shadow Foreign Affairs spokesman at a particularly sensitive time, as the Rhodesian situation moved towards the unilateral declaration of independence (UDI) by Ian Smith, which Home always referred to as a 'revolt against the Crown'. He wrote to Macmillan, 'The more I think of it the surer I am that Smith can't wait long – a melancholy end to a problem that perhaps was scarcely soluble.'[42] The Brighton conference showed how perceptions of him had changed in the rank and file of the Party, always prone to outbursts of remorse and guilt, particularly towards those felt to have had a rough deal from the political fates. Many thought that Home had been badly treated: encouraged to come forward as leader at the cost of his ancient title, he had now been unceremoniously bundled on to the sidelines of convenience. As a result there was an outpouring of enthusiasm wherever he appeared, and Heath had to break off his speech at the mention of Home to allow the applause to run its natural course, hardly the best baptism for the new leader.

There was serious disagreement at the conference on the question of sanctions against Southern Rhodesia, in the event of UDI. Home's 'firmness' on Rhodesia much impressed Tony Benn, who was hardly one of his natural supporters. After the statement by Harold Wilson, eleven days after UDI, the fissures in the Tory Party were plain to see. Benn wrote, 'Home and Selwyn Lloyd are really running the Tory Party now and are much firmer on Rhodesia than Heath.'[43]

After his narrow victory in the general election, Wilson chose his moment wisely for the next contest. Parliament was dissolved on 10 March 1966 and polling day fixed for 31 March. At 1 year, 5 months and 13 days, it had been the shortest Parliament of the century; the election was also the first March contest of the century. Labour had been soldily ahead in the opinion polls since September 1965. The marginal constituency of Hull, which Labour retained in January 1966 on a swing of 4.5 per cent, was seen as a crucial pointer. Although Hull was won in the wake of the decision to build the Humber Road Bridge, described as 'the most notorious election bribe in recent memory',[44] the momentum was clearly with Wilson and the Tories had little expectation of overall victory. The Conservative Manifesto was called *Action Not Words*, which led Home to ask at one planning meeting whether 'ideas' might not also be included. If the 1964 Election was the 'one that got away', that in 1966 was 'the one that never was', leading to the second largest working majority in the Labour Party's history. Many Conservatives, as they awakened on that April Fool's Day, must have pondered that Wilson was well on his way to making Labour 'the natural party of government'.

Of necessity, Alec Home's contribution was more low-key than in October 1964. He spent much of his time in his Kinross and West Perthshire constituency, where he faced a three-cornered contest. The figures, declared on 1 April, were: Sir Alec Douglas-Home (Unionist) 14,466; Andrew Donaldson (Scottish Nationalist) 4,884; Brian Parnell (Labour) 4,461, giving a Unionist majority of 9,582. It was a relaxed contest, with none of the frenetic attention of the 1963 by-election, or the post-election controversies over the Grieve petition. But nationally the Conservatives faced a long haul and no guarantee that they would be able even then to end the Wilson hegemony. In this difficult situation, 'Home was a model of loyalty and discretion in serving his successor both in opposition and office for the next eight years'.[45] In the opinion of many of his Party associates, the way he departed the leadership and behaved towards his successor were his finest hour.

Following the March 1966 defeat, Heath could now shape his own shadow Cabinet and three important figures emerged: Anthony Barber, who had returned to the House at a by-election in February 1965; Geoffrey Rippon; and Peter Walker, epitome of the new classless meritocracy. At his request, Selwyn Lloyd stepped down from Commonwealth Affairs, responsibility for which devolved upon Alec Home when the deputy leader, Reginald Maudling, moved to shadow Foreign Secretary. Despite this infusion of new blood, Alec Home (and Quintin Hogg, who became the new Home Affairs spokesman) retained their positions of influence, more so in many respects than Reginald Maudling, whose influence was seen in some quarters as on the wane. Maudling was not offered the Foreign Secretaryship in 1970. Home took an active part in shadow Cabinet meetings, but was not one of the inner circle who attended policy discussions in Heath's Albany rooms. He travelled widely with Elizabeth on shadow Cabinet business, and was kept in touch with political events back home by his private secretary, Angela Bowlby, in her unique style. 'Will try and remember all gossip', began one typical letter. 'Jay has got into trouble with Wilson for coming out strongly against going into the Common Market ... Wilson is having a fearful row with the *Express* because they published a report about censoring overseas cables which apparently contravened two "D" notices (whatever they are!).'[46] Marcia Williams, Harold Wilson's secretary, played a high profile role in the Downing Street team, which led to some wry comments from Angela Bowlby. 'Have just been told that Marcia is writing her life story in the *News of the World*! What do you imagine she will get paid? I am sorely tempted!'[47]

Despite his status as a former Prime Minister, Alec Home preferred to travel anonymously and with the minimum of fuss. On a visit to Mexico in February 1967, Alec and Elizabeth Home booked ordinary tickets for the long flight, but when identified he was immediately upgraded at no extra cost. 'The second leg of our flight was again 1st Class', wrote Elizabeth Home to Angela Bowlby. 'Alec says it's all very awkward and we can never go "Economy" again if BOAC thinks it *infra dig* and has to move us.[48] During a long visit to South Africa in February 1968, Angela Bowlby reported what came to be known as the Coalition Plot. 'Over the weekend an idea was put about that we should have a Coalition government – bypassing Wilson and Heath – and having as the three king-pins, Lord Robens, Cecil King and Jo Grimond! Cecil King denied on TV yesterday that he had been approached! Food for thought – and the press are feeding well!' Later in the same letter she told the Homes that three Labour-held by-elections were scheduled for the week after the Budget, adding, 'So I suppose the family allowances must be going up!'[49] Angela Bowlby and Elizabeth Home gave cryptic references to HH in these letters, after one grandchild said of an afternoon visit Alec Home was making to 10 Downing Street, 'He's not going to have tea with Horrid Harold, is he?' Although Home felt Wilson was very far from being 'horrid', HH became private family code.[50]

Harold Wilson also knew the value of Alec Home as a figure who commanded respect on both sides of the House. On 10 August 1966, Wilson stated that an inter-party group of privy counsellors would consider proposals for a new range of official histories covering selected periods of peace-time history, a prelude to the relaxation of the Fifty to the Thirty Year Rule covering official documents in 1967. Alec Home was nominated to be the Conservative Party figure on this body, and with Patrick Gordon Walker and Lord Ogmore (representative of the Liberal Party), became a key figure in the opening up of archive material, though he believed that Thirty Years should mean Thirty Years. 'I do not quite see the point of the 30 years rule', he wrote to Edward Heath, 'if Official Historians have access to all the material long before it is up.'[51]

In September 1966, Alec Home's mother, Lilian, Countess of Home, died in her eighty-fifth year. She was buried beside her husband, the 13th Earl, at Lennel Churchyard. Two years later, her grandson, Robin Douglas-Home, took a fatal overdose at the age of thirty-six. Another break with the past was the death in 1967 of Anne Chamberlain, a correspondent to the end. Two years later Home played a prominent part in the marking of the Chamberlain centenary year. 'It's never safe', Home said of his former master, 'to assume that a man's public posture is what he really is.'[52] It could have been the epitaph for his own career.

Home took on many new responsibilities. None promised so much, yet caused such disappointment, as his presidency of the MCC in 1966. Cricket had always been one of the great loves of his life. To be governor of I Zingari cricket club or patron of the English Schools Cricket Association was a joy, never a duty. He was always ready to contribute forewords to books on such figures as Harry Altham (by Hubert Doggart) and Gubby Allen (by E.W. Swanton).[53] As the only Prime Minister to have played first class cricket his role in the MCC should have been the culmination of his cricketing life. Only once before had a former Prime Minister accepted the Presidency of the MCC and that was Stanley Baldwin in 1938. During his visits to Lord's, Baldwin arranged that Committee meetings should be held at 4 p.m. and gave strict instructions that tea was to be served at 4.30 p.m. promptly, so that 'close of play' was predetermined.[54] Home had agreed to take on the job on condition that there was nothing political in the offing. But the late 1960s were one of the unhappiest periods in English cricket and his term of office was blighted by bitter controversies. When he succeeded Sir Oliver Leese on 1 October 1966, letters of congratulation poured in, one from Colin Cowdrey that began 'Dear Sir Alec', to which he replied 'You can drop the "Sir", if you ever drop anything.'[55] No sooner had he accepted office than several contentious issues arose; the two most damaging were the Basil d'Oliveira affair, when the England cricket tour of South Africa was cancelled following the host nation's refusal to accept d'Oliveira, a Cape Coloured, as one of the touring party, and the dropping of Brian Close as England captain, following alleged time-wasting in a Warwickshire–Yorkshire county match. It was useful for the MCC that they had a figure of Home's stature to chair contentious meetings, but it was hardly what he had anticipated. The ramifications of the d'Oliveira affair persisted for years, and Alec Home found himself cast in the role of intermediary between deeply entrenched factions, a task more difficult than many he had faced as Foreign Secretary, such were the passions aroused.

The first mention of what became known as the Basil d'Oliveira affair was at a meeting on 1 February 1967. Basil d'Oliveira had first been selected for England in the summer of 1966, and had patently justified his selection, becoming a regular member of the side. The South African tour, due in 1968, was edging closer, and articles were already appearing in the press raising d'Oliveira's status. At a committee meeting in April 1967, Home said that it would be advisable 'to check that any coloured member of the MCC team would be free to attend hotels, cinemas etc. on the same basis as other players'. He undertook personally to see the South African ambassador in London and it was agreed that no press statement would be made. At the Annual General Meeting on 3 May a vote of thanks was proposed to the President 'wishing him a happy cricket season with plenty of sunshine'. Over the summer Home represented the MCC at the International Cricket Conference, and his last committee meeting as President was on 24 August, when the Brian Close affair blew up out of a seemingly clear sky. During the Warwickshire–Yorkshire county match at Edgbaston from 16 to 18 August, Close employed what were considered delaying tactics to deny Warwickshire victory, and Committee voted by fourteen votes to four to remove him from the England captaincy, replacing him with Colin Cowdrey for the forthcoming tour of the West Indies. The d'Oliveira affair was one of race; the Close affair raised issues of class, the Gentlemen versus Players divide. Cowdrey was portrayed as the Tonbridge-educated Oxbridge Gentleman, and Close as the gritty, self-made Yorkshireman, whose bravery in fielding at silly point with Garfield Sobers in full flight with the bat, was seen as the kind of stubborn bravado England needed if victory was to be achieved in the winter tour. Again the press fed well and the MCC Committee were portrayed as being out-of-touch with the modern world. One letter of great anguish came to Home from the Duke of Norfolk, imploring him to call all the county captains to a meeting at Lord's to discuss the future. Although this meeting did not take place, it was an indication of the way different factions turned to Alec Home to resolve their difficulties.[56]

If anything, Alec Home's role in MCC matters increased after the nominal ending of his term as president in October 1967. He intended to visit South Africa in February 1968, in his capacity as an opposition spokesman, to discuss the Rhodesian rebellion, but it was also a perfect opportunity to sound out the South African government about their attitude to the forthcoming tour. The MCC had written to the South African Cricket Association in January 1968 'asking for an assurance that no pre-conditions would be laid on their choice of players'.[57] Home found little comfort on either topic – Prime Minister Vorster refused to apply economic sanctions on Rhodesia or to give any guarantees over the acceptability of an as yet unselected MCC touring party.

On the way back from South Africa Home met Ian Smith and Sir Hugh Beadle, the Rhodesian Chief Justice, in Salisbury and told Smith that he wanted a settlement as soon as possible as time was running out. He hoped that Smith would enable him to take suggestions back to the Prime Minister in Britain which might serve as a foundation for resumed negotiations. The main importance of the meeting was to underline the bi-partisan approach at the most senior level in Britain. Wilson had accepted at the 1966 Lagos Commonwealth Prime Ministers' Conference that there could be no independence before majority rule – NIBMAR – and this remained the sticking point for many years. Beadle saw Home as a useful intermediary with the Wilson Government, and wrote to him in the aftermath of this February meeting.[58]

On his return, Home brought little comfort to the shadow Cabinet and was frankly pessimistic about Vorster's attitude to the forthcoming MCC tour. He felt sure that there was more chance of the selected side being accepted if the MCC waited until selection was actually known before confronting the South African government. No reply had been received to the MCC's letter in January to the South African Cricket Association. This was still the position in the summer when the First Test was played at Old Trafford, Manchester, in June against the visiting Australian side. Although Australia won this match by 159 runs, on the last day there was a splendid rearguard innings by d'Oliveira, who made 87 not out. Afterwards, at a meeting with Colin Cowdrey, about the South African tour, Home was quite clear that the team should be picked on merit, without any compromise because of possible political implications. He advised that the MCC should not press for a reply to their January letter, but let events take their course. D'Oliveira was called into the side for the final test against the Australians at the Oval when one player dropped out because of a viral infection and his innings of 158 contributed to a famous victory. On 27 August the selectors chose their party to tour South Africa; it did not include d'Oliveira.[59] The public interpretation was that the MCC had backed off from a confrontation with the South African authorities and a prolonged and bitter controversy followed. Within days, however, d'Oliveira was included in the touring party when the original choice of all-rounder, T.W. Cartwright, had to step down on medical grounds. Vorster cancelled the tour, claiming that the team had been forced upon South Africa by people 'with certain political aims'. The matter did not end there. A group of MCC members, led by the Reverend David Sheppard (later Bishop of Liverpool), critical of the handling of the whole affair, sought an extraordinary general meeting of the club and a motion of no confidence in the Committee. It was felt that Alec Home should act as spokesman for the Committee's actions during the previous eighteen months and 'that there was a chance that the protesting Members might see the difficulties with which the MCC had been faced and consequently the need for a Special General Meeting might be averted'. Home later met Sheppard's group and 'outlined the salient points in the situation leading up to the selection of the team to tour South Africa'. He detailed the various courses open to the Committee 'and explained the reasons for the Committee taking the course they did'. He emphasised the importance of not pressing for answers prior to selection as the best way of saving the tour.

A special general meeting of the MCC was held on 5 December in the Assembly Hall of Church House. A motion was put by the dissident group 'That the members of MCC regret their Committee's mishandling of affairs leading up to the selection of the team for the intended tour of South Africa in 1968–1969'. The essence of the MCC's position was explained by Dennis Silk when he said, 'Sir Alec Douglas-Home, a diplomat of some experience, knowing the idiosyncrasies of South Africa, advised us then simply to press our basic principle, which was that whatever else happened we would pick the side we wanted to pick on cricketing merit.' From the floor of the house, it was said with some passion, 'I would like to know who amongst Mr Sheppard and his friends is qualified to pit his judgment against the judgment of Sir Alec

Douglas-Home', a remark greeted with great applause. The resolution was defeated by 4,357 to 1,570.[60] But it was, in the words of Colin Cowdrey, 'the saddest controversy in cricket'.[61] The episode, however, remains an important one in perceptions of Alec Home's career. His integrity was held up as the mitigating element in the MCC's actions, and all were agreed that he did not compromise himself, but found time to help the MCC, even when he was already heavily involved in work on Rhodesia, Gibraltar and Czechoslovakia, all the subjects of major Foreign Affairs debates that summer.

Another development in late 1968 brought shadows from the past, in this case the Scottish Office years. After a period of relative quiescence, Scottish nationalism was once more on the march, and the break-up of the United Kingdom became an issue for the first time since the Irish troubles of the 1920s. The Scottish Nationalists' most spectacular success came in November 1967, when Winifred Ewing won the Hamilton by-election, one of the safest Labour seats in the country. The shock of this reversal was greater to the Westminster establishment than the Liberal victory at Orpington in March 1962, for that was a threat to one party only. 'Wilson and Heath decided that a bit of Home Rule, a toy parliament, albeit with working and satisfactorily noisy parts, would end the Scottish tantrum', Andrew Marr has written, adding, 'devolution did stop the SNP bandwagon, which was its primary purpose.'[62] Mrs Ewing was thus the 'onlie begetter' of a great deal of constitutional shenanigans, with the Labour MP for West Lothian, Tam Dalyell, eventually asking why he should be 'able to vote on the most delicate issues of housing, health, education and local government finance for the West Midlands but not for West Lothian, which I represented'[63] (the so-called 'West Lothian question'). Scotland raised a different problem for the Conservatives, one of which Alec Home was acutely aware. Over his political lifetime he had seen Unionist representation north of the border slump from 57 in 1931 to 20 in 1966; in the previous ten years, the total had virtually halved. In May 1968, in the so-called 'Declaration of Perth', Heath shocked the Scottish Conservative and Unionist conference by saying that he had decided to respond to the clamour for change in Scotland, and in effect committed the Party to a directly elected Scottish Assembly. 'Let there be no doubt about this,' Heath concluded, 'the Conservative Party is determined to effect a real improvement in the machinery of government in Scotland, and it is pledged to give the people of Scotland genuine participation in the making of decisions that affect them all within the historic unity of the United Kingdom.'[64] In August 1968 he set up a Committee of Inquiry, under Alec Home's chairmanship, to 'examine the possibilities of the devolution of greater political responsibilities to Scotland and to report in particular whether there is a place in a reformed system of government for a Scottish Assembly with a legislative function'.[65]

Alec Home assembled a veritable galaxy of the 'great and the good' for this committee, and set up an office in Edinburgh.[66] For the next eighteen months he chaired meetings every four weeks, in addition to travelling the length and breadth of the country, seeking evidence for the Report. More than a thousand witnesses were interviewed. Distinguished experts in their field, Professor A.L. Goodhart, and the former Lord Chancellor, Lord Dilhorne, were invariably impressed by Home's grasp of the material and the careful preparation he had undertaken before meetings.[67] The report was published on 20 March 1970 and nobody could deny the thoroughness of Home's approach. Many Scottish Conservatives had resented the way the Party had been presented with a *fait accompli* at the Perth conference in 1968. This was particularly the case in the West of Scotland, and Home took all these factors into consideration. The report contained thirty-four recommendations, of which the most important were a 'Scottish Convention' with an optimum size of approximately 125 members and the replacement of the old 'Goschen' formula for financing Scotland's government.[68]

The committee's findings evoked a muted response – one cartoon showed a Scotsman carrying a copy of the report from a bookshop with the caption, 'Ah asked for the New English Bible an' look what she gied me!'[69] It was accepted by the Scottish Conservatives at their 1970 conference, and its main recommendations were included in the Conservatives' manifesto for the 1970 general election. After the Conservatives had won that election, the issue was pushed to the back-burner.

With their work on the Constitutional Committee completed, Home wrote to all those who had served over the previous eighteen months: 'I would like to thank you for all the trouble that you took as a member of the Constitutional Committee on Scotland's Government. It was for me a happy and rewarding experience, especially as I was able to preside over people who were so patient and good-tempered. I am grateful for your contribution. At our final meeting we decided that it would be nice to give a lunch or dinner to Ted Heath who was responsible for our coming together. He could manage a luncheon in London on Tuesday, 2nd June. I do hope that you will be able to join us on this occasion. It would be a very pleasant way of winding up our proceedings.'[70] Accordingly, a lunch was held for Edward Heath on 2 June to mark the end of the Committee. Seventeen days later, he became Prime Minister.

Few Prime Ministers of the modern era have prepared so assiduously for eventual responsibility as Edward Heath. He did this against a background of criticism from his own Party, who after the euphoria of the initial honeymoon period never warmed to their leader as a personality. Indeed as Labour did well in the local elections in April and the Conservatives slipped behind Labour in the polls in May, there was even a whispering campaign among backbenchers to bring back Alec Home as leader.[71] By its very nature such stirrings were not documented on paper, nor did they ever reach Alec Home. Had they done so, he would have given the conspirators short shrift.[72] The talk was summer madness, temporarily scotched by Wilson's announcement on 18 May of the dissolution of Parliament.

At the end of January 1970, the shadow Cabinet met at Selsdon Park, a country house hotel near Croydon, to finalise strategy for the general election. 'Selsdon Man' (a phrase coined by Wilson to disparage the gathering) entered the mythology of the Conservative Party; according to some, Selsdon Park was where the Party took a decisive rightward step against the post-war consensus. In fact, it was a co-ordination of many aspects of recent political thinking, particularly from the Steering Group that was working on the manifesto, *A Better Tomorrow*. Discussions centred on questions such as immigration, trade union reform and incomes policy, and the press portrayed the meeting as atavistic – not least on 'law and order'. This was not entirely to the Tory Party's disadvantage: nobody could now claim that the two main parties were interchangeable.

Buoyed up by the opinion polls in May, and exuding confidence as he spoke to the BBC's Political Editor, Hardiman Scott, in the garden at 10 Downing Street, Harold Wilson announced a general election for 18 June. It did not pass unnoticed that the chosen date was Waterloo Day. The result was a severe reversal to public confidence in the ability of the pollsters to predict the result, although the volatility of the electorate made the 1970 campaign a particularly difficult one to assess with great accuracy.

As the campaign got underway, Home was increasingly seen as one of the 'big beasts in the Tory jungle', together with Maudling, Macleod, Whitelaw and Barber.[73] Like many of his colleagues, notably Selwyn Lloyd, he was not optimistic about the outcome. The Scottish

Conservative Party conference took place just before Wilson's announcement, and Home was mainly concerned with presenting his Committee's report on Scotland's government. Off the record, however, he was frank with delegates: 'In Scotland swings are less than in England, so at least we won't do as badly up here.' In another remark reminiscent of Haig in the bleakest days of the First World War, he said, 'In the Conservative Party, we always do our best with our backs to the wall. And all I can say is that it's a damned great wall we're up against now.'[74]

He devoted five days to campaigning in marginal constituencies and was one of the most popular Tory speakers, regularly drawing audiences in excess of 500. There was no doubt, at least, about the outcome in Kinross and West Perthshire, where the figures were: Sir Alec Douglas-Home (Unionist), 14,434; Mrs Elizabeth Whitley (Scottish Nationalist), 4,670; Donald Leach (Labour), 3,827; John Calder (Liberal), 2,228; giving a Unionist majority of 9,764. Overall, the Conservatives won 330 seats; Labour 287, and the Liberal total halved to six. In one fell swoop, the Tories had overturned the incumbent government and achieved a working majority for the incoming government.

On Sunday 14 June (the day that England lost in the World Cup) a general mood of despondency had settled on the Conservative high command. Heath had been recording television interviews, with the advice of Gordon Reece. The inner circle had then patched together a series of private *ad hoc* supper parties to mull over what was to be done after what seemed inevitable Conservative defeat on Thursday. The scenario was plain for all to see. Heath would lose the election on Thursday, and would then be compelled to stand down, indeed it was assumed that he would wish to do so. Into this vacuum would then appear the brooding presence of Enoch Powell, who had put down his marker in the 1965 contest. The question was 'Who could stop Enoch Powell taking over the Conservative Party?'[75] To this hypothetical question, the only answer, even if for the short term, was Alec Home, who was then telephoned at the Hirsel. The feeling of the meeting was communicated to him, and his response was one of understandable caution. The line from the London end was adamant, but Home felt answers should not be sought until events had shown what the questions might be. So it was arranged that Willie Whitelaw would drive over to the Hirsel from his home near Penrith on the Friday after the election defeat and that Reginald Maudling would fly up from London to assess the position. They would take it from there.[76] An awkward follow-up to this 'conspiracy' arose when with a confidence bordering on the hubristic, Heath asked Whitelaw to come to Downing Street on the Friday afternoon 'to help choose the government'. Whitelaw knew that his arrangements for that day were to discuss choosing the new leader.[77]

History records a different outcome. Against all the odds Heath won the election and the principal shadow spokesmen gathered in the lobby to the Cabinet room at 10 Downing Street as they waited their call to office. Alec Home said rather impishly to some of his colleagues, 'And we were due to be meeting at the Hirsel this afternoon!'[78] Six years of opposition were over. The electorate had also decided that it was 'the right moment to change'.

16

Return to the Foreign Office

If the Conservatives had been defeated at the 1970 election, there was an outside possibility that Alec Home could have been brought back as leader of the Party. 'You mean temporarily, as an undertaker?' asked one grandee. 'The word usually used', he was told, 'is caretaker.'[1] There was nothing of the caretaker about his second term at the Foreign Office. His experience on the Foreign and Commonwealth front (and it was to the Foreign *and* Commonwealth Office he now returned[2]) was without equal in contemporary British politics. Lord Rosebery once said that to have an ex-Prime Minister in a Cabinet was 'a fleeting and dangerous luxury'.[3] For Heath the move was not a luxury, but an essential buttress to his administration. Home's seniority gave him a place at the heart of the Heath administration, though he was never one of the inner circle.

Edward Heath and Alec Home were personalities of a very different stamp, but their relationship was one of fruitful harmony and produced its own alchemy, for two reasons: Home's great generosity of spirit towards his successor, and the fact that their interests complemented rather than overlapped each other. With Heath's absorption in the European movement, Home was free to concentrate on East–West relations, Africa, the Middle and the Far East. The warmth of the letters he received from embassies around the world indicated the regard in which he was held. He resumed the tenancy of Dorneywood, for which he and Elizabeth had a special affection, more so than for either Chequers or 10 Downing Street.

Although Maudling had been shadow Foreign Secretary and had hopes of the post, Home's claims were stronger. His experience went back many years and Heath saw the advantages of one who was known to the leading players on the world scene. Had he not been Foreign Secretary, his placing in Cabinet would have been problematic, added to which Heath owed Home a debt of gratitude for his loyalty over the years and it would hardly be a unifying act to retire him at this stage. Maudling went to the Home Office, but the knock-on effect of this appointment was that another post had to be found for Quintin Hogg, the shadow Home Affairs spokesman. A ready solution was to hand: Hogg's father had been Lord Chancellor in pre-war days; Hogg was touched to be offered the Woolsack and threw himself wholeheartedly into the work.[4]

The crucial post was widely seen to be that at the Treasury. Macleod had been shadow Chancellor since August 1965. His preparations for Number 11 Downing Street had been as thorough as Heath's for Number 10 and he was duly appointed on 20 June. At the head of Heath's government were now the two ministers who, in the 1960s, had so often been at odds with each other. With Heath's rival for the leadership at the Home Office, the balance of the triumvirate promised much. Tragically, however, Macleod was denied his inheritance. The first signs of illness came on 20 June, the day of his appointment. On 7 July, after making his only speech in the House of Commons as Chancellor of the Exchequer, he was taken to St George's Hospital for an immediate operation, but on the night of 20 July, had a heart attack and died. He was only fifty-six years old. It could be argued that the Heath government never fully recovered from this blow.

Alec Home was shocked by the news, which was given to him at once. He did not intrude, knowing that Edward Heath and Willie Whitelaw were dealing with all the manifold problems for Macleod's widow, Eve. Apart from the personal sufferings, he realised that Macleod's death would unbalance the Cabinet that Heath had so carefully constructed. A team that contained himself as Foreign Secretary and Macleod as Chancellor, particularly after their differences in 1963, had wide political appeal. For all his qualities, Macleod's successor, Anthony Barber, did not make a similar impact on the public consciousness. As Barber had served as both Economic and Financial Secretary in the Macmillan years, the appointment was natural and had the advantage of avoiding an extensive reshuffle. Geoffrey Rippon now inherited the Duchy of Lancaster, with special responsibility for Europe, and the Home–Rippon team oversaw the central achievement of the Heath government: entry into the European Economic Community on 1 January 1973. Home was by far the oldest member of the administration (he was sixty-seven on 2 July 1970), the average age of which was forty-seven. Many of the dominating figures of the next generation of British politics came to prominence for the first time – Peter Walker, Keith Joseph, James Prior, Geoffrey Howe, Michael Heseltine and, of course, Margaret Thatcher. (Within a year, Alec Home told one of his family that Margaret Thatcher and Neil Kinnock would eventually lead their respective parties.)[5] Robert Carr, a former PPS to Anthony Eden, had the crucial job of masterminding the Industrial Relations Bill. In July 1972 he was to take over the Home Office on the resignation of Reginald Maudling. (Later he was to be the caretaker Leader of the Party at the time of Heath's downfall.) Willie Whitelaw became Lord President of the Council, though his unofficial role as Heath's mentor was possibly more rewarding. He also became one of Home's closest colleagues, a frequent visitor to the Hirsel and Douglas over many years. Nine members of Home's Cabinet of 1964 were in the Cabinet that took office in June 1970.

Home's team at the Foreign Office was one of the most harmonious he had ever worked with. His Minister of State, loyal and dependable, was Joseph Godber. In November 1972 the team was augmented by Julian Amery and Lord Balniel, a fellow Scot. Amery, Macmillan's son-in-law, was a figure Home much admired. Biographer of Joseph Chamberlain, he represented a strand of Conservatism, which though a little out of fashion in the brave new Heathite world, had much care and valour.[6] Among the Under-Secretaries were the Marquess of Lothian, and Anthony Royle, who was to serve for the full term. On 12 November 1970, the Ministry of Overseas Development was subsumed into the Foreign Office; at its head was Richard Wood, third son of the former Foreign Secretary, Lord Halifax. The Permanent Under-Secretary was Sir Denis Greenhill, who was the last to travel widely with the Foreign Secretary. The role became more London-based when the Foreign Secretary was abroad. The respect in which Home held Greenhill was reciprocated in full measure. 'The greatest blessing the Foreign Office can have is an experienced Secretary of State, admired in his own country, respected abroad by friend and foe and gifted with an instinct for foreign affairs,' Greenhill wrote. 'Alec Home combined these with politeness, charm and humour in the daily conduct of business. Ruff's Guide to the Turf always lay on his desk within reach of his right hand and gave an assurance of interests beyond affairs of state.'[7] Further evidence of this was when, at the height of the Icelandic cod war, Home was handed a huge file on the arcane origins of the dispute, with a note suggesting, 'You might care to look at this while at

Douglas' for the weekend. In his spidery hand, Home had added, 'A kindly thought, but an erroneous one'.[8]

Home's Principal Secretary in the Private Office was John Graham, whose experience of the Foreign Office went back to the Eden days. John Graham noted the informality that characterised Home's approach. He liked to walk in from Carlton Gardens, through St James's Park, and start on the paperwork early. Whenever possible he preferred to lunch quietly at the Turf Club. At the end of 1972, one of the great partnerships was forged when Antony Acland, son of his old Christ Church contemporary Peter Acland, who had been his assistant secretary in the early 1960s, became his Principal Private Secretary. Acland scaled the heights of the Foreign Office world, rising to Permanent Under-Secretary and the Washington embassy, before becoming Provost of Eton. Another important figure from 1972 was Michael Alexander, a future Overseas Affairs Secretary to Margaret Thatcher in Downing Street, and Ambassador to NATO. One of the most interesting appointments was beyond the confines of the Civil Service: Miles Hudson, who had been in charge of Rhodesian affairs in the Conservative Central Office from the time of the rebellion, became Home's foreign affairs adviser, with a desk in the Private Office, a pre-echo of the arrangement Home's successor James Callaghan was to have with Tom McNally. They were a happy band, welcoming back one of their own. One sign of the regard in which a Secretary of State is held in the Private Office, notably among the typists, is the display of pictures and cuttings of former masters. 'In the rapid turnover of Foreign Secretaries which occurred in the years immediately after 1963, many a new Minister found, on visiting this room [the Private Office] for the first time, that he had to run the gauntlet of Sir Alec Douglas-Home's features, so enduring was his hold upon their Private Office staff.'[9] His lack of pomposity and general approachability, especially after George Brown, were much appreciated.

Morale was not high when Home returned in the summer of 1970. The Duncan Report on Overseas Representation in 1969 had proposed a time of retrenchment which many felt profoundly misguided.[10] It was shelved after the general election, but one of its recommendations – enhanced provision for the News Department – did bear fruit and John Leahy became one of Home's constant and much respected aides as head of that department.[11] Another key figure in the team was John McDonnell, a past President of the Oxford Union, who joined the Diplomatic Service from the Conservative Research Department to become the Assistant Private Secretary with responsibility for speeches. His legal background was also of great help in avoiding unnecessary ambiguity. Home's draft speeches of this time are an insight into the way in which the office worked: an initial outline would be prepared and typed up, on which Home would make his emendations, often by drawing an oblong around unsatisfactory paragraphs, scoring them out and inserting new, and invariably shorter ones alongside. This process would be repeated several times until he was satisfied with the overall shape and detail. 'Mr McDonnell: It might be an idea to follow up the above thoughts' was a typical post-script to the initial scribblings.[12]

Home's predecessor but one, George Brown, had caused tremendous offence in the service by his calculated rudeness, most notoriously to Lady Reilly, the wife of Sir Patrick Reilly, Ambassador in Paris from 1965 to 1968, whom he twice accused at a dinner for Prime Minister Pompidou at the French Embassy in London of being unfit to be an Ambassador's wife. But his successor, Michael Stewart, whom Sir Nicholas Henderson has described as 'an unsung Foreign Secretary',[13] was a stolid, if not stylish Chief. With the advent of Home, morale continued to improve. Brown had inhabited a Forsterian world of 'telegrams and anger'; Stewart and Home were a welcome return to a more effective and traditional way of conducting business. Indeed, nothing more symbolised the return of courtesy than Alec Home's first representational duty in June 1970, to host a reception that had been arranged by Michael Stewart, when he invited Stewart to be alongside him in the receiving line.[14] Home and Stewart had, in fact, much in common, and both had that invaluable quality of bringing out the best in people. During Michael Stewart's time, the key word officials remembered was 'Mankind'; with Alec Home, it was 'Reconciliation'. The two concepts contributed to a sense of continuity, on which James Callaghan was able to build in 1974.

The first Cabinet meeting of the new administration was on 23 June, and one of its major problems was the question of arms sales to South Africa. On his visit to Vorster in 1968, Home had pledged the resumption of sales, the abandonment of which he said was contrary to the Simonstown Agreement of 1954. The arms would be limited to weapons needed for the maritime defence of the sea-routes. This decision led to the first row of the Heath administration and a serious alienation of Commonwealth opinion. The problem arose because Britain's realigned foreign policy came into conflict with established Commonwealth policy. In a lecture to the Ditchley Foundation on 19

July 1968, Home had emphasised that access to South African ports under the Simonstown Agreement 'will be of great value in terms of the defence of Western Europe from interference with her oil supplies and that it will in effect become an informal extension of the NATO defences'.[15] Accordingly he announced in the House of Commons on 21 July that Britain planned to resume arms sales to South Africa for external defence of the sea-routes, but only after consulting the Commonwealth. He had expected a furore, but not to the extent that actually occurred. Macmillan privately suggested a Commonwealth Defence Conference of Foreign Ministers so that Home could emphasise the importance of the Commonwealth in the defence of the East from Russia and China. Macmillan felt that whatever was then decided about South Africa and Simonstown would be seen in the context of a much wider framework, making it easier for some of the African leaders to content themselves with mild protests rather than leaving the Commonwealth, which President Nyerere of Tanzania had threatened in a meeting with Heath at Chequers on 11 October.[16]

The decision to resume arms sales was taken in Downing Street; Home's task was to implement the policy, with which he fully agreed but, unlike the sale of Leyland buses to Cuba, based entirely on commercial considerations, the South African issue had wider implications. As different factions occupied increasingly entrenched positions, Home made it clear that Britain was not going to be told what to do by African Commonwealth countries, though he conceded that no decision would be announced until Parliament reassembled in October. The problem was brought into the open at the Commonwealth Prime Ministers' Conference in Singapore from 14 to 22 January 1971. Milton Obote, President of Uganda from 1966 until the military coup that brought Idi Amin to power later in 1971, was especially incensed and there were difficult meetings between Obote and Heath at this Conference. (One of the consequences was that Britain initially reacted to Amin far more favourably than later events justified. Home was horrified in July 1971 when Amin invited himself to Britain and told the Foreign Secretary, at a Number 10 dinner, that he was thinking of sending bombers to raid Tanzania, where Obote was in exile.)[17] A formula was agreed, but it was a tortuous compromise. Douglas Hurd, Heath's secretary, recorded the outcome. 'There was to be a study group to examine the security of trade routes in the South Atlantic and the Indian Ocean. There was to be a declaration of Commonwealth Principles, ruling out racial discrimination. Britain was not bound to withhold arms from South Africa while the study group was at work; nor were the African states bound to stay in the Commonwealth if such arms were supplied.'[18] There was an element of bravado in the government's action. The resumption was not a manifesto commitment, and 'It stirred up emotions which were better left quiet'.[19] Part of the controversy arose because the officials were unusually passive. It was just after the election and there was no desire to 'manage' a new government. Had it arisen at a different time in the electoral cycle, there would have been greater resistance and warning of the dangers at an early stage.[20] For the first few months in office Home was under pressure to do a lot of backtracking, particularly from liberal Tories such as David Lane, a future Chairman of the Race Relations Board. An early day motion had been put down in July 1970 by a dissenting group of younger Conservative backbenchers, mainly from the recent intake, urging that, should it be necessary to supply South Africa with equipment for the defence of the Cape route, 'then Her Majesty's Government should ensure that no equipment is supplied which might be used for the furtherance of apartheid or to the detriment of Great Britain's Commonwealth partners north of the Zambesi, and should make it clear that any such supplies imply no approval of South Africa's policy of apartheid'.[21] Some of the signatories wrote directly to the Foreign Secretary. Overall it was a difficult beginning to the second term.

Controversy was the background to much of the four years of the Heath government. The parliamentary atmosphere, which Home had found alien in 1963, was even more confrontational seven years later. He regretted most the decline in courtesy and good manners. As the House of Commons frequently sat through the night, Home, who was now in his late sixties, had the burden of all-night sessions in addition to his inevitable round of representational and diplomatic meetings. The paperwork had also increased out of all proportion; incoming telegrams in 1962 had totalled 75,391, and outgoing ones 155,020; by 1972 the figures were 231,269 and 391,859.[22] Such a burden would have taken its toll of a much younger man, and until he had worked out a *modus vivendi*, he seemed tired and listless.

The Foreign Office was in a state of transition on Alec Home's return, in the wake of the Plowden and Duncan Reports. In the immediate post-war period the Foreign Secretary was in the business of 'doing' things at a time when Britain was still clinging tenuously to its superpower status. Post Suez, the role was more selectively interventionist, though Home always believed that Britain, 'present at the creation' of the post-war world, should punch above its weight. This was not a question of being at the top table or on the front row for photo calls. Twenty years later few television news broadcasts would be complete without footage of the Foreign Secretary of the day disembarking at some far-flung airport and rushing to the negotiating table (stocked with neat rows of unopened bottles of mineral water and soft drinks) before appearing at a news conference. Alec Home had no time for such summitry. He simply did not believe that the international treadmill was the best place for the Foreign Secretary. Yet, ironically, one of the reasons his staff respected Home was because he had been on personal terms with world figures for the best part of twenty years; he spoke their language and knew the niceties.

Home did not inherit an easy legacy, but few foreign ministers do. The Labour government's commitment to reduce forces east of Suez led to many anxious dealings with the Shah of Iran, over which Home took immense care. At such meetings, he preferred to take decisions after hearing advice from more junior staff than was customary, so that the Office as a whole were involved in policy and understood its direction, an approach Lloyd had favoured and which was still remembered. Home drew on experts wisely, respecting their deeper knowledge of the background and the technicalities, which he did not go into unnecessarily.

His main aims now were the reduction of tension in the Middle East and paving the way for an eventual settlement in Rhodesia. Both were seemingly intractable problems and Britain's ability to make a valid contribution, particularly in the Middle East, was open to question in many quarters. Home saw his task as being to balance the European emphasis of the Heath government with a close relationship with the recently elected Nixon administration in Washington. He had known and admired Nixon for many years, an admiration which survived Watergate.[23] With the emphasis on Europe at 10 Downing Street, Home became the contact for Dr Henry Kissinger, whose global influence after his appointment as America's Secretary of State in July 1973 was of special significance. Remembering the role Lord Harlech had played, Home recommended the appointment of the Earl of Cromer, former Governor of the Bank of England, as Ambassador to succeed John Freeman in Washington in November 1970. Cromer was invaluable in persuading the Americans that Britain's European commitment would stimulate, not hinder, transatlantic commercial ties.[24]

When Home took office in the summer of 1970, the Six Day War (5–10 June 1967) was a recent memory, its political consequences still uncertain, despite UN Resolution 242 having been adopted as the basis for a permanent settlement. Nasser's position as acknowledged leader of Arab nationalism was gravely weakened by the Six Day War and the Middle East remained a crucible of conflict and mistrust. Home decided that one of his first pronouncements on foreign affairs should be a survey of the Arab–Israeli situation. It was planned that he would deliver this speech at a meeting in Harrogate on 31 October and over the summer the Near Eastern Department of the Foreign Office worked on the background material. Four weeks before Home was due to speak in Harrogate, Nasser died of a heart attack while mediating in the Jordanian civil war.

Home had attended many funerals in his official capacity, but none in his memory equalled Nasser's in its combination of chaos, hysteria, grief and danger.[25] The British party consisted of the Secretary of State, Sir John Graham, the PPS and John McDonnell, who was working on the Harrogate speech. At the last moment George Brown asked if he could have a lift in the Foreign Office plane. As a former Foreign Secretary, renowned for his pro-Arab stance, Brown could hardly be refused and Home's response was of the cheerful 'good to have you aboard' type. Nevertheless with folk memories still strong of Brown's behaviour at the time of Kennedy's death, and his recent unofficial Middle East tour which had left a trail of recrimination and controversy, there was a certain apprehension as he boarded the plane.[26] But he played only a walk-on role in the ensuing drama. The British party, badly affected by the injections they had been given, were transported through deserted streets to the Cairo embassy in a rickety army jeep. Shepheard's Hotel had been taken over by the military and food and water were in short supply outside the diplomatic compound. Security was non-existent.

The funeral the next day on an island in the Nile went on for hours, and eventually the British delegation had to make their way back to the embassy as best they could through keening mobs. They passed a hefty policeman sobbing by his motor-bike at the side of the road and found a tent and a queue that Home thought was the opportunity to say goodbye to their Egyptian hosts. By the time it transpired that it was Yasser Arafat and Colonel Gaddafi holding court for their followers, it was too late to withdraw, though it is doubtful if the two leaders were aware that they had silently shaken the hand of Her Britannic Majesty's Principal Secretary of State for Foreign Affairs. George Brown was separated from the main party and there were fears for his safety. Eventually Nasser's coffin was helicoptered on to the island by the Russians, by which time the Secretary of State was sitting on the terrace of the embassy with his drink, the sun beginning to dip below the horizon. A death's head moth splattered itself into oblivion on the windows of the embassy: 'Will the spirit of Nasser forever haunt the British?' asked the Ambassador. That evening the party flew back to Britain, ensuring that George Brown, who by this time was much the worse for wear, was safely on board. The plane put down briefly in Morocco, where there had just been an unsuccessful *coup*, with shootings at a garden party. (Later when asked for arrangements for a Moroccan delegation, Home insisted 'No garden parties!') On arrival at Heathrow, George Brown came down the steps of the aircraft, embracing the reception party on the tarmac, as he set foot on British soil again. For many reasons, it had been an unforgettable two days.[27]

The importance Alec Home attached to his speech in Harrogate can be gauged from the fact that he printed it in full as an appendix to his memoirs.[28] He began by saying that the most difficult and dangerous of all the problems facing the government was the conflict between Israel and her Arab neighbours; 'the oldest battlefield in the world' was still the meeting point of irreconcilables. The Arab–Israeli struggle seemed intractable: 'Both sides believe that force is legitimate and necessary for them to achieve their goals. And so the dispute drags on from crisis to crisis, with all the waste and bloodshed that involves ...' Implementation of UN Resolution 242 offered the best hope, based as it was on 'the inadmissibility of the acquisition of territory by war, and the need for a just and lasting peace, in which every State in the area is guaranteed the right to live in security'. This would entail the withdrawal of the Israeli forces from the occupied territories, but Home recognised that no outsider could prescribe where the recognised boundaries should be. Even if a settlement were achieved, the problem of Jerusalem would remain. But if the opportunity for lasting peace were lost, 'we may face another twenty years of tension and strife ... and with the risks of confrontation between the major Powers increasing'.[29]

The importance of the speech was that in the course of it a British Foreign Secretary outlined a serious and deeply considered strategy. It was far removed from the simplistic jingoism that Party conferences encouraged – a return to the kind of comprehensive survey Eden had given to the San Francisco conference in April 1945 or Bevin to the United Nations in Paris in September 1948.[30] Home was aware that the Israelis would take offence at his suggestion of withdrawal and that the Foreign Office would as usual be accused of pro-Arab bias. But his belief was that a longer perspective was needed. In an article entitled 'The World Sir Alec Finds', *The Economist* commented that 'his chief asset is his ability to see the international scene as a whole: to relate the day-to-day problems of the Foreign Office to a longer term picture of what Britain should be doing in the world'.[31] In July he was much concerned to improve relations with Spain, as Lord Mountbatten wrote in a letter to Prince Juan Carlos: 'Last night at a dinner party I talked to our new Foreign Secretary Alec Douglas-Home and our ambassador at Madrid John Russell together about future policy vis-a-vis Spain and we all three agreed relations between our countries would greatly improve once the Gibraltar blockade was lifted, however quietly and discreetly this was done.'[32]

The same day as Mountbatten's letter, Home flew to Paris for talks with his opposite number, Maurice Schumann, on reviving the British application to join the EEC. There were metaphorical and actual bouquets all round – 'such as had hardly been exchanged since General de Gaulle returned to power in 1958'.[33]

On 6 September, however, Heath's government faced a dangerous international crisis, when the Popular Front for the Liberation of Palestine hijacked four aircraft. One of these, an Israeli El Al flight en route for New York, put down at Heathrow after one of the hijackers was killed, and an Arab woman, Leila Khaled, was arrested and held under the Aliens Order. Other hijackings followed, including that of a BOAC VC-10, bound from Bombay to London, which was taken with its 113 passengers to Dawson's Airfield in Jordan, in the midst of the civil war. A decision on whether Khaled should be prosecuted depended on whether she came under the jurisdiction of the British courts, but political and humanitarian issues complicated the legal and moral dilemma. On 12 September, after taking advice from the British embassy in Amman, Home decided that the hostages would be at greater risk if the prosecution went ahead. On 27 September, the decision was taken not to prosecute, and three days later the British hostages were released. 'We are beset with hi-jackers of all kinds,' Home wrote at the time.[34]

In December 1970, in a debate on foreign affairs, Home outlined the British government's feelings about the worsening situation in Vietnam.

President Nixon had put forward cease-fire proposals in October, as well as ideas for an Indo-China peace conference, Home had asked Gromyko if he would, as co-chairman, join in reconvening the Geneva Conference, but Gromyko had given a dusty answer about the time not being appropriate.[35]

Home's frustration with Gromyko became clear in the expulsion of 105 Russian spies on 24 September 1971, one of the most important episodes of his second spell at the Foreign Office. Many of his advisers had misgivings about the extent of Russian retaliation, but Home was convinced that a stand had to be taken on the *scale* of Russian spying in Britain, which he regarded as contempt of the host country. The considerable increase in Soviet accreditation, especially at the Trade Delegation in Highgate, was confirmed as being espionage-linked by a KGB officer, Oleg Lyalin, who defected from the Delegation. Upwards of 300 'officials' (out of a total of 550) were actively engaged in espionage activities. Home saw Gromyko privately to convey the view that the brazen extent of such activity was unacceptable. When this produced no results, he gave Gromyko two written warnings. The first letter on 3 December 1970 referred back to their meeting in October over F.D. Kudashkin:

> The case of F.D. Kudashkin is by no means isolated, and it is with regret that, after the enjoyable and constructive discussions I had with you in London, I find myself constrained to write to you about the scale and nature of the intelligence activities conducted by Soviet officials in this country and about the frequency of the attempts which have been made in recent months to introduce into this country officials who, in the past, have been engaged in such activities.
>
> In 1970 alone we have refused visas to more than half a dozen Soviet officials assigned to this country because we had every reason to suspect, on the basis of what we know about their previous activities, that if they were admitted to this country they would not restrict themselves to work which we regard as legitimate and conducive to the maintenance and development of good relations.

Home went on to detail specific examples of transgression by members of the Soviet Trade Delegation. Adopting the Robert Kennedy tactic of always allowing an opponent an opportunity for a dignified climb-down without loss of face, Home ended in an emollient tone.

> When you were in London, you said that Anglo–Soviet relations could not be described as bad, but that more could be done for their development and improvement.
>
> In this letter I have indicated a field which is becoming an increasing obstacle to the development of our relations, and with regard to which the kind of improvement of which you spoke would be most welcome . . . I hope that this personal letter to you will be handled in the spirit of your opening remarks to the Prime Minister and yourself during your visit to London.[36]

There was no reply to this communication. A further letter was delivered on 4 August 1971. If the first letter had been the footballing equivalent of the yellow card, this second letter was be the red card. After further detailing the large-scale Soviet espionage in Britain, Alec Home continued:

> This is not the first time that I have had occasion to bring such matters to your attention. I spoke to you on the subject during your visit to London in October 1971.
>
> I did so in a manner which would have permitted the question to be pursued in a non-polemical way. You suggested that I should write you a letter and on 3 December I did so.
>
> To this date to my surprise I have received no reply, nor even an acknowledgement. Meanwhile inadmissible Soviet activities in this country continue unabated.
>
> I ask you to reflect upon this and to consider the extent to which these activities are obstructing the development of Anglo–Soviet relations . . . I trust that you will now feel able to reply to my original letter and to this one which I send in the hope that you will say that you are ready immediately to terminate such activities.[37]

No reply was received to this letter. Accordingly, Sir Denis Greenhill summoned Ivan Ippolitov, the Soviet Charge d'Affaires, to the Foreign Office to be given the names of the 105 Russians who would not be allowed to remain in Britain. When the expulsions were enacted, the Soviet ambassador in London did not (as was usual) ask for details on each case, though Home had explicit evidence for all 105 names. Had there been significant retaliation from Moscow, Home had an even longer list for a second expulsion and Soviet intelligence was aware of this. The operation was described by Peter Wright as 'a brilliant coup'[38] and Colonel Mikhail Lyubimov, chief of the KGB's anti-British operations in the early 1970s, later admitted, 'The station of the KGB was really destroyed.'[39]

There was a feeling that the Wilson government had let things slip; the Russians regarded Britain as a pushover. The main objective in expelling the 105 spies was that longer-term relations could be clarified and made more productive. The expulsions coincided with a change of British ambassador in Moscow, with the retirement of Sir Duncan Wilson, and Home was well aware that this could cause difficulties for the new ambassador Sir John Killick, who took over on 9 September 1971, a fortnight before the balloon went up. The resolve of Sir John and Lady Killick, under what was to be severe provocation, was a vital contribution to the success of the operation. The main obstacle was to carry the Cabinet, where Home met with much scepticism, especially from Reginald Maudling, the Home Secretary. Once the expulsions had been accomplished, Britain was taken more seriously, especially in the newly established CSCE (Conference on Security and Co-operation in Europe).

Alec Home was quite unmoved by the press and public excitement following the expulsions, and flew the next day to New York, where Gromyko confronted him in an angry meeting and warned that it was very dangerous for Britain to threaten the Soviet Union. Gromyko expected a conciliatory response or belligerence, which could have led to further difficulties. Home's reaction was neither of these; he burst out laughing. 'Do you really think', he asked Gromyko through the interpreter 'that Britain can "threaten" your country? I am flattered to think that this is the case.' He felt no personal animosity, he said, as obviously Gromyko did not know what the KGB were doing and he had hoped to be helpful in letting him know who all these KGB people were. The combination of politeness and put-down deflated Gromyko, making him appear a mere functionary who was not *au fait* with the USSR espionage programme.[40] Gromyko never quite knew at such times whether Home was speaking tongue-in-cheek, as on the occasion when the ballerina Natalia Makarova defected to the American Ballet Theatre, and Home told him that this was what cultural exchanges were all about.

One aspect of the expulsions that most pleased Alec Home was the fact that in Russia, where the KGB's hold on the best flats, transport and restaurants was resented by ordinary Muscovites, the expulsions raised no glimmer of protest. In truth, many Russians, in so far as they heard the full details, were delighted that this body had received such a public rebuff. In expelling 105 diplomats Alec Home made it clear that the zero option was one the British Government were prepared to countenance. In the long term, relations were soon back to normal, and in December 1973 Home was invited on an official visit to Moscow. The whole episode, an epitome of Alec Home's approach, considerably enhanced Britain's position and encouraged other European governments to stand out against Soviet infiltration. At the time many in the Foreign Office marvelled at Home's nerve, one figure comparing him to Ernie Bervin, neither of them intellectuals, but both with an innate commonsense and the ability to speak out clearly. There was no accommodation for 'Emperor's clothes' in their FO.

In one other 'espionage' matter Home showed this same directness. J.C. Masterman, his tutor at Christ Church, who had been chairman of the Twenty (or 'Double-Cross') Committee during the Second World War, had written his memoirs, *The Double Cross System*, a quarter of a century earlier and wanted to publish them. Official permission had been consistently withheld, most recently by the Labour government in April 1970, on grounds of national security. Masterman then sought an American publisher, taking the risk of prosecution in Britain. Sir Dick White, the former head of MI5, and the Permanent Under-Secretary, Sir Denis Greenhill, met Alec Home to decide the course of action. Ironically, all three had been pupils of Masterman. Alec Home's reaction, which infuriated White, was 'If I can't trust my old tutor, who can I trust?'[41] Home also held a tripartite meeting with Masterman and the Home Secretary, Reginald Maudling, when it was explained to Masterman that the matter would be resolved by the legal opinion of the Attorney-General. Eventually the book, which was described by Ronald Lewin as 'a record of the double agent story unequalled in its authority',[42] was published in America in February 1972; when the British edition followed, the government took 50 per cent of the royalties.

While he was in America that autumn, Alec Home indulged in a little 'spying' of his own. On 30 September he was having substantive talks on Laos with President Nixon and Dr Henry Kissinger in the Oval Office, and was surprised that no notes were being taken. His deduction was that the meeting was being taped, and discreet enquiries revealed this was so. The British government had uncovered the taping system which led to Nixon's downfall.[43]

Home returned from the United Nations for the debate on British entry to the EEC. Heath announced that Conservative MPs would be allowed a free vote, though Home, together with Carrington and Maudling, felt such an arrangement was far from ideal in a matter of such national importance.[44] Although Home is often seen as playing a secondary role in the EEC applications of 1961 3 and 1970–2, his commitment to entry, especially his firm line as opposition leader, gave Heath a base to build on, and as chairman of the European Policy Committee, he had co-ordinated Rippon's work, and played a part in the build-up to the decisive vote by opening the debate. The voting on 28 October 1971 (appropriately the first night of Sadler's Wells Opera's new production of Verdi's *The Force of Destiny*) resulted in a government majority of 112 (356 to 244), even though 39 Conservative MPs voted against entry and two abstained. The 69 votes from Labour MPs gave Heath a comfortable margin. He won the vote, but was never to win the hearts of British people on the issue, least of all a determined anti-European wing of his own party. On the day that Heath signed the Treaty of Accession at the Egmont Palace in Brussels, with Alec Home on his right and Geoffrey Rippon on his left, he was spattered with ink by a German protestor, an unhappy reminder of his entry into Downing Street on 19 June 1970 when paint was thrown over him. Although the protest was not about the EEC, the incident marred the day. The ceremony was delayed whilst Heath changed, and then almost had to be delayed further when Alec Home could not be found. With all the attention given to Heath, who had suffered a direct hit, Home had quietly found a room in the palace to take off and clean his own spattered shirt. He was eventually tracked down and the ceremony proceeded. On 17 February 1972, the second reading was treated as a vote of confidence, and with the Labour MPs returning to their fold, the government whips had to draw on all their resources; Alec Home was even called back from the Far East. Although the government survived by a majority of 8 (309 to 301), 15 Conservative MPs voted against the Bill, and four abstained. Britain formally joined the EEC on 1 January 1973, and Home busied himself studying the requirements of the Council of Ministers; he was critical of many of the bureaucratic arrangements. He believed, for instance, that the policy of a six-month presidency of the Council did not give sufficient time to settle into the job. When his advisers pointed out that this was an unavoidable by-product of the increased number of member countries and that Britain would not get her 'turn' again during his political lifetime, he replied, 'Well, I could be back in ten years.' It was not an entirely flippant remark.[45]

The major concern of Home's second term at the Foreign Office was Southern Rhodesia, which he had been dealing with in September 1964, just before leaving Downing Street. Rhodesia to the Conservative Party was the equivalent of ancient territories marked 'Here be dragons'; dissent from both right and left of the Party bedevilled Home's efforts to reach a solution. At the Commonwealth Prime Ministers' Conference in Lagos in January 1966, Wilson had unwisely said that 'the cumulative effects of the economic and financial sanctions might well bring the rebellion to an end within a matter of weeks rather than months'.[46] Yet an agreement with Smith had evaded the Wilson government, despite the two series of talks on *HMS Tiger* in December 1966 and *HMS Fearless* in August 1968, not least because the two Prime Ministers could not establish any personal rapport.

Both Heath and Home wanted to resolve one of the last of the great colonial problems and the task of finding a basis for fresh negotiations was a high priority. As with the South African arms controversy, Home had discussions with Macmillan over courses of action, and both agreed that preliminary soundings would be a prerequisite, the origin of the various missions by Lord Goodman, who had worked in a similar capacity for Wilson. Though initially Macmillan had felt that his former PPS, Freddie Bishop, might be a suitable emissary, or a South African businessman such as Harry Oppenheimer (Chairman of the Anglo-American Corporation), Home's first choice for the role was Evelyn Baring, the former Governor of Southern Rhodesia and of Kenya; but he declined the Foreign Secretary's invitation.[47] The question was what to do in the event of complete failure. Macmillan felt that a formal report to the UN Sanctions Committee giving practical proof that no country except Britain attempted to apply sanctions, would be an essential preliminary to giving them up on the grounds that nobody worked them. But even if sanctions then ended, the problem of our relations with Rhodesia would remain. Macmillan did not hold out high hopes, believing that Britain would have to admit that she had lost the contest. An Act of Parliament could then follow, declaring that the crown no longer claimed any authority in Rhodesia and the situation would be analagous to that when South Africa left the Commonwealth. It was a pessimistic scenario, but a realistic one Home felt. He did not go into the Rhodesian negotiations of 1971 with any false expectations, but he felt that the government could not neglect a problem because it seemed intractable.[48] In any event, the 1970 election manifesto had pledged action. Miles Hudson, his Political Adviser, was asked to prepare background papers. His assessment laid stress on the attitudes the government would face from their own supporters:

> There is a strong political case for us being as forthcoming as possible in the initial correspondence with Mr Smith without prejudicing our bargaining position. It would be a pity if negotiations never got off the ground at all because Mr Smith thought that we were prepared to make no concessions of any kind over and above what the Labour government was prepared to do, and in particular if he thought that we were not prepared to take his present constitution as a starting point to be adapted to meet the five principles. We would be in a stronger position with our right wing were you to have met Mr Smith and to have failed to reach agreement than if you were not to have met him at all. Mr Smith will clearly not reveal his hand in the preliminary exchanges and it is possible that he might be prepared to concede in a face to face meeting more than is immediately apparent now. If he is, well and good: if he is not, we will not have lost anything provided that we have not conceded any points of principle in the initial correspondence. We would be able to argue that we had made a real effort.[49]

Home felt that this assessment summed up his options succinctly and fairly. In May 1969, following the failure of the *HMS Fearless* talks, Smith had introduced a constitution based on white supremacy, far removed from the Five Principles over which Home and Smith had engaged in 1964, and it was on this constitution that much of the discussions would hinge. One of the strengths Home brought to the fresh round of talks came from his preparedness to admit that if things had gone wrong previously, they should be put right. Although Home was felt to be straightforward, he was ready to consider all the options on the political chessboard. He was not politically naive over Rhodesia and knew that many of his difficulties would come from his own Party (23 Conservative MPs had voted against the government motion to renew sanctions on 9 November 1970)[50], but he played subtly upon the underlying sympathy the Party felt about the way he had been treated in the months after October 1964. He was thus able to achieve by persuasion what might have been denied to another despite the three-way split in the Tory Party.[51] Of all British politicians of that time, he was the one best placed to achieve a settlement with Smith. Smith respected Home as an 'outdoor' sort of person, one whose word could be trusted, unlike some other Conservatives of whom he was very critical. For his part, Home remembered Smith's bravery as an RAF pilot during the Second World War and felt that he was the prisoner of hardliners in his own party. Home was given a free hand to deal with Rhodesia as he felt best. In November 1970 Smith had begun a secret correspondence with Home, in which he emphasised that, in any forthcoming talks, Rhodesia would not be negotiating out of weakness. Nevertheless, he was keen to get the issue settled, as long as the terms were acceptable.[52] On the basis of this correspondence, Lord Goodman went to Salisbury to resume negotiations in April 1971. Goodman's involvement in the Rhodesian negotiations dated back to 1968, when he had paved the way (together with Sir Max Aitken) for the talks on *HMS Fearless* between Wilson and Smith. On the understanding that he was working not for any political party but for the country, Goodman, again accompanied by Aitken, accepted the government's invitation to visit Rhodesia in April 1971, as a preliminary to possible negotiations. This was the first of four meetings that year before the final visit in November, when Home headed the British team. For Smith, Wilson was the archetypal school swot ('Please, sir, you haven't set the prep') and there was always an underlying clash of personalities, something absent in Smith's dealings with Home.

Goodman's initial talks centred once more on the Five Principles, which the British Parliament had laid down as the necessary framework for a settlement. These principles stated that there should be unimpeded progress to majority rule as stated in the 1961 Constitution; guarantees against retrogressive amendment of the constitution; an immediate improvement in the political status of the African population; progress towards ending racial discrimination; and that the basis for independence should be acceptable to the people of Rhodesia as a whole.

Despite the demands of the Rhodesian Front (the white ruling party led by Smith) in October 1971 that attempts at a settlement with the British be abandoned, Smith insisted that final talks begin on 15 November. Home's first task, before leaving for Rhodesia, was to find a chairman as head of the Commission which would test the acceptability of the proposals in the event of an agreement between himself and Smith. This did not prove an easy task, as November was not the best of times to assemble a team at short notice. Home's initial preference had been for Lord Radcliffe, the epitome of 'the great and the good', first chairman of the Broadcasting Committee established by the post-war Labour government, and more recently of the Vassall Tribunal in 1963 and a member of the Committee of Privy Councillors in the 'D' Notice Enquiry of 1967. But he was unavailable, as was Lord Denning, who headed the inquiry into the Profumo Case in 1963. Goodman would have preferred the former Lord Chancellor, Lord Dilhorne.[53] Home finally chose Lord Pearce, a Lord of Appeal in Ordinary, and wrote to him on 11 November. Of the outline terms of reference, Home said:

> We shall not of course wish to impose these on you but we have naturally been giving some thought to the matter. We will give you all possible support, so please let me know if there is anything you think is needed ... I cannot be sure that we will be able to reach an agreement; and of course if we do not all this will fall through. If, however, as I hope, we can get a settlement, I shall be in touch with you again to confirm formally your appointment and terms of reference.[54]

Elizabeth accompanied Alec Home to Rhodesia on 14 November. The party included Lord Goodman; Sir Peter Rawlinson, the Attorney-General; Sir Denis Greenhill, the Permanent Under-Secretary; Martin Le Quesne, the Deputy Under-Secretary, together with Philip Adams, Assistant Under-Secretary; Philip Mansfield, Head of the Rhodesian Department, and Jeremy Varcoe, later Deputy Secretary-General on the Pearce Commission. As the plane was bound for a country regarded as a pariah by the international community, a long circuitous flight of great discomfort, avoiding various countries, followed. Although Alec and Elizabeth Home were given bunks in a cabin, others had to make the best of whatever mattresses were available, an arrangement that caused some trepidation to Peter Rawlinson who was billeted close to 'the vast bulk of Lord Goodman' and 'prayed that the pilot had a steady hand and would have no need suddenly to bank'.[55] Home was taken to Mirimba House, the British High Commissioner's residence in Salisbury until UDI, where he was to meet many of the African leaders during his ten days in Rhodesia.

Within a few hours of arriving, the teams went into the first plenary session of talks held at the Cabinet Office of Smith's government. The main participants were Alec Home for the British government, together with Goodman, Rawlinson and Greenhill, with, on the Rhodesian side of the table, Smith, Jack Howman, his Minister for Foreign Affairs, and Desmond Lardner-Burke, the Justice Minister. The atmosphere was tense, with both sides feeling their way, and the intellectual imbalance between the delegations at once apparent. Smith relied almost entirely on the advice of his Attorney-General, Jack Gayland, and preferred face-to-face meetings with Home in his own small office, rather than the plenary sessions. Home's contribution smoothed the way. 'In the negotiations, Alec showed exemplary patience, was devoid of partisan feeling, dispassionate and represented his government's viewpoint without fear or favour', Lord Goodman later recalled.[56] It was largely owing to Home's advocacy that the British delegation were allowed to meet some of the African leaders. Joshua Nkomo, leader of the Matabele, was brought in a Black Maria van from prison to meet Home on the lawns of the High Commissioner's house. What struck the British as Nkomo emerged was that he completely dominated by force of personality his white Rhodesian guards. Nkomo at the time was regarded as the African most likely to emerge in the long term, rather than Robert Mugabe, the left-wing leader of the Shona people, first Prime Minister and later President of the independent Zimbabwe from 1980. The visit of Nkomo emphasised to Alec Home the personal circumstances of many of the black leaders; this was the first time he had met a person serving a custodial sentence since his visit to William in Wakefield gaol during the war. Nkomo's first request was to be allowed to retire to the lavatory. When he did not return after some time, there was a momentary thought that he had perhaps absconded, but when he eventually rejoined the party on the High Commissioner's lawns he said that he had wanted to savour every moment of freedom – in prison he had an escort everywhere. Over many hours of talks, both on this visit and later, Nkomo reiterated that no solution short of NIBMAR (No Independence Before Majority Rule) would be acceptable, whereas Home argued that a compromise settlement with Smith which would lead to NIBMAR should be grasped as the only alternative to a bitter war. Home was in no doubt that he was in the presence of a big man in every sense of the word. When Nkomo was taken back to prison, it took two strong men to prise the legs of the steel chair on which he had sat, from the grip of the lawn, so deeply had it sunk into the ground.[57] Other African leaders voiced their dissent, including the leader of the Methodist Church, Bishop Abel Muzorewa. The Reverend Ndabaningi Sithole, leader of ZANU (Zimbabwe African National Union), who was serving a six-year sentence, was not permitted to see Home but smuggled a message to him which left no doubt of ZANU's uncompromising rejection of any weakening of British policy: white minority rule would never advance the political status of the African majority.

The fine print was pored over by both sides, until it became clear that they were in sight of agreement within the terms of the Five Principles. On 19 November, the *Mercury News*, published in Bulawayo and Salisbury, reported that a settlement was imminent, but warned that both African leaders and extreme right-wing whites feared a 'sell-out'.[58] 'Well, that's it I suppose,' said Smith, as the last point was agreed. 'I suppose it is,' replied Home.[59] The agreement was announced on 24 November, to acclamation from the white population. Goodman had returned to London and Home wrote to him immediately. 'We concluded only a few minutes after you left ... The final product is as good as I think we had any right to expect and a good deal better than often seemed possible.' He thanked Goodman for his 'tireless energy and unmatched ingenuity'.[60]

However, the problems were just beginning. Smith had conceded the principle of majority rule, but the timetable for this goal would never be acceptable to the African population – and their mistrust of Smith was total. Clauses about a Declaration of Rights and a commission to investigate racial discrimination did not alter the fact that the basis of the settlement was an amended version of Smith's 1969 constitution. The white population were of course in favour, but the African leaders – Nkomo, Mugabe, Muzorewa and Sithole – were united in their opposition. Smith's belief, shared by Home, that the agreement would be acceptable to the African population was unrealistic. In December, the hitherto antagonistic parties, ZANU and ZAPU (Zimbabwe African People's Union) joined forces to campaign against the settlement.

On his return to London, Home announced the appointment of Lord Pearce to head the commission to test acceptability. Following the debate in the House of Commons on the issue, Home wrote to Pearce on 3 December:

> After the debates in Parliament it will now be possible for the Commission which you are to chair to tell the people of Rhodesia that the proposals in the White Paper are the decisive recommendation of the British government. I recall that in the case of the explanations given to the Africans in respect of the Central African Federation the first question always asked was what is the view of Her Majesty's government? At that time those who were giving the information were told by the Secretary of State of the day that they should not disclose the government's view. I would like

> you to be certain from the start that my feeling is exactly the opposite, namely that all those who will be talking to Africans should say quite clearly that the proposals are sponsored by Her Majesty's Government who consider them just and fair. I thought that on this point you would like to know my view.[61]

Many of those who had been out in Rhodesia believed that the commissioners should have returned on the same plane. However, there were those, particularly on the right wing of the Conservative Party, who felt that the Africans had been given time to organise resistance to the proposals and that this tactical advantage played into the hands of the nationalist forces who had fermented opposition. Alec Home also felt that the intervention of Christmas was a crucial delay, and did not believe in premature celebrations. 'We must wait for the test of acceptability before we can say that the fish is on the bank', he wrote presciently on the day of his return.[62] But it took time to assemble the rest of the team, and other more moderate voices in Britain asked why it was wrong to allow the Africans time to make up their minds. Up to the last minute, names were being added, and it was not until 10 January that the commission finally set foot in Rhodesia. Before they flew out, Home wrote to Lord Harlech:

> Just one point on Rhodesia before you go. I agreed with Ian Smith when I was in Salisbury that neither of us would try to estimate a time-scale for parity and majority rule. If I speculated and put it lowish (as I believe is justified) Smith would do the opposite and an awful and totally confusing dog-fight would ensue. So much depends on the Africans taking up their chances, industrial and educational, that it is really impossible to calculate the time to parity. We gave it a lot of thought but concluded that to make any shot at it was really too dangerous. The statisticians during our calculation were haywire! I thought you would like to know this ... PS I am glad you are getting on with the job. I think that it is vital.[63]

The terms of reference given to the commission were 'To satisfy themselves that the proposals for a settlement as set out in Annex B to Command Paper 4835 have been fully and properly explained to the population of Rhodesia; to ascertain by direct contact with all sections of the population whether the people of Rhodesia as a whole regard these proposals as acceptable as a basis for independence; and to report to the Foreign and Commonwealth Secretary accordingly.'[64]

The next two months saw Lord Pearce conducting an enquiry in the best traditions of the British judicial system. Impeccably impartial, thorough and dispassionate, it was not what was required for a settlement at that time. The Pearce Commission gave direct answers to direct questions, yet many matters were shaded in tones of grey; there was no attempt to indulge in persuasive *realpolitik*. Wherever the commissioners went, African National Council supporters followed them crying 'No', and angry Africans ripped up copies of the simplified version of the settlement proposals, wrote 'No' on the scraps and pushed them under the commission's locked doors.[65] Garfield Todd, the liberal-minded former Southern Rhodesian Prime Minister, and his daughter were arrested by the Rhodesian Front government and held in prison 120 miles apart, which led to a stormy debate in Westminster. Home sent Philip Mansfield out to investigate and asked Smith to explain the arrests. On 24 January, Home announced that there was evidence that elements in Rhodesia were set on disrupting the work of the Pearce Commission by encouraging nationwide disorder and a further batch of 'intimidation' commissioners were sent out to investigate the complaints. Philip Mansfield acted throughout as intermediary between Pearce and Home, and Home wrote to Pearce assuring him of Parliament's support: 'I realise that as things have turned out your task has proved to be even more formidable than we supposed at the time when you took it on. The patient and determined way in which you and your colleagues have tackled it filled us all with admiration. I was asked in the House of Commons on 24 January to convey to you that the House is entirely behind you in your work and this I gladly do. As I have said on more than one occasion, I very much hope that you will be able to complete your task.'[66]

He also wrote a personal letter to the Bishop of Edinburgh, Kenneth Carey, which gives an insight into his feelings and worries at this time:

> I simply do not know what Pearce will say or how he will have to react. We will have to judge by what he finds. He might say he cannot really find out the real opinion because of intimidation on both sides! I do not think so because he is a determined character. What is quite clear to me is that the Africans have been given a first-class chance to get their foot in the door and push it open. Would it be moral to invite them not to try and push it open bit by bit till it was wide? I sometimes fear those who advocate the best and will not look at the second best … The Africans in Rhodesia have no chance of asserting themselves without a blood-bath so I

> must advise them to take it gradually or not at all. I will weep for them if they turn down the chance.[67]

Pearce personally saw as many of the leaders of African opinion as he could; other members of the commission went into the bush to meet the villagers. Such meetings did not endear him to the Rhodesian right wing, who 'suspect I am a "Trojan Horse" to spy out the economic situation of Rhodesia'.[68]

Their two months in Rhodesia came to an end, and Pearce and his commissioners returned to Britain to begin work on their report. Pearce presented his conclusions to Alec Home on 4 May and the Report was published on 23 May. The crucial paragraph was No. 420:

> We are satisfied on our evidence that the Proposals are acceptable to the great majority of Europeans. We are equally satisfied, after considering all our evidence including that on intimidation, that the majority of Africans rejected the Proposals. In our opinion the people of Rhodesia as a whole do not regard the Proposals as acceptable as a basis for independence.[69]

'I think that Rhodesia is the only real disappointment which I take away with me,' Home wrote to Miles Hudson on relinquishing office, 'but even then in a lurking hope that 1970 will not be too wide of the mark when the settlement comes.'[70] Arnold Smith, Secretary-General of the Commonwealth, recorded: 'He thought the whole situation would now polarise, with the Rhodesian whites moving further into the South African pattern. He had little confidence in sanctions being effective, especially with the United States lifting its embargo on Rhodesian chrome.'[71] In announcing the verdict to the House of Commons, Home said the best atmosphere for constructive discussion and advance would be provided if sanctions were maintained. There was much criticism of the continuation of sanctions and in a debate on the Pearce Report on 15 June, ten backbenchers tabled a critical amendment, though 'By comparison with other backbench dissent expressed during the session', Philip Norton has written, '[that] expressed on the decision to continue sanctions was very light indeed'.[72] Home's influence undoubtedly swayed many backbenchers, though he was always aware of a hard-core of implacable opponents to the sanctions order.

Despite his disappointment, Home spoke generously and with warmth of the work the Pearce Commission had done. It not only was fair, it was seen to be fair, and it would be a failure of understanding of

African politics to perceive it otherwise. There was no attempt to deal separately with Smith in the aftermath of the Pearce Report. Home's acceptance of the Report showed the Rhodesian Africans that there was now no fundamental difference between the Labour and the Conservative approach. The real loser was Smith, for time was not on his side, something he tacitly recognised. The Rhodesian problem festered for another eight years; in 1980 an independent Zimbabwe was born during Thatcher's first year in office. Home's team played their part in paving the way for that later settlement, not least in impressing upon Smith that the time would come when events would overtake him and further concessions would be needed. By the end of the decade, the final settlement was built on their vital preliminary work.

Despite their unexpected victory at the polls in June 1970, the Conservative Party was often in a fractious and dissenting mood in the early 1970s. Home found this over Rhodesia sanctions, and he was to find it again in a related problem; the Ugandan Asian refugees. In August 1972 Idi Amin began expelling Asians with British passports from Uganda. The House was about to rise for the summer recess, but Home reiterated that Britain had a special obligation to those who were British passport holders. Together with Robert Carr, the Home Secretary, he faced a group of dissenting Conservatives from West Midlands constituencies, where there was a high incidence of immigration; he also persuaded Canada and India to accept a proportion of the expelled Asians (28,000 eventually settled in Britain).

On 31 August, Home made a nationwide television broadcast, explaining the government's policy, a speech described by the chairman of the right-wing Monday Club as 'moonshine'.[73] An ugly debate followed at the Party conference in October, but Home's action ensured that the Commonwealth Conference in 1973 was a very different occasion from the Singapore meeting. Home spent one break at Douglas that August, writing to Macmillan on his return, 'At Douglas we averaged 90 brace a day for 10 days. I would like to have had Amin through the butts upwind!'[74]

As Home settled into his responsibilities at the Foreign Office, there were some important family occasions. In October 1970, a memorial to the Alingtons was unveiled at Durham Cathedral, and on 21 November, Elizabeth Home was appointed as the first Lady Fellow (member of the governing body) of Eton College, where her down-to-earth advice on many aspects gave a new perspective. So successful was Elizabeth Home's spell on the governing body that the Fellows considered in

1994 whether it was not time to appoint another lady to help with their counsels.[75] But the most important event came in 1972 with the engagement of David Douglas-Home to Jane, the younger daughter of Colonel John Williams-Wynne of Merioneth, a tonic after the result of the Pearce Commission, as many papers described the news. The wedding was at St Margaret's, Westminster on 10 October. The reception broke new ground, as the Queen had given special permission for the Banqueting House in Whitehall to be used for the first time. Alec Home took a quiet pleasure in the marriage, and the eventual addition of new grandchildren to the family circle, as well as David's burgeoning career with Morgan Grenfell.[76]

Despite his reluctance to travel the world unnecessarily, Home found that many commitments – the CENTO meeting in Ankara in April 1971, his tour of Australia in 1972 when he spoke on the Five Power Defence Arrangements, the journeys to Moscow and Peking in 1973 – were now inseparable from the post of Foreign Secretary; there were even some murmurings in Kinross and West Perthshire that he was neglecting constituency surgeries, that they could not always obtain a personal interview, as the Foreign Secretary was so often abroad.

Hospitality abroad was always an area of potential embarrassment – sometimes through ignorance of the local gastronomic traditions or because of conversational *faux-pas*. At a dinner in the Indian sub-continent, Alec Home found himself next to a taciturn, but bemedalled general, who apparently operated in the remoter regions of the north-west frontier. All attempts at conversation failed, until, as a last diplomatic effort, the Foreign Secretary enquired what his companion's country was renowned for. 'Mr Home,' replied the general, brightening, 'our country is renowned for three things. First, it is renowned for its friendship; second for its hospitality; and finally, for revenge. And the greatest of these is revenge.'[77]

The war in 1971 between India and Pakistan led to the recognition of Bangladesh and the emergence of Ali Bhutto as President of West Pakistan; it caused a considerable cooling in Anglo–American relations. At the time Heath was much concerned to improve relations between Britain and India, but President Nixon saw India as the aggressor and supported Pakistan. Home agreed with Nixon; for him India practised too often the 'double standards' he had criticised in his Berwick-on-Tweed speech eleven years earlier. She had annexed Goa by force in 1961, but had been a consistent critic of Britain during the Suez crisis. He also perceived India as a conduit for Soviet penetration, as did

Nixon. The situation was complicated by the fact that Nixon was about to make his first visit to China, the protector of Pakistan.

Unlike Presidents Kennedy and Johnson, who had their 'special relationships' with Macmillan and Wilson, there was no warmth between Nixon and Heath. This made Alec Home, who had always met Nixon on his visits to London, an important touchstone in Britain for the Republican administration, who liked his uncompromising stance on communism. At a conference on 'Britain in the World', held in London in March 1995, the former Secretary of State, Dr Henry Kissinger, reminded his audience of what the Special Relationship – 'vital for the creation of the post-war international system' – had meant in the early 1970s. 'You would not say that President Nixon, nor I, were excessively sentimental men, but we often found ourselves in the habit of calling the Foreign Secretary on a whole series of issues.'[78] These issues ranged over the continuing agonies in Vietnam until the cease-fire in January 1973, détente, arms limitation and the Middle East. Yet Home's most successful transatlantic partnerships were forged with William Rogers, Kissinger's predecessor as Secretary of State, and George Bush, then US ambassador to the UN. Kissinger was never a soul-mate; there was something about the acerbic directness and intellectual clarity of the American lawyer which rather discomfited Alec Home.

When Denis Greenhill retired as Permanent Under-Secretary in November 1973, Home wrote, 'I think that if I had to select one particular field of activity for which you will be remembered, it is in the vital area of defence and our relations with the Americans'[79] – a reflection of Home's own priorities and the support Greenhill had given.

Home's visit to China in October–November 1972 was at the invitation of the Chinese Foreign Minister, Chi P'eng-fei, and was the first by a British Foreign Secretary. Indeed, until 1972, no Foreign Minister from a developed capitalist country had visited China since the Chinese People's Republic had been formally proclaimed in October 1949. However, by 1972, five such visits had taken place, including William Rogers's visit with Nixon in February. Anthony Royle, Parliamentary Under-Secretary at the Foreign Office, had made a preliminary visit between 30 May and 6 June, during which he had ten hours of talks with Mr Ch'iao, senior Vice-Minister of Foreign Affairs.

Apart from going to the Great Wall of China, the Ming Tombs and the Forbidden City, a full programme of visits to agricultural communes and other economic projects was planned for Alec and

Elizabeth Home. When he visited one Chinese museum in the Hidden City he was shown an ancient farm inspector's hat with strange flaps. It was explained that in ancient times when the inspector had had enough explanations he put the flaps down. 'That would be very useful for the House of Commons,' he said to his bemused hosts.[80] His aim was to consolidate the improved relations between the two countries, to build trade and cultural links and to brief the Chinese Foreign Minister on the latest developments in the European community. The Chinese really took to Home. He met Chou En-lai – a privilege not normally granted to Foreign Ministers – and walked farther along the Great Wall than Nixon, which impressed his hosts. The visit ended with a fourteen-course banquet in the Great Hall of the People's Republic in Peking, during which the strains of the Eton Boating Song were heard in that communist redoubt.

One of the last events Greenhill masterminded as Permanent Under-Secretary was the celebration of Alec Home's seventieth birthday on 2 July 1973. Edward Heath gave a dinner at 10 Downing Street, where messages were read out from, among others, Dean Rusk and Andrei Gromyko. The guests were from all areas of the celebrant's life, including Sir John Masterman, who had tutored both Home and Greenhill at Christ Church. The Foreign Office staff and heads of mission had given considerable thought to their gift. Antony Acland suggested thay they should give the Secretary of State a plant, tree or shrub from every country Home had visited in Commonwealth and Foreign Office days, to be planted at the Hirsel. Over ninety specimens were prepared, including *Magnolia Wilsonii*, a rare plant from Western China, to which Home responded appropriately: 'I know it well, it hangs upside down and is red at the centre!' He thanked all those who had contributed: 'They catered exactly for my overwhelming vice of horticulture and will give enormous pleasure to me and Elizabeth for the rest of our lives and to our children thereafter.'[81]

The latter part of 1973 saw Home drawn into two areas of policy not hitherto prominent concerns – Northern Ireland and Energy. He was one of the principal delegates at the tripartite talks at Sunningdale, between the British and Irish governments and the Northern Ireland party leaders which resulted in the formation of an overall Council of Ireland, and a new power-sharing Executive which took office in Stormont in January 1974. But it was yet another false dawn in Anglo–Irish relations, and for the Conservatives an electoral nightmare:

the pro-Sunningdale Unionists failed to win a single seat in the general election of 1974, with disastrous consequences for Heath.

The Yom Kippur War also had grievous consequences for the Heath government, though their extent was not immediately appreciated. Although a cease-fire was agreed on 22 October by implementation of the UN Resolution 242, the threat to oil supplies was the Damoclean sword hanging over western governments. Britain and France did not suffer the embargo imposed upon Holland, but were accused by Israel of being concerned only with their own interests. Home replied that Britain's approach had been even-handed: Home had endorsed an embargo on arms supplied to both sides. Centurion tanks on their way to Israel had even been held in a customs shed. With passions rising ever higher, an adjournment debate was held in the House of Commons, during which it seemed that the government might fall. Walking over to the debate, one Foreign Office official asked Home what would happen tomorrow if the debate was lost. 'Then there won't be a tomorrow', he replied, so uncertain was the outcome.[82] Defending the arms embargo in a speech on 18 October, Home said that it would be kept under continuous review, especially if the existence of Israel appeared to be at risk. But the dilemma remained – how to reconcile Israel's requirements for security with the demands of its neighbours for the return of their territories. He stuck resolutely by the officials who had implemented the arms embargo decision and found time, at the end of a hectic three weeks, to express his gratitude on paper. 'I am very well aware of the great pressure under which you and the departments which you supervise have been working during these past weeks since the Middle East war and the oil crisis flared up', he wrote on 25 October to Anthony Parsons, who was in charge of Middle East operations at the Foreign Office. 'I wish that I could foresee a significant let up in the pressure. I fear however that we are at the beginning of a long period of considerable activity; but I wanted to send my thanks now for the excellence of your work and help to me.'[83]

The subsequent hike in oil prices had the most profound effects upon living standards in the West, and in the combination of the inflationary wages–prices spiral and the threat to oil supplies lay the genesis of the government's downfall. The crisis also dealt a blow to the fragile unity of the nine European member countries at the EEC heads of state summit in Copenhagen in December. It was agreed that the nine would in future bargain collectively, though Heath refused to allow the North Sea Oil fields off Britain to be part of the equation, to avoid the isolation experienced by member countries such as the Dutch with the Arab embargo following the Yom Kippur War. Heath had set great store by the EEC Regional Development Fund for Britain's depressed areas, but German unwillingness to agree to the three-year funding Heath had wanted led to Home threatening to veto the Copenhagen energy policy if regional funding was not forthcoming. There was also doubt about whether there had been a joint understanding between America and Britain regarding the use of nuclear weapons, as it transpired that US forces in Germany had been put on nuclear alert. In a letter to Kissinger, Home said that it would not be much use if Britain supported America unflinchingly on everything, even when there was underlying disagreement.[84]

Home's visit to Moscow in December 1973 was plain sailing by comparison, in spite of its taking place under the shadow of the expulsions of September 1971, and the worsening domestic situation following the miners' overtime ban on 12 November. A State of Emergency had been declared on 13 November, owing to the energy crisis in the wake of the Yom Kippur War and on 19 November Peter Walker, the Energy Secretary, announced a 10 per cent cut in fuel and petrol supplies, followed a week later by the decision to issue petrol rationing books by post, as a contingency measure. The atmosphere attending the visit was one of reconciliation. 'We flew to Moscow on Sunday 2 December 1973', Miles Hudson wrote. 'Arriving in the dark we were met by Gromyko and many Russians, all indistinguishable in their long coats and fur hats. It was very cold.'[85] The fact that Gromyko came to the airport to welcome Alec Home was itself a sign of improved relationships between Russia and Britain. The delegations discussed moves towards peaceful co-existence, and banquets, reminiscent of the Test Ban Treaty celebrations, were held. Gromyko toasted his British guests at every opportunity: it was as though the 1971 expulsions had never taken place.

Home was accompanied on the Moscow trip by the new Russian-speaking Permanent Under-Secretary, Sir Thomas Brimelow, his unexpected choice for Head of the Foreign Service in November 1973. Home believed that key promotions should be based on 'horses-for-courses', not Buggins's turn. The surprise at Brimelow's appointment was nothing to do with his abilities, which were acknowledged, but that at fifty-eight he could expect only two years in the post. Brimelow had been reluctant to accept it, suspicious of the attendant flummery of the job, but Home persuaded him. Home took a discreet but deep interest in promotions, always keeping a weather eye open for suitable postings for the brightest people. On the way back from a CENTO conference in Tehran with Anthony Parsons, he spoke of how interesting Tehran was. Parsons thought he was making conversation, but it led to a question: 'How would you like Iran as your next posting?' So began one of the most significant of post-war ambassadorships. Sir Murray MacLehose's outstanding governorship of Hong Kong was also of Alec Home's choosing. He took great care to see ambassadors and thank them personally when tours ended, as when Sir David Hunt retired from Brazil in 1973.[86]

The appointment of a new Permanent Under-Secretary is one of the major, if intermittent, responsibilities of the Secretary of State. As with the appointment of Harold Caccia in 1962, he called in all the senior ambassadors, who were themselves nearing the compulsory retirement age of sixty to seek advice, before sending his recommendation for Brimelow through to Downing Street. Home was in no doubt that Brimelow was the correct choice. Not only had he served in Moscow and in the consulate-general in New York, he was a fluent linguist, and acceptable to both front benches. (After his ennoblement on retirement, Brimelow was to sit on the Labour benches in the Upper House.) Home had an intuitive feeling in the autumn of 1973 that the Conservatives might not be in office much longer. He was confident that with Brimelow in charge, the Foreign Office would cope with the transition to a new administration, an example of how Home looked beyond the immediate move on the board. No one could claim that this quiet, profoundly intelligent northerner could be seen as Carlton Browne of the FO and that mattered to Home.

The general election was not due until the summer of 1975, but Heath had begun preparing the manifesto as early as September 1971. On 20 September he invited Home to be a member of the Steering Committee on Election Strategy. Accepting Heath's invitation on 6 October 1971, he wrote:

> It is, of course, difficult to forecast now precisely what problems we will face at the time of the next election, whenever that may be, but undoubtedly we will be confronting a new situation in the sense that we will be in the Community.
>
> We are giving urgent study to the institutions of the Community and in what direction we would like to see them develop. We are also considering the future of external policies and problems of the

> enlarged Community and its individual members in order to identify how our interests will be served by common or co-ordinated action. As you know, we are actively considering our defence policies within Europe and the Alliance.
>
> We are also making studies of the issues likely to arise at a European security conference, and of the new situation which will be created by the admission of China to the United Nations.
>
> We are taking part in the inter-departmental review of the aid programme and are working with other departments on oil policy.
>
> When the outcome of the Rhodesian negotiations becomes clear I expect to consider again the general outline of our policies towards Africa.[87]

Not only had Home been a regular contributor to steering commitee meetings from 1971 onwards, but he had been one of the inner ministerial circle considering election strategy in December 1973 (before the beginning of the three-day week on 1 January 1974).[88] As the domestic situation worsened in January 1974, the Cabinet divided into two camps, one pressing for an early election to resolve the situation, the other advising caution. Home was away for much of the time, but was in the latter group. When the decision was taken on 6–7 February, and the general election announced for 28 February, Home was visiting Kenya and did not know of the dissolution, a confusion that led to an Osbert Lancaster cartoon of bemused witchdoctors receiving a signal over the tom-toms ('Douglas-Home. Most immediate. Alec where art thou? Love Ted. End of message'), begging the Foreign Secretary to return to the fold.[89]

The interval between dissolution and polling day was as short as possible, for it was not in Heath's interest for a single issue campaign on 'Who Governs?' to drag on. Alec Home knew that this would probably be his last general election as a candidate, and his position was not under threat. Nevertheless he took nothing for granted. There was still the memory of the 'surgeries controversy', as well as the nascent Scottish National Party. He began his campaign (with the faithful John Robertson in attendance) at Blair Atholl on 14 February, but as in 1966 and 1970 travelled the country. Many of the lessons of the past had been learned. A big rally at Glasgow's Kelvin Hall on 25 February was an all-ticket affair, so there was no repeat of the Birmingham Bull Ring fiasco of 1964. One nostalgic visit was to his old constituency of Lanark, held by Judith Hart for Labour since the redrawing of the boundaries in 1959. The turn-out at Kinross and West Perthshire (77.5 per cent) was

A PRIME MINISTER'S ROUND

Rab Butler, the Foreign Secretary, and the Prime Minister at talks in London with the West German Chancellor, Ludwig Erhard, 15 January 1964

The Prime Minister and President Johnson at the White House, 12 February 1964. Despite outward courtesies, there were many disagreements between the two leaders

In Lagos, 19 March 1964: 'Colourful ceremonial not experienced since the days of his visit to Queen Salote's Tonga as Commonwealth Secretary'

The Prime Minister at a constituency fête, 22 August 1964

Signing autographs whilst electioneering in Kinross and West Perthshire

The Prime Minister speaking for Christopher Soames in Bedford, 7 October 1964, during the General Election. It was whilst visiting Soames in hospital that he promised him the Foreign Secretaryship in the event of a Conservative victory

The State Opening of Parliament, 3 November 1964:
Harold Wilson and Alec Douglas-Home leading the Commons to hear the Queen's speech

IN OPPOSITION

Edward Heath acknowledges the applause at his first Party Conference as Conservative leader, 16 October 1965

Alec Douglas-Home with King Olav of Norway, May 1965. Born on the same day in 1903, they were installed together as Knights of the Thistle in July 1962

Alec Douglas-Home in talks with Richard Nixon in London, 1969. Even after Watergate Alec Douglas-Home never joined in the denigration of the former American President

RETURN TO
THE FOREIGN OFFICE

Alec of Arabia, September 1971

With Ian Smith, 24 November 1971, after the Rhodesian Agreement

The ink-throwing episode at the Egmont Palace, 25 January 1972

In Madrid with Prince Juan Carlos and Antony Acland, who was to give the address at Alec Home's memorial service in January 1996

Osbert Lancaster cartoon,
8 February 1974:
'Douglas-Home.
Most immediate.
Alec where art thou?
Love, Ted.
End of message'

The February 1974 General Election was to bring to an end Alec Douglas-Home's ministerial career. Returning to the House of Lords as Lord Home of the Hirsel, his was a customary presence on the front bench with Lord Boyd-Carpenter and the Earl of Stockton, as on the day when the debates of the Upper Chamber were televised for the first time on 23 January 1985

LAST THINGS

Alec Home with his daughter Caroline and Sir Douglas Bader at the opening of the Hirsel Golf Course, 10 August 1980

The Hirsel in the summer of 1995

The last photograph of Elizabeth and Alec Home, Castlemains, September 1990

Malcolm Rifkind gives Alec Home a present from the Cabinet on his 90th birthday, 2 July 1993; Diana and Meriel look on from behind their father

Alec Home in benign old age

the highest of all the campaigns he fought. The figures were: Sir Alec Douglas-Home (Unionist), 14,356; Duncan Murray (Scottish Nationalist Party), 6,274; David Barrie (Liberal), 3,807; Danus Skene (Labour), 2,694; giving a Unionist majority of 8,082.

The national result was a devastating blow to Heath, all the more so for being unexpected. For the second general election in succession, the predictions of politicians, pollsters and public were confounded. Labour won 301 seats, the Conservatives 297, the Liberals 14, the Scottish Nationalists 7, Plaid Cymru 2.[90] The position of the twelve Northern Ireland members and two Independents would be crucial in the horse-trading which now followed. Heath attempted in vain to seek accommodation with the Liberal Party, while Harold Wilson waited for what he saw as the inevitable call to the Palace. As he observed to waiting news reporters, it might not be clear who had won the election, but it was certainly clear who had lost it. Home therefore stayed in office until James Callaghan was appointed Foreign Secretary on 5 March.

It was a melancholy weekend in London: Carlton Gardens was a shuttered place and the clubs in Pall Mall were closed. The Aclands invited the Homes to stay and they took long walks in Richmond Park as they waited for the political situation to clear. 'I'm afraid it's the end of the road,' Home said to Antony Acland, as they walked by the Isabella Plantation, 'but it's been great fun.' He hoped Callaghan would be his successor at the Foreign Office; he believed this would be the best appointment.[91] On Monday 4 March, when it became clear that the Liberals would not join him, Heath went to the palace to tender his resignation. When Harold Wilson was invited to form an administration, Alec Home's Foreign Secretaryship was over. With Elizabeth, he cleared his belongings from Dorneywood; six days later the press reported that he was to retire from the Commons. He was never to hold public office again.

To some critics, Home's second term as Foreign Secretary was seen as a reactionary time, punctuated by the sale of arms to South Africa, the expulsion of the Russian spies, and a feudal approach to the problems of Lagos. Some felt he did not have an awareness of how things had altered, nor was there a feeling for fundamental change. He was a reactive, not a creative Secretary of State. But, to others, he possessed the two key attributes of a Foreign Secretary: judgment of men and judgment of affairs. He was the solid ballast of the Heath government, as the ship of state hit choppy waters. His term of office saw no major errors of judgment. He came at the end of a particular chapter in diplomacy, when foreign policy was still conducted from London by a Foreign Secretary, supported by his Permanent Under-Secretary, and he saw his job as keeping the machine running smoothly, creating an atmosphere conducive to good management. He was totally without vanity, one of the abiding scourges of Foreign Secretaries, yet was strong and independent in character. Like his counterpart Gromyko, he was the great survivor. He had clear beliefs and inspired trust among those with whom he worked. During his second spell at the Foreign Office, he was at the peak of his influence; it was undoubtedly the culmination of his career.

'Search the world over, hunt history from beginning to end, and you will conclude as the result of your labours that the great Foreign Minister is the rarest bird that flies.'[92] So wrote F.S. Oliver in *The Endless Adventure* in 1935, citing Palmerston and Salisbury as the only truly great Foreign Secretaries since Castlereagh. The pantheon of great twentieth-century Foreign Secretaries traditionally encompasses Sir Edward Grey, Ernest Bevin and Sir Anthony Eden. It would be unrealistic to include Alec Home in their company, not least because of the reduced role that Britain occupied in the world when he was in King Charles Street, yet he had much in common with all three: Grey's courtesy, length of service and innate countrymen's values; Bevin's intuitive common-sense and directness; and Eden's steadfastness in adversity, together with the determination to pursue unpopular courses of action in which he profoundly believed. Unlike them, however, he had to preside over what Wellington considered the most difficult test of a general, namely the conduct of a successful retreat. For his skill in that role above all, in the post-war list of Foreign Secretaries, Alec Home has an assured and special place. From his time at the Commonwealth Relations Office in April 1955 until his retirement from the Foreign Office in March 1974, he was at or near the centre of Britain's imperial retreat. Few other politicians could have managed that process with fewer traumas, whilst at the same time inspiring the affection of both the service he headed and of those on the wider stage, who may have disagreed with the emphasis of his policy, but never doubted the integrity that lay behind it.

17

Last Things

The Conservative defeat at the February 1974 general election marked an important turning-point in post-war British history, the true significance of which was not immediately apparent. Edward Heath's position as Conservative leader was not under immediate threat, largely because a further poll seemed inevitable within a few months. His fate was ultimately decided by the election of 10 October 1974, his third defeat in four contests. Although the Conservatives had polled marginally more votes in February than Labour, the rise in the Liberal share of the vote by 11.8 per cent denied Heath the victory he had expected. Post mortems centred on the timing of the contest, and the wisdom of trying to limit the campaign to the single issue of 'Who Governs Britain?', which turned into a referendum on Heath's stewardship of the country. Some ministers felt that polling day should have been on 7 February (the day of the announcement of the election), while others, including Alec Home, who remembered Walter Elliot's dictum that the best way to lose a general election was to hold one, were not convinced that there should have been a campaign at all. Too many imponderables and a skilful widening of the arguments by Wilson, cost the Conservatives dearly, and less than eleven months after Edward Heath's loss of office, Margaret Thatcher succeeded him as Conservative leader.

In the immediate aftermath of the February defeat, Alec Home knew that the time had come to retire from the Commons, though he was reappointed shadow Foreign Secretary by Heath. He had already had talks in Dunblane the previous October with D. A. McNeill, his chairman in Kinross and West Perthshire, about the most appropriate time to bow out, so that a new candidate could be in place for the next election, expected to be in the autumn of 1974 or, more likely, the spring of 1975. As these discussions coincided with the Foreign

Secretary's impending visit to Russia, McNeill agreed that no statement would be made at that autumn's AGM of the Constituency Association, and that it would be better to wait until after Christmas before making a formal announcement. McNeill felt that though it was impossible to know the exact timing of the next election, it would be reasonably far enough ahead to introduce the future chosen candidate to the members of the Association in due course. When events overtook them however, Home willingly agreed to defend the seat in the sudden and unexpected February campaign. He issued a press statement on 22 March 1974 in the form of a message to his Constituency Association:

> Before Christmas I had a conversation with our chairman about the future. I told him then that should the 1970 Parliament run on for a reasonable time that I would not seek re-election for the following Parliament. Events then took charge and we were faced with a general election in January or February. I think you will agree that in those circumstances I could do nothing else than stand by the constituency and the party.
>
> The political situation today is still very uncertain and in these circumstances I will not of course let you down. But I think it is prudent that a successor to me should have time to play himself in for Kinross and West Perthshire, so I have asked Mr McNeill to start the process of finding such a person now.
>
> I am very grateful to you for your sustained support but the records tell me that I am approaching 71![1]

Alec Home remembered the uncertainties that had marked Churchill's last years as member for Woodford and ultimate retirement from the Commons, and had no wish to outstay his welcome. So he went before people began asking when he would be going. But in case there was a snap election, the press were told that he would defend the seat if a new candidate had not been adopted before the Dissolution. Eventually the Association chose Nicholas Fairbairn, a future Solicitor-General for Scotland, and a colourful figure in the House of Commons, dressed more often than not in his own tartan designs, and who could always be relied upon for a lively and unconventional quotation, such as his famous entry under recreations in *Who's Who*, 'making love, ends meet and people laugh'. Home backed Fairbairn resolutely as his successor: 'I send to Nicholas Fairbairn my good wishes for a decisive victory,' said Home's message in October 1974. 'With your help we can hold the seat with a good majority over all comers.' In a contest where the SNP vote had its largest percentage increase in the whole of Scotland, Fairbairn won by a mere 2 per cent (53 votes), compared with Home's margin in February of 29.7 per cent – an indication of his strong personal vote. Fairbairn nevertheless sent a telegram to the Hirsel announcing his 'Decisive victory'.[2]

However, Home was no passenger in Edward Heath's shadow Cabinet for the next seven months. His successor, James Callaghan, kept in close touch with him and included the Homes in Foreign Office invitations. Callaghan wanted to build trade links with Russia following Home's recent visit, and to examine why the French and the Germans seemed to do better with the USSR than Britain. Continuity was helped by Antony Acland's being Callaghan's Private Secretary. Callaghan always made it clear to Acland how much he respected Home's contributions, exempting Home from criticisms he made at one early meeting and turning to Acland to say, 'That wasn't just for your benefit.'[3]

Although Home already chaired the Foreign and Commonwealth Affairs Committee, Heath asked him on 4 April if he would serve on a Policy Group on Devolution under the chairmanship of James Prior. He might have been excused for thinking this the small change of political life in opposition, but he threw himself into work which he judged would be of importance in an era of narrow Westminster majorities. On 23 April, he sent Prior a memorandum:

> I have been thinking about Devolution and Scotland. I think that the choices which we have to make are basically three:
> 1 Is the Assembly to be directly elected or indirectly elected from the Regional Councils and Districts?
> 2 Is the Assembly to receive the monies voted by Parliament as a lump sum and then distribute them to the Regions? This would certainly be a substantial move and would allow Scotsmen to look at the Scottish picture as a whole. But would the Regions like it? I think they would have to be consulted before we could commit ourselves. Fear of domination by the industrial belt is real.
> 3 Should the Assembly have any legislative function? Teddy Taylor's preference is that it should have the chance to comment on all Scottish legislation and, as I understand, the Estimates. There is a lot to be said for that. It is clear and there would be no confusion or rivalry between Westminster and Edinburgh. There would be no reason either to lessen the number of Scottish MPs at Westminster.
>
> My doubt as to whether we should stop there derives less from

> Scottish sentiment than from the desirability of decentralisation from Westminster with the consequent relief to Scottish members if a number of Bills were delegated each year.
>
> The Taylor proposal might not detach enough moderate Scottish SNP supporters – the alternative might. It is this, I think, on which we should concentrate when we meet.[4]

Alec Home brought a lifetime of knowledge of Scottish affairs to the deliberations of the Policy Group, as Heath knew he would, and the subsequent Report bore the marks of his input.

Heath also drew on Home's advice for the line to be taken on State Funding for Opposition Parties. Although Home had always felt that there should be an official residence for the leader of the opposition, he was uncertain about the acceptability of a general subsidy to political parties. He wrote to the Opposition Chief Whip, Humphrey Atkins, on 11 June 1974:

> I have been giving some thought to the subject of financial help for opposition parties.
>
> My instinct is against the proposal and I believe it will be unpopular with our supporters who already tend to think that the country pays enough for its politicians.
>
> However, if something is to be done, I would far rather see the money applied to the leader's office and the whips' office. That the leader should be properly served can properly be argued, likewise the whips.
>
> I would far rather see a staff round the leader on which other 'Shadows' could draw, rather than supply a research man to each shadow minister.[5]

In 1975 an Opposition Parties Finance Grant was introduced, but it was limited (as Home preferred) to helping opposition parties fulfil their Westminster responsibilities, rather than financing extra-parliamentary activities.

The prospect of an election concentrated the minds of the Conservatives on their strategy. Heath held the first meeting on the manifesto on 18 March. A sub-committee, chaired by Michael Fraser, worked on the initial outline, reporting back to Heath's Steering Committee, with Home as its senior figure.[6] On 1 May Home spoke on Defence policy, and two days later introduced a paper on the state of the Party. There had recently been too much bickering and there was now a need to reaffirm the theme and philosophy of Conservative policy – it was important to build on the idea of a 'property-owning democracy', and on the need for choice and variety in education. His plea to end the bickering came from the heart, as he knew the pressures under which Heath was now operating from his own experience in 1964–5. On 3 June he spoke on Northern Ireland policy and the repercussions for Scotland of any break-up of the United Kingdom. Over the actual manifesto (eventually published as *Putting Britain First*), Home paid close attention to the wording of key passages, stating that the draft should talk of the government working *with* people, rather than *for* them.[7] One of his most important contributions was over the possible referendum on the EEC, trailed by Harold Wilson as a device to resolve the divisions in his own ranks, and which also threatened to highlight differences on the Conservative benches. In March 1974, Home had accepted Jean Monnet's invitation to join an action committee for a United States of Europe and withdrawal was not an option for him. He wrote to Heath on 27 June:

> I have been giving some thought to our attitude towards a referendum on the question of coming out of the EEC or staying in.
>
> I feel that we should give no encouragement to the idea. Were we to do so we would, if we won the election, be saddled with having a referendum. In such a case I do not believe that the socialists would support us. I believe that we shall not suffer politically if we say that we do not believe that referenda should be part of the constitution, but that if the Labour Party ever bring in an act to provide one we will make our point of view known at the time.
>
> We are in the Community and intend to lead in the way we want to go.[8]

At this time, the Conservative Party in the Wirral asked Home for his opinions on the Referendum, as their Member, Selwyn Lloyd, was Speaker and could not get involved in political controversy. He sent a considered reply, pointing out that two world wars had divided western Europe this century and the European Community was an insurance against this happening again. He also stressed that all Commonwealth countries were now in favour of Britain staying in.[9] Although Home did not take a high profile part in the eventual Referendum campaign, he made it clear that he was firmly against any question of rejecting the terms Wilson had renegotiated. On 5 June, 67 per cent of those voting were in favour of staying in the Community.[10]

Following in Home's footsteps, Heath visited China in May 1974; while he was away, Home chaired the meetings of the Consultative Committee and generally 'minded the shop'. Most of the work concerned Conservative reaction to Callaghan's renegotiation proposals for the EEC. On 25 June, he chaired the meeting of the Foreign and Commonwealth Affairs Committee at the House of Commons to hear Heath's report on his visit to China. He had been received by the eighty-two-year-old Chairman Mao, an occasion of great significance for experts in Chinese politics, who were anxious to know from the seating arrangement for this meeting, who was in line of succession for the Chairman's job.[11] Heath reported that the Chinese mistrusted the British Labour party because they could not honestly accept that British socialists believed themselves to be socialists, whereas they knew exactly where the Conservative Party stood. In the public mind, the most important outcome of the visit was the gift of two giant Chinese pandas for London Zoo.

As a former Prime Minister and Foreign Secretary, Home was also much in demand on the international conference circuit, and publishers now began enquiring about rights to his memoirs. 'I am thinking, rather vaguely, of writing something', he said in a letter to Macmillan, who at once suggested a meeting to help in working out the scheme and method.[12] Macmillan had just completed his six-volume history of his life and times, but felt that Home would be better advised to aim for a single volume of a personally anecdotal nature.

On 18 September, Wilson announced that he had sought a dissolution of Parliament and that a general election would be held on 10 October. At six months and twelve days, this had been the shortest Parliament of the century, sitting on only 87 days. Six days before Wilson's announcement the 1922 Committee of Conservative backbenchers, peers and candidates had met to hear Heath's outline of election strategy. The Executive later decided to hold their next meeting on 14 October at the chairman's house; it was to prove the wake for Heath's leadership.

Freed of responsibilities in Kinross and West Perthshire, Home embarked during the next three weeks on his most vigorous campaign since 1964. He spoke at 28 meetings, travelled over two thousand miles by road, had several sorties by helicopter and spoke in marginal seats. He made four separate appearances on behalf of Nicholas Fairbairn. Of the twelve Conservative MPs who were not seeking re-election, Home, at seventy-two, was by far the oldest, so his contribution was particularly noteworthy.[13] As a former Prime Minister, he drew large crowds and received a warm welcome, 'Good old Alec' as one voter called out.

The Conservative strategy, tacitly admitted in inner circles, was one of damage limitation. Voters were bored with both Wilson and Heath, who had now fought more head-to-head campaigns than Gladstone and Disraeli. Labour had a lead of 14.6 per cent in September's National Opinion Poll and many Tories feared a landslide defeat. But for the third time in a row, the volatility of the electors returned an unexpected result in the dullest campaign since May 1955. Labour won 319 seats, the Conservatives 277, and the Liberals 13. With an overall majority of 3, Harold Wilson was in a similar position to his first administration in October 1964. For the second time in succession, he had won office on less than 40 per cent of the popular vote. The Conservatives had fared little better. It seemed 'A curse on both your houses'.

Although his defeat was narrow, Heath's position as Conservative leader was now widely seen as untenable, if not immediately by himself. Balfour and Home accepted the inevitable in 1911 and 1965, their voluntary retirements lancing the boil of discontent and enabling the party to move on to a new phase. Heath was prepared to fight to maintain his position. Apart from Willie Whitelaw, there was no obvious heir, but as at earlier moments of crisis, unexpected candidates emerged. Edward du Cann was deputed by the Executive of the 1922 Committee to see Heath informally and tell him that 'an election for the leadership must be held, not necessarily at once but in the foreseeable future'.[14] This message was no more welcome to Heath than Macmillan's nudges to Churchill in 1954. On Tuesday 15 October, the Executive of the 1922 Committee met at the Milk Street offices of Keyser Ullmann, the merchant bank chaired by du Cann. Even though they made every effort to arrive unobtrusively (the change of venue was to avoid drawing attention to their meeting), within hours the *Evening Standard* was on the streets with its news of the 'Milk Street Mafia'. The battle to succeed Heath was already well underway.

Parliament met on 22 October. Alec Home was not a member of the House of Commons; on 7 November, it was announced that a life peerage had been conferred and he would be ennobled as Baron Home of the Hirsel, of Coldstream in the County of Berwickshire, the title by which he would be known until his death. Heath believed that the precariousness of the Labour government's overall majority, the forthcoming EEC Referendum and the absence of an agreed successor, precluded a change of leadership at this time. The rules established in July 1965 applied only to a situation where there was a vacancy; there was no provision for a challenge to a leader who had simply outstayed his welcome. The Executive of the 1922 Committee pressed for a revision of the rules. Confident that he would prevail whatever system was adopted, Heath agreed to their request as a means of defusing the situation.

On 14 November, at a crowded meeting of the 1922 Committee, Heath announced that he had asked Lord Home of the Hirsel (it was the first occasion on which his new title had been used) to chair a committee to examine the Party's rules for electing its leader. The choice of Home was both obvious and highly popular; he was now an elder statesman, above the heat and dust of battle. But if Heath thought Home's committee would produce an anodyne revision, he was in for a rude awakening. The whole point of the revisions was to enable a leader who had lost the support of the Party to be challenged. Home went to work with his usual alacrity and the changes were announced before Christmas. On 4 February 1975, after the first ballot under the new rules, Heath announced his retirement. He had been Conservative leader for just under ten years.

Home's Committee had many echoes of October 1963, in that all elements of the Party had an input into the final decision-making process, and he believed that the new rules should fulfil two requirements. First, a contest should in its initial stage answer the question of whether the Party wanted a change. Heath believed the answer to that question would be in the negative, and consequently his position would be strengthened, as when John Major invited a contest in the summer of 1995 by resigning the leadership, subsequently defeating his challenger, John Redwood. The second function should be that if the first ballot indicated a change was wanted, subsequent ballots (there was provision for three) should identify the candidate most likely to bring unity to the Party.[15]

Home's Committee decided on a significant number of changes to the 1965 rules after considering submissions from interested parties, including the Executive of the 1922 Committee. One of the questions was whether there should be an extension of the electoral college, beyond the Parliamentary Party in the Commons, and there were those who felt that a small number of peers and members of the National Union (about fifteen in each category) would be a welcome broadening. Home had regretted the narrowing of the franchise to MPs alone in July

1965, but had accepted it as a way of satisfying the demands for a simple, readily understandable electoral system.

The Home Committee decided against extending the franchise, though they provided that consultation of the extra–parliamentary party should be on a more formal basis. Some MPs were to take little notice of this provision before casting their votes, but others conscientiously saw themselves as bound to consult widely in their constituency before casting their vote, as Elizabeth Peacock, MP for Batley and Spen, was to do in November 1990. A more substantive change was their recommendation that an incumbent leader be subject to annual re-election within four weeks of the opening of a new session of Parliament; in the case of a new Parliament the election would be held not sooner than three or later than six months from the date when Parliament first met.[16] A challenger required only two secret nominations, a condition changed later to prevent 'frivolous' stalking horses. (Ten per cent of the parliamentary Party must now write to the Chairman of the 1922 Committee to back the nomination, otherwise the contest cannot proceed.) Although it went largely unnoticed at the time, the possibility of an annual challenge was not confined to periods when the party was in opposition, a loophole that effectively ended Mrs Thatcher's premiership. Unlike some members of the Party, Home was always aware that one day this could be the case.[17] Another provision was that, if the contest went to a third ballot, the result would be determined by single transferable vote. In 1965, to win on the first ballot, a candidate had to have an absolute majority (i.e. not over anybody else, but over *everybody* else) and be ahead of the nearest challenger by a margin of 15 per cent *of the votes cast*. This was now changed to a 15 per cent margin *of all those entitled to vote* (rather than of the votes cast), an important change that meant abstentions were no longer neutral. The hurdle to be cleared by the incumbent leader was now much higher, as Mrs Thatcher found in November 1990, when her total of 204 votes (against Michael Heseltine's 152) on the first ballot was 4 short of the majority of 56 needed under the revised 15 per cent provision. The leader had to win and win well, failure to do so leading to a second and even a third ballot. The longer it took to assert numerical ascendancy, the less likely was survival. Although he deprecated the use of the phrase, the new 15 per cent rule became known as 'Alec's revenge'.[18]

Taken as a whole, this package was a timebomb for an unpopular leader. It was no longer the 'men in grey suits' who advised a leader to step down; the rank and file would withdraw legitimacy by secret ballot, even if that leader was (as in 1990) Prime Minister. It was a return to the golden age of the backbencher. 'The House of Commons is an electoral chamber,' wrote Walter Bagehot in 1867, 'it is the assembly which chooses our president.'[19]

Heath accepted the recommendations of the Home Committee on 25 January 1975; not only did he accept them, he announced a timetable for a contest, the implicit understanding being that, once the Conservatives had new rules, they would want to test them at once. Nominations for the leadership would close on 30 January and the ballot (he did not expect a second) would be held on 4 February. Home received a massive correspondence from the general public, many suggesting that as he had formulated the rules, he was to blame for Heath's difficulties. He replied to them all personally before the vote took place.

> No one can stop people challenging a leader of the party if they want to do so. If challenges are to come it is necessary to have machinery. If a leader can win a decisive victory that is the best answer, so if Mr Heath can beat his nearest rival by 42 (out of 276) that is that. If he doesn't, and he didn't last time, there is always the opportunity for the runner-up to withdraw, which Mr Maudling did, and again that is that. But if it is a close election no one can stop others coming in and again there has to be machinery which is orderly. I hope that Mr Heath can win.[20]

The names of various possible candidates had already been trailed, including Willie Whitelaw, who was unwilling to stand while Heath was in possession of the field; Keith Joseph, though the reception to his recent controversial speeches on unemployment and contraception had persuaded him not to run; Edward du Cann, but his City connections militated against him. In December 1974, Lord Alport had proposed Richard Wood as a 'transitional' leader of the party on the grounds that Wood was a north country member, had served in both home and overseas departments, was not seeking the post, and whose election would allow a younger man to emerge. He asked Alec Home for advice, who replied on Christmas Eve: 'I have the highest opinion of Richard but surely it is not fair to cast him in this role and to press him to consider it. It is the most awful job because you can only "talk", not "do", and Richard's particular strength has been out in the field, particularly Asia and Africa.

It is, of course, for him to judge his health but I have been close to him for years now and I think that this would kill him in no time.

Anyhow there is time as it must be long odds against anyone who is elected Leader in February actually taking the Tories into the General Election.'[21]

When nominations closed, Heath faced two challengers: Margaret Thatcher, his former Education Secretary, now shadow Spokesman on the Environment, and Hugh Fraser, the right-wing MP for Stafford and Stone. Thatcher had powerful, hard-working backers, who organised her campaign with military precision; by comparison, Heath's efforts were lack-lustre. The result of the ballot was Margaret Thatcher 130, Edward Heath 119, Hugh Fraser 16, Abstentions 11.[22]

The first question – do the Party want a change of leadership? – had been decisively answered. By 6 p.m. Heath had announced he would not stand in the second ballot. Home was sad for Heath personally, but felt that the rules had provided the machinery for the party to remove a successor who did not intend to go quietly.

Attention now turned to the subsequent ballots, when – under the rules – fresh candidates can enter the fray, the so-called 'coward's charter'. Once Heath had stood down somebody would emerge to carry the banner. That person was Willie Whitelaw, who might well have become Prime Minister eventually had he stood in the first ballot. The problem was that Margaret Thatcher had now secured the momentum, as Whitelaw recognised only too clearly. 'I never felt particularly enthusiastic in the circumstances', he was to write later, 'especially since Margaret Thatcher, having had the courage to stand against the existing Leader and defeat him, clearly had a strong bandwagon rolling for her.'[23] She had only failed by 9 votes to win outright on the first ballot. Hugh Fraser withdrew and urged his supporters to vote for Whitelaw. Maurice Macmillan was pressed to stand, as was his brother-in-law Julian Amery, though in the end both declined to do so.[24] Geoffrey Howe, James Prior and John Peyton eventually entered the lists, but Margaret Thatcher's hour had come. The vote took place on 11 February in the same Committee Room. The figures were: Margaret Thatcher 146, William Whitelaw 79, Geoffrey Howe 19, James Prior 19, John Peyton 11, Abstentions 2. Margaret Thatcher won an absolute majority on the second ballot. 'Margaret Thatcher will lead us with authority and style, humanity and common-sense,' said Home. 'May she be the first woman Prime Minister, and the sooner the better.'[25]

Home wrote to congratulate Margaret Thatcher, and her reply was the beginning of a fascinating correspondence, in which she frankly admitted her inexperience in the field of foreign affairs and turned increasingly to Home for guidance. The tone of the letters is one of humility and gratitude on Mrs Thatcher's side, understanding and humour on Alec Home's. The first letter from the new Leader of the Opposition read:

> My dear Alec,
>
> Please forgive the long delay in replying to your kind letter of congratulation. Like the best wine the most important letters were left to the last so that I could find time to answer them properly myself. Easter gives me just a brief respite from the ceaseless round which you know so well.
>
> The pressures of the last few weeks have been enormous. There was no time to prepare for the changeover and very few staff to cope. As always the press want instant comments and instant new policies on everything. I have had to tell them that that way lies disaster and it is my task to find the path to success. I sometimes think that we got our policies too detached in 1969–1970, so much so that we didn't realise the nature of some of the problems had already changed.
>
> I much enjoy meeting foreign statesmen, but some of the problems seem even more difficult than economic ones. At least, the answers are sometimes clear if only the people would accept them!
>
> When you are in London may we talk? I should so much value your advice – especially on the whole Foreign Affairs and defence fronts.[26]

Alec Home replied from the Hirsel on 4 April: 'Thank you for your letter. It was very nice of you to write in your own hand. I will get in touch with your Private Office one day.

'I would like to talk about our franchise. I do not believe that the moderate majority opinion, which is surely there, is adequately represented in recent election results.

'No answer. I will propose myself for a talk before long.'[27]

After the Easter recess, Home began a series of informal meetings with Margaret Thatcher in her office at the House of Commons, and she was always grateful for his help on a wide range of issues, especially East–West relationships in the light of the forthcoming Helsinki summit, and checking the drafts of speeches, notably one Thatcher made in Kensington Town Hall on 26 July 1975.[28] She had written to

Alec Home well in advance: 'It is time I made a comprehensive speech about "Britain's Place in the World". I wonder if you would give me some advice about it. If so – could we meet one day soon when you are in the House of Lords?'[29] The influence of Home can be seen in many passages, notably on the denial of freedom implicit in a repressive communist system. Margaret Thatcher thanked him for his help: '... thank you first for providing the framework for the foreign affairs speech and then for going through it so carefully. It gave me all the confidence I should otherwise have lacked. And thank you for your lucid remarks and wise judgment on the early morning broadcast today.'[30] Home replied: 'Thank you for your kind note. You were absolutely right to make the foreign affairs speech and if you compare what you said with the speech of President Ford you will find that your thinking is very close ... One always hopes that the communists will change their spots but they have not done so yet, and until there is firm evidence of change people must be warned. I hope you will take other opportunities, and the outrageous Berlin Wall is probably one of which you can speak at first hand. It is ... an absolute denial of civilisation. Luckily the communists are showing a pretty nasty hand in Portugal and Angola.'[31]

In the next few months their talks covered Mozambique, the Nuclear Non-proliferation Treaty in Geneva and the veto of the South African arms embargo. Whenever a particularly difficult problem arose, Alec Home was one of the first to whom Margaret Thatcher turned.

In the wake of the Labour Party's hardening attitude towards the House of Lords in 1976, Mrs Thatcher asked Lord Home to chair a Conservative committee of MPs and peers on proposals for the reform of the Upper Chamber. In 1977 a document was approved by the Labour Party conference stating: 'Should we become the Government after the next General Election, we intend to abolish the House of Lords.'[32] Home's committee contained the constitutional expert and historian, Robert Blake; Baroness Young, a future Leader of the House of Lords; and Kenneth Baker, a future Chairman of the Party. Their report was published in March 1978. It regretted 'the drift towards a unicameral form of parliamentary government', and acknowledged that the Upper Chamber 'may be swept away by government impatient of the modest checks it imposes on the passage of legislation'. This would be a regressive move. 'The case for radical reform of the House of Lords is thus effectively the case for stronger constitutional safeguards ... In such a situation only a second chamber with very strong moral authority could be expected to provide an effective constitutional check. In the present moral climate that moral authority could only come from the direct election of its members.' Accordingly, the committee proposed various ways in which an elected Upper Chamber could be established, preferring a hybrid system of election and nomination, with a total membership of 400, 60 per cent being elected either indirectly or directly, and 40 per cent being recruited from the House of Lords. But with the Labour Party's defeat in the 1979 election, the issue of abolition faded from the political agenda.

Work on his memoirs occupied much of Alec Home's time in 1975, though he did take on membership of the cross-party committee of Privy Counsellors, established to consider proposals for official histories of peace-time events.[33] Macmillan had given him much inside knowledge on the publishing world, including the importance of choosing an appropriate title. He eventually remembered a comment one of the estate workers had made to a journalist when he had succeeded Macmillan: 'Oh, the Home boys always seem to know which way the wind blows.' *The Way the Wind Blows* was published by Collins in October 1976. As it was his first literary project, he had taken great care to have the drafts checked at each stage, much of the help and advice coming from Miles Hudson, who sent him detailed comments, particularly on the Rhodesian section, saying that he found the book 'totally absorbing and full of wisdom'.[34] *The Way the Wind Blows* sold 27,000 copies in the first week and went to the top of the bestseller list. The book eventually sold more than 70,000 copies in hardback; a paperback edition which did even better followed in 1978. Alec Home was pleased to note that Harold Wilson's *The Governance of Britain* made the bottom half of the bestseller list only fleetingly. Some reviews were waspish. Enoch Powell, who referred to it privately as 'Gone with the Wind', wrote, 'When a politician who throughout his life has gone "the way the wind blows", and actually chooses that phrase as the title for his autobiography, it is difficult to know whether one is in the presence of fantastic candour or fantastic innocence.'[35] But Kenneth Rose described it as an 'evocative, wonderfully good-natured autobiography' that was 'remarkable for generosity towards political opponents'.[36] This was the case with Home's attitude towards Powell's review. For some it would have been the cause of a bitter rift, but that was not in Alec Home's nature. His attitude remained one of amused tolerance. When told by one colleague that the book showed he was better at writing about the dead than the living, he replied, 'I never did care for vivisection.'[37]

Much of the book was about his country interests and gave an insight into a vanished way of life, fascinating to the general reader. Its tone was self-effacing, despite the photographs showing him with the world leaders of half a century. No comprehensive survey of the major political developments of his time was attempted, and there were some surprising omissions such as the Cuban missile crisis. Nor did he draw attention to the significance of the changes he proposed in 1965 and 1975 for the choosing of the Party leader. Showing Home on the cover with his fishing rod, it was 'a good read', not a specialist study. Rab Butler kept a copy at his country home, Spencers, in Great Yeldham and he would sometimes offer it to weekend guests as they retired with the comment, 'Would you care to look at this book on fishing?'[38]

His publishers were delighted with the success of the book and pressed Home to write more. He obliged in 1979 with *Border Reflections*, which was 'chiefly on the arts of shooting and fishing'. Although again aimed at the general reader, this book was a valuable compendium of country ways; it, too, reached the bestseller list. He also helped the historians of the time, being an important witness for Dilks's biography of Chamberlain in 1984,[39] and assisting Nigel Fisher on his study of the Tory leaders (1977) and of Macmillan (1982). Home was always a ready contributor to serious historical documentary programmes, most notably Christopher Jones's *No. 10 Downing Street: The Story of a House* (BBC 1985), and Robert Harris's reassessment of Munich, *God Bless You Mr Chamberlain*, for the fiftieth anniversary in 1988. The last historian to benefit from his first-hand accounts was Andrew Roberts for his life of Halifax in 1991. He could, however, be sharp when he felt that authors showed ignorance of their subject matter. In 1977 Robert Lacey published *Majesty*, a study of the Queen, which had details of country life on the royal estates. '"Alive with the cry of mating partridges"? – possible in January, but unlikely', Home minuted on the proofs sent to him. 'Salmon don't rise in the evening cool. Better to say "where the salmon might come to the fly in the evening light".'[40] He also commented on some of the political assumptions in the script. 'I enclose a copy of my latest exchange with Mr Lacey,' he wrote to the Queen's Private Secretary, 'I somehow don't think I should like to be next to him on the moors!'[41]

Home's literary career eventually took the road of 'Grow old along with me! The best is yet to be.'[42] He conceived the idea of a series of letters to his grandson, Matthew Darby, on some of the episodes he had been involved in, including the Cuban missile crisis. He had often spoken to the Eton Political Society and he knew intuitively at what level he should pitch his reminiscences. *Letters to a Grandson* was published by Collins in 1983 and it remains the most enduring and endearing of his three books, a kind of political *Screwtape Letters*. Just as Anthony Eden produced his literary masterpiece, *Another World 1897–1917* in 1976, almost as a postscript to his three volumes of memoirs, so Alec Home expressed himself most memorably in this last volume, a classic of its kind. In twenty-one letters, he covers his career from the First World War, never condescending to his audience. The early letters, with accounts of Edward Grey and Rosebery, have the immediacy and vividness of Churchill's *Great Contemporaries*. Of Baldwin's appearances in the Commons, he writes that Baldwin would 'smack kisses on the Order Paper as though he were starved of affection!'[43] He wrote to his grandson's history tutor at Eton about his intentions in choosing such a format: 'I was lately struck by how little two Edinburgh undergraduates knew of modern history, and thought I would write something in readable form. I chose Matthew as he is the same age as I was when at Eton in the First World War, and I trust his generation will avoid the pitfalls into which we fell.'[44]

Another sign that Alec Home was now an elder statesman came with his appearance on *Desert Island Discs* in April 1977. One of his predecessors as Foreign Secretary, Herbert Morrison, had pressed in vain for an invitation to appear on the programme,[45] but to Alec Home an invitation came unsolicited. His choices reflected his love of Scotland and cricket and hinted at the more reflective and religious side of his nature. He chose Harry Lauder singing 'Roaming in the gloaming', the Alec Bedser calypso from the coronation Ashes series of 1953, the song 'I sit in the sun' from *Salad Days*, Handel's 'Water Music', a duet from *The Magic Flute* and Orfeo's lament from Gluck's *Orfeo ed Euridice*, Handel's Coronation Anthem 'Zadok the Priest' and the 23rd Psalm to the tune of 'Crimond'. His book choice was Bannerman's *History of British Birds* and, for his luxury, a pair of field glasses 'to widen the horizon'.[46]

On 16 March 1976, his old adversary Harold Wilson unexpectedly announced his intention to step down as Prime Minister. In the subsequent election for Labour leader, James Callaghan was chosen to succeed him. Callaghan's successor as Foreign Secretary was Anthony Crosland, but he died on 19 February 1977 and was succeeded by the thirty-eight-year-old Dr David Owen, the youngest Foreign Secretary since Anthony Eden in 1935. One of the first letters Owen wrote after his appointment was to Alec Home. 'Don't hesitate to offer your advice and guidance at any time and I will be always delighted to have a chat.'[47] With the death of Anthony Eden on 14 January 1977, and the arrival at the Foreign Office a few weeks later of the youthful Owen, Home was a link between two ages, and was deeply touched that the new Foreign Secretary should have written in these terms.

On 22 February 1977, Callaghan's government was defeated on the Scotland and Wales Bill, a turning point for his administration since he could no longer depend on the Scottish and Welsh Nationalists for support, when any immediate prospect of devolution vanished. The Lib-Lab Pact, a short term measure that kept Labour in office, was concluded between David Steel and James Callaghan on 23 March 1977, and the No Confidence motion tabled by Mrs Thatcher was defeated on the same day by 298 votes to 322. Despite this set-back for the Conservatives, there was a feeling that time was running out for the Labour government. Callaghan knew that a sea-change was coming over British politics and at the beginning of 1979 it seemed only a matter of weeks before the fragile alliances that kept Labour in office would finally break. Just as Harold Wilson caught the tide of public imagination in 1964, so now it seemed that Mrs Thatcher's hour had come. With the general expectation of a Conservative Government, Home nevertheless felt Callaghan had played the hand that political fate had dealt him with dignity and skill. He also hoped that Peter Carrington would be appointed Foreign Secretary when the Conservatives came to power.[48]

The years saw the inevitable thinning of the ranks of his old friends and colleagues. Eden's death in 1977 was a distinct break with the past, and, as Home set off for Robert Menzies's funeral in Australia in May 1978, he heard of the death of Selwyn Lloyd, whose career had overlapped so much with his own. Home flew back from Australia to give the address at Lloyd's funeral, and the words he chose could have applied to himself. 'He never courted the crowd – he shunned it. He never tried the showmanship of oratory – he disdained it.'[49] There were family bereavements also: his sister Bridget died in March 1980 and that summer, his brother Henry died. Alec Home became sought after for memorial addresses, a difficult genre that he raised to an art form. The one he gave on Alan Lennox-Boyd on 3 May 1983 was a model of its kind, though afterwards he said that the most difficult thing was that the acoustics in Westminster Abbey were worse than those in King's Cross Station.[50] In 1987, he gave the address at the televised memorial service for Harold Macmillan, a gesture that greatly touched the Macmillan family, for he was by then in his eighty-fourth year. For Harold Macmillan, memorial services were the cocktail parties of the geriatric set; for Alec Home they were the opportunity to tell the truth in a kindly way.

The general election of May 1979 was a controversial episode towards the end of Home's career. In a speech in Edinburgh in February on the eve of the referendum vote on the Labour government's proposals for Scottish devolution, he advised that Scotland should vote 'No for a better bill'. As the bill stood, it would lead to a separatism analogous to that of the Basques in Spain or the Walloons in Belgium. BBC Scotland then ran a television interview with Home in which these views permeated far beyond Edinburgh. He claimed the Conservatives would introduce a better bill once they were in office; this intervention was thought to have tilted the balance against the necessary vote for devolution especially when Thatcher issued a statement on 28 February which promised 'A No vote does not mean the devolution question will be buried'.[51] But when the Conservatives took office the much-vaunted 'better bill' was not forthcoming. Home was unrepentant, but his enthusiasm for Thatcher cooled somewhat in the aftermath of the 1979 election. 'The Act as drafted was divisive. It would have resulted in too much power for the central belt, and it would have alienated other regions like the Borders and the Highlands. More important, it didn't tackle the central difficulty of striking the balance between an assembly in Edinburgh and a Parliament at Westminster which has still not been solved. I'm sure it was right to vote against it.'[52]

Home's intervention in the devolution debate can be seen as one of the straws that broke the back of the Callaghan government. When the referendum was held on 1 March 1979, the Labour government's proposals were overwhelmingly defeated in Wales, whereas in Scotland only 51.2 per cent voted in favour, well short of the 40 per cent hurdle *of the entire population* needed to carry the day.[53] The Scottish Nationalists then put down a censure motion on the government's failure to bring in immediate devolution. The opportunity for the overthrow of the government was at hand and in the No Confidence debate on 28 March, it was defeated by 311 votes to 310.[54] A general election was called for 3 May, and five and a quarter years of Labour government were at end.

As Home had hoped, Lord Carrington was appointed Foreign Secretary by Thatcher in the Conservative government that now took office. That Carrington took office without any criticism in May 1979 was a tacit admission that a Foreign Secretary in the Upper House was not a constitutional anomaly. As in 1960, a Cabinet Minister was appointed to answer for the Foreign Office in the House of Commons, when Sir Ian Gilmour became Lord Privy Seal. Carrington was at the heart of the final settlement in Rhodesia in 1980. He chaired the Lancaster House conference, which led to independence in 1980. Robert Mugabe's ZANU Party won the elections and he became the first Prime Minister of an independent Zimbabwe; one of the longest roads in Britain's imperial retreat was at an end.

Alec Home followed this process closely, as he did all international developments. The various news bulletins were always fixed points in his day at the Hirsel, Douglas or his flat in London. He received many anxious letters from the public about future prospects for Zimbabwe, all of which he answered in his own hand. 'The great question is Can Mugabe be a Kenyatta?' he wrote in one such reply. 'Bishop Muzorewa deserves a place of honour in the records of Rhodesia, for he started the whole action which led to majority rule', he wrote in another. 'It is of course very difficult to foresee the future, but Mugabe is orientated to Chinese philosophy rather than to Chinese Marxism. He is also pragmatic and will want a prospering economy.' It was not only to members of the public that he wrote. With his Christmas message to Sir Roy Welensky that year, he added: 'Christopher Soames was much impressed by Mugabe's ability, and I am glad to hear that you confirm this. If he really feels able to clear up the arms (a difficult thing to do) that ought to make a decisive difference to the prospect ahead.'[55]

Margaret Thatcher kept in touch with the former Prime Minister, not only out of courtesy. He was informed of the decision to announce the identity of Anthony Blunt as the 'Fourth Man' on 15 November 1979. In explaining the decision to grant Blunt immunity from prosecution in the House of Commons, the Prime Minister stated that the decision had been taken in 1964 at a meeting between Peter Brooke, then Home Secretary, and the Attorney-General, Sir John Hobson, after extensive discussions in Whitehall. She confirmed that Sir Alec Douglas-Home, Prime Minister and Head of the Security Services, had not been privy to the decisions. The view of the Director-General of MI5, Sir Roger Hollis, was 'that the Prime Minister might refuse to compromise the Queen [Blunt was the Surveyor of The Queen's pictures] and that any successful debriefing depended upon Blunt retaining his status in the Palace',[56] which spoke volumes about Alec Home.

When the Falklands war broke out in April 1982, Home was again kept in the picture by Downing Street and received an extensive correspondence. The news of Lord Carrington's resignation as Foreign Secretary in the wake of the Argentine invasion of the islands came on 5 April, the morning of the Memorial Service to Rab Butler, who had died on 7 March. Home attended the service, travelling to Westminster Abbey in the same car as Harold Macmillan. Carrington read the first lesson at the service, as news began to spread that he was no longer, as described in the service sheet, 'Secretary of State for Foreign and Commonwealth Affairs'.

Home was in no doubt that the government took the right course of action over the Falklands, as he stated to correspondents: 'Aggression cannot be condoned, or no one would be safe. Any number of countries have historical claims to parts of others, but force must not be used. The authors of the Charter of the UN put "non-interference by one country in the affairs of another" at the centre of international relations and peace. They were right. The trouble is that the UN has no machinery to enforce its will, hence we have to try and protect those for whom we are responsible and uphold international law. It is costly, but we have done it before, and the Falklands should be within our capacity.'[57] So it proved and, though Home was relieved at the outcome, he was disturbed by some of the elements of triumphalism that accompanied the return of the troops from the South Atlantic. He attended the Service of Thanksgiving at St Paul's Cathedral in July after the cessation of hostilities. The Archbishop of Canterbury, Robert Runcie, preached a sermon that disappointed some members of the congregation, but which struck a sympathetic chord with Alec Home. 'War is a sign of human failure and everything we say and do in this service must be in that context', said the Archbishop. 'In our prayers we shall quite rightly remember those who are bereaved in our own country and the relatives of the young Argentinian soldiers who were killed. Common sorrow could do something to reunite those who were engaged in this struggle. A shared anguish can be a bridge of reconciliation.' 'I sympathised with Runcie in St Paul's!' wrote Home to the Bishop of Lincoln. 'He was very good.'[58]

The 1980s saw a decrease in the pace of Lord Home's activities, though he still attended the House of Lords on a regular basis, where he sat on the front bench next to Quintin Hailsham and John Boyd-Carpenter, and, after February 1984, Harold Macmillan, ennobled as the first Earl of Stockton. His last major speech was on 4 December 1989, when he spoke against prosecuting war criminals resident in Britain. On 8 March 1983 Mrs Thatcher spoke at the ceremony when a bust of Lord Home was unveiled in the House of Lords. 'Of all the tasks that have fallen to me since I became Prime Minister, none has given me greater happiness than today's ceremony,' she said. 'There are statues already to fourteen Prime Ministers who sat in the House of Lords, today we add a fifteenth. The way the wind blows, it is unlikely that there will be another.'[59] Mrs Thatcher hosted a lunch at Chequers for his eightieth birthday on 2 July 1983, and the Earl of Bessborough arranged a gala cricket match in Sussex as part of the celebrations. But the most important anniversary during the 1980s was Alec's and Elizabeth's golden wedding on 3 October 1986. The Queen sent congratulations and the family gave them fifty golden plants for the Hirsel grounds.

Life at the Hirsel was unhurried and informal, as David Steel found. 'With such a huge house and estate I expected at least footmen and silver trays,' he recorded of one visit. 'On the contrary we blundered about the deserted, darkened basement while he found some beer, and drank it quickly in his frozen library.'[60] Those who helped, like Mrs Greenshields who came in every weekday, lived on the estate, or in the case of Miss Anthea Montgomery, who cooked and gardened for many years, in a flat in the big house. It was a world of gumboots and labradors, the latest political biographies on the tables, and walks by the lake, where the Homes would talk to visitors to the grounds or golfers on the Hirsel course.[61] A craft centre was opened, with places for children to play, and a car park, though there were no tickets for admission, just an unattended box by the gate. Each day had its rituals: at breakfast in the bay window of the large dining room, the morning's copies of *The Times* and the *Daily Mail* were scoured for the racing news, and by 9.30 Alec would have spoken on the telephone with his brother William to compare notes on the day's prospects. In the school holidays, grandchildren were staying, and other guests found themselves swept into the day's activities, particularly picnics, which continued in waterproofs even when it rained. Lunch was at one, though often delayed for a few minutes to catch the latest headlines. After his stroke in November 1990, he liked to go down to the riverbank, where a special chair was set for him, to watch and enjoy the day's sport, and even to land the occasional fish himself, including a 16lb salmon in September 1992. At 4.30, people gathered for tea in the smoking room, a favourite time of day for the young, with home-made scones, bannock and cakes. The evening was a time for talk, board games for the children, reading after dinner. The house was rarely without visitors for long. Christmas meant a gathering of all the family, with services at St Mary and All Souls, Coldstream, and presents around the dining-room table, though one grandchild once declared that she no longer believed in Father Christmas, who 'shops at the same shops as Grandmummy'.[62]

The first months of 1990 were busy ones. Alec Home presided at the luncheon in February held at the Savoy for the fortieth anniversary of Edward Heath's election to Parliament, and made the main speech. Their first great-grandchild, Harry Wolfe Murray, was born in March 1990 and his christening party in the summer was one of the last family events attended by both Alec and Elizabeth Home. On 21 June, Bernard Weatherill, Speaker of the House of Commons, hosted a dinner for Members who had been elected before the Second World War. There were nineteen survivors, including Quintin Hailsham, Michael Foot and George Strauss. Alec Home was the only former Prime Minister. The Homes then journeyed north: the second week in August marked the start of the annual Douglas holiday, when the family gathered in Lanarkshire with friends for the shooting. Alec Home had always hoped that Elizabeth would outlive him, but it was not to be. A stroke had weakened her and she found it difficult to stand for long. On 3 September, while Alec Home was out on the moors, Elizabeth collapsed and died two months before her eighty-first birthday.

Alec Home never recovered from this blow in the five years of life that were left to him. 'He and Elizabeth were a team to such an extent that one cannot really separate them in any assessment of their impact,' Miles Hudson wrote after Alec Home's death. 'She supported him, and he her, with total commitment and love. One could not really consider them as two separate beings. They were one.'[63] One of the first calls was from Margaret Thatcher, who wrote the next day:

> My dear Alec,
>
> We spoke on the telephone about Elizabeth, but I wanted also to write to express our sorrow and grief. Goodness and kindness radiated from Elizabeth to all the people she came in contact with. It was a real joy to be with her and hear her words of encouragement

> and cheer. She was a tower of strength not only to you and your family but to its many causes in which she took an interest.
>
> There will be such a gap in your life now. All the countless daily things and kindly words that one takes so much for granted are gone – they are the bread of life, the daily habits together.
>
> You will be sustained by your faith and the sympathy of thousands and thousands of friends the world over. And by many happy memories of a golden life so deeply shared.[64]

Alec Home received letters from all over the world. Each one was individually answered.

A Service of Thanksgiving was announced for 22 November at St Margaret's, Westminster, but so many people wished to attend that the celebration was held in Westminster Abbey. The address was given by Lord Charteris, who began by reading out the first words that Elizabeth Home had written in her Commonplace Book, when still a young girl: 'I shall pass through this world but once. Any good thing therefore that I can do or any kindness that I can show to any fellow creature, let me do it now. Let me not defer or neglect it for I shall not pass this way again.'[65]

Lord Home planned to speak that afternoon in the House of Lords debate on the worsening situation in the Gulf, but the service had taken a heavy toll, so he simply took his place on the front bench between John Boyd-Carpenter and Quintin Hailsham for what was his last appearance at Westminster.[66]

From London, he went to stay with his brother William and his wife at Kilmeston, where he was low and unduly taciturn. On the morning of Sunday 25 November, however, he went out with William and his son-in-law to a local farm to see some pigs. On the way back he collapsed, and suffered another small stroke in the night. Although he had not mentioned it, for fear of missing Elizabeth's Memorial Service, he had suffered two turns in Scotland before travelling south. He was now taken to a nursing home in Winchester, where he stayed until just before Christmas. His stay was enlivened by his brother William, who referred to his MOT, and by a series of increasingly scabrous seaside postcards from Brian Johnston ('And here's one for Matron'), which led to a certain horrified amusement among the staff.[67]

One of his first worries on returning to the Hirsel was the full-time nurses who would now be necessary, for his memories of the 1940s and Springhill were still vivid. But a succession of young nurses, mainly from Australia and New Zealand, looked after him over the next five years; gradually he recovered, though he could only move when supported by someone, and took his old interest in political news and sport, though reading became more difficult. During the Gulf War, when he was kept in touch with the news by Douglas Hurd, then Foreign Secretary, both these interests coalesced when he saw Saddam Hussein in curious garb on a television bulletin. Looking at the multi-coloured neck-wear, he commented, 'Rum fellow that Saddam, he's wearing an Eton Rambler's tie!'[68] His life was now spent at the Hirsel with visits to Douglas and he never came to London again.

He wrote his last letters to *The Times* (on 9 October 1991) on socialism in Eastern Europe and to *The Scotsman* (on 18 May 1992) on the union between England and Scotland. Despite opinion polls suggesting the contrary, he was confident that John Major would prevail in the general election of 9 April 1992, the 24th of his lifetime. 'What a splendid result last night', he wrote.[69] Other events in 1992 were not so happy. The death of his brother William in September 1992 seemed to take some time to register; he retreated into silence and his condition declined. On 2 July 1993 he celebrated his ninetieth birthday, marked by a presentation from the Cabinet by Malcolm Rifkind, then Defence Secretary, of John Gould's *Monograph of the Pittidae*. The inscription read 'Presented to Lord Home of the Hirsel on the occasion of his 90th Birthday with affection and best wishes from the Cabinet' and was signed by them all. Twenty-five members of the family gathered at the Hirsel for the celebrations. After lunch he watched the test match against Australia at Trent Bridge, where he had once faced the bowling of Harold Larwood.

For some prime ministers the departure from Downing Street is the final curtain. 'It is tempting, perhaps, but unrewarding', wrote Harold Macmillan, 'to hang about the green room after final retirement from the stage', an ironic observation in the light of his Indian summer as the nonagenarian Earl of Stockton.[70] In the three decades after leaving Downing Street Alec Home was more than a conventional elder statesman; as Walter Scott had written, 'Old age ne'er cools the Douglas blood.'[71] In May 1995 two of Alec Home's associates died within a few days of each other: Arnold Goodman, on 12 May and a fortnight later, Harold Wilson. The next day Alec Home's old constituency of (now) Perth and Kinross fell to the Scottish Nationalists in the by-election following the death of Nicholas Fairbairn. Home's health deteriorated over the long summer of 1995. There was one last visit to Douglas in August.

Alec Home died peacefully on 9 October 1995 at his beloved Hirsel, surrounded by his family. He was described as 'the quiet aristocrat of British politics'[72] and the lesson of his career that 'politics and honour are by no means incompatible'.[73] At the end of a day of tributes from around the world, Nigel Lawson, interviewed on *Newsnight*, said that if he was faced with a difficult decision, he only had to ask himself, 'How would Alec Home have behaved in similar circumstances?' Alec Home, he said, was the most remarkable person he had ever known. For Lady Thatcher, he was the wisest of men, and 'represented all that was best in his generation'.

The coverage in the press included editorials in *The Times* and the *Daily Telegraph*. Of Rab Butler's death in 1982, Anthony Howard had written that *The Times* had yielded Butler 'the ultimate accolade of carrying no other obituary'.[74] When Home died, Anthony Howard was the obituaries editor of *The Times*; it carried no other obituary.

By one of the ironies of history, delegates were arriving at Blackpool for the start of the Conservative Party Conference when news of Alec Home's death broke, just as they had been doing in strangely similar circumstances in 1963. Labour were ahead in the opinion polls, the Labour leader of the day had just made a keynote speech to his conference, and the Conservatives were trying to cope with the political fall-out of the actions of their former Member of Parliament for Stratford-upon-Avon, John Profumo in 1963, and Alan Howarth, who had just anounced his defection to the Labour Party in 1995; 9 October was also the day that Macmillan had let the Queen know of his intention to resign, had given Home the letter to read to the Conference, and urged him to allow his name to go forward for the leadership. When the 1995 Conference began, the delegates stood in silence to remember their former leader. Thirty-two years earlier to the day, the same hall had been silent as Alec Home read the letter announcing Macmillan's retirement. In the Prime Minister's suite in the Imperial Hotel, Home's portrait was hung with black. A fortnight later I Zingari met to celebrate its 150th anniversary. Before dinner, the members stood in silence 'in memory of Lord Home of the Hirsel, Governor 4th Wicket down'.[75]

The funeral was a private family gathering in Coldstream on Saturday 14 October, a golden autumnal day with butterflies in the hazy air. 'It was the one brilliant day in seven', said the Duke of Buccleuch in his address at the Service of Thanksgiving in St Giles Cathedral, 'and it seemed that nature too had come to salute an exemplary countryman.'[76] The service was conducted by the Bishop of Edinburgh and Primus,

Richard Holloway and the parish priest of St Mary and All Souls, the Reverend Gordon Tams. The bidding prayer, which had been written by Caroline, Meriel and Diana, spoke of their father's 'Humour and contentment in family life, the smile that lit his face and the gentle way he dealt with the exuberance of youth'. Of the five brothers, who 'knew which way the wind blew', only Edward survived him. The music included Alec's old favourite, the 23rd Psalm. His grandsons, Rory Wolfe Murray and Matthew Darby, read from *The Way the Wind Blows* and Caroline read the Old Testament lesson, Psalm 121: 'I will lift up my eyes to the hills, from whence cometh my help.' The New Testament lesson from St John was read by David: 'Let not your heart be troubled, neither let it be afraid.' So ended the simple tributes to a much loved man. After the service Alec Home was laid to rest beside Elizabeth in Lennel Churchyard, in sight of the Cheviot Hills, as hundreds of pink-footed geese flew overhead across a cloudless blue sky.

Appendix I

The Douglas-Home Procedure for the Selection of the Leader of the Conservative and Unionist Party, February 1965.

1. There shall be a ballot of the Party in the House of Commons.
2. The Chairman of the 1922 Committee will be responsible for the conduct of the ballot and will settle all matters in relation thereto.

Nominations and Preparation of the Ballot

3. Candidates will be proposed and seconded in writing. The Chairman of the 1922 Committee and a body of scrutineers designated by him will be available to receive nominations. Each candidate will indicate on the nomination paper that he is prepared to accept nomination, and no candidate will accept more than one nomination. The names of the proposer and seconder will not be published and will remain confidential to the scrutineers. Nominations will close twenty-four hours before the first and second ballots. Valid nominations will be published.
4. The scrutineers will prepare a ballot paper listing the names of the candidates and give a copy to each voter at a meeting called by the Chairman of the 1922 Committee for the purpose of balloting and consisting of all Members of the House of Commons in receipt of the Conservative and National Liberal Whips.

First Ballot

5. For the first ballot each voter will indicate one choice from the candidates listed, and hand the ballot paper to the scrutineers who will count the votes.
6. If as a result of this ballot one candidate *both* (i) receives an overall majority *and* (ii) receives 15 per cent more of the votes cast than any other candidate, he will be elected.

7. The scrutineers will announce the number of votes received by each candidate, and if no candidate satisfies these conditions a second ballot will be held.

Second Ballot

8. The second ballot will be held not less than two days and not more than four days after the first ballot, excluding Saturdays and Sundays. Nominations made for the first ballot will be void and new nominations, under the same procedure as for the first ballot, will be submitted for the original candidates if required and for any other candidate.
9. The voting procedure for the second ballot will be the same as for the first, save that paragraph 6 above shall not apply. If as a result of this second ballot one candidate receives an overall majority he will be elected.

Third Ballot

10. If no candidate receives an overall majority, the three candidates receiving the highest number of votes at the second ballot will be placed on a ballot paper for a third and final ballot.
11. For the final ballot each voter must indicate two preferences amongst the three candidates by placing the figure '1' opposite the name of his preferred candidate and the figure '2' opposite the name of his second choice.
12. The scrutineers will proceed to add the number of first preference votes received by each candidate, eliminate the candidate with the lowest number of first preference votes and redistribute the votes of those giving him as their first preference amongst the two remaining candidates in accordance with their second preference. The result of this final count will be an overall majority for one candidate, and he will be elected.

Party Meeting

13. The candidate thus elected by the Commons Party will be presented for election as Party Leader to the Party Meeting constituted as at present.

Appendix II

Lord Home's address at the Memorial Service for Harold Macmillan, Westminster Abbey, 10 February, 1987

In the early days of the year, the funeral service of Harold Macmillan, Lord Stockton, was held in the small and beautiful church of St Andrew in Horsted Keynes, in Sussex and near his home, and that was fitting because it was there that he and Lady Dorothy and their children used to worship every Sunday when he could be at home; for the self-discipline and the witness of church-going was part of his code of conduct, and he was always ready to testify that from his Christian faith he drew the strength for the daily round. The congregation that day consisted of relations and neighbours from the village and the local countryside and that, too, was fitting for Harold Macmillan was a family man who believed in the loyalties of kinship, and that the example of close family life strengthened the fabric of society. He valued friendship and he practised it. Essentially, he was a private man, happy when he could lose himself in intimate and easy conversation with a few friends and happiest, perhaps, in the company of his books. Today it is equally fitting that in this great Christian and national shrine a company widely representative of the nation should recall the public man, the patriot, parliamentarian, master of both Houses, the statesman of national and international reputation, the scholar, the thinker and always, in whatever role he was cast, the man of style.

He was brought up as a boy in the company of men of letters and when he arrived at school at Eton his scholarship was already marked, and in no mean company, for many of his contemporaries were to become household names. Partly by custom and certainly by his strong preference, he went for his own education to the classics, to the philosophers of ancient Greece and Rome, men wise in their generation, pioneers in the arts of politics and statecraft, in which profession he hoped in due course to take up and to contribute to the unfinished business of building democracy. Ever afterwards, one of the most attractive aspects of his exposition of politics was his ability to place current events in the perspective of history. To the end of his life, he expressed gratitude to Eton and Balliol for having introduced him to wise men from whom he learned and never forgot that politics is essentially about people, and that democracy is all about the relationship of the individual citizen with the law. It was in the classics that he found his philosophy of life.

Two convulsive events in early manhood engaged his deep emotions and gave point and direction to his thinking. The first, the death of so many of his contemporaries and potential leaders of men in the trench fighting of the 1914 war. 70,000 casualties in one week in the Battle of Loos in which he fought with exemplary courage; the slaughter which he would wryly remind us is now called 'conventional' war. The second event is the human waste in terms of poverty and unemployment which followed the economic depressions of the late 1920s and early 1930s. Those who had returned with him from fighting had been promised a land fit for heroes to live in, and Stockton, which he represented in Parliament, was not like that. Curiously, it was to take another war and the high political responsibility given to him by Winston Churchill in North Africa and the Mediterranean before this serious, well-equipped young man gained the confidence in himself to do things, and to realise that he could command a following in doing them. The story has been so often repeated lately that it must be told in shorthand: as Minister of Housing, he sensed a human need; he set a target for building, cut the red tape and, by emphatic drive, he reached the goal. The success earned him the familiar superlatives, he dismissed the flattery as an impostor. He was never, as the lesson at his funeral service reminded us, never puffed up. He exploited the publicity, and why not when all of it was free, and when it gave him the opportunity to further his economic and social and political aims, in the objects of which he believed. He was the first to recognise that an increasingly educated electorate would look for government by explanation and he knew he could provide it. An actor? yes; an advocate? certainly, and very persistent and convincing in his advocacy. It was the sustained wisdom and wit and style of his interpretation of the meaning and conduct of Britain's parliamentary democracy which kept him at the centre of the political stage for so many years.

The office of Prime Minister gave him the wide screen. A second war in his lifetime had aroused his anger at the folly of men who acquiesced in the suicidal repetition of wars for political gain, and he resolved to act. Always the realist, he understood that so long as the security of Europe and the Atlantic was poised on a balance of power, America held the key to peace. He therefore laid himself out to exercise all the personal magnetism at his command on the young President of the United States, to convince him that the interests of the United States and the democracies of Western Europe were identical in the prevention of wars and that this justified a commitment of power in peace time to demonstrate beyond doubt that any breach of the peace would involve America and Europe from the start; not one or the other, as it had been in previous wars but both Europe and the United States. His advocacy was a success. Always the idealist, he sought to persuade President Kennedy that Britain and America should at least launch the process of control of the new dimension of power which was the nuclear arm. The Nuclear Test Ban Treaty against the odds was virtually Harold Macmillan's doing. Historians will be certain to find that the accord between the older and the younger leaders and statesmen has deep significance for the peace and security of the free democracies.

Foresight is not conspicuously man's most successful piece of equipment, but Macmillan had it. He foresaw, following India's independence, the rampant advance of nationalism. Here he could only warn and hope that others would take the warning in time. Every historic sense that he had insisted on the partnership of Britain and Europe, for this he had to wait, but he lived to see his dream come true. Those who have lately seen parts of his life replayed on the television programmes will recognise the quality and the extraordinary versatility of the man. Nothing in his presence could ever be dull. The flavour cannot be recaptured at secondhand, and I would only dare to give one illustration. I once received a message from the Foreign Office that the Prime Minister would like to meet me at my convenience. It was in the middle of some stubborn international crisis. Thinking of Number Ten, or the House of Commons or, possibly, Birch Grove, I asked my Private Secretary, Did the Prime Minister suggest when and where? Yes, was the answer, before luncheon on the 18th green at Gleneagles! His instinct was right – the clear Highland air swept all the cobwebs away, and the international crisis was solved. So, today, there is nothing for tears, and everything for rejoicing and thanksgiving for a life courageously, richly and fully lived to the very end of a long and testing journey. For him we may be content that of this he was sure, totally sure, that when the time came to die he would receive at the hands of his Lord and Saviour love, and mercy and justice.

Bibliography

Private Papers

1 *Home papers*

The principal papers of the Douglas-Home family and estates are divided between the Hirsel, Coldstream, and HM General Register House, Edinburgh (The National Register of Archives, Scotland).

The private and political papers consist of 111 boxes, together with loose uncatalogued material. The bulk of the catalogued material relates to the post-war period, particularly 1960–74, though the labelling on the boxes is only a general guide to the wealth and variety of material within. As in due course this material will be fully catalogued, any attempt at detailed identification of file would be unhelpful and even confusing to later researchers. Material from these boxes is indicated as Hirsel Archive (HA).

In addition to the 111 boxes is a collection of 108 scrapbooks, covering the years from 1928 to 1990. Scrapbook is an inadequate description for the volumes collected over 62 years by Lady Home. Each volume is a substantial hard-backed record, interweaving family material with national and international developments. Volume 37, for instance, is devoted to the General Election campaign of October 1964. These volumes give a unique insight into Lord Home's family and public life. Material from these 108 scrapbooks is indicated as Scrapbook (SB), together with the number, viz., SB/37.

The Estate papers, relating principally to Douglas and the Hirsel, consist of 185 boxes ('Box 1, Bundles 1–3 Parcel Writs, 1502–1708, of lands'). The full catalogue for this collection is available at HM General Register House, Edinburgh, as are some of the items. The majority of the boxes remain at the time of writing at the Hirsel.

Also at the Hirsel are volumes of family memorabilia, including photographic records (in particular those taken by the Hon. George Douglas-Home before the war), ornithological, game and fishing records, draft manuscripts and proofs of Lord Home's three books, various journalism and occasional writings, together with broadcasting transcripts.

2 *Other private papers*

Royal Archives, Windsor Castle (by gracious permission of Her Majesty the Queen)

Earl Alexander of Tunis (Public Record Office)
Earl of Avon (Birmingham University Library, courtesy of the Countess of Avon)
Sir William Becher (courtesy of Sir William Becher, Bt)
Lord Butler of Saffron Walden (Trinity College, Cambridge)
Lady Butler of Saffron Walden (private record of the events of October 1963, courtesy of Lady Butler of Saffron Walden)
Dr David Butler (private papers on 1964 General Election, courtesy of Dr David Butler)
Sir Alexander Cadogan (Churchill College, Cambridge)
Viscount Caldecote (Churchill College, Cambridge)
Neville Chamberlain (Birmingham University Library)
Lord Chandos (Churchill College, Cambridge)
Sir John Colville (Churchill College, Cambridge)
Lord Crookshank (Bodleian Library, Oxford)
Sir Knox Cunningham (courtesy of the late Sir Knox Cunningham)
Mr John Dickie (private record of the events of October 1963, courtesy of Mr John Dickie)
Sir Thomas Dugdale (courtesy of Lord Crathorne)
Lady Emmett (Bodleian Library, Oxford)
Sylvia Goodfellow (Trinity College, Cambridge and private possession)
Lord Fanshawe (courtesy of Lord Fanshawe)
Lord Gordon Walker (Churchill College, Cambridge)
Sir William Gorell Barnes (Churchill College, Cambridge)
Sir Eldon Griffiths (courtesy of Sir Eldon Griffiths)
Lord Hailes (Churchill College, Cambridge)
R.M. Hamilton records of Douglas and Angus estates (courtesy of the late Mr R.M. Hamilton)
Lord Hankey (Churchill College, Cambridge)
Lord Hore-Belisha (Churchill College, Cambridge)
Miles Hudson (courtesy of Mr Miles Hudson)
John F. Kennedy (John F. Kennedy Library, Boston)
Robert F. Kennedy (John F. Kennedy Library, Boston)
Lord Kilmuir (Churchill College, Cambridge)
Alan Lennox-Boyd (Bodleian Library, Oxford)
Ramsay MacDonald (Public Record Office, Kew)
John McDonnell (courtesy of Mr John McDonnell, QC)
Harold Macmillan (courtesy of the Macmillan Trustees)
Viscount Margesson (Churchill College, Cambridge)
Sir Derek Mitchell (courtesy of Sir Derek Mitchell)
Earl Mountbatten of Burma (University of Southampton)
Lord Monckton (Bodleian Library, Oxford)
Viscount Norwich (Churchill College, Cambridge)
Sir Anthony Parsons correspondence (courtesy of the late Sir Anthony Parsons)
Lord Pearce (courtesy of Mrs Ian Ball and Mr Edward Pearce)
Sir Patrick Reilly (courtesy of Sir Patrick Reilly)
Lord Reith diaries (unpublished material, BBC Written Archives, Caversham)
John Robertson (courtesy of Mr John Robertson)

Kenneth Rose (courtesy of Mr Kenneth Rose)
Lord Selwyn-Lloyd (Churchill College, Cambridge)
Lord Sherfield (courtesy of Lord Sherfield)
Sir Harold Smedley (courtesy of Sir Harold Smedley)
Viscount Simon (Bodleian Library, Oxford)
Lord Strang (Churchill College, Cambridge)
Lord Swinton (Churchill College, Cambridge)
Viscount Thurso (Churchill College, Cambridge)
Lord Vansittart (Churchill College, Cambridge)
A.W. Whitworth family (courtesy of Mr Compton Whitworth)
Sir Horace Wilson (Public Record Office)
Lord Woolton (Bodleian Library, Oxford)

3 *Oral History Transcripts* (John F. Kennedy Library, Boston)
Henry Brandon
David Bruce
McGeorge Bundy
Chester Cooper
Sir Alec Douglas-Home (later Lord Home of the Hirsel)
William Douglas-Home
Lord Gore-Booth
Averell Harriman
Benjamin H. Read
Lord Redmayne
Sir Patrick Reilly
Dean Rusk
Lord Thorneycroft
Sir Humphrey (later Lord) Trevelyan
Sir Michael Wright

Public and Institutional Records

1 *State Papers* (Public Record Office, Kew)
Individual files are listed in the footnotes

2 *American State Papers* (John F. Kennedy Library, Boston)
President's Office Files (POF)
National Security Files (NSF)

3 *Other Records*
BBC Written Archives (Caversham Park, Reading)
Eton College
Ludgrove School, Wokingham
Marylebone Cricket Club, Lord's
Mass Observation files (Sussex University)
Oxford University Calendar, 1922–1926 (Clarendon Press, Oxford)
Keesing's Contemporary Archives, 1945–1979
Who's Who 1932–1995, (A. & C. Black)

Who Was Who 1897–1980, (A. & C. Black)
Wisden Cricketers' Almanack, 1922–1970

4 *Published Official and Party Documents*

A Better Tomorrow (The Conservative Manifesto 1970), Conservative Central Office
Annual Register
Conservative Party Archives (Bodleian Library, Oxford)
Correspondence respecting Czechoslovakia (September 1938), Cmd. 5847
Further Documents respecting Czechoslovakia including the agreement concluded at Munich on September 29, 1938 (October 1938), Cmd. 5848
The Denning Report, Cmd. 2152 (September 1963)
Hansard (House of Commons Debates, House of Lords Debates) – 1931 to 1995
The Next Five Years (The Conservative Manifesto 1959), Conservative Central Office
Prosperity with a Purpose (The Conservative Manifesto 1964), Conservative Central Office
Report of the Advisory Commission on the Review of the Constitution of Rhodesia and Nyasaland (The Monckton Commission), (October 1960), Cmd. 1148
Report of the Nyasaland Commission of Inquiry (The Devlin Report), (July 1959), Cmd. 814
Report of the Review Committee on Overseas Representation (The Duncan Report) (July 1969), Cmd. 4107
Report on Social Insurance & Allied Services (December 1942), Cmd. 6404
Rhodesia: Report of the Commission on Rhodesian Opinion under the Chairmanship of the Right Honourable the Lord Pearce (May 1972), Cmd. 4964
Royal Commission on the Constitution, 1969–73, (October 1973), Cmd. 5460
Safety in Coal Mines, Report of Royal Commission under Lord Rockley (December 1938), Cmd. 5890
Scotland's Government: The Report of the Scottish Constitutional Committee, Edinburgh, The Scottish Constitutional Committee, 1970
Scottish Affairs, 1952–54, *Report of Royal Commission (Chairman: Lord Balfour)* (July 1954), Cmd. 9212
Scottish Financial and Trade Statistics, Report of the Committee (Chairman Lord Catto) (July 1952), Cmd. 8609
Scottish Control of Scottish Affairs (Scottish Unionist Party), 1949
Scottish Valuation and Rating Committee Report (Chairman: Lord Sorn) (August 1954), Cmd. 9244
The Treaty Banning Nuclear Weapon Tests in the Atmosphere, in Outer Space and under Water, done at Moscow on the 5th of August 1963, Cmd. 2118

Published Works by Lord Home

1 *Books*

The Way the Wind Blows, Collins, 1976
Border Reflections: chiefly on the arts of shooting and fishing, Collins, 1979
Letters to a Grandson, Collins, 1983

2 *Other Published Works*
'An International Weather Forecast', lecture at the Ditchley Foundation, 1968.

Secondary Sources

1 *Published Works*
(All books are published in London unless otherwise indicated)

Dean Acheson, *Present at the Creation*, Hamish Hamilton, 1970.
R.J.Q. Adams, *British Politics and Foreign Policy in the Age of Appeasement, 1935–1939*, Macmillan, 1993.
Paul Addison, *The Road to 1945*, Jonathan Cape, 1975.
——, *Churchill on the Home Front 1900–1955*, Pimlico edition, 1993.
Jonathan Aitken, *Nixon: A Life*, Weidenfeld & Nicolson, 1993.
Princess Alice, Duchess of Gloucester, *Memories of Ninety Years*, Collins & Brown, 1991.
Cyril Alington, *Crime on the Kennet*, Collins, 1939.
Stephen Ambrose, *Eisenhower The President Volume 2, 1952–1969*, Allen & Unwin, 1984.
Noel Annan, *Our Age: Portrait of a Generation*, Weidenfeld & Nicolson, 1990.
R.L. Arrowsmith and B.J.W. Hill, *The History of I Zingari*, Stanley Paul, 1982.
Sidney Astor, *Anthony Eden*, Weidenfeld & Nicolson, 1976.
Earl of Avon, *The Memoirs of the Rt. Hon. Sir Anthony Eden K.G., P.C., M.C: Full Circle*, Cassell, 1960.
——, *Facing the Dictators*, Cassell, 1962.
——, *The Reckoning*, Cassell, 1966.
A.J. Ayer, *Part of My Life*, Collins, 1977.

Walter Bagehot, *The English Constitution*, Fontana edition, 1963.
Mary Banham and Bevis Hillier (eds.), *A Tonic to the Nation: The Festival of Britain 1951*, Thames & Hudson, 1976.
David A. Bannerman, *The Birds of the British Isles*, 12 volumes, Oliver & Boyd, Edinburgh & London, 1953–1963.
James Barber, *The Prime Minister since 1945*, Blackwell, Oxford, 1991.
John Barnes and David Nicholson (eds.), *The Empire at Bay: the Leo Amery Diaries 1929 1945*, Hutchinson, 1988.
Michael Bar-Zohar, *The Armed Prophet: A Biography of Ben Gurion*, Arthur Barker, 1967.
Mark Bence-Jones, *The Viceroys of India*, Constable, 1982.
David Benedictus, *The Fourth of June*, Anthony Blond, 1962.
David Ben Gurion, *Israel: Years of Challenge*, Anthony Blond, 1964.
Tony Benn, *Out of the Wilderness: Diaries 1963–1967*, Hutchinson, 1987.
——, *Office without Power: Diaries 1968–1972*, Hutchinson, 1988.
——, *Against the Tide: Diaries 1973–1976*, Hutchinson, 1989.
——, *Conflicts of Interest: Diaries 1977–1980*, Hutchinson, 1990.
——, *Years of Hope: Diaries, Papers and Letters 1940–1962*, Hutchinson, 1994.
Alan Bennett, *Forty Years On*, Faber, 1969.
Jill Benton, *Naomi Mitchison: A Biography*, Pandora, 1990.
Humphry Berkeley, *Crossing the Floor*, Allen & Unwin, 1972.

Michael R. Beschloss, *Mayday: Eisenhower, Khrushchev and the U2 Affair*, Faber, 1986.
——, *Kennedy v Khrushchev: The Crisis Years 1960–1963*, Faber, 1991.
Reginald Bevins, *The Greasy Pole*, Hodder, 1965.
Earl of Birkenhead, *The Prof in Two Worlds: the official life of Professor F.A. Lindemann, Viscount Cherwell*, Collins, 1961.
——, *Halifax: The Life of Lord Halifax*, Hamish Hamilton, 1965.
——, *Walter Monckton: The Life of Viscount Monckton of Brenchley*, Weidenfeld & Nicolson, 1969.
Andrew Birkin, *J.M. Barrie and the Lost Boys*, Constable, 1979.
Robert Blake, *The Unknown Prime Minister: The Life and Times of Andrew Bonar Law*, Eyre & Spottiswoode, 1955.
——, *Disraeli*, Methuen paperback edition, 1969.
——, *The Conservative Party from Peel to Thatcher*, Methuen, 1985.
——, *A History of Rhodesia*, Eyre Methuen, 1977.
——, *The Decline of Power 1915–1964*, Granada, 1985.
Robert Blake and Wm Roger Louis (eds.), *Churchill: A Major New Assessment of His Life in Peace and War*, Oxford University Press, Oxford, 1993.
Robert Blake and C.S. Nicholls (eds.), *The Dictionary of National Biography 1971–1980*, Oxford University Press, Oxford, 1986.
——, *The Dictionary of National Biography 1981–1985*, Oxford University Press, Oxford, 1990.
Wilfred Blunt, *Slow on the Feather: Further Autobiography 1938–1959*, Michael Russell, Salisbury, 1986.
Vernon Bogdanor, *The Monarchy and the Constitution*, Clarendon Press, Oxford, 1995.
Vernon Bogdanor and Robert Skidelsky (eds.), *The Age of Affluence*, Macmillan, 1970.
Alan Bold (ed.), *The Letters of Hugh MacDiarmid*, Hamish Hamilton, 1984.
Christopher Booker, *The Neophiliacs: The Revolution in English Life in the Fifties and Sixties*, Pimlico edition with a new introduction, 1992.
Lord Boothby, *My Yesterday. Your Tomorrow*, Hutchinson, 1962.
——, *Recollections of a Rebel*, Hutchinson, 1978.
Tom Bower, *The Perfect English Spy: Sir Dick White and the Secret War 1935–1990*, Heinemann, 1995.
Francis Boyd, *Richard Austen Butler*, Rockcliff, 1956.
John Boyd-Carpenter, *Way of Life: The Memoirs of John Boyd-Carpenter*, Sidgwick & Jackson, 1980.
Jack Brand, *The National Movement in Scotland*, Routledge & Kegan Paul, 1978.
Henry Brandon, *Special Relationships: a foreign correspondent's memoirs from Roosevelt to Reagan*, Macmillan, 1989.
Asa Briggs, *The History of Broadcasting in the United Kingdom, Volume 5: Competition 1955–1974*, Oxford University Press, Oxford, 1995.
Douglas Brinkley, *Dean Acheson: The Cold War Years 1953–1971*, Yale University Press, New Haven, 1992.
Samuel Brittan, *The Treasury under the Tories*, Secker & Warburg, 1964.
George Brown, *In My Way*, Gollancz, 1971.

Alan Bullock, *Ernest Bevin: Foreign Secretary 1945–1951*, Oxford University Press, 1985.

Ivor Bulmer-Thomas, *The Growth of the British Party System: Volume 2, 1924–1966*, John Baker, 1967.

Trevor Burridge, *Clement Attlee: A Political Biography*, Jonathan Cape, 1985.

David Butler, *The British General Election of 1951*, Macmillan, 1952.

——, *The British General Election of 1955*, Macmillan, 1955.

David Butler and Dennis Kavanagh, *The British General Election of February 1974*, Macmillan, 1974.

——, *The British General Election of October 1974*, Macmillan, 1975.

——, *The British General Election of 1979*, Macmillan, 1980.

David Butler and Anthony King, *The British General Election of 1964*, Macmillan, 1965.

——, *The British General Election of 1966*, Macmillan, 1966.

David Butler and Michael Pinto-Duschinsky, *The British General Election of 1970*, Macmillan, 1971.

David Butler and Anne Sloman, *British Political Facts 1900–1975*, Macmillan, 1975.

Lord Butler, *The Art of the Possible*, revised edition, Penguin Books, Harmondsworth, 1973.

——, *The Art of Memory: Friends in Perspective*, Hodder, 1982.

Mollie Butler, *August and Rab: A Memoir*, Weidenfeld & Nicolson, 1987.

Ronald Butt, *The Power of Parliament*, Constable, 2nd edition, 1969.

Sir Alec Cairncross (ed.), *The Robert Hall Diaries, Volume II 1954–1961*, Unwin Hyman, 1991.

James Callaghan, *Time and Chance*, Collins, 1987.

John Campbell, *The Goat in the Wilderness*, Jonathan Cape, 1977.

——, *Nye Bevan and the Mirage of British Socialism*, Weidenfeld & Nicolson, 1987.

——, *Edward Heath: A Biography*, Jonathan Cape, 1993.

Alan Campbell Johnson, *Anthony Eden: A Biography*, Robert Hale, 1938.

David Cannadine, *The Decline and Fall of the British Aristocracy*, Yale University Press, 1990.

——, *G.M. Trevelyan: A Life in History*, Fontana Press edition, 1993.

Tim Card, *Eton Renewed: A History from 1860 to the Present Day*, John Murray, 1994.

David Carlton, *Anthony Eden: A Biography*, Allen Lane, 1981.

Lord Carrington, *Reflect on Things Past: The Memoirs of Lord Carrington*, Collins, 1988.

Michael Carver, *Out of Step: The Memoirs of Field Marshal Lord Carver*, Hutchinson, 1989.

Lord Casey, *Australian Foreign Minister: The Diaries of R.G. Casey 1951–1960*, Collins, 1962.

——, *The Future of the Commonwealth*, Frederick Muller, 1963.

Lord Chandos, *The Memoirs of Lord Chandos*, The Bodley Head, 1962.

Laurence Chang and Peter Kornbluh (eds.), *The Cuban Missile Crisis 1962: A*

National Security Archive Documents Reader, The New Press, New York, 1992.
John Charmley, *Duff Cooper: The Authorized Biography*, Weidenfeld & Nicolson, 1986.
——, *Chamberlain and the Lost Peace*, John Curtis, Hodder & Stoughton, 1989.
Randolph S. Churchill, *The Rise and Fall of Sir Anthony Eden*, MacGibbon & Kee, 1959.
——, *The Fight for the Tory Leadership*, Heinemann, 1964.
Winston S. Churchill, *Lord Randolph Churchill: Volume Two*, Macmillan, 1906.
William Clark, *From Three Worlds: Memoirs*, Sidgwick & Jackson, 1986.
Peter Clarke, *A Question of Leadership: Gladstone to Thatcher*, Hamish Hamilton, 1991.
Michael Cockerell, *Live from Number 10: The Inside Story of Prime Ministers and Television*, Faber & Faber, 1988.
Richard Cockett, *Twilight of Truth: Chamberlain, Appeasement and the Manipulation of the Press*, Weidenfeld & Nicolson, 1989.
Rex Collings (ed.), *Reflections of a Statesman: The Writings and Speeches of Enoch Powell*, Bellew Publishing, 1991.
John Colville, *Footprints in Time: Memories*, Collins, 1976.
——, *The Churchillians*, Weidenfeld & Nicolson, 1981.
——, *The Fringes of Power: Downing Street Diaries 1939–1955*, Hodder, 1985.
——, *Those Lambtons! A Most Unusual Family*, Hodder, 1988.
Sir Arthur Conan Doyle, *The Valley of Fear*, edited by Owen Dudley Edwards, Oxford University Press, Oxford, 1993.
Cyril Connolly, *Enemies of Promise*, Penguin edition, Penguin Books, Harmondsworth, 1961.
Chris Cook, *Sources in British Political History 1900–1951*, 5 volumes, Macmillan, 1973.
Chris Cook, Jane Leonard and Peter Leese, *The Longman Guide to Sources in Contemporary British History: Volume 2 Individuals*, Longman, 1994.
Chris Cook and John Ramsden, *By-Elections in British Politics*, Macmillan, 1978.
Duff Cooper, *Old Men Forget*, Hart-Davis, 1953.
Colin Coote, *A Companion of Honour: The Story of Walter Elliot*, Collins, 1965.
Patrick Cosgrave, *R.A. Butler: An English Life*, Quartet, 1981.
Colin Cowdrey, *M.C.C.: The Autobiography of a Cricketer*, Hodder & Stoughton, 1976.
Maurice Cowling, *The Impact of Labour 1920–1924*, Cambridge University Press, Cambridge, 1971.
——, *The Impact of Hitler: British politics and British policy 1933–1940*, Cambridge University Press, Cambridge, 1975.
Bernard Crick, *George Orwell: A Life*, Penguin edition, Penguin Books, Harmondsworth, 1980.
Anthony Crosland, *The Future of Socialism*, Jonathan Cape, 1980.
J.A. Cross, *Sir Samuel Hoare: A Political Biography*, Jonathan Cape, 1977.
——, *Lord Swinton*, Clarendon Press, Oxford, 1982.
Richard Crossman, *The Backbench Diaries of Richard Crossman*, edited by Janet Morgan, Hamish Hamilton & Jonathan Cape, 1981.

David Daiches, *Edinburgh*, Granada, 1980.
Tam Dalyell, *Dick Crossman: A Portrait*, Weidenfeld & Nicolson, 1989.
J.C. Dancy, *The Public Schools and the Future*, Faber & Faber, 1963.
Danny Danziger (ed.), *Eton Voices*, Viking, 1988.
Russell Davies and Liz Ottaway, *Vicky*, Secker & Warburg, 1987.
Robin Day, *Grand Inquisitor*, Weidenfeld & Nicolson, 1989.
——, *But With Respect: Memorable TV Interviews*, Orion paperback edition, 1994.
Richard Deacon, *'C': A Biography of Sir Maurice Oldfield*, Macdonald, 1984.
Gerard J. de Groot, *Liberal Crusader: The Life of Sir Archibald Sinclair*, Hurst & Company, 1993.
Lord Denning, *The Denning Report: The Profumo Affair*, Pimlico edition, 1992.
Duchess of Devonshire, *The House: A Portrait of Chatsworth*, Macmillan, 1982.
John Dickie, *The Uncommon Commoner: A Study of Sir Alec Douglas-Home*, Pall Mall Press, 1964.
——, *Inside the Foreign Office*, Chapmans, 1992.
——, *'Special No More': Anglo-American Relations – Rhetoric and Reality*, Weidenfeld & Nicolson, 1994.
David Dilks (ed.), *Curzon in India* Rupert Hart-Davis, 1969.
——, *The Diary of Sir Alexander Cadogan 1938–1943*, Cassell, 1971.
——, *Neville Chamberlain Volume I: Pioneering and Reform, 1869–1929*, Cambridge University Press, Cambridge, 1984.
Piers Dixon, *Double Diploma: The Life of Sir Pierson Dixon*, Hutchinson, 1968.
Sir Douglas Dodds-Parker, *Political Eunuch*, Springwood Books, Ascot, 1986.
Hubert Doggart (ed.), *The Heart of Cricket: A Memoir of H.S. Altham*, with a foreword by Sir Alec Douglas-Home, Hutchinson and The Cricketer, 1967.
Frances Donaldson, *Edward VIII*, Weidenfeld & Nicolson, 1974.
Bernard Donoughue, *Prime Minister: The Conduct of Policy under Harold Wilson and James Callaghan*, Jonathan Cape, 1987.
Bernard Donoughue and G.W. Jones, *Herbert Morrison: Portrait of a Politician*, Weidenfeld & Nicolson, 1973.
Fyodor Dostoevsky, *Devils*, translated by Michael R. Katz, Oxford University Press, Oxford, 1992.
Charles Douglas-Home, *Evelyn Baring: The Last Proconsul*, Collins, 1978.
Henry Douglas-Home, *The Birdman*, Collins, 1977.
William Douglas-Home, *Mr Home pronounced Hume: An Autobiography*, Collins, 1979.
——, *Sins of Commission*, Michael Russell, Salisbury, 1985.
——, *Old Men Remember*, Collins & Brown, 1991.
David Dutton, *Austen Chamberlain: Gentleman in Politics*, Ross Anderson Publications, Bolton, 1985.
——, *Simon: A Political Biography of Sir John Simon*, Aurum Press, 1992.

Anthony Eden, *Full Circle*, Cassell, 1960.
D.H. Elletson, *Chequers and the Prime Ministers*, Robert Hale, 1970.
Nicholas Elliott, *Never Judge a Man by his Umbrella*, Michael Russell, Salisbury, 1991.
Harold Evans, *Downing Street Diary: The Macmillan Years 1957–1963*, Hodder, 1981.

Keith Feiling, *The Life of Neville Chamberlain*, Macmillan, 1946.
Nigel Fisher, *Iain Macleod*, André Deutsch, 1973.
——, *The Tory Leaders: Their Struggle for Power*, Weidenfeld & Nicolson, 1977.
——, *Harold Macmillan*, Weidenfeld & Nicolson, 1982.
Hugh Foot, *A Start in Freedom*, Hodder & Stoughton, 1964.
E.M. Forster, *Abinger Harvest*, Edward Arnold, 1956 edition.
Joseph Frankel, *The Making of Foreign Policy*, Oxford University Press, Oxford, 1963.
——, *British Foreign Policy 1945–1973*, Oxford University Press, Oxford, 1975.
Michael Fry, *Patronage and Principle: A Political History of Modern Scotland*, Aberdeen University Press, Aberdeen, paperback edition, 1991.

Joe Garner, *The Commonwealth Office 1925–1968*, Heinemann, 1978.
Raymond L. Garthoff, *Reflections on the Cuban Missile Crisis*, The Brookings Institution, Washington, D.C., 1987.
John S. Gibson, *The Thistle and the Crown: A History of the Scottish Office*, Her Majesty's Stationery Office, 1985.
Martin Gilbert, *The Roots of Appeasement*, Weidenfeld & Nicolson, 1966.
——, *Winston S. Churchill: Volume V 1922–1939*, Heinemann, 1976.
——, *Finest Hour: Winston S. Churchill 1939–1941*, Heinemann, 1983.
——, *Road to Victory: Winston S. Churchill 1941–1945*, Heinemann, 1986.
——, *Never Despair: Winston S. Churchill 1945–1965*, Heinemann, 1988.
Lord Gladwyn, *The Memoirs of Lord Gladwyn*, Weidenfeld & Nicolson, 1972.
Peter Godwin and Ian Hancock, *Rhodesians Never Die: The Impact of War and Political Change on White Rhodesia, c. 1970–1980*, Oxford University Press, Oxford, 1993.
Grace Wyndham Goldie, *Facing the Nation: Television and Politics 1936–1976*, Bodley Head, 1977.
Philip Goodhart, *The 1922: The Story of the Conservative Backbenchers' Parliamentary Committee*, Macmillan, 1973.
Arnold Goodman, *Tell Them I'm On My Way: Memoirs*, Chapmans, 1993.
Patrick Gordon Walker, *The Cabinet*, 2nd edn, Jonathan Cape, 1972.
Paul Gore-Booth, *With Great Truth and Respect*, Constable, 1974.
Denis Greenhill, *More by Accident*, Wilton 65, York, 1992.
Eldon Griffiths (ed.), *Peaceful Change*, Arthur Barker, 1964.
Richard Griffiths, *Fellow Travellers of the Right: British Enthusiasts for Nazi Germany 1933–1939*, Constable, 1980.
Jo Grimond, *Memoirs*, Heinemann, 1979.
Andrei Gromyko, *Memoirs*, Hutchinson, 1989.

Lord Hailsham, *The Door Wherein I Went*, Collins, 1975.
——, *A Sparrow's Flight: The Memoirs of Lord Hailsham of St Marylebone*, Collins, 1990.
Ian Hamilton, *The Taking of the Stone of Destiny*, Corgi edition, 1992.
Kenneth Harris, *Attlee*, Weidenfeld & Nicolson, 1982.

Ralph Harris, *Politics without Prejudice: A Political Appreciation of the Rt. Hon. Richard Austen Butler*, Staples Press, 1956.
L.P. Hartley, *The Go-Between*, Penguin Books, Harmondsworth, 1958.
John Harvey (ed.), *The Diplomatic Diaries of Oliver Harvey, Volume 1, 1937–1940*, Collins, 1970.
Sir William Hayter, *A Double Life*, Hamish Hamilton, 1974.
G.W.F. Hegel, *Philosophy of Right*, trans. T.M. Knox, Clarendon Press, Oxford, 1942.
Sir Nevile Henderson, *Failure of a Mission*, Hodder, 1940.
Sir Nicholas Henderson, *The Private Office*, Weidenfeld & Nicolson, 1984.
——, *Mandarin: The Diaries of an Ambassador, 1969–1982*, Weidenfeld & Nicolson, 1994.
Peter Hennessy, *Whitehall*, Secker & Warburg, 1989.
——, *Never Again: Britain 1945–1951*, Jonathan Cape, 1992.
Peter Hennessy and Anthony Seldon (eds.), *Ruling Performance: British Governments from Attlee to Thatcher*, Blackwell, Oxford, 1987.
S.J. Hetherington, *Katherine Atholl: Against the Tide*, Aberdeen University Press, Aberdeen, 1989.
J.D. Hoffman, *The Conservative Party in Opposition, 1945–1951*, MacGibbon & Kee, 1964.
Alistair Horne, *Macmillan 1894–1956: Volume 1 of the Official Biography*, Macmillan, 1988.
——, *Macmillan 1957–1986: Volume 2 of the Official Biography*, Macmillan, 1989.
Anthony Howard, *R.A.B.: The Life of R.A. Butler*, Jonathan Cape, 1987.
——, *Crossman: The Pursuit of Power*, Jonathan Cape, 1990.
—— (ed.), *The Crossman Diaries: Selections from the Diaries of a Cabinet Minister 1964–1970*, Hamish Hamilton and Jonathan Cape, 1979.
Anthony Howard and Richard West, *The Making of the Prime Minister*, Jonathan Cape, 1965.
T.E.B. Howarth, *Prospect and Reality: Great Britain 1945–1955*, Collins, 1985.
Miles Hudson, *Triumph or Tragedy? Rhodesia to Zimbabwe*, Hamish Hamilton, 1981.
Spike Hughes, *Glyndebourne: A History of the Festival Opera*, Methuen, 1965.
Douglas Hurd, *An End to Promises: A Sketch of Government 1970–1974*, Collins, 1979.
George Hutchinson, *The Last Edwardian at No. 10*, Grafton Books, 1980.
Aldous Huxley, *Antic Hay*, Grafton Books edition, Grafton Books, 1977.

Lord Ismay, *The Memoirs of General the Lord Ismay*, Heinemann, 1960.

Alan James, *Britain and the Congo Crisis 1960–1963*, Macmillan, Basingstoke, 1996.
Douglas Jay, *The Socialist Case*, Faber, 1937.
Roy Jenkins, *Asquith*, Collins, 1964.
——, *Nine Men of Power*, Hamish Hamilton, 1974.
——, *Truman*, Collins, 1986.
——, *Baldwin*, Collins, 1987.
——, *Gallery of 20th Century Portraits*, David & Charles, Newton Abbot, 1988.

——, *A Life at the Centre*, Macmillan, 1991.
——, *Portraits and Miniatures*, Macmillan, 1993.
Thomas Jones, *A Diary with Letters 1931–1950*, Oxford University Press, 1954.

Michael Kennedy, *Britten*, J.M. Dent, 1981.
Robert F. Kennedy, *13 Days: The Cuban Missile Crisis*, Macmillan, 1969.
Earl of Kilmuir, *Political Adventure: The Memoirs of the Earl of Kilmuir*, Weidenfeld & Nicolson, 1964.
Sir Ivone Kirkpatrick, *The Inner Circle: Memoirs of Ivone Kirkpatrick*, Macmillan, 1959.
Henry Kissinger, *Years of Upheaval*, Weidenfeld & Nicolson/Michael Joseph, 1982.
——, *Diplomacy*, Simon & Schuster, New York, 1994.
Keith Kyle, *Suez*, Weidenfeld & Nicolson, 1991.

Richard Lamb, *The Failure of the Eden Government*, Sidgwick & Jackson, 1987.
——, *The Drift to War 1922–1939*, W.H. Allen, 1989.
——, *The Macmillan Years 1957–1963: The Emerging Truth*, John Murray, 1995.
P.S.H. Lawrence (ed.), *Grizel: Grizel Hartley Remembered*, Michael Russell, Salisbury, 1991.
John Lawton, *1963: Five Hundred Days*, Hodder & Stoughton, 1992.
Zig Layton-Henry (ed.), *Conservative Party Politics*, Macmillan, 1980.
Colin Leach, *A School at Shrewsbury: The Four Foundations*, James & James, 1990.
Shane Leslie, *The Oppidan*, Chatto & Windus, 1922.
Bernard Levin, *The Pendulum Years: Britain and the Sixties*, Jonathan Cape, 1970.
Ronald Lewin, *Ultra Goes to War: The Secret Story*, Arrow Books, 1980.
Selwyn Lloyd, *Suez 1956: A Personal Account*, Jonathan Cape, 1978.
Lord Longford, *A History of the House of Lords*, Collins, 1988.
Charles Lysaght, *Brendan Bracken*, Allen Lane, 1979.
Oliver Lyttelton, Viscount Chandos, *The Memoirs of Lord Chandos*, Bodley Head, 1962.

R.B. McCallum and Alison Readman, *The British General Election of 1945*, Oxford University Press, Oxford, 1947.
Malcolm Macdonald, *Titans and Others*, Collins, 1972.
Robert McKenzie, *British Political Parties: The Distribution of Power within the Conservative and Labour Parties*, Heinemann, revised paperback edition, 1967.
J.P. Mackintosh, *The British Cabinet*, 3rd edition, Stevens & Sons, 1977.
——, (ed.), *British Prime Ministers of the Twentieth Century, Volume 2: Churchill to Callaghan*, Weidenfeld & Nicolson, 1978.
Denis Mack Smith, *Mussolini*, Granada, 1983.
Iain Macleod, *Neville Chamberlain*, Muller, 1961.
Harold Macmillan, *Winds of Change 1914–1939*, Macmillan, 1966.
——, *The Blast of War 1939–1945*, Macmillan, 1967.
——, *Tides of Fortune 1945–1955*, Macmillan, 1969.
——, *Riding the Storm 1956–1959*, Macmillan, 1971.
——, *Pointing the Way 1959–1961*, Macmillan, 1972.

——, *At the End of the Day 1961–1963*, Macmillan, 1973.
——, *The Past Masters: Politics and Politicians 1906–1939*, Macmillan, 1975.
Nicholas Mansergh, *The Commonwealth Experience*, Weidenfeld & Nicolson, 1969.
David Marquand, *Ramsay MacDonald*, Jonathan Cape, 1977.
Andrew Marr, *The Battle for Scotland*, Penguin Books, Harmondsworth, 1992.
Paul Martin, *The London Diaries 1974–1979*, edited by William R. Young, University of Ottawa Press, Ottawa, 1988.
J.C. Masterman, *The Double Cross System*, Yale University Press, 1972, and Oxford University Press, 1975.
Stuart Matthew, *The Knights and Chapel of the Most Ancient and Most Noble Order of the Thistle*, Eaglebank Publications, Edinburgh, 1988.
Reginald Maudling, *Memoirs*, Sidgwick & Jackson, 1978.
Robert Menzies, *Afternoon Light: Some Memories of Men and Events*, Cassell, 1967.
Martin Meredith, *The Past is Another Country: Rhodesia 1890–1979*, André Deutsch, 1979.
Keith Middlemass, *Power, Competition and the State, Volume One: Britain in Search of Balance, 1940–1961*, Macmillan, 1986.
——, *Power, Competition and the State, Volume Two: Threats to the Post-War Settlement, Britain 1961–1974*, Macmillan, 1990.
Keith Middlemass and John Barnes, *Baldwin: a biography*, Weidenfeld & Nicolson, 1969.
T.B. Millar (ed.), *Australian Foreign Minister: The Diaries of R.G. Casey 1951–1960*, Collins, 1972.
Sir David Milne, *The Scottish Office: and Other Scottish Government Departments*, Allen & Unwin, 1957.
James Mitchell, *Conservatives and the Union: A Study of Conservative Party Attitudes to Scotland*, Edinburgh University Press, Edinburgh, 1990.
D.E. Moggridge, *Maynard Keynes: An Economist's Biography*, Routledge, 1992.
Geoffrey Moorhouse, *The Diplomats: the Foreign Office Today*, Jonathan Cape, 1977.
Austen Morgan, *Harold Wilson*, Pluto Press, 1992.
Janet Morgan (ed.), *The Backbench Diaries of Richard Crossman*, Hamish Hamilton and Jonathan Cape, 1981.
Kenneth Morgan, *The People's Peace: British History 1945–1989*, Oxford University Press, Oxford, 1990.
Kenneth and Jane Morgan, *Portrait of a Progressive: The Political Career of Christopher, Viscount Addison*, Clarendon Press, Oxford, 1980.
James Morris, *Farewell the Trumpets: An Imperial Retreat*, Faber, 1978.
Charles Mott-Radclyffe, *Foreign Body in the Eye*, Leo Cooper, 1955.
C.L. Mowat, *Britain between the Wars*, Methuen, 1956 edition.

H.G. Nicholas, *The British General Election of 1950*, Macmillan, 1951.
Harold Nicolson, *Diaries and Letters: 1930–1962*, edited by Nigel Nicolson, 3 volumes, Collins, 1966, 1967, 1968.
Philip Norton, *Conservative Dissidents: Dissent within the Parliamentary Conservative Party 1970–1974*, Temple Smith, 1978.
David Nunnerly, *President Kennedy and Britain*, Bodley Head, 1972.

Anthony Nutting, *No End of a Lesson: The Story of Suez*, Constable, 1967.
——, *Nasser*, Constable, 1972.

F.S. Oliver, *The Endless Adventure*, Macmillan, 1935.
George Orwell, *The Collected Essays, Journalism and Letters of George Orwell, Volume 4, 1945–1950*, Penguin Books, Harmondsworth, 1970.

Anthony Parsons, *From Cold War to Hot Peace: UN Interventions 1947–1994*, Michael Joseph, 1995.
Peter Paterson, *Tired and Emotional: The Life of Lord George-Brown*, Chatto & Windus, 1993.
Henry Pelling, *Winston Churchill*, Macmillan, 1974.
A.D. Peters, *Anthony Eden at the Foreign Office 1931–1978*, Gower Publishing, Aldershot, 1986.
Sir Charles Petrie, *The Chamberlain Tradition*, Lovat Dixon, 1938.
——, *The Life and Letters of the Rt. Hon. Sir. J. Austen Chamberlain*, 2 volumes, Cassell, 1939–1940.
Ben Pimlott, *Harold Wilson*, Harper Collins, 1992.
Chapman Pincher, *Their Trade is Treachery*, Sidgwick & Jackson, 1981.
J. Enoch Powell, *Joseph Chamberlain*, Thames & Hudson, 1977.
James Prior, *A Balance of Power*, Hamish Hamilton, 1986.
Alan Pryce-Jones, *The Bonus of Laughter*, Hamish Hamilton, 1987.
R.M. Punnett, *Selecting the Party Leader: Britain in Comparative Perspective*, Harvester Wheatsheaf, 1992.

John Ramsden, *The Age of Balfour and Baldwin 1902–1940*, Longman, 1978.
Peter Rawlinson, *A Price Too High: An Autobiography*, Weidenfeld & Nicolson, 1989.
David Reynolds, *Britannia Overruled: British Policy and World Power in the 20th Century*, Longman, 1991.
Robert Rhodes James (ed.), *Chips: The Diaries of Sir Henry Channon*, Weidenfeld & Nicolson, 1967.
——(ed.), *Memoirs of a Conservative: J.C.C. Davidson's Memoirs and Papers, 1910–1937*, Weidenfeld & Nicolson, 1969.
——, *Churchill: A Study in Failure*, Weidenfeld & Nicolson, 1970.
——, *Anthony Eden*, Weidenfeld & Nicolson, 1986.
——, *Bob Boothby: A Portrait*, John Curtis, Hodder & Stoughton, 1991.
Peter Riddell, *Honest Opportunism: The Rise of the Career Politician*, Hamish Hamilton, 1993.
Andrew Roberts, *The Holy Fox: A Biography of Lord Halifax*, Weidenfeld & Nicolson, 1991.
——, *Eminent Churchillians*, Weidenfeld & Nicolson, 1994.
Frank Roberts, *Dealing with Dictators: The Destruction and Revival of Europe 1930–1970*, Weidenfeld & Nicolson, 1991.
C.H. Rolph (ed.), *The Trial of Lady Chatterley: Regina v. Penguin Books Limited*, Penguin Books, Harmondsworth, 1961.
Kenneth Rose, *Superior Person: A Portrait of Curzon and His Circle in Late*

Victorian Britain, Weidenfeld & Nicolson, 1969.
——, *Kings, Queens & Courtiers: Intimate Portraits of the Royal House of Windsor from its foundation to the present day*, Weidenfeld & Nicolson, 1985.
Stephen Roskill, *Hankey: Man of Secrets, Volume III 1931–1963*, Collins, 1974.
Victor Rothwell, *Anthony Eden: A Political Biography 1931–1957*, Manchester University Press, Manchester, 1992.
A.L. Rowse, *A Cornishman at Oxford*, Jonathan Cape, 1965.

Anthony Sampson, *The Anatomy of Britain*, Hodder & Stoughton, 1962.
——, *Macmillan: A Study in Ambiguity*, Allen Lane, 1967.
——, *The New Anatomy of Britain*, Hodder & Stoughton, 1971.
Avi Schlaim, Peter Jones and Keith Sainsbury, *British Foreign Secretaries since 1945*, David & Charles, Newton Abbot, 1977.
Arthur Schlesinger, *A Thousand Days: John F. Kennedy in the White House*, André Deutsch, 1965.
Thomas J. Schoenbaum, *Waging Peace and War: Dean Rusk in the Truman, Kennedy & Johnson Years*, Simon & Schuster, New York, 1988.
David Scott, *Ambassador in Black and White: Thirty Years of Changing Africa*, Weidenfeld & Nicolson, 1981.
Sir Walter Scott, *The Monastery*, Adam and Charles Black, Edinburgh, 1862.
——, *The Poetical Works of Sir Walter Scott, Bart*, 2 volumes, Adam and Charles Black, Edinburgh, 1864.
Anthony Seldon, *Churchill's Indian Summer: The Conservative Government 1951–1955*, Hodder & Stoughton, 1981.
Anthony Seldon and Stuart Ball (eds.), *Conservative Century: The Conservative Party since 1900*, Oxford University Press, Oxford, 1994.
Michael Shanks, *The Stagnant Society: A Warning*, Penguin Books, Harmondsworth, 1961.
Robert Shepherd, *A Class Divided: Appeasement and the Road to Munich 1938*, Macmillan, 1988.
——, *The Power Brokers: The Tory Party and Its Leaders*, Hutchinson, 1991.
——, *Iain Macleod*, Hutchinson, 1994.
Philip Short, *Banda*, Routledge & Kegan Paul, 1974.
Evelyn Shuckburgh, *Descent to Suez: Diaries 1951–1956*, edited by John Charmley, Weidenfeld & Nicolson, 1986.
Viscount Simon, *Retrospect: The Memoirs of the Rt. Hon. Viscount Simon*, Hutchinson, 1952.
Adam Sisman, *A.J.P. Taylor: A Biography*, Sinclair-Stevenson, 1994.
Michael Sissons and Philip French (eds.), *Age of Austerity: 1945–1951*, Penguin Books, Harmondsworth, 1964.
Noel Skelton, *Constructive Conservatism*, Blackwood, Edinburgh, 1924.
Robert Skidelsky, *Oswald Mosley*, Macmillan, 1975.
Arnold Smith, *Stitches in Time: The Commonwealth in World Politics*, André Deutsch, 1981.
Mary Soames, *Clementine Churchill by her daughter*, Cassell, 1979.
Gerald Sparrow, *RAB: Study of a Statesman*, Odhams, 1965.
Tom Stannage, *Baldwin Thwarts the Opposition: The British General Election of*

1935, Croom Helm, 1980.
David Steel, *Against Goliath: David Steel's Story*, Weidenfeld & Nicolson, 1989.
Michael Stewart, *Life and Labour: An Autobiography*, Sidgwick & Jackson, 1980.
James Stuart, *Within the Fringe: An Autobiography*, Bodley Head, 1967.
C.L. Sulzberger, *The Last of the Giants*, Weidenfeld & Nicolson, 1970.
Earl of Swinton, *Sixty Years of Power*, Hutchinson, 1966.

A.J.P. Taylor, *Beaverbrook*, Penguin Books, Harmondsworth, 1974.
Margaret Thatcher, *The Downing Street Years*, Harper Collins, 1993.
——, *The Path to Power*, Harper Collins, 1995.
Alan Thompson and John Barnes, *The Day Before Yesterday: an illustrated history of Britain from Attlee to Macmillan*, Sidgwick & Jackson, 1971.
Neville Thompson, *The Anti-Appeasers: Conservative opposition to appeasement in the 1930s*, Clarendon Press, Oxford, 1971.
A.A. Thomson, *Hirst and Rhodes*, Epworth Press, 1959.
Andrew Thorpe, *The British General Election of 1931*, Clarendon Press, Oxford, 1991.
D.R. Thorpe, *The Uncrowned Prime Ministers: A Study of Sir Austen Chamberlain, Lord Curzon and Lord Butler*, Darkhorse Publishing, 1980.
——, *Selwyn Lloyd*, Jonathan Cape, 1989.
Michael Tracey, *A Variety of Lives: A Biography of Sir Hugh Greene*, Bodley Head, 1983.
G.M. Trevelyan, *History of England*, Longman, 1952.
Humphrey Trevelyan, *Worlds Apart: China 1953–5, Soviet Union 1962–5*, Macmillan, 1971.
John Turner, *Macmillan*, Longman, 1994.

Peter Vansittart, *In the Fifties*, John Murray, 1995.

Peter Walker, *Staying Power: An Autobiography*, Bloomsbury, 1991.
Dennis Walters, *Not Always with the Pack*, Constable, 1989.
Gerald Warner, *The Scottish Tory Party: A History*, Weidenfeld & Nicolson, 1988.
Alan Watkins, *A Conservative Coup: The Fall of Margaret Thatcher*, Duckworth, second edition, 1992.
Harold Watkinson, *Turning Points: A Record of our Times*, Michael Russell, Salisbury, 1986.
Sir Roy Welensky, *Welensky's 4000 Days: The Life and Death of the Federation of Rhodesia and Nyasaland*, Collins, 1964.
Nigel West, *Molehunt: The full story of the Soviet Spy in MI5*, Weidenfeld & Nicolson, 1987.
John W. Wheeler-Bennett, *King George VI: His Life and Reign*, Macmillan, 1958.
——, *Munich: Prologue to Tragedy*, Macmillan, 1963 edition.
William Whitelaw, *The Whitelaw Memoirs*, Aurum Press, 1989.
L.G. Wickham Legg and E.T. Williams (eds.), *The Dictionary of National Biography 1941–1950*, Oxford University Press, 1959.
E.T. Williams and Helen H. Palmer (eds.), *The Dictionary of National Biography 1951–1960*, Clarendon Press, Oxford, 1971.

E.T. Williams and C.S. Nicholls (eds.), *The Dictionary of National Biography 1961–1970*, 1981.

Philip Williams, *Hugh Gaitskell: A Political Biography*, Jonathan Cape, 1979.

—— (ed.), *The Diary of Hugh Gaitskell 1945–1956*, Jonathan Cape, 1983.

Raymond Williams, *Culture and Society 1780–1950*, Penguin Books, Harmondsworth, 1961.

Roger Wilmut (ed.), *The Complete Beyond the Fringe*, Methuen, 1987.

Harold Wilson, *Memoirs: The Making of a Prime Minister 1916–1964*, Weidenfeld & Nicolson/Michael Joseph, 1986.

John Wilson, *CB: A Life of Sir Henry Campbell-Bannerman*, Constable, 1973.

J.R.T. Wood (ed.), *The Welensky Papers: A History of the Federation of Rhodesia and Nyasaland*, Graham Publishing, Durban, 1983.

C.M. Woodhouse, *British Foreign Policy since the Second World War*, Hutchinson, 1961.

Lord Woolton, *The Memoirs of the Rt. Hon. the Earl of Woolton*, Cassell, 1959.

Peter Wright, *Spycatcher: The Candid Autobiography of a Senior Intelligence Officer*, Viking, New York, 1987.

Kenneth Young, *Rhodesia and Independence: A Study in British Colonial Policy*, Dent, revised edition, 1969.

——, *Sir Alec Douglas-Home*, Dent, 1970.

Michael Young, *The Rise of the Meritocracy*, Penguin Books, Harmondsworth, 1961.

Philip Ziegler, *Melbourne: A Biography of William Lamb 2nd Viscount Melbourne*, Collins, *1976*.

——, *Mountbatten: the official biography*, Collins, 1985.

——, *Harold Wilson: the authorised biography*, Weidenfeld & Nicolson, 1993.

Solly Zuckerman, *Monkeys, Men and Missiles: An Autobiography 1946–1988*, Collins, 1988.

2 *Articles, Essays, Lectures and Pamphlets*

R.K. Alderman and Martin J. Smith, 'Can British Prime Ministers be given the push by their Parties?', *Parliamentary Affairs*, July 1990.

Dr Stuart Ball, 'The Politics of Appeasement: The Fall of the Duchess of Atholl and the Kinross and West Perthshire By-Election, December 1938', *Scotttish Historical Review*, 69 (1990).

Humphry Berkeley, 'Choosing a Leader', The Berkeley Memorandum, December 1964.

R.A. Butler, *Fundamental Issues*, Conservative Political Centre, 1946.

Christopher Coker, *Who Only England Know: Conservatives and Foreign Policy*, Institute for European Defence & Strategic Studies, 1990.

Ian Colvin, 'The Pearce Commission and After', *South Africa Society paper No 9*, 1972.

Professor David Dilks, 'The Office of Prime Minister in Twentieth-Century Britain', 18 November 1992, Hull University Press, 1993.

——, 'From Trustee to Partner: The British Government & Empire in the

1950s', six lectures to mark the tenure of the Colonial Office by Alan Lennox-Boyd, 1st Viscount Boyd of Merton, Rhodes House, Oxford, 1993.
——, 'Communications, The Commonwealth and the Future', 10 May 1994, Hull University Press, 1994.
——, 'De Gaulle and the British', 22 June 1994, Paris, printed privately.
Sir Michael Fraser, 'The Conservative Research Department & Conservative Recovery after 1945', circulated privately, August 1961.
Jo Grimond, 'Hanging too long on the bell', *Sunday Telegraph*, 15 July 1990.
Sir Edward Heath, 'Home's belief in devolution', letter in the *Daily Telegraph*, 27 October 1995.
Professor Peter Hennessy, 'Searching for the "Great Ghost": The Palace, the Premiership, the Cabinet and the Constitution in the Post-war Period', Queen Mary and Westfield College, 1 February 1994.
Anthony Howard, 'Monarch of Glencoe', *New Statesman*, 20 July 1962.
——, 'Mr Home and Mr Hogg?', *New Statesman*, 14 December 1962.
Douglas Johnson, 'The Fall of the Mighty', *History Today*, February 1992.
Gerald Kaufman, 'The cheap gibes that can be so costly', *Evening Standard*, 10 January 1995.
Michael Knipe, 'Verdict on the Pearce Commission', *The Times*, 13 March 1972.
Keith Kyle, 'The British and Cyprus in 1963', *Report* (Friends of Cyprus Magazine), 1994.
Magnus Linklater, 'With sweet Home at the Hirsel', *The Times*, 10 October 1995.
Robert McKenzie, 'Has Macleod Really Proved His Case?', *Observer*, 19 January 1964.
Iain Macleod, 'The Tory Leadership', *Spectator*, 17 January 1964.
Peter MacMahon, 'Quiet believer blamed for referendum defeat', *The Scotsman*, 10 October 1995.
Michael Melford, 'The d'Oliveira Case: Cancellation of South African Tour', *Wisden 1969*, Sporting Handbooks Limited, 1969.
Ministry of Information, Salisbury, 'Where did Pearce Go Wrong? A brief appreciation of the Pearce Report', June 1972.
Sarah Newman, 'The Commonwealth and the Suez Crisis of 1956', *Contemporary Review*, October 1991.
Julius K. Nyerere, 'After the Pearce Commission', privately printed in Tanzania, 1972.
Christopher Patten, 'R.A. Butler – What We Missed', Inaugural R.A. Butler Lecture, Coningsby Club, 25 May 1994.
William Rees-Mogg, 'The Right Moment to Change', *Sunday Times*, 18 July 1965.
Robert Rhodes James, 'Here's to the Class of '59', *The Times*, 14 March 1995.
Laurence Thompson, 'Man in the Red', five articles on R.A. Butler, *News Chronicle*, September 1955.
'The World Sir Alec finds', *The Spectator*, 27 June 1970.
'Under the Umbrella' (centenary tribute to Neville Chamberlain), *Spectator*, 27 March 1969.
Hugo Young, 'The First Gentleman of the Cold War', *Sunday Times*, 3 October 1971.

3 *Unpublished Theses, etc*

Sir Knox Cunningham, 'One Man Dog: the Memoirs of Harold Macmillan's Private Secretary', in the possession of the Drapers' Company.

Sylvia Goodfellow, 'R.A. Butler and the Conservative Party Committee on Post-War Problems', Private memorandum.

Dr. Susan Onslow, 'Conservative Backbench Debate and its influence on British Foreign Policy 1948–1956', PhD thesis, University of London/London School of Economics.

Dr. A.L. Teasdale, 'Interpreting the Crisis of October 1963', PhD thesis, Nuffield College, Oxford.

Broadcast material

1 *Radio*

Transcripts in BBC Written Archives, Caversham.

'Into the Darkness', Radio 5, 21 July 1994.

'The Makers of Modern Politics. 3: Rab Butler – Artist of the Possible' by Anthony Howard. Radio 4, 27 April 1995.

'A Countryman in Downing Street', Professor Peter Hennessy. Radio 4, 9 October 1995.

2 *Television*

'At the End of the Day', Harold Macmillan/Robert McKenzie interview, BBC TV, 1973.

'The Day Before Yesterday', Thames Television, 1971.

'End of Empire', Granada Television, 1985.

'God Bless You, Mr Chamberlain' by Robert Harris, BBC Television, 23 September 1988.

Lord Home interview with Robert Kee, Tyne Tees Television, 22 October 1974.

Lord Home profile, BBC *Panorama*, 2 July 1973

'The Night of the Long Knives', BBC Television, 27 July 1989.

'No. 10 Downing Street: The Story of a House', by Christopher Jones, BBC Television, 1985.

'Reputations: R.A. Butler' by Anthony Howard, BBC Television, 13 July 1983.

'The Twentieth Century Remembered', interviews with Professor David Dilks, BBC Television, 13, 22, 29 July and 5 August 1982.

'Westminster's Secret Service', a report by Michael Cockerell on the world of the Government Whips, BBC Television, 21 May 1995.

3 *Video material*

Unbroadcast interviews of Sir Alec Douglas-Home by Robin Day (in the possession of Sir Robin Day).

4 *Gramophone recordings*

'British Prime Ministers: 1924–1964'. BBC Records, REB 39M, 1969. Contains Harold Macmillan's speech to the United Nations, 29 September 1960 and two extracts from Sir Alec Douglas-Home's speech at the Lord Mayor's Banquet, 11 November 1963.

Notes

Chapter 1.

1. The late William Douglas-Home to the author, 17 July 1990.
2. John Colville, *Footprints in Time: Memories*, Collins, London, 1976, p. 74. David Margesson was government Chief Whip; Thomas Dugdale was a junior Lord of the Treasury; Sir John Colville was successively Private Secretary to Clement Attlee, Princess Elizabeth and Sir Winston Churchill. Colville's letter no longer exists but Home vividly remembered receiving it on becoming Prime Minister. I am grateful to Sir David Hunt for drawing my attention to this episode.
3. Cyril Connolly, *Enemies of Promise*, Penguin Books, Harmondsworth, 1961, p. 245.
4. George, 1st Viscount Goschen of Hawkhurst (1831–1907), Chancellor of the Exchequer 1886–92. His acceptance of the Treasury in 1886 on the resignation of Lord Randolph Churchill helped to keep the Unionist government in office.
5. Sir Knox Cunningham, Parliamentary Private Secretary to Harold Macmillan, wrote to the author on 6 March 1975, 'You are well aware that it is thought that Harold Macmillan made a personal recommendation of his successor in 1963 with a view to preventing Rab from becoming Prime Minister. This is not true. Recently a reference to this appeared in the Press (one can never kill a story such as this).'

   The records – including the Royal Archives, the Stockton Papers, and the Home Papers – show that Macmillan was a conduit for a wide canvass of opinions. On 19 October 1963 he wrote to John Morrison, then Chairman of the 1922 Committee, 'The Press has tried to represent that Alec Home was my personal choice. You know well the immense trouble I took to get the views of the Cabinet, the House of Commons, the House of Lords and the Conservative Party generally. I think if you can help to get this about among Members it will do a lot of good. I was not really anything more than a convenient recipient of this information, and the means by which this advice could be given to the Queen.' (Stockton Papers, Box 009.)
6. Douglas Hurd to Lord Home, 26 November 1990. Hirsel Archive (hereafter HA).
7. John Ramsden, *The Age of Balfour and Baldwin 1902–1940*, Longman, 1978, p. 91.

8. Selwyn Lloyd recorded his impressions of a lunch at No. 10 shortly after Home had become Prime Minister. 'Menu: Haddock, Prunes and Rice Pudding. Elizabeth [Lady Home] said if she had known I had been coming she would have had a grand lunch, but that was what Alec liked.' SELO 61 (6). Selwyn Lloyd Papers. (Churchill College, Cambridge.)
9. Quoted by Bernard Donoughue, *Prime Minister: The Conduct of Policy under Harold Wilson and James Callagahan*, Jonathan Cape, 1987, p. 191.
10. Jo Grimond, *Memoirs*, Heinemann, 1979, p. 216.
11. The late Baroness Elliot of Harwood to the author, 13 November 1991. Baroness Elliot was one of the foursome.
12. J. Enoch Powell, *Joseph Chamberlain*, Thames & Hudson, 1977, p. 151.
13. *Sunday Times*, 18 July 1965.
14. Cited in D.R. Thorpe, *The Uncrowned Prime Ministers: a Study of Sir Austen Chamberlain, Lord Curzon and Lord Batler*, Darkhorse Publishing, 1980, p. 237.
15. David Butler to Lord Blakenham, December 1964, Conservative Party Archives, File CRD 3/22/10 (1). (Bodleian Library, Oxford).
16. In a parallel with the Labour Party's battles of the mid-1950s, Anthony Howard saw Alec Home as the Gaitskell to Hailsham's Bevan and Butler's Morrison. *New Statesman*, 11 October 1963.
17. George Eliot, *Middlemarch*, 1871–2, Penguin edition, Harmondsworth, 1965, chapter 38, p. 419.
18. Private information.
19. A.J.P. Taylor, *Beaverbrook*, Penguin edition, Harmondsworth, 1974, p. 846.
20. Harold Macmillan diary, 18 January 1964. (Stockton Papers).
21. PREM 11/4147. Public Record Office (hereafter PRO).
22. Private information.

Chapter 2.

1. Sir Walter Scott, *The Monastery*, Adam and Charles Black, Edinburgh, 1862, chapter 25, p. 174.
2. Lady Caroline Douglas-Home to author, 12 April 1991.
3. NC 18/1/1071. Neville Chamberlain papers. (Birmingham University Library.)
4. Sir Walter Scott, *Marmion: A Tale of Flodden Field*, 1808, Canto V, Verse IV.
5. *Ibid.*, Canto VI, Stanzas XXXIII and XXXIV. I am grateful to Caroline Douglas-Home for taking me both to the ruin of Hume Castle and to an annual Flodden Day Memorial Service at Branxton Hill. Flodden Field is clearly visible from the ramparts of Hume Castle.
6. G.M. Trevelyan, *History of England*, Longman, 1952 edition, p. 382.
7. *Macbeth*, I. iv. 41–2.
8. Quoted by Lord Home of the Hirsel in *The Way the Wind Blows*, Collins, 1976, p. 14; these were tracts of land between the Esk and the Sart rivers.
9. The original Douglas Castle was destroyed by fire in 1755 and, though

restored, was demolished in 1938 due to subsidence from newly discovered local coal seams.

10. Lord Home, *op. cit.*, p. 16.
11. Speech in the House of Lords, 11 March 1952, about the removal of the Coronation Stone from Westminster Abbey. *Hansard* (House of Lords Debates, 11 March 1952, Col. 606). Record in CAB 21/3876 (PRO).
12. Lord Home, *op. cit.*, p. 250.
13. Andrei Gromyko, *Memoirs*, Hutchinson, 1989, p. 158.
14. *Scotland's Magazine*, December 1966.
15. Kenneth Young, *Sir Alec Douglas-Home*, Dent & Sons, 1970, p. 10.
16. *Recollections of Louisa, Countess of Antrim*, privately published, 1937. Cited by Kenneth Young, *op. cit.*, p. 6.
17. Sir John Colville, *Those Lambtons!*, Hodder & Stoughton, 1988, p. 88.
18. Lord Boothby to Lord Home, 20 October 1963. HA.
19. James Morris, *Farewell the Trumpets: An Imperial Retreat*, Penguin Books, Harmondsworth, 1979, p. 96.
20. Lord Curzon to Lord George Hamilton, 9 July 1903. Cited David Dilks, *Curzon in India, Volume 1*, Rupert Hart-Davis, 1969, p. 237.
21. The Earl of Home to the Rev. Peter Wild of Northern Rhodesia, 28 November 1962. HA.
22. A.J. Balfour to Austen Chamberlain, 17 January 1906. Austen Chamberlain Papers. Birmingham University Library. Cited D.R. Thorpe, *The Uncrowned Prime Ministers: a Study of Sir Austen Chamberlain, Lord Curzon and Lord Butler*, Darkhorse Publishing, 1980.
23. John Galsworthy, *In Chancery*, Penguin Books, Harmondsworth, 1962 edition, p. 268.
24. Ludgrove, Eton and Christ Church were to become the educational pattern of the Douglas-Homes. Ludgrove was the 'family' preparatory school, attended by his son David, by which time it had moved to Wokingham in Berkshire.
25. In 1913 the total estate acreage was 134,671, producing rental income of £98,035. SB/9.
26. Thomas Hughes, *Tom Brown's Schooldays*, London, 1857, chapter 4.
27. Mr Gerald Barber to author, 13 June 1994. I am indebted to Mr Barber and the boys at Ludgrove for research into details of Alec Douglas-Home's career between 1913 and 1917.
28. G.O. Smith to Lady Dunglass, 31 March 1917. HA.
29. Details of Alec Douglas-Home's Eton career, unless specified otherwise, are from the College Archives, Eton (courtesy of Dr W.E.K. Anderson, headmaster, 1980–94).
30. First Hundred was the generic name for Block A, the top block in the school below Sixth Form. The term was first used in 1870. Lectures to the Sixth Form were called First Hundred Lectures. Tim Card, *Eton Renewed: A History from 1860 to the Present Day*, John Murray, 1994, p. 305.
31. Sir Roger Cary, Bt, letter to author, 7 September 1990.
32. Cyril Connolly, *Enemies of Promise*, Penguin Books, Harmandsworth, 1961,

p. 188. *Enemies of Promise* (Chapters 19–24) gives an unforgettable portrait of the Eton Alec Dunglass experienced from 1917 to 1922. Orwell actually had a term at Wellington before taking up a place at Eton on 3 May 1917, the day Alec Dunglass also entered the College. George Orwell, 'Such, Such were the Joys', in *The Collected Essays, Journalism and Letters of George Orwell, Volume 4, 1945–1950*, Penguin Books, Harmondsworth, 1970, p. 417.

33. P.S.H. Lawrence (ed.), *Grizel: Grizel Hartley Remembered*, Michael Russell, Salisbury, 1991, p. 110, a line from a letter of condolence to Julia Coleridge, 27 August 1982, on the death of her husband, Fred Coleridge. Fred Coleridge, latterly Vice-Provost, was David Douglas-Home's housemaster from 1957 to 1962, and a frequent holiday guest at Douglas.
34. Letter from A.W. Whitworth, 18 October 1963. Undated reply from Lord Home. HA.
35. Memoirs of B.J.W. Hill, *Eton Remembered 1937–1975* quoted by Tim Card, *op. cit.*, pp. 224–5. Corner House, its exterior a copy of the old building, was eventually rebuilt on the same site, overlooking the graveyard. Today it serves as a 'colony' for bachelor masters.
36. Lord Home interview in Danny Danziger (ed.), *Eton Voices*, Viking, 1988, p. 141.
37. *Eton College Chronicle*, 17 May 1917.
38. George Orwell, *op. cit.*, p. 409.
39. Tim Card, *op. cit.*, p. 141.
40. Danziger, *op. cit.*, p. 139.
41. Lord Home to Mr Compton Whitworth, 24 June 1976. (Whitworth papers.)
42. George Lyttelton and Rupert Hart-Davis, *The Lyttelton Hart-Davis Letters: Volumes Three and Four 1958–1959*, John Murray, paperback edition 1986, pp. 39, 101.
43. The story, a famous Eton legend, is variously told. I have followed the version given by Lord Home, *op. cit.*, p. 56.
44. Bernard Crick, *George Orwell: A Life*, Penguin Books, Harmondsworth, 1980, p. 100.
45. E.M. Forster, *Abinger Harvest*, Edward Arnold, 1956 edition, p. 13.
46. Lord Home, *op. cit.*, p. 29.
47. Lord Home to Sir William Becher, Bt, 2 July 1987, on his eighty-fifth birthday, thanking Sir William for a gift from I Zingari marking his long governorship of the club.
48. Lord Home, *op. cit.*, p. 32.
49. A.A. Thomson, *Hirst and Rhodes*, Epworth Press, 1959, p. 188.
50. Cyril Connolly, *op. cit.*, p. 252.
51. Lord Home, *op. cit.*, p. 35.
52. A.W. Whitworth to the Earl of Home, July 1922. HA.
53. J.C. Masterman, 8 July 1973. SB/74.
54. The late Brigadier Peter Acland to the author, 10 December 1991.
55. Lord Sherfield to author, 20 June 1994.
56. Roger Makins, diary, 19 September 1925 (courtesy of Lord Sherfield).
57. *Ibid.*, 1 October 1925.

Chapter 3.

1. Katharine, Baroness Elliot of Harwood, DBE, 1903–94; her papers contain many valuable insights into the world of Scottish Unionist politics.
2. R.L. Arrowsmith and B.J.W. Hill, *The History of I Zingari*, Stanley Paul, 1982, with a foreward by Lord Home of the Hirsel. Hill was housemaster of Corner House during his career at Eton. Arrowsmith, a long-serving housemaster at Charterhouse, was another of the many cricketer–schoolmasters with whom Alec Home had a long-standing friendship.
3. At one I Zingari fixture in the 1980s he asked to be introduced to a promising young cricketer who had just scored a sparkling fifty. 'I'm Home,' he said by way of introduction. 'Hugh who?' was the response. Private information.
4. David Daiches, *Edinburgh*, Granada, 1980, p. 62.
5. In 1990 the late William Douglas-Home showed the author examples of his brother's paintings; the 1926 book was particularly attractive.
6. The photograph albums of the Hon. George Douglas-Home are in the Hirsel archives.
7. R.M. Hamilton, letter to author, 15 February 1995.
8. Lord Home, *The Way the Wind Blows*, Collins, 1976, p. 42.
9. Very Revd. Dr Ronald Selby Wright to the author, 18 March 1992.
10. *Hansard*, 22 July 1936, Vol. 315, column 595. Cited by John Campbell, *Nye Bevan and the Mirage of British Socialism*, Weidenfeld & Nicolson, 1987, p. 51. Disraeli used his phrase about 'the Two Nations' in *Sybil* (1845), Book II, Chapter 5.
11. C. L. Mowat, *Britain between the Wars*, Methuen, 1956 edition, p. 469.
12. Andrew Marr, *The Battle for Scotland*, Penguin Books, Harmondsworth, 1992, p. 55.
13. Robert Skidelsky, *Oswald Mosley*, Macmillan, 1975, p. 129.
14. Miles Hudson, *Triumph and Tragedy: Rhodesia to Zimbabwe*, Hamish Hamilton, 1981, p. 90.
15. *Observer*, 16 September 1962. Although this remark was partly tongue-in-cheek, Alec Home considered it one of his most damaging mistakes, an unmitigated gift to his opponents and one which had a significant influence on the outcome of the 1964 general election. Together with Harold Wilson's 'pound in your pocket' broadcast about devaluation (20 November 1967) and Edward Heath's pledge to reduce 'prices at a stroke' in a press release about the wage/price spiral (16 June 1970), the 'matchsticks' interview is one of the prime post-war examples of an unguarded and isolated remark entering the political language and returning to haunt its perpetrator. Lord Home, conversation with the author.
16. Archibald Noel Skelton (1880–1935) is one of the forgotten figures of Conservative politics. Yet with the publication of *Constructive Conservatism* in 1924 he was seen as a possible future leader of the Party and had he not died of cancer in 1935 would undoubtedly have played a prominent role in national politics. Among his protégés and close friends were two future Conservative prime ministers, Anthony Eden and Alec Home.

17. Noel Skelton, *Constructive Conservatism*, Blackwood, Edinburgh, 1924.
18. Maurice Cowling, *The Impact of Labour 1920–1924*, Cambridge, Cambridge University Press, 1971, p. 1.
19. Skelton, *op. cit.*, p. 17.
20. Skelton, 'The Conservative Task: A Property Owning Democracy', *Yorkshire Post*, 23 January 1930. This was the third of four articles looking at the practical applications of Conservative policy-making. Copies in the papers of the late Baroness Elliot of Harwood.
21. Papers of the late Baroness Elliot of Harwood.
22. Earl of Avon to Sir Alec Douglas-Home, 28 September 1964. Avon papers. AP 23/27/35. (Birmingham University Library.)
23. Private information.
24. King Edward VIII, speech in South Wales, 18 November 1936.
25. John Campbell, *The Goat in the Wilderness*, Jonathan Cape, 1977, traces the influence of Lloyd George in the twenty-three years after his fall from office.
26. Sir Alec Douglas-Home, 18 December 1963. HA.
27. Lloyd George, Free Trade Hall, Manchester, 12 April 1929.
28. Former miners in BBC *Panorama* seventieth-birthday profile of Lord Home, 2 July 1973.
29. Gerald Warner, *The Scottish Tory Party: A History*, Weidenfeld & Nicolson, 1988, p. 192.
30. Lanark Unionist Association Minute Books, 1949.
31. Mowat, *op. cit.*, p. 412.
32. When Dunglass first won Lanark, the electorate was 39,389 (20,727 women and 18,662 men). Lanark Unionist Association Records.
33. John Dickie, *The Uncommon Commoner: A Study of Sir Alec Douglas-Home*, Pall Mall Press, 1964, p. 30. George Collingwood was the last butler at Douglas and the Hirsel. His loyal eccentricities were the basis for a memorable portrait of the independently minded family retainer in William Douglas-Home's play, *The Chiltern Hundreds*. At the Hirsel Collingwood kept a shot-gun in the breakfast room, from where he would shoot rabbits as the need arose. When war came in September 1939, Collingwood telegraphed from Douglas to the Hirsel, 'As the emergency has broken out I am making my way back to The Hirsel across country overnight.'
34. Andrew Thorpe, *The British General Election of 1931*, Clarendon Press, Oxford, 1991, p. 279.
35. See Peter Riddell, *Honest Opportunism: The Rise of the Career Politician*, Hamish Hamilton, 1993, for an examination of this change of emphasis. Recalling his first years in Parliament, Harold Macmillan wrote, 'The great majority of Members had no desire for Office. They sat, often unopposed, in Parliament after Parliament, for constituencies which had elected their fathers and grandfathers. Many, of course, were the eldest sons of peers.' Harold Macmillan, *The Past Masters: Politics and Politicians 1906–1939*, Macmillan, 1975, p. 16.
36. Viscount Boyd of Merton papers, MSS. Eng C. 3432 (Bodleian Library, Oxford). Lennox-Boyd had been elected MP for mid-Bedfordshire in 1931. A contemporary of Alec Dunglass at Christ Church, he became a close personal

and political ally.
37. BBC interview, 2 July 1973. HA.
38. One of Lloyd George's comments about Samuel at this time is reputed to have been 'When they circumcised Sir Herbert Samuel they threw away the wrong bit'.
39. Neville Chamberlain letter to Stanley Baldwin, 16 August 1923. Cited Keith Feiling, *The Life of Neville Chamberlain*, Macmillan, 1946, p. 107.
40. J.A. Cross, *Sir Samuel Hoare: A Political Biography*, Jonathan Cape, 1977, pp. 165–6.
41. Draft of talk for BBC Radio 3 for the centenary of Churchill's birth in November 1974. HA.
42. Details of Lord Dunglass's maiden speech are in *Hansard*, 15 February 1932; Hirsel Archives and John Dickie, *op. cit.*, pp. 30–3.
43. Gerard J. de Groot, *Liberal Crusader: The Life of Sir Archibald Sinclair*, Hurst, 1993, p. 96.
44. Thurso papers. THRS 8/2. THRS 9/2. (Churchill College, Cambridge.)
45. John S. Gibson, *The Thistle and the Crown: A History of the Scottish Office*, HMSO, Edinburgh, 1985, pp. 68, 72–3.
46. *Ibid.*, p. 76. The debate is recorded in *Hansard*, 24 November 1932, Cols. 235–360.
47. Sir David Milne, *The Scottish Office: And Other Scottish Government Departments*, Allen & Unwin, 1957.
48. The late Sir William Murrie to author, 23 January 1991.
49. Undated cutting from the mid-1930s from SB/6.
50. Foreword by Sir Alec Douglas-Home in James Stuart, *Within the Fringe: An Autobiography*, Bodley Head, 1967, p. xiii. Robert Boothby had many clashes with Stuart. See Robert Rhodes James, *Bob Boothby: A Portrait*, John Curtis, Hodder & Stoughton, 1991, for a critical view of James Stuart.
51. Lord Home to author, 10 April 1991.
52. Viscount Whitelaw to author, 11 April 1991.
53. Colin Coote, *A Companion of Honour: The Story of Walter Elliot*, Collins, 1965, p. 148.
54. The late Baroness Elliot of Harwood to author, 13 November 1991.
55. Cited by Lord Crathorne in his obituary of Baroness Elliot, *The House Magazine*, 24 January 1994.
56. Lanark Unionist Association Records.
57. Tom Stannage, *Baldwin Thwarts the Opposition: The British General Election of 1935*, Croom Helm, 1980, p. 245.
58. PREM 1/194 (PRO).
59. A.W. Whitworth papers.
60. Private information.
61. William Douglas-Home, *Old Men Remember*, Collins & Brown, 1991, p. 35. It is a story which grew over the years. Johnston remembered the remark being made in a corridor in the headmaster's house. The late Brian Johnston to author, 4 January 1991.
62. Lanark Unionist Association Records.
63. Lord Home, *op. cit.*, p. 55.

64. *The Times*, 5 September 1990.
65. Alistair Horne, *Macmillan 1957–1986: Volume II of the Official Biography*, Macmillan, 1989, p. 687. Many of those to whom the author spoke inquired who was writing the biography of Elizabeth Home.
66. Dr Eric Anderson to the author, 4 October 1990.

Chapter 4.

1. David Dilks, *Neville Chamberlain: Volume 1, 1869–1929*, Cambridge University Press, Cambridge, 1984, pp. 360, 528. See also Lord Hailsham, *A Sparrow's Flight: The Memoirs of Lord Hailsham of St Marylebone*, Collins, 1990, pp. 71–4 for Hogg's appointment and its effect upon Quintin Hailsham's political prospects.
2. John Colville, *The Fringes of Power: Downing Street Diaries 1939–1955*, Hodder & Stoughton, 1985, p. 37.
3. Anne Chamberlain to Lord Baldwin of Bewdley, 15 December 1940. NC13/19/2/34. (Birmingham University Library.)
4. Robert Rhodes James (ed.), *Chips: The Diaries of Sir Henry Channon*, Weidenfeld & Nicolson, 1967, p. 194.
5. *The Times*, 16 July 1994.
6. NC 18/1/947 (Birmingham University Library).
7. Lord Baldwin to Selwyn Lloyd, 20 October 1947. Selwyn Lloyd papers, SELO 104 (1), (Churchill College, Cambridge).
8. *Sunday Times*, 5 August 1990. Private information.
9. James Stuart, *Within the Fringe: An Autobiography*, The Bodley Head, 1967, p. 83.
10. Lord Reith diaries. Entry for 6 May 1938. BBC Written Archives, Caversham.
11. Correspondence between Sir Alec Douglas-Home and William Whitelaw, November 1964. HA.
12. After spells at the Home Office (1915–16 and 1935–7) and the Foreign Office (1931–5) this meant that Simon became the first politician of modern times to hold all three of the 'great' offices of State. Only R.A. Butler and James Callaghan have matched this record. Callaghan is unique in also having held the office of Prime Minister.
13. Undated press cutting of May 1937, SB/6. HA.
14. Lord Home to Lord Blake, 30 November 1980. HA. The notice was written by Lord Armstrong, Cabinet Secretary, 1979–87.
15. In 1948 Sir John Colville (1915–87) married Lady Margaret Egerton, one of the six daughters of Lord Ellesmere, brother-in-law to the Countess of Home. He was thus distantly related to Alec Dunglass. His book *Those Lambtons!* is an invaluable guide to the intricate network of Douglas-Home and Lambton ancestry. Sir John's contribution to British public life had many unique touches, not least in the trust he inspired in a disparate trio of prime ministers – Chamberlain, Churchill and Attlee. Few Chamberlainites supped at Chartwell, but Colville was one of them.
16. Colville, *The Fringes of Power*, pp. 31, 35.

17. Robert Rhodes James, *Anthony Eden*, Weidenfeld & Nicolson, 1986, p. 174.
18. SB/7.
19. John Harvey (ed.), *The Diplomatic Diaries of Oliver Harvey, Volume 1, 1937–1940*, Collins, 1970, p. 63.
20. The Earl of Birkenhead, *Halifax: The Life of Lord Halifax*, Hamish Hamilton, 1965, p. 368.
21. The Countess of Avon to the author, 17 December 1990.
22. One of the central enigmas of the Home–Butler relationship is why Munich was held against Butler in later years by sections of the Conservative Party, whereas Home largely escaped censure. Colleagues of both men have attributed this to Butler's 'executive' capacity, whereas Home's was a 'bag-carrying' one. Truth, as Oscar Wilde has noted, is rarely pure, and never simple. For Conservatives antipathetic to Butler's claims in the 1950s and 1960s, Munich was a convenient stick to beat back his ambitions. See Chapter 9.
23. Neville Chamberlain to King George VI, 24 February 1938. PREM 5/206 (PRO).
24. Anthony Eden to Neville Chamberlain, 20 February 1938. PREM 5/158 (PRO).
25. Iain Macleod to the Earl of Avon, 10 August 1961. Avon Papers. AP 23/47/1. (Birmingham University Library.)
26. Private information.
27. He later much admired Dan Quayle, Vice-President of the United States from 1989 to 1993, whom he considered undervalued and misunderstood.
28. Simon papers. MS Simon 7 (Bodleian Library, Oxford). The diary entry gives the date, incorrectly, as 28 August. Details of the visit are also in the Lanark Unionist Association Records and in the Hirsel papers. Simon gives an account in *Retrospect: The Memoirs of the Rt. Hon. Viscount Simon*, Hutchinson, 1952, pp. 244–5.
29. Simon papers. MS Simon 7 (Bodleian Library, Oxford).
30. Sir Horace Wilson, 'Papers on Munich', T 273/404, PRO. Seven dated files outline the main developments.
31. *Scottish Daily Express*, 29 August 1938. A former miner from Baillieston, and a delegate of the Lanarkshire Miners' Union, P.J. Dollan was Lord Provost of Glasgow, 1938–41, where he had been chairman of the Labour Council Group and a member of Glasgow Corporation 1913–46. Knighted in 1941. His high regard for his local Unionist MP was an example of the cross-party relationships which characterised this stage of Dunglass's career.
32. In discussing his career, the sharpest and most detailed recollections of Lord Home were invariably associated with the events of September 1938, the outbreak of war and the fall of Chamberlain as Prime Minister. Dunglass never forgot those eighteen months; otherwise unattributed details in this account of Munich and its aftermath are from conversations between Lord Home and the author and from SB/7 & 8. HA.
33. Neville Chamberlain to Ida Chamberlain, 11 September 1938. Neville Chamberlain papers. NC 18/1/1068. (Birmingham University Library.)
34. Neville Chamberlain to King George VI, Royal Archives, Windsor. RA GVI 235/02.

35. Lord Dunglass's copy of the three-line whip is in SB/7.
36. Sir John Simon diary, 28 September 1938. MSS Simon 10 (Bodleian Library, Oxford). Accounts are also included in the diaries of Sir Harold Nicolson and Sir Henry 'Chips' Channon and all the memoirs of the period, notably Duff Cooper's (*Old Men Forget*, Hart-Davis, 1953, pp. 240–1). Simon's account, which is as dramatic as any, has been unaccountably neglected. The common factor in all is that hindsight had not yet dampened the sense of relief which greeted Chamberlain's statement.
37. SB/7.
38. Martin Gilbert, *Winston S. Churchill: Volume V 1922–1939*, Heinemann, 1976, p. 987.
39. Rhodes James, *Chips*, *op. cit.*, p. 172. Bill Astor (1907–66) had entered the House of Commons in 1935, and visited Berlin, the Sudetenland, Austria, Czechoslovakia and France in the wake of the Munich agreement. His subsequent report gave Chamberlain too optimistic a view of Hitler's thoughts and intentions, as Chamberlain reported to his sister Ida in a letter of 10 November 1938. NC 18/1/1130 (Birmingham University Library).
40. Lord Home, in 'I was There' series, 14 January 1968. BBC Written Archives, Caversham.
41. The late Brian Johnston to author, 4 January 1991. Brian Johnston's memory of Heston airport was of the blackness of Lord Halifax's homburg and the smallness of the plane.
42. Simon papers. MS Simon 274 (Bodleian Library, Oxford). *Evening News*, 29 September 1938.
43. Evidence of Bill Dockrell, flight engineer. *Daily Telegraph*, 26 August 1992.
44. When the aircraft bringing Manchester United home from a European cup tie crashed at Munich Airport in 1958 with great loss of life, some commentators drew a companion with Chamberlain. The parallel, some said, was clear: Munich was an unlucky place.
45. Goebbels diary, 29 September 1938. *Sunday Times*, 12 July 1992.
46. 'Memories of 1938/1939'. SB/104.
47. Cited by John W. Wheeler-Bennett, *Munich: Prologue to Tragedy*, Macmillan, 1963, p. 172.
48. Lord Home to author, 9 August 1990.
49. Lord Home, 'I was There' series.
50. Chamberlain note of 30 September 1938. CAB 23/95 (PRO).
51. BBC Written Archives, Caversham. Munich file, R 28/297. The Munich Agreement was formally 'negated' by the British Prime Minister, John Major, and President Havel of Czechoslovakia on 27 May 1992.
52. The original, with its clearly visible fold marks, is on public view at the Imperial War Museum, London.
53. Cited in Iain Macleod, *Neville Chamberlain*, Muller, 1961, p. 256.
54. Record of Neville Chamberlain's talk with Herr Hitler, 30 September 1938. PREM 1/266A (PRO).
55. Lord Home, 'I was There' series.
56. Wheeler-Bennett, *op. cit.*, p. 180. *God Bless You, Mr Chamberlain*, BBC Television, 23 September 1988.

57. *Daily Herald*, 1 October 1938. Further details of Chamberlain's return journey to Downing Street, via Heston and Buckingham Palace, are from this source, a comprehensive contemporary record.
58. BBC Written Archives, Caversham. Czechoslovak Crisis General File. R 34/325.
59. The runway has long since disappeared. Since 1967 the site has been occupied by Heston Services, part of the Granada Services on the M4.
60. King George VI to Neville Chamberlain, 30 September 1938. Royal Archives, Windsor. RA GVI 235/15.
61. Royal Archives, Windsor. RA GVI 03348/297.
62. BBC Written Archives, Caversham. Czechoslovak Crisis General File. R 34/325.
63. Neville Chamberlain to Ida Chamberlain, 2 October 1938. NC 18/1/1070. (Birmingham University Library.)
64. Cited by Robert Blake, *Disraeli*, Methuen paperback edition, 1969, p. 664.
65. *Daily Herald*, 1 October 1938.
66. There are contradictory accounts of the circumstances of Duff Cooper's resignation. See Duff Cooper, *Old Men Forget*, Hart-Davis, 1953, p. 242; John Charmley, *Duff Cooper: the Authorized Biography*, Weidenfeld & Nicolson, 1986, pp. 125–6; A.J.P. Taylor, *Beaverbrook*, Penguin edition, Harmondsworth, 1974, p. 501. Cooper's resignation was accepted and the letter appeared in the *Evening Standard* on 1 October 1938.
67. Nevile Henderson, *Failure of a Mission*, Hodder, 1940, p. 167.
68. SB/7.
69. Neville Chamberlain to Ida Chamberlain, 2 October 1938. NC 18/1/1070. (Birmingham University Library.)
70. Lady John McEwen to Duff Cooper, 11 October 1938. Norwich papers. DUFC 2/15. (Churchill College, Cambridge.)
71. Neville Chamberlain to Ida Chamberlain, 2 October 1938. NC 18/1/1070. (Birmingham University Library.)
72. Details and photographs are in SB/8.
73. Neville Chamberlain to Ida Chamberlain, 9 October 1938. NC 18/1/1071. (Birmingham University Library.)
74. Neville Chamberlain to Hilda Chamberlain, 15 October 1938. NC 18/1/1072. (Birmingham University Library.)
75. Robin Douglas-Home (1932–64) was the eldest son of Henry and Margaret Douglas-Home. Talented musician, photographer and author of the novel *Hot for Certainties*, his suicide in 1964 was a grievous blow to the family. His former wife, Sandra, later married Michael Howard, Home Secretary in the Major administration.
76. Neville Chamberlain to Lady Home, 22 October 1938. HA.
77. Katharine Marjory Ramsay, Duchess of Atholl (1874–1960) had been Conservative MP for Kinross and West Perthshire since 1923, though at the general elections of 1931 and 1935 she had stood under the Independent Unionist label.
78. Dr Stuart Ball, 'Local Conservatism and Party Organisation', in *Conservative Century: The Conservative Party since 1900*, edited by Anthony Selden and

Stuart Ball, Oxford University Press, Oxford, 1994, p. 267. The Duchess of Atholl was the most prominent inter-war example of such a breakdown between local MP and constituency organisation. See also Ball's 'The Politics of Appeasement: The Fall of the Duchess of Atholl and the Kinross and West Perth By-Election, December 1938', *Scottish Historical Review*, 69 (1990), pp. 49–83.

79. Robert Rhodes James, *Bob Boothby: A Portrait*, John Curtis, Hodder & Stoughton, 1991, pp. 187–8.
80. Ball, 'The Politics of Appeasement', *op. cit.*, p. 50.
81. SB/8. Record of 17 December 1938.
82. *Perthshire Advertiser*, 21 December 1938.
83. Ball, 'The Politics of Appeasement', *op. cit.*, p. 77.
84. Mass Observation MSS, Box 2, File D, Sussex University.
85. Private information. Details of the by-election are in Chris Cook and John Ramsden, *By-Elections in British Politics*, Macmillan, 1973, Chapters 1 and 6, and p. 371.
86. Robert Rhodes James, *Churchill: A Study in Failure*, Weidenfeld & Nicolson, 1970, p. 340.
87. Dr Ball to author, 24 October 1994, writing with knowledge of the private Atholl papers on the by-election.
88. Earl of Birkenhead, *op. cit.*, p. 430.
89. Neville Chamberlain to King George VI, 17 January 1938. PREM 1/327, PRO.
90. Sir Henry Channon, in Rhodes James, *Chips*, *op. cit.*, entry for 28 March 1939, p. 191.
91. *Ibid.*, p. 198
92. Viscount Cranborne to Harold Macmillan. Macmillan Papers. Box 052 (Birch Grove classification).
93. FO 800/317. Fol 82. PRO.
94. Harold Nicolson, *Diaries and Letters: 1930–1962*, Collins, 1966–8, 2 September 1938.
95. One of the most dramatic (and bitter) re-creations of the scene is in Alan Bennett, *Forty Years On*, Faber & Faber, 1969, pp. 73–5.
96. BBC Sound Archives, Caversham.
97. Lord Home of the Hirsel, *The Way the Wind Blows*, Collins, 1976, p. 72.
98. Patrick Gordon Walker diary, 3 September 1939 and 21 September 1939. GNWR 1/1 (Lord Gordon-Walker Papers). Churchill College, Cambridge.
99. John Colville diary, *op. cit.*, 15 December 1939, p. 57.
100. SB/8. In retrospect, Lord Home was amused by these Civil Service instructions, when they were discovered among his papers. They were not uncommon in his experience. In later Commonwealth Office days, a punctilious secretary advised Elizabeth Home to take 'sensible shoes' for a visit to the Victoria Falls.
101. NC 2/24A. (Birmingham University Library.)
102. For Chamberlain's thoughts on the visit see Neville Chamberlain to Ida Chamberlain, 20 December 1939. NC 18/1/1135. (Birmingham University Library.) Details of Lord Dunglass's uniform and the menus are in SB/8.

103. CAB 65/2 PRO.
104. Neville Chamberlain diary, 24 December 1939. NC 2/24A. (Birmingham University Library.)
105. SB/9.
106. Charles Douglas-Home, *Evelyn Baring: The Last Proconsul*, Collins, 1978, p. 87.
107. Admiral Sir Roger Keyes was National Conservative MP for North Portsmouth, 1934–43. His dramatic intervention in the Norwegian Debate on 7 May, when he appeared in the uniform of an Admiral of the Fleet, complete with six rows of medals, contributed to Chamberlain's fall.
108. Lord Dunglass memorandum for Neville Chamberlain, 29 April 1940. PREM 1/418, PRO.
109. Channon diary, in Rhodes James, *Chips*, *op. cit.*, 25 April 1940, p. 242.
110. Charles Douglas-Home, *op. cit.*, p. 87.
111. Leo Amery diary, 8 May 1940. John Barnes and David Nicholson (eds.), *The Empire At Bay: The Leo Amery Diaries 1929–1945*, Hutchinson, 1988, pp. 610–11.
112. *Ibid.*, p. 594.
113. King George VI diary, 10 May 1940, John Wheeler-Bennett, *op. cit.*, p. 444. The Peerage Act, which allowed peers to disclaim their titles, became law on 31 July 1963. In the King's suggestion is the genesis of what later transformed Lord Home's life. See also Robert Blake, 'How Churchill became Prime Minister', in *Churchill: A Major New Assessment of His Life in Peace and War*, eds. Robert Blake and Wm Roger Louis, Oxford University Press, Oxford, 1993, p. 263, 266.
114. Lord Halifax diary, 9 May 1940. Earl of Birkenhead, *op. cit.*, pp. 454–5.
115. John Colville diary, 10 May 1940, p. 122.
116. *Ibid.*,12 May 1940, p. 124.
117. Charles Lysaght, *Brendan Bracken*, Allen Lane, 1979, p. 176.
118. Nancy Dugdale to Thomas Dugdale, 20 June 1940. Crathorne Papers.
119. Evelyn Baring to Molly Baring, 11, 12, 14, 23, 30 May 1940. Charles Douglas-Home, *op. cit.*, pp. 87–9.
120. Nancy Dugdale to Thomas Dugdale, 20 June 1940. Crathorne Papers.
121. SB/9.
122. Lord Dunglass to Neville Chamberlain, 29 July 1940. NC 7/11/33/60. (Birmingham University Library.)
123. Neville Chamberlain to Lord Dunglass, 10 August 1940. HA.
124. Undated press cuttings, SB/9.
125. Neville Chamberlain to Lord Dunglass, 19 October 1940. HA.
126. Mrs Neville Chamberlain to David Margesson, undated letter. Margesson papers MRGN 1/4. (Churchill College, Cambridge.)
127. Martin Gilbert, *Finest Hour: Winston S. Churchill 1939–1941*, Heinemann, 1983, p. 902. Churchill's complete speech is reprinted as an appendix in Iain Macleod, *op. cit.*, pp. 303–5.
128. Lord Dunglass to Mrs Neville Chamberlain, 19 November 1940. NC 13/19/2/272. (Birmingham University Library.)

129. 13th Earl of Home to Mrs Neville Chamberlain, 11 November 1940. NC 13/19/2/271. (Birmingham University Library.)
130. Draft notes for talk on BBC Radio 3; Churchill Centenary, 30 November 1974. HA.
131. Lord Home of the Hirsel to Cornelius Mawby, 30 September 1985. HA.
132. Lord Home, 'I was There' series.
133. *The Scotsman*, 2 July 1993.
134. Cited by D. E. Moggridge, *Maynard Keynes: An Economist's Biography*, Routledge, 1992, p. 611, from the 'Social, Political and Literary Writings', 84 JMK, XXVIII, 62.
135. The late Colonel Terence Maxwell to the author, 5 August 1974.

Chapter 5.

1. Sir Horace Wilson to Sir Thomas Dugdale, 28 September 1940. Crathorne Papers.
2. Nancy Dugdale to Thomas Dugdale, 31 October 1940. Crathorne Papers.
3. Lady Diana Wolfe Murray, *Daily Mail*, 30 November 1994.
4. Jonathan Aitken to the author, 18 May 1993.
5. Colin Coote, *A Companion of Honour: The Story of Walter Elliot*, Collins, 1965, pp. 222–3.
6. Lord Dunglass to Mrs Walter Elliot. Undated letter of 1943. Baroness Elliot of Harwood papers, Harwood, Bonchester Bridge.
7. Churchill referred to Halifax's mission in America as a 'high and perilous charge' in a letter of 19 December 1940, cited Earl of Birkenhead, *Halifax: The Life of Lord Halifax*, Hamish Hamilton, 1965, p. 467.
8. R.A. Butler to Lord Dunglass, 8 October 1941. Butler papers, G13 (164). (Trinity College, Cambridge.) The post-Prague speech is on p. 400 of Keith Feiling, *The Life of Neville Chamberlain*, Macmillan, 1945. Sylvia Goodfellow, private secretary to R.A. Butler at this time, remembers how he assiduously juggled the responsibilities of the Board of Education and the Post-War Problems Central Committee, and how uneasy he was about obscurantist Conservative opposition. 'He wasn't comfortable with the wartime Conservatives and maybe that remained the trouble to the end.' (Conversations with Miss Goodfellow and letter to author, 26 September 1994.) John Barnes and Richard Cockett, 'The Making of Party Policy', *Conservative Century: The Conservative Party since 1900*, edited by Anthony Seldon and Stuart Ball, Oxford University Press, Oxford, 1994, p. 364.
9. Lord Dunglass, letter to *Scotsman*, 25 September 1941.
10. Mrs Edna Berresford to the author, 17 January 1991.
11. John Stuart Mill, *Autobiography*, chapter 1.
12. A.N. Wilson, 'True Confessions', *Daily Telegraph*, 29 January 1994.
13. Lord Home, *Letters to a Grandson*, Collins, 1983.
14. Baroness Thatcher to author, 11 November 1992.
15. The bookshelves at the Hirsel contain every major political biography of the

past century, invariably well thumbed. Until failing eyesight in the 1990s made reading difficult, current publications found their way on to tables in the drawing room and smoking room, to be taken up when time permitted. The multiple volumes (together with their companion volumes of documents) on Churchill by Randolph Churchill and Martin Gilbert were all read as they appeared, together with the volumes on his contemporaries. Works by David Dilks and Kenneth Rose were particular favourites. The last book he attempted seriously before yielding to failing eyesight was Andrew Roberts's *The Holy Fox: A Biography of Lord Halifax* (1991).

16. William Douglas-Home, *Mr Home pronounced Hume: An Autobiography*, Collins, 1979, pp. 58–9.
17. Leo S. Amery, 'John Amery, An Explanation', privately printed 1946. Reprinted in *The Empire at Bay: The Leo Amery Diaries 1929–1945*, edited by John Barnes and David Nicholson, Hutchinson, 1988, pp. 1071–5. The release of government papers at the PRO on 7 February 1995 revealed the disquiet felt in many quarters about the executions of Amery and William Joyce (Lord Haw-Haw).
18. Private information. Dunglass knew of the impact the death of Norman Chamberlain in the Great War had upon his cousin, Neville. So much of what Chamberlain later attempted was so that Norman's sacrifice was not wasted.
19. Undated newspaper cutting, SB/9.
20. Lanark Unionist Association Records.
21. *Ibid.*
22. Lady Caroline Douglas-Home to author, 13 September 1994.
23. Mrs Anne Chamberlain to the Countess of Home, 22 February 1943. HA.
24. Mrs Edna Berresford to author, 17 January 1991; Lady William Scott to author, 10 August 1990.
25. The conduct of elections for the party leader (under various versions of the original Douglas-Home rules) has been in the hands of the Chairman of the 1922 Committee since 1965. The standard history is Philip Goodhart, *The 1922: The Story of the 1922 Committee*, Macmillan, 1973. See also, Philip Norton, 'The Parliamentary Party and Party Committees' in *Conservative Century: The Conservative Party since 1900, op. cit.*, pp. 97–144.
26. Goodhart, *op. cit.*, p. 131.
27. Speech at the Military Academy, West Point, USA, 5 December 1962.
28. *Hansard*, 24 May 1944.
29. The reference to man, the great amphibium, can be found in Sir Thomas Browne, *Religio Medici*, 1642, Part 1, Section 34.
30. *Hansard*, 24 May 1944.
31. House of Commons Debates, *Hansard*, 28 and 29 September 1944.
32. The first of these summits had been held at Tehran (28 November–1 December 1943) and the third was to be held at Potsdam, west of Berlin (16 July–2 August 1945). Stalin, Roosevelt and Churchill attended the Tehran and Yalta Conferences. After Roosevelt's death on 12 April 1945, President Truman represented the US at Potsdam, and after Churchill's

defeat in the general election, Clement Attlee led the British delegation.
33. Frank Roberts, *Dealing with Dictators: The Destruction and Revival of Europe 1930–1970*, Weidenfeld & Nicolson, 1991, pp. 75–6.
34. James Stuart to Anthony Eden, FO telegram 512, 15 February 1945. FO 945/20, PRO.
35. 1922 Committee minutes, 14 February 1945, cited by Goodhart, *op. cit.*, p. 134.
36. House of Commons Debates, *Hansard*, 27 February 1945.
37. *Ibid.*
38. Guy Eden to Lord Dunglass, 27 February 1945. HA.
39. John Colville diary, 27 February 1945, *op. cit.*, p. 565.
40. Harold Nicolson diary, 27 February 1945: *Harold Nicolson: Diaries and Letters, Volume 2*, 1939–1945, (ed. Nigel Nicolson) Weidenfeld & Nicolson, 1967, p. 437.
41. *New Statesman*, 2 October 1948. 'He may have been thinking of Lord Dunglass,' wrote Taylor's biographer, 'an appeaser before the War, he was now advocating a very firm line against Russia.' Adam Sisman, *A.J.P. Taylor: A Biography*, Sinclair-Stevenson, 1994, p. 183*n*.
42. Manuscript of broadcast of 30 November 1974 (BBC). HA.
43. John Keats to George and Georgiana Keats, 14 February 1819: *The Letters of John Keats*, ed. Maurice Buxton Forman, Oxford University Press, 1952, p. 335.
44. Appointment of caretaker government. PREM 5/215 (PRO).
45. Manuscript of broadcast of 30 November 1974 (BBC). HA.
46. *Ibid.*
47. Lanark Unionist Association Records, Lanark.
48. Information from the family.
49. SB/9. HA.
50. Lanark Unionist Association Records.
51. Anthony Howard, 'We are the Masters now: The General Election of 5 July 1945', in Michael Sissons and Philip French (eds.) *Age of Austerity: 1945–1951*, Penguin Books, Harmondsworth, 1964, pp. 15–16. The late Lord Butler to the author, 20 November 1975.
52. *Daily Worker*, 8 August 1945
53. Avon papers. AP 33/6. (Birmingham University Library.)
54. J.D. Hoffman, *The Conservative Party in Opposition, 1945–1951*, MacGibbon & Kee, 1964, remains the best guide to these years and to Butler's role as a latter-day Peel formulating new Tamworth Manifestos.
55. Lanark Unionist Association Records.
56. *Ibid.*
57. Lord Dunglass to *The Times*, 12 March 1946.
58. *Hamilton Advertiser*, 30 July 1948.
59. This was one of the main recommendations of the Selwyn Lloyd Report into Party Organisation in 1963.
60. Lanark Unionist Association Records; private conversations with former constituents.

Chapter 6.

1. *The Diary of Hugh Gaitskell 1945–1956*, ed. Philip M. Williams, Jonathan Cape, 1983, 27 January 1950, p. 161.
2. J.C. Teesdale to the Earl of Home, 21 October 1963. HA.
3. Douglas Jay, *The Socialist Case*, Faber, 1937, p. 258.
4. Michael Cockerell, *Live from Number 10: The Inside Story of Prime Ministers and Television*, Faber, 1988, p. 8. H.G. Nicholas, *The British General Election of 1950*, Macmillan, 1951, p. 125.
5. Nicholas, *ibid.*, p. 295, pp. 82–3., p. 227.
6. Although later polls were reflecting the shift away from Dewey. Roy Jenkins, *Truman*, Collins, 1986, p. 133.
7. Nicholas, *op. cit.*, pp. 1–9.
8. Nigel Fisher, *Iain Macleod*, André Deutsch, 1973, p. 72.
9. Lanark Unionist Association Records.
10. In 1964, when Douglas-Home was Prime Minister, he was horrified to hear that Attlee had been seen in full evening dress at a Green Line bus stop waiting for public transport after an official dinner. 'My dear Clem,' he wrote, '... if you should at any time want to have the use of a Government Car Service car and driver for such official functions in the Metropolitan area of London you have only to call on the Government Car service. Will you let me know if you would like these arrangements.' Sir Alec Douglas-Home to the Rt Hon. Earl Attlee, 29 July 1964. In his retirement, Lord Home eschewed his right to a government car, until Mrs Thatcher insisted following a mugging incident in Piccadilly. HA.
11. Anthony Eden to Sir Alexander Cadogan, 4 August 1945. Avon Papers. AP 33/6. (Birmingham University Library.)
12. Disraeli had subtitled his novel *Sybil* (1845) 'The Two Nations'. The original 'One Nation' group of MPs included Robert Carr, Edward Heath, Iain Macleod, Angus Maude and Enoch Powell.
13. Lord Carr of Hadley to the author, 13 October 1987.
14. Selwyn Lloyd diary, 3 January 1968. SELO 124 (2). Selwyn Lloyd Papers. (Churchill College, Cambridge.)
15. The Peerage Act of 31 July 1963 was passed after a determined and courageous three-year campaign by Tony Benn to have the law changed. This directly enabled Lord Home to be a candidate for the premiership later that year. See Tony Benn, *Out of the Wilderness: Diaries 1963–1967*, Hutchinson, 1987, pp. 2–54.
16. House of Commons Debates, *Hansard*, 9 March 1951; 29 November 1950.
17. Lanark Unionist Association Records.
18. Kenneth Harris, *Attlee*, Weidenfeld & Nicolson, 1982, pp. 484–94.
19. The majority of 17 in October 1951 was then considered a dangerously narrow margin. It was exactly the same majority the Conservatives had after the loss of the Newbury and Christchurch by-elections in 1993.
20. Lady William Scott to the author, 10 August 1990.
21. James Stuart, *Within the Fringe: An Autobiography*, Bodley Head, 1967, p. 162.
22. The *Scotsman*, 27 October 1951.

23. Sir David Pitblado to the author, 18 November 1990.
24. George Pottinger, *The Secretaries of State for Scotland 1926–1976*, Scottish Academic Press, Edinburgh, p. 133.
25. *Ibid.*, p. 138.
26. The late Ian Robertson to the author, 9 April 1991.
27. *Scotsman*, 2 November 1951.
28. Andrew Marr, *The Battle for Scotland*, Penguin Books, Harmondsworth, 1992, pp. 66–97.
29. House of Lords Debates, *Hansard*, 11 March 1952, Cols. 606–7.The debate is filed in DO 35/5126 (PRO). The Sword of State was carried by Lord Home when the Queen went to St Giles Cathedral on 24 June 1953 for the Presentation of the Honours of Scotland.
30. *The Times*, 29 November 1949. Filed in CAB 21/3328 (PRO).
31. Ian M. Robertson, CB, LVO (1918–92), was a familiar and elegant figure on the Edinburgh scene, in the Scottish Office, the New Club and in the artistic world, and became a close friend of the Homes.
32. The late Ian Robertson, letter to author, 12 April 1991.
33. The *Scotsman*, 20 November 1951. Filed in CAB 21/3329 (PRO).
34. When the author was researching this section, the New Club was almost always suggested as the place for a meeting by the civil servants of the 1950s; the portrait by Allan Sutherland dates from 1977.
35. From the obituary notice of Viscount Muirshiel, *Daily Telegraph*, 21 August 1992.
36. SOE 11/19 (PRO).
37. John S. Gibson, letter to author, 16 March 1991.
38. House of Lords Debates, *Hansard*, 20 November 1951 (Cols. 383–4); CAB 21/3329 (PRO).
39. House of Commons Debates, *Hansard*, 21 November 1951 (Col. 482) and CAB 21/3329 (PRO).
40. *Ibid.* (Col. 522).
41. House of Lords Debates, *Hansard*, 20 November 1951. Cols. 392–4. Filed in CAB 21/3329 (PRO).
42. SEP 12/22. Scottish Record Office.
43. Lady Mitchison served on the Advisory Panel 1947–65 and on its successor, the Highlands and Islands Development Consultative Council, 1966–76; letter to author, 15 July 1991.
44. Minutes Book of the Highlands and Islands Advisory Panel, 25 January 1952. File SEP 12/22. Scottish Record Office.
45. SEP 12/2. Scottish Record Office.
46. Professor Nigel Walker to author, 27 March 1991.
47. Private information.
48. *Ibid.*
49. *Ibid.*
50. Details from SEP 12/99. Scottish Record Office.
51. *News Chronicle*, 2 June 1953.
52. Letter in the possession of the Earl of Home. His father carried the Sword of Spiritual Justice at the Coronation, which is why a page had to be in

attendance.

53. Sir Arthur Penn (1886–1960), Private Secretary and later Treasurer to Queen Elizabeth the Queen Mother, was not discomfited by the Coronation marbles alone. Once, when a guest at Douglas for the shooting, he saw Alec Home's black labrador breaking cover and vanishing over the horizon. Home did not worry about his dogs behaving badly, as it put his guests at ease if their dogs behaved badly. On this occasion, however, Penn covered his own dog's eyes and said, 'Don't look Sable, don't look.' (Private information.)
54. Kenneth Rose, *Kings, Queens and Courtiers: Intimate Portraits of the Royal House of Windsor from its foundation to the present day*, Weidenfeld & Nicolson, 1985, p. 169.
55. Stanley Cursiter (1887–1976) had been appointed HM Painter and Limner in Scotland by King George VI. Kenneth Rose, 'Tactful Orcadian', *Sunday Telegraph*, 9 August 1987.
56. One still stands in Edinburgh's Regent Terrace, outside the home of a civil servant involved in the original decision.
57. DD 17/13. (Scottish Record Office.)
58. Report of the Committee on Scottish Financial and Trade Statistics, July 1952, Cmd. 8609. James Mitchell, *Conservatives and the Union: A Study of Conservative Party Attitudes to Scotland*, Edinburgh University Press, Edinburgh, 1990, p. 33.
59. The late Harold Macmillan to author, 23 April 1975.
60. John Colville, *The Churchillians*, Weidenfeld & Nicolson, 1981, p. 171.
61. Nigel Walker to author, 27 March 1991.

Chapter 7.

1. The Earl of Home to Sir Anthony Eden, 7 April 1955. PREM 5/228 (PRO). Eden had received the Order of the Garter on 20 October 1954.
2. Lord Home of the Hirsel to Lord Plowden, 11 December 1985. HA.
3. Dr David Butler to author, 25 January 1995. Unemployment showed a year-on-year decrease and during the Churchill administration, particularly from 1953, there was an increase in real terms in social expenditure. See Anthony Seldon, *Churchill's Indian Summer: The Conservative Government 1951–1955*, Hodder & Stoughton, 1981, pp. 244–5; Kenneth Morgan, *The People's Peace: British History 1945–1989*, Oxford University Press, Oxford, 1990, pp. 116–18; Paul Addison, *Churchill on the Home Front 1900–1955*, Pimlico edition, 1993, p. 429. A more recent example of a campaign influencing the succeeding election was the 1992 American presidential election when Bush's 'Read my lips' taxation pledge from 1988 was recalled by his opponents.
4. Memorandum by the Earl of Avon, 4 September 1969. AP 23/27/42A. Avon Papers. (Birmingham University Library.)
5. Private information.
6. Douglas Dodds-Parker, *Political Eunuch*, Springwood Books, Ascot, 1986, p. 82.
7. Macmillan diary, 6 April 1955. (Stockton Papers.)
8. Private information; see Dodds-Parker, *op. cit.*, p. 80.

9. Frank Roberts, *Dealing with Dictators: The Destruction and Revival of Europe 1930–1970*, Weidenfeld & Nicolson, 1991, p. 138. The CRO existed as an independent body until October 1968, when it was merged into the enlarged Foreign and Commonwealth Office. The Earl of Home was the longest-serving of its nine Secretaries of State. Technically, he returned to it in his second spell as Secretary of State for Foreign and Commonwealth Affairs from 1970–4.
10. Viscount Boyd of Merton Papers. File Mss. Eng. C. 3432. (Bodleian Library, Oxford.) Professor David Dilks, 'From Trustee to Partner: The British Government & Empire in the 1950s', a series of lectures in 1993 to mark the tenure of the Colonial Office by Alan Lennox-Boyd, also stressed the importance of the relationship of Lennox-Boyd and Home in this matter.
11. This was completed in 1959. 'Marlborough House as a whole will be under the control of the Commonwealth Relations Office,' wrote Norman Brook, 14 December 1959. CAB 21/3894 (PRO).
12. CAB 128/28 (PRO).
13. Internal CRO memorandum, 10 March 1960. DO 35/9543 (PRO).
14. The Republic of Ireland left the Commonwealth in 1949, Pakistan in 1972 (rejoining in 1989), and Fiji proclaimed a republic in 1987 after an internal coup. South Africa rejoined in 1994.The main additions during Alec Home's spell at the CRO and his first spell at the Foreign Office were Cyprus and Nigeria in 1960; Sierra Leone and Tanganyika (Tanzania) in 1961; Jamaica, Trinidad and Tobago, and Uganda in 1962.
15. Sir Frank Roberts to the author, 1 July 1992.
16. Speech in Washington, February 1956.
17. The functions of the CRO are outlined in DO 35/9543 (PRO).
18. Viscount Chandos to Earl of Home, 2 December 1958, reporting on conversations with his nephew, Viscount Cobham, Governor-General of New Zealand 1957–62. CHAN II 4/7 Chandos Papers. (Churchill College, Cambridge.)
19. Harold Smedley (b. 1920) joined the Dominions Office in 1946. He served in a variety of posts before becoming Private Secretary to Lord Swinton in 1954. In 1957, he moved to the British High Commssion Office in Delhi. His career overlapped again with Home's when he was appointed Secretary-General of the Pearce Commission on Rhodesia in 1971–2.
20. Lord Home to author, 31 March 1993.
21. The late Sir Henry Lintott to author, 26 August 1992.
22. Private information from several sources.
23. Joe Garner, *The Commonwealth Office 1925–1968*, Heinemann, 1978, p. 285.
24. CAB 128/29 (PRO).
25. Sir Anthony Eden to Earl of Home, 27 April 1955. AP 20/20/6. Avon Papers. (Birmingham University Library.) Malcolm MacDonald was about to take up his post as High Commissioner in India (1955–60), where he helped to improve Anglo–Indian relations after Suez. His successor as Commissioner-General was Sir Robert Scott.
26. *The Times*, 17 May 1955.
27. CAB 129/75–76 (PRO).

28. Patrick Gordon Walker to C.R. Attlee, 2 October 1950. GNWR 1/9. Gordon-Walker Papers. (Churchill College, Cambridge.)
29. J.A. Cross, *Lord Swinton*, Clarendon Press, Oxford, 1982, pp. 280–1.
30. Earl of Home to Sir Anthony Eden, 13 April 1955; Earl of Home to Sir Michael Adeane, 21 April 1955. DO 35/6512 (PRO).
31. *Ibid.* Correspondence, May–July 1955.
32. Unless otherwise noted, quotations are from Harold Smedley's diary, 30 August–4 November 1955 (courtesy of Sir Harold Smedley).
33. CRO Minute, 28 July 1955. FO 800/665 (PRO).
34. Earl of Home to Harold Macmillan, 25 July 1955. FO 800/665 (PRO).
35. *The Times*, 24 October 1955.
36. Krishna Menon (1896–1974), Indian High Commisioner in London 1947–52, Indian delegate to the United Nations, and a Minister in Nehru's Cabinets from 1956, was a controversial figure, even in India where he had many enemies.
37. Smedley's diary, 30 August–4 November 1955.
38. Robert Menzies, *Afternoon Light: Some Memories of Men and Events*, Cassell, 1967, p. 189.
39. CRO, record of tour, DO 35/6513 (PRO).
40. CAB 129/77 (PRO).
41. Private information.
42. Andrew Roberts, *Eminent Churchillians*, Weidenfeld & Nicolson, 1994, p. 239. Kilmuir's Report, presented to the Cabinet on 11 July 1956, a fortnight before the Suez Crisis broke, prevaricated by saying that 'control will eventually be inescapable; but that the balance of advantage lies against imposing it now', a conclusion from which Salisbury alone dissented. CAB 128/29 (PRO). Cabinet Minutes, 11 July 1956. CAB 128/30 (PRO).
43. Sir Anthony Eden to Earl of Home, 10 December 1955. DO 35/6513 (PRO).
44. Sir Roger Makins to the Earl of Home, 8 March 1956. DO 35/6513 (PRO).
45. Harold Macmillan to Sir Anthony Eden, 24 October 1955. (Stockton Papers.) This letter was sent two days before Butler's additional October budget.
46. Cabinet Minutes, 31 January 1956. CAB 128/30 (PRO).
47. Harold Smedley diary, 9 and 15 May 1956.
48. Earl of Home to Selwyn Lloyd, 1 June 1956. PREM 11/1477 (PRO).
49. Private information.
50. 'The owner of one of the loudest and most totally sincere laughs in the United Kingdom' was Colville's description of Makins. John Colville, *The Fringes of Power: Downing Street Diaries 1939–1955*, Hodder, 1985, p. 766.
51. Interview with C.L. Sulzberger, 10 December 1963. Cited Sulzberger, *The Last of the Giants*, Weidenfeld & Nicolson, 1970, p. 1036.
52. Sir Henry Lintott (1908–95) was a member of the team preparing Britain's first application to join the Common Market. A great Commonwealth Office stalwart, he contributed to Joe Garner's official history of the department. In later years he returned to Cambridge, where he renewed his friendships with other retired CRO figures, such as Sir James Hennessy and Dame Eleanor

Emery. Home had the highest regard for his abilities.

53. Cabinet Memorandum CP (56) 141, submitted to Cabinet 14 June 1956. CAB 128/30 (PRO).
54. Cabinet Minutes, 28 June 1956. CAB 128/30 (PRO).
55. Countess of Home diary, 26 July 1956. Unless otherwise acknowledged, all quotations about the Suez crisis are from this diary. HA.
56. Private information. Cited D.R. Thorpe, *Selwyn Lloyd*, Jonathan Cape, 1989, p. 211.
57. The most comprehensive account of the origins, course and consequences of the Suez crisis is Keith Kyle, *Suez*, Weidenfeld & Nicolson, 1991.
58. Harold Macmillan diary, 27 July 1956. (Stockton Papers.)
59. Earl of Avon's description of Alec Douglas-Home's main characteristics. Press release of 20 October 1963. AP 23/27/26. Avon Papers. (Birmingham University Library.)
60. Private information.
61. Ironically, Krishna Menon and Robert Menzies have adjoining notices in the *Dictionary of National Biography: 1971–1980*, edited by Lord Blake and C.S. Nicholls, Oxford University Press, Oxford, 1986, pp. 560–5.
62. Record of Secretary of State's meetings with the Commonwealth High Commissioners, 27 July 1956. DO 35/6317 (PRO).
63. Anthony Eden, *Full Circle*, Cassell, 1960, p. 425.
64. Lord Home to Selwyn Lloyd, 1 August 1956. DO 35/6317 (PRO).
65. Lord Home to Sir Anthony Eden, 11 September 1956. DO 35/6314 (PRO).
66. Cited by Sarah Newman, 'The Commonwealth and the Suez Crisis of 1956', *Contemporary Review*, October 1991.
67. Lord Home to Sir Anthony Eden, 15 August 1956; response through Downing Street Secretariat, 16 August 1956. DO 35/6314 (PRO).
68. Earl of Home to Sir Anthony Eden, 17 August 1956. Sir Anthony Eden to the Earl of Home, 19 August 1956. DO 35/6314 (PRO).
69. UK High Commission, Pakistan, Telegram 1769 to Commonwealth Relations Office, 3 November 1956 (because of the time differential, the telegram was received in London on 2 November) and Telegram 1770, 5 November 1956. ADM 116/6119 (PRO).
70. Suez File MB/N108A. Mountbatten note for 'Correspondence about Suez books', 1965. Mountbatten Papers. (University of Southampton Library.)
71. Sir Anthony Eden to Duncan Sandys, 22 August 1956. PREM 11/1152. (PRO).
72. Earl of Home to Sir Anthony Eden, 22 August 1956. PREM 11/1152 (PRO).
73. Lord Home to Sir Anthony Eden, 24 August 1956.The envelope, marked Personal the Prime Minister, and signed H, shows signs of having been ripped open. PREM 11/1152 (PRO).
74. See D.R. Thorpe, *Selwyn Lloyd*, *op. cit.*, pp. 236–44, for Sèvres and its aftermath.
75. Mrs Anne Chamberlain to the Countess of Home, 3 November 1956. HA.
76. SELO 129 (2). Selwyn Lloyd Papers. (Churchill College, Cambridge.)
77. CAB 128/30 (PRO).

78. Lord Home to Sir Anthony Eden, 5 November 1956. PREM 11/1154 (PRO).
79. For Macmillan's crucial role in this decision, see Alistair Horne, *Macmillan 1894–1956: Volume II of the Official Biography*, Macmillan, 1988, p. 440.
80. Lady Home's Suez diary, 26 July–25 November 1956, ends at this point. HA.
81. House of Lords Debates, *Hansard*, 12 December 1956.
82. Earl of Home to the Marquess of Lothian, 13 December 1956. DO 35/5422 (PRO).
83. Lord Selwyn-Lloyd to Lord Home of the Hirsel, 6 December 1977. SELO 254 (5). Selwyn Lloyd Papers. (Churchill College, Cambridge).
84. Sir Alec Douglas-Home to the Earl of Avon, 19 June 1967. AP 23/27/42B. Avon Papers. (Birmingham University Library.)
85. The Earl of Home to Sir Anthony Eden, 10 January 1957. AP 9/1/113. Avon Papers. (Birmingham University Library.)
86. Sir Anthony Eden to the Earl of Home, 16 January 1957. AP 9/1/114. Avon Papers. (Birmingham University Library.)

Chapter 8.

1. Robert Rhodes James, *Anthony Eden*, Weidenfeld & Nicolson, 1986, p. 595.
2. Eden Memorandum, 11 January 1957. AP 20/33/12A. Avon Papers. (Birmingham University Library.)
3. HAIS 4/12. Hailes Papers. (Churchill College, Cambridge.)
4. Lord Boothby, quoted in Alan Thompson and John Barnes, *The Day Before Yesterday: an illustrated history of Britain from Attlee to Macmillan*, Panther and Sidgwick & Jackson, 1971, p. 161. Late Lord Boothby to author, 13 December 1974.
5. Martin Gilbert, *Never Despair: Winston S. Churchill 1945–1965*, Heinemann, 1988, p. 1227.
6. With hindsight Butler considered his best chance of the premiership to have been in June 1953 when both Churchill and Eden were laid low by illness.
7. Alistair Horne, *Macmillan 1957–1986: Volume II of the Official Biography*, Macmillan, 1989, p. 4.
8. Lord Home to Harold Macmillan, 3 April 1957. PREM 5/230 (PRO).
9. Harold Macmillan to Lord Home, 22 December 1957. (Stockton Papers.)
10. Lord Home to R.A. Butler, 14 January 1957. RAB B27 (99). Butler Papers. (Trinity College, Cambridge.)
11. Lord Home to author, 9 August 1990. He was at the Commonwealth Relations Office for 5 years, 3 months and 20 days. His two spells at the Foreign Office were 3 years, 2 months and 22 days, and 3 years, 7 months and 13 days.
12. Cabinet meetings, 21 August 1956–8 January 1957, CAB 128/30 (PRO). Joe Garner, *The Commonwealth Office 1925–1968*, Heinemann, 1978, pp. 334–5. Charles Douglas-Home, *Evelyn Baring: The Last Proconsul*, Collins, 1978, chapters XVII and XVIII, *passim*.
13. Lord Home to Harold Macmillan, 17 February 1959. PREM 11/2910 (PRO).

14. Lord Salisbury to Harold Macmillan, 11 January 1957. PREM 5/230 (PRO).
15. *Evening Dispatch*, 5 April 1957.
16. Lord Home to Harold Macmillan, 3 April 1957. PREM 5/230 (PRO).
17. *Ibid.*, 9 December 1959.
18. Secretary of State's visit to Australia and New Zealand, 1957. DO 35/6110 (PRO).
19. Minutes of Commonwealth Prime Ministers Meeting, June–July 1957. DO 35/4757 (PRO).
20. Lord Home's visit to the Central African Federation, 1957. The Earl of Home to Harold Macmillan, 24 June 1957, Official Memo, DO 35/4829 (PRO).
21. Sir David Cole to author, 4 December 1990.
22. Private information from several sources.
23. Professor David Dilks, 'From Trustee to Partner: The British Government and Empire in the 1950s', a series of six lectures at Rhodes House, Oxford to mark the tenure of the Colonial Office by Alan Lennox-Boyd, February–March 1993.
24. Sir Roy Welensky, *Welensky's 4000 Days: The Life and Death of the Federation of Rhodesia and Nyasaland*, Collins, 1964, pp. 81–2; CAB 129/89 (PRO).
25. *Report by the Secretary of State for Commonwealth Relations on his visit to the Federation of Rhodesia and Nyasaland*, October 1957. DO 35/4829 (PRO).
26. Harold Macmillan, diary, 13 July 1959. (Stockton Papers.)
27. The Earl of Home to Alan Lennox-Boyd, 27 July 1959. Mss Eng C. 3395. Boyd Papers. (Bodleian Library, Oxford.)
28. Alistair Horne, *op. cit.*, p. 183.
29. The Earl of Home to Alan Lennox-Boyd, 14 October 1959. Mss Eng C. 3393. Boyd Papers. (Bodleian Library, Oxford.)
30. John Barnes and Richard Cockett, 'The Making of Party Policy', in *Conservative Century: The Conservative Party since* 1900, edited by Anthony Seldon and Stuart Ball, Oxford University Press, Oxford, 1994, pp. 371–2. Robert Shepherd, *Iain Macleod: A Biography*, Hutchinson, 1994, p. 144. Nigel Fisher, *Iain Macleod*, André Deutsch, 1973, p. 135.
31. Harold Macmillan to the Earl of Home, 7 September 1959. (Stockton Papers.)
32. Nigel Fisher, *op. cit.*, p. 150.
33. Robert Shepherd, *op. cit.*, p. 147.
34. The late Lord Fraser of Kilmorack to author, 6 April 1995.
35. *The Next Five Years*, the Conservative Manifesto 1959, 'Policy for Progress', Conservative Central Office. The old and inadequate Carlisle–Glasgow road ran past the Douglas estate and was a notorious accident black spot. In September 1961 a coach crashed and the injured were taken to Douglas where they received first aid from Lady Home and Lady Caroline Douglas-Home. SB/23 HA.
36. Michael Cockerell, *Live from Number 10: The Inside Story of Prime Ministers and Television*, Faber & Faber, 1988, p. 72.
37. Harold Macmillan diary, 11 October 1959. (Stockton Papers).

38. Philip M. Williams, *Hugh Gaitskell: A Political Biography*, Jonathan Cape, 1979, pp. 526–7. In April 1991, the author was in the smoking room at the Hirsel with Lord Home, who stood up to collect a book. Crisp, the last in a long line of black labradors, awakened from his slumbers by the fireplace and made for the door. 'Crisp thinks he's going for a walk,' I commented. 'Gaitskell thought he was going to win the 1959 Election,' came the reply.
39. Alistair Horne, *op. cit.*, p. 195.
40. Harold Macmillan to the Earl of Home, 9 February 1960. DO 35/7564 (PRO).
41. *Report of the Advisory Commission on the Review of the Constitution of Rhodesia and Nyasaland*, October 1960, Cmnd. 1148.
42. Lord Home, cited in Lord Casey, *The Future of the Commonwealth*, Frederick Muller, 1963, p. 143.
43. CAB 128/34 (PRO).
44. Harold Macmillan to the Earl of Home, 19 June 1960. PREM 5/233 (PRO).
45. Harold Macmillan to the Countess of Home, 27 November 1962. (Stockton Papers.)
46. Private information.
47. Late Lord Butler to author, 20 November 1975.
48. *Daily Mirror*, 28 July 1960.
49. *Evening Standard*, 25 July 1960; *Scottish Daily Express*, 27 July 1960.

Chapter 9.

1. Selwyn Lloyd diary, 4 November 1959. SELO 308(1). Selwyn Lloyd Papers. (Churchill College, Cambridge.)
2. *Ibid.*, 22 November 1959.
3. *Ibid.*, 24 May 1960.
4. SB/19.
5. Private information.
6. Selwyn Lloyd diary, 30 May 1959.
7. *Ibid.*, 11 June 1960.
8. John Campbell, *Edward Heath: A Biography*, Jonathan Cape, 1993, p. 112.
9. Private information from a Foreign Office official present at the dinner.
10. Selwyn Lloyd diary, 28 July 1960.
11. Harold Macmillan diary, 30 July 1960. (Stockton Papers.)
12. Philip M. Williams, *Hugh Gaitskell: A Political Biography*, Jonathan Cape, 1977, pp. 684, 948, n.142. House of Commons Debates, *Hansard*, 28 July 1960, Cols. 1997–8.
13. *Sunday Express*, 24 July 1960. *Scottish Sunday Express*, 24 July 1960. SB/19.
14. Harold Macmillan to the Earl of Home, 29 July 1960.The Earl of Home to Harold Macmillan, 29 July 1960. PREM 5/23 (PRO).
15. The 'New Oxford Group' was particularly critical of the contrast between the 'progressive' openness of America and the 'stuffiness' of hidebound, class-ridden Britain, epitomised by the appointment of figures such as Alec Home. 'Mr Macmillan's fondness for aristocrats – again regardless of the fact that many of them justified their appointments by their performance – could

hardly have been better calculated to confirm the New Oxford Group's most fondly held prejudices.' Christopher Booker, *The Neophiliacs: The Revolution in English Life in the Fifties and Sixties*, revised Pimlico edition, 1992, p. 162.

16. *Daily Mail*, 23 June 1961.
17. Avi Shlaim, Peter Jones and Keith Sainsbury, *British Foreign Secretaries since 1945*, David & Charles, Newton Abbot, 1977, p. 149. Ann Dunn, secretary to Mr Rusk, has written of 'his high regard for Lord Home'. Ann Dunn to author, 22 February 1995.
18. Dean Rusk to Edward Heath, 20 June 1973. Copy in HA.
19. Anthony Howard, *R.A.B: The Life of R.A. Butler*, Jonathan Cape, 1987, p. 280.
20. Private information. Late Lord Butler to author, 20 November 1975.
21. Lord Hailsham, *A Sparrow's Flight: The Memoirs of Lord Hailsham of St Marylebone*, Collins, 1990, pp 326–7. Harold Macmillan diary, 17 June 1960. (Stockton Papers.)
22. Tony Benn, *Years of Hope: Diaries, Papers and Letters 1940–1962*, Hutchinson, 1994, p. 259.
23. American State Department Papers. NSF Box 166 a, 21 December 1961. John F. Kennedy Presidential Library, Boston, Massachusetts.
24. John Colville to Lord Home, 28 July 1960. SB/8.
25. Alan Bullock, *Ernest Bevin: Foreign Secretary 1945–1951*, Oxford University Press edition, Oxford, 1985, p. 833.
26. Sir Ivone Kirkpatrick, *The Inner Circle: Memoirs of Ivone Kirkpatrick*, Macmillan, 1959, p. 258.
27. Evidence from Foreign Office staff of the time.
28. Lady Home to M.J. Wilmshurst, 31 July 1960; to Antony Acland, undated letter of September 1961. HA.
29. Lord Stockton to Lord Home, 21 July 1986. HA.
30. Private information.
31. 'When he returned here in 1951,' the Countess of Avon said when unveiling a bust of Anthony Eden in the Foreign Office on 20 June 1994, 'it was like a man coming home.'
32. Private information.
33. Lord Home to Sir George Labouchère, British ambassador to Spain 1960–6, 12 December 1960. FO 371/153114 (PRO).
34. House of Lords Debates, *Hansard*, 29 June 1960.
35. Speech to the National Press Club, Washington, 19 September 1960. HA.
36. Foreign Secretary Press Cuttings: Volume 1 1960. HA.
37. Anthony Parsons, *From Cold War to Hot Peace: UN Interventions 1947–1994*, Michael Joseph, 1995, p. 85.
38. Professor Alan James, author of *Britain and the Congo Crisis 1960–1963*, Macmillan, Basingstoke, 1996, to author, 16 April 1995.
39. *Ibid.*, 23 April 1995.
40. Lord Home to Lord Avon, 4 December 1961. AP 23/27/10. Avon Papers. (Birmingham University Library.) Eden had taken the title of 1st Earl of Avon in July 1961.
41. Minute by Antony Acland of the Secretary of State's views, 6 September

1961. FO 371/154944 (PRO).

42. Lord Home, memorandum 'UN Debates and Resolutions', 1 December 1961. CAB 127/107 (PRO).
43. Minute of 28 November 1961. FO 371/155107 (PRO).
44. The significance Home attached to the speech can be gauged from the fact that in his memoirs, which contain no mention of the Cuban missile crisis, he allocates five pages to long extracts from the 'double standards' speech. *The Way the Wind Blows*, Collins, 1976, pp. 160–5.
45. Lord Home to Harold Macmillan, 19 September 1960. FO 371/153632 (PRO).
46. Foreign Secretary Press Cuttings: Volume 1 1960. HA.
47. Nigeria gained its independence on 1 October 1960. The four years between 1960 and 1964 saw a wave of decolonisation as the Commonwealth doubled in size. British Somaliland also became independent in 1960, followed by Cyprus, Sierra Leone and Tanzania in 1961; Jamaica, Trinidad and Tobago and Uganda in 1962; Kenya in 1963; and Malawi and Malta in 1964.
48. Harold Macmillan speech to the United Nations, 29 September 1960. 'British Prime Ministers: 1924–1964', BBC Records REB 39M, 1969.
49. FO 371/152109 (PRO).
50. *Boston Massachusetts Christian Science Monitor*, 20 September 1960.
51. *News of the World*, 25 September 1960.The Olympic Games, held in Rome that summer, had not been a success for Britain.
52. Private information.
53. Andrei Gromyko, *Memoirs*, Hutchinson, 1989, p. 158.
54. FO 371/152109 (PRO). Alec Home's favoured interpreter when dealing with Khrushchev and Gromyko was E.E. (Ted) Orchard, a former lecturer in Russian at Oxford and later an official in the British embassy in Moscow and the FCO. Orchard had been the interpreter for Bulganin and Khruschev's visit in 1956 and was well versed in the ambiguities of Khrushchev's speech.
55. Speech at the Conservative Party Conference, 13 October. Foreign Secretary Press Cuttings: Volume 1 1960. HA.
56. House of Lords Debate, *Hansard*, 2 November 1960.
57. Thomas J. Schoenbaum, *Waging Peace and War: Dean Rusk in the Truman, Kennedy & Johnson Years*, Simon & Schuster, New York, 1988, p. 384.
58. Benn, *Years of Hope, op. cit.*, p. 356. See pp. 353–419 for the account of his campaign to renounce his title.
59. *Ibid.*, p. 360.
60. The principal tours in Home's first year as Foreign Secretary included Bonn (10 August 1960), Washington and New York for the United Nations General Assembly (17 September–8 October), Rome (21–24 November), Paris for NATO meeting (15–18 December), Milan (30–31 January 1961), Nepal and Iran (24 February–6 March), Bangkok (24–29 March), Washington (3–9 April), Ankara for CENTO Meeting (26–29 April), Italy (29 April–5 May), Geneva (11–19 May), Lisbon (25–28 May), Madrid (29–31 May), Geneva (11–12 June), Washington, Boston and Chicago (13–17 June) and Paris (4–8 August). At the Scottish Conservative Party Conference at Ayr on 20 April 1961, he said, 'I have concluded that this perambulation is seriously overdone

and interferes with the continuity and direction of British foreign policy.' In June 1961, the Homes moved into 1 Carlton Gardens. SB/22.

61. See, Robert Shepherd, *Iain Macleod*, Hutchinson, 1995, pp. 224–7; Nigel Fisher, *Iain Macleod*, André Deutsch, 1973, pp. 170–3; and Anthony Sampson, *Anatomy of Britain*, Hodder & Stoughton, 1962, pp. 80–2.
62. Private information.
63. Peter Goldman (1925–87) had one of the unluckiest careers among post-war Conservatives. Not only did he write the second half of Macleod's book on Chamberlain, but he largely ghosted Rab Butler's *The Art of the Possible*, without ever getting due acknowledgment for either collaboration. Chosen for the 'safe' Conservative seat of Orpington, he was on the receiving end of one of the most stunning electoral reverses, at the hands of Eric Lubbock, later Lord Avebury, who turned a Conservative majority of 14,760 into a Liberal one of 7,855. A progressive figure in the Noel Skelton mould, his premature death was widely mourned.
64. Harold Macmillan to Ava, Lady Waverley, 19 August 1960. Cited by Alistair Horne, *Macmillan 1957–1986: Volume II of the Official Biography*, Macmillan, 1989, p. 311.
65. David Nunnerley, *President Kennedy and Britain*, Bodley Head, 1972, p. 43.
66. Sir David Ormsby-Gore to the Earl of Home, 19 September 1962. PREM 11/4166 (PRO). There is further correspondence in the John F. Kennedy Presidential Library in Boston and in the archive at the Hirsel.
67. Telegram of 17 September, 1961. FO 371/160508 (PRO).
68. Lord Home to Dean Rusk, 19 August 1961. FO 371/160511 (PRO).
69. Lord Home memorandum on Berlin, 21 November 1961. CAB 129/107 (PRO).
70. Late Harold Macmillan to author, 23 April 1975.
71. CAB 129/107 (PRO).
72. PREM 11/3782 (PRO). The Oder-Neisse line had been established at Yalta as the dividing line of the post-war German state.
73. Statement by Sir Alec Douglas-Home, 17 March 1965. Oral History files, John F. Kennedy Presidential Library, Boston, USA.
74. Lord Home to author, 6 August 1992.
75. Harold Macmillan to Lord Home, 15 April 1962. PREM 11/3778 (PRO).
76. Harold Macmillan diary, 22 October 1962. (Stockton Papers.)

Chapter 10.

1. Thomas Hardy, *In Tenebris*.
2. President John F. Kennedy's Radio and Television Report to the American People on the Soviet Arms Buildup in Cuba, 22 October 1962. The full text of this broadcast is reprinted in Robert F. Kennedy, *13 Days: The Cuban Missile Crisis October 1962*, Pan books paperback edition, 1969, pp. 129–39.
3. Signatories to the Warsaw Pact, the 'Eastern European Mutual Assistance Treaty' of 14 May 1955, were Albania, Bulgaria, Czechoslovakia, the DDR, Hungary, Poland, Romania and the Soviet Union. Its genesis was as a response to West German membership of NATO.

4. Information from declassified Pentagon Papers discovered by Mr Maurice Frankel of the Freedom of Information Campaign in Washington. *Daily Telegraph*, 23 December 1992.
5. CAB 128/36 (PRO).
6. *Ibid.*
7. Sir Herbert Marchant (1906–90) joined the diplomatic service on the outbreak of the Second World War. His penultimate posting was as ambassador to Cuba (1960–63). Alec Home regarded him as one of the unsung heroes of the Cuban crisis.
8. Sir David Ormsby-Gore to the Earl of Home, 13 November 1961. PREM 11/4166 (PRO).
9. Sir David Ormsby-Gore to the Earl of Home, 4 December 1961, 15 December 1961. PREM 11/4166 (PRO).
10. Sir Frank Roberts to the Earl of Home, 5 January 1962 and 3 March 1962. FO 371/166212 (PRO).
11. PREM 11/3997 (PRO).
12. Sir Frank Roberts to the author, 1 July 1992.
13. Private information.
14. Harold Macmillan diary, 24 October 1962. (Stockton Papers.) In *Beyond the Fringe*, Alan Bennett was closer to reality than he perhaps realised when in the sketch 'Civil War' he asked what would happen if the Americans fired a missile by mistake. 'It could not happen,' he said. 'You see, before they press that button they've got to get on the telephone to number 10 Downing Street, and say, "Now look, Mr Macmillan, Sir, can I press this button?" And Mr Macmillan will say "yes" – or "no" as the mood takes him … Now, there is a flaw in this argument … and I can see one of you seems to have spotted it. What if Mr Macmillan is out? Perfectly simple! Common sense, really – we'd ask Lady Dorothy.' Roger Wilmut (editor), *The Complete Beyond the Fringe*, Methuen, 1987, p. 81. Macmillan, who had enjoyed the revue more than many of its intended victims, acknowledged the parallel in his diary at the moment of greatest danger in the whole crisis. For Her Majesty the Queen's visit to *Beyond the Fringe*, see Chapter 11.
15. Herbert Marchant to the Earl of Home, 23 October 1962. FO 371/162376 (PRO). Sir Frank Roberts to the Earl of Home, 23 October 1962 and 24 October 1962. FO 371/162375 and FO 371/162376 (PRO).
16. Herbert Marchant to the Earl of Home, 24 October 1962. FO 371/162377 (PRO).
17. Speech to National Committee of the International Chamber of Commerce, 23 October 1962. Foreign Secretary Files, HA.
18. Private information.
19. CAB 128/37 (PRO).
20. Sir Harold Caccia to Sir Frank Roberts, 24 October 1962. PREM 11/3690 (PRO).
21. Chester L. Cooper Oral History Transcript, 16 May 1966, John F. Kennedy Presidential Library.
22. Harold Macmillan diary, 22 October 1962. (Stockton Papers.)
23. McGeorge Bundy, Oral History Transcript, John F. Kennedy Presidential

Library.

24. Lord Redmayne, Oral History Transcript, John F. Kennedy Presidential Library.
25. Lord Thorneycroft, Oral History Transcript, John F. Kennedy Presidential Library.
26. Lord Home to the author, 9 August 1991.
27. *The Listener*, 30 January 1969. Transcript of BBC TV programme of 29 January 1963.
28. CAB 128/36 (PRO). The eventual addition to the Queen's Speech read: 'My Government were gravely concerned at the dangers of the recent introduction of offensive missiles into Cuba. They have played their full part, in close consultation with my allies, in efforts to deal with the critical situation which arose.' By this time, the main threat was removed. PREM 11/3691 (PRO).
29. Foreign Office telegram to 'Certain of Her Majesty's Representatives', 24 October 1962. FO 371/162378 (PRO).
30. CAB 129/111 (PRO).
31. PREM 11/3690 (PRO).
32. FO 371/162379 (PRO).
33. The Earl of Home to Harold Macmillan, 27 October 1962. Prime Minister's Minute PM/62/140. PREM 11/3690 (PRO). The Soviet view was also that there was no legal justification for the blockade, as they said frequently to Sir Frank Roberts during the crisis, forgetting that the British had often been rather lax on this point in past centuries. Sir Frank Roberts, letter to the author, 10 July 1995.
34. Harold Macmillan diary, 24 October 1962. (Stockton papers.)
35. Minute by the Earl of Home for the UK Mission in New York, 24 October 1962.FO 371/162378 (PRO).
36. Harold Macmillan to John F. Kennedy, 25 October 1962.Harold Macmillan diary, 24 October 1962. (Stockton Papers.)
37. *Ibid.*, 25 October 1962.
38. CAB 128/36 (PRO).
39. Herbert Marchant to the Earl of Home, 25 October 1962. FO 371/162380 (PRO).
40. Summary of record of Foreign Secretary's meeting with the Soviet Chargé d'Affaires, 25 October 1962. PREM 11/3690 (PRO).
41. Harold Macmillan diary, 26 October 1962. (Stockton Papers.)
42. Sir Frank Roberts to the Earl of Home, 26 October 1962. Herbert Marchant to the Earl of Home, 26 October 1962. FO 371/162381 (PRO).
43. Sir David Ormsby-Gore to the Earl of Home, 26 October 1962. FO 371/162381 (PRO).
44. Lord Thorneycroft, Oral History Transcript, John F. Kennedy Presidential Library.
45. Nikita Khrushchev to John F. Kennedy, 28 October 1962, cited in Michael R. Beschloss, *Kennedy v. Khrushchev: The Crisis Years 1960–1963*, Faber & Faber, 1991, p. 541. So urgent was the message that it was broadcast on Moscow Radio. The final sections of the letter had not been fully drafted when the opening section was broadcast.

46. Harold Macmillan diary, 28 October 1962. (Stockton Papers.)
47. The Earl of Home to Sir David Ormsby-Gore, 29 October 1962. PREM 11/3691 (PRO).
48. This report was circulated above Home's signature, 31 October 1962.FO 371/162393 (PRO).
49. Sir Frank Roberts to the Earl of Home, 29 and 31 October 1962. PREM 11/3691 (PRO).
50. FO 371/162398 (PRO).
51. PREM 11/3691 (PRO).
52. Memo of 6 November, 1962. FO 371/162398 (PRO).
53. Sir Michael Adeane to Harold Macmillan, 31 October 1962. PREM 11/3691 (PRO).
54. Speech to the Conference of the Institute of Directors, 31 October 1962. HA.
55. *Hansard*, House of Lords Debates, 1–2 November 1962.
56. Transcript of John F. Kennedy–Harold Macmillan Telephone Conversation, 15 November 1962. (Stockton Papers.) Copies are also in the John F. Kennedy Presidential Library.
57. Harold Macmillan diary, 25 November 1962. (Stockton Papers.)
58. Harold Macmillan to Sir David Ormsby-Gore, 31 October 1962. PREM 11/3691 (PRO).
59. Henry Brandon, *Special Relationships: a foreign correspondent's memoirs from Roosevelt to Reagan*, Macmillan, 1989, p. 160.
60. Sir Alec Douglas-Home interview, 17 March 1965. John F. Kennedy Oral History Statement, John F. Kennedy Presidential Library.
61. Memorandum, 'Visit of the Prime Minister and Foreign Secretary to the Soviet Union' (Reilly papers).
62. David Bruce, Oral History Transcript, John F. Kennedy Presidential Library.
63. Sir Alec Douglas-Home, Oral History Statement, 17 March 1965, John F. Kennedy Presidential Library.
64. PREM 11/4147 (PRO).
65. *Ibid.*
66. Lord Home of the Hirsel to Professor Keith Sainsbury, 12 June 1975. HA.
67. Harold Macmillan diary, 28 January 1963. (Stockton Papers.)
68. The Earl of Home to Sir Pierson Dixon, 28 December 1962. PREM 11/4147 (PRO).
69. Harold Macmillan diary, 1 January 1963. (Stockton Papers.)
70. The Earl of Home to President John F. Kennedy, 7 January 1963. Kennedy Papers. President's Office Files (POF), Box 127, Folder 5. John F. Kennedy Presidential Library.

Chapter 11.

1. Robert Blake, *Disraeli*, Methuen paperback edition, 1969, p. 270.
2. Roger Wilmut (editor), *The Complete Beyond the Fringe*, Methuen, 1987, p. 20. *Beyond the Fringe* had first been performed at the Edinburgh Festival on 22 August 1960. After touring, it opened on 10 May 1961 at the Fortune

Theatre, London, where with various casts it ran until September 1966. Its irreverent and witty humour was a talisman of the age. Ironically, its popularity was particularly marked among the political class it mocked. Alec Home's mentor, James Stuart, gave a nod in its direction when he called his memoirs *Within the Fringe*.

3. Samuel Brittan, *The Treasury under the Tories*, Secker & Warburg, 1964, p. 208.
4. Anthony Crosland, *The Future of Socialism*, Jonathan Cape, 1980 edition, p. 161. The book was originally published in 1956 in the wake of Labour's defeat at the 1955 general election.
5. Michael Young, *The Rise of the Meritocracy*, Penguin Books, Harmondsworth, 1961.
6. Michael Young traced the first use of the word 'Meritocrat' to the 1860s 'in small circulation journals attached to the Labour Party'. Henry Fairlie, political correspondent of *The Spectator*, had used the term 'Establishment' in a pejorative sense in September 1955, in connection with what he saw as the cover up of the Burgess and Maclean affair. Christopher Booker's *The Neophiliacs: The Revolution in English Life in the Fifties and Sixties*, Collins, 1969, introduced the concept of the neophiliac, 'those afflicted by a morbid love of the new'.
7. Sir Shane Leslie, *The Oppidan*, Chatto & Windus, 1922. David Benedictus, *The Fourth of June*, Anthony Blond, 1962.
8. Speech at Bedford, 20 July 1957. *The Times*, 22 July 1957. The second half of the quotation, usually omitted, shows that Macmillan's real concern was one of warning, not celebration.
9. Cited by Anthony Sampson, *Anatomy of Britain*, Hodder & Stoughton, 1962, p. 175.
10. Memorandum of 26 December 1962. PREM 11/4412 (PRO). Philip Woodfield was to be the most important link for the Douglas-Home Administration with this celebrated inner circle.
11. Selwyn Lloyd, 'Memorandum on the events of July and August 1962'. SELO 88 (3). Selwyn Lloyd Papers. (Churchill College, Cambridge.)
12. Harold Macmillan diary, extracts from the period 2 January–22 September 1962. (Stockton Papers.)
13. PREM 11/4218 (PRO).
14. The late Harold Macmillan to the author, 23 April 1975.
15. Stuart Matthew, *The Knights and Chapel of the Most Ancient and Most Noble Order of the Thistle*, Eaglebank Publications, Edinburgh, 1988, pp. 60, 64, 98, 100, 110. Alec Home became Chancellor of the Order in 1973.
16. The only good thing about it was that it happened here before the Thistle service which I am sure brought it on, as he was excited and longing to go to it, but at the same time was pretty apprehensive.' Lady Caroline Douglas-Home, letter to the author, 6 June 1991.
17. On 4 September 1964, three weeks before the Dissolution of Parliament, Sir Alec Douglas-Home attended the opening of the Forth Road Bridge by the Queen, one of his last official representational duties as Prime Minister. Prime Minister's Diary. HA.

18. Lord Home, record of the State Visit of King Olav of Norway (16–19 October 1962), 3 December 1962. PREM 11/3898 (PRO).
19. *Keesing's Contemporary Archives*, 1962.
20. *Observer*, 16 September 1962.
21. Of the devaluation of sterling on 20 November 1967, Harold Wilson said, 'It does not mean, of course, the pound here in Britain in your pocket or purse or in your bank has been devalued.' At a Conservative Party press conference on 16 June 1970, a press release (G.E. 228), stated 'This would, at a stroke, reduce the rise in prices, increase productivity and reduce unemployment.' The words were never delivered by Heath, but were later attributed to him. 'Crisis, what crisis?' (*Sun*, 11 January 1979) was also fathered upon Callaghan, who said on his return from a meeting in Guadeloupe, 'I don't think other people in the world would share the view there is mounting chaos.'
22. Speech at the Labour Party Conference, 1 October 1963.
23. Professor David Dilks, 'De Gaulle and the British', lecture delivered in Paris, 22 June 1994. Privately printed.
24. Philip Goodhart, *The 1922: The Story of the Conservative Backbenchers' Parliamentary Committee*, Macmillan, 1973, p. 191.
25. Harold Macmillan to Viscount Kilmuir, 22 April 1961. PREM 11/4395 (PRO).
26. See Chapter 12 for the influence of this article on Home's actions between December 1962 and October 1963.
27. Lord Home to the author. Lord Hailsham, *A Sparrow's Flight: The Memoirs of Lord Hailsham of St Marylebone*, Collins, 1990, p. 349.
28. PREM 11/4396 (PRO). Lord Home to the author on several occasions.
29. CAB 128/37 (PRO).
30. PREM 11/4396 (PRO).
31. Prime Ministerial Minute M 218/63. (Stockton Papers.)
32. Lord Hailsham, *op. cit.*, p. 348.
33. T.J. Bligh to Harold Macmillan, 4 July 1963. (PRO).
34. CAB 128/37 (PRO).
35. Lady Butler of Saffron Walden to the author, 20 July 1995.
36. CAB 128/37 (PRO).
37. Charles Dickens, *Nicholas Nickleby*, Chapter XXX.
38. Asa Briggs states that Lord Home hosted the party. Asa Briggs, *op. cit.*, Oxford University Press, Oxford, 1995, p. 353.The Royal Archives show that the host was in fact Lord Scarborough. *Beyond the Fringe* paved the way for programmes that were intrinsically less amusing and which depended instead on the gratuitously offensive. On an edition of *Not So Much a Programme More a Way of Life*, which went out on BBC television between 13 November 1964 and 11 April 1965, Bernard Levin described Alec Douglas-Home as 'a cretin'. Levin's remark brought a written apology to Home from Sir Hugh Greene, Director-General of the BBC, after a hurriedly convened Governors' meeting. The files at the BBC Written Archives Centre at Caversham show how seriously this episode was taken at the highest level of the BBC. File R 41/286/1. BBC Written Archives Centre, Caversham.

'Levin's impudent outburst about Sir Alec Douglas-Home was quite the worst behaviour I have yet seen televised' was one of the milder letters of complaint from the public.

39. Earl of Home to Harold Macmillan, 21 May 1963. (Stockton Papers.)
40. Mrs John F. Kennedy to Harold Macmillan, 22 June 1963. (Stockton Papers.)
41. PREM 11/4586 (PRO).
42. See Harold Macmillan, *At the End of the Day 1961–1963*, Macmillan, 1973, pp. 471–5; and Richard Lamb, *The Macmillan Years 1957–1963: The Emerging Truth*, John Murray, 1995, pp. 363–7.
43. Alistair Horne to the author, 13 February 1992.
44. In April 1975, almost twelve years after the visit, Harold Macmillan took the author to the site of the helicopter pad in the gardens and spoke, with tears in his eyes, of the last time he had seen Kennedy before the assassination. The site, beyond the April daffodil fields, is now subsumed in a Japanese financed Birch Grove Golf Course development.
45. Memorandum by the Prime Minister on the visit of President Kennedy to Birch Grove. (Stockton Papers.)
46. Harold Macmillan to President John F. Kennedy, 4 July 1963. PREM 11/4593 (PRO).
47. Sir David Ormsby-Gore to President John F. Kennedy, 2 August 1963. Kennedy Papers (President's Office Files POF 6/26/22). John F. Kennedy Presidential Library.
48. PREM 11/5123 (PRO).
49. Private information. The passage was from *Mark* 9:50. John Dickie to the author, 17 October 1991. John Dickie, Home's pioneering biographer, was present at the service in his capacity as Diplomatic correspondent of the *Daily Mail*. Commonwealth unity was emphasised when the second lesson was read by the Canadian Ambassador, Arnold Smith, later the first Commonwealth Secretary-General.
50. FO 371/173327 (PRO).
51. Douglas Hurd diary, 4–6 August 1963. Douglas Hurd to the author, 25 July 1994.
52. Earl of Home to Harold Macmillan, 7 August 1963. Sir Alec Douglas-Home to Nikita Khrushchev, 5 August 1964. PREM 11/5123 (PRO).
53. FO 371/171229 (PRO).
54. Private information.
55. Harold Macmillan diary, 6 October 1963. (Stockton Papers.)

Chapter 12.

1. Avon Papers. AP/23/44/56. (Birmingham University Library.)
2. Robert McKenzie, *British Political Parties: The Distribution of Power within the Conservative and Labour Parties*, Heinemann, revised paperback edition, 1967, p. 594*n*.
3. Cited by Philip Ziegler, *Melbourne: A Biography of William Lamb, 2nd Viscount Melbourne*, Collins, 1976, p. 170.

4. *Eton College Chronicle*, 10 November 1961.
5. Only Austen Chamberlain (March 1921–October 1922) served a shorter spell as leader.
6. Until July 1995 conventional wisdom had it, that the Douglas-Home rules showed the party in a more 'democratic' light, but after the leadership contest of July 1995, the feeling grew that no incumbent Prime Minister should be subject to such challenge; that the constitutional way to remove him or her should be through the ballot box at a general election or through a loss of confidence in the House of Commons.
7. PREM 11/4221 (PRO).
8. Harold Macmillan diary, 18 September 1963. (Stockton Papers.)
9. Private information.
10. Sir Philip Goodhart, letter to the *Daily Telegraph*, 4 July 1995.
11. Sir Philip Goodhart, *The 1922: The Story of the Conservative Backbenchers' Parliamentary Committee*, Macmillan, 1973, p. 191.
12. The late Reginald Maudling to the author, 4 September 1975.
13. Private information.
14. Harold Macmillan to Her Majesty Queen Elizabeth II, 15 October 1963. (Stockton Papers.) This was indeed accomplished in the Stockton Papers and the Royal Archives. The Home Papers and those of Selwyn Lloyd confirm the accuracy of material that overlaps with the Stockton Archive. The following outline is based on this material, as well as conversations with the principal participants, especially Harold Macmillan, Lord Home and Lord Butler.
15. Harold Macmillan to R.A. Butler, 14 October 1963. Prime Minister's Minute 360/63. Copy in Stockton Papers, marked on the top in red in Macmillan's hand IMPORTANT. Lord Chelmer was chairman of the Executive Committee of the National Union in 1963 and Mrs Margaret Shepherd was chairman of the conference at Blackpool.
16. The late Sir Knox Cunningham to the author, 8 April 1975. Professor A.W. Bradley confirmed this evidence in a letter to *The Times*, 16 January 1987. See Vernon Bogdanor, 'The Selection of the Party Leader', in *Conservative Century: The Conservative Party since 1900*, edited by Anthony Seldon and Stuart Ball, Oxford University Press, Oxford, 1994, pp 69–96.
17. Harold Macmillan to Earl St Aldwyn, 19 October 1963. Harold Macmillan to John Morrison, MP, 19 October 1963. Harold Macmillan, note of 22 March 1976. (Stockton Papers.) Sir Knox Cunningham to the author, 6 March 1975. The unpublished manuscript of Sir Knox Cunningham, 'One Man Dog: the Memoirs of Harold Macmillan's Private Secretary', is now in the possession of The Drapers' Company in London. D.R. Thorpe, *The Uncrowned Prime Ministers: a Study of Sir Austen Chamberlain, Lord Curzon and Lord Butler*, Darkhorse Publishing, 1980, which I was then researching, is a study of the failure of Sir Austen Chamberlain, Lord Curzon and Lord Butler to achieve the premiership. On 23 April 1975 Harold Macmillan went through the Knox Cunningham memorandum with the author at Birch Grove. Humphry Berkeley was later to play a significant role in the campaign for a change in the system of choosing a Conservative leader. *See* Chapter 15 and

Alan Watkins, 'The Importance of Mr Berkeley', in *A Conservative Coup: The Fall of Margaret Thatcher*, Duckworth, 2nd edition, 1992, pp. 156–77.

18. Francis Bacon, 'Of Church Controversies', *Essays*, 1625.
19. The Earl of Home to Harold Macmillan, 8 October 1963. (Stockton Papers.)
20. *The Spectator*, 17 January 1964.
21. Alistair Horne, *Macmillan 1957–1986: Volume II of the Official Biography*, Macmillan, 1989, p. 542 and pp. 540–44.
22. David Badenoch, letter to *The Times*, 12 January 1994.
23. Private information.
24. The Earl of Home to Lady Dorothy Macmillan, 8 October 1963. (Stockton Papers.)
25. Harold Evans, *Downing Street Diary: The Macmillan Years 1957–1963*, Hodder & Stoughton, 1981, pp. 296–7.
26. PREM 11/4410 (PRO).
27. *Daily Mail*, 9 October 1963. *Evening Standard*, 9 October 1963.
28. Private information.
29. Private information. 'They all agreed that this was the right procedure and I thought you would like to know this', Butler wrote to Macmillan after this Cabinet. R.A. Butler to Harold Macmillan, 15 October 1963. (Stockton Papers.) Sir Philip Woodfield served as Private Secretary to three Prime Ministers, Harold Macmillan, Alec Douglas-Home and Harold Wilson between 1961 and 1965.
30. Lady Butler of Saffron Walden file on the events of October 1963. File L114. Butler Papers. (Trinity College, Cambridge.)
31. Anthony Trollope, *The Prime Minister*.
32. The method of selection employed clearly conditions the result. If the 1963 leadership had been decided under the later formal rules, there would in all probability have been three declared candidates, Butler, Hailsham and Maudling. With voting limited to MPs in the Commons, Hailsham could well have been eliminated on the first ballot. In a second ballot, Butler – in the view of many who would have been eligible to vote – would probably have prevailed over Maudling.
33. Undated holograph, PREM 11/4410.The letter was written on the evening of 8 October, but never sent. The 'problems' referred to the closing speech at the conference: should it be cancelled or should Butler deliver it?
34. Harold Macmillan, *At the End of the Day, 1961–1963*, Macmillan, 1973, p. 496.
35. Nigel Fisher, *Iain Macleod*, André Deutsch, 1973, p. 169.
36. *Dictionary of National Biography 1971–1980*, edited by Robert Blake and C.S. Nicholls, Oxford University Press, Oxford, 1986, p. 546.
37. Private information.
38. *Daily Mail*, 10 October 1963.
39. John Boyd-Carpenter, *Way of Life: The Memoirs of John Boyd-Carpenter*, Sidgwick & Jackson, 1980, p. 176.
40. Foreign Office File 1960–63. HA.
41. Harold Macmillan letter for the Party conference, 9 October 1963.
42. Foreign Office File 1960–63. HA.

43. Vernon Bogdanor, 'The Selection of the Party Leader', *op. cit.*, pp. 75, 76.
44. H.S. Boyne, *Daily Telegraph*, 10 October 1963.
45. See Lord Hailsham, *A Sparrow's Flight: The Memoirs of Lord Hailsham of St Marylebone*, Collins, 1990, pp. 348–59, for his recollections of the events of October 1963.
46. Dennis Walters, *Not Always with the Pack*, Constable, 1989, p. 125.
47. Unattributable interview. Hailsham bitterly resented the way the 'baby food' episode was used against him, as though he were exploiting his family. Lord Hailsham, *op. cit.*, pp. 353–4. For Conservatives of that generation, however, the proper person to be dispensing such attention was the nanny – and in private.
48. See Anthony Howard, 'Mr Home and Mr Hogg?',*New Statesman*, 14 December 1962.
49. *Ibid.*
50. Lord Curzon, 'Notes for a Biography', cited by Kenneth Rose, *Superior Person: A Portrait of Curzon and His Circle in Late Victorian England*, Weidenfeld & Nicolson, 1969, p. 29.
51. Lady Butler of Saffron Walden to the author, 20 June 1995.
52. Private information. The article was an old-fashioned scoop in that it disclosed that sitting peers might be able to disclaim from the moment of the royal assent, information passed to Anthony Howard by Charles Pannell, a Labour member of the Committee that was investigating peerage law. Anthony Howard to the author, 10 July 1995. One of the underlying ironies of the article, which certainly contributed to the actions that Home then took, was that it was written by Butler's eventual biographer.
53. *Sunday Times*, 13 October 1963.
54. 'Westminster's Secret Service', a report by Michael Cockerell on the world of the Government whips, BBC Television, 21 May 1995.
55. David Bruce to Dean Rusk, Telegram 5130, 19 June 1963. Department of State Papers, John F. Kennedy Presidential Library.
56. It is worth noting here that John Major's resignation of the Conservative leadership on 22 June 1995, to trigger a leadership contest, was an attempt to keep the initiative in the Prime Minister's hands under a system where the result would be determined by the votes of the Parliamentary party. By calling an election at a time of his choosing, he thus excluded from the contest the heavyweight Cabinet colleagues who could have been his real challengers. It was the one occasion in the history of the Douglas-Home rules when an incumbent leader under pressure from a substantial section of his party used the system to legitimise his position.
57. The Earl of Home to Harold Macmillan, 16 June 1963. (Stockton Papers.)
58. Tim Bligh to Sir Edward Ford, 9 October 1963. PREM 11/5008. (PRO).
59. Lord Fanshawe, memorandum on the leadership contest of October 1963, recording discussion with Lord Margadale of Islay, formerly John Morrison, on 5 July 1989. (Fanshawe Papers.)
60. *Ibid.*
61. Private information.
62. Sir Robin Day to the author, 26 April 1994; an arcane reference to the Duke

were nonplussed when Lord Home appeared on the political scene – as if from nowhere. His startling characteristics soon became obvious.' Of the assassination, Mr Robinson wrote, 'Words cannnot describe the enormity of that event at that time and how inadequate any words about it would be ... Sir Alec simply showed everyone how it should be done.' Peter Robinson to the author, 26 June 1995.

63. See Peter Paterson, *Tired and Emotional: The Life of Lord George-Brown*, Chatto & Windus, 1993, pp. 146–64.
64. John F. Kennedy Condolence Mail. John F. Kennedy Presidential Library.
65. Sir Alec Douglas-Home to R.A. Butler, 23 November 1963. PREM 11/4582. The service was held on 1 December.
66. PREM 11/4408 (PRO).
67. SB/30.
68. Private information.
69. The Duchess of Devonshire, *The House: A Portrait of Chatsworth*, Macmillan, 1982, p. 114. The Duchess of Devonshire presented Alec Home with a copy of this book, apologising for not asking permission to include the story.
70. It hangs in a corridor of the Hirsel.
71. Cabinet Minutes, 28 November 1963. CAB 128/38 (PRO).
72. Sir Alec Douglas-Home to Sir David Ormsby-Gore, 2 December 1963. PREM 11/4408 (PRO).
73. Lord Hailsham, *A Sparrow's Flight: The Memoirs of Lord Hailsham of St Marylebone*, Collins, 1990 p. 357.
74. Sir Burke Trend to Sir Alec Douglas-Home, 19 November 1963. PREM 11/4115 (PRO).
75. Lord Thorneycroft's evidence in Michael Cockerell's film, 'The Night of the Long Knives', BBC TV, 27 July 1989, gives an indication of these feelings.
76. Private information.
77. Robert Rhodes James, *Anthony Eden*, Weidenfeld & Nicolson, 1986, p. 614.
78. Earl of Kilmuir, *Political Adventure: The Memoirs of the Earl of Kilmuir*, Weidenfeld & Nicolson, 1964, p. 273.
79. PREM 11/4115 (PRO).
80. *Ibid.*
81. 'Rab had no one to blame but himself. Many at that time considered that his habit of publicly hedging his political bets was too great a weakness and this had accordingly damaged his position both in the Conservative hierarchy and in the parliamentary party.' Viscount Kilmuir, *op. cit.*, p. 286.
82. Sir Robert Rhodes James letter to *The Spectator*, 15 August 1992.
83. Iain Macleod to Martin Redmayne, 6 January 1964. PREM 11/4805 (PRO).
84. Nigel Fisher, *Iain Macleod*, André Deutsch, 1973, p. 253.
85. Iain Macleod, 'The Tory Leadership', *The Spectator*, 17 January 1964.
86. Private information.
87. Harold Macmillan diary, 18 January 1964. (Stockton Papers.)
88. *Sunday Telegraph*, 26 January 1964.
89. *The Times*, 22 July 1970.
90. Cabinet Minutes 17 January, 1964. 'Extra Releases.' CAB 128/40 (PRO). Macleod had sent Butler advance proof copies of the article. Anthony

Howard, *R.A.B: The Life of R.A. Butler*, Jonathan Cape, 1987, p. 331.

91. Sir Alec Douglas-Home to Randolph Churchill, 17 January 1964. PREM 11/4805 (PRO).
92. *The Times*, 20 January 1964.
93. *South Wales Evening Post*, 20 January 1964.
94. Oliver Wright to Sir Alec Douglas-Home, undated memo of January 1964. PREM 11/5196 (PRO).
95. Sir David Ormsby-Gore to R.A. Butler, 29 January 1964. PREM 11/5196 (PRO). Robert Kennedy was also fatally shot, in Los Angeles on 6 June 1968 whilst campaigning for the Presidency.
96. Sir Burke Trend to Harold Macmillan, 24 September 1963. PREM 11/4697 (PRO).
97. John Dickie, *'Special No More': Anglo-American Relations – Rhetoric and Reality*, Weidenfeld & Nicolson, 1994, p. 134.
98. PREM 11/4794 (PRO).
99. Oliver Wright to Sir Alec Douglas-Home, 11 February 1964. PREM 11/4794 (PRO).
100. Speech of 11 February 1964. PREM 11/4794 (PRO).
101. Sir Henry Lintott to Sir Saville Garner, 14 February 1964. PREM 11/4794 (PRO).
102. PREM 11/4697 (PRO).
103. Sir Alec Douglas-Home to Lyndon Baines Johnson, 14 February 1964. PREM 11/5199 (PRO).
104. Harold Macmillan to Sir Alec Douglas-Home, 12 February 1964. HA.
105. Statement on Cuban bus deal, February 1964. FO 371/174260 (PRO).
106. R.A. Butler, *The Art of the Possible*, revised edition, Penguin Books, Harmondsworth, 1973 edition, p. 256. R.A. Butler to Sir Alec Douglas-Home, 29 April 1964. PREM 11/4789 (PRO).
107. Evidence from the Private Office.
108. Anthony Howard, *op. cit.*, p. 330.
109. Memorandum, 2 January 1964. CAB 129/116 (PRO).
110. Quoted by Keith Kyle, 'The British and Cyprus in 1963', *Report* (The Friends of Cyprus Magazine), 1994.
111. Sir Alec Douglas-Home to Nikita S. Khrushchev, 8 February 1964. PREM 11/5126 (PRO).
112. Sir Alec Douglas-Home to Sir Humphrey Gibbs, 8 June 1964. HA.
113. Sir Alec Douglas-Home to Ian Smith, 4 June 1964. HA.
114. Sir Alec Douglas-Home to Sir Humphrey Gibbs, 10 July 1964. HA.
115. Briefing memorandum for the Commonwealth Conference, 12 June 1964. CAB 133/201 (PRO).
116. *The Times*, 19 February 1964.
117. Harold Macmillan to Sir Alec Douglas-Home, 1 April 1964. (Stockton Papers.)
118. Harold Macmillan to Sir Alec Douglas-Home, 2 April 1964. (Stockton Papers.)
119. Statement of 9 April 1964. HA.
120. Lord Home to the author, 8 April 1991. Khrushchev fell from office on

15 October and news was received of the Chinese test of a nuclear device.

121. PREM 11/4752 (PRO).
122. SELO 61(3). Selwyn Lloyd Papers.
123. John Campbell, *Edward Heath: A Biography*, Jonathan Cape, 1993, p. 151.
124. Sir Edward Heath to the author, 26 September 1991.
125. Edward Heath to Sir Alec Douglas-Home, 17 December 1963. Sir Alec Douglas-Home to Edward Heath, 18 December 1963. Martin Redmayne to Timothy Bligh, the Prime Minister's Secretary, 20 December 1963.Reginald Maudling to Sir Alec Douglas-Home, 24 December 1963. PREM 11/5154 (PRO).
126. Cabinet minutes, 14 January 1964. CAB 128/38 (PRO).
127. Selwyn Lloyd to Sir Alec Douglas-Home, 14 February 1964. PREM 11/5154 (PRO).
128. Francis Pearson to Sir Alec Douglas-Home, 14 February 1964. PREM 11/5014 (PRO).
129. Edward Heath to Sir Alec Douglas-Home, 19 February 1964. CAB 129/117 (PRO).
130. John Morrison to Sir Alec Douglas-Home, 12 March 1964. PREM 11/4991 (PRO).
131. Ronald Butt, *The Power of Parliament*, Constable, 2nd edition, 1969, p. 272. Chapter 9 – 'Resale Price Maintenance: a Study of Backbench Influence' – remains the classic analysis of the power of dissident backbenchers to scrutinise the passage of contentious domestic legislation.
132. John Boyd-Carpenter, *Way of Life: The Memoirs of John Boyd-Carpenter*, Sidgwick & Jackson, 1980, p. 185.
133. John Campbell, *op. cit.*, p. 157.
134. D.E. Butler and Anthony King, *The British General Election of 1964*, Macmillan, 1965, p. 23.
135. Keith Middlemass, *Power, Competition and the State, Volume Two, Threats to the Postwar Settlement, Britain, 1961–1974*, Macmillan, 1990, p. 88.
136. *Sunday Times*, 27 February 1994.
137. Sir Alec Douglas-Home to Lord Crathorne, 28 June 1964. (Crathorne Papers.)
138. Peter Walker, *Staying Power: An Autobiography*, Bloomsbury, 1991, p. 33.
139. Speech on the death of Lord Beaverbrook. HA.
140. Cabinet memorandum, 10 August 1964. CAB 129/118 (PRO).
141. PREM 11/5066 (PRO).
142. Quoted in Kenneth Young, *Rhodesia and Independence: A Study in British Colonial Policy*, Dent, 1969 edition, pp. 150, 154.
143. Mary Soames, *Clementine Churchill by her daughter*, Cassell, 1979, p. 485.
144. *Ibid.*, pp. 484–5.
145. Sir Alec Douglas-Home to the office of the Duke of Norfolk, 4 September 1964. PREM 11/4715. Churchill died on 24 January 1965, the seventieth anniversary of his father's death, and a State Funeral was held at St Paul's Cathedral on 30 January before the private interment at Bladon in Oxfordshire.

146. Her Majesty the Queen to Sir Alec Douglas-Home, 14 October 1964. HA.

Chapter 14.

1. Christopher Booker, *The Neophiliacs: The Revolution in English Life in the Fifties and Sixties*, revised Pimlico edition, 1992, p. 173.
2. Home's uneasiness on television can be exaggerated. He was aware of the techniques for the new medium and asked pertinent questions of his interviewers before transmissions, quickly assimilating their advice. Those who interviewed him frequently noted how he had improved out of all recognition in the months leading up to the campaign. Sir Robin Day to the author, 26 April 1994.
3. H.G. Nicholas, *The British General Election of 1950*, Macmillan, 1951, p. 126.
4. See Michael Cockerell, *Live from Number 10: The Inside Story of Prime Ministers and Television*, Faber & Faber, 1988, pp. 100–2.
5. Asa Briggs, *The History of Broadcasting in the United Kingdom, Volume 5: Competition 1955–1974*, Oxford University Press, Oxford, 1995, p. 440.
6. Sir Alec Douglas-Home to Lord Blakenham, 14 August 1964. HA.
7. Speech at the Cumberland Hotel, 5 September 1964. HA.
8. PREM 11/4754 (PRO).
9. Sir Alec Douglas-Home to Her Majesty The Queen, 8 September 1964. HA.
10. Sir Alec Douglas-Home to Christopher Soames, 10 September 1964. PREM 11/4756 (PRO).
11. Private information. See Anthony Howard, *R.A.B.: The Life of R.A. Butler*, Jonathan Cape, 1987, p. 333.
12. C.M. Grieve to Professor B.C. Knight, 14 October 1964. General Election File. BBC Written Archives, Caversham. Cited in Alan Bold (ed.), *The Letters of Hugh MacDiarmid*, Hamish Hamilton, 1984, p. 670.
13. Scheme of Organisation, Kinross and West Perthshire Constituency, October 1964. (Robertson Papers.)
14. Transcript of interview with Kenneth Harris on *Election Forum*, 24 September 1964. HA.
15. D.E. Butler and Anthony King, *The British General Election of 1964*, Macmillan, 1965, p. 113.
16. *Ibid.*, p. 115.
17. The Prime Minister's meeting was at the spot where Leo Colston had met Marian Maudsley in L.P. Hartley's novel *The Go-Between.*
18. SB/37.
19. *The Times*, 9 October 1964.
20. Sir Alec Douglas-Home to Sir John Masterman, 8 October 1964. HA.
21. *Daily Express*, 9 October 1964.
22. Private information from several sources.
23. Sir David Ormsby-Gore to Sir Alec Douglas-Home, 16 October 1964. HA.
24. House of Commons Debates, *Hansard*, 4 November 1964.
25. Sir Alec Douglas-Home to Patrick Gordon Walker, 27 September 1964. PREM 11/4891. See A.W. Singham, 'Immigration and the Election' in D.E. Butler and Anthony King, *op. cit.*, pp. 360–8, for further consideration of this issue.

26. Graham C. Greene to the author, 13 July 1992.
27. The 1964 General Election was characterised by many narrow victories, five with majorities below 30. Apart from Brighton Kemptown, Labour won Ealing North by 27 votes. The Conservatives won Reading by 10, Eton and Slough by 11 and Preston North by 14.
28. Lord Home to the author, 9 August 1991.
29. Tam Dalyell in his obituary notice of Dennis Hobden, the *Independent*, 22 April 1995.
30. Robert Rhodes James, 'Here's to the class of '59', *The Times*, 14 March 1992.
31. Mrs Jacquetta James, letter to *The Times*, 25 March 1992, in response to the above article.
32. Asa Briggs, *op. cit.*, pp. 447–8. Michael Cockerell, *op. cit.*, p. 107.
33. Michael Tracey, *A Variety of Lives: A Biography of Sir Hugh Greene*, Bodley Head, 1983, p. 266.
34. Prime Ministerial Deadlock File, PREM 11/4756 (PRO).
35. Prime Minister's speeches, October 1964. HA.
36. Dennis Skinner interview on BBC 'Breakfast with Frost', 13 March 1994.
37. Record of general election day, 1964. (Robertson Papers.)
38. Sir Alec Douglas-Home to Anthony Barber, 28 October 1964. HA. In the 1970–4 Conservative government, Home and Barber served alongside each other as Foreign Secretary and Chancellor of the Exchequer respectively. Geoffrey Rippon had special responsibility for Europe, as Chancellor of the Duchy of Lancaster, in Home's Foreign Office team.
39. Sir Alec Douglas-Home to Harold Wilson, 16 October 1964. HA.
40. Prime Minister's speeches, June 1964. HA. See Gerald Kaufman, 'The cheap jibes that can be so costly', *Evening Standard*, 10 January 1995.
41. Jo Grimond, *Memoirs*, Heinemann, 1979, pp. 216–17.Grimond was referring to Quintin Hogg's comment at the Conservative Central Office press conference on 12 October 1964, when he said of Labour's policy, 'If the British public falls for this, I say it will be stark, staring bonkers.' See also, Jo Grimond, 'Hanging too long on the bell', a review of Lord Hailsham's memoirs, *A Sparrow's Flight, Sunday Telegraph,* 15 July 1990.
42. Lady Home to the author, 8 August 1990.
43. Tony Benn, 27 February 1989. Cited in John Lawton, *1963: Five Hundred Days*, Hodder & Stoughton, 1992, p. 307.
44. Lord Reith diary, 15 October 1964. File BBC 560/5/16. BBC Written Archives.
45. The Archbishop of Canterbury to Sir Alec Douglas-Home, 28 October 1964. HA.
46. Peter Hennessy, *Whitehall*, Secker & Warburg, 1989, p. 174.
47. PREM 11/4834 (PRO).
48. Memorandum by J.C.C. Davidson for Neville Chamberlain, May 1937. Robert Rhodes James (ed.), *Memoirs of a Conservative: J.C.C. Davidson's Memoirs and Papers, 1910–1937*, Weidenfeld & Nicolson, 1969, p. 421.
49. Sir John Colville to Sir Alec Douglas-Home, 24 July 1965. HA.

Chapter 15.

1. William Deedes to Sir Alec Douglas-Home, 21 October 1964. HA.
2. Humphry Berkeley (1926–94) was Conservative MP for Lancaster from 1959 to 1966. He later espoused both the Labour and Social Democratic cause, standing against Teddy Taylor at Southend East in 1987. His 'Berkeley memorandum', proposing a formal system of electing Conservative leaders, ensures him a place in the history of the post-war Conservative Party. See, for example, 'The Importance of Mr Berkeley', in Alan Watkins, *A Conservative Coup: The Fall of Margaret Thatcher*, Duckworth, second edition, 1992, pp. 156–77.
3. Humphry Berkeley to Sir Alec Douglas-Home, 1 January 1964. HA.
4. Sir Alec Douglas-Home to Humphry Berkeley, 14 January 1964. HA.
5. Sir Alec Douglas-Home to Humphry Berkeley, 12 November 1964. HA.
6. Secret Draft on Possible Methods for Selecting a Leader of the Party', 20 November 1964. CRD 3/22/10. 'Conservative Party Archive.' (Bodleian Library, Oxford.)
7. James Douglas to Martin Redmayne, 27 November 1964. CRD 3/22/10. Such prior consultation before voting was scrupulously observed by Elizabeth Peacock, MP for Batley and Spen, before voting for Michael Heseltine in the leadership election of November 1990.
8. CRD 3/22/10.
9. Dr David Butler, undated letter of December 1964. The letter was discussed at the meeting on 9 December and was acknowledged on 10 December. CRD 3/22/10.
10. Iain Macleod to Sir Alec Douglas-Home, 15 December 1964. CRD 3/22/10.
11. Minutes of meeting of 22 December 1964. CRD 3/22/10.
12. The full correspondence between Berkeley and Douglas-Home is published in Humphry Berkeley, *Crossing the Floor*, Allen & Unwin, 1972, Appendix I, pp. 149–57. The Berkeley Memorandum is in Appendix II, pp. 158–61.
13. The late Humphry Berkeley to the author, 4 July 1991.
14. *Ibid.*, 29 May 1991.
15. Reprinted in Appendix I.
16. Procedure for the Selection of the Leader of the Conservative and Unionist Party, February 1965. HA.
17. The figures were Margaret Thatcher 130, Edward Heath 119 and Hugh Fraser 16, with 11 abstentions. Heath and Fraser withdrew from the second ballot, but Margaret Thatcher (with 146 votes in the next round) had the vital momentum and the four new candidates – William Whitelaw (79), James Prior (19), Sir Geoffrey Howe (19) and John Peyton (11) – were unable to deny her victory. There were two abstentions.
18. Sir Martin Redmayne to Sir Alec Douglas-Home, 26 January 1965. HA. Patrick Gordon Walker had lost the specially created by-election of Leyton on 21 January 1965 by 205 votes.
19. Michael Fry, *Patronage and Principle: A Political History of Modern Scotland*, Aberdeen University Press, 1991 edition, p. 232. David Steel, *Against Goliath: David Steel's Story*, Weidenfeld & Nicolson, 1989, pp. 28–43, gives an account of the Roxburgh, Selkirk and Peebles by-election. David Steel

came to know Sir Alec very well in the next decade through many shared train journeys between Berwick and London; he gives an affectionate and perceptive portrait of Douglas-Home's informality in his memoirs.
20. R.A. Butler to Sir Alec Douglas-Home, 29 January 1965. HA.
21. Mary Soames, *Clementine Churchill by her daughter*, Cassell, 1979, p. 490.
22. Private information.
23. *Hansard*, 25 January 1965.
24. BBC File on 26 March episode of *Not So Much a Programme, More a Way of Life*, R 41/286/1. BBC Written Archives, Caversham.
25. Selwyn Lloyd to the Earl of Avon, 14 April 1965. SELO 309 (1). Selwyn Lloyd Papers. (Churchill College, Cambridge.)
26. *Sunday Times*, 18 July 1965.
27. D.E. Butler and Anthony King, *The British General Election of 1966*, Macmillan, 1966, p. 170.
28. Sir Alec Douglas-Home to Peter Thorneycroft, 19 July 1965. HA.
29. Selwyn Lloyd Diary, 22 July 1965. SELO 60 (202). Selwyn Lloyd Papers. (Churchill College, Cambridge.)
30. Speech to the 1922 Committee, 22 July 1965. HA.
31. Private information.
32. *The Times*, 23 July 1965.
33. The Earl of Avon to Sir Alec Douglas-Home, 26 July 1965. HA. The significance of the date did not escape Alec Home: it was the ninth anniversary of Nasser's nationalisation of the Suez Canal.
34. Lord Butler of Saffron Walden to Sir Alec Douglas-Home, 25 July 1965. HA.
35. Harold Macmillan to Sir Alec Douglas-Home, 26 July 1965. Macmillan–Home correspondence file. (Stockton Papers.)
36. Sir Alec Douglas-Home to Harold Macmillan, 26 July 1965.
37. Selwyn Lloyd diary, 25 July 1965. SELO 60 (202). Selwyn Lloyd Papers. (Churchill College, Cambridge.)
38. D.R. Thorpe, *Selwyn Lloyd*, Jonathan Cape, 1989, pp. 394–5.
39. Speech at Church House, Westminster, 2 August 1965. HA.
40. Speech at Heriot-Watt University, 20 April 1966. HA.
41. The others were from Oxford (1960), Harvard (1961), Edinburgh (1962), Aberdeen (1966), Liverpool (1967), and St Andrews (1968). In 1962, he was made an Honorary Student (Fellow) of Christ Church.
42. Sir Alec Douglas-Home to Harold Macmillan, 17 October 1965. Macmillan-Home Correspondence file. (Stockton Papers.)
43. Benn diary, 22 November 1965. Tony Benn, *Out of the Wilderness: Diaries 1963–1967*, Hutchinson, 1987, p. 354.
44. John Campbell, *Edward Heath: A Biography*, Jonathan Cape, 1993, p. 207. Home, it will be remembered, had been accused of using the opening of the Forth Road Bridge in September 1964 for electoral advantage.
45. *Ibid.*, p. 213.
46. Angela Bowlby to Sir Alec Douglas-Home, 22 February 1967. HA. Douglas Jay was one of the most prominent anti-Common marketeers in the Labour Party. A D-Notice is a request by the Joint Services, Press and Broadcasting

Committee of the House of Commons to journalists to refrain from publishing matters regarding national security. The controversy at this time led to Wilson saying on 2 March 1967 that 'Every dog is allowed one bite', what came to be known as the 'Dog Licence' speech.

47. Angela Bowlby to Sir Alec Douglas-Home, 21 February 1967. HA.
48. Lady Douglas-Home to Angela Bowlby, 2 February 1967. HA.
49. Angela Bowlby to Sir Alec and Lady Douglas-Home, 20 February 1968. HA. Cecil King was the chairman of the International Publishing Corporation, publishers of the *Daily Mirror*. Lord Robens, chairman of the National Coal Board, had been a Labour Minister in the Attlee governments of 1945–51. An account of the so-called 'Coalition Plot' can be found in Tony Benn, *Office Without Power: Diaries 1968–1972*, Hutchinson, 1988, pp. 29–37.
50. Private information.
51. Sir Alec Douglas-Home to Edward Heath, 9 August 1967. HA.
52. 'Under the Umbrella', *Listener*, 27 March 1969.
53. 'I was, of course, aware of Alec before 1967, but it was in that year that I invited him as President of the M.C.C. to write a foreword for *The Heart of Cricket*, the collection of writings both about and by Harry Altham that I edited, at the request of the family. He responded with a delightful piece which evoked to a "t" Harry's passion for cricket and young people, and the way that cricket kept breaking into his conversation. At the same time he reflected Harry's interest in the classics, Chinese pottery and Winchester cathedral. It was a most sympathetic foreword, and Alec took the trouble to come to the book's launching and to delight others who came with his ease of manner and total lack of pomposity.' Hubert Doggart to Sir William Becher, 16 June 1991, for onward despatch to the author. (Becher Papers.)
54. Lord Home to the author, 5 August 1991.
55. Sir Alec Douglas-Home to Colin Cowdrey, undated letter of 1966. HA.
56. Minutes of MCC Committee. (The Library, Lord's Ground.) The Duke of Norfolk to Sir Alec Douglas-Home, 13 August 1967. HA.
57. Michael Melford, 'The d'Oliveira Case: Cancellation of South African Tour', *Wisden 1969*, Sporting Handbooks Limited, 1969, p. 75. The article (pp. 74–9) is a dispassionate account of the origins and course of the controversy.
58. Record of meeting at Government House, Salisbury, 26 February 1968. Home–Beadle Correspondence, 1968. HA.
59. The reasons for this decision are outlined in Colin Cowdrey, *M.C.C.: The Autobiography of a Cricketer*, Hodder & Stoughton, 1976, pp. 193–201. Melford also discusses the issue.
60. All details from minutes of MCC Committee. (The Library, Lord's Ground.)
61. Colin Cowdrey, *op. cit.*, p. 204.
62. Andrew Marr, *The Battle for Scotland*, Penguin Books, Harmondsworth, 1992, pp. 121–2.
63. Tam Dalyell, *Dick Crossman: A Portrait*, Weidenfeld & Nicolson, 1989, p. 224. Dalyell was Crossman's Parliamentary Private Secretary in May 1968.
64. Speech to the Scottish Conservative and Unionist Party Conference, 18 May 1968. HA.
65. Preface to *Scotland's Government: The Report of the Scottish Constitutional*

Committee (Chairman: The Rt. Hon. Sir Alec Douglas-Home, KT, MP), Edinburgh, The Scottish Constitutional Committee, 1970, p. v.

66. Lord Home listed the members of the Constitutional Committee in full as Appendix D in *The Way the Wind Blows*, Collins, 1976, p. 313.
67. The Very Revd Dr Ronald Selby Wright to the author, 30 March 1992.
68. Paragraphs 205–28 of *Scotland's Government.*
69. *Scots Independent*, 28 March 1970.
70. Sir Alec Douglas-Home, letter to all members of the Scottish Constitutional Committee, 1 April 1970. Scottish Constitutional Committee Records 1968–70. HA.
71. John Campbell, *op. cit.*, p. 269.
72. Lord Home to the author, 8 August 1991.
73. David Butler and Michael Pinto-Duschinsky, *The British General Election of 1970*, Macmillan, 1971, p. 156.
74. *Ibid.*, p. 136.
75. On 21 April 1968 Enoch Powell had made a speech on immigration to a Conservative political central meeting in Birmingham, in which he said, 'Like the Roman, I seem to see "the river Tiber foaming with much blood".' Heath then dismissed Powell from his defence post in the shadow Cabinet. See John Campbell, *op. cit.*, pp. 239–46 for a full account.
76. Private information from several sources.
77. Private information from the Nuffield College Conference on the Heath government, Nuffield College, Oxford, 25 February 1984.
78. Private information.

Chapter 16.

1. *Spectator*, 27 June 1970.
2. The amalgamation of the two, long anticipated, had been finalised on 17 October 1968.
3. A reference to Balfour, who became Foreign Secretary in 1916.
4. Apart from following his father as Lord Chancellor, he made another piece of constitutional history by becoming the first former hereditary peer to return to the upper chamber as a life peer (as Baron Hailsham of St Marylebone), a route Alec Home was also to follow after his life peerage of 7 November 1974. Alec Home was reintroduced into the Upper House as Baron Home of the Hirsel by Lord Balerno and Lord Carrington on 22 January 1975. With typical modesty, Home failed to appreciate why the Upper Chamber was so full on this occasion. 'It is very odd,' he said, 'in 1963 rarely more than 80 peers turned up even for a quite important debate. This afternoon there was nothing much on the order paper, but there must have been at least 300 peers in the chamber.' Kenneth Rose to the author, 25 March 1991, and in the 'Albany' column in the *Sunday Telegraph*, 15 October 1991.
5. Private information. Margaret Thatcher became Leader of the Conservative Party in February 1975. Neil Kinnock entered the House of Commons as MP for Bedwellty in June 1970 and became Leader of the Labour Party in 1983.

6. Lord Home to the author, 8 August 1991.
7. Denis Greenhill, *More by Accident*, Wilton 65, York, 1992, p. 144.
8. Private information.
9. Nicholas Henderson, *The Private Office*, Weidenfeld & Nicolson, 1984, p. 10.
10. *Report of the Review Committee on Overseas Representation* (The Duncan Report), July 1969, Cmd. 4107.
11. Both Home and Sir John Leahy were members of the Cook Society, which Sir Robert Menzies had founded to further Anglo–Australian co-operation.
12. As in the first draft for a speech at Devizes on 17 July 1971. I am grateful to Mr John McDonnell QC for allowing me to see the boxes of draft speeches of this period.
13. See Nicholas Henderson, *op. cit.*, Chapter 8 *passim*, pp. 97–110.
14. Private information.
15. 'An international weather forecast', lecture to the Ditchley Foundation, 19 July 1968. HA.
16. Record of talks between Harold Macmillan and Sir Alec Douglas-Home on the Simonstown Agreement. HA.
17. Private information.
18. Douglas Hurd, *An End to Promises: Sketch of a Government 1970–1974*, Collins, 1979, p. 55.
19. *Ibid.*, p. 52.
20. Evidence from the Private Office.
21. Early day motion, 16 July 1970. Cited by Philip Norton, *Conservative Dissidents: Dissent within the Parliamentary Conservative Party 1970–1974*, Temple Smith, 1978, p. 41.
22. Foreign Office Records. HA.
23. See Jonathan Aitken, *Nixon: A Life*, Weidenfeld & Nicolson, 1993, p. 1.
24. See Earl of Cromer obituary, *Daily Telegraph*, 18 March 1991.
25. Lord Home to the author, 8 August 1991. See also Anthony Nutting, *Nasser*, Constable, 1972, p. 476, for an account of contemporary Egyptian feeling.
26. For an account of George Brown's Middle East tour in January 1970, see Peter Paterson, *Tired and Emotional: the Life of Lord George Brown*, Chatto & Windus, 1993, pp. 238–40.
27. Private information. Alec Home told the author that he had once planned to write a monograph on public funerals he had attended. The principal section was to be on Nasser. Lord Home to the author, 8 August 1991.
28. Lord Home, *The Way the Wind Blows*, Collins, 1976, pp. 296–301.
29. Speech by the Right Hon. Sir Alec Douglas-Home, KT, MP, Secretary of State for Foreign and Commonwealth Affairs, to Yorkshire Provincial Area Meeting (Conservative Party) at Harrogate on Saturday, 31 October 1970. HA.
30. See Sidney Astor, *Anthony Eden*, Weidenfeld & Nicolson, 1976, pp. 86–7; also Alan Bullock, *Ernest Bevin: Foreign Secretary 1945–1951*, Oxford University Press, Oxford, paperback edition, 1985, pp. 604–6.
31. *The Economist*, 27 June 1970.
32. Earl Mountbatten of Burma to Prince Juan Carlos of Spain, 15 July 1970.

Mountbatten Private Correspondence, File S232, Broadlands Archive. Prince Juan Carlos, grandson of King Alfonso XIII of Spain, was nominated by General Franco on 22 July 1969 as his eventual successor, a transition that occurred peacefully on 30 October 1975, three weeks before Franco's death. I am grateful to Lord Brabourne for arranging access to Home material among the Mountbatten correspondence in papers held at Broadlands.

33. *Daily Telegraph*, 16 July 1970.
34. Undated memo. HA.
35. House of Commons Debates, *Hansard*, 9 December 1970.
36. Sir Alec Douglas-Home to Andrei Gromyko, 3 December 1970. HA.
37. Sir Alec Douglas-Home to Andrei Gromyko, 4 August 1971. HA.
38. Peter Wright, *Spycatcher: The Candid Autobiography of a Senior Intelligence Officer*, Viking, New York, 1987, p. 345.
39. Colonel Mikhail Lyubimov, 'Today' programme, BBC Radio 4, 25 February 1994.
40. Private evidence from a diplomat present at the meeting.
41. Private information.
42. Ronald Lewin, *Ultra Goes to War: The Secret Story*, Arrow Books paperback edition, 1980, p. 304.
43. See Jonathan Aitken, *op. cit.*, pp. 494–7.
44. Professor John Young, 'The Heath Government and British Entry into the European Community', typescript draft of December 1994, p. 20. I am grateful to Professor Young for allowing me to see this draft.
45. Private information.
46. Final communiqué of Commonwealth Prime Ministers' Conference, Lagos, 12 January 1966.
47. Charles Douglas-Home, *Evelyn Baring: The Last Proconsul*, Collins, 1978, p. 318.
48. Record of Macmillan–Home discussions on Rhodesia, September 1970. HA.
49. Miles Hudson to Sir Alec Douglas-Home, 26 November 1970. HA and Hudson Papers.
50. See Philip Norton, *op. cit.*, pp. 45–8, 98–100, and 124–6 for Conservative divisions on Rhodesia in the 1970–4 Parliament.
51. On 17 October 1965 the central body of the Conservative Party abstained on the issue of oil sanctions and blockading the port of Beira in Mozambique (the official line); 50 right-wing Conservatives voted against, and 31 on the left of the Party voted with the Wilson government.
52. Martin Meredith, *The Past is Another Country: Rhodesia 1890–1979*, André Deutsch, 1979, p. 76.
53. The late Lord Goodman to the author, 10 January 1991.
54. Sir Alec Douglas-Home to Lord Pearce, 11 November 1971. Pearce papers.
55. Peter Rawlinson, *A Price Too High: An Autobiography*, Weidenfeld & Nicolson, 1989, pp. 167–8.
56. The late Lord Goodman to the author, 10 January 1991.
57. Private information.
58. *Mercury News*, 19 November 1971.
59. Miles Hudson, *Triumph or Tragedy? Rhodesia to Zimbabwe*, Hamish Hamilton, 1981, p. 98.

60. Sir Alec Douglas-Home to Lord Goodman, 25 November 1971. HA.
61. Sir Alec Douglas-Home to Lord Pearce, 3 December 1971. Pearce papers.
62. Sir Alec Douglas-Home to Ian Colvin, 25 November 1971. HA.
63. Sir Alec Douglas-Home to Lord Harlech, 23 December 1971. HA.
64. *Rhodesia: Report of the Commission on Rhodesian Opinion under the Chairmanship of the Right Honourable, the Lord Pearce*, Cmd. 4964, May 1972, p. 2. HMSO.
65. *Guardian*, 17 January 1972.
66. Sir Alec Douglas-Home to Lord Pearce, 4 February 1972. Pearce papers.
67. Sir Alec Douglas-Home to the Bishop of Edinburgh, 7 February 1972. HA. He also had many private talks with the Archbishop of Canterbury at this time on the moral issues involved.
68. Lord Pearce to Lady Pearce, 11 February 1972. Pearce papers.
69. *Rhodesia: Report of the Commission ... op cit.*, p. 112.
70. Sir Alec Douglas-Home to Miles Hudson, 7 March 1974. Hudson papers.
71. Arnold Smith, *Stitches in Time: The Commonwealth in World Politics*, André Deutsch, 1981, pp. 74–5.
72. Philip Norton, *op. cit.*, p. 100.
73. *Ibid.*, p. 109.
74. Sir Alec Douglas-Home to Harold Macmillan, 7 September 1972. HA.
75. Douglas Hurd to the author, 25 July 1994.
76. The Earl and Countess of Home have three children, Iona, Mary, and Michael. With the birth of Michael on 30 November 1987, the male line was secured to the second generation. This brought the number of grandchildren to eight – Kate and Matthew Darby; Fiona, Rory and Clare Wolfe Murray; and Iona, Mary and Michael Douglas-Home. Until the birth of Michael Douglas-Home, the presumptive heir to the Earldom was Sholto Douglas-Home, son of his late nephew, Robin Douglas-Home. Alec Home groomed Sholto into his possible future responsibilities. *Daily Mail*, 19 October 1995. For an account of the present Earl of Home's business career, see 'Quiet climber with a key role in Kuwait', *Scotsman*, 6 August 1991.
77. Private information.
78. *Daily Telegraph*, 30 March 1995.
79. Sir Alec Douglas-Home to Sir Denis Greenhill, 7 November 1973. HA.
80. Private information.
81. Message to the Foreign Service, 2 July 1973. HA.
82. Private information.
83. Sir Alec Douglas-Home to Anthony Parsons, 25 October 1973. Parsons papers.
84. Sir Alec Douglas-Home to Dr Henry Kissinger, 29 November 1973. HA.
85. Miles Hudson record, 2 December 1973. Hudson papers.
86. Private information.
87. Sir Alec Douglas-Home to Edward Heath, 6 October 1971. HA.
88. The others were Anthony Barber, Robert Carr, Peter Carrington, James Prior and Willie Whitelaw. David Butler and Dennis Kavanagh, *The British General Election of February 1974*, Macmillan, 1974, p. 25.

89. The original is at the Hirsel.
90. Labour won four more seats than the Conservatives, but on a slightly smaller total of the popular vote – 11,639,243 against 11,868,906. This was a reversal of the pattern in the October 1951 election when 13,717,538 votes produced 321 seats for the Conservatives, and 13,948,605 votes produced 295 seats for Labour.
91. Private information.
92. F. S. Oliver, *The Endless Adventure*, Macmillan, 1935, p. 204.

Chapter 17.

1. Statement to the Kinross and West Perthshire Unionist Association, 22 March 1974. HA.
2. October 1974 general election file. HA. The figures in Kinross and West Perthshire in October 1974 were: Nicholas Fairbairn (Unionist), 11,034; D. Cameron (SNP), 10,981; D.A. Barrie (Liberal), 2427, and D.G. Skene (Labour), 2028; Unionist Majority, 53.
3. Private information.
4. Sir Alec Douglas-Home to James Prior, 23 April 1974. HA. Teddy Taylor, then MP for Glasgow Cathcart, was later described as 'the leading bare-knuckle anti-devolutionist'. Andrew Marr, *The Battle for Scotland*, Penguin Books, Harmondsworth, 1992, p. 154.
5. Sir Alec Douglas-Home to Humphrey Atkins, 11 June 1974. HA.
6. The other members were Willie Whitelaw, James Prior, Robert Carr, Lord Carrington, Peter Walker, Francis Pym, Sir Geoffrey Howe, Ian Gilmour, Humphrey Atkins and Lord Windlesham. David Butler and Dennis Kavanagh, *The British General Election of October 1974*, Macmillan, 1975, p. 65.
7. Steering Committee Records, 1974. HA.
8. Sir Alec Douglas-Home to Edward Heath, 27 June 1974. HA.
9. Referendum file. HA.
10. The overall figures for the whole of the United Kingdom were 17,378,581 in favour, and 8,470,073 against.
11. Private information.
12. Sir Alec Douglas-Home to Harold Macmillan, 13 November 1974 Stockton papers.
13. David Butler and Dennis Kavanagh, *op. cit.*, p. 209.
14. Nigel Fisher, *The Tory Leaders: Their Struggle for Power*, Weidenfeld & Nicolson, 1977, p. 148.
15. Lord Home to the author, 8 August 1991.
16. In the revision that took place in 1991, after Mrs Thatcher's fall, those timings were changed to fourteen days, with the cut-off point in a new Parliament set at three months.
17. Lord Home to the author, 8 August 1991.
18. Alan Watkins, *A Conservative Coup: The Fall of Margaret Thatcher*, revised Duckworth edition, 1992, p. 175.
19. Walter Bagehot, *The English Constitution*, Fontana edition, 1963, p. 150.

20. Lord Home of the Hirsel to Mr O. Wilson, a correspondent from Cheshire, 29 January 1975. HA.
21. Lord Home of the Hirsel to Lord Alport, 24 December 1974. HA.
22. One of Heath's principal supporters, James Prior, was delayed on his return to London by train from the East Midlands and unable to vote, though a total of 120 would not have saved Heath. James Prior, *A Balance of Power*, Hamish Hamilton, 1986, p. 100.
23. William Whitelaw, *The Whitelaw Memoirs*, Aurum Press, 1989, p. 142.
24. The author was interviewing Julian Amery at 112 Eaton Square on the evening of 5 February 1975 in connection with the research for *The Uncrowned Prime Ministers*, an interview punctuated by constant telephone calls as MPs urged him to stand. There was a poignant irony in the fact that we were discussing the events at Blackpool in October 1963 at the time.
25. Message to the Chief Whip, Humphrey Atkins, 15 February 1975. HA.
26. Margaret Thatcher to Lord Home of the Hirsel, 2 April 1975. HA.
27. Lord Home of the Hirsel to Margaret Thatcher, 4 April 1975. HA.
28. See Margaret Thatcher, *The Path to Power*, Harper Collins, 1995, pp. 348–53, for details of the speech and reactions to it.
29. Margaret Thatcher to Lord Home of the Hirsel, 23 June 1975. HA.
30. Margaret Thatcher to Lord Home of the Hirsel, undated letter of July 1975. HA.
31. Lord Home of the Hirsel to Margaret Thatcher, 13 August 1975. HA. Gerald Ford had become President of the United States on 9 August 1974 following Richard Nixon's resignation over Watergate.
32. Lord Longford, *A History of the House of Lords*, Collins, 1988, p. 181.
33. His fellow members were Lord Gordon-Walker (Labour) and Lord Ogmore (Liberal). HA.
34. Miles Hudson to Lord Home of the Hirsel, 10 April 1976. HA.
35. Cited in the *Independent*, 6 November 1991.
36. *Sunday Telegraph*, 10 October 1976.
37. Kenneth Rose to the author, reporting a comment of Alec Home's in May 1977, 25 March 1991.
38. Private information.
39. David Dilks, *Neville Chamberlain; Volume One, Pioneering and Reform, 1869–1929*, Cambridge University Press, Cambridge, 1984. The second volume of this study is still awaited.
40. Lord Home of the Hirsel to Robert Lacey, 31 August 1976. HA.
41. Lord Home of the Hirsel to Sir Martin Charteris, 2 September 1976. HA.
42. Robert Browning, *Rabbi ben Ezra*, i.
43. Lord Home, *Letters to a Grandson*, Collins, 1983, p. 29.
44. Lord Home of the Hirsel to Patrick Croker, 12 September 1983. I am grateful to Mr Croker for letting me see this correspondence.
45. Bernard Donoughue and G.W. Jones, *Herbert Morrison: Portrait of a Politician*, Weidenfeld & Nicolson, 1973, p. 559.
46. Desert Island Discs file. HA.
47. Dr David Owen to Lord Home of the Hirsel, 24 February 1977. HA.
48. Paul Martin, *The London Diaries, 1974–1979*, edited by William R. Young,

University of Ottawa Press, Ottawa, 1988, pp. 376–7.

49. D.R. Thorpe, *Selwyn Lloyd*, Jonathan Cape, 1989, p. 436.
50. Private information.
51. David Butler and Dennis Kavanagh, *The British General Election of 1979*, Macmillan, 1980, p. 114. See also Peter MacMahon, 'Quiet believer blamed for referendum defeat', *The Scotsman*, 10 October 1995; and 'Home's belief in devolution', letter by Sir Edward Heath, *Daily Telegraph*, 27 October 1995.
52. Lord Home made these remarks to Magnus Linklater, editor of *The Scotsman*, at a lunch at the Hirsel on 1 April 1992. This was eight days before the general election of 1992 when the issues of devolution were again to the fore. See Magnus Linklater, 'With sweet Home at the Hirsel', *The Times*, 10 October 1995.
53. The figures were 1,1230,937 in favour (33 per cent of those entitled to vote), and 1,153,502 against.
54. It was only the second occasion in the twentieth century when a government had fallen on a vote of No Confidence in the House of Commons. The first was on 8 October 1924 on a Liberal amendment by Sir John Simon on the failure of Ramsay MacDonald's Labour government to prosecute J.R. Campbell, editor of the communist journal the *Workers' Weekly*, under the Incitement to Mutiny Act, over an article in its issue of 25 July 1924, inciting soldiers not to act against strikers when ordered to do so. The amendment was carried by 364 votes to 198.
55. Lord Home of the Hirsel to Michael Barrett, 13 March 1980; to A. Foxall, 19 March 1980; and to Sir Roy Welensky, 27 November 1980. HA.
56. Tom Bower, *The Perfect English Spy: Sir Dick White and the Secret War 1935–1990*, Heinemann, 1995, p. 325. Blunt had been appointed Surveyor of the King's Pictures in 1952, shortly before the death of George VI.
57. Lord Home of the Hirsel to T. Labey, 27 March 1980. HA.
58. Lord Home of the Hirsel to the Right Reverend Simon Phipps, Bishop of Lincoln, 18 July 1982. HA.
59. Speech by Margaret Thatcher, 8 March 1983. SB/91.
60. David Steel, *Against Goliath: David Steel's Story*, Weidenfeld & Nicolson, 1989, p. 45.
61. Originally nine holes to the right of the drive by the lodge, the course was extended to eighteen in the 1990s.
62. Private information and personal knowledge.
63. Miles Hudson, letter to *The Times*, 17 October 1995.
64. Margaret Thatcher to Lord Home of the Hirsel, 4 September 1990. HA.
65. Address by Lord Charteris, Westminster Abbey, 22 November 1990. I am grateful to Lord Charteris for giving me the full text of his address.
66. The author was present in the Gallery during the Debate. Alec Home was attentive to all the speeches to the end.
67. Private information. The postcards survive at the Hirsel.
68. Comment made to the author.
69. Lord Home to the author, 10 April 1992.

70. Harold Macmillan, *At the End of the Day 1961–1963*, Macmillan, 1973, p. 520.
71. Sir Walter Scott, *Marmion: A Tale of Flodden Field*, 1808, Canto VI, Verse XV.
72. BBC Radio 4 Bulletins, 9 October 1995.
73. Huw Edwards, BBC Political Correspondent, on BBC TV news bulletins, 9 October 1995.
74. Anthony Howard, *R.A.B.: The Life of R.A. Butler*, Jonathan Cape, 1987, p. 363.
75. *The Times* and the *Daily Telegraph*, 25 October 1995.
76. Address by the Duke of Buccleuch, KT, St Giles Cathedral Edinburgh, 4 December 1995. A second Service of Thanksgiving was held at Westminster Abbey on 22 January 1996, at which the address was given by Sir Antony Acland.

Index

The following abbreviations are used:

AE	Sir Anthony Eden	JFK	John Fitzgerald Kennedy
BEF	British Expeditionary Force	MP	Member of Parliament
C of E	Chancellor of the Exchequer	MCC	Marylebone Cricket Club
CRO	Commonwealth Relations Office	NC	Neville Chamberlain
FO	Foreign Office	PM	Prime Minister
f-n	footnote	PPS	Parliamentary Private Secretary
FS	Foreign Secretary	RAB	R. A. Butler
H	Sir Alec Douglas-Home	RPM	Resale Price Maintenance
H of C	House of Commons	WSC	Sir Winston Churchill
HM	Harold Macmillan	UN	United Nations

Abdication (1936), 66–67
Acheson, Dean, 121; & West Point Speech (1962), 257
Acland, Sir Antony, 407, 437, 441
Acland, Brigadier Peter, 407; view of H at Christ Church, 31
Action Not Words, 393
Adams, Sir Philip, 423
Adeane, Sir Michael (*later* Baron), 163, 300, 310, 313, 360; & 1957 succession, 189; & Cuban Missile Crisis, 242, 247; consults H on constitutional procedures, 292; asks Lady H privately if H would accept Premiership, 293–4
Adenauer, Konrad, 228, 252, 254
Adoula, Cyrille, 217
'Affair of the Handbag', The (June 1953), 150–151
Aitken, Jonathan, 110, 256
Aitken, Sir Max, 422
Aitken, Sir William, 110, 256
Aldington, Lord (*formerly* Sir Toby Low), 286, 292, 312
Alexander, A.V. (*later* Earl Alexander), H's view of, 136
Alexander, Field Marshal, Harold (*later* Earl), xvii, 122, 175
Alexander, Sir Michael, 407
Alington, Dr. Cyril, 25–27, 36, 60–62; as preacher, 26; as Dean of Durham, 62; officiates at daughter's wedding, 62; as detective story writer, 114; death, 162; memorial in Durham Cathedral, 429
Alington, Elizabeth (*later* Lady Dunglass; Countess of Home; Lady Douglas-Home; and Lady Home of the Hirsel), *see* entry under Douglas-Home, Lady (Elizabeth)
Alington, Giles, 162
Alington, Hester, 26; religious beliefs, 26–27
Alington, Lavinia, 126; marriage to Roger Mynors, 130
All Souls College, Oxford, 207
Allen, Sir George ('Gubby'), 35, 395
Alport, Lord, 448
Alsop, Joe, 339
Altham, Harry, 395
Amery, John, 117
Amery, Julian (*later* Baron Amery), 263, 268, 449; & 1963 succession, 272–273, 286; H's admiration for, 406
Amery, Leopold, 32, 79, 96, 117; & Norwegian Debate (1940), 101
Amin, Idi, 409, 429
Amory, Viscount (*see* Heathcoat Amory, Derick)
Anders, General, 119
Anderson, Sir John (*see* Waverley, Viscount)
Anstruther-Gray, Sir William (*later* Lord Kilmany), 386
Arafat, Yasser, 412
Ashton-Gwatkin, Frank, 82, 83, 84; accompanies NC to Munich, 80
Aspidistra Society, 31–32, 173
Asquith, H. H. (*later* Earl of Oxford and Asquith), 5, 38, 323
Asquith, Margot (*later* Countess of Oxford and Asquith), 34
Assheton, Ralph (*later* Lord Clitheroe), 38
Atholl, Katharine, Duchess of ('The Red Duchess'), & Kinross and West Perthshire By-Election (1938), 90–93
Atholl, Duke of, 92–93

Atkins, Sir Humphrey (*later* Baron Colnbrook), 442
Attlee, Clement (*later* Earl Attlee), 32, 79, 95, 133, 138, 140, 142, 157, 162, 212, 254; & H's view of, 136
Avon, 1st Earl of, (*see* Eden, Sir Anthony)
Ayer, Sir Alfred Jules, 26

Bacon, Francis, 276
Badenoch, Alec Williams, 278
Badenoch, David, 278
Bagehot, Walter, 75, 448; & *The English Constitution*, 318
Baker, Kenneth (*later* Baron Baker), 451
Baldwin, Stanley (*later* Earl Baldwin of Bewdley), 2, 4, 30, 39, 50, 59, 64, 188, 226, 319, 322, 381, 389, 395, 454; & 1929 Election, 44–45; as PM, 57, 306; & 1931 Election, 58; & Ottawa Conference (1932), 63; & Abdication, 66–67; retirement as PM, 69
Balfour, Arthur James (*later* Earl of Balfour), 4, 5, 6, 63, 116, 271, 389; misses putt at North Berwick, 5; favours change in Conservative Party name, 46
Balfour Commission on Scottish Affairs (1954), 144
Ball, George, 235
Balliol College, Oxford, 162, 391
Balniel, Lord, 406
Band, David, 108, 109
Banda, Dr. Hastings, 195, 197, 201, 282
Bandaranaike, Solomon, 183, 203
Barber, Anthony (*later* Baron Barber), 323, 373, 393, 401; as C of E, 405
Baring, Evelyn (*later* Baron Howick of Glendale), 31, 97, 100, 102
Baring, Lady, 102
Barrie, David, 437
Bartlett, Vernon, 90
Batista, Fulgercio, 231
Beadle, Sir Hugh, 397
Beaverbrook, Lord, 314, 359; attack on H in *Sunday Express*, 172–173; & H's appointment to FO, 208; believes H has 'the loaves and fishes', 7, 313–314
Becher, Sir William, 28
Beck, Colonel, 119
Beeching Report (1962), 327
Bell, Mr (gamekeeper), 36
Bell, Mrs (HM's cook), objects to de Gaulle's blood in Birch Grove fridge, 228
Benn, Tony (*formerly* 2nd Viscount Stansgate), 211, 316, 355; & campaign to renounce peerage, 224–225, 259, 288; on H's appeal, 375, 392
Bennett, Sir Reginald, 282
Berchtesgaden, NC's visit to, 77
Berlin Conference (1878), 112
Berlin Crisis, 226–228, 229, 230, 234, 239, 240, 246
Bermuda Conference (1961), 228, 337
Berkely, Humphrey, 276; & procedures for the selection of the Leader of the Conservative Party, 378–379, 381–382
Berwick-upon-Tweed, 8, 9, 332, 430
Bessborough, 10th Earl of, hosts cricket match for H's 80th birthday, 459
Better Tomorrow, A, 401
Bevan, Aneurin, 37, 129, 149; & 'the Class of 1950', 136
Beveridge Report (1942), 112
Bevin, Ernest, 131, 137, 157, 212, 438
Beyond the Fringe, 253, 262; H arranges Queen's visit to, 262
Bhutto, Ali, 430
Birch, Nigel (*later* Baron Rhyl), 289; & resignation (1958), 192
Birch Grove, 228, 263–264, 272, 337; & JFK's visit (1963) 263–264
Bird, W. S., 22
Bishop, Sir Frederick, 420
Blair, George, 258
Blair, Patrick, 90–91, 93
Blake, Robert (*later* Baron Blake), 254, 451
Blakenham Viscount (*formerly* John Hare), 6, 307, 323, 363–364, 368; dubbed 'the March Hare', 343; & draft of Leadership Selection rules, 379
Bligh, Sir Timothy, 262, 321, 338, 340; & 1963 leadership context, 282, 293, 298, 304–305, 306
Blunt, Anthony, 457
Boer War, 1
Bogdanor, Professor Vernon, 285, 311
Bonnet, Georges, 77
Booker, Christopher, 362
Boothby, Robert (*later* Baron Boothby), 40, 59, 91, 96, 102, 189
Bowes-Lyon, Sir David, 17, 36
Bowes-Lyon, Lady Elizabeth (see Elizabeth, Queen, Consort of King George VI)
Bowlby, Angela, 328, 394
Boyd of Merton, Viscount (*see* Lennox-Boyd, Alan)
Boyd-Carpenter, John (*later* Baron Boyd-Carpenter), 461; & Blackpool Conference (1963), 284; & RPM, 357
Boyle, Sir Edward, (*later* Baron Boyle of Handsworth), 307, 314; & resignation (1956), 183
Boys' Brigade, The, & H's work for in Lanarkshire, 37
'Boys' Brigade, The', group of young Conservative MPs, 73
Boyne, Harry, 259
Bracken, Brendan (*later* Viscount Bracken), 102, 103; H's views on, 102
Bradman, Sir Donald, H witnesses record Test innings of, 55
Braid, James, 56
Branxton Hill, site of Battle of Flodden, 7
Bridges, Sir Edward (*later* Baron Bridges), 70
Bridgwater By-Election (1938), 89–90
Brimelow, Sir Thomas (*later* Baron Brimelow), as Permanent Under Secretary at FO, 434–435; H's regard for, 435
British Broadcasting Corporation, 82, 324, 337, 347, 362–363, 370, 386; & 1963 leadership contest, 279, 281, 288, 295, 296
Brittan, Sir Samuel, 253
Britten, Benjamin (*later* Baron Britten of Aldeburgh), coronation opera of not appreciated by gala audience (1953), 150; H attends première of, 150
Brooke, Henry (*later* Baron Brooke of Cumnor), 305
Brooke, Sir Peter, 457
Brown, Bunco, 21
Brown, Ernest, 91
Brown, George (*later* Baron George-Brown), 317, 343; & broadcast after JFK's assassination, 337–338; as Foreign Secretary, 407–408; attends Nasser's funeral with H, 412–413
Browne, Sir Thomas, H electioneers by statue of, 367
Bruce, David, 232, 239, 249, 289, 346; analysis of Conservative leadership prospects (1963), 289–291; reports on H's return to H of C (1963), 335–336
Buccleuch, 7th Duke of, 18
Buccleuch, 9th Duke of, gives address at H's memorial

service in St. Giles Cathedral, 463
Buchan, John (*later* Baron Tweedsmuir), 32, 116
Buchan-Hepburn, Patrick (*later* Baron Hailes), 189; & Suez crisis, 183
Buchanan, George, 39, 51
Bulganin, Nikolai, & visit to Britain, 172
Bundy, McGeorge, 239
Burgess, Guy, 172
Burns, Robert, 9, 37, 266; H quotes at opportune moment in Moscow, 266
Bush, President George, 431; H's fruitful political relationship with, 431
Butler, Dr. David, 329; on electoral effects of RPM, 358; advises H on procedures for electing Conservative leader, 6, 380–381, 383
Butler of Saffron Walden, Baroness (Mollie), 280, 296, 318, 347
Butler, Richard Austen (*later* Baron Butler of Saffron Walden), xvi, 3, 4, 101, 158, 170, 175, 204, 214, 251, 261, 271, 329, 335, 338, 453; as Under Secretary at FO, 73; view of Churchill as PM (1940), 101; war-time correspondence with H, 111–112; compares NC to Saul and Pitt the Younger, 112; on post-war reconstruction, 112, 127, 130; & December 1955 re-shuffle of Cabinet, 171; & Suez Crisis, 180–181; as candidate for Premiership (1957), 188–190; as Party Chairman, 201; offered Commonwealth Relations Office, 211; wariness of Tony Benn's campaign to alter peerage law, 224; & Cuban Missile Crisis, 245; & 1963 leadership contest, 273–276, 280–281, 283–284, 286–288, 290, 295–298, 302–310, 312–314, 318, 321; candidature compared to H's, 318–319; as Foreign Secretary (1963–1964), 72, 340, 341–342, 346, 350, 354; & Macleod's *Spectator* article on 1963 leadership contest, 345; & visit to Washington with H (1964), 347–350; & 1964 Election, 368–369; & Mastership of Trinity College, Cambridge, 376; generous tribute on H's retirement as leader, 388–389; relationship with H, 169–170, 319–320, 376; death, 463

Caccia, Sir Harold (*later* Baron Caccia), 238, 242, 243, 265, 317
Cadogan, Sir Alexander, 70, 78, 129
Calder, John, 402
Callaghan, James (*later* Baron Callaghan of Cardiff), 330, 336, 407; on sea-changes in politics, 4–5; tagged with 'Crisis, what crisis?' remark, 257; as Foreign Secretary, 437, 441; as PM, 454–455; & 1979 Election, 456; admiration for H, 441
Campbell, Dr. John, xvi, 207; & Heath's campaign for RPM, 356, 357, 358
Canongate Kirk, Edinburgh, 31, 35
Carey, Bishop Kenneth, 427
Carlin, W., 57
Carlos, Prince Juan, of Spain (*later* King Juan Carlos), 414
Carlton Club, 8, 221; H dines Gromyko at, 8
Carr, Robert (*later* Baron Carr of Hadley), 406, 429
Carrington, Lord, 193, 335, 346; as Foreign Secretary, 208, 323, 457; favours Lords involvement in selection of post-1965 Conservative leaders, 381
Cartwright, T. W., 398
Castro, Fidel, 219, 231; & Cuban Missile Crisis (1962), 234–236, 246; social policies of, 236
Carr, Mr (gamekeeper), 36
Cary, Sir Roger, 22–23
Casey, Richard (*later* Baron Casey), 193
Castlereagh, Robert, Viscount, 438
Cecil, Lord Robert, 16, 32
Central African Federation, 174, 193, 195–197, 202, 262
Chamberlain, Mrs Anne, 64, 68, 71, 72, 85, 86, 97, 104, 119, 182, 395
Chamberlain, Sir Austen, xviii, 4, 33, 59, 322; literary works, 116; Sir Charles Petrie's life of, 116; & 1911 leadership contest, 271; death, 68
Chamberlain, Hilda, 88
Chamberlain, Ida, 11, 89
Chamberlain, Dame Ivy, 70
Chamberlain, Joseph, 406; J. L. Garvin's life of, 116; Julian Amery's life of, 116
Chamberlain, Neville, xv, xviii, 2, 4, 5, 30, 33, 60, 108, 120, 122, 131, 137, 170, 188, 225–226, 239, 327–328, 381, 395, 453; early life, 111; MP for Ladywood, 63; as Postmaster General, 63; as Minister of Health, 41, 50, 63; as C of E, 50, 58, 63, 66; & Import Duties Bill (1932), 52, 63; admires H's maiden speech, 53; appoints H as PPS, 58–59; view of H, 65; use of newsreels, 63, 99; view of King Edward VIII, 65; view of Baldwin, 67; as PM, 63, 69; team at No 10, 69; relationship with Eden, 70, 72, 106; relationship with H, 71; closeness to H family, 72; view of Halifax, 73; 69th birthday, 74; & Mussolini, 74; flies to Germany, 75, 77; uncertain health, 76, 77, 89; meetings with Hitler, 77–84; signs Munich Agreement and 'piece of paper', 83–84; triumphant return to London, 84; reception at Buckingham Palace with H, 84–85; return to Downing Street, 85–86; repeat's Disraeli's words, 86; visit to Hirsel (October 1938), 10–11, 87–89; visit to Rome (January 1939), 93–94; outbreak of war, 95–97; visit to BEF (December 1939), 98–99; downfall as PM, 99–101, 357; as Lord President, 103–104; final illness & death, 104; funeral, 107; *Characteristics*: 64–65, 67, 71, religious beliefs, 64; love of countryside, 64; love of Scotland, 68, 75; sensitivity, 71
Chandos, Viscount (*see* Oliver Lyttelton)
Channon, Sir Henry ('Chips'), 65, 95, 97, 101
Charteris, Sir Martin (*later* Baron Charteris of Amisfield), f-n xvii, 453; & 1963 leadership contest, 280; gives address at Lady Home's memorial service (November 1990), 461
Chataway, Sir Christopher, 363
Chatham Club, 32
Chelmer, Lord, 300, 306, 307
Chequers, 71, 87, 371, 378, 404, 409
Ch'iao, Mr., 431
China, H's visit to (1972), 431–432
Chips with Everything (Arnold Wesker), as reflection of early 1960s, 257
Christ Church, Oxford, 3, 16, 26, 28, 30–33, 35, 38, 41, 116, 147, 162, 256, 322–324, 407, 418
Christ, George, 329, 330, 334
Churchill College, Cambridge, H attends opening of, 358
Churchill, Clementine, Lady, 385
Churchill, Diana, death of, 321, 361; H's sympathy over, 321
Churchill, Lord Randolph, 3, 115
Churchill, Randolph, 8; 1963 leadership contest, 286, 294; & *The Fight for the Tory Leadership*, 341, 343, 346

Churchill, Sir Winston, xv, 4, 59–60, 63, 74, 79, 90, 100, 111, 112, 122, 125, 128, 129, 140, 141, 158, 188, 189, 264, 272, 309, 321, 341, 381, 389, 440, 445, 454; opposes Conservative Party's India policy, 51; & Kinross & West Perthshire By-Election (1938), 91; quarrel with James Stuart, 93; & NC's death, 104, 107; & *World Crisis, The*, 116; & Yalta Agreement, 123–125; & 1945 Caretaker Government, 126–127; & 1945 Election defeat, 129–130; & Iron Curtain speech, 131; & Suez Base Agreement (1954), 175; & 80th birthday, 152; retirement, 152; leaves H of C (1964), 360–361; H and contingency plans over WSC's possible death during 1964 Election, 360; death and funeral, 385
Ciano, Count, 66, 70, 78, 94
Clarendon, 6th Earl of, 84
Close, Brian, 396
Coatbridge & Airdrie, 58; H's candidacy at (1929), 43, 45, 46
Coldstream, 116, 329, 385, 445, 463
Coldstream, Sir George, 241
Cold War, 1, 249
Cole, Sir David, 193, 194, 203
Cole, Lady, 203
Cole, G. D. H., & *How to Conquer Unemployment*, 44
Coleridge, Samuel Taylor, 49
Collingwood, Mr George (butler), 48
Collins, Sir Godfrey, 53, 54, 55
Collins, Norman, 371
Colville, Sir John (Secretary of State for Scotland; *later* 1st Baron Clydesmuir), 91
Colville, Sir John ('Jock'), 2, 65, 97, 101, 127, 152, 288, 377; & Yalta Agreement, 124; congratulates H on becoming FS, 211–212; summing up of H as PM, 376–377
Common Market, 155, 159, 202, 209, 228, 248, 250, 255, 405, 418–419; de Gaulle's veto on British entry, 252, 258; 1975 Referendum on, 443, 445
Congo, 216–218, 223, 229, 230, 237
Connolly, Cyril, xvi, 2–3, 24, 29
Conservative and Unionist Party, 38, 39, 46, 120, 127, 131, 136, 291, 439, 445; & 1929 Election, 44; & 1931 Election, 48, 49; & 1935 Election, 57; & Margate Conference (1936), 106; & Blackpool Conference (1963), 268, 272, 277–298, 334, 340; & Brighton Conference (1965), 392
Conservative Party Leadership Contests: (1911), 4, 7, 271, 390; (1922), 7; (1923), 2, 4, 188, 271, 383; (1940), 2, 4, 101; (1957), 4, 188, 189, 271, 275, 303; (1963), 3, 8, 259, 268–269, Ch. 12 *passim*, 383; (1965), 271, 374, 382, 386–388; (1975), 271, 288, 383, 444–449; (1989), 383; (1990), 271, 288, 382, 447; (1995), 446
Commonwealth Relations Office, Ch. 7 *passim*, 190–203
Cooper, Chester, 239
Cooper, Duff (*later* 1st Viscount Norwich), 51, 78, 124; as 1st Lord of the Admirality, 69; resignation after Munich, 80
Co-operative Movement, 49
Cornhill-on-Tweed, 9
Coulson, Phyllis, 113
Countryman, The, 64
Cowdrey, Sir Colin, 395–397, 399; 'You can drop the "Sir"' says H 'if you ever drop anything', 395
Crabb, Commander, 172
Cranborne, Viscount (*see* Salisbury, 5th Marquess of)
Crawley, Cosmo, 36
Cripps, Sir Stafford, 355
Cromer, Lord, 411
Crookshank, Harry (*later* Viscount Crookshank), 203
Crosland, Anthony, 454
Crossman, Richard, 65, 317
Cuban Missile Crisis (1962), 227, 230, Ch. 10 *passim*, 254, 288, 453
Cunningham, Sir Charles, 54
Cunningham, Sir Knox, & 1963 leadership context, 276, 282, 283, 306–307, 313, 327
Cursiter, Stanley, 151
Curzon, George Nathaniel, Marquess of Kedleston, 4, 18, 204, 288, 320; passed over for Premiership (1923), 2, 306.
Cyprus, 172, 173, 191, 193, 344, 346, 348, 350–351; & Cyprus Conference (1960), 193

Daily Express, 368
Daily Herald, 316
Daily Mail, 210, 280, 459
Daily Telegraph, 104, 160, 259, 273, 463
Daily Worker, 134
Daladier, Edouard, 77, 84, 98
Dale, David, 49
Dalhousie, 16th Earl of, 195
Dalton, Hugh (*later* Baron Dalton), 121
Dalyell, Tam, 65; & 'West Lothian' question, 399
Dance to the Music of Time, A, 116
Darby, Adrian, H's son-in-law, 329
Darby, Matthew, H's grandson, 454, 464; as dedicatee of *Letters to a Grandson*, 115
Darby, Lady Meriel, H's daughter, 213, 328, 464; birth, 97
Darkness at Noon (Arthur Koestler), 115
Day, Sir Robin, 295–297, 353, 363, 366
Decline and Fall (Evelyn Waugh), 116
Deedes, William (*later* Baron Deedes), 307, 327, 378
de Gaulle, President Charles, 228, 248, 250, 251, 255; vetoes British application to join Common Market, 252, 258
Denning Report (1963) 346
Devils, The (Fyodor Dostoevsky), 115
Devizes By-Election (1964), 359
Devlin, Lord, & Report on Nyasaland (1959), 197
Devonshire, Victor Cavendish, 9th Duke of, 129, 304
Devonshire, Andrew Cavendish, 11th Duke of, 333; & JFK's funeral, 338–339
Devonshire, Deborah, Duchess of, & JFK's funeral, 338–339
Dewey, Governor, 135
Dexter, Ted, 336
Dickens, Charles, 116, 262
Dickie, John, xvi, 329, 336
Dilhorne, Viscount (*formerly* Sir Reginald Manningham-Buller), 400; & Cuban Missile Crisis, 241–242; & 1963 leadership contest, 275, 277, 283, 298, 306–312; as possible dark-horse candidate for leadership, 283
Dilks, Professor David, 453
Dimbleby, Richard, 337
Ditchley Foundation, 408–409
Disraeli, Benjamin (*later* 1st Earl of Beaconsfield), 4, 29, 82, 86, 112; & 'Peace with Honour', 86; Monypenny & Buckle's life of, 115

Dixon, Sir Pierson, 252
Dobrynin, Anatoly, 235
Dodds-Parker, Sir Douglas, 156
Doggart, Hubert, 395
d'Oliveira, Basil, 395–399
Dollan, P. J., view of H, 76
Donaldson, Arthur, 334, 393
Donaldson, Mrs (cook), 114, 120
Douglas, xvii, 1, 13–14, 16, 30, 34, 35, 36, 43, 48, 60, 118, 213, 221, 226, 363, 391, 406, 407, 457, 460; HM visits, 169, 203, 248, 250; H's last visit to, 462
Douglas Castle, 13, 21, 28, 30, 34, 36, 38, 131, 140, 248
Douglas family, early history of, 13–15
Douglas, Sir James ('The Good'), 13–14
Douglas, James, & methods of choosing Party leader, 380–381, 384
Douglas, Lady Jane, 15
Douglas, Isabel (2nd Lady Home), 11
DOUGLAS-HOME, SIR ALEXANDER FREDERICK (*variously* Viscount Dunglass; the 14th Earl of Home; and Lord Home of the Hirsel); ancestry, 10–18; birth, 1, 18; childhood, 18–23; Christian upbringing, 20, 21; *education*: at Ludgrove School, Barnet, 20–23; at Eton College, 23–30; at Christ Church, Oxford, 30–35; *early career*: visit to South America, 35; commitments in Lanarkshire, 36–37; in Lanarkshire Yeomanry, 37, 98, 108; impact of Lanarkshire unemployment, 37–38, 42; political allegiance, 38–39; influence of Noel Skelton, 40–42, 50; & Scottish Unionism, 40, 42; as candidate at Coatbridge and Airdrie (1929), 43–45; as platform speaker, 44–45, 47–48; candidate for Lanark (1931), 46–48; *pre-war Parliamentary career*: elected MP for Lanark, 48; as backbench MP, 49–50; Parliamentary Secretary to Noel Skelton, 50; maiden speech, 51–52; at Scottish Office, 53; as constituency MP, 56–57, 76, 94; as PPS to Colonel Anthony Muirhead, 57–58; at Ministry of Labour, 57–59; & 1935 General Election, 57; as PPS to NC, 58–61; Chapter 4 *passim*; similarities to NC, 64–65, 68; & admiration of NC, 65, 71, 95; declines Under-Secretaryship in Scottish Office, 65; & work at 10 Downing Street, 2, 69–103; & Sir Horace Wilson, 69; aware of differences between NC and AE, 72; & war clouds in Europe, 74–80; & Sir John Simon's speech in Lanark, 75–77; & NC's statement in H of C, 28 September 1938, 78–80; flies to Munich with NC, 80–87, 166; view of Hitler, 81, 84; goes to Buckingham Palace with NC on return from Munich, 84–85; regrets NC's echo of Disraeli, 85–86; co-hosts NC's visit to the Hirsel (October 1938), 87–89; & Kinross and West Perthshire By-Election (1938), 89–93, 106; & visit to Rome (January 1939), 93–94; & outbreak of war, 95–97; visit to BEF (December 1939), 97–99; & fall of Neville Chamberlain as PM, 99–101; & view of Churchill in May 1940, 101–102; & mistrust of Brendan Bracken, 101–102; & NC's death, 103–104, 107; & letter of condolence to Mrs Anne Chamberlain, 104; assessment of years with NC, 105–107; *during Second World War*: illness, 108–120; tuberculosis operation, 109, & extensive reading, 114–116; & life at Springhill, 109, 113–114; & white feather episode, 117; & resumption of constituency work, 118–120; & war-time correspondence with R. A. Butler, 111–112; & Keith Feiling's life of NC, 112–113; & visits of Count Starzenski, 119; & feelings towards Communism, 115–116, 120–122, 451; & views on Russia, 122, 131–132, 184–185; 'second' maiden speech, 121; & Yalta debate, 123–124; as member of Caretaker Government, 121, 125–128; & 1945 Election, 128–130; & defeat at Lanark, 129; *in opposition*: retained as candidate in Lanark, 130; & work in Lanark, 132–133; & 1950 Election, 133, 134, 135–136; re-elected to H of C, 135; inherits Earldom of Home (July 1951), 139; *as Minister of State in Scottish Office*: 11, 34, 142–153; & Scottish Nationalism, 142–143; & work with Ian Robertson, 143; & theft of Stone of Scone, 142–143; H's place in organisation of Scottish Office, 144–145; Highlands & Islands Panel work, 145–148; maiden speech in House of Lords, 146; & Forth Road Bridge, 142, 148, 152; & Calton Hill routine, 148–149; & Coronation of Queen Elizabeth II, 149–150; & 'The Affair of the Handbag', 150–151; & work in 1954–1955, 151–152; & Churchill's 80th birthday, 152; *Commonwealth Relations Office*: 34, 40; appointed to CRO, 152–153; & relations with AE, 154–156; & relations with Sir Gilbert Laithwaite, 156, 160, 163–164; & relations with FO, 157, 194–195; & process of decolonisation, 158–159; & work with Harold Smedley, 160; & routine at CRO, 160–161; & Commonwealth Tour (1955), 164–168; & views on immigration, 169; & Canada tour (1956), 171–174; & Suez Crisis (1956), 174–186; & work with Henry Lintott, 174; & Eden's resignation, 186–187; favours HM for the Premiership, 189; & relations with HM, Ch. 8 *passim*.; & Seretse Khama, 190–191; & Cyprus, 191–192; becomes Leader of House of Lords & Lord President, 192; & African tour (1957), 193–194, 195–196; & work with David Cole, 193; & Commonwealth Prime Ministers' Conference (1957), 193–194; & contacts with Royal family, 194; & Alan Lennox-Boyd, 196–197; & Iain Macleod, 198–199; & 1955 Election, 199–200; & farewell party, 203; & assessment of time at CRO, 202–204; *Foreign Office 1960–1963*: 18, 73; appointment & controversy over, 205–209; & relationships with HM, 209, 213; & work with Edward Heath, 209; & organisation of FO, 212–214; & mistrust of excessive travel, 214–215; & Kennedy administration, 215, 223; & United Nations, 216–223; & Congo, 216–217; & 'double standards speech', 218; & Khruschev, 218–220; & Gromyko, 220–222; & House of Lords reform, 224, 259–261; & Iain Macleod, 225–226; & Berlin, 226–228; & Bermuda Conference (1961), 228–230; & Cuban Missile Crisis (1962), Ch 10 *passim*; & de Gaulle, 250–251; & Rambouillet meeting (1962), 250; & Nassau (1962), 250–252; & Laos, 255; & State Visit of King Olav (1962), 256–257; & 'matchsticks' comment, 257–258; & Hailsham, 259–261, 267–268; arranges Queen's visit to *Beyond the Fringe*, 262; & Central African Federation, 262–263; & Test Ban Treaty (1963), 263, 265–267; & JFK visit to Birch Grove (1963), 263–264; & talks with HM on Conservative leadership, 268, 272; *1963 Conservative Leadership Contest*, Ch 12 *passim*; H's views on leadership contests, 271; advises HM, 272–274; offers to sound Cabinet opinion, 277; writes to Lady Dorothy Macmillan, 279; visits HM in hospital, 280, 298–299, 300–301; considers candidacy, 282–289; announces HM's intention to resign to

Conservative Conference, 284–285; & private conversations with Michael Adeane (June 1963), 292; urged to stand by senior figures, 293–294; & last day at Party Conference, 295–297; urged to stand by Lord Woolton, 299–300; undergoes medical examination, 302; given advance notice of his recommendation to the Queen, 310–311; & 'midnight meeting' at Enoch Powell's house, 312–313; & audience at Buckingham Palace, 313–314; & appointment as PM, 314–315; *PRIME MINISTER* (1963–1964): 23, 67; & reactions to appointment, 316–317; & relations with RAB, 72, 318–320, 388–389; & methods of, 320–322; & appointment of Cabinet, 321–322; & work with Burke Trend, 324–326; & reform of Cabinet Committee system, 253, 326–327; & Downing Street team, 327–330; & Kinross & West Perthshire By-Election, 330–335; & takes seat in H of C, 335–336; & assassination of JFK, 336–340; & first meetings with LBJ, 338–339; & Kilmuir memoirs, 341–343; & choice of election date, 343, 353–355; & Macleod's *Spectator* article, 343–345; & RPM, 346, 354, 355–358; & Leyland bus controversy, 347–350; & Cyprus, 350–351; & Rhodesia, 351–352, 360; & Commonwealth, 352–353; & opening of Forth Road Bridge, 360, 364; & retirement of Churchill, 360–361; & Queen's letter on Election, 361; *1964 General Election*: Ch 14 *passim*; style of campaigning, 362–363, 365–368, 371–372; & controversy over 'donations', 366; & Hardy Spicer, 366–367; & RAB's pessimistic forecast, 368–369; & Gordon Walker, 369–370; & loss of Brighton Kemptown, 370; & preparation of 'Deadlock File', 371; & polling day, 372; & resignation as PM, 373; assessment of Premiership, 375–377; *in opposition*: as Leader of the Opposition, 67, 378–391; instigates new procedures for selecting the Party leader, 378–384; & 1975 revisions to procedures, 446–449; & Roxburgh, Selkirk and Peebles By-Election (1965), 384–385; & death of Churchill, 385; & Rees-Mogg article on his leadership, 387; steps down as Conservative leader, 387–388; votes for Heath as his successor, 390; as Shadow Foreign Secretary, 391; as Shadow Commonwealth Secretary, 393; & elder statesman rôle, 391–395; as President of MCC, 395–399; & Rhodesia, 397; & Scottish devolution, 399–401; & 1970 Election, 401–403; seen as short-term leader after Heath's expected defeat, 402–403; *Foreign Secretary* (1970–1974): Ch 16 *passim*; appointment to FO, 404; & work with Heath, 404–405; & team at FO, 406–407; & South African Arms sales, 408–410; & relations with American administrations, 411–412, 414–415, 431; & Nasser's funeral, 412–413; & Harrogate speech (1970), 413–414; & Common Market, 414, 418–419; & expulsion of Russian spies, 221, 415–418; & Rhodesia, 420–429; & Pearce Commission, 422–423, 425–429; & Ugandan Asians, 429; & China visit (1972), 431–432; & Northern Ireland, 432–433; & Yom Kippur War (1973), 433–434; & visit to Moscow (1973), 434–435; & February 1974 Election, 435–437; leaves FO for the last time, 437; retires from H of C, 437, 440; assessment of second period at FO, 437–438; *late years*: & Scottish devolution, 441–442, 455–456; & 1975 referendum, 443, 445; returns to Lords, 445; & 1975 leadership contest, 446–449; consulted by Margaret Thatcher over Foreign Affairs, 449–451, 457, 458; & literary activities, 452–453; & Falklands War, 458; death of Lady Home, 460–461; last appearance in Lords, 461; final years, 461–462; death and funeral, 462–464. *Characteristics*: informality, 220, 459; lack of pomposity, 27, 392, 455; love of local roots, 36–37; mistrust of Scottish 'Lairdism', 56; methods of working, 161; & regard for experts, 28, 34–35, 54; religious beliefs, 20, 37, 62, 110; sense of propriety, 149, 338; *family life*: engagement to Elizabeth Alington, 61–62, marriage, 62, 162; birth of children, 71, 109, 120; in wartime, 116–117, 120; 21st birthday, 36, 40th birthday, 120, 70th birthday, 209, 211, 432, 80th birthday, 459; 90th birthday, 462; *recreations*: birdlife, 96; cricket, 22, 28–29, 35, 54, 395; crosswords, 27; fishing, 20, 36; fives, 29; horse-racing, 32, 148, 459; music, 28; reading, 20, 114–116, 161; *residences*: Chequers, 404; Chester Square, 83, 94; Dorneywood, 163, 202, 213, 335, 402, 404, 437; Hirsel, 140, 255; Roebuck House, 373, Springhill, 114, 140

Douglas-Home, Lady Bridget (H's sister), 18, 20, 109, 117, 316; death of, 455

Douglas-Home, Lady Caroline (H's eldest daughter), 71, 72, 113, 118, 119, 316, 464

Douglas-Home, Hon. David (H's son, *formerly* Viscount Dunglass, *later* 15th Earl of Home), 254, 256, 323, 464; birth, 120; as father's page at Coronation (1953), 149–150; marriage, 430; career, 430; family, 541

Douglas-Home, Hon. Edward (H's brother), 18, 26; as Prisoner of War, 116, 126

Douglas-Home, Lady Elizabeth (H's wife, *variously* Elizabeth Alington, Lady Dunglass, Countess of Home, Lady Douglas-Home, and Lady Home of the Hirsel), xv, xviii, 6, 27, 36, 122, 132, 139, 164, 171, 172, 186, 194, 213, 220, 221, 312, 318, 336, 338, 347, 387, 389, 390–391, 394, 404, 432, 437, 464; engagement and marriage, 60–62; and Mrs Anne Chamberlain, 71; births of children: Caroline, 71; Meriel, 97; Diana, 109; David, 120; at Springhill in war, 114; & white feather episode, 117; & CRO, 171; & Suez, 174–175, 182–184; & H's appointment to FO, 207; compiles 108 scrapbooks (1936–1990), 86–87, places Anthony Howard article on possible H premiership in scrapbooks, 289; privately consulted by Queen's secretary on H's possible candidacy for Premiership, 293–294, 300; at 10 Downing Street, 328; & Kinross and West Perthshire By-Election (1938), 332, 334; & 1964 Election, 367, 374; as Fellow of Eton College, 429–430; Golden Wedding, 459; death, xvii, 460; memorial service in Westminster Abbey, 461

Douglas-Home, Hon. George (H's youngest brother), 18, 20, 126; as photographer, 36; war service with RAF, 116; death on active service, 117, 120

Douglas-Home, Hon. Henry (H's eldest brother), 18, 20, 21, 35, 60, 96–97, 116, 316

Douglas-Home, Jane (H's daughter-in-law, *later* Countess of Home), 430

Douglas-Home, Lady Rachel (H's sister, *later* Lady William Montagu Douglas Scott), 18, 20, 36, 60; marriage, 68

Douglas-Home, Robin, 89, 395

Douglas-Home, Sholto, as putative heir, 541

Douglas-Home, Hon. William (H's brother), 18, 20, 60, 61, 71, 126, 140, 424, 459, 461; war service, 116; & Le

Havre, 116–117
Douglas Home Rules on Selection of Party Leader, reprinted in Appendix 1 in 1965 version, 6, 7, 376, 378–384, 446–448
Dover House, Whitehall, 53, 149
Doyle, Sir Arthur Conan, 13
Drummond-Moray, Major Andrew, 332, 334
du Cann, Sir Edward, 391; & 1975 leadership contest, 445, 448
Dudley, 9th Lord, 12
Dugdale, Blanche, 116
Dugdale family, 74
Dugdale, Nancy (*later* Baroness Crathorne), 102, 103, 108, 109
Dugdale, Thomas (*later* Baron Crathorne), 2, 59, 66, 359
Dulles, John Foster, 161, 173, 178, 181, 182, 187, 215
Duncan Report (1969), 407, 410
Dundee, 11th Earl of, 208
Dunglass, Viscount Alexander (*see* Sir Alexander Douglas-Home)
Dunglass, Viscount Charles (*see* 13th Earl of Home)
Dunglass, Viscount David (*see* Hon. David Douglas-Home, *later* 15th Earl of Home)
Dunglass, Viscountess Elizabeth (*see* Lady Elizabeth Douglas-Home)
Dunn, Arthur, 21
Durham, 1st Earl of ('Radical Jack'), 1, 14
Durham, 4th Earl of (H's grandfather), 1
Durham Report (1840), 1, 348

Eden, Sir Anthony (*later* 1st Earl of Avon), xvi, xviii, 3, 5, 32, 33, 41, 51, 63, 64, 131, 132, 137, 138, 212, 303–304, 320, 324, 325, 341–343, 381, 386, 391, 407, 414, 438, 454–455; as Foreign Secretary (1938), 69; & resignation, 72–74; & Munich, 79; as War Secretary, 102; & Neville Chamberlain, 106; as Foreign Secretary (1940), 111; & Yalta Agreement, 125; as Foreign Secretary (1945), 127; & 1945 Election, 129–130; as Prime Minister, 90, 154, 155, 156, 159, 163, 164, 170, 171, 203; & 1955 Election, 162; & view of H, 169; & Suez Crisis (1956), 174–186; & resignation, 186–187, 188; & 1965 Leadership context, 388, 390
Eden, Clarissa, Lady (*later* the Countess of Avon), 187, 390
Eden, Guy, 124
Edinburgh, 9, 12, 40, 45, 108, 109, 122, 147, 150–151, 256, 427
Edinburgh, Duke of, 152, 338–339, 358
Edward I, King, 9
Edward VIII, King, 42, 65–66; & Mrs Simpson, 62
Eisenhower, President Dwight D., 137, 177, 219, 220, 229, 231, 250; re-elected as President, 184
Elizabeth, Queen, Consort of King George VI, 75; & NC's return from Munich, 85, 87; visits NC at Heckfield, 104
Elizabeth II, Queen, 3, 148, 152, 186, 188, 203, 240, 247, 453, 457, 459; & Coronation, 149–150; & Honours of Scotland, 150–151; attends performance of *Beyond the Fringe*, 262; & 1963 Conservative Party leadership: 268, 274–276, 281, 285, 292, 297, 301, 303, 304, 306, 308, 310, 311, 314–315; & visit to Canada (1964), 360–361; & 1964 Election, 354, 364–365, 371
Elliot, Kay (*formerly* Kay Tennant, *later* Baroness Elliot of Harwood), 33, 110; & Lord North Street salon, 56; marries Walter Elliot, 56
Elliot, Walter, 34, 50, 54, 111, 130; as MP for Lanark, 47, 49; accident at Hawick Station, 110–111; as influence on Scottish Conservatism, 130
Emrys-Evans, Paul, 100
Emslie, George (*later* Baron Emslie), 334
Enemies of Promise, 2–3
Enemy of the People, An (Henrik Ibsen), 106
Engels, Frederick, & Communist Manifesto, 115
Erhard, Ludvig, 339
Erroll, Frederick (*later* Baron Erroll of Hale), 206, 232, 312
Eton Boating Song, performed in Great Hall of the Peoples' Republic of China, 8
Eton College, 2–3, 4, 7, 22–30, 57, 61, 125, 136, 162, 253–254, 256, 270, 344, 391, 407, 429
Eton Ramblers, 61, 321; Saddam Hussein thought to be wearing tie of, 462
Eton Society ('Pop'), 29
Evans, Sir Harold, 279, 338
Evening Standard, 280, 366, 445
Everest, Mount, 149, 165
Ewing, Winifred, 399

Fairbairn, Sir Nicholas, as H's successor in Kinross and West Perthshire, 440–441, 444, 462
Falklands War (1982), 458
Fawzi, Dr M, 219
Feeney, Mr (gardener), 113
Feiling, Sir Keith, 30, 226; sees H about his life of NC, 111–113
Feisal of Iraq, King, 174, 176
Festival of Britain (1951), 253
Fettes College, 367
Field, Winston, 351
Fight for the Tory Leadership, The (Randolph Churchill), 8, 341, 343
Fingleton, Jack, 165
First World War, 16, 22, 24, 34
Fisher, Sir Nigel, 344, 453
Flodden, Battle of (1513), 9, 10, 11, 12
Foot, Sir Hugh (*later* Baron Caradon), 193
Foot, Michael, 460
Ford, Sir Edward, 274, 276, 280, 293
Ford, President Gerald, 451
Ford, Lionel, 26
Foreign Office, 3, 287–288, 407; Chapters 9, 10 and 16 *passim*
Forrester, Andrew, 334
Forster, E. M., 27, 408
Forth Road Bridge, 147, 148, 161, 199, 256, 360
Fourth of June, The (David Benedictus), 254
Fox, C. J., 101
Fox, Paul, 337
Fraser, Sir Hugh, 449
Fraser, Sir John, 109
Fraser, Sir Michael (*later* Lord Fraser of Kilmorack), 136, 286, 329, 330, 376, 442; & procedures for Selection of the Party Leader, 379, 381
Freeman, John, 411

Gaddafi, Colonel, 412
Gaitskell, Hugh, 171, 177; & 1959 Election, 512–513; & H's appointment to FO, 208; view of H, 208; death, 252, 254
Gale, George, & 1964 Election, 368–369

Gamelin, General, 98
Gayland, Jack, 424
General Elections: (1832), 130; (1906), 4, 130; (January 1910), 4; (December 1910), 4; (1924), 43; (1929), 41, 43, 44, 58; (1931), 40, 47, 48, 58; (1935), 57, 58; (1945), 46, 58, 124, 128–129, 135; (1950), 55–56, 133–135, 136, 137, 362; (1951), 139–140; (1955), 162, 305; (1959), 198, 200, 288, 305, 354, 365, 374, 512–513; (1964), 5, 259, 271, 277, 325, 332, 334–344, 353–355, 360–361, Ch 14 *passim*; (1966), 392–393; (1970), 401–403; (February 1974), 5, 435–437, 439; (October 1974), 444–445; (1979), 4, 456; (1992), 462
General Strike (1926), 37
George, Sir John, 327, 331, 332
George VI, King, 75, 126, 129, 253; coronation of, 66; receives NC after Munich Agreement, 84–85; & choice of PM in 1940, 101; visits NC at Heckfield, 104
Gibbs, Sir Humphrey, 351–352
Gibson, Sir John, 331
Gibson, J., 48, 57
Gilmour, Sir Ian (*later* Baron Gilmour), 457
Gilmour, Sir John, 40, 43, 45, 50
Gladstone, William Ewart, 3, 218; Morley's life of, 115
Glamis Castle, 36
Glasgow Woodside By-Election (1962), 254
Gleneagles, 226–227
Go-Between, The (L. P. Hartley), 16, 533
Godber, Frederick Joseph (*later* Baron Godber), 323, 406
Godesberg, NC's visit to, 77
Goering, Hermann, at Munich, 81
Goldman, Peter, 226, 286; career, 516
Goodfellow, Sylvia, 502
Goodhart, Professor A.L., 400
Goodhart, Sir Philip, 273
Goodman, Lord, & Rhodesia talks, 420, 422–425; death, 462
Gordon Walker, Patrick (*later* Baron Gordon-Walker), 97, 163, 395; & loss of Smethwick seat, 369–370; & loss of Leyton By-Election (1965), 384; & H's view of, 137
Goschen, George, Viscount, 3; & Goschen formula, 400
Gow, A. J., 28
Graham, Sir John, 407, 412
Great Reform Bill (1832), 1
Great Train Robbery (1963), 259
Greene, Sir Hugh Carleton, 370, 386
Greenhill, Sir Denis (*later* Baron Greenhill of Harrow), 406, 418; & view of H, 406–407; & expulsion of Russian spies, 416; retirement, 431; & H's 70th birthday, 432
Greenshields, Mrs (cook), 459
Greenwood, Arthur, 96
Grey, Sir Edward (later Viscount Grey of Falloden), 137, 438, 454
Grierson, John, & documentary films, 49
Grieve, C. M. (*also* Hugh MacDiarmid), & Kinross & West Perthshire, 365; & election petition of, 393
Griffiths, Sir Eldon, 329
Griffiths, Peter, 369–370
Grigg, Sir Edward, (*later* 1st Baron Altrincham), 59
Grimond, Jo (*later* Baron Grimond), 5, 337, 338–339, 361, 394; as Liberal leader, 162
Gromyko, Andrei, 14, 215; dines at Carlton Club, 8; & son's shooting ability, 221; relationship with H, 220–222; penchant for long-johns, 221; & Cuban Missile Crisis, 244, 246; & Test Ban Treaty, 250, 266, 267, 272, 301; & expulsion of Russian spies, 415–418; & H's 1973 visit to Moscow, 434
Gromyko, Mrs, 221
Groves, John, 327
Guinness, Sir Alec, 346
Gulf War, xv, 461
Gwynne Jones, Alun (*later* Baron Chalfont), 337

Haig, Douglas, Field Marshal (*later* Earl Haig), 5, 16, 402; visits Hirsel, 98
Hailes, Baron (*see* Patrick Buchan-Hepburn)
Hailsham, 1st Viscount (*formerly* Douglas McGarel Hogg), elevated to peerage, 63; death, 138
Hailsham, 2nd Viscount (*formerly* Hon. Quintin Hogg, *later* Quintin Hogg, *later* Baron Hailsham of Saint Marylebone), xvi, 102, 138, 199, 203, 211, 224, 227, 259, 260, 261; & Test Ban Treaty, 263–265, 267–268; & 1963 leadership contest, 272, 280, 282, 283, 284, 287, 290, 293, 297, 298, 300, 301, 302, 303, 304, 305, 306, 307, 308, 309, 310, 314, 381, 460–461; & daughter Kate, 286; & H's Cabinet, 321–323; & return to H of C, 340; as Shadow Home Affairs Spokesman, 393; & *A Sparrow's Flight*, 283
Halifax, Viscount, *later* 1st Earl of (1944), 2, 4, 204, 406; & visit to Hitler, 72; as Foreign Secretary, 73, 75, 77, 80, 94, 96, 98; as Ambassador to Washington, 111
Hamilton, Duke of, 15
Hammarskjöld, Dag, 216, 217, 219; & Suez, 175; death of, 217
Hankey, Sir Maurice (*later* Baron Hankey), 70
Hartley, Grizel, 23
Hansard, 51, 114
Hardy, Thomas, 231
Hardy Spicer controversy, 366–367
Hare, 1st Viscount (*see* John Blakenham)
Harlech, Baron (see Sir David Orsmby-Gore)
Harriman, Averell, 239, 267; & Test Ban Treaty, 263–265; & view of Lord Hailsham, 267
Harris, Kenneth, 366; & 'matchsticks' interview, 257, 288; & '14th Mr Wilson' interview, 323
Harris, Robert, makes film on NC, 453
Harrogate Speech (1970), 412–413
Harrow School, 24, 26, 28
Hart, Judith (*later* Baroness Hart of South Lanark), 130, 436
Hartington, Lady, 263
Hartwell, Baron, 343
Harvey, Sir Oliver (*later* Baron Harvey of Tasburgh), 72
Haselrig, Governor of Lanark, 48
Head, Antony (*later* 1st Viscount Head of Throope), 175
Headlam, G. W. ('Tuppy'), 27
Heath, Sir Edward, xvi, 4, 90, 203, 257, 259, 327, 362, 366, 378, 460; as Lord Privy Seal, 73, 207, 209, 213; as Chief Whip, 171, 189, 200; as Minister of Labour, 201; relationship with H, 209, 404; & Cuban Missile Crisis, 245; & Test Ban Treaty, 265–266; & 1963 leadership contest, 283, 286, 290, 293, 300, 301, 303, 305–306, 307, 310; as Trade Secretary, 322; & RPM, 355–358; & 1965 leadership contest, 386, 390–391; as Conservative leader, 395, 400–401; & Declaration of Perth (1968), 399; plot to oust as leader, 402–403; & victory in 1970 Election, 70, 403; as PM, 404–406, 409–411, 414, 419–420, 431–437; as Leader of the

Opposition, 441–445, 446; & 1975 rule changes for selecting Party leader, 6, 382–383, 448–449; visits China, 444; as Balliol man, 391; character of, 391
Heathcoat Amory, Derick (*later* 1st Viscount Amory), 3; & Suez Crisis, 181; as C of E, 201; effects of retirement of, 202, 205, 210–211
Heathcoat Amory, Richard, 31
Hegel, G. W. F., 320
Helsby, Sir Laurence, 336
Henderson, Arthur, 47, 182
Henderson, Dr. John (H's doctor), 293, 302
Henderson, Sir Nevile, 96
Henderson, Sir Nicholas, 318, 408
Hennessy, Professor Peter, 301
Henry VIII, King, 12
Herter, Christian, 220
Heseltine, Michael, 4, 406; challenges Mrs Thatcher for Party leadership, 6, 447
Heston Aiport, 80, 84, 166
Highlands and Islands Panel, 144, 145, 146–148
Hill, Herbert, 367
Hill, Kathleen, 104
Hillary, Sir Edmund, 165
Hirsel, The (H family home and estate), xviii, 10, 13, 16, 21, 34, 35, 36, 64, 117, 119, 140, 214, 252, 316, 363, 376, 403, 406, 445, 457, 461–462; NC's visit to (1938), 87–89; life at, 459–460
Hirst, George, 28
Hoare, Sir Samuel (*later* 1st Viscount Templewood), 51, 59–60, 100, 129
Hobden, Dennis, 370
Hobson, Sir John, 457
Hogg, Hon. Douglas, 256; & Christ Church, 324
Holland, Sir Sidney, 165, 178
Hollis, Sir Roger, 457
Holloway, Bishop Richard, officiates at H's funeral, 463–464
HOME FAMILY: origins 10–11; early history of, 12–16
Home, Sir Alexander, 11
Home, Sir Alexander (1st Lord), 11
Home, Sir Alexander (2nd Lord), 11
Home, Sir Alexander (3rd Lord), 11, 12
Home, William, 11, 12
Home, George (4th Lord), 12
Home, Alexander (5th Lord), 12, 13
Home, Alexander (6th Lord and 1st Earl of), 12
Home, Mary (1st Countess of), 12
Home, James (2nd Earl of), 10, 15
Home, 2nd Countess of, 35
Home, James (3rd Earl of), 10, 15; & family of, 15
Home, Jean (3rd Countess of), 10
Home, Sir John, 11
Home, Sir Thomas, 11
Home, Alexander, 4th Earl of, 15
Home, James, 5th Earl of, 15
Home, Charles, 6th Earl of, 15
Home, Alexander, 7th Earl of, 15
Home, Alexander, 8th Earl of, 15
Home, Alexander, 9th Earl of, 15
Home, Alexander, 10th Earl of, 15
Home, Elizabeth, 10th Countess, 15
Home, Cospatrick Alexander, 11th Earl of, 15–16
Home, Lucy Elizabeth, 11th Countess of, 15
Home, Charles Alexander, 12th Earl of (H's grandfather), 16, 34; family of, 17
Home, Charles, 13th Earl of ('the Unlucky Earl') (H's father), 1, 15, 19, 21, 105, 117, 126, 130, 146, 316; at Gallipoli, 22; as Chairman of British Linen Bank, 35; & NC's visit to the Hirsel, 88; death of, 37, 139
Home, Lilian, 13th Countess of (H's mother), 1, 17, 119, 140; family of, 17–18; thought RAB deserved Premiership, 316; death of, 395
Home, Alexander Frederick, 14th Earl of (*see* Sir Alexander Frederick Douglas-Home)
Home, Elizabeth, 14th Countess of (*see* Lady Douglas-Home)
Hoover, Herbert, Jr., 173
Hore-Belisha, Leslie (*later* Baron Hore-Belisha), 69
Horne, Alistair, xvi, 264, 307; & HM's role in 1963 leadership contest, 278
Howard, Anthony, xv, 129, 463; sees H as future candidate for Premiership, 260, 287, 289; & analysis of 1963 leadership context, 287, 288
Howard, Greville, 388
Howarth, Alan, 463
Howe, Sir Geoffrey (*later* Baron Howe), 406, 449
Howman, Jack, 423
Hoyer Millar, Sir Frederick (*later* 1st Baron Inchyra), 206, 213
Huddersfield, H visits Harold Wilson's home town, 359
Hudson Miles, 330, 420, 427, 434, 452; letter on Lady Home's death, 460
Huggins, Godfrey (*later* 1st Viscount Malvern), 196
Hull By-Election (1966), 393
Hume Castle, 10
Hunt, Sir David, 435
Huntly, Earl of, 11–12
Hurd, Douglas, xv, 213, 288, 409; on disadvantage of being old Etonian in 1990 leadership contest, 4; & Test Ban Treaty (1963), 265–266
Hussein, King of Jordan, 220
Hussein, Saddam, H suspects of wearing Eton Ramblers' tie, 462
Huxley, Aldous, portrait of Dr Alington in *Antic Hay*, 26

Import Duties Bill (1932), 58, 64
India Bill (1935), 51
Ippolitov, Ivan 416
Iran, Shah of, 411
Ironside, Sir Edmund (*later* Baron Ironside), 104
Irvine, Robert, 45
Ivanov, Captain Yevgeny, 238
I Zingari, 28, 395, 463

James III, King of Scotland, 12
James V, King of Scotland, 141
James VI, King of Scotland, *later* James I, King of England, 12, 256
James, David, & loss of Brighton Kemptown (1964), 370
James, Henry, 327
Jay, Douglas (*later* Baron Jay of Battersea), 394
Jellicoe, 2nd Earl of, 323
Jenkins, Roy (*later* Baron Jenkins of Hillhead), 116, 130
Jinnah, Mahomed Ali, H visits tomb of, 167
John XXIII, Pope, 254
Johnson, President Lyndon Baines, 317, 363, 431; H's first meetings with, 338–339; view of H, 340; & February 1964 talks, 344, 346, 347–350
Johnson, Dr Samuel, xvii, 126
Johnston, Brian, 61, 80, 461

Jones, Christopher, 453
Jones, Dr Thomas, 326
Joseph, Sir Keith (*later* Baron Joseph of Portsoken), 286, 300, 305, 406
Joyce, James, 116
Junior Imperial League, 42, 94

Kasavubu, President, 216
Kaunda, Kenneth, 195, 197
Kennedy, Mrs Jacqueline, 263, 339
Kennedy, President John Fitzgerald, 213, 226, 227, 228, 254, 301, 317, 349, 431; elected President, 211, 223; H's view of, 229; & Cuban Missile Crisis (1962), 231–236, 238–240, 242–246, 248–249, 251–252; visits Birch Grove, 263–264; & assassination of, 255, 336–337; funeral of, 338–339
Kennedy, John F., Jr., 339
Kennedy, Robert, 415; & Cuban Missile Crisis, 235; visits London (1964), 346; H's admiration for, 340
Kennedy, Mrs Robert, 346
Kent, Duke of (1902–1942), 78
Kenyatta, Jomo, 195, 457
Ker, Nichola (2nd wife of 2nd Lord Home), 11
Kerr, Sir John, 10
Kerr, Philip, (*later* 11th Marquess of Lothian), 32
Keyes, Admiral Sir Roger (*later* Baron Keyes), 99, 100, 101
Keynes, J. M. (*later* Baron Keynes), 44, 107
KGB, 415, 416, 417
Khaled, Leila, 414
Khama, Seretse, 190–191
Khama, Tshekedi, 191
Khrushchev, Nikita, 205, 218–219, 220, 226, 227, 228, 229, 350; & visit to Britain (1956), 172; & meeting with H at United Nations (1960), 222–223; & shoe-banging incident, 368; & Cuban Missile Crisis, 234–236, 238, 240, 242, 244–247, 249, 255; & Test Ban Treaty, 263, 265–266; & fall of, 372, 375
Killick, Sir John, 338, 417
Killick, Lady, 417
Kilmuir, 1st Earl of (*formerly* Sir David Maxwell Fyfe), 158, 255, 259, 260, 319; & 1948 Conservative Party organisational reforms, 135, 199; & Suez crisis, 183; & 1957 leadership contest, 188–189; & controversy over memoirs, 341–343
King, Professor Anthony, 329, 358
King, Cecil, 394
King-Lewis, Dr Lionel, 268, 276
Kinnock, Neil, 406
Kinross and West Perthshire By-Election (1938), 89–93, 106
Kinross and West Perthshire By-Election (1963), 3, 261, 271, 282, 297, 330–335
Kipling, Rudyard, 20, 238
Kirkpatrick, Sir Ivone, 212
Kirkwood, David, 39
Kissinger, Dr Henry, 411, 412, 431
Korean War, 138
Kotelawala, Sir John, 166
Kudashkin, F. D., 415
Kuznetsov, Vasily, 246
Kyle, Keith, & *Suez*, 175

Labour Party, 39, 40, 43, 95, 136, 273, 318, 439, 445, 463; & early growth of, 19; & 1931 Election, 47, 48; & 1935 Election, 58; & 1945 Election; & Suez Crisis, 183
Labour, Ministry of, 58–59
Lacey, Robert, 453
Laithwaite, Sir Gilbert, 163, 164; & character of, 160; as defender of CRO interests, 194
Lambton, Lady Lilian (H's mother, *see* Home, 13th Countess of)
Lanark, 37–38, 42, 46, 47, 48–49, 52, 54, 56–57, 58, 75–77, 130, 132, 331
Lanark Constituency organisation, 61, 118, 128–129, 130, 136, 139
Lanarkshire Yeomanry, 37, 108, 116
Lancaster, Sir Osbert, 436
Lansdowne, 8th Marquess of, 208
Laos, 223–224, 229, 230, 248, 255, 418
Lardner-Burke, Desmond, 423
Larwood, Harold, H faces bowling of, 462
Lascelles, Sir Alan, 150
Lauder, Harry, 122, 454
Lane, Sir David, 410
Law, Andrew Bonar, 4, 188, 325, 390; & 1911 leadership contest, 271
Lawrence, D. H., 71
Lawson, Nigel (*later* Baron Lawson of Blaby), 329, 330, 334, 363, 463
Leach, Donald, 402
League of Nations, 16
Leahy, Sir John, 407
Leburn, Gilmour, 330; & death of, 261
Leese, Sir Oliver, 395
Legge-Bourke, Sir Harry, 293
Leicester North By-Election (1962), 254
Le Quesne, Sir Martin, 423
Lennox-Boyd, Sir Alan (*later* 1st Viscount Boyd of Merton), 147, 151, 162, 174, 196, 199, 300, 455; on pre-war backbenchers, 50; & relations with H, 158, 198; & Hola Camp, 197; & 1959 Election, 200
Leopold, King, 101
Levin, Bernard, 386
Lewin, Ronald, 418
Lewis, Geoffrey, xvi
Lewis, Tony, 294
Leyland Bus controversy, 347–350, 409; & genesis of, 246
Leyton By-Election (1965), 384, 386
Liberal Party, 5, 38–39, 43, 50, 127, 199, 439, 445; & unemployment, 44; & 1931 Election, 47, 48; bed at Chatsworth could accommodate entire Parliamentary party, 340
Lindemann, Professor Frederick ('The Prof', *later* 1st Viscount Cherwell), 38
Lindsay, A. D. (*later* Baron Lindsay of Birker), 90
Lintott, Sir Henry, 174, 347–348
Llewelyn Davies, Nico, 29
Lloyd George, David (later 1st Earl Lloyd-George of Dwyfor), 2, 4, 5, 30, 38, 50, 120; & 1929 Election, 44; & 1931 Election, 47; & Norwegian Debate, 101; as author, 116
Lloyd, Geoffrey (*later* Baron Geoffrey-Lloyd), 286, 314; & 1964 Election, 368
Lloyd, John Selwyn Brooke (*later* Baron Selwyn-Lloyd of the Wirral), xvi, 170, 203, 209, 212, 255, 262, 268, 269, 386, 387, 392, 393, 401, 443; H's view of, 137; as Defence Secretary, 155, 156, 157, 162, 168; as Foreign Secretary, 171, 172, 175–177, 182, 183, 185, 186, 194,

249; & Suez book, 185; moves to Treasury, 205–207; as C of E, 253; & 1963 leadership contest, 270, 291, 294, 300, 304–305, 312, 314, 323, 336, 341, 344, 355; & RPM, 357; & 1964 Election, 367; & 1965 leadership contest, 387, 390; death, 455; H gives address at funeral of, 455
Loginov, Mr, 243, 250
London Gazette, 331
Long, Walter (*later* 1st Viscount Long of Wraxall), 271
Lothian, 12th Marquess of, 185, 406
Lovat, 17th Baron, 127
Ludgrove School, 20–23, 28, 163
Lumumba, Patrice, 216
Luton By-Election (1963), 334
Lyalia, Oleg, 415
Lyttelton, 4th Lord, 26
Lyttelton, George, 26
Lyttelton, Oliver (*later* 1st Viscount Chandos), 189, 199; & low opinion of CRO staff, 159–160
Lyubimov, Colonel Mikhail, 406

Macbeth, 12
MacDiarmid, Hugh (*see* C. M. Grieve)
MacDonald, Malcolm, 161, 167
MacDonald, Ramsay, 50, 63, 93; & 1931 Election, 47
McDonnell, John, 407–408, 412
McEwen, Bridget, Lady, 87
McEwen, Sir John, 87
McGovern, James, 39, 51
MacGregor, John, 329, 330
McKenzie, Robert, 287, 297, 324; & assessment of Iain Macleod, 270, 345
Maclay, John (*later* 1st Viscount Muirshiel), 144, 206
Maclean, Donald, 172
Maclean, Sir Fitzroy, 333
MacLehose, Sir Murray (*later* Baron MacLehose of Beoch), 435
Macleod, Dame Flora, 148
Macleod, Eve (*later* Baroness Macleod of Borve), 405
Macleod, Iain, xviii, 169, 202, 203, 259, 318, 329, 331, 378, 401; relationship with H, 169–170, 199; biography of NC, 74, 225–226; as Minister of Labour, 170, 198, 200; as Colonial Secretary, 170, 198; as Leader of H of C, 225; & attack by Lord Salisbury, 225; & 1963 leadership contest, 277, 282, 283, 286, 301, 303, 305, 307, 311, 312, 384; refuses to serve in H's Cabinet, 322; & *Spectator* article, 8, 343–344, 381; & new procedures for selecting the Party leader, 381; & 1965 leadership context, 390; as C of E, 405; & death of, 405; effect of death on Heath's administration, 405
Macmillan, Lady Dorothy, 248, 279, 517
Macmillan, Harold (*later* 1st Earl of Stockton), xvi, xviii, 3, 4, 5, 7, 8, 50, 102, 116, 191, 213, 222, 223, 254, 261, 263, 318, 320, 325–327, 328, 329, 331, 340, 376, 391, 429, 452; as Chancellor of Oxford University, 32, 207; sees 1931 intake of Conservative MPs as 'temporary gentlemen', 50; & first meetings with H, 56; & respect for Lady Douglas-Home, 62; exaggerated reputation for unflappability, 70, 353; & Oxford By-Election (1938), 90; as Foreign Secretary, 156, 168; welcomes H's appointment to CRO, 157, 169; visits H at Douglas, 169, 203, 248, 250; & relations with AE, 170–171; & Suez Crisis, 175, 181; & 1957 leadership contest, 184, 188–189; & appointment as PM, 189; & resignation of Lord Salisbury, 191–192; & support for H at CRO, 192–193; & 'Winds of Change' speech, 197, 201; & Central African Federation, 196–198; & 1958 Steering Committee, 198–199; & 1959 Election, 200; appoints H Foreign Secretary, 203–204, 205–206, 207–208; & relations with H, 213, 230–231, 250, 255; & appointment of Ormsby-Gore to Washington Embassy, 204; refers to Dean Rusk as 'the biscuit man', 210; & 1960 Paris summit, 210; & relations with RAB, 211; at UN (1960), 218–220; & Khrushchev's shoe-banging, 219, 368; at Gleneagles during Berlin crisis, 226–227; & Bermuda Conference (1961), 228; & view of de Gaulle, 228; & Cuban Missile Crisis (1962), 230, Ch. 10 *passim*; & Nassau Conference (1962), 250–252; & Rambouillet meeting, 250; on prospects for 1963, 252; & 'never had it so good', 254; & Eton College, 254, 344; & Europe, 258; & Portland Spy Ring, 258; & Profumo Affair (1963), 259, 291; & possible retirement, 259, 265, 267, 272–274; & JFK visit to Birch Grove, 263–264; sends Stilton cheese to Khrushchev, 265; & illness, 268–269, 276; & 1963 leadership contest, 272–313; & decision to retire, 278, 281, 462; & memorandum for the Queen, 301–302, 311–312; & advice to H on 1964 Election date, 325, 343, 353–354; & Night of the Long Knives (1962), 341; & Randolph Churchill's *The Fight for the Tory Leadership*, 343–344; & advice to H over Macleod's *Spectator* article, 344; & JFK, 349, 431; & Leyland bus crisis, 349; as Balliol man, 391; advises H on South African arms controversy (1970), 409; & Rhodesia, 420; & advice to H on writing memoirs, 392, 452; in House of Lords, 459; memorial service, 456; H's address at, Appendix II.; & view of H, 8, 194, 213, 231, 301–302, 311–312
Macmillan, Maurice, 268, 286, 449
McNally, Tom, 330, 407
McNeill, D. A., 439–440
Mabane, Sir William, 127
Magdalen College, Oxford, 57
Maitland, Patrick, Master of Lauderdale, as H's successor in Lanark constituency, 139, 162
Maitland-Gardiner, David, 331
Major, John, 4, 288, 382, 446
Makarios, Archbishop, 193, 195, 350
Makarova, Natalie, 417
Makins, Roger (*later* 1st Baron Sherfield), 30–32, 99, 100; as Ambassador in Washington, 169, 173
Malkin, W., 80
Mansfield, Sir Philip, 423, 427
Mao, Chairman, 444
Marchant, Sir Herbert, & Cuban Missile Crisis (1962), 233, 236–237, 244
Margaret, H.R.H., Princess, Countess of Snowdon, 339
Margesson, David (*later* 1st Viscount Margesson), 2, 51, 64, 78, 99
Marjoribanks, Charles, 9, 10
Marlborough House, 158, 353
Marples, Ernest, (*later* Baron Marples), 307
Marr, Andrew, 38
Marten, Miss, & unpalatable pudding, 25
Mary, Queen of Scots, 12, 14, 370
Mary, Queen, Consort of King George V, xviii, 78, 158
Marylebone By-Election (1963), 340
Marylebone Cricket Club, 395–399
Marx, Karl, & *Das Kapital*, 115

Masarik, Dr Hubert, 82
Massie, Alan, 106
Masterman, Sir John, 30, 418; & view of H, 31; consulted by H, 322; & RPM, 356; & 1964 Election; H allows memoirs to be published, 448
Mastny, Dr. Voytech, 82
Maudling, Reginald, 259, 262, 265, 268, 316, 353, 362, 378, 402, 404–406, 417–418, 448; as President of Board of Trade, 201; & 1963 leadership contest, 273, 280–281, 283, 286, 290, 295, 297, 301, 303, 306, 307–309, 311–312, 314; H regards as vital buttress for his administration, 314; & 1964 Budget, 355; & RPM, 356; & 1964 Election, 366; & 1965 leadership contest, 386, 390–391, 393
Maugham, William Somerset, 116
Maxton, James, 39, 51; & friendship with H, 54
Melbourne, Lord, 116, 270, 271
Menon, Krishna, 167, 177, 179
Menzies, Sir Robert, 161, 165, 168, 255; & H's view of, 165, 178; & 'robustness', 168; & Suez Crisis (1956), 175, 177, 203
Messina Conference (1955), 154, 170
Meyer, Sir Anthony, & challenge for Conservative leadership (1989), 6
Middlesborough West By-Election (1962), 254
Mikoyan, Anastas, 339
Mill, John Stuart, 114
Millar, Duncan, 330
Milne, Sir David, 54, 144
Ministry of Labour, 57
Mitchell, Sir Derek, 328
Mitchell, Stephen, 46
Mitchison, Naomi, 147
Mobutu, Joseph, 216
Monckton Commission (1960), 197, 202, 211
Monckton, Sir Walter, (*later* 1st Viscount Monckton of Brenchley), 203; as Minister of Defence, 171; & misquiet over Suez, 179–182
Monk, General, 9
Monnet, Jean, 443; & European ideal, 159
Monograph of the Pittidae (John Gould), Cabinet's 90th birthday present to H., 462
Montgomery, Anthea, 459
Moore, Dudley, 253
Morgan, Charles, 116
Morris, James (*later* Jan Morris), 18
Morris, 'Old' Tom, 56
Morrison, Hon. Sir Charles, 359
Morrison, Herbert (*later* Baron Morrison of Lambeth), 102, 149, 454; & H's view of, 136
Morrison, Sir John (*later* 1st Baron Margadale of Islay), 189, 386; & 1963 leadership contest, 273, 275, 283, 291, 293
Moscow, H's visit to (1973), 474
Mosley, Sir Oswald, 39
Mott-Radclyffe, Sir Charles, 280, 293
Mountbatten, Louis, Earl Mountbatten of Burma, 414; & Suez, 179
Mugabe, Robert, 424–425, 457
Muirhead, Colonel Anthony, 57, 58, 125
Munich Agreement (1938), 10, 65, 77, 81–83, 86, 87, 89, 90, 91–92, 93, 105, 106, 160, 234, 453
Murray, Duncan, 437
Murrie, Sir William ('Stuart'), 54
Mussolini, Benito, 66, 70, 74, 78, 82, 86, 93, 94, 95; & H's view of, 94
Muzorewa, Bishop Abel, 424–425, 457
Mynors, Sir Roger (H's brother-in-law), 126, 130, 162

Nassau Conference (1962), 248, 250, 251, 337
Nash, Sir Walter, 203
Nasser, President Gamal Abdel, 176, 177, 184, 219, 255; & nationalisation of the Suez Canal, 175; death & funeral, 412–413
Nehru, Pandit Motilal, 159, 167, 168, 185, 203, 255; & funeral of, 353
New Club, Edinburgh, 35, 143, 148
New College, Oxford, 162
New English Review, The, 131
'New Lanark', 49
New Society, 329
New York Times, 294
Nicholas, H. G., 362
Nicolson, Sir Harold, 79, 96, 124
Nicolson, Nigel, xvii
Nixon, President Richard Milhaus, 411–412, 430–431
Nkomo, Joshima, 424–425
Nkrumah, Dr Kwame, 193, 195, 220
Noble, Commander Allan, 307
No End of a Lesson, 175
Norfolk, Bernard Marmaduke, FitzAlan-Howard, 16th Duke of, & H's view of, 150; & Coronation, 150; & Kennedy assassination, 336–337; & MCC furore, 396
Norrie, Lord, 165
North Berwick, 5, 34, 76, 118
Norton, Professor Philip, 428
Norwegian Debate (May 1940), 99–101
Not so Much a Programme, More a Way of Life, 386
Nuffield College, Oxford, 6, 358
Nutting, Sir Anthony, 175, 186, 362; & resignation, 183; & *No End of a Lesson*, 175
Nyerere, President Julius, 409

Obote, President Milton, 409
Observer, 39, 288, 324, 345
Oedipus Rex, Harold Wilson favours for election night television, 370–371
Ogmore, 1st Baron, 395
'Old Gang', The, 73; Sir John Simon as key figure in, 76
Old St Bride's Church, Douglas, 13–14
Olav V, King of Norway, birth of, 19; sharer of H's birthday, 1903, 19; as Knight of the Thistle, 256
Oliver, F. S., & *The Endless Adventure*, 438
O'Neill, Captain Terence (*later* Baron O'Neill of the Maine), 336
Oppenheimer, Harry, 420
Oppidan, The (Sir Shane Leslie), 254
Orchard, E. E., 234
Ormsby-Gore, Sir David (*later* 5th Baron Harlech), 204, 265, 267, 316–317, 339, 340, 346, 369, 411; as Ambassador to Washington, 204, 227; & Cuban Missile Crisis (1962), 233–234, 244–245, 247; & Lord Hailsham's role in Test Ban Treaty talks, 267–268; & Lord Hailsham's candidacy for Premiership, 298–301; & Rhodesia, 426
Orpington By-Election (1962), 254, 516
Orwell, George (Eric Blair), 24–25, 27
Other Club, The, xv
Owen, Dr David (*later* Baron Owen), as Foreign Secretary, 455; consults H, 455

Owen, Robert, establishes 'New Lanark', 49
Oxford By-Election (1938), 89
Oxford University (*see* under individual colleges)

Palmerston, Lord, as Foreign Secretary, 438
Pandit, Mrs Vijaya Lakshmi, 176–177; assures H that airport kiss for Krishna Menon has no political implication, 177
Paris Peace Treaty (1919), 60
Parliament Bills (1911), 2, 18; (1949), 18
Parnell, Brian, 393
Parsons, Sir Anthony, 216, 433, 435
Parsons, Jane, & work at 10 Downing Street, 328
Peace of Berlin (1878), 86
Peacock, Elizabeth, 447
Pearce, Edward Holroyd, Baron, & Rhodesia, 423, 427–429; & Pearce Commission, 423, 427–429; & Pearce Report (1972), 428–429
Pearson, Sir Francis, as PPS to H, 327–328, 357
Pearson, Lady, 328
Pearson, Lester, 173, 178, 203, 348
Peel, Sir Robert, 47, 116
Peerage Act (1963), 3, 259, 260–262, 288, 290, 323
P'eng-fei, Chi, 431
Penkovsky, Col Oleg, 231, 250
Penn, Sir Arthur, 150; shoots at Douglas, 507
Peoples' Budget (1909), 2
Pepdie family, 11
Perth, 16th Earl of, 78
Perth, 17th Earl of, 157, 208, 225
Petrie, Sir Charles, 116
Peyton, John (*later* Baron Peyton of Yeovil), 449
Philby, Kim, 259
Philpott, Ellen, killed at Springhill, 114
Phouma, Prince Souvenne, 224
Pimlott, Professor Ben, xvi, xviii
Pineau, Christian, 175
Pinkie, Battle of (1547), 12
Pirandello, Luigi, 323
Pitt, William the Younger, 101, 112
Plowden Report (1961), 410
Polaris Missile, 229, 251, 335
Poole, Oliver (*later* 1st Baron Poole of Aldgate), 189, 261; & 1963 leadership contest, 275, 291–292, 305, 306, 307, 308, 309, 310, 329
Potsdam Conference (1945), 128
Powell, Anthony, 116
Powell, Enoch, xviii, 5, 259, 322, 323; & resignation (1958), 192; & 1963 leadership contest, 276–277, 300, 301, 311, 312, 313; & H's olive branch towards, 375, 378; & 1965 leadership contest, 390–391; thought of as possible leader in 1970, 402; reviews H's memoirs, 452
Primrose League, 42; H speaks at, 43
Prior, James (*later* Baron Prior of Bampton), 406, 449
Private Eye, 262, 373; described by Selwyn Lloyd as 'the working man's Erskine May', 262
Profumo, John, 204, 258, 259, 264, 287, 289, 291, 292, 326, 346, 388, 463; & resignation, 256, 267
Prosperity with Purpose, 365

'Q' Buttons, as dispensed by Randolph Churchill at Blackpool Conference, 286, 299; not favoured in White House, 317
Quayle, Vice-President Dan, H's view of as example of reluctance to follow conventional opinion, 497

Radcliffe, Cyril, 1st Viscount, 422
Raikes, Victor, 123
Raleigh Club, 32
Rambouillet Summit (1962), 248, 250
Ramsay, Lord James Huber (son of 16th Earl of Dalhousie), asks Sir Roy Welensky why he gave up driving a train for political career, 195
Ramsey, Dr Michael, (*later* Baron Ramsay of Caterbury), 207, 375
Rawlinson, Sir Peter (*later* Baron Rawlinson of Ewell), 423
Reading, 1st Marquess of, 50, 204
Redmayne, Sir Martin (*later* Baron Redmayne), 106, 361, 364, 384; & 1963 leadership contest, 275, 286, 289, 291, 294, 298, 300, 302–303, 306, 308, 309, 312, 327, 336, 343; & RPM, 357
Redwood, John, 446
Reece, Sir Gordon, 402
Rees-Mogg, Sir William (*later* Baron Rees-Mogg of Hinton Blewitt), 6, 286, 316; & 'Right Moment to Change', 387
Reid, James, 130
Reid, Malcolm, 328
Reilly, Sir Patrick, 213, 249, 408
Reilly, Lady, insulted by George Brown, 408
Reith, Sir John (*later* 1st Baron Reith), 67, 375
Representation of the People Act (1948), 135
Resale Price Maintenance, 346, 355–358
Rhineland, German occupation of (1936), 59
Rhodesia, 333, 351–353, 360, 364, 392, 397, 399, 411, 420–429, 436
Rhodes House, Oxford, 190
Rhodes James, Sir Robert, xvi; & Kilmuir's memoirs, 341, 343
Ribbentrop, Joachim von, 81, 94
Richardson, Sir John (*later* Baron Richardson of Lee), 268, 278; HM refers to as his 'caddy', 526
Rifkind, Malcolm, & H's 90th birthday celebrations, 462
Rippon, Sir Geoffrey (*later* Baron Rippon of Hexham), 144, 373, 393, 405, 419
Rizzio, David, 14
Robbins Report on Higher Education (1963), 326
Robens, Alfred, Baron Robens of Woldingham, 394
Robert the Bruce, King of Scotland, 13
Roberts, Andrew, H helps over biography of Lord Halifax, 453
Roberts, Sir Frank, & Cuban Missile Crisis (1962), 233–236, 238, 244, 246
Robertson, Ian, 143, 144
Robertson, John, as H's agent in Kinross and West Perthshire, 365–366; & Kinross and West Perthshire By-Election (1963), 331, 333
Robertson, Norman, & Suez, 178–179
Robertson, Una, 331
Robins, Commander, & flight to Munich, 80
Robinson, Peter, on H's tribute to JFK, 337, 529–530
Robson, Edna (*later* Mrs Berresford), & memories of war-time Springhill, 114
Rochdale By-Election (1958), 199
Rogers, William, 431
Roosevelt, President Franklin, D., 123, 264, 338; & Yalta, 125
Rose, Kenneth, 150, 452

Rosebery, Archibald Primrose, 5th Earl of, 32, 404, 454
Ross, William (*later* Baron Ross of Marnock), 142
Rowse, A. L., 30
Roxburgh, Selkirk and Peebles By-Election (1965), & effect of H's leadership, 384–385
Royle, Sir Anthony (*later* Baron Fanshawe of Richmond), 406, 431
Rucker, Arthur, 70
Runcie, Most Rev. and Rt. Hon. Robert, (*later* Baron Runcie of St Albans), H admires St Paul's Cathedral address of on Falklands, 458
Runciman, Sir Walter (*later* 1st Viscount Runciman of Doxford), & mission to Prague, 74
Rusk, Dean, 210, 215, 227, 230, 232, 272, 289, 301, 338, 349; nicknamed 'the biscuit man' by HM, 210; tribute to H, 210; & Cuban Missile Crisis (1962), 245, 247, 249; & Nuclear Test Ban Treaty (1963), 250, 263, 264, 265–266
Rushton, William, 297, 330
Russell, Lord John, as PM, 313
Russell, Sir John, as Ambassador to Spain, 414
Rycroft, Sir Benjamin, 302

Safeguarding of Industry Act (1921), 52
St. Aldwyn, 2nd Earl of, 275, 304, 306, 307, 308
St Giles Cathedral, Edinburgh, 150–151; H's memorial service at, 463
St Mary & All Souls, Coldstream, as H family church, 20; H's funeral at, 463–464
Salisbury, Robert Gascoyne-Cecil, 3rd Marquess of, 1, 3, 438
Salisbury, Robert Arthur Gascoyne-Cecil ('Bobbety'), 5th Marquess of, *formerly* Viscount Cranborne, 203, 207, 288, 291, 300; as Leader of Lords, 162; & Suez Crisis (1956), 176, 181, 183; & 1957 leadership contest, 188–189; as Commonwealth Secretary, 190; & resignation (1957), 191–192; & attack on Iain Macleod as 'too clever by half', 225
Salote, Queen of Tonga, 150, 353
Samuel, Sir Herbert (*later* 1st Viscount Samuel of Mount Carmel and Toxteth), 38, 47, 50; & Suez, 177; Lloyd George's opinion of, 495
Samuel, Ian, 213
Sandys, Duncan (*later* Baron Duncan-Sandys), 203, 211; & Suez Crisis (1956), 180; as Commonwealth Secretary, 202; favours H for Premiership, 300, 305, 307
San Francisco Conference (1945), 158, 414
Savoy Hotel, stocks hampers for NC's flight to Munich, 80
Scarborough, 11th Earl of, accompanies Queen to performance of *Beyond the Fringe*, 262
Schumann, Maurice, 414
Scotsman, The, 113, 462
Scott, Hardiman, 401
Scott, Sir Walter, 9, 11, 12, 13, 49, 256, 462; H's liking for, 462
Scott, Lord William Montagu Douglas, H's brother-in-law, 68
Scottish Control of Scottish Affairs (1949), H's joint authorship of, 140, 143
Scottish Daily Express, 88
Scottish devolution, 399–401, 441–442, 455–456
Scottish Nationalism, 39, 40, 126, 133, 142–143, 150–151, 440–462
Scottish Office, 206, 256, 286; in 1930s, 53–57; Ch 6 *passim*
Scottish Unionism, 34, 40, 45, 46, 90, 130, 131, 330, 400; & blight of 'Lairdism', 56
Second World War, 58, 96–97, 108–128
Seely, Colonel John (*later* Baron Mottistone), 332
Seldon, Dr Anthony, & H's career, xvi
Selkirk, 10th Earl of, 157
Selsdon Park Meeting (1970), 401
Sèvres, Protocol of (1956), 182
Shakespeare, William, 12
Sharpeville Massacre (1960), 202
Shepherd, Dame Margaret, & 1963 leadership contest, 275, 285, 306, 307
Sheppard, Rt. Rev. David, 398
Shooting Party, The (Isabel Colegate), 16
Shrimpton, Daphne, 330, 338
Shuckburgh, Sir Evelyn, 213; & Cuban Missile Crisis (1962), 245
Silk, Dennis, 398
Silkin, 1st Baron, 182
Simon, Sir John (*later* 1st Viscount Simon of Stackpole Elidor), 32, 78–79, 80, 94, 100, 132; & speech at Lanark (1938), 75–76; as Foreign Secretary, 50; as C of E, 69; & character of, 75–76
Simonstown Agreement (1954), 408–409
Simpson, Mrs Wallis (*later* Duchess of Windsor), 66
Sinclair, Sir Archibald (*later* 1st Viscount Thurso), 50, 53, 54, 55
Sithole, Rev. Ndabaningi, 424–425
Six Day War (1967), 412
Skelton, Noel, 40–42, 45, 50, 53, 54, 125, 128, 325; influence on H, 42; influence on AE, 41; character of, 40–41; invites H to be his PPS, 50; & death of, 57
Skene, Danus, 437
Skybolt Missile, 229, 250, 251
Smedley, Sir Harold, 160, 172, 184, 193; & diary of Commonwealth tour (1955), 164–168
Smith, Arnold, 353, 428
Smith, F. E. (*later* 1st Earl of Birkenhead), xv
Smith, G. O., 21, 22, 28
Smith, Ian (Prime Minister of Rhodesia), 333, 392, 421–422, 425; as PM of Rhodesia, 351–352, 364, 397; & view of H, 421–422
Smith, Ian, & Kinross and West Perthshire By-Election (1963), 334
Snadden, W. McNair, 91–93
Snadden, Lady McNair, 333
Snow, C. P., (*later* Baron Snow), H's admiration for novels of, 116
Soames, Sir Christopher (*later* Baron Soames), 304, 307, 319, 353, 390, 457; H offers reversion of Foreign Secretaryship to in event of Conservative victory (1964), 365
Soames, Lady Mary, 361, 385
Sorenson, Reginald (*later* Baron Sorenson), vacates Leyton seat for Patrick Gordon Walker, 384
Sorenson, Theodore, 339
Soskice, Sir Frank (*later* Baron Stow Hill), 241
South Africa, 163; leaves Commonwealth, 230, 352; & arms sales to (1970), 408–410
South Dorset By-Election (1962), 254
South Wales Evening Post, 346
Spectator, The, 41, 343; Iain Macleod's article in (1964), 8, 298, 344

Springhill, 19–21, 64, 88, 107, 120, 148, 164; H's childhood at, 19–21; father's wedding present to H, 62; wartime life at, 113–116
Stagnant Society, The (Michael Shanks), 253
Stalin, Joseph, & Yalta, 123–125
Stanley, Oliver, 51, 54
Stannage, Tom, 58
Stansgate, 1st Viscount, death of, 224, 288–289
Stansgate, 2nd Viscount (*see* Tony Benn)
Starzenski, Count, 119, 122
Steel, Sir David, 330, 384–385; & Lib–Lab pact, 455; surprised by informality of Hirsel, 459
Steele, Tom, 128, 129, 130, 133, 134; & 1950 election, 134–135
Steering Committee (1958–1959), H's membership of, 198–199
Steering Committee (1971), 435
Steptoe & Son, as threat to Labour vote if broadcast on 1964 election night, 370
Stevenson, Adlai, 232; & Cuban Missile Crisis (1962), 246
Stewart, Michael (*later* Baron Stewart of Fulham), 408
Stone of Scone, 142–143
Stonehouse, John, 356
Strang, Sir William (*later* 1st Baron Strang of Stonesfield), 80
Strauss, George (*later* Baron Strauss), 460
Strauss, Henry (*later* Baron Conesford), 124
Strutt, Sir Austin, 150
Stuart, James (*later* 1st Viscount Stuart of Findhorn), 55, 64, 67, 90, 123, 126, 127, 138, 140, 141, 169, 203, 272; & Kinross & West Perthshire By-Election (1938), 93; as Secretary of State for Scotland, 142–145, 149–151; & 1963 leadership contest, 306, 307
Suez Crisis (1956), 159, 168, 174–186, 239, 341–342, 411, 430; effects of, 184
Sunday Express, 206
Sunday Telegraph, 329
Sunningdale Talks (1973), 432
Sutherland, 5th Duke of, 95
Swanton, E. W., 395
Swinton, 1st Earl of (*formerly* Philip Lloyd-Greame, & Philip Cunliffe-Lister), 160, 163; & antipathy to Nehru, 159
Syers, Sir Cecil, 70, 166, 347; & Munich trip, 80, 166
Syers, Lady, 166

Talleyrand-Périgord, Charles, 160
Taylor, A. J. P., 124
Taylor, Sir Teddy, 441–442
Teesdale, J. C., 134
Telfer, Mr (gamekeeper), 36
Temple, W., 62
Tennant, Sir Charles, 34
Tennant, Kay (*see* Elliot, Baroness of Harwood)
Test Ban Treaty (1963), 261, 263–267, 272, 301, 339, 434; & effects of, 267
Test Oath (1682), 48
Thant, U., 348
Thatcher, Margaret (*later* Baroness Thatcher of Kesteven), 320, 406; & Community Charge, 55; & WSC's life of Lord Randolph Churchill, 115–116; & 1975 Conservative leadership contest, 449; as Leader of the Opposition (1975–1979), 449–451; & 1979 Election, 455–456; as PM, 457; challenged as Conservative leader (1989), 6, 383; & 1990 Conservative leadership contest, 383, 447; resigns as PM, xv, xvi, 4, 5; & Lady Home's death, 460–461; consults H over Foreign Affairs, 449–451; view of H, 463
That Was The Week That Was (TW3), 262, 330
Thistle, Order of, 8, 256
Thomas, Dylan, 346
Thomas, J. P. L. (*later* 1st Viscount Cilcennin), 162, 179, 180
Thomas, Peter, (*later* Baron Thomas of Gwydir), 283
Thorneycroft, Peter (*later* Baron Thorneycroft of Dunston), 203, 346, 387, 390; & resignation, 192; & Cuban Missile Crisis (1962), 240, 245; & Nassau Conference (1962), 251; & 1963 leadership contest, 286, 303
Times, The, 61, 104, 131, 162, 170, 276, 316, 345, 353, 459, 462, 463
Tito, President, 219
Todd, Hon. Sir Garfield, 196, 427
Todd, Judith, 427
Travellers' Club, 160
Trend, Sir Burke (*later* Baron Trend), 280, 347; & view of H as PM, 320, 324; as Cabinet Secretary, 324, 326; & Kilmuir's memoirs, 341–342
Trethowan, Sir Ian, 297, 337
Trevelyan, George Macaulay, 12
Trevelyan, Sir Humphrey (*later* Baron Trevelyan), 265
Trinity College, Cambridge, 385
Turner, J. M. W., 49
Tweedsmuir, Lady Priscilla (*later* Baroness Tweedsmuir of Belhelvie), 333

United Nations, 177, 182, 185, 214, 216, 217, 218, 223, 229, 237, 283, 288, 306, 348, 350; & H's 'double standards' speech, 218, 430

Valley of Fear, The (Sir Arthur Conan Doyle), 13
Vansittart, Sir Robert (*later* Baron Vansittart), 70
Varcoe, Jeremy, 423
Vassall Affair, 252, 258, 327
VE Day, 126
Verneuil, Battle of (1424), 11
Verwoerd, Dr H. F., 201, 352
Vicky (Victor Weisz), 257; & cartoon on 'donations', 366
Victoria, HM Queen, 313
Victoria Falls Conference (1963), 262, 273
Vorster, Dr. John, 397–398, 408

Walker, Professor Nigel, 144; unknown to Dame Flora Macleod, 148; & H's appointment to CRO, 153
Walker, Peter (*later* Baron Walker of Worcester), 359, 393, 406, 434; & Edward Heath's 1965 leadership campaign, 390
Wallace, William, 48
Walsh, James C., 44, 45
Ward, Dr Stephen, 238, 259
Walters, Sir Dennis, 286, 294
Warner, Sir Pelham ('Plum'), 35
Warsaw Pact, 230
Washington Post, 339
Waterloo, Battle of (1815), 26
Watson, Miss Edith, 74, 97, 288, 315, 376; predicts in 1939 that H will one day be PM, 2; prediction comes

true, 315; relegated to back room at 10 Downing Street (May 1940), 101–102; & character of, 70
Waugh, Evelyn, 116
Waverley, Viscount (*formerly* Sir John Anderson), 189
Weatherill, Bernard (*later* Baron Weatherill), 460
Welensky, Sir Roy, 160, 193, 195–197, 201–202, 203, 217, 457
Wellington, 1st Duke of, 26, 438
Westminster Abbey, 142–143, 150, 463
Westminster School, 30
Wheatley, John, & Housing Act (1924), 41
White, Sir Dick, 418
Whitelaw, William (*later* 1st Viscount Whitelaw of Penrith), 68, 106, 256, 288, 401–403, 405, 445, 448; & Kinross and West Perthshire By-Election (1963), 334; & 1975 Conservative leadership contest, 449
Whitley, Mrs Elizabeth, 402
Whitworth, Mrs Alice, 27, 36; rôle in H's engagement to Elizabeth Alington, 60–61
Whitworth, Aymer W., 23, 24, 25, 27, 36; & view of H, 25, 30; as godfather to Caroline Douglas-Home, 71
Wilford, Sir Michael, 213
Wilkes, John Vaughan (H's brother-in-law), 162
Williams, Marcia (*later* Baroness Falkender of West Haddon), 394
Williams-Wynne, Jane (H's daughter-in-law), *see* 15th Countess of Home
Williams, Ruth, 190
Wilmshurst, Michael, 213
Wilson, Sir Harold (*later* Baron Wilson of Rievaulx), 32, 257, 258, 310, 316, 319, 320, 321, 323, 324, 325, 328, 329, 330, 337, 340, 354, 361, 363, 365, 374, 386, 387, 388, 391, 393, 394, 401, 417, 431, 432, 455; & 1964 Election, 366–367, 369, 370, 371, 373; & offer of Mastership of Trinity to RAB, 385; & D Notices, 394; as PM, 162; & Rhodesia talks, 420–421; & 1970 Election, 401–402; as PM in February 1974, 437; as PM in October 1974, 445; & *The Governance of Britain*, 452; resigns as PM, 454; HM's view of, 252; & death, 462
Wilson, Sir Horace, 76, 77, 78, 100; as member of NC's Downing Street team, 69–70; influence diminishes in May 1940, 101–102
Wilson, Sister, 113
Winchester College, 162
Winterton, 6th Earl, 59
Wolfe Murray, Lady Diana (H's daughter), 464; birth of, 109
Wolfe Murray, Fiona (H's grand-daughter), 328; & christening of, 354
Wolfe Murray, Harry (H's great-grandson), 460
Wolfe Murray, James, (H's son-in-law), 256
Wolfe Murray, Rory, (H's grandson), 464
Wolsey, Cardinal, 207
Wood, Sir Kingsley, 54
Wood, Hon. Richard, 406; considered as possible Conservative leader, 448
Woodfield, Sir Philip, 280
Woolf, Virginia, 116
Woolton, Frederick Marquis, 1st Earl of, 203, 323; as Minister of Food, 102; urges H to be a candidate for the Premiership, 299–300
Worcester College, Oxford, 322, 367
Wordsworth, William, 20, 49
Worsley, Sir Marcus, 373
Worsthorne, Sir Peregrine, 345
Wort, Richard, 334
Wright, Matt, 28
Wright, Sir Oliver, 213, 328, 346, 348
Wright, Peter, & *Spycatcher*, 416
Wyndham, John (*later* 1st Baron Egremont and 6th Baron Leconfield), 328, 376

Yalta Agreement (1945), 119, 123–125; & H's speech against terms of, 123–124
YMCA (Conservative supporters of Eden), 73
Yom Kippur War (1973), 433–434; & effects on energy prices, 433–434
Young, Janet, Baroness Young of Farnworth, 451
Young, Kenneth, xvi
Young, Michael (*later* Baron Young of Dartington), 253
Young, Thomas, 270
Younger, 1st Viscount of Leckie, 331
Younger, George (*later* Baron Younger of Prestwick), 261, 384; & Kinross and West Perthshire By-Election (1963), 331–332; & 1964 Election, 362, 372

ZANC (Zambian African National Congress), 197
ZANU (Zimbabwe African National Union), 425, 457
ZAPU (Zimbabwe African People's Union), 425
Zeebrugge Raid (1918), 99
Ziegler, Philip, xvi
Zorin, Ambassador, 232
Zulueta, Sir Philip de, 307, 311, 338; & JFK's visit to Birch Grove (1963), 264

THE ARTIST'S HANDBOOK

Arcturus Publishing Ltd
26/27 Bickels Yard
151–153 Bermondsey Street
London SE1 3HA

Published in association with
foulsham
W. Foulsham & Co. Ltd,
The Publishing House, Bennetts Close, Cippenham,
Slough, Berkshire SL1 5AP, England

ISBN 0-572-02866-0

British Library Cataloguing-in-Publication Data: a catalogue record for this book is available from the British Library

Editor: Rebecca Panayiotou
Designer: Adam Renvoize
Illustrator: Alison Barratt
Cover Photography: Thomas Mitchell and James Ellerker

Printed in Poland

THE ARTIST'S HANDBOOK

A complete professional guide to materials and techniques

Pip Seymour

ARCTURUS

Contents

INTRODUCTION 10

PIGMENTS 15

Pigments: An Introduction 15
Key to Pigment Information 17
Pigment Types 22
Particle Size of Pigments 24
Artists' Pigments 25
Permanence of Artists' Pigments 28
Pigment Tables 31
Miscellaneous Pigments 180

DRAWING MATERIALS 191

Dry Drawing Tools 192
Wet Drawing Tools 200

EGG TEMPERA PAINTING 203

Supports for Panel Painting with Egg Tempera 203
Natural Wood 204
Preparation of the Panel, Prior to Applying Gesso Ground 205
Application of the Painting Ground 206
Glue 207
Preparing the Panel with Gesso 211
Preparation of Pigments for Egg Tempera Painting 214
Egg Yolk as a Binder 215
Palette for Egg Tempera Painting 219
Procedure for Painting 224
Tempera and Oil Paint, Egg-Oil Emulsions 226
Varnishes for Tempera Paintings 227
Tempera and Gilding 229

OIL PAINTING 233

Supports for Oil Painting 233
Sizing and Priming Supports for Oil Painting 248

Properties of Oil Paints 258
Hand-Made Oil Colour 273
Manufactured Oil Colour 289
Building an Oil Painting 294
Drying Rates of Oil Colours 300
Oil Painting Whites 304
The Oil Painting Palette Explained 307
Oil Paint Mediums 309
Picture Varnishes 326
Solvents for Oil Painting 331
Clean-Up of Oil Paint, Palette and Brushes 333

WATERCOLOUR AND GOUACHE PAINTING **335**
Watercolour 335
Historical Background 335
Properties of Watercolour 337
Commercially Manufactured Watercolours 342
Hand-Prepared Watercolours 343
Lightfastness and Permanence 346
Supports for Watercolour Painting 346
Papermaking 347
Stretching Watercolour Paper 350
Care and Storage of Watercolours 352
Auxiliary Materials 353
Painting Additives 354
Combining Watercolour and Other Media 355
Gouache 356
Artists' Gouache and Designers' Gouache 357
Hand-Made Gouache Colours 358
Application 361
Supports 361
Preservation and Storage of Work 361
Alternative Water-Based Binding Agents 362

SOFT PASTEL PAINTING **371**
Supports for Pastel Painting 372
Binding Agents for Pastel 381
Filler Material 381
Formation of Colour Ranges 381
Basic Recipes for Making Soft Pastels 384
Procedure for Hand-Making Soft Pastels 390
Working with Pastels 394
Manipulating Pastel 395
Fixing and Storage of Pastel Paintings 396

ACRYLIC PAINTING **400**
Acrylic Paint Systems 400
How Acrylic Paint Works 400

Acrylic Paints 402
Hand-Preparation of Acrylic Paints 404
Health and Safety Information 410
Manufactured Acrylic Paints 411
Acrylic Painting Mediums 413
Why Artists Sometimes Mistrust Acrylic Paint 419
Priming Information for Acrylic Paint Systems 422

ENCAUSTIC PAINTING **427**
Supports for Encaustic Painting 427
Equipment for Encaustic Painting 428
Composition and Use of Encaustic Paints 429
Wax Types 430
Suggested Palette for Encaustic Painting 432
Painting Techniques 433
Glazing with Encaustic 435
Working in Layers 435
Presentation of Finished Encaustic Paintings 435
Safe Clean-Up of Encaustic Paint 436

LIME-FRESCO PAINTING **437**
Health and Safety Precautions 438
Supports for Lime: Preparing Walls and Other Substrates for Application of Lime 439
Pigments for Lime-Fresco 448
Whites in Lime-Fresco 450
Application of Colours 452
Fresco Secco 453
Protection of Fresco Paintings 455
Alternative Wall Painting Binders 455

BRUSHES **459**
Brushes for Oil Painting 459
Brushes for Acrylic Painting 464
Brushes for Watercolour Painting 466
Brushes for Gouache Painting 470
Brushes for Priming 470
Brushes for Varnishing 472
Brushes for Soft Pastels 473
Brushes for Fresco Painting 473

STORAGE AND PRESERVATION OF FINISHED ARTWORKS **475**
Oil Paintings 475
Acrylic Paintings 478
Works on Paper 478
Pastel Paintings 480

BIBLIOGRAPHY **481**

INDEX **488**

About the Author

Pip Seymour is a painter and writer, who lives in England and Italy. He studied Fine Art at Bradford College of Art, Winchester School of Art and Brighton Polytechnic and has been a practising artist since the mid-1980s.

He teaches about the use of painting materials at a number of institutions in the United Kingdom, including the Prince's Foundation, London; Camberwell College of Art & Design, London; the Colour Museum, Bradford and Abbot Hall Art Gallery, Kendal, Cumbria.

Pip Seymour is a member of the Society of Dyers and Colourists.

Acknowledgements

I would like to thank the following people for their help and co-operation:

Sue Petheridge and Quentin Burkenshaw at the Society of Dyers and Colourists, Bradford, West Yorkshire (for Colour Index information, especially in relation to historical pigments). Dr Georg Kremer and Uta Williams, at Kremer Pigmente, Aichstetten, Germany. Yvonne Hindle at University of Central England, Birmingham. Sarah Miller, Technical Advisor, Winsor & Newton. Dr. Mike Roberts, DEFRA. Susan Ward-Booth, Alison Barratt, Jo Wooding, Arif Ozakca, Mary Gregis-Walker, Kathrin Kinseher, Kate Dineen.

Introduction

In relation to the activity of painting, the application of technique can be a crucial factor in the complete realisation of painted images.

For many artists, the role of technique in painting is somehow missing. In recent years, the teaching of Fine Art has concentrated more on the development of ideas than on the provision of information relating to the properties of painting materials. Despite this, many artists require technical information about their materials in order to progress and develop their work.

My own students have frequently asked for more information than is possible to transmit in the teaching environment, often the type of detailed information that pertains to an individual path of development. The need to provide this has prompted me to attempt to put into book form everything I have learnt about painting materials and practice over the last fifteen or so years.

The aim of this book is to collate, in one comprehensive volume, information that would otherwise require cross-referencing from many different publications, from various time periods.

The book is intended as a resource for painters, and covers practically all the accepted paint media in some depth. In many senses, this book is a personal response to the choice and use of materials. This information has been gleaned from my own painting practice; through discussion with other artists, students, fellow tutors, paintmakers and conservation specialists.

The information included in this book is not intended to be prescriptive: some of the opinions about materials expressed here relate to my own practice, and my understanding of the working properties of the materials discussed. Nevertheless, this information has been hard won: just like any other painter, one makes mistakes along the way and one continues to make mistakes. Indeed, some of the most interesting paintings come by accident, or through experimentation with materials.

The recipes, formulas and technical advice can be considered as a starting point for any artist who is interested in developing their technique. To this end, the raw materials used in painting are discussed at length, along with some practical advice as to how best to incorporate these raw materials into paints, mediums, primers, varnishes, etc.

The importance of understanding the nature of the materials one uses in painting cannot be underestimated. Without some basic knowledge of the working properties of materials, artists may not fully develop and progress with their work.

The materials at the disposal of the modern-day artist are perhaps wider in scope than at any other time in history. However, because many of these materials are presented in ready-to-use form (e.g. tube oil colours), many artists do not know how their paints and associated materials are manufactured, and where, why and how those materials came to be used in the first place. This book attempts to provide information on just these aspects, by giving some historical background in relation to the use of a material (e.g. the date of introduction of a pigment) and suggestions on how best to use it.

At the beginning of the 21st century, we find ourselves in the strange position of having available not only modern, industrially made pigments but also a revived selection of historical colours.

For the modern artist, the choice is not just between different brands of paint, but also between hand-made paint systems and manufactured paint ranges. As a consequence, this book focuses strongly on the properties of pigments and their incorporation into a variety of different binding agents.

When an artist selects a pigment, it is often possible to use that pigment with the whole family of binding agents available. However some pigments are not stable in certain mixtures. In order to help facilitate good working practice, each pigment is identified with the appropriate binding system(s), conforming to the notion that artists should make their work with longevity in mind.

Similar information is provided in relation to the working properties of binders, resins, waxes, gums, and all the other materials commonly used in artists' paints. The correct choice of priming for example, is fundamental to the execution of both the image and longevity of the finished artwork. Wherever information is available in relation to a material, it is given in order to provide as thorough a background as possible to all of the materials used in painting.

Information on the permanence of pigments is included, with the proviso that this was accurate at the time of going to press. The supply of artists' materials, like any other material, is in constant flux: as a consequence, specifications relating to a material may change.

The historical information on pigments (and other materials) comes mainly from the Western European tradition: the same materials may be handled and prepared in different ways in some other cultures, most noticeably in Oriental painting.

Our understanding of the use of painting materials changes and develops with time. Thanks to modern conservation techniques, the composition of historical paint layers has begun to be successfully identified. With this development, some previously obsolete colours, such as smalt and lead-tin yellow have come back into the palettes of contemporary artists. Similarly, historically important paint binders, such as lime-fresco and encaustic have been revived.

For many artists, the choosing of colours remains a daunting task without some supervision. For each paint media, a selection of basic colours is suggested. These can be adopted as a starting point: there will be many others to explore. Again, the pigment section provides a link between colour and appropriate binding agent.

Modern artists' paint ranges offer the opportunity to work with pigments that have a high permanence to both light and air. Most artists' materials companies offer their own permanence ratings in their catalogues and on colour charts/tube labelling. In the pigment section, an indication of permanence according to independent authorities (Blue Wool Scale/ASTM) is provided where available.

Some artists continue to use older colours, sometimes of a less-permanent nature. The pigment section contains much relevant information about all the pigments that are currently available to the market. The choice of colours listed relates to my own travels within the last few years, through Europe and North America. The section includes all the pigments I have found listed as being available in current artists' supply catalogues and associated literature.

Similarly, other materials (oils, gums, resins, waxes, etc) are included because one can find them on the market today. While some of the techniques discussed have historical importance (e.g. egg tempera painting), all media are considered and given value. For example, the properties of acrylic paint systems are discussed at length, with the aim of giving the reader a clear overview of how best to use this relatively new medium.

In making this book as comprehensive as possible, my aim has been to provide information on each material commonly used in painting practice, from which artists can choose the appropriate materials for their own work.

My hope for this book is that it becomes a standard resource for all artists, providing a practical link between material and practice.

Pip Seymour, London. 2003

Pigments

Pigments: An Introduction

The colouring substances employed in paint manufacture are derived from many sources. In simple terms, colour can be presented in the form of pigments (composed of finely divided particles) or dyestuffs (which dissolve when introduced to water or alcohol to form coloured liquids). In most instances, dyestuffs are not used in paint manufacture, because they are a) resoluble, b) without body/solidity and c) liable to fade when exposed to the ultra-violet light rays contained within sunlight.

By contrast, pigments always have a particle structure, even when the particle size is minuscule. Consequently, pigments are easier to control when mixed with binding media and create stable pastes of colour, which can be expressed by brushing or spreading on to a surface. In addition, pigments usually have a greater resistance to fading on exposure to sunlight when compared to dyestuffs.

A simple way to check the quality of a pigment is to place a small quantity of powdered pigment (e.g. 20g) into a glass jar (100ml). Fill the jar with cold water, stir, and then leave to stand for 2-3 days. After this time, all the pigment particles (being heavier than water), will have settled at the bottom of the jar, leaving the water clear. If the pigment contains an addition of dyestuff, the water may remain coloured, even after being left to settle for many days or weeks.

The pigments used in the manufacture of the best quality of artists' colours are carefully chosen, to provide optimum results.

The ideal pigment for use in an artists' colour would be:

- **Fast to light. Does not lose its brilliance when exposed to sunlight.**
- **Permanent to atmospheric conditions (e.g. some lead-based pigments are known to darken when exposed to sulphurous compounds in the air).**
- **Regular in particle size, helping to provide a uniform/stable paint paste.**
- **Free of impurities: some earth pigments have inclusions of "foreign" matter, which can cause difficulties in the mixing process, when preparing colours.**
- **Free of additives: some pigments are topped up with filler material (low tinting strength white pigments, such as blanc fix, or chalk), or admixed with other pigments.**

In practice, there are some pigments in use which do not conform to this wish list, simply because they have always been used by tradition. Alizarin crimson, a synthetic organic pigment first introduced in the mid-19th century, is a good example. Despite the fact that it is known to fade when applied as a glaze (a thin, transparent layer), it has remained in artists' colour assortments because artists still demand it, even though there are a number of modern alternatives which could easily be substituted.

Similarly, many artists dislike modern synthetic iron oxides (e.g. mars red, mars yellow), because, although they have similar colour values to the traditional earth pigments, they lack character. Synthetic iron oxides are super-opaque, absolutely regular in particle size and do not tend to alter from one batch of pigment to another. By contrast, natural ochre pigments, dug from the earth, are always irregular in terms of particle size and can alter in shade from batch to batch, due to inclusions of varying amounts of chalk and silica. When prepared into paint form, such earth pigments tend to be slightly gritty in texture and may take longer to mix into an acceptable paint paste. Despite this, or perhaps because of it, artists often choose such colours, because they show character, idiosyncrasy and contrast when compared with modern, industrial products.

It is this facet in regard to the raw colouring material that makes the understanding of pigments so vital to anyone learning to paint, or involved in the practice of painting.

The character of each pigment is different. The way that each pigment is mixed with a binder to form a paint paste can be different. It is also true that as artists, we express each colour differently on to the painting support, according to the characteristic of that particular colour. For example, viridian is a bright, cold green which shows great transparency when applied as a glaze. When mixed with other colours, it loses its influence within that mixture (i.e. it has a low tinting strength). Why is this? How can we recognise this? In practice, we find such information through trial and error: by taking each colour in turn and working with it; mixing it with white to see how it behaves as a tint; applying it to white grounds and to black grounds to see how transparent it is (very transparent pigments hardly show at all when applied to black grounds).

This section aims to provide in-depth information about the characteristics of all the pigments that are commonly used in artists' materials, or that have been used in painting practice. In addition, a number of historic pigments are mentioned because in recent years they have become available to the market again, especially in dry pigment form.

Key to Pigment Information

For each pigment, a table has been created to provide as much information as is currently available. The tables are laid out in the following format:

Colour Index Name

The Society of Dyers and Colourists have assigned many colouring substances an index name and number as a means of identification. Such information is used by the paint industry to identify ingredients and is also often included on the labelling of artists' colours or associated product information. For example, lead white is known as PW 1 (Pigment White Number 1).

Colour Index Number

The Colour Index Number is a further means of identification used within the paint industry. For example, lead white is Colour Index Number CI 77597.

A complete up-dated list of all colouring matter is available from the Society of Dyers and Colourists in the form of both book and CD-Rom (see Bibliography).

Common Names

The traditional colour name (e.g. venetian red, is the common name for a natural red earth pigment with a slightly pink-violet undershade). Other commonly accepted names for the same pigment are included (e.g. ultramarine is often referred to as french ultramarine. This relates to its development in the 19th century, where it was first patented in France).

Origin

A description of the manufacturing process and/or where the raw material is sourced. An outline of the use of each pigment in painting practice citing, in some cases, specific use by individual artists.

Composition

The accepted chemical formula for a pigment. For example, lead white is basic lead carbonate ($2PbCO_3$).

Tinting Strength

The relative tinting strength of a pigment (e.g. when admixed with white).

Shade

A description of the shade (warm, cold, bluish, reddish, etc) of each pigment.

Suitability to Media

Certain pigments are not compatible with some of the binding agents used for paint making. For example, lead-based pigments do not work well in acrylic binders, because they are too heavy to remain stable in the acrylic resin dispersion binder.

Opacity/Transparency

Pigments can give either transparent or opaque paint films, depending on the particle size and structure. For each pigment, the relative transparency/opacity is indicated – a useful aid when selecting colours.

Defects

Some colours cannot be intermixed, or may change appearance on exposure to light/atmosphere. In some cases, this can be countered by selection of specific binding media (e.g. lead white is less prone to sulphurous compounds when prepared as an oil paint than when prepared in a water-based binder, because the oil film protects the pigment from exposure to the atmosphere).

Availability/Cost

The relative availability of a pigment through regular suppliers of artists' materials is mentioned and, where noteworthy, reference is made to its cost (e.g. rock-mineral based pigments tend to be quite costly, whereas modern, industrial iron oxides are inexpensive). The cost of the raw material (pigment) may have some influence on the buying price of a paint product.

Special Comments

If a pigment requires a wetting agent in order to aid dispersion into the chosen paint binder, this is indicated. The choice of correct wetting agent is vital. The following wetting agents are commonly used in the manufacture of artists' paints:

Wetting Agent for Oil Colours

Mineral (white) spirit. It is not advised to use turpentine, because this solvent takes longer to evaporate than mineral spirit. Special dispersion formulations may be available for oil colours, under brand names (e.g. "Disperse aid").

Wetting Agent for Acrylic Colours

Special synthetic wetting agents are available, usually in the form of very dilute detergent (e.g. "Orotan", "Disponil"). Check with supplier as to the most appropriate wetting agent when purchasing acrylic resins.

Wetting Agent for Watercolours/Gouache

Alcohol, or ox-gall. Ox-gall is normally sold as a dilute liquid, sometimes deodorised. Neat ox-gall may be over-strong (causing too much wetting, dispersion of paint paste) and prone to the release of bad odour. Alcohol should be 99% water-free and non-coloured. It may be wise to dilute the alcohol with a little water, prior to use.

Wetting Agent for Hand-made Soft Pastels

Alcohol, diluted with water in the ratio one part alcohol to ten parts water.

Wetting Agent for Egg Tempera

Alcohol.

Wetting Agent for Casein Binder and Animal Skin Glue Binders

Alcohol.

Where applicable, further information is provided on the special characteristics of some pigments. For example, some of those derived from minerals, such as the semi-precious stones malachite and azurite, need careful preparation. When such pigments are mixed for too long, the particle size can be altered: as the particle size reduces, so the colour becomes paler and paler. Consequently, it is normal with these two pigments to mix them with the relevant binding agent using a slightly coarser particle size than would be the case with other pigments.

Drying Rate (in Oil Paint)

Some pigments have a catalytic effect on the vegetable oils used as binders for artists' oil colours. For example, raw umber (containing manganese deposits) will cause linseed oil to dry out in perhaps a day, or even less. As a consequence, it is often employed for underpainting (the first "sketching-in" coat of paint). Such fast-drying colours can be admixed with other pigments to improve their drying rate. This fast-drying action is only seen in oil-based paint systems.

Heath & Safety Information

Some pigments can be potentially injurious to the user, especially in their dry, powdered form. All dry, powder-form pigments represent a hazard in that they can be classed as nuisance dusts. It is imperative when handling dry pigments that the user wears an appropriate dust mask, protective gloves and protective clothing. An indication is given of the relative health hazard of each pigment.

The supplier of each material may offer further information on its correct use. It is prudent to request up-to-date information on all the materials discussed, as the available information is always changing.

Pigment Types

Pigments can be derived from two distinct sources:

1. Inorganic Pigments.
2. Organic Pigments.

Inorganic Pigments

Colouring matter that is derived from compounds that were never part of living matter are considered to be inorganic pigments. Within this category there are coloured compounds that are formed as a) earth deposits, b) mineral/rock, c) treated metallic compounds and d) fused metallic compounds.

Some Examples of Inorganic Pigments

Earth Deposit	Yellow ochre. Mix of clay with silica, tinted by iron deposits which oxidise to give a coloured earth.
Earth Deposit (naturally calcined)	Pompeii red. A natural earth pigment, given a red tinge through contact with heat from volcanoes.
Earth Deposit (artificially calcined)	Burnt sienna. Natural (raw) sienna is a special type of ochre, which contains a high proportion of silica (a translucent material). Raw sienna gives a relatively transparent paint film, when applied as a glaze. When raw sienna is calcined (heated) in a closed furnace or kiln, it changes shade to give a

	fiery-red colour. This calcining process also creates a slightly more transparent effect when the resultant paint paste is applied as a glaze.
Mineral/Rock	Cinnabar. A red rock, fused from mercury with sulphur, normally within volcanoes. It may also contain other aggregates such as sandstone, quartz, etc. The rock is pulverised in a pestle and mortar, then put through a fine sieve to separate the different particle sizes in order to gain a red pigment with a regular particle size. This pulverised form of cinnabar is known as vermilion (*"the little worm"* – Old French and Latin).
Treated Metallic Compound	Lead white. When sheets of lead are exposed to vinegar, the metal corrodes to form carbonate of lead. This simple white pigment is one of the oldest manufactured inorganic pigments, dating back to antiquity.
Fused Metallic Compounds	Cobalt blue. When two metallic compounds are burnt together (fused), they can be employed to create a new material. Cobalt blue, for example, is a fusion of cobalt and aluminium oxides.

Organic Pigments

Colouring matter that is derived from living substances or substances which were once part of living things, can be ascribed as organic pigments. Within this category, pigments may be composed from a) animals, b) plants or c) synthetic treatment of plantstuff.

Animal	Bone black. A simple black pigment can be produced by calcining cattle bones, which are then pulverised to a fine grain powder.
Plant	Madder red lake. Many plant roots, fibres or leaves can be used to make colouring substances. In the case of madder red, the roots of the madder plant are warmed with water that has been treated with potash. This produces a red dyestuff, which is then fixed to a metallic substrate (e.g. rock alum, a type of salt) to form a pigment with a particle structure.
Synthetic Organic	Alizarin crimson. Crude oil is converted into petroleum products. The solvents created through this process can be developed, through modern organic chemistry, into a wide range of coloured dyes. Some of these dyes can be converted into pigment form (attached to a particle structure). These "synthetic" organic pigments provide very strong, bright colour and are now widely employed within the paint industry as colourants.

Particle Size of Pigments

Pigments are rated according to the size of the individual (molecular) particles from which they are composed. The measurements are given in microns (μ).

The relationship between particle size and the binding agent used can be a factor in the making of coherent paint films. For example, the micron size of natural earth pigments (naturally occurring oxides of iron) may vary from between 20-50 microns and the particle structure may be irregular. By contrast, synthetic iron oxides (artificial oxides of iron) may have a particle size as small as 10 microns. In addition, the regular form of such manufactured pigments can make them easier to incorporate within the chosen binding system.

The micron size is represented by the symbol μ. The term "grind size" is also sometimes used in connection with particle size.

Comparative examples of micron size in pigments (sizes vary according to manufacturer and processing of the original material):

Natural Earth Pigments	20-50μ
Synthetic Iron Oxides	10μ
Synthetic Organic Pigments	0.1-5μ
Titanium White	5-15μ
Azurite	10-120μ (larger particle size shows greater colour)
Glass Pigments	63-125μ (larger particle size shows greater colour)

The combination of larger particle size pigments with smaller particle size pigments may lead to a loss of colour resonance in the resultant paint film. Rather than intermixing pigments with widely differing particle sizes, it may be better to overlay one colour on top of another to gain the optimum effect.

Artists' Pigments

The following index of pigments includes information on both historic and modern colours. Wherever possible permanence information is included. However, the reader should bear in mind that such information is always in flux and liable to revision over time. Where a pigment has been mentioned, its inclusion indicates its use in the fine arts, it does not necessarily confirm permanence or recommend use in permanent works of art.

Pigments Classification

When purchasing artists' colours, the colour name given on the product label may or may not relate to the pigment(s) used in its manufacture. It is important that artists understand the composition of the paints they use, to ensure a full understanding of a) the working properties of the paint chosen, b) the composition of the raw materials of that paint and c) the potential toxicity of the paint. The artists' materials industry often assigns names to paints that do not reflect their chemical composition. For example, sap green is often a combination of two or more pigments. Within published information (e.g. colour charts), the manufacturer may indicate the pigment composition of the paint. Increasingly, many companies show the pigment composition on tube or can labelling. However, this approach has not been adopted by all manufacturers: as a consequence, artists may need to do some research before selecting their materials. Where the manufacturer does indicate the pigment composition of their paints, identification is made by use of the relevant Colour Index Name and/or Number.

The Colour Index (C.I.) is the internationally recognised system for the identification of pigments and dyes. It is published jointly by the Society of Dyers and Colourists in the United Kingdom and the Association of Textile Chemists and Colorists in the United States. The Colour Index includes technical information and classification of all coloured materials, including pigments and dyes that may be found in artists' materials.

The complete Colour Index identification comprises two separate items:

a) The Colour Index Name

An example of a Colour Index Name would be "C.I. Pigment Violet 23".

The Colour Index Name comprises three different parts:

1. Use. What the colourant is used for (e.g. "Pigment", or dye class such as "Acid" or "Reactive").
2. Colour. Pigments are classified into ten colour groups, which are abbreviated as follows:

PB pigment blue, PBk pigment black, PBr pigment brown, PG pigment green, PM pigment metal, PO pigment orange, PR pigment red, PV pigment violet, PW pigment white, PY pigment yellow. NR = natural red, NY = natural yellow, etc (for colours based on plant or other organic source).

3. A Number. This number was assigned sequentially as the substance was added to the Index and has no chemical or constitutional significance.

b) The Constitution Number

C.I. Constitution Numbers are assigned by chemical class and run from 10000 to 77999. From this number, the exact formula and structure of most dyes and pigments can be found. While this information may not be required by most artists, it may assist identification of colours. At the very least, an understanding of these classifications allows artists to recognise what pigments may have been used in the paints they choose.

The full Colour Index Name and Constitution Number for a pigment commonly found in artists' materials, alizarin crimson, is:

Colour Index Name	Constitution Number	Common Name
C.I. PR 83	C.I. 58000	alizarin crimson

The American Society for Testing and Materials (ASTM) is often quoted by manufacturers and in technical literature with regard to artists' pigments. Their ratings refer to the performance of selected pigments when ground in a variety of vehicles, for example oil, gum arabic (watercolour), acrylic. ASTM ratings relate to pigment mixed with a binder (e.g. linseed oil) rather than proprietary brands of paint. Manufactured colours may contain the pigments listed on the tube or in technical information but can also include other undisclosed materials, which could in theory reduce permanence.

ASTM Lightfastness Ratings for oil paints have been based on testing done of the chosen pigment(s), let down with titanium white to a pastel-like tint at approximately 40% reflectance.

The pigments mentioned may fall into the following categories (in relation to oil colours):

ASTM I	Excellent lightfastness
ASTM II	Very good lightfastness
ASTM III	Not satisfactory (may be satisfactory when applied full strength)

Note: ASTM ratings are continually updated, any information supplied in this text may be subject to change.

Permanence of Artists' Pigments

The Blue Wool Scale

In the textiles industry, dyed cloth is measured for fastness against light according to the Blue Wool Scale. Samples of wool are dyed with eight different grades of blue dye and exposed to sunlight for a set period (e.g. twelve months, south facing Florida sunlight). The eight separate dyes show fading to different degrees: the dye with the strongest resistance to light is graded no.8 (no change after 12 months exposure), while the dye that fades the most is graded no.1. (complete or virtually complete fading after 12 months).

Other colours (both dyes and pigments) can be exposed to sunlight and measured against this scale. With regard to artists' pigments, colours that are graded 7-8 on the blue wool scale may be considered permanent (being more or less equivalent to pigments accorded the rating ASTM I, ASTM II under the ASTM rating system). Many plant-based colours, along with the earlier varieties of synthetic organic pigments may fall below this benchmark. For example, pigments that measure 6 or lower on the blue wool scale, may perform less well when exposed to strong sunlight, or when strongly mixed with white pigments.

The information supplied by manufacturers of artists' materials and by suppliers or manufacturers of dry pigments is assumed to be correct and diligently researched. However, "home" testing of batches of paint or dry pigment may become appropriate for specific processes. For example, a number of publications have been produced in recent years that attempt to test and evaluate the performance of proprietary brands of watercolour paint. Such evaluations often seem highly subjective, but it may be a useful exercise for artists to make their own, similar tests. Such tests can provide a useful record of, for example, the way a particular paint brushes out, or perhaps the degree of granulation observed when pigment is simply mixed with gum arabic and applied to paper as a wash. A register of paint-out samples would be a useful resource for any professional artist's studio, showing paint-outs of favourite colours and perhaps admixtures between different colours. It may also be useful to expose such paint-outs to south-facing light for a period of weeks or months, to ascertain any change in terms of fading.

For such tests, the chosen paint should be applied on to a support which is the same as that normally used for painting. For oil colours, it could be an off-cut of primed canvas, or perhaps a series of primed panels. For watercolour, a suitable paper is selected. For each paint sample, the colour needs to be applied at full strength; admixed with 10% white (admixture with perhaps more than one variety of white could be considered); admixed with white in the ratio one part colour, to nine parts white; applied diluted (as a wash in watercolour); applied combined with a chosen paint medium (e.g. in oil paint, co-mixed with a 10% addition of stand oil-dammar medium). The finished paint samples are left exposed to sunlight (preferably in a south-facing window). One half of each sample can be covered up, so that it is preserved and thus acts as a "standard" against which the exposed sample can be compared. After one month, the paint sample is inspected for any changes, then re-positioned for another month, and so on. After a period of perhaps six months, any significant changes are noted and recorded for future reference. Although this procedure may seem lengthy and pedantic, it may help individual artists to recognise subtle differences of quality between one paint brand and another. In the case of dry pigments, to make a colour sample, the chosen pigment is milled into a specific binder. For example, a simple gum arabic solution can be used to make basic watercolours. This is especially useful when selecting pigments for watercolour painting, where qualities such as the staining or granulation properties of a pigment are better understood.

Staining Pigments

Some small/fine particle size pigments, such as the synthetic organic pigments and also prussian blue, tend to give a staining effect when used in water-based techniques. This is partially due to the very high tinting strength of such pigments, but is also connected to their fine particle size. These staining colours tend to be difficult to wash out of brush hairs, especially soft sable hair brushes. They may also cause running or bleeding when applied to the painting surface (e.g. painting on paper in watercolour technique), when one wet colour contacts with another.

An addition of gum water (gum arabic solution) with such colours may help to give more control in terms of application (the colour is slower to disperse). In some gouache paint ranges, colours may be based on dyes rather than pigments, which will have a strong staining effect, or rather, bleeding – where colour is easily redissolved and reactivated on the surface when re-wetted.

Granulation (in Watercolour)

The particle structure of a pigment may cause the applied paint to show an effect referred to as "granulation", where the particles partially settle out in the paint mixture, to give a granular effect. This granulation of applied colour can be aesthetically pleasing, especially in the context of watercolour painting, where the grainy particles settle out in the pits/grain of the paper. Examples of these granulation pigments include cobalt blue, cobalt violet, cerulean blue, manganese blue, cobalt green, natural earths, natural madder, stil di grain, natural indigo, viridian, ultramarine violet. Alongside these colours, most of the mineral-based pigments show granulation due to their crystalline structure. The large particle size of such pigments may mean that they require greater binding strength than finer particle sized pigments.

Pigment Tables

WHITE PIGMENTS

LEAD WHITE PW 1

Colour Index Number	77597
ASTM/BWS Rating	ASTM I
Common Names	Kremnitz white, krems white, cremnitz white, nottingham white, london white, genoa white, silver white, ceruse white, snowflake, or flake white. The term flake white is often used in tube oil paint to describe lead white admixed with zinc white. It is common for lead white oil colours also to include additions of blanc fix (barium sulphate), which is incorporated to improve the paint consistency.
Composition and Origin	$2PbCO_3.Pb(OH)^2$. Artificial mineral pigment. Basic lead carbonate. Used since antiquity. Krems is a town in Austria, where lead white pigment was produced.
Tinting Strength	Good reducing power when mixed with other colours.
Shade	Pure white, not over bright. A warmish white as oil colour.
Opacity	Fairly good – titanium white has greater hiding (covering) power.
Suitability to Media	Not suitable for use in water-based media. Lead white is a heavy pigment, which settles out in water-based media. The pigment is more prone to darkening upon exposure to sulphurous compounds in the environment, when used in water-based techniques. In oil paint and also when carefully bound in egg yolk for tempera, lead white performs well.
Drying Rate (in oil)	Fast.
Defects	In oil, lead white yellows with age, especially if kept in the dark during drying. Can blacken on exposure to (sulphur) polluted atmospheres, although this tendency is reduced when the pigment is locked in an oil binder.

Availability/Cost	Withdrawn from use in most industrial paints in Europe and the US. Current EU legislation has made it more costly and prohibitive for artists' colour-makers to produce lead white as an oil paint. As a consequence, prepared white lead oil colour has become expensive. Similarly, the dry pigment is now more expensive and more difficult to purchase. Demand from artists for this pigment is still high. The availability of lead white is limited by current UK regulations. It is available for the restoration of works of art and buildings upon application to the relevant authority. In the UK, this has been The Council for Museums, Archives and Libraries, who inherited this responsibility from the Museums and Galleries Commission. This situation is apparently due to change, however, and DEFRA (Department of Environment, Fisheries and Rural Affairs) can advise as to the appropriate authority henceforth.
Comments	As an oil colour, lead white can be prepared to provide a rich, buttery texture, ideal for mixing down with other colours. Add to other colours to speed drying in underpainting. Most flexible of all whites, with a smooth, pasty consistency, often preferred for admixing and modifying consistency of other colours.
Special Note	Lead sulphate (PW 2/C.I. 77633) is sublimed lead carbonate and not permanent for works of art - was formerly used in industrial paints.
Health & Safety Information	Toxic, contains lead. Wear gloves and dust mask when handling dry pigment. Wash hands thoroughly after using pigment or paint. Lead can be ingested through the skin - wear a barrier cream, applied to hands and forearms to ease cleaning and prevent pigment/paint from resting in contact with skin.

ZINC WHITE PW 4

Colour Index Number	77947
ASTM/BWS Rating	ASTM I
Common Names	Zinc oxide, chinese white (originally a special grade used to make body colour for watercolour painting), permanent white (not to be confused with blanc fix, which is also sometimes afforded this name).
Composition and Origin	ZnO. An artificial mineral pigment, pure zinc oxide. Developed from 1746 onwards, introduced to artists in the 1830s (by Winsor & Newton: chinese white, as a watercolour paint).
Tinting Strength	Good.
Shade	Cold, bluish white.
Opacity	Semi-opaque, admix with other colours to gain pastel shades.
Suitability to Media	Stable in oil, watercolour, gouache, tempera, but not advised for outdoor mural painting using acrylic, where the paint surface can chalk.
Drying Rate (in oil)	Very slow.
Defects	Forms brittle paint films in oil, especially when applied thickly.
Availability/Cost	Widely used.
Comments	Thick passages of paint may form hard, brittle films, leading to a danger of cracking.
Special Note	Zinc sulphate (PW 7/C.I. 77975) is formed when zinc oxide is exposed to hydrogen sulphide. Although zinc sulphate is a similar white colour to zinc oxide, it is rarely used in the preparation of artists' colours, but finds use in industrial products. It is also used in the manufacture of lithopone, where it is co-precipitated with barium sulphate. Zinc sulphate is not stable in acidic mixtures. Exposure to heat causes release of toxic hydrogen sulphide gas.

	with barium sulphate. Zinc sulphate is not stable in acidic mixtures. Exposure to heat causes release of toxic hydrogen sulphide gas.
Health & Safety Information	–

LITHOPONE PW 5

Colour Index Number	77115
ASTM/BWS Rating	Not tested.
Common Names	Lithopone silver, ponolith, carlton white, griffith's patent zinc white, jersey lily white, orr's zinc white.
Composition and Origin	$BaSO_4$ + ZnS. An artificial mineral pigment. First produced in England in the 1870s. Early lithopones had a tendency to darken when mixed with oil. The modern pigment (dating from 1926) is stable. A co-precipitate of zinc sulphide and barium sulphate.
Tinting Strength	Stronger than zinc white, with more hiding power due to better opacity.
Shade	Similar to zinc white, a bright, coldish white.
Opacity	Semi-opaque.
Suitability to Media	Oil, watercolour, gouache, tempera – although in oil it shows a certain yellow-greenness.
Drying Rate (in oil)	Very slow.
Defects	–
Availability/Cost	Inexpensive, sometimes used to bulk out other white oil paints.
Comments	–
Special Note	–
Health & Safety Information	–

TITANIUM WHITE PW 6

Colour Index Number	77891
ASTM/BWS Rating	ASTM I
Common Names	Titanox, titanium dioxide.
Composition and Origin	TiO_2. An artificial mineral pigment, Titanium dioxide is derived from ilmenite, black titanium ore. Introduced in the 1920s.
Tinting Strength	High.
Shade	Very bright pure white.
Opacity	Very opaque.
Suitability to Media	Stable to all media.
Drying Rate (in oil)	Slow. Hand-ground oil colour can take months to dry out.
Defects	Dries to a brittle film (when ground in oil). For this reason, it is not recommended for oil priming, or for thick passages of oil painting.
Availability/Cost	Inexpensive, widely used.
Comments	An inert, non-toxic pigment with the highest tinting strength of all whites and very high refractive power.
Special Note	-
Health & Safety Information	-

A Note on Pearlescent Pigments

In Japanese painting, iridescent or nacreous pigments are traditionally produced by grinding the inside of mother of pearl sea shells. This technique is still in use and Japanese art materials catalogues detail various iridescent white and pearl pigments, which are mixed with a skin glue binder in the traditional Japanese painting technique on paper. Mica, called muscovite, or muscovy glass, (hydrous potassium aluminium silicate) $H_2K\ Al_3\ (SiO_4)_3$, is a type of natural quartz, which occurs in the form of compressed thin sheets or plates that divide easily.

Mica has been used as a pigment in painting and the decorative arts. When ground into a fine powder, it acts like the Japanese ground-shell pigments, giving a slight iridescent effect. Mica is available in a variety of grades, from fine powder to sequin-size platelets. They retain their lustre best when mixed with water-based binders, especially acrylic dispersion, but also with animal glue (distemper), or gum arabic.

Mica is used as the substrate for the modern pearlescent pigments. In a costly process, the fine mica plates are coated with metal oxides. The pearlescent pigments are extremely lightfast and stable in all the usual paint binders: oil, acrylic, gum arabic, casein, lime, etc. The pearlescent pigments can be divided into three distinct groupings: Pearlescent, Iridescent and Interference.

Pearlescent types

Fine particles of mica are coated with a very thin layer of titanium white pigment (titanium dioxide, TiO_2), to produce pearlescent and silver, or rather silver-white shades. These are generally referred to as pearlescent pigments. Examples of these are the Ekaton types. They have a metallic surface sheen and brush out to a transparent glaze when prepared with medium (e.g. acrylic polymer dispersion).

Iridescent types

Iridescent pigments (for example, Colibri types) are very similar, in that they are derived from mica, which is coated with iron oxide and titanium white, or just iron oxide, to provide a range of yellow gold, orange gold and copper shades. However, they are less transparent when compared with pearlescent pigments and give a very good approximation to shades of real gold, copper and bronze. These iridescent gold, copper and bronze shades can be mixed from the dry pigment to imitate gilding effects, or in many cases, bought ready-dispersed into a binding medium.

These shades are already available in the form of acrylic and oil paint. The iridescent pigments can be mixed with animal glue binder to replicate fine water gilding effects but are perhaps closest to gold, or shell gold, when mixed into an acrylic polymer dispersion.

By contrast to similar shades available as bronze powder, the iridescent pigments show a greater subtlety with a softer finish, are stable to light and do not tarnish or oxidise.

Interference types

Interference pigments (for example, Chroma types) differ from the pearlescent and iridescent types in that the combination of refraction and reflection of light upon the titanium white coatings produces an interference effect, rather like the rainbow colours visible when looking at a thin film of oil upon the surface of water. With interference pigments, mica is coated with titanium white to a specific thickness, which allows only a narrow band of light to reflect. As a result, the eye sees just one colour of the spectrum, yellow for example. The pigment is structured so that it edits out other colours in the spectrum, which are then not seen by the eye. The resultant interference colour is best seen when the painted surface is tilted, or viewed at an angle. The colour is also more visible when painted out against a dark ground.

By contrast, when looking at pearlescent pigment types, the only colour seen is a lustrous white, or silver-white. This is because the coating of titanium white is very thin and light wavelengths are reflected as white only.

IRIDESCENT WHITE (MICA/PEARL LUSTRE)
PW 20 or PW 26 (natural mica) +PW 6 (titanium white)

Colour Index Number	77019, 77718 + 77891
ASTM/BWS Rating	Not tested.
Common Names	Pearlescent white, mica white, glimmer white.
Composition and Origin	-
Tinting Strength	When mixed with transparent pigments, the resulting colour takes on a pearlescent appearance.
Shade	Bright, pearl white.
Opacity	Translucent.
Suitability to Media	Stable in all media. In oil, the colour of the oil used may show strongly. Tends to make poor paint pastes when combined with drying vegetable oils such as poppy oil or linseed oil. Better suited to combination with alkyd resin.
Drying Rate (in oil)	Normally presented in oil colour ranges with fast-drying alkyd resin as binder.
Defects	Difficult to make into a paste without additions of wax paste. Best used as required, into glaze mediums, etc.
Availability/Cost	Expensive but intense, now available in some paint ranges and as dry pigment.
Comments	-
Special Note	-
Health & Safety Information	-

BLANC FIX PW 21 (artificially prepared), PW 22 (natural mineral barytes, heavy spar)

Colour Index Number	77120
ASTM/BWS Rating	Not tested.
Common Names	French: blanc fix; English: permanent white, constant white, barytes, heavy spar.
Composition and Origin	Barium sulphate, $Ba(SO_4)$. Occurs naturally, but can also be manufactured by precipitation of barium chloride with sulphuric acid. The manufactured form was introduced by Kuhlmann (Lille, France) in 1830.
Tinting Strength	Poor. Blanc fix has little tinting strength.
Shade	When mixed with cold water only, blanc fix appears as a perfect snow white, having a high reflectance in light. However, when mixed into any binding agent, it takes on a dull white appearance, especially so with oil binders.
Opacity	Has some opacity: when admixed with other opaque pigments, it can be used to emphasise or enhance opacity. In water-based systems it retains an opaque effect. When used as an additive in oil colours, blanc fix will enhance opacity when added in quantity, but when used sparingly, as an addition to coloured glazes, it enhances the transparency of such glazes.
Suitability to [illegible]dia	Stable to all media, most often used as a filler material in oil paints and opacifier in gouache paints. When used in water-based paints, blanc fix shows as a brightish white, especially so with binders that remain water clear (e.g. klucel).
[illegible] oil)	Slow.
	If prepared alone as an oil colour, blanc fix would show a great tendency towards yellowing, due to weak tinting strength.

Availability/Cost	Inexpensive and widely used as an additive in artists' paints.
Comments	Blanc fix is primarily used as a filler/extender in paint systems. When added to pigments milled in linseed oil, blanc fix provides opacity but also adds bulk and weight to the paint mixture. This weight can prove to be deceptive when used in larger quantities to extend paints: the resultant tube of paint may be heavy in weight and thus seemingly appears to indicate a high pigment load. However, the inclusion of excess blanc fix will render the paint mixture rather stodgy and make the colour value somewhat dull. It is best used in small amounts to improve the consistency and regulate the opacity of the pigments with which it is mixed. In gouache paints, blanc fix may be used alone as an alternative to white. It is also commonly used in gouache paints to achieve a regular opacity across a range of colours, giving a paint paste that has body and will dry to leave a matt paint film.
Special Note	-
Health & Safety Information	Contains barium.

ALUMINIUM HYDRATE PW 24

Colour Index Number	77002
ASTM/BWS Rating	Not tested.
Common Names	Alumina hydrate, aluminium hydroxide.
Composition and Origin	$Al(OH)_3$. A metallic soap, aluminium hydrate is manufactured by mixing soda ash or potash with a solution of aluminium sulphate.
Tinting Strength	Very low, almost negligible. It is often used as a transparent extender for paint systems, notably oil colours.
Shade	Soft, bright white as dry powder. When mixed with any binder it takes on the coloration/hue of that binder. When milled with linseed oil, it creates a dull yellow-orange paste, which if applied as a paint dries to show intense yellowing/darkening.
Opacity	Has little or no hiding power when used in any binder, but especially so in oil.
Suitability to Media	Inert, can be used as a filler/extender in any paint system but most commonly with oil colours. Aluminium hydrate quickly forms a pleasant buttery paste when mixed with linseed oil. It is often added to oil colours to improve consistency. However, overuse (e.g. more than 5-10%) will leave the resultant paint unworkable, smeary in consistency. The inclusion of small amounts of aluminium hydrate in oil paints may help to break up light as it hits the paint surface, so enhancing colour resonance. Overuse will cause the paint film to become dull and lacking in luminosity.
Drying Rate (in oil)	Slow. When added to oil colours, aluminium hydrate will act to retard drying times.
Defects	When overused as an extender/filler, it encourages yellowing/darkening of the paint film. Cheaper artists' oil colours may contain larger quantities, and as a consequence may show excessive yellowing upon drying. Overuse of aluminium hydrate makes the paint paste unworkable and matts the dried paint film. Due to its very high oil absorption rate, aluminium hydrate,

	when added in quantity will encourage wrinkling or shrivelling of the drying oil paint film. In good-quality oil colours it is added sparingly, no more than 5-10% of the whole. This is especially important when adding to transparent pigments with a high oil absorption rate. Overuse of this filler in such circumstances will increase the likelihood of yellowing and may weaken the structure of the paint film.
Availability/Cost	Widely used in all artists' oil colours, but its use is governed by the quality of the paint. Ideally it is only added in small quantities.
Comments	Avoid paint mediums based on aluminium hydrate milled into linseed oil: their use will encourage darkening of the overall paint film. When hand-making oil colours, it is useful to add a small amount of aluminium hydrate (5-10%): this not only helps to stabilise consistency but will also help to prevent separation of oil from pigment when filling the paint paste into empty metal tubes.
Special Note	-
Health & Safety Information	-

YELLOW PIGMENTS

HANSA YELLOW **(types)**

RN = PY 65 - $C_{18}H_{18}N4O_6$
GX = PY 73 - $C_{17}H_{15}ClN_4O_5$
5GX = PY 74 - $C_{18}H_{18}N_4O_6$
10G = PY 3 - $C_{16}H_{12}Cl_2N_4O_4$
G = PY 1 - $C_{17}H_{16}N_4O_4$

Colour Index Number	PY 65/11740, PY 73/11738, PY 74/11741, PY 3/11710, PY 1/11680
ASTM/BWS Rating	ASTM I (except PY 3, PY 1 = ASTM II)
Common Names	Brilliant yellow, hansa yellow light, hansa yellow dark, arylide yellow, monoazo yellow, azo yellow.
Composition and Origin	Synthetic organic pigment. Originally dates from early 1900s, although the modern equivalents have been improved. These pigments are often adulterated in cheaper paint ranges by the addition of extenders. The high tinting strength allows for a greater amount of extender to be incorporated without losing colour strength. However, such additions tend to cause problems in terms of stability of consistency and loss of transparency. In oil, the slow drying rate makes hansa yellow unsuitable for any technique that involves a degree of impasto, as the paint film may wrinkle upon drying.
Tinting Strength	Good.
Shade	Bright yellow, cool to warm shades, from light to dark.
Opacity	Tends towards transparency.
Suitability to Media	Stable in all media.
Drying Rate (in oil)	Slow.
Defects	When too much extender is added, hansa yellow loses its tendency towards transparency.

Availability/Cost	Fairly inexpensive and widely used, especially in cheap paints to imitate expensive cadmiums.
Comments	New types have improved lightfastness.
Special Note	Requires wetting agent. Hansa yellows tend to show little or no yellowing when ground in oil.
Health & Safety Information	–

BARIUM LEMON YELLOW PY 31

Colour Index Number	77103
ASTM/BWS Rating	Not tested.
Common Names	Lemon yellow, barium yellow, yellow ultramarine, permanent yellow.
Composition and Origin	An artificial mineral pigment. Barium chromate, ($BaCrO_4$). Discovered by Vauquelin, 1809. Used in wider industry as ingredient in anti-corrosive paints.
Tinting Strength	Weak.
Shade	Dull, pale, yellow.
Opacity	Slightly transparent as glaze.
Suitability to Media	Stable in all media, but liable to turn greenish in oil.
Drying Rate (in oil)	Medium.
Defects	Upon ageing, becomes slightly greenish in oil paint.
Availability/Cost	Hard to find in manufactured ranges. Usually replaced with non-toxic nickel titanium yellow. The pigment is available from specialist pigment suppliers.
Comments	-
Special Note	-
Health & Safety Information	Toxic, barium chromate.

CHROME YELLOW PY 34

Colour Index Number	77600, 77603
ASTM/BWS Rating	Not tested.
Common Names	Primrose yellow.
Composition and Origin	A group of artificial mineral pigments. Lead chromate, $PbCrO_4$. Developed by the French chemist, Nicholas Louis Vauquelin (1763-1829), after studying the properties of a Russian mineral called chrocoite, which could be processed to give yellow, green and red precipitates. The discovery of French sources of chrocoite led to the industrial production of chrome-based pigments, both in France and England. Found in paintings from early 1800s. Chrome yellow was formerly used widely in industry and artists' colours. Due to its relative toxicity, EU directives have reduced the availability of the chrome pigments. Chrome yellows can darken on exposure and with age. In recent years, chrome yellows have been developed in which the particles have been silica encapsulated, so preventing darkening upon exposure and with age. When these pigments were in wider use, it would be quite common to find chrome yellows, with barium sulphate (blanc fix) as a bulking agent. Similarly, chrome yellows were often mixed with yellow ochres to brighten the appearance of the natural earth colour.
Tinting Strength	Very good, as a pure tint (i.e. without extender).
Shade	Lemon, light, mid-yellow, deep to orange shades.
Opacity	Good.
Suitability to Media	Oil (but can turn dark on exposure to atmosphere and show a greenish tinge, when too much oil is used in the milling process).
Drying Rate (in oil)	Fast (lead-based). Sometimes used in oil gilding, co-mixed with oil to act as a mordant.
Defects	Turns greenish or brownish with age, especially in oil films, where contact with acid in the oil can turn the lemon and pale yellow varieties to a greenish tinge very quickly.

Availability/Cost	Until recently, this pigment was cheap and available in many paint ranges. Withdrawn from colour ranges in the early 1990s and now difficult to obtain through pigment suppliers.
Comments	Strontium yellow (PY 32/C.I. 77839), strontium chromate, is similar to chrome yellow, with a bright lemon shade ($SrCrO_4$). This pigment has been hard to find in recent years, due in part to the toxicity of its manufacture. Strontium yellow may also appear under the name "ultramarine yellow".
Special Note	An important artists' pigment. No longer available (from most sources in Europe), due to EU legislation. Chrome green (PG 15) is formed from a mixture between prussian blue and chrome yellow and may vary in shade according to a) the amount of prussian blue to yellow b) the tone of the chrome yellow used (e.g. lemon, mid, deep, etc).
Health & Safety Information	Toxic, lead chromate.

CADMIUM YELLOW (shades)

LIGHT PY 35 - CdSZn
MEDIUM PY 37 - Cds
DEEP PY 37 - CdS
ORANGE PO 20 - CdS. x CdSe

Colour Index Number	PY 35/77205, PY 37/77199, PO 20/77202
ASTM/BWS Rating	ASTM I
Common Names	Cadmium lemon, cadmium yellow pale/light, cadmium yellow medium, cadmium yellow deep/dark, cadmium orange.
Composition and Origin	CdS. The metal cadmium was discovered in 1817 and first used by artists in England in the 1840s. However, due to the scarcity of the material, it was not fully developed as a pigment for artists until the early 20th century. An artificial mineral pigment, pure cadmium sulphide is sometimes mixed with cadmium selenide. Cheaper cadmium pigments may be co-precipitated with barium sulphate. According to ASTM, the pigment can include up to 15% barium sulphate. PO 20:1 is cadmium orange blended with barium sulphate (cadmium lithopone orange, CdS. x $CdSe.yBaSO_4$). The purest grades are derived only from cadmium sulphide and this is generally reflected in the price.
Tinting Strength	Good.
Shade	Cool lemon, light yellow, mid yellow, dark yellow to orange shades.
Opacity	Tends towards transparency in extremely thin layers, otherwise opaque.
Suitability to Media	Stable in all media. Exterior application is not advised, because when cadmium is exposed to damp and/or air, it changes to cadmium carbonate, showing a degree of discoloration.
Drying Rate (in oil)	Slow.
Defects	Can fade, when exposed in combination to damp and sunlight.
Availability/Cost	Expensive but widely used.
Comments	-

Special Note	Mixtures with lead-based colours are not recommended, although mixtures with lead white tend to remain unchanged. Aurora yellow was a patented form of cadmium yellow, developed by Winsor & Newton in 1889. Their catalogue of 1925 suggests that this yellow vies with chrome yellow in terms of opacity and brightness. Orient yellow is a deeper shade of aurora yellow.
Health & Safety Information	Contains cadmium.

ZINC YELLOW PY 36

Colour Index Number	77955
ASTM/BWS Rating	Not tested.
Common Names	Zinc chrome yellow, primrose yellow, citron yellow.
Composition and Origin	An artificial mineral pigment, zinc chromate, $ZnCrO_4$. Developed by Vauquelin, 1809.
Tinting Strength	Weak.
Shade	Cold pale yellow, almost lemon in shade.
Opacity	Semi-opaque.
Suitability to Media	Stable in oil, but reduced in permanence when admixed strongly with white. In water-based media, zinc yellow remains partially soluble and is soluble when in contact with alkalis (i.e. avoid in lime-fresco).
Drying Rate (in oil)	Fast.
Defects	Sensitive to moisture and alkalis.
Availability/Cost	No longer widely available in pigment form: still offered by some Italian manufacturers as prepared oil colour and dry pigment.
Comments	Was formerly used in the production of mixed greens, such as zinc green (with prussian blue). In some cases, such admixtures were further complicated by the inclusion of blanc fix. The author has in recent years bought a variety of zinc greens from old pigment stores in Italy (which were closing down), showing a wide range of colours, from light, acid greens, to murky, subdued shades.
Special Note	-
Health & Safety Information	Toxic.

ORPIMENT PY 39

Colour Index Number	77085
ASTM/BWS Rating	Not tested.
Common Names	Kings yellow (denotes the artificial product).
Composition and Origin	As_2S_3, mineral containing a naturally occurring sulphide of arsenic. It can be prepared artificially from arsenic trichloride and sodium thiosulphate. Due to its extremely poisonous nature, orpiment is used with great caution. Also, because it is sulphide-based, it can react with other pigments.
Tinting Strength	Good.
Shade	Bright yellow, similar to cadmium yellow light or medium.
Opacity	Not especially transparent.
Suitability to Media	Stable in egg tempera, and when used in oil-resin mixtures where the pigment is protected from exposure to the atmosphere and other pigments.
Drying Rate (in oil)	-
Defects	-
Availability/Cost	Expensive as dry pigment.
Comments	-
Special Note	In historical paintings, sometimes found admixed with blue (e.g. lapis, azurite) to make green shades.
Health & Safety Information	Toxic, contains arsenic.

COBALT YELLOW, AUREOLIN PY 40

Colour Index Number	77357
ASTM/BWS Rating	ASTM II
Common Names	Sunshine yellow.
Composition and Origin	$CoK_3(No_2)^6].H_2O$. Artificial mineral pigment, from cobalt salts and potassium nitrate - Potassium cobaltinitrite. Introduced as an artists' pigment in the 1860s, primarily as a watercolour.
Tinting Strength	Good.
Shade	A pure golden yellow, similar to true indian yellow when applied as a glaze. When ground in oil, it takes on a slightly greenish cast at full strength but appears as a true yellow when thinned to a glaze.
Opacity	Almost transparent as a glaze colour.
Suitability to Media	Stable in all media, except lime-fresco.
Drying Rate (in oil)	Slow.
Defects	-
Availability/Cost	Very expensive. Available in many paint ranges, in all media.
Comments	-
Special Note	-
Health & Safety Information	-

NAPLES YELLOW PY 41

Colour Index Number	77589
ASTM/BWS Rating	ASTM I
Common Names	Antimony yellow.
Composition and Origin	$Pb_3(SbO_4)$. An artificial mineral pigment. Lead antimoniate (lead and antimony oxides). Often confused with lead tin yellow in historical paint samples.
Tinting Strength	Good.
Shade	Lemon, mid-yellow to reddish-yellow shades.
Opacity	Good hiding power, opaque. Heavy powder makes thick paint pastes with stiffish consistency.
Suitability to Media	Stable in oil, lime, casein, egg but some varieties may be liable to darkening (on exposure to sulphurous compounds) in water-based media. Also, in water-based media the heavy powder tends to settle out in mixtures.
Drying Rate (in oil)	Fast (contains lead). Can also be used to speed up drying time of pigments intermixed with it.
Defects	-
Availability/Cost	Hard to find in manufactured ranges, although the pigment is still available from specialist pigment suppliers.
Comments	Naples yellow in modern colour ranges usually refers to the shade rather than the true pigment. Excellent for flesh tints. Avoid using steel palette or painting knives with the dry powder, as this can cause a greenish/darkening effect.
Special Note	Jaune brilliant is a mixed colour, originally based on naples yellow with cadmium yellow, vermilion and lead white. Modern examples may be based on admixtures of lead white (or other whites) with cadmium red and cadmium yellow.
Health & Safety Information	Toxic, contains lead.

LEAD TIN YELLOW, TYPE I PY 46

Colour Index Number	77577
ASTM/BWS Rating	Not tested.
Common Names	Giallorino (as mentioned by Cennini).
Composition and Origin	Pb_2SnO_4, lead stannate, prepared from a heated mixture of lead dioxide with tin dioxide. Thought to be a by-product of the glass-making industry in former times. Two distinct shades can be produced in this manner; at temperatures of around 700-800°C, a cold lemon yellow is achieved. At lower temperatures, a slightly warmer shade is created. Lead tin yellow was often incorrectly identified as either naples yellow or *massicot* in historical paintings. In 1941, the Doerner Institute in Munich identified the presence of tin in lead-based yellow historical paint samples. The pigment was subsequently remade according to chemical analysis, the development of cool lemon and warm yellow shades being effected in the early 1960s.
Tinting Strength	Weak. Best used alone, or as very pale yellow when admixed with lead white.
Shade	Pale lemon, or warm mid-yellow.
Opacity	Both pale lemon and warm shades are milky and opaque when mixed into binder. Lead tin yellow is sometimes found in old paintings as an underpaint, subsequently overpainted with a green glaze (copper resinate), to achieve bright, strong green shades.
Suitability to Media	Stable in oil, tempera and oil-tempera emulsions.
Drying Rate (in oil)	Dries fast (contains lead).
Defects	Can turn black in watery binders (e.g. gum arabic), where the lead content darkens on contact with sulphur in the atmosphere.

Availability/Cost	Available as dry pigment.
Comments	-
Special Note	-
Health & Safety Information	Contains lead, toxic.

LEAD TIN YELLOW, TYPE II PY 46

Colour Index Number	77577
ASTM/BWS Rating	Not tested.
Common Names	Giallorino.
Composition and Origin	Lead and tin oxides, with the inclusion of free tin oxide and silicon (quartz). As with type I, type II may originate from glass colouring fabrication. It is a yellow lead-glass pigment, most probably a by-product of lead crystal glass manufacturing. The inclusion of quartz effects a degree of transparency to the pigment, making it possible to use in glaze techniques. The colour is warmer and stronger than type I. The pigment is sifted through a fine mesh to provide a grind size suitable for use in oil, tempera and egg-oil painting.
Tinting Strength	Weak.
Shade	Warm, translucent yellow.
Opacity	Transparent.
Suitability to Media	Oil, egg-oil emulsions, egg tempera. The grainy particle size makes it unsuitable for use in very thin paint films where the paint film can show a textured finish.
Drying Rate (in oil)	Fast drying.
Defects	May discolour (darken) in aqueous media.
Availability/Cost	Available as dry pigment.
Comments	A transparent glazing pigment with a warm hue.
Special Note	-
Health & Safety Information	Contains lead, toxic.

MASSICOT PY 46

Colour Index Number	77577
ASTM/BWS Rating	Not tested.
Common Names	Litharge (pale varieties); massicot (warmer varieties). Lead monoxide may be named according to the country of origin. For example in France, pigments based on lead oxide are known as "*massicot*".
Composition and Origin	PbO. Manufactured inorganic pigment, derived from lead monoxide (PbO). Manufactured by oxidisation of lead, at temperatures of 500-700°C. At one stage, pale yellows in old paintings were identified as being forms of massicot. However, this is due in part to the fact that while lead was identified in such paint samples, no tests were done to identify the presence of tin. In 1941, the Doerner Institute in Munich identified tin in many paint samples previously thought to contain only lead (such as forms of lead-tin yellow).
Tinting Strength	Weak.
Shade	Pale yellow to warm yellow-orange.
Opacity	Milky, opaque.
Suitability to Media	More stable in oil than other media, but still liable to darken upon contact with sulphides in the atmosphere. Also unstable in dry form, turning paler when exposed to air.
Drying Rate (in oil)	Fast. Often used as a drying agent in old paint medium recipes.
Defects	Unstable in all media (tends to darken), especially in any water-based binder. Due to its particularly heavy nature, tends to settle out in paint mixtures.
Availability/Cost	Inexpensive but never used in artists' paints due to toxicity and instability.
Comments	Discarded as a pigment for most techniques. May have some practical relevance as a drying agent when added to paint mediums or varnishes. For example, in the manufacture of sun-thickened linseed oil, an inclusion of perhaps 10% massicot into the oil bath may impart fast-drying properties to the resultant oil.
Special Note	-
Health & Safety Information	Contains lead, toxic.

NICKEL TITANIUM YELLOW PY 53

Colour Index Number	77788
ASTM/BWS Rating	ASTM I
Common Names	Nickel yellow, lemon yellow (hue), naples yellow (hue).
Composition and Origin	(Ti,Ni,Sb)O_2. A group of artificial mineral pigments, developed since the 1960s. Oxides of nickel, titanium and antimony. Available in a variety of shades of cool lemon yellow, yellow-green.
Tinting Strength	Fairly strong.
Shade	Similar to barium lemon yellow, or naples yellow light/lemon.
Opacity	Good.
Suitability to Media	Stable in all techniques.
Drying Rate (in oil)	Slow.
Defects	When mixed with other colours, the opacity of nickel titanium yellow tends to transfer to the co-mixed pigment. This is especially so with transparent pigments, which tend to become lost within mixtures. However, the opacity and bulky nature of paint pastes made with nickel titanium make this pigment an ideal substitute for barium lemon yellow and naples yellow.
Availability/Cost	Widely used (especially in acrylic paints) as lightfast, permanent and safe to use alternatives to barium lemon yellow and genuine naples yellow.
Comments	Soft, fluffy powder, easy to hand-grind into oil colour.
Special Note	-
Health & Safety Information	-

PYRAMID YELLOW PY 108

Colour Index Number	68420
ASTM/BWS Rating	ASTM I/ BWS 8
Common Names	Anthrapyrimidine yellow.
Composition and Origin	$C_{30}H_{15}N_3O_4$. Synthetic organic pigment.
Tinting Strength	Good.
Shade	Warm, mid-yellow, with slightly mustard shade at mass tone. As a thinned glaze, shows a warmer tinge.
Opacity	Tends towards transparent (semi-opaque).
Suitability to Media	Not stable to lime.
Drying Rate (in oil)	Medium.
Defects	-
Availability/Cost	-
Comments	Permanent to light.
Special Note	Requires wetting agent.
Health & Safety Information	-

IRGAZINE YELLOW PY 110

Colour Index Number	56280
ASTM/BWS Rating	ASTM I/ BWS 7-8
Common Names	Isoindolinone yellow, chromophtal yellow.
Composition and Origin	Synthetic organic pigment, tetrachloroisoindolinone. Introduced 1960s.
Tinting Strength	High.
Shade	Bright, warmish yellow, similar to cadmium yellow mid-deep.
Opacity	Good, similar to cadmium pigment.
Suitability to Media	Stable in all media, including lime.
Drying Rate (in oil)	Slow.
Defects	-
Availability/Cost	-
Comments	-
Special Note	Requires wetting agent.
Health & Safety Information	-

PALIOTOL YELLOW PY 139

Colour Index Number	56298
ASTM/BWS Rating	ASTM I
Common Names	Isoindoline yellow.
Composition and Origin	$C_{16}H_9N_5O_6$. Synthetic organic pigment, introduced 1960s.
Tinting Strength	Good.
Shade	Warm yellow-orange, reddish yellow.
Opacity	Semi-transparent.
Suitability to Media	Not stable to lime.
Drying Rate (in oil)	Slow.
Defects	-
Availability/Cost	-
Comments	Similar in tone to cadmium yellow deep but with more transparency.
Special Note	Requires wetting agent.
Health & Safety Information	-

PRIDERITE YELLOW PY 157

Colour Index Number	77900
ASTM/BWS Rating	Not tested.
Common Names	Nickel barium, titanium primrose.
Composition and Origin	Artificial mineral pigment. A complex matrix of nickel, barium and titanium.
Tinting Strength	Medium.
Shade	A bright lime green-yellow (similar in shade to the old chrome based cinnabar green hue).
Opacity	Good.
Suitability to Media	Stable in all media.
Drying Rate (in oil)	Slow.
Defects	-
Availability/Cost	Available as dry pigment.
Comments	-
Special Note	-
Health & Safety Information	-

BISMUTH-VANDATE YELLOW PY 184

Colour Index Number	11777
ASTM/BWS Rating	Not tested.
Common Names	Bismuth yellow, bristol yellow, sicopal yellow.
Composition and Origin	Artificial mineral pigment, mixed crystal of the bismuth-vanadium oxide system. Stable and lightfast. Introduced 1980s. A new class of bismuth-based pigments, known as bristol yellows have recently been introduced.
Tinting Strength	Good.
Shade	Very pure, strong bright lemon shade. Bristol yellows are also available, ranging in shade from light yellow, mid-yellow to reddish yellow. Bristol yellows are opaque, permanent colours which offer a good alternative to zinc yellow, chrome yellow or cadmium yellow.
Opacity	Good - use in mixtures with transparent synthetic organic pigments to create opaque mixtures.
Suitability to Media	Stable in all media.
Drying Rate (in oil)	-
Defects	Lemon shades may appear greenish when poorly mixed with oil.
Availability/Cost	Becoming available in paint ranges.
Comments	-
Special Note	-
Health & Safety Information	-

INDIAN YELLOW GENUINE

Colour Index Number	-
ASTM/BWS Rating	Not tested.
Common Names	-
Composition and Origin	$C_{19}H_{16}MgO_{11}$. $6H_2O$. Magnesium salt of euxanthic acid. True indian yellow is derived from the urine of cows fed on mango leaves. The urine is mixed with a clay base to make a purée, which is then dried out and ground into a lightfast powder. It is now banned on grounds of cruelty. Indian yellow was formerly imported from Calcutta to London, the pigment being produced at Monghyr, in the Indian state of Bihar.
Tinting Strength	Good.
Shade	A strong, warm yellow orange.
Opacity	Excellent transparency.
Suitability to Media	Stable in all media but destroyed by alkalis, so never used in lime-fresco.
Drying Rate (in oil)	Slow.
Defects	-
Availability/Cost	No longer available, except perhaps in the trade of antique pigments between collectors.
Comments	Modern synthetic organic pigments such as Indian Yellow Substitute (PG10) can make a reliable alternative. Earlier synthetic organic pigments such as tartrazine lake are less permanent, especially when mixed with whites and exposed to direct light.
Special Note	By 1925, Winsor & Newton record that the genuine colour being "no longer available", was replaced at that time by a coal tar yellow with a similar shade.
Health & Safety Information	-

GAMBOGE Natural Yellow 24

Colour Index Number	-
ASTM/BWS Rating	Not tested.
Common Names	Camboge, gomma gutti (Italian).
Composition and Origin	Gamboge is a tree resin, from the species *Garcinia*, found in India and South East Asia. In the crude "pipe" form, the resin, or sap is tapped from the tree, collected into a mould and left to dry. The resin contains both pigment and binding agent. With just a brush and water, one can take colour from the solid resin and apply the resultant "paint" to paper as a watercolour (i.e. it requires no binding medium). Gamboge is sold in lump form or as a powder.
Tinting Strength	Weak when admixed with other pigments, although in watercolour mixed greens can be made by combination with small amounts of prussian blue or indigo.
Shade	A warm orange-yellow.
Opacity	Very transparent, often used as a colouring agent for alcohol (sandarac/shellac) varnishes, in the toning of furniture or musical instruments.
Suitability to Media	The resin partially dissolves in water to form a sticky, resinous form of watercolour (i.e. does not require the addition of gum arabic to adhere to paper). Gamboge can also be dissolved in alcohol and warm turpentine and thus used as a colouring agent for transparent warm-yellow varnishes, such as those employed over silver leaf, to imitate gold.
Drying Rate (in oil)	Soluble in oil, therefore unsuitable.
Defects	Not fast to light (fugitive).
Availability/Cost	Available in powder or resin form.
Comments	Substitute with cobalt yellow.
Special Note	-
Health & Safety Information	Toxic.

STIL DE GRAIN

Colour Index Number	-
ASTM/BWS Rating	Not tested.
Common Names	Brown lake, yellow lake, persian lake, buckthorn lake, dutch pink, yellow carmine, italian pink.
Composition and Origin	$C_{16}H_{12}O_7$. Plant-based pigment, derived from unripe buckthorn berries. Similar yellow "lake" pigments could be processed from quercitron bark and fustic. The plant berries are steeped in a lye (potash), then precipitated with alum to create a translucent yellow "lake" pigment. Some yellow pigments derived from plant material (e.g. weld) may be struck on to opaque substrates such as finely ground marble dust.
Tinting Strength	Weak.
Shade	Warmish yellow, can vary from batch to batch of pigment.
Opacity	Very transparent, especially in oil.
Suitability to Media	Compatible with all media, except lime, but liable to fade on exposure to sunlight.
Drying Rate (in oil)	Slow.
Defects	Fugitive to light.
Availability/Cost	Available as dry pigment, also as dried berries which can be hand-treated with potash and alum to create a pigment.
Comments	Sometimes used as overpaint, on top of blue underpaint, to achieve a green colour. However, may partially or wholly fade when used in this manner. In oil, the binder saturates the pigment to give very dark, almost brown-yellow character; in watercolour, the pale, warm yellow hue is preserved. In old watercolour ranges, various mixed hues were prepared using stil de grain as an ingredient: Olive green – stil de grain, indian yellow genuine, indigo Olive lake – stil de grain, bone black (brown shade), ultramarine.

Special Note	Sap green is also obtained from buckthorn berries, but is expressed from the ripe (dark) fruit. By tradition it is prepared as a watercolour paint by immersing the berries into a warm solution of alum and water. To ease the process, the berries may be left to steep in water for a few hours, drained and then crushed in a pestle and mortar before placing in the alum-water bath. The alum-water solution with the berries in it is slowly stirred over a gentle heat for 15-30 minutes. The resulting liquid is strained through muslin to form a thick syrup or jelly, which is applied in this semi-liquid state as a watercolour paint. When first applied, the colour is a warmish green, turning a warm yellow-brown upon drying. Sap green in this form is very unstable to light, bleaching out quickly when exposed to sunlight, turning a poor green-brown. Genuine sap green is no longer available in this form, other than by processing the berries by hand. Early 20th century substitutes for this colour were derived from non-lightfast coal tar colours, such as alizarin green. In recent years, sap green is usually a mixed colour, based on more permanent synthetic organic pigments.
Health & Safety Information	-

INDIAN YELLOW (SUBSTITUTE) PG 10

Colour Index Number	12775
ASTM/BWS Rating	ASTM I
Common Names	Nickel azo yellow.
Composition and Origin	Nickel-based synthetic organic pigment. A reliable alternative to genuine Indian yellow (not available in Europe since the 1920s).
Tinting Strength	Good.
Shade	Greenish as mass tone, gives a transparent yellow when used as glaze.
Opacity	Gives perfect transparent glazes.
Suitability to Media	-
Drying Rate (in oil)	Slow.
Defects	-
Availability/Cost	Relatively expensive, but high tinting strength means a little goes a long way as a glaze colour.
Comments	-
Special Note	Requires wetting agent. Has a more greenish tone than genuine indian yellow.
Health & Safety Information	-

ORANGE PIGMENTS

CINQUASIA YELLOW GOLD PO 48

Colour Index Number	–
ASTM/BWS Rating	ASTM I
Common Names	Quindo gold, quinacridone gold.
Composition and Origin	$C_{20}H_{12}N_2O_2$. Synthetic organic pigment.
Tinting Strength	Good.
Shade	Warm yellow-orange, similar to raw sienna but with higher tinting strength.
Opacity	Tends towards transparent.
Suitability to Media	Difficult to disperse without a wetting agent, paint film may not remain consistent over time. In all other respects, stable to all media.
Drying Rate (in oil)	Medium-slow.
Defects	Some uncertainties remain with regard to stable film formation, more likely to become apparent in cheaper paint ranges, where less time has been spent on mixing.
Availability/Cost	Available in some acrylic ranges and as dry pigment.
Comments	–
Special Note	Requires wetting agent
Health & Safety Information	–

CINQUASIA RED GOLD PO 49

Colour Index Number	-
ASTM/BWS Rating	ASTM I
Common Names	Quindo red gold, quinacridone red gold, quindo gold deep.
Composition and Origin	$C_{20}H_{12}N_2O_4$. Synthetic organic pigment.
Tinting Strength	Good.
Shade	Warm red-orange, yellow-orange, similar to burnt sienna but with higher tinting strength.
Opacity	Tends towards transparent.
Suitability to Media	Difficult to disperse without a wetting agent, paint film may not remain consistent over time. In all other respects, stable to all media.
Drying Rate (in oil)	Medium-slow.
Defects	Some uncertainties remain with regard to stable film formation, more likely to become apparent in cheaper paint ranges, where less time has been spent on mixing.
Availability/Cost	Available in some acrylic ranges and as dry pigment.
Comments	-
Special Note	Requires wetting agent.
Health & Safety Information	-

PALIOTOL ORANGE PO 59

Colour Index Number	12075
ASTM/BWS Rating	ASTM II/ BWS 8
Common Names	Permanent orange, dinitraniline orange.
Composition and Origin	$C_{16}H_{10}N_4O_5$. Organic synthetic monoazo pigment.
Tinting Strength	Good.
Shade	Bright red-orange.
Opacity	Tends towards transparent.
Suitability to Media	Stable to all media (may streak or run when in contact with mineral solvents).
Drying Rate (in oil)	Medium.
Defects	-
Availability/Cost	-
Comments	-
Special Note	Requires wetting agent.
Health & Safety Information	-

HOSTAPERM ORANGE PO 60

Colour Index Number	11782
ASTM/BWS Rating	ASTM I
Common Names	Benzimidazolone orange HGL.
Composition and Origin	Synthetic organic pigment. Monoazo benzimidazolone.
Tinting Strength	Good.
Shade	Warm orange as mass tone, thins to warm orange glaze.
Opacity	Good transparency.
Suitability to Media	Stable to all media.
Drying Rate (in oil)	Slow.
Defects	-
Availability/Cost	-
Comments	-
Special Note	Requires wetting agent.
Health & Safety Information	-

ISOINDOLINE ORANGE PO 61

Colour Index Number	11265
ASTM/BWS Rating	BWS 8
Common Names	Chromophtal orange.
Composition and Origin	Synthetic organic pigment.
Tinting Strength	Good.
Shade	Warm, dark orange as mass tone, takes on a colder hue when diluted to a thin glaze.
Opacity	Good transparency as glaze.
Suitability to Media	-
Drying Rate (in oil)	Slow.
Defects	-
Availability/Cost	Available as dry pigment and in some updated oil colour ranges.
Comments	Good glazing colour.
Special Note	Requires wetting agent.
Health & Safety Information	-

IRGAZINE ORANGE PO 73

Colour Index Number	-
ASTM/BWS Rating	BWS 8
Common Names	Pyrrol orange, irgazine orange DPP (Di-Keto-Pyrrolo-Pyrrol).
Composition and Origin	Synthetic organic pigment, introduced 1980s.
Tinting Strength	Good.
Shade	Warm, deep orange.
Opacity	Relatively opaque - glazes when thinned right down with binder/medium.
Suitability to Media	Stable in all media, including lime.
Drying Rate (in oil)	Slow.
Defects	The raw pigment tends to form together in clumps. Before combining into binder, break the particles down and separate them by wetting first with alcohol (watercolour, casein); a disperse agent for acrylic such as orotan (acrylic); mineral spirit (oil).
Availability/Cost	Available as dry pigment.
Comments	Offers an excellent alternative to cadmium pigments, with a similar opacity.
Special Note	Requires wetting agent.
Health & Safety Information	-

RED LEAD PR 105

Colour Index Number	77578
ASTM/BWS Rating	Not tested.
Common Names	Minium, saturn red, orange mineral.
Composition and Origin	Red tetroxide of lead, Pb_3O_4. Manufactured by heating either lead white or litharge (massicot) over a prolonged period at a constant temperature of 480°C. If the temperature varies during manufacture, the colour can be ruined. Lead red is often found in gilding, as an underpaint and as a mordant for oil gilding. Its fast-drying characteristic is also utilised for the coating of iron exterior structures (e.g. bridges).
Tinting Strength	Good.
Shade	Bright red-orange.
Opacity	Good.
Suitability to Media	Not stable in any medium, especially water-based binders.
Drying Rate (in oil)	Fast.
Defects	Turns brown in oil (on reaction to acidic compounds); turns black in water-based media (on reaction to sulphides). When ground in oil, tends to harden quickly when packed into tubes.
Availability/Cost	Inexpensive, in pigment form only.
Comments	Replaced by more reliable pigments (e.g. cadmium orange, irgazine orange).
Special Note	-
Health & Safety Information	Toxic, contains lead.

TITANIUM ORANGE PBr 24

Colour Index Number	77310
ASTM/BWS Rating	Not tested.
Common Names	Chrome titanate orange, ironstone brown.
Composition and Origin	An artificial mineral pigment. Cr-Sb-Ti, mixed phase system.
Tinting Strength	Moderate (weak in mixtures with other colours).
Shade	Dull orange.
Opacity	Good.
Suitability to Media	Found in some acrylic paint ranges but may also be useful in the making of gouache colours, due to its opacity.
Drying Rate (in oil)	Slow.
Defects	-
Availability/Cost	Available as dry pigment and in some paint ranges.
Comments	-
Special Note	-
Health & Safety Information	-

REALGAR

Colour Index Number	-
ASTM/BWS Rating	Not tested.
Common Names	Arabic name: *Rahj al ghar* "powder of the mine".
Composition and Origin	Sulphide of arsenic, similar to orpiment, naturally occurring in mineral form. Can also be prepared artificially. As_2S_2. Often found in nature in conjunction with or alongside orpiment. Sometimes confused with red lead, which is a similar colour.
Tinting Strength	Poor, due to crystalline structure.
Shade	Solid orange-red.
Opacity	Good.
Suitability to Media	Often found in egg tempera paintings, sometimes admixed with blues to make greenish shades.
Drying Rate (in oil)	-
Defects	-
Availability/Cost	Expensive.
Comments	-
Special Note	-
Health & Safety Information	Toxic, contains arsenic.

RED PIGMENTS

STUDIO RED PR 3

Colour Index Number	12120
ASTM/BWS Rating	BWS 7
Common Names	Helio red, lithol red, scarlet lake*, imitation vermilion, monoazo red, hansa red, toluidine red.
Composition and Origin	Synthetic organic pigment (based on organic dyestuff). Introduced early 1900s.
Tinting Strength	Good, although cheaper grades may be premixed with extender which gives a more subdued effect.
Shade	Variety of shades: mid-red to deep red, particularly shades close to vermilion.
Opacity	As pure pigment, transparent: when admixed with extender, less so.
Suitability to Media	-
Drying Rate (in oil)	Slow.
Defects	-
Availability/Cost	Often used in place of cadmium reds, or as substitute for vermilion, especially in cheaper paint ranges.
Comments	When mixed strongly with white, prone to fading.
Special Note	Requires wetting agent. Scarlet lake is an old colour name, referring to the preparation of alizarin crimson with vermilion, or vermilion with natural madder lake or carmine (as commonly used in 18th and 19th century portrait painting practice).
Health & Safety Information	-

PERMANENT RED/CARMINE PR 5/PR 170/PR 9/PR 7/PR 194

Colour Index Number	PR 5/C.I. 12490, PR 170/C.I. 12475, PR 9/C.I. 12460, PR 7/C.I. 12420, PR 194/C.I. 71100
ASTM/BWS Rating	PR 5 - ASTM II - Napthol Red ITR - $C_{30}H_{31}ClN_4O_7S$ PR 170 - ASTM II - Napthol Red/Crimson - $C_{36}H_{22}N_4O_4$ PR 9 - ASTM II - Napthol Red AS-OL - $C_{24}H_{17}Cl_2N_3O_3$ PR 7 - ASTM I - Napthol Red AS-TR - $C_{25}H_{19}Cl_2N_3O_2$ PR 194 - ASTM I - Perione/Permanent Red Dark GOLO
Common Names	Formerly: para red (PR 1/C.I. 12070); updated: permanent red/carmine, napthol red, napthol crimson.
Composition and Origin	Synthetic organic group of pigments, with variable permanence (despite the name!). Early permanent reds (e.g. para red) were based on azo-napthol synthetic dyestuffs and prone to fading on exposure to light. These colours performed satisfactorily when used neat. When admixed with white, their tendency to fade made them suitable only for cheaper paints. The modern equivalents to these colours have better permanence and are widely used, as relatively stable alternatives to the expensive cadmium pigments. The naming of these colours is rather confusing: some napthol red pigments are not reliably permanent to light. Choose the more lightfast varieties, as recommended above - look for the Colour Index Name on tube labelling and in catalogues.
Tinting Strength	Good.
Shade	Mid-red, deep red to crimson, carmine shades.
Opacity	Very transparent, especially when compared to cadmium reds.
Suitability to Media	-
Drying Rate (in oil)	Slow.
Defects	-
Availability/Cost	Offered in most paint ranges, as alternative to cadmium reds.
Comments	The new carmine shades have great intensity.
Special Note	Requires wetting agent.
Health & Safety Information	-

CADMIUM RED VERMILION ORANGE PO 23 - CdS. x HgS
RED PR 113 - CdS. x HgS
LIGHT PR 108 - CdS. x CdSe
MEDIUM PR 108
DEEP PR 108

Colour Index Number	PO 23/77201, PR 113/77201, PR 108/77202
ASTM/BWS Rating	ASTM I
Common Names	Selenium red, cadmium scarlet, cadmium vermilion, cadmium red pale/light, cadmium red medium, cadmium red deep/dark, cadmium bordeaux, cadmium brown.
Composition and Origin	An artificial mineral pigment, produced by heating cadmium sulphide with the element selenium. Cadmium vermilion orange is a solid solution of mercury sulphide in cadmium sulphide. Introduced for artists in the 1920s - a permanent replacement for vermilion.
Tinting Strength	Good.
Shade	Warm orange, through bright vermilion tone to deep red, purple-red (bordeaux), red-brown.
Opacity	Good.
Suitability to Media	Stable to all media, in lime-fresco suitable for indoor work only.
Drying Rate (in oil)	Slow.
Defects	-
Availability/Cost	Expensive but widely used.
Comments	More opaque than the synthetic organic red pigments, which are often used to imitate cadmium red. The best grades are pure, but some varieties may include up to 15% barium sulphate as an extender (PR 108:1).
Special Note	-
Health & Safety Information	Contains cadmium.

ALIZARIN CRIMSON PR 83

Colour Index Number	58000
ASTM/BWS Rating	ASTM III, as oil colour
Common Names	Madder lake synthetic, alizarin carmine, crimson lake, alizarin madder lake.
Composition and Origin	$C_{14}H_8O_4$. A synthetic organic pigment, based on the dyestuff alizarin. Alizarin is the most lightfast of the colourants derived from natural madder root. (Madder root was previously processed to produce natural madder lake). Alizarin was first separated from the other colourants in madder root, in 1826. The dyestuff alizarin was subsequently synthesised in 1868.
Tinting Strength	Dark shades quite strong.
Shade	Blue-red, some varieties are a bright red (alizarin crimson light).
Opacity	Transparent.
Suitability to Media	Not stable to lime fresco.
Drying Rate (in oil)	Slow - thick paint dries with wrinkling.
Defects	Drying problems. Can fade against white grounds and in mixtures with whites. Performs better when applied over darker ground colours.
Availability/Cost	Widely used, fairly inexpensive.
Comments	Use as thin glazing colour.
Special Note	Requires wetting agent. In some paint ranges, alizarin crimson is offered with the name permanent alizarin crimson. This may relate to the use of anthraquinone red (PR 177/C.I. 65300) - $C_{28}H_{16}N_2O_4$, which is stable and lightfast in all media, although in tints with white it may exhibit lower stability to light. To mix a lightfast approximation of alizarin crimson, the following colours can be combined: quinacridone red (PV 19, red-shade), perylene red (PR 149) and ultramarine blue (PB 29).
Health & Safety Information	-

CHROME RED PR 104

Colour Index Number	77605
ASTM/BWS Rating	Not tested.
Common Names	Chromate red, molybdate of lead, chinese red.
Composition and Origin	$Pb_2(OH)^2CrO_4$. Artificial mineral pigment, developed since 1820s.
Tinting Strength	Good. Lead chromate red.
Shade	Bright pillar-box red, also in shades of orange red*, red-orange, mid-red, deep red.
Opacity	Good.
Suitability to Media	Previously used in oil colours. However, not permanent in any media.
Drying Rate (in oil)	Fast.
Defects	Turns dark in oil, sometimes with a greenish or brownish cast.
Availability/Cost	Sometimes still available as a dry pigment.
Comments	Withdrawn from use due to toxicity of manufacture and exposure to end user.
Special Note	Satisfactory substitutes can be found among the cadmium reds or irgazine reds. *Chrome orange is a co-mixture of chrome yellow and chrome red.
Health & Safety Information	Contains lead, chrome. Toxic.

VERMILION PR 106

Colour Index Number	77766
ASTM/BWS Rating	ASTM I
Common Names	Cinnabar (technically refers to the mineral form of the pigment), chinese vermilion, scarlet vermilion, orange vermilion, pale vermilion, etc.
Composition and Origin	HgS. An artificial mineral pigment, based on mercuric sulphide. The natural mineral (cinnabar, mercury ore) produces a darker, brownish pigment and has been used as a painting material from classical times. In Chinese painting, the pigment dates back to prehistory. In Europe, mineral cinnabar was formerly mined in Almaden, Spain and Monte Amiata in Italy. The artificial "wet" and "dry" processes for producing vermilion date from the 13th century, although industrial production began in the late 18th century. The permanence of vermilion is disputed: for many decades, the appearance of random black areas on paintings made with vermilion was blamed on a defect of the pigment. Recent studies seem to indicate that this blackening effect may be caused by admixtures with chrome red or red lead pigment. Curiously, vermilion is rated ASTM I as an oil paint. In the meantime this important pigment has disappeared from most oil colour ranges. Despite the confusion surrounding vermilion, it is still sought after by artists and retains its historic significance within the painters' palette.
Tinting Strength	Good.
Shade	Warm, bright red, sometimes slightly pinky. Darker shades can have a dusky appearance.

Opacity	Good.
Suitability to Media	Oil, tempera, watercolour. In lime-fresco it is generally safely applied in fresco secco (bound in animal glue, egg or casein and applied over dried layers of lime), although examples of fresco paintings survive that are painted entirely into lime.
Drying Rate (in oil)	Very slow.
Defects	Some varieties of processed vermilion are prone to reverting to black mercuric sulphide.
Availability/Cost	Expensive. Vermilion has all but vanished from modern oil colour ranges due to its reputed toxicity and apparent impermanence, coupled with its scarcity in pigment form. Specialist pigment suppliers offer the dry pigment in light and dark shades. The mineral form is also available.
Comments	A soft, warm red with unique qualities.
Special Note	Vermilion can be considered stable in lime-fresco techniques, when saturated in lime-water and left to dry, then re-powdered (in a pestle and mortar), and re-saturated with lime-water. This process, when undertaken five times (or more), will help encapsulate the pigment particles and so avoid contamination with atmospheric pollutants. After the fifth saturation with lime-water, the material is re-ground to a powder and added as normal (with water only) and applied to fresh intonaco.
Health & Safety Information	Contains mercury.

QUINACRIDONE PINK/RED (Permanent Rose)

MAGENTA PR 122 - $C_{22}H_{16}N_2O_2$
RED PR 192
SCARLET PR 207 - $C_{20}H_{12}N_2O_2$
VIOLET PV 19 - $C_{20}H_{12}N_2O_2$

Colour Index Number	PR 122/73915, PR 192/NA, PR 207/NA, PV 19/73900
ASTM/BWS Rating	ASTM I
Common Names	Quinacridone red, quinacridone scarlet, quinacridone violet.
Composition and Origin	A group of synthetic organic pigments, introduced from 1950s.
Tinting Strength	Very high.
Shade	Bright pink-red, with violet tinge, shades available from mid-red, to pink-red, violet-red, violet.
Opacity	Very transparent.
Suitability to Media	Stable to all media.
Drying Rate (in oil)	Slow, usually has drier added in tube oil colour.
Defects	-
Availability/Cost	Expensive but very strong, can be extended considerably in cheaper paint ranges. Other synthetic reds, such as perylene red and paliogen maroon are less expensive and may become easier to obtain.
Comments	Dark red/crimson/rose shades offer a lightfast alternative to alizarin crimson, which can be applied in glazes against pale grounds, or in admixtures with white.
Special Note	Requires wetting agent. PV 19 can be sold as either a red, red-violet or violet shade, according to manufacturer.
Health & Safety Information	-

PERYLENE RED PR 149

Colour Index Number	71137
ASTM/BWS Rating	ASTM I
Common Names	Anthraquinone red, perylene red BL.
Composition and Origin	$C_{40}H_{26}N_2O_4$. Synthetic organic pigment.
Tinting Strength	Strong.
Shade	Bright warmish red. Tints with white tend towards pink-red.
Opacity	Transparent, excellent for glazing.
Suitability to Media	Stable in all media, except lime-fresco.
Drying Rate (in oil)	Medium.
Defects	-
Availability/Cost	Becoming available in updated paint ranges.
Comments	-
Special Note	-
Health & Safety Information	-

SCARLET RED PR 168

Colour Index Number	58300
ASTM/BWS Rating	ASTM II
Common Names	Anthranthrone red, anthraquinone red or scarlet.
Composition and Origin	$C_{22}H_8Br_2O_2$. Synthetic organic pigment. Brominated anthranthrone, introduced from 1913 onwards.
Tinting Strength	Good.
Shade	Bright red, similar to cadmium vermilion shade.
Opacity	Good transparency.
Suitability to Media	Stable to all media.
Drying Rate (in oil)	Medium-Slow.
Defects	-
Availability/Cost	-
Comments	-
Special Note	Requires wetting agent.
Health & Safety Information	-

PALIOGEN MAROON PR 179

Colour Index Number	71130
ASTM/BWS Rating	ASTM I
Common Names	Perylene maroon, indanthrene red, palamid bordeaux.
Composition and Origin	$C_{26}H_{14}N_2O_4$. Synthetic organic pigment. Perylene. Production dates from 1959: introduced in artists' colours in recent years.
Tinting Strength	Good.
Shade	Warm, deep crimson. Similar to alizarin crimson but deeper in shade.
Opacity	Good transparency.
Suitability to Media	Stable in all media.
Drying Rate (in oil)	Slow.
Defects	Difficult to disperse, may take longer to mull than other pigments, in order to create a smooth paint paste.
Availability/Cost	Available as pigment and in some updated oil colour ranges.
Comments	A lightfast alternative to alizarin, with a warmer tone.
Special Note	Requires wetting agent.
Health & Safety Information	-

POTTER'S PINK PR 233

Colour Index Number	77301
ASTM/BWS Rating	Not tested.
Common Names	Pink colour, chrome-tin pink.
Composition and Origin	An artificial mineral pigment, from either roasted chromium and zinc oxides (pink colour), or roasted chromium and tin oxides (potter's pink), or roasted chromium, aluminium and tin. Discovered in the 1790s in connection with English pottery in Staffordshire, both forms of this deep pinkish colour were formerly used in the ceramics industry.
Tinting Strength	Weak.
Shade	Dull, deep pink, available in light and dark shades.
Opacity	Opaque.
Suitability to Media	Used in watercolour painting during the 18th and 19th centuries. Stable to lime.
Drying Rate (in oil)	-
Defects	Weak tinting strength and heavy, dumpy powder renders this pigment unsuitable to manufactured paints.
Availability/Cost	Expensive and only available in pigment form.
Comments	A subtle, dull pink, of particular interest to fresco painters and also to artists working with strong water-based binders such as casein applied to strong paper.
Special Note	-
Health & Safety Information	-

CARMINE Natural Red 4 (carmine from cochineal), Natural Red 3 (kermes red lake)

Colour Index Number	75470 (carmine from cochineal) 75460 (kermes red lake)
ASTM/BWS Rating	Not tested.
Common Names	Carmine lake, cochineal (Coccus cacti).
Composition and Origin	$C_{18}H_{12}O_9$ or $C_{22}H_{20}O_{13}$. Red lake pigments date back to antiquity. Prior to the introduction of carmine derived from the cochineal insect (after the discovery of the Americas by Columbus in 1492), red lakes processed from the kermes insect (*Kermesillicis*) were widely used in Europe. The colouring matter, kermes acid, is extracted from the female insects, by boiling with potash, then precipitation on to an alum base to make a "lake" pigment. The kermes insect was common in the Mediterranean countries of southern Europe, feeding on oak trees. A similar insect, *Coccus polonicus,* in northern Europe (especially Poland) was also used for making red lakes. By contrast to carmine lakes from cochineal, Kermes lakes have less tinting strength and a weaker colour. Kermes was once a celebrated and important dyestuff for textiles, at times more important than madder. Since the introduction of the cochineal insect to Europe in the 1500s it fell out of favour both as a dyestuff and as a colour for painting. The discovery of the new world in 1492 by Christopher Columbus, heralded the introduction to Europe of a very important colouring agent: carmine red lake from the cochineal insect. The colour is derived from the bodies of the insects, which have been fed exclusively on the nopal cactus. Initially, Spain had exclusive rights over the importation to Europe of cochineal. However, eventually, the process was copied in India, where the same type of cactus plant was specially imported to enable cultivation. Today, cochineal is still farmed on the Spanish Canary Islands and in Peru and Chile. The pigment is formed from an initial dye base. The liquid dye is attached to a substrate (e.g. alumina) by precipitation. In the trade, naccarat carmine is the most applicable form for use in oil paints and varnishes.
Tinting Strength	Good.

Shade	Carmine from cochineal is a strong red-crimson.
Opacity	Excellent transparency.
Suitability to Media	Poor permanence: fades in strong sunlight.
Drying Rate (in oil)	Slow.
Defects	Fugitive to light.
Availability/Cost	Expensive, but still found in some oil paint ranges.
Comments	–
Special Note	Requires wetting agent. Burnt carmine is an old colour, prepared by calcining carmine pigment. Indian purple is a fugitive preparation of carmine on a copper base (obsolete).
Health & Safety Information	–

NATURAL MADDER Natural Red 9

Colour Index Number	75330
ASTM/BWS Rating	ASTM II
Common Names	Madder lake, rose madder, rose dore, etc.
Composition and Origin	$C_{14}H_8O_4$. Dyestuff from the roots of the madder plant have been used since antiquity for the dyeing of cloth and for the preparation of colour for painting. The dye extract can be struck on to a substrate to provide a pigment. The exact methods used to gain pigment from the madder plant is open to interpretation: a great many recipes could be quoted and all may have credence. Until the mid-19th century, the production of dyestuffs from madder was of great importance: all over Europe, but especially in France, madder cultivation and processing was common. Often, the dye was used to colour tunics worn by the military and, as a consequence, the madder industry was buoyant. Madder has been employed as pigment since the time of the Egyptians. In some periods, the use of scale insects such as kermes may have been more prevalent than that of madder. In some instances, makers derived the colour not from the actual roots of the madder plant, but from waste cuttings of dyed cloth, the cast-offs from textile production. Such dyed fabrics were immersed into a mordant bath to recover the dyestuff, the liquid then being processed into pigment by mixture with alum. Madder contains purpurin with ruberythric acid: from these dyestuffs, a more stable, reliable dyestuff, known as alizarin (1,2 dihydroxyanthraquinone) is extracted from the plant roots, by treatment with dilute sulphuric acid (3-4%). The dyestuff is then precipitated on to a base of alum, then washed thoroughly to create a stabilised "lake" pigment. Natural madder lake pigments tend to contain some residual quantities of purpurin: this gives natural madder lakes their characteristic warm tinge. Purpurin is understood to be less lightfast than alizarin: in practice this may lead to a loss of brilliance of depth of a paint film, or in some cases, partial fading of the colour in the paint film. By contrast to natural madder

	lakes, modern, synthetic alizarin pigment has a cold, sharp edge. In 1868, the principal colouring matter from madder, alizarin, was first commercially synthesised, precipitating the demise of the madder industry. There is some debate as to the relative lightfastness of synthetic alizarin and natural madder lake. It is suggested by some colourmakers that natural madder is more lightfast than alizarin crimson. This seems to be confirmed by ASTM ratings. As with alizarin crimson, natural madder is prone to fading when admixed with white, or when applied as glaze on to pale ground colour.
Tinting Strength	Weak.
Shade	Warm light pink (as powder); dark crimson (as oil colour).
Opacity	Very transparent as glaze.
Suitability to Media	Stable in all media, but liable to fade in lime-fresco.
Drying Rate (in oil)	Very slow.
Defects	Liable to fade on exposure to sunlight.
Availability/Cost	Expensive. Still offered as prepared paint and in pigment form. The production of madder lake is a costly, time-consuming business.
Comments	A simple method to gain pigment from madder root: take 1kg of dried madder roots (from plants that are 2-3 years old, grown in chalky soil). Place in a heat resistant glass vessel (e.g. pyrex). Immerse into enough cold water to cover the roots. Add 200g, powdered potash (K_2CO_3), stir. Potassium dichromate can be used in place of potash: this is available in the form of pastilles which dissolve into cold water. Potassium dichromate can be affected by light and needs to be stored in a dark brown glass bottle, or in a closed cupboard. Potash is wood ash and this is what would have been used in old recipes for madder lake; the modern product is synthetically produced. Place on a low heat (ideally in a double boiler). Do not let contents boil. Simmer for 1-2 hours. A deep red-purple colour will be extracted from the roots, in the form of a gloopy syrup. The longer the liquid is left to boil, the greater

its viscosity. It is possible to make madder lake without resorting to any heat whatsoever, but heating does however give a more controllable, concentrated liquid that is easier to manipulate.

Pour the liquid into a new container, strain the roots and other debris so that you are left with a coloured liquid solution. This "dyestuff" can then be fixed on to a base of rock alum. Take 500g alum $K_2Al_2(SO_4)$, pour into the liquid dyestuff and leave to steep for 2-3 days. Pour off the coloured water that collects above the settled sediment. Keep the sediment, and dry it by first pouring on to filter paper to remove any remaining dye, then spreading on to a porous surface. A brick is an ideal surface, or perhaps a concrete paving slab - any stone structure with a little porosity. Alternatively, spread the colour paste over a sheet of blotting paper, overlaid with a piece of fine mesh muslin. The muslin stops the alum particles from absorbing into the paper. Once dry, the coloured alum can be scraped from the muslin into a pestle and mortar. Pulverise the coloured alum, to reduce the particle size. Place the dried powder/pieces into a container and fill with cold water to cover. Leave to settle for 2-3 days, pour off the resulting coloured liquid and again, spread the alum paste on to a porous surface. This process is repeated 3-4 times, until the alum paste stops giving out dye (i.e. the water in which the alum-paste is steeped remains colourless upon settlement). This process is very lengthy, perhaps taking 5-6 weeks to produce thoroughly washed pigment. After each washing and drying, the "pigment" should be ground in the pestle and mortar, to gain a fine grain size.

The final product, madder lake, is ideally a warm, deep red-crimson. However, the exact colour will alter from batch to batch so that it is extremely difficult to obtain matches. Some recipes call for the inclusion of ground egg shells (calcite), or very fine chalk (e.g. calcium carbonate, whiting chalk, with mesh size 20) or fine marble dust with the alum: this may reduce transparency but increase the brilliance of the colour.

Special Note	Requires wetting agent. Obsolete forms of natural madder (the particular hue indicated here is sometimes matched in modern paint substitutes): Rose dore – a variation of madder, with a scarlet tinge Brown madder – warm red-brown Madder carmine – rich deep red madder lake Ruben's madder – warm orange-brown.
Health & Safety Information	–

DRAGON'S BLOOD Coloured Natural Resin

Colour Index Number	-
ASTM/BWS Rating	Not tested.
Common Names	-
Composition and Origin	A tree resin from Indonesia, from the palm, *Calamus draco*. The best quality is that which is tapped from the tree, then left to set into a round ball, or square/rectangular form. To signify high quality, these "lump" forms of dragon's blood are stamped with a gold seal. The resin has a strong red-brown tinge and, when formed into a solution, provides a clarified (varnish) film, with pink-red or orange-red colour.
Tinting Strength	Weak.
Shade	Pink-red or red-orange, according to source.
Opacity	Transparent.
Suitability to Media	Soluble in alcohol only, making it suitable as a glaze over dried layers of egg tempera paint, or as a varnish over gold, silver or tin leaf to enhance/warm the surface colour. Dragon's blood is partially soluble into turpentine, when oil of spike lavender is added. In this form it can be used as a coloured varnish (for aged effects) on to dried oil paint.
Drying Rate (in oil)	-
Defects	Dragon's blood fades in direct sunlight, showing as a dull red-brown.
Availability/Cost	Available in lump (resin) form, or as a pulverised powder.
Comments	-
Special Note	-
Health & Safety Information	Toxic.

GUBBIO RED PBr 23

Colour Index Number	-
ASTM/BWS Rating	BWS 8
Common Names	-
Composition and Origin	Synthetic organic pigment.
Tinting Strength	Strong.
Shade	Deep red-brown.
Opacity	Transparent when expressed as a glaze.
Suitability to Media	Stable in all media.
Drying Rate (in oil)	-
Defects	-
Availability/Cost	-
Comments	-
Special Note	Requires wetting agent.
Health & Safety Information	-

EARTH PIGMENTS

The production of pigment from earth deposits is of great value to many artists. Natural earth pigments tend to be irregular in terms of their particle size. This can mean that from one batch of pigment to another, there are discrepancies in terms of the exact colour and grind size. To the manufacturer of artists' paints, this can be something of a problem, because each time a pigment is prepared into paint, it needs to be checked against previous makings, and the formula may have to be adjusted accordingly. This can lead to extra costs and delays in processing. Also, natural earth pigments are not suited to the acrylic paint making process, due to inconsistencies in the particle size and the possibility of contamination/impurities being present. In oil paints and watercolours, this is less problematic, but in the case of acrylic, it may upset the balance of other raw ingredients used. Consequently, it is far simpler for a manufacturer to use modern synthetic iron oxides, which have regular particle sizes and tend to be consistent from batch to batch. However, the nuance of colour provided by synthetic iron oxides is different from that of the natural earth pigments. The synthetic iron oxides are strong and opaque by comparison. Natural earth pigments tend to be subtle in shade and create beautiful transparent glazes when diluted or when manipulated with the addition of a paint medium. The supply of earth pigments is another factor. The traditional core colours – raw sienna, burnt sienna, raw umber, burnt umber, green earth, venetian red – may not be derived from their original sources in the current market. In order to obtain natural earth pigments more cheaply, it may be necessary to look outside Western Europe. In any case, the processing of natural earth pigments may be less thorough than in previous times.

Just as the mineral pigments produced from semi-precious stones have to be worked in a specific manner to gain the best colour, so the processing of earth deposits involves considerable work. The raw material needs to be washed and freed from impurities such as plant debris. It can then be dried, pulverised and sieved through a fine mesh to gain particular grind sizes.

In the UK, the author has recently visited a producer of ochre pigments in Gloucestershire, at Clearwell. This former iron mine has long been a source for yellow, orange, red and purple ochre pigments. Indeed, the term "English Red" is often cited as having originated from Clearwell, in the Forest of Dean. Today, the mine is effectively a part of the heritage industry. Guided tours can be made underground, with exhibits of mining equipment and an explanation of the geology of the area. In the old mine workings, small pockets of ochre are still found and are sold by the company through their own on-site shop, in small quantities. Although such deposits could never be used in a manufacturing context, to an individual artist, familiar with the preparation of pigment into binding media, such colours have a special nature and significance. Another example of English ochre was that dug from open pits in Oxfordshire (Shotover Hill near Oxford). This colour is referred to as "oxford ochre" and is a particularly orange cast.

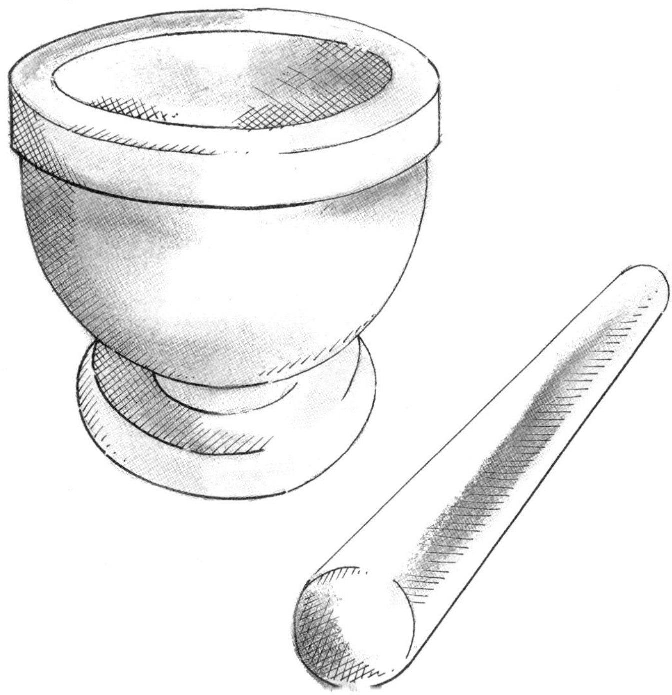

Pestle and Mortar

Examples of Earth Pigment Deposits

Limonite – Cyprus

The term limonite can be ascribed to all forms of hydrated ferric oxide (natural oxides of iron). In terms of clarity of colour and paleness, limonite deposits in Cyprus have always been highly prized.

French ochres – Rousillon, Le Luberon, France

A rich variety of natural ochres in yellow, orange and red shades. These ochres are washed, sieved and levigated in the traditional manner to produce the best quality colour, free of impurities.

English red – Clearwell Caves, Gloucestershire, England

This ancient iron mine continues to yield very strong ochres in colours varying from yellow, orange and red to purple and brown. The colour is found in loose, clumpy powder form and is dug out from small cavities between sedimentary layers of limestone. It is first steeped in water to remove plant debris and other impurities. The pigment is then stirred and the finest particles, while in suspension in water, are floated off and left to dry out over a period of days. They are then pulverised to form a fine powder, suitable for paint making or for adding into lime mortars for house painting.

In industrial terms, english red relates to a form of synthetic iron oxide (PR 101), usually with a yellowish shade. However, true english red may refer back to any number of native red earths found in England, but perhaps most importantly those found within the Forest of Dean, at Clearwell Caves.

Raw sienna – Arcidosso, Tuscany, Italy

Prior to the 1930s, sienna was dug from open pits near the town of Arcidosso. The yellow earth was carefully washed and sieved to provide pigment of the strongest colour and optimum transparency. The raw product was calcined to create burnt sienna.

Sienna should always have a degree of transparency. It differs from ochres (which are milky, opaque) in that the clay base of raw sienna means that it has a high proportion of silica (which is translucent and affords good light refraction).

Haematite – "Ruddle" Florence Mine, Egremont, Cumbria, England

The west coast of Cumbria was once an important source of pig iron, used in the manufacture of steel. Rich iron ore seams (haematite) lie in between layers of limestone. Mining for iron ore in Cumbria dates back to Roman times but was developed industrially at the end of the 19th century, to serve the shipbuilding yards at Barrow-in-Furness. Florence mine was first worked in 1914 and at the height of production in 1924 was producing over 4,000 tons of pure grade haematite per week. Although the mining of iron ore is today much reduced, Florence mine is still producing iron oxide pigment for use in the paint and cosmetics trades, and the mine is also open to visitors, who can take a tour underground. The rich red haematite derived from Cumbria is known locally as "ruddle" and in former times was used for sheep-marking. It has a very strong red-violet shade, but the pulverised rock retains a little grittiness when hand-processed using a pestle and mortar.

Armenian Bole

$Al_2O_3.SiO_2+Fe_2O_3.$

By tradition, the soft, clay-rich red coloured ground applied below gilded surfaces is taken from a type of red earth from Armenia, and commonly referred to as armenian bole. This description, while perhaps not viable in the present market is still often applied, to denote that the pigment has a soft texture, suitable for binding with animal glue size as a ground for gold leaf. In practice, armenian bole may be used to describe any earth-tone pigment used for this purpose (PR 102), including artificially prepared iron oxides.

Brown Ochre (PY 43)

Dull, fawn ochres are often referred to in old manuals on painting practice as "brown ochre". The colour is derived from the natural product, although it is possible to calcine varieties of yellow ochre, or even green earth to provide similar soft brown shades.

Burnt Ochre

Any yellow or pale orange ochre, or other forms of PY 43 (e.g. raw sienna) can be calcined to give darker hues. This process, (as with burnt sienna) reduces the water-content of a pigment and makes the resultant colour slightly more transparent in nature. The author has deposited samples of various ochres into a kiln, heated to approximately 600°C, to gauge this colour change. It was observed that the strong yellow ochres from France turned a fiery orange-brown, while a sample of pale Italian brown ochre simply became a shade darker. See also: light red.

Burnt Green Earth, Veronese Brown (PG 23/C.I. 77009)

Fe, K, Mn, Al.

As with the ochres, samples of green earth, when calcined, transform to rich red-brown shades. These burnt green earths have great transparency and vary in shade according to the type of green earth used. It is vital that the calcined green earth be pure, rather than co-mixed with industrial pigments, which is often the case.

Caledonian Brown

A deep, rich red-brown, containing oxides and/or hydrates of iron and manganese, the latter giving good drying properties in oil. It usually contains some residual moisture and thus requires air-drying prior to use. By calcination, caledonian brown provides a deep black-brown shade. An imitation shade can be easily prepared by mixing burnt sienna with van dyke brown or burnt umber.

Cappagh Brown, Mineral Brown

The original source for cappagh brown was at Skibbereen, County Cork in Ireland, on the estate of Lord Audley, who began producing the pigment in 1814. When this original source was closed, the remaining stock was purchased by Winsor & Newton, from whom it was still available in 1925. The high manganese content of the original pigment made this a fast-drying colour when prepared as oil paint. It is a similar red-brown shade to caledonian brown but may contain trace elements of humus (decomposed plant matter, peat). Prior to use, the pigment is required to be air-dried to become free of moisture.

Davy's Grey (PBk 19)

Powdered slate, sometimes including portions of soft clay in powdered form, provides a variety of soft, warmish grey, blue-grey and green-grey pigments, which can be used with care in strong water-based binders such as casein. As oil colour, the finer grades of davy's grey make excellent neutral tones when admixed to transparent colours, providing tints towards darkness, due in part to the pigment's weak tinting strength and good transparency. In oil, davy's grey dries fast and evenly. Some dry pigment samples can have an uneven texture, due to inclusions of impurities and may therefore be difficult to process. Pulverisation in a pestle and mortar of the dry pigment can help to free any clumping of particles and reduce grittiness. It may also be advisable to leave the dry pigment to air, so that it loses a little residual moisture, prior to use with oil binders.

Manufactured oil and watercolour paints can include examples of davy's greys formed from admixtures of other pigments. The colour is named after artist Henry Davy (1780-1833), who recommended its use to the colourmaker Winsor and Newton.

In watercolour, "neutral tint" can be prepared by mixing davy's grey with red ochre and ultramarine. An earlier (and more fugitive) formula for neutral tint was derived from carmine, lamp black and indigo.

Gulf Red, Persian Red Oxide (PR 102)

Red earth pigments are found all over the world, but can vary widely in terms of texture and colour. The red native earths of the Persian Gulf have a hard texture, similar to that of a mineral pigment (i.e. crystalline) and tend to contain almost 100% pure iron oxide. As a consequence, the colour can be much heavier, tending towards violet, when compared to many European red earths.

Sinopia is another name commonly applied to any number of natural red earth pigments (originally from the ancient city of Sinope). In fresco painting, sinopia is the colour used to make the cartoon underdrawing. Cinabrese as a flesh-tint used in fresco painting, is composed of two-thirds sinopia to one-third bianco san giovanni.

Indian Red (PR 101)

Today, indian red refers to a shade of synthetic iron oxide, usually with a cold, blue-violet tinge. It is a by-product of other iron-related industries, produced from the calcination of ferrous sulphate. The native earth, imported to Britain in the 19th century would have contained over 90% pure red iron oxide, and possessed a similar violet tinge to the modern product.

Light Red (PR 102)

The modern product is a synthetic iron oxide red with a warm shade. The original pigment was prepared by heating selected yellow ochre, the colour being arrived at according to the heat applied and the colour of the original ochre material.

Pompeii Red (PR 102)

The name refers to the pigment of antiquity from Pompeii, being an orange-red earth pigment, with a degree of transparency as a glaze. As with other similar red earths, the low colour strength is due to the ratio of iron oxide to clay. The modern product may be based on a mixture of red earth pigments and may or may not contain artificial iron oxides.

Pozzuoli Red

True pozzuoli red is a soft, delicate red from volcanic earth deposits and was processed, through pulverisation and washing, at Pozzuoli in the Bay of Naples until the 1930s. As with pompeii red, the modern product may be based on a mixture of red earth pigments and may or may not contain artificial iron oxides. Pozzuolana earth may refer to a pale natural earth still produced at Pozzuoli, but which contains a high proportion of silica and is used for its natural, fast-setting, cement-like properties in building restoration.

True native red earths are intrinsically linked to volcanic activity, the coloration caused when yellow-orange iron bearing rock and earth is exposed to intense heat from active volcanoes.

Spanish Red (PR 102)

An old colour name, spanish red refers to soft orange-red ochre pigments, from Castille in Spain.

Terra Rosa (PR 101)

An old trade name for a natural red earth pigment from Italy, similar in shade to venetian red (pinkish).

Turkey Umber, Turkey Brown (PBr 7)

Turkey umber is raw umber, whose deposits were originally those in Cyprus or the Turkish Mediterranean region.

Venetian Red (PR 101)

Venetian red in its original form is a partially hydrated natural iron oxide with a characteristic pinkish shade, especially when admixed with whites. When used with animal skin glue in combination with chalk in a dilute consistency, it makes a fine, translucent pink ground colour over gesso.

The modern product is manufactured by calcination of ferrous sulphate with chalk (calcium carbonate). The proportion of colour to chalk varies from source to source, but is typically somewhere in the region of 20-30% iron oxide to 70-80% calcium carbonate, thus giving a relatively weak tinting strength with a pinkish hue – less brown than with light red, and less violet when compared to indian red.

"Neutral orange" is an old Winsor & Newton colour name for a preparation of venetian red with cadmium yellow.

RAW UMBER PBr 7

Colour Index Number	77492
ASTM/BWS Rating	ASTM I
Common Names	Cyprus umber, turkey umber, green umber.
Composition and Origin	$Fe_2O_3.MnO_2.nH_2O+Si+al_2O_3$. Natural earth pigment, derived from natural iron oxide ore, with varying amounts of manganese and aluminium silicate.
Tinting Strength	Good.
Shade	From yellow-brown and green-brown to olive-brown, can be cool to warm in tone.
Opacity	Deeper shades more transparent.
Suitability to Media	Stable to all media but may be difficult to disperse into acrylic binders.
Drying Rate (in oil)	Fast. Strong catalytic effect, use in admixtures during underpainting and for toned grounds.
Defects	Rapid drying can cause cracking if applied over slower drying colours. Darkens with age.
Availability/Cost	Inexpensive, widely used.
Comments	Useful for underpainting. Because it darkens appreciably in oil, use carefully. Requires high oil content (up to 80%) – may absorb oil from subsequent paint layers if overpainted when wet.
Special Note	-
Health & Safety Information	-

BURNT UMBER PBr 7

Colour Index Number	77492
ASTM/BWS Rating	ASTM I
Common Names	Brown iron oxide.
Composition and Origin	$Fe_2O_3.MnO_2.nH_2O + Si + Al_2O_3$. Natural burnt earth pigment. Calcined raw umber.
Tinting Strength	Good.
Shade	Variety of shades, from red-brown to dark brown, generally with a stronger, warmer tone than raw umber.
Opacity	Fairly transparent, more transparent than raw umber.
Suitability to Media	Stable to all media but may be difficult to disperse into acrylic binders.
Drying Rate (in oil)	Fast.
Defects	-
Availability/Cost	Inexpensive, widely available. Often used in mixtures with other reliable pigments to give imitations of unreliable antique colours such as van dyke brown.
Comments	-
Special Note	-
Health & Safety Information	-

RAW SIENNA PBr 7

Colour Index Number	77492
ASTM/BWS Rating	ASTM I
Common Names	Sienna, natural sienna, raw sienna.
Composition and Origin	$Fe_2O_3.nH_2O + Mno_2 + Al_2O_3.SiO_2.2(H_2O)$. Natural earth pigment, a mixture of iron oxide and silica. Known since antiquity.
Tinting Strength	Good.
Shade	Warm, deep golden yellow, darker than yellow ochre due to higher silica content. Although dark as a mass tone, raw sienna brushes out to a bright transparent yellow.
Opacity	Tends towards transparent.
Suitability to Media	Stable to all media but may be difficult to disperse into acrylic binders.
Drying Rate (in oil)	Fast to medium.
Defects	High oil absorption, tends to darken when ground in oil.
Availability/Cost	Inexpensive, widely used.
Comments	-
Special Note	-
Health & Safety Information	-

BURNT SIENNA PBr 7

Colour Index Number	77492
ASTM/BWS Rating	ASTM I
Common Names	Burnt sienna.
Composition and Origin	$Fe_2O_3.nH_2O + al_2O_3$. Calcined raw sienna. Burnt sienna and other calcined natural earths are thought to date back to antiquity.
Tinting Strength	Good.
Shade	Deep and bright red-brown.
Opacity	Very good glazing colour.
Suitability to Media	Stable to all media but may be difficult to disperse into acrylic binders.
Drying Rate (in oil)	Fast-Medium.
Defects	Darkens with age in oil, may harden when ground with poppy oil.
Availability/Cost	Inexpensive, widely used.
Comments	-
Special Note	-
Health & Safety Information	-

VAN DYKE BROWN   Natural Brown 8 or PBr 9

Colour Index Number	PBr 9/77430
ASTM/BWS Rating	Not tested.
Common Names	Cassel brown, cologne earth (usually a calcined form of van dyke brown).
Composition and Origin	$Fe_2O_3.nH_2O$. Where manganese deposits are found in brown coal (lignite), a brown pigment, commonly known as van dyke brown is formed. It is still of interest to painters because of its excellent transparency: when mulled into linseed oil, it gives a deep black-brown colour, that can be drawn out to a thin glaze. However, van dyke brown never completely dries successfully, tending to remain in a semi-soluble state as a paint film. Although it contains some manganese, it is a very poor drier in oil, tending to slow down the formation of a closed paint film indefinitely. Where the pigment is used in water-based binders, or when underbound in oil-based paints, it has a tendency to turn greyish upon exposure to air. When mixed in small quantities into an oil-resin medium, it is less problematic and slightly more stable over time.
Tinting Strength	–
Shade	In oil, a deep brown-black, sometimes with a warm shade. In watercolour, has a slight violet-brown tinge.
Opacity	Transparent in all media, but shows a slight graininess in water-based binders.
Suitability to Media	Unsuitable in all media. In oil, it dries very poorly, often causing cracking and wrinkling of the paint film. In water-based techniques, it turns grey on exposure to air.
Drying Rate (in oil)	Slow – never completely dries.
Defects	Instability to light in water-based media and poor-drying characteristics in oil make this pigment unsuitable for all media.
Availability/Cost	Inexpensive, rarely found in modern paint ranges. Substitute with mixtures of burnt umber with blacks for stable alternative.

Comments	When van dyke brown is added in very small quantities to a glaze medium, it can be used for final coatings in oil painting, with some success.
Special Note	-
Health & Safety Information	-

YELLOW OCHRE PY 42, PY 43

Colour Index Number	77492
ASTM/BWS Rating	ASTM I
Common Names	Gold ochre, light ochre, roman ochre, brown ochre, also calcined variety, burnt ochre, a red-brown, similar to burnt sienna.
Composition and Origin	Fe_2O_3. x H_2O. A natural earth pigment, varying in shade according to source. Formed by the coloration of silicate (clay) and/or calcium carbonate (chalk) by iron oxide, in conjunction with water. Found on cave, rock, wood support paintings dating back to antiquity.
Tinting Strength	Varies according to source, generally paler than raw sienna but less transparent.
Shade	Pale, warm yellow: other ochres available in shades from yellow, through orange and red to brown.
Opacity	Tends to be more opaque than sienna.
Suitability to Media	Stable in all media.
Drying Rate (in oil)	Medium to slow.
Defects	High oil absorption if the pigment contains large amounts of clay.
Availability/Cost	Inexpensive, widely used, on a small scale there is a continuing supply from original sources (e.g. Rousillon, France).
Comments	Ochre with more clay content will be softer in texture than ochre containing a larger proportion of chalk.
Special Note	-
Health & Safety Information	-

GREEN EARTH (Terre Verte) PG 23

Colour Index Number	77009
ASTM/BWS Rating	ASTM I
Common Names	Terre verte, terra verde, verona green earth, bohemian green earth (often named according to source).
Composition and Origin	Fe, Mg, Al, K. A natural earth pigment, clay, coloured by iron silicate, containing glauconite and/or celadonite. Known since antiquity, offering different shades according to source. For example, the original shade of verona green, sourced at Bentonico, on Mt. Baldo, near Verona is a delicate, pale grey-green. By contrast, aegrine from Malawi is very dark in colour, and has a pronounced, needle-like structure, which is best preserved in casein or glue binders on to stiffish paper. Bohemian green earth, from the Czech Republic, is a brilliant pale green, similar to malachite. Green earth from Cyprus has a cool blue-green shade. Deposits are also found in the Baltic States and parts of Russia.
Tinting Strength	Low.
Shade	Cold, pale greenish-grey.
Opacity	Very transparent.
Suitability to Media	Stable to all media but may be difficult to incorporate into acrylic binders due to inclusion of impurities. In lime-fresco, avoid mixed green earths containing small quantities of prussian blue.
Drying Rate (in oil)	Medium to slow. Forms a very soft paint film, especially when applied with any impasto.
Defects	High oil content (up to 100%), darkens with age.
Availability/Cost	Inexpensive, widely available, although the "original" grades, such as bohemian and verona green earth are more expensive.
Comments	Best applied in thinned glazes.
Special Note	When calcined, green earth gives a red-brown colour with some transparency, "burnt green earth".
Health & Safety Information	-

SYNTHETIC IRON OXIDES

MARS COLOURS (Synthetic Iron Oxides) (shades)
YELLOW PY 42/C.I. 77492
ORANGE PY 42/C.I. 77492
RED PR 101/C.I. 77491
RED PR 102/C.I. 77492
VIOLET PR 101/C.I. 77015
BROWN PBr 6/C.I. 77499
BLACK PBk 11/C.I. 77499

Colour Index Number	PY 42, PR 102/77492, RED PR 101/77491, VIOLET PR 101/77015, PBr 6, PBk 11/77499
ASTM/BWS Rating	ASTM I
Common Names	Mars yellow, mars orange, mars red, mars violet (caput mortuum red, or caput mortuum violet), mars brown, mars black, light red, venetian red (true venetian red has long been replaced with synthetic iron oxide). Colcothar is an old term for mars red.
Composition and Origin	Fe_2O_3. A group of artificial mineral pigments, hydrated ferric oxides, which effectively replace in terms of performance some of the natural earth pigments. Derived from the oxidation of metallic iron, or iron salts. Commercial manufacture dates from the mid-1800s.
Tinting Strength	Strong.
Shade	Yellow, orange, red, red-purple earth shades, plus brown and black.
Opacity	Good.
Suitability to Media	Stable to all media.
Drying Rate (in oil)	Medium.
Defects	Often deemed too opaque when compared to natural earth pigments.
Availability/Cost	Inexpensive, widely used.

Comments	Alternative to natural earths, free of impurities. Many brands also now include a range of transparent iron oxides, which are luminous and bright. Mars black is a useful and cheap alternative to other black pigments, being opaque and therefore possible to use in mild impasto oil paint applications, without undue shrinkage upon drying.
Special Note	-
Health & Safety Information	-

TRANSPARENT IRON OXIDE (shades)
YELLOW PY 42/C.I. 77492
ORANGE PY 42 PR 101/C.I. 77492-77491
ORANGE-RED PR 102/C.I. 77492
RED PR 101/C.I. 77492

Colour Index Number	YELLOW PY 42, ORANGE-RED PR 102, RED PR 101/77492, ORANGE PY 42 PR 101/77492-77491
ASTM/BWS Rating	ASTM I
Common Names	Transoxide red, yellow, etc; translucent iron oxide red, yellow, etc.
Composition and Origin	A special class of synthetic iron oxide, where the pigment particle shape is altered (micronised) so that more light transmits through the paint film. The resulting colour is similar in transparency to the natural earths raw sienna and burnt sienna, but with a more glowing intensity.
Tinting Strength	Strong.
Shade	Yellow, orange, orange-red, red.
Opacity	Very transparent, or rather translucent.
Suitability to Media	-
Drying Rate (in oil)	Medium.
Defects	Over-strong when compared to transparent natural earth pigments, thereby lacking subtlety.
Availability/Cost	Available as pigment and in many updated oil colour ranges. Some ranges use transparent iron oxides to replace similar natural earths, such as burnt sienna.
Comments	The transparent iron oxides are luminous and bright and make ideal glazing colours. They appear dull and grainy in dry pigment form, but once worked into oil, they become clear, bright, translucent and warm in tone.
Special Note	-
Health & Safety Information	-

SPINEL PHASE PIGMENTS (shades)
BROWN LIGHT PY 119
BROWN DARK PY 119
BLACK-BROWN PG 17

Colour Index Number	PY 119/77496, PG17/77288
ASTM/BWS Rating	Not tested.
Common Names	Zinc iron brown light, zinc iron brown dark, zinc iron chrome brown light, haematite-chrome oxide black-brown.
Composition and Origin	Spinel pigments are man-made minerals, manufactured by calcining an intimate mixture of metal oxides at high temperatures. During this process a compound is formed with its own chemical structure. The desired colour is produced by selecting specific metals such as chrome, nickel, antimony, titan, manganese, cobalt, aluminium, zinc, iron, copper, etc. The compound is then ground to particle size.
Tinting Strength	Good.
Shade	Shades of brown, similar to the iron oxides but with more warmth and subtlety of colour.
Opacity	Good.
Suitability to Media	-
Drying Rate (in oil)	Fast.
Defects	-
Availability/Cost	-
Comments	A new choice of strong colours, perfect for application in oil painting.
Special Note	-
Health & Safety Information	-

BLUE PIGMENTS

PHTHALOCYANINE BLUE PB 15/C.I. 74160 METAL FREE PB 16/C.I. 74100

Colour Index Number	PB 15/74160, PB 16/74100
ASTM/BWS Rating	ASTM I
Common Names	Heliogen blue, monestial blue, monastral blue, thalo blue.
Composition and Origin	$C_{32}H_{16}CuN_8$ = PB 15, $C_{32}H_{18}N_8$ = PB 16. A synthetic organic pigment, copper phthalocyanine. Invented in 1928 and introduced to the market in the 1930s.
Tinting Strength	Very high.
Shade	Very bright, intense deep blue, lighter than prussian blue, available in various shades (e.g. blue shade, green shade, red shade, etc).
Opacity	Very transparent but covers well.
Suitability to Media	Stable in all media.
Drying Rate (in oil)	Medium to slow.
Defects	Difficult to wet: prepare a paste with white spirit before grinding with oil.
Availability/Cost	Widely used, often to imitate cobalt or cerulean, in mixes with white and phthalocyanine green.
Comments	A high tinting strength colour, often reduced in power with additions of blanc fix or aluminium hydrate to meet the hue of traditional pigments. When used at full strength, the dried paint film may show a bronze-copper sheen, especially in water-based paint systems.
Special Note	Requires wetting agent.
Health & Safety Information	Contains copper, very fine particles tend to stain skin and clothing. Always wear a dust mask and gloves when handling pigment, or when applying paint.

PRUSSIAN BLUE PB 27

Colour Index Number	77510
ASTM/BWS Rating	ASTM I
Common Names	Milori blue (softest powder, easiest to hand-grind), berlin blue, paris blue, chinese blue, iron blue.
Composition and Origin	$Fe_4(Fe[CN]_6)^3$. Artificial inorganic pigment, based on ferric chloride and potassium ferrocyanide (ferric ferrocyanide). Discovered by accident in Berlin, in 1704 and subsequently introduced as an artists' pigment.
Tinting Strength	Very high.
Shade	Bluish-black in mass tone.
Opacity	Very transparent, ideal glazing colour.
Suitability to Media	Darkens in oil, sensitive to alkalis and therefore never used in fresco.
Drying Rate (in oil)	Fast: wrinkles when applied thickly.
Defects	Sensitive to alkalis. It is never used in the preparation of acrylic colours, where it would react with the alkaline nature of acrylic resin binders. In acrylic paint ranges, a hue replacement for prussian blue can be prepared by mixing phthalocyanine blue with a small addition of lamp/carbon black. Prussian blue may darken in tone when finished paintings are stored away from light. Can turn brown as oil paint. In watercolour, it can fade when admixed with a large percentage of zinc white.
Availability/Cost	Inexpensive, widely used.
Comments	Good mixing colour: a little goes far.
Special Note	Requires wetting agent. "Hooker's green" is an old colour name that usually refers to a mixture of prussian blue with natural gamboge, presented as a watercolour paint. On exposure to light, the gamboge fades somewhat, leaving a blue cast to the paint layers. Old watercolours may show this defect. In some cases, natural gamboge

	is mixed with indigo, where both colours fade to an extent when exposed to light. Modern paints that include hooker's green tend to be prepared from mixtures of prussian blue (or phthalocyanine blue) with a permanent type of synthetic organic yellow, or with a cadmium yellow. Sometimes, the less permanent nitroso green pigment is used for hooker's green. "Prussian green" usually denotes a mixed colour, formerly prepared with (fugitive) natural gamboge or stil di grain, with prussian blue. Modern preparations of this colour tend to include mixtures of prussian (or phthalocyanine blue) with synthetic organic yellows. "Antwerp blue" is a weaker tint of prussian blue, containing aluminium hydrate, as is "brunswick blue". "Brunswick green" is a co-mixture of brunswick blue with chrome yellow. "Cinnabar green" is a co-mixture of chrome yellow deep, prussian blue and raw sienna. Updated paint ranges featuring cinnabar green tend to replace chrome yellow with a synthetic organic yellow, such as hansa yellow (PY 3). "Cyanine blue" as oil colour usually refers to a combination of prussian blue with cobalt blue. Another name for this mixture is "leitch's blue". "Prussian green" as oil colour was formerly based on a mixture of prussian blue with either zinc yellow or chrome yellow. Later mixtures tend to be based on prussian blue with a synthetic organic yellow, such as hansa yellow (PY 1).
Health & Safety Information	Very high tinting strength, tends to stain skin and clothing. Wear gloves and a mask when using pigment or paints.

COBALT BLUE PB 28

Colour Index Number	77346
ASTM/BWS Rating	ASTM I
Common Names	Thenard's blue.
Composition and Origin	$CoAl_2O_4$. An artificial mineral pigment, derived from calcined cobalt oxide and aluminium oxide (cobalt aluminate). Discovered in the 1770s but developed by Thenard commercially, from 1804.
Tinting Strength	Weak.
Shade	Light to deep varieties.
Opacity	Good transparency, when expressed as a glaze.
Suitability to Media	Stable in all media, very lightfast.
Drying Rate (in oil)	Fast.
Defects	Delicate blues yellow significantly in linseed oil. Cobalt blue performs better when ground in paler but slower-drying poppy oil.
Availability/Cost	Relatively expensive, widely used.
Comments	-
Special Note	-
Health & Safety Information	-

LAPIS LAZULI PB 29 (from semi-precious stone)

Colour Index Number	77007
ASTM/BWS Rating	Not tested.
Common Names	Natural ultramarine (oltremare – Italian, "from over the seas").
Composition and Origin	$3Na_{20}.3Al_2.6SiO_2.{}_2Na_2S$. Natural ultramarine, in pigment form, is derived from the semi-precious stone, lapis lazuli. The stone is composed of the blue mineral, lazurite, with additions of calcspar and iron pyrite. The original source for lapis lazuli lies in the valley of the Kokcha river, at Sar-e-sang (place of stones) in the province of Badakshan, north-eastern Afghanistan. These lapis mines were mentioned by Marco Polo in 1271, who noted that the stones were processed to make colour. Lapis lazuli from Afghanistan was imported into Europe through Venice, the main trading port between Europe and the East. While azurite had a dominant role in the development of painting in northern Europe, in the south and especially in Italy, lapis lazuli was extensively used through the Renaissance and during the golden period of Venetian painting in the 1600s. Lapis is today still mined by hand, and the stones that are brought to the surface are sorted into three basic qualities: "*rang-i-ob*" (colour of water); "*rang-i-sabz*" (green colour) and "*surpar*" (red feather). Surpar is considered the highest quality blue stone and has a deep blue-violet colour. The pigment is extracted from the stones by means of a complex process. After pulverisation, the resultant powder is mixed with a combination of molten wax, resin and oil. This mass compound is then wrapped in muslin cloth and immersed in a bath of lye (provided by wood ashes, potash, dissolved in water). The compound is kneaded under the surface of the water (which is in turn hot), whereby the blue particles of lazurite mineral are washed out from the compound. The particles settle out at the bottom of the vat: the water

	is then poured off and the particles are allowed to dry out thoroughly. The compound is washed a number of times in this manner, until almost no blue particles are left. The final washings produce a soft blue-grey colour, known as "ultramarine ash", which contains a high proportion of non-coloured particles. If the original stone is simply crushed to a fine powder and used as a pigment it will have a similar faint, blue-grey tinge. Poorer quality stones were formerly used to make a pale blue-grey with translucent properties, known as "mineral grey".
Tinting Strength	All mineral-based pigments are low in tinting strength, because when admixed with other colours, they lose their influence.
Shade	Best grades (often referred to as fra angelico blue) show a deep, blue-violet tinge.
Opacity	Good transparency, especially in oil glazes.
Suitability to Media	In water-based media (glue, gum arabic, egg), the true blue colour is beautifully shown. In oil, the colour is a deeper blue-violet. Often found in oil paintings as a thin glaze over an azurite or ultramarine ash underpaint. In oil, a small addition of lead white will provide a more covering, solid blue.
Drying Rate (in oil)	-
Defects	-
Availability/Cost	Expensive, although a new source in Chile has provided a reliable alternative to the Afghanistan variety, at a slightly lower cost.
Comments	Often employed with red lake pigments such as carmine or madder, to gain purple/violet mixtures. Also possible to lay down lapis as an underpaint, then overpaint with transparent glaze of red lake to gain purple/violet.
Special Note	Ask to see samples of pigment prior to purchase to ensure the colour strength and particle size is that required.
Health & Safety Information	-

ULTRAMARINE BLUE (shades)
BLUE PB 29/C.I. 77007 - $Na_{6-8}Al_6Si_6O_{24}S_{2-4}$
RED PV 15/C.I. 77007 - $H_2Na_{(4-6)}Al_6Si_6O_{24}S_2$
VIOLET PV 15/C.I. 77007 - $H_2Na_{(4-6)}Al_6Si_6O_{24}S_2$

Colour Index Number	PB 29, PV 15/77007
ASTM/BWS Rating	ASTM I
Common Names	French ultramarine, synthetic ultramarine, ultramarine red/pink (violet), ultramarine violet (available in three or more shades of violet), see also ultramarine green.
Composition and Origin	An artificial mineral pigment, made by heating clay, soda, sulphur and coal (sodium aluminium silicate-polysulphide). Commercially produced in France and Germany from the 1830s onwards, replacing natural ultramarine, lapis lazuli.
Tinting Strength	High.
Shade	Deep blue, grades from green-blue to red-violet.
Opacity	Transparent. Glazing pigment.
Suitability to Media	Stable in most media, but sensitive to alkalis, especially in lime-fresco. Some qualities of ultramarine blue are now prepared and sold as being stable to lime.
Drying Rate (in oil)	Medium to slow.
Defects	Difficult to grind by hand into a stable consistency. Add 2% wax or a stabilising additive such as aluminium stearate.
Availability/Cost	Inexpensive blue, widely used. A fraction of the price of lapis lazuli and much more intense.
Comments	Does not keep well when hand-ground and placed in collapsible tubes, tending to harden or revert to a stringy consistency.
Special Note	"New blue" is a pale variety of ultramarine, formerly prepared at Backbarrow, on the River Leven in the Lake District of England. The plant was known by the locals as the "Blue Factory", as all the buildings in the village were coated in blue, as were the trees and rocks. A recent visit (2001) found the site reused as a tourist hotel, no trace of blue remaining.

	"Payne's grey", as an oil colour or watercolour is usually prepared by combining ultramarine blue with lamp black, davy's grey and iron oxide red. The name relates to the English artist and lecturer William Payne (1760-1830), who passed on this mixing formula to many students and fellow artists.
Health & Safety Information	-

AZURITE PB 30

Colour Index Number	77420
ASTM/BWS Rating	Not tested.
Common Names	Copper blue, blue malachite, chessylite, mineral blue, mountain blue.
Composition and Origin	$2CuCO_3$,$Cu(OH)^2$. A basic copper carbonate, formed naturally within copper ore, often found in association with green malachite, another copper carbonate mineral. Azurite can be found in many parts of the world: early European sources of this pigment were located in the south of Germany, Hungary, Czech Republic, France and the Austrian Tyrol. It is likely that azurite was important within the context of Egyptian painting, but also in the tradition of wall painting in central Asia. It has been widely used in Japanese painting. The pigment is processed from the stone mineral by pulverisation, washing, levigation and sieving. The various particle sizes after pulverisation are separated from large to small, through sieving. The larger particles have the strongest colour. The more that the particles are crushed, the paler the colour becomes. Consequently, the large particle size format of this pigment, giving a strong blue, blue-green colour is most commonly used, despite its granular appearance.
Tinting Strength	Very weak: when admixed with other colours, it becomes insignificant within the mixture. A small amount (perhaps 5%) lead white, or zinc white admixed with azurite will give a reasonable pale blue, where the small white pigment particles close in between the larger azurite particles, so forming a more or less even paint film.
Shade	Dark blue, or blue-green, with crystalline structure.
Opacity	Slightly transparent.

Suitability to Media	For watercolour, bind with gum arabic solution; into tempera, use egg white, or apply in very thin films with egg yolk (to reduce the yellowing effect of the egg yolk); stable in casein, glue. Not stable in lime, unless mixed and used immediately. In oil, the acidity of the oil binder discolours the azurite, showing as a dirty green-blue. If the individual pigment particles are coated in protein (e.g. egg yolk), then dried and re-crushed to a powder, the resultant coated particles can be ground in oil without change. Azurite can change colour to green, reverting to malachite, when exposed to damp or humidity. This is especially poignant in water-based mediums that remain hygroscopic (e.g. rabbit glue). When incorporated into a thin glaze medium, azurite can be used as a final coating over dried oil paint. In historical paint technique, azurite is often found in tempera underpaintings, which may be overpainted with lapis lazuli.
Drying Rate (in oil)	-
Defects	Tendency to turn green when exposed to prolonged damp.
Availability/Cost	Expensive, available only in dry pigment form, in a variety of grind sizes. The paler shades equate to the smallest particle sizes.
Comments	-
Special Note	-
Health & Safety Information	-

EGYPTIAN BLUE PB 31

Colour Index Number	77437
ASTM/BWS Rating	Not tested.
Common Names	Copper silicate blue, blue frit, pompeiian blue, pozzuoli blue (the Egyptian process for making egyptian blue was brought to Italy through the port of Pozzuoli, according to Vitruvius).
Composition and Origin	$CaCuSi4O_{10}$. Derived from quartz, which is boiled together with copper and calcium at high temperatures (up to 1000°C). An artificially made pigment, dating from antiquity, egyptian blue was known through the Egyptian and Roman dynasties and into the middle ages. As a glass frit, egyptian blue is absolutely stable, as witnessed by its use and preservation on many Egyptian artefacts and wall paintings. Egyptian blue is a synthesis of the naturally occurring rare mineral cuprorivaite.
Tinting Strength	Weak, especially when admixed with other colours.
Shade	The exact shade of egyptian blue depends on the grind size of the particle: smaller particles tend towards pale, whitish blue, whereas the larger particles reveal a striking blue colour, similar to modern cobalt blue light or cerulean blue.
Opacity	Transparent, especially in oil glazes.
Suitability to Media	Stable in all media.
Drying Rate (in oil)	-
Defects	-
Availability/Cost	Now revived as a dry pigment but also available in a variety of shades as a glass pigment, the colour shade governed by the grind size of the particle (small particle size is very pale).
Comments	-
Special Note	-
Health & Safety Information	-

SMALT PB 32

Colour Index Number	77365
ASTM/BWS Rating	Not tested.
Common Names	Saxon blue, royal blue.
Composition and Origin	K,Co (Al) – potash silicate (glass) with cobalt oxide. Blue glass powder, a form of cobalt silicate. When cobalt salts are heated to a temperature of 1150°C, they melt to form a blue glass with a deep blue-black colour. The glass is quenched in water and pulverised to form a fine powder. Smalt dates from the 1500s, when sources of cobaltite and smaltite minerals were located in Saxony and Bohemia. Glass-makers took these minerals and found that, when heated to high temperatures, they could be used to colour glass blue. Smalt is also associated with the glass-makers of Murano, Venice and was used in many Venetian paintings during the 1600s, most often admixed with lead white, to create sky colours.
Tinting Strength	Weak when admixed with other colours; the transparency of the material causes it virtually to disappear. Best used alone, in thin oil glazes, so preserving the strong blue colour.
Shade	Deep blue with a purple tinge.
Opacity	Transparent. Glass.
Suitability to Media	Works best in water-based media. In oil, the blue colour becomes almost invisible: glass has a similar refractive index to dried linseed oil, as a consequence the eye does not register the colour. This phenomenon is only observed in dried paint films: when the paint is freshly applied, the blue colour remains visible. This effect can be countered by admixing smalt with a little lead white, which breaks up the way that light transmits within the paint film.
Drying Rate (in oil)	Very fast. Smalt has a catalytic effect on oil, indeed it has often been cited as a siccative agent for drying vegetable oils.
Defects	Can turn grey or pale on exposure to air.

Availability/Cost	Available in various grind sizes as a dry pigment. Best used when made up into a paint film, then applied. The large particle size tends to settle out, especially in water-based media, if left to stand for a long period.
Comments	-
Special Note	-
Health & Safety Information	-

MANGANESE BLUE PB 33

Colour Index Number	77112
ASTM/BWS Rating	ASTM I
Common Names	Manganese-cerulean blue.
Composition and Origin	$BaMnO_4BaSO_4$. An artificial mineral pigment. Barium sulphate - permanganate. Introduced as an artists' colour in the 1930s. The pigment was widely used to colour cement and within the ceramics industry. The toxicity of manganese blue seems to have played a part in its downfall. Sadly, production (in Europe) of this valuable pigment ceased in the late 1980s.
Tinting Strength	Best used independently as a glaze.
Shade	Very bright, cold blue with a greenish cast.
Opacity	Transparent.
Suitability to Media	Stable in all media, but liable to settle out in water-based paint systems. However, this phenomenon in watercolour (referred to as "granulation"), can be pleasing.
Drying Rate (in oil)	Fast.
Defects	Heavy, tends to settle out in mixtures, especially water-based paint-pastes.
Availability/Cost	No longer manufactured but may still be available through specialist art suppliers. Until recently, this brilliant, lightfast blue pigment was relatively cheap to buy. Although some suppliers still have stocks, the cost of the pigment has obviously increased since its manufacture ceased. Currently still found in some oil colour ranges.

Comments	A valuable pigment, of great interest to artists. Imitations of manganese blue, derived from mixtures between phthalocyanine blue and zinc white have recently come on to the market. They lack the characteristic hue and granular texture of the original pigment. Additions of spar or quartz mica into water-based combinations of phthalocyanine blue and zinc white may help to imitate the surface qualities provided by manganese blue.
Special Note	"Manganese green" is simply a greenish shade of manganese blue, now obsolete. It was also known as cassel green.
Health & Safety Information	Contains barium, toxic.

CERULEAN BLUE PB 35

Colour Index Number	77368
ASTM/BWS Rating	ASTM I
Common Names	Coeruleum blue, cobalt-cerulean blue.
Composition and Origin	$CoO.n(SnO_2)$. An artificial mineral pigment, made by roasting cobalt sulphate, tin salts and silica (cobalt stannate). Originally introduced in 1821, although the pigment was not widely used until Rowney & Co. introduced the pigment under the name coeruleum blue, in 1860.
Tinting Strength	Weak.
Shade	Bright but weak greenish-blue.
Opacity	Semi-transparent, slightly less so than cobalt blue.
Suitability to Media	Stable to all media but may show a tendency towards green when milled with linseed oil, where the yellow of the oil takes precedence over this pale and delicate blue. Pale poppy oil can be used instead, the fast-drying properties of cerulean blue assist rapid film formation of poppy oil.
Drying Rate (in oil)	Medium.
Defects	-
Availability/Cost	Found in most paint ranges. Expensive.
Comments	Manganese-cerulean blue previously formed an inexpensive alternative to cobalt-cerulean blue. Sadly, production of manganese blue has now ceased and as a result, the pigment is very expensive or unobtainable.
Special Note	-
Health & Safety Information	-

COBALT TURQUOISE PB 36

Colour Index Number	77343
ASTM/BWS Rating	ASTM I
Common Names	Cobalt turquoise light/dark, cobalt blue greenish.
Composition and Origin	$Co(Al, Cr)_2O_4$. A group of artificial mineral pigments, associated with cobalt blue and cerulean blue. May be derived from fusions of cobalt-chrome-lithium-titanium- and/or zinc oxides.
Tinting Strength	Similar to cobalt blue. The high key of cobalt turquoise is perhaps best used independently from other colours.
Shade	A range of shades: bright blue-turquoise, deep blue-turquoise, deep blue/green-turquoise.
Opacity	Semi-transparent.
Suitability to Media	Stable in all media, but may show a tendency towards green when milled in linseed oil.
Drying Rate (in oil)	Fast.
Defects	-
Availability/Cost	Available as pigment and in some oil colour ranges. Expensive.
Comments	Mixtures of phthalocyanine blue and green, with zinc white can produce similar shades, which are useful, if not as subtle.
Special Note	-
Health & Safety Information	-

INDANTHRONE BLUE PB 60

Colour Index Number	69800
ASTM/BWS Rating	ASTM I
Common Names	Paliogen blue, chromophtal blue, anthraquinone blue, indanthrene blue.
Composition and Origin	$C_{28}H_{14}N_2O_4$. Synthetic organic pigment. Introduced in the 1950s.
Tinting Strength	Good - not as strong as other synthetic organic pigments.
Shade	A warmer, paler alternative to prussian blue and synthetic indigo, with less tinting strength.
Opacity	Transparent.
Suitability to Media	Stable in all media.
Drying Rate (in oil)	Medium to slow.
Defects	-
Availability/Cost	Available as pigment and in some updated oil colour ranges.
Comments	A lightfast alternative to natural and synthetic indigo.
Special Note	Requires wetting agent.
Health & Safety Information	-

BLUE VERDITER

Colour Index Number	-
ASTM/BWS Rating	Not tested.
Common Names	Mountain blue, blue bice.
Composition and Origin	$CuO + nH_2O$. An artificial copper-calcium carbonate pigment, a synthetic version of azurite. In manufacture, copper nitrate is mixed with chalk, or precipitated from copper sulphate in solution, in combination with ammonia and lime paste. During preparation, if the temperature becomes too warm, a green shade develops (green verditer). The author has samples of various makings, showing colours from blue, through blue-green (turquoise) to green. In England, verditer pigments were formerly manufactured in Sheffield, Yorkshire. Blue verditer was important in wall decoration during the 1600s and 1700s and also used on a small scale in easel painting.
Tinting Strength	Weak.
Shade	Pale blue, similar to cerulean blue and pale forms of azurite.
Opacity	Slightly transparent.
Suitability to Media	Works best in water-based binders. In oil, the copper reacts with acidity in the oil and turns green (copper oleate).
Drying Rate (in oil)	-
Defects	Turns green in oil.
Availability/Cost	Available as a dry pigment. Recommended as a useful pigment when hand-making watercolours.
Comments	-
Special Note	"Bremen blue" is prepared from copper hydroxide with copper carbonate and has a blue or green-blue shade.
Health & Safety Information	-

INDIGO

Colour Index Number	-
ASTM/BWS Rating	Not tested.
Common Names	Woad (European version of indigo).
Composition and Origin	$C_{16}.H_{10}.N_2O_2$. A natural vegetable pigment, derived from the leaves of the Indian plant, *Indigofera tinctoria.* The leaves are immersed in water and left to ferment, then dried, oxidising to indigo. This residue is then washed, boiled in water, air-dried and formed into small cakes or lumps. The cake form is then pulverised to form a fine, but slightly grainy powder, which can be further ground as required. In Europe, the woad plant, *Isatis tinctoria*, was formerly used to prepare a similar colour, important in both textiles and paint technique. In France, this colour was known by the term "pastel". Imports to Europe from India began in the 1600s.
Tinting Strength	Good.
Shade	Deep blue-black.
Opacity	Transparent.
Suitability to Media	Historically, indigo has been used in oil and watercolour technique. However, because it fades on exposure to sunlight, it can be replaced by mixtures between prussian blue or phthalocyanine blue and various black pigments.
Drying Rate (in oil)	Dries slowly in oil, especially in fat applications.
Defects	Fades in sunlight. Historical mixtures between indigo and yellow pigments to provide green are common. However, where the indigo has been exposed to light, the blue component may fade from the mixture, changing the nature of the green. Where indigo is not exposed to prolonged sunlight (e.g. in a closed portfolio), its deep velvet blue hue is preserved. Destroyed by alkali or acid exposure.
Availability/Cost	No longer available as a ready-made paint, but available in pigment form.

Comments	A special form of indigo, "maya blue" is now available, where the particles are mingled with attapulgite (a fibrous clay), magnesium silicate, which partially inhibits the passage of light rays to the blue pigment. In this manner, the colour is preserved, or rather degrades at a slower rate than natural indigo. Synthetic indigo is a form of dye (Vat Dye number 1) and is chemically similar to natural indigo. $C_9H_7NO_4$. Synthetic indigo was developed and patented by Bayer in the 1890s. Synthetic indigo is fugitive to light, but enjoyed considerable popularity in the early decades of the 20th century, when the price of both natural and synthetic indigo reduced dramatically, due to the manufacturers of these rival colours entering a protracted trade conflict.
Special Note	Requires wetting agent.
Health & Safety Information	-

SODALITE

Colour Index Number	-
ASTM/BWS Rating	Not tested.
Common Names	-
Composition and Origin	$Na_8Al_6Si_6O_{24}Cl_2$. A semi-precious stone, sodalite has a crystalline structure. Sodium-aluminium-silicate. Found among alkali-rich volcanic rocks such as phonolite. Related to lazurite (the blue colouring in lapis lazuli stones).
Tinting Strength	Weak.
Shade	Translucent, pale white-blue grainy powder.
Opacity	Transparent.
Suitability to Media	Best suited to strong protein binders such as casein on to stiff paper, where the translucent character of this subtle pale blue is preserved.
Drying Rate (in oil)	-
Defects	Only available in larger particle size (when ground finely, the colour is lost).
Availability/Cost	Expensive.
Comments	Use carefully on to gesso panel (with glair binder), or with casein on to stiff paper.
Special Note	-
Health & Safety Information	-

PURPURITE

Colour Index Number	-
ASTM/BWS Rating	Not tested.
Common Names	-
Composition and Origin	Purpurite is a natural form of iron-manganese-phosphate. The pulverised stone has a crystalline structure, which has a slight glinting effect when bound in casein or glue. Paler varieties, from powdered slate coloured by iron and manganese (*cote d'azur* violet).
Tinting Strength	-
Shade	Similar to natural *caput mortuum*, a deep but bright purple.
Opacity	Slight transparency in glazes.
Suitability to Media	Useful in tempera and other water-based media.
Drying Rate (in oil)	-
Defects	-
Availability/Cost	Expensive, available as pigment only.
Comments	-
Special Note	-
Health & Safety Information	-

ALIZARIN VIOLET PV 5

Colour Index Number	58055
ASTM/BWS Rating	BWS 7-8
Common Names	Purple madder lake, alizarin purple.
Composition and Origin	Synthetic organic pigment. Dihydroxyanthraquinone: related to alizarin crimson. Can fade when admixed with white, or painted as glaze against pale ground. Some varieties can run (seep) in oil glazes.
Tinting Strength	Similar to alizarin crimson.
Shade	Deep red-violet with a cold edge.
Opacity	Good transparency.
Suitability to Media	-
Drying Rate (in oil)	Very slow.
Defects	Some varieties may bleed in oil. As with alizarin crimson, avoid using in thick layers to prevent paint film from wrinkling.
Availability/Cost	Available as pigment and in some oil colour ranges. Largely replaced by other synthetic pigments with better permanence.
Comments	-
Special Note	Requires wetting agent.
Health & Safety Information	-

COBALT VIOLET DEEP PV 14

Colour Index Number	77360
ASTM/BWS Rating	ASTM I
Common Names	Cobalt violet dark.
Composition and Origin	$Co_3(PO_4)^2$. An artificial mineral pigment. Anhydrous cobalt phosphate. Manufacturing process discovered in 1859. The pigment is slightly coarser than cobalt violet light but is stable and lightfast in oil.
Tinting Strength	Better than cobalt violet light.
Shade	Deep red-violet.
Opacity	More transparent than cobalt violet light.
Suitability to Media	Stable to all media.
Drying Rate (in oil)	Fast.
Defects	-
Availability/Cost	Cobalt violet light and dark are offered in many paint ranges. Because the pigment is so expensive, the intensity of prepared colour ranges can vary widely, according to the amounts of extender added to the paint.
Comments	-
Special Note	-
Health & Safety Information	Contains cobalt.

MANGANESE VIOLET PV 16

Colour Index Number	77742
ASTM/BWS Rating	ASTM I
Common Names	Permanent violet, mineral violet.
Composition and Origin	$H_4O_7P_2.H_3n.Mn$. An artificial mineral pigment. Manganese dioxide-ammonium phosphate. Introduced as an artists' colour, 1890. Often overlooked, due to its poor tinting strength and dull character.
Tinting Strength	Weak, best used independently.
Shade	Dull, dark violet, with a reddish tinge.
Opacity	Semi-opaque.
Suitability to Media	Stable to all media.
Drying Rate (in oil)	Fast.
Defects	-
Availability/Cost	Cheaper than cobalt violet, although not as intense or bright.
Comments	-
Special Note	In oil colour may sometimes include an addition of ultramarine blue, to give a bluish tinge.
Health & Safety Information	Contains manganese.

DIOXAZINE VIOLET (shades)
Red Shade PV 23 RS/C.I. 51319
Blue Shade PV 23 BS/C.I. 51319

Colour Index Number	51319
ASTM/BWS Rating	PV 23 RS – ASTM I, PV 23 BS – ASTM II
Common Names	Dioxazine purple, purple red, permanent violet.
Composition and Origin	$C_{34}H_{22}Cl_2N_4O_2$. Synthetic organic pigment. Carbazole dioxazine. The blue shade is more liable to some fading when mixed with white. Developed in Germany, dates from 1929.
Tinting Strength	Good.
Shade	Saturated, almost black as a powder. When mixed as a paint, thins to blue or red purple glaze, according to shade.
Opacity	Good transparency.
Suitability to Media	Stable to all media – permanence to light reduced in strong admixtures with white.
Drying Rate (in oil)	Slow-Medium.
Defects	–
Availability/Cost	Common in many modern oil colour ranges, also as dry pigment. Expensive.
Comments	–
Special Note	Requires wetting agent.
Health & Safety Information	–

COBALT VIOLET LIGHT PV 47

Colour Index Number	77363
ASTM/BWS Rating	Not tested.
Common Names	Cobalt violet pale.
Composition and Origin	An artificial mineral pigment. Calcined cobalt arsenate (therefore toxic). Dates from the early 1900s. The particular hue of cobalt violet light cannot be matched through mixing other colours. Despite the high price, it is still an important colour for artists. Cobalt violet light has a tendency to darken slightly when ground as an oil colour (due to high oil absorption).
Tinting Strength	Weak.
Shade	Pale violet.
Opacity	Semi-opaque.
Suitability to Media	Stable in oil and watercolour. Not usually prepared as acrylic colour, as the pigment tends to settle out in aqueous mixtures.
Drying Rate (in oil)	Fast.
Defects	-
Availability/Cost	Expensive, although common to most paint ranges.
Comments	Weak tinting strength – best used alone, or carefully mixed down with zinc white.
Special Note	-
Health & Safety Information	Contains cobalt-arsenate. Toxic.

COBALT VIOLET LIGHT (BRILLIANT) PV 49

Colour Index Number	77362
ASTM/BWS Rating	Not tested.
Common Names	Cobalt violet brilliant.
Composition and Origin	An artificial mineral pigment.
Tinting Strength	Weak.
Shade	Very bright, brilliant purple-violet. Brighter than PV 47.
Opacity	Semi-opaque.
Suitability to Media	Stable in oil and watercolour.
Drying Rate (in oil)	Fast.
Defects	-
Availability/Cost	Expensive, available as dry pigment.
Comments	-
Special Note	-
Health & Safety Information	-

GREEN PIGMENTS

PHTHALOCYANINE GREEN PG 7, PG 36

Colour Index Number	74260 - PG 7 (green-blue shade) 74265 - PG 36 (brominated copper phthalocyanine - yellow shade)
ASTM/BWS Rating	ASTM I
Common Names	Heliogen green, monastral green, monestial green, thalo green.
Composition and Origin	$C_{32}H_{16}CuN_8Cl_{15}$ = PG 7, $C_{32}Br_6Cl_{10}$ CuN_8 = PG 36. A synthetic organic pigment, phthalocyanine. Developed, with phthalocyanine blue, since 1927.
Tinting Strength	Very high.
Shade	Very bright, cold green-blue. Available as cold blue-green (PG 7) or yellow shade (PG 36).
Opacity	Very transparent but covers well.
Suitability to Media	Stable to all media. Fine particle size means that dispersion can be difficult without prior wetting. Sometimes sold in a water-paste to ease dispersion.
Drying Rate (in oil)	Medium to slow.
Defects	Difficult to wet: prepare a paste with white spirit before grinding with oil.
Availability/Cost	High tinting strength guarantees strong colour: widely used in many paint systems but often combined with filler material to reduce tinting strength.
Comments	Sometimes appears in cheaper ranges to imitate costly viridian.
Special Note	Requires wetting agent.
Health & Safety Information	Contains copper.

NITROSO GREEN PG 8

Colour Index Number	10006
ASTM/BWS Rating	ASTM III (as Artists' Acrylic)
Common Names	Naphthol green, hooker's green, but may also be used to make imitation sap green.
Composition and Origin	$C_{30}H_{18}FeN_3O_6$.Na. Synthetic organic complex (1-nitroso-2-naphthol), in reaction with ferrous sulphate and sodium hydroxide.
Tinting Strength	Good.
Shade	Dark green.
Opacity	Transparent.
Suitability to Media	Water-based binders (not lime-fresco).
Drying Rate (in oil)	Medium.
Defects	Not stable in acid-containing mixtures. Not wholly permanent, especially when expressed as a wash in watercolour or acrylic, or when strongly mixed down with white.
Availability/Cost	Available in some paint ranges, but more often superseded by more permanent mixed colours.
Comments	May be found in some lower quality watercolours and designer's gouache.
Special Note	Requires wetting agent.
Health & Safety Information	-

QUINDO GREEN GOLD PG 10

Colour Index Number	12775
ASTM/BWS Rating	ASTM I
Common Names	Green gold lake, golden green lake, irgazine yellow (green).
Composition and Origin	$C_{30}H_{18}Cl_2N_6NiO_4$. A synthetic organic pigment. Nickel azo. Developed late 1940s, recently introduced to artists' ranges.
Tinting Strength	Good.
Shade	Warm, dark green in mass tone. When thinned to glaze, takes on a golden yellowish cast.
Opacity	Good transparency as a glaze.
Suitability to Media	Stable in all media.
Drying Rate (in oil)	Medium-Slow.
Defects	-
Availability/Cost	Introduced to updated oil colour ranges, also available as dry pigment.
Comments	-
Special Note	Requires wetting agent.
Health & Safety Information	Contains nickel.

CHROME OXIDE GREEN PG 17

Colour Index Number	77288
ASTM/BWS Rating	ASTM I
Common Names	Chromium oxide opaque.
Composition and Origin	Cr_2O_3. An artificial mineral pigment, derived from potassium dichromate, sulphur and charcoal, or by heating viridian (hydrated ferric oxide). Introduced in 1809, widely available by the middle of the 19th century.
Tinting Strength	Good.
Shade	Dull, cool olive-green.
Opacity	Good.
Suitability to Media	Stable to all media.
Drying Rate (in oil)	Fast-Medium.
Defects	-
Availability/Cost	Inexpensive, widely used.
Comments	Chrome oxide green is often overlooked by artists because of its dull shade. It has very high tinting strength and excellent covering power.
Special Note	-
Health & Safety Information	Contains chromium.

VIRIDIAN PG 18

Colour Index Number	77289
ASTM/BWS Rating	ASTM I
Common Names	Hydrated chromium hydroxide, guignet's green, transparent oxide of chromium.
Composition and Origin	Cr_2O_3. $2H_2O$. An artificial mineral pigment. Derived from bichromate and boric acid, calcined then washed. Discovered by Guignet in 1859, available commercially since the early 1900s.
Tinting Strength	Good.
Shade	Bright, deep green with bluish tinge.
Opacity	Very transparent, typical glazing colour.
Suitability to Media	Stable in all media.
Drying Rate (in oil)	Slow.
Defects	Dries with wrinkling when applied in any thickness.
Availability/Cost	Expensive, widely used.
Comments	Although phthalocyanine green is less subtle in shade, it may provide a cheaper alternative. Viridian green possesses a subtlety that is hard to match, especially in tints with zinc or lead white.
Special Note	"Victoria green" is an obsolete composition pigment, based on a mix of viridian, zinc yellow and zinc or lithopone whites. "Academy blue" denotes a mixture of viridian with ultramarine, prepared as an oil colour (Winsor & Newton catalogue of 1925).
Health & Safety Information	Contains chromium.

VERDIGRIS SYNTHETIC PG 20

Colour Index Number	-
ASTM/BWS Rating	Not tested.
Common Names	Copper acetate, copper resinate (when mixed with a balsam).
Composition and Origin	$Cu(CH_3COO)^2.2H_2O$. An artificial mineral pigment. Copper (II) acetate, 1- hydrate. Verdigris dates from antiquity. Originally prepared from copper plates or shavings, exposed to vinegar. The modern product is treated with acetic acid. In the original process, grape skins are left to decompose, lying on copper sheet, in the presence of mild warmth. After 4-5 weeks, a greenish-blue deposit develops, which is then pulverised to form a fine powder, taking on a green hue in the process. Verdigris tends to turn brown in oil, especially when admixed with pigments containing sulphur. Traditional recipes call for the combination of verdigris, locked within a resin-oil, or balsam (Venice turpentine) paint medium, to prevent the pigment contacting with the atmosphere and with other pigments. Verdigris takes the form of a crystalline powder and has a pronounced, gritty structure, which is difficult to mask in paint mixtures. Best used locked into an oil-resin paint medium.
Tinting Strength	When applied as a glaze on its own, verdigris gives a strong, dark green-blue glaze.
Shade	Dark green-blue.
Opacity	Transparent (although the particle structure tends to show).
Suitability to Media	Difficult to prepare in aqueous binders, especially acrylic. Best suited to preparation in animal glue size or casein binder, or prepared as copper resinate for use in oil paint technique.

Drying Rate (in oil)	Fast.
Defects	Verdigris is highly acidic, so assists the deterioration of paper fibres when applied in water-based binders.
Availability/Cost	Available as pigment, or premixed as "copper-resinate": $Cu(CH_3CO)^2.2Cu(OH)^2.nH_2O\text{-}Cr_2O_7.nH_2O$.
Comments	-
Special Note	-
Health & Safety Information	-

ULTRAMARINE GREEN PG 24

Colour Index Number	77013
ASTM/BWS Rating	Not tested.
Common Names	*Oltremare verde* (Italian).
Composition and Origin	$2Na_2Al_2Si_2O_6.NaS_2$. Calcined kaolin with soda, sulphur and carbon, in a process similar to that of ultramarine blue, except that a lower temperature is required. Available since 1827.
Tinting Strength	Weak.
Shade	Cold, green with slight bluish undershade.
Opacity	Transparent.
Suitability to Media	Stable in all media, except lime-fresco (similar to ultramarine blue).
Drying Rate (in oil)	Similar to ultramarine blue.
Defects	Poor tinting strength, dull appearance. Not stable in mixtures with lead-based pigments.
Availability/Cost	Not widely available, sometimes found as dry pigment, especially in Italy.
Comments	-
Special Note	-
Health & Safety Information	-

COBALT GREEN (DARK) PG 50

Colour Index Number	77377
ASTM/BWS Rating	ASTM I
Common Names	Cobalt bottle green.
Composition and Origin	Co_2TiO_4. An artificial mineral pigment, formed from calcined oxides of titanium and cobalt.
Tinting Strength	Medium.
Shade	Deep, cool green.
Opacity	Semi-opaque, tending towards opaque.
Suitability to Media	Stable in all media.
Drying Rate (in oil)	Fast.
Defects	-
Availability/Cost	Expensive.
Comments	-
Special Note	-
Health & Safety Information	Contains cobalt.

COBALT GREEN PG 26

Colour Index Number	77343
ASTM/BWS Rating	Not tested.
Common Names	Cobalt green-blue oxide, cobalt blue-green oxide.
Composition and Origin	Cr_2O_3. CoO. Al_2O_3. An artificial mineral pigment, prepared by calcination or precipitation of cobalt carbonate with hydrated chromium oxide. Developed during the late 19th century.
Tinting Strength	Medium, stronger than cobalt green light.
Shade	Two distinct shades are available: grass green, or blue-green.
Opacity	Semi-opaque, tending towards opaque.
Suitability to Media	Stable in all media.
Drying Rate (in oil)	Fast.
Defects	-
Availability/Cost	Expensive and not always found in artists' colour ranges.
Comments	-
Special Note	-
Health & Safety Information	Contains cobalt.

COBALT GREEN LIGHT PG 19

Colour Index Number	77335
ASTM/BWS Rating	ASTM I
Common Names	Rinman's green, cobalt blue-green light.
Composition and Origin	CoO.ZnO. An artificial mineral pigment, oxides of cobalt and zinc. Cobalt green was first developed in Sweden by Rinman in 1780, but not introduced to the market until the 1830s. Modern varieties can be based on a complex of cobalt, zinc and ammonium.
Tinting Strength	Weak.
Shade	Pale blue-green with a delicate presence in mixtures with other pigments.
Opacity	Semi-opaque.
Suitability to Media	Stable to all media but modern varieties (based on a complex of cobalt, zinc and ammonium) may not be stable in lime-fresco techniques.
Drying Rate (in oil)	Fast.
Defects	Weak tinting strength in admixtures.
Availability/Cost	Expensive, the peculiar hue of cobalt green-blue light is difficult to match through mixing.
Comments	Shows granulation when expressed as a wash in watercolour techniques.
Special Note	The exact shade of PG 19 can vary from manufacturer to manufacture.
Health & Safety Information	Contains cobalt.

MALACHITE

Colour Index Number	-
ASTM/BWS Rating	Not tested.
Common Names	Mineral green, mountain green.
Composition and Origin	Mineral pigment, natural copper carbonate, $CuCO_3.Cu(OH)^2$. Often found in association with blue azurite, to which it is closely related. Malachite is prepared by crushing, sieving and levigating the resultant powder. The particles are sorted into different grind sizes, according to the depth of colour and exact particle size required. In fresco, larger particles can be utilised, to preserve the strongest colour value.
Tinting Strength	Weak.
Shade	Pale green with bluish cast. Chrysocolla (copper silicate, $CuSiO_3.nH_2O$) is a blue-green form of malachite, a dull turquoise.
Opacity	Tends towards opaque.
Suitability to Media	Not suitable in oil binders, where it takes on a greenish appearance. Best used fresh in fresco, as malachite will change colour when left to steep in water. In water-based binders such as glair (egg white), casein and gum arabic, the true pale green quality of malachite can be preserved.
Drying Rate (in oil)	-
Defects	Poor tinting strength in mixtures.
Availability/Cost	Available in a variety of grind sizes: the finer grades are progressively weaker in colour, according to the smallness of the particle size.

Comments	In historical paintings, malachite is sometimes admixed with organic greens from plant stuff, such as the yellow colour derived from weld. Similarly, green earth was sometimes enhanced in colour by admixture with malachite.
Special Note	-
Health & Safety Information	Contains copper.

MALACHITE (SYNTHETIC)

Colour Index Number	-
ASTM/BWS Rating	Not tested.
Common Names	Copper carbonate, mountain green, green bice.
Composition and Origin	$CuCO_3Cu(OH)_2$. Copper carbonate. An artificial mineral pigment. Chemically similar to natural malachite (basic copper carbonate). A bright, soft powder. This is a modern, industrially made equivalent to the historic pigment green verditer, in the form of a finely divided powder (less coarse than historic green verditer).
Tinting Strength	Medium.
Shade	Cool green-blue, more intense than natural malachite.
Opacity	Good.
Suitability to Media	-
Drying Rate (in oil)	-
Defects	-
Availability/Cost	Available as pigment. Malachite "hues" appear in paint ranges, which are mixtures of other pigments.
Comments	-
Special Note	-
Health & Safety Information	-

CADMIUM GREEN

Colour Index Number	-
ASTM/BWS Rating	Not tested.
Common Names	Cadmium green light, cadmium green dark.
Composition and Origin	An artificial mineral pigment: mixture of a) synthetic ultramarine and cadmium yellow; b) viridian and cadmium yellow, or similar mixtures of reliable, permanent pigments. Introduced as a standard artists' colour in Germany, during the 1920s.
Tinting Strength	High.
Shade	Bright lime green/grass green (light and dark shades).
Opacity	The inclusion of ultramarine or viridian gives a semi-opaque quality.
Suitability to Media	-
Drying Rate (in oil)	Slow.
Defects	-
Availability/Cost	-
Comments	Various mixtures approximate cadmium green light and dark, in manufactured paint ranges. The dry pigment is also commonly available, usually in two shades - light and dark.
Special Note	-
Health & Safety Information	-

GREEN VERDITER

Colour Index Number	-
ASTM/BWS Rating	Not tested.
Common Names	Mountain green, cendres green, green bice.
Composition and Origin	$CuCo_3.(OH)^2$. Basic copper carbonate pigment, formed by the precipitation of copper sulphur, from a combination of potassium and lime (or in England, chalk), with copper sulphate and ammonium chlorate. Developed since the 17th century and widely used in decorative paints, although today considered an obsolete colour. Larger particle size when compared to synthetic malachite.
Tinting Strength	Weak.
Shade	Pale green-blue, especially in water-based binders.
Opacity	Semi-opaque, powder usually has a crystalline structure.
Suitability to Media	Unstable in all media, especially oil, where it turns dark green.
Drying Rate (in oil)	-
Defects	Discolours in oil (darkens).
Availability/Cost	-
Comments	-
Special Note	-
Health & Safety Information	-

VOLCHONSKOITE GREEN

Colour Index Number	-
ASTM/BWS Rating	Not tested.
Common Names	Russian green, wolchonskoite green.
Composition and Origin	$Ca_{0,3}(Cr^{+3},Mg,Fe^{+3})_2(Si,Al)_4O_{10}(OH)_2 4H_2O$. Natural clay-containing mineral pigment, the colour formed by natural chromium oxide. Sources located only in the former Soviet Union (Perm Basin, Okhansk, but also found in the Ural mountains). The pigment is named after the 19th century Russian Imperial Court minister, Prince Volkonskoi.
Tinting Strength	Good, far superior to green earth.
Shade	Dark green pistachio colour, but available in a variety of shades, from darkish olive green-brown to bright earth green, or even emerald.
Opacity	Good transparency.
Suitability to Media	Stable in all media, especially oil, where its low oil absorption rate (15-25g) makes it far superior to green earth.
Drying Rate (in oil)	-
Defects	Unavailable to the general market, but found in Russian paint ranges.
Availability/Cost	Available in Russian paint ranges and as dry pigment.
Comments	A valuable and unique pigment, especially beautiful when mixed with small amounts of zinc white, to form cool olive green shades.
Special Note	-
Health & Safety Information	-

SCHWEINFURT GREEN

Colour Index Number	-
ASTM/BWS Rating	Not tested.
Common Names	Emerald green (manufactured form), also mittis green, imperial green, vienna green, scheele's green, paris green, veronese green, etc.
Composition and Origin	$CaCu(AsO_4)(OH)$. Conichalcite is a natural mineral copper-arsenic-carbonate compound. A natural mineral pigment containing arsenic, and therefore toxic. The name - Schweinfurt - relates to the town where the brighter, artificial form (emerald green) was first manufactured, in 1814. Emerald green (PG 21/C.I. 77410) is basically copper aceto-arsenate, derived from verdigris which is combined with a boiling water-solution of white arsenic. An earlier form, dating from 1778 and known as scheele's green (PG 22/C.I. 77412), is copper arsenite, bearing an excess of copper oxide.
Tinting Strength	-
Shade	The natural pigment is a dark, crystalline green, similar to green earth. The prepared pigment is a bright acid-green colour, similar to emerald.
Opacity	Emerald green is more opaque than scheele's green.
Suitability to Media	Unstable, especially in water-based binders.
Drying Rate (in oil)	-
Defects	In watercolour, copper-arsenate pigments quickly darken, while in oil, admixtures with any sulphide containing pigments turn brown or black.
Availability/Cost	Highly toxic, no longer supplied in paint form.
Comments	-
Special Note	Considered obsolete but may be required in relation to painting conservation.
Health & Safety Information	Toxic.

BLACK AND BROWN PIGMENTS

LAMP BLACK PBk 6

Colour Index Number	77266
ASTM/BWS Rating	ASTM I
Common Names	Furnace black, gas black, blue black, carbon black.
Composition and Origin	C (amorphous carbon). Use of lamp black dates back to antiquity. Originally, lamp black was made from the soot from oil lamps/fireplaces. Modern lamp black is produced from partially combusted mineral and/or vegetable oil. Pure carbon. Oily residue is removed during the manufacturing process. The dry pigment is very light and forms a soft powder.
Tinting Strength	Good.
Shade	Intense blue-black, with a cold tinge. As an oil colour, gives a deep, velvety black.
Opacity	Very transparent.
Suitability to Media	Stable in all media.
Drying Rate (in oil)	Very slow.
Defects	Very high oil absorption: use in thin layers only (thick layers tend to wrinkle and take forever to dry out). Difficult to combine with oil: wet the pigment first with white (mineral) spirit to form a stiff paste.
Availability/Cost	Common to most oil paint ranges.
Comments	-
Special Note	Requires wetting agent.
Health & Safety Information	-

IVORY BLACK
(Black from charred bones) PBk 9

Colour Index Number	77267
ASTM/BWS Rating	ASTM I
Common Names	Bone black.
Composition and Origin	Natural pigment from animal origin ($C, Ca_3 (PO_4)^2$). Originally from calcined ivory but now commonly from charred bones. Genuine ivory black contains more carbon than the modern product and has a higher tinting strength.
Tinting Strength	Good.
Shade	Slight brown or grey tinge.
Opacity	Not transparent but thins to a glaze.
Suitability to Media	-
Drying Rate (in oil)	Very slow drier, forming relatively soft, brittle films. To be avoided in underpaintings, unless admixed with fast-drying pigments such as lead white or raw umber and applied as a thin coating.
Defects	Slow drying can cause matting/sinking of paint film. Grind thoroughly to combine oil and pigment particles.
Availability/Cost	Inexpensive, replaces genuine ivory black.
Comments	Additions of painting medium can help counter sinking/matting of paint film.
Special Note	"Bone brown" is a variation of ivory black, which gives a gentle, transparent brown colour, ideal for use in watercolour mixed colours (e.g. "olive lake", with stil de grain and ultramarine).
Health & Safety Information	-

MARS BLACK PBk 11

Colour Index Number	77499
ASTM/BWS Rating	ASTM I
Common Names	Iron oxide black, mineral black.
Composition and Origin	$FeO.Fe_2O_3$. An artificial mineral pigment - see synthetic iron oxides. Ferro-ferric oxide. Production of mars black dates back to the 1920s.
Tinting Strength	Good.
Shade	Deep black (not as saturated as ivory black), also brown and blue-black shades.
Opacity	Good.
Suitability to Media	Stable in all media.
Drying Rate (in oil)	Medium.
Defects	Opacity may render mars black slightly less subtle than transparent blacks, when intermixing with other transparent colours to gain neutral tints.
Availability/Cost	Cheap, easy to use from dry pigment. Found in most oil colour ranges.
Comments	-
Special Note	-
Health & Safety Information	-

MANGANESE BLACK PBk 14

Colour Index Number	77728
ASTM/BWS Rating	Not tested.
Common Names	Manganese grey, manganese brown, according to shade.
Composition and Origin	MnO_2. Manganese dioxide natural mineral pigment. Has been used sporadically by artists since the early 1900s.
Tinting Strength	Strong.
Shade	Neutral black-grey.
Opacity	Semi-opaque.
Suitability to Media	-
Drying Rate (in oil)	Very fast.
Defects	-
Availability/Cost	Not widely used in tube oil colours, although the pigment is relatively inexpensive.
Comments	A useful, fast-drying black.
Special Note	-
Health & Safety Information	-

SPINEL BLACK PBk 26

Colour Index Number	77494
ASTM/BWS Rating	Not tested.
Common Names	Manganese ferrite spinel black, cobalt black.
Composition and Origin	An artificial mineral pigment. Spinel: procedure similar to manufacture of cobalt pigments. Recently introduced.
Tinting Strength	Very good – multiple glaze layers give the deepest blacks.
Shade	Deep, slightly blue-black.
Opacity	Good transparency as glaze.
Suitability to Media	-
Drying Rate (in oil)	Fast.
Defects	-
Availability/Cost	Expensive, available as pigment and in some updated oil colour ranges.
Comments	-
Special Note	-
Health & Safety Information	-

SEPIA Natural Brown 9

Colour Index Number	-
ASTM/BWS Rating	Not tested.
Common Names	-
Composition and Origin	$CaCO_3$. The ink sac of the cuttlefish provides a dark brown-black pigment. In nature, when the fish is attacked, it releases a jet of ink into the water, to confuse prey. This ink sac can be dried, washed free of salt water and carefully dried, then pulverised to form a powder and then boiled with lye (potassium hydroxide). The resultant coloured liquid is precipitated with hydrochloric acid, washed and then left to dry out thoroughly. Today, the term, "sepia" is often used to describe browns, brown-blacks and red-browns in ranges of inks and paints. As a consequence, the exact colour of sepia is known to few people. The true colour of sepia is a very dark brown, virtually black, that possesses a slight transparency when diluted, or when added to glazing media. From the late 1700s, sepia was widely used as an ink and wash colour for works on paper. Old recipes mention two distinct forms of sepia: a) sepia used alone, as a simple black-brown colour; b) sepia admixed with red madder lake to give a warmer tone. During the 19th century it was sometimes used as a pigment for oil painting, although it is not lightfast enough for this purpose.
Tinting Strength	High.
Shade	Deep brown black, turning slightly warmer (redder) in hue when exposed to light. Modern pigment mixtures called sepia often have this warm red-brown appearance. The dark colour is preserved somewhat if finished artworks are stored in closed portfolios and only shown in subdued lighting. "roman sepia" is a warm red-brown formed when sepia is admixed with a red lake such as carmine or madder.
Opacity	Semi-transparent.
Suitability to Media	Best suited to gum arabic, or shellac-borax binders, applied to paper.
Drying Rate (in oil)	Not stable in oil.

Defects	Fugitive to light.
Availability/Cost	Best quality sepia is presented as dry pigment, washed and divided into three distinct grind sizes.
Comments	-
Special Note	Requires wetting agent. In the 19th and early 20th centuries, artists' watercolours were commonly prepared with carefully processed natural sepia. However, the pigment is unusable in oil, where mixtures of natural earths (e.g. cologne earth with bone brown) can be used.
Health & Safety Information	-

FRUIT STONE BLACK

Colour Index Number	–
ASTM/BWS Rating	Not tested.
Common Names	Peach black, nut black, cork black, etc.
Composition and Origin	C (carbon + various impurities). A simple carbon black, produced by calcining fruit stones (walnuts, peach, cherry, pear, almond, chestnut, or even cork). The colour produced varies from deep brown to velvet black, according to the type of stone and length of exposure to heat. The author has prepared pigment from peach stones, forming a warm deep brown. The stones require pulverisation to form a fine powder.
Tinting Strength	Poor.
Shade	Brown to black.
Opacity	Tends towards transparency.
Suitability to Media	Formerly found in oil and watercolour paint systems.
Drying Rate (in oil)	–
Defects	–
Availability/Cost	Formerly available in French and Russian paint ranges or as dry pigment.
Comments	Peach black is often confused with vine black, both being basic charcoals.
Special Note	The Leningrad Paint Plant (now St. Petersburg Paint Plant) of the former Soviet Union include genuine peach black (catalogue of 1991) in their list of oil colours, the colour described as being "deeply bluish black, obtained [from] peach stones [by] calcinations".
Health & Safety Information	–

ATTRAMENTUM

Colour Index Number	-
ASTM/BWS Rating	Not tested.
Common Names	Iron scale black.
Composition and Origin	Attramentum is made by reacting the tannic acid of oak bark with iron salts. This produces a deep black with a violet tinge (as a glaze).
Tinting Strength	Strong, in oil.
Shade	Deep black with violet undershade.
Opacity	Semi-opaque.
Suitability to Media	In oil, forms a deep, velvet black, which is stable. Lightfast.
Drying Rate (in oil)	-
Defects	In water-based media, attramentum can have a corrosive effect on paper supports.
Availability/Cost	Available as dry pigment.
Comments	-
Special Note	-
Health & Safety Information	-

BISTRE

Colour Index Number	-
ASTM/BWS Rating	Not tested.
Common Names	-
Composition and Origin	C_nH_{2n+2}. The soot from burning beech wood or birch wood has a tar-like quality. It can be washed, sifted and pulverised to form a slightly bituminous pigment known as bistre. Bistre is known to fade or become pale in strong light, through oxidisation. Many ink and wash drawings from the 1600s were made with inks based on bistre mulled into gum arabic, or shellac soap (shellac and borax). Bistre is a deep-blackish brown with some transparency. When the pigment is steeped in turpentine it forms a sticky mass, similar to bitumen in consistency. It can be used to tint oil-resin mediums with a clear-transparent brown effect, but dries poorly.
Tinting Strength	Poor.
Shade	Cold brown-black in water-based media, shows some warmth when ground in oil.
Opacity	Good transparency.
Suitability to Media	Best suited to liquid ink, using a shellac-borax based binder (water-thinnable but insoluble when dry).
Drying Rate (in oil)	Poor drier in oil.
Defects	Fugitive to light.
Availability/Cost	Available as a dry pigment and as ready-made "bistre ink".
Comments	-
Special Note	Requires wetting agent.
Health & Safety Information	-

PRUSSIAN BROWN

Colour Index Number	-
ASTM/BWS Rating	Not tested.
Common Names	Berlin brown.
Composition and Origin	$Fe_4[Fe(CN)_6]^3$. Prussian brown (available from 1704) is a by-product of prussian blue. A stable, transparent brown can be processed from prussian blue (ferric ferrocyanide). The blue pigment is calcined while exposed to air, turning to cyanogen (manufacturing of prussian brown is hazardous, which to some extent explains the limited use of this pigment) and ferric oxide.
Tinting Strength	Medium.
Shade	Dull, neutral brown, enhanced in oil-resin glazes.
Opacity	Transparent.
Suitability to Media	Stable in oil and watercolour.
Drying Rate (in oil)	-
Defects	-
Availability/Cost	Rarely available, sometimes as dry pigment.
Comments	-
Special Note	-
Health & Safety Information	-

BITUMEN

Colour Index Number	-
ASTM/BWS Rating	Not tested.
Common Names	Asphaltuum.
Composition and Origin	C_nH_{2n+2}. Asphaltuum, formed after the evaporation of petroleum. Bitumen or asphaltuum, occurs naturally in low-lying or sub zero level locations such as the Dead Sea in Israel/Syria, Peru, Albania, and Gilsonite in the United States. In nature it is found as a black, tarry substance which is collected, for example from the surface of the Dead Sea, then dried and pulverised. In former times it was also found in Sicily and is sometimes even referred to as Sicilian Oil. It can also be artificially prepared from brown coal and coal tar. It tends to dissolve in drying vegetable oils such as linseed oil but may also be dissolved in (warm*) turpentine to form a simple, tacky mass that can be used as a transparent brown glaze. As bitumen is carefully dissolved, then diluted with turpentine, it reveals a clear, warm brown colour, which can be brushed out to form a thin glaze. By contrast, undiluted it has a thick, viscous tarry presence and is unpleasant to work with in both smell and consistency. Bitumen, despite its pleasing warm-brown colour is a technical nightmare: it never completely dries as a paint film and remains susceptible to temperature changes. For example, in the summer, paint films may re-open and become tacky. As a consequence, in oil paint technique bitumen has no practical importance, unless used to tint an oil-resin glaze, where its pronounced detrimental properties are slightly reduced. * Warm turpentine in a warm water bath - not direct heat source. Turpentine and all solvents are highly flammable.
Tinting Strength	Poor - does not mix well with other pigments.
Shade	Warm, rich brown-black.

Opacity	Transparent.
Suitability to Media	Not stable in any media.
Drying Rate (in oil)	Does not dry.
Defects	Poor drying.
Availability/Cost	Available as a paste, or in dry powder form and still in some oil paint ranges.
Comments	Best avoided – but remains of importance to painting conservation and to those interested in painting techniques of the past.
Special Note	-
Health & Safety Information	-

VINE BLACK

Colour Index Number	-
ASTM/BWS Rating	Not tested.
Common Names	French vine black, blue black.
Composition and Origin	C (pure carbon). A natural vegetable pigment: made from charred vines. Pure carbon. Dates from antiquity.
Tinting Strength	Medium.
Shade	Cold grey-black.
Opacity	Good transparency.
Suitability to Media	-
Drying Rate (in oil)	Very slow.
Defects	-
Availability/Cost	Common to many paint ranges: a variety of vine blacks are available as dry pigment.
Comments	Pigment as powder has a mild grainy presence, which can be smoothed to some degree by extra grinding in a pestle and mortar.
Special Note	Requires wetting agent.
Health & Safety Information	-

Miscellaneous Pigments

Pigments that may have advantageous or interesting properties for special techniques

This section includes a number of pigments that may now be considered obsolete (i.e. no longer available).

Alizarin Green

Early coal tar dye colour. Not permanent. Alizarin green progressively darkens on exposure to light, moving towards black. Obsolete.

Alizarin Brown, $C_6H_4(CO)^2C_6H_2(OH)^2$

Also known as brown madder. Has similar properties as alizarin crimson, but is no longer in general manufacture. Some shades of natural madder may also share this name. Obsolete.

Aloe

A brown, with a warm tinge can be prepared from the juice of aloes, native to South Africa (Port Elizabeth) and India. The dried aloes are steeped in alum-rich water (similar to the making of sap green) and the resultant sticky colour can be used as a simple watercolour paint on to paper. Fugitive to light.

Antimony Orange, Antimony Gold, Antimony Vermilion. Goldschwefel in German. Sb_2O_3

Unstable in mixtures with lead-based pigments, antimony orange is a trisulphide of antimony. It is available in a number of shades, from dark yellow-orange through to orange-red. Developed in the 1840s in Scotland, by Murdock & Co and C. Himly in Germany.

The pigment is dull in appearance in powdered form but becomes rather more glowing and brighter when mixed with a binding agent. Inclusion of free-sulphur in the manufacturing process leaves antimony orange rather unstable, especially when in contact with lead-based pigments.

Antimony Oxide White, Sb_2O_3

Antimony oxide is sometimes found in industrial paints. It darkens when in contact with hydrogen sulphide. As a consequence, it is prepared by co-mixing with zinc oxide (which is able to absorb hydrogen sulphide). Alone, antimony oxide white is very opaque, similar to titanium white. Developed in the 1920s but of no practical importance as an artist's material. Obsolete.

Bismuth White, PW 17, $BiOnO_3.H_2O$

Less toxic than lead white. Bismuth white (bismuth nitrate) was used as an alternative to lead white in the early 19th century, prior to the introduction of zinc white. It is affected by sulphurous compounds and has a tendency to turn black on exposure, at a more accelerated rate than is the case with lead white.

Bone Ash (tricalcium phosphate)

The white-grey ashes from burnt bones can be used with animal skin glue binder, or casein binder to give a ghostly grey-white colour. Bone ash is more commonly used as an addition in metalpoint/silverpoint grounds and as a thickening agent in lime-fresco.

Brazilwood, $C_{15}H_{12}O_5$

A red-brown lake can be prepared from yellowish brazilwood chippings, by boiling in water, then straining the resultant coloured dye and allowing it to form a dry residue, which is then pulverised to a powder.

This red-brown lake was commonly found on painting from the middle ages, when the source for the colour came from Sri Lanka.

The same wood was also discovered in South America and lends its name to the modern country of Brazil. Fugitive to light.

Coloured Marble Dusts

Coloured marble dust in the form of chips, sized between 0.7-4.0mm can be used to create textured effects in a variety of binders, especially when incorporated into fresco techniques. It can also be safely used with various acrylic binders. The different chip size provides a variation of hue, with the palest shades resulting from chips of the smallest size. Coloured marble dusts are available in colours ranging from white, cream/ivory, pale ochre-like yellow, brown-pink, green, red-pink and black.

These coloured marble dusts can also be used with strong protein glue binders, especially casein-ammonium carbonate (see Lime-Fresco chapter, for binder recipe). Other coloured rocks such as quartz chips (orange-red), granite (grey) and basalt (black/grey) can be used in a similar fashion and offer specialised textured effects, especially when used in fresco ground layers.

Fluorescent Colours

These "pigments" may be produced by combining fluorescent dyes with fast-setting resin. The hard resin is then pulverised to a powder form to enable paint to be made. These fluorescent or "dayglo" colours have been formulated to encourage reflectance of UV light and are supplied in the following shades: white, blue, green, lemon yellow, golden yellow, orange, brick red (pink), flame red, magenta red.

The fluorescent colours show best light reflectance when painted on to white primed grounds and better still when lit only by UV lights. They are not permanent and will lose their brilliance in a matter of months when exposed to daylight. Some colours appear more fluorescent than others. For example, the pink, red and lemon yellow shades do seem to glow. By contrast, the blue is slightly dull when painted out and compared to manganese blue pigment.

Special UV light absorbing varnishes are available which can be applied over the fluorescent colours, they do not stop the fading of fluorescent pigments but will slow down the rate of change. These varnishes are normally based on acrylic resin formulations.

In practice, the fluorescent colours work best into acrylic binders. For best light reflectance, they should be mixed with the acrylic resin binder and expressed on to the painting surface immediately (i.e. not left to stand). To increase light reflectance, co-mix with hollow glass beads – this has the effect of increasing luminosity. If any filler material is included in the basic paint mixture, the resultant colour will not appear particularly fluorescent. This is especially so with cheaper acrylic brands that include fluorescent colours. In oil, the fluorescent colours appear rather dull.

Glass Pigments

Coloured ground glass is manufactured by fusing lead crystal glass and other metals (e.g. cadmium, copper, nickel, cobalt, selenium) to create a spectrum of colours. These coloured ground glass pigments are widely used in the glass-blowing industry, especially in Venice and the Czech Republic. The technology surrounding the development of coloured glass pigments has a long history. In Venice, for example, as early as 1292, the city had gathered all glassware production on the island of Murano, and even today, Murano remains an important centre for glassmaking.

Although coloured glass is normally associated with these centres of glass-blowing and glassware production, when a smaller particle size is created, coloured glass can be used in various paint binders with some success. The base material is first pulverised, then graded according to micron (grind) size. The particle size of such glass pigments may thus range from 63m to 125m, the size of the particle determining the exact shade of colour – a very fine particle size gives a much paler hue. This represents the same phenomenon exhibited by smalt, but also relates to the crystalline mineral pigments (e.g. malachite, azurite), where in order to achieve a strong colour, the pigment is required to be used in a grittier particle size. This somewhat limits the use of coloured glass pigments in terms of painting, unless one is happy for the paint film to include a textured surface. Pale or waterclear binders show the colour of the glass to best effect. As a consequence, acrylic binders may be the most suitable, in particular, acrylic gel mediums, which possess body and clarity. In such systems, the glass is encapsulated in the acrylic gel film, so guaranteeing good adhesion to the support. However, encapsulation within an acrylic binding somehow lessens the colour effect, because light is effectively swallowed into the acrylic resin paint film. By contrast, when the glass pigments are carefully used in oil binders, they can provide both colour saturation and transmission of light. The best policy with oil is to use a pale sun-bleached linseed oil, combined with a slightly warm addition (perhaps 20-30%) of Venice turpentine. The Venice turpentine deepens the gloss of the pigment but also helps light to pass through the paint film. The pale sun-bleached linseed oil does not show yellowing and creates enough binding with the Venice turpentine to hold the glass pigment to the support. The Venice turpentine needs to be slightly warm (place container in a warm water bath before applying) in order for this oleo-balsam to flow sufficiently to be able to brush out. Careful use of these glass pigments in this oleo-balsam formula will give rich, glossy, luminous paint coatings, where the granular particle size is partially hidden in the thickness of the binding.

Although the coloured glass pigments can be construed as toxic when burnt, giving off noxious fumes, in their powdered state they are relatively inert. Even so, because they contain lead and other heavy metals it is advisable not to breathe in dust when working with the loose powder. Glass pigments are stable to light and protected from damage by air pollutants. They can be used with any binder, although in fresco techniques they may cause surface problems such as blooming. In short, glass pigments represent one of the best possible forms of pigment, in that all colours react identically to any binder and particle sizes are sorted into different grind sizes, so the artist can adopt whichever is most suitable. If one drawback with these pigments is their weak colour when used at the small grind size, then another problem is the range of colours available. As already stated, the colours are only strong in large particle format, so one tends towards making paintings that show pale tints. Also, the colours cannot be successfully intermixed: they need to be laid over each other to gain any kind of colour transformation, although not all glass pigments are absolutely transparent. They are best used alone, with colours being placed size by side, using different grind sizes to apportion control of lights and darks.

Inert Fillers

Low tinting strength whites such as blanc fix and aluminium hydrate can be used in painting practice, with care, as colours in their own right (see White Pigments section). A number of other white or off-white inert pigments/fillers can also be considered.

Into animal skin glue binders, white chalk can be used as a pure white pigment: whiting (calcium carbonate) or gypsum (calcium sulphate) are examples. Kaolin and china clay (PW 19) are forms of aluminium silicate and are often used as extender/filler material, especially in school paints and some industrial paints. Kaolin is the brightest white form of china clay. Both forms are used for their cohesive properties in the manufacture of soft pastels, graphite pencils and coloured pencils. However, due to their fast-setting properties when admixed with cold water, they have been used successfully to make temporary wall drawings.

Logwood, $C_{16}H_{12}O_6$

A plant colour, giving a red colour when boiled in water, but can be reacted with various metal mordants (tin, alum, etc) to give different dye colours, especially black, or brown-black and blue-black. It can also be developed as a "lake" in a process similar to that for natural madder. Fugitive to light.

Luminous Pigments

Luminous or phosphorescent pigments are based on heat-fusions of heavy metal sulphides such as cadmium or zinc, in combination with small trace elements of other minerals. Such pigments glow or luminesce in the dark. They store light when exposed to strong light sources, then when placed in the dark, the pigment emits this light, usually showing a white-green effect. Gradually the phosphorescent effect wears down, and even after re-exposing to strong light, the glowing effect becomes progressively weaker. As a consequence, such pigments cannot be considered for permanent works of art but may be successful in the context of installation work, or for decorative purposes.

Some phosphorescent pigments only emit this glowing effect when shown in black light (i.e. a room devoid of natural light and lit only by UV light).

Magenta, $C_{20}H_{20}N_3Cl$

Also known as fuschin, magenta is a red-purple dyestuff, developed from 1856 and named after an Italian town. Along with mauve, it was used during the 19th century, particularly in watercolour and gouache paints. May still be used in some cheaper water-based paints, although this colour can be readily matched by a number of permanent quinacridone pigments.

Mauve, $C_{27}H_{25}N_4(SO_4)$

The first synthetically made dyestuff, discovered accidentally by William Perkin in 1856. Mauve is an aniline dye, prepared from a distillation of coal tar. It was used in watercolour paints in the 19th century, but its fugitive nature and tendency to bleed render it unsuitable as an artists' material. Obsolete.

Metal Powders

Some powdered metals can be considered permanent for painting purposes. For example, stainless steel powder can be used in linseed oil to effect a dense, metal grey. Similarly, carborundum powder, a grit normally used for re-grinding the texture on the base of glass mullers, is stable in oil and makes a heavy metal black-grey. Metal powders have no intrinsic tinting strength: when admixed with opaque pigments they disappear, perhaps leaving only their texture behind. Some metal powders are prone to change upon exposure to atmosphere: for example, aluminium does not tarnish as some metals do, rather it corrodes, developing an unhealthy pale, dull grey appearance. Similarly, copper powder gives a bright, bronze finish, but this effect changes on exposure to acids, where the copper turns bright green. This patination may be aesthetically pleasing, but it indicates instability and of course more changes can occur after the initial tarnishing.

When such metal powders are bound in acrylic, they may have a better chance of remaining intact. However, such mixtures should be made and used at once. Acrylic-metal combinations containing water may discolour/tarnish rapidly if left to stand. Some proprietary brands of acrylic colour include metal hues, which may be based on metals such as aluminium, copper and stainless steel. For correct use of these colour types, refer to the manufacturers' instructions. Caution is recommended in the use of metal powders: not only are some metals highly toxic, but because of the heavy nature of the material they should never be ingested through inhalation. Always wear a dust mask when working with such products in dry form.

Examples of Metal Powders

Aluminium, in powdered form, Pigment Metal 1/C.I 77000

Bronze powder, Pigment Metal 2/C.I 77400

Bronze powders can be mixed alloys of the following:

a) zinc, aluminium, copper, tin

b) iron, zinc, copper

c) zinc, copper (sometimes with other metals)

d) copper

Bronze powders are presented as coarse particles, of varying size, according to quality and end use. The four shades indicated can vary widely from brand to brand and many other intermediary shades are available. Fusion with synthetic organic pigments and/or synthetic dyestuffs, were previously available under the name of "blitzer bronze". As indicated, metal powders – especially the bronze powders – are susceptible to tarnishing or oxidisation and as a consequence, are rarely considered for use in permanent works of art.

Gold, in powder, leaf or foil, Pigment Metal 3/C.I. 77480

Chemical formula: Au. Gold can be used in water-based binders in powdered form. The raw gold powder is carefully combined with gum arabic solution, or solutions of gum tragacanth, isinglass, or acacia (clear, pouring) honey. In such preparations it has been used in the context of illuminated manuscript painting, but also finds use in gilding techniques, when patching in broken areas of gold leaf. The high cost of gold in powdered form limits its use in painting, but it has successfully been employed in miniature painting and is effectively stable in all binding systems (but works best into clear water-based binders as indicated).

Tin, in powder or foil, Pigment Metal 5/C.I 77860.

In early panel paintings, tin foil was often used to imitate gold. The leaf was applied as per gold leaf, then varnished with a warm yellow-coloured lacquer, such as that obtained from the plantstuff saffron ($C_{20}H_{24}O_4$). Unlike silver, tin does not tarnish or discolour with age. Tin powder has a soft silverish colour and can be mixed with oil, oil-resin paint medium or alkyd resin, to make a thin paint film, which is best applied as a top coat over dried layers of paint.

Mica

Natural forms of mica are available. They have less sheen when compared to pearlescent pigments (which are usually based on a manufactured fusion between mica and other pigments such as titanium white), and tend to respond differently, according to the type of binder used. For example, muscovy glass, also known as muscovite mica, is the simplest form of potassium aluminium silicate, sold in the form of small platelets or pulverised to a fine grain powder. This form of mica will give a soft sheen when used with pale, water-based binders such as dilute animal skin glue, isinglass or very dilute acrylic resin binders. When used with oil, it forms a mushy paste which shows only the colour of the oil used. Some forms of mica such as phlogopite have a definite colour, in this case, a bronze-grey, again seen to its best advantage in pale water-based binding media.

As with pearlescent pigments, the micas show best when painted against dark grounds.

Mosaic Gold ("purporino")

PY 38/C.I. 77878. An artificially made pigment, stannic (tin) sulphide, Sn S2. Small yellow scales, similar in appearance to bronze metal powder. Mosaic gold can be used to give imitation gilding effects and is stable in most binding systems. Toxic when ingested. Obsolete.

Mummy

The Egyptian practice of embalming dead bodies of humans and sacred animals in asphaltuum (bitumen) was, for a short period the source for a dark, transparent brown, known as "mummy brown", or "caput mortuum" (literally "dead-head"). The embalmed body, including bones, was simply ground to a fine powder.

The composition is more stable than asphaltuum, because a great portion of the volatile hydrocarbons normally present in asphaltuum have evaporated over time. The pigment was used in the 19th century and has been recorded as being on sale right into the 1920s. It was a particularly useful colour in oil painting, providing excellent glazing properties. Obsolete.

Modern caput mortuum may be synthetic iron-oxide red-violet (mars violet), or may indicate a red-violet, or brown-violet shade of naturally occurring iron oxide/haematite.

Pumice

A glass, comprising elements of potassium and aluminium silicate. A type of volcanic ash, available as a gently coarse powder, or in small lumps or "stones". Pumice is found in many areas of the world, close to recent volcanic activity, especially the Lipari islands off the coast of Sicily.

The stones can be used to abrade the surface of raw linen, to remove any knots or faulting, prior to the application of sizing/priming. The powdered form of pumice is useful in certain painting grounds, especially for soft pastel, providing a toothy support. The preparation of soft pastels using pigment, china clay, etc with an addition (perhaps 10%) of pumice powder, provides a pastel stick which is easy to break against a similarly toothy support surface. Pumice can also be combined with gum arabic and pigment, to make a gouache paint with a slightly granular texture. Pumice can be incorporated into acrylic gels and mediums to give a variety of textured effects.

Silver Glitter

When thin aluminium sheets are coated in epoxy resin, then stamped to produced a variety of different sized platelets, a new material, silver glitter is formed. These silver glitter pigments do not corrode through oxidisation, as is normally the case with aluminium. Additionally, they can be used in conjunction with acrylic binders, co-mixed with synthetic organic pigments to create glowing, luminous coloured flakes within a paint film. Some experimentation is required in terms of fluidity of medium with these flakes of glitter, but with careful manipulation it is possible to lay down even paint films with a glittering nature.

Turner's Yellow, Mineral Yellow, Patent Yellow, $PbC_{12}7PbO$

Lead oxychloride. Patented by William Turner in 1781, but first developed by Carl Wilhelm Scheele in the 1770s. Formerly available in shades from yellow through to orange. Turns black on exposure. Not permanent. Obsolete.

Tyrian Purple, Imperial Purple, $C_{16}H_8Br_2N_2O_2 + SnO_2 . nH_2O$

A purple colour from a species of Mediterranean molluscs, *Murex trunculis* or *Murex brandaris,* was once used to colour the robes of Roman emperors. To gain a strong colour, millions of these small whelks are required. For example, tests made by Friedlander in 1908, required over 12,000 *Murex brandaris* to provide just over a gram of dye. Pliny mentions that this colour was produced at Tyre, hence the name. It is possible that this purple colourant was used throughout the Mediterranean and even Atlantic seacoasts up until the middle ages. Although its chief use seems to have been in textiles, it is thought to have been used in the production of illuminated manuscripts.

Drawing Materials

Drawing materials can be dry or wet: both types are used to design or outline form. The exact nature of drawing is a difficult thing to pin down. In the past, drawing was generally related to the production of paintings, and in many cases drawing would have taken place below the applied layers of paint, as a kind of guide. In more recent times however, drawing has taken on a more independent role whereby the result of drawing can be seen by the viewer as a finished artwork.

The dry types of drawing material include familiar items such as pencils and charcoal, but also more unusual, or seemingly outmoded tools, such as silverpoint. Similarly, materials commonly used for drawing that are in liquid form, can include ink, but also dilute forms of many paint types (e.g. watercolour, acrylic).

The exact identity of a drawing material may be hard to define, especially when some of the same materials are used to paint, however, it is the intention of the drawn mark which makes the crucial difference. With drawing, there is always the sense of finding form through expressed marks, whereas with paint, other considerations – particularly form through colour – are important. It is perhaps wisest to say that drawing reaches into painting, when required.

The choice of drawing materials today is wide, as are the types of support applicable to drawing. In considering each drawing "tool" in turn, suitable supports have been suggested. This is by no means a prescriptive list, there may be other ways to employ drawing materials and artists are as always encouraged to experiment.

Dry Drawing Tools

Graphite

Graphite is an allotrope of carbon, occurring in a semi-crystalline, brittle form, which is found in many parts of the world. In industry it has long been used as a lubricant, due to its greasy nature. Most commercial supplies of graphite today are from Sri Lanka. However, graphite was mined in the English Lake District, from the 1660s. At Borrowdale, a graphite mine was worked for many years, supplying drawing and writing tools. The precious nature of graphite was such that it was given an armed escort on its way to London from the mine. The crudest lump form of graphite can be used as a drawing tool, although the mark given out by such pieces can be uneven and even scratchy, depending on the type of paper support used. However, lump graphite can also be supplied in a shiny, smooth form, which easily glides over the surface of paper. Check the consistency of a graphite lump before purchasing.

In general, graphite in lump form is best applied to a paper that has a very slight tooth. Perhaps the ideal support is a smooth/hot pressed 300gsm watercolour paper, which has been coated with one thin layer of rabbit glue size and fine pumice powder. When dry, this surface is slightly toothy, catching the mark of the gently applied graphite lump. This type of support will also mean that little or no fixative need be sprayed on to the drawing surface to preserve it intact. The rabbit glue size needs to be dilute and somewhere in the ratio of one part glue grains to 30 parts of water. This should be left to soak for 30 minutes, then gently warmed through by sitting the vessel containing the glue in a warm water bath for five to ten minutes. Once formed into a clear solution, a pinch of pumice powder is slowly sprinkled into the glue (about 10-20% powder to the volume of glue). When dry, the grainy particles of pumice stand up slightly in the glue layer, forming a kind of toothy grip coat. Once applied to the support, pure lump graphite can be easily smudged into the support surface to create tonal effects. It can also be erased using proprietary brands of putty rubbers or gum erasers, or by taking some soft white bread, forming it into a ball and impressing it into the drawing surface.

Graphite is also sold in the form of powder, in both a silver-grey and a black-grey colour. Both types have a certain sheen or glimmer, especially silver graphite. Care should be taken when using raw graphite powder, as the particles are rather large and when breathed-in can represent a health risk, causing internal scarring in the worst cases. As with all dry powders and pigments, wear a dusk mask when handling.

A common technique with graphite powder, is to rub the raw powder into the surface of the drawing, and then apply a spray fixative. This gives a certain looseness to the working technique, but can present difficulties when fixing, as the spray of the aerosol fixative may dislodge the fine graphite powder. An answer to this may be to prepare the paper support with a solution of egg white (glair). This is done by first whisking the egg white to a froth, then leaving to stand (cover the glass bowl of egg white with a damp cloth) overnight. After leaving to stand for 12 hours, the froth and liquid separate out. Throw the froth away and use the liquid egg white: it contains a high percentage of protein and will thus be less water resoluble than the complete egg white. Apply the egg white liquid with a flat brush to the paper support and leave to dry for 20-30 minutes. After this time, the drawing is made, using graphite rubbed into the paper surface or dispersed into water and brushed on to the surface. When the drawing is complete (no longer than 4-5 hours after the egg white was applied to the paper), the paper surface is fixed by exposing to steam – a boiling kettle can be used for this. This steam-fixing causes the egg white to harden, encapsulating the graphite particles and binding them to the paper surface in the egg white binder. Once dried thoroughly, the drawing surface is fixed and will not smudge unless reactivated with water or more steaming.

Graphite can also be offered in the form of hexagonal sticks, like large crayons. These crayons are simply graphite powder, cooked with clay and then formed into a mould without the wood casing. They tend to be large in diameter (perhaps 2cm wide) and therefore very useful for making expressive marks.

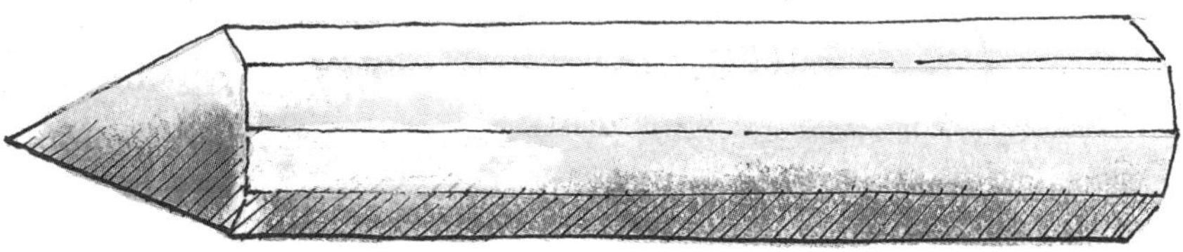

Graphite Crayon

Pencil

Graphite was in former times referred to as plumbago, or black lead, because it closely resembled raw lead pieces and indeed, until the 18th century was thought to be a form of lead. Because of this, pencils are sometimes erroneously called "lead pencils", when they in fact have nothing to do with that odious metal. The first pencils were formed by cutting lump graphite into thin slivers that were then placed between wooden or metal callipers (port-crayon) to form a drawing tool. The same procedure was carried out with other lump materials used for drawing, such as pieces of red chalk or black shale.

The pencil as we know it today relates to a modified form of graphite, where graphite powder has been cooked (calcined) with china clay or kaolin, to form thin but durable rods of graphite. The clay content in a pencil governs its hardness. For example, a 9B pencil will be very soft because it contains virtually no clay, whereas a 9H is very hard because it contains a high proportion. The cooked rods of graphite and clay are subsequently encased in wood, usually soft cedar wood.

Pencil offers a great number of possibilities, not least because it is such a direct medium: the mark is made in a controlled and direct manner, and by combining different hardness and softness of pencil, a variety of tonal marks can be achieved.

Pencil lends itself well to sturdy, smooth drawing papers, especially when detail is called for. However, experimentation is important: the paper chosen for a soft pencil may not work as well with a hard pencil and vice versa.

Charcoal

Wood that has been slowly charred in an enclosed environment, produces charcoal. During this process, the supply of air is virtually excluded, but just enough is permitted to allow the wood to continue burning slowly. The best drawing charcoal has a velvety feel as it contacts with the paper surface and can subsequently be smudged, or gently taken back, using an eraser, putty rubber or paper stump (a tightly rolled piece of paper, which forms a gentle type of eraser, ideal for making soft tonal marks with charcoal). Charcoal can be made from many different types of wood. Most drawing charcoal is made from charred willow twigs, but other woods such as hazel, alder, poplar and beech may also be used. Harder woods such as oak produce charcoal that is hard and scratchy, requiring the paper support to be first prepared with a toothy ground such as rabbit glue and pumice, as described for graphite.

Charcoal is offered in a variety of formats, from thin sticks for detailed drawing, to wider sticks ("scene-painters' charcoal"), large twigs, blocks or stumps. All give a variety of mark and should be tried on to a number of different paper supports.

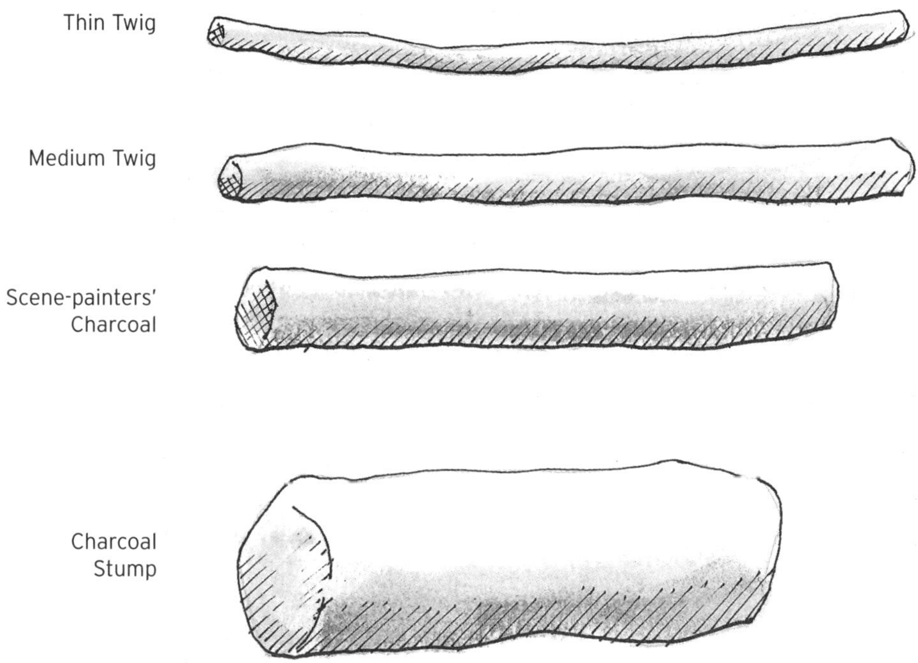

Varieties of Charcoal

Oil Charcoal

When charcoal is soaked in vegetable oil for a prolonged period, it slowly absorbs the oil and thereby gives a greasy, saturated black line when used as a drawing material. Take slow-drying poppy or safflower oil and immerse charcoal twigs/sticks into it, then leave in a closed container for about one week. After this time, each stick is carefully blotted with absorbent paper to get rid of any residual oil and then wrapped in aluminium foil, to prevent the oil drying. Oil charcoal can be applied to any support which has been given a nominal layer of rabbit glue size, or gelatine size. Alternatively, it can be used on to supports that have been acrylic primed. If used directly on to paper, the oil in the charcoal will leech out and stain the paper surface. Oil charcoal will take between one to two weeks to dry out once applied.

Compressed Charcoal

When charcoal is mixed with oil, then reduced to a slurry and fed through an extruding machine, the result is compressed charcoal. This is a dense, saturated black drawing stick which smudges very easily and gives a slightly greasy mark. Compressed charcoal is normally sold in the form of cylindrical or square end sticks. The amount of oil in the charcoal is much reduced compared to that of oil charcoal and as such, compressed charcoal can be applied to any type of paper support.

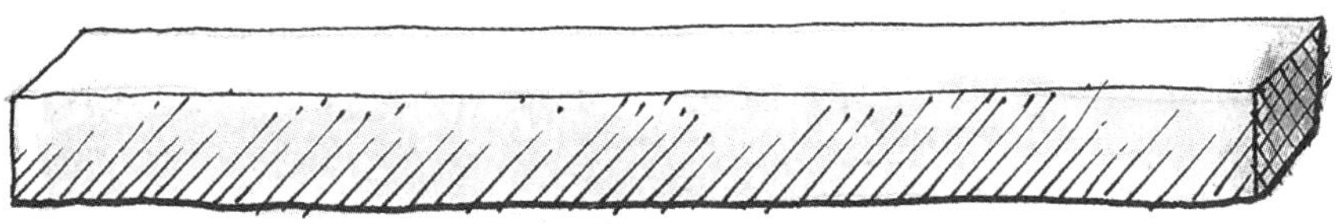

Compressed Charcoal

Soft Pastel

Soft, velvety pastel sticks make excellent drawing tools: they are supplied in a vast array of delicate tones and have a consistency that is ideal for smudging and blending. They offer a subtlety that is often lacking in other drawing materials. For example, if one uses a range of soft pastel in greys from dark to light, perfect modulation of tonality is possible. Soft pastel can also make a good contrast when applied alongside other drawing media. (For further information, see the chapter on Soft Pastel Painting.)

Oil Pastel

Linseed oil, beeswax and animal fat (tallow) may be used to form oil pastels. By contrast to soft pastel, oil pastels are heavy and saturated in colour terms, but the drawn mark may be rather greasy and difficult to smudge or manipulate once applied. Oil pastel can be applied to glue-sized paper or acrylic primed paper, but with unsized papers, oil pastel can gradually leech out oil into the paper fibres. Another drawback with oil pastel is that the tallow used in some brands leaves a paint film which may be virtually non-drying. Some oil pastels can remain slightly greasy and moist indefinitely. Some brands are based on vegetable oils which have a very long curing (drying) time, perhaps between one to two years; only after this may finished works be framed. If oil pastel paintings or drawings are framed under glass before completely dry, the paint film can remain slightly humid, thereby fogging-up the inside of the glass. However, if the finished artwork were to be left unglazed, it may be susceptible to attack by microbes (in the case of oil pastels containing tallow) and can also attract dust on to the soft surface. One French manufacturer offers a special spray varnish for oil pastel, which protects the applied surface.

Oil pastels are available in a variety of colours and sizes. Check the permanence of oil pastel sticks before purchasing, as some brands may be less stable to light and atmosphere.

Oil Sticks

Linseed oil (or stand oil), carnauba wax and beeswax can be used to form an oil stick, in combination with pigment. These oil or pigment sticks are rather better than oil pastels in terms of use, because they do dry effectively and allow the artist to apply colour directly to the chosen support. As with any oil-containing media, oil sticks need to be applied to primed surfaces. The applied mark remains flexible, so can be used on to acrylic primed stretched canvas, but also glue-sized papers. Oil sticks can be manipulated once applied, by a brush either dry or loaded with paint medium or solvent. In a sense, oil sticks create a bridge between drawing and painting: colour can be applied directly without use of brushes, but can be subsequently manipulated to give changed effects as required. Soft beeswax is combined with a proportion of harder carnauba wax to provide a dry paint film which has a good degree of durability. Any paint/drawing medium containing wax however, is sensitive to heat. Beeswax melts at 62°C, so finished artworks need to be displayed or stored away from heat sources (even domestic radiators) and never displayed in direct sunlight.

Crayon

Square-format crayons, as developed by Nicolas Jacques Conté (1755-1805) in France, are formed by heating pigment with clay (in a similar fashion to that of pencil making). The resultant crayons are harder than soft pastel but can be used in a similar way. These crayons can give harder edged lines and detail, and may form a useful contrast to soft pastel when used in combination. For life drawing, a special range of colours is produced: sanguine, sepia, grey, black and white.

Metalpoint

Silver or other soft metals may be used for metalpoint drawing. By tradition, such drawings are made on to a specially prepared support. Gesso panel can be used, or gypsum with rabbit glue applied to any type of paper. Bone ash is sometimes used in the place of gypsum, or admixed with it in the formation of the gesso ground. Bone ash gives a soft cushion, which reacts well when contacted with metalpoint. On a gesso panel, the drawn mark will appear as a dull grey: the mark made by the soft metal re-depositing itself on to the white ground. With silver, at first the mark is greyish, but over time it tarnishes to a red-brown colour, reminiscent of many Old Master drawings.

Natural Chalks

Coloured earths, usually clays tinted by iron oxides, have long been used as drawing materials. With Old Master drawings, terms such as "red chalk" and "black chalk" are often cited, relating to just such materials. Red chalk, sanguine (the colour of dried blood) is typical of these natural drawing "chalks", being composed of soft sandstone coloured by iron deposits, changed from yellow to red during exposure to heat from volcanic activity and found in the form of compressed lumps. This sanguine chalk gives out a soft earth-red mark which is easy to smudge. The best quality varieties of this can be carefully sawn into thin slivers and used for making detailed marks. These sawn slivers are best placed into a port-crayon for ease of use. Lumps of raw ochre from the South of France or sienna from Italy, may also be used as drawing tools, giving a soft yellow mark.

Black chalk, from soft shale can be used for drawing and similarly cut to form drawing tips. Natural black chalks are found in many parts of the world. Historically, "Bideford Black" was an important source of soft black cliff chalk from Devon, England.

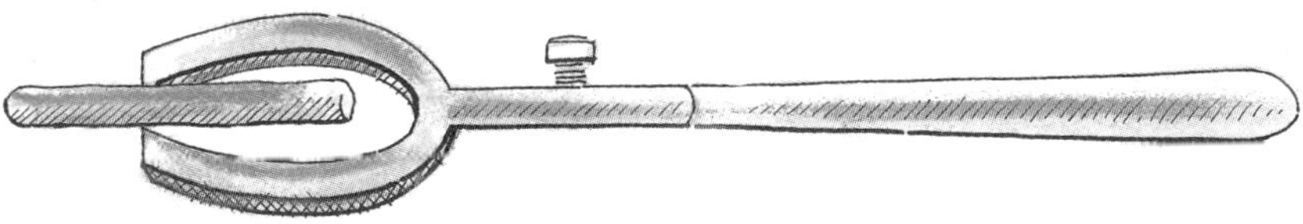

Port Crayon for Holding Natural Chalks

Calcium carbonate (white chalk) in lump can also be used as a drawing material. Kaolin can be formed into a white drawing chalk, by simply mixing the powdered kaolin with cold water and allowing to set. The kaolin is naturally setting and dries out to form a consistent chalk. Adding a little neat alcohol to the water helps to form a more compressed lump when the material is kneaded together before drying.

Wet Drawing Tools

Inks

Ink is a general term that seems to refer to any drawing medium which is applied in a liquid form.

The simplest form of ink, often used more for writing than drawing, was that made from gall nuts (oak apples). The diseased gall nuts of the oak tree are collected and immersed into water which is rich in iron salts. For example, old rusty nails, left to steep in cold water for a week will suffice. Otherwise, pure iron salts in granular form can be used. The oak galls react with the iron-infused water to produce a deep black with a slight bluish tinge. This iron-gall ink does not require any binder, as the ink itself has a slightly corrosive nature: gently embedding itself into the fabric of the paper support. When kept away from sunlight, iron-gall ink will last and last. However, on exposure to sunlight, it can fade perceptibly. For this reason, inks for drawing tended to be prepared with other raw materials.

Ink Stone

In Chinese art technique, a water-soluble gum is compounded with the black soot from a chimney (the equivalent of modern-day lamp black). The lamp black pigment has such a fine particle size, that the resultant ink paste appears to be very strong and saturated. Traditionally the ink paste is left to dry out in a stone well or reservoir. It forms a hard cake, which only gives back a black colour when re-wetted with water and the surface agitated against the small hard ink stone. The gums used for making such inks were resoluble (e.g. gum acacia, gum tragacanth, cherry gum) and in a sense were very similar to cakes of watercolour paint. In Japanese painting, similar ink stones or sticks are still used today, known as Sumi ink. These vary in intensity of tone and have variations of granularity upon drying.

Ink, with Gum Arabic Binder

Pigments, especially those with a fine particle size, can be carefully mixed with a thick solution of gum arabic to create hand-made coloured inks. These can be diluted with water, but will remain water-resoluble, even when dry on the paper surface.

Indian Ink

Lamp black can be combined with a special binder, which is water-diluting but water-insoluble upon drying. This type of ink is commonly known as "Indian Ink" or "India Ink". The binder is a mixture of shellac resin, with borax. The borax is gently heated until dissolved in a quantity of water, then shellac is slowly introduced and left to simmer. The resultant syrup provides a water-insoluble binder upon drying. When applied neat, the ink dries slightly shiny: ideally, these inks are diluted during use, so that they dry to form a neutral sheen. Indian Ink and pigmented inks based on this shellac-borax binder can be applied to most paper surfaces, or to gesso panels (e.g. to map out underdrawing with a liquid ink), but are less successful on to stretched canvas, where the shellac forms a very brittle paint film.

Shellac-Borax Inks

This same formulation of shellac-borax can be used with dry pigment to create individual inks of character. This also allows the artist to govern the strength of the ink. Proprietary brands of shellac-borax inks tend to be rather dilute. Many ink ranges in this category are also based (partially at least) on coloration by dyes rather than pigments. As a consequence, such dyes cannot be seen to be wholly permanent. It may be better practice to take a range of permanent dry pigments and prepare them with the shellac-borax binder. The first stage of this process is to wet the chosen pigment on a glass slab. A small amount of distilled water is added to the quantity of pigment used, just enough to create a stiffish paste. This paste is mixed, using a palette knife or glass muller, so that all the particles of pigment are saturated with water. Once this is done, about 30-40% shellac-borax binder is introduced and thoroughly mixed through. The resultant ink-paste can be stored for a week or so in a closed glass container. This brackish ink-paste can be further diluted with water as required while drawing. It should be possible to use such diluted ink with dip pens, cut quills, brushes, or feather tips.

Sepia Ink (from the cuttlefish ink sac)
Bistre Ink (from birch or beech soot)

These two inks have long been used by artists to create deep brown tones. Both are fugitive to light but remain of great interest. Finished works should be kept in closed portfolios and only displayed in subdued lighting. Both can be prepared by mixing the authentic dry pigment into the shellac-borax binder.

Many sepia "tints" or imitations are available commercially, often prepared with fugitive dyes, but none have the subtlety of true sepia ink.

Ink, with Acrylic Binder

Proprietary brands of acrylic-based inks are available, which tend to have a higher gloss when dry than shellac-based inks. However, acrylic-based inks should be far more flexible and, as such, have found favour with many artists who wish to use them on to stretched canvases, perhaps in mixed media techniques. Acrylic-based inks may be presented in very thin, fluid format, where often the pigment content filters out to the bottom of the pot. Before use, such inks need to be stirred to redistribute the contents. It may make more sense to choose strong acrylic paints and simply dilute them with water when required for ink techniques.

Egg Tempera Painting

Supports for Panel Painting with Egg Tempera

Painting supports can be divided into two basic types:

1. Rigid support; panel, board.
2. Flexible support; canvas, paper.

By tradition, rigid supports are adopted for egg tempera painting, due to the relative inflexibility of the dried paint film. Over time, egg yolk (as a binder) gradually hardens. Although the paint film is extremely durable, it loses what flexibility it may have initially possessed. As a consequence, egg tempera paint, when applied to flexible supports such as canvas, tends to show cracking or flaking to some extent, over time. However, many historical examples of egg tempera painting made on to canvas exist, where careful (i.e. thin) application of paint helps to reduce the degree or likelihood of this cracking/flaking.

The ideal support for egg tempera is a rigid panel or board, carefully prepared in the time-honoured tradition, by laying down many coats of gesso ground. This gesso ground has a gently absorbent surface, which partially sucks the first paint layers into itself, providing a perfect bonding between painting ground and paint layer.

The panels or boards used for egg tempera vary according to source and quality. Modern, compressed fibre boards (e.g. medium density fibreboard) offer a suitable alternative to panels of natural wood. Compressed fibre boards are manufactured from exploded wood fibres, which are mixed with a resin-based glue and put under pressure, thus compacting to form a solid, stable "wood-like" panel. Because heat is used in the compression of the fibres, the surfaces of such boards tend to be flat and smooth. By contrast, the edges of the panels are slightly fibrous, more so when such panels are cut at the wood yard. This fibrous edge needs to be carefully sealed during the priming stage, so that moisture cannot work its way into the panel (which could induce swelling).

The thickness of the panel is crucial: thin panels will tend to warp when the priming ground is applied. Thinner panels may also show a fibrous surface, which interferes with the smoothness of applied painting grounds. By choosing thicker panels (12, 15 or even 20mm), the risk of warping is reduced. However, any larger size panels (for example, larger than one metre square) may need to be braced on the reverse, to prevent warping. Such bracings, made with wooden batons glued to the reverse with strong wood glue, will also increase the overall weight of the panel.

Other types of manufactured panels, such as hardboard (masonite) are less-suited as supports for egg tempera, due to their thinness and subsequent tendency to warp.

Natural Wood

A great many historic examples of panel paintings made with egg tempera have survived, executed on to various types of natural wood. With the benefit of hindsight, it can be seen that some of the woods chosen for painting panels have shown remarkable defects. For example, the Italian painters of the *quattrocento* made extensive use of poplar wood as their painting support. Poplar is a very fibrous, absorbent wood, which quickly takes up moisture in damp conditions. As a consequence, many panel paintings from this period exhibit cracking within the paint film; the wood itself has swollen and contracted over time, thereby exerting pressure on to the paint film. By contrast, in Northern Europe, painters worked on harder panels, constructed from oak, which do not absorb moisture so readily. Such hard-quality panels were often used by Rubens, for example. His panel paintings show remarkably few cracks or imperfections that relate to the support.

Natural wood is always prone to moisture. As a consequence, wood used to make painting panels should be thoroughly dried (seasoned) before use. This drying process necessitates that the wood be air-dried for a long period (1-3 years) in a stable environment.

It is also important that the wood is cut in the autumn (when it is most dense in structure), rather than at other times of the year. In particular, wood cut in the spring will be more "open" to moisture than that cut in the autumn.

In practice, painters would benefit by locating specialist wood suppliers (e.g. for cabinet making) rather than bulk wood merchants.

Preparation of the Panel, Prior to Applying the Gesso Ground

Before applying any priming material, wooden panels or boards should be degreased thoroughly. During handling and cutting, greasy residues are often transferred on to the panel surface. These will inhibit the application of sizing and priming layers.

Ensure that the sides of the panel are relatively smooth. Gently sand down any fibrous residue from the sawing process. It is not advisable to sand the surface of the panel, as this will open the pores of the wood. When sizing/priming (i.e. moisture) is applied to such a surface, it will tend to increase the chances of the panel expanding. A soft, lint-free cloth is used to wipe the panel of any dust or loose fibrous residue. Another cloth is then soaked with a little methylated spirit (alcohol) and wiped over the board surface, its sides and reverse. This treatment will dislodge any small greasy residues. The panel will need to be left to dry after this treatment, before application of the priming material. During this process it may help to sit the panel on small wooden blocks, so that it is raised off the ground, allowing air to circulate.

It is always advisable to prepare a series of panels at one time, so providing consistency from one support to another. Start by preparing six smallish panels, using the same treatment. This saves time and provides a uniform and coherent end result.

Application of the Painting Ground

The traditional ground for egg tempera painting is referred to as "gesso", usually a combination of animal skin glue with a type of chalk. The term originates from Italy, being the Italian word for gypsum. In simple terms, gesso painting grounds fall into two basic types:

1. Gesso ground, based on gypsum (calcium sulphate).
2. Chalk ground, based on whiting chalk, or champagne chalk (calcium carbonate).

The gesso ground (gypsum) tends to be found on old paintings made in Italy (south of the Alps), while chalk grounds (whiting, champagne chalk) can be found in old paintings made in Northern Europe. This generalisation is somewhat confused due to the movement of artists between Italy and the rest of Europe, although until the 20th century, most artists used only materials that were available locally. By contrast, artists working in the first decade of the 21st century have access to virtually any type of material imaginable. This practice is perhaps best seen in the United States, where the use of historical artists' materials (especially painting grounds) still follows the European tradition. An artist working in New York for example, will be able to find all the traditional materials of the Renaissance, through specialist art supply stores. This could include animal hide/skin glues; Bologna chalk (an original type of gypsum) and even horsetail plant which can be used as an abrasive, in the place of modern sandpaper.

The chief difference between gypsum (calcium sulphate) and chalk (calcium carbonate) relates to the degree of absorbency. Gypsum grounds tend to absorb paint films evenly; the applied paint film gently percolates down through it. By contrast, grounds prepared with chalk-based gesso tend to absorb applied paint slightly unevenly, with a sponge-like effect. As a consequence it can be easier to gain regular, even paint films with gypsum based gesso grounds.

Glue

Traditionally the glue used for applying gesso on to panels is based on animal skin. It is sometimes referred to as "hide" glue. Good quality modern skin glues (for example rabbit-skin glue) differ from the glues of earlier periods in that they are clean (refined) and swell very quickly when soaked in cold water.

Recipes from the 1300s and 1400s mention the use of parchment clippings (the waste from the production of goatskin vellum parchment, used for illuminated manuscripts). Goatskin parchment clippings have to be soaked for at least 24 hours before they begin to swell. Similarly, in former times, skin glues were prepared in the form of thin sheets. These need to be soaked in cold water for about 24 hours before they swell. By contrast, some high quality, clean, modern glues will swell in 30 minutes.

In some cultures (Russian for instance), other glues were commonly used for preparing panels. Isinglass, a glue made from the swim bladder of the Russian Sturgeon is a good example. As with parchment clippings from goatskin, isinglass produces a very pale, almost clear glue, which is somewhat less-prone to darkening than animal skin glues. Although glues such as isinglass and parchment clippings are more difficult to find in today's market, artists may wish to consider using them, not only because of their pale colour, but also because they remain very flexible over time. For example, isinglass is often used as an adhesive in the repair or conservation of textiles, where a great degree of flexibility is required.

The quality of animal skin glue available to artists today is a matter of some concern. Where possible, artists should use glues that are clean, free of waste products and which swell readily. Modern glues tend to be sold in the form of grainy powder, or small rough granules. An easy test for the quality of a glue is to place a quantity of it into a glass jar. Fill the jar with clean, cold water and allow the contents to settle for a few hours. If any debris forms on the surface of the water, this is an indication that the glue may include foreign matter.

In some cases, glues have a dark brown appearance in their dry, powdered state. This can also be an indication that the glue is dirty. Ideally, animal skin glue should form an almost clear solution, perhaps with a very pale straw colour. If it is orange-brown, or has a residual scum on the surface, it may not be of the best quality.

The strength of the glue is a further consideration, which is the cause of much consternation among artists of a discerning nature. In the furniture-repair trade, animal bone glues are often employed. These need never be considered for use in painting, as they tend to be rather dark in colour and quite inflexible. However, these glues are sometimes sold to artists for sizing canvas, preparing panels, etc. It is important that artists wishing to work using refined techniques (such as tempera, oil painting), check the quality of the materials they intend to use prior to use, in order to facilitate the best possible outcome for the proposed artwork.

In relation to this, the ideal glue for preparing gesso on to panels needs to be:

- Flexible
- Clean
- Pale in colour
- Sufficiently strong to adhere the chalk/gypsum to the panel surface.

An additional factor when considering glue, is to remember that such natural products are prone to fluctuation. As a consequence, the exact quality of a glue may change from batch to batch. Because artists tend to use very small amounts of these raw materials at any one time, it is quite possible that in the time period between one purchase and another, the quality of a product could fluctuate. As a consequence, it is unwise in the context of this book to give an exact recipe for making glue, because the relative strength of a glue can vary from one supplier to another, and also between time periods.

For panels, the strength of the glue may be higher than that used for the sizing of canvas. Rigid supports such as wooden panels tend to flex to a lesser degree and less often than would be the case with stretched canvas. As a consequence, it is suggested that for panels, the glue can be prepared with less water than one would use for a glue being applied to canvas.

The following recipe, as already stated, relates to one particular brand of animal skin glue. It may be necessary to adjust the recipe according to the nature of the glue being used.

Standard Recipe for Animal Skin Glue (for Panels)

Animal skin glue	1 part
Cold water	15 parts

The glue, usually supplied in the form of a rough powder, or grains, is measured (e.g. with a spoon) and placed into a clean glass vessel. The required amount of cold water is slowly introduced, then finally stirred, so that all the glue is covered and wet. The glue tends to sink to the bottom of the vessel. Leave this mixture to stand for at least 30 minutes. Stir once or twice, to distribute the glue in the water; if the glue is left unstirred, it tends to clump together. After 30 minutes, the glue will have swollen in the cold water to create a mushy paste.

In order to form this into a solution, it requires warming. During this process, the glue changes from a slightly opaque/frosty paste to a clarified, translucent liquid. It needs to be warmed through very carefully. Ideally, the glue is applied to the panel surface when it is still warm, if it becomes too cold, it will turn back to a firm jelly. The best way to warm the glue, is using a hot water bath. Firstly boil a kettle and pour its contents into a large pan. The glue vessel is then placed into this hot water bath: after 1-2 minutes, the glue should be sufficiently warmed to form a clarified solution. The hot water bath will stay warm enough to retain the glue in solution for another 10-15 minutes. If the glue has started to set into a jelly, simply replace the hot water with more boiled water. In this manner, the glue can be kept warm but not too hot.

The worst method for warming the glue is to keep the vessel it is in over a direct heat, or in a double boiler placed on a direct heat. If the glue is heated too much, the water content will be driven off and as a consequence, the glue will become stronger and stronger. When layers of glue are applied with different strengths (e.g. a strong layer over a weak layer), a discrepancy in the relative tension of each layer is created. In the worst case, this leads to warping of the panel, or could cause one layer (of gesso) to pull away from the layer on to which it has been painted.

A good way to check the strength of the glue is to warm it through, then leave it to cool and set to a jelly. When the jelly is parted by forcing it to break between the thumb and forefinger, it should ideally collapse slightly (giving an "apple-sauce" consistency). If when parted, the glue jelly cleaves cleanly, it is a sign that it is overstrong. If one feels that the glue is too strong it can be re-warmed with a little more water added. Keep a note of the recipe used for each batch of glue.

Another factor relating to glue is atmospheric condition. In hot weather, glue will stay in solution more readily than in cooler weather. In the northern hemisphere, glue will tend to cool rapidly in the winter, especially if one is working in a large, un-heated studio space.

Preparing the Panel with Gesso

The procedure for applying the ground, whether using gypsum or chalk, is essentially the same. A first "grip" coat is applied to the panel surface, followed by a series of between 4-10 coats of gesso.

The grip coat consists mainly of glue, with a pinch of gypsum or chalk (about 10% dry powder to 90% volume of liquid glue). This small addition of gypsum or chalk provides a key to which further coats can attach themselves.

The first coat is applied to the face of the clean panel and allowed to dry. Some artists choose to apply the grip coat and subsequent coats to the sides and reverse of the panel, at least in the first few layers. This seals the vulnerable edges of the panel, and coats applied to the reverse help to equalise tension across it. However, on examining many panel paintings over the years, made during different time periods, the author suggests that this practice of gessoing the sides and reverse is a modern fashion and largely unnecessary.

The grip coat also seals the pores of the wood, so that subsequent layers of gesso can be laid down evenly and smoothly on to the equalised first coat. With all primings, the first coat laid down has some influence on subsequent ones. If the first coat is coarse, then following coats will repeat the unruly pattern, providing an incoherent, bobbly surface. If the grip coat contains only a small amount of gypsum/chalk, it will be enough to form a key with the next coat but will not interfere with the smoothness of the priming.

Once dry, the grip coat is overlaid with subsequent coats of gesso (gypsum/chalk with glue). Again, there are many recipes for making gesso: it is advised that the following standard recipe is used and then changed according to the requirements of the artist and the type of surface.

Recipe for Gesso

Gypsum	1 part
Liquid glue	1 part

Always add the gypsum (or chalk) to the glue, never the other way round. An equal volume of liquid glue to gypsum is a good starting point. The gypsum is lowered into the glue and allowed to fall beneath the surface, spoon by spoon. Allow the gypsum to absorb into the warm glue slowly and by its own gravity. Try to avoid stirring, as this will introduce unwanted air bubbles into the mixture. The best method is to deposit the gypsum into the glue and leave it for 15-20 minutes, until it all falls down to the bottom of the vessel. Do not worry if the glue cools and forms a jelly during this period. It can be readily re-warmed, by replacing in a hot water bath.

When ready to apply to the panel surface, stir very slowly (again, to avoid air bubbles), to distribute the gypsum within the glue solution. The gesso should have the consistency of single cream: if too thick, dilute slightly with some warmish water and stir slowly before using. The gesso is applied to the panel using a 4-5cm width flat hog-hair brush (regularly sold as varnishing brushes). Dip the brush into the gesso mixture, slowly draw it against the side of the vessel, so that only a small amount of the liquid is retained in the brush. Again, this helps to free air bubbles. The gesso is then applied to the surface of the panel, working quickly but carefully over the whole panel in one direction, and carefully wiping back any residue at the panel edges, with the brush. Allow the first coat to dry for 10-15 minutes before applying a second. Allow each coat to dry before putting on the next, in this way, between 4-10 coats can be applied to build up the priming surface. The number of coats applied is a personal decision but remember that the greater number of coats, the greater the tension across the panel from the glue.

Once all the coats have been applied, the panel is left to dry for a few hours, so that all dampness has gone from the panel and the gesso layers. Preferably leave overnight to dry out thoroughly.

Once dry, the gesso surface can be sanded to a smooth, ivory-like finish. Choose finer, rather than coarse sandpaper, or use dried horsetail plant. The stem of the horsetail is cut in half and flattened, then slightly dampened. This causes the plant fibre to swell slightly and, because the texture of the stem is abrasive, it can be used in place of sandpaper.

It is also possible to sand the gesso between each dried layer. This will ensure a very smooth surface between each layer and make the final sanding easier.

If air bubbles formed during the laying down of the gesso, this usually indicates that it was too hot when applied, or that air was stirred into the mixture. Through practice, such annoyances can be eradicated.

The recipe above relates to the use of fine gypsum mixed with glue. In many historical texts, other grades of gypsum or chalk are mentioned. In Italian technique for example, there are two basic forms of gypsum used for preparing panels:

1. *Gesso grosso* - larger particles, giving a rough surface.
2. *Gesso sottile* - very fine particles, giving a smooth surface.

By tradition, the gesso *grosso* would be employed for the first coats, especially where two panels were to be joined together, or faults in the wood had to be disguised. The larger particles would form a thicker cushion, over which the gesso *sottile* would be applied. Nevertheless, the gesso *grosso* would need to be abraded to give a smooth finish, once the joints or discrepancies in the panel were covered over. In some cases, it was used in conjunction with strips of linen cloth, employed to cover over joints between panels. The gesso layers would be used to adhere the linen cloth to the panel and then overpainted with subsequent coats, until the linen was not visible.

Modern gypsum and chalk is sold according to a mesh number. This relates to the size of the mesh used when sieving the raw material. The smaller the mesh number, the finer the grains of gypsum/chalk. The finest grades are also used by gilders, for the preparation of gilding grounds and are therefore sometimes referred to as "Gilders' Whiting", or "Gesso *d'oro"* (gesso for gold).

As already mentioned, it is wise to prepare a number of panels at any one time for the sake of consistency.

Preparation of Pigments for Egg Tempera Painting

Tempera painting relies on the mixing of pigments (colour) with a water-thinnable binding agent. Upon drying, this binding agent becomes insoluble and permanent. However, while damp, or very recently dried, it is possible to rework the paint film. The term "tempera" may refer to the notion of "tempering" colours prior to painting. Within the fresco painting technique, colours are simply mixed in water and applied to a wet ground of plaster. This plaster, being composed of fast-setting lime, fixes the water-borne pigments to the painting surface (typically a wall structure). In this way, with fresco painting, colours are never mixed with a binding agent, rather they are attracted to the wet plaster surface, which in effect acts like a cement: attracting the pigment particles into a fixed position.

By contrast, with tempera painting, pigments are specifically mixed with a binding agent prior to application to the painting support (usually a gessoed wooden panel). This process can thus be referred to as the tempering of colour, in readiness for painting.

Egg is the most famous of these binding agents and the terms "tempera" and "egg tempera" have become inextricably linked. However, other forms of tempera paint exist and require some discussion. Among the other water-based binding agents sometimes referred to in the context of tempera painting are:

Gum tempera	gum arabic, dextrin, or gum tragacanth solutions (plant protein binders), mixed with pigment (see Gouache Painting section)

Glue tempera	animal skin glue, or isinglass (fish glue), mixed with pigment and applied as a paint, while kept warm
Casein tempera	curd cheese (or dried "skimmed" milk), mixed with pigment
Glair	egg white, mixed with pigment.

Egg Yolk as a Binder

The characteristic finish of an egg tempera painting has a low, slightly glossy sheen. The binding agent responsible for this is egg yolk, a natural protein-rich emulsion: a mixture of albumen, water and fatty oils. This slightly greasy substance has a characteristic warm yellow colour and a certain viscosity. It can be readily diluted with water to form a thinner consistency as required. As already mentioned, once thoroughly dry, egg yolk paint films become extremely hard and durable and remain water-insoluble. There is a window of solubility, perhaps somewhere between one and six months, when the paint surface can be disturbed if thoroughly agitated, prior to complete curing (drying).

Preparing the egg yolk for tempering with pigment is an important procedure: the white of the egg must first be removed, followed by the sac of the yolk, so that only the liquid portion of the yolk is retained for use. After cracking the egg and separating the white from the yolk by carefully passing from one hand to another, pinch the yolk in its sac between thumb and forefinger and carefully slice the sac with a scalpel. Collect the liquid yolk, which will slowly drain out of the sac, into a clean glass or ceramic vessel. It may help to strain the liquid yolk through a fine sieve to remove any other debris.

The resultant yolk is ready to use for painting, although it is a good idea to add between 30-40% cold water to reduce the consistency.

This allows the yolk to flow freely and mix more readily with the dry pigments. When water is added, the yolk becomes cloudy/milky in appearance. This cloudiness disappears upon drying to reveal a thoroughly translucent paint film.

Because egg yolks decompose rapidly, it is advised not to mix up quantities of pigment with the yolk. Far better practice is to prepare the chosen pigments with purified or distilled water, making them into stiffish pastes. These damp pastes can then be incorporated with the egg yolk as and when required for painting. It is wise only to prepare enough egg yolk for each painting session. After 1-2 days, the yolk will begin to give off an odious sulphur smell.

The character of the eggs used in painting may also be of some influence. Factory-laid eggs may be pale in colour, or weak and watery in consistency. By contrast, farm eggs tend to be very warm in colour and thick in consistency. It is preferable to work with freshly laid eggs that are free from any additives or colourings.

Before painting, each chosen pigment needs to be mixed with purified or distilled water, rather than mineral-containing tap water, which can react with some delicate metal-based pigments (e.g. genuine naples yellow). Another possibility, is to mix the pigment with pure alcohol (methylated spirit). The alcohol rapidly saturates the pigment particles but will quickly evaporate. Better practice is to make a mix of part alcohol, part water, which gives a more balanced paste. Alcohol as a wetting agent is very useful for certain pigments, namely those with a very small particle size. Normally when such pigments (e.g. alizarin crimson) are mingled with water, the water does not readily mix. The addition of a drop of alcohol into the water helps to break water tension, so that the water-pigment paste can be prepared. Older recipes call for the use of spirits of wine to perform this wetting task, but industrial methylated spirit (water-clear), or denatured methyalted spirit (which has a pale pink or violet colour) are readily available today.

The procedure for making the water-pigment pastes is as follows:

On a glass slab (with a sand-blasted surface, which catches the pigment particles and prevents them from dancing across the surface), grind the required amount of pigment with a tiny amount of purified/distilled water. Add enough water to create a stiff, brackish paste, using a straight palette knife for mixing. Take this paste as a whole, or divide it into small portions, and begin to mix it thoroughly using a glass muller (also known as a glass runner). This, is a round, heavy glass "paper-weight" shaped object, sometimes with a tall glass handle, or perhaps a doorknob style handle.

It is used to mix pigments thoroughly into binding agents, or in this case, with water, so that all the particles are divided and saturated by the water. This process ensures a smooth paint film. In fact, the more the pigment is mixed in this way, against the glass plate, the better the colour may be. It is normal to move the glass muller across the glass plate in a figure of eight motion, trapping the particles under the muller and forcing them to combine into the water, to divide from each other (to stop clumping together) and gradually to form a smooth paste. As one proceeds, it may be useful to add a few more drops of water to lubricate the mixture, but beware of adding too much as this could give a sloppy consistency. If pigment catches on the edge of the glass muller, reposition it with the palette knife back on to the glass plate, so that it can be reworked. It is easier to work with small amounts of pigment at a time, than to try and mix everything at once. There is no need for excessive force when using the glass muller: it is merely a case of introducing the pigment into the water, then, once it is freely moving around in the water, the glass muller should move easily over the glass plate. Once a smooth paste has been achieved, where all the particles are saturated with water and forming a coherent paste, put this into a small air-tight glass jar (e.g. 60ml). In this form, the pastes can be stored indefinitely. If they should dry out, re-constitute the pastes with a little more purified/distilled water and remix on the glass plate, before using for painting.

When ready to paint, put a little bit of the water-paste out on to the palette. A glass plate works very well as a palette, with a sheet of white paper underneath to give an accurate colour reading. Alternatively, a ceramic palette or ceramic plate could be used, or a slab of marble.

Into the water-paste, add a small quantity of the slightly diluted egg yolk binder. The exact amount will be different for each pigment, according to its particle shape and size. For example, some earth pigments (e.g. green earth) have large, irregular forms and as such need more binding agent than pigments with a regular, small particle form. Make test paint-outs of each colour before painting properly. When the test paint is dry, it should ideally be sleek, slightly glossy and provide a smooth, even coating on to a well-prepared gesso panel.

If the mixture contains too much egg yolk binder, it will be over-glossy and fat-looking, with a warmish hue, due to the yellow colour of the yolk (most noticeable when used with whites, yellows and pale blues). If the mixture has too little egg yolk binder, the surface will look rough, matt and chalky. Too little binding may cause the paint film to lose adhesion to the support. Getting the pigment to egg yolk ratio right is crucial with the first coat of paint. This is because the gesso ground has a gently absorbent quality which is highly desirable for tempera painting: the first coat percolates into the painting ground and forms a bond within its structure. It also equalises the surface of the paint film, so that subsequent coats lie flat and even.

If the paint mix is too egg yolk-rich, it may be possible to dilute the mixture quickly with water to gain an even finish. In practice, it takes time and patience to learn the exact mixtures of binder to pigment paste for each colour.

The paint is traditionally applied with small, soft hair, brushes. Kolinsky sable is purported to be the best hair for such painting: it is soft, subtle, yet has great resilience and also a natural "spring" to its tips, which helps to retain its shape. For painting, round tipped brushes are commonly used, but for larger, flat areas, filbert or flat sables are sometimes employed. It is also possible to paint egg tempera using other soft, hair brushes such as those made with ox hair, or even synthetic filament brushes.

The paint is applied in small hatching strokes, whereby form is gradually built with many applications of small amounts of paint. However, there is no exact formula for tempera painting, rather a conflict of styles and applications, often seen within the same painting. In order to obtain the best results with this paint-type, remember that the egg-yolk has a wonderfully translucent effect upon drying, which makes it ideal for making intricate, delicate glazes, or shifts between colours.

During the *quattrocento* period in Italy, the technique of egg tempera painting was refined beyond the confines of Byzantine painting. In part this was due to a more exacting method of preparation in the gesso layers, but also to the fact that the Italian painters did not varnish their tempera paintings in the same way as the Byzantine artists. In the Byzantine technique, an oil varnish (referred to as "Olifa" in many texts) is painted over the finished work. Such varnishes are often composed of a drying vegetable oil (e.g. linseed oil) which has been cooked with a metallic drying agent such as lead acetate. This oil varnish layer saturates the colour values and unifies the painting, with a warm, glowing effect. However, over time, the varnish layer discolours, turning a warm, dark brown, which may obscure some finer details. In many Italian paintings, this oil varnish layer is not applied, or it appears as a very thin veil of varnish, most often made without any oil in the mixture (e.g. a solution of a tree resin such as sandarac into alcohol, providing a very thin, almost colourless but slightly glossy sheen). It is difficult to generalise about such practice but it is obvious to see that egg tempera paintings made without the addition of heavy varnishes over the painted surface retain a clarity, lucidity and freshness, which is difficult to imitate in any other technique.

Palette for Egg Tempera Painting

In the context of egg tempera painting, perhaps more than with other media, it is possible to work with historic pigments. This is because only small quantities of pigment tend to be used, worked up in a careful manner. In other words, costly mineral pigments such as azurite and lapis lazuli tend not to be wasted when working with egg tempera. It is an exacting medium, calling for a measure of patience and careful use of materials. As a consequence, many historic (some would argue obsolete) pigments are mentioned here, along with notes on their use in the context of tempera painting.

List of Historic Colours

This basic list of colours for tempera accords to those pigments mentioned in "The Craftman's Handbook" (*Libro dell'Arte*), by Cennino Cennini (original manuscript of 1437) – see Bibliography.

Lead tin yellow, type I

Lead tin yellow, type II - Soft, pale yellow, for highlights, type I is milky and opaque. Type II is coarser and warmer in hue, based on a silicone matrix which affords some transparency. Toxic, contains lead.

Stil de grain - a warm, transparent yellow, for glazing over blues to make greens. Fades in sunlight.

Orpiment - bright, solid yellow, coarse texture. Toxic, contains arsenic.

Yellow ochre - milky, opaque earthy yellow, varies in shade according to source.

Raw sienna - translucent earthy yellow, for glazing.

Lead red - opaque red-orange, blackens on exposure to atmosphere. Toxic, contains lead.

Realgar - yellow-orange, opaque, coarse in texture. Toxic, contains arsenic.

Madder lake - warm crimson, transparent. Often glazed over vermilion to deepen red shade. Fades in sunlight.

Carmine - coldish crimson, transparent. Often glazed over vermilion to deepen red shade. Fades in sunlight.

Red ochre - earth red, milky, opaque.

Venetian red - earth red, with pinky shade.

Burnt sienna - warm red earth, highly transparent.

Morellone (haematite) - strong red-violet earth. Added to white for pinkish tints.

Vermilion - solid red, opaque, bright red. Toxic, contains mercury/sulpher. Available as mineral (coarse texture) or processed (smooth texture) types.

Red jasper - coarse textured pink-red from mineral rock.

Raw umber - greenish tinge, opaque.

Burnt umber - deep warm brown, transparent.

Verdigris - needle shape particles. Not to be mixed with egg yolk. Prepare instead with just warm animal glue. Discolours over time, to give brownish tinge.

Malachite - pale cold green, from mineral rock. When pulverised to small particle size becomes extremely pale in tone.

Green earth - very transparent, cool, olive green. Needs a lot of yolk binder to work successfully but consequently tends to have a greasy, slimy presence.

Ultramarine ash - coarse texture, very pale blue. By-product of lapis lazuli. Often used for underpainting, before working on top with more expensive blues.

Lapis lazuli (natural ultramarine) - costly pigment derived from lapis lazuli mineral rock. Coarse texture, with violet tinge. Often used over base coat of ultramarine ash or azurite.

Azurite - from mineral rock, coarse texture, with greenish tinge.

Indigo - dark cold blue from plant source. Often used admixed with yellows to give green. Transparent.

Vine black - neutral black, very transparent.

Lamp black - blue-black, very transparent..

Lead white – heavy texture, makes fattish paint paste. Only white available pre-1700s.

Flesh Tints

For flesh tints, a series of mixtures are commonly used, as follows:

1. "Verdaccio". Underpaint for flesh tint. Either a) green earth, or b) verdaccio is applied as an underpaint for further flesh tints. Verdaccio is a mixed colour, sometimes made with raw umber, yellow ochre and vine black, or simply using a raw umber with a greenish tinge. This verdaccio is also sometimes admixed into a series of intermediary tints with lead white.

2. "Cinabrese". Overpaint for flesh tint. Either a) cinabrese made with vermilion and lead white, or b) cinabrese made with a red earth (e.g. haematite) and lead white. Sometimes such mixtures could include both vermilion and a red earth, with white. The cinabrese flesh tint overpaint is strongly diluted with binder and water until it shows some transparency. When applied over the verdaccio underpaint, some of the green colour can be seen through the semi-transparent cinabrese layer. This gives a two

tone effect, similar to the composition of flesh as seen when observing the back of one's hand.

Modern Colours for Tempera

A comparative selection of modern pigments suitable for egg tempera.

O Nickel titanium yellow

T Intensive yellow

O Cadmium yellow

O Iron oxide yellow

T Transparent iron oxide yellow

O Cadmium orange

O Cadmium scarlet

T Quinacridone pink

T Quinacridone red

O Iron oxide red, light

O Iron oxide red, middle

T Transparent iron oxide red

O Iron oxide violet

O Cadmium red

O Cadmium brown

O Iron oxide brown light

O Iron oxide brown dark

T Phthalo green

T Viridian

SO Chrome oxide

T Ultramarine blue

SO Cobalt blue

T Prussian blue

SO Spinel black

T Lamp black

SO Zinc white

For verdaccio: chrome oxide green+iron oxide brown light+zinc white

For cinabrese: cadmium red+zinc white

T = Transparent

O = Opaque

SO = Semi-opaque

Procedure for Painting

With tempera painting, a set series of applications may be followed. While this procedure may not suit all artists, it is a worthwhile exercise to undertake in order to familiarise oneself with the medium of egg tempera.

1. **Gesso ground**

   The surface is smoothed with sandpaper to an ivory-like finish. By tradition, this can be done by dusting the surface with fine charcoal dust. After sanding, when the surface is level, all the charcoal dust will have been sanded off.

2. **Charcoal cartoon**

   On to the smooth gesso ground, a cartoon, or drawing can be made using charcoal, but not fixed. In this way, the composition can be established and re-worked easily by dusting off.

3. **Ink cartoon**

   The charcoal cartoon is gently dusted with a soft brush, or feather, so that only a trace of the drawing is visible. Over this faint design, the cartoon is re-established using a permanent ink, such as Indian ink, diluted to give a pale grey wash.

4. **Coloured glaze**

   Over the "fixed" ink cartoon, a glaze can be applied, using a transparent pigment mixed with the egg yolk binder (e.g. green earth).

5. **Flesh tone - verdaccio**

   The green underpaint for the areas of flesh can be applied, bound with egg yolk. The colour can be solid or transparent as required. This verdaccio layer can be used to create form and depth within the flesh areas.

6. **Flesh tone - cinabrese**

   Over the verdaccio, a semi-transparent veil of cinabrese is applied, to confirm and embellish the form already made with the verdaccio underpaint.

7. **Painting in general**

   Other areas are completed with flatter applications, sometimes overpainted with glazes or details, as required.

Tempera and Oil Paint, Egg-Oil Emulsions

Tempera makes a perfect underpaint for oil painting. If one were to work straight on to gesso panel with oil paint, the first applications of oil colour would readily sink into the absorbent gesso surface, leaving the applied oil colour extremely lean, matt and perhaps even underbound. By contrast, if a tinted ground is painted in egg tempera on to a smooth gesso panel, it provides a well-balanced support surface on to which oil paint can be applied. The first layer of oil colour on to such a ground would only slightly absorb into the tempera layer, but enough to form a good bond between paint layer and ground.

Consequently, many examples of oil paint over tempera underpaints can be found in paintings of the past. Indeed, even though tempera is perceived to be too brittle for use on to stretched, flexible canvas, there are many examples of paintings made in this way, which have been overpainted in oil colour. Sometimes artists worked directly on top of an egg tempera underpainting, at other times a form of emulsion was made, between egg and oil. This provides a more flexible, glossier paint than straight oil colour, but with the advantage of being water-diluted. As with normal tempera painting, the binder will spoil after a few days, so colours need to be prepared and used within the same painting session. It may be possible to keep the emulsion in a refrigerator for a few days, but the ingredients soon start to separate and are never quite the same when they are remixed.

Formula for Egg-Oil Emulsion

Whole egg (yolk/white)	2 parts
Linseed oil (with drying agent)	1 part

Break the shell of an egg(s) and put the liquid contents into a glass vessel. The egg is shaken until completely intermingled and then poured through a sieve to get rid of any waste material. Put the quantity of egg(s) with half the amount of linseed oil. Ideally this should be linseed oil with a drying agent such as cobalt siccative, sometimes referred to as "linseed oil varnish" (the modern equivalent of "Olifa", as previously mentioned). The resultant mixture needs to be shaken so that it forms an emulsion, to which water can be added (up to about 40%) to create a dilute consistency. This will dilute further when brushed out with water.

Pigments can be mixed directly with this binding agent and diluted with water as required. By contrast to normal egg tempera, the paint film is slightly thicker and glossier. If required, thin dammar varnish or mastic varnish can be added to the egg-oil emulsion to create an enamel-like finish. Although this emulsion is more flexible than normal egg tempera, it is not as flexible as oil paint. Once a painting has been begun with this egg-oil emulsion, one must continue to use it on all subsequent layers to avoid cracking.

There are many variations on this recipe which may be worth investigating. For example, walnut oil is often used in place of linseed oil; it has a glassy sheen and is very hard-wearing. Walnut oil is also a paler oil than linseed oil, so may be useful when painting in egg-oil emulsion using pale colours.

Varnishes for Tempera Paintings

Whenever a varnish is applied to a matt paint film, the sheen is radically altered. With egg tempera, the finished paint film has some gloss, but this is not excessive. If a varnish is applied, it tends to saturate colour values (i.e. deepens them), because the tempera paint film is slightly absorbent. Working with proprietary brands of varnish may be a mistake with tempera painting, because they tend to be too thick, or too glossy. By contrast, if one takes a glossy varnish and dilutes it with the appropriate solvent, a fine, thin film of varnish may be applied, which acts to protect the painting surface from dirt, dust, and atmospheric pollutants. However, the best policy may be to leave tempera paintings unvarnished, to preserve their unique presence.

Varnishes – Historic

Shellac flakes, solved into pure alcohol	(pale yellow-orange colour)
Sandarac resin, solved into pure alcohol	(very pale straw colour)
Mastic resin, solved into pure alcohol	(pale straw colour)
Egg white (glair)	(colourless, but turns "frosty" after a few years)
Cooked linseed oil ("Olifa")	(red-brown colour, becomes darker with age)

Varnishes – Modern

Dammar varnish, solved into turpentine	(pale straw colour)
Ketone resin, solved into white spirit	(colourless, may yellow slightly with age)
Paraloid B-72, solved into shellsol A	(colourless, may yellow slightly with age)
Plexisol P 550-40, solved in white spirit	(colourless, may yellow slightly with age)

The practice of tempera painting is at times slightly confusing, because traditionally certain colours are not applied bound in egg yolk, but with other binders such as size, glair (egg white), or in varnish form.

To follow, some examples of colours that are often found in egg tempera paintings but which may not be bound in egg yolk:

Verdigris - bind with animal glue size, or isinglass
Dragon's blood - dissolve into pure alcohol to make a coloured resin varnish
Gamboge - dissolve into pure alcohol to make a coloured resin varnish
Pale blues - sometimes bound with glair (egg white)

The inclusion of such colours gives a particular dilemma when considering which varnish to apply, as some of the colours would re-dissolve if varnished over. For example, if one were to glaze shellac varnish over a layer of dragon's blood, the dragon's blood, being sensitive to alcohol, could re-dissolve.

Some modern varnishes may offer a good solution in that they can be diluted to extremely thin films, almost to the point where they give no perceptible change in sheen to the surface of the painting. In dilute solutions, varnishes such as paraloid B-72 can also be spray applied, thereby avoiding any mechanical contact with the painting surface.

Tempera and Gilding

Gold as a colour has played a very important role in the history of Western art. Principally, gold signifies a heavenly, celestial space. It is therefore found in backgrounds/backdrops to many sacred paintings, especially during the Italian Renaissance. Gold is normally applied alongside egg tempera in the form of extremely thin leaves of gold. Because gold as a metal is extremely soft and malleable it is possible to beat small pieces of it into very fine sheets or leaves. This "gold leaf" can also be applied on to gessoed panels, to give an impression of solid gold colour. The gold leaf is applied over a special ground, known as "bole". This is similar to gesso in that it is formed principally of animal skin glue mixed with a coloured pigment. To impart softness to this special bole ground, an addition of china clay or kaolin is added to the glue-pigment mixture. Other softening agents may also be included. Graphite was extensively used in English gilding as a sure-fire method to achieve a smooth polished surface. The mix of bole is applied over the smoothed gesso surface, usually in 2 or 3 coats. The first coat may be a yellow colour – yellow ochre or raw sienna – followed by 1 or 2 coats of red, made with a soft earth red, known as red bole, armenian bole (after one of its historic sources) or sinopia. The combination of yellow and red bole layers provides a warm orange ground colour. The bole layers are applied in thin, transparent veils, with animal skin glue as the binding agent. The glue is important because when polished with an agate burnisher, it produces a delicate sheen. The inclusion of china clay in the bole also helps to create this burnished, polished effect.

Before the gold leaf is applied to the bole surface, it may be polished with an agate burnisher or gently abraded with very fine wire wool. This gives a very smooth surface upon which the gold can be laid. The gold leaf itself is slightly transparent, so that light can transmit through the leaf to the coloured bole ground below. The general effect is to give a warmth to the gold. Alternatively, cold colours can be used in the bole layers (e.g. green earth), to impart a cool tinge to the gold.

The gold leaf is applied by means of a flat brush made with squirrel hair, known as a gilder's tip. The hair is made slightly greasy, usually by brushing against the human cheek, just enough to lift the fine gold leaf from the gilding cushion. Before application, the gold is transferred from an interleaved book (gold leaf is sold in booklets of 25 leaves, interleaved with non-greasy paper), first by blowing it gently against the edge of a special knife, the gilding knife. This should be made of stainless steel and have one sharp edge and one blunt edge. The knife is usually about 20-25cm long and 2-3cm wide. Care needs to be taken that fingers do not come into contact with the blade of the knife, or greasy residues could be deposited which would quickly attach and ruin the fine, sensitive gold leaves. Against the knife, the gold leaf (about 8cm x 8cm) is gently lifted from the booklet and placed on to a special gilding cushion. This is rectangular in shape, about 12cm x 30cm, consisting of pig skin stretched over a wooden base. This cushion is packed tightly with a fine layer (about 1cm deep) of horsehair, which gives a firm but gentle cushion, against which the gold can be cut with the knife. The gold leaf is cut into small strips, which are then carefully raised from the cushion using the gilder's tip.

To adhere the gold to the bole surface, the gilder gently dampens the bole surface with a little water, using a small, flat or filbert shape soft, hair brush (e.g. ox or sable). The water used for this purpose, the "gilding water", has a small addition of animal skin glue (about 5% liquid glue) and also a drop or two of alcohol, which degreases the surface of the bole as the water is brushed on. This process of dampening the bole with the gilding water partially reactivates the glue in the bole layer, this assures that the gold leaf adheres firmly to it. Strips of gold are laid over the painting surface where required using this technique. It is imperative when gilding to work in a room where there is no draught, so that the precious gold leaf does not fly away. Once the gold is applied to the desired areas and dried thoroughly for a few hours, it can be burnished to a high polish with an agate burnisher. The gold thereby takes on a delicate sheen and gives the impression of solid metal.

In the context of tempera painting, gold leaf is applied on to areas that have been clearly marked out prior to painting. Areas of gold should not be overpainted with tempera, as light will refract differently and contrast with areas where paint has been applied on to gesso. To protect the gold leaf, a fine layer of shellac or sandarac varnish is applied. Alternatively, a varnish made with beeswax, dissolved in cold turpentine could be used, although this will give a matt effect.

Oil Painting

Supports for Oil Painting

Suitable supports for oil painting fall into two categories:

1. Flexible support: cotton canvas, linen canvas, paper.
2. Rigid support: panel, board, or canvas faced on to panel or board.

Flexible Supports

Canvas is a loose term, indicating a painting support usually derived from cotton (e.g. cotton duck canvas), although it may also be used to describe other natural fabrics (flax, linen), or synthetic fabrics such as polyester.

Cotton Duck Canvas

Cotton duck canvas is generally thought to be not as strong and durable as linen canvas, although some heavier weights have proven to be extremely stable. It varies in quality, according to weight and closeness of weave. Generally, a cotton duck canvas with a loose weave and of a light weight (9-10oz) will shrink (tighten) when stretched and sized. The combination of loose weave and light weight produce a fabric that is too easy to pull in opposing directions. When such a canvas is stretched up, the tensions caused by the stretching process may render it unstable as a painting support. When rabbit skin glue has been used for sizing, fluctuations of temperature and humidity may cause the fabric to shrink and expand greatly. Layers of paint applied on to this type of canvas, if at all brittle or underbound, may over time become fragile and show defects such as cracks, or may lose adhesion to the support.

Cotton duck canvases of 12oz and above are available. The heavier weights, especially those with a close weave (no pin-prick holes) and a reasonable texture are recommended. Heavier weights of cotton duck are relatively more expensive but will remain stable and less prone to shrinkage when stretched up. Good quality cotton duck canvas does not have to be pre-shrunk before stretching up, although it can go a little floppy once sized and/or primed. This is especially the case when priming with acrylic, which does not seem to cause the fabric to tighten up very much.

Linen/Flax

Linen, most of which is woven in Belgium or Ireland, has been used for oil painting for many centuries. It is made from fibres of the flax plant and the best grades have great durability, strength and stability. Linen is sometimes referred to as "flax", this may indicate a heavier, coarse weave fabric. The best grades are those that are "wet spun", resulting in a smooth surface. Some "dry spun" linens have a hairy surface.

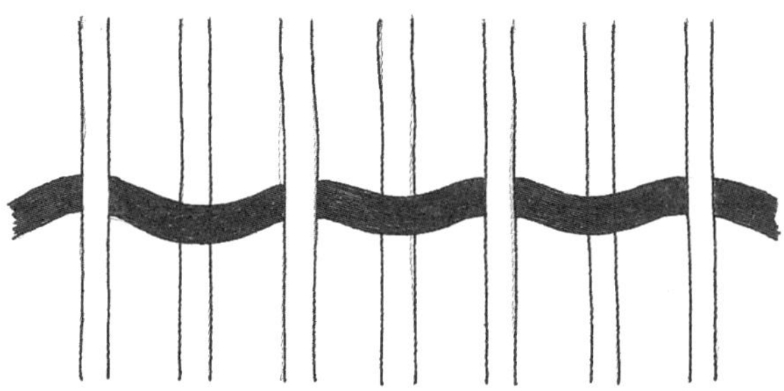

Diagram to Show Warp and Weft Thread

The warp thread runs the length of the canvas. It is pulled tightest during weaving. When stretching up linen, the warp thread should pull across the shortest distance possible, as it is likely to shrink more acutely than the weft thread, when wetted. Ideally, the weft thread forms the length of the stretched fabric. It is likely to shrink less than the warp when wetted.

When linen is removed from the loom, it contracts ("crimps"). Before use for painting, linen can be treated to counteract the crimping effect and straighten the weave of the fabric, by wetting before stretching and sizing. The wetting process is best done by tacking the fabric on to the painting stretcher, quite loosely. The warp should pull across the shortest distance. The fabric is then sprayed with water (use a garden sprayer), or has water painted on to it with a large flat brush. This will also remove any compressed folds. The fabric is left to dry out thoroughly and tightens up as a result.

The degree to which linen will shrink in this process depends upon the nature of the fabric. Lightweight, closely woven fabrics shrink less than heavier fabrics, with a loose weave.

Linen is preferred by many artists because after careful preparation of the ground, the texture of the canvas surface can still be seen and incorporated into the building of the paint layers. Linen is often described as having a "coarse", "medium" or "portrait" (smooth) appearance, this refers to the texture of the canvas surface and the feel of the weight. "Portrait" linen is often preferred by artists working in a detailed manner.

Some fabrics are composed of a mixture of cotton and linen threads: these are prone to unpredictable fluctuations when stretched up, sized and painted upon. Similarly, fabrics composed of linen/polyester mix, or cotton/polyester mix are liable to pull with opposing tensions. The restoration trade has successfully used polyester fabrics for relining paintings. In the future, artists are liable to paint on to polyester flexible supports more and more. Unlike cotton and linen, they are virtually non-moving when paint, primer or size are applied and they retain tension. Their construction is very regular and the rate at which they deteriorate is likely to be less than that of plant-fabrics. Some brands of pre-primed canvas include polyester types.

Pre-Primed Canvas

Linen, cotton duck and polyester painting fabrics come in ready-primed form. Generally supplied by the roll, they are available with a variety of priming preparations and relative quality. The quality of pre-primed canvases needs to be checked prior to purchase. During the priming process, the priming may have been spray-applied, which gives a different finish compared to primer that has been brush-applied by hand. By tradition, canvases were prepared by hand, using lead-oil primer, applied on to glue-sized canvas with long, flat spatulas. In practice, very few companies prepare canvases in this way today. It is far more economical to spray-apply a non-toxic, water-based acrylic priming. It should be borne in mind that the market for pre-primed canvases relates very strongly to the hobby market, where discerning values are less of a concern. For the professional artist looking to work on to a high grade painting ground, the choice of suitable pre-primed canvases is reduced to a handful of specialist companies. The author has found, even in recent years, samples of pre-primed canvases which conform to older traditions, where the canvas fabric has been carefully prepared with a number of special coatings to give painting grounds that are resilient yet gently absorbent, providing a suitable surface on to which oil paint can be applied. Companies offering such canvases often work at a local rather than national or international level, and tend to exist in centres where painting is still a key activity among professional artists. For example, one of the key outlets for artists' materials in Florence still offers linen canvases prepared with special grounds, which approximate to the types of grounds used by artists of previous generations. Similarly, in the south of Germany, a supplier of primed canvases prepares their painting grounds with recipes that approximate to those suggested by Max Doerner. These are acrylic preparations which mimic the gentle absorbency of the older glue-chalk-pigment grounds advocated by Doerner (see Bibliography).

Because pre-primed canvases are supplied in rolls, normally 10 metres in length, perhaps 210cm wide, it is incorrectly assumed by many artists, that such canvas can easily be re-rolled. The opposite may be the case, especially with regard to oil-primed canvas which shows a tendency towards brittleness when rolled or stressed. This is due to the fact that in general, oil-primed canvases are prepared using titanium white as the basic white colourant in the priming. All paint films containing titanium white in oil tend towards brittleness and this is especially the case when the support is rolled or stressed. For example, when stretching such pre-primed canvas, it is very easy to over-pull it and thus cause the priming to crack as it is pulled over the edge of the stretcher using a pair of canvas pliers. Oil-primed canvas may also have a glossy or semi-gloss finish, which can make it difficult for oil paint to adhere to it. For this reason, in recent years, most firms supplying primed canvas have switched to acrylic preparations, which are not only easier for the manufacturer to apply, but also more flexible when stressed. It is possible to apply acrylic primer and achieve a surface that is not too shiny, nor too matt, and which also provides the desired degree of absorption when oil paint is applied.

Pre-primed canvases tend to be more rigid when compared to raw linen or cotton. Because of this, stretching up pre-primed canvas can be more taxing. A pair of canvas pliers is used to hold the painting fabric against the stretcher frame, while tacks or staples are applied to the reverse to fix. It is often necessary to fix tacks or staples to the side edges of the painting when working with pre-primed canvas, in order to gain a tight and even tension across the canvas.

In addition to checking the relative flexibility and gloss of pre-primed canvas it is also advisable to make sure that the fabric has been coated with enough layers of priming to prevent strike-through when oil paint is applied. In the worst case scenario, oil paint, especially when strongly diluted, can sometimes absorb too much into the priming layer and transfer through the priming to the reverse side of the fabric. In such cases, the priming is insufficient and a further coat or two may need to be applied. However, it is better practice not to use such cheaply-made pre-primed canvas. Usually, artists' materials suppliers will have sample swatches of primed canvas which can be checked prior to purchase. The optimum quality of pre-primed canvas will remain flexible when stressed, show durability in use and not allow applied paint to strike-through to the reverse.

Stretching Canvas

Stretcher frames for flexible supports vary greatly in quality and suitability. Mitred stretcher bars are usually made of seasoned pine, or other woods that are reasonably resistant to warping. The wood itself must be free of knots, imperfections and also sap (which will ooze out into the canvas). Imperfections can be isolated by applying "knotting" to the wood. (Knotting varnish is also known as button polish – shellac-based varnish.)

The front edge of the stretcher bars are usually slightly raised, so that the canvas when stretched up does not press directly against the frame or crossbar. Larger paintings will require a crossbar to help stabilise the stretcher frame: for paintings over 36" in any direction it is a good idea to include at least one. Always check that bought stretcher bars are warp-free. Wooden stretchers can warp after purchase. Many artists work in damp, cold studios, where temperature changes can lead to seemingly perfect stretcher bars warping.

The mitred corners of stretcher bars have slot and tenon joints, which fit together. The joints are knocked together with a hammer (preferably a wooden or rubber mallet with a soft head), to form a basic rectangle. Wedges or "keys" can be inserted into the mitred corners to tighten up the fabric, once stretched. This is best done after sizing and priming, where the canvas surface has gone a little limp. "Wedging-out" with the keys will tighten the fabric gently.

The diagonal measurement of the resultant rectangle is checked to ensure that the frame is square, i.e. the diagonal measurement should be equal. The required amount of canvas is cut and laid on to the floor or table top. It is advisable to lay down a clean sheet (e.g. polythene) to prevent studio floor dirt, or paint residue affecting the fabric. The canvas is cut with enough over-lap (at least 2 inches) around the frame. Canvas is attached to the stretching frame using either a staple gun, or tacks. Staples are easiest to attach: choose a robust staple gun, with strong, non-rusting staples. The canvas threads run parallel with the edge of the frame during stretching. The fabric overlaps the sides and back of the stretcher and is then tacked down, all the way round. The tacks are placed parallel to the top edge of the stretcher frame, about two-thirds of the way from the edge.

Procedure for Stretching Canvas

This method aims to reduce the potential stress placed upon the weave of the canvas when wetted with size and/or primer, by evenly distributing the stress throughout the whole canvas area. It also reduces the degree to which the canvas fibres can pull, so that over time, effects of shrinkage or expansion due to humidity/temperature are kept to a minimum. The weave of the canvas is placed parallel to the running edge of the stretcher frame. The warp thread (identified as the length of the canvas, when pulled from the roll) should ideally travel over the shortest distance. For example, on a stretcher frame measuring 20 inches x 40 inches, the warp thread should pull across the 20 inch measurement.

Procedure for Stretching Unprimed Linen

1. Place one tack or staple in the centre of each length.

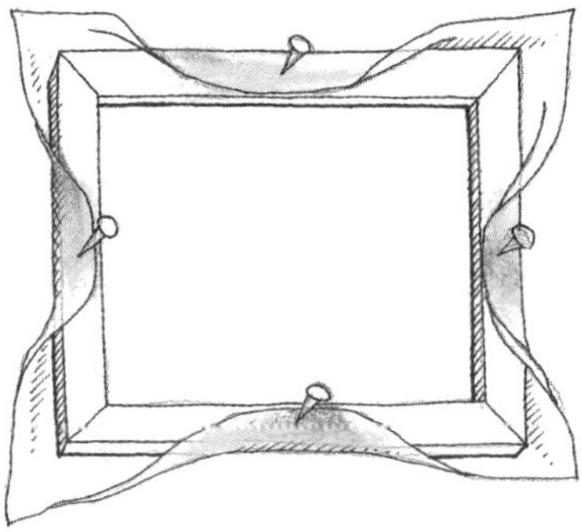

2. The fabric is pulled gently and fastened at each corner. A tack or staple is placed just short of either side of the corner.

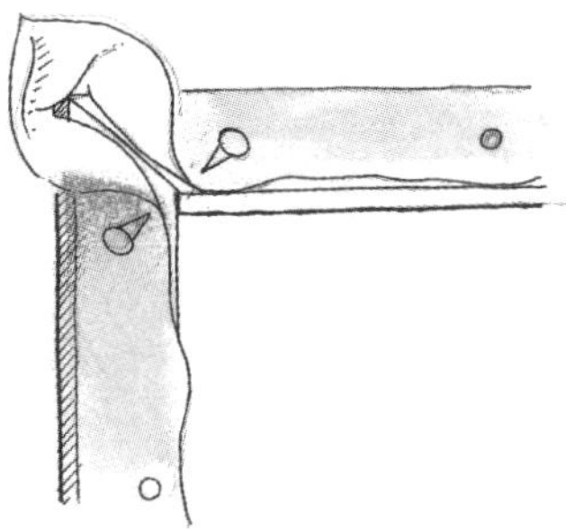

3. The half points are fastened. This can be done by going across one edge, then the opposing edge. This is done on all sides.

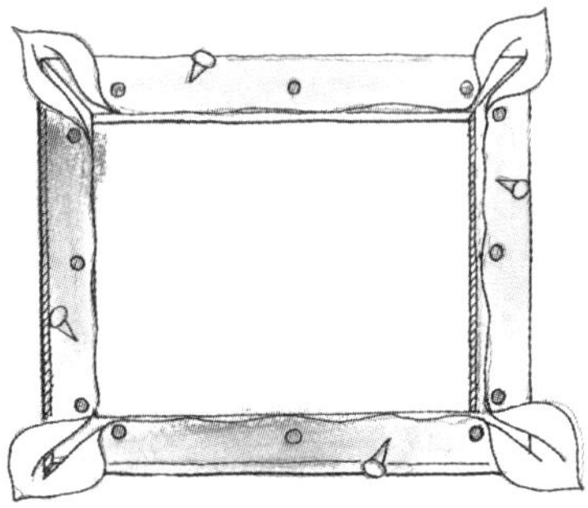

4. The procedure is continued, by fastening the next set of half points. Keep an even distance between each staple/tack. Aim to achieve an even tension over the whole canvas surface.

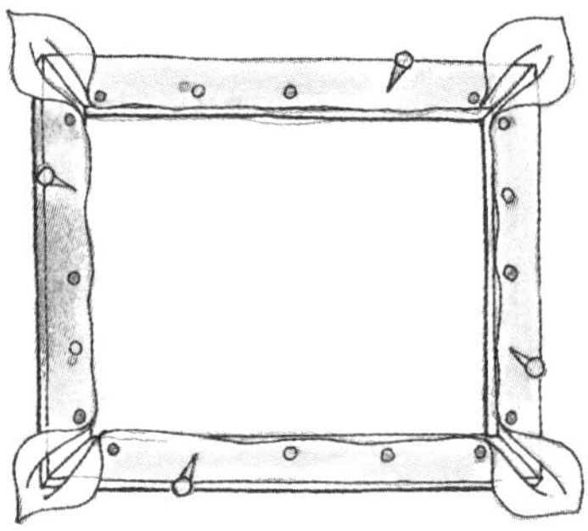

5. Continue fastening the half points.

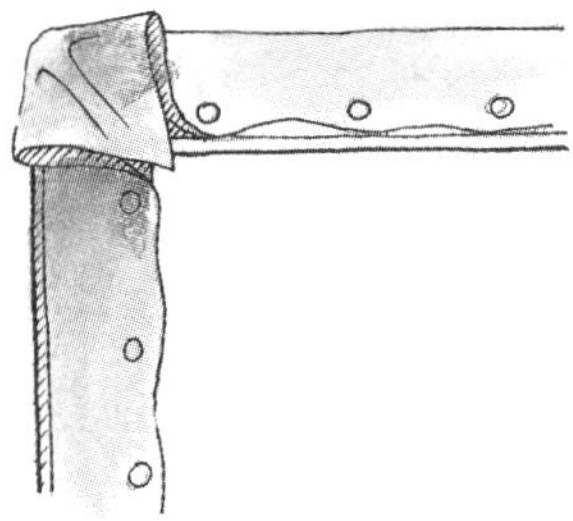

6. Fold over the corner flaps and fasten.

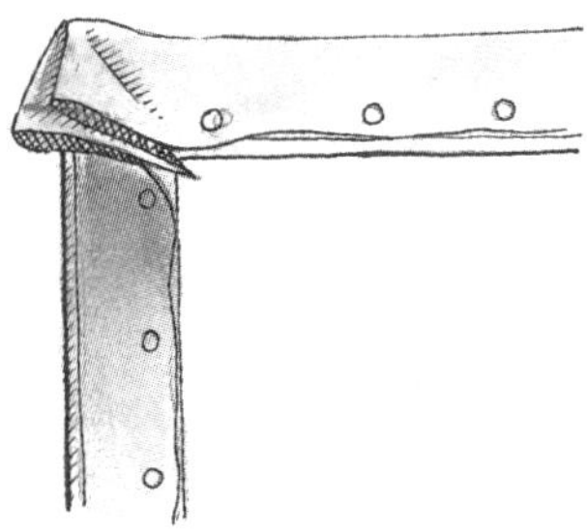

7. Finally, fasten the corner flaps down.

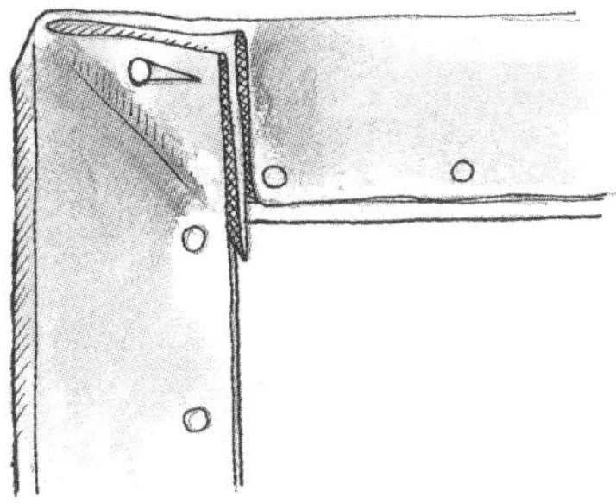

Paper

Paper as a support for oil painting is not widely recommended. However, heavy watercolour papers (300gsm or preferably even heavier) could be used. The paper should be robust. Choose papers with 100% cotton rag content.

Before painting, the paper is given a coat of rabbit skin glue (1 : 15, left to soak, then a further 15 parts water added before warming through to gain solution). This acts as an isolating layer between the absorbent paper fibres and the actions of oil paint and its solvents. The glue size penetrates the surface of the paper but ideally does not build up a mechanical layer. In the extreme, a thicker layer of glue size may prevent oil paint from bonding successfully with the paper surface. Oil paintings made on paper should be treated with care during storage (as per watercolour paintings), being kept flat at all times. When oil paint is applied on canvas in thin layers, it becomes brittle with age. It follows that when thick oil paint is applied to a thin support such as sized paper, the paint may lose adhesion with the support upon drying out. When painting on paper with oils, it is advised only to paint thinly, in a sketching manner, perhaps for ideas, or try-outs for later paintings on canvas.

The best choice of paper would be a Rough surface watercolour paper of a heavy weight, providing a "key" for oil paint to adhere to, again, prepared with glue size. This procedure provides a support which uses to advantage the texture of the paper. Alternatively, an acrylic ground can be used, which changes the texture of the paper but provides a relatively cheap oil painting support. The best combination may be a layer of acrylic size, to seal the paper surface, followed by an application of a semi-absorbent acrylic gesso. The first coats of oil paint are absorbed slightly into the gesso priming, forming a strong bond between the ground and paint layers. The paper used for such a preparation could be a NOT 300gsm watercolour paper, with just a slight texture. During the preparation process it is necessary to stretch the paper up against a board, using brown gum-strip, to reduce the effects of cockling upon applying the acrylic materials. Once dried, the paper may still show some cockling: simply re-stretch the paper before painting on it.

Commercially Prepared Canvas Paper and Boards

Canvas paper tends to be rather unsatisfactory: it can become very brittle, or be too absorbent. Available brands vary widely. It is probably best to use such materials for sketches only.

Prepared painting boards vary in quality too. They tend to consist of cheap cotton canvas prepared with an acrylic ground and can be overpainted with oil or acrylic paints. The canvas is backed on to a compressed pulp-board/card-board. These backing boards are prone to absorbing moisture, upon which they warp badly. Although certain brands are superior, it is better practice to face rigid supports with canvas as described and use prepared boards for sketches only.

Rigid Supports

Wood

Solid panels made from oak (hard) or poplar (soft) have long been used for painting, although they are rarely employed by artists today. Modern compressed fibre-boards perform quite well by comparison and have the advantage of being available in large sheet format, free of knots and not prone to warping with age, if prepared carefully. Wood absorbs moisture: as it releases moisture it shrinks. This process in turn leads to dimensional instability of the support, resulting in the warping of the surface of the board and subsequent cracking of the applied ground and paint layers. Soft woods, such as poplar, absorb the most moisture - up to 200%. Such panels were employed widely by the Italians during the early Renaissance, being the most readily available source of wood. Oak panels, more commonly used in Northern Europe from the early Renaissance onwards, have more dimensional stability, being cut from harder wood. These types of panels were prepared for painting using a gesso ground, composed of gypsum (Italy) or chalk (Northern Europe) mixed with animal skin glue, to form a tough, hard, yet absorbent ground, ideally suited for egg tempera painting. Developments in painting techniques, to include emulsions of egg tempera with oil and subsequently, the employment of oil alone as a binder for pigments, were matched by modifications to the painting support. Often, underpaintings were made with egg tempera on to an absorbent gesso ground, on which subsequent layers of oil paint could sit without sinking. Alternatively, gesso supports were rendered less absorbent by applying a thin layer of animal skin glue, or an isolating varnish (for example shellac varnish) over the final layer of gesso. To alleviate some of the problems of dimensional stability with wooden panels, strips of cloth (usually linen) were incorporated into the first coat of gesso.

Preparation of Wooden Panel for Oil Painting Using Gesso Ground

Gesso is composed of whiting chalk (calcium carbonate) or gypsum (calcium sulphate), with an animal skin glue, such as rabbit skin glue, or gelatine. There are many different types of chalk available which can be incorporated into gesso grounds. For example, different grades of coarseness of marble dust could be used to obtain a degree of tooth on the painting surface. Such additions are probably best achieved by admixing with a fine chalk such as whiting, gypsum or champagne chalk.

Recipe for Gesso

Prepare a rabbit skin glue solution (1 : 15). Add 15 parts of cold water (by volume) to 1 part of powdered glue. Leave to soak for 30 minutes, until swollen. Warm the glue into a solution in the top pan of a double boiler (or empty food can). This acts as a stock solution for preparing rigid gesso grounds. The strength of animal glues can vary. As a general guide, the glue solution for gesso can be stronger than that normally used for sizing canvas. However, over-strong glue will make the gesso too hard and reduce its absorbency and may cause problems with the dimensional stability of the panel. The first layer of glue solution can be diluted with a further 15 parts of water and requires a small addition of chalk (sprinkle a handful into the solution). This adds a very slight tooth, giving the first coat proper some texture to bond with. Solid wood panels may require a light sanding to make the surface slightly absorbent, so that the glue forms a good bond with the support.

The sealing coat is applied to the face, sides and reverse of the panel, so as to equalise any dimensional tensions caused by the glue. On thin panels, glue applied only to one side may cause the wood to shrink in on itself. When this first sealing coat is dry, the first coat proper is applied. To the warm glue, add slowly, through a sieve (to eradicate lumps) roughly an equal amount by volume of chalk to glue. Wait for all the chalk to disappear under the surface before stirring the mixture. Stirring induces air bubbles to form and needs to be done with patience. The gesso mixture should have a creamy consistency and be free of lumps. This is applied in thin layers with a flat hog varnish brush, or a round "house" style hog sash brush. The hog hair needs to be strong but not too hard, or it will leave behind brush marks. The first coat proper is applied and left to dry for a few moments. When the coat of gesso appears to go dull, a second coat can be applied. If the preceding layer "picks-up", leave to dry a little longer. Five to eight coats can be added to form a tough, thick structure on the panel. The coatings of gesso are applied at right angles to each other to gain a thoroughly bonded ground. The top coat is sanded for a smooth finish.

Thin strips (i.e. off-cuts) of linen can be incorporated into the first layer of gesso. The linen is dipped into the gesso, then placed flat on to the dried "sealing" coat, already applied to the panel. These linen strips are overpainted with layers of gesso which hide their presence. The inclusion of linen strips gives the ground greater dimensional stability.

Oil paint, applied to gesso tends to sink, leaving a very matt paint film. Rather than applying a thin layer of size to reduce absorbency, artists could consider underpainting in egg tempera, followed by subsequent layers of oil, or egg-oil emulsion. The egg tempera underpainting forms a perfect bond with the gesso and provides a matt and slightly absorbent painting surface for oil paint.

Plywood

Thin boards (panels) exert less power when warping than thick panels. Plywood is composed of several thin panels (veneers) glued together, with each sheet glued across the grain of the previous one. Plywood can be rotary cut (to give sheets up to five feet wide), or flat cut, sliced directly from the log. Both types are susceptible to degrees of shrinkage and expansion through swelling. These effects show as fine cracks on the surface of the ply and can permeate through applied ground and paint layers. This problem can be reduced by applying the painting ground over a layer of canvas, glued to the board. Three-ply birch or poplar sheets are recommended. Sizes over two feet in any direction can be reinforced to offset warping by fastening battening to the reverse. Ply is less prone to destruction by wood boring insects than wooden panels of oak and poplar.

Facing Ply with Canvas

Stick a piece of canvas down on to the face and sides, with flaps glued over on to the reverse. Use cotton canvas with an open weave, which prevents the glue from being trapped under the fabric surface. Apply a solution of rabbit skin glue (1 : 15) to the face, sides and reverse (the whole of the back) of the ply and stick the fabric down, smoothing out any trapped pockets of air. A layer of size (diluted a further 15 parts with water) should be coated over the fabric once dry, to isolate it from the priming layer. Over this facing of fabric, two types of ground can be applied:

- Gesso ground, as described for solid panels
- Oil Ground. This could be lead primer, or a reliable brand of alkyd primer.

Acrylic Priming for Plywood or Blockboard

Alternatively, plyboard can be prepared with acrylic primer, using the following procedure. The board is faced with lightweight cotton canvas, or linen. The overlaps are tacked to the reverse with staples. Acrylic primer can be painted straight over the fabric (does not need to be sealed as is the case with oil priming).

Reinforcing Rigid Supports

Strong adhesives based an acrylic polymers can be used for fixing batons to the reverse of rigid supports. The glue is applied as thinly as possible. Wood glues, for example a PVA Scotch glue, or casein based glues could also be used. It is important that the glue does not come into contact with the painting surface or ground. Avoid using screws or nails, which may rust or cause splits in the wood surface. Animal glues should also be avoided due to their tendency to fluctuate according to humidity, and become brittle with age.

While the glue is drying the frame is clamped tight: batons of wood are interleaved between metal clamp and board, to protect the surface. The glue is left to dry for at least 24 hours. The supporting frame is made from seasoned wood (i.e. thoroughly dried out) of a similar thickness and nature to standard stretching frames. The frame can take the form of simple batons, stuck down to the reverse, or a stronger jointed structure.

Masonite (also known as Hardboard)

Hardboard is made by exploding wood fibre with steam, compressed into sheets under great pressure. It is available in two basic forms, tempered and untempered. The untempered variety is best, as tempered hardboard is treated with paraffin oil, which leaves a greasy residue. This can resist priming or sizing applications if not carefully degreased with methylated spirits (alcohol). The reverse side of hardboard has a rough "wove" appearance, which can also be used for painting. However, this face of the board has a more fibrous nature and should be prepared for painting using a primer that contains the least amount of moisture. Neat acrylic primer is probably best.

Sanding the smooth side of untempered hardboard to give a slight tooth, before application of sizing/priming, disturbs the fibres on the surface of the ground. Moisture allowed to absorb into the board can cause the fibres to expand, affecting its dimensional stability. The smooth surface should be degreased prior to application of sizing/priming. This is done with methylated spirits (alcohol), applied with a clean cotton rag on to the surface and left to dry thoroughly. Hardboard is prone to deteriorate if too much moisture penetrates the surface (for example, dilute acrylic primer). It may also warp if stored in a damp area. It is often recommended that alkyd based primers be applied neat to hardboard but these can leave a very shiny, slippery surface if undiluted. Acrylic primer can be applied neat to degreased hardboard. Without degreasing, the acrylic primer may not adhere to the surface.

Hardboard is prone to warping in larger sizes. A supporting frame can be attached to alleviate this problem. Hardboard can also be faced with canvas, as described for ply and blockboard. Many artists like to face hardboard with muslin, a light cotton fabric with a very loose weave. This gives an interesting texture, is inexpensive and is highly suited to making "on the spot" sketches, where paint is required to be fluid, yet needs to catch the painting surface lightly.

Medium Density Fibreboard (MDF)

Another type of exploded fibreboard. The wood fibres are compressed to form a compact, homogenous surface. MDF forms a highly stable painting support, which is warp resistant (choose a thickness over 12mm). It can be prepared with traditional gesso, animal size and oil primer, or acrylic grounds. MDF is also quite moisture resistant, although the edges tend to be more absorbent. It does not crack as do natural woods, ply and blockboard.

MDF can be difficult to obtain, cut to preferred sizes, due to the inclusion in its manufacture of urea-formaldehyde resins, which are thought to be carcinogenic in nature. This is not such a problem to the artist using a cut piece of board but rather to the timber merchant, whose cutting machinery releases the wood fibres into the working environment. However, a new specification of MDF, "Zero Formaldehyde" (ZF) is available, using a polyurethane resin in place of urea-formaldehyde. Canvas can be faced to MDF, to provide a cheap and rigid alternative to buying stretcher pieces. A piece of canvas is cut with 2-3 inch overlaps and the MDF sheet laid down on to the canvas. The canvas is then tacked to the reverse of the board. An archival, acrylic adhesive can be applied to the reverse of the board to assist the process of stretching and tacking. The canvas is tacked down with staples while the glue is drying but these are applied only to the reverse, not the sides. When the canvas has been pulled tight all the way round, the face of the canvas is coated with one or two layers of neat acrylic primer.

Honeycomb Aluminium Panel

Lighter than similar sized boards, aluminium panel with a honeycomb centre is warp resistant and can be prepared successfully as a support for oil painting. The face of the panel is first degreased, then lightly abraded to give a slight key. Acrylic primer can be applied directly to the panel and subsequently sanded to give a smoother finish. This type of rigid support may be preferred when using brands of paint with less flexibility than artists' oil colours. For example, household oil-based paints often contain less flexible oil components, additions of varnish, chalk and drier which can leave the paint film brittle. Painting on to a well-prepared rigid ground with such materials will reduce the degree to which the paint flakes and embrittles, although the surface is temperature sensitive and rather easily dented.

Sizing and Priming Supports for Oil Painting

Some sources of raw canvas are sold as being pH neutral, affording some resistance to ageing. Recent research into the ageing properties of painting fabrics[1] suggests that the life of a canvas can be extended by pretreating with a de-acidification agent.

Rabbit Skin Glue

Rabbit skin glue or gelatine can be used to size canvas, prior to applying a coat of oil or alkyd primer. The glue impregnates the

1. Stephen Hackney and Torben Ernst, "The Applicability of Alkaline Reserves to Painting Canvases." *Measured Opinions*, UKIC.

canvas weave, forming a barrier between the fabric and the layer of primer. Sizing prevents the ground (priming) layers of paint from seeping through to the back of the canvas. Rabbit skin glue, like other animal skin glues, is a hygroscopic material: it reacts to extremes of moisture and humidity by swelling and contracting. When this occurs, brittle priming layers applied over canvas sized with skin glue may be prone to crack or blister. It is therefore advisable to choose a primer that is flexible, such as lead white primer. However, acrylic primings are more flexible and easier to use and may be more appropriate in the long term. Rabbit skin glue should be applied to canvas in one thin layer, while it is still warm but never hot. Do not try to re-use animal glue once made up: although it will keep for a few days in the fridge, it will not have the same adhesive strength when re-warmed.

Recipe for Rabbit Skin Glue for Sizing (1 : 30), for Canvas (Flexible Support)

Rabbit skin glue grains	1 part (by volume, i.e. 1 x tablespoon)
Cold water	15 parts

Add the water to the glue in a suitable container. A double boiler is best but an empty food tin (washed thoroughly) can be used. A double boiler comprises two pans, the lower one filled with water is in direct contact with the heat source. The upper pan sits inside the lower pan, allowing animal glues to be warmed through without being scorched. If a double boiler is unattainable, use an old pan, into which an empty food can is placed. Leave the glue to soak for half an hour, during which time it swells up to form a sloppy paste. Add a further 15 parts water to the mixture. To form a solution, the glue has to be warmed through in a double boiler.

Place the glue in the upper pan of a double boiler. The lower pan is half-filled with water. The glue has to be warmed through gently, if it is allowed to boil it will lose some adhesive strength. The warmed solution should be free of lumps. When left to cool, the set jelly should ideally break with a ragged fracture when pressed with a finger.

Animal skin glues can be hardened by the addition of alum (aluminium potassium sulphate), to reduce the extent to which they are resoluble. However, this makes the sizing very brittle and the alum can attack the canvas fabric. Powdered alum (available from pharmacies and some art suppliers) is soaked overnight and warmed through, if necessary, to form a clear solution. Use one part by volume of alum to ten parts of glue. The alum is soaked in the water to be used for making the glue solution. Rabbit skin glue is sold in powder form, in small, flaked grains and in the form of sheets (sheets should be left to swell overnight).

Rabbit skin glue is a natural product, prone to fluctuations in quality and therefore different batches of glue may have a variety of strengths. Good animal skin glue appears pale as a powder and has only a pale straw-yellow colour when made into a clear solution. Darker glues should be avoided, as they may be more brittle and may darken even more when warmed through. The glue size is applied to the face of the stretched fabric. Care should be taken to apply it to the edges, flaps and especially the corner overlaps of the canvas. Subsequent layers of primer should also follow this rule. The glue size is applied while just warm. The action of sizing the fabric will make it become taut as the water in the glue solution causes the fabric to tighten up. If the glue is too strong, the canvas will become as tight as a drum. While this might seem to be an advantage, giving a strong support, strong glue size, being very hygroscopic is more prone to fluctuations later from the effects of humidity.

Some authorities advise glue size to be applied cold, with a spatula, although this does not penetrate to the fibres of the yarn and can form a brittle skin, prone to cracking.

Gelatine

Gelatine is derived from collagen, which is found in animal bones and skin. It is carefully refined to form a pure, virtually colourless glue, usually sold in the form of thin sheets. The high standards demanded by the food industry mean that gelatine is usually very pure and not as affected by fluctuations in quality as can be the case with rabbit skin glue. Industrial grades have a slight yellow colour, due to the sheets' thickness. Gelatine is left to dissolve until a clear solution forms. It dissolves quickly in cold water, swelling appreciably but does not have to be left as long as rabbit skin glue. According to Wehlte[2], "gelatine has good adhesive properties, the jelly is relatively firm, and the warm solution has a high viscosity".

As a guide, around one part gelatine (by volume, roughly one-eighth of a sheet) is immersed in 40-50 parts water. When the solution is clear, as with rabbit skin, the glue is warmed through and brushed on to the canvas, in one or two thin applications. When used in recipes for gesso on to rigid supports, the strength of the gelatine glue could be higher.

Brushes for Applying Size to Canvas

Hog varnishing brushes can be used for sizing canvas. Flat brushes, with short handles, of a good width (3-4 inches) and with a length out of $1^1/_2$ inches hold a good amount of liquid, enabling size to cover large areas of unprimed canvas rapidly. Thicker household type brushes can be used, but be careful when selecting them that the hair does not come loose from the ferrule. Flat hog hair brushes with a shorter hair length out from the ferrule ($^1/_2$ - $^3/_4$ inches), for example, a "straight mottler" can be used to good effect for applying cold size, where the glue needs to be pushed out across the canvas and also into its pores.

Flat hog varnish brushes can also be used for applying primer, those with slightly stiff hair work well, enabling the primer to be applied in thin layers, stroked into the canvas weave.

Priming

Sizing is applied to reduce the absorbency of the fabric so that subsequent applications of primer and paint are less prone to sinking. The priming layer is required to fill the pores of the canvas weave to provide a stable and integrated bonding surface for oil paint.

If the sizing has been applied too thickly, the primer cannot properly combine with the weave of the fabric. Because of this, it is

2. Kurt Wehlte, *The Materials and Techniques of Painting (Werkstoffe und Techiken der Malerei),* Otto Maier Verlag, 1967

advisable to apply not more than two, thin and even coats of size to the fabric. The priming coat is applied to form a tough, durable ground on which to work. Primer alters the absorbency of the fabric, its texture, colour and stiffness.

Some artists choose to sand in between coats of primer, to achieve a smoother, flat surface, which shows the canvas weave.

Lead White Primer

Lead-based pigments in artists' paints can constitute a considerable danger to health if used improperly. Their use in industry is increasingly limited due to their toxicity. Lead white can be extremely toxic and should not be handled without thorough precautions. Artists should be aware of the associated dangers before considering using these pigment types. Lead white primer has been widely used as a suitable primer for oil painting on stretched canvas, over a dried application of glue size. It is the most flexible of white pigments in oil and dries thoroughly to form a durable paint film.

Primers made with zinc or titanium white, or mixtures of zinc and titanium in oil, can be more brittle. In respect to this, avoid household primers and undercoats. These are designed to endure for only a limited time scale and may contain unknown additions of drier, varnish, etc.

Lead white primer is sold in cans, usually as a thick paste, which is thinned down slightly with turpentine or white spirit, so that it can be brushed out easily. Alternatively the neat primer can be spread out on to the sized canvas using a metal spatula. Lead white primer can also be prepared from the dry pigment with linseed oil on a glass slab, mixed to a stiff paste and then thinned with turpentine so that it can be brushed out evenly.

Lead white pigment is toxic. Great care should be taken when using the dry powder. Wear protective gloves and a high quality particle filter mask, and further protect skin from contact with the pigment by applying a barrier cream. Wash hands thoroughly after use. Never eat, smoke or drink when in contact with this, or other dry pigments.

Recipe for lead white oil primer

Cremnitz white pigment (basic lead carbonate, lead white)	1kg
Refined linseed oil	approx. 250ml

Wet the pigment with enough oil to form a stiff paste on a glass or marble slab. A palette knife can be used to mix the pigment and oil together. Store the mass of the mixture to one side of the palette, then gradually mull small portions of it, moving the glass muller in a figure of eight motion. Mull the whole batch of primer, then leave to rest on absorbent paper for an hour or so. Repeat the process, so that the final primer mixture is smoothly mulled. The resultant stiff paste can be applied neat with a spatula, or thinned down a little with rectified turpentine. Lead white primer is applied to canvas that has been prepared with glue size as described. The primer should be applied in thin coats to the edges, overlaps and corner flaps for maximum protection of the fabric. Two thin coats will suffice; leave the first coat to dry for a week before applying the second. After the second coat, the primed canvas should be left to cure thoroughly, for 4-6 months before being painted on. This long drying time is required because oil paint applied to the priming ground during the curing process would be absorbed into the primer. Curing draws oil from applied paint layers, leaving it underbound and making it too dry to adhere to the support sufficiently.

Once the priming coat is thoroughly cured, lead white primer provides an ideal ground for oil painting: it is lean (low oil content) and slightly absorbent.

The linseed oil in which lead white is ground turns the priming coat yellow if stored away from light (i.e. in a cupboard). The white colour is restored upon exposure to sunlight, although it remains yellow behind the visible surface coat.

Comparison of Primings for Oil Paintings

Titanium white, when carefully prepared in an alkyd resin is fast drying and thought to stay flexible, while acrylic primings are by comparison very flexible, fast drying and not prone to yellowing. Both alkyd and acrylic primings are non-toxic.

The use of casein gesso, animal glue gesso and half oil and egg-oil grounds provide relatively brittle primings when applied to stretched canvas. However, in historical terms, such grounds have been important and some artists continue to use them today.

One common complaint with modern acrylic primings, is that the colour of the ground (derived from titanium white, with calcium carbonate in an acrylic polymer emulsion) is too bright a white. With older painting grounds, for example lead white ground in oil, the colour is more subtle and slightly warmish. Similarly, painting grounds based on water-dilutable mixtures tend to give a more subtle colour to the ground.

Chalk Grounds for Oil Painting

Early oil paintings would have been primed with similar materials to those used on wooden panels, namely gesso, composed from an animal glue mixed with chalk. Such mixtures tend towards brittleness when applied to flexible supports like canvas. However, if only one or two coats of this gesso are applied, with the priming being worked into the weave of the canvas fabric so that there is no significant build-up of priming, a workable ground may be achieved. By contrast to the glue formula for rigid panels, the glue strength needs to be somewhat dilute, perhaps one part rabbit glue to 30 parts water. After being left to soak for 30 minutes to one hour, the swollen glue-paste is gently warmed through to a solution and applied while just warm. The temperature of the glue becomes more important when applying to canvas. If the glue is hot, or boiling, it will introduce more tension across the painting fabric. Subsequent changes in humidity will affect the glue and cause the fabric either to tighten or relax. When the glue is applied just warm enough so that it can be brushed out (i.e. not re-forming into a jelly), much less tension is present in the glue film. Prior to the application of the gesso, the canvas is treated with two coats of glue size (again, at 1 : 30 glue strength). Rabbit glue size is commonly used today, but prior to the 19th century, hide glues from cattle would have been used, or goatskin glue, derived from parchment clippings. In practical terms it is probably best to use rabbit glue, as this provides a good degree of flexibility and, where high grades of glue have been chosen, it is pale in colour and free from impurities.

The canvas is attached to the stretcher frame before the glue size is applied. Each coat of glue size is left to dry. Between coats, it may be useful to abrade the surface lightly with a pumice stone, to remove or reduce any knots or anomalies in the structure of the painting fabric. It is also advisable to "wash" linen fabric before stretching. This process removes any residual starch in the cloth, and reduces the degree to which it will shrink when sizing is applied. Once the first two coats of glue size have been applied, the canvas is dry and the surface smooth, subsequent coatings of gesso can be added. Best practice is to apply as few coats as possible, with each priming being worked into the canvas surface with a soft hog varnish brush. This procedure allows the structure of the canvas weave to remain visible and also produces a relatively thin, even application of priming. To the stock glue solution, an equal volume of chalk* is added, which is left to soak into the glue and drop to the bottom of the mixture, prior to stirring. This helps to alleviate air-bubbles.

If the gesso mixture returns to a jelly, simply stand it in a bath of hot water (from a recently boiled kettle) and use when brushable. White pigment can be added to the gesso. Historically, this would be lead white, but other whites such as zinc white, titanium white or permanent white (blanc fix) could also be used. The addition of white pigment produces a brighter white ground, but may alter the relative absorbency of the priming.

Many artists experimented with gesso primings, in the hope that they could be made more flexible by the inclusion of plasticising agents. These would have included honey, starch glues, soap and oil. All these additives create some degree of flexibility but tend to cause problems over time. For example, the addition of soap leaves the painting ground too greasy for applications of oil colour to adhere properly. Honey remains hygroscopic (water-reactive), while the addition of oil to gesso tends to give a painting ground that possesses uneven absorption. Perhaps the most successful of these

* The type of chalk used is a personal decision. Historically, gypsum (calcium sulphate) was used in Southern Europe, while whiting or champagne chalk (calcium carbonate) was used in Northern Europe.

additives is wheat starch glue, which is thought to have been used during the golden period of Venetian painting in the 1600s. The wheat starch glue provides a degree of flexibility without unduly altering the absorbency of the gesso ground.

Gesso can be rendered more flexible by the addition of linseed oil, drop by drop into the warm chalk-glue mixture. A small addition of oil, perhaps 15-20% provides enough flexibility to give a priming that will move with the painting fabric and renders the gesso mixture dilutable with water (it forms a kind of emulsion). Such grounds are often referred to as half-oil, or half-chalk grounds. The addition of the oil is a difficult process: it must be added slowly, drop by drop, in the manner of making mayonnaise, until it forms a suspension within the warm gesso. The author has found that if the gesso mixture is left to cool so that it forms a jelly, the oil can then be worked into this on a sheet of glass using a spatula. When warmed through, the resulting solution tends to stay in suspension. The addition of linseed oil makes the resulting ground thicker and it will take longer to dry. If one uses refined linseed oil, a thin coat of the ground will dry in perhaps 2-3 days. It is important when applying such a ground that the priming is worked into the canvas structure (i.e. it is a smooth, even, thin film). This half-oil ground needs to be applied on top of 1-2 coats of glue size.

For small scale paintings (perhaps up to 50cm x 50cm), a special smooth ground can be made using a mixture of gesso (glue size + chalk) which is mixed with an equal volume of egg. The whole egg is added into the warm gesso and they are mixed together thoroughly. The resultant ground is somewhat shiny in appearance at first, but upon drying leaves a satin sheen. This ground needs to be applied over 1-2 coats of glue size. It works best on to fine/portrait linen, where thin applications of the ground help provide a flat, even working surface, which allows the structure of the linen fabric to be seen. Only one coat should be applied to guarantee a consistent finish.

Larger size paintings are more difficult with this egg-gesso ground, as it is more difficult to achieve evenness over a larger surface. Also, the ground is relatively brittle upon drying and becomes increasingly more so over time, thereby being more affected by flexing of the canvas.

Alkyd Primer

A fast drying primer based on an oil-modified alkyd resin. The advantage of using such a primer is that it has low toxicity and dries quickly. Each coat can be overpainted after 24 hours. Alkyd primer is applied to canvas that has been prepared with a coat of glue size. It can also be applied directly (without pre-sizing with glue size) to wood and hardboard, for overpainting with oil colours. This primer can be diluted in strength as required with white spirit/ turpentine. Alkyd primings can dry to give a glossy coating, which may be too slippery for oil painting, although the degree of gloss can be manipulated by thinning the primer.

Acrylic Primer

Primers based on acrylic polymer resin thinned with water, are flexible, durable and dry to become water-insoluble. They are also non-hazardous to use. Such primers can be applied directly to stretched raw canvas and dry thoroughly in only a few hours (preferably leave to dry overnight). They are variously described as acrylic, universal or acrylic gesso primer. The term "gesso" is misleading, as such primings may not have the same absorbency as traditional gesso grounds prepared with animal glue and chalk. The absorbency of commercially available acrylic primers will vary from brand to brand.

Ideally, an acrylic primer should have some absorbency and not be too shiny on the surface as this would be too slippery for oil colour to adhere to properly. The primer should allow the weave of the canvas to be apparent and enable oil colour to become absorbed into the surface texture slightly, to achieve a good bonding. Acrylic primers can be thinned down with water, although, when very heavily diluted, acrylic primer may become too absorbent. On to linens, acrylic primers applied to the raw fabric tend to penetrate through to the back. To counter this, acrylic size or water-thinned acrylic matt medium can be applied, to impregnate the surface and prevent sinking of the priming coat. Acrylic size is a milky white soft paste which dries clear. The soft formulation of acrylic size does not interfere with the texture of the canvas weave, or clog up the pores of the fabric. Other acrylic mediums could be used: for example, a flowing matt acrylic medium, diluted 30% with water to avoid applying a coating that is too thick. Gloss mediums tend to build up too much of a surface and have little or no absorbency. PVA is best avoided: it is prone to yellowing and embrittlement with age. Animal glue sizing underneath acrylic primings is not recommended, as the glue becomes increasingly hard and brittle with age, while the acrylic remains durable and flexible.

Acrylic primer can be applied neat to wooden panels and hardboard. However, the water content tends to swell wood fibres. Prime the edges first to reduce the risk of swelling and apply without water-dilution if possible. Such surfaces should always be dirt and grease-free, to aid adhesion. Methylated spirits (alcohol) can be used to degrease the surface: this is always recommended, as wooden boards are invariably handled when being cut and sold.

Properties of Oil Paints

Oil paint is made by combining a drying vegetable oil such as linseed oil with high quality pigments, to form a cohesive paint paste. During the manufacturing process, certain additive materials may be included to enhance the brushing quality (rheology) of the paint, alter the consistency and control the drying time.

The manufacturing process for oil paint can differ from one brand of paint to another. It would be true to say that there is no accepted standard for making artists' oil paints. By contrast, each manufacturer (rather like individual artists) has their own philosophy as regards what would constitute the optimum oil colour. As a consequence, there are a great many differences between paint brands. Some are stiff in consistency, some are very glossy, others matt, and so on. There is no "best" oil paint, as such, to recommend; each individual artist will adopt an oil paint that suits the context of their own work. This is an important facet to understand about oil paint: if one goes through life using the same brand, from school, through art school and into professional practice, one may end up not making the most of one's potential. The best advice as regards choosing oil paints is to try more than one brand, and to compare and contrast between brands before settling on one particular make. In practice, many artists work with a variety of brands within the same palette.

Manufactured oil colours are sold from colour charts, which may identify aspects such as the mass tone, undertone, transparency, opacity and permanence of each colour. Some also show how each colour admixes with white. There is no industry standard for the production of these colour charts, so they tend to vary according to the manufacturer. If possible, refer to a hand-painted colour chart as printed charts are always made within the bounds of commercial colour printing, so that the colours shown are a guide only. The best way to judge an oil colour is to buy a few tubes and try them against what you already have. In particular, some attention should be paid to whites. Often, cheaper, or poorly made oil colour whites can show a great deal of yellowing (darkening) after a relatively short period of time. Also, by admixing a colour (e.g. ultramarine blue) with a white, some indication of its relative strength can be ascertained and compared to the same colour in another brand. Tinting strength alone may not be such an important aspect: look also at how the paint brushes out, its consistency, glossiness, drying time, etc.

A number of terms are often applied in the context of artists' oil paints, which require some explanation.

Oil to Pigment Ratio

Each pigment requires a different recipe in order to make a balanced oil paint paste. In order to keep oil paint stable in a metal tube, certain additives are required, which can in turn alter the working characteristics of the paint, when compared to an oil paint made simply by hand, combining only pigment with oil. One governing factor in the manufacture of stable, balanced tube oil colours, is the ratio of oil required to the quantity of pigment and other dry materials. If too much oil is included in the mixture, the paint may be sloppy, or over time, the excess oil may leak out of the mixture. This usually becomes apparent when the cap of the oil paint tube is bursting with oil, or where oil has leached from the base of the tube.

Each pigment absorbs oil in a different way from the next. If the particle size is large and irregular (as is the case with green earth), it will require a larger proportion of oil than a pigment with a small particle size and a regular form. Consequently, manufacturers have to adopt a different recipe for each colour. This partly explains the high cost of artists' oil colours: not only are the raw material costs a factor, but the processing time and "aftercare" is also an issue. Most manufacturers will keep a record of each batch of paint, for cross reference. Also, when testing each paint batch, the manufacturer may compare the paint to batches from previous makings. In this way, small changes can be made to retain consistency from year to year.

Drying Time

According to the philosophy of each manufacturer, an optimum drying time for a paint range may be agreed upon. In some cases, this means adding no drying agent at all: allowing the paint to dry naturally. In other cases, all colours may have a drying agent added, so that they all dry within a specific time window. In the case of refined linseed oil for example, a thin coating of this will dry in about 2-3 days when mixed with pigment. However, some pigments, such as raw umber and lead white, have a catalytic effect on the oil, causing the paint film to dry out (cure) at a faster rate (perhaps 1-2 days). By contrast, other pigments have a retarding effect on the oil in which they are ground. Alizarin crimson and genuine vermilion will take a prolonged period to dry out thoroughly. From an artist's point of view, the best kind of paint is probably that which takes a little longer to dry out, affording them more time to rework passages of paint. This is a dilemma in present times, as the mass market for artists' materials has moved progressively towards supplying the amateur artist and hobbyist. For that market, a quick drying time is preferred. By contrast, the professional artist may be more discerning when considering the drying time of oil colours. A longer drying period may be preferred. The table of drying times for pigments hand-ground in linseed oil, shown on pages 301-304 is a good reference point and will give an indication of the drying times for specific pigments. However, this does not allow for the inclusions of drying agent that a manufacturer may adopt within a paint range. In short, there is no way to gauge the drying time of a manufactured paint other than by using it and noting how long it takes to dry. Another factor to consider with the drying time of colours, relates to the atmospheric conditions present when the painting is made. For example, a painting made in winter, in England during a damp, cold spell, will dry far slower than a painting made during a warm period in late spring. Also, paintings made in an ambient temperature (e.g. a modern house that is centrally heated) may dry a lot quicker than a painting made in a cold, draughty and possibly damp studio space. All these factors need to be considered.

In the manufacturing process, a number of drying agents are used. The principal choice for most manufacturers is cobalt siccative, also known as cobalt drier. This is based on cobalt (metal) salts in a liquid form and a small amount is added to the paint mixture during the mixing process. With cobalt siccative, the paint film dries first on the surface, then slowly through to the core. When paints containing cobalt siccative are packaged into tins, they tend to skin over on the surface very quickly. While the paint underneath the surface remains serviceable, a quantity of paint will become unusable, having formed a substantial skin. The same process can take place on the painting, where paint is applied thickly: the core of the paint may stay wet and squidgy, while the surface is dried to a hard skin. Other drying agents such as manganese and lead driers may also be found, but due to their relative toxicity are less and less common in manufactured paints.

Some manufacturers publicise the fact that they do not add drying agents. Such paints are worth examining, especially if working in a dry, warm environment.

Consistency

Tube oil colour is often a thick, buttery paste, which squeezes readily from the tube and is subsequently easy to dilute or admix with solvent and/or paint medium. However, there is no standard consistency for oil colours, it can differ from brand to brand and even within one brand, according to the character of the pigment used. If a paint range exhibits differences in consistency between one colour and another, this is not necessarily a disadvantage, it may be intended. A plus point for many artists when working with oil colours can be when a colour conforms to the characteristic of the pigment used. For example, cerulean blue is a metal-based pigment, with a slightly grainy character. When brushed out to a thin film, the particle size tends to show with a mattish finish, which can be attractive from an aesthetic point of view. If a paint is made to embellish and heighten this facet, it can be said to conform to the characteristic of the pigment used. By contrast, some brands of oil colour exhibit the same consistency and film finish, regardless of the pigment used. In such circumstances, the manufacturer has opted for a uniform, homogenised finish to all the colours across the range. This may be of interest to the system painter or to someone who paints as a hobby and wants all the colours to behave the same. However, it may be a source of frustration to the serious artist who values the exact differences of nuance between one pigment and another.

The consistency of the paint is governed to some extent by the manufacturing process and the inclusion of various additives. For example, the milling process of some brands of oil colour involves the formation of a gel consistency, achieved by putting linseed oil with aluminium stearate, a type of metal soap. This "gel" consistency affords a similar, "uniform" consistency to each colour and perhaps cuts down on processing time. However, the traditional way to make oil paint is to afford each colour a separate recipe, which will also involve different amounts of additive material, according to the nature of the pigment or pigments used to make the colour.

The inclusion of small amounts of additives can help provide stabilised paint pastes with optimum light refractive qualities. An overuse of additives may lead to a cheapening or deadening of the colour value and may also ruin the stability of consistency. For example, aluminium hydrate is often included in oil paints to give a firm, buttery consistency. Because this filler/additive is a low tinting strength white, with great transparency, it is often used with pigments of a transparent nature. However, when overused, the consistency turns to a mushy paste rather like margarine, and the colour also loses its brilliance, giving a frosty/matt finish to the dried paint film. A precise and calculated inclusion of an additive/filler material can improve a paint, but this may be costly and again, is reflected in the high price of good quality artists' oil colours.

The choice by manufacturers of a stiffish, buttery paint paste relates more to the fact that it is packaged into metal tubes, than to the consistency desired by the artist. It is true that an artist like Van Gogh found the possibility of squeezing colour direct from the tube on to the painting surface attractive. However, many artists prefer to put colour out on to a palette, or into some kind of vessel, and then admix the paint with solvent or a paint medium to alter the consistency of the oil colour. There is therefore a strong argument for the supply of oil colour in a more liquid form. Sadly, because this type of oil colour would dry out on the surface and skin over, such paints remain at the idea stage, although artists hand-making their own oil colours can certainly achieve this kind of consistency, as long as they make the paint and use it directly.

In modern times we have become very accustomed to the notion that we paint with ready-made paints and paint mediums. How different the situation would have been for artists working prior to the invention of the collapsible metal tube in the 1840s, when oil colours had to be hand-ground (perhaps by an apprentice if one was lucky) and used within a day or so. Some artists were able to keep oil paints for a few weeks or months, stored in a tied-up pig's bladder, but by and large this was a woefully impractical system. For most artists, the preparation of colours on to the palette was an important part of the painting process itself. As a consequence, it can be argued that it is good practice for all artists to learn how to hand-make oil colours, as this is perhaps the best way to learn the working properties of individual pigments.

Rheology

The brushing quality of a paint is referred to in terms of its rheology. Some paints are prepared so that they brush out smoothly once squeezed from the tube. Others may be in the form of a very stiff paste, which the artist has to manipulate further with solvent or paint medium. Paints based on refined linseed oil tend to show brush marks, whereas those based on cold-pressed linseed oil tend to hide them, because the paint itself has a self-levelling character. When choosing oil colours, these factors may become important: if one does not want to see directional brushmarks or brushstrokes, then choose a paint based on cold-pressed linseed oil. Alternatively, any oil paint can be manipulated by admixing with a small amount of a paint medium such as stand oil, which imparts a self-levelling characteristic into the paint film. Some paints are manufactured as basic "paint pastes" and actually work better when admixed with a specific paint medium. With each brand of paint it makes sense not only to look at the colour chart in terms of the actual colour, but also to look for information from the manufacturer relating to the best working methods. Some manufacturers publish small handbooks which explain how to get the best results from a paint.

Mass Tone and Undertone

The mass tone can be said to relate to the paint when painted without dilution (neat). The undertone relates to when a paint is diluted or brushed out strongly, to reveal any transparency. With some pigments, the mass tone and undertone can indicate a difference of colour. For example, nickel azo yellow has a mustard tinge when applied neat as a mass tone but becomes a warmer yellow when brushed out to a glaze.

Binding Media for Oil Paint

Oil paints are based on combinations of pigment(s) into drying vegetable oils such as linseed oil. It is best to understand the properties of these oils before beginning to work with oil colours, or when hand-making oil colours. Oil paints dry through a complex process of oxidisation, whereby the paint film gradually hardens to form, in the case of linseed oil, a leathery, durable film. During this process, oxygen is attracted to the open, wet fresh oil paint surface but paradoxically, expelled from the mixture at the same time. This continues for a prolonged period, until finally more oxygen is coming out than going in. Typically, the surface of the paint film dries first, partially trapping oxygen underneath. This trapped oxygen slowly leaks out until the paint film hardens in the core. As a consequence, it can be seen that paint films that are thin, dry much quicker than fat paint films.

(N.B. Because some pigments seem to retard the drying/oxidisation process, it is not possible to use them to paint thickly if one expects the paint film to dry successfully. As a guide, for thicker passages of oil paint, it is wise to use opaque colours with a regular particle shape such as the cadmium yellows and reds, or the synthetic iron oxides. Another factor to consider with thicker passages of oil paint, is that when the paint takes a long time to dry, it is more than likely that the sheen of the paint will become slightly matt. This can be countered somewhat by admixing a small amount of paint medium – e.g. stand oil/dammar varnish – to help retain an even gloss.)

Different oils give different paint film sheens. Where linseed oil tends to form a hard, leathery skin, poppy oil, which dries slowly, gives a matt, slightly frosted sheen. Choice of the appropriate oil when hand-making oil colours can be crucial to the paint film appearance.

Refined Linseed Oil

The most commonly used oil for modern artists' colours is refined, or heat-expressed linseed oil. As the name suggests, the seeds of the flax plant are pressed using a heat process, through metal rollers. The resultant oil is a dark orange-brown colour but is bleached to provide a pale straw colour. Over time, this pale colour reverts to its original darker shade, thereby introducing a warm brownish tinge to all the colours with which it has been ground to make paint. While this defect is alarming to many artists, the very patina of age that oil paints exhibit is of great value to the auction house. If an oil painting has the characteristic warm glow of aged linseed oil, then it does indeed look old. It can be argued that the responsibility of the artist is to the image, not to the final care, storage and exhibition of the artwork. However, many artists are concerned that the images they paint should remain in a similar condition once the painting leaves the studio. Refined linseed oils have a low acid value, which shows in the paint film in the form of directional brushmarks. This is also known as the "suede-effect", being similar to the brushing of suede in one direction, then another, to reveal two different marks or shades. This tendency to show brushmarks can be countered by adding a small amount of a paint medium that is self-levelling (e.g. stand oil, alkyd medium). Linseed oil is produced extensively in the Low Countries and the Baltic States of

Europe, where sunlight tends to filter through low cloud for a large part of the year, offering ideal growing conditions for the flax or linseed plant.

Refined linseed oil dries quickly (perhaps 2-3 days), sometimes causing the surface of the paint film to skin-over or wrinkle if applied too thickly. Poor quality refined linseed oil may dry even quicker: industrial products may have an inclusion of drying agent such as cobalt siccative, which may be appropriate for industrial paints, but is not desirable for artists' colours. The addition of excessive drying agent into a paint mixture causes the applied paint film to dry out too aggressively: once the paint film has seemingly dried, the drying agent continues to act on the oil until eventually, the paint film turns chalky and becomes underbound. This is not such a problem with industrial paints, where periodically, the object that has been painted requires re-painting. When the paint film turns slightly chalky, it can be easily overpainted, the mattness of the remaining paint coating providing a good grip for the new coat of paint. With artists' colours, this would be a disaster: the paint film becomes embrittled and fragile.

Herein lies the argument for purchasing artists' materials from specialist suppliers rather than hardware stores or industrial suppliers as they are more likely to offer the best quality and most appropriate choice of materials.

Cold-Pressed Linseed Oil

In the food industry, cold-pressed oils such as olive oil are highly prized and afforded the term "extra-virgin", which refers to the pedantic nature involved in pressing oil from the olive fruit. In a similar fashion, in the context of artists' materials, cold-pressed linseed oil is also produced using an exacting method, which in turn increases the cost price and limits availability to a degree. The term "cold-pressed" refers to the method of oil extraction from the seeds of the flax plant. The seeds are crushed between milling stones (as with the old method of producing flour inside a windmill) and the oil is expressed without any heat whatsoever. This form of pressing produces an oil that has a higher acid value than refined linseed oil. It is of great importance to artists wishing to prepare their own oil colours, as this high-acid value oil readily absorbs powdered pigments, so assisting the paint-making process. The pressed oil usually contains plant mucilage and other debris, so has to be cleaned before offering to the market. This is traditionally done by adding a quantity of fuller's earth into the oil vat. This diacatamous earth has a very large particle size, in a form similar to a horseshoe: this peculiar shape tends to attract debris and drags it down to the bottom of the vat, as it falls with gravity. In this way, the oil is cleaned, partially clarified and free of impurities. When the fuller's earth has settled out at the bottom of the vat, the clear oil is poured off into another vessel, then packaged. An alternative method for cleaning the oil is to mix it 50 : 50 with cold water, into an air-tight vessel. The contents are then shaken vigorously, so that the oil and water are combined. After repeated shaking, perhaps for 15-30 minutes in total, the vessel is left to stand for a period of approximately 1-2 weeks. Upon standing, the oil and water separate out: the clean oil rises to the top, while the water remains at the bottom. In between, a layer of mucilage forms. By letting the mixture stand for a prolonged period, it will be observed that more and more mucilage forms in between the oil and water. After 1-2 weeks, the clean oil is carefully poured into a new container. The whole process can be repeated a number of times, until the oil has absolute clarity. In order to remove the oil from the mucilage and water without contamination, the mixture can be frozen. The water and mucilage will freeze before the oil does. As a result, the clean oil can be poured out of the vessel without contamination.

This lengthy process results in oil that has a surprising clarity, which may help to realise brighter colour resonance.

Whereas refined linseed oil is a modern, industrial product, extensively used by other industries, cold-pressed linseed oil is utilised by artists' material companies and health food suppliers; a tiny, niche market. As a consequence, the quality of cold-pressed linseed oils available to the market may vary from brand to brand, depending on the source of production. The colour may vary, as may the debris content and acid content. The best quality oils currently on the market are sourced from Scandinavia and Germany, although the author has seen samples from Australia, United Kingdom and North America. In general, cold-pressed linseed oil has a golden yellow or yellow-orange colour. As with all vegetable oils, a colour change takes place over time, leading to a general darkening of the dried paint film, although this is not as pronounced with cold-pressed linseed oil, as with the refined type, which darkens alarmingly.

The real advantage of cold-pressed linseed oil is that it readily accepts dry powders (pigments, additive/filler material) and that when brushed out on to the painting surface, brushmarks tend to level out. Cold-pressed linseed oil will take longer to dry than refined linseed oil (perhaps 3-4 days for a thin paint film) but has a superior gloss and hardness once dried.

Upon drying, linseed oil has a tough, leathery film, with a good gloss, which should sustain over time. With certain pigments, there may be a matting, or sinking effect. This usually happens where not enough oil has been incorporated into the paint mixture: when the paint is first applied to the painting surface, it may be glossy, but upon drying it becomes less so. The best way to counter this is to add a small proportion of a painting medium to the paint (see Oil Painting Mediums), but it may be an indication that the paint itself is not particularly well made. In practical terms, such defects are rarely seen until a few months after the painting is complete. It may be wise therefore, to make a sample chart of paint-outs of one's usual palette, applied to a canvas prepared in the usual way, upon which one can easily check the performance, with age, of specific colours. The incorrect amount of pigment to oil is most usually noticed with black pigments. They may seem to be sleek and glossy when first painted, but may lose their glossiness in a short space of time and turn matt. To counter this, always add a little painting medium to black oil colours.

All oil paint films yellow (darken) with age. To an extent this is unavoidable. In the case of pale colours: whites, yellows, certain blues such as cerulean blue, it is often advised to use pale coloured oils such as poppy or safflower oil. In the short term, this can be desirable, because the paint film will be truer to the hue of the pigment used. However, over time, all the vegetable oils used as binders for oil paint tend to turn dark. While linseed oil always forms a hard, durable and glossy paint film, other oils may form less desirable films: often, the pale oils form matt films, which may attract dirt and dust. As a consequence, it may be wise to use only linseed oil, even if this means that with pale colours, the natural yellow of the linseed oil has some presence in the paint mixture.

With white pigments, this yellowing tends to show the most, especially if the paint is poorly made. If there is too much oil to the quantity of pigment, upon drying, the pigment will settle out in the mixture, leaving a thin skin of oil over the pigment surface, which reads to the eye as being yellow. This phenomenon is greater when a painting is stored in the dark, or stored away from daylight (i.e. stacked with the paint surface hidden from view). While this darkening can be countered by re-exposing the paint surface to strong sunshine for a week or so, it is an inevitable defect seen in oil paintings, especially when large amounts of white have been used.

The natural yellow-orange colour of cold-pressed linseed oil will have some presence in the paint film, even if the paint is very well made. Refined linseed oil, which has been bleached to give a very pale colour, may in the short term not effect the colour in the paint film, but over time it turns progressively darker. It may as a consequence be wiser to continue to use cold-pressed linseed oil, safe in the knowledge that although all colours will be warmed up slightly by the natural colour of the oil, they will not dramatically alter over time.

This situation is further confused by claims from some artists' material companies that their refined linseed oils do not darken excessively or change over time. The best advice for artists is to test some different oils and leave them for an extended period (perhaps 4-5 years) to gauge which option is best. While this may not seem like a practical solution, for a young artist at art school, this is easy enough to do. By the time one has finished art school, the result of the experiment is more or less complete. It would make sense if more art schools encouraged their students to experiment and test painting materials early in their courses, so that information such as that available in "text" books like this one, can be thoroughly explored and challenged where appropriate.

Refined Linseed Oil with Siccative (Oil Varnish)

As mentioned, some industrially produced refined linseed oils may already contain a drying agent such as cobalt siccative. These oils are sometimes referred to as linseed oil varnish. When used as a binder, such oils should only ever be applied thinly, as fatter passages of paint will tend to wrinkle and shrivel on the surface. Such oils may be useful for making very quick drying oil colours, where the paint needs to dry in a short period (perhaps 1-2 days). Because the manufacturer has incorporated the drying agent into the oil, such oil may be useful when making paint mediums. Rather than adding neat driers to an oil paint medium, it may be wiser to use a proprietary brand of drying oil, where the same quantity of drying agent is added to the oil, in each batch produced. Adding neat drying agent to paints and paint mediums is rather unpredictable. Unless one does this in a scientific way, with accurate measurement of the liquid drier, it is more than likely that such additions will lead to cracking or over-drying of the paint film.

Modern Stand Oil

Modern stand oil is produced by heating linseed oil in a vacuum. This process thickens the oil to the consistency of heavy syrup. It also partially oxidises the oil, so that it dries a little quicker, forms a self-levelling film and does not darken excessively. As a consequence, stand oil is often used as an addition to painting mediums, but rarely as a binder for oil paints. As a binder, it is rather difficult to manipulate, being thick and viscid in nature. While this type of thickened oil is today referred to as stand oil, it is really a type of polymerised oil, or blown oil. Somewhere along the way it was given the name stand oil, probably because in some way it resembles the historic sun-bleached or sun-thickened oils of the past.

Historic Stand Oil

Linseed oil which has been left to "stand" for a period while exposed to sunlight, is true stand oil. This is also sometimes referred to as sun-bleached oil, because upon exposure to sunlight, the colour becomes very pale and clear. The consistency of this historic form of stand oil is similar to ordinary linseed oil, it can be poured easily and is excellent for making paints. It is still available, though is highly priced, due in part to the lengthy process involved in its manufacture.

Sun-Thickened Linseed Oil

When linseed oil is exposed to both air and strong sunlight, it will become pale in colour but will also thicken to a heavy syrup consistency (similar, somewhat confusingly, to modern stand oil). This glossy, rich oil is excellent as an additive to painting mediums, especially when cold-pressed linseed oil has been used, which has been cleaned of impurities (see Cold-Pressed Linseed Oil). Sun-thickened linseed oil is prepared by pouring a quantity of oil into a flat glass tray, which in turn is exposed to strong sunlight for a period of days or weeks. During this exposure, the oil needs to receive air: a glass lid is placed over the tray, with props to let air circulate. A fine gauze or muslin can be stretched over the tray to keep insects and debris out (although these impurities can always be strained at a later stage). The oil needs to be stirred once a day for a period of perhaps 1-2 weeks. Stirring helps to stop the oil from thickening on the surface only. The oil produced in this way is light in colour but viscous: it can be incorporated into oil painting medium recipes (for example, in the place of modern stand oil). Sun-thickened linseed oil imparts a glossy, enamel-like sheen to oil colours, is self-levelling and less prone to darkening than cold-pressed or refined forms of linseed oil.

The drying time of sun-thickened linseed oil is quickened when the oil is exposed to lead during the thickening process. This can be done by laying a strip of lead in the bottom of the glass tray, with the oil covering it. Lead has a catalytic effect upon the oil. Alternatively, 10% by volume of massicot pigment is left to settle at the bottom of the tray of oil. This lead mono-oxide pigment will also impart a drying action to the oil.

Poppy Oil

Poppy oil is a delicate pale colour, with a thinner consistency than cold-pressed linseed oil. Both refined and cold-pressed varieties may be found on the market. The French painters of the 19th century used oil colours prepared with poppy oil, in part because this was the fashion of the day but also because the longer drying time (4-5 days for a thin film) enabled paintings to be worked on over longer periods. This can be seen to be especially useful when working out of doors, from nature, where a fresh, wet paint surface can be re-worked over a period of days. Because it is so pale, poppy oil reveals the true colour of each pigment ground into it. This can be especially useful with regard to pale colours: whites, blues, yellows. While this clarity of colour may be useful during the painting process, poppy oil - as with all the other drying vegetable oils used in oil painting - will become darker over time.

Oil paints prepared with poppy oil tend to form a stiffish, short buttery paste very readily. This can be helpful when learning to hand-make oil colours, as each pigment can be seen at its best (because of the pale colour of the oil) and the paint paste is quickly achieved. Also, because of the slower drying time, hand-made oil colours based on poppy oil will remain fresh for longer on the palette, or perhaps in air-tight glass jars, than would be the case with linseed oil based paint. The author has examples of slow drying colours (e.g. genuine carmine, genuine vermilion), which were hand ground into poppy oil, and which remained wet and workable for over a year when stored in an air-tight glass jar.

A particular defect of poppy oil is the matt quality of the paint film. This tends to cause the initial gloss of the paint to edge away, as the matt/dry nature of the resultant paint film is rather attractive to dust and dirt. Paintings made with poppy oil need to be stored while drying, as close to the ceiling as possible (away from dust, which gathers at floor level). The Victorians in Britain built their art schools with drying racks, high up above the studio workspace. This was not just an ingenious and rational use of space, it had the desired effect of allowing paintings to dry without coming into contact with excessive dirt and dust.

Poppy oil forms a less durable paint film when compared to linseed oil. Indeed, fat passages of oil paint made with poppy oil as the binder tend to crack rather easily when stressed.

Safflower Oil and Sunflower Oil

Safflower and sunflower oils are sometimes used within oil paint ranges, especially for white pigments. However, they suffer similar defects as poppy oil, forming relatively matt films and giving weaker paint films (especially when applied thickly), than linseed oil based paints. They dry at a similar slow rate as poppy oil.

Walnut Oil

Oil pressed from walnuts was used to a great extent in the past, especially in the context of Italian oil painting and later, in the work of artists such as Van Dyke. Because of its very pale colour and brilliant gloss, it was often preferred over linseed oil. The clarity of this oil was greatly respected, because colours ground in it revealed their true shade. Walnut oil was also important as an ingredient in egg-oil emulsions. Despite these attractive qualities, walnut oil is seldom used today for oil painting, in part because it becomes rather brittle upon drying, making it somewhat unsuitable for using on to stretched canvas (flexible support). On to rigid supports such as wooden panels, walnut oil may be an excellent binder for oil colours. It remains glassy, glossy and hard-wearing over time, lending colours excellent saturation and depth. Freshly cold-pressed walnut oil can quickly turn rancid upon exposure to air. Walnut oil dries a little faster than poppy oil (3-4 days).

Hand-Made Oil Colour

Before using proprietary brands of oil colour, it is useful to learn the process of paint-making. The factory processing of oil colours is in truth a mechanised copy of hand-made paint. Prior to the 1840s, and the invention of the collapsible metal tube, artists were required to hand-prepare their colours, perhaps even every day. In many ways, this paint-making process was an integral part of the activity of painting as a whole.

The genesis of oil painting technique can be traced back to the workshop tradition of medieval artists, where a team of apprentices or assistants would work under a "master". All facets of painting production were achieved in such workshops, from the correct preparation of the painting ground, through the precise preparation of colours, down to the execution of the painting.

During the early 19th century in France, especially Paris, dedicated suppliers of colours and other materials for artists began to emerge, with the advent of the Industrial Revolution. On a small scale, individual suppliers began to diversify their trade to cater for a growing demand for ready-made artists' materials. This would have included hand-stretched canvases, but also the hand-preparation of oil paints. Often such paints were prepared according to the demands of an individual artist, rather than conforming to some ideal "standard" form of oil paint. As a consequence, today we have a myriad of oil paint ranges, which differ from one brand to another, dependent to some degree on the philosophy and history of production of the factory concerned. This individuality has in recent years become less distinct, with many companies pushing through products that meet the common demand, rather than the peculiar demand of individual artists.

The author has had many intriguing conversations with artists over the years regarding the notion of the ideal oil paint. In truth, this would seem to relate more to the foibles of the artist concerned than to any higher truth. In practice, any artist can take a batch of pigment, some oil and a few other additives and make a superior quality oil paint. There is no secret to the making of oil colours, it is not necessarily a high art. It is the high cost of the raw materials used in the manufacture of oil colours that causes most artists to shy away from experimenting with hand-made oil paint: one does not want to waste money and materials. Another factor that prevents artists from experimenting with raw materials is time. The artist is preoccupied (rightly so) with achieving the image, rather than dabbling about with pigments in the hope of finding the answer to a seemingly elusive quest.

However, it can be argued that even a cursory amount of time spent paint-making can open the artist's mind to a world of possibility with colour. The best way to form an opinion about colour (and the vehicle/binders) is to take the raw materials used in painting and put them to work.

For making oil colours it is advised that a space is made within the studio which is dedicated to this activity. In effect, this entails clearing the area required and keeping it dirt and dust free. Cleanliness and organisation is paramount in this matter, as will become apparant once such work is undertaken. A table or worktop is required, positioned just above waist height, so that as little stooping as possible is necessary. On to this level worktop, the following items can be carefully laid out, so that they are easily accessible:

- Selection of dry pigments (see list - stored in air-tight glass jars, and labelled)
- Glass muller
- Glass slab, with slight tooth (sandblasted glass), or a marble slab with a slightly rough surface
- Cold-pressed linseed oil (and other oils as preferred)
- Odourless mineral spirit
- Sunflower oil (for cleaning)
- Methylated spirit (alcohol)
- Beeswax paste
- Aluminium hydrate (transparent filler)
- Blanc fix (opaque filler)
- Empty metal tubes (60ml, or 100ml)
- Paper roll for cleaning
- Waste bin
- Disposable gloves
- Dust mask

Tools and Ingredients

Dry Pigments

This basic selection of pigments offers a starting point. All the colours have good permanence, are relatively straightforward to prepare and are not too costly to procure. If possible, keep the original labels for each colour, so that in the case of an accident, the supplier can be contacted. It will also be useful for keeping a record of each colour, so that when new supplies are required, the same colour name, code number or colour index name can be quoted.

Nickel titanium yellow

Cadmium yellow light

Hansa yellow light

Cadmium yellow deep

Hansa yellow deep

Cadmium orange

Cadmium red middle

Permanent red

Cadmium red deep

Quinacridone red (permanent rose)

Ultramarine blue

Ultramarine violet

Indanthrone blue

Cobalt blue

Cerulean blue

Heliogen (phthalo) blue

Quinacridone violet

Dioxazine violet

Heliogen (phthalo) green

Viridian green

Chrome oxide green

Cadmium green

Terre verte

Oxide (mars) yellow

Raw sienna

Burnt sienna

Raw umber

Burnt umber

Oxide (mars) red

Oxide (mars) violet

Oxide (mars) brown

Oxide (mars) black

Carbon black (ivory black)

Lamp black

Titanium white

Zinc white

Glass Muller

The glass muller, or glass runner, is a round, bulbous piece of heavy glass, with a flat bottom. It may have a tall glass handle, or sometimes a "door-knob" shaped handle. The base is flat and is usually abraded (sandblasted). This grainy surface corresponds to the sandblasted surface of the glass slab, so that pigment powder caught in-between these two pitted surfaces does not dance around on the glass surface.

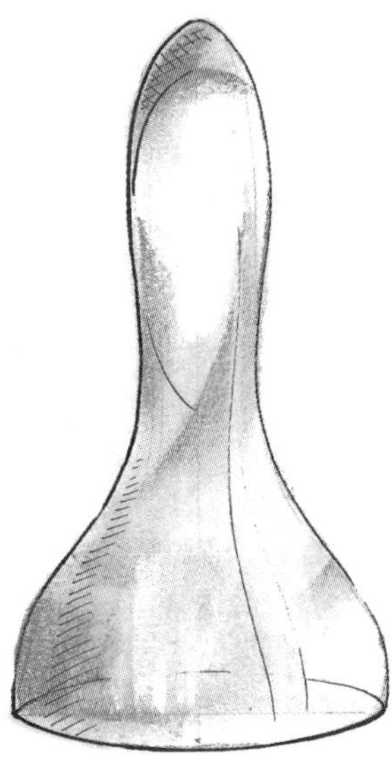

Glass Muller

Glass (or Marble) Slab

The slab, with its pitted, sandblasted surface, allows the paint mixture to be moved around without spreading out all over the glass. The pigment particles get lodged in the pits of the glass surface. The slab needs to be thick enough to withstand a certain amount of pressure. An ideal size format for the glass slab is 40 x 60cm: this is big enough to work up small quantities of pigment and is relatively portable.

Straight Palette Knives

Stainless steel palette knives, with a length of about 12-14cm are perfectly serviceable, it is not necessary to have large palette knives. The palette knives are used to help combine the initial mix of pigment and oil, and to help gather up the paint once it has been milled.

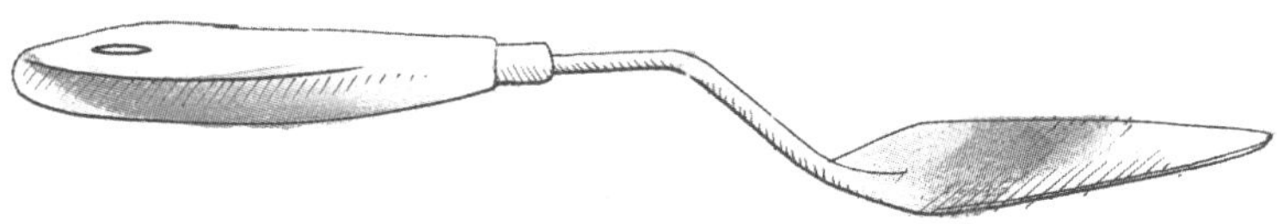

Painting Knife

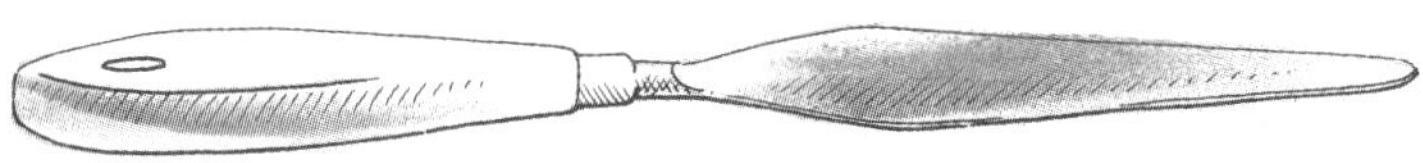

Pallete Knife

Cold-Pressed Linseed Oil

The choice of oil is a personal one. It is suggested that to begin with, cold-pressed linseed oil is used as a standard binder. Other oils can then be contrasted with it.

Odourless Mineral Spirit

White spirit is now available in a form that has little or no smell. This can be used to help free pigment particles from the glass, when cleaning up.

Sunflower Oil

Cheap sunflower oil, or other vegetable oils for cooking can be obtained from food stores. These can be used to clean the slab, muller, knives etc, without the introduction of a solvent. This helps to make the workspace more pleasant and is much kinder to hands than solvent.

Methylated Spirit

This can be used to clean the glass slab and muller properly after working. A little methylated spirit will remove any residual pigment, especially with strong staining colours, such as the synthetic organic pigment phthalocyanine blue.

Beeswax Paste

This paste is used as an additive in the paint-making process, to assist the consistency of the paint and to help keep the pigment and oil adhered together. A small percentage (2%) is added to the paint mixture. If more beeswax paste is added, the paint will become waxy, thick and matt.

The paste is made by taking:

Refined beeswax	1 part
Distilled turpentine	2 parts (by volume)

The wax is left to dissolve in the turpentine for 2-3 days, until it forms a smooth paste (similar to Vaseline). No heat is required for this process. If too thick, add a little more turpentine, mix and leave to solve again for a few days.

Aluminium Hydrate and Blanc Fix

Fillers can be added to oil paint mixtures in small quantities, to improve their light refraction (light is helped to break up on the surface) and the consistency of the paint. Too much filler will leave the paint in a stodgy, unmanageable paste and create mattness and dryness in the paint film. A small amount, perhaps between 2-10% of the whole paint mixture is advised. This will vary from pigment to pigment.

Aluminium hydrate can be used with transparent colours (e.g. phthalocyanine green), while blanc fix is a heavier, slightly opaque material, which can be used with opaque colours (e.g. cadmium red). Both "fillers" are actually white pigments that possess low tinting strength.

Empty Metal Tubes

Collapsible metal tubes are sold with open ends. These can be crimped after being filled with paint, using a pair of pliers. Before putting the paint mixture into the tube, lubricate the inside walls with a little alcohol: this will help the paint to slip down the tube. The size of the tube is open to question: in practice slightly larger tubes (60 or 100ml size) are useful, because they allow enough space for the palette knife to deposit paint in through the open end.

Paper Roll

Kitchen roll, or industrial paper roll should be on hand, so that any waste residue can be quickly removed during cleaning, etc.

Waste Bin

The waste bin should be closeable, so that the waste roll or waste rags are contained at all times.

Disposable Gloves

While handling dry pigment, always use a barrier cream on the hands and forearms, so that pigment does not come into contact with the skin. It is advised to always wear disposable gloves when working with dry pigment and when processing paint. This avoids any skin contact and makes cleaning up much easier.

Dust Mask

Similarly, a dust mask needs to be worn when handling dry pigment. Because the specification for dust masks is always changing, consult the supplier as to the most appropriate. For pigments, ask for a dust mask which inhibits nuisance dusts with a very fine particulate size. Treat all pigments as potentially hazardous.

Paint-Making Procedure

The pigment is first mixed roughly into a stiff paste with the oil, using the palette knife, combining all the pigment, and so "wetting" all the particles. Difficult pigments that are fluffy or fly-away due to their light weight and fine particle size (e.g. the synthetic pigments, such as quinacridones), need wetting before they can be ground with oil. This is done by saturating the pigment with odourless mineral spirit, until all the powder is wet. Once this is done, leave to dry out a little on some absorbent paper, before mixing to a paste with the oil. The pigment/oil mixture is then ground on the slab with a glass muller in a figure of eight motion. The aim is to achieve a smooth paint, free of lumps, where all pigment particles are bound in the oil. The oil surrounds and coats each pigment particle, so that it links the paint film together.

It is best to mull a little pigment at a time, placing each freshly milled amount to the edge of the slab. When the desired amount has been milled, repeat the process. The finished paint should be "short", i.e. it stands up when manipulated with a palette knife. If the paint levels out or is too runny, simply mull in more pigment. To the oil, it is possible to add a small percentage of beeswax (2%) to give the paint a more buttery texture and stop pigment-oil separation if being stored in a tube. However, the addition of wax will matt the paint sheen and stiffen the consistency. Poppy oil produces a shorter paint, removing the need to add wax as a stabiliser.

The choice of oil to use for grinding is decided according to the drying properties of a specific pigment (see drying times). Slow drying pigments can be ground with cold-pressed linseed oil (which dries alone in up to 4 days as a thin coat). Fast drying pigments can be ground with slow drying poppy oil (5-8 days), thus achieving a balance of drying times. Poppy, safflower and sunflower oils are often used for grinding with pale yellows, delicate blues and whites. They are paler than linseed oil and less prone to yellowing, although they dry slowly and produce less durable paint films.

Some pigments, for example ultramarine blue are difficult to grind to a good, thick consistency. In such cases it is better to grind up the amount of colour needed for the painting session, then use immediately, rather than try to store it in a tube. The addition of a painting medium can enhance the adhesion of hand ground paints. A good way to do this is to place the freshly milled colour on to a sheet of absorbent paper (newsprint, newspaper, etc.) and leave for an hour or so. Excess oil is leached out of the paint mixture, leaving a lean oil paint. This can then be fattened slightly by mixing in a small amount of a glaze medium (no more than 10%), derived from stand oil/dammar varnish/turpentine.

The final paint mixture should be stiff in consistency but easy to brush out and dilute with turpentine. If the paint is too stiff, it may harden in the tube; if too sloppy, the pigment/oil may separate out, so that when the tube cap is opened, an excess of oil spurts out.

A small addition of aluminium hydrate as an extender/filler may be incorporated. This will help give the paint a homogenous, buttery texture but will increase its transparency. Up to 2% (by weight) could be added to the paint mixture. An excess will leave the paint dry and crumbly, and more prone to yellowing. Metallic soaps such as aluminium hydrate can cause oil films to become spongy and brittle with age.

The freshly mulled oil paint is best used straight away but can if preferred be stored in empty collapsible tubes. These should be labelled for identification and a small swatch of colour painted out on canvas paper, as a record for the future.

Oil Absorption

Pigments absorb oil to varying degrees. The amount of oil needed to make a stable paint paste will vary from one pigment to another. For example, the oil required to form a stable paint paste with green earth may be around 80% or more, while that of zinc white is lower, at around 15-25%. The percentage is approximate, because the product may vary in its absorption from one source to another. The percentage of oil to pigment can be expressed as the relative volume of oil to dry pigment powder required to make a stable paint paste. It follows that pigments that require more oil to form such a paint paste will exhibit a propensity to turn dark/yellow with age, due to the addition of a larger amount of oil. The dried paint film may also remain softer for longer, especially when paint is applied in any thickness. Artists wishing to work in a technique where the paint is applied with a little impasto should therefore choose colours that require the least quantity of oil in their composure.

The following outline list of common pigments found in oil paint ranges can be regarded as a starting point. When hand grinding colours, it may be wise to let each batch of paint rest on an absorbent paper for a few minutes, then remix to form a paste: if the resultant paint is too matt when dried, it then follows that more oil is required. In this way, by trial and error, one can find the right balance between pigment and oil required for a specific colour.

Where relevant, a specific oil is mentioned, as in the case of whites, where pale oils such as poppy oil may be more desirable to reduce the degree of yellowing. Otherwise, it can be assumed that the percentage figure relates to the required amount of linseed oil.

Pigment	Colour Index Number	Approximate Oil Required in % with Dry Pigment
White Pigments		
Lead white	PW 1	20% + (poppy oil, safflower oil)
Zinc white	PW 4	15-25% + (poppy oil, safflower oil)
Lithopone	PW 5	10-20% + (poppy oil, safflower oil)
Titanium white	PW 6	15-20% + (poppy oil, safflower oil)
Blanc fix	PW 21	10-20% + (poppy oil, safflower oil)
Alumina hydrate	PW 24	*

* Never used alone for paint making, as it shows the colour of the oil too readily and gives too soft a paint paste. Only added as a filler/extender, in small quantities (e.g. up to 10% of whole paint mix).

Pigment	Colour Index Number	Approximate Oil Required in % with Dry Pigment
Yellow Pigments		
Massicot	PY 46	25%+
Cadmium yellow	PY 35, 37	40-60% +
Hansa yellow	PY 1, 3, 65, 73, 74	50% +
Chrome yellow	PY 34	30-60%+ (poppy oil, safflower oil)
Cobalt yellow	PY 40	30-40% + (poppy oil, safflower oil)
Naples yellow	PY 41	20-40% + (poppy oil, safflower oil)

Nickel Titatium yellow	PY 53	15-20%
Zinc yellow	PY 36	40% +
Lemon yellow	PY 31	15-20% + (poppy oil, safflower oil)

Pigment	Colour Index Number	Approximate Oil Required in % with Dry Pigment
Red Pigments		
Red lead	PR 105	20% +
Studio red	PR 3	50-70%
Chrome red	PR 104	40% +
Carmine	NR 4	60-80% +
Madder	NR 9	60-75% +
Alizarin crimson	PR 83	60-75% +
Cadmium red	PR 108, 113, PO 23	40% +
Vermilion	PR 106	25% +

Pigment	Colour Index Number	Approximate Oil Required in % with Dry Pigment
Earth Pigments		
Raw umber	PBr 7	70% + tends to vary according to type
Burnt umber	PBr 7	70% + tends to vary according to type
Raw sienna	PBr 7	100% + tends to vary according to type
Burnt sienna	PBr 7	50-200% + tends to vary according to type

Yellow ochre	PY 42, 43	50-60% + tends to vary according to type
Green earth	PG 23	80% + tends to vary according to type
Van dyke brown	NB 8	200-250% +

Pigment	Colour Index Number	Approximate Oil Required in % with Dry Pigment
Synthetic Iron Oxide Pigments		
Mars yellow	PY 42	65-70% +
Mars red, violet	PR 101, 102	30-70% +
Mars black	PBk 11	50-60% +

Pigment	Colour Index Number	Approximate Oil Required in % with Dry Pigment
Blue Pigments		
Phthalo blue	PB 15, 16	30-50% +
Prussian blue	PB 27	60-120% + (poppy oil, safflower oil)
Cobalt blue	PB 28	120-140% + (poppy oil, safflower oil)
Ultramarine blue	PB 29	30-50% + (poppy oil, safflower oil)
Manganese blue	PB 33	30% + (poppy oil, safflower oil)
Cerulean blue	PB 35	120-140% + (poppy oil, safflower oil)
Cobalt violet dp.	PV 14	100% +
Manganese violet	PV 16	20-30%+
Cobalt violet lt.	PV 47	100% +
Cobalt violet br.	PV 49	100% +

Pigment	Colour Index Number	Approximate Oil Required in % with Dry Pigment
Green Pigments		
Chrome oxide	PG 17	30% +
Phthalo green	PG 7, 36	30-45% +
Cobalt green	PG 26	70% + (poppy oil, safflower oil)
Viridian	PG 18	50-100% +

Pigment	Colour Index Number	Approximate Oil Required in % with Dry Pigment
Black and Brown Pigments		
Lamp black	PBk 6	100-800% + *
Ivory black	PBk 9	50% +
Manganese black	PBk 14	30% +
Vine black		50-120% +

* Particle size is extremely small and therefore may require excessive amounts of oil to provide a stable paint film. It follows that lamp black only successfully dries when applied in flat layers, rather than with impasto.

Working With Pigments

When handling dry pigments, take care not to breathe in pigment dusts (wear a dust mask) and avoid using toxic pigments without adequate protection (mask and gloves).

Take particular care when handling lead-based pigments, such as lead white.

Do not eat, smoke or drink when working with dry pigments. Keep all materials out of the reach of children. Prepare materials only for intended use. Before handling dry pigments and also solvents, rub a good quality barrier cream into the hands and wrists. This will help prevent absorption of pigments into the skin and will assist when cleaning colour from hands and skin after painting, etc. If possible, wear protective gloves when preparing pigments into the binding medium to help prevent contact between pigment powder and skin. Label all dry pigments, so that they can be identified in case of accident. Keep a record of the supplier, code number and supplier phone number and address. When cleaning up residue of paint pigment after working, wipe excess on to absorbent cloth or paper. Avoid emptying waste paint, etc into sink, as this can clog and contaminate drainage. It is also a potential offence to dispose of coloured and/or possibly toxic materials in this manner. Dispose of all toxic materials, (including old tubes, containers, bags) responsibly. Contact local authority for further advice on disposal.

Toxicity of Pigments

This table covers some pigments mentioned in the text but includes others that are available either as prepared oil colour and/or as dry pigment. Due caution is advised when handling any pigment in dry form.

Pigment	Potentially Toxic Composition
Chrome yellow	chromate of lead
Naples yellow	lead
Indian yellow imit.	nickel
Nickel titanium yellow	nickel
Cadmium yellow, orange	cadmium sulphide. Cadmium is toxic when burnt. Cadmium pigments can also contain a percentage of barium sulphate
Cadmium red	cadmium sulpho-selenide. Cadmium is toxic when burnt. Cadmium pigments can also contain a percentage of barium sulphate
Lead red	lead tetroxide

Vermilion	mercuric sulphide
Manganese blue	barium manganate
Cobalt blue	cobalt oxide
Phthalocyanine blue/ green	copper
Cobalt violet	cobalt oxide
Manganese violet	manganese
Cerulean blue	cobalt oxide
Cobalt green	cobalt
Lead white	lead carbonate
Lithopone white	barium
Blanc fix (extender)	barium

Further advice on use of materials may be available from the supplier or manufacturer.

Manufactured Oil Colour

Oil colours are sold according to a curious form of grading. High quality colours may be referred to as "Professional" or "Classic" oil colours; "artists' quality" is another term applied to high quality oil colour. By contrast, the determination of lower quality colours is more difficult to explain. "Student" or "Sketching" oil colours are sometimes referred to. This calls into question the role of the student: does every student have to work with poor quality materials? No, this is a kind of insult for all students, many of whom aspire to work with the best (or perhaps most appropriate) materials. Similarly it is not a crime to make a sketch, so perhaps the term "Sketching colours" is similarly invalid.

The proof of the pudding is always in the eating. In practice, there are many differing qualities of oil colour on the market: some high priced paints are not good when compared to some lower priced products, and so on. The only true test is to procure a number of colours from different brands and to place them against each other, admixing each with white and noting the results.

Manufactured oil colours tend to be of a higher quality dependent on:

- **Quality of raw materials used (pigment, binder, additive)**
- **Length of time spent processing the raw material**
- **Exactitude of balance between the raw materials used**
- **Intention within the marketplace**

Wherever possible, only the highest quality pigment is used in the manufacture of artists' quality oil colours. This determines that fugitive pigments, or pigments that are reactive, are excluded from the paint range. There are some notable exceptions to this. For example, the author continues to use factory-made genuine vermilion, because of its particular colour quality, despite the fact that vermilion is known to darken in certain circumstances. Many artists still use alizarin crimson, despite the fact that it is known to fade and that superior equivalent pigments are also available (e.g. quinacridone red). Where the market continues to demand the use of questionable pigments, some manufacturers continue to supply. Just like any other industrial product, there are good and bad qualities of pigment. Some, which are classified as permanent, may be sold strongly diluted in tinting strength, because the manufacturer is selling them into a market that does not require absolute permanence. For example, gloss house paints need not last forever, they are periodically replaced. Some pigments may be adulterated with dye, or filler material. In the case of poorer quality oil colours, often excessive filler is introduced to make the colour go further. Because aluminium hydrate is relatively transparent when used as a filler, it can be employed to cheapen a colour, providing bulk quantity but not quality. Sometimes, the raw pigment is mixed with a filler material before it is sold.

In an ideal world, high quality artists' paints are made using only high quality pigments and other materials of a similar bias. As a consequence, the cost of these raw materials may be a factor in the pricing of the end product. For some manufacturers, the problems of maintaining the supply of traditional pigments (e.g. earth pigments, expensive metal-based colours such as cadmiums, cobalts, etc) have led them to re-align their colour ranges to make best use of modern, inexpensive pigments. For example, phthalocyanine blue and phthalocyanine green (also known as phthalo blue/green) are extremely strong pigments in terms of their tinting strength. They can be used to make reasonable imitations of cobalt blue and viridian, two relatively expensive metal-based pigments.

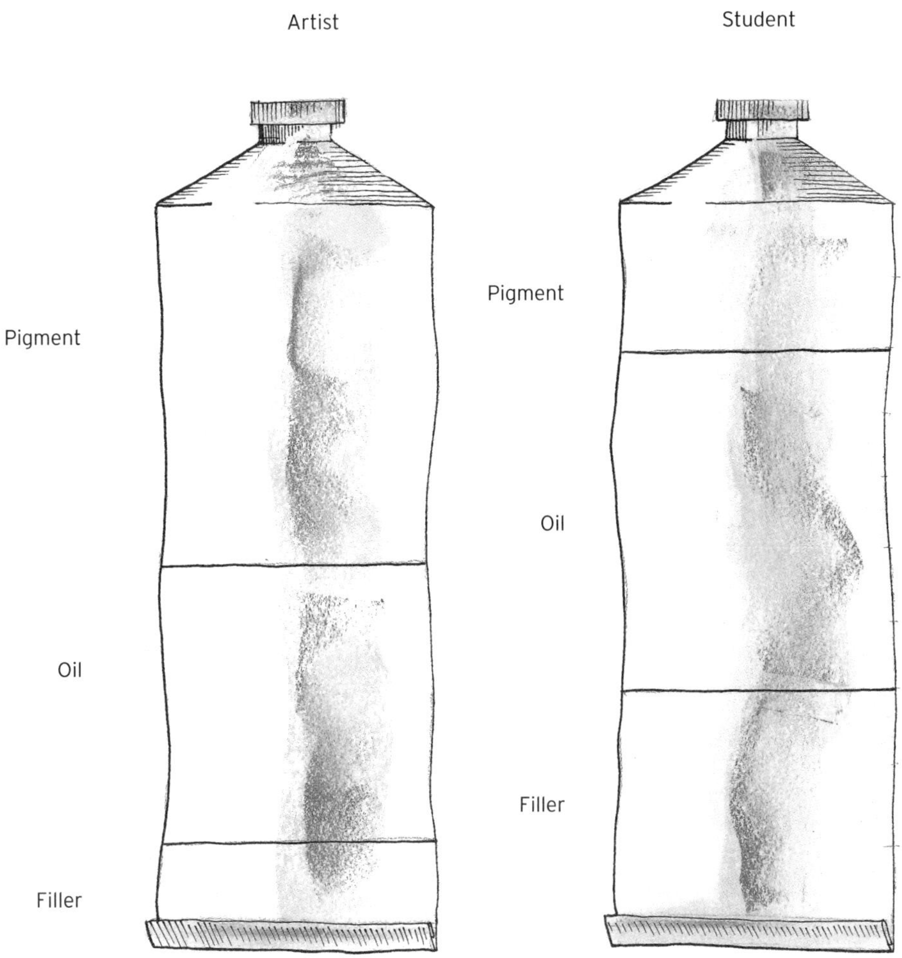

Comparison of Artist and Student Oil Colours

This is especially the case with lower quality oil colours, where labels often refer to "cadmium yellow hue", or "cobalt blue hue". Such colours, referred to with "hue" or "imitation", are matches to the original colour using other pigments. In this way, manufacturers have created a whole palette of "nearly" colours – ones that look a little bit like some traditional colours. These do offer the artist an alternative to high-priced colours, but rather detract from the potentially interesting qualities of the modern pigments that have been used. For example, at full strength, phthalocyanine blue is deep, saturated, extremely intense, almost a blue-black in the mass tone. However, when used to imitate cobalt blue, it is usually admixed with a little ultramarine blue and zinc white, and may include a filler such as aluminium hydrate to reduce its supreme tinting power.

By tradition, artists' oil colours are processed in factory conditions on a special milling machine, referred to as a triple roll mill. This consists of three cylindrical drums, ideally made from granite, which rotate at different speeds and in opposing directions. Prior to processing through the triple roll mill, the raw materials are combined together loosely, in a large vat, where the contents are slowly stirred together. This pre-mixing ensures that all the dry raw ingredients are dispersed into oil before being put through the roll mill. A quantity of colour (the loosely mixed paint paste) is deposited on to the top cylindrical roller; two other rollers are positioned below. The gap between the three milling cylinders is extremely small, perhaps a few millimetres. The rotation of the rollers causes the paint to be forced down between them, finally dropping out into a collection vat positioned below. Each time the paint mix is passed through the rollers, the mixture becomes finer and smoother. In effect, this milling process imitates the action of the glass muller when hand-making oil paint. Each pigment particle becomes coated with oil and any clumping together of dry material is eradicated, so that pigment particles are evenly spread within the paint mixture. After being passed through the rollers perhaps 3-5 times, the paint mixture takes on a regular, buttery consistency and the pigment particles cannot be seen by the naked eye within the oil and other additive ingredients.

It is the case with some brands and for certain colours, that special swelling agents are added to the paint mixture. One of these is a product known as Tixogel, a form of bentonite. Tixogel swells in linseed oil, forming a fat, short paste consistency. The use of Tixogel and similar products is not uncommon in the manufacture of oil colours: it is very useful to be able to create a thick, stable paint consistency by adding a small amount of such an additive to the other raw materials. Another additive used to control the paint paste during manufacturer is aluminium stearate, a metallic soap, which forms a kind of gel when worked with linseed oil. Again, this "gel" formula provides a balanced consistency, counteracting the nature of pigments that do not readily form into a workable painting paste. In cheaper colour ranges, the use of such additives may be more pronounced, so that the consistency of all the colours in the paint range are governed by the use of this gel formula, or by the addition of a swelling agent. A fundamental division can be made between high quality oil colours, (where the use of additives is kept to the bare minimum) and cheaper colour ranges, whose consistency, tinting strength and permanence is controlled (perhaps compromised) by an excessive use of additive material. Within high quality oil colour ranges, the aim is to work with each pigment to provide the optimum realisation of that particular pigment. In this context, the amount of additive material included is carefully controlled, in order to ensure that the quality of the final colour is true to the nature of the pigment used.

In many paint ranges, a number of colours may be based on admixtures of more than one pigment. If two pigments are put through the triple roll mill to make a mixture, that mixture will always be more intimate and therefore colour-resonant than one made on the palette between two colours. In effect, when two pigments are processed through rollers, they are cleaved together, so that the pigment particles mingle together in extremely close contact. This is best seen with mixtures based on whites, especially zinc white. Because zinc white affords a certain transparency to paint films, it can be put with other pigments to make subtle tints, especially with other transparent or semi-transparent pigments. Such mixtures have a degree of brilliance and radiance about them. Indeed, in some paint ranges they are referred to as "radiant" tints.

With reference to colour theory, mixtures of light rays are deemed to be additive mixtures. By contrast, mixtures with coloured particles (i.e. pigments) are designated as being subtractive mixtures. Whenever two or more pigments are mixed together, the result is a subtractive mixture. In real terms, these tend towards dullness, greyness. This is best seen when four or five pigments are combined, especially when opaque white, or other opaque pigments are included in the mixture. This effect is more pronounced when hand-mixing colours on the palette. Nevertheless, it follows that most manufacturers keep mixed colours (using more than one pigment) to a minimum of two or three individual pigments, in order to retain a degree of brilliance and radiance in the paint film.

Oil Paint in Stick Form

A number of brands of oil paint in stick form have recently been introduced to the market. A drying oil is combined with pigment and a blend of waxes, to form a crayon which can be applied to the painting support directly, held in the hand. Some oil sticks are based on a combination of beeswax and synthetic waxes, while others may be based on a beeswax and carnauba (plant) wax. Some oil sticks contain drying agents, so that the tip of the crayon skins over when not in use. However, other brands are available which do not contain drying agents, being affected only by the properties of the pigment used. This type may be more suitable, when intermixing with hand-ground oil colours with comparable drying rates. The wax-oil formulation is designed to be flexible, so that oil sticks can be applied to stretched canvas. In theory, they can be used in conjunction with oil paints, although as mentioned, the drying properties of the chosen brand of oil sticks may be a concern. It may be prudent to remember when mixing with oil colour, that the wax content in the oil stick is soluble in turpentine and white spirit. Oil colour mixtures that include these solvents can disturb adjacent applications of oil stick. Similarly, the application of picture varnishes containing turpentine or white spirit, can disturb dried layers of oil stick.

Building an Oil Painting

Because there are no standards or rules for making an oil painting, it would be unwise to suggest that artists have to follow any particular method in order to achieve the desired image. However, there are a number of concepts, common within oil painting practice, that are held with some trust both by artists and the conservation world. In short, oil paint layers are required to correspond to each other, this includes the connection between the painting ground and support; painting ground and first layer of oil paint; first layer and second, and so on. If one of these layers is inconsistent with the layer to which it connects, it may lead to a weakness or incompatibility within the structure of the painting. For example, if a thin layer of paint is applied over a thick layer, where the thick layer is still wet, upon both layers drying, the top (thin) layer may crack. This is because the thicker layer, as it dries out may change in density and elasticity, and the attached top (thin) layer moves with the thicker one. If the thin layer is so stressed, it may crack or split eventually. Such fine divisions between paint applications may be hard to gauge and control while working. As a consequence, it is advised that certain basic concepts are held on to during the working process, so that paint is applied according to sound technique.

The ideal structure for an oil painting involves a careful consideration of the painting ground and the support on to which it is applied. The ideal surface is a priming ground which equalises the surface of the support. In the case of canvas, this would involve losing the grain or texture of the canvas, so that oil paint layers applied over the painting ground lie down flat and evenly. The choice of priming and its application will alter depending on the nature and texture of the painting support (canvas, panel, etc). In ideal terms, the painting ground is even in its application, equalises the support and has a slightly absorbent surface. This absorbency is a key ingredient in the context of paint technique. For example, if the painting ground (priming) is non-absorbent, oil paint will stay on the surface and over time, will become more likely to shear away (cleave) from the ground. Ideally, the first coat of oil paint needs to absorb slightly into the painting ground, to provide a locked, keyed surface. As a consequence, many brands of acrylic primer on the market today, aim to imitate the nature of traditional semi-absorbent historical painting grounds. For example, products that are sold as "acrylic gesso primer" may be relatively more absorbent than those marked as "acrylic primer". The term "gesso" usually implies that the priming has some absorbency (in the same way that gesso made from chalk and glue is absorbent). However, there are no hard and fast rules relating to such priming and artists need to satisfy themselves that a priming is semi-absorbent prior to overpainting with oil colours. The best way to do this, is to take a teaspoon of artists' quality oil colour and dilute it with one teaspoon of solvent (e.g. turpentine). The thinned oil paint is then applied to the painting ground, using a flat hog varnish brush. Make a number of tests in this manner on to different painting grounds. Ideally, the paint should absorb slightly, leaving the finished paint film slightly matt, but not chalky matt. If the ground is too absorbent, the paint may appear very matt, even underbound and powdery. By contrast, if the painting ground has little or no absorbency, the paint film will stay glossy and show brushmarks, because it has not been allowed to sink slightly into the painting ground.

A perfect ground for oil painting, is to apply one coat of egg tempera over a traditional chalk-glue gesso priming. On to this surface, oil paint slightly absorbs, forming a solid bond between the oil paint and tempera layer. Because underpainting in tempera is a technique from the past and often a nuisance, or irrelevant to modern artists, few artists today bother with such a formula. However, for the sake of comparison, if one has time, it may be a good idea to try this method once. In practical terms, if the modern (e.g. "acrylic gesso") painting ground has the desired degree of absorbency, then oil paint layers can be successfully applied in an integrated manner.

If the first coat of oil paint is applied to the painting ground in a slightly dilute form (mixed down with a solvent such as turpentine), subsequent paint layers may contain less solvent. By tradition, one works from lean to fat paint. This concept, "fat over lean" relates to the oil, or oil-medium content within the paint. For example, the first layer is usually diluted with a solvent. This corresponds to a "lean" layer of oil paint, in that it is both thin and dilute. Consequently, this layer dries with a relatively matt finish, especially when applied to a gently absorbent ground. Whenever solvent is added to neat oil paint, it takes away some of the natural sheen/gloss of oil colour. In effect, the oil content is diluted, controlled in such a way as to lose its greasiness, its glossy sheen. In the first paint layer, this lack of gloss is an advantage: it means that the next coat has a slightly matt surface to grip to and matt coats provide better adhesion than glossy coats. Linseed oil as a binder is a poor adhesive, when layers are gently laid down on to each other they will form a consistent whole. However, if a thinned, dilute layer of oil paint is applied on to a fatter, glossier layer (without dilution), there is a discrepancy between one layer and another in terms of its adhesion. Consequently, it is advised to work from lean (dilute, thin) layers up to fatter (oil rich, oil-medium rich) layers. Each time a layer with progressively more oil or oil-medium is applied over a previous layer containing less oil a degree of stability is imparted into the paint film.

In practice, this works best if one keeps to the following procedure of layering:

1. Oil paint over ground layer: dilute with solvent 1:1.
2. Neat oil paint, without dilution.
3. Neat oil paint, plus 10% oil-medium (e.g. dammar/stand oil based medium).

In combination with this procedure, colours that are naturally fast drying, such as lead white or raw umber can be used in the first layers of oil paint. These layers will dry quickly, providing a sound foundation over which further coats can be applied. Where slow drying colours are used, these need to be limited to top coats, or combined with a paint medium that has a siccative (drying) effect on the paint layer.

Most problems occur when the first layers are too dilute, or when the first layer takes too long to dry and is applied too thickly. If the first layer is extremely dilute, it can become underbound, so that the paint film is actually powdery on the surface. This may happen if the painting ground is too absorbent, or if the paint film is too strongly diluted. To counter this, before painting, make a series of test paintings on to different grounds, using the same oil paint diluted with different amounts of solvent and wait to see how each one dries, before proceeding.

The problem of the first layer being too thick is easily countered, by astute dilution with solvent. Each colour may behave differently, according to its consistency and how it brushes out. Some oil paints are very stiff and require some manipulation prior to application. Others are ready to use from the tube and dilute readily. In truth, both situations may occur even within the same paint range, so one has to be prepared to manipulate the paint at all times. In any case, it is better practice to administer some control over the paint mixture before application to the painting, rather than applying paint and then trying to re-work it on the painting surface.

The table of drying rates of pigments (see pages 301-304) gives an indication of the relative drying times of pigments ground in oil. From this table it can be understood that faster drying colours need to be employed in the first layers of the painting, so that once dry, they can be safely overpainted without leading to cracking or splitting of the paint film. However, many modern oil paint ranges dry within a specific time period. The manufacturer may have added drying agent to all colours, so that they possess a similar drying time ratio. The only way to establish this, is to make some test paint-outs and to record how long they take to dry. Even when drying agent has been added to a paint, some caution is required in terms of the application of colour. True, all colours may dry in a specific time period (e.g. 7 days), but this drying time will relate to oil paint applied in relatively thin, or rather "flat" layers. Paint applied in fat, thick layers will always take longer to dry and this needs to be borne in mind at all times. Also, thicker passages of paint will dry on the surface before they dry through at the core. Consequently, pigments that have no drying effect on the oils they are ground with (e.g. alizarin crimson) may stay wet and squidgy under the surface for a considerable time. It is important in these instances not to overpaint such fat layers with faster drying colours.

Upon drying thoroughly, linseed oil changes to form linoxin, a hard, dry, but still flexible film. While drying, the oil remains susceptible to disturbance by solvent action. This is most commonly seen when one (undried) layer is overpainted with a solvent-rich layer, perhaps where the brush used in this process somehow agitates the previous paint layer, allowing solvent to re-activate it. This is seen by the eye as a leaking of colour from one layer to the next. This tends to happen when one layer is part-dried or seemingly dried but below the core is still slightly wet.

To counter this, artists can choose two options:

1. Wait for each paint layer to dry before proceeding.
2. Only work wet into wet oil paint "*alla-prima*" (at the first).

Option 1 conforms to the perfect model of an oil painting, where each layer is allowed to dry out before overpainting. This works well when working in thin, flat and even layers, especially where a reliable oil paint medium is added progressively into each layer. Some oil paint mediums that contain a drying agent can be particularly useful in this context. For example, alkyd resin based mediums, containing a percentage of drying agent, make excellent fast-drying paint mediums. Alkyd resins tend to give flat, even, self-levelling paint films and can also control the relative drying time of each paint layer. Once each thin layer of paint alkyd medium is dry, it can be overpainted successfully. Because the drying time is short (perhaps 3-4 hours), it is possible to work quickly, building up thin, even layers.

Option 2 is slightly more hit and miss, but basically affords the possibility to make paintings in one working session which can involve different thicknesses and drying times, without subsequent defects such as cracks or splits within the paint film(s). When paint is applied *alla prima*, in theory all colours join together and dry together: they are locked together and work with each other. However, if further layers are overpainted, perhaps after one or two days, there will be a discrepancy between the first mass of paint and subsequent ones. *Alla prima* painting refers to paintings that are made at one sitting. This is an ideal solution for portrait painting, where paint is applied during a working day of perhaps 6-7 hours. Similarly, to the landscape artist, working outdoors, colour can be applied quickly and freely, without fear of technical problems later. However, if an *alla prima* sketch or study is then worked over at a later stage, there may be a lack of consistency between the paint applied *alla prima* and that applied later. A variation on this technique, is to use hand-ground oil paints, where all pigments have been prepared with poppy oil, which takes longer than linseed oil to dry off. This provides a longer open working time to finish the painting and allows one to come back to the painting for a series of days or sessions, rather than having to complete the painting in one session. Be wary however, of manufactured oil colours prepared with poppy or other slow drying oils such as safflower. Often the paint has a drying agent included and the oil has been used more for its pale colour than its slow drying properties.

Another solution to the drying time question, is to underpaint with colours based on linseed oil and then work on later layers using colours based on poppy oil: in this way, the final layers will take longer to dry out than the underpainting.

Upon complete drying, oil paint films close over and prevent oxygen from entering the paint layer. Once completely dry, it is often suggested that oil paintings be given a coat of varnish, which acts as a protective layer, but this may also change the sheen appearance of the paint film.

The application of varnishes is fraught with problems and it is suggested that instead of applying varnish to oil paintings, artists instead consider using a paint medium during the painting process, which contains a resinous component. This will impart some gloss and also a degree of protection to the final paint layers. In the context of the ideal painting, such oil paint mediums are applied in small concentrations (about 10%) to the paint paste. This is enough to impart a degree of change in sheen appearance, perhaps also a little flexibility to the paint layer and to harmonise the visual impact of the paint layer.

Drying Rates of Oil Colours

Some pigments (e.g. raw umber) act upon the drying oils in which they are ground, speeding up the drying process. Conversely, other pigments (e.g. zinc white) have no drying action whatsoever. To accommodate these extremes, paint manufacturers may add small amounts of drying agents to paint formulae, so that all their colours are touch dry within a certain period.

Other colourmakers prefer to adhere to the characteristics of the pigments used, adding no drying agents and allowing the artist to decide when to apply certain colours and introduce drying mediums during painting. The manner in which oil colours dry governs their application. Oil paint can be applied in thin layers: each layer needs to dry out before subsequent ones are applied unless the painting is made *alla prima*. When oil colour is applied over previously layers that are still drying, there is a danger that the top coat will sink. This sinking process can continue for months or years after application - oil paintings can take up to 100 years (and longer, depending on the thickness of application) to dry thoroughly. Similarly, fast drying colours applied over slow drying colours may take months or years to show defects. To counter these problems, an understanding of the drying effect of the pigments used in oil painting is useful. Sound practice is to begin painting with lean colours (i.e. oil paints with a low oil content), which are fast drying. Avoid the use of 'fatty' mediums during underpainting. Raw umber and lead white linseed oil colours dry quickly, they also have a catalytic effect on other colours. Underpainting can be carried out by admixing either of these two colours with other fast drying oil colours. The following table of drying rates refers primarily to the characteristic of the pigment when ground in linseed oil only, rather than prepared oil colours. A manufacturer may add drying agents and other additives to the formulae, or introduce slower drying oils in some cases, to obtain a paint range with appealing drying qualities.

COMPARATIVE DRYING RATES OF OIL COLOURS

FAST (ideal for underpainting, or admixtures in underpainting)

Chrome yellow

Naples yellow (genuine)

Raw umber

Burnt umber

Lead white

Prussian blue

FAST TO MEDIUM

Manganese blue

Cobalt turquoise

Cobalt violet deep

Manganese violet

Cobalt violet light

Cobalt green

Cobalt bottle green (dark)

Manganese black

Cobalt blue*

Chrome oxide

Burnt sienna

Raw sienna

Spinel black

Spinel phase pigments

Priderit yellow

* Pigments containing compounds of cobalt, manganese (raw umber) and lead are good driers in oil. However, when a colour is prepared with a slow drying oil, as can be the case with cobalt blue (often ground in poppy oil), the drying effect is not as apparent. Whites and blue pigments are often ground in pale, less yellowing oils such as poppy, safflower and sunflower oils.

MEDIUM

Barium lemon yellow

Mars colours

Transparent iron-oxides

MEDIUM TO SLOW

Green earth

Yellow ochre

Ultramarine blue

Phthalocyanine blue

Phthalocyanine green

Quinacridones

Cerulean blue

Viridian

SLOW

Cobalt yellow

Alizarin crimson

Titanium white

Hansa yellow

Cadmium yellow

Nickel titanium yellow

Irgazin yellow

Paliotol yellow

Indian yellow (imitation)

Hostaperm orange

Isoindoline orange

Titanium orange

Studio red

Permanent red/Permanent carmine

Scarlet red

Paliogen maroon

Indanthrone blue

Alizarin violet

Dioxazine violet

Cadmium green

Quindo green gold

SLOW - VERY SLOW

Zinc white

Lithopone

Cadmium red

Natural madder

Vermilion

Lamp black

Vine black

Ivory black

Oil Painting Whites

Most manufacturers sell more white than any other colour, especially in the case of oil paint. The use of white in colour mixtures is very common among artists, yet many have little understanding of the merits of each white and why one should be used as opposed to another.

A simple test is to take titanium, zinc and lead white and mix a small quantity of each, in turn, with ultramarine blue. The relative transparency/opacity of each white is then easily understood. Keep this colour mix sample in the studio as a point of reference.

Titanium White

Despite only being available to artists since the late 1920s, titanium white is commonly used and accepted. It is a strong true white, with incredible brilliance, when used alone. However, when other colours are admixed with titanium white, they tend to become muddy, dead in appearance. This deadening effect is due to the fact that titanium white is an intense, covering (hiding) pigment. It tends to take over in colour mixtures, being dominant and devaluing the subtleties of other colours. This is especially so with transparent colours, which all but disappear when mixed with it.

Used alone, however, titanium white affords brilliant reflectance. It is the ideal white for use in painting grounds, where it provides the optimum bright white background, upon which light rays refract strongly. When thin veils of transparent colours are overpainted on primings made with titanium white, light rays pass through the transparent applied colour and hit the bright white ground. The light rays are then rebounded back through the transparent applied colour to the eye, affording maximum luminosity to the perceived colour of the paint layer.

Titanium white, when ground with linseed oil forms a relatively brittle paint film, especially so when applied thickly.

Zinc White

By contrast to titanium white, zinc white is semi-opaque: it has a degree of transparency. As such, when admixed with other colours, it tends to make subtle half-tints, pastel shades, where the original colour has a great presence. This is especially so with transparent pigments, whose delicate nuances of hue remain intact when carefully combined with zinc white. It has a slightly bluish tinge, which may give a certain coldness when used alone, or when mixed with pale colours.

Zinc white, when ground with linseed oil forms a relatively brittle paint film, especially when applied thickly, where the paint film may form characteristic "slash" cracks upon drying. In any case, zinc white is best used in thinner applications, to make subtle glazes with other colours.

Lead White

If zinc and titanium whites form relatively brittle paint films, by contrast, lead white provides more flexible films, even when applied with a slight impasto (perhaps up to 1cm thick). Lead white has a warm tinge when ground in linseed oil, which can be helpful when mixing with other colours to make half-tints. Although not as transparent in nature as zinc white, lead white does make acceptable admixtures with other pigments. Also, because it dries quickly in linseed oil, lead white can act as a carrier for slow drying colours. If one makes a series of half-tints based on lead white (e.g. with lamp black, indanthrene blue, cadmium yellow, cadmium red, etc), those half-tints will dry off quickly (perhaps 1 day for a thin coat). This makes lead white ideal as an underpainting white, where all colours mixed with it will take on its characteristic. The paste consistency of lead white oil paint is also desirable: it is a soft, buttery paste, which is especially useful for admixing with transparent colours that are oil-rich (e.g. green earth), to control their paste-consistency. Lead white is especially prized among portrait painters, where a good paste quality, quick drying time and kind harmonious strength with other colours is required. It can be seen in historical paintings that areas of paint that contain lead white tend to contract, or shrivel, less than areas that do not contain it. This is especially so in areas of impasto: where these parts are modelled with lead white, there is little change in the shape or form of the paint film. By contrast, areas of thick paint, which are made just with colour, may have changed shape and form dramatically.

Despite its toxicity, lead white is still asked for by artists and remains a crucial component colour in the traditional painting palette.

When lead white is ground with linseed oil, it is often referred to as underpainting, or foundation white. In linseed oil it dries quickly: as a consequence it is sometimes used for the priming ground, or to make a tinted ground with another colour, which will be fast drying.

The term "flake white" is also often used in connection with lead white. Flake white is the name most often used when lead and zinc white are mixed together.

Lead white may darken on exposure to sulphurous compounds in the atmosphere. While this was a common problem in the 19th century and early 20th century, due to the amount of coal fires being used in cities, today this is less of a problem. To protect oil paintings from exposure to sulphurous fumes, paintings were often varnished so that the paint film was closed off from the environment. This may partially explain a neurosis among artists that all paintings have to be varnished upon completion. The opposite may be more true today: because sulphurous compounds in the air are now minimal in Western Europe, paint films need not be so comprehensively protected from the immediate environment.

In accordance with EU law, lead white is now sold according to certain restrictions, which are liable to change with time. While at present this pigment is still available to artists, this is a situation that may change. Because of its historical importance, artists wish to continue to use lead white: it is a pigment that possesses many preferred qualities and remains an integral part of many artists' palettes.

The Oil Painting Palette Explained

The genesis of the painting palette is worth some consideration prior to beginning work. The organisation of colours on to the palette is a matter of some importance. Prior to the invention of the collapsible metal tube in the 1840s, artists were required to pre-mix and lay out the colours required for each painting session. In these circumstances, the exact layout and order of preference for each colour was important. For example, core colours could be laid out around the top edge of the palette, while half-tints and special mixtures might be laid along the bottom edge. A study of artists' palettes through the ages would reveal a myriad of possibilities for arrangement. Despite this, most artists laid out their colours according to the demands of the subject. For example, portrait painters would be required to have ready-mixed flesh tints to hand once the painting session began. In this way, no time would be wasted adjusting colours while the sitter was present in the studio. In accordance with this, many artists adopted a rationalised approach to the layout of their colours: perhaps 4-5 pale flesh tints, followed by a similar series of darker tints, some tints for highlights and so on. The crucial element here is that prior to painting, the artist would have all these tints pre-mixed and they would be placed at strategic points within the palette, rather like a piano keyboard.

For the modern artist, the situation is different: modern tube colours can be readily squeezed out as required. However, most colour ranges feature very few pre-mixed half-tints, so before working, the raw, neat colour requires some manipulation (e.g. with white) prior to painting. Some facets of previous times remain within paint ranges. For example, most ranges feature a "flesh tint", yet the exact shade of this flesh tint will be different from brand to brand. In practice, rather than relying on the idea of a colour as governed by the paint factory, the artist is required to take the neat pure colour and make mixtures to afford the colours required.

The main difference is that in previous times, the artist would prepare the colours from the raw materials, or, if lucky an apprentice would do this task. As a consequence, the artist made enough paint for that painting session - this could entail making a composite colour, which included more than one pigment, oil and also a paint medium. In this system, all the raw materials are combined at the beginning, rather than is the practice of today, where tube colours are put with each other, then admixed with a paint medium. The main practical differences here seem to be the resonance of the mixed colour: it is always better to hand-grind pigments together with oil, rather than mix two tube colours together. One can make a truer, more intimate mixture using the former technique. Also, one preserves the exact nature of an individual pigment. With modern paints, the "colour" may in fact contain more than one pigment, plus filler/additive material.

The palette is by tradition a kidney-shaped or rectangular shaped piece of wood, normally a hardwood such as mahogany. Some palettes were weighted at one edge, so that when standing to paint, they could be easily held. Traditionally, palettes have a thumb hole in their structure so that they can be held, supported by the forearm and hand, against the body of the artist. Modern wooden palettes are often simply varnished plywood, dyed to imitate the appearance of harder woods. In practice the raw wood should be treated with linseed oil, so that it becomes non-absorbent. This involves applying perhaps 3-4 coats of oil, rubbed into the surface to gradually reduce its absorbency.

The dark colour of the wood may be a disadvantage to modern artists, who tend to work on to bright white grounds, rather than the dull toned grounds of the past. For this reason and also for reasons of practicality, it may be more relevant to the modern artist to use a sheet of glass as a palette. The glass sheet or plate needs to have sanded edges, so that there is no risk of cuts to the hands. It is placed on to a worktop, with a sandwich of white paper between the glass and the work surface. This imitates the white ground of the painting support, thereby allowing colour mixtures to approximate how they will look when applied on to the painting.

Simple Palette Suggestion for Portrait Painting

The following colours need to be hand-ground and laid out in the following sequence:

Lead white+yellow ochre; lead white+vine black (make a very pale grey, almost white); lead white+vermilion (make 3 tints of varying strength); pure vermilion; yellow ochre+vine black+lead white; yellow ochre+vine black; burnt sienna; vine black; vermilion+vine black+lead white (make 2 tints); vine black+lead white (mid grey); lead white+naples yellow (very pale yellow).

This palette accords to late 18th-century portrait palettes of the English school.

Simple Palette Suggestion for Landscape Painting

Lead white (set to one side, for making admixtures and half-tints); zinc white (set to one side, for making admixtures and half-tints, especially with transparent colours); viridian; yellow ochre; orange ochre; raw sienna; indian red; burnt sienna; ivory black; ultramarine blue; cobalt blue; cadmium yellow.

This palette accords to late 19th-century French landscape palettes.

Oil Paint Mediums

The use of oil painting mediums is crucial to the realisation of the image by the artist. The simplest way to modify a paint film is to dilute it with a solvent such as turpentine. This will allow the paint to brush out freely and create more transparency within the paint film. However, dilutions of oil paint that rely on solvent alone tend to leave the dried paint film less glossy and, in the worst cases, underbound. Over dilution of paint with solvent can cause the paint film to break down and become too matt, underbound and liable to "chalk" if rubbed, ultimately leading to loss of the paint film in the most extreme circumstances.

The key reason to add oil paint medium to oil colour, is to retain the inherent sheen of oil colour when diluting or thinning the paint so that it can be spread out over a large area, for example, when glazing.

Manufactured oil colours are formulated to give a specific finish when applied undiluted. The exact appearance of the dried paint film will differ from one manufacturer to another. Some oil paints are made to be oil-rich, others have a more matt finish. It may therefore be advisable to incorporate a paint medium into the painting process, to modify the final appearance of the applied paint film.

In general, paint mediums are employed to maintain the original finish of the paint film, or to change the appearance of the paint film. The most common desire among artists is to achieve a high gloss finish, regardless of the dilution of the paint. In such cases, a small addition of a glossy paint medium (e.g. dammar varnish with stand oil), perhaps 10% to the amount of oil paint present, is sufficient. This creates a glossy sheen when applied undiluted, but retains gloss, even when the mixture of oil paint plus medium is subsequently diluted with a solvent. In practice, the oil paint medium retains a glossy structure, regardless of dilution. In this manner, a relatively thick formulation of the oil paint medium can be added in small amounts to the oil colour, then subsequently diluted with a solvent to the thickness/thinness required.

Problems with paint mediums tend to arise when too much medium is added – so the inclusion of paint medium is best done in moderation. If for example, 50% paint medium is added to oil colour, then the resultant paint film has less to do with oil paint than with the properties of the medium used.

Oil paint mediums can be composed of fusions of drying vegetable oils with dissolved tree resins, but may also be derived from synthetic resins, such as alkyd resin. It would be useful to understand the relative properties of these raw materials before opting to use mediums based on them.

Oils and Modified Oils

Modern Stand Oil

A relatively non-yellowing form of linseed oil. Stand oil is linseed oil that has been thickened by heating in a vacuum. This process causes partial polymerisation of the oil, which in turn means that it does not yellow (darken) to the same extent as regular cold-pressed or refined linseed oil. For this reason it can be used as an addition to oil colours, without causing excessive darkening within the oil paint film. Stand oil is also self-levelling (does not show brush marks) and highly elastic when compared to regular linseed oils.

Sun-Thickened Linseed Oil

By exposure to air and strong sunlight, linseed oil can be thickened to produce a highly viscous form of oil, similar in consistency to modern stand oil. Sun-thickened linseed oil is self-levelling (does not show brush marks), very glossy and does not yellow (darken) with age when compared to regular linseed oil.

Sun-Bleached Linseed Oil (Historic Stand Oil)

Oil that is left to "stand" in strong sunlight for 3-4 weeks (without exposure to air) takes on a pale colour, which does not yellow (darken) with age when compared to regular linseed oil.

Cold-Pressed Linseed Oil

Reduces the effect of brush marks (self-levelling) when added to oil colours, but has a strong golden yellow colour, which may be noticeable when used with pale colours and whites.

Refined Linseed Oil

When added to regular oil colour, refined linseed oil will darken progressively over time and also show brushmarks.

Alkyd Resin

When acid and alcohol are combined to create an ester, a material known as alkyd resin is formed. In order to create a paint binder, this ester is modified with an addition of soya bean oil, (or other vegetable drying oils), to impart flexibility. The ratio of ester to oil may be in the region 40:60, but this will vary according to the type of product and its end use. Alkyd resins dry through oxidisation, in a process similar to that of drying vegetable oils such as linseed oil. However, with alkyd resin, the drying time is usually shorter, owing to the particular film-forming properties of the resin. Additions of drying agent may also be incorporated into alkyd resin binders, to give very quick drying properties.

Alkyd resins are widely employed in the manufacture of industrial and decorating paints, where their thixotropic properties and fast drying characteristics are exploited. Alkyd-based paints were introduced during the 1950s and today almost completely replace oil as the chief binder in industrial and decorating paints. Some manufacturers of artists' colours offer lines of paint using alkyd resin as a binder. These paints tend to dry quickly and as such have been successfully used for quick-drying underpainting. Care must be taken in such applications that the alkyd paint is thinned a little with solvent so that the dried paint film is slightly matt (i.e. if undiluted, the dried glossy paint film may offer a poor surface for subsequent layers of oil colour to adhere to). Some special colours, such as the pearlescent pigments and metal-based pigments may be presented in paint ranges as being milled in alkyd resin. Such formulations help to provide a more stable paint consistency, although they will tend to dry much more quickly (perhaps in only a few hours) than regular oil-based paints. Industrial or decorating alkyd paints often include a large amount of filler material which tends to make the dried paint film rather brittle, especially after prolonged drying (six months or more). As a consequence, industrial grades of alkyd resin and alkyd paints may not be suitable for working on to flexible supports. Similarly, these paints may not perform well over time on to rigid supports, although it tends to be the case that industrial/decorating alkyd paints may show defects in terms of colour (i.e. the pigments used are not lightfast), rather than deterioration of the paint film. Some alkyd paints, which are formulated for use on ships, may be used on metal panels, such as honeycomb aluminium panel. Reassurances in relation to pigment content may be advisable in the case of such applications. It may be preferable to prepare dry pigment into an appropriate alkyd resin binder when working on to metal panel supports, where the permanence of the chosen pigment can be determined by the artist.

Alkyd resins have a warm yellow-orange colour. They can be formulated to create a flowing, self-levelling paint film when added to oil colours. In most manufactured paint mediums, alkyd resin has been treated with a drying agent, so that each paint film mixed with it will dry within a few hours, allowing multiple coats to be applied quickly. The colour of alkyd resin may progressively darken, especially with pale colours and whites, and especially if too much alkyd resin (i.e. more than 10-15%) is added to oil colour. Alkyd resins are presented in the form of free-flowing liquids, syrup consistency and also as gels. They share a property referred to as being "thixotropic": this refers to the fact that the alkyd is static before manipulation. Once the alkyd resin is agitated with a brush or painting knife, the resin begins to flow, enabling it to be spread out over a wide area easily. Alkyd resins can be reduced in consistency by the addition of a solvent (e.g. turpentine, white spirit, odourless thinner) to create thinner, finer films. Alkyd resins remain flexible when applied as thinish films but may become more inflexible when applied thickly. Those formulated as a gel are intended to be mixed with the desired quantity of oil colour and then applied flat to form a thinner, even paint film. If the alkyd is applied as an impasto gel, it will dry with a degree of wrinkling or shrivelling. In practice, it dries quickly on the surface but remains squidgy underneath and is therefore unstable. Alkyd gels applied in this fashion may also remain temperature sensitive. For example, thick alkyd gels appear to regain some stickiness in extremely hot weather.

Some manufacturers offer alkyd gels that have an inclusion of silica. This helps to maintain the structure of the gel, effectively allowing it to be applied with some impasto (perhaps 5-10mm thickness) without undue shrinkage or shrivelling upon drying. Similarly, some manufacturers suggest using additions of synthetic wax (microcrystalline wax) to help maintain impasto. It is advised to refer to individual manufacturers' recommendations in this respect.

Waxes

Beeswax

The most flexible of all the natural waxes, beeswax is offered in two forms:

- raw beeswax, yellow beeswax
- refined beeswax, bleached beeswax

The refined product has been cleaned and has a white colour. It is normally supplied in small pellets which are easy to melt, or dissolve in solvent. Over time, the pale colour of refined beeswax reverts back to yellow. The raw, yellow beeswax is slightly more flexible than the refined product, but the dark yellow colour may compromise mixtures involving pale colours and white. Yellow beeswax is also supplied in small pellet form or in the form of larger, raw lumps.

Beeswax is easily dissolved to a soft paste by leaving to steep in rectified turpentine as follows:

Beeswax pellets	1 part
Rectified turpentine	3 parts

Leave in an air-tight container for 3-4 days, stir occasionally until free from lumps, forming a soft gel paste, similar in consistency to Vaseline. Alternatively, beeswax can be melted under heat, then while still warm, added into oil paint mediums (see recipes).

Beeswax will darken over time. It remains temperature sensitive, indefinitely. If too much beeswax is added to oil colour, the whole paint film will take on this characteristic. As with all paint medium additives, wax is added sparingly.

Carnauba Wax

This plant wax is often used in paint mediums to create hardness within a paint film. Carnauba wax is offered in natural (grey colour) or refined (yellow) form. It is normally melted then added in very small quantities (perhaps 5%) to paint mediums that already contain a beeswax element. This small addition is enough to impart toughness to the dried paint film. The dried film may also be buffed with a soft cloth to a polish. It is not flexible enough to use on to stretched canvas but forms a tough, durable film on to panels. Fusions of beeswax with carnauba wax are used when making oil paint in stick form. Usually such sticks also include stand oil as the binding agent. This formulation gives a thick, waxy stick of colour, which can be freely applied to any suitable oil painting support but especially to rigid supports which provide a degree of physical support to the applied stroke of oil stick.

Synthetic Wax

Microcrystalline waxes tend to be more brittle than natural waxes, despite their pale colour. They are dissolved in white spirit/odourless thinner, in a similar fashion to natural beeswax. Small additions of this wax may be possible when oil painting on to rigid supports, although it is far too brittle for use with stretched canvas.

Other synthetic waxes, such as paraffin wax are even less desirable because they are even more brittle and possess a very low melt point.

Natural Resins

Many types of tree, especially coniferous ones yield sticky resinous liquids that, when hardened form into "resin" material. When such resins are immersed into the appropriate solvent, they form solutions, which provide glassy, transparent films and are commonly employed as varnishes, or as the varnish component of a paint medium. In truth, many recipes for varnishes and painting mediums are based on fusions of different resins, in association with drying vegetable oils. The reliability and appropriate use of such varnishes and painting mediums has been called into question, especially in the last 30-40 years. However, there is still a demand from artists to use traditional recipes for varnishes and painting mediums and for this reason, it is worth considering the working properties and characteristics of historically important resins and other raw materials which have been used in oil paint technique.

Resins are often used to impart glossiness to paint films: by careful dilution and admixture with oils, etc, the exact gloss and depth of the paint film coating can be adjusted as required. In general terms, wherever a resin is employed in a paint medium recipe, its relative brittleness (lack of flexibility) is countered by the addition of a quantity of drying vegetable oil, such as linseed stand oil. This fusion between resin and oil affords the combined product with a degree of flexibility and a change in the gloss/colour saturation of the final paint film. Resins, dissolved in the appropriate solvent alone, when added to oil paint, would tend to give rather brittle paint films.

In the case of oil painting, most of these resins are employed after they have been solved into turpentine and mixed with vegetable oils, so that they form oil resin mediums. By contrast, some of the resins may be dissolved into alcohol. These alcohol-based varnishes (or "spirit varnishes") cannot be admixed with oil paints, because the alcohol prevents dilution/admixture with oil-based material. In historical paint technique, sometimes alcohol-based varnishes have been used as isolating coats between layers of oil-based paint. Such coats form a barrier between oil paint layers. Alcohol will not disturb oil paint layers, nor will oil paint layers applied on to dried alcohol-based varnish disturb the varnish layer. The turpentine used to dilute oil paint films will not redissolve dried alcohol-based varnishes. In theory, this sounds like an excellent system of isolating one area of dried oil paint from another. In practice, alcohol-based varnishes tend to be very brittle and prone to cracking (e.g. sandarac, shellac). As a consequence, they form a weak link in the structure of the painting and should be avoided.

Dammar

Dammar is one of the softest tree resins used in paint media. It has a pale, almost white colour, is sold in small lumps and is usually dusty on the surface but breaks to reveal a translucent core. Dammar dissolves wholly in turpentine to form a pale, star-coloured varnish. In this form it can be mixed, without any heat, with drying vegetable oils and is especially suited to admixture with stand oil, where it forms an excellent, glossy and relatively flexible paint medium.

Mastic

Tree resin from Chios, a Greek island (but also from other sources in Greece and North Africa) derived from a species of pistaccio. The bark is incised in springtime and the resultant sap collects into tiny beads and then hardens. These characteristic hardened "tears" of pale yellow mastic resin are then harvested in late summer. Mastic readily dissolves into alcohol. With turpentine and spike lavender oil the resin dissolves readily when placed in a warm water bath at the beginning of the solving process. Subsequent stirring is also advised to give a quick-forming resin solution. Mastic is a soft resin with some elasticity. While in solution and mixed with other resins, it aids the adhesion of other resins to the support.

Mastic has been employed in many historical paint mediums, usually cooked with a drying oil. For example, the dry resin is heated until molten; warmed linseed oil is then added to the molten resin and the two are combined over heat to form a unified mixture. The end result is a thick syrup, slightly cloudy and golden yellow in appearance. When a small amount of this concoction is added to oil paint (about 10% medium to paint), the resultant paint film is glossy and enamel-like. In some cases, a drying agent would be added to the oil, to increase the speed of drying. This drying agent may have been based on a metal salt, such as cobalt siccative or manganese drier, or could be the result of having steeped a lead-rich pigment in the oil. For example, if massicot (lead mono-oxide) is left to steep, covered with linseed oil, for a period of 2-3 weeks, it imparts a drying action into the oil. The liquid oil is filtered from the pigment and only the clear oil is used in the manufacture of the paint medium. Because such mixtures involve the use of toxic, lead-based raw materials, they have all but disappeared from paint material catalogues as prepared mediums. However, the raw materials are still offered by some specialist companies and as such, it is important to mention their existence.

Sandarac

Derived from the sap of a variety of pine found in North Africa, especially Morocco, sandarac is a pale, straw coloured resin, formed in the shape of long droplets. The sap is harvested from the tree bark by incision, the hardened droplets are later gathered. The resin fractures easily and usually has a slightly dusty, grainy powder surface. Sandarac can be solved into alcohol completely to make a spirit (alcohol) varnish which is softer (less friable) than shellac. Such alcohol-based varnishes have been employed in oil painting as isolating coats between layers of oil paint.

It can also be partially solved into warm turpentine (the residue must be filtered) but will dissolve completely into spike lavender oil, allowing it to be used with various drying vegetable oils. Whenever spike lavender oil has been used in oil paint media, take great care! Spike lavender oil has a solvent action when applied on to dried oil paint: it may act like a paint stripper, dislodging previous layers, percolating into them and making them soft or sticky. As a consequence, the use of spike lavender oil (and lavender oil) is perhaps less than wise. It may be admissible in a final paint layer, where the previous layers have completely dried. Sandarac was used in the past as a final varnish coating, because it has a slightly paler, clearer finish than shellac. Its relative inflexibility makes it more suitable as a varnish coating for rigid supports than flexible ones. It may be used as a final varnish for tempera, where it will deepen and saturate colour values, without causing excessive darkening or yellowing of the finished paint film appearance.

By contrast to mastic, sandarac is slightly harder (more brittle) as a varnish coating.

Colophony

Where pine trees are used for turpentine production, colophony is the term used to describe the solid residue left behind when turpentine is distilled. This resin has a very high acid content and is extremely brittle. When incorporated into oil paint mediums or varnishes, it tends to lead to cracking or splintering. As a consequence it is advised not to use colophony at all for permanent oil paint techniques. Colophony dissolves readily into turpentine but also with alcohol.

Copal

A family of tree resins derived from fossilised, or partially fossilised plant material. Copals are hard and give glossy coatings. "Congo Copal" is the most highly desired of this resin group, dug from fossilised trees, typically lying beneath swamps. The difficulties of extraction, coupled with the fact that such resins are no longer required by industry (where modern alkyd resins are now used) mean that fossilised copal resins are now hard to find on the market. In order to put copal into solution, it is first "run", by heating until it melts and forms a solution. This hot bath of resin can be fused with linseed oil, or other drying oils, to make a thick syrup. The mixture can be diluted with turpentine to the desired consistency.

Copal oil mediums, based on a heated fusion of congo copal resin with linseed oil, were previously used in oil paint technique, to give a very glossy, enamel-like finish to paint films. When a small amount, perhaps 10% is added to oil paint, the resultant mixture is shiny and transparent. Such mixtures were employed to a great extent during the 19th century, especially in England. The defect of copal in oil paint mediums is that it forms a hard but brittle film. It also darkens excessively, changing pale colours to an orange-brown glow over time. Some paint manufacturers continue to offer copal-based mediums, despite these known drawbacks. Such mediums may typically be fusions of copal with thickened linseed oil (modern stand oil), in the form of a thickish syrup, which can be thinned with turpentine as required, or even a gel formula "Megilp".

Other forms of copal are often mentioned but are not suitable in oil paint technique: "Kauri Copal" is a partially fossilised resin from New Zealand, which is soluble in alcohol only; "Manila Copal", confusingly, is not from fossilised resin. It derives from a type of conifer native to Manila and actually imparts a softish varnish film when solved into alcohol to make a spirit varnish.

Amber

Another type of fossil resin, amber is collected from open pits or from shore deposits in the Baltic States, where it is often washed up along the coastline. Amber is a solid resin, and extremely hard and glassy. As a consequence, it is very difficult to form into a solution. It melts at 290°C and in this state can be solved into linseed oil to form a permanent liquid varnish. Because of the very high temperature involved, the utensils used in manufacture are likely to be unusable afterwards, being caked in hard, cooled resin. The vapours given off are rather noxious and the burning of amber should always be done out of doors and using appropriate protective equipment. Spike lavender oil is sometimes added to the linseed oil to help keep the resin liquid but this leads to a coating with a longer drying (curing) time. Artists have found amber-oil mediums useful in terms of their extreme gloss and enamel-like finish. Mediums based on fusions of amber with linseed oil or walnut oil may be useful for the laying down of multiple glazes, without pick-up from one layer to another. Such amber-oil mediums shift from wet to tacky rapidly, allowing subsequent coatings to be applied while still tacky but no longer in a fluid, liquid state.

In recent years, there has been a revival of interest in amber as an oil painting medium and some specialist companies have begun to offer various formulations based on amber to the market. However, in practical terms, their high cost precludes their use for most artists.

Gum Elemi

Elemi, the best types of which are procured from Manila, is

collected as a soft-resinous mass, containing many impurities. If left exposed to air, it hardens and is then unusable. It can be dissolved into warm turpentine to form a solution, which is then strained to gain a straw coloured (but slightly cloudy) liquid. Elemi is very soft and can be incorporated into oil paint medium recipes as a plasticiser. However, over-use may provide films that are rather sticky and possess a certain cloudiness.

Tree Balsams

A number of trees yield sap residues which are collected in this form and kept as thick, viscous liquids. These tree balsams, or "oleo-resins" are highly prized for their clear films and brilliant sheen. When warmed slightly, they flow better than in the cool state. They are sometimes added in small proportions (e.g. 5-10%) to other oil paint mediums to increase the gloss and brilliance of the final paint film.

Venice Turpentine

From the European Larch, this tree balsam (it is collected as a liquid sap and used as such) is often used as an additive to varnishes to impart flexibility and extra gloss. Good varieties do not discolour because they do not contain abietic acid (as is the case with colophony and some other pine resins, which take on a dark yellow-orange colour that can become progressively darker with age). As a consequence, venice turpentine is highly prized by oil painters (especially so in the golden period of Venetian painting, hence the name of the material). The best quality of venice turpentine is collected from larch trees in the Austrian Tyrol. The best sap is located at the heart of the tree and this is collected by drilling into the tree's centre. This perhaps explains the high cost of the material. Small amounts of venice turpentine are added to other ingredients to impart luminosity and brilliance, to gain an enamel-like surface. It may also be used to impart flexibility to harder resins. Modern venice turpentine tends to be very thick in consistency and has to be placed in a warm water bath to gain fluidity, from which point it can be diluted with a little turpentine to provide a permanently fluid formulation. In earlier times, venice turpentine was probably less viscous and easier to brush out without warming. Sometimes this material is sold under the name "Venetian Turpentine". This can be the same material, but more commonly, it infers that the true venice turpentine has been adulterated with colophony, thereby giving a more brittle film upon drying.

Strasbourg "Silver-Fir" Turpentine

Often mentioned in historic texts, the so-called "Silver-Fir" or "Strasbourg Turpentine" is similar to venice turpentine but has a paler colour. It is sourced from silver-fir trees in the Vosges region of France but also, and perhaps more importantly, it has been derived from silver-fir trees in the Italian Tyrol, often mentioned in old texts as *"olio d'Abezzo"*. The balsam is collected from openings in the bark caused by natural blistering. It is used in a similar way to venice turpentine and is particularly useful for coating pigments that are susceptible to degrading when exposed to atmospheric conditions: the balsam envelopes the pigment, thereby offering protection.

Copaiva Balsam

Derived from Latin America, this balsam contains volatile (essential) oils which can have a solvent effect. The balsam has a red-brown colour and dries to form a glossy finish. However, the essential oils remain active in the varnish/paint film and can cause previous layers to dissolve or pick-up when brushing. Similarly, top coats will be affected by the undercoat. As a consequence, it is used with some caution.

Canada Balsam

Found in Europe from the 18th century onwards, canada balsam is from a species of pine tree native to northeastern North America. The bark of the tree yields a very pale balsam, not unlike strasbourg turpentine but slightly paler. The balsam only occurs where the bark has blistered: as a consequence, collection of the material is protracted and difficult, lending this material a high price in the market. It is used in a similar way to venice and strasbourg turpentine.

Sample Recipes for Oil Painting Mediums

There are a selection of "standard" recipes for painting mediums. Variations on these and many other recipes are possible. The following recipes can be seen as a starting point for further experimentation and exploration.

GLAZE MEDIUM (Resin-Oil Medium)

To improve the brilliance of oil colour and to help avoid oil colour sinking, a simple glaze medium can be introduced. This medium will help extend transparent colours without their losing adhesion or luminosity.

Recipe for Glaze Medium

Dammar varnish (1 part dammar resin to 3 parts turpentine, see Varnish Recipes)	50ml
Linseed stand oil	50ml
Double rectified turpentine	200ml

The varnish and oil are stirred together, before adding turpentine. Stir each time used. Less turpentine will give a more viscid medium. This glaze medium is flexible and keeps for a long time in a sealed bottle.

Scumbling

The glaze medium can also be used for scumbling of oil colour. The amount of turpentine is reduced, so that the medium is thicker and more importantly, slower in consistency. This more viscid medium is mixed with colour on the palette and then scumbled with brushes, rags, fingers or painting knives across the painting surface. The effect is to slow down the flow of oil paint, effectively dragging the colour. A combination of glazes and scumbles can be built up to form a unifying whole: such applications can be re-worked while still wet, scraped off, or worked over with fatter paint mixtures. Always, when applying mediums, scumbles and glazes refer to the Fat over Lean principle. Fatter layers always sit on top.

Impasto Mediums

Oil paint has a bad tendency to wrinkle and dry in on itself when applied neatly (without additions) in thick impasto. This is particularly the case with glazing colours such as alizarin crimson, which takes such a long time to dry when applied thickly, that the surface dries out first and shows wrinkling. Extenders such as blanc fix could be introduced but this would change the colour and also make the paint rather underbound and heavy. Better practice is to introduce a wax-based medium. Beeswax is the most flexible of waxes and combines well with the drying oils and with oil paint. It is dissolved to a soft paste with turpentine. When adding wax to oil paint never add more than about 5%. Beeswax tends to cause adhesion problems, there is also the possible risk of the paint film remaining soluble in white spirit or turpentine. Beeswax paste alone would be too soft and attract dust and dirt to the picture surface. Beeswax remains vulnerable to the solvent action of turpentine or white spirit. To overcome this and to impart more flexibility, oil can be added to the wax paste.

Beeswax Medium

Beeswax, natural yellow (refined bleached beeswax turns yellow with age, so is no advantage)	100g
Linseed stand oil	75ml
Double rectified turpentine	300ml

Method 1

1. Place beeswax in a saucepan.
2. Melt beeswax on low heat. Take off heat, pour oil into liquid wax, stir. Place back on heat until clarified.
3. Remove from heat, add turpentine. Leave to cool, to form a paste.

Method 2

1. Place 100g beeswax in pan. Cover with 300ml turpentine.
2. Leave to soak for 2-3 days until dissolved.
3. Stir oil into soft beeswax paste. Place in a warm water bath if necessary, to gain homogeneous mixture.

Carnauba, a plant wax, can be added to beeswax mediums to impart hardness but only when applied to rigid supports.

Resin-Oil-Wax Medium

Wax-based oil mediums can give a less matt finish by admixing with resin-oil.

Beeswax	100g
Linseed stand oil	50ml
Turpentine	300ml
Dammar varnish (100g resin to 300ml turpentine)	50ml

1. Dissolve the beeswax in turpentine and add oil (as per beeswax medium).
2. Stir in dammar varnish, with container placed in warm water bath.

Imparts lustre and a tougher sheen to beeswax medium. Add more turpentine if too thick, or to reduce to a softer gel consistency.

Manufactured Paint Mediums

Variations upon the mediums described are sold through the art materials trade. Preparation of painting mediums from the raw materials is advised simply so that the artist gains control over the ingredients employed. Manufactured mediums are never universal or standard, each make of "glaze medium" may contain a great variety of ingredients, the properties of which should be understood before incorporating into paintings. Manufacturers' technical notes in catalogues and brochures give advice on the contents and uses for specific painting mediums.

Alkyd resin based oil paint mediums have been widely used by manufacturers. Alkyd is a synthetic resin that has been oil-modified and is compatible with oil colours. It is often prepared with a siccative to give fast drying and comes in a variety of consistencies, from a liquid, soft gel, jelly, to a rubbery gel. The thicker varieties are often used by artists to create thick impasto passages of paint. These thick gels tend to dry in on themselves when applied very thickly. It is probably better practice to use alkyd mediums in flat glazes only, where the medium is levelled out and dries at an even rate. Too great an addition of oil paint medium may impair the adhesion of paint layers.

Other prepared painting mediums include fast drying, fluid mediums. These contain drying agents but are preferable to the addition of neat siccative such as cobalt drier to oil paint, as the prepared drying medium is (hopefully) always made to the same recipe. An artist adding neat drier has always the potential to add too much to the paint mixture, causing bad cracking of the paint film.

Picture Varnishes

Final varnish for oil painting is applied when the painting is absolutely dry. The drying process takes from one year to one hundred years, or even longer, depending on the thickness of the paint, its constituent parts (e.g. added mediums) and the conditions in which it has dried. Varnishing a painting before it is properly dried out leads to cracking of the varnish film and the possibility that the varnish is absorbed into the drying paint film, leaving an uneven final varnish film on the surface. Varnish is applied to protect the painting from atmospheric pollution, dirt, smoke, humidity and dust. The varnish film can become stained by these elements. Restorers prefer a varnish that is removable, so that before it becomes dirty, or cracks, it can be replaced.

The ideal varnish would be removable (i.e. able to be re-dissolved with solvents by a trained picture restorer), non-yellowing, non-cracking and flexible. No picture varnish on the market completely fulfils these expectations. The natural resin varnishes, mastic and dammar are often used for varnishes. Mastic gives a very fine varnish when dissolved in turpentine, although it yellows appreciably and is prone to embrittlement and blooming. Dammar yellows to a lesser degree but is more friable and gives a softer finish. Previously, varnishes based on copals (very hard resin) and colophony were used as picture varnishes. However, such resins produced hard, glossy films, that were very prone to darkening and in the case of colophony, cracking and embrittlement.

Synthetic resin picture varnishes, such as "ketone N" are often preferred to natural resin varnishes. Ketone is thought to yellow very little but may become brittle and difficult to remove with age. New varnishes, based on acrylic resins, are available and these may become more important in the future as final picture varnishes.

Varnishes can be tinted with pigment to achieve certain effects as desired. The addition of oil colour to a varnish mixture renders it less re-soluble. A better approach may be not to varnish at all but to work in a resin-oil technique, building up coloured glazes and scumbles as previously described, so that all layers of the painting and especially the final layers are effectively bound and protected from atmospheric pollution and have a reasonable lustre. Paintings under glass (glazed) are better protected from the atmosphere, dirt and dust.

Varnish Recipes

Dammar Varnish

Dammar resin	100g
Double rectified turpentine	300ml

Place the resin in an improvised bag made from muslin (or old tights), and tie the top with string. Immerse the bag in the turpentine and leave (covered) for 2-3 days to dissolve.

The resultant varnish can then be used as a painting medium ingredient (see recipes), or thinned further with turpentine, to make a varnish. Final picture varnish should be thin enough not to change the appearance of the painting too much. Dammar varnish that is too thick will remain sticky and soft on the picture surface.

Procedure for Making Dammar Varnish

Lumps of dammar resin

Dammar resin wrapped in muslin bag

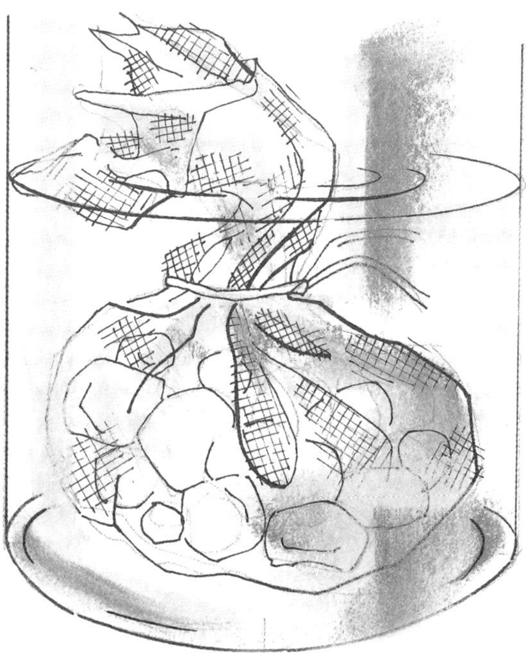

Dammar resin is suspended in rectified/distilled turpentine

The resultant varnish is filtered through muslin then bottled

Mastic Varnish

Mastic resin	100g
Double rectified turpentin	300ml

Dissolve as per dammar varnish. Mastic can be used to achieve a very fine picture varnish by dilution with turpentine.

Mastic varnish should be prepared in dry conditions, without humidity or damp cold air, which could induce "blooming" into the varnish/paint film. This manifests itself as a slight clouding in the dried varnish film which cannot be removed. As a consequence, varnish making in Northern Europe is best done on warm spring and summer days.

Matt Dammar Varnish

Dammar varnish	100g
Beeswax	25g
Double rectified turpentine	300ml

Dissolve the beeswax to a soft paste in a proportion of the turpentine, then add to the rest of the varnish. The wax should be warmed (place bottle/can in warm water bath) before pouring into the varnish. When cooled, the wax tends to collect at the bottom of the mixture: heat in warm water bath before each application. This varnish imparts a satin-matt finish (slightly cloudy effect) to the picture surface, softening colour relationships.

Ketone N Resin Picture Varnish

Ketone N resin	100g
Double rectified turpentine, or white (mineral) spirit	300ml

Dissolve as per dammar varnish. The can containing the mixture is placed in a warm water bath to aid the beginning of the dissolving process. The mixture is stirred/agitated from time to time while dissolving. Produces a water white, non-yellowing picture varnish.

Solvents for Oil Painting

When used to thin oil colour, the solvent should ideally evaporate cleanly without leaving a residue. Take care when handling oil paint solvents. Prepare hands with a good quality barrier cream before working and wash thoroughly with soap and water if in contact with solvent. Ensure good ventilation in the studio when working with solvents.

Turpentine

Turpentine, distilled from pine is of great value to the artist as a solvent for oil colours but also as an essential ingredient in painting mediums and varnishes. Turpentine has a sweet aromatic smell. The best grade is that which has been double rectified. This means that the gummy residue contained in pure gum turpentine has been removed. This residue converts into a sticky mass when exposed to light, making it unsuitable for painting purposes. As a consequence, double rectified turpentine is preferred, as it is free of this gummy deposit. Turpentine should be kept in closed metal cans or brown bottles, away from sunlight, to avoid discoloration and thickening. Turpentine thickens when in contact with air: keep stored with the cap tight. Always use as fresh a supply of turpentine as it is possible to obtain.

Turpentine evaporates from paint mixtures at an even rate, reducing the chances of colour sinking unevenly when thinned out. It has a more oily presence than mineral (white) spirit. Turpentine is preferred when dissolving resins such as dammar, when making varnishes and oil painting mediums. It has a stronger solvent action than white spirit.

White (Mineral) Spirit

A petroleum solvent, distilled directly from coal. It has a drier presence and evaporates more rapidly and more unevenly than turpentine. It is much cheaper than turpentine and can be used for brush and palette cleaning. White spirit is made more stable as a painting thinner by admixing with a small amount of stand oil. This should be done fresh for each painting session: the oil helps the spirit settle out more evenly. Low odour mineral spirit (OMS) is also available and may be preferred by many artists.

Low Odour Thinner/Odourless Mineral Spirit

A low odour solvent, where the proportion of aromatic hydrocarbons present has been significantly reduced. Shellsol T is a typical example of a low odour thinner. It evaporates at a similar rate to turpentine, leaving oil paint with an even finish. Shellsol T and other OMS – odourless mineral spirits - tend to evaporate over a period of a number of hours. Typically, the release of solvent vapour takes place towards the end of the evaporation period (for example after perhaps 6-8 hours from application).

Gum Turpentine

This type of non-rectified turpentine contains a gummy residue, which can interfere with paint mixtures. It also becomes more sticky and yellows when exposed to light and heat. The gummy residue is related to colophony, or rosin, which is the by-product of turpentine production. Colophony in solution forms a very brittle, unstable film and should be avoided at all costs unless the artist desires a brittle, cracking paint film.

Over-thinning of oil colour may cause paint to lose adhesion. A characteristic of this is when the paint breaks up into tiny rivulets, leaving behind underbound islets of pigment.

Clean-Up of Oil Paint, Palette and Brushes

Painters are prone to bad studio practice: the image is everything and a tidy workplace is far from the mind while working. However, a few simple procedures can be followed to make cleaning-up easier and the studio a more pleasant place to be.

The most important step is to make sure your working space is clean and obstacle-free before starting. When painting we often forget where we are, so lessen the chances of accidental spillage etc, by spending a few minutes before starting work, reorganising the studio using common sense. Have a good supply of clean-up materials to hand in case of spillage.

Painters often douse brushes in mineral spirit/double-rectified turpentine/OMS to loosen oil paint from the bristles. This process inevitably dries out the brush hair and makes it brittle. Try immersing brushes in mineral (Vaseline) oil to free oil paint from bristles, then wipe on to a soft rag. You could also try cheap sunflower/vegetable oil from the supermarket. The process of immersing brush tips into these oils helps loosen the oil colour, so that it can be largely removed from the brush hairs by gentle rubbing on to a soft rag.

To cleanse brush hairs thoroughly, use olive oil soap, supplied in grated flakes. Take a handful of soap flakes and put into an empty, clean food container. Pour boiled water from a kettle over the flakes and leave for 10-15 minutes, stirring every now and then to gain a smooth gel consistency. The resultant gloopy gel of soap can be used to clean oil colour completely from brush hairs. The soap naturally restores oil back into the brush hairs, so helping to prolong the life of the brush. Once all oil colour residue has been freed from the brush hair, rinse under warm water to rid the brush hair of any soap residue. Leave the brushes to dry overnight before re-using. If you can, hang the brush so that the hair points down (i.e. handle at top), so that any remaining water/paint residue follows gravity, rather than collecting in the ferrule of the brush (the commonest cause of split hairs with brushes!).

When working with oil colours/dry pigments/solvents, always try and wear protective gloves, so that skin does not come into contact with potentially harmful materials. If you treat all pigments as being potentially harmful, it will quickly become standard practice to treat all the materials you use with respect.

Solvent Disposal and Dispensation

Solvents used in the studio require dispensing from one source. Ideally, this is a lockable cabinet. Individual solvent dispensing units (plunger cans) are also available.

It makes very good sense to limit the types of solvent used in the studio to one. The most suitable solvent currently available is odourless mineral spirit (OMS).

Never throw solvents down sinks or discard them carelessly. Try and be as sparing as possible with solvents: if you use them to dilute oil colour, only decant what you need for each painting session. Preferably use a prepared paint medium to dilute paint mixtures. Mediums take longer for the solvent content to evaporate, so the vapours are less pronounced while working.

If you have waste solvent, pour it into a container filled with fuller's earth (rottenstone), or fine cat litter, which is very absorbent. When the solvent has evaporated after 2-3 days, the residual powder can be disposed of safely.

Waste rags also need to be carefully disposed of. Ideally, the studio will have an oil waste can (with a closing lid). This prevents rags, soaked with linseed oil from causing fires through self-combustion.

Watercolour and Gouache Painting

WATERCOLOUR

Historical Background

The origins of watercolour spring from the cake colours of the Chinese and Japanese. These were compressed cakes of colour, which re-dissolved with water. The binder for these paints was often fish or animal glue size. Such paints were widely employed on fine textiles, such as silk, as well as paper made from bark or rice. The closest likeness to this paint available today are the compressed Chinese inks, which give out colour when rubbed against an ink stone in the presence of water. In Japan, watercolour paints are still available based on pigments bound in deer skin glue.

In medieval Europe, water-based paints, bound with resoluble gum, glair (egg white) or animal size were used for painting illuminated manuscripts. Albrecht Durer (1471-1528) was one of the earliest artists to liberate gum tempera (i.e. aqueous gum binder + pigment in place of egg + pigment) from being a decorative medium. During the 17th century, the Dutch began to develop watercolour painting further, through landscape painting. The British championed the use of watercolour at the close of the 18th century, to record the "Grand Tour" of Europe, taking in the ancient and modern sights of Italy and the extreme landscapes of the Alps.

Initially, watercolour was used merely in the form of tints over pen line drawings. This application gradually developed to a more personal use of transparent watercolour by early pioneers such as

Thomas Girtin (1775-1802) and Frances Towne (1740-1816). Each summer Girtin made tours of Britain, making landscape studies which would be developed during the winter in the studio. He began to employ broad washes of colour, restraining the use of descriptive detail. Often this would take the form of bold washes of watercolour over monochromatic underpainting, descriptive details being touched in with fine brushes. Frances Towne made a tour of Italy in 1780-81, returning to Britain via the Alps. His Alpine studies show his technique well: striking pen and ink drawings, complemented by flat washes of harmonious colour.

While Girtin's paintings emerged from the applied notion of watercolour, the study of nature, topography and so on, his friend and rival J.M.W. Turner (1775-1851) stood such tradition on its head. Although his first works in watercolour were topographical in nature, his experience of working in oils led to the production of powerful and atmospheric landscapes, characterised by a complicated yet direct and ambitious use of both watercolour and body colour. His most lucid works were spontaneous sketches made directly in the landscape and from drawings executed on the spot. His larger exhibition watercolours were rather more flamboyant and exaggerated in style, pushing the medium to the absolute limits.

Watercolour painting became a popular pastime among the English gentry. In response, the early colour makers, Rowney and Winsor & Newton began to produce “moist” watercolours, which could be easily re-dissolved and carried in small painting boxes on sketching expeditions. Previously, watercolours had been available in compressed, hard cakes, which gave out very flat, matt, dry washes.

In the early part of the 20th century, the German Expressionist Emil Nolde (1867-1956) used watercolour in a more experimental fashion. Nolde's work is characterised by a use of bold, saturated colour. He used unmixed colour, dissolved from tube watercolour and kept in large pots. These pure colours he would then apply to highly absorbent Japanese papers (papers made with little or no sizing), so that the saturated colour would also saturate the paper.

Colourmakers today offer their watercolours in formats that will suit most approaches to watercolour painting: in a variety of sizes of sketching boxes, in the form of pans or tubes and in good capacity tubes for larger, studio-based work. Similarly, the range of supports, brushes and auxiliaries matches the demand from artists: papers for example are offered as tiny pads for outdoor work, or in the form of rolls for larger works. Artists also demand that their colours have good lightfastness and perform well. Manufacturers have begun to offer more information in this area, through their catalogues, labelling and retail outlets.

Properties of Watercolour

Watercolour painting relies upon pure pigments dispersed into a binding agent which is resoluble with water. Watercolour is unusual among painting media in that it is named after its diluting agent, water, rather than binding agent, as is the case with media such as oil paints (linseed oil) or acrylic paints (acrylic polymer emulsion).

The pigments used in watercolour are carried in an aqueous binder, usually a solution of gum arabic. The binder can be diluted heavily with water to make fine washes of thinned, transparent colour, without losing adhesion to the support. The transparent nature of watercolour allows the artist to build tonal values through layers of colour. Watercolour is a highly responsive medium, providing the artist with a direct yet delicate means of building colour, tone and form.

The main criteria for watercolour painting include:

- Fine particle size pigments
- Good transparency (although some important colours are opaque)
- Resoluble binding agent
- A matt film when dry
- Resolvability of colour on palette and on paper
- Easy "lift-off" of colour from pan or palette
- Good flow when diluted with water.

Fine Particle Size Pigments

The pigments used for watercolour painting ideally have a fine particle size, allowing for extreme dilution with water, without the paint film breaking down. Pigments with a larger particle size can break up the paint film when heavily diluted, showing a granulated effect. Traditionally, watercolour pigments are transparent when diluted with water into a wash. However, some opaque colours such as oxide of chromium green, are indispensable to the artist and are thus used in combination within the watercolour palette.

Watercolour is the most sensitive medium regarding stability to light. Because the pigments are applied in thin, transparent washes, direct sunlight can pass through the paint film, to the white of the paper support. Therefore, any fugitive pigments may be bleached out. Previously, watercolours would have been kept in portfolios and shown only under subdued light, to counter the effects of direct exposure to the UV rays in sunlight. However, the modern watercolour palette (see pigment tables in chapter on pigments) can provide the artist with a relatively stable range of colours.

Good Transparency

Traditional watercolour techniques call for pigments with a tendency towards transparency, such as the "lake" pigments. These were formerly vegetable dyes, such as madder derived from madder roots, or stil de grain yellow, derived from buckthorn berries. These natural plant dyes were then struck on to a transparent chalk base. The lake pigments tend to be rather fugitive (although natural madder survives today and is still prepared and used in watercolours by some manufacturers). In the late 19th century, organic dyes made from coal tar were introduced. This group of pigments are chemically similar to the fugitive natural dyes but possess greater tinting strength. The first coal tar dyes proved to be largely fugitive too, although some colours such as alizarin crimson are still widely used in artists' quality paints. The natural madder pigment prepared from madder root contained two dyestuffs: purpurine and alizarin. Purpurine is quite fugitive but alizarin is reasonably lightfast. Synthetically produced alizarin was introduced in 1868. Problems with lightfastness of coal tar dyes led to a meeting of artists and industry in 1908 which decided that all pigments based on coal tar dyestuffs should be at least as lightfast as alizarin crimson.

In the early part of the 20th century, superior coal tar colours such as the azo and indanthrone groups were introduced and are still in use today. Special grades of these pigments have been updated and as a result have better permanence. Later colours, derived from chemical fusions of by-products of the petro-chemical industries such as the quinacridones have even better permanence and have been readily incorporated into artists' paint ranges.

All the synthetic organic pigments used by artists are essentially colourant struck on to a transparent base, giving them similar properties to the original "lake" pigments. Their high tinting strength and good transparency provide intense, clear washes of colour, making them ideal for watercolour painting. The only drawback to these colours is their capacity to stain the paper, making lift-out of mistakes more difficult. Examples of staining watercolour pigments include phthalocyanine blue and phthalocyanine green.

Resoluble Binding Agent

The binder for watercolour is usually gum arabic, from the Acacia tree, species of which are found all over the Near and Middle East, Central Africa and India. Sudan is the principal supplier of high grade gum arabic, the best quality, from the Kordofan region is generally found in artists' watercolour and gouache paints.

The gum is collected during the dry season between October and May: the tree is "tapped" by carefully incising the bark. The tree has to reach a maturity of six years before it will yield gum. The exuded gum forms into hard, translucent irregular lumps or balls. The dried balls or droplets of gum are collected and graded according to their clarity. The paler varieties are considered most suitable for watercolour painting and should be free of impurities. Cheaper varieties are also available but these may provide a more brittle paint film and often include impurities such as bits of bark, and the pieces of gum can be a variety of shades from dark to light. Gum arabic is sold in the raw form, as lumps or balls but also in grain form (smaller pieces) and crushed as a fine powder. The gum is prepared for use as the binding agent for watercolour painting by dissolving in water (see Hand-Prepared Watercolours).

Other gums that have been used in water-based paints include cherry gum (more brittle but more glossy than gum arabic); gum tragacanth (gives a very hard, matt paint film), dextrin (starch) and methylcellulose (converted starch). Dextrin or methylcellulose are sometimes judiciously used in commercial watercolours to improve their consistency, or in the place of gum arabic, in school paints.

A Matt Film When Dry

Traditional watercolour technique demands that the paint film dries to a matt sheen. This allows the finished painting to be viewed without any glare on the painting surface and shows the true depth of tone of the pigments used.

A paint that dries to a high sheen contains too much gum. This high sheen effect may be pleasing for some artists and it is possible to add gum water to your watercolour paints to improve the gloss of the paint film. Gum arabic is sold in a prepared solution, often slightly diluted and containing preservative and plasticising agent. It can be readily diluted with water as required. Bear in mind however, that by introducing more gum solution, the paint mixture may have a more brittle film when dry.

For the finished painting to be perfectly matt, the paint employed should be as short as possible. This means that it should contain the least amount of binder to pigment possible but enough binder to facilitate dilution of the paint without losing adhesion to the support. Some brands of watercolour fulfil this requirement perfectly, while other makes will be gum-rich. The make-up of any paint has to be experienced by the artist at first hand in order to determine its suitability: some artists will prefer a rich, moist watercolour to a very short paint.

Resolvability of Colour on the Palette and on Paper

Gum arabic is a water-resoluble material. Watercolour can therefore be reconstituted when dry, both on the palette and when applied to watercolour paper. Good watercolour should be easy to re-dissolve when dry. Some brands use different formulae in their tube and pan watercolours, for example, adding more glycerine to pan colours to make them more moist. This can mean that colour squeezed from the tube is not so easy to re-constitute, once dry, when compared to pan colours.

The degree to which watercolour can be lifted out of paper when dry depends to some extent on the nature of the pigment in a specific colour. Some colours, as mentioned, have a capacity to stain the paper. Another consideration is the quality of the watercolour paper used. To assist the removal of dried washes of colour, paper should be robust enough to withstand a degree of scrubbing or rubbing with a brush loaded with water, or a wet sponge.

Easy "Lift-Off" of Colour from Pan or Palette

Watercolours are presented in pans or tubes. Pans are square (small/half pan size) or rectangular (large/whole pan) in shape. Presented in this form, the watercolour is either poured into the pan and left to set, or cut from strips of colour and pressed into the pan. There is much debate as to the relative merits of both procedures. Essentially pan watercolours should be compact yet moist compressed cakes of colour. The paint should be easy to lift off, at the touch of a wet brush. The pan should have some tack on the surface but should not be too sticky. This would signify an excess of plasticiser and/or moisturising agent.

Colour in tubes may have a different formula to that of the equivalent pan colour. When squeezed from the tube, the colour should readily dilute to make even washes.

Good Flow when Diluted with Water

Watercolour should flow readily when water is introduced, to provide even washes when brushed out on to good paper. Flow can be improved by an addition of oxgall to the painting water. This liquid, obtained from the gall bladder of the ox helps disperse washes of colour.

Stabilising agents and transparent filler can also be introduced to aid the consistency and shelf-life of commercially prepared watercolours. Such additions, along with careful use of wetting agents (oxgall or synthetic equivalents, for example, disponil) may also assist the flow of the watercolour when diluted with water.

Commercially Manufactured Watercolours

Manufactured watercolours are available in three main formats:

- 1/2 pans
- whole pans
- tubes

Generally, watercolour tubes come in small sizes – 5ml, 6ml and 7.5ml – designed to fit into travelling watercolour boxes. However, some manufacturers produce large size tubes of 15-20ml, which are more economical.

Watercolour boxes are sold complete, or as empty boxes. There is a great variety of folding watercolour boxes available for outdoor work. The best-quality boxes are enamelled to prevent rusting. Wooden studio boxes are also produced, often with elaborate mixing trays and storage compartments, which are influenced by the grandiose watercolour boxes produced in the Victorian era. Although buying the empty box and filling this up with a preferred colour range can be more expensive, it does allow the artist to select only the most necessary colours. Often this choice is based on the artist's eye and preference for certain colours.

While printed shade cards are readily available at regular art shops, always ask to see a hand-made actual colour chart. Most stores will have a copy of this chart which shows the colour neat and as a gradated wash. It is useful to prepare a similar chart of your favourite colours to keep in the studio. This can help aid identification of colours, and over a period of time will show how well the chosen colours have stood up to exposure to sunlight. It may also be useful to keep a swatch of colours in the window, with half of each colour paint-out covered and half exposed. This may show if a colour is prone to fading.

Variety in Quality and Price

"Artists' Quality" watercolours are generally sold in different price series and each manufacturer may have a different price structure. "Second Grade", or "Student Quality" watercolours tend to have one price across the range, offering the beginner a reasonable selection of colours at an affordable price.

In second grade colours the expensive cadmium and cobalt pigments tend to be replaced with mixtures, frequently using synthetic organic pigments. Often, second grade watercolours are prepared with a different binder, generally a mixture of gum arabic with dextrin (a water resoluble starch). Dextrin is used in minimum amounts as an addition to watercolour, to improve the smoothness of the paint. Excess will make the paint too dry and crumbly, providing less adhesion to the support. Cheap poster paints (which readily crack and crumble when applied in any thickness) are often prepared with dextrin. The lightfastness of second grade watercolours may not be sufficient to serve for permanent painting: check manufacturers' catalogues for details of lightfastness ratings.

Hand-Prepared Watercolours

Gum arabic is prepared for use as the binding agent for watercolour painting by dissolving in water. This is done by taking one part (by volume) of gum arabic pieces and placing in a pan or glass jar. Six parts (by volume) of boiling water are poured over the gum and this is then left to soak for two to three days. The gum will begin to dissolve within a few minutes but takes a few days to dissolve completely. The dissolved gum solution should be strained through muslin before use to eradicate any impurities. The resultant solution is fairly thick and syrupy. When painted out in this neat form, it has a brittle film.

A plasticising agent is introduced to give the paint film more flexibility. To make the paint lift easily when wetted with a water-loaded brush, a moisturising agent is also added. These additions are usually hygroscopic substances such as hydromel (honey dissolved in water), sugar syrup (sugar dissolved in water) and glycerine.

Hydromel as plasticiser, in combination with glycerine to make the colours moist, can be added to the gum solution. Hydromel makes the paint film more flexible, also aiding the smoothness of the paint mixture. Glycerine also aids flexibility but essentially keeps the watercolour paint moist, making it easy to lift the prepared colour. This is especially important in the commercial manufacture of watercolours in pan form, where the artist needs to be able to touch the wet brush on to the surface of the watercolour pan and lift off colour readily.

For hand-made watercolours, small additions of hydromel and glycerine can be added to the prepared gum solution. The precise measure for each pigment colour will be different: make tests before painting. If the dried colour stays moist, then add less glycerine. Should the dried paint film crack, add more honey. Excess of these materials makes the paint too sticky. The plasticising and moisturising agent can be added to the gum solution, or to the paint mixture later. The gum solution will keep for a few days before spoiling. Specialist artists' pigment suppliers may be able to supply preservatives for water-based paints (e.g. preventol, metatin).

Hand-made watercolour paints can be prepared using this stock solution of gum. Firstly, the dry pigment is combined with distilled water using a glass muller on a toothed glass slab, to form a smooth but thick paste. Distilled water is used, as tap water may contain minerals, typically salts, which can form a cloudy layer on the picture surface. Water that is rich in acids will break down certain pigments but will also have a detrimental effect on the paper support. Distilled water is formed from steam and is therefore relatively pure.

The ground pigment paste can be stored in closed glass jars until required. A little distilled water can be reintroduced should the paste dry out. The wet pigment paste is combined with the gum solution, again using a glass muller. Before painting, make tests on to a good quality watercolour paper. If the test colour is too dry (i.e. chalks when rubbed with the finger), add more gum solution to the pigment paste. If the mixture is too rich, the paint will appear over shiny. Traditionally, watercolours are transparent with a matt sheen when dry.

It is best to make up enough paint for each painting session, rather than try to store the finished colour. It will dry out, or the pigment will separate from the gum solution if put into an empty tube. You can press the paint paste into empty (clean) sea shells. The paste will dry out but remain water-resoluble.

Commercially made watercolours counter such problems by using a different recipe of pigment to binder for each colour. Some colours are still prepared exclusively by hand in watercolour: for example, one firm still hand grind certain colours such as carmine. The high cost of the pigment (a red colourant extracted from the cochineal insect) and the subsequent small paint batches needed, require careful hand grinding of the colour.

Materials for Hand-Prepared Watercolours

- Dry pigments
- Glass muller
- Glass slab, or marble slab
- Gum arabic, crystals, or in solution
- Distilled water
- Empty glass jars, for storing distilled water-pigment pastes
- Glycerine
- Hydromel (honey, dissolved 1:3 in hot water)
- Palette knife
- Kitchen towel
- Empty pans, or sea shells
- Dust mask
- Disposable gloves

Health & Safety Note – treat all pigments with due caution and wear a dust mask when preparing the dry powder into the binding medium. Wear disposable gloves and/or a barrier cream when handling dry pigments.

Lightfastness and Permanence

The permanence of watercolour paintings is an area of much debate among both artists and conservators. In general, watercolour paintings are best kept stored or displayed away from direct sources of sunlight. Because the paint film is thin and transparent, more light transmits through the paint film than is the case with oils or acrylics. As a consequence, pigments that are fugitive (liable to fade), are more likely to show signs of change upon exposure to light. The permanence of a paint does not only concern stability to light: exposure to certain atmospheric conditions (e.g. sulphur in industrial areas), can have a detrimental effect upon some pigments. The chapter on pigments contains more detail of specific instances where this can occur.

In some cases, the permanence of a paint may also be affected by its composition. For example, in second grade paints, additions of filler material could (in theory) reduce the fastness to light of some pigments (typically, some synthetic organic yellows can be rendered less stable to light when over-mixed with whites, including inert whites used as filler). Many manufacturers now include permanence information in their literature along with health and safety information, although there is no obligation to do this.

Supports for Watercolour Painting

Early supports for gum-based painting included parchment made from dried goatskin and also thin ivory plaques. The first papers generally used as a support for aqueous media were made from linen cellulose fibres. While this paper is often thought to be superior, its expense largely precludes its manufacture. Before 1750, in Europe, only laid papers were available, these had a marked ribbed pattern formed from a special wire grid motif on the paper mould. At the close of the 18th century many watercolourists began to prefer wove papers, which had a smoother appearance, close to woven fabric. Tinted papers were often used, or those which were hand coloured by the artist with a ground wash.

Watercolour paper is made with two main constituents, water and cellulose fibres (present in all plants). Cotton and woodpulp are the main sources of cellulose for the production of artists' watercolour papers. Cotton fibres provide the best paper for watercolours, giving a surface that is strong yet durable. The highest grade 100% cotton papers will be free of optical brightners and acid free, so avoiding yellowing or embrittlement with age. Because a paper is acid free, this does not guarantee that over time it will not become affected by acids. Some high grade papers are also buffered with calcium carbonate to help resist the effects of acids. To establish good working practice for watercolour painting always work, if possible, on to 100% cotton rag papers, preferably those that are sold as being buffered with calcium carbonate and state "acid-free" on packaging. "Acid-free" describes papers with a neutral pH (around 6.5), thus giving a fine balance between acids and alkalis.

Papers that contain an acid presence (e.g. newsprint, brown wrapping paper, decorative papers) are prone to deteriorate over time. Often such papers are included within an artist's work (for example in collage) without thought as to their effect on the stability and appearance of the work.

Papermaking

Watercolour paper can be hand-made or mould (machine) made. The first stage in the paper making process is to break down the cellulose fibres with water into a pulp. To do this requires a close supply of pure, reliable water.

A good example is St. Cuthbert's Paper Mill, in Somerset, England. This company produces the Saunders Waterford range of 100% cotton rag watercolour papers, using water drawn from the River Axe. The source of the river is close by, so the quality of the water is reliably constant. This mill uses cotton cellulose fibres which are supplied from farmed, renewable crop plants. To the pulp, sizing agents are introduced, this provides the paper with an internal sizing, which gives artists a support that can withstand its surface being broken, so preventing the cross-bleeding of washes beneath the paper surface.

The fibre and water pulp is then pumped into a vat in which a cylinder, covered with a porous mesh is present. The action of water draining through the mesh pulls the fibre on to the wire and a mass of fibre builds up to form the paper sheet as a continuous length. At this stage, the paper is given an identification watermark, which is produced by fixing wire to the mould cover on which the paper is made. This mark indicates the "right" side of the paper to paint on. Some papers can be painted on both sides, others show a pronounced difference on each surface. The cellulose fibres are distributed randomly in mould made paper production, this helps the structure of the paper, making it stronger. This method imitates the procedure for making hand-made papers, where the fibres are totally random.

The fibres used in the production of commercial machine made papers follow the direction of the movement of the machine, which does not give the paper as much strength as mould made or hand-made papers.

The wet paper sheet is transferred from the cylinder on to woven woollen felts by a process known as "couching" (meaning "to lay down"). The texture of the felt determines the surface of the paper. There are three basic surfaces used for artists' papers: Rough, NOT and Smooth.

Rough (French-Torchon) has the most texture: when watercolour is applied, the pigment settles in the gently pitted surface of the paper. Here, a rough, woven felt has been used to couch the paper from the cylinder.

NOT, or Cold Pressed paper (meaning not pressed with heat) is formed by couching with a random textured felt.

Smooth or Hot Pressed paper (French-Satine) is formed using the same felt but the paper is also passed through hot metal rollers to achieve the smooth surface.

The paper passes through a system of heated rollers to help the drying process (after couching, the paper comprises 80% water content), before being surface sized with a gelatine solution. Gelatine is a refined animal glue, which prevents delicate watercolour paint from sinking into the paper but which is sensitive to the artist's application of colour on to the paper. This process where the paper is dipped into a bath of hot gelatine, forming a skin over the paper surface, is known as "tub" sizing. Mould made papers tend to have two deckle edges (rough, uneven) and two torn or cut edges.

Papers are sold by weight, which is determined by the speed of the rotating cylinder in the production of mould made papers. The weight is expressed in two forms: lb, showing the weight of each ream (500 sheets) of paper, or gsm, giving the number of grams per square metre of paper.

Comparison of Weights of Watercolour Paper

Grams per square metre	**lbs/weight per ream (gsm) (per 500 sheets)**
150-160	72
180-200	90
285-300	140
410-425	200
600-640	300
850	400

Papers of 300gsm/140lb tend to be robust enough to accept watercolour without stretching, although saturation and wet in wet washes may cause some cockling of the paper. If in doubt, stretch the paper!

Woodpulp is a cheaper source of cellulose than cotton and therefore provides cheaper artists' paper. However, the strength and durability of such papers can be less than those of 100% cotton rag papers. Some brands contain a mix of the two types.

The best woodpulp papers are those known as "woodfree" paper, composed of chemical woodpulp. Here, the acidic lignin content has been taken out, making yellowing and deterioration of the fibres less likely.

Hand-made papers are prepared by mixing cellulose fibres and sizing agents together in a vat. A mesh frame is lowered into the vat and collects the pulp, with the fibres placed at random. The mesh frame is then pressed against another mesh (the deckle frame) and excess water is forced out. The fibres settle roughly at the four edges, producing the characteristic "deckle" edge. The paper sheets are then left to dry. Sometimes a coating of gelatine surface size is added, although some hand-made papers contain little or no size. The production of hand-made papers continues on a small scale, often meaning that the paper maker will produce a range of tinted papers (by introducing pigment to the paper vat), or may include a mix of other plant fibres, to give added decoration and/or texture to the paper.

Some hand-made papers, due to their surface and lack of size, can seem very absorbent for watercolour painting, seemingly sucking the wet washes into the fibre. This can be partially alleviated by coating the paper with a thinned gelatine solution, which can be bought prepared (expensive) or made up from sheet gelatine (cheap).

Gelatine Solution Recipe for Unsized Papers

One part gelatine (1/8 of a sheet) is immersed in 60-70 parts (by volume) of water. Gently warm the solution in a double boiler, until it becomes clear. Apply while just warm, before the gelatine begins to form a jelly. This solution will spoil in 2-3 days. Adjust the strength of the gelatine to control the absorbency of the paper as required.

Stretching Watercolour Paper

Use a drawing board that is slightly bigger than your sheet of paper. Soak the paper in a bath filled with a couple of inches of cold water. When it is thoroughly immersed, take out of the bath, run off any excess and then lay the paper down on to the board. Take a dry sponge around the edge of the paper where the gum strip is to be placed, this will remove any excess water. Cut strips of brown gum strip to the correct lengths for the paper, then with a slightly damp sponge, make the gum tacky. Stick the gum strip down, with an equal proportion of paper to board covered. Run a dry sponge round the fixed down gum strip to take off any excess water. Leave to dry: a hairdryer can be used to speed this process.

Once dry, the paper is ready to paint on and should be free of cockles, providing a tight drum surface, although saturation with water will relax the paper somewhat.

At this stretched stage, it is possible to hand tint white watercolour papers, by using pigment mixed into a thinned gum solution, or you can apply a layer of thinned watercolour. Flat, even washes can be obtained by using a wide, flat ox hair varnish brush, or a similar size flat synthetic hair brush.

Watercolour paper is sold in sheet form. Full Imperial sheet size is usually 560mm x 760mm/22 x 30 inches, although larger sheet sizes are also available. In addition, many mills can supply their papers in roll form (more economical) and in the form of pads, quarter sheets and tear-off blocks. Watercolour blocks are very useful when working outdoors, as the paper is already stretched and remains stretched while working. Despite being an expensive and perhaps lazy approach, it does allow the artist to concentrate wholly on painting.

Good quality watercolour paper should be able to withstand a good deal of brush scrubbing and sponging. Often, a wash will need to be lifted out: this can be done by flooding the paper with water and applying a dry natural sea sponge which will suck up the colour. It should be possible to apply firm pressure to the paper in this manner, to lift out colour. The same procedure can be done with a sable or squirrel hair brush, by wetting the paper then lifting out with a dry brush into the damp paper. Watercolour should re-dissolve when wet, with the exception of certain synthetic organic pigments, which tend to leave a stain behind on the paper.

Care and Storage of Watercolours

Cleaning Dirt from Watercolour Paintings

Dust and dry dirt particles can be removed from watercolour paper by using a soft dry brush only. A soft eraser may also be useful but this may damage the paint surface. It is unwise to introduce any solvents or chemicals: take the painting to a trained paper conservator if further treatment is required.

Choosing Framing Materials

Use only archival grade mounts, adhesives, adhesive tapes and backing boards when framing watercolours. Cheap materials that contain acids can turn yellow-brown but may also migrate to the painting, leading to possible discoloration of the paper and infiltration of the paper fibres.

Storage

Watercolours should be carefully stored flat and away from damp. Mold growth is the most common result of exposure to damp, resulting in foxing (brown stains) that look like spots of iron on the paper. These can be treated by a trained paper conservator but preservation is always better than cure.

If possible, paintings should be stored in a portfolio or closed plan chest, away from extremes of direct sunlight and heat. It is preferable to show watercolour paintings under subdued light, although this is not always practical. Prolonged exposure to daylight should be avoided and especially to direct sunlight. Avoid the use of colours which you know are prone to fade, in transparent washes against white grounds or in admixtures with white, where the colour will be bleached out. Colours such as alizarin crimson may last longer when painted out over a dark underpainting than when applied thinly over a bright white ground.

Auxiliary Materials

Natural Sponge

Natural sponges, usually from Greece are important to the watercolourist, for lifting out unwanted colour, dabbing, smearing and soaking up water from the paper surface. Sponges are sold in sizes ranging from 1 to 4 inches in diameter, although larger flat "Elephant Ear" and round "Wool" sponges are also available from specialist suppliers.

Sponges should be soft enough to meet the delicate surface of paper without scratching. Blotting paper may also serve well for lifting out washes and spilt water.

Scalpel

Useful tools for scratching the paper surface, to create highlights through the paint surface, scalpels are sold in a variety of shapes. Other sharp knives, such as penknives can be utilised, or other abrasive materials, such as sand (glass) paper.

Palettes

Ceramic palettes, usually available in a variety of sizes and shapes are considered best for watercolour painting. They are superior to plastic types because staining colours can be cleaned completely from the ceramic surface. Enamelled metal palettes are also perfect as they too can be easily cleaned. Many painters prefer to improvise, especially when working on a large scale. Plastic baker's trays for example are good for making up large amounts of wash.

Painting Additives

Oxgall

A liquid that is added to painting water to improve the flow of watercolours, enabling colour to disperse readily. Add sparingly. Usually sold in clarified form, suitably diluted. Neat oxgall is also available although this is rather smelly!

Gum Water

Basic gum arabic solution in water. Sometimes has additions of hydromel or sugar syrup to aid flexibility. Added to watercolour paint to introduce lustre to paint film, or diluted further with water to improve flow.

Impasto Gels

Painting thickly with watercolour goes against the traditional technique of application in thin layers. However, many artists wish to use their watercolours with impasto. Some manufacturers offer pasty gel-type mediums specifically for watercolour, which act as thickening additives to watercolour or gouache.

Prepared Size

Used to reduce the absorbency of watercolour paper. Apply to the surface of the paper and leave to dry before painting. Made from gelatine, available in a prepared solution, or in dry sheet form.

Masking Fluid

A latex solution, which can be applied to paper to give a water-impervious film, to protect selected areas when applying colour in broad washes. It can be removed from suitable papers (make tests first) by peeling or rubbing gently. It should not be applied on top of water resoluble colour, as it may lift the paint on removal. Supplied in colourless or tinted form. Brushes used to apply masking fluid need to be washed straight away in warm, soapy water, as once dry, the masking fluid is virtually impossible to remove from brush hairs.

Varnishes

Varnishing is not appropriate to watercolour painting, as this would destroy the matt film of the paint surface. Paintings should instead be kept in the correct storage environment.

A light spray of archival standard fixative will afford invisible protection without altering colour tones or the appearance of the paint sheen.

Diluent

The solvent or diluent for aqueous paint media is water, or preferably distilled water. Avoid saltwater and tap water, which contain potentially harmful mineral elements. Distilled water can be admixed with a small proportion of gum water solution to help retain the lustre of watercolour in extreme washes. An addition of oxgall (a couple of drops only) to painting water aids flow and dispersion.

Combining Watercolour and Other Media

Watercolour is often used with other media. For example, charcoal, pencil or pastel are frequently used in combination with watercolour. If drawn marks are to be overpainted without smudging, it is a good idea to give the paper surface a light coat of an archival spray fixative. This will stabilise the drawn area, so that washes of watercolour do not dislodge the drawn marks. Sometimes, soft pastel is applied on top of dried watercolour paint. Because pastel grips best to a toothy support, Rough watercolour papers are a good choice for this method of working. The fixative mentioned is recommended because it does not build up a sheen, is very flexible, water-clear and can be overpainted with almost any art medium.

Acrylic Materials and Watercolour

Acrylic colours can be used to imitate watercolour technique. When strongly diluted with water, acrylic paints can be used to apply thin washes of colour on to any dirt and grease-free support. It is possible to use acrylics in combination with watercolour, although it is best to leave coats of applied paint to dry thoroughly before overpainting (i.e. do not intermix acrylic and watercolour, as the two materials have different drying characteristics.) To achieve a finish as close as possible to traditional watercolour, matt acrylic paint, or acrylic paint mixed with a matt medium is recommended. Sometimes it is useful to introduce a specific acrylic colour to achieve an effect that is difficult in true watercolour. For example, most acrylic paint ranges include iridescent or interference colours, which are not available in watercolour ranges. These pearlised colours give a lustre sheen and work best on to dark backgrounds.

GOUACHE

The term "gouache" is the French equivalent of the Italian "*a guazzo*", meaning literally, "a muddy pool". In English, traditionally, gouache paints are also known as "body colour", being watercolour with a heavier body, where all colours are rendered with equal opacity.

Typically, gouache paints are derived from a mixture of pigment and gum arabic, with a filler such as blanc fix admixed to certain colours, to achieve opacity, and to help register a flat, velvety matt dried paint film. In recent years, some manufacturers have introduced gouache paint systems based on acrylic polymer emulsion mixed with a starch binder, thus providing a more flexible dry paint film.

In essence, we can think of gouache colour as being opaque watercolour. In true watercolour technique, sometimes chinese white is admixed to transparent colours to render them more opaque, to give them "body". This idea is taken a step further with gouache colours, where all the colours in each range will have been admixed with a low tinting strength white (blanc fix, also known as permanent white, barium sulphate). The resultant paint dries to a matt, velvety finish, light being absorbed rather than transmitted, as would be the case with transparent watercolour.

Of course it is more than possible to combine watercolour and gouache technique, thus fusing transparent and opaque areas. Because gouache is a water-thinning paint system, one can always thin out colour towards transparent glazes as required, although the resultant chroma of the dried paint film will be less glowing, less intense than a watercolour.

The origins of gouache painting stem from true tempera painting. While egg tempera painting was perhaps best suited to application on to solid, gessoed panels, a simple tempera paint made from pigment and a water-resoluble gum (gum arabic, gum cherry) could be used on parchment, or more recently paper, with similar results to egg tempera. This "gum tempera" was a little easier to prepare than true egg tempera, as the colour could be reconstituted on the palette when dry, so that mixed-up colour could be used and re-used as required.

Artists' Gouache and Designers' Gouache

Tubed gouache colours tend to be presented in two formats, as artists' (permanent) colours, or as designers' colour (for reproduction work). With designers' gouache, the need for lightfastness is not as acute, because the kind of work undertaken may only need to last a relatively short time: camera-ready artwork may require very bright colours, often based on dyes that can be replicated by commercial printing techniques. As a consequence, often designers' gouache ranges contain colours based on fugitive pigments or dyes. A good example are the fluorescent pigments, which are very liable to fading when exposed to daylight. These are often found in designers' gouache ranges, but one should try to avoid using them for permanent artworks. Often, designers' ranges include colours based on dyes that are not only liable to fading, but which "run" when re-wetted on the paper, often staining/bleeding into other colours. While ranges marked as designer gouache do contain more permanent colours, one needs to read the colour chart carefully before choosing paints, to ascertain the permanence of the colours. The colour chart usually has a star rating guide for lightfastness: choose only those with the best resistance to fading.

Artists' gouache ranges by contrast provide relatively permanent colours, where the paint has been manufactured with permanent artworks in mind. Even so, one should still look at the colour chart and pick out those with the best lightfastness. This is essential, because it is likely that each pigment will have been reduced in tinting strength due to the admixture with a filler (e.g. blanc fix). For some pigments (e.g. alizarin crimson), this admixture of white pigment can reduce the fastness to light and encourage fading upon exposure to daylight.

A simple way to test the resistance to fading of gouache colour, is to make some paint-outs on to paper: one application of neat colour, then another, admixed 50/50 with white. When dry, cover one half of each painted-out strip of colour, and place the paper or card against a window, facing daylight. Leave for about one month and then see if there is any perceptible change in hue. Gouache colours based on dyes or fugitive pigments tend to lose their brilliance, or in the most extreme cases, fade out altogether.

Hand-Made Gouache Colours

Gouache colours are fairly easy to prepare using dry pigment, because the pigment and binder do not need to be mulled expertly to achieve a good paint. This is because each colour is admixed with blanc fix, which absorbs the chosen pigments and helps to provide a soft, stiff paste.

Methods for Making Gouache Paints

On to a glass slab, with a straight palette knife, mix a stiff paste of distilled water and dry pigment. To this, add about 15-20% blanc fix, adding a little water as required. The resultant paste should be stiff rather than sloppy. This mixture can be stored for few days but is best used straight away, so make only enough colour for each painting session. To the pigment paste, add a quantity of binder, just enough to wet the pigment and make it glossy in this wet state. Make some tests before painting: if the paint dries glossy then too much binder has been added; on the other hand, if the dry paint is chalky and rubs off when rubbed lightly with a finger, a little more binder is required. It is a delicate balance. However, it is very good practice to prepare your colours in this way, as one quickly learns how each pigment behaves. The binder for making gouache paints is normally a gum arabic solution. Each manufacturer of watercolour usually provides a gum arabic based paint medium, which can be used as the basic binder in gouache paint. Alternatively you can prepare it yourself from the dry gum arabic.

Take one part (by volume) of gum arabic pieces, place in a container (e.g. glass jar). Pour into the container 12 parts of boiled water from the kettle. Stir every 15 minutes for a few hours, then leave to soak overnight. The next day, the gum will have dissolved to a brackish, honey-like consistency. This mixture should be strained/sieved to remove any impurities from the gum pieces, and can then be stored for a few days before spoiling. Some recipes call for the use of dextrin (starch) in conjunction with gum arabic. This simple starch solution (it dissolves quickly in warmish-water) renders the paint more resoluble and also improves the matt quality of the dried paint film.

Alternatively, a resoluble acrylic binder can be used when making gouache or watercolour paints by hand. One advantage of using this is that the binder keeps indefinitely and remains water-resoluble when dry, so that colours can be kept for longer periods.

Another method for making gouache paints uses the same binders as already discussed, but utilises pre-prepared pigment pastes, or colour pastes. These liquid pastes consist of pigment suspended in water, with a biocide and flow agents. In this method, the colour paste will not spoil, so has a very long shelf life. To the colour paste, 15-20% of blanc fix is added. The binder is then added as required.

For both methods, the author has found that a cup-cake baking tray is the best palette for keeping colours. The deep wells allow for a plentiful quantity of prepared paint-paste, while the intervening ridges can be used for colour mixing.

Suggested Pigments for Hand-Made Gouache Paint

This list of pigments concentrates on naturally opaque colours. To these opaque pigments only a small amount of blanc fix needs to be added. To the transparent colours (marked *), a greater proportion of blanc fix is added to achieve opacity.

Cadmium yellow lemon
Cadmium yellow medium
Cadmium orange
Cadmium red medium
Cadmium bordeaux (a deep rich, red-violet)
Cadmium brown (a deep red-brown)
Chrome oxide green
Phthalocyanine green* (with blanc fix, tends towards emerald green)
Phthalocyanine blue* (with blanc fix, tends towards sky blue)
Ultramarine blue*
Ultramarine violet*
Quinacridone red* (for a bright fuschia pink)
Titanium orange
Mars (iron oxide) yellow
Mars (iron oxide) red
Mars (iron oxide) violet
Mars (iron oxide) brown
Mars (iron oxide) black
Titanium white

Application

Traditionally, gouache colours are broken against each other, to accentuate the contrast between them. However, it can be equally effective to mix the colours on the paper (truly a muddy pool of colour). Because the paint is thicker than watercolour, having a denser structure, it is ideal for pushing about on the surface. Diluting the colour just a touch when applying, allows it to slip off the brush rather than dragging across the paper. A slick consistency, which does not show brushmarks when dry, is ideal. Obviously, everyone has their own technique and preferences. Some will prefer to dab, others to apply thinner paint, etc.

When overpainting, wait for each layer to dry before proceeding. It should be possible to overlay colour without picking up from the previous layer. However, if one agitates the surface of the dry layer with a wet brush, it will of course reconstitute that layer of paint. One can learn to utilise these properties judiciously in the working process.

Supports

Supports suitable for gouache include the standard watercolour papers: 300gsm papers, or preferably heavier weights, to give a more card-like structure are ideal. For example, 600gsm Saunders Waterford NOT paper, provides a slightly pitted surface and a very strong, durable support, which does not cockle when wet colour is applied. Other possible supports include parchment vellum, matt acrylic gesso primed paper, board or canvas fixed to a rigid support. If you use an acrylic priming, make sure that it is very matt when dry, as the glossy types tend to resist applied gouache paint.

Preservation and Storage of Work

Like watercolour, gouache paintings are relatively fragile artworks. They should be stored away from direct sunlight, preferably in a closed portfolio. A sheet of acid-free tissue paper will protect the matt paint surface from scratches or marking, when stored flat. Finished work can be glazed for best protection. Varnishing is not recommended, as this can change the matt, velvety paint finish. A light spray of fixative will preserve the paint surface without darkening the tones too much.

Alternative Water-Based Binding Agents

A number of protein glues and starch-glues can be used with dry pigment to create new binding systems, which do not correspond readily to manufactured paints. However, they should be considered by artists because they may offer a cost-effective way to make simple paintings, usually on to paper, which emphasise the characteristics of the pigments used.

Gum Tragacanth

Natural tree gums have been used by artists for many centuries. Gum tragacanth swells in water but does not completely dissolve.

Typical Recipe for Gum Tragacanth Solution

Gum tragacanth, powder	1 part
Cold water	20 parts

Ideally, the cold water needs to be distilled water, or water from a boiled kettle left to cool. Tap water tends to promote mould growth.

The powdered gum is left to soak in the water for 1-2 days. The gum swells and forms a kind of suspension, which is quite lumpy, or gel-like. After 2 days, press the whole mixture through muslin, leaving behind most of the lumps/gel. The strained liquid can then be prepared with dry pigments to make a very matt watercolour, which gives a dry, velvety paint film. Gum tragacanth is commonly used as a binder for soft pastels, due to its soft, forgiving qualities.

For pastel making, even weaker solutions of gum can be used: just enough to hold the pigment together in a rolled stick-form.

Because tragacanth solution spoils quickly, it needs to be made then used. The exact amount of pigment to binder required for making a simple watercolour will vary from pigment to pigment. Even when the amount of binder to pigment is very high, the paint film tends to dry to be dead-matt rather than glossy. As a consequence, artists can make a simple paint using tragacanth solution which has far more binder to pigment, without too much trouble. The resultant paint can be applied to any watercolour paper.

Dextrin

To make a very simple water-based paint, dextrin (starch powder), is mixed with water.

Dextrin, powder	1 part
Hot water	20 parts

Boil a kettle, then leave to stand for 5-10 minutes. Pour this hot water over the dextrin powder, in a clean vessel. Leave to stand for 10-15 minutes, stirring every now and then to free any lumps. The resultant thin syrup can be used as a basic binder for pigments and the paint produced in this way can be applied to any watercolour paper. If the syrup is too rich in binder, it will feel slightly sticky when dry on the paper. If this happens, simply dilute the stock solution as required. Dextrin is an economic alternative to gum arabic and gum tragacanth.

Methylcellulose (Tylose)

This type of converted starch is sold in powder form and swells when mixed with water to provide a lump-free solution, which can be used as a binder for making watercolours, gouache, or soft pastels. It is offered in a variety of thicknesses, according to end use. For paint making, methylcellulose with a low viscosity (e.g. MH

300) is recommended. It has little or no binding power, so resultant paint films may be dusty, requiring an application of fixative spray, once dried.

Methylcellulose	1 part
Cold water	30 parts

Leave this mixture to stand for 1-2 days, stir occasionally. Once the mixture forms a clear solution, free of lumps, it can be used as a simple binder. It can also be added to raw acrylic resin dispersions in small amounts (10-15%), to give a matt, gently absorbent acrylic paint. Solutions of methylcellulose tend to absorb pigment powder readily, so can be used to make quick, economic paints. The solution remains very resoluble with water once dried and needs to be kept away from damp. Soft pastels can also be made with methylcellulose (see the chapter on Soft Pastel Painting).

Casein

A dried milk product, casein is a high protein binder for pigments. The powder only forms a solution (or rather an emulsion) in water, when ammonium carbonate is added to the mixture. This emulsifying agent allows the casein to take up the water to form a swollen paste. This paste is further diluted to a single cream consistency. Casein has a high glue strength: as a consequence, it provides a very durable, hard-wearing matt paint film. Sadly, solutions of casein tend to spoil within days, so need to be prepared and used immediately. The dried paint film is effectively non-resoluble with water, so is nominally damp-resistant.

Recipe for Simple Casein Paint

Casein powder (lactic acid)	2 parts
Cold water	8 parts
Ammonium carbonate, powder	1 part

Add the water to the casein powder. Slowly stir in the ammonium carbonate. Leave to stand for one hour, stir occasionally. The mixture swells to form a brackish paste. Add a further 8 parts of water slowly, stirring all the while, to achieve a smooth single cream consistency. Add more water as required. The mixture and resultant paint can be further diluted with water.

To the casein solution, add the desired quantity of pigment. Because casein is such a strong binder, it can be overloaded with pigment to some extent while still adhering to the support. Casein paint can be applied thinly to watercolour paper, or on to panels prepared with gesso made with animal glue and chalk. Multiple coats of casein paints tend to be unsuccessful, due to the extreme strength of the binder. Make sure that subsequent coats are weaker (diluted) to counter this defect. Casein is a quick, economic pigment binder, which can be used to show how pigments behave (i.e. transparency and opacity are clearly seen when mixed with the casein binder).

Casein paint can be applied to stiff watercolour papers, or on to panels prepared with casein gesso (where casein is used as the binding agent for chalk). Care must be taken during the preparation of casein gesso, to ensure that the glue strength of the base coat is stronger than that of subsequent coats (i.e. each successive coat is required to be slightly more dilute than the previous, to prevent the gesso layers shearing away from each other). Applied layers of paint follow the same basic principle, as already mentioned.

Egg White, Glair

In medieval illumination, the white of the egg was commonly used as a binder for pigment. This egg white, or glair, is almost wholly protein based and forms a strong, thin binding, which is especially useful for pale colours. To prepare, the egg white is whisked until the liquid becomes a foaming froth. The quickest way to do this is with an electric food mixer. Once the egg white turns entirely to a froth, it is left to stand for 2-3 hours. After this time, part of the mixture will be liquid, part will still be froth. Pour off the liquid into a clean container: this is the binder, “glair”. Throw away the remaining froth.

The glair can be mixed with pigment and applied to watercolour paper, or gesso panels. The original support for glair-based paint would have been goatskin parchment (vellum), where a thin coat of a gesso-like preparation was used as a ground on the areas to be painted (e.g. letter capitals on illuminated manuscripts etc).

Klucel (Hydroxi-propyl-cellulose)

Klucel is a modern, clean starch-based binding agent, sold in a variety of viscosities. The thicker types may be unusable as paint binders, being too viscous to manipulate successfully.

Klucel can be solved 10% powder to cold water, to form a clear, viscous liquid. Leave to stand for 1-2 days then strain through mesh to remove any lumps. Klucel made up this way (using distilled cold water) keeps for many months before spoiling (it does not attract microbes). It can be further diluted with cold water as required.

Add the klucel solution to dry pigment and stir well. Normally, the pigment is readily absorbed into the klucel binder. A little alcohol can be added to improve wetting of pigment, especially when using the synthetic organic pigments. Pigments can be first mulled with distilled water on a glass plate with glass muller to improve their wetting, as required.

It is recommended to prepare pigments into klucel using the 10% concentration, then dilute later to achieve thinner paint films. Klucel dries to a flat, neutral finish: excessive use of binder does not increase the gloss of the paint film, especially when filler (e.g. blanc fix) is added. Paints made with mixtures of klucel/pigment/filler tend to give flat, matt, paint films. The dried paint film is insoluble with warm water, but will pick-up when cold water is applied and agitated on to the paint surface. This system allows dried, or recently dried colours to be overpainted without discoloration or disturbance.

Klucel-based paints can be applied to stiffish watercolour papers and to gesso-primed panels. Klucel also dissolves into alcohol, to make a consolidant often used in paper conservation.

Animal Skin/Bone Glues

Any type of protein/starch glue can be used to bind pigments, but the characteristic properties of the chosen binder may affect the longevity of the artwork.

In the case of animal skin/bone glues, the dried glue film remains water-receptive (hygroscopic) and sensitive to moisture. If agitated with warm water, a paint film based on this glue may become reconstituted (or at least slightly sticky). Such paint films are also very prone to deterioration from damp and need to be stored in a dry, ambient atmosphere. Examples of paintings made on to stretched linen canvas using animal skin glue bindings have survived many hundreds of years. However, the initial rich gleam produced by animal skin/bone glue paint films soon becomes dull, matt in appearance. Over time, the paint film becomes very dry and progressively harder (less flexible). As a consequence, chalking of the paint film is common with age.

Weak solutions of animal skin glues (e.g. rabbit glue) can be prepared and used to bind dry pigment. Such binders readily absorb most pigments, especially earth pigments, mineral pigments and other large-particle size pigments. With finer particle pigments, a 5% addition of water-free alcohol acts as a wetting agent (e.g. with alizarin crimson, prussian blue). When the binding is relatively dilute (e.g. one part glue to 30 parts water), the paint film is more or less water-clear. Stronger glues have a slight brownish cast, depending on the quality of glue used. Laying down multiple layers of such glue bindings can be rather tricky, as the previous layer will want to "pick-up" if agitated. However, careful brushing of thin glazes can avoid this. As with casein, the glue strength is of great importance. The first layer needs to be slightly stronger than the next, and so on. This requires the addition of a small amount of water at each layer stage. To keep animal skin or bone glues in a fluid solution form, it is best to keep the glue bath just warm. Rather than contacting with a direct heat source, the glue container simply stands in a larger bath/vessel containing water from a recently boiled kettle. This method will keep the glue warm for 10-15 minutes at a time: as the glue returns to a jelly, simply re-boil the kettle and replace the hot water.

Animal glues may be sourced from skins (hides), usually from cattle, or from bones and hooves (gelatine). While rabbit glue requires warming to form a solution, gelatine swells readily in cold water and requires only modest heat (10°C) to form a solution. Gelatine is usually more refined than grains or cubes of animal skin glue, with a paler colour and contains fewer impurities. Recipes vary according to the intended use, a simple glue is made in the ratio of one part gelatine (by volume) to 10 parts of water. Upon swelling and forming a solution, then cooling, this ratio should provide a softish-jelly. When working with pale and delicate colours (e.g. mineral blues such as lapis lazuli, or azurite), using gelatine as a binder, rather than heavier coloured bindings (e.g. egg yolk), helps to preserve subtle colour values. Although gelatine can be considered less strong than skin glue as a binder, it should have greater flexibility.

Isinglass

In the Russian icon tradition, the glue used in the preparation of the painting ground (gesso) and also in some cases, the pigment binder, is derived from isinglass, a pale, almost colourless glue from the swim bladder of the sturgeon fish. Since the fall of the Soviet Union, the supply of isinglass has become rather limited, although at present, Andrei Andreev has procured an ongoing source of bladders, which are collected at the mouth of the Volga river once a year, dried and sold by weight. The best quality "Salianski" glue is unrefined and has a pale yellow-brown colour. This pale colour is negligible in terms of its use as a binder or glue for painting grounds. Unrefined isinglass has greater flexibility than the cleaned-refined type (which appears as a translucent white membrane). Some isinglass on the market may be from other sources, usually from South American sturgeon fish.

Isinglass has greater binding strength than gelatine and skin glues. To form into a usable solution, it is left to soak for 3-4 hours in distilled water. At this stage, the glue mass swells. The glue is removed from the water and carefully wrung to remove excess water. Wrap the glue mass in cotton muslin, and gently squeeze to remove as much water as possible. The remaining mass of glue is then placed in a double boiler and left to warm through on a low heat (no more than 60°C), so that the glue forms a clear solution. Once the glue is clarified, strain through muslin to remove impurities. In this form, the isinglass glue can be used, while still just warm, and makes a fine, almost water-clear binding for pigments. Between each applied layer, leave the glue to dry off, or pick-up may occur. The stock solution of isinglass will keep for a few days and can be stored in a fridge at about 6°C. The cooled gel can be re-warmed as required, although this process tends to give progressively weaker glue. Isinglass has excellent flexibility and is the chosen glue for repairing tapestry work due to its almost invisible colour and elasticity.

Starch Pastes

Starch, in the form of powder can be obtained from wheat, rye, rice or arrowroot. These powders are prepared into starch paste by combination with cold water, just enough to form a brackish, viscous paste. To this paste, an equal quantity of recently boiled water (i.e. very hot) is added and stirred together to form a syrup with the consistency of double cream. This simple starch paste is most often used in the repair of paper artefacts (the starch contains no sulphur or nitrogen, so acts as a neutral adhesive). However, the glue strength is not high and as a binder for pigment, such pastes are less than reliable. The resultant paint film is very dry (can rub off easily), although this method does show the exact nuance of the pigment used. It may be possible to use starch+pigment to execute the painting on to paper, then, once dry to apply a spray fixative to help hold the fragile surface to the paper support. In this way, starch paste can be combined with soft pastel painting techniques to give a similar appearance.

Simple pigment-starch pastes are often used in printmaking techniques, for woodblock printing. In this instance, fat (thick) starch pastes, containing a small amount of pigment are ideal for pressing against incised woodblocks to gain an embossed impression. During the application of pressure, excess water in the starch paste is pushed out and a soft, fine layer of colour is transferred on to the (usually delicate, soft) paper. In the restoration trade, old recipes for the relining of canvas mention the combination of starch glues (wheat, rye, etc.) with venice turpentine, to make a tacky adhesive.

Soft Pastel Painting

When dry pigment is combined with an extremely weak binding agent, cylindrical sticks of pastel, usually referred to as "soft pastel" can be formed, thereby allowing the artist to apply colour directly to a specially prepared paper support.

The degree of softness of the pastel stick is governed by the strength of the binding agent used but also the exact combination of dry raw materials. If the binding agent is too strong, the resultant pastel stick is hard, possibly unworkable over the paper support. Some pastel brands are softer in feel than others: this is more often than not a conscious decision by the manufacturer. Just as different brands of oil colour will have different consistencies, colour strengths, degree of matt or gloss, so the various brands of pastel colours on the market can vary in texture. Similarly, if the binding agent is too weak, the pastel stick may crumble easily when moderate pressure is applied.

Pastel sticks are made by combining a number of dry raw materials into a weak binder. For example, pigment is often admixed with china clay and/or talc to help produce a soft, velvety mark, when the resultant pastel stick is applied to the support. Without the addition of these dry filler materials, the pastel stick may be too hard and scratchy to work well. As a consequence, the manufacturing of pastel sticks is not always straightforward: each individual pigment will require a separate recipe, in order to produce a pastel stick with the optimum qualities of softness and colour strength.

From the recipes given in this chapter, artists can prepare their own pastel sticks for pastel painting. The recipes provide a starting point, and it should be noted that the strength of binder and exact combination of raw material differs from one colour to another. Because pigments vary from source to source, the recipes given here are a guide only, from which one expects that adjustments may need to be made in order to create the desired effect when painting.

Supports for Pastel Painting

In many ways, the softness of the pastel stick relates directly to the type of support used. If very soft pastel is applied to a highly abrasive ground, then the pastel stick will be quickly used up: in the worst case, it will simply crumble into the paper surface. As a consequence, the choice of support is crucial.

If one uses smooth paper, when the pastel stick is applied to the surface, the pigment particles have little or nothing to catch on to. Ideally, the applied pastel colour becomes caught in the structure of the support. For this reason, mildly abrasive grounds, for example, those prepared with pumice powder in a water-based glue are quite successful. Similarly, papers with a pronounced grain (e.g. rough watercolour paper, or special pitted surface pastel papers) are commonly employed. The degree to which the pastel pigment is caught on the surface of the support also governs the amount of "fixing" required. Many theories exist as to the best way to "fix" the particles of pigment to the support surface. It is probably best to use the minimum amount of fixative, in order to avoid a change in colour tones. Whenever fixative is applied to pastel paintings, it saturates the pigment dust, coating the particles with resin. Consequently, the colour tones may darken, thereby negating the appearance of the painted image.

The best solution seems to be to apply only the minimum amount of fixative, in combination with pastel applied to a relatively toothy support, where much of the pigment dust is held in place by the texture of the support.

Another factor to consider, is the best way to exhibit pastel paintings. In order to protect the fragile painting surface, they are usually shown behind glass (glazed). This prevents the pigment dust from being disturbed but at the same time introduces a change in the way light falls on the surface (i.e. it has to pass through the glass before hitting the painting surface). It is possible to attach the painting (for example if done on paper) to a second support, such as an MDF panel, and to show the painting without glass protection. This obviously makes handling and display more of an issue. It may also be necessary to fix the surface more comprehensively when showing work in this manner.

While the surface of the pastel painting is fragile and requires careful handling, so the type of support used needs to conform to notions of longevity and durability. The best choice is to work on to acid-free papers, which do not discolour over time or promote the activity of acid compounds. Similarly, when choosing abrasive supports, ensure that the substrate on to which the abrasive ground is applied is acid-free and of archival quality. In respect to this, sand paper (glass paper) from the hardware store is wholly unsuitable. The thick card backing to such papers is extremely acid-rich and will discolour over time. This discoloration can spread to the face of the painting and influence colour tones. Such acidic papers may also decompose readily, especially in combination with mild damp.

Commercial Pastel Papers

Commercially prepared pastel papers tend to have a degree of texture, but this is not particularly pronounced. As a consequence, most commercially prepared papers catch and hold less pigment dust than hand-prepared ones, leading, inevitably to the application of multiple coats of fixative. While the surface of such papers tends to be slightly pitted, rather than abrasive, they may serve perfectly well for studies made in pastel where minimal amounts of colour are applied - for example in the context of a life drawing class, where perhaps only two or three colours are used during the drawing/painting process.

Commercial pastel papers are often sold in pads or blocks, with each page interleaved with a sheet of tissue or glassine paper to help prevent smudging of the applied pastel.

Pastel paper is often marketed in a range of colours, to provide a tinted ground. However, the permanence of coloured papers is not always disclosed by the manufacturer. Often such papers are coloured by dyes that have a tendency to fade. This may be especially so with strong, bright colours.

Flock/Velour Paper

In French pastel painting, a special support based on velvet flocking, glued to a paper backing has long been used. This surface has a soft, velvety texture which catches pastel dust successfully but also allows for a large degree of blending and smudging on the painting surface. With such papers, often the paper and the flocking have been coloured to give a tinted ground. Again, the exact properties may not be disclosed by the manufacturer. For example, the colouring may be dye-based and thereby more liable to fade upon exposure to light.

Cork Boards

Finely ground cork can be mixed with glue and applied to a thick paper or cardboard backing to provide a suitable support for pastel painting. In the author's experience, such grounds should not come into contact with water (i.e. not suitable for mixed media, with additions of watercolour, gouache, etc), nor should they be rubbed aggressively, as the cork soon detaches itself from the backing.

Hand-Made Supports

The easiest pastel support to hand prepare is that which is made from pumice powder (pulverised volcanic pumice stone), mixed into a solution of rabbit glue. This support is slightly toothy, thereby allowing the pastel pigment particles to be attached to the surface and subsequently reducing the need for excessive fixing upon completion of the painting.

Recipe for Pumice-Glue Ground

The glue is first prepared into a solution:

Rabbit glue, grains	**1 part**
Cold water	**15 parts**

The glue is placed in a clean vessel (e.g. glass jar), to which the cold water is slowly added. Leave the glue to soak for 30 minutes or so. During this time, the glue swells slightly but does not form a clear solution. Boil a kettle and deposit the boiled water into another (larger) container, into which the glue vessel is placed (i.e. a warm-water bath). The action of the boiled water on the glue vessel causes the glue to clarify and form a solution. Into the now warm glue solution, a percentage of pumice powder (perhaps 20-30% pumice to the volume of glue solution) is added. Stir vigorously, so that the glue saturates the pumice particles. The mixture is then applied using a wide hog varnish brush (40-50mm wide), on to the chosen paper surface. The pumice-glue mixture needs to be applied while still warm: if it cools too much, the glue will set as a jelly. If this happens, simply sit the mixture in a bath of warm water again to re-constitute.

Each time the glue-pumice mix is applied to the paper surface, it is imperative that the mixture is stirred to keep the pumice particles in suspension, thereby producing a relatively even film of application over the paper surface. Upon drying, check that the pumice particles are firmly attached to the paper surface. Wait 24 hours to do this, so that all moisture has evaporated. If the pumice particles are not properly attached to the paper surface, try adding more glue the next time, or reducing the amount of pumice used. One thin application is best, so that the pumice powder stands up against the surface of the paper just enough to catch the pastel pigment particles. This pumice-glue ground can be modified by the addition of a small amount of dry pigment, to give a tinted ground. If no pigment is added, the colour is a soft beige or beige-grey, depending on the colour of the pumice. By adding small amounts of dry pigment (e.g. a natural earth pigment such as yellow ochre), the dull colour of the pumice is hidden. If too much pigment is added, the tooth of the pumice may become lost.

Some pigments have a toothy nature and can be applied in place of the pumice to act as both a colourant and give an abrasive quality. For example:

- Green quartz, fuchsite
- Aergirine (iron silicate green)
- Azurite
- Malachite
- Sodalite
- Basalt
- Iron glimmer (iron ore, ranging from 0-150 micron size)
- Cast iron powder
- Stainless steel powder
- Glass pigments (which range from 0-125 micron size)
- Many types of earth pigment have coarse structures

All these coarse textured pigments could be combined with the glue solution to give coloured pastel grounds.

Coarse Pastel Ground

In order to bind large, coarse pigments or other material (e.g. coarse marble dusts, quartz chips), a stronger water-based protein glue, such as casein could be used. Casein has great adhesive strength and dries fast to a neutral, mattish finish.

Recipe for Casein as an Adhesive for Large Particle Size Pigments/Filler:

Casein (lactic acid)	2 parts
Ammonium carbonate	1 part
Cold water	8 parts

The powdered casein and water are combined together. The ammonium carbonate is slowly stirred into this mixture and acts as an emulsifying agent, to create a smooth mixture. The ammonium carbonate tends to cause swelling or effervescence. Upon being left to stand for 30 minutes or so, the mixture calms down to give a smooth, thick paste. In this form, the casein can be used as a strong glue, especially when attempting to adhere large particulate structures to stiff paper (e.g. quartz chips). The mixture can be diluted with more cold water as required. The casein solution is good for 2-3 days before it begins to turn rancid and becomes smelly.

When combining with aggregates such as marble dust or quartz chips, apply only one coat of the casein to the support. Multiple coats may delaminate from the support, as the casein glue is so strong that the top coat will stick to the first coat and upon drying want to shear away from the support. Multiple coats may also lead to cracking. Upon drying, casein always has a neutral, dry finish. This makes it especially suitable for use with larger particle size aggregates such as marble dust and quartz chips, where the applied material will dry off to give a stone-like effect. The application of such aggregates obviously adds weight to the support. It may therefore be more appropriate to apply such pastel grounds on to boards (e.g. MDF panel of 15mm + thickness). If working on to paper, choose heavy watercolour paper (425 to 640gsm) that is rigid enough to take thick applications of painting ground.

It is also possible to combine aggregates and abrasive powders into acrylic binding media. Indeed, many manufacturers offer ready-to-use pastel primer which involves the combination of pigment and abrasive into an acrylic binder to give a coloured pastel ground.

Sometimes, such combinations appear slightly glossy when compared to grounds prepared using rabbit glue or casein. However, one advantage of acrylic pastel grounds is their relative flexibility. This may mean that such grounds can be applied to stretched canvas supports, thereby enabling the artist to work on a larger scale.

Acrylic texture or modelling pastes are also manufactured, which may find use as grounds for pastel painting. Such pastes tend to be white, or off-white in colour and may be tinted by admixture with acrylic colour to give a coloured ground. Alternatively, the off-white paste can be applied to the support, then when dry overpainted with a thin glaze of acrylic colour. If the colour is applied too thickly, it may inhibit the abrasive nature of the texture paste.

Choice of Paper, When Hand-Preparing Pastel Grounds

Archival, acid-free papers are best suited as supports for pastel painting. The advantage of such papers is that they remain resilient when exposed to acid compounds and do not discolour readily, or decompose when exposed to mild damp. Such papers are often treated during manufacture with a calcium carbonate (chalk) buffer, which resists acids to an extent: it will prevent the paper from deteriorating in normal conditions (i.e. when not exposed to damp or humidity, or left in excessively acidic environments).

In terms of stability while painting with pastel, a durable, sturdy paper is preferred. For example, papers of 300gsm or above are suggested, as they do not cockle excessively if water is applied to them. By the same token, such papers have a degree of stability and firmness which may assist the application of pastel, where at times the paper surface is stressed by the pressure of the application. Watercolour papers are sold with a variety of surfaces. If one is applying a special ground (as outlined), it may be best to begin with a smooth (satin) surface watercolour paper of 300gsm weight or above. The smooth paper will provide a level surface on to which the pastel ground can be brushed. Consequently, the particles of pumice (or other abrasive) will stand up within the dried glue or casein film. Because the particles lie in this slightly exposed structure, the applied pastel pigment will catch on to this surface and the pigment dust will hold on, without the need to apply excessive coats of fixative.

The use of hand-prepared pastel grounds also allows the artist to experiment with a wide variety of papers, such as hand-made papers with rough deckle edges. In this way, the support can become an integral part of the painting itself.

Dralon Fibre as a Pastel Ground

Nylon dralon fibres, presented in the form of short, fluffy lengths can be mixed with a very dilute solution of acrylic binder (e.g. Primal AC 35), to give a synthetic version of the older Velour paper surface. The dralon fibres are carefully mixed into the dilute acrylic binder and then spread over the chosen paper surface. Upon drying, the fibres stick up and have a soft, velvety texture. If the surface is not dry/velvety enough, simply dilute the acrylic binder with more water and try again. To gain the optimum surface, the acrylic binder needs to be strong enough to bind the fibre, but not over strong, so that it creates a plastic surface.

Cork Particles

Dried, ground cork can be intermixed with rabbit glue (recipe as with pumice) to give a support for pastel painting. The resultant ground is slightly springy in nature but gently absorbent, where the pastel pigment dust is gently rubbed into the cork surface. If the surface is abraded too much when applying colour, the cork begins to disintegrate. As a consequence, cork offers a very sensitive (bark coloured) support.

Egg White (Glair) as Binding Agent for Pastel Grounds

Egg white hardens upon exposure to steam, to produce a water-insoluble binding. When pumice powder is incorporated into glair, a thin veil of this mixture can be applied to paper to give a pastel ground. The glair-pumice mixture is required to be applied freshly, then left to dry for perhaps 2-3 hours. After this time, the pastel painting is made on to the abrasive pumice ground. Immediately upon completion, the painting requires fixing with steam, so that the egg white hardens to a durable film. If the painting is not quickly fixed, it becomes impossible to harden the egg white and the surface becomes prone to attack from microbes.

Recipe for Egg White (Glair)

Take 3 egg whites
Put in food blender and whisk until foamy
Leave for 2-3 hours
Pour off liquid, throw away foam.

This procedure removes the non-adhesive component from the egg white, leaving the liquid portion, which is high in protein and adhesive strength. For pastel ground, the liquid portion is combined with the pumice powder and brushed out on to the paper surface.

After the ground has dried and the painting has been executed, the face of the painting is exposed to steam from a kettle. Due to this exposure to steam, the egg white hardens, trapping the pigment particles from behind and fixing the colour into the ground. Be careful not to add too much pumice into such a ground, as the colour of the pumice itself may show strongly once the painting is fixed. The egg white, when fixed, tends to deepen the colour values of the pastel pigment particles to a degree. This system overcomes the need to fix the painting by spray fixative.

Binding Agents for Pastel

A number of protein-type adhesives can be used for preparing soft pastel sticks. The degree of softness/hardness of a pastel stick is to some extent determined by the strength of the binding agent used, but these different binders inherently influence the relative hardness/softness of the pastel stick. For example, by tradition, the binder for soft pastels is often gum tragacanth. Pastels based on this binder tend to be very soft in nature, with a velvety mark. By contrast, pastels prepared using gum arabic tend to have a certain hardness. Water-swelling gums from small fruit trees, such as gum arabic, gum cherry and gum tragacanth are most commonly employed in the manufacture of pastels, although a number of other binders are often cited. For example, stale beer has a weak binding strength and may be used with many colours. In some modern pastel ranges, methylcellulose is used. This binder is of great importance, especially to the making of hand-prepared pastel sticks, because unlike natural binders it tends to keep for a period of months rather than days, before spoiling. A manufacturer may make use of all of these binding agents in order to create the optimum pastel stick for each pigment/colour offered.

It is also possible to make pastel sticks with some pigments without using any binding agent whatsoever. This is especially the case with clay-containing earth pigments, which may readily form into a solid stick just by mixture with water. Upon drying, the adhesive clay content of the pigment allows the pastel stick to remain in one piece.

Filler Material

Into manufactured pastels (and hand-made ones), a number of additives may be incorporated. For example, china clay (Pigment White 19, hydrated aluminium silicate) is often used to help impart softness to the pastel stick. The cohesive nature of china clay, when mixed with water, is also important: it helps to keep the pigment together in solid stick form, but gives way under gentle pressure, as the pastel stick contacts with the painting ground. The addition of filler material into any paint system is done judiciously: too much china clay for example will create a pastel stick that dries too hard and breaks easily. The exact amount of china clay used in each colour will vary, according to the degree of softness/hardness required. Kaolin is another form of china clay (normally whiter in colour), originally derived from China.

Talc (hydrous magnesium silicate) is also known as soapstone and French chalk. It may be used in some pastel sticks, where its soft nature can help produce a highly velvety mark. It is similar to china clay but tends to form more crumbly pastel sticks. As a consequence it is best used in very small quantities, perhaps along with china clay, to improve the softness of pastels derived from pigments with very small particle sizes (e.g. synthetic organic pigments).

Chalk, also known as whiting, is natural calcium carbonate (Pigment White 18). It has a harder, coarser nature than talc and china clay but is sometimes used in pastel making to give a harder, more durable pastel stick. Overuse of chalk may cause the pastel stick to become brittle, snapping when pressure is applied. Chalk works best when combined with earth pigments that naturally set when combined with water. The addition of a little chalk may help allow the particles to break up as they contact with the paper surface, so distributing colour to the painting ground.

Formation of Colour Ranges

Unlike paints based on liquid formulations, pastel relies on pigment applied in a dry form. As such, it is not easy to blend and mix colours on the painting surface. Some pastels are extra soft, so that some degree of blending can be achieved. However, the traditional method of working with pastel is to have each colour available in a series of pure tones, tints towards black and tints towards white. In the case of each manufacturer, this can vary and there is no set standard presentation of pastel colours.

In general terms, pastel ranges are organised in the following manner:

1. Pure Colour - where one pigment is represented.

2. Tints Towards White - where one colour is presented admixed with white to form a series of tints, moving towards white (pale, light tints). The choice of white used is crucial. Zinc white gives gentle gradations of the original colour, but adds a slightly cold tinge which becomes particularly apparent when the tint comprises white with just a trace of colour (very pale tints). By contrast, titanium white tends to give a deadening effect when admixed with colour, producing duller mixtures, where the white effect may be over strong.

3. Tints Towards Black - where one colour is presented admixed with black to form a series of tints, moving towards black (neutral, dark tints). Choice of black pigments is also crucial. Ideally, a neutral black (e.g. ivory black) is used, one that possesses a little transparency and therefore allows the original colour to have a presence in the mixture. This effect works best when both the black pigment and the colour being admixed are transparent in nature.

There are many variations on this format, but for practical reasons, this should suffice as an introduction.

Whenever two or more pigments are mixed, there is an inevitable loss of colour resonance. Also, admixtures are dependent upon particle size: pigments with larger particle size tend to dominate in mixtures.

Basic Recipes for Making Soft Pastels

The following recipes were prepared during the late spring in North Yorkshire, England, during a dry spell of weather. Each pastel stick took some 3-4 days to air-dry thoroughly when left in a dry room, without any central heating. It would be an advantage to prepare pastels during hot dry weather rather than at times of cold and damp. It is important to let pastels dry naturally: if too much heat is applied to the drying pastel sticks, they can split or crumble during the drying process. It also makes sense to prepare a batch of sticks at any one time, (perhaps six sticks of each colour) to save time and effort.

These recipes are intended to form a starting point for anyone interested in making their own soft pastels. It may be advisable to be prepared to change the recipe ingredients, in order to make the exact colour required (i.e. to add white to the core colour, etc).

Measurements : tbs = level tablespoon
tsp = level teaspoon

N.B. Tylose MH300 is a brand of methylcellulose.

Cadmium yellow lemon

Pigment:	cadmium yellow lemon	9 tbs
	+ china clay	2 tsp
Binder: Tylose MH300	1:60	

Cadmium yellow deep

Pigment:	cadmium yellow	9 tbs
	+ china clay	2 tsp
Binder: Tylose MH300	1:60	

Permanent yellow (hansa yellow)

Pigment:	permanent yellow	3 tbs
	zinc white	1 tbs
	+ china clay	2 tsp
Binder: Tylose MH300	1:60	

Cadmium orange

Pigment:	cadmium orange	4 tbs
	+ china clay	1 tsp
Binder: Tylose MH300	1:90	

Cadmium red medium

Pigment:	cadmium red	4 tbs
	+ china clay	1 tsp
Binder: Tylose MH300	1:90	

Permanent red PR 170 Neutral Red B

Pigment:	permanent red	3 tbs
	zinc white	1 tbs
	+ china clay	2 tsp
Binder: Tylose MH300	1:60	

Ultramarine blue deep

Pigment:	ultramarine blue deep	1 tbs
	+ china clay	4 tsp
Binder: Tylose MH300	1:60	

Cobalt turquoise light

Pigment:	cobalt turquoise light	3 tbs
	+ china clay	1 tsp
Binder: Tylose MH300	1:60	

Kings blue (mixed)

Pigment:	heliogen green	1 tbs
	+ china clay	2 tsp
Binder: Tylose MH300	1:60	

mixed with

Pigment:	titanium white	6 tbs
	+ china clay	2 tsp
Binder: Tylose MH300	1:90	

Cinnabar green (mixed)

Pigment:	nickel titanium yellow	2 tbs
	+ china clay	1/2 tsp
Binder: Tylose MH300	1:90	

mixed with

Pigment:	chromium oxide green	1 tbs
	+ china clay	1/2 tsp
Binder: Tylose MH300	1:90	

Chromium oxide green

Pigment:	chromium oxide green	3 tbs
	+ china clay	1 tsp
Binder: Tylose MH300	1:90	

Olive green (mixed)

Pigment:	green earth, burnt	1 tbs
	+ china clay	1/2 tsp
Binder: Tylose MH300 1:90		

mixed with

Pigment:	chromium oxide green	1/2 tbs
	+ china clay	1/4 tsp
Binder: Tylose MH300	1:90	

Ivory black

Pigment:	ivory black	1 tbs
	+ china clay	1/2 tsp
Binder: Tylose MH300	1:60	

Silver graphite

Pigment:	silver graphite powder	3 tbs
	+ china clay	2 tsp
Binder: Tylose MH300	1:30	

Mars yellow

Pigment:	iron oxide yellow	3 tbs
	+ china clay	7 tsp
Binder: water	+ a drop of Tylose MH300	
	1:90, to moisten	

Raw sienna

Pigment:	raw sienna	3 tbs
	+ china clay	4 tsp
Binder: water		

Burnt sienna

Pigment:	burnt sienna	4 tbs
	+ china clay	2 tsp
Binder: Tylose MH300	1:90	

Burnt green earth

Pigment:	green earth, burnt	1 tbs
	+ china clay	1/2 tsp
Binder: water		

Venetian red

Pigment:	venetian red	3 tbs
	+ china clay	1 tsp
Binder: water		

Pozzuoli red

Pigment:	pozzuoli red	3 tbs
	+ china clay	1 tsp
Binder: water		

Caput mortuum

Pigment:	caput mortuum synthetic	4 tbs
	+ china clay	2 tsp
Binder: Tylose MH300	1:60	

Burnt umber

Pigment:	burnt umber	3 tbs
	+ china clay	1 tsp
Binder: water		

Davy's grey

Pigment:	davy's grey, grey-green	3 tbs
	+ china clay	1 tsp
Binder: Tylose MH300	1:60	

Iron oxide glimmer

Pigment:	iron oxide glimmer grey	10 tbs
	+ china clay	6 tsp
Binder: Tylose MH300	1:60	

Titanium white

Pigment:	titanium white	3 tbs
	+ china clay	2 tsp
Binder: Tylose MH300	1:90	

Pearlescent pink – Use white pearlescent pigment, admixed with any transparent pigment, to create similar pearlescent tones. For pearlescent white, use a combination of equal parts zinc white/pearlescent white.

Pigment:	permanent red	3 tbs
	zinc white	1 tbs
	pearlescent white	1 tbs
	+ china clay	2 tsp
Binder: Tylose MH300	1:60	

Binding Agents

The binder, other than water for these recipes is methylcellulose, a converted starch glue, sold under the name "Tylose MH300". It dissolves completely in water and remains resoluble when made up into pastels, or when drawn marks are washed over with water. The dilute solutions suggested here make relatively soft pastels, when compared to those made with gum tragacanth or gum arabic.

Pastels made from the given recipes were prepared during the summer months. The temperature and humidity conditions at the time of making can greatly affect the amount of time you need to allow the pastel sticks to dry out before using. A little preservative (e.g. Preventol) added to the water used in manufacture may help to prevent pastel sticks from going mouldy. It is always a good idea to keep hand-made soft pastels away from damp conditions where mould can occur. When preparing the pastel sticks, always leave them to dry out thoroughly before use. If you put them close to a heat source whilst drying, this can sometimes make the sticks bend out of shape and split. It seems better to just leave them to dry out naturally, over a period of 1-2 days, or longer in colder, damp conditions.

Recipe for Stock Solution of Tylose MH300

Tylose MH300	1 part (i.e. 1 level teaspoon)
Water	60 parts

Add water to the powder and leave to stand for 1-2 days, until completely dissolved. Dilute the solution as required (e.g. 1 : 90), for weaker binding strength.

For some pigments, you need only use water to facilitate the formation of the stick.

Recipe for Stock Solution of Gum Tragacanth

Gum Tragacanth (powder)	1 part
Water	30 parts

Leave to soak for 1-2 days. The gum tragacanth powder will partially dissolve, leaving a thick residue. Sieve the liquid solution and throw away the residue. Dilute to give a weaker binding strength (e.g. 1:60, 1:90).

Gum tragacanth makes velvety soft pastels but the mixture quickly spoils without a preservative and, when compared to tylose, it is more fiddly to prepare.

Recipe for Stock Solution of Gum Arabic, or Gum Cherry

Gum arabic, or gum cherry	1 part
Water	30 parts

Gum arabic and gum cherry are supplied as translucent pieces, with an amber colour. Gum cherry is the harder of the two.

Place the required amount of dry gum into an empty glass jar. Boil a kettle. Pour the correct measure of boiling water over the gum and leave to stand for 1-2 days, until completely dissolved. Dilute the mixture as required, 1:60, 1:90, etc. With these harder binders, a weak solution will give a softer pastel.

Procedure for Hand-Making Soft Pastels

Before starting to prepare soft pastels by hand, ensure that you have the following list of materials (see page 392). It is especially important to wear disposable gloves and a dust mask when handling dry pigments. Check also that the pigments you intend to use are non-toxic, or that necessary precautions are taken when working with potentially toxic pigments.

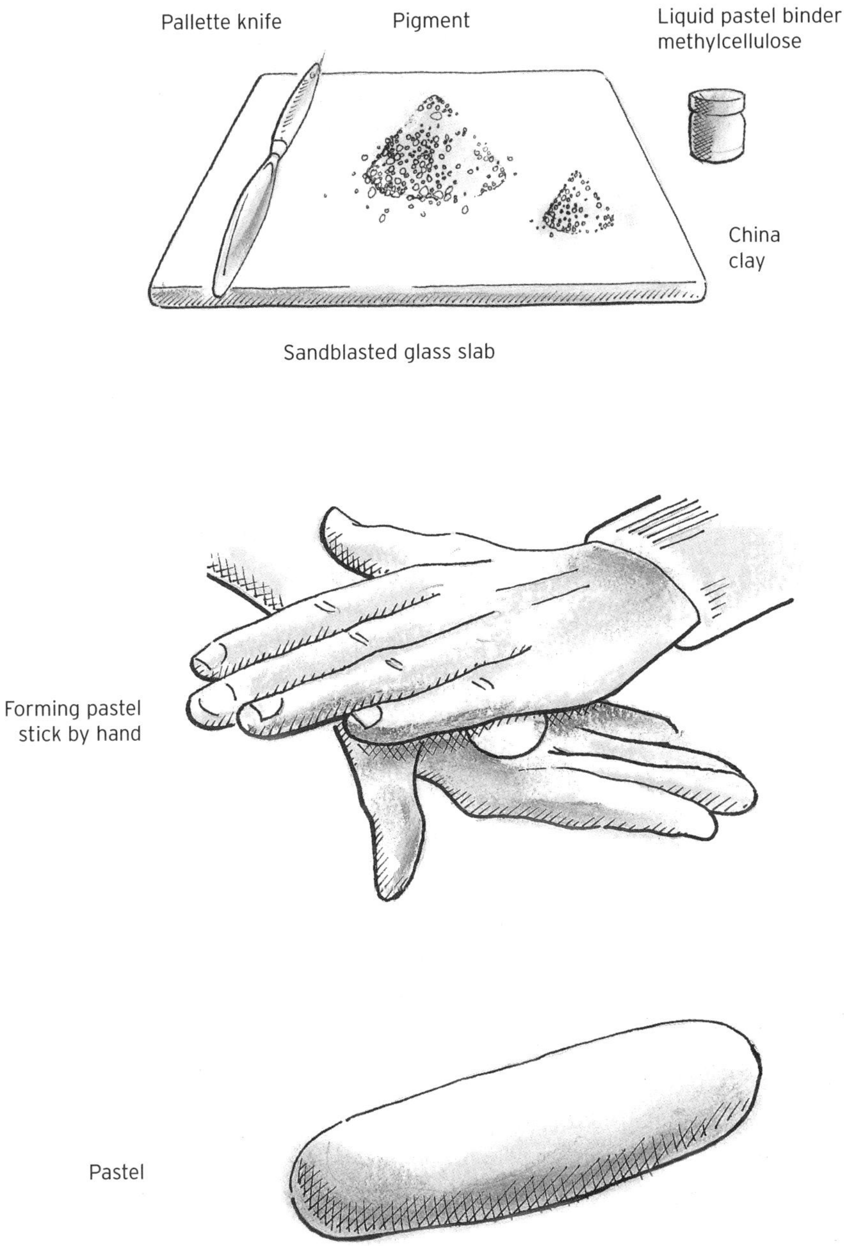

Procedure for Hand-Making Soft Pastels

Checklist of materials:

- Empty jars
- Palette knives
- Slab
- Dust mask, gloves
- Recipes
- Pigments
- China clay
- Whiting
- Champagne chalk
- Tylose (methylcellulose), stock solutions of 1:30, 1:60, 1:90
- Gum tragacanth, gum arabic, or gum cherry stock solutions of 1:30, 1:60, 1:90
- Newspaper
- Paper towels
- Metal bowl
- Teaspoon
- Tablespoon

The recipes indicated cover a basic range of colours, there are hundreds of other pigments you could use. It is important to remember that the recipes are guidelines only: you may prefer to make harder or softer pastel sticks, in which case, the ingredients can be modified until you have the right texture for your work. When making pastels, it is worth making up perhaps three different strengths of binder for each colour. This will give three sticks of the same colour, all with different degrees of hardness/softness. By doing this, you can discover which recipe is right for your work.

It is usual to work on a large glass (or marble) slab and/or a large glass or metal bowl. The first step is to wet the pigment and make it into a paste with water only. Ideally distilled water is used, because it is pure but you could use a still mineral water, water from a boiled kettle which has cooled, or plain tap water and hope for the best.

To make the paste, measure out the desired amount of pigment and form into a cone on the slab, or in the bowl. Make a little depression in the top of the cone and pour on some water, enough simply to wet the pigment into a stiff paste. If you add too much water, then correct this by adding more pigment. If making a large quantity of colour, use a bowl for pre-mixing, as the water and pigment can be combined without flying everywhere. The pigment and water can be worked, until thoroughly combined, with a flexible palette knife. Some pigments can be difficult to wet. The synthetic organic pigments (e.g. phthalocyanine green) can be difficult to disperse into water. Try adding a drop of wetting agent, such as alcohol or ox-gall to the water.

To the pigment-water paste, add the recommended solution of tylose and china clay. The china clay usually soaks up the wetness, so that you are left with a dough-ball mixture, which can be readily rolled between the hands into a round ball, then subsequently into round pastel sticks. Wearing latex gloves is usually beneficial not just in terms of protection of the skin, but also to facilitate easy rolling of the pastel stick. Once the stick is formed it is carefully placed on to a sheet of absorbent paper (e.g. newspaper) and left to air-dry thoroughly before use. Leave at least one week between making and using the pastel, to ensure that all moisture has evaporated.

It is possible to add a small percentage of pumice powder (perhaps 10-15% of the total quantity of colour pigment) during the mixing stage. This creates a pastel stick that easily deposits colour on to the pastel support, especially when that support is also prepared with a toothy pumice surface, as already described. Adding too much pumice into the pastel stick will make it more likely to crumble: this system seems to work best when used with larger particle size pigments such as the earths.

Working with Pastels

Because the pigments used in pastel painting tend to become distributed into the environment of the space where the painting is made, it is very important to wear some protective clothing when working with pastels and to take some elementary steps to limit exposure to pigment dust. Manufactured pastel ranges tend to avoid any pigments that are considered to be toxic. For this reason, lead-based pigments as well as cadmium and cobalt pigments tend to be excluded.

First of all, it is imperative to wear protective gloves: this prevents pigment dust from becoming encrusted in nails and the flesh of the hands. Secondly, a dust mask should be worn, to prevent inhalation of pigment dust. Thirdly, it is wise to dampen the air in the studio prior to working. This can be done by applying water from a plant sprayer into the air, every 15-30 minutes. This dampens the air and causes any airborne dust to fall quickly to floor level. Ensure that the floor is washed after each painting session, to remove pigment dust. Better still, have a vacuum cleaner on hand to remove dusts periodically. If one insists on applying the pastel without wearing gloves, then at least use a barrier cream on the hands, wrists and forearms to prevent prolonged contact with pigment dust.

After use, store pastels in a closed box, to contain dust. If the sticks get dirty during use, they can be cleaned by placing into a Tupperware box full of dry rice which is then shaken so that the rice takes off the dirty top layer of pigment dust.

While working, the pastel sticks can be laid out in colour sequence on a worktop. This will allow the artist to pick and choose tints of colour as required. It makes sense to order the colours into pure tone, tints towards black, tints towards white and so on, so that each colour is readily available as required.

Manipulating Pastel

During the painting process, colour is normally applied to the painting support by holding the pastel stick between thumb and forefinger. Pastels are sold in a variety of stick formats. Sometimes they are offered in the form of thin cigarette sticks (5mm), but are also available as thicker sticks (10mm) and even fat sticks (20-30mm). The thickness of the stick governs the type of mark expressed. In French pastel painting, the tradition is to use fine, thin sticks. By contrast, in recent years in Britain and North America, artists have preferred to work with fatter sticks, which show a more expressive mark. Fashions change, but all that matters to the artist is that the pastel stick chosen deposits colour evenly on to the paint support. With some brands, the pastel stick is formatted to work with a specific type of painting support, usually manufactured by the same company. This is especially the case with some harder pastels, which only work on very toothy supports.

With some pastel brands, the applied colour can be further worked into by adding water to the painting. When the binder is readily resoluble (e.g. methylcellulose) this is more than possible. By keeping a solution of methylcellulose at hand, this can be used to re-work passages of the painting. Although this changes the pastel from a dry form of painting to a liquid one, the methylcellulose solution dries back to a similar matt film to that of the applied pastel stick.

Fixing and Storage of Pastel Paintings

Another method of manipulating applied colour is to work into the surface with soft brushes, such as those made with squirrel or ox hair. These brushes (often referred to as "mop" brushes) are soft enough to re-distribute or blend the pastel pigment particles, without scrubbing them from the surface. Special wound and bound paper blending tools, known as "torchons" can also be used to soften the effect of applied colour. This is especially useful when portrait painting, where pale tints need to be blended and fused into each other. These torchons (also known as "paper stumps") can be firmly applied to the pigment particles without completely erasing the colour from the surface. It is useful to use such implements to gain a varied finish to the painting. Similarly, putty rubbers/erasers can be used to soften lines, although they may leave a greasy mark or residue on the painting surface. A piece of fine sandpaper may also be useful to sand away part of the paint surface if a course ground, such as those made with pumice or quartz chips, has been used.

Multiple layers of pastel can be applied, but this is very dependent upon the type of ground used. A toothy support will provide a better key for multiple applications than smoother surfaces, allowing more pigment dust to be despatched on to the painting surface.

As already noted, fixing of pastel paintings is a cause of concern. Various formulations are available for this purpose. Perhaps the best solution is not to fix at all, but instead to prepare the pastel ground carefully so that good amounts of pigment dust can attach to the ground without the need of fixing. The process of steam fixing with egg white is another possibility, but as this needs to be done soon after completion of the painting, it may not suit some working methods (e.g. if one keeps on painting over a period of months).

Careful and skilful application of spray fixatives can also be effective, but overuse of such fixatives can lead to saturation of the paint surface and possible discoloration over time. Modern aerosol fixatives are based on solutions of synthetic resins (e.g. Paraloid B-72, a light and age-resistant type of acrylic resin) which dry to a neutral finish when applied to pastel pigment dust. If such fixatives are overused, the resin begins to build up a saturated effect, thereby slightly altering colouring relationships. The key to this problem is careful and judicious applications of spray fixative. Following the manufacturers' recommendations, the fixative is sprayed at a set distance from the picture surface in an even and consistent manner. Avoid using heavy applications, for example after the painting is finished, where the whole picture is saturated with a large dose of fixative. It is far more successful to apply very thin layers of fix as each application of pastel is put down. In this manner, any colour shift can be seen during the period of painting and subsequent layers of pastel laid down with this in mind.

Fixatives based on alcohol-based resin varnishes such as sandarac or shellac may be less successful in that they darken with age and can crack when applied in multiple layers or with any thickness. Such liquid varnishes need to be applied with an atomiser or hand-held spray-diffuser and inevitably leave less consistent fixative layers than aerosol fixatives.

Finished pastel paintings can be shown under glass (glazed), or stored in closed portfolios. When storing, interleave each painting (on paper) with sheets of acid-free tissue paper, or glassine paper (a coated translucent paper which resists picking up pastel pigment dust). Any pressure applied to pastel paintings may cause the surface to become disturbed. As a consequence, stored paintings need to be kept carefully, away from wind sources and need to be handled with clean hands, as any greasy residue will transfer into the matt, dry paint surface.

It is imperative to paint using pigments that are stable to light and air. For this reason, lead-based colours are never used for pastel painting, as they tend to darken upon exposure to air. Similarly, colours that are fugitive to light should be avoided, because the particles of pigment are not bound and as such lie exposed on the painting support and are therefore liable to fading upon exposure.

Acrylic Painting

Acrylic Paint Systems

Acrylic paint is based on an emulsion of synthetic resins, suspended in water. Although the term "synthetic resin" is often used, acrylic resin is based on natural materials which have been chemically altered by means of modern technology, into a new type of raw material. This new basic material, acrylic resin, is presented for ease of use, in the form of clear beads or droplets. It is the basis for a number of "plastic" products, including Plexiglas (synthetic glass) and has many uses in industry. To make a binding agent for paints, the acrylic resin has to be made into a fluid solution. This is achieved by the polymerisation of acrylic and methacrylic acid, to form a milky solution, which dries perfectly clear. This product is referred to as an acrylic emulsion, or acrylic dispersion. The first acrylic products were developed in Germany during the 1920s and '30s: the first artists' acrylic paints (based on water-borne acrylic emulsion) became available in the 1950s and have been subsequently updated and improved up to the present day.

The first acrylic paints for artists were actually based on a solution of the acrylic resin (polybutyl methacrylate, under the trade name "Acryloid F-10") into turpentine, by the American company, Bocur, in the early 1940s. The paint was sold under the brand name "Magna". Both Leonard Bocur and Sam Golden, who co-produced this early type of acrylic paint, had strong links with many leading artists working in New York in the late 1940s. Together, they ran a store for artists' colours, which was frequented by artists such as De Kooning, Newman, Louis, Noland, Lichtenstein and Rothko.

Magna was developed in conjunction with Rhom and Haas, manufacturers of raw acrylic resins, to provide a paint that had a degree of viscosity before dilution, but upon dilution could be painted out in flat, even applications. The dilution of the paint with turpentine or mineral spirit was a key element with Magna: the paint could be diluted in this manner yet retain high colour resonance. This was in part due to the high pigment concentration of these early acrylics, but also to the rheological properties of the paint binder itself.

Because the acrylic resin was dissolved into turpentine, the dried paint layer remained re-soluble with turpentine or mineral spirit upon drying. This meant that the application of multiple layers of paint became difficult, because the top layer would soften the previous one, making it sticky and giving the possibility of the applied layers blending or fusing together. As a consequence of this, Bocur developed a special isolating varnish that was resistant to turpentine or mineral spirit. This system proved useful for artists working in a planned manner, but was less useful to those wishing to paint in a spontaneous fashion.

Magna is no longer manufactured, but other companies who specialise in acrylic paint systems continue to offer similar systems. For general use, these acrylic-solvent paint systems have a substantial drawback with regards to health and safety for the user, and adequate ventilation is required when working with such products. The use of acrylic resins into solvent has also been widely employed in conservation programmes, where the clarity of film provided and resistance to discoloration of acrylic resin films are highly regarded.

How Acrylic Paint Works

The acrylic dispersion is not soluble with water, but the addition of surfactants emulsifies the mixture of acrylic and water, so that it can be painted out and further diluted with water. The paint dries by evaporation of the water constituent. In turn, as the water evaporates into the atmosphere, capillary action forces the water out and the acrylic polymers bond together. As the water content is reduced, so the polymers form a regular, hexagonal pattern, trapping the pigment (colour) particles and producing a clear, flexible and durable dry paint film.

In their wet state, acrylic paints are a little lighter (milky in appearance) than when dry. This means that there is a subtle colour shift from wet paint to dry paint. This is because the acrylic emulsion is a milky-white colour when wet but dries to become completely clear. It takes a little time to get used to this process. It is probably best at this stage to think of acrylic as a paint system in its own right and not to compare it unfairly with oil paint. Because oil paint remains virtually unchanged in terms of gloss and colour depth, from wet to dry, it is tempting to argue that acrylic paint is inferior, because the artist has to compensate for the slight colour shift upon drying. Balance this advantage of oil paint with the advantages of acrylic paint:

Oil Paint

Colour remains constant upon drying
Long drying time
Risk of cracking and wrinkling of paint film
Long term: oil paint becomes brittle, harder
Long term: oil paint yellows / darkens
Long term: oil paint becomes more transparent with age
Dilution: solvents such as turpentine and white spirit, which may be uncomfortable for user

Acrylic Paint

Very quick drying time, subsequent coats can be applied speedily without fear of cracking
Paint film remains very flexible, regardless of thickness of application
Long term: acrylic paint remains flexible
Long term: acrylic paint does not yellow or darken
Long term: acrylic paint does not become transparent with age, remains constant
Dilution: water, non-hazardous

Upon drying the paint film becomes water-insoluble. The drying process is relatively quick compared to oil colours: a thin layer of acrylic paint will dry in just a few moments. The true curing (complete drying) time is a little longer but usually, acrylic paint can be overpainted as soon as it is surface dry, without fear of cracking. This represents enormous advantages to the artist when compared to the perilous nature of oil paints, where cracking can occur at any time.

Another great advantage for the user, is that acrylic paints are thinned only with water, or extended with a combination of water and paint medium. No potentially harmful solvents are involved. This is a great advantage, particularly for artists working outdoors, or those working in a confined space.

Acrylic Paints

Acrylic paints are available in a variety of formats, which can represent different consistencies and/or qualities. The acrylic emulsion or dispersion (the basic binder for the paint) is presented as a fluid, milky solution. There are many different types of acrylic resin suitable for making artists' paints. In manufactured paint ranges, often these basic acrylic resins are modified - with flow agents, matting agents, stabilising agents, etc - to assist the overall working properties of the paint paste. In the case of the best quality acrylic colours, the basic resin may be modified with a great number of additives, the sum of which combine to produce a paint paste with characteristic properties. For example, some brands dry to show a satin-matt sheen, whereas other brands may dry with minimal colour shift, from wet to dry: these facets are governed by the type of resin(s) used and their formulation with various additive materials.

One consequence of the high number of component materials normally incorporated in artists' acrylic paints is that hand-made acrylic colour is somewhat lacking in finesse. By contrast to hand-mixed oil colours, acrylic colours tend to be very variable in consistency and film sheen when prepared by hand. Without the close calculations of additives used by manufacturers of acrylic paint, the individual artist is somewhat at the mercy of the properties of the acrylic resin binder chosen. However, if the paint is prepared by hand and used within a short space of time, reasonable results can be achieved. This is especially so, if one considers the comparative working properties of the different acrylic binders available and adjusts the paint making process in accordance with those properties. For example, each different resin possesses a different amount of solid resin, when presented in dispersion/emulsion form with water. In the following list of commonly available resins (in water-borne dispersion/emulsion form), the solid resin content is indicated by the letters FK. If the solids content is high, it follows that the resultant paint paste will include a smaller amount of water, which upon evaporation tends to cause less shrinkage of the paint film than would be the case with high-water content acrylic resin dispersions. As a consequence, such dispersions, which typically make a short, stiff paint paste, are more often applicable to making paint where a degree of impasto is required. It follows that dispersions with a higher water content are better suited to making paints intended to be used brushed flat into glazes.

Typical Acrylic Resin Dispersions and Their Basic Characteristics

This is by no means a comprehensive list: indeed, the specification and availability of these dispersions is always in flux. These are types of dispersion that are commonly available in Western Europe.

(MFT= minimum temperature required to form a coherent paint film*)

(FK= solids content)

* Acrylic paints need to be protected from frost

Primal AC 35 MFT 9°C FK 46.5%
High binding power, tough, durable. Fluid, milky consistency

Dispersion K6 Gloss MFT 11°C FK 60.5%
Glossy, very hard finish, very durable, elastic

Dispersion K6 Matt MFT 8°C FK 60%
Matt, slightly milky dispersion

Plextol B-500	MFT 7°C	FK 49-50%
Good pigment binder for acrylic paints, low-tack		
Plextol D-498	MFT 5°C	FK not available
Clear, medium gloss. Thicker consistency than that of Primal AC 35		

All these acrylic dispersions have different qualities. Upon drying, some are soft, some hard, some are more glossy, others less so. The manufacturer takes the raw acrylic polymer emulsion and adds various agents to aid its flow and brushing qualities; prevent it from spoiling; prevent it from freezing in cold climates.

Hand-Preparation of Acrylic Paints

There are many ways to prepare acrylic paints by hand and each supplier of the raw materials required may be able to supply recipe information. The processes outlined represent the simplest way to prepare colour into paint form. It is intended that these simple paint pastes are prepared and then used within one painting session, rather than stored for a longer period. Storage is difficult, because the raw materials may separate or coagulate upon standing, leaving a paint with a poor viscosity.

A supply of clean plastic pots or air-tight glass jars is useful to place the prepared paint paste into. It is usually better practice to prepare a milky, semi-fluid paint paste than one that is free flowing or extremely stiff in nature.

Suggested Basic Palette for Acrylic Paint Making

The following pigments can be assumed to be non-hazardous and relatively easy to prepare. Where a pigment may require a wetting agent, an asterix * denotes this. If possible, try to obtain these colours already dispersed in water (colour pastes).

Titanium white	PW 4
Cadmium lemon	PY 35

Zinc white †	PW6
Hansa yellow*	PY 74
Yellow iron oxide	PY 42
Nickel titanium yellow	PY 53
Intensive yellow	N/A
Cadmium orange	PO 20
Transparent orange-red oxide	PR 102
Permanent red*	PR 170
Paliogen maroon*	PR 179
Caput mortuum (violet iron oxide)	PR 42
Phthalocyanine blue*	PB 15
Ultramarine blue	PB 29
Chrome oxide green	PG 17
Irgazine yellow (green shade)*	PG 129
Iron oxide black	PBlk 11

† – Zinc white is not stable in acrylic dispersions for use on outdoor murals, where the paint film may break down and chalk. It is common practice among acrylic paint manufacturers to prepare zinc white with an addition of titanium white (perhaps 15-20%) to help stabilise the paint mixture.

The following basic procedure can be followed to make such a paint:

Prepare dry pigment with distilled water, in a paste, which should be stiff. Each particle of pigment is required to be wet before incorporation with the chosen binder. In some cases, this cannot be done by simply mixing water and pigment together. An addition of wetting agent (e.g. disponil or orotan, in the ratios indicated, see Additives for Acrylic Paint Systems) may be required with some pigments, especially the synthetic organic ones. It may be advisable to purchase the synthetic organic pigments in the form of ready-dispersed water-pigment pastes. These pastes contain a biocide to prevent spoiling and a flow agent to assist brushing, and provide a ready-to-use colour paste to add to the acrylic dispersion binder.

The stiff pigment-water paste needs to be thoroughly mixed before incorporation with the acrylic dispersion binder. In the first place, the dry pigment and water are brought together on a ground glass slab, using a flat, long bladed palette knife. Once all the pigment is absorbed into the water to form a wet paste, this needs to be mulled, with a glass muller, using a figure of eight motion (as would be the case with oil colour). This process helps to divide the pigment particles from each other and encourage saturation by the water. The longer this is done, the smoother the end paint paste should be. If the water dries off during this process, add a tiny bit more to re-wet. It is best to keep a supply of distilled water nearby, in a dispenser bottle, so that small droplets can be added if and when the pigment-water paste becomes too dry. To the stiffish water-pigment paste, a small addition of Mowiol 4-98 (up to 10%) is slowly added to gain a slightly smoother, richer wet paste. This resoluble acrylic resin helps to stabilise the consistency of the paste but has minimal binding power. It is possible to make a very simple resoluble paint using mowiol as the binding agent, although the dried paint film will remain water-soluble indefinitely. It is preferable to use mowiol as an additive rather than a binding agent. Into the water-pigment-mowiol paste, a small amount of a filler material may be added to provide a shorter (stiffer) consistency. For this purpose, aluminium hydrate can be combined with pigments which show transparency, whereas for opaque pigments, blanc fix is used. Overuse of such filler will make an unstable paint film and may cause cracking. No more than 5-10% filler is normally required to provide optimum results.

To the resultant paste, the binder is added to create a paint that will dry to form a cohesive, insoluble film. The choice of binder, as already indicated, depends on the intended use. For example, to create a flowing, easy to brush-out paint, an acrylic resin dispersion with a low solids content is selected. The dried sheen of the chosen binder may also be of consequence. Some dispersions are offered which already contain a matting agent, thereby producing satin-matt effects upon drying. Otherwise, special matting agents can be added to the dispersion (e.g. aerosil, a fine white powder that imparts mattness, or fine scotchlite, very small hollow plastic bubbles) to give a more matt sheen. Some experimentation is called for: it would be wise to paint out a number of different acrylic resin dispersions (without pigmentation) on to a sheet of clean glass, and leave them to dry. Upon drying, one can gauge the relative gloss/mattness of the paint film, its transparency and whether or not it cracks or wrinkles upon drying. Sometimes, if too much water is added to an acrylic dispersion, it may dry unevenly - in the worst case, forming some kind of cracks or splits. The addition of a matting agent to an acrylic dispersion will lead to a loss of transparency and in some cases may cause the acrylic to have a slight yellow appearance. One can see that with acrylic paint making, the smallest thing can upset the balance of the paint paste.

The exact quantity of acrylic resin dispersion to pigment (+ other additives) needs to be judged on a pigment-to-pigment basis. Some pigments will need a larger quantity of binder than others. In general, those with a larger particle size will require more binder than those of a very fine particle size. However, again experimentation is required prior to application on to the painting surface. It should also be borne in mind that the drying time of each paint layer may be variable, compared with manufactured paints, especially when the original paint paste is diluted with extra water. Some care should be exercised when painting: for example, leave each layer to dry off before overpainting.

The hand-preparation of pigment into an acrylic resin dispersion allows the artist to judge the intensity of the resultant paint. It also enables them to prepare colours that are not normally available in acrylic paint ranges. For example, it is difficult for manufacturers to use earth pigments in their colour ranges, because these tend to include impurities, may have a degree of grittiness and irregular particle size. In particular, the particle size, and the way it reacts to water can make paint making nigh on impossible in terms of a commercial acrylic paint. Some earth pigments swell when in contact with water, and will only form a stable mixture when gently coaxed by hand-mixing. As a result, the use of these pigments is omitted by most acrylic paint manufacturers. However, with care, they can be used to make simple hand-made paints, which are prepared and then applied immediately. Once dry, the applied paint will quickly show if it has enough binding power. If the resultant paint application is too matt, simply add more binder; if it is underbound and delaminating from the support, again add more binder. A slightly thickened acrylic resin dispersion may also assist in this regard. In such cases, the original acrylic resin dispersion is thickened mildly (i.e. not as much as when making an impasto gel). The resultant fat dispersion will help to adhere larger particles to the support. This can also be useful when working with other large particle dry colours or additives such as mica flakes, silver glitter, marble dusts and chips, coloured ground glass and with crystalline mineral pigments such as azurite and malachite. In fact any dry material that does not readily make a simple paint paste will benefit from being prepared in this way.

Additives for Acrylic Paint Systems

When using dry pigments to make acrylic paints, the following additives may be useful. They are all commonly in use in Western Europe, but their specification/properties are always in flux, due to developments within the paint and coatings industry, for which they are formulated. Exact use of these additives may depend on the context and type of work undertaken. Check with the supplier for further details.

Disponil 286 (Wetting Agent)

When making acrylic paints from dry pigment, add 0.5% disponil to the water used to make the pigment paste. This synthetic wetting agent helps to saturate the pigment particles, making it easier for the binder (e.g. Plextol D-498) to combine readily, to make a smooth paint paste. Some acrylic binders may already contain similar wetting / flow agents: check with the supplier.

Orotan 731 K (Dispersing Agent)

To acrylic paint paste, add 1% orotan, to facilitate easy brushing/flow of paint.

Mowiol 4 - 98 (Stabilising Agent)

Add 10% mowiol to acrylic paint paste to stabilise the consistency (so that contents do not settle out) and slightly retard the drying time of the paint film. Over use of this additive may leave the paint film resoluble/prone to swelling when in contact with water.

Preservative

It is not recommended to add a preservative agent to hand-made acrylic paint systems. Such preservatives (e.g. sodium-2-phenylphenolate) tend to be harmful to the environment when released into the water supply and are toxic to use. In any case, it is better practice to make and use hand-made acrylic paints, so that the contents do not separate, or become unworkable after standing for a prolonged period. If only distilled water is added to paint mixtures, this may help to alleviate mould growth. Manufactured paints may already contain a biocide as preservative. However, it is vital that water is not stirred back into manufactured paints and left to stand, as it invariably attracts microbes and starts to smell or become infected with mould.

Thickener for Acrylic Paint Systems (e.g. Rohagit SD 15)

When added in very small quantities (no more than 10%) to acrylic paint pastes, or directly into acrylic binder, this thickening agent causes swelling. By careful addition of thickener, acrylic gels can be made. However, even with careful notation of the amounts used, it is difficult to repeat this process so that each time a consistent gel is created.

Using these additives to make acrylic paints may lead to a further understanding of the complexities involved in the manufacture of acrylic paint systems. Proprietary brands either already contain similar additives, or such additives are available separately and can be used to further modify the manufactured brand (e.g. impasto gel to create thicker passages).

Dry Additives Materials

Because acrylic is such a good adhesive, many dry materials can be experimented with to achieve texture, change of sheen, etc. For example, any inert filler can be incorporated to give more bulk and/or texture to the paint paste. Marble, quartz, basalt, granite in grit or sand form could be utilised. Before use, apply the mix of dry material with the chosen binder on to a sheet of glass and judge how well it dries. It follows that incorporation into a thick gel impasto will be more successful, where the large particles of the additive(s) are dispersed into a viscous, fat paste of acrylic. This could be done by incorporation into a manufactured acrylic impasto gel, or by thickening a basic acrylic resin dispersion, as already indicated.

Glass Beads

Glass beads in a variety of sizes, from 0.5mm diameter upwards are available and can be incorporated into acrylic dispersions. While such inclusions create some texture/granulation on the surface of the painting, they also act to encourage light refraction. In effect, light is bounced around between the pigment content and the glass beads, causing a more brilliant effect. This is especially useful with fluorescent colours and with the synthetic organic pigments, in both cases, exaggerated luminosity results.

Scotchlite - Hollow Plastic Bubbles

Can be used in very small additions, to increase matting of the paint film. In larger quantities, it can be useful in creating lightweight texture pastes when combined with acrylic resin dispersion with a high solids content. However, thorough mixing is imperative in such combinations to ensure no dry materials are left unbound. It is best to do this by combining the plastic bubbles and acrylic dispersion in some kind of food blending machine, to create a thorough mixing. However, the apparatus must obviously never be used for food preparation again!

Health and Safety Information

Acrylic paints are water-based emulsions. Clean-up is with water. For general use, there are no specific hazards involved. However, some pigments used in the manufacture of acrylic paints are labelled as not suitable for spray-applying (e.g. cadmium pigments), to conform to US/EU labelling requirements. Also, some additives to acrylic paints may be hazardous when used in large quantities, when spilled, etc. Check with the supplier on the nature and properties of each component mat making. Some acrylic dispersions (and very small solvent additives, to speed drying ing paint ntain

Dust Masks

All pigments in dry powder form can be assumed to be nuisance dusts. As a consequence, while working with dry powders, appropriate dust masks should be worn. The exact specifications for dust masks change according to new research. Within the EU, protective dust masks are accorded a P rating, which relates to their suitability to specific tasks. For example, masks P1, P2 and P3, may be adequate for use with small amounts of nuisance dusts. Always check with the supplier and read product information, before using in a given situation. Remember that a mask designed for use with dry powders may not be suitable for use with wet applications (e.g. spraying paint). The information relating to choice of dust mask is in constant flux and it would unwise to recommend a specific mask for a specific situation. The dust mask manufacturer may be able to recommend the most suitable one for a particular purpose.

Gloves

Protective gloves are appropriate when working with dry powders. Caution is advised when choosing these items. Some gloves (e.g. latex type) may cause a skin reaction for some people. The manufacturer of the equipment should be able to provide up-to-date information.

Manufactured Acrylic Paints

It is good policy to use only one brand of acrylic paint. Try to avoid intermixing of brands and mediums. This is because each brand may use slightly different resins, or even if the same acrylic resin is used, it could be modified to a different consistency. In the worst case scenario, intermixing can lead to differing drying rates and

...es of flexibility in the paint film. Acrylic paint manufactures can opt to make any of the following types of paint:

1. A fluid paint (i.e. same consistency as the raw acrylic polymer emulsion).

2. A gel paint, with a thick buttery paste consistency, similar to that of oil paint.

3. A modified fluid paint (can be thinner, as with acrylic "inks").

In order to make a fluid acrylic paint, the manufacturer simply mixes the pigment into the binder. To provide the best possible paint (i.e. where the pigment is evenly distributed into the binding medium), the mixture is put through a triple roll mill. Often, the mixture is re-milled and sometimes sieved to remove any lumps, etc. This process may be different for different colours, depending on the nature of the pigments used.

Many acrylic paint ranges employ the synthetic organic pigments, which may be bought by the manufacturer in the form of wet pastes. These pastes, or pigment dispersions may reduce the need for milling (mixing) with the binder, therefore reducing the overall cost of production.

To make a gel consistency paint, the acrylic polymer emulsion has to be made fat by the addition of a thickening agent. The emulsion and pigment may already be mixed together, before the thickening takes place. The resultant paint is short in consistency (meaning that when manipulated with a brush or palette knife, the paint does not spread out, unless diluted with medium or water). It has a thick, buttery-paste consistency, ideal for application by painting knife or short dabbings with a brush. The thick consistency allows for an impasto technique, to build relief and texture. Because the manufacturing process takes a little longer than with fluid colours, so the cost of the product may be higher. Generally, artists' quality acrylics are presented in this thick gel-form. This probably has more to do with the notion that acrylic paint should feel like oil paint. It does not mean that all fluid form acrylics are inferior: indeed, the fluid acrylics are closer to the raw material than the mechanically thickened gel-type acrylics. Some ranges are marketed as artists' quality paints, even though they have a fluid, flow formula.

Sometimes, the acrylic polymer emulsion is further modified by dilution so that it has a consistency which is even more fluid, so that when colour is introduced, an ink-like paint is produced.

Modified Paint Ranges

There are many different types of acrylic paint on the market and it is impossible to describe them all here. True artists' quality acrylics contain good pigment, finely dispersed into a high quality acrylic polymer elusion binder. Extenders, or rather "carriers" may be employed, so that the resultant paint brushes out evenly. The exact use of extender, or filler material can help to produce paint with a high chroma; overuse of them can lead to duller colour values and a weaker paint film. Some colour ranges contain maximum pigment content to acrylic resin, with no extender at all. In theory, this gives a paint with maximum tinting strength: in practice, each colour in the range has a slightly different finish. Some pigments require more binding medium than others, with the result that the paint film is either saturated (glossy), or matt (dull) in appearance. This system provides the artist with strong colour: the finish can be further manipulated by the addition of gloss or matt mediums for coherence. Alternatively, the finished painting can simply be given a unifying coat of varnish.

Acrylic Painting Mediums

A huge variety of mediums is available for acrylic paint. The addition of a medium can be used to change the surface finish or texture, or both. Similarly, there is an ever-increasing number of primers and painting grounds, so that the initial painting support can be made absorbent, semi-absorbent, glossy, textured, etc. All these products provide an expanding range of possibilities for the acrylic painter.

Mediums and varnishes can be loosely divided into the following formats:

1. Fluid medium, available in matt, gloss and satin finishes. Used in place of, or in conjunction with water, to thin/extend colour. Using

a medium instead of water to dilute acrylic paint will give a more consistent paint finish. Sometimes, if water is used to dilute, the paint can dry too matt, or uneven in areas of matt and gloss. The matt mediums tend to be slightly cloudy upon drying; gloss mediums dry water-clear.

2. Gel medium, thick impasto pastes, available in gloss or matt. Mix together for a satin finish. These fat pastes are mixed with colour to build impasto and remain flexible upon drying. The matt mediums tend to be slightly cloudy upon drying, giving an appearance a little like wax. By contrast, good quality gloss mediums will appear clear when dry. The addition of gloss gel to acrylic paint tends to produce a very heavy glossiness. Although these gels are designed to help impart impasto to the paint surface, as with any material they have their limitations. Impasto is best built up by applying multiple layers of gel, rather than one thick wodge. Over-thick applications of gel may dry to show some shrinkage as the water content evaporates. In the worst cases, this leads to a great loss of volume in the paint film (the gel when first applied appears as a high impasto but on drying levels down). During this drying out process, it is possible that the gel will split or shrivel, so compromising the paint film.

For each manufacturer's product, the extreme of impasto capable by their gel will differ. Some companies produce gels with a very high solids content which hold better when applied thickly. However, such gels may cause applications on to stretched canvas to sag considerably. It may therefore be advisable to apply such gels on to rigid supports only. Normal practice is to tint the gel with a quantity of colour before application. This is best done by thorough mixing in a plastic cup, using a plastic palette knife, gradually adding the required colour concentration into the gel. Once mixed thoroughly, the gel can be applied, by brushing, palette or painting knife, fingers, spatulas, sponge, etc. When applied to a thickness of about 3cm, most gels will dry without undue shrinkage. Over the dried layer of gel, further applications can be made of a similar thickness. However, it is vital to wait for each layer to dry thoroughly before proceeding. It is likely that such layered applications of paint and gel will create a paint film that becomes progressively more inflexible. Again, some testing is advisable before use in permanent artworks.

The variety of gels available may appear confusing at first to most artists. It is vital when working with a brand of paint, to stick with gels that are formulated for use with that specific brand. Most companies now offer information sheets or charts indicating when and where a gel can be used to best advantage. For example, some gels have a high gloss sheen, while others may be self-levelling. It is normal to presume that acrylic colour can be mixed into a gel in any ratio (unlike oil paint mediums, where a maximum of 10% medium to paint is advised), although reference to manufacturers' information may give clearer guidelines. By adding colour into gel, a large volume of paint can be achieved. Although this gel-paint will be weaker in colour strength (according to the amount of paint added), it may be a useful shortcut, when working on a large scale.

Hand-made gel (i.e. acrylic dispersions, plus thickening agent) should be used with great caution. They should work well with hand-made paint formulations that are based on the same acrylic resin dispersion as that which has been thickened, but may not work well with brand acrylic paints, due to differing formulations. In the worst case, admixtures of different brands and/or hand-made paint/medium may cause blistering, cracking or non-film formation. Intermixed brands, or brand paint plus hand-made paint may also begin to smell when the component parts are not compatible.

3. Texture pastes can be added to colour, or used in conjunction with primer. These are often based on mixtures of acrylic with quartz, marble dust, or synthetic materials such as dralon fibres, or scotchlite (hollow plastic bubbles). All should remain flexible and can be mixed into paint, or laid down on top of the dried priming coat, to give a textured ground. Some texture pastes may reduce the flexibility of the paint film. Some can be mixed with primer/gesso, to give a gently toothed or absorbent surface. The texture pastes tend to show some colour when dry (usually an off white), which should be borne in mind when mixing with colour. Texture or "moulding" pastes tend to dry with less shrinkage than is the case with gels, due to a lower water content. Also, the composition may include inert fillers such as quartz or marble dust, which help create great stability. However, flexibility is an issue with these pastes, especially when they are applied very thickly. Best practice is to build impasto slowly by adding layers of texture paste (perhaps 3cm thick) and waiting for each layer to dry before proceeding with the

next. Many oil painters have used these texture moulding pastes to create an impasto underpainting (in acrylic), which when dry can be safely overpainted with oil colours. While such pastes tend to have reduced absorbency compared with acrylic gesso, they normally have enough texture to allow oil-based paints to grip to the surface adequately.

4. Varnishes are available for acrylics in two distinct formats:

i) Water-thinnable varnish, which can be mixed with the paint to give a harder finish (scratch-proof), or as a final coating, to change, or homogenise the appearance of the final paint layers. The gloss varieties of these varnishes tend to dry to give a clear coating. The matt or satin varieties may slightly frost the surface of the painting, so altering the sheen appearance: in some cases this may mean that delicate parts of the painting are obscured. When brushing these varnishes, care should be taken to avoid the inclusion of air bubbles into the varnish film. This is because the varnish dries so quickly that any air bubbles will tend to form and dry before they can be brushed out. An addition of water (perhaps 20%) may help to keep the varnish wet on the surface while being brushed out. With some water-based acrylic varnishes, dilution with water is always necessary because the neat varnish is too thick to brush out successfully. Testing is wise in such instances, to gauge the brushing properties of the chosen varnish. Use soft hog hair varnish brushes, with gently shaped tips (rather than cut tips), working the applied varnish in one direction across the painting surface. It should be possible to brush out any residual hairs or other impurities while the varnish is still wet, by changing direction of stroke. The exact brushing technique for varnish application will vary according to the type of finish required.

Because these water-based varnishes dry to become insoluble, they are very difficult for conservators to remove when cleaning or repairing a painting, without damaging the paint surface. As a consequence, it is recommended that such varnishes are used to enhance the sheen of the final layers of the painting, i.e. colour is worked into the varnish to apply coloured glazes which will impart a matt/satin or gloss sheen to the painting surface. If varnish needs to be applied to the dried painting in order to protect the surface, or merely to change the sheen of the finished painting, it may be more appropriate to apply a solvent-based varnish, which can be removed without damaging the paint surface.

ii) Solvent-based varnishes are only ever used over dried acrylic paint. A final protective coat of varnish can be applied to dried acrylic paintings with such varnishes. These varnishes are formed by solving acrylic resin (sometimes a combination of resin types) into an active high polar solvent (e.g. toluene, benzene, etc). There are many resin types on the market, and some debate as to which resin performs best over time. Each manufacturer may publish information relating to the relative qualities of the resins or resin formulations used in their varnishes.

To follow are some examples of acrylic resin in solvent varnishes (where information permits, the solvent type is indicated, although this is not a guarantee of the formulation, as manufacturers may change constituents without notice). Such combinations are often used by conservators, although the exact formulas may change according to the designated use:

- MS2-A resin in Shellsol A
- Paraloid B-72 in Shellsol A
- Paraloid B-72 in ethylacetate
- Regalrez 1094 in Shellsol D 40, with addition of Kraton G 1650, as softening agent (e.g. 2g Kraton to 100g Regalrez)
- Regalrez 1126 in Shellsol A, with addition of Kraton G 1650, as softening agent (e.g. 2g Kraton to 100g Regalrez)
- Paraloid B-67 in white spirit
- Plexisol P 550-40 in white spirit
- Mowilith 35/73 in ethylacetate
- Ketone N resin, in turpentine or white spirit

(N.B. The product codes and identifications may change from those indicated here.)

Correct choice of such varnishes may be dependent on the type of work to be varnished. For example, a dried acrylic painting on canvas will require a solvent-based varnish that is flexible. With mural acrylic paintings, a less flexible varnish may suffice. It is vital to seek sound technical advice prior to undertaking varnishing of finished paintings. It is also important to ensure that the acrylic paint layers are completely dry before over-varnishing with any product containing solvent. If the painting is not wholly dry (cured), the solvent in the varnish may cause bleeding or disturbance in the paint film. In such cases, it is advised to wait for 14 days after the painting has dried, so that any residual moisture is emitted from the paint surface and it is thoroughly dried.

When preparing raw acrylic resin into solvent, it is normal to agitate the mixture at the beginning of the process to encourage the resin to dissolve. If the contents are simply left unstirred in a container, little or even no solving may take place. Placing the raw resin/solvent mixture container into a warm water bath may also encourage the resin to dissolve more readily. For artists, it is always recommended that a proprietary brand of solvent-based acrylic varnish is used, because the types of solvents required to dissolve the resin are usually too noxious to use in normal studio conditions.

The chosen resin is dissolved to form a colourless liquid with some viscosity (according to the solids content). It is usual that such varnishes are further diluted by using mineral (white) spirit, or another appropriate solvent as a thinning agent. Such less-active solvent additions tend to evaporate at a slower rate than the active type, thereby providing a balanced drying time: allowing enough time for the varnish to be brushed out over the painting surface. Low odour thinners (odourless mineral spirit) are not normally used for such varnishes, because they are not active/strong enough to combine with the varnish properly.

A common procedure in the varnishing of an acrylic painting may be to apply a coat of water-based acrylic varnish over the dried painting first to form a sealing or isolation coat. Upon drying, a coat of the appropriate solvent-based acrylic varnish is then applied. This varnish will, technically, be removable, so that it can be replaced should any yellowing/discoloration of the final varnish occur. Such solvent-based varnishes afford protection to paint surfaces from atmospheric pollutants in addition to changing the sheen of the painting surface.

Both water-based and solvent-based acrylic varnishes are now available which contain a UV absorbing material. These do not totally inhibit UV light from acting on the paint film, but may delay the rate of any action. As a consequence, their use is often recommended in the context of outdoor mural paintings, which are exposed to strong sunlight. They may also help to stop the oxidisation of metallic acrylics (those containing copper), thereby preventing tarnishing of the dried paint film.

Some of the acrylic resin examples may be suitable for using as binding agent for pigment, when prepared with solvent: the early acrylic paints followed this idea. Paraloid B-67, solved in white spirit provides a simple acrylic resin solution, which can be pigmented as required. In order to incorporate the pigment into the acrylic resin solution, it is advisable to wet the pigment with white spirit, to form a stiffish paste. This paste is carefully stirred into the viscous acrylic resin solution. If the acrylic resin solution is too thin (too much solvent), the resultant "paint" will be difficult to control. This type of acrylic resin-pigment combination is best applied in flat layers, with the colour being brushed out on to the painting surface. Subsequent coats will tend to pick-up (re-dissolve) the first layer, especially if the surface is agitated. However, this property could be used to produce interesting fused effects. If such acrylic resin-pigment applications are made too thickly, or with multiple layers, cracking may result. However, such systems for painting could be very useful, in so much as the paint is re-soluble with white spirit once dry. This means that dried-up hand-made colours can be re-worked by stirring white spirit back into the container in which they are kept. This re-solubility becomes less easy over time, but is not usually problematic within the first few months of preparation.

Some proprietary brands of acrylic resin in solvent are available, in varying forms: as a viscous syrup; free-flowing varnish consistency; or in aerosol form. Particular care needs to be taken with the latter, as the solvents used to propel the resin during spraying are likely to be very fast to evaporate and as such hazardous to use, should any vapours be inhaled. As always, one should refer to the manufacturers' exact instructions and take any recommended precautions prior to use.

Why Artists Sometimes Mistrust Acrylic Paint

Many claims have been made for acrylic paint: it is permanently flexible, non-yellowing, durable and age-resistant. However, a number of artists are worried that these claims cannot be substantiated, because acrylic paint has not been around for very long. Articles have appeared from time to time in the press, relating to the deterioration of old acrylic paintings. All this adds to the hysteria about acrylic paint: is it really trustworthy and should we use it? After all, we know what happens to oil paint and, despite its defects, oil paint is still preferred by many artists.

There is a danger that acrylic paint is being unfairly damned. It is true that some acrylic paintings have not lasted well, but it appears to be the case that this is more to do with bad practice on the part of the artists, than with the drawbacks of the medium. If we start with the premise that artists intending to produce permanent works use only the best materials, it follows that their work should last the longest. In some of the most celebrated cases where acrylic paint has been seen as the cause of deterioration, it transpires that the artist may have used poor quality materials. In the early days of acrylic painting, often, the cheaper polyvinyl materials were incorrectly assumed to be just the same as true acrylics. Vinyl is a cheaper and simpler material than true acrylic. Vinyl emulsions were, and are still, widely used to make house paints (e.g. matt vinyl emulsion) and as the binder for some childrens' paints. In the confusion over what "acrylic" really means, painting grounds were often made by using a white vinyl emulsion paint as the primer. This type of paint is not designed to be flexible (it is intended for painting walls) and it is quite absorbent. In the DIY trade, it is assumed that people redecorate their houses every 3-5 years: as a consequence, some of their products are designed to last for relatively short periods. It therefore follows that, if you use a non-flexible paint, with minimum binding power, on to a flexible canvas, it is likely that at some point in the future it will begin to deteriorate. Typically, this leads to cracking and/or chalking (dryness) of the paint film. It also has a different flexibility compared with, for example, an overpainting of true acrylic paint: the acrylic paint is more flexible, the white emulsion less so. At some stage, this discrepancy may show itself - when the painting is moved or knocked, parts of the paint layers may become damaged.

Similarly, artists used vinyl-based (PVA - Polyvinyl acetate) paints and mediums for their paintings, sometimes mixing them with true acrylic paints. The PVA-based mediums and paints can embrittle and yellow with age, so it should be no surprise that their use in painting leads to problems. This is still an issue today: lack of resources for students and practising artists, often means that the cheapest materials are used. While this may be unavoidable, it is a great sadness. Not only does this lead to artists making paintings that have a short life-span, it also encourages a bad use of materials and a bad understanding of technique. Part of the blame for this state of affairs lies with education, but it could also be argued that manufacturers should have drawn more attention to the distinctions between true acrylic paint and cheaper PVA/vinyl paints. The main distinctions are as follows:

Acrylic Paint

Paint film remains very flexible, regardless of thickness of application
Long term: acrylic paint remains flexible
Long term: acrylic paint does not yellow or darken
Long term: acrylic paint does not become transparent with age, remains constant
Dilution: water, non-hazardous

PVA/Vinyl Colours

Paint film becomes brittle with age
PVA/vinyl colours have less binding strength than true acrylic paints
Long term: PVA/vinyl colours lose their flexibility
Long term: PVA/vinyl colours can yellow with age

One of the intentions of this text is to persuade artists not to use any PVA-based materials. Often, artists use clear PVA, from a builders' yard, or that intended as a glue for children's artwork, as a transparent sealing coat for canvas. They may also use it to bind dry pigments. This can lead to problems later. Moreover, there are acrylic materials that will do these jobs and which will last.

It can be argued that acrylic paints have a bad name because, in their early use, they were often combined with inferior materials. Artificial ageing tests done by respected conservation specialists, have revealed that high quality acrylic paint is lightfast (non-yellowing), flexible, durable and possesses high binding strength. The words "high quality" are paramount here. Just as in earlier times vinyl-based colours did an injustice to true acrylic paints, so today, there are inferior acrylic paints on the market. They are made with the minimum of fuss, using a true acrylic resin but with the addition of an excess of fillers. Instead of mixing the binder and pigment on a triple mill, costs are cut by simply stirring the ingredients together, so that they form a paint but one which lacks subtlety of consistency and colour. Cheaper pigments are used in minimal quantities. Some of the modern synthetic organic pigments can be extended a long way and still give the impression of colour saturation. However, when such colours are intermixed, instead of giving good mixtures, colour values tend to be muddy. In addition, these economical paints dry quickly on the surface but remain soft at the core for long periods. Ideally, acrylic paint should dry right through to the core at an even rate.

Of course, price is always important to the user: it may be that students will find these cheaper colours ideal for making trial paintings in acrylic. However, the author would suggest that even those new to acrylic should at least try a high quality paint, so that they can judge the differences. Often an expensive, pigment-rich paint can be extended by addition with mediums and/or water, to give much more colour in terms of volume, than is the case with bulk quantity, cheaper acrylic paint.

Priming Information for Acrylic Paint Systems

The choice of priming material for acrylic painting can be crucial. Generally, acrylic primer can be applied to any dirt and grease-free surface. Typically, boards that have been cut at the wood-yard, are prone to having dirty finger marks/residue from cutting. The simplest way to de-grease a surface, such as MDF (medium density fibreboard), hardboard or plywood, is to clean it with a soft rag dampened in alcohol (methylated spirit). The alcohol de-greases the board surface and evaporates rapidly from it. This process should also be applied to the sides of the board and the reverse, so that the object is in effect "clean". Hands can also be cleansed prior to working with acrylic primer, to reduce the possibility of dirt/grease getting back on to the board surface.

Other supports suitable for painting with acrylic primer can include cotton duck canvas, linen, polyester fabric and paper. It may not be necessary to prime paper supports, as acrylic paint will sit comfortably on the paper surface. In general, papers with a surface sizing are desirable, because the acrylic paint does not sink into the fibres of the paper. However, it is dangerous to be too prescriptive about this, because the choice of papers available is so wide and the relative absorbency is also great.

The quality of priming materials for acrylic paint systems varies a great deal from brand to brand. It is impossible to identify one brand as being the best, because that description rather relies on the judgement of the artist. For example, a priming that leaves a very absorbent ground may be exactly what is required by one artist, while another may need a primer with no absorbency. The only way to assess these qualities is to purchase small amounts of different brands and carry out tests. As with all the materials discussed in this text, the same process can be applied: ultimately it is for each individual artist to choose which is the most suitable material for the work in hand.

Generally, acrylic primers fall into two distinct categories:

1. **Non-absorbent primer.**
2. **Absorbent primer, or "gesso".**

Both types tend to be manufactured using a blend of titanium white pigment, calcium carbonate (whiting chalk) and acrylic emulsion. The exact absorbency of a primer is dependent upon the ratio of pigment to calcium carbonate. For the most absorbent primer, typically, a greater amount of calcium carbonate is used. The term "gesso"* usually refers to a primer that has more absorbency. However, this is not a standard within the artists' materials trade. It can sometimes simply refer to the fact that it is an acrylic primer. Acrylic primer can also be termed as "universal primer" (signifying that it is suitable for overpainting in any paint media). This confusion of nomenclature is of little help to the artist.

* *Gesso* is the Italian word for gypsum (calcium sulphate). In Italian panel painting, grounds are usually based on a combination of gypsum and animal glue, which tends to be referred to as "traditional gesso". In Northern Europe, artists made a similar ground using animal glue and calcium carbonate (whiting, chalk). Both types of "filler" produced painting grounds that were gently absorbent but suitable only for rigid supports, as they produced paint films that were too brittle for stretched canvas. Modern acrylic-based gesso, should be flexible enough for stretched canvas but can also be used on rigid supports.

As already stated, the choice of the best materials still resides with the artist. By comparing brands, one can find the most suitable material. Ideally, within the painting workshop/dedicated space, a selection of examples of primers should be available, so that sample paint-outs can be made.

The quality of an acrylic primer can be related to the process of manufacture. Economical primers tend to be crudely mixed together, and may not be suitable for further dilution with water. It is essential for the artist to obtain as much technical information as possible about these materials before using them. Manufacturers often produce information sheets about their products, with guidance on their use. Some brands are labelled implicitly with instructions not to be further diluted with water (i.e. they are ready-to-use/pre-diluted). Similarly, check that the primer is suitable for the chosen support. Some primers are labelled as not being suitable for stretched canvas, indicating that they may not be flexible on such supports. The wording on the label may refer to a list of supports for which the primer is suitable, but not mention surfaces for which it should not be used. If in doubt, check with the manufacturer: most have technical support, even if it means talking to more than one person to ascertain the information required. Ideally make a note of the answer given for future reference.

The process of manufacture often governs the pricing of these materials. The longer a material is worked on, the more expensive it may be. For example, some primers are milled thoroughly, more than once, sieved, milled again, then re-sieved. This process removes lumps of material and provides a smooth, fine priming paste. Other primers may be mixed crudely and perhaps not sieved at all. In general, primers that dry to a slightly chalky, matt finish tend towards brittleness. This can be a problem when they are applied to large stretched canvas, where the fabric is under stress. In the worst cases, the weakness of the painting ground (primer) can inform subsequent paint layers (i.e. they crack when stressed). The best quality acrylic primers stay flexible and durable. They may have a higher price but tend to be more cost-effective, because a) they can often be diluted up to 40-50% and b) they do not crack, even when applied dilute.

To achieve the best possible surface (i.e. smooth), there are a number of methods with which the artist can experiment. One aspect to consider is that of brushes. Often, a cheap, decorating brush is used, which gives out a distinct mark. Such brushes also tend to shed hairs badly, contributing to a "bad" surface. Soft hog hair varnish brushes can be used, where the hair is shaped at the tip, so that primer is released slowly from the brush hairs. Sharply cut flat brushes tend to retain brushmarks when applied to a surface. By diluting the priming material with water, to a consistency where it flows off the brush tip, a relatively smooth application of primer can be realised. Typically, a dilution with water of the primer by 25-30% may give a single cream consistency, which flows from the brush tip evenly. As suggested, for each material used, as with each support chosen, some adjustment of proportions may be necessary due to variations between brands etc.

In some instances, primer can be applied and then sanded, either between each coat, or after the final coat. Before doing this, it is advisable to test a number of different primers, to see how successfully they sand down. Generally, the more absorbent acrylic gesso will sand down with greater ease than straight acrylic primer. Some artists use a mixture between acrylic primer and a light acrylic modelling paste, as this helps fill the pores of the canvas fabric, to give an even surface, and can also be gently sanded to provide a smooth finish. Each manufacturer of acrylic material can advise on the best type of light modelling paste to use for this purpose.

In principle, the best acrylic primings stay flexible and provide a cushion for subsequent paint layers. Some brands also produce coloured acrylic primer or gesso. However, it is also possible to admix white acrylic primer or acrylic gesso, with acrylic paint, to achieve a tinted ground.

For some supports, such as linen, a pre-primer may be required. A number of clear, neutral "sizing" agents are available on the market. These can be called "acrylic size", "canvas sealer", "clear acrylic sealant", etc. This acrylic size acts as a sealing agent for absorbent supports, such as linen, where the weave of the fabric is slightly open. When acrylic primer is applied direct to linen, it tends to soak through in places, leaving an uneven surface on the front and reverse. To counter this, the acrylic size is applied, normally in two thinned coats (again refer to directions on product information). This sizing coat penetrates into the weave of the fabric and helps to achieve a homogenous surface when the primer is subsequently applied.

The acrylic size has a matt, virtually neutral quality, which allows subsequent coatings of primer to adhere well. It does not increase tension when applied to stretched canvas, in the same way that animal skin glue sizings tend to.

For best results, canvas is lightly tacked to the stretcher. Two coats of acrylic size are applied, allowing the first coat to dry before proceeding with the second. The first coat can be more dilute than the second. Dilution allows the acrylic size to penetrate successfully into the fabric.

Once dry, the acrylic size can be overpainted with acrylic primer or acrylic gesso as required. If the colour of the canvas needs to be visible, acrylic paint can be applied directly to the acrylic sized surface. However, a third or even fourth coating of acrylic size may be desirable, to ensure that the acrylic paint does not sink into the surface of the painting fabric.

The amount of acrylic size and subsequent coats of acrylic primer can vary, according to the type of fabric used. It is important to make some distinction between priming methods for acrylic paint systems as opposed to oil paint; one method of priming will not suffice for every media. Although acrylic primer can be used for oil painting, it is often necessary to apply more coats of it to avoid strike through.

Encaustic Painting

The term "encaustic" is originally Greek, meaning "to burn in". It is applied to the use of wax as a binding medium, where no solvent is present. In effect, encaustic painting relies on pigments mixed with a blend of beeswax and natural resin (such as dammar resin). Colour is expressed on to the painting surface by making the pigment-wax-resin mixture molten (fluid) enough to manipulate, with brushes or special tools. The applied paint film quickly cools and sets hard, whence it can be gently buffed with a soft cloth to give a mild polish. Once set and dried, encaustic paints are extremely durable, they do not attract dirt or dust and can be easily cleaned with a soft dusting cloth as required.

N.B. True encaustic painting is applied with heat and never in combination with solvents of any kind (highly flammable). Special oil-pigment sticks for direct painting with colour, are mentioned in the context of oil painting.

Supports for Encaustic Painting

Beeswax is a relatively flexible wax but is not really flexible enough to apply on to stretched canvas. As a consequence, encaustic colour is applied to a rigid panel, prepared with an animal skin glue-chalk mixture (as per panels for use with egg tempera painting). This type of painting ground is porous (absorbent) enough for the encaustic colour to grip on to. Linen, cotton canvas or muslin scrim, stuck to board with animal skin glue could also be used as a support, either with or without a gesso ground.

Acrylic and oil-based primers do not have enough porosity of surface to allow the wax layers to grip on to them.

The support panel must be rigid enough to withstand warping: larger paintings would need to be braced on the reverse to prevent this.

Equipment for Encaustic Painting

Heat is essential for encaustic painting. The paint itself is sold in solid lump form, which needs to become molten before application to the support.

Specialist suppliers of encaustic painting materials can provide the basic equipment, including:

- Thermostat controlled hot plate. Beeswax becomes molten at around 62-66°C. A thermostat controlled hot plate will enable this temperature to be reached easily and kept constant, without over-heating. This is vital, as the temperature must remain constant but never rise above 93°C. Above this temperature, beeswax gives off potentially noxious fumes as do certain pigments (e.g. cadmiums) when strongly heated. It is also the case that some pigments are sensitive to colour change - the ochres and raw siennas are especially prone to this (changing from yellow to red) when strongly heated. In any case, a controlled temperature is advised, so that there is no danger of fire. It is advisable to keep a fire extinguisher within easy reach when working with encaustic, as a precaution.

- Heated spatulas (in a variety of head shapes, for flat applications, smoothing, sculpting, etc). These electronic spatulas provide heat to the tip, so that paint surfaces can be modelled while molten and re-modelled as required once set. A variety of shaped-tips are available.

- Aluminium-steel alloy tins (cake tins, cupcake tins) for holding molten colour. On to the warm hotplate, encaustic colour is deposited into a metal receptacle, such as a cake tin, or baking tin for small cup cakes. Protective oven gloves should be worn when moving the hot tins.

Once softened into a molten, liquid state, the encaustic colour can then be applied to the surface using hog bristle brushes or metal spatulas.

Composition and Use of Encaustic Paints

Encaustic paints rely on a fusion of pigment into molten beeswax and dammar resin. The dried paint film is resistant to moisture, thus providing a very stable final painting. The only caution with finished encaustic paintings is that they be stored away from direct heat sources such as radiators or open fires. They should also be kept away from sources of strong (hot) sunlight during the summer months.

Beeswax is available in both lump and pellet form. In its raw state, natural beeswax has some flexibility, but this is somewhat reduced in refined products. With the artists' materials market, most beeswax can be considered as being refined to some extent. The refined product is sold in a yellow or bleached form. The latter has a white colour and is seemingly more useful when combining with pigment. In practice, the colour of the wax is of little importance, as the bleached wax will revert to the same colour shade as the yellow wax over time. Raw natural beeswax, procured from the bee-keeper, will be more plastic (flexible) and higher in resin content than the refined forms. The raw product is also less likely to be adulterated: some refined beeswax may have inclusions of synthetic waxes. However, raw natural beeswax may have a stronger colour (typically yellow-brown), which may have some drawbacks when being used with pale colours and whites.

In an enamel pan, the beeswax is melted on a hotplate, together with an inclusion of perhaps 30% dry dammar resin. Choose the palest pieces of dammar available and pick through it before use, to remove any plant impurities and other foreign matter. If too much is added, the encaustic paint will be too sticky when molten. Experimentation is called for in this respect. The inclusion of dammar gives the resultant encaustic paint more gloss and better hardness upon drying. During the melting process, the contents of the enamel pan are stirred to ensure fusion between the two ingredients. When adding pigment to colour the wax-resin, it is advisable to take the pan off the heat, stir in the dry pigment (while still hot) so that all the dry powder is incorporated into the wax-resin, then place back onto the heat source and stir until the pigment is freely distributed in the wax-resin. The longer this stirring can continue, the better the mixing of the ingredients will be. Some pigments with larger particle size, such as the natural earths, will take longer to mix in than those with smaller particle grain size.

When the ingredients are thoroughly combined, the mixture can be poured into small empty bread tins or cupcake tins and left to cool and harden. When each colour is required, it is simply re-melted in its tin and used. It is possible to mix colours by melting the required colours, then combining while still hot, into a new receptacle. It is much easier to mix colours this way, than to try and mix colours on the painting surface. Once the chosen palette has been decided upon, it may be appropriate to make up some half-tints with white, or perhaps neutral tints towards black, by the addition of a transparent black such as lamp black.

Wax Types

Beeswax is the most useful wax for encaustic, being slightly flexible and easy to melt and re-melt. The other waxes can be experimented with, but may cause more problems than they solve - with the possible exception of carnauba wax.

Carnuaba Wax

Carnuaba wax melts at 83-86°C. A natural plant wax, from South America, it can be incorporated into encaustic colours to impart toughness and durability to the paint sheen. An addition of perhaps 5-10% of the wax content in the encaustic block will produce a wax paint that melts at a higher temperature but will bring a certain hardness to the cooled paint film. The importance of using a thermostat controlled hotplate becomes crucial when adding this higher melt-point wax to beeswax. Carnauba wax is sold in a grey (natural) form, or a pale white-yellow colour (refined).

Paraffin Wax

Paraffin wax melts at around 50-60°C. It is a by-product of the petro-chemical industry. Paraffin wax is too brittle to use in encaustic paints and, with a low melt point, would make the cooled paint surface very susceptible to change in warm environments.

Microcrystalline Wax

Microcrystalline wax is related to paraffin wax, but may have a higher melt point, according to the grade selected (e.g. 73-77° C). It may be more flexible than paraffin wax, however, some cheaper grades may be even more inflexible!

A special grade of microcrystalline wax, called "Cosmoloid" wax has a higher melt point (around 80-100°C), which may be useful, but only when used in relatively thin layers and with pigments that don't give off noxious fumes at high temperature.

Other waxes are available (none of which are commonly used in encaustic technique):

Candelilla wax (melt point, 67-71°C). A brown plant wax. Similar hardness to carnauba wax.
Insect wax (melt point, 79-83°C). Yellow-white in colour, harder than beeswax.
Japan wax (melt point, 50-52°C). Very soft, sticky insect wax, which remains soft upon cooling. Pale yellow colour.
Montan wax - ozokerite (melt point, 76-130°C). Brown-black wax from bitumen.
Ceresin wax (melt point, 61-80°C). Derived from bitumen, ceresin wax is a refined form of brown-black ozokerite mineral wax, with a pale, yellow colour. More flexible than paraffin or microcrystalline waxes.

Stearin wax (melt point, 69-71°C). Animal fat wax, pale white-yellow colour, soft. Most often used as an additive (adulterant) in candle making or cosmetics.

Spermaceti wax (melt point, 41-44°C). Brittle, white wax, from the sperm whale.

Suggested Palette for Encaustic Painting

It is vital that the pigments used in the composition of encaustic paint are not heated to high temperatures. As previously indicated, beeswax must never be heated beyond 93°C, to avoid wax fumes.

It is also crucial to keep the temperature constant and always below 93°C, because some pigments can a) give off toxic fumes when overheated (e.g. cadmiums) and b), change colour when strongly heated (e.g. natural earths). If kept at a stable, gentle temperature (around 66°C), the following list of pigments can be used:

Cadmium lemon
Cadmium yellow light
Cadmium yellow medium
Cadmium yellow deep
Cadmium orange
Cadmium red light
Cadmium red medium
Cadmium red deep
Cadmium maroon
Cadmium green
Cobalt yellow
Cobalt violet light
Cobalt violet deep
Cobalt blue
Cobalt turquoise
Cerulean blue
Cobalt green
Synthetic iron oxides: yellow-orange-red-violet, brown, black
Nickel titanium yellow

Paliogen maroon

Quinacridone red, pink, violet

Manganese violet

Ultramarine violet

Ultramarine blue

Prussian blue

Phthalocyanine blue

Phthalocyanine green

Ultramarine green

Viridian

Chrome oxide green

Green earth

Natural earths: raw sienna, burnt sienna, raw umber, burnt umber

Ivory black

Lamp black

Titanium white

Zinc white

N.B. Avoid all lead-based pigments in encaustic technique.

Painting Techniques

In the soft, molten state, encaustic can be applied to the painting surface in a number of ways. From the hot tin in which the encaustic has been melted, the contents can be poured out on to the surface, or applied with hog bristle brushes, or painting knives, spatulas, etc. Some improvisation is called for in terms of application. Speed is of the essence, as the encaustic colour soon cools and hardens. If the encaustic cools before the surface of the paint has been manipulated, it can be re-worked with a flat head heated spatula. It is also possible to move the painting close to a heat source (e.g. a hot radiator), to soften the paint surface for re-working. If paint needs to be taken off, it can simply be melted with a hot spatula and scraped off.

It is advisable to work in relatively thin layers, slowly building up translucent layers of wax. The strength of the colour used can be controlled by admixture with more beeswax and resin. This is best done by preparing a block of colourless encaustic paint, containing only melted beeswax and dammar resin. The resultant block can be made molten with heat and poured into tins containing strong colour, as a kind of diluent or extender. If too much wax-resin is contained in a paint mixture, the resultant paint sheen may take on a frosted/obscured appearance, where the thickness of the wax-resin in comparison to the pigment content subdues colour resonance. Some experimentation is called for in these circumstances. Of course, once cool, any difficult areas can be quickly overpainted, or re-melted and removed as required.

Never add solvents into encaustic paints: the low flash points of solvents such as white spirit and turpentine would make fire a distinct possibility. Encaustic is best used alone, rather than in combination with other media. However, an 18th century formula for working with wax involved the covering of a wooden panel with a thick (3cm plus) layer of beeswax, poured on to the surface and worked over with heat to gain a flat, level surface. On to the cooled wax surface, gouache paint is applied (without dilution with water), to create an image. Once dry, the finished gouache on wax painting is taken close to a heat source and exposed to heat for a few moments. This can be done by hovering over the paint surface (laid flat) with a heat gun. The heat gently melts the wax, and the gouache paint is quickly absorbed into it. Once cool again, it is found that the paint layers have become embedded in the wax, so providing a stable and durable paint surface. If the wax is melted too quickly, the painted image may separate or crack, although in abstract painting terms, this may be of some benefit. The cooled wax surface can be gently buffed to give a soft polish. Alternatively, subsequent layering of encaustic can be applied over this "underpainting".

Glazing with Encaustic

Wax has a frosting effect on paint films, when it is applied in any thickness. By contrast, when encaustic is applied in relatively thin layers, translucency within the paint film is preserved. As a consequence, pigments that are normally transparent in other binding media, will retain their transparent properties when applied in relatively thin layers of encaustic, but will exhibit an opaque, solid presence when applied thickly.

Working in Layers

When applying multiple layers of encaustic, it is important to heat the whole painting gently after completion, to ensure that all the layers bond together. This gentle heating is best done with a heat gun, held perhaps 40-50cm from the painting surface. The heat gently warms the paint surface until it becomes soft and just molten. This process (known as "fusing") softens the various layers so that they all fuse together, ensuring correct bonding between layers. The painting is laid flat during this process, so that the wax layers do not start to run. If the painting is not fused in this way, either upon completion, or while working, it is possible that one layer may shear off from another.

As with most paint systems, encaustic is best applied in multiple thin layers rather than thick wodges. However, the durability of encaustic when applied to a rigid support does allow for some degree of impasto and indeed, applied paint layers can be worked into with heated spatulas in order to part-sculpt the paint surface.

Presentation of Finished Encaustic Paintings

Encaustic paintings do not need to be varnished: the surface, once buffed with a soft cloth, will resist collection of dirt and dust. The surface is also resistant to water, so can be wiped with a damp cloth to clean. For exhibition, encaustic paintings can be shown without glazing, indeed, putting encaustic paintings under glass would somewhat detract from the paint's inherent qualities.

Safe Clean-Up of Encaustic Paint

As already indicated, some precautions are necessary with encaustic technique. Aside from the use of a thermostat controlled hot plate, a fire extinguisher should be kept close at hand. In addition, heat resistant gloves should be worn when handling hot paint tins, etc. Used brushes can be cleaned by rinsing in a tin of molten wax. This should free the encaustic paint from the brush hairs. However, in practice it may be better to nominate each colour a specific brush, so that cleaning is unnecessary. In this case, the brush need only be re-dispersed in the same colour in the molten state. It is also possible to clean brushes by rinsing in a molten solution of (cheaper) synthetic wax, such as paraffin wax. However, the synthetic waxes are never used for encaustic painting itself, because they generally have a lower melt point and are more prone to cracking/splitting upon cooling.

Lime-Fresco Painting

Fresco (literally "fresh") refers to the practice of painting using pigments dispersed into water, on to a base of wet lime plaster. True fresco (*buon fresco*) is applied in this way, relying on the setting properties of lime to capture pigment particles worked on to the lime plaster (*intonaco*) surface.

Lime is calcium oxide, prepared by burning calcium carbonate (e.g. limestone, marble, etc) in a brick kiln. Not all varieties of lime are suitable for use in fresco painting. Ideally, the lime is free of magnesium and not tinted by iron oxides. Not all sources of limestone concur with these requirements. Additionally, commercial suppliers of lime deal almost exclusively with the building trade and building restoration trade, where the need for very finely sieved, high white colour lime may not be as important as it is for fresco painting.

When lime is introduced to water, it provokes a strong reaction, being an aggressively caustic alkali. On immersion into water, heat is generated and the material is formed into a new substance, calcium hydroxide, also referred to as "slaked lime". The best qualities of slaked lime are derived from lime that has been left to "rot" in tanks of water. This process of ageing the soaked lime, provides the best possible adhesion to the support and coherent setting of the lime paste. During this process, the wet slaked lime settles out in the tank: the finest particles stay at the top of the wet lime slurry, while the larger, coarse particles descend towards the bottom. The tank must be dug into the ground, ideally below the surface so that frost cannot develop, as this would injure the setting properties of the lime. The tank must also be covered at night, to prevent frost from developing.

In the traditional use for lime - the white-washing of houses and the preparation of lime plaster - the slaked lime need not be of a uniform consistency. However, for use as an artists' paint system, the smoother the lime paste, the better, in terms of achieving fine results.

When applied on to the correct substrate, the slaked lime (calcium hydroxide) changes back to calcium carbonate on exposure to carbon dioxide in the air. As the applied slaked lime dries with the evaporation of the water content, it gradually reverts back to calcium carbonate, in reality, a chemical change occurs to the original material (e.g. limestone, marble, etc). Upon hardening, the dried lime layer becomes as hard as rock; the individual particles of lime being strongly bonded to each other. It follows that when pigments are mixed with distilled water to form a liquid paste, then applied to the fresh lime layer, the pigment particles become trapped within the structure of the re-forming calcium carbonate, thereby resulting in a hard-set and durable paint film.

Health and Safety Precautions

Lime is a caustic, alkaline material, which can burn the skin and is especially dangerous when in contact with the eyes. As a consequence, it is advised that at all times, preventative measures are taken.

Wear protective eye goggles, gloves, barrier cream (applied to hands, forearms, face and neck - any part of the skin which could be exposed) and a dust mask when working with dry pigments. Never eat or drink in the studio when working with lime. The clothes worn while working with lime must be removed on leaving the studio, as residual dried lime dust can easily be brushed off on to skin, etc. It is imperative to wear eye goggles, because the wet lime paste is prone to a certain amount of splashing, when pouring, painting, etc.

Once absolutely dry, fresco paintings become relatively inert.

Supports for Lime: Preparing Walls and Other Substrates for Application of Lime

The wall structure is prepared so that it will take subsequent coats of mortar. Preparation will vary according to the structure in question. For example, an old, aged plaster coating over brick may be simply hacked all over to provide a grip coat. If the wall structure is clean, aged brick, the bricks themselves will possess enough porosity to allow the first scratch coat to form a bonding. In the case of walls they must be free from any minerals, especially salt residues. Preferably, the wall should be specially constructed, including an air cavity between the wall to be painted on and the structural wall of the building. It is advised that this air cavity be designed to allow air to circulate (i.e. it is not a simple void of trapped air, there are holes that allow the air space to "breathe"). It is also advisable to ensure that any wall structure is free from damp and does not contain any residual moisture prior to painting.

Once the wall is prepared, before application of the scratch coat, the wall is soaked with cold water, the purpose being to penetrate the porous wall, so that the scratch coat partially absorbs into the wall itself to form a coherent bonding. The wall is repeatedly soaked, as evenly as possible, until it will not absorb any more water. At this point, the scratch coat is applied.

For portable panels, the procedure is simpler, as described later in this section.

The Mortar Layers

The following aggregates are suggested for use in lime mortars:

Marble dust, white offered in a variety of grind sizes, μ, for example:

Finest	32μ or less (marble flour)
Fine	32μ

Middle 90µ
Coarse 200µ
Extra coarse 150-300µ

Marble chips, sold in a variety of colours and grind sizes (use white for mortar layers):

Sand texture	0.7-1.2mm
Grit texture	1.8-2.5mm
Gravel	2.5-4.0mm

(In practice, a mix between marble chips and dust may be preferable, but experimentation is called for at all stages with lime-fresco painting.)

Quartz chips (white river sand, free of mica), in grind sizes from 0.15mm to 0.5mm.

These aggregates are presented in different "grind", or "grain" sizes (particle size format). In true fresco, the wall is prepared by combining coarse aggregates into lime putty in the first coat, followed by subsequent coats that may contain a higher proportion of lime, and increasingly less-coarse inclusions of aggregates. There is some evidence that in the first coats (*trulisatio, arenato*) a mix of coarse and medium grind aggregates is advantageous. While this provides a relatively gritty and coarse structure, the in-fill is completed with smaller sized particles. These help to keep the mortar structure slightly damp, when residual water from the intonaco layer percolates down into the mortar, thereby giving a longer working period for application of colour to the intonaco layer.

According to traditional Italian techniques, the support layers of mortar are applied to the prepared wall surface, in the following sequence:

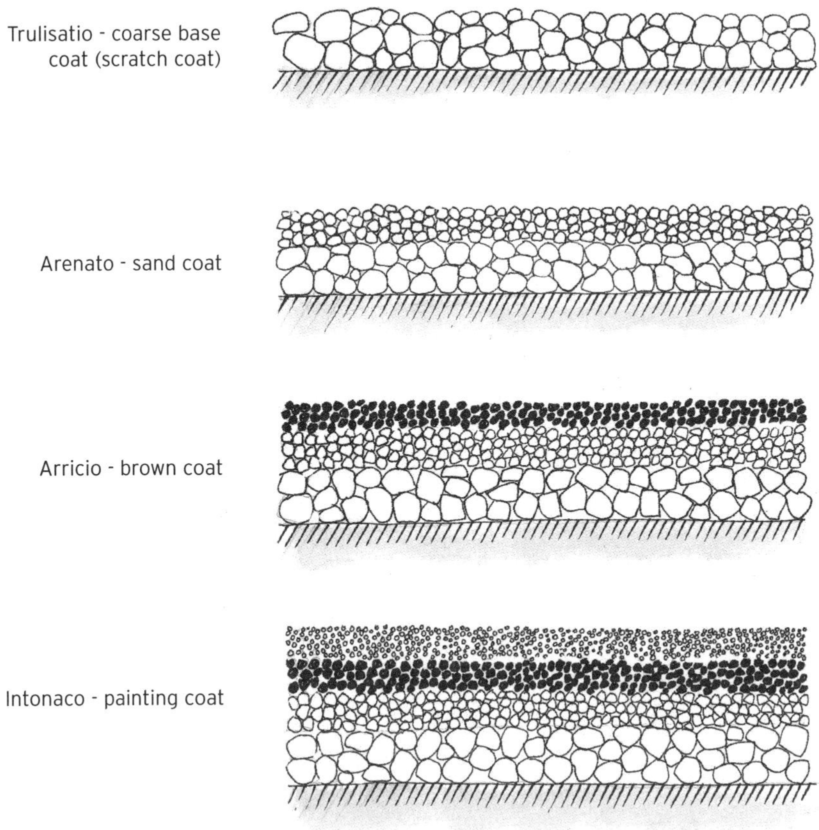

Mortar Layers for Fresco Painting

Trulisatio - coarse base coat, or scratch coat, containing larger-sized aggregates (white river sand/quartz chips, or coarse marble dust). For example, take marble dust chips, sized 2.5-4.0mm and combine 3 parts marble dust chips with 1 part lime putty. The use of aggregates helps to form a solid and stable working surface. By including these coarse materials, the mortar coats tend to dry with minimum shrinkage. The large grain marble dust chips/quartz chips will stand out proud from the dried mortar to some extent: this gives a kind of grip coat for the next layer of mortar. By gradually adding finer grain size aggregate to larger inclusions of lime putty, the "wall" structure of the mortar is brought to a smooth, relatively even finish.

Arenato - consolidation coat, or sand coat, applied over the trulisatio layer: a mixture of 1 part lime to 2 parts marble dust chips, 0.7-1.2mm grind size.

Arriccio - underpainting coat, or brown coat, applied over the arenato coat. It is composed of fine quartz sand or marble dust with an equal quantity of lime putty.

Intonaco - the painting coat, usually made with fine lime putty. While still damp, pigments mixed with distilled water are applied to the intonaco layer. The pigments are driven into the surface of the layer upon evaporation of the water content, becoming intrinsically bonded into the structure. While the intonaco layer is still damp (but not saturated with wetness), colour can be safely applied and a bonding can be assumed. However, once the intonaco layer is dry, applied colour will not form a reaction with the lime and little or no bonding will occur. As a consequence, large-scale work is usually undertaken with some planning, the intonaco layer only being applied to an area that can be worked on comfortably before drying out.

The preparation of the previous mortar layers can be crucial to the way the intonaco layer operates. The mortar layers are applied loosely (i.e. without undue pressure being applied during trowelling of the mortar) and the material is not especially compacted during this process. This leaves the underlayers of lime-mortar relatively porous, so that when the intonaco layer is applied, some dampness percolates into the mortar layer and remains within it for a protracted period, thus allowing a longer working time on to the freshly applied intonaco layer. However, if the mortar layer is too porous, too much water will be sucked out of the intonaco layer. By tradition, the coarse layers of mortar are applied by throwing the mixed mortar at the wall surface, from a metal trowel. Once they have contacted with the wall structure, the trowel is used if necessary to gently form a level coating of mortar. In the first stages, the material is not compacted down on to the support structure: it is gently levelled, but not aggressively pushed against the support. This method of application allows the mortar to retain a little porosity. If the mortar were to be strongly compacted, too smooth a layer would result. This layer would also be less liable to retain moisture, when the final intonaco layer is applied.

The mortar is then left to dry for 20-30 minutes before the next coat is applied. Allow this amount of time so that the mortar is still slightly wet but not sopping. A good method for testing at this stage is to press the thumb against the mortar layer gently. One should be able to leave a firmish thumb impression in it: if the mortar gives way (goes to a sludge), then more drying time is required. If the mortar coats are laid down in this manner (i.e. without complete drying between each coat), then theoretically the different coats are better bonded together. However, some experimentation may be required and it should be borne in mind that different atmospheric conditions may cause the mortar layers to dry out at variable rates.

However, with the final intonaco layer, the trowelling is followed by compaction of the surface, to gain a hard, smooth finish. To avoid "popping" of the surface (the rising of air bubbles and water through the final coat), it is worked over with a special lime or chalk brush, which helps to free any residual pockets of air or water, so creating an even and unpock-marked surface.

Portable Panels

The preparation of wall structures for lime-fresco painting is a somewhat protracted and technical matter, which may require consultation prior to working with an appropriate authority. By contrast, artists can prepare a form of portable panel, which allows smaller scale work to be undertaken in lime-fresco.

There are two basic types of portable panel that can be used:

1. Support layers on to wood panel.
2. Support layers on to plaster panel.

Wood Panel

MDF (medium density fibreboard), of at least 15mm thickness can be used to make small panels, up to 50cm square (larger size formats will tend to warp and would require significant bracing). The preparation of the panel gives a synthesis of a wall-mortar, but is arrived at by the inclusion of casein (milk glue), as a strong bonding agent. The casein allows the coarse particles of quartz/marble to grip on to the panel, and the top layers to be painted in lime only. Casein is a very strong protein glue, which will enclose and grip larger particle aggregates in the mortar layers. Because it is so strong, the intonaco coat of lime will not pull away from the mortar layers. Also, casein is a porous glue, which allows moisture from the intonaco layer to percolate down into the mortar layers, as with traditional fresco. However, it is important to ensure that each layer of mortar is slightly weaker than the last (in terms of the strength of the casein glue), to prevent the strong nature of the glue from shearing away from previous coats. This is simply done, by preparing the mortar coats with increasingly dilute additions of casein binder.

For the first coat – the grip or scratch coat - take 3 parts coarse marble chips ("gravel", 2.5-4.0mm) to 1 part of lime putty. Mix these thoroughly. To this paste, add about 30-40% casein binder. The casein is prepared into a stock solution as follows:

Lactic casein	2 parts
Cold water	8 parts

Add the water to the casein. Then add 1 part (i.e. 1 level tablespoon) of powdered ammonium-carbonate, which acts as an emulsifying agent, allowing the casein and water to form a thick paste. Leave to stand for 15-30 minutes, stir to free any lumps. To this paste, slowly add a further 8 parts of cold water, stir again until free from lumps. Sieve if necessary. It may be advisable to leave this to stand for an hour or so, to allow the ammonium carbonate to settle. It eventually effervesces out of the mixture, so plays little or no part in the formation of the dried paint film. Once sieved and in a free flowing, but thick solution, the casein is ready for use. At this dilution it is added to the lime-aggregate paste, as already suggested.

Before applying to the panel, make sure that the panel is dirt and grease-free. If necessary, de-grease the surface of the panel with alcohol. Leave to dry for at least 3-4 hours after preparation with alcohol. The first mortar coat is then applied, by brush to the panel. A large round hog fresco brush (*muccino*) is used. This ensures that the first coat contacts with the panel and that no air pockets or gaps are left. While the mortar-casein mix is still wet, work the brush over the surface to give an even distribution of the aggregates. Leave this first coat to dry completely, perhaps for 2-3 hours.

The second coat is applied in the same manner, but this time a mix of 2 parts marble chips ("grit" texture 1.8-2.5mm) is mixed with 1 part of lime. To this paste, 30-40% casein binder is added. However, with this coat, the casein binder is diluted with another 8 parts water, to make its glue strength relatively weaker than the first scratch coat.

Once dry, the third coat is applied, this time using an equal mixture of marble chips ("sand" texture 0.7-1.2mm) to lime putty. In this third coat, again the casein binder is added about 30-40%, but again it has to be diluted with a further 8 parts of cold water. During application, it may be useful to run a smooth spatula over the surface to create an even texture, or this can be done by careful brushing. In practice, the author has also found it possible to wait for this third coat to dry, then abrade with glass paper to achieve a smoother surface.

Once this third coat is dry, the intonaco layer can be applied (1 part lime putty to 1 part fine marble flour/marble dust). It is useful to do this using a trowel and patting the surface of the lime, so that it is compacted against the mortar coats. As with normal fresco technique, the intonaco layer can also be smoothed by brushing flat, this will eradicate any air or water trapped in the surface. It is best to leave the applied intonaco a few minutes before doing this, to allow the surface to settle out. Into the damp intonaco layer, pigment-water paste can be applied, and the paint film will dry out as expected, with the pigment particles bonded into the lime intonaco.

Plaster Panel

Plaster of Paris is a form of gypsum, where the material has been calcined so that a large portion of its inherent water of crystallisation has been eradicated. Upon mixing with cold water, such plaster is driven to set extremely quickly. During setting, the plaster hardens before it loses all the water that has been mixed with it, so allowing a firm set, without undue shrinkage. As a consequence, such plaster is used for casting in sculptural techniques, but it can also be used to make a thick, flat panel, suitable for applying mortar layers on to.

Choose a fine grade plaster, which is quick setting. This is usually a hard white, finely and evenly divided powder. Use cold water, slowly stirring it into the dry plaster, to form a smooth paste. This procedure must be undertaken quickly. In practice, the best way to incorporate the water into the plaster is to mix by hand. First, apply a barrier cream to the hands and forearms, then wear some protective gloves, so that the plaster does not come into contact with skin. Slowly combine the water with the plaster and stir, using the hand like a paddle to form a smooth, air bubble-free paste. This paste is then quickly poured out into the panel mould.

It is suggested that the plaster panel be small in size, no bigger than 50cm square. Cut a strong piece of wood to this size, to act as a kind of backing. This will ensure that the back of the panel is completely smooth. Cut strips of strong cardboard, or thin wood to act as a mould, and go around the edge of the wooden panel with these strips, so that the plaster can be poured over the wood panel and kept in this reservoir by the retaining walls of cardboard/wood strips. Hold the strips in place by going around the outside with strong adhesive packing tape. Into this reservoir, place a thin sheet of polythene to act as a barrier between the plaster and the wood panel and edge strips. Once the mould is secured, pour in the freshly mixed plaster, quickly spreading it across the inside of the mould using the hand, or a flat hog brush. The plaster should come up to a thickness of between 6-8cm. As long as the plaster is mixed to a fine slurry and free from air bubbles, it should form a strong base panel. Such panels tend to take a long time to cure (dry out), as water is pushed out to the top of the mixture as the material starts to harden. This process can be quickened, by drawing off excess water as it collects on the surface, or even by carefully soaking the excess water on to an absorbent paper and lifting out.

Once completely dried, the mould is removed and the panel is ready for use. Before applying the mortar coats (as described for normal walls), the surface of the plaster panel can be abraded using very coarse glass paper, or even by grating using a metal file, or any implement that will make many shallow incisions into the plaster. It is vital to do this, to ensure that the mortar coats have something to grip to and bond with.

It is also possible to include some aggregate into the wet plaster, although this does make the formation of a consistent panel rather more difficult. Another possibility is to lay a coarsely woven piece of hessian, jute or linen into the setting plaster, or to lay down one coat of plaster, overlay the fabric, then while everything is still fresh, apply another coat of plaster on top. The inclusion of this kind of fabric tends to give a stronger panel. Alternatively, fine horse hair can be mixed with the plaster to achieve a similar toughening of the plaster base.

Pigments for Lime-Fresco

The best pigments for use in lime-fresco are those that are chemically inert, or at least not sensitive to alkalis. This precludes the use of typically alkali-destroyed pigments such as prussian blue. The air in the environment may also cause pigments that are affected by acidity to become altered. Care should be taken when working on outdoor fresco paintings, to choose only those pigments that are stable in all conditions.

Basic Palette of Fresco Pigments

The following list of pigments provides a starting point, as a basic palette. Further information on use of pigments in lime-fresco is touched on in the pigment section. In truth, it is impossible to guarantee the safe use of any pigment in lime-fresco technique, due to the possibility that during manufacture, even the most inert pigments may have impurities or additives which can cause reactions when in contact with lime. It is advisable to confer with manufacturers/suppliers of fresco materials to determine their appropriate use in this technique.

On to a test panel (e.g. a panel prepared with plaster as previously described), make up small batches of pigment-distilled water pastes and apply these on to a layer of fresh intonaco. Leave this sample panel to dry for at least six months. During this period, any reaction should show: for example, effervescence on the surface; discoloration, or fading (leave panel exposed to south facing sunlight).

By tradition, each pigment is carefully mixed with cold distilled water into a paste, then applied to the wet (or rather damp) lime plaster surface. It is also possible to admix lime with the water paste to improve adhesion, although this will cause the dried colour to take on a pastel shade, rather than full tint strength. Some pigments are sold as prepared water pastes, which can be used directly on to wet or damp lime plaster, although some dilution with water prior to use may be advised, so that the applied colour is not streaky. These water-pigment pastes are especially useful in connection with the synthetic organic pigments, which have a very fine particle size and can be difficult to disperse into water.

This list is intended as a starting point and many other pigments may be used, as confirmed by the relevant supplier, etc.:

White	Bianco san giovanni (smooth white lime, partially carbonised) Slaked lime (always as a wet paste) Zinc white Titanium white
Yellow	Synthetic iron oxide yellows (mars yellow) Natural yellow earths: ochre, sienna, etc. Nickel titanium yellow Permanent yellow (PY 154) Cadmium yellow (for interior use only)
Red	Synthetic iron oxide reds (mars red) Natural red earths: burnt sienna, etc. Irgazine red (PR 254) Paliogen maroon (PR179)
Blue	Cobalt blue Cerulean blue Azurite (when applied freshly - if left to stand in water, will turn greenish) Phthalocyanine blue (PB 15) Indanthrene blue (PB 60)
Green	Viridian Cobalt green Green earth Chrome oxide green Phthalocyanine green (PG 7)

Black	Synthetic iron oxide black (mars black)
	Spinel black
	Manganese black

In the case of the synthetic organic pigments, the Colour Index name is given to aid identification.

Whites in Lime-Fresco

The intonaco layer and the mortar layers are normally prepared using a good quality aged lime putty. For example, putties that have been left to steep in water (slaked) for at least three years, possess the best setting characteristics. New lime putty (less than six months) will not set as quickly or as thoroughly. In fact, such lime putties tend to form cracks or surface deposits upon drying. While it may be impractical for individual artists to prepare their own lime, in recent years there has been a revival of interest in fresco painting, and a number of specialist suppliers now offer aged lime putties. In practical terms, the longer the lime has been left to slake, the better its setting qualities become.

The white colour of lime can be utilised as a colour during painting. Pigment-distilled water paste can be co-mixed with lime putty to achieve pastel tints. However, such applications tend to have a slightly dull appearance, compared with very thin applications of pigment applied over the damp intonaco layer. This is because, when pigment is mixed directly into the lime putty, the larger particles of lime tend to take a more prominent position in the mixture. So much so, that some pigments with a small particle size will virtually disappear. This is especially the case with the synthetic organic pigments, which are composed of extremely fine particles. As a consequence, fresco painters tend to shy away from the use of pigment mixed with lime putty. Indeed, this technique is more common in the decoration of buildings, where a tint of colour (e.g. an earth pigment) is produced by admixture with lime putty.

A more successful way of using pigment with lime white, is to mix the pigment-water paste into lime-water (sometimes referred to as "milk of lime"). Lime-water can be said to be the residual water that forms on the surface of the lime putty. In the formation tank, this water tends to clarify readily once the lime has been left to age for a few months. In practice, unless one has access to a tank of aged lime, this lime-water is best obtained from aged lime putty, which is sold in large quantities (e.g. 25 litre, or 50 litre bucket). On opening these buckets of aged lime, it will be observed that clear water settles out at the top of the mixture. This can be carefully drawn off and used as lime-water. Because lime dissolves (over time) into cold water, even though the lime-water looks clear, upon evaporation of the water content it will reveal a slight white residue. However, this residue is minimal and does not unduly affect colours it is mixed with, especially large particle pigments (e.g. earth pigments, synthetic iron oxides). If a paste of pigment-water is introduced to an equal volume of lime-water, it can be used to effect thin glazes of colour over the damp intonaco. The added lime in the lime-water creates extra bonding of the pigment into the carbonised lime putty structure upon drying, so forming a very hard-wearing bond. In practice, the pigment particles become as one with the newly formed calcium carbonate structure of the dried intonaco layer. Thus, the resultant painting is age and weather-resistant to a great degree.

Bianco san giovanni is a form of lime that has been exposed to air and is therefore closer to carbonisation than normal lime putty. By tradition, the finest grain-size basic lime putty is taken from the top of the lime pit and formed into small cakes, then left to dry for 3-4 months in a dust-free environment. When used as pigment, mixed again with distilled water, then applied to the damp intonaco layer, it dries to becomes extremely hard and fast-setting. The best quality bianco san giovanni will also have been finely sieved, so that only the finest powder is used.

Blanc fix is sometimes used in fresco as a white. Indeed, when used as a water-pigment paste, applied on to the intonaco layer, blanc fix shows as a brilliant white. This is not the case when blanc fix is used with other binding agents, where the colour and thickness of film of the binder tends to mask the whiteness of the pigment.

Titanium and zinc whites can be used in fresco safely, although these colours (being relatively late in terms of their introduction to the painter's palette) bear no relation to the whites used in traditional fresco painting.

It should be obvious that lead white can never be used in true fresco techniques, as all lead-containing pigments are inevitably changed upon exposure to air. This is especially true in the case of fresco, where the pigment particles are merely trapped in the dried calcium carbonate structure: air can still act on these pigment particles and so it follows that atmospheric pollutants will quickly make their presence known. For this reason, fresco painters are best advised to work with inert pigments, especially if the completed work is situated outdoors. There is some evidence that sulphide containing pigments, such as the cadmiums, can be safely used for indoor fresco painting but tests should be made prior to execution.

Bone ash is sometimes used as pigment in fresco painting. It has a soft grey colour in the dry state. It is also used in fresco to thicken the consistency of water-pigment pastes: because it has very little tinting power, it can be used (add 10-20% bone ash) to make a fat paste with pigments that have small sized particles (e.g. synthetic organic pigments). This will make such pigments easier to spread out over the surface, without changing the colour value too much.

Application of Colours

Before painting, it is common to execute a cartoon underpainting on to the wet/damp intonaco layer. By tradition, this is done with a natural red earth pigment, sinopia. This cartoon drawing or underpainting can be used as a guide for later painting. Once the cartoon is dry, a new intonaco coat (which remains slightly transparent, allowing the basic cartoon design to be followed) is painted over the top, on to which the actual painting is made. This final intonaco layer over the cartoon may be derived from lime only, compacted on to the surface by trowel application and further smoothed using a brush as previously described.

The pigment-distilled water pastes are spread over the surface of the (top coat) wet/damp intonaco layer, usually with brushes. The surface of the intonaco is gently absorbent and allows some of the colour to percolate down into the mortar structure. Correct preparation of the mortar and intonaco is therefore crucial. Again, it is advisable to make some test panels, keeping a note of the exact recipes used for each mortar layer, prior to undertaking major paintings. As already suggested, the use of lime-water with the pigment and distilled water pastes, will help adhesion and film formation. Admixture with lime-water may also assist larger particle size pigments (such as the historic, mineral pigments) to be spread out over the surface, allowing the particles to be dispersed, rather than clustered together. With pigments such as malachite and azurite, this technique helps to show the crystalline nature of the colour, as light catches on the exposed particles.

Because the intonaco layer is still damp during the paint process it is susceptible to disturbance. For this reason, the brushing on of pigment-distilled water paints is done with some care. It helps if the intonaco layer has been applied firmly, where the material has been compacted with a trowel and subsequent brushing, as previously described. Again, trial and error through experimentation is called for. Another tip with fresco, is to remember to be patient. The dried surface is only truly dry when all the water has evaporated. This can take many days. During this period, the surface of the painting is not always fixed (i.e. it may look dry, but the image can be dislodged with gentle rubbing). The complete carbonisation of the intonaco layer is required for fixing of the image. If the surface remains in a smudgeable/moveable state after complete drying, this may indicate that the mortar layers are simply too absorbent, or too thick.

Fresco Secco

Fresco secco (dry technique) is applied to the same substrate, but after the intonaco layer has thoroughly dried. With fresco secco, pigments are then mixed with a protein binder such as casein (milk glue) and applied to the dried intonaco layer. The resultant finish bears a close resemblance to true fresco but is not as weather and age resistant. Fresco secco allows certain fragile pigments to be applied, which would be destroyed by the caustic, alkaline nature of wet lime. For example, plant based pigments, such as stil de grain or madder, are quickly affected by lime. When used 'a secco', such pigments do not react with the dried intonaco layer. Also delicate colours, which would show as a tint only when used in true fresco technique, may benefit from fresco secco application.

Casein is perhaps the best binder for this technique and it is prepared as follows:

Casein	2 parts
Cold water	16 parts
Ammonium carbonate	1 part

The casein powder and water are combined, the ammonium carbonate added to aid emulsification. After stirring and leaving to stand for 30 minutes or so, a solution is formed. A further 16 parts water is added to the basic solution, to form a single cream consistency. It is advised that pigment is mixed into this solution and then diluted further with water, to achieve a thin paint film - the thinner the better. If the casein is over strong, it may pull at the lime substrate and cause weaknesses in the mortar/intonaco layer.

Other types of protein glue have been found on old fresco secco paintings. For example, egg yolk, isinglass and animal skin glue. In practice, casein is the most suitable, because the dried paint film remains slightly porous, allowing the mortar structure below to breathe. If a continuous film is applied over mortar/intonaco, this closes off air circulation and increases the possibility of damp/moisture causing faults in the structure. Moisture usually shows on the surface of the painting, where residues (usually simple mould, or mineral effervescence) gather, in the form of whitish crusts, or powdering. Casein also hardens quite well when kept away from moisture, becoming nominally moisture-resistant with age. By contrast, animal glues remain hygroscopic over time and when in contact with moisture tend to re-swell and/or attract microbes.

Protection of Fresco Paintings

In the past, frescoes were often varnished with a concoction known as "beverone", a simple solution protein binder such as animal hide glue, egg yolk, or egg white. This was used to impart a glossy-gleam to the surface of fresco paintings, with a look similar to that of oil paint. However, with age, such applications tend to turn dark and attract dirt and dust. So much so, that the visual image is obscured, or takes on an aged "brown" appearance. The application of beverone is normally not associated with the artist, rather with later generations who undertook to protect the fresco surface with protein binder glue/varnish. Rather than periodically removing and replacing these varnishes, practice tended towards overpainting of the original beverone with yet more of the same, resulting in a disastrous build up of dust-friendly varnish.

Removal of such varnishes is also difficult, because these protein binders tend to penetrate into the porous surface of the fresco. As a consequence, when such varnishes are removed it is all too easy to take with them a portion of the fresco surface. These protein binders also become progressively harder and less easy to remove with age, especially when multiple coats have been impacted on top of each other.

In practice, if a fresco painting has been undertaken using tried and trusted techniques, it should not require any protective varnish, especially in the case of interior work. It can also be argued that the use of varnish on to fresco painting is detrimental to the aesthetic look of the finished paint surface and therefore not necessary.

Alternative Wall Painting Binders

Waterglass

An alkaline solution of potassium silicate is known as waterglass, and is used as a binding agent for pigments applied to plaster mortar. As with lime-fresco, the pigments used should be inert if possible, so that upon drying they are not affected by atmospheric pollutants. Painting with waterglass is also known as "Stereochromy" and became popular in the mid-19th century. Waterglass is sold as prepared paint, where the pigments are ready-bound in waterglass with the required filler materials for use in building decoration. For artistic purposes, it is far more suitable to take a solution of waterglass (typically 28% potassium silicate, dissolved in water) and to combine this clear binder with pigment-distilled water pastes to form a stiff paste. This mixture is left to dry back to a solid form (sets hard) and then pulverised to re-form a powder. The resultant powder is then mixed with an equal volume of waterglass and can be applied to any clean plaster surface, in fact any surface suitable for fresco painting. Perhaps the most suitable and easiest support would be the ground described for wooden panels, using a blend of casein and lime putty, with aggregates. In order to gain a better working consistency for the waterglass-pigment mix, it is sometimes necessary to include some filler material. Aluminium hydrate, finely ground glass, zinc white or fine marble dust may be used to achieve a better paint paste. However, such additions will tend to show when used with weaker or pale colours.

Prior to painting, the surface of the plaster intonaco is saturated with a very dilute solution of waterglass (10% waterglass to water) and the waterglass-pigment combination is applied into this wet/damp ground. This process aids adhesion. Upon drying, the paint layer reflects the colouring properties of the pigment, almost as if the painting were made without binder. In this sense, waterglass has the potential to show the best effects of invidual pigments. Once the painting is complete, ideally it is sprayed with another dilute solution of waterglass, the intention being to drive more of the binding medium into the porous crevices of the painting surface. Repeated spraying of waterglass is recommended to achieve complete fixing of the paint layer. The extent to which this fixing is done is connected to the porosity of the support.

Acrylic

Modern acrylic paint systems are sometimes designed for use in mural painting. These flow-formula acrylic paints are designed to brush out flat and have an equalised paint sheen (typically, satin-matt). Acrylic paints can be applied to any dirt and grease-free support, but care must be taken in the case of brick walls and plastered walls, to ensure that no moisture residue remains inside the wall. Unlike fresco, acrylic paints form a coherent, continuous film, thereby trapping any residual moisture behind the paint layer. This can become a problem if the wall support has not been adequately prepared prior to painting. Also, if damp penetrates the wall at any time, it becomes trapped behind the paint layer and can, in the worst case scenario, burst through the paint layer, causing cracking or blistering of the paint film.

When preparing walls for use with acrylic paints, it is vital to follow the manufacturers' recommendations as regards wall preparation and priming. It cannot be overstated that the correct choice of primer is vital in this instance. For example, the use of poorly bound white emulsion paint as a priming for acrylic murals is never recommended. Such emulsion paints have a much weaker binding strength than acrylic paints and may in fact shear off from the support if stressed (e.g. in contact with damp). Such emulsion paints are also prone to chalking after a period of a few years, indeed many are designed to do just that, so that they can be easily overpainted (for house decoration). By contrast, high quality acrylic primings are available which have strong binding strength and may even be formulated for use as priming for wall paintings.

Care must also be taken that the selected acrylic paint range meets the requirements of the wall. For example, if the mural is outside, check that the colours used are permanent to light, weathering and atmospheric conditions. Some pigments, such as zinc white, tend to break down in acrylic binders when exposed to prolonged weathering. Similarly, some synthetic organic pigments are much reduced in permanence to light when strongly admixed with white.

Acrylic paintings may be less permanent when situated in a damp environment. For example, a mural alongside a swimming pool may degrade more quickly when painted in acrylic than when carefully and correctly prepared with fresco. Any moisture that finds its way into the support wall will become trapped behind the acrylic paint film. For the same reason, acrylic paints are not advised for use in bathroom wall decorations.

Unlike fresco, acrylic-painted murals can be varnished without any problems. The acrylic resin varnishes may be water-diluting, or solvent-based. In both cases, they form continuous paint films which will render the dried paint film water-washable. In effect they can be used to seal the painting from atmospheric pollutants, as well as change the gloss or mattness of the dried paint film.

Brushes

One of the key tools for applying paint is the brush. Brushes come in all manner of sizes, hair types and qualities. For artists' use, brushes are required to have a finesse which may not be the case with household brushes. However, some brushes that are manufactured for the decorating trade may also be of interest to artists and should not be overlooked. Brush making follows different traditions according to the country/culture of manufacture. For example, Italian and French decorating brushes tend to be of a much higher quality than similar products made in the United Kingdom. However, many artists are unaware of this and overlook the possibility of using such brushes. As with all materials, a degree of experimentation is encouraged, and this can extend to trying out a range of brushes to ascertain the correct choice of brush for the type of work undertaken.

The manufacturing of artists' quality brushes mirrors the expertise and high standards exemplified in high quality artists' paints. As a consequence, many brushes have a high cost price to the artist. However, with careful use and maintenance, expensive brushes can be made to last for many years.

Brushes for Oil Painting

Oil painting requires brushes that have a degree of resilience. For example, hog bristle brushes will withstand abrasion on contact with the painting support and immersion in solvents such as turpentine. By contrast, softer hair brushes, such as sable or ox hair have less resistance to such applications. Nevertheless, many artists need to use soft hair brushes in oil painting, in order to create the exact mark required. The key to using brushes in connection with oil paint, is to clean and maintain them fastidiously. In this way, softer hair brushes will last longer.

Hog Bristle Brushes

The best quality bristle brushes for oil painting are made with hair from chinese hog. The hair is carefully selected and cleaned of grease and other residues or impurities, before being shaped and fitted into the metal ring (ferrule) that clamps the brush hair on to the brush handle. The best quality hog bristle brushes will be made from specially selected hair, and the brushmaker will shape the brush tip, often by hand, to the required formation. In many cases, the work of the brushmaker is a finely honed craft, carried out by small teams of makers, or even individuals. Some European manufacturers have in recent years given their brush making over to mechanised production, which may have contributed to a lowering of quality generally in the market.

The tips of good quality hog bristle brushes are specially designed to gain a better shape during use by the artist. The hair has a minute "tree" (also known as "flags") at its tip. This "tree" of small hairs tends to grip to adjoining hairs, forming the brush tip to a coherent point. With use, these trees (or flags) associate with each other more and more, giving the brush a characteristic tip shape, which should remain constant, provided the brush is carefully washed after each use.

On first using a hog brush, often a few stray hairs may dislodge: with good quality brushes, this becomes less over time and need not be a worry. Cheaper brushes tend to continue to shed hairs and will also lose their shape. The worst kind of brush has a tip that is simply cut, rather than being carefully formed to the required shape. Such brushes will inevitably splay upon use, making controlled work impossible. Hog brushes should also be firmly packed into the metal ferrule which holds the hairs in place. If the hairs are loose in the ferrule, they are more likely to loosen further when the brush is stressed through use.

Oil painting brushes tend to have long handles, which enable the artist to stand away from the painting while working, in order to be able to judge colour mixing and make observations of the subject, etc. In most cases, the brush handle is lacquered. It would be preferable if brush handles (for all media) were made with raw wood, as quite often the lacquer from the handles splinters with time and can fall into paint pots and on to palettes, etc. However, the author has seen few examples of this type, save perhaps for brushes made for the ceramics industry.

Hog oil painting brushes are manufactured in a range of shapes: flat, long flat, round, filbert (cat's tongue) and fan. By tradition, round brushes are employed for detailed areas (with small size

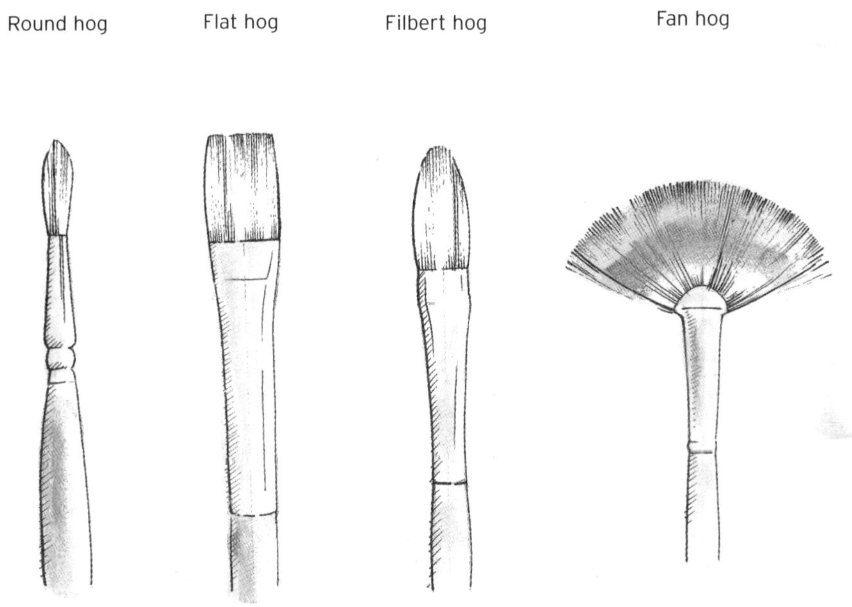

Oil Painting Bristle Brushes

brushes), whereas the flat types can be used for short or long dabbing strokes. Filbert brushes, which have a characteristic tongue shape tip, are excellent for blending colour, the larger sizes offer a kind of hybrid between round and flat brushes. Fan brushes can be used for blending colours wet into wet and for gently lifting out unwanted paint applications.

Because hog brushes are relatively stiff, the marks they make tend to be rather evident in the paint film. This "gestural" type of mark may be required and has a certain aesthetic appeal. However, if one wants to lose brushmarks, softer hair brushes may be more suitable.

As with all brushes, the shape and size of the brush belly governs the amount of paint which it can hold. Many artists opt for larger round or filbert brushes to load up paint, for expressive painting. Similarly, many artists choose large round Italian house-painting brushes when needing to apply large amounts of paint. However, the larger the brush tip, the more cleaning needs to be done after painting. Typically, residual oil colour gets trapped at the base of the hair, where it fits into the ferrule. This part of the brush therefore requires particular attention when cleaning. If the paint is left in this area, it will tend to clog up the brush (make it stiffer). It may also cause the hair to splay, or stick together. As brushes are expensive, often costing more than tubes of oil colour, it makes sense to clean them regularly and carefully.

Soft Hair Brushes

For detailed or subtle applications of oil colour, softer hair brushes may be required. Included in this category, one may find brushes made with sable, ox, polecat or mongoose hair.

Ox hair brushes, made from hair obtained from the ears of cattle, give a degree of resilience yet possess great softness when used for oil painting. The hair behaves rather like sable, although it is not as soft. It has enough spring to re-form into the correct shape after proper cleaning and will help when making detailed paint marks. Ox hair brushes are supplied in a similar range of tips as with hog hair brushes, although long haired "rigger" brushes (used by sign writers) may be especially useful for applying long lines of colour and thin detailed marks. Larger size ox hair round brushes are considerably cheaper than the equivalent sable brushes and may be very useful when applying large amounts of oil colour, which then needs to be manipulated (flattened) on the painting surface. Ox hair brushes perhaps work best in connection with thinned oil colour, where the paint has been modified with an addition of oil paint medium or solvent, to create thin paint films. In glazing techniques, ox hair brushes allow paint to be applied, brushed out and then further manipulated, without revealing strident brush marks, especially when the paint medium used (e.g. dammar-stand oil) is inherently self-levelling.

Polecat and mongoose hair brushes tend to be slightly less subtle when compared to ox, although this can vary from one manufacturer to another.

Sable hair is often considered to be too soft for use with oil paint, especially when applied to linen canvas with a pronounced weave texture. Such brushes will tend to wear down quickly. However, if paint is applied in loose glazes, where the paint has been modified with the addition of a paint medium, the paint mixture will slip gently off the brush tip on to the painting surface. Problems tend to arise when soft hair brushes are used to scrub into the painting surface. They tend to shed hairs when used in this way and the ferrules will become clogged up with paint. Sable brushes are available with long handles, for use in oil painting technique, in round, flat and filbert shapes. Some manufacturers also offer fan shaped sables, which can be extremely useful for softening and blending applied paint.

For large-scale painting, soft hair brushes made with badger hair may be useful. These are normally supplied with a flat shape, up to widths of four inches. Such brushes are referred to as "badger softeners", as they are designed for use in house painting, where scumble glazes are required to be modified after application. In Fine Art painting, they can be used for a similar purpose: to push down applied paint layers, to brush such applications out, and for blending and smudging of paint.

In practice, most artists experiment with a variety of brushes before finding an adequate group of brushes to form a kind of reliable armoury.

Cleaning Brushes After Use with Oil Paint

During painting, regularly dip the brush tip into vegetable oil, or Vaseline oil. This will free unwanted paint from the brush hairs. Any residue can be carefully wiped from the brush with soft rag or paper.

Take care not to immerse brushes into solvent unless absolutely necessary, as such contact tends to make natural brush hairs embrittle over time. Vegetable oil or Vaseline (mineral) oil will suffice for cleaning. For strong staining colours such as phthalocyanine blue, repeated cleansing may be called for. In an ideal world, artists would have a complete range of brushes to match the colours on their palette.

At the end of the painting session, brushes can be completely washed and thereby maintained, by immersing into a warm solution of olive oil soap (also known as Marseilles soap). This vegetable soap restores natural oils to bristle brushes (and to soft hair brushes) and will also free residual paint from around the ferrule. During cleaning, the brush tip is worked against the palm of the hand, in a soapy lather. The author has found it useful to wear disposable latex gloves when doing this, both to protect hands and also to facilitate the washing process. After cleaning with this soap, brushes need to be rinsed with warm (not hot) water, then left to dry out completely before re-use. If the brush has lost its shape, the soap can be used to re-shape the tip. Leave to dry after re-forming, then wash through with warm water after 2-3 days.

The soap is available in grated flakes, which form a solution when mixed with water from a boiled kettle, to make a soupy gel. Alternatively, olive oil soap is available in block form, which releases a soapy lather when in contact with warm water. While olive oil soap works best in connection with oil paint, it can also be used to wash brushes after painting with acrylic, for watercolour brushes after using strong staining colours, or to clean palettes, hands, wrists, etc.

Brushes for Acrylic Painting

The same hog brushes used for oil painting can easily be transferred into acrylic painting, although they tend to reveal brush marks to a greater degree than with oil colour.

The hairs of hog brushes tend to splay more with thick acrylic paint, when paint residue gets trapped in the base of the hairs where they meet the metal ferrule. As a consequence, it is essential to clean brushes thoroughly after each colour application. With hog hair, staining colours such as the synthetic organic pigments tend to discolour the brush hairs. This can mean that cleaning is difficult and one may have to be content to have permanently tinted brush hairs.

Perhaps the best policy with brushes when using acrylic paint, is always to add a little water to the paint mixture: this keeps the paint slightly fluid, so that it comes away from brush hairs more easily. This applies particularly to soft hair brushes such as sable and ox hair. Careful cleaning, using olive oil soap will also help to thoroughly clean and shape brushes after use.

Special brushes made with a synthetic filament are available and may be most appropriate for use with acrylic paints. These synthetic (a form of nylon) brushes tend to have a softness akin to sable brushes but are slightly more snappy or springy. Brush manufacturing has developed steadily in the area of artists' brushes, so much so that today synthetic hair brushes can be designed for specific applications. For example, round synthetic brushes can be made that mimic the performance of natural sable hair but which are much easier to clean, and in the case of acrylic paints, provide brushes that are much more resilient. Some synthetic brushes tend to splay when in contact with very hot water: as with all brushes, use olive oil soap in a gently warm soapy solution to gain optimum cleaning results.

Some synthetic brushes are specifically made for use with acrylic paint: they tend to have similar handling qualities to hog oil painting brushes in that the brush tips are formed into shapes that are retained and even improved with use. Synthetic brushes are usually a white colour when first manufactured, but then tinted to take on the appearance of natural hair. Sometimes, synthetic hair is admixed with sable or other natural hairs, to make a kind of hybrid brush. These may offer a good alternative to sable brushes, because they will possess a similar softness and suppleness.

The dilution or admixture of acrylic paint with paint medium can govern the way in which paint flows off the brush. It is important to make tests with brushes on to a variety of support surfaces, prior to painting, in order to ascertain the best dilution for a paint mixture. For example, a fluid acrylic paint usually flows well without the need for extra dilution with water. The brush chosen to apply such mixtures should conform to the paint effect desired. For example, a large flat synthetic hair varnish brush may work very well when applying large areas of flat colour where the paint has been slightly diluted with a mix of paint medium and water. The shape and density of the brush hairs will govern how the paint runs off the brush. As with hog hair varnish brushes, if the hair is shaped (rather than just cut) at the tip, it will assist in laying down flat glazes.

Because acrylic paint is water-diluted, care needs to be taken that the ferrules of brushes are not left in water pots for too long, as this may cause rusting of these metal parts. Perhaps the most useful brushes with acrylic paint are string bound fresco brushes, which are commonly available in Italy. The string binding allows the brush to be left in water to soak for long periods without deterioration. These brushes tend to be made with chinese hog hair and are offered in various sizes in round format, or in long, tapered ("Riga") round format.

Brushes for Watercolour Painting

Watercolour painting relies strongly on the application of diluted paint on to semi-absorbent paper surfaces. The way in which the brush contacts with the paper can be crucial. As a consequence, the choice of brush becomes integral to the type of mark required. The best brushes for applying even flat washes of dilute paint are those made with very soft natural hair, such as sable.

Sable is often cited as being the best type of natural hair because it is both strong yet supple. It has a natural spring or "snap" which enables the brush tip to re-form readily after use. The best quality sable brushes are made from the hair of sable animals living in the coldest parts of Russia. In fact, the colder the conditions, the better the hair quality. Sable can be divided into two distinct categories in terms of quality:

1. Kolinsky sable.
2. Red sable.

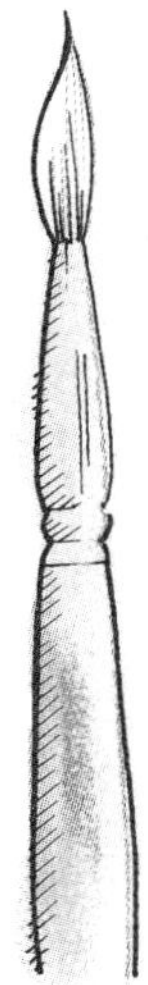

Round Kolinsky
Sable Brush

Kolinsky sable brushes are made with hair taken from the tails of the kolinsky, a type of mink, similar to the marten or weasel. The name is derived from the region of Kola in north-east Russia where they originate. The hair is a warm red-yellow colour. It is cut from the tail, then sorted into different lengths, before cleansing, de-greasing and removal of impurities. It is then sold through special agencies to brushmakers. The price of kolinsky sable is relatively high, partly due to the scarcity of the material but also because the length of the hair (up to 2 inches or more) allows for the production of rather large brush tips. The best hair is taken by the brush manufacturer, skilfully inserted into the ferrule and crimped. The main skill here is to shape the hair without resorting to cutting it. Each hair is teased until it forms a perfect shape for the desired brush tip. The best type of watercolour brush will fit tightly into the ferrule and possess a full "belly" (the main body of the brush), tapering down to a perfect pointed tip, in the case of round brushes.

The full belly of hair allows paint to be held in this "reservoir" and then slowly released as it contacts with the paper surface. The brush tip, when wet, retains a certain degree of spring and shape during application. When the painting is finished, clean the brush in cold water, rinsing thoroughly. Afterwards, the brush can be re-pointed by quickly flicking it while it is loaded with water. This should bring the brush hair back to a perfect shape.

Cheaper sable brushes tend to remain slack or floppy under this test. Many art supply stores fear the moment when watercolour painters enter their premises to test their sable brushes, requesting a pot of water and the finest no.14 sable. However, because these expensive brushes are hand-formed, one may differ in quality to another, even within the same brand. As a consequence, it is essential for the discerning artist to test their brushes prior to purchase. Kolinsky sables are sold in sizes ranging from 5/0 (very fine) up to size no.12 or no.14 (United Kingdom sizes).

Cheaper sable brushes are often sold as "red sable" or "selected red sable". These may be from the same animal or from other animals of the same group, but the hairs tend to have less spring and snap. However, the larger sizes of these brushes may be an adequate alternative for the beginner. Some red sable brushes also include mixed hairs, for example, an inclusion of ox hair, which again will lessen the working properties of the brush.

While round sables are essential for most watercolour artists, sable brushes are also available in flat "one-stroke" format, or flat "varnish" format. Both types are useful for laying down large areas of flat colour wash.

In order to stop moths from attacking sable hair, the best quality brushes are sold with a protective sachet of camphor. Sable brushes should be left to dry hanging down if possible (so that all water drains down, rather than gathering in the ferrule), and allowed to dry out thoroughly before being stored flat, alongside a sachet of camphor for safe-keeping. If the brush is properly cleansed after each use and carefully stored afterwards, it should last for many decades.

"Sable spotters" or "retouching brushes" can be used for fine detailed painting. These are designed specifically for in-painting and retouching in the restoration of paintings. However, the watercolourist, especially botanical artists and miniaturists will find these brushes very useful. In this format, the brush has a reasonable belly but a short point. These brushes are generally sold in sizes from 00000 (smallest) up to size 6 or 8.

Flat sable brushes are much sought after by watercolour painters. These are known as "one strokes" and are fine for laying in horizontal and vertical strokes: to bring a horizontal wet wash down the paper for example.

Long hair sable brushes are sometimes useful for laying in long strokes of colour. These "rigger" type brushes frequently have long handles (which may need to be cut down). French and English quill sables have this longer hair and are fitted into shorter handles. Italian brush makers produce a compromise brush, usually in cheaper ox hair, with a very fat belly, from which a grouping of longer hair emerges. The colour is stored up in the belly and drawn out through the longer hairs to make long, thin lines of paint. Italian brushmakers also produce regular round tipped brushes (similar to round sables) in ox hair. These offer an alternative to expensive sables.

Flat ox hair brushes are also popular for laying in washes, being available in widths up to 100mm across. For laying in even larger washes, goat hair "hake" brushes can be used. These originate from Japan and China and have even softer hair, which makes them good for working wet into wet, moving colour about across the paper surface gently. These brushes are generally string bound rather than ferrule bound and their pure white hair is quickly stained by certain strong synthetic organic colours.

Squirrel hair mops, frequently fixed into place with an old-fashioned "quill" ferrule, make a good alternative to large size sable wash brushes. They are not quite as firm and able to retain their shape but they hold a good amount of liquid, so can be very useful for carrying large washes.

Synthetic hair based on a variation of nylon is often used in place of the expensive sable brushes, or in mixtures with sable. The synthetic hair is generally coloured to imitate sable and has good control and pointing. The main advantage of these brushes seems to be that they are easy to clean and very durable compared with natural hair brushes. They are also inexpensive when compared to some sables.

Brushes for Gouache Painting

Because gouache contains some extra filler/inert white, it tends to wear down soft hair brushes more than watercolour. As a consequence, sable brushes should be employed with care. A better option may be to use synthetic (nylon) brushes, which are more resilient, or ox hair brushes, which are still soft but stand up to such vigorous use. As with watercolour, a good selection of round brushes is essential, but it is also very useful to have some flat (one-stroke) brushes, for laying in flat areas of colour. One can use flat varnish brushes, made with soft hog hair, or ox or squirrel hair for this purpose.

When the painting session is over, wash brushes carefully. Because gouache contains some extra filler/inert white, this tends to get lodged in the base of the brush hair, where it meets the ferrule. If this is not carefully washed out while the hairs are still damp, it can cause them to splay.

Brushes for Priming

When applying coats of sizing or priming to canvas and boards, it is vital to use brushes that will help to transmit the fluid on to the surface of the support. Flat brushes that are carefully shaped at the tip, give an even distribution of paint, whereas brushes with cut ends will tend to deposit paint too quickly. The ideal brush for priming is one that slowly releases the liquid paint mix on to the support surface, assisting the formation of an even coating. Correct dilution of the sizing/priming is also important. Manufactured brands tend to show a variety of consistencies: if the chosen primer is thick, then dilution with water (in the case of acrylic primer) is necessary to achieve a consistency similar to single cream. It is better to apply multiple coats of thin primer/size, than to deposit heavy, dragging coats, which tend to show up imperfections within the weave of painting fabrics. When priming layers are being applied, a first coat of size (with acrylic primer, one must only ever use an acrylic sizing) is advisable, in order to equalise the surface of the painting fabric. This is less important when applying size to boards, although dilution usually results in a more even application of the sizing material.

The dilution of sizing and primer material needs to be matched to the relative softness of the brush used. For acrylic-based sizing and priming materials, hog varnish brushes, perhaps 2-3 inches wide are recommended. The best quality brushes have shaped tips rather than cut tips and allow paint films to be laid down carefully and evenly. While these brushes are designed for the application of varnish coats, they also work very well for applying coats of sizing and primer. Softer brushes, such as flat brushes made with ox hair may also be useful when trying to achieve a very smooth surface, but the suppleness of these brushes will require the sizing/primer used to be strongly diluted, to stop the paint from dragging. Similarly, synthetic hair brushes tend to flop when used with primer, quickly losing their shape. The thickness of the brush used for priming is also of consequence. For example, brushes with a thickness of more than 5mm may quickly collect primer residue, causing the hairs to splay or the brush hair body to bulge in the ferrule.

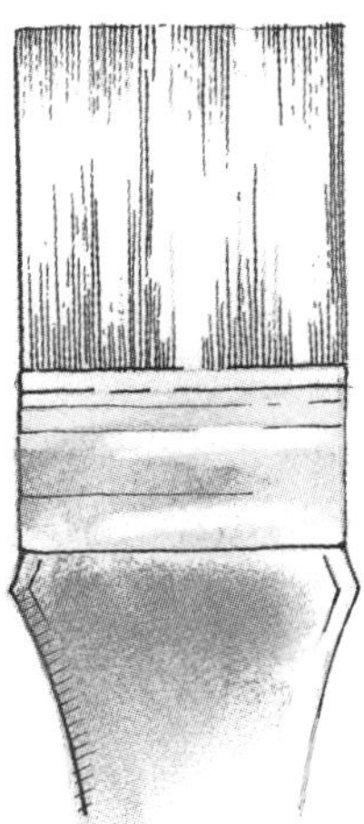

Flat Hog Varnish/Priming Brush

Because primers tend to contain chalk in their make-up, it is wise to wash brushes immediately after use, rather than leaving them to stand in water. If brushes are not completely cleaned, some residue of priming can collect at the base of the hair, where it fits into the metal ferrule. These ferrules will also begin to rust when left standing in water, although some brands are made with non-rusting ferrules. In any case, it is not advised to leave brushes standing in water, as prolonged immersion may affect the glue used to fix the base of the hairs on to the paint brush handle.

Hog hair varnish brushes are available in sizes from 1/2" inch to 4", although larger widths may also be available, up to 6 or 8 inches wide. These wider brushes tend to give less control than the smaller widths when applying primers, simply because the 1/2 hand is more prone to wavering when applying the material to the support. It is important to retain control over the brush and its contents when applying sizing/priming, as an even application is crucial to a smooth finish. The brush is held at about a 45° angle against the support and then slowly worked in one direction over the support surface. By diluting the material so that it runs slowly but freely off the brush tip, an even coating is easier to obtain. However, careful brushing after application will help to squash down the sizing/primer, so achieving an even finish. While the sizing/primer is still wet on the surface, further brushing can be effected: working the brush in one direction, then leaving to dry. The next coat can then be applied with the opposite right-angled stroke, and subsequent coats varied in a similar fashion.

Brushes for Varnishing

When applying coats of varnish to dried oil paintings and dried acrylic paintings, a simple hog varnish brush, as previously described, should suffice. Varnishes for oil paintings tend to be sold ready-diluted for application, and will have a consistency similar to milk. Before applying, some tests should be undertaken on to a similar support, to see how easily the varnish brushes out. If the varnish drags, it can be diluted a little with the same solvent used in its manufacture (e.g. ketone resin tends to be solved into white spirit, so use white spirit). Water-based acrylic varnishes tend to be slightly thicker, typically a little thicker than single cream. With these varnishes, a degree of dilution may also be required in order for the varnish mixture to slip off the brush.

As with priming, the brush needs to be cleaned after each use, so that it remains supple and retains its shape. Hog varnish brushes should be cleaned with olive oil soap, followed by a thorough rinsing with warm water. If possible, the brush should then be hung, with the hairs facing down, so that any paint residue falls down and out of the hairs. Often these brushes have a small hole in the handle to allow them to be hung in this way.

Brushes for Soft Pastels

Although pastel is applied directly to the painting support, special soft brushes can be used to distribute and manipulate colour once it has been applied to the painting surface. Keep the brush hairs dry at all times, using soft strokes to mix, fuse and blend colours with gentle pressure only. Suitable brushes may be those made with squirrel hair (e.g. squirrel mops), pony hair, mongoose hair, ox hair or sable hair. If this technique proves successful, it may be prudent to keep a number of brushes to hand, so that basic colours can be dealt with separately.

Brushes for Fresco Painting

Fresco painting requires the use of special brushes, which allow for a degree of control while at the same time being resilient. By tradition, string bound brushes are used, so that the brush can be kept wet while not in use, by depositing in a bucket of water. In this way, the brush hair does not dry out and become brittle and any residual lime in the hairs slowly soaks off while immersed in water. Some metal ferrules may have resistance to rusting when placed in water, if handled with care, so ferrule bound brushes may also be used for fresco painting.

Traditional fresco brushes are made with white chinese hog hair, in two distinct formats:

1. Muccino - round shape.
2. Riga - long round shape, with tapered tip.

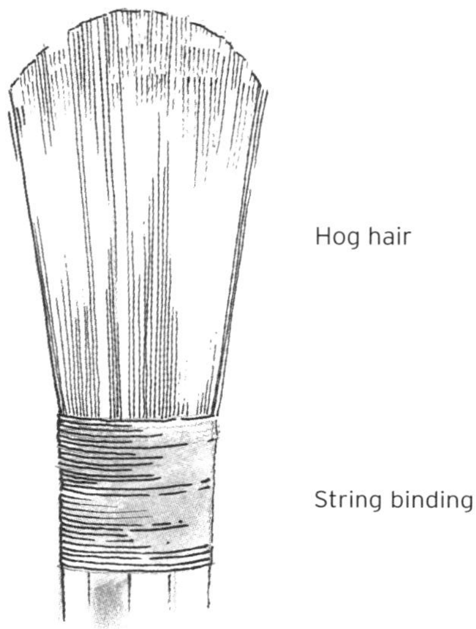

String Bound "Muccino" Fresco Brush

Storage and Preservation of Finished Artworks

When handling works of art, for example, when bringing them in and out of storage, it is a good idea to wear some soft cotton (lint-free) gloves. These will stop greasy finger mark residues and also encourage the wearer to take extra special care. This could be vital when moving larger works, or delicate paintings (e.g. pastel on to paper).

Oil Paintings

The ideal drying place for a finished oil painting, is to be hung high up on a wall (above dust levels), facing out, so that the paint surface receives daylight. However, this daylight should not be direct (i.e. not in a south facing window). Paintings that are left to dry in such a position tend not to yellow excessively, especially when they have been left to dry for six months or more in such a position. By contrast, newly finished paintings that are immediately stacked away from light, or in a closed dark room or cupboard, will show yellowing (darkening) much sooner. The quality of paint used may also have some bearing on the yellowing/darkening of a paint film. Cheaper paints, which often include too much oil in their composition, will show yellowing, whereas higher quality products tend not to. Hand-made oil paints will always have a tendency to yellow, simply because the incorporation of oil to pigment is not done in a specific measured way. As a consequence, paintings made with hand-milled colour should ideally be exposed to light upon completion. Paintings that have yellowed can be restored to some degree by facing into direct sunlight for a period: some aspect of the darkening of the paint film may be rectified, as the oil film is gently bleached by sunlight. However, such treatment can never return for example, a passage of white paint back to being a pure white area.

The use of paint mediums may also contribute towards the darkening of oil paint films, especially when large additions of such mediums have been made. For example, alkyd resins can cause a darkening of the paint film when used in concentrations above 10%, especially when added to whites or pale colours. Similarly, the natural resins dammar and mastic, both of which are commonly used in painting mediums, are known to darken over time to some extent.

To a degree, this darkening of the paint film can be accepted, because it reveals a natural patination/ageing of oil paintings. In the auction house, this aspect is highly prized: old oil paintings can reach higher prices at auction when they show this characteristic "aged" appearance. For the artist, such inevitable chemical changes within the oil paint film may compromise the appearance of the image. In order to minimise the natural darkening of oil paints, it is therefore vital to adhere to good practice while painting, especially in the judicious addition of oil paint mediums. It is recommended that before using an oil paint medium, some aspects of the properties of the component parts are understood. For example, beeswax may impart a beautiful sheen to oil colours, but it also leaves the paint film matt (attractive to dust) and vulnerable to heat (the wax can re-melt if exposed to strong heat). These properties must be understood before the decision to use this is taken.

Many artists assume that the varnishing of dried oil paintings is essential. However, if a small addition of a paint medium has been used during painting, it may be completely unnecessary to apply a final picture varnish. Doing so would only alter the appearance of the painting and may make it too gloss, or too matt, depending on the type of varnish applied. Varnishes can also cause more harm than good. The solvent content of a varnish can percolate into recently dried (or still drying) oil paint layers. In the worst case scenario, the solvent reconstitutes the paint layer, causing bleeding from one layer to another. Applying a layer of varnish over paint that appears to be dry (but is in fact only touch dry on the surface) may cause eventual cracking, when the paint film completely dries out. Applications of varnish may also cause a colour change in the appearance of the painting. The natural resin varnishes (dammar, mastic) turn yellow-brown after many years, giving a dark film over the painting surface, which may obscure details in the painting. Also, some natural resin varnishes, notably dammar, stay slightly tacky on the surface, attracting dirt and dust.

When a dried oil painting is stored or is to be shipped, it may be appropriate to protect the painting. For shipping, ideally oil paintings are crated in wooden boxes, specially built for this purpose. Avoid wrapping an oil painting if at all possible. If a dried painting has to be wrapped (for example when being stored), thick polythene sheeting may be used with some caution. If the paint film is even mildy soft, it may adhere to the sheeting, causing damage. It is important to avoid using bubble-wrap-plastic, as the air-filled pockets tend to adhere to oil paint surfaces, even when seemingly completely dry. This is especially so in the case of oil paintings with additions of paint medium, for example dammar-stand oil medium. The dammar remains slightly soft and a little tacky and will want to adhere to other surfaces. In the case of bubble-wrap, the pattern of the bubbles is often transferred on to the paint film. If paintings need to be rolled to be shipped, cracking may result. The painting must be rolled with the paint surface facing out, to minimise contraction. As wide a cardboard roll as possible should be used (e.g. a carpet roll), with the painting being faced with acid-free tissue paper, or glassine paper as it is rolled. If a painting is rolled soon after completion and drying, it tends to resist cracks: by contrast, older oil paintings become increasingly harder with time, and when rolled can crack easily, especially where impasto areas of paint are present. Paintings that have been varnished may also crack more easily, as the varnish film may have less flexibility than the paint layers.

Oil paintings need to be stored in ambient temperature conditions. Never store paintings in damp, or excessively cold rooms. This is especially important when the painting has sizing made with an animal glue. Such glues remain moisture sensitive and will soften in damp or humid conditions, often resulting in mould growth, and/or changes in tension on the painting fabric. Damp and humidity may also cause rusting of staples or tacks used to fix the painting fabric to the support. Paintings made on to wooden panels must also be kept away from sources of moisture to prevent warping.

Acrylic Paintings

High quality acrylic paints remain flexible upon drying and may be safely rolled with care. However, acrylic paintings made with heavy impasto may have reduced flexibility. Hand-made acrylic paints may also have reduced flexibility, especially when heavy applications have been made, or where there are inclusions of gritty materials. Paintings made with heavy gels or texture pastes can also lose adhesion to the support if rolled.

Acrylic paintings, once dried, are virtually impervious to water. As a consequence, dust and dirt can be gently cleaned from the surface of the painting, by treating with a very mild detergent and a lint-free cotton cloth. Often, it is enough simply to dust the surface of the painting. Never clean acrylic paintings with alcohol, or any product that contains alcohol, as this will re-swell the acrylic paint film, causing blisters or cracking.

Works on Paper

Watercolours and gouache paintings made on to paper should be stored in closed portfolios, away from sources of direct sunlight. Similarly, framed paintings should be hung on walls that receive a diffused or subdued light source. This is especially so in the case of watercolours made using pigments with reduced permanence (e.g. plant-based pigments such as madder). Avoid hanging works of art on paper in direct sunlight, especially in south-facing windows.

The paint film with watercolour and gouache paintings, is more liable to atmospheric pollutants than with oil or acrylic paints, where pigments are effectively locked into the binding system. As a consequence, watercolour or gouache paintings made with unstable pigments are more liable to change. For example, massicot (lead mono oxide) is a pale yellow, which quickly turns greenish or even black when exposed to air, especially when bound in gum arabic, or casein. In order to stop this rapid colour change, such pigments can only be used in binders that effectively coat and therefore protect the pigment particles. Klucel binders can be used with some success in such instances: this thick syrupy paste encapsulates the pigment particles and affords better protection to air, yet gives a similar matt-neutral sheen when dry, as standard watercolour or gouache binders.

The particular defects of certain pigments are alluded to in the pigment section: an understanding of how pigments perform in different binders can be useful, especially when using water-based paints.

Paper as a support is also not without its difficulties. It is prone to deterioration on contact with acid compounds in the air. Many papers are sold as being acid-free: that is, at the point of manufacture, they are pH balanced. However, over time their acidity can alter, depending on the environment in which they are stored. Some papers are buffered with chalk (calcium carbonate), which may help to resist the action of acid compounds. Paper is also prone to deterioration on exposure to damp, whereby mould can develop. It therefore follows, that any works of art on paper should be stored in a closed portfolio, away from damp or humidity. Contact with metals should also be avoided, where for example, rust spots can quickly develop when in contact with damp or humidity.

Pastel Paintings

Where a pastel painting has been fixed, a reduced amount of pigment dust will become dislodged if the paint surface is disturbed. However, in practice, all pastel paintings, whether fixed or not, can easily be disturbed and damaged unless carefully handled. For storage, pastel paintings can be interleaved with acid-free tissue paper, so that the delicate surface has a nominal protection. Pastel paintings are best stored flat, for example in a plan chest, away from dust and draft sources. The application of fixative may change colour values and as a consequence, fixing is normally kept to an absolute minimum.

Bibliography

AMOROSI, Luca. *Colori e Materiali per l'Arte e il Restauro.* Bologna, Zanichelli Editore SpA, 1991.

ARPAGUS, Elizabeth. *Aegypten.* Essen, Arpagus-Hotzel, 1996.

ASSOCIATION OF BRITISH PICTURE RESTORERS (ABPR). *Varnishing: Theory & Practice* (Conference paper). London/Bristol, ABPR, 1993.

ASTM. 1993 *Annual Book of ASTM Standards – Paints, Related Coatings, and Aromatics.* Philadelphia, ASTM, 1993.

BALL, Philip. *Bright Earth – The Invention of Colour.* London, Penguin Books, 2002.

BARDWELL, Thomas. *Practical Treatise on Painting in Oil Colours.* London, B&J White, 1795.

BETTI, Cesare and PAGANI, Giancarlo. *Minerali del Senese.* Siena, Protago Editori Toscani, 2000.

BOMFORD, David and ROY, Ashok. *Colour.* London, National Gallery Publications, 1998.

BOMFORD, David, DUNKERTON, Jill, GORDON, Dillian and ROY, Ashok. *Italian Painting Before 1400.* London, National Gallery Publications, 1989.

BOMFORD, David, KIRBY, Jo, LEIGHTON, John and ROY, Ashok. *Impressionism – Art in the Making.* London, National Gallery Publications, 1990.

CENNINI, Cennino d'Andrea. *The Craftman's Handbook.* "Il Libro dell'Arte". New York, Dover, 1933.

CHURCH, A.H. *The Chemistry of Paints and Painting.* London, Seeley & Co, 1892.

CROOK, Jo and LEARNER, Tom. *The Impact of Modern Paints.* London, Tate Publishing, 2000.

DALESSO, Marc. *Studio Handbook, Charles H. Cecil Studios.* Florence, Charles H. Cecil Studios, 1998.

DELAMARE, Francoise and GUINEAU, Bernard. *Colour – Making & Using Dyes & Pigments.* London, Thames & Hudson, 2000.

DIETHELM, Alois K. *Painting with Lascaux Colours.* Brüttisellen, Alois K. Diethelm AG Farbenfabrik, 1997.

DOERNER, Max. *The Materials of the Artist* (English text). San Diego/New York/London, First Harvest/HBJ, 1984.

FAIRBURN, Linda. *Paint & Painting.* London, Tate Publishing/Winsor & Newton, 1982.

FELLER, Robert L. *Artists' Pigments Vol.1.* Cambridge, Cambridge University Press, 1986.

FELS, Donald. *The FELS System of Painting in Oil.* Hillsville, Alchemist Paints & Varnishes, 1999.

FIELD, George. *Chromatography.* London, Tilt & Bogue, 1841.

FINLAY, Victoria. *Colour – Travels Through the Paintbox.* London, Hodder & Stoughton, 2002.

FLORENCE MINE HERITAGE CENTRE. *Florence Mine.* Cumbria, Florence Mine Heritage Centre, 2000.

FRUMESS, Richard. *R&F Handmade Paints* (catalogue). New York, R&F Handmade Paints, 2000.

GAGE, John. *Colour & Culture.* London, Thames & Hudson, 1993.

GAGE, John. *Colour & Meaning.* London, Thames & Hudson, 1999.

GAMBLIN, Robert and BERGMAN-GAMBLIN, Martha. *Gamblin Color Book.* Portland, Gamblin Artists Colors Co., 1996.

GETENS, Rutherford J. and STOUT, George L. *Painting Materials – A Short Encyclopedia.* New York, Dover, 1966.

GHEROLDI, Vincenzo. *Varnishes & Very Curious Secrets.* Cremona, Cremona Books, 1999.

GOLDEN ARTISTS COLORS. *Product Information Binder.* New York, Golden Artists Colors, 2000.

GOTTSEGEN, Mark D. *The Painter's Handbook.* New York, Watson-Guptill, 1993.

HACKNEY, JONES and TOWNSEND. *Paint & Purpose: A Study of Technique in British Art.* London, Tate Publishing, 1999.

HACKNEY, Stephen and ERNST, Torben. "The Applicability of Alkaline Reserves to Painting Canvases". *Measured Opinions.* London, United Kingdom Institute of Conservators (UKIC), 1988.

HAMMERL, Josef and HAMMERL, Reiner. *Violin Varnishes.* Bayreuth, J&R Hammerl, 1990.

HARLEY, Rosamund. *Artists' Pigments, c.1600-1835.* London, Butterworth Scientific, 1982.

HILLS, Paul. *Venetian Colour.* New Haven/London, Yale University Press, 1999.

HINDLE, Yvonne, ROSSOL, Monona, KINSEHER, Kathrin and SEYMOUR, Pip. *Paint Theory, Paint Practice.* London, Lee Press/University of Central England, 2001.

HOOD, Peter. *Lead Paint of the Older Tradition.* Cumbria, Hood & Stilling, 1997.

INDUNI, Bruce and INDUNI, Liz. *Using Lime.* Swanage, Induni, 1994.

KREJCAREK, Antonio. *Preparations for Artistic Painting.* Decin, Umton Barvy, 1996.

KREMER, Dr Georg. *Kremer Pigmente* (Catalogue). Aichstetten, Kremer Pigmente, 2003.

LE BLON, J.C. *Coloritto – The Harmony of Colours.* London, J.C. Le Blon, 1723.

LENINGRAD PAINT PLANT. *Painter's Paint.* Leningrad, Leningrad Paint Plant, Division of Research Institue for Technical and Economical Studies, 1991.

MANN, W. *Gouache Painting with Designer's Gouache.* London, Winsor & Newton, 1964.

MASSEY, Robert. *Formulas for Painters.* New York, Watson-Guptill, 1967.

MAYER, Ralph. *Dictionary of Art Terms & Techniques.* New York, Harper Collins, 1991.

MAYER, Ralph. *The Artist's Handbook of Materials and Techniques.* Boston/London, Faber & Faber, 1991.

MAYER, Ralph. *The Painter's Craft.* London, Penguin, 1979.

McKIM-SMITH, Gridley. *Examining Velazquez.* New Haven/London, Yale University Press, 1988.

MOLLET, J.W. *Illustrated Dictionary of Words Used in Art and Architecture.* London, Sampson, Low, Marston, Searle and Rivington, 1883.

MONTAGNA, Giovanni. *I Pigmenti.* Florence, Nardini Editore, 1993.

PAVEY, Don and STAPLES, Peter. *The Artists' Colourmen's Story.* London, Winsor & Newton/Reckitt & Coleman, 1984.

PETUKHOVA, Tatyana. *Preventative Care of Graphic Art on Paper.* New York, Cornell University Press, 2001.

PIVA, Prof Gino. *Manuale Pratico di Tecnica Pittorica.* Milan, Ulrico Hoepli Editore SpA, 1980.

RONCHETTI, Giuseppe. *Pittura Murale*. Milan, Ulrico Hoepli Editore SpA, 1983.

ROSSOL, Monona. *The Artist's Complete Health & Safety Guide*. New York, Allworth Press, 1990.

SENNELIER, J. *Sennelier Catalogue, 1993*. Paris, Sennelier, 1993.

SEYMOUR, Pip and NIEDRING, Anja. *Making Soft Pastels* (English-German text). London, Lee Press, 1999.

SEYMOUR, Pip. *A Short Book About Oil Painting*. London, Lee Press, 1995.

SEYMOUR, Pip. *Alternatives to Gold Leaf*. London, Lee Press, 1998.

SEYMOUR, Pip. *Colours for Violin Varnish*. London, Lee Press, 2002.

SEYMOUR, Pip. *Pigment Register*. London, Lee Press, 2002.

SEYMOUR, Pip. *Watercolour Painting*. London, Lee Press, 1997.

SHULMAN, Ken. *Anatomy of a Restoration: The Brancacci Chapel, Florence*. New York, Walker Publishing Company, 1991.

SKELTON, Helen. "A Colour Chemist's History of Western Art". *Review of Progress in Coloration*. Society of Dyers and Colorists, 1999.

SOCIETY OF DYERS & COLOURISTS. *Colour Index International*. Bradford, Society of Dyers & Colourists, 1997.*

STALKER, John and PARKER, George. *A Treatise of Japanning and Varnishing, 1688*. London, Alec Tiranti, 1960.

THOMAS, Anabel. *The Painter's Practice in Renaissance Tuscany.* Cambridge, Cambridge University Press, 1995.

TOWNSEND, Joyce. *Turner's Painting Techniques.* London, Tate Gallery Publications, 1993.

TURNER, Silvie. *Which Paper?* London, Estamp, 1991.

WINSOR & NEWTON. *Notes on the Composition and Permanence of Artists' Colours.* London, Winsor & Newton, 1925, 1928, 1980, 2003.

*Available in CD-Rom format from:

Society of Dyers & Colourists

Perkin House, 82 Grattan Road

Bradford, West Yorkshire BD1 2JB

England

OR

American Association of Textile Chemists and Colorists

PO Box 12215

Research Triangle Park, North Carolina 27709

USA

Useful contacts:

ASTM

1916 Race Street, Philadelphia

PA 19103-1187

USA

Index

A

abietic acid 321
absorbent primer 423-426
acid-free paper 378-379
acrylic dispersion 399, 400, 403-404
acrylic emulsion 399
acrylic gesso primers 257, 295, 296
'acrylic inks' 412
acrylic materials, watercolour paint 356

acrylic paint 400-413
- *additives 408-410*
- *dry additive materials 409-410*
- *hand-preparation 404-410*
- *lime-fresco painting 457-458*
- *manufactured 411-413*
- *modified ranges 413*
- *preservative 409*
- *thickener 409*
- *wetting agents 20*

acrylic painting 399-426
- *absorbent primer 423-426*
- *acrylic dispersion 399, 400, 403-404*
- *acrylic paints 400-404*
- *brushes 464-466*
- *dust masks 411*
- *fluid mediums 413-414*
- *gel mediums 414-415*
- *gesso 423-426*
- *glass beads 410*
- *gloves 411*
- *hollow plastic bubbles 410*
- *mediums 413-419*
- *mistrust 419-422*
- *non-absorbent primer 423-426*
- *oil painting comparison 401*
- *palette 404-408*
- *polyvinyl materials 420*
- *preservation 478*
- *priming 422-426*
- *PVA-based materials 420-421*
- *quality 419-422*
- *safety 410-411*
- *scotchlite 410*
- *solid resin content 403*
- *storage 478*
- *synthetic resin 399*
- *systems 399-400*
- *texture pastes 415-416*
- *universal primer 423*
- *varnishes 416-419*
- *vinyl-based paints 420-421*

acrylic primers 246, 253-254, 257, 295
acrylic-based inks 202

agate burnisher 230, 231
alcohol-based varnishes 316
alizarin 93-94
alizarin brown 180
alizarin crimson 16, 24, 27, 79, 82, 86, 89, 94, 142, 180, 216, 260, 290, 298, 338, 358
alizarin crimson light 82
alizarin green 68, 180
alizarin madder lake 82
alizarin purple 142
alizarin violet 142
alkyd medium 265
alkyd primings 253-254, 257
alkyd resin 312-313
alkyd resin based mediums 298-299
alkyd resin based oil paint mediums 325
alla-prima 298, 299, 300
aloe 180
alum 250
alumina hydrate 42
aluminium hydrate 42-43, 184, 262, 280, 282-283, 290
aluminium hydroxide 42
aluminium potassium sulphate 250
aluminium powder 187
aluminium stearate 262, 292
aluminium-steel alloy tins 428-429
amber 320
American Society for Testing Materials (ASTM) 27-28
animal bone glues 208, 367-368
animal glue gesso 254
animal skin glue 207-210, 215, 367-368
animal skin glue binder as wetting agent 21
animal skin glue for panels recipe 209-210
anthranthrone red 88
anthrapyrimidine yellow 60
anthraquinone blue 136
anthraquinone red 82, 87, 88
anthraquinone scarlet 88
antimony gold 180-181
antimony orange 180-181
antimony oxide white 181
antimony vermilion 180-181
antimony yellow 54
antwerp blue 121
arenato 441, 442
armenian bole 102, 230
arriccio 441, 442
artists' gouache 357-358
artists' quality
oil colours 289-290
watercolour paint 343
arylide yellow 44
asphaltuum 177, 188-189
Association of Textile Chemists and Colorists 26
ASTM Lightfastness Ratings 28
attramentum 174
aurora yellow 50
availability of pigments 19-20
azo yellow 44
azurite 21, 52, 127-128, 159, 183, 219

B

badger softener brushes 463
barium lemon yellow 46, 59
barytes 40
beeswax 282, 314, 430
beeswax medium recipe 324
beeswax paste 279-280
beeswax paste recipe 279-280

bentonite 292
benzimidazolone orange HGL 73
berlin blue 120
berlin brown 176
bianco san giovanni 451
bibliography 481-487
bideford black chalk 199
binders, alternative for lime fresco paintings 455-458

binding agents
- *egg tempera painting 214-219*
- *soft pastel painting 381, 388-390*
- *water-based 362-369*
- *watercolour paint 339-340*

binding media for oil paint 264-273
- *alkyd medium 265*
- *blown oil 270*
- *cold-pressed linseed oil 266-269*
- *drying and oxidisation process 264-265*
- *heat-expressed linseed oil 265-266*
- *historic stand oil 270*
- *linseed oil varnish 269-270*
- *modern stand oil 270*
- *polymerised oil 270*
- *poppy oil 271-272*
- *properties of oil paints 264*
- *refined linseed oil 265-266*
- *refined linseed oil with siccative 269-270*
- *self-levelling 265*
- *stand oil 265, 270*
- *sun-bleached oil 270*
- *sun-thickened linseed oil 271*
- *sunflower oil 272*
- *walnut oil 273*

bismuth nitrate 181
bismuth white 181
bismuth yellow 64
bismuth-vandate yellow 64
bistre 175
bistre ink 175, 202
bitumen 177-178, 188-189

black and brown pigments 166-179
- *asphaltuum 177*
- *attramentum 174*
- *berlin brown 176*
- *bistre 175*
- *bistre ink 175, 202*
- *bitumen 177-178*
- *blue black 166, 179*
- *bone black 24, 67, 167*
- *bone brown 167*
- *carbon black 166*
- *cobalt black 170*
- *cork black 173*
- *french vine black 179*
- *fruit stone black 173*
- *furnace black 166*
- *gas black 166*
- *iron oxide black 168*
- *iron oxide red 126*
- *iron scale black 174*
- *ivory black 167*
- *lamp black 126, 166, 201*
- *lead black 305*
- *manganese black 169*
- *manganese brown 169*
- *manganese ferrite spinel black 170*
- *manganese grey 169*
- *mars black 168*
- *mineral black 168*
- *nut black 173*
- *oil required in mix with dry pigment 287*
- *peach black 173*
- *prussian brown 176*
- *roman sepia 171*
- *sepia 171-172*
- *sicilian oil 177*
- *spinel black 170*
- *vine black 173, 179, 222*

black chalk 199
black lead 194
black pigments, painting medium addition 268
blanc fix 31, 33, 40-41, 184, 280, 358, 451
bleached beeswax 314
bleeding pigments 30
blitzer bronze 187
blooming 184
blown oil 270
blue bice 137
blue black 166, 179
blue frit 129
blue malachite 127
blue pigments 119-147
- *academy blue 152*
- *alizarin purple 142*
- *alizarin violet 142*
- *anthraquinone blue 136*
- *antwerp blue 121*
- *azurite 21, 52, 127-128, 159, 183, 219*
- *berlin blue 120*
- *blue bice 137*
- *blue frit 129*
- *blue malachite 127*
- *blue verditer 137*
- *bremen blue 137*
- *brunswick blue 121*
- *cassel green 133*
- *cerulean 119*
- *cerulean blue 134, 261-262, 268*
- *chessylite 127*
- *chinese blue 120*
- *chromophtal blue 136*
- *cobalt 119*
- *cobalt blue 23, 121, 122, 290, 291*
- *cobalt blue greenish 135*
- *cobalt turquoise 135*
- *cobalt turquoise dark 135*
- *cobalt turquoise light 135*
- *cobalt violet 144*
- *cobalt violet brilliant 147*
- *cobalt violet dark 143*
- *cobalt violet deep 143*
- *cobalt violet light 146*
- *cobalt violet light (brilliant) 147*
- *cobalt violet pale 146*
- *cobalt-cerulean blue 134*
- *coeruleum blue 134*
- *copper blue 127*
- *copper silicate blue 129*
- *cyanine blue 121*
- *dioxazine purple 145*
- *dioxazine violet (blue shade) 145*
- *dioxazine violet (red shade) 145*
- *egyptian blue 129*
- *french ultramarine 125*
- *heliogen blue 119*
- *indanthrene blue 136, 305*
- *indigo 67, 138-139*
- *iron blue 120*
- *lapis lazuli 52, 123-124, 125, 219*
- *leitch's blue 121*
- *manganese blue 132-133*
- *manganese green 133*
- *manganese violet 144*
- *manganese-cerulean blue 132, 134*
- *maya blue 139*
- *milori blue 120*
- *mineral blue 127*
- *mineral grey 124*
- *mineral violet 144*
- *monastral blue 119*
- *monestial blue 119*
- *mountain blue 127, 137*
- *natural ultramarine 123*
- *new blue 125*

oil required in mix with dry pigment 286
oltremare 123
paliogen blue 136
paris blue 120
permanent violet 144, 145
phthalocyanine blue 119, 133, 135, 279, 290, 291-292, 339
pompeiian blue 129
pozzuoli blue 129
prussian blue 48, 51, 120-121, 176
purple madder lake 142
purple red 145
purpurite 141
royal blue 130
saxon blue 130
smalt 130-131, 183
sodalite 140
synthetic indigo 139
synthetic ultramarine 125, 162
thalo blue 119
thenard's blue 122
ultramarine 67, 152, 167
ultramarine (synthetic) 162
ultramarine ash 124
ultramarine blue 82, 155, 282, 291
ultramarine blue (shades) 125-126
ultramarine pink 125
ultramarine red 125
ultramarine violet 125
woad 138

blue verditer 137
Blue Wool scale 28-30
body colour 356
bohemian green earth 114
bole 230
bologna chalk 207
bone ash 181, 452
bone black 24, 67, 167
bone brown 167
brazilwood 181-182
bremen blue 137
brilliant yellow 44
bristol yellow 64
bronze powder 187
brown iron oxide 108
brown lake 67
brown madder 96, 180
brown ochre 102, 113
brown pigments *see* black and brown pigments
brunswick blue 121
brunswick green 121

brushes 459-474
acrylic painting 464-466
applying size to canvas 251
badger softeners 463
cleaning 333
cleaning after oil paint use 463-464
egg tempera painting 218-219
fan hog 461
filbert 218
flags 460
flat hog varnish 295
flat hog-hair 212
flat sable 218
gilder's tip 230
gilding 231
gouache painting 470
hog bristle 460-462, 464-466
hog hair varnish 471, 472-473
kolinsky sable 218, 467
lime-fresco painting 473-474
marseilles soap 464
mineral oil 333
mongoose hair 463, 473
muccino 474
nylon 470
oil painting 459-464
oilve oil soap 333, 464

one stroke 469
ox hair 218, 462, 469, 473
polecat hair 463
pony hair 473
priming 470-472
quality 459
red sable 467, 468
retouching 468
riga 474
round tipped 218
sable hair 463, 466-467, 469, 473
sable spotters 468
small soft hair 218
soft hair 462-463
soft hog varnish 255
soft pastel painting 473
soft sable hair 30
squirrel hair 230, 469, 473
squirrel mops 469, 473
straight mottler 251
synthetic 465-466, 469, 470
synthetic filament 218
tree 460
varnishing 212, 472-473
vaseline oil 463
watercolour painting 466-469
buckthorn lake 67
buon fresco 437
burnt carmine 92
burnt green earth 103, 114
burnt ochre 102, 113
burnt sienna 22-23, 110
burnt umber 108

C

cadmium bordeaux 81
cadmium brown 81
cadmium green 162
cadmium green dark 162
cadmium green light 162
cadmium lemon 49
cadmium orange 49, 76
cadmium red 280, 305
cadmium red dark 81
cadmium red deep 81
cadmium red light 81
cadmium red medium 81
cadmium red pale 81
cadmium red red 81
cadmium red vermilion orange 81
cadmium reds 79, 80
cadmium scarlet 81
cadmium vermilion 81
cadmium yellow 49-50, 162, 305
cadmium yellow dark 49
cadmium yellow deep 49, 62
cadmium yellow light 49
cadmium yellow medium 49
cadmium yellow pale 49
calcium carbonate 185, 199, 255
calcium sulphate 185, 255
caledonian brown 103
camboge 66
canada balsam 322
candelilla wax 431
cappagh brown 103
caput mortuum 188-189
caput mortuum red 115-116
caput mortuum violet 115-116
carbon black 166
carborundum powder 186
carlton white 35
carmine 79, 91-92, 124, 272
carmine (kermes red lake) 91-92
carmine from cochineal 91-92
carmine lake 91
carnauba wax 315, 324, 430-431
cartoon underpainting 452-453
casein 90, 364-365
casein as an adhesive for large particle size pigments recipe 377-378
casein as binder for lime-fresco painting recipe 454

casein binder 21
casein gesso 254
casein paint recipe 364-365
casein tempera 215
cassel brown 111
cassel green 133
cendres green 163
ceresin wax 431
cerulean 119
cerulean blue 134, 261-262, 268
chalk ground 206-207
chalk grounds for oil painting 254-256
chalks 199, 382
champagne chalk 206-207, 255
charcoal 194-196
chessylite 127
china clay 185, 230, 382
chinese blue 120
chinese red 83
chinese vermilion 84
chinese white 33
chrocoite 47
Chroma type pigments 38
chromate red 83
chrome green 48
chrome orange 83
chrome oxide green 151
chrome red 83
chrome titanate orange 77
chrome yellow 47-48, 83, 121
chrome yellow deep 121
chrome-tin pink 90
chromium oxide opaque 151
chromophtal blue 136
chromophtal orange 74
chromophtal yellow 61
cinabrese 222, 225
cinnabar 23, 84
cinnabar green 63, 64, 121
cinquasia red gold 71
cinquasia yellow gold 70
citron yellow 51
classic oil colours 289
cleaning
brushes after oil paint use 463-464
encaustic painting 436
oil painting 333-334
watercolour painting 352
coal tar dyes 338
coal tar yellow 65
coarse pastel ground 376-378
cobal violet deep 143
cobalt 119
cobalt black 170
cobalt blue 23, 121, 122, 290, 291
cobalt blue greenish 135
cobalt blue-green light 158
cobalt blue-green oxide 157
cobalt bottle green 156
cobalt drier 261
cobalt green 157
cobalt green (dark) 156
cobalt green light 158
cobalt green-blue oxide 157
cobalt siccative 261, 266, 269, 317
cobalt turquoise 135
cobalt turquoise dark 135
cobalt turquoise light 135
cobalt violet 144
cobalt violet brilliant 147
cobalt violet dark 143
cobalt violet light 146
cobalt violet light (brilliant) 147
cobalt violet pale 146
cobalt yellow 53
cobalt-cerulean blue 134
cochineal (Coccus cacti) 91
coeruleum blue 134
colcothar 115-116
cold pressed paper 348
cold-pressed linseed oil 263, 266-269, 278, 311

Colibri type pigments 37-38
collapsible metal tubes 280
cologne earth 111
colophony 319, 322
Colour Index (C.I.)
  Constitution Number 27-28
  name 26-27
colour index name 17-18
colour index number 18
coloured marble dusts 182
colourless mineral spirit 279
colours, historic, for egg tempera painting 220-222
colours, modern, for egg tempera painting 223-224
colphony 332
commercial pastel papers 373-374
commercially prepared canvas board 242
commercially prepared canvas paper 242
common names of pigments 18
composition of pigments 18, 26
compressed charcoal 196
compressed fibre board 203-204
congo copal 319
consistency of oil paint 261-263
constant white 40
copaiva balsam 322
copal 319-320
copper acetate 153
copper blue 127
copper carbonate 161
copper powder 186
copper resinate 153, 154
copper silicate blue 129
cork black 173
cork boards 374
cork particles 379
cost of pigments 19-20
cotton duck canvas 233-234
couching 348
crayon 198
cremnitz white 31
crimson lake 82
curd cheese 215
cyanine blue 121
cyprus umber 107

D

dammar 317
dammar resin 427
dammar varnish 227, 282, 310, 326
dammar varnish recipe 327-329
davy's grey 103-104, 126
dayglo colours 182-183
de-acidification agent 248
dead-head 188
defects of pigments 19
designers' gouache 357-358
dextrin 214, 363
dextrin recipe 363
dinitraniline orange 72
dioxazine purple 145
dioxazine violet (blue shade) 145
dioxazine violet (red shade) 145
'Disperse Aid' 20
'Disponil' 20, 405, 408
disposable gloves 281
dragon's blood 97, 229
dralon fibre 379

drawing materials 191-202
  dry drawing tools 191-199
  wet drawing tools 191, 200-202

dried goatskin 346
dried skimmed milk 215

dry drawing tools
  bideford black chalk 199
  black chalk 199
  black lead 194
  calcium carbonate 199

chalks 199
charcoal 194-196
compressed charcoal 196
crayon 198
graphite 192-193
graphite lump 192
graphite powder 192-193
graphite sticks 193
kaolin 199
lead pencil 194
metalpoint 198
natural chalks 199
oil charcoal 195-196
oil pastel 197
oil sticks 197-198
pastel sticks 196-197
pencil 194
plumbago 194
port-crayon 199
red chalk 199
sanguine chalk 199
scene-painters' charcoal 195
soft pastel 196-197
white chalk 199

drying agent 260-261
drying and oxidisation process 264-265
drying rate of pigments 21
drying rates of oil colours 297-298, 300-304
drying time for oil paint 260-261, 300-304
Durer, Albrecht 335
dust mask 281
dutch pink 67

E

earth pigment deposits
armenian bole 102
brown ochre 102
burnt green earth 103
burnt ochre 102
caledonian brown 103
cappagh brown 103
davy's grey 103-104, 126
english red 99, 101
french ochre 101
gulf red 104
haematite 101-102, 222
indian red 104
light red 105
limonite 100
mineral brown 103
persian red oxide 104
pompeii red 22, 105
pozzuoli red 105
raw sienna 101, 121
ruddle 101-102
spanish red 105
terra rosa 105
turkey brown 106
turkey umber 106
venetian red 106
veronese brown 103

earth pigments 99-114
bohemian green earth 114
brown iron oxide 108
brown ochre 113
burnt green earth 114
burnt ochre 113
burnt sienna 22-23, 110
burnt umber 108
cassel brown 111
cologne earth 111
cyprus umber 107
deposits 100-106
gold ochre 113
green earth 114, 160, 218, 222, 259
green umber 107
light ochre 113
natural sienna 109
oil required in mix with dry pigment 285-286
oxford ochre 100
raw sienna 109
raw umber 21, 107, 222, 260,

297, 300
red earth 222
roman ochre 113
sienna 109
synthetic iron oxides 99
terra verde 114
terre verte 114
turkey umber 107
van dyke brown 108, 111-112
verona green earth 114
yellow ochre 22, 113, 222

egg tempera painting 203-232
binding agents 214-219
brushes 218-219
colours not to be bound in egg yolk 229
colours, historic 220-222
colours, modern 223-224

egg yolk as binder 215-219

egg-oil emulsions 226-227
flesh tints 222-223
gesso preparation for panels 211- 214
gilding 229-232
glue 207-210
importance of set method 224-225
natural wood supports 204-205
painting ground application 206-207
palette 219-220
panel preparation 205-206
panel preparation with gesso 211-214
pigments preparation 214-215
procedure for painting 224-225
supports for panel painting 203-204
unvarnished 228
varnishing 219, 227-229
wetting agents 21

egg white 365-366
egg white as binder 215
egg white as binding agent recipe 380
egg yolk as binder 215-219
egg-gesso grounds 256
egg-oil emulsion 226-227
egg-oil emulsion recipe 226-227
egg-oil grounds 254
egyptian blue 129
Ekaton type pigments 37
elemi 320-321
emerald green 165

encaustic painting 427-436
aluminium-steel alloy tins 428-429
beeswax 430
candelilla wax 431
carnauba wax 430-431
ceresin wax 431
clean-up 436
equipment 428-429
glazing 435
heated spatula 428
hot plate 428
japan wax 431
layers 435
microcrystalline wax 431
palette 432-433
paraffin wax 431
pigments 432-433
presentation 435-436
safety 436
spermaceti wax 432
stearin wax 432
supports 427-428
techniques 433-434
wax 430-432

encaustic paints
composition 429-430
use 429-430
english red 99, 101
'extra-virgin' term 266

F

fan hog brushes 461
fast-drying action 21
'fat over lean' concept 296, 323
fibreboard 247-248
filbert brushes 218
filbert hog brushes 461
fish glue 215
FK abbreviaiton 403
flags (brushes) 460
flake white 31, 306
flat hog varnish brushes 295
flat hog-hair brushes 212
flat sable brushes 218
flax 234-235
flesh tints, egg tempera painting 222-223
flexible supports 233-242
flock paper 374
flourescent colours 182-183
fluid mediums 413-414
foundation white 306
framing watercolour paint 352
french chalk 382
french ochre 101
french ultramarine 125
french vine black 179
french-satine paper 348
french-torchon paper 348
fresco secca 453-454
fruit stone black 173
fuller's earth 267
furnace black 166
fuschin 185

G

gamboge 66, 120-121, 229
gas black 166
gel mediums 414-415
gelatine 250-251
gelatine solution for unsized paper recipe 350
genoa white 31
gesso d'oro 214
gesso for egg tempera painting recipe 212
gesso for wood as a support recipe 243-244
gesso grosso 213
gesso ground 203, 206-207, 243
gesso in acrylic painting 423-426
gesso panel 198
gesso preparation for panels 211-214
gesso sottile 213
giallorino 55, 57
gilders' tip brushes 230
gilding 187, 213-214, 229-232
  brushes 231
  cushion 231
  egg tempera painting 229-232
  knife 231
  water 231
  whiting 214
Girtin, Thomas 336
glair 215, 365-366
glair as binding agent recipe 380
glass beads 410
glass muller 217, 277
glass palette 308
glass pigments 183-184
glass runner 217, 277
glass slab 278
glaze medium 282
glaze medium recipe 323
glazing in encaustic painting 435
glimmer white 39
glue tempera 215
glue, egg tempera painting 207-210
glycerine 344
goatskin glue 254

goatskin parchment clippings 207-208
gold foil 187
gold leaf 187, 230-232
gold ochre 113
gold powder 187
golden green lake 150
goldschwefel 180-181
gomma gutti 66
gouache painting 356-362
- *application 361*
- *artists' gouache 357-358*
- *background 356-357*
- *brushes 470*
- *designers' gouache 357-358*
- *hand-made colours 358-359*
- *paper 361*
- *preservation 361-362, 478-479*
- *storage 361-362, 478-479*
- *supports 361*
- *tempera painting 357*
- *wetting agents 20*

'Grand Tour' 335
granulation 30, 132
graphite 192-193
graphite lump 192
graphite powder 192-193
graphite sticks 193
green bice 161, 163
green earth 114, 160, 218, 222, 259
green gold lake 150
green pigments 148-165
- *brunswick green 121*
- *cadmium green 162*
- *cadmium green dark 162*
- *cadmium green light 162*
- *cendres green 163*
- *chrome green 48*
- *chrome oxide green 151*
- *chromium oxide opaque 151*
- *cobalt blue-green light 158*
- *cobalt blue-green oxide 157*
- *cobalt bottle green 156*
- *cobalt green 157*
- *cobalt green (dark) 156*
- *cobalt green light 158*
- *cobalt green-blue oxide 157*
- *copper acetate 153*
- *copper carbonate 161*
- *copper resinate 153, 154*
- *emerald green 165*
- *golden green lake 150*
- *green bice 161, 163*
- *green gold lake 150*
- *green verditer 161, 163*
- *guignet's green 152*
- *heliogen green 148*
- *hooker's green 120-121, 149*
- *hydrated chromium hydroxide 152*
- *imitation sap green 149*
- *imperial green 165*
- *irgazine yellow (green) 150*
- *malachite 21, 159-160, 183*
- *malachite (synthetic) 161*
- *mineral green 159*
- *mittis green 165*
- *monastral green 148*
- *monestial green 148*
- *mountain green 159, 161, 163*
- *naphthol green 149*
- *nitroso green 149*
- *oil required in mix with dry pigment 287*
- *oltremare verde 155*
- *paris green 165*
- *phthalocyanine green 119, 135, 148, 152, 280, 290, 339*
- *quindo green gold 150*
- *rinman's green 158*
- *russian green 164*
- *sap green 26, 68, 180*
- *sap green (imitation) 149*
- *scheele's green 165*
- *schweinfurt green 165*
- *synthetic malachite 161*

thalo green 148
transparent oxide of chromium 152
ultramarine green 125, 155
verdigris 229
verdigris synthetic 153-154
veronese green 165
victoria green 152
vienna green 165
viridian 17, 152, 162, 290
volchonskoite green 164
wolchonskoite green 164
zinc green 51

green umber 107
green verditer 161, 163
griffith's patent zinc white 35
grind size 25
grip coat 211
gubbio red 98
guignet's green 152
gulf red 104
gum arabic 214, 339-340
gum arabic recipe 390
gum cherry recipe 390
gum elemi 320-321
gum tempera 214, 335
gum tragacanth 362-363
gum tragacanth recipe 389-390
gum tragacanth solution recipe 362-363
gum tragacanth solutions 214
gum turpentine 332-333
gum water 354
gypsum 185, 198, 206-207, 255

H

haematite 101-102, 222
haematite-chrome oxide black-brown 118
half-chalk grounds 256
half-oil grounds 254, 256

hand-made colours
acrylic painting 404-410
gouache painting 358-359
oil painting 263, 273-289
soft pastels 390-393
watercolour 343-346

hand-made paper 349-350
hand-made soft pastels, wetting agents 20
hansa red 79
hansa yellow 44-45, 121
hansa yellow dark 44
hansa yellow light 44
hardboard 204, 246-247
Health and Safety information on pigments 21
heated spatula 428
heavy spar 40
helio red 79
heliogen blue 119
heliogen green 148
hide glue 207, 254
historic stand oil 270, 311
historical background 11
hog bristle brushes 460-462, 464-466
hog hair varnish brushes 471, 472-473
hollow plastic bubbles 410
honeycomb aluminium panels 248, 313
hooker's green 120-121, 149
horsetail plant 207
hostaperm orange 73
hot plate 428
hot pressed paper 348
'hue' 291
hydrated chromium hydroxide 152
hydromel 344
hydrous magnesium sillicate 382
hydroxi-propyl-cellulose 366

I

imitation sap green 149

imitation vermilion 79
impasto gels 354
impasto mediums 324
imperial green 165
imperial purple 190
indanthrene blue 136, 305
indanthrene red 89
indanthrone blue 136
india ink 201
indian ink 201
indian purple 92
indian red 104
indian yellow genuine 65, 69
indian yellow substitute 65, 69
indigo 67, 138-139
inert fillers 184-185
ink stone 200
ink with acrylic binder 202
ink with gum arabic binder 201
inks 200
inorganic pigments
earth deposit 22
earth deposit, artifically calcined 22
earth deposit, naturally calcined 22
fused metallic compound 23
mineral 23
rock 23
treated metallic compound 23
interference pigments 38
intonaco 437, 441, 442, 452-453
irgazine orange 75, 76
irgazine orange DPP 75
irgazine yellow 61
irgazine yellow (green) 150
iridescent pigments 37-38
iridescent white (mica lustre) 39
iridescent white (pearl lustre) 39
iron blue 120
iron oxide black 168
iron oxide red 126
iron scale black 174
iron-gall ink 200
ironstone brown 77
isinglass 207-208, 215, 368-369
isoindoline orange 74
isoindoline yellow 62
isoindolinone yellow 61
italian pink 67
ivory black 167
ivory plaques 346

J

japan wax 431
jaune brilliant 54
jersey lily white 35

K

'Kaolin' 185, 199, 382
kauri copal 320
kermes red lake 91
ketone N 326
ketone N resin picture varnish recipe 330-331
kings yellow 52
klucel 40, 366
kolinsky sable brushes 218, 467
kremnitz white 31
krems white 31

L

lamp black 126, 166, 201
landscape painting palette 309
lapis lazuli 52, 123-124, 125, 219
lavender oil 318
layers in encaustc painting 435
layers of oil paint 294-300
lead black 305
lead monoxide 58
'lead pencil' 194
lead tin yellow 54, 58
lead tin yellow type I 55-56
lead tin yellow type II 57
lead white 23, 31-32, 127, 222, 252, 260, 287

lead white oil primer recipe 253
lead white primer 252-253
lead-based pigments 19, 252, 287, 433
leitch's blue 121
lemon yellow 46, 59
light ochre 113
light red 105, 115-116
lime plaster surface 437
lime putty 450

lime-fresco painting 437-458
- *acrylic paint 457-458*
- *arenato 441, 442*
- *arriccio 441, 442*
- *background 437-438*
- *bianco san giovanni 451*
- *binders, alternative 455-458*
- *blanc fix 451*
- *brushes 473-474*
- *cartoon underpainting 452-453*
- *casein 454*
- *fresco secca 453-454*
- *intonaco 441, 442, 452-453*
- *lead white 452*
- *lime putty 450*
- *lime-water 451*
- *marble chips 440*
- *marble dust 439-440*
- *medium density fibreboard (MDF) 444-446*
- *milk of lime 451*
- *mortar layers 439-443*
- *palette 448-450*
- *pigments 448-450*
- *plaster panel 446-447*
- *portable panels 443-444*
- *protection of paintings 455*
- *quartz chips 440*
- *safety 438*
- *sinopia 452*
- *supports 439-447*
- *trulisatio 441-442*
- *walls, preparing 439-447*
- *waterglass 455-456*
- *whites 450-452*
- *wood panels 444-446*

lime-water 451
limonite 100
linen 234-235
linoxin 298
linseed oil 21
linseed oil varnish 227, 269-270
litharge 58, 76
lithol red 79
lithopone 33, 35, 152
lithopone silver 35
logwood 185
london white 31
low odour thinner 332
luminous pigments 185

M

madder 124, 338
madder carmine 96
madder lake 93, 94-95
madder lake pigment recipe 94-95
madder lake synthetic 82
madder red lake 24
magenta 185-186
'magna' 399-400
malachite 21, 159-160, 183
malachite (synthetic) 161
manganese black 169
manganese blue 132-133
manganese brown 169
manganese ferrite spinel black 170
manganese green 133
manganese grey 169
manganese violet 144

manganese-cerulean blue 132, 134
manila copal 320
manufactured mediums 325-326
marble chips 440
marble dust 182, 439-440
marble slab 278
mars black 115-116, 168
mars brown 115-116
mars colours 115-116
mars orange 115-116
mars red 115-116
mars violet 115-116, 189
mars yellow 115-116
marseilles soap 464
masking fluid 354-355
masonite 204, 246-247
mass tone 264
massicot 55, 58, 76, 271, 317
mastic 317
mastic varnish 227, 326
mastic varnish recipe 330
matt dammar varnish recipe 330
mauve 186
maya blue 139
media suitabililty of pigments 19
medium density fibreboard (MDF) 247-248, 444-446
meglip 319
mesh number 213-214
metal powders 186-188
metal tubes 280
metalpoint 198
methylated spirit 216, 279
methylcellulose 363-364, 395
mica 37-38, 188
mica white 39
microcrystalline wax 313, 431
micron size 24-25
milk of lime 451
milling machine 292
milori blue 120
mineral black 168
mineral blue 127
mineral brown 103
mineral green 159
mineral grey 124
mineral spirit 332
mineral violet 144
mineral yellow 190
minium 76
miscellaneous pigments 180-190
alizarin brown 180
alizarin green 180
aloe 180
aluminium powder 187
antimony gold 180-181
antimony orange 180-181
antimony oxide white 181
antimony vermilion 180-181
asphaltuum 188-189
bismuth nitrate 181
bismuth white 181
bitumen 188-189
blitzer bronze 187
bone ash 181, 452
brazilwood 181-182
bronze powder 187
brown madder 180
caput mortuum 188-189
carborundum powder 186
coloured marble dusts 182
copper powder 186
dayglo colours 182-183
dead-head 188
flourescent colours 182-183
fuschin 185
glass pigments 183-184
gold foil 187
gold leaf 187
gold powder 187
goldschwefel 180-181
imperial purple 190
inert fillers 184-185
logwood 185
luminous pigments 185
magenta 185-186
marble dusts 182

mars violet 189
mauve 186
metal powders 186-188
mica 188
mineral yellow 190
mosaic gold 188
mucovite mica 188
mummy brown 188-189
muscovy glass 188
patent yellow 190
phlogopite 188
phosphorescent pigments 185
potassium aluminium silicate 188
powdered metals 186-188
pumice 189
purporino 188
saffron 188
silver glitter 189-190
stainless steel powder 186
synthetic iron-oxide red-violet 189
tin foil 187-188
tin powder 187-188
turner's yellow 190
tyrian purple 190
mittis green 165
modern stand oil 270, 310-311
moist watercolour paint 336
moisturising agent 344
molybdate of lead 83
monastral blue 119
monastral green 148
monestial blue 119
monestial green 148
mongoose hair brushes 463, 473
monoazo red 79
monoazo yellow 44
mortar layers 439-443
mosaic gold 188
mountain blue 127, 137
mountain green 159, 161, 163
mowiol 408
muccino brushes 474
mucovite mica 188
mummy brown 188-189
muscovite 37
muscovy glass 37, 188

N

naccarat carmine 91
naphthol green 149
naples yellow 54, 55, 59, 216
naples yellow lemon 59
naples yellow light 59
napthol carmine 80
napthol red 80
natural chalks 199
natural madder 93-96
natural madder lake 79
natural ochre pigments 16
natural resins 315-321
natural sienna 109
natural sponge 353
natural ultramarine 123
natural wood supports 204-205
'nearly' colours 291
new blue 125
nickel azo yellow 69, 264
nickel barium 63
nickel titanium yellow 59
nickel yellow 59
nitroso green 149
Nolde, Emil 336
non-absorbent primer 423-426
not paper 348, 361
nottingham white 31
nuisance dusts 21, 281, 411
nut black 173
nylon brushes 470

O

oak 205
obsolete pigments 180-190
alizarin brown 180
alizarin green 68, 180

- *antimony oxide white 181*
- *brown madder 180*
- *caput mortuum 188-189*
- *dead-head 188*
- *imperial purple 190*
- *mauve 186*
- *mineral yellow 190*
- *mosaic gold 188*
- *mummy brown 188-189*
- *patent yellow 190*
- *purporino 188*
- *turner's yellow 190*
- *tyrian purple 190*

odourless mineral spirit (OMS) 332, 334
oil absorbtion 283-287
oil charcoal 195-196
oil colour manufactured 289-294

oil colour paint making 273-289
- *aluminium hydrate 280, 282-283*
- *beeswax 282*
- *beeswax paste 279-280*
- *black and brown pigments 287*
- *blanc fix 280*
- *blue pigments 286*
- *cold-pressed linseed oil 278*
- *collapsible metal tubes 280*
- *colourless mineral spirit 279*
- *dammar varnish 282*
- *disposable gloves 281*
- *dry pigments 275-277*
- *dust mask 281*
- *earth pigments 285-286*
- *glass muller 277*
- *glass runner 277*
- *glass slab 278*
- *glaze medium 282*
- *green pigments 287*
- *hand-made 273-289*
- *historic 273*
- *ingredients 275-281*
- *marble slab 278*
- *metal tubes 280*
- *methylated spirit 279*
- *oil absorbtion 283-287*
- *palette knives 278*
- *paper roll 280*
- *poppy oil 282*
- *procedure 281-283*
- *process, importance 273*
- *red pigments 285*
- *safety 287-288*
- *safflower oil 282*
- *stand oil 282*
- *sunflower oil 279, 282*
- *synthetic iron oxide pigments 286*
- *tools 275-281*
- *toxicity of pigments 288-289*
- *turpentine 282*
- *waste bin 281*
- *white pigments 284*
- *white spirit 279*
- *yellow pigments 284-285*

oil paint mediums 309-326
- *abietic acid 321*
- *alcohol-based varnishes 316*
- *alkyd resin 312-313*
- *alkyd resin based 325*
- *amber 320*
- *beeswax 314*
- *bleached beeswax 314*
- *canada balsam 322*
- *carnauba wax 315, 324*
- *cold pressed linseed oil 311*
- *colophony 319, 322*
- *congo copal 319*
- *copaiva balsam 322*
- *copal 319-320*
- *crucial importance 309-310*
- *dammar 317*
- *dammar varnish 310*
- *elemi 320-321*
- *fat over lean concept 323*
- *gum elemi 320-321*
- *historic stand oil 311*

honeycomb aluminium panels 313
impasto mediums 324
kauri copal 320
lavender oil 318
manila copal 320
manufactured mediums 325-326
mastic 317
meglip 319
metal-based pigments 312
microcrystalline wax 313
modern stand oil 310-311
modified oils 310-313
natural resins 315-321
oilo d'Abezzo 322
oils 310-313
oleo-resins 321-322
paraffin wax 315
pearlescent pigments 312
raw beeswax 314
recipes 323-325
refined beeswax 314
refined linseed oil 311
sandarac 316, 318
scumbling 323
shellac 316
silica 313
silver-fir turpentine 322
spike lavender oil 317, 318, 320
spirit varnishes 316
stand oil 310-311
strasbourg turpentine 322
sun-bleached linseed oil 311
sun-thickened linseed oil 311
synthetic wax 315
thixotropic property 313
tree balsams 321-322
turpentine 309
underbound 309
venice turpentine 321-322
waxes 314-315
yellow beeswax 314

oil paint properties 258-273
binding media 264-273
cobalt drier 261
cobalt siccative 261
consistency 261-263
drying agent 260-261
drying time 260-261, 300-304
hand-made oil colours 263
manufacturing process 258-259
mass tone 264
oil to pigment ratio 259-260
ready-made paints 263
rheology 263-264
tube oil colour 261
undertone 264

oil painting 233-334
acrylic painting comparison 401
alla-prima 298, 299, 300
brushes 459-464
clean-up 333-334
concepts of building a painting 294-300
drying rates of oil colours 297-298, 300-304
egg-oil emulsions 226-227
fat over lean concept 296
flexible supports 233-242
gum turpentine 332-333
layers 294-300
low odour thinner 332
mediums 309-326
mineral spirit 332
odourless mineral spirit (OMS) 332, 334
oil colour manufactured 289-294
oil colour paint making 273-289
painting ground 294-300
palette 307-309
priming supports 251-258
properties 258-273
rigid supports 242-248
sizing supports 248-251

solvents 331-333
stick form 294
supports 233-248
tempera underpaint 226
turpentine 331-332
varnishes 299-300, 326-331
wet into wet approach 298, 299
wetting agents 20
white spirit 332
whites 304-307

oil paintings
preservation 477-478
storage 475-478
transporting 477

oil pastel 197
oil sticks 197-198
oil to pigment ratio 259-260
oilo d'Abezzo 322
oleo-resins 321-322
olifa 227
olive green 67
olive lake 67, 167
olive oil 266
olive oil soap 333, 464
oltremare 123
oltremare verde 155
one stroke brushes 469
opacity of pigments 19
opaque white 293
orange mineral 76

orange pigments 70-78
benzimidazolone orange HGL 73
cadmium orange 76
chrome orange 83
chrome titanate orange 77
chromophtal orange 74
cinquasia yellow gold 70
dinitraniline orange 72
hostaperm orange 73
irgazine orange 75, 76
irgazine orange DPP 75
ironstone brown 77
isoindoline orange 74
minium 76
orange mineral 76
paliotol orange 72
permanent orange 72
pyrrol orange 75
quido gold deep 71
quinacridone gold 70
quinacridone red gold 71
quindo gold 70
quindo red gold 71
rahj al ghar 78
realgar 78
red lead 76, 78
saturn red 76
titanium orange 77

orange vermilion 84

organic pigments 23-24
animal 24
plant 24
synthetic 24

organic yellows 121
orient yellow 50
Oriental painting 12
'Orotan' 20, 405, 408
orpiment 52
orr's zinc white 35
ox hair brushes 218, 462, 469, 473
ox-gall 20
oxford ochre 100
oxgall 354

P

paint making *see* oil colour paint making
paint pastes 264
paint-out samples 29-30
painting ground 206-207, 294-300
palamid bordeaux 89
pale blues 229
pale vermilion 84

palette
acrylic painting 404-408
egg tempera painting 219-220
encaustic painting 432-433
glass 308
historic arrangement 307
landscape painting 309
lime-fresco painting 448-450
oil painting 307-309
portrait painting 309
watercolour painting 353

palette knives 278
paliogen blue 136
paliogen maroon 86, 89
paliotol orange 72
paliotol yellow 62
panel preparation for egg tempera painting 205-206
panel preparation with gesso 211-214

paper
acid-free 378-379
cold pressed 348
commercial pastel 373-374
flock 374
french-satine 348
french-torchon 348
gouache painting 361
hand-made 349-350
hot pressed 348
not 348, 361

preservation of completed works 478-479
rough 348
smooth 348
soft pastel painting 378-379
stetching 350-351
storage of completed works 478-479
unsized 350
velour 374
weights 349
woodfree 349-350
woodpulp 349-350

paper as a support
oil paintings 241-242
watercolour painting 346-347

paper roll 280
paper stetching for watercolour 350-351
papermaking for watercolour 347-350
para red 80
paraffin wax 315, 431
paraloid B-72 229
parchment clippings 207-208, 254
paris blue 120
paris green 165
particle size of pigments 24-25
pastel painting *see* soft pastel painting
pastel sticks 196-197, 371-372
pastel sticks recipes 384-390
patent yellow 190
payne's grey 126
peach black 173

pearlescent pigments
Chroma types 38
Colibri types 37-38
Ekaton types 37
interference types 38
iridescent types 37-38

pearlescent types 37
pearlescent white 39
pencil 194
permanence of artists' pigments 28-30
permanent alizarin crimson 82
permanent carmine 80
permanent orange 72
permanent red 80
permanent violet 144, 145
permanent white 33, 40
permanent yellow 46
persian lake 67
persian red oxide 104

perylene maroon 89
perylene red 82, 86, 87
perylene red BL 87
phlogopite 188
phosphorescent pigments 185
phthalocyanine blue 119, 133, 135, 279, 290, 291-292, 339
phthalocyanine green 119, 135, 148, 152, 280, 290, 339

pigments
- *artists' 25-28*
- *availability 19-20*
- *black 166-179*
- *bleeding 30*
- *blue 119-147*
- *Blue Wool scale 28-30*
- *brown 166-179*
- *classification 25-28*
- *Colour Index (C.I.) 26-28*
- *colour index name 17-18*
- *colour index number 18*
- *common names 18*
- *composition 18, 26*
- *cost 19-20*
- *defects 19*
- *dry, for oil colour making 275-277*
- *drying and oxidisation process 264-265*
- *drying rate 21*
- *earth 99-114*
- *encaustic painting 432-433*
- *gouache hand-made paint 360*
- *granulation 30*
- *green 148-165*
- *Health and Safety information 21*
- *historic 25*
- *ideal 16*
- *information key 17-22*
- *inorganic 22-23*
- *introduction 15-17*
- *lead-based 19, 252, 287, 433*
- *lime-fresco painting 448-450*
- *metal-based 312*
- *miscellaneous 180-190*
- *natural ochre 16*
- *obsolete 180-190*
- *oil required in mix with dry pigment 283-287*
- *opacity 19*
- *orange 70-78*
- *organic 23-24*
- *origin 18*
- *paint-out samples 29-30*
- *particle size 24-25, 338*
- *particle structure 15*
- *pearlescent 37-43, 312*
- *permanence 28-30*
- *preparation for egg tempera painting 214-215*
- *quality check 15*
- *quinacridones 281*
- *red 79-98*
- *shade 19*
- *staining 30*
- *suitability to media 19*
- *synthetic iron oxides 115-118*
- *testing at home 29-30*
- *tinting strength 19*
- *toothy nature 376*
- *toxicity 288-289*
- *transparency 19*
- *types 22-24*
- *unstable in some mixtures 12*
- *wetting agents 20-21*
- *white 31-36*
- *yellow 44-69*

pillar-box red 83
pink colour 90
plaster panel 446-447
plasticising agent 344
plumbago 194
plywood 245-246
polecat hair brushes 463
polymerised oil 270
polyvinyl materials 420
pompeii red 22, 105

pompeiian blue 129
ponolith 35
pony hair brushes 473
poplar wood 204
poppy oil 268, 271-272, 282
port-crayon 199
portable panels 443-444
portrait painting palette 309
potassium aluminium silicate 188
potter's pink 90
powdered alum 250
powdered metals 186-188
pozzuoli blue 129
pozzuoli red 105
pre-primed canvas 236-237
prepared size 354

preservation
- *acrylic paintings 478*
- *finished artworks 475-480*
- *gouache paintings 478-479*
- *oil paintings 477-478*
- *soft pastel painting 480*
- *watercolour paintings 478-479*

priderite yellow 63

priming 251-258
- *acrylic 253-254, 257, 295*
- *acrylic gesso 295, 296*
- *acrylic gesso primer 257*
- *acrylic painting 422-426*
- *alkyd 253-254, 257*
- *animal glue gesso 254*
- *applying glue size 255*
- *brushes 470-472*
- *casein gesso 254*
- *chalk grounds 254-256*
- *comparison (for oil paintings) 253-254*
- *egg-gesso grounds 256*
- *egg-oil grounds 254*
- *gesso experiments 255-256*
- *goatskin glue 254*
- *half-chalk grounds 256*
- *half-oil grounds 254, 256*
- *hide glue 254*
- *lead white 252*
- *lead white primer 252-253*
- *parchment clippings 254*
- *rabbit glue size 254-255*
- *titanium white 253*
- *universal primer 257*
- *wheat starch glue 256*

priming supports 251-258
primrose yellow 47, 51
procedure for egg tempera painting 224-225
professional oil colours 289
prussian blue 48, 51, 120-121, 176
prussian brown 176
prussian green 121
pumice 189
pumice-glue ground recipe 375
purple 124
purple madder lake 142
purple red 145
purporino 188
purpurin 93
purpurine 338
purpurite 141
PVA-based materials 420-421
pyramid yellow 60
pyrrol orange 75

Q

quartz chips 440
quido gold deep 71
quinacridone gold 70
quinacridone magenta 86
quinacridone pink 86
quinacridone red 82, 86, 290
quinacridone red gold 71
quinacridone scarlet 86
quinacridone violet 86
quinacridones 281
quindo gold 70

quindo green gold 150
quindo red gold 71

R

rabbit glue size 254-255
rabbit skin glue 207-210, 248-250, 367-368
rabbit skin glue for sizing for canvas recipe 249-250
'radiant' tints 293
rahj al ghar 78
raw beeswax 314
raw sienna 101, 109, 121
raw umber 21, 107, 222, 260, 297, 300
ready-made paints 263
realgar 78

recipes
- *animal skin glue for panels 209-210*
- *beeswax medium 324*
- *beeswax paste 279-280*
- *casein as adhesive for large particle size pigments 377-378*
- *casein as binder for lime-fresco painting 454*
- *casein paint 364-365*
- *dammar varnish 327-329*
- *dextrin 363*
- *egg white as binding agent 380*
- *egg-oil emulsion 226-227*
- *gelatine solution for unsized paper 350*
- *gesso for egg tempera painting 212*
- *gesso for wood as a support 243-244*
- *glair as binding agent 380*
- *glaze medium 323*
- *gum arabic 390*
- *gum cherry 390*
- *gum tragacanth 362-363, 389-390*
- *kentone N resin picture varnish 330-331*
- *lead white oil primer 253*
- *madder lake pigment 94-95*
- *mastic varnish 330*
- *matt dammar varnish 330*
- *oil paint mediums 323-325*
- *pumice-glue ground 375*
- *rabbit skin glue for sizing for canvas 249-250*
- *resin-oil-wax medium 325*
- *soft pastel sticks 384-390*
- *tylose MH300 stock solution 389*
- *varnishes 327-331*

red bole 230
red chalk 199
red earth 222
red lake 124
red lead 76, 78

red pigments 79-98
- *alizarin carmine 82*
- *alizarin crimson 16, 24, 27, 79, 82, 86, 89, 94, 142, 180, 216, 260, 290, 298, 338, 358*
- *alizarin crimson light 82*
- *alizarin madder lake 82*
- *anthranthrone red 88*
- *anthraquinone red 82, 87, 88*
- *anthraquinone scarlet 88*
- *brown madder 96*
- *burnt carmine 92*
- *cadmium bordeaux 81*
- *cadmium brown 81*
- *cadmium red 280, 305*
- *cadmium red dark 81*
- *cadmium red deep 81*
- *cadmium red light 81*
- *cadmium red medium 81*
- *cadmium red pale 81*
- *cadmium red red 81*
- *cadmium red vermilion orange 81*

cadmium reds 79, 80
cadmium scarlet 81
cadmium vermilion 81
carmine 79, 91-92, 124, 272
carmine (kermes red lake) 91-92
carmine from cochineal 91-92
carmine lake 91
chinese red 83
chinese vermilion 84
chromate red 83
chrome red 83
chrome-tin pink 90
cinnabar 23, 84
cinnabar green 63, 64
cochineal (Coccus cacti) 91
crimson lake 82
dragon's blood 97, 229
gubbio red 98
hansa red 79
helio red 79
imitation vermilion 79
indanthrene red 89
indian purple 92
kermes red lake 91
lithol red 79
madder 124, 338
madder carmine 96
madder lake 93, 94-95
madder lake synthetic 82
madder red lake 24
molybdate of lead 83
monoazo red 79
naccarat carmine 91
napthol carmine 80
napthol red 80
natural madder 93-96
natural madder lake 79
oil required in mix with dry pigment 285
orange vermilion 84
palamid bordeaux 89
pale vermilion 84
paliogen maroon 86, 89
para red 80
permanent alizarin crimson 82
permanent carmine 80
permanent red 80
perylene maroon 89
perylene red 82, 86, 87
perylene red BL 87
pillar-box red 83
pink colour 90
potter's pink 90
quinacridone magenta 86
quinacridone pink 86
quinacridone red 82, 86, 290
quinacridone scarlet 86
quinacridone violet 86
rose dore 93, 96
rose madder 93
ruben's madder 96
scarlet lake 79
scarlet red 88
scarlet vermilion 84
selenium red 81
studio red 79
toluidine red 79
vermilion 79, 81, 84-85, 222, 260, 272, 290

red sable brushes 467, 468
refined beeswax 314
refined linseed oil 263, 265-266, 311
refined linseed oil with siccative 269-270
reinforcing rigid supports 246
resin-oil-wax medium recipe 325
retouching brushes 468
rheology 263-264, 400
riga brushes 474
rigid supports 242-248
rinman's green 158
rohagit 409
roman ochre 113
roman sepia 171
rose dore 93, 96
rose madder 93
rough paper 348

round tipped brushes 218
royal blue 130
ruben's madder 96
ruddle 101-102
russian green 164

S

sable hair brushes 463, 466-467, 469, 473
sable spotters brushes 468
safflower oil 268, 272, 282
saffron 188
sandarac 219, 232, 316, 318
sanguine chalk 199
sap green 26, 68, 180
sap green (imitation) 149
saturn red 76
saxon blue 130
scalpel 353
scarlet lake 79
scarlet red 88
scarlet vermilion 84
scene-painters' charcoal 195
scheele's green 165
schweinfurt green 165
scotchlite 410
scumbling 323
seasoned wood 205
second grade watercolour paint 343
selenium red 81
self-levelling paint medium 265
sepia 171-172
sepia ink 202
seruse white 31
shades of pigments 19
shellac 232, 316
shellac-borax inks 201-202
short paint 340
sicilian oil 177
sicopal yellow 64
sienna 109
silica 313
silver glitter 189-190
silver white 31
silver-fir turpentine 322
silverpoint 191
sinopia 230, 452
sizing supports 248-251
sketching oil colours 289
small soft hair brushes 218
smalt 130-131, 183
smooth paper 348
snowflake 31
soapstone 382
Society of Dyers and Colourists 17, 18, 26
sodalite 140
soft hair brushes 462-463
soft hog varnish brushes 255
soft pastel painting 196-197, 371-398
- *binding agents 381, 388-390*
- *brushes 473*
- *coarse pastel ground 376-378*
- *colour ranges 382-383*
- *commercial pastel papers 373-374*
- *cork boards 374*
- *cork particles 379*
- *dralon fibre 379*
- *egg white as binding agent 380*
- *filler material 381-382*
- *fixing 396-398*
- *flock paper 374*
- *glair as binding agent 380*
- *hand-made supports 374-380*
- *hand-making soft pastels 390-393*
- *manipulating pastel 395*
- *paper choice 378-379*
- *pastel sticks 371-372*
- *pastel sticks recipes 384-390*
- *preservation 480*
- *safety 394*
- *storage 480*
- *storing 396-398*
- *supports 372-380*

velour paper 374

soft sable hair brushes 30
solvent dispensation 334
solvent disposal 334
solvents for oil painting 331-333
spanish red 105
spermaceti wax 432
spike lavender oil 317, 318, 320
spinel black 170
spinel phase pigments black-brown 118
spinel phase pigments brown dark 118
spinel phase pigments brown light 118
spirit varnishes 316
squirrel hair brushes 230, 469, 473
squirrel mops 469, 473
staining pigments 30
stainless steel powder 186
stand oil 264, 265, 270, 282, 310-311
starch pastes 369
stearin wax 432
stetching paper 350-351
stick form of oil paint 294
stil de grain 67-68,121, 167

storage
acrylic paintings 478
finished artworks 475-480
gouache paintings 478-479
oil paintings 475-478
soft pastel painting 480
watercolour paint 352
watercolour paintings 478-479

straight mottler brushes 251
strasbourg turpentine 322
stretching canvas 238-241
strontium chromate 48
strontium yellow 48
student oil colours 289
student quality watercolour paint 343
studio good practice 333-334
studio red 79
suede effect 265
sumi ink 200
sun-bleached linseed oil 311
sun-bleached oil 270
sun-thickened linseed oil 271, 311
sunflower oil 272, 279, 282
sunshine yellow 53

supports
commercially prepared canvas board 242
compressed fibre board 203-204
cotton duck canvas 233-234
dried goatskin 346
egg tempera painting 203-204
encaustic painting 427-428
fibreboard 247-248
flax 234-235
gouache painting 361
hardboard 204, 246-247
honeycomb aluminium panel 248
ivory plaques 346
lime-fresco painting 439-447

linen 234-235
masonite 204, 246-247
medium density fibreboard (MDF) 247-248
natural wood 204-205
oil painitng 233-248
oil painting, flexible 233-242
oil painting, rigid 242-248
panel painting 203-204
panel thickness 204
paper 241-242, 346-347
plywood 245-246
pre-primed canvas 236-237
priming 251-258
reinforcing rigid supports 246
rigid 203-204
sizing 248-251
soft pastel painting 372-380
stretching canvas 238-241
watercolour painting 346-347
wood 242-245

swelling agents 292
synthetic brushes 465-466, 460, 470
synthetic filament brushes 218
synthetic indigo 139

synthetic iron oxides 16, 99, 115-118
caput mortuum red 115-116
caput mortuum violet 115-116
colcothar 115-116
haematite-chrome oxide black-brown 118
light red 115-116
mars black 115-116
mars brown 115-116
mars colours 115-116
mars orange 115-116
mars red 115-116
mars violet 115-116
mars yellow 115-116
oil required in mix with dry pigment 286
red-violet 189
spinel phase pigments black-brown 118
spinel phase pigments brown dark 118
spinel phase pigments brown light 118
translucent iron oxide orange 117
translucent iron oxide orange-red 117
translucent iron oxide red 117
translucent iron oxide yellow 117
transoxide orange 117
transoxide orange-red 117
transoxide red 117
transoxide yellow 117
transparent iron oxide orange 117
transparent iron oxide orange-red 117
transparent iron oxide red 117
transparent iron oxide yellow 117
venetian red 115-116
zinc iron brown dark 118
zinc iron brown light 118
zinc iron chrome brown light 118

synthetic malachite 161
synthetic resin 399
synthetic ultramarine 125, 162
synthetic wax 315

T

talc 382
tempera painting 357
terra rosa 105
terra verde 114
terre verte 114
texture pastes 415-416
thalo blue 119

thalo green 148
thenard's blue 122
thixotropic property 313
tin foil 187-188
tin powder 187-188
tinting strength of pigments 19
titanium dioxide 36
titanium orange 77
titanium primrose 63
titanium white 31, 36, 181, 253, 304-305, 452
titanox 36
tixogel 292
toluidine red 79
Towne, Frances 336
translucent iron oxide orange 117
translucent iron oxide orange-red 117
translucent iron oxide red 117
translucent iron oxide yellow 117
transoxide orange 117
transoxide orange-red 117
transoxide red 117
transoxide yellow 117
transparency of pigments 19
transparency of watercolour paint 338-339
transparent iron oxide orange 117
transparent iron oxide orange-red 117
transparent iron oxide red 117
transparent iron oxide yellow 117
transparent oxide of chromium 152
transporting oil paintings 477
tree (brushes) 460
tree balsams 321-322
triple roll mill 292
trulisatio 441-442
turkey brown 106
turkey umber 106, 107
turner's yellow 190
Turner, J M W 336
turpentine 20, 177, 184, 282, 309, 331-332
tylose 363-364
tylose MH300 384
tylose MH300: stock solution recipe 389
tyrian purple 190

U

ultramarine 67, 152, 167
ultramarine (synthetic) 162
ultramarine ash 124
ultramarine blue 82, 155, 282, 291
ultramarine blue (shades) 125-126
ultramarine green 125, 155
ultramarine pink 125
ultramarine red 125
ultramarine violet 125
ultramarine yellow 48
underbound 297, 309
underpainting 21, 226, 296, 306
undertone 264
universal primer 257
unsized paper 350

V

van dyke brown 108, 111-112
varnishes
acrylic painting 416-419
alcohol-based 316
brushes 212, 472-473
dammar varnish 326
egg tempera painting 219, 227-229
historic for egg tempera painting 228
ketone N 326
mastic varnish 326
modern for egg tempera painting 228-229

oil painting 299-300, 326-331
recipes 327-331
sandarac 316
shellac 316
spirit 316
watercolour painting 355

varnishing brushes 212, 472-473
vaseline oil 463
velour paper 374
venetian red 106, 115-116
venice turpentine 184, 321-322
verdaccio 222, 225
verdigris 229
verdigris synthetic 153-154
vermilion 79, 81, 84-85, 222, 260, 272, 290
verona green earth 114
veronese brown 103
veronese green 165
victoria green 152
vienna green 165
vine black 173, 179, 222
vinyl-based paints 420-421
violet 124
viridian 17, 153, 162, 290
volchonskoite green 164

W

walls, preparing 439-447
walnut oil 227, 273
waste bin 281
water-based binding agents 362-369
water-pigment pastes 216-218

watercolour paint
acrylic materials 356
additives 354-355
binding agent 339-340
combining with other materials 355-356
commercial manufacture 342-343
diluent 355
flow when diluted 342
framing 352
glycerine 344
half pans 342-343
hand-prepared 343-346
hydromel 344
lift-off of colour 341
moist 336
moisturising agent 344
pans 342-343
particle size 338
plasticising agent 344
quality 343
resolvability 341
short 340
storing 352
transparency 338-339
tubes 342-343
wetting agents 20

watercolour painting 335-356
auxiliary materials 353
brushes 466-469
care 352
cleaning 352
criteria 337
historical background 335-337
lightfastness 346
palette 353
paper stretching 350-351
papermaking 347-350
permanence 346
properties 337-342
supports 346-347
varnishing 355

watercolour paintings
preservation 478-479
storage 478-479

waterglass 455-456
waxes as oil paint mediums 314-315
weld 67, 160

wet drawing tools
acrylic-based inks 202

bistre ink 202
india ink 201
indian ink 201
ink stone 200
ink with acrylic binder 202
ink with gum arabic binder 201
inks 200
iron-gall ink 200
sepia ink 202
shellac-borax inks 201-202
sumi ink 200
wet into wet approach 298, 299

wetting agents
acrylic colours 20
animal skin glue binder 21
casein binder 21
egg tempera 21
gouache 20
hand-made soft pastels 20
oil colours 20
watercolours 20
wheat starch glue 256
white chalk 199

white pigments 31-36
alumina hydrate 42
aluminium hydrate 42-43, 184, 280, 282-283, 290
aluminium hydroxide 42
barytes 40
blanc fix 31, 33, 40-41, 184, 280, 358, 451
carlton white 35
ceruse white 31
chinese white 33
constant white 40
cremnitz white 31
flake white 31
genoa white 31
glimmer white 39
griffith's patent zinc white 35
heavy spar 40
iridescent white (mica lustre) 39
iridescent white (pearl lustre) 39
jersey lily white 35
kremnitz white 31
krems white 31
lead white 23, 31-32, 127, 222, 252, 260, 287, 297, 305-307, 452
lime-fresco painting 450-452
lithopone 33, 35, 152
lithopone silver 35
london white 31
mica white 39
nottingham white 31
oil paint 304-307
oil required in mix with dry pigment 284
orr's zinc white 35
pearlescent white 39
permanent white 33, 40
ponolith 35
silver white 31
snowflake 31
titanium dioxide 36
titanium white 31, 36, 181, 253, 304-305, 452
titanox 36
zinc oxide 33
zinc white 33-34, 35, 127, 133, 135, 291, 293, 300, 305, 306, 405, 452

white spirit 279, 332
whiting 185, 382
whiting chalk 206-207, 255
woad 138
wolchonskoite green 164

wood as support
egg tempera painting 204-205
oil painting 242-245

wood panels as support
lime-fresco painting 444-446

woodblock printing 369
woodfree paper 349-350
woodpulp paper 349-350

Y

yellow beeswax 314
yellow bole 230
yellow carmine 67
yellow lake 67
yellow ochre 22, 113, 222
yellow pigments 44-69
anthrapyrimidine yellow 60
antimony yellow 54
arylide yellow 44
aurora yellow 50
azo yellow 44
barium lemon yellow 46, 59
bismuth yellow 64
bismuth-vandate yellow 64
brilliant yellow 44
bristol yellow 64
brown lake 67
buckthorn lake 67
cadmium lemon 49
cadmium orange 49
cadmium yellow 49-50, 162, 305
cadmium yellow dark 49
cadmium yellow deep 49, 62
cadmium yellow light 49
cadmium yellow medium 49
cadmium yellow pale 49
camboge 66
chrome yellow 47-48, 83, 121
chrome yellow deep 121
chromophtal yellow 61
cinquasia red gold 71
citron yellow 51
coal tar yellow 65
cobalt yellow 53
dutch pink 67
gamboge 66, 120-121, 229
giallorino 55, 57
gomma gutti 66
hansa yellow 44-45, 121
hansa yellow dark 44
hansa yellow light 44
indian yellow (substitute) 69
indian yellow genuine 65, 69
indian yellow substitute 65
irgazine yellow 61
isoindoline yellow 62
isoindolinone yellow 61
italian pink 67
jaune brilliant 54
kings yellow 52
lead monoxide 58
lead tin yellow 54, 58
lead tin yellow type I 55-56
lead tin yellow type II 57
lemon yellow 46, 59
litharge 58, 76
massicot 55, 58, 76, 271, 317
monoazo yellow 44
naples yellow 54, 55, 59, 216
naples yellow lemon 59
naples yellow light 59
nickel azo yellow 69, 264
nickel barium 63
nickel titanium yellow 59
nickel yellow 59
oil required in mix with dry pigment 284-285
orient yellow 50
orpiment 52
paliotol yellow 62
permanent yellow 46
persian lake 67
priderite yellow 63
primrose yellow 47, 51
pyramid yellow 60
sicopal yellow 64
stil de grain 67-68, 121, 167
strontium chromate 48
strontium yellow 48
sunshine yellow 53
titanium primrose 63

ultramarine yellow 48
yellow carmine 67
yellow lake 67
yellow ultramarine 46
zinc chrome yellow 51
zinc yellow 51, 121, 152

yellow ultramarine 46

Z

zinc chrome yellow 51
zinc green 51
zinc iron brown dark 118
zinc iron brown light 118
zinc iron chrome brown light 118
zinc oxide 33
zinc white 33-34, 35, 127, 133, 135, 291, 293, 300, 305, 306, 405, 452
zinc yellow 51, 121, 152